SAGE
Premium
Video

BOOST COMPREHENSION. BOLSTER ANALYSIS.

- SAGE Premium Video **EXCLUSIVELY CURATED FOR THIS TEXT**

- **BRIDGES BOOK CONTENT** with application & critical thinking

- Includes short, auto-graded quizzes that **DIRECTLY FEED TO YOUR LMS GRADEBOOK**

- Premium content is **ADA COMPLIANT WITH TRANSCRIPTS**

- Comprehensive media guide to help you **QUICKLY SELECT MEANINGFUL VIDEO** tied to your course objectives

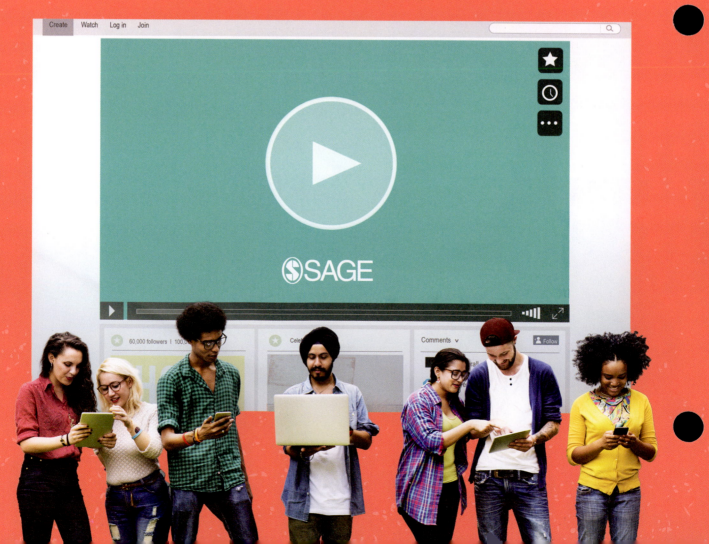

The Hallmark Features

Learning tools throughout the text help your students make sense of the dynamics and complexities of American politics. Learning objectives set clear expectations, "What Have I Learned?" quizzes and Chapter Review sections keep students on track, and the features prompt critical thinking and deeper learning.

- Two new **PRACTICING POLITICAL SCIENCE** boxes in every chapter help students become more capable and critical readers of arguments made through data, images, and text.

- **NEW CASE STUDIES** keep students engaged by connecting key concepts to recent events, such as the Standing Rock pipeline protests in a chapter on civil liberties and discussion of "fake news" in the media chapter.

- Up-to-date **2018 MIDTERM ELECTION** coverage and analysis, particularly in the chapters on Congress, the American Presidency, and Political Parties, provide students with a current snapshot of the results and an overview of the bipartisan battle for Congress.

PRACTICING POLITICAL SCIENCE

USING MAPS TO EXPLORE THE CONSEQUENCES OF PRIMARY AND CAUCUS SCHEDULES

Geographical representations of data can be useful tools in exploring important topics in political science. We have discussed the fact that the schedule of state caucuses and primaries can and does have important political consequences. One of the issues with this scheduling involves the degree to which voters in states that participate early in the cycle may be advantaged in selecting eventual nominees. Figure 9A displays the month of a state's primary or caucus in the 2016 presidential elections.

Keeping Figure 9-A in mind, consider Figure 9-B, which displays counties in which racial or ethnic minorities constituted a majority of voters in 2014. While the data are county based, focus on the patterns between states.

connecting these population patterns to the data presented in Figure 9-A.

What Do You Think?

One of the criticisms of the current caucus and primary schedule is that it disadvantages members of racial and ethnic minorities by bringing states with larger minority populations into the nomination process later in the process, when many campaign narratives have already been constructed or reconstructed. Do you think these data support that argument? What other data might you want to investigate this issue further?

▼ **FIGURE 9-A**
Frontloading: Presidential Primary and Caucus Scheduling by State, 2016

THE MEDIA
Truth, Power, and American Democracy

CHAPTER 8

Fake Donald Trump tweets are shown in a Twitter timeline in February 2017. In China, a site that generates fake tweets that look as if they were generated by U.S. president Donald Trump is being used to mock the president.

140

View 11 new Tweets

4m.

...orting FAKE NEWS again. So ...ot nice!

Donald J. Trump ✓
@realDonaldTrump
45th President of the United S...

WHAT HAVE I LEARNED?

1. Apportionment refers to ____.
   a. the allocation of seats in the House of Representatives
   b. the allocation of seats in the Senate
   c. congressional committee assignments
   d. the number of candidates who may run in a congressional election
   c. protect incumbents in the House of Representatives
   d. concentrate the opposing party's voters in a small number of districts

2. Partisan gerrymandering is designed to ____.
   a. spread your own party's voters out as much as possible
   b. encourage the representation of members of minority groups

3. Why do incumbents have such an advantage in congressional elections? Do you think that the nation should consider any electoral reforms to give challengers a better chance? If so, what might these be?

Answer Key: 1. a; 2. a; 3. Answers should describe specific characteristics of theories of the incumbency advantage.

CONCLUSION: POLITICS AND AMERICA'S CHANGING LANDSCAPE

While the Latino vote may not have proved decisive in the 2016 presidential race, there were several lessons to be learned. First, the concept of a singular "Latino vote," as we have explored, masks a great deal of complexity within Latino communities. While the majority of Latinos voted for Clinton, for example, Trump appeared to do well with Cuban Americans, helping him win Florida. In addition, the inevitability of demographic change will continue to press candidates to try to connect with these growing communities.

The 2018 midterm elections resulted in an increasing diversity across many identities in the Congress that would convene in January (Chapter 12). Texas, for example, elected its first two Latina congresswomen, Sylvia Garcia and Veronica Escobar, both Democrats. Alexandria Ocasio-Cortez (D-NY) became the youngest woman ever elected to serve in the House of Representatives.

Exit poll data collected on voting day indicated perhaps record-breaking Latino turnout, with immigration as one of the key issues mentioned by nearly all voters. While detailed turnout analyses were yet to come, these are early indications that Latinos could represent the highest percentage of total turnout ever for this group of voters in a midterm election." As the election took place, a caravan of asylum-seeking group of Central American and Mexican individuals was making its way to the U.S. border, and President Trump vowed that they would not be allowed to cross.

The combination of the geographical distribution of Americans of diverse identities, the division of partisan support between urban and rural areas of the nation, and the structure of Congress established as a result of the Great Compromise in the Constitutional Convention are likely to act as powerful forces in shaping congressional political outcomes going forward.

In the 2018 midterms—as part of their successful effort to reclaim the House of Representatives—Democrats "flipped" the last remaining "purely urban" House district in Republican hands, one covering Staten Island and parts of Brooklyn, New York. Urbanization and demographic change benefit the Democrats in coming House elections. Republicans, however, benefit from the mapping of congressional and rural voters onto a larger number of ...

$SAGE edge
for CQ Press

For my family

In memory of Bobby

AMERICAN GOVERNMENT

Second Edition

•••• STORIES OF A NATION

The Essentials

Rawpixel.com/Shutterstock

WE MADE A DIFFERENCE

SCOTT F. ABERNATHY

University of Minnesota

FOR INFORMATION:

CQ Press

An Imprint of SAGE Publications, Inc.

2455 Teller Road

Thousand Oaks, California 91320

E-mail: order@sagepub.com

SAGE Publications Ltd.

1 Oliver's Yard

55 City Road

London EC1Y 1SP

United Kingdom

SAGE Publications India Pvt. Ltd.

B 1/I 1 Mohan Cooperative Industrial Area

Mathura Road, New Delhi 110 044

India

SAGE Publications Asia-Pacific Pte. Ltd.

18 Cross Street #10-10/11/12

China Square Central

Singapore 048423

Executive Publisher: Monica Eckman

Editorial Assistant: Sam Rosenberg

Content Development Editors: Elise Frasier,
Scott Harris

Production Editor: Tracy Buyan

Copy Editor: Rachel Keith

Typesetter: C&M Digitals (P) Ltd.

Proofreader: Lawrence W. Baker

Indexer: Maria Sosnowski

Cover Designer: Anthony Paular

Marketing Manager: Erica DeLuca

Library of Congress Cataloging-in-Publication Data

Names: Abernathy, Scott Franklin, 1966- author.

Title: American government : stories of a nation / Scott F. Abernathy, University of Minnesota, USA.

Description: Second Essentials Edition. | Washington, D.C. : CQ Press, a DIVISION OF SAGE, [2019] | First Essentials Edition: 2017. | Includes bibliographical references and index.

Identifiers: LCCN 2018032593 | ISBN 9781544327617 (Paperback : acid-free paper)

Subjects: LCSH: United States—Politics and government—Textbooks.

Classification: LCC JK31 .A23 2019 | DDC 320.473—dc23
LC record available at https://lccn.loc.gov/2018032593

This book is printed on acid-free paper.

19 20 21 22 23 10 9 8 7 6 5 4 3 2 1

BRIEF CONTENTS

PREFACE   XXII

ACKNOWLEDGMENTS   XXXII

ABOUT THE AUTHOR   XXXVI

PART I: FOUNDATIONS

CHAPTER 1.   AMERICAN POLITICAL STORIES: CLAIMING RIGHTS, DEMANDING TO BE HEARD   2

CHAPTER 2.   THE CONSTITUTION OF THE UNITED STATES: A NEW VISION OF REPRESENTATIVE
             GOVERNMENT   30

CHAPTER 3.   FEDERALISM: THE CHANGING BOUNDARIES BETWEEN THE NATION AND THE STATES 62

CHAPTER 4.   CIVIL LIBERTIES: BUILDING AND DEFENDING FENCES   92

CHAPTER 5.   CIVIL RIGHTS: HOW EQUAL IS EQUAL?   122

PART II: POLITICAL BEHAVIOR AND MASS POLITICS

CHAPTER 6.   POLITICAL PARTICIPATION: CARRY THAT WEIGHT   154

CHAPTER 7.   PUBLIC OPINION: HOW ARE AMERICANS' VOICES MEASURED, AND DO THEY MATTER?   182

CHAPTER 8.   THE MEDIA: TRUTH, POWER, AND AMERICAN DEMOCRACY   210

CHAPTER 9.   POLITICAL PARTIES: THE INSURGENTS VERSUS THE ESTABLISHMENT   236

CHAPTER 10. CAMPAIGNS AND ELECTIONS: CANDIDATES AND VOTERS IN AN ERA OF
             DEMOGRAPHIC CHANGE   266

CHAPTER 11. INTEREST GROUPS AND SOCIAL MOVEMENTS: COLLECTIVE ACTION, POWER,
             AND REPRESENTATION   296

PART III: INSTITUTIONS

CHAPTER 12. CONGRESS: REPRESENTATION, ORGANIZATION, AND LEGISLATION   322

CHAPTER 13. THE AMERICAN PRESIDENCY: INSTITUTIONS, INDIVIDUALS, AND POWER   356

CHAPTER 14. THE FEDERAL BUREAUCRACY: PUTTING THE NATION'S LAWS INTO EFFECT   384

CHAPTER 15. THE FEDERAL JUDICIARY: POLITICS, POWER, AND THE "LEAST DANGEROUS" BRANCH   412

APPENDIXES   442

GLOSSARY   474

NOTES   486

INDEX   516

Carl Juste/Miami Herald/TNS via Getty Images

DETAILED CONTENTS

PREFACE   XXII

ACKNOWLEDGMENTS   XXXII

ABOUT THE AUTHOR   XXXVI

PART I: FOUNDATIONS

CHAPTER 1. AMERICAN POLITICAL STORIES: CLAIMING RIGHTS, DEMANDING TO BE HEARD   2

AMERICAN STUDENTS CLAIM THEIR RIGHTS   4

AMERICAN POLITICAL CULTURE IS BUILT ON A SET OF SHARED IDEAS   6

Equality Is About Having the Same Rights or Status   7

Inalienable Rights Exist above Any Government Powers   7

Liberty Involves Both Freedom from Interference and Freedom to Pursue One's Dreams   8

● **Practicing Political Science: Millennials and the American Dream**   9

The Pursuit of Happiness Is at the Core of the American Dream   9

American Political Culture Has Many Roots   9

American Exceptionalism Flows from the Nation's Historical Development   10

POLITICS AND POLITICAL ACTION SET THE STAGE FOR REVOLUTION   11

Colonial Settlements Establish a Precedent for Independence   11

A Global War Forces Change in Colonial Policy   12

Economic Conflicts Grow between Great Britain and Its Colonies   12

The Idea of Independence Is Given Voice in Political Propaganda   13

Revolutionaries Take Action, Their Eyes on Increasing the Powers of Colonial Legislatures   14

The Institution of Slavery Denied the Natural Rights of African Americans   16

Revolutionary Women, Though Excluded, Built Institutions of Their Own   17

Indigenous Peoples in North America Challenged Colonization   18

Independence Becomes Institutionalized   19

The American Revolution Is Still under Construction   20

THE STRUCTURE OF INSTITUTIONS AFFECTS HOW CITIZENS PARTICIPATE   21

DR. MARTIN LUTHER KING JR.'S "LETTER FROM BIRMINGHAM JAIL" LINKS THE CHALLENGE AGAINST RACIAL SEGREGATION TO CORE AMERICAN IDEALS   23

White Clergy Members Urge Moderation   24

Dr. King's Letter Affirms Natural Rights for African Americans   24

● **Practicing Political Science: The Power of the Media**   25

CONCLUSION: THE AMERICAN EXPERIMENT CONTINUES, AND YOU ARE PART OF IT   26

CHAPTER REVIEW   27

Chip Somodevilla/Getty Images

CHAPTER 2. THE CONSTITUTION OF THE UNITED STATES: A NEW VISION OF REPRESENTATIVE GOVERNMENT — 30

JAMES MADISON PLANS FOR A REPUBLIC THAT WILL LAST — 31

THE CONFEDERAL SYSTEM MADE COORDINATION BETWEEN THE STATES DIFFICULT — 33

The Articles of Confederation Attempted to Unite the States While Preserving Their Authority — 34

Under the Confederal System, States Had Sovereignty and Equal Representation — 34

The Confederal Government Was Designed to Be Weak — 35

The Prospect of Changes to the Systems of Slavery and Representation Sowed Unrest — 37

Fears of Unrest and Rebellion Worried State Governments — 37

Rebellion Began — 38

From Shays' Rebellion Came New Opportunity — 38

● Practicing Political Science: Image as a Political Tool — 39

DELEGATES REACH A COMPROMISE AT THE CONSTITUTIONAL CONVENTION — 40

Delegates Look to America's State Constitutions for Models, Good and Bad — 41

Delegates Debate Forms of Representation and the Powers of the National Government — 41

The Virginia Plan Outlines a System of Proportional Representation for the States — 42

The New Jersey Plan Maintains Equal Votes in the Legislature — 42

The Great Compromise Calls for a Bicameral Legislature with Different Methods of Representation in Each Chamber — 43

DELEGATES WORK OUT DETAILS OF THE NEW GOVERNMENT — 45

The Legislative Branch Is Made the Most Powerful — 45

The Executive Branch Is Initially Less Thoroughly Planned Out — 45

The Judiciary Is Designed to Interpret Constitutional Conflicts — 46

Separation of Powers Allows for Checks and Balances on Government — 47

Delegates Address the "Unfinished Parts" but Leave the Problem of Slavery Behind — 47

● Practicing Political Science: Slavery, Population, and the Balance of Power between Southern and Northern States — 50

The Constitution Is Finished but Not Yet Made the Law of the Land — 51

FEDERALISTS AND ANTI-FEDERALISTS FIGHT OVER RATIFICATION — 52

Federalists and Anti-Federalists Debate the Dangers of Power in a Large Republic — 54

Federalists and Anti-Federalists Debate Where Power Should Be Concentrated — 56

A Bill of Rights Is a Key Issue in the Ratification Debates — 56

CONCLUSION: THE MOTIVES OF THE FRAMERS AND THE EFFECTS OF THE CONSTITUTION ARE STILL BEING DEBATED — 58

CHAPTER REVIEW — 59

AP Photo/Ben Margot

CHAPTER 3. FEDERALISM: THE CHANGING BOUNDARIES BETWEEN THE NATION AND THE STATES — 62

THE FIGHT FOR ACCESS TO MEDICAL MARIJUANA REVEALS TENSIONS BETWEEN STATE AND FEDERAL LAW — 63

In *Gonzales v. Raich*, the Supreme Court Sides with Federal Law — 64

THE CONSTITUTION DIVIDES POWER BETWEEN THE NATION AND THE STATES — 66

There Is More Than One Way to Divide Power between Levels of Government — 66

The Supremacy, Necessary and Proper, and Commerce Clauses Are the Keys to American Federalism — 67

The Constitution Describes the Powers Belonging to the Nation and the States — 68

● Practicing Political Science: Interpreting Graphs and Charts: Americans' Views of Federal, State, and Local Governments — 70

FOR MUCH OF AMERICAN HISTORY, THE BOUNDARIES BETWEEN THE NATION AND THE STATES WERE SHARPER THAN THEY ARE TODAY — 72

Early Supreme Court Decisions Shape the Division between State and National Power — 72

The Era of Dual Federalism Separates the Powers of the Nation and the States — 73

PRESIDENT FRANKLIN ROOSEVELT'S RESPONSE TO THE GREAT DEPRESSION RESHAPES AMERICAN FEDERALISM — 77

President Roosevelt Greatly Expands the Role of the National Government — 78

The Supreme Court Pushes Back against President Roosevelt's New Deal Expansions — 78

President Roosevelt Strikes Back with a Court-Packing Plan — 80

In the New Deal, Cooperative Federalism Replaces Dual Federalism — 80

MODERN AMERICAN FEDERALISM REMAINS COOPERATIVE BUT FACES CHALLENGES — 81

● Practicing Political Science: Reading and Studying Supreme Court Decisions — 82

President Lyndon Johnson's Great Society Expands Cooperative Federalism — 83

With New Federalism Comes Devolution and Attempts to Roll Back National Power — 84

State Governments Have Several Tools to Preserve Their Interests — 85

CONCLUSION: THE EVOLUTION OF FEDERALISM CONTINUES — 88

CHAPTER REVIEW — 89

CHAPTER 4. CIVIL LIBERTIES: BUILDING AND DEFENDING FENCES — 92

STANDING ROCK: WATER PROTECTORS CLAIM THEIR RIGHTS AND FREEDOMS IN NORTH DAKOTA — 94

Interaction of the Protesters with Law Enforcement Officials Brings Other Civil Liberties into Question — 95

● Practicing Political Science: Examining How Issues May Cut across Party Lines — 96

Rainer Jensen/picture-alliance/dpa/AP Images

THE BILL OF RIGHTS ESTABLISHES PROTECTIONS FOR AMERICANS' CIVIL LIBERTIES 98

The Bill of Rights Takes Center Stage in the Ratification Debates 98

The Bill of Rights Establishes Civil Liberties Protections, and Selective Incorporation Applies Them to the States 99

The Relationship between Members of Indigenous Nations and the Bill of Rights Has Evolved over Time 100

THE FIRST AMENDMENT'S FIRST TWO PROTECTIONS BOTH INVOLVE RELIGION 102

The Establishment and Free Exercise Clauses Ensure Separation of Church and State 102

THE FIRST AMENDMENT ALSO PROTECTS EXPRESSION: SPEECH, PRESS, ASSEMBLY, AND PETITIONING THE GOVERNMENT 106

Free Expression Was Challenged in the Early Years of the Republic 106

Courts Have Attempted to Balance Political Expression against the Needs of National Security 106

Courts Have Weighed Press Freedoms against National Security 107

Symbolic Speech Is Protected as a Form of Political Expression 108

Other Forms of Expression Have More Limited Protection 108

Freedom of Assembly Is Broadly Protected 109

THE CONSTITUTION ALSO PROTECTS INDIVIDUALS INVOLVED WITH THE CRIMINAL JUSTICE SYSTEM 110

The Fourth Amendment Protects Against Unlawful Search, Seizure, Warrants, and Evidence 110

● **Practicing Political Science: The Second Amendment, "Philosoraptor," and Internet Memes** 111

The Fifth Amendment Guarantees the Accused Certain Procedures for Their Defense 112

The Sixth Amendment Guarantees the Accused Certain Rights to Trials and Representation 113

The Eighth Amendment Guards against Cruel and Unusual Punishment 113

THE NINTH AND TENTH AMENDMENTS HELP SHAPE FREEDOMS IN THE NATION AND ACROSS THE STATES 114

The Defense of Marriage Act Restricts the Rights of Same-Sex Couples to Marry 114

The Ninth Amendment and Privacy, a Right Not Enumerated 115

The Tenth Amendment Is Intended to Protect State Powers 117

The Final Blow to DOMA 117

CONCLUSION: CIVIL LIBERTIES INVOLVE FENCES STILL UNDER CONSTRUCTION 118

CHAPTER REVIEW 119

CHAPTER 5. CIVIL RIGHTS: HOW EQUAL IS EQUAL? 122

PROTESTERS ACT TO SECURE RIGHTS FOR AMERICANS WITH DISABILITIES 123

The Americans with Disabilities Act Expands Protections for People with Disabilities 126

CIVIL RIGHTS AMENDMENTS EMERGE FROM THE CIVIL WAR—BUT PROVIDE ONLY IMPERFECT PROTECTION — 127

The Supreme Court Denies Citizenship Rights to African Americans, Helping to Spark a War That Splits the Nation — 127

Secession Ensues, and Then Civil War — 128

Constitutional Amendments Abolish Slavery and Affirm Voting and Citizenship Rights for African Americans during Reconstruction — 129

Racial Oppression Continues despite New Protections — 130

Opponents of Jim Crow Attempt to Use the Judiciary to Challenge It, but Fail — 131

CHALLENGES TO LEGAL SEGREGATION FACE SUCCESSES AND FAILURES — 132

Thurgood Marshall and the NAACP Devise a Strategy to End School Segregation — 132

The Supreme Court Rules That "'Separate but Equal' Has No Place" — 134

The South Resists Desegregation — 135

Citizens Engage in New Forms of Civil Disobedience and Protest — 136

● Practicing Political Science: Can the Supreme Court Effect Social Change? — 137

The Court Delivers New Rules Aimed at Strengthening Civil Rights — 139

The Court Tests the Limits of Equal Protection for African Americans — 140

AMERICAN WOMEN WORK TO SECURE THEIR CIVIL RIGHTS — 142

Women's Early Civil Rights Efforts Focused on Enfranchisement — 142

● Practicing Political Science: Considering Contrasting Opinions and Arguments—Frances Ellen Watkins Harper on Women's Rights, Racism, and American Society — 145

The Second Wave Focuses on Ongoing Inequalities — 146

The Supreme Court Uses Different Standards of Scrutiny on Gender Discrimination and Sexual Harassment — 147

AMERICANS CONFRONT OVERLAPPING FORMS OF DISCRIMINATION — 148

Civil Rights Challenges Persist for Other Groups as Well — 149

CONCLUSION: HAVE AMERICANS' CIVIL RIGHTS BEEN SECURED? — 150

CHAPTER REVIEW — 151

PART II: POLITICAL BEHAVIOR AND MASS POLITICS

CHAPTER 6. POLITICAL PARTICIPATION: CARRY THAT WEIGHT — 154

TWO PERSPECTIVES ON CAMPUS CARRY OF FIREARMS IN RESPONSE TO SEXUAL VIOLENCE ON COLLEGE CAMPUSES — 155

POLITICAL PARTICIPATION CAN TAKE MANY FORMS — 160

Americans' Civic Engagement Can Be Fluid — 162

THE DECISION TO VOTE OR NOT VOTE INVOLVES MANY FACTORS — 163

● Practicing Political Science: Comparing American Voter Turnout with That of Other Nations — 164

Individual Factors Shape Electoral Participation   165

Legal and Institutional Factors Enable and Constrain Voter Turnout   168

Election-Specific Factors Also Affect Voter Turnout   170

ANOTHER RESPONSE TO CAMPUS SEXUAL VIOLENCE HIGHLIGHTS THE FLUIDITY OF PARTICIPATION   171

A Personal and Public Protest Catalyzes Change   171

Elected Officials Take Action   172

● **Practicing Political Science: The Use of Images in Political Protest and Mobilization**   173

Survivors Engage the Political Process through Title IX   173

The Debate Reaches the Highest Levels of Government   174

Individuals Organize to Teach Others How to Personally Intervene in Campus Sexual Assaults   175

ARE YOUNG ADULT AMERICANS REALLY DISCONNECTED FROM THE POLITICAL PROCESS?   176

CONCLUSION: CARRYING THE WEIGHT OF SELF-GOVERNANCE   178

CHAPTER REVIEW   179

CHAPTER 7. PUBLIC OPINION: HOW ARE AMERICANS' VOICES MEASURED, AND DO THEY MATTER?   182

PUBLIC OPINION MAY BE MOVED BY IMPORTANT EVENTS LIKE FERGUSON   183

Public Opinion Reflects Different Fergusons   184

● **Practicing Political Science: Looking for a "Break in Trend" in Data and Drawing Conclusions over Time**   186

PUBLIC OPINION IS THE SUM TOTAL OF INDIVIDUAL BELIEFS AND ATTITUDES   187

There Are Competing Views About the Meaning of Public Opinion   188

PUBLIC OPINION IS TRANSMITTED AND MEASURED IN SEVERAL WAYS   191

Citizens' Opinions Are Transmitted to Public Officials through Direct and Indirect Channels   191

● **Practicing Political Science: Analyzing Editorial Choices in Presenting Visual Information**   192

Scientific Polling Is Based on Efforts to Accurately Sample Representative Populations   193

Public Opinion Survey Validity Varies by Type   193

How Public Opinion Surveys Are Constructed Affects Their Validity   195

Individual Opinions Vary According to Direction, Intensity, Stability, and Salience   195

Polls Are Used for Commercial, Academic, and Political Purposes   196

POLITICAL SOCIALIZATION AND POLITICAL IDEOLOGY SHAPE PUBLIC OPINION   197

Political Socialization Shapes Individual Attitudes   197

Partisan Identification, Individual and Group Identities, and Elite Attitudes Inform Our Views   198

Government and Media Influence Public Opinion   201

FERGUSON AND THE EFFECTS OF PUBLIC OPINION ON DEMOCRATIC REPRESENTATION   202

Donald J. Trump

CONCLUSION: HOW MEANINGFUL IS PUBLIC OPINION?	206
CHAPTER REVIEW	207

CHAPTER 8. THE MEDIA: TRUTH, POWER, AND AMERICAN DEMOCRACY — 210

CAN A FOREIGN GOVERNMENT CHANGE A PRESIDENTIAL ELECTION? HOW POWERFUL ARE THE MEDIA?	211
THE EVOLUTION OF AMERICAN MEDIA SHOWS THAT ISSUES OF POWER AND TRUSTWORTHINESS ARE NOT NEW	213
Early Newspapers and Pamphlets Shape a New Nation	213
Freedom of the Press Becomes Enshrined in the Constitution through the Bill of Rights	214
The Media Go "Mass" with the Penny Presses in the Eighteenth and Nineteenth Centuries	214
Journalists Become Investigators and Activists in the Nineteenth Century	215
The Twentieth Century Brings Radio and TV News Directly into Americans' Homes	215
New Media Have Reinvented the Media Landscape	217
● Practicing Political Science: Drawing Conclusions from Data: Do the Media Make Us Smart (or Not So Smart)? Or Do We Make Them Look Good (or Not So Good)?	219
QUESTIONS OF BIAS CHALLENGE AMERICANS' TRUST IN THE MEDIA'S OBJECTIVITY	221
The News Can Function as Entertainment	222
Bias and the Perception of Bias Are a Problem in Media Coverage	222
Contemporary Pressures Affect How the Media Cover Campaigns and Elections	224
MEDIA OWNERSHIP AND CONTENT ARE SUBJECT TO REGULATION	225
Regulation Affects Who Owns the Media and How We Consume It	225
Regulation Affects Media Technologies and Ownership	226
Regulation Also Affects Content	227
● Practicing Political Science: Evaluating Arguments: In Defense of Deregulation	228
THE POWER OF THE MEDIA TO AFFECT THE PUBLIC IS TESTED	229
Scholars Have Differed on the Media's Effects	230
Americans May Be Separated by a Digital Divide	231
CONCLUSION: DEBATES ABOUT THE POWER OF THE MEDIA CONTINUE	232
CHAPTER REVIEW	232

CHAPTER 9. POLITICAL PARTIES: THE INSURGENTS VERSUS THE ESTABLISHMENT — 236

TWO PRESIDENTIAL CANDIDATES SHAKE UP THE FIELD . . . AND CONVENTIONAL WISDOM ABOUT THE POWER AND COHESION OF THEIR PARTIES	237
Bernie Sanders Challenges Fellow Democrats to Focus More on Income Inequality	238

AP Photo/John Locher

Donald Trump Challenges Fellow Republicans on Policy and with Controversial Remarks   239

Sanders and Trump Share in a Basic Challenge to Their Parties' Establishment   240

PARTIES ACT TO IDENTIFY, SUPPORT, AND NOMINATE CANDIDATES FOR ELECTED OFFICE   **241**

Parties Unite People as Organizations   242

Parties Shape Elections by Recruiting and Supporting Candidates   242

● **Practicing Political Science: Using Maps to Explore the Consequences of Primary and Caucus Schedules**   **245**

PARTIES PROVIDE LABELS TO CANDIDATES TO ASSIST VOTERS IN MAKING THEIR CHOICES   **248**

Party Identification Helps Candidates Connect with Voters   248

Americans' Identification with Either of the Two Major Political Parties Is Changing   249

THE PRESIDENTIAL ELECTION OF 2016 THROWS CONVENTIONAL WISDOM OUT THE WINDOW   **251**

Sanders's Supporters Cry "Foul!"   251

● **Practicing Political Science: A Political Cartoon Depicts Bernie Sanders's Campaign**   **252**

Donald Trump's Campaign Benefits in Unexpected Ways from Republican Rules   253

Both Major Parties Continue to Wrestle with Insurgencies   254

POLITICAL POLARIZATION, GRIDLOCK, AND TWO-PARTY DOMINANCE ARE THE DEFINING FEATURES OF PARTIES IN GOVERNMENT TODAY   **255**

Polarization Leads to Gridlock in American Governance   255

While the Landscape of Parties in Government Has Changed, It Has Historically Been Dominated by Two Major Parties   256

America's Electoral System Leads to Two-Party Dominance   259

Minor Parties May Challenge the Two Major Parties   260

CONCLUSION: HOW WILL THE PARTIES RESPOND?   **262**

CHAPTER REVIEW   **263**

CHAPTER 10. CAMPAIGNS AND ELECTIONS: CANDIDATES AND VOTERS IN AN ERA OF DEMOGRAPHIC CHANGE   **266**

PRESIDENTIAL CANDIDATES ADDRESS LATINO VOTERS IN 2016   **267**

Republican Hopefuls Adopt Very Different Approaches   267

Democratic Hopefuls Face Their Own Challenges   269

Demographic Changes in the American Electorate Will Impact Future Political Campaigns   269

Could a Growing Latino Vote Alter the Party Landscape?   270

NATIONAL ELECTIONS SERVE TO HOLD OFFICIALS ACCOUNTABLE, BUT REGULATING THEM IS NOT ALWAYS EASY   **274**

Elections Help Hold Elected Officials Accountable   275

Elections Are Expensive   275

Holly Pickett/Bloomberg via Getty Images

PRESIDENTIAL ELECTIONS HAVE MANY STAGES AND MOVING PARTS   **277**

Candidates Lay the Foundations for Their Campaigns Long before
Formal Nomination   277

Candidates Try to Secure Their Party's Nomination   278

Nominees Compete in the General Election   278

The Rules of the Electoral College Decide the Presidency   278

● **Practicing Political Science: "My Story | Dulce Candy" and
Self-Presentation in the Twenty-First Century**   **280**

A FIRST-TIMER RUNS FOR CONGRESS, WINS, AND THEN TURNS TOWARD REELECTION   **281**

Newcomers Choose the Right Time to Jump In   281

Candidates Must Navigate the Electoral Rules   282

Candidates Raise Money and Secure Endorsements   284

The First Day on the Job Begins the Next Campaign   285

**THE DETAILS OF CONGRESSIONAL ELECTIONS DIFFER BY STATE, BUT MANY
OF THE RULES ARE THE SAME**   **286**

In Congressional Elections, Constituency Is Key   286

Redistricting and Gerrymandering Shape Constituencies and
Elections in House Races   287

● **Practicing Political Science: The Representational Consequences
of the Great Compromise**   **289**

Congressional Incumbents Have Significant Institutional Advantages   290

CONCLUSION: POLITICS AND AMERICA'S CHANGING LANDSCAPE   **292**

CHAPTER REVIEW   **293**

**CHAPTER 11. INTEREST GROUPS AND SOCIAL MOVEMENTS:
COLLECTIVE ACTION, POWER, AND REPRESENTATION**   **296**

A HOUSING BUBBLE BURSTS, AND INTEREST GROUPS POP OUT   **297**

Wall Street Responds to a National Financial Crisis   297

Financial Engineering Sows the Seeds for a Major Crisis   298

The Lobbyists' Pressure Play Begins   298

Counterpressure Arises from Outside Groups   300

The Bailout Begins   300

**AMERICANS FACE CHALLENGES IN ACTING COLLECTIVELY IN A
REPRESENTATIVE DEMOCRACY**   **301**

Theories of Interest Group Formation Focus on the Challenges of Faction   302

Theories of Interest Group Formation Also Explore the Challenges
of Collective Action   304

INTEREST GROUPS VARY BY TYPE AND TACTIC   **306**

● **Practicing Political Science: 2016 Campaign Contributions
by Economic Sector**   **307**

"Inside" Interest Groups Lobby to Influence Policymaking   308

Grassroots Lobbying and Political Protesters Act from "Outside" to
Influence Policy   313

Interest Groups Face Challenges in Representation   313

Andrew Innerarity/For The Washington Post via Getty Images

OCCUPY WALL STREET ILLUSTRATES THE STRUGGLES, SUCCESSES, AND FAILURES OF SOCIAL MOVEMENTS — **314**

● Practicing Political Science: Depicting Income Inequality in the United States — **315**

SOCIAL MOVEMENTS EMPLOY DIFFERENT TACTICS FROM INTEREST GROUPS TO MAKE CHANGE AND EDUCATE — **317**

The Success of Social Movements Is Difficult to Measure — 318

CONCLUSION: ORGANIZING IN AMERICAN POLITICAL LIFE — **319**

CHAPTER REVIEW — **320**

PART III: INSTITUTIONS

CHAPTER 12. CONGRESS: REPRESENTATION, ORGANIZATION, AND LEGISLATION — 322

THE ELECTIONS OF 2018 HIGHLIGHT THE CONNECTIONS AMONG PARTISANSHIP, INSTITUTIONS, AND IDENTITIES IN CONGRESS — **323**

In 2018, Women Ran in Historic Numbers — 324

THE CONSTITUTION DEFINES CONGRESS'S SHAPE AND POWERS — **326**

The House and Senate Serve Different Roles — 326

Congress Has Three Key Powers: Lawmaking, Budgeting, and Oversight — 327

CONGRESS IS ORGANIZED AROUND FORMAL AND INFORMAL RULES — **331**

Political Parties Shape How Congress Is Structured — 331

The Work of Congress Is Done through the Committee System — 333

Congressional Staff and the Congressional Bureaucracy Help Members Represent Their Constituents — 333

Norms Are Informal Contributors to Congressional Organization — 334

THE LEGISLATIVE PROCESS IS COMPLEX BY DESIGN — **335**

The First Step Is Bill Introduction — 335

Referral to Committee Involves Political Strategy — 337

The House and Senate Resolve Differences between Their Bills — 339

Bills Go Back to the Floor for Reconsideration — 339

The President Takes Action — 339

GETTING TO CONGRESS INVOLVES PERSONAL, PROFESSIONAL, ELECTORAL, AND FINANCIAL FACTORS — **340**

A Singular Event Galvanizes a New Field of Candidates — 341

Political Ambition Launches Careers — 341

● Practicing Political Science: Gender and Metaphors of Power in Image — **342**

Constituency, Incumbency, and Other Electoral Factors Lay the Groundwork — 342

Experience and Money Legitimize Candidates — 343

Alex Wong/Getty Images

MEMBERS REPRESENT CONSTITUENTS BY HOW THEY ACT AND WHO THEY ARE   **345**

Acting in Congress Involves Visible and Invisible Legislative Work   345

Descriptive Representation Is About Who Members Are   348

● **Practicing Political Science: Representing Representation**   **349**

Substantive Representation Connects How Members Act and Who They Are   351

CONCLUSION: REPRESENTATION REMAINS COMPLEX, BUT THE LANDSCAPE CONTINUES TO CHANGE   **353**

CHAPTER REVIEW   **354**

CHAPTER 13. THE AMERICAN PRESIDENCY: INSTITUTIONS, INDIVIDUALS, AND POWER   **356**

ONE PRESIDENT'S WARS: A WEEK IN THE ADMINISTRATION OF DONALD TRUMP   **357**

President Trump Fights Wars Abroad   357

Trump Fights Wars at Home   358

Is President Trump at War with Conventional Wisdom?   360

THE CONSTITUTION OUTLINES THE POWERS OF THE AMERICAN PRESIDENCY AND PLACES LIMITS ON THOSE POWERS   **361**

Delegates Settle Questions of Selection, Qualifications for Office, and Length of Terms   361

The President Is Granted Considerable Powers   362

The Powers of the Presidency Are Also Constitutionally Limited   364

INSTITUTIONS AND OTHER INFORMAL SOURCES OF POWER SHAPE THE MODERN EXECUTIVE BRANCH   **366**

The Vice Presidency Plays a Limited but Important Role   366

The Cabinet and the Executive Branch Bureaucracy Help Advise the President   367

The Executive Office of the President Assists the President with Policy   367

The First Spouse Can Help the President Connect   369

Political Parties Influence the Executive Office   369

● **Practicing Political Science: The Media and the Risks of the Photo Op**   **370**

The President Tries to Use the Media to Shape Public Opinion   370

Americans' Evaluations of Presidential Performance Can Affect the President's Policy Agenda   371

PRESIDENTS HAVE PUSHED THE LIMITS OF THEIR POWER TO PRESERVE NATIONAL SECURITY   **372**

Abraham Lincoln Suspends Habeas Corpus during the Civil War   374

THE PRESIDENT HAS SEVERAL TOOLS FOR UNILATERAL ACTION   **377**

Presidential Character Affects the Success of a Presidency   379

● **Practicing Political Science: The Problem of Small Numbers in the Study of the Presidency**   **380**

CONCLUSION: THE PARADOXES OF THE PRESIDENCY CONTINUE   **381**

CHAPTER REVIEW   **381**

Joe Raedle/Staff

CHAPTER 14. THE FEDERAL BUREAUCRACY: PUTTING THE NATION'S LAWS INTO EFFECT — 384

FEDERAL BUREAUCRATIC ACTION CONSISTS OF MANY ACTORS AND EVOLVES OVER TIME — 385
Hurricanes Harvey, Irma, and Maria Test the Federal Response — 386
Katrina Provides Uncomfortable Lessons About the Federal Response — 387
Did the Bureaucracy Learn from Katrina? — 389

THEORIES OF BUREAUCRATIC ORGANIZATION FOCUS ON RULES, PEOPLE, AND TASKS — 390
Weber's Theory Focuses on Rules — 391
Barnard's Theory Focuses on People — 391
Wilson's Theory Focuses on Tasks — 392

THE BUREAUCRACY HAS DEVELOPED IN RESPONSE TO DEMANDS AND CRISES — 393
The Founders Were Skeptical Of, and Unclear About, the Role of the Bureaucracy — 393
The Jacksonian Era Saw the Rise of Political Patronage — 396
Post–Civil War, the Bureaucracy Grew Along with the Nation's Territories — 396
Bureaucratic Expansion in the Progressive Era Focused on Labor and Eliminating Patronage — 397
Twentieth-Century Crises Expanded Clientele Agencies and the Military Bureaucracy — 398
In the Mid-Twentieth Century, the Social Safety Net Grew — 398
The Late Twentieth Century Brought Reform and Scaling Back — 399
● Practicing Political Science: The Growth of the Federal Bureaucracy — 400

A FUNCTIONING BUREAUCRACY DEPENDS UPON EFFECTIVE ORGANIZATION — 400
The Federal Bureaucracy Is a Web of Organizations — 401
Bureaucratic Authority Is Hierarchical — 402
The Core Tasks of the Bureaucracy Are Implementation, Rulemaking, Advising, and Representation — 402

THE BUREAUCRACY IS CONSTRAINED BY OVERSIGHT AND REFORM — 404
Separation of Powers Makes Overseeing the Bureaucracy Difficult — 405
Reform Efforts Involve Devolution, Deregulation, Reinvention, and Privatization — 406
● Practicing Political Science: Analyzing Congressional Testimony — 408

CONCLUSION: WHAT DOES A "GOOD" BUREAUCRACY LOOK LIKE? — 408

CHAPTER REVIEW — 409

CHAPTER 15. THE FEDERAL JUDICIARY: POLITICS, POWER, AND THE "LEAST DANGEROUS" BRANCH — 412

THE POLITICS OF SUPREME COURT CONFIRMATIONS PLACE NOMINEES ON "TRIAL" — 413
Sonya Sotomayor's "Trial" Highlights the Role of Lived Experience in Judicial Decision Making — 413

Drew Angerer/Getty Images

Robert Bork's "Trial" Highlights the Role of Politics in Confirmations   415

One Nominee Gets His "Trial," the Other Does Not: Merrick Garland
and Neil Gorsuch   416

THE CONSTITUTION CASTS THE JUDICIARY AS THE WEAKEST BRANCH   417

The Constitution Grants the Federal Judiciary Supremacy
over Lower State Courts   417

During Ratification, Concerns About Judicial Abuse of Power
Are Addressed   418

Congress Fills in the Blanks with the Judiciary Act of 1789   418

● **Practicing Political Science: Different Visuals, Different Stories:
The Presentation of the Supreme Court**   419

THE "TRIAL" OF JOHN MARSHALL ESTABLISHES THE PRINCIPLE OF JUDICIAL REVIEW   420

The Election of 1800 Gives Rise to a Federalist Judicial Strategy   420

Chief Justice John Marshall Confronts Politics and the Power
of the Supreme Court   421

Marbury v. Madison Leads to the Establishment of
Judicial Review   422

THE AMERICAN LEGAL SYSTEM IS DEFINED BY FEDERALISM   424

Cases Are Divided into Criminal and Civil Types   424

State Courts Handle the Majority of Cases in the United States   425

Most of the Impactful Cases Are Handled by the Federal Judiciary   426

Cases Involving Federal Questions Proceed through
the Federal Judiciary   428

Appointment to the Federal Judiciary Is Often Political   430

JUDICIAL REVIEW RAISES QUESTIONS OF CONSTITUTIONAL INTERPRETATION AND JUDICIAL DECISION MAKING   433

Justices Take Several Approaches to Constitutional Interpretation   433

Justices Exercise Degrees of Judicial Restraint and
Judicial Activism   434

The Supreme Court Acts as National Policymaker   435

● **Practicing Political Science: Analyzing Data across Time:
Judicial Review and the Political Ideologies of Justices**   436

CONCLUSION: THE TRIAL OF THE SUPREME COURT CONTINUES   439

CHAPTER REVIEW   440

APPENDIX 1: ARTICLES OF CONFEDERATION   442

APPENDIX 2: DECLARATION OF INDEPENDENCE   446

APPENDIX 3: CONSTITUTION OF THE UNITED STATES   450

APPENDIX 4: *FEDERALIST* NO. 10   460

APPENDIX 5: *FEDERALIST* NO. 51   464

APPENDIX 6: POLITICAL PARTY AFFILIATIONS IN CONGRESS AND
    THE PRESIDENCY, 1789–2017   466

APPENDIX 7: SUMMARY OF PRESIDENTIAL ELECTIONS, 1789–2016   470

GLOSSARY   474

NOTES   486

INDEX   516

PREFACE

REAL PEOPLE, REAL POLITICS, REAL STORIES

ENGAGING STUDENTS FOR POLITICAL PARTICIPATION

The story of American politics is at its heart a story about people: the ways they engage the political system, the strategies they form to shape political outcomes, their collective efforts to build and change institutions over time. It is also about how individuals' experiences and choices are molded by the political system, how the contingencies surrounding their actions have altered the political outcomes, and how they have responded to the struggles they have faced. When people *act* to confront injustices, advocate for policies they care about, and rally support for their causes, the political world around them can be *transformed*.

This book, *American Government: Stories of a Nation*, focuses on the many ways individuals have participated in the political life of the United States. By sharing real narratives about real people across each chapter, students learn precisely *how* others have used the tools of political engagement to bring about change. Rather than merely exhorting students to become involved, the extended profiles shine a spotlight on the steps others have taken, providing a richer foundation for students' own political engagement. In that sense, the book is very much a guidebook for students as they wrestle to define their place in the American political landscape, to make their own voices heard, and add their own threads to the quilt of American representative democracy. The narratives told in this book can help students better grasp the core ideas, political dynamics, and institutions that underlie American government—and they will also engage and inspire students to take action themselves.

A RICHER UNDERSTANDING OF POLITICAL DYNAMICS Anyone who has taught American politics knows that there is a chasm between how basic political dynamics can be described on paper and how they exist in the real world. With this approach, students will better understand that political outcomes are not predetermined but are instead the results of strategic choices made by political actors, usually undertaken in an uncertain environment, often amid unequal relationships of power. The approach in this book is designed to show students how others have wrestled with questions of power, action, and change, whether in very different times and circumstances or in situations ripped from today's headlines. They witness how some have succeeded, others failed, but, more importantly, how many have operated in the space between success and failure, adjusting their strategies along the way.

The chapter on civil liberties, for example, begins with a study of oil pipeline protests by members of the Standing Rock Sioux Nation and their supporters in 2016–2017. By engaging in depth with these protests and law enforcement's responses to them, students not only explore the exercise of First Amendment rights and freedoms but also come to understand how civil liberties do not exist in isolation—from each other or from the political landscape in which they are exercised. As the protests grew, there were widespread accusations that law enforcement officials were violating protesters' civil liberties, rights that protect those accused of criminal offenses, from evidence gathering to bail and trial. Exploring these accusations allows students to see the protection of civil liberties as a current and ongoing process of delineation and action.

Subsequent sections then cover the first ten amendments, the process of selective incorporation, and the challenges of balancing national security and civil liberties. Along the way, we refer back to the Standing Rock narrative to connect the story to those core political science concepts. We conclude with two additional narratives about civil liberties—the stories of Edie Windsor and James Obergefell, whose efforts to pursue judicial strategies reshaped federal policy toward same-sex marriage and how full faith and credit is interpreted among the several states in the area of marriage, shedding light on the implications of the Ninth Amendment and its statement that rights and freedoms not textually listed are not necessarily excluded. Together these narratives form a thread that connects people from a wide range of backgrounds and places to a set of political actions and outcomes that have profoundly shaped the country.

STRONGER CONNECTIONS WITH THE POLITICAL WORLD A second benefit is that the stories are *interesting* to students. Class-testing has shown that they *actually read and relate to the chapters*. Your students will be able to step into the shoes of the people about whom they are learning, and in doing so they will be doing much more than skimming for key terms or IDs. By combining the deep dives into one or a few key stories in each chapter with solid research-backed core content, *American Government: Stories of a Nation* will guide your students to a genuine engagement with the material, the theories that try to explain political outcomes, and the enduring questions of American representative democracy. And they will connect the dots between those elements.

The first chapter of the book, for example, clearly identifies and explains the founding ideals of American democracy—liberty, equality, natural rights, the American Dream, American exceptionalism. But those ideas are each situated within a set of vivid stories about people and groups coming from different times, places, and experiences who claimed their rights as citizens. Starting on page one, students learn about Bridget Mergens, a high school student who wanted to start a Bible club at her high school. They then read about a group of high school students in Kentucky who—using the same set of rights—wanted to start a gay-straight alliance club. Later in the chapter, they pick up the narrative thread again to hear how Thomas Jefferson went about arguing for natural rights in drafting the Declaration of Independence and the revolution of ideas that followed. As important, they learn what he and others left out. They hear the voices of people like Lemuel Haynes and Esther DeBerdt Reed, who spoke on behalf of African Americans and women in colonial America. Finally, at the chapter's end, readers conclude the journey in the twentieth century to witness Martin Luther King Jr. take up the language of natural rights to advance rights for African Americans. Together, these stories help students understand so-called "key terms" in ways no ordinary descriptive text can.

GREATER INSTRUCTIONAL FLEXIBILITY Third, *American Government: Stories of a Nation* is adaptable to the approach you want to use. This is not a book that pushes a specific perspective or one that envisions a teacher as a repository of fact. These narratives allow for an emphasis on institutions, behavior, or a combination of both. For example, two stories are used to present the core concepts underlying a study of interest groups and social movements—one of the efforts of lobbyists in the wake of the financial crisis of 2008, the other of Occupy Wall Street and its efforts to call attention to economic inequality in the years following. They can be used to highlight the ways in which institutions structure political action, the ways in which individuals make strategic choices in their efforts to solve problems of collective action, or both. In addition to allowing for analytical flexibility, the book also consciously strives to avoid weighing in on one side or another of heated debates but instead guides students to use their own engagement with them to more deeply understand American politics.

The chapter on the media, for example, begins with an in-depth exploration of a topic very much on students' minds as well as on those of the nation as a whole: fake news. By exploring what Secretary Hillary Clinton called "weaponized information"—referring to allegations of Russian use of media, especially social media, to sway the outcome in Donald Trump's favor—students gain a deeper understanding of citizens' roles as receivers and shapers of the media. Rather than focusing on whether or not the Russian government successfully "hacked" the presidential election of 2016, we ask what the *potential that they did* means for conclusions about the power of the media and Americans' abilities to critically receive their products.

By concluding with a case study of a fake Martian invasion broadcast over the radio in 1938, students come to understand that these questions—though different in the era of social media—are not new. Evaluating Americans' competencies to sift through the bombardment of media aimed at drawing them in, entertaining them, and shaping their knowledge and attitudes—all at the same time—is as old and relevant as the media themselves. As active participants in the American political process, students need and demand these key skills.

GREATER INCLUSIVENESS The fourth reason you and your students will find this book useful is just as important and closely connected to the politically engaged approach in this book, and the tools used to achieve it. This book embraces inclusivity throughout, both so that *all students* will find their identities and voices validated and because an inclusive approach also reinforces core concepts and skills. In this book, diversity is not a list of boxes to check off. Americans' diverse identities have powerfully shaped political processes and outcomes even when not successful in any given struggle.

For example, an exploration of political campaigns and elections becomes more immediate through a thoughtful examination of the ways in which political parties are struggling to attract the Latino/a vote (and questioning the existence of such a monolithic entity), and efforts by Latino candidates themselves, in an era of profound demographic change. The chapter on Congress focuses on two election years that have been called "the year of the woman": 2018 and 1992. Not only does a focus on women running for, joining, and navigating Congress allow for a deeper analysis of congressional representation than more formulaic approaches, but it also reinforces and makes relatable traditional coverage of constituency, congressional rules and institutions, and the legislative process.

Through the power of narrative, my goal is that all students reading and using this book will find that they are also a part of the American experience, whether or not their voices have been heard. They will also be assisted in understanding the complexities of American government in ways that will endure once the semester is long over.

ORGANIZATION OF THE BOOK

TOOLS FOR REAL-WORLD ENGAGEMENT

By now you've noticed that *American Government: Stories of a Nation* approaches American politics a little bit differently than other introductory textbooks. Still, if you look at the table of contents, you'll see that the text covers everything you'd expect and require in a book that primes your students for future engagement in the political world, or, perhaps, future study in the field. You'll also notice that this book covers topics having to do with political participation and behavior before it covers institutions, which is a natural outgrowth of the fact that we highlight the role that real people have played in the development of our government—although the chapters could certainly be assigned out of order to suit your preferences.

Part I, Chapters 1 through 5, therefore, covers foundations, beginning with an introduction to the central themes in American politics (Chapter 1), then covering the Constitution (Chapter 2), federalism (Chapter 3), civil liberties (Chapter 4), and civil rights (Chapter 5). Chapters 6 through 10, Part II, "Political Behavior and Mass Politics," covers participation (Chapter 6), public opinion (Chapter 7), the media (Chapter 8), parties (Chapter 9), campaigns and elections (Chapter 10), and interest groups and social movements (Chapter 11). The chapters in Part III cover political institutions: Congress (Chapter 12), the presidency (Chapter 13), bureaucracy (Chapter 14), and the judiciary (Chapter 15).

THE CASE STUDIES: DEEP DIVES INTO REAL POLITICS

As you'll soon discover, this textbook harnesses the power of stories, both in the service of engaging students with the core concepts and skills and in showing them how others—in times present and past—have charted their own courses to shape and reshape American government.

One of the key tools in this goal is the use of case studies, extended narrative sections focusing on real-world action in American politics, in each chapter, each with clearly defined learning objectives to guide students in their reading. These narratives are not used as marginal introductory elements that serve only as gateways into the main material, nor just as examples that extend the lessons, but as key elements of the text itself. As a teacher of undergraduates for many years here at the University of Minnesota, my experience has been that students often read right past the chapter-opening vignettes in their textbooks. I'll bet you have had that same, frustrating experience. It's not because those brief intros are poorly written or boring, either; it's that students know these supplemental narratives are, by design, peripheral and might be skipped to get to the real testable content. That is a real missed opportunity for them to learn and remember core concepts but also to understand how individual choices shape outcomes.

Narratives are powerful things. They help shape the political world in which we each live. They help define who we are as individuals and as a people. And stories are also excellent teaching tools, making the material relatable, memorable, and real. This book harnesses the full power of narrative to draw students into the study of American politics, highlighting the unpredictable outcomes of people's actions and strategies—both of individuals and of groups of individuals acting together.

How does this approach work in practice? In the chapter on public opinion, I focus the narrative on the aftermath of the fatal police shooting of Michael Brown in Ferguson, Missouri, in 2014. The basic questions are these: Has public opinion about the way African Americans are treated by police changed since that event and others related to it? And, if so, does public opinion, or changes in public opinion, matter to American public policy?

The chapter begins by setting up the story, focusing on the one-year anniversary of the tragic event. Learning objectives guide students to a full set of issues that political scientists consider when presenting the topic of American public opinion—assessing the components and formation of opinions, ways of measuring it, patterns of change in people's attitudes, and the larger meaning and impact of public opinion in American democracy.

The nuts-and-bolts sections of the chapter—each, like the case study, with attached learning objectives (see below)—explore debates over the stability, coherence, and meaning of public opinion, the ways in which public opinion is measured, its importance to representative democracy, and the challenges inherent in scientific polling, and political socialization. Like every chapter, this one also has a comprehensive guide for review that connects the learning objectives, take-home points of the stories, major political science themes, and key terms to help students confirm that they have fully comprehended the chapter.

The exploration of public opinion concludes by bringing the discussion of Ferguson and its effects into the present with an examination of public opinion on the tragic events of Charlottesville, Virginia, in 2017 as well as the national anthem protests by Colin Kaepernick and other players in the NFL. Students examine how the lens of the events of Ferguson may or may not have changed how Americans viewed police–community relations.

As you can see, no political science content gets "lost" at the expense of the case studies—and with plenty of built-in guidance, no student gets lost in the narrative.

"PRACTICING POLITICAL SCIENCE" FEATURE BOXES: CRITICALLY CONSIDERING DATA, IMAGE, AND TEXT IN POLITICAL PERSUASION

This book acknowledges the challenges of dealing with the political world that students will inevitably have to confront in their own lives. To that end, it also provides students with specific skills with which to bring the deeper understandings they will develop to bear on their own political realities. Each chapter includes two "Practicing Political Science" boxes designed to assist students in becoming more capable and critical readers of arguments made through data, image, and text.

In an increasingly data-driven world, the ability to act as a critical interpreter of data, and perhaps most importantly of the stories told based on the sometimes-competing interpretations of those data, is a fundamental skill. Data, and their interpretation, constitute an exercise of power. Students will critically reflect on how the data were obtained, how they were interpreted and displayed, and how political narratives were constructed around them. In doing so, students will engage with the use of data to advance a particular political objective and become more thoughtful and critical readers of the stories constructed around numbers and statistics.

In the data-based "Practicing" feature in the chapter on public opinion, called "Looking for a 'Break in Trend' in Data and Drawing Conclusions over Time," for example, I present data from the Pew Research Center on perceptions of how important it is for the nation to make changes to secure equal rights. The data are broken down by respondents' racial identities. Between 2014 and 2015, immediately following Ferguson and related protests, both African American and white public opinion appeared to shift toward increasing support for needed changes. The "What Do You Think?" section asks students to reflect upon what other kinds of evidence might be useful to confirm that the events of 2014–2015 caused the apparent shift in opinion. In doing so, students are guided to reflect on possible "breaks in trend" in longitudinal survey data.

Image literacy is as crucial to the pedagogical objectives of this book as textual literacy. Instead of offering images solely as illustrative enhancements to the text, the book also examines the ways in which images themselves have played and continue to play a role in the development of American government and politics. Political stories are told not only through text, especially in a political space increasingly driven by social media. Through a critical presentation of the use of images, students will gain skills in interpreting images as they gain a deeper understanding of the political world of which they are part, and which they will help to shape.

As an example, the second "Practicing" feature box in the chapter on public opinion, subtitled "The *St. Louis Post-Dispatch* Changes Its Cover Photo," explores the changes the editors and publishers of that paper made to its front-page photograph within a few hours on the one-year anniversary of Michael Brown's shooting and the protests on that day. Because of another shooting of a young African American man on the evening following the peaceful demonstrations, those in charge chose to dramatically alter the next day's front page. The feature's "What Do You Think?" section asks students to place themselves in the position of a newspaper editor covering a highly controversial event in order to encourage them to think about the social and political ramifications of these decisions that are made every day.

Finally, students are guided in critical analyses of text and text-based arguments. For example, in the chapter on the bureaucracy, which focuses on the federal response to twenty-first century hurricanes, students hear and respond to the congressional testimony of residents of New Orleans in the aftermath of Katrina wherein they leveled accusations that the government's response was inequitable and biased especially against poor, black residents.

Each chapter in the book includes one "Practicing" feature focusing on data analysis and one focused on either the use of image or text—including counternarratives that challenge "conventional wisdom."

OTHER FEATURES THAT REINFORCE THE FUNDAMENTALS

Several other features of the book also serve to reinforce the nuts-and-bolts materials and also help students understand why the chosen narratives will help them gain a deeper and more memorable understanding of this material.

- **Learning Objectives** at the start of each chapter guide students' reading of and engagement with the material, signposting the goals and setting clear expectations for what they will master. Each main section of the chapter is attached to a specific learning objective. While the nuts-and-bolts sections are accompanied by learning objectives designed to signpost key terms and concepts, those associated with the case studies link to the deeper concepts associated with the material.

- Each section ends with a brief **What Have I Learned?** quiz (with an answer key) so that students can gauge their comprehension, ensure they understand concepts, and know they are making connections between key terms and broader questions.

- **Chapter Review** sections conclude each chapter by offering students additional opportunities to review core concepts, connect them to the stories, think critically about the issues, and master key terms—all helpfully framed around the chapter's learning objectives. The chapter reviews conclude with "Think" subsections designed to encourage discussion and reflection and to help students place themselves within the considerations raised in the chapter.

AN APPROACH THAT WORKS FOR TEACHERS AND STUDENTS

I have had the privilege of teaching incarcerated youths, homeless adolescents, fourth graders, seventh graders, undergraduates, and graduate students. Across all of these experiences, I have learned that narrative is a powerful educational tool. People are born to be storytellers and story-hearers; it seems to be in our makeup. We are wired to respond to narrative and its ability to convey the contingency, complexity, and uncertainty of collective human action, and the hopes of what might be accomplished if it succeeds. Our students care about these stories. They are also already talking about them—all the time. My goal, in this book, is to give students both a framework and a set of tools with which to discuss the complexities and contradictions of American government and politics. The stories told within this book will resonate with and engage your students. They are not sugarcoated. This book does not shy away from the difficult issues with which your students are already dealing.

Over the last few years, we have taken the time to ask hundreds of college students to respond to a set of survey questions after conducting a class-test of several draft chapters of the book and receiving feedback from adopters of the first edition. Here is what just a handful of students have said about how well they thought the book's approach works. Note that these are unedited—real students' own words:

I want to keep reading

I LOVED how I could relate more to the examples or there were more recent issues on public opinion that I saw first-hand like the news, such as the Ferguson incident. I would say the biggest strengths of this book are keeping the readers engaged. It does not feel like an ordinary American Government textbook . . . which is very important if you want your students to actually read.

It was very easy for me to connect the stories to the overall concepts of the chapter which is critical in a textbook. Student are usually not thrilled about being forced to read chapter after chapter of information on American Government but this approach lightens that burden. Bravo.

I was very engaged with this approach. I thought it was extremely helpful and interesting. I agree one hundred percent with the stories and this method because it got my attention.

This textbook excites me as it speaks of issues that have happened recently that I have actually lived to experience.

The stories (specially as a woman and a minority) most definitely helped me connect the concept to the story. I like the stories that were used because they were interesting and I haven't heard of them before.

[I] enjoyed this approach. It made this book more pleasurable to read. I could put myself in the shoes of these women [in Congress] at the time and get a better understanding of the mindset of the time. It's encouraging to read the stories and see that though the odds were against them, they didn't give up. They're not made up stories but real women with real issues and had the drive to push forward despite the obstacles.

Stories that are devoid of people, their actions, aspirations, and mistakes are not very interesting. Fortunately, as teachers of American government, we rarely encounter stories like that. The political world that we teach our students about is vibrant, fascinating, and charged. The description of the chapter content above and a glance at the table of contents of the book show that this book takes up stories that emerge directly from that political world, stories that will draw your students into a real understanding of their political world, and their place in it.

That is why stories are such powerful things.

SUPPORTING YOUR TEACHING

This textbook comes with a host of resources to help both instructors and students get the most out of this class. For some, the book alone will provide a rich and engaging experience. But, more likely, you may want to avail yourself of some of the following.

SAGE edge is a robust online environment featuring an impressive array of tools and resources for review, study, and further exploration, keeping both instructors and students on the cutting edge of teaching and learning. SAGE edge content is open access and available on demand. Learning and teaching has never been easier! We gratefully acknowledge Jeneen Hobby, Cleveland State University; Andrew Levin, Harper College; Hyung Lae Park, El Paso Community College; Nick Pyeatt, Penn State Altoona; John Seymour, El Paso Community College; and Theresa Marchant-Shapiro, Southern Connecticut State University, for developing the ancillaries on this site.

SAGE edge for Students at **http://edge.sagepub.com/abernathy2e** provides a personalized approach to help students accomplish their coursework goals in an easy-to-use learning environment.

- **Chapter summaries** with **learning objectives** reinforce the most important material.

- Mobile-friendly **eFlashcards** strengthen understanding of key terms and concepts, and make it easy to maximize your study time, anywhere, anytime.

- Mobile-friendly practice **quizzes** allow you to assess how much you've learned and where you need to focus your attention.

- Carefully selected **video resources** bring concepts to life, are tied to learning objectives, and make learning easier.

- **Exclusive access to influential SAGE journal and reference content** ties important research and scholarship to chapter concepts to strengthen learning.

SAGE edge for Instructors at **http://edge.sagepub.com/abernathy2e** supports teaching by making it easy to integrate quality content and create a rich learning environment for students.

- The **Test bank**, built on Bloom's taxonomy (with Bloom's cognitive domain and difficulty level noted for each question), is created specifically for this text, with references to chapter learning objectives (and page numbers) and ExamView test generation. It includes more than 1,500 multiple-choice, short-answer, essay, fill-in-the-blank, and true/false questions, as well as the opportunity to edit any question and/or insert personalized questions to effectively assess students' progress and understanding.

- **Sample course syllabi** provide suggested models for structuring your course.

- Editable, chapter-specific **PowerPoint® slides** offer complete flexibility for creating a multimedia presentation for the course, so you don't have to start from scratch but can customize to your exact needs.

- An **instructor's manual** features chapter overviews and learning objectives, lecture starters, ideas for class activities, and discussion questions.

- A set of all the **graphics from the text**, including all the maps, tables, and figures in PowerPoint, PDF, and JPG formats, are provided for class presentations.

- Carefully selected chapter-by-chapter **video and multimedia content** enhances classroom-based exploration of key topics.

ENRICHED LEARNING THROUGH TECHNOLOGY

Students today are connected, wired, and networked in ways previous generations could not have imagined, and they process information in ways that go way beyond reading the printed word on a paper page. To keep up with them and their quickly evolving world, *American Government: Stories of a Nation* is also a fully integrated multimedia experience. When students purchase a new print copy of the book, they receive **FREE access** to an enhanced eBook. This interactive eBook uses the VitalSource Bookshelf®, where students can read the eBook online, on any device, and download it to read offline. They can also share notes and highlights with instructors and classmates, and "follow" friends and instructors as they make their own notes and highlights. Through a series of annotated icons on select pages, students can quickly link to multimedia on the page where a topic is discussed, connected to articles and background pieces, to audio clips of interviews, to video clips of news stories or satirical commentary, to reference and biography material, to CQ Researcher policy backgrounder reports, and to important current data on such topics as approval ratings and public opinion polls.

In addition to the curated multimedia content discussed above, two exciting types of **SAGE Premium Video** truly set this eBook apart:

- **Topics in American Government** videos recap the fundamentals of American politics in every chapter—from the Bill of Rights to voter turnout to the powers of the presidency. Each animated video is paired with chapter learning objectives and tied to assessment in our SAGE coursepacks, offering a more complete way to **reinforce mastery of key concepts** while meeting your students' diverse learning styles.

- **American Government News Clips** bring extra coverage of current events into the book, connecting multiple two- to four-minute news clips to core chapter content. With multiple-choice assessment in **SAGE coursepacks**, these clips offer an ideal way for students to practice using higher-level analysis and application skills to apply chapter concepts to recent political events.

All together, these resources allow students to explore an important topic or idea while reading—a reinforcing exercise as well as vetted content that provides depth and added context. It's an enhanced, enriching, and interactive learning experience.

SAGE COURSEPACKS FOR INSTRUCTORS

The **SAGE coursepack** for *American Government: Stories of a Nation* makes it easy to import our quality instructor materials and student resources into your school's learning management system (LMS), such as Blackboard, Canvas, Brightspace by D2L, or Moodle. Intuitive and simple to use, **SAGE coursepack** allows you to integrate only the content you need, with minimal effort, and requires no access code. Don't use an LMS platform? You can still access many of the online resources for *American Government: Stories of a Nation* via the **SAGE edge** site.

Available SAGE content through the coursepack includes:

- Pedagogically robust **assessment tools** that foster review, practice, and critical thinking and offer a more complete way to measure student engagement, including:

  ○ Diagnostic chapter **pretests and posttests** that identify opportunities for improvement, track student progress, and ensure mastery of key learning objectives.

  ○ **Test banks** built on Bloom's taxonomy that provide a diverse range of test items with ExamView test generation.

  ○ **Activity and quiz options** that allow you to choose only the assignments and tests you want.

  ○ **Instructions** on how to use and integrate the comprehensive assessments and resources provided.

- **Chapter-specific discussion questions** to help launch engaging classroom interaction while reinforcing important content.

- **Assessment questions for SAGE Premium Video** from the interactive eBook that offer high-quality video assignments and test students on comprehension as well as analysis and application.

- **Assignable data exercises** in each chapter that help students build essential data literacy skills using interactive data visualization tools from **SAGE Stats** and **U.S. Political Stats**. Drawing on key data series ranging from demographic patterns to state budgets to voting behavior, these exercises offer students a dynamic way to analyze real-world data and think critically about the stories behind the numbers.

- Additional **video resources** that bring concepts to life, are tied to learning objectives, and make learning easier.

- EXCLUSIVE, influential **SAGE journal and reference content**, built into course materials and assessment tools, that ties important research and scholarship to chapter concepts to strengthen learning.

- Editable, chapter-specific **PowerPoint®** slides that offer flexibility when creating multimedia lectures so you don't have to start from scratch but can customize to your exact needs.

- **Integrated links to the interactive eBook** that make it easy for your students to maximize their study time with this "anywhere, anytime," mobile-friendly version of the text. The eBook also offers access to more digital tools and resources, including **SAGE Premium Video**.

- **All tables and figures** from the textbook.

A number of instructors helped guide the development of the above resources. We appreciate the time and thought our reviewers put into their feedback, which has helped us refine the material and ensure that we provide content useful to both instructors and students. We offer special thanks to Kathleen Cole, Metropolitan State University; Justin S. Vaughn, Boise State University; and to:

Richard A. Almeida, Francis Marion University

John A. Aughenbaugh, Virginia Commonwealth University

Madelyn P. Bowman, Tarrant County College, South Campus

Marla Brettschneider, University of New Hampshire

Mark A. Cichock, University of Texas at Arlington

Amy Colon, SUNY Sullivan

Victoria Cordova, Sam Houston State University

Kevin Davis, North Central Texas College

Michael J. Faber, Texas State University

Terry Filicko, Clark State Community College

Patrick Gilbert, Lone Star College

Andrew Green, Central College

Sally Hansen, Daytona State College

Alyx D. Mark, North Central College

David F. McClendon, Tyler Junior College

Michael P. McConachie, Collin College

Patrick Moore, Richland College

Tracy Osborn, University of Iowa

Carl Palmer, Illinois State University

Melodie Pickett, Tarleton State University

Daniel E. Ponder, Drury University

Nicholas L. Pyeatt, Penn State Altoona

Paul Rozycki, Mott Community College

Deron T. Schreck, Moraine Valley Community College

Tony Wohlers, Cameron University

The journey to retaining and applying course content differs for every student. To successfully navigate this journey, course goals should remain clear, consistent, and constructive. For instructors, the ability to track and measure individual progress is vital to ensuring student success.

SAGE | CQ Press is invested in mapping measurable course outcomes to chapter-level learning objectives for all of our introductory textbook offerings through **SAGE course outcomes**. Each of our titles is crafted with specific course outcomes in mind, vetted by leading advisors in the field, and adapted from renowned syllabi from across the country.

AMERICAN GOVERNMENT

COURSE OUTCOMES
for **AMERICAN GOVERNMENT.**
Upon successful completion of this course, students will be able to:

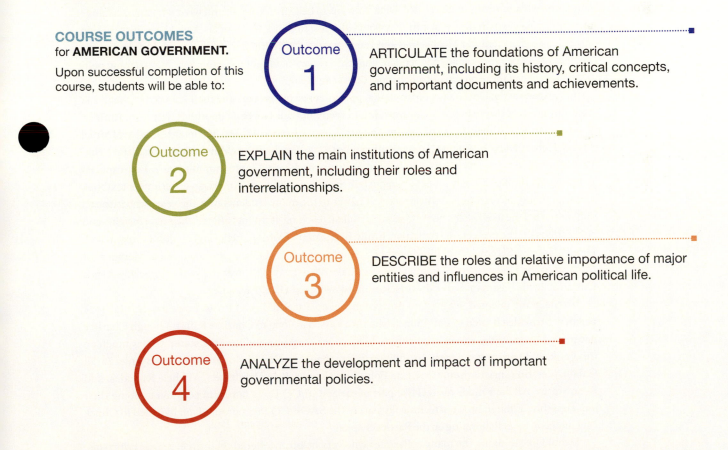

Outcome 1
ARTICULATE the foundations of American government, including its history, critical concepts, and important documents and achievements.

Outcome 2
EXPLAIN the main institutions of American government, including their roles and interrelationships.

Outcome 3
DESCRIBE the roles and relative importance of major entities and influences in American political life.

Outcome 4
ANALYZE the development and impact of important governmental policies.

FOR STUDENTS, understanding the objectives for each chapter and the goals for the course is essential for getting the grade you deserve!

FOR INSTRUCTORS, being able to track your students' progress allows you to more easily pinpoint areas of improvement and report out on success.

Tracking student progress can be challenging—promoting success should never be.

Want to see how these outcomes tie in with this book's chapter-level objectives?
Visit us at **https://edge.sagepub.com/abernathy2e** for complete outcome-to-objective mapping.

ACKNOWLEDGMENTS

There are many, many people who have helped to make this book a reality, some of whom probably have, or had, no idea that they did so. I am grateful to all of them. Just as the Ninth Amendment makes it clear that Americans' fundamental rights and freedoms can never be fully enumerated, this will be a necessarily incomplete statement of my gratitude.

First, I would like to thank some of my teachers over the years. I owe a great debt to William S. Kilborne Jr. for teaching me how to write and to William Voss and Sharon Foster for inspiring a group of middle-school students to explore the natural and social worlds and to embrace the wonderful uncertainly of being outside of our comfort zones. I would like to also thank David Schaafsma for teaching me why stories matter and how they can change the world, as well as Sisters Luke and Priscilla from the Missionaries of Charity in Calcutta and Ellen Maling of Bridge Over Troubled Waters in Boston, who taught me what it means to do service, what it means to be a professional, and what it means to change the world, one very small step at a time. I would also like to thank R. Douglas Arnold, my dissertation adviser, as well as Jennifer Hochschild and Larry Bartels for their mentorship. John J. DiIulio Jr., in a small conference room for an independent study at Princeton, taught me American bureaucratic politics. I owe each of these professors much more than I can repay.

Colleagues at the University of Minnesota, past and present, have offered their knowledge, feedback, and support over the years: Teri Caraway, John Freeman, Paul Goren, Timothy R. Johnson, Andrew Karch, Daniel Kelliher, Howard Lavine, Nancy Luxon, Joanne Miller, Michael Minta, C. Daniel Myers, Robert Nichols, August Nimtz, Kathryn Pearson, Wendy Rahn, Martin Sampson, Peter Seim, Paul Soper, Joe Soss, Dara Strolovitch, John Sullivan, and Joan Tronto, among many. I owe special thanks to W. Phillips Shively for not trying to talk me out of writing an American government textbook and supporting me throughout the process. Thanks to the many students over the years who inspired and motivated me to write the book. Graduate student teaching assistants offered their own insights and suggestions on the project, in particular: Emily Baer, Adam Dahl, Ashley English, John Greenwood, Daniel Habchi, Serena Laws, Eli Meyerhoff, Zein Murib, Adam Olson, and Paul Snell. Members of the staff in the Department of Political Science have been invaluable over the years, especially Alexis Cuttance, Jessie Eastman, Kyle Edwards, Rose Miskowiec, and Becky Mooney.

To the many talented, warm, and professional people at SAGE/CQ Press, I owe much. The book began with an idea floated to Earl Pingel, who then passed it along to Charisse Kiino. Though Charisse has moved on from the role of acquisitions editor to other responsibilities, her stamp is very much on this book, and I am grateful for it. In addition, many thanks to Gail Bushman, Matthew Byrnie, Sarah Calabi, Kerstin Christiansen, Christina Fohl, Eric Garner, Jade Henderson, Michele Rhoades, and Rose Storey. All have made me feel like part of the SAGE/CQ Press family in addition to doing their jobs superbly. Though he is not technically part of the SAGE/CQ Press group, I am indebted to Chuck McCutcheon for collaborating on the Parties chapter.

I would like to thank the many colleagues who very helpfully offered their time, praise, criticisms, and support throughout the process of writing this book. They offered feedback in reviews, surveys, focus groups, and class testing. In addition to several who wish to remain anonymous, they include:

Milan Andrejevich, Ivy Tech Community College

Stephen Anthony, Georgia State University

Juan Arzola, College of the Sequoias

Yan Bai, Grand Rapids Community College

Kathleen Barrett, University of West Georgia

Patricia Bodelson, St. Cloud State University

Seth Bordner, Kent State University

Christopher Borick, Muhlenberg College

Madelyn Bowman, Tarrant County College South

Mark Brewer, University of Maine

Jeffrey Brown, Wayne County Community College

Susan Burgess, Ohio University

Timothy Campbell, Labette Community College

Mary Carver, Longwood College

Kimberly Casey, Northwest Missouri State University

LaTasha Chaffin, College of Charleston

Ben Christ, Harrisburg Area Community College

Dewey Clayton, University of Louisville

Diana Cohen, Central Connecticut State University

Kathleen Cole, Metropolitan State University

Todd Collins, Western Carolina University

Michael Coulter, Grove City College

Kevin Davis, North Central Texas College

Chris Deis, DePaul University, Lincoln Campus

Joseph S. Devaney, East Georgia State College

Richardson Dilworth, Drexel University

Agber Dimah, Chicago State University

Cristina Dragomir, SUNY Oswego

Lauren Elliott-Dorans, Ohio State University

Bond Faulwell, Johnson County Community College

Daniel Franklin, Georgia State University

John Frendreis, Loyola University of Chicago

Maria Garcia-Acevedo, California State University Northridge

Sarah Gershon, Georgia State University

Tobias Gibson, Westminster College

Patrick Gilbert, Lone Star College

Andra Gillespie, Emory University

Frederick Gordon, Columbus State University

George Gordon, Illinois Wesleyan University

Andrea Graff, Lincoln Land Community College

Greg Granger, Northwestern State University of Louisiana

Matthew Gritter, Angelo State University

Gloria Guevara, California State University Northridge

Homer Guevara, Northwest Vista College

Paul Henri Gurian, University of Georgia

Mel Hailey, Abilene Christian University

Therese M. Hammond, Pennsylvania State University Lehigh Valley

Jeneen Hobby, Cleveland State University

Tom Hoffman, Spring Hill College

Michael Hoover, Seminole Community College

Jennifer Hopper, Washington College

JoyAnna Hopper, University of Missouri

Tony Horton, Arkansas State University

Mark Jendrysik, University of North Dakota

Caitlin Jewitt, Virginia Tech

April Johnson, University of Illinois at Chicago

Gabe Jolivet, Ashford University

Jeff Justice, Tarleton State University

Mily Kao, Mesa Community College

Kimberly Keenan, City College of San Francisco

Christopher Kelley, Miami University

Athena King, Eastern Michigan University

John Klemanski, Oakland University

Lisa Krasner, Truckee Meadows Community College

Andrew Levin, Harper College

La Della Levy, College of Southern Nevada Henderson Campus

Eric Lomazoff, Villanova University

Benjamin Lundgren, Santa Clara University

James Malone, Hillsborough Community College

Mack Mariani, Xavier University

Alyx Mark, North Central College

Shane Martin, Fitchburg State University

Wendy Martinek, Binghamton University

Valerie Martinez-Ebers, University of North Texas

Michael McConachie, Collin College

Karen McCurdy, Georgia Southern University

Mary McHugh, Merrimack College

Stephen Meinhold, University of North Carolina, Wilmington

Melissa Merry, University of Louisville

Keesha Middlemass, Trinity University

Mark Miller, Clark University

Patrick Moore, Richland College

Samantha Mosier, Missouri State University

Brian Naples, Panola College

Sharon A. Navarro, University of Texas at San Antonio

Brian Newman, Pepperdine University

Timothy Nokken, Texas Tech University

Hyung Park, El Paso Community College

Sara Parker, Chabot College

Scott Parker, Sierra College

Lisa Perez-Nichols, Austin Community College

Robert Peters, Western Michigan University

Clarissa Peterson, DePauw University

William Pierros, Concordia University Chicago

Blayne Primozich, El Paso Community College

Elizabeth Prough, Madonna University

Nicholas Pyeatt, Pennsylvania State University, Altoona

Judd Quarles, Tyler Junior College

Andree Reeves, University of Alabama, Huntsville

Ted Ritter, John Tyler Community College

Joseph Robbins, Shepherd University

Jason Robles, Colorado State University

Michelle Rodriguez, San Diego Mesa College

Jon Ross, City Colleges of Chicago

Paul Rozycki, Mott Community College

Mikhail Rybalko, Texas Tech University

Ray Sandoval, Richland College

Erich Saphir, Pima Community College

Scot Schraufnagel, Northern Illinois University

Deron Schreck, Moraine Valley Community College

Eric Schwartz, Hagerstown Community College

Allen Settle, California Polytechnic State University

John Seymour, El Paso Community College

Brent Sharp, University of Central Oklahoma

Amy Shriver Dreussi, University of Akron

Abha Singh, University of Texas, El Paso

Sue Ann Skipworth, University of Mississippi

Nate Steffen, Bismarck State College

Gwyn Sutherland, Elizabethtown Community and Technical College

Bob Switky, Sonoma State University

Barry Tadlock, Ohio University

Chris Thuot, SUNY Onondaga Community College

Anip Uppal, Central New Mexico Community College

Troy Vidal, Columbus State University

Danny Vyain, Ivy Tech Community College

Kimball Waites, Big Bend Community College

Adam Warber, Clemson University

Jessica Webb, Kalamazoo Valley Community College

Zach Wilhide, Tidewater Community College

Mark Williams, St. Charles Community College

Claire Wofford, College of Charleston

Tony Wohlers, Cameron University

Patrick Wohlfarth, University of Maryland

Laura Wood, Tarrant County College

Tyler Young, Collin College

Kimberly Zagorski, University of Wisconsin–Stout

Penultimately, I am deeply grateful to the other members of our little band: Rachel Keith, on copyediting; Tracy Buyan, on production; Erica DeLuca and Jennifer Jones, on marketing and warning me about playing Texas Hold'em with Michele Sordi (senior vice president); Scott Harris, on digital production and pedagogy, often in ways unexpected; Monica Eckman, on publishing, vision, and faith in and advocacy for the project; and Elise Frasier, on development editing, llama communications, and being a "human/genius."

This book is theirs as much as it is mine.

Finally, I would like to thank friends and family: Mark Dailey, Erik Ness, and other buttheads. Also, the members of the Knox Block ring. They are my friends; their kids are like cousins to mine, and fire pits rule. My family, Mom, Julie, and Jeannette, to whom I am deeply thankful, and at times apologetic for randomly timed phone calls seeking support and discussing the history of central Asia and/or the Dallas Cowboys. Russell and Sadie, who have grown—too quickly—into wonderful and wonderfully different people. And lastly my wife, Sara: In spite of the hours, days, and weeks away from you and the kids, I am still here, and I am still yours.

Scott
Minneapolis, Minnesota
November 2018

ABOUT THE AUTHOR

Scott F. Abernathy was born and raised in Fort Worth, Texas. While an undergraduate at Dartmouth College, he volunteered for three months with Mother Teresa's Missionaries of Charity in Calcutta, India. After graduation, hoping to do service work closer to home, Scott worked as an on-street counselor with homeless adolescents in Boston, Massachusetts.

Scott then received a master of curriculum and Instruction and taught fourth and seventh grades in Wisconsin public schools. Hoping to learn more about the underlying systems that drove the educational outcomes he was trying to change, Scott completed an MPA in domestic policy and then a PhD in politics from Princeton University. Scott is now an associate professor of political science and a University Distinguished Teaching Professor at the University of Minnesota. He is also the author of *School Choice and the Future of American Democracy* and *No Child Left Behind and the Public Schools*, both from University of Michigan Press.

His current research explores the ways in which members of interest groups and social movements use narrative in text, speech, and image to reframe and socially reconstruct their populations in the service of agenda setting and policy implementation. The work focuses on disability rights policy in the United States.

While Scott says that being a street outreach worker was the most transforming job he ever had, he admits that the chance to teach students, not in a subway stop or a squat, but through the writing of this textbook, is pretty cool as well.

AMERICAN

Second Edition

GOVERNMENT

The Essentials

CHAPTER 1

AMERICAN POLITICAL STORIES

Claiming Rights, Demanding to Be Heard

▼ Hearing-impaired new U.S. citizen Willy Theodorice (left), 26, born in Haiti, stands alongside sworn-in citizens in Miami in December 2015. Their stories of immigration are part of the American political story: people claiming their constitutional rights and asking to be counted.

Carl Juste/Miami Herald/TNS via Getty Images

In my undergraduate Introduction to American Government course here at the University of Minnesota, on the first day of class, I tell my students, "I don't care *what* you think," which does tend to generate some uncomfortable silence. But I mean it. Before things get too out of hand, though, I quickly follow up with, "However, I care very much about *how* you think. That is what this course is about."

This book is no different. My hope is that you will use this book to question what everyone tells you that you *should* know or think, to become more confident in making your own ideas known, and to sharpen your ability to interpret for yourself the political world around you. This book uses stories to help accomplish those goals. These stories are very much a central part of the book's structure and objectives. In each chapter, you will be presented with stories that illustrate important concepts in the study of American politics. They are meant to make those ideas come to life—to help you understand that American government is not something that exists apart from you. And because they are *real* stories, in all their messy, complicated glory, they will also encourage you and your classmates to think in ways that are not either/or and to walk in the shoes of people who may be very different from you.

This book, therefore, is going to be difficult at times, although not in the sense of being difficult to read and follow—far from that, I hope. I mean that many of the stories don't have clear heroines, heroes, or villains. Hardly any of them have tidy endings. In this book, I will quote individuals whose words or ideas some will strongly disagree with, maybe even find objectionable. This book will not offer any one political, theoretical, or academic perspective. There will be no magic wand waved in the final chapter of this book that announces, "Here! We've got it!" Welcome to the world of American politics and government.

Read the stories; absorb the nuts-and-bolts facts and concepts that emerge along the way in these chapters. Most importantly, however, connect the two. Use the stories to more deeply understand the complexity of American politics, then and now. Use them to understand the diversity of the voices that are a part of the national conversation. Use the stories to make your own voices stronger, better informed, more politically savvy, and more effective.

LEARNING OBJECTIVES

By reading this chapter, you will be able to do the following:

 1.1 Explain how diverse Americans have been able to use the same political tools to achieve their own distinct visions of good government.

1.2 Define the key elements of American political culture.

 1.3 Identify the political, social, and economic events and institutions that gave rise to the American Revolution and reflect upon what was and was not achieved.

1.4 Describe the core features of American political institutions.

1.5 Consider the ways in which the "Letter from Birmingham Jail" draws upon core American ideals.

In this chapter and in the book generally, we raise fundamental questions when we try to define what we mean by a "good government" or a bad one. Whose rights get protected? Whose get restricted? How do these questions get resolved? Who gets to decide? The stories told in this book illustrate how big questions like these are resolved, revisited, and reresolved through **politics**, the process of influencing the actions and policies of a **government**. Politics and government are closely connected, but they are not the same thing. Politics describes processes; government describes the rules and institutions that arise from political action and conflict and that structure future political action. Throughout the book, we'll hear from people who have engaged with those institutions and who have taken part in those processes.

We will begin with two stories: one about a young woman in Nebraska who fought for the right to establish a Christian Bible study group at her school and the other about a group of Kentucky students who claimed their right to establish a gay-straight alliance (GSA). We will then go back in time to the American Revolution and Thomas Jefferson's drafting of the Declaration of Independence, and conclude by fast-forwarding to Dr. Martin Luther King Jr.'s "Letter from Birmingham Jail."

politics
the process of influencing the actions of officials and the policies of a nation, state, locality, or community.

government
a system of rules and institutions that defines and shapes the contours of public action.

What could these stories possibly have in common? In them we will witness the efforts of vastly different people who have wrestled with what fundamental rights mean in American democracy and see how they as individuals and groups have tried to answer that question, staking their own claims upon their rights.

AMERICAN STUDENTS CLAIM THEIR RIGHTS

• **Explain how diverse Americans have been able to use the same political tools to achieve their own distinct visions of good government.**

Bridget Mergens walked into the office of her school principal in Omaha, Nebraska, with a request. She wanted to start a student group—a Christian Bible study club.

"I thought he liked me and I was sure he'd say yes," Mergens later recounted.[1] As one reporter noted, "Principal James Findley did like her . . . but he didn't say yes. 'An informal get-together over lunch at the cafeteria would be fine,' Findley [recalled] saying, 'but a school-sponsored club? Don't ask me that, Bridget, because I have a problem with that.'"[2]

Mergens's high school sponsored many other extracurricular clubs, including a photography club and a scuba diving club. Was her proposal fundamentally different from these sanctioned student groups?

This became a question with which her principal and her local school board had to wrestle, and they ultimately denied her request. To Mergens, the school board's arguments were fundamentally flawed.

The legal basis of Mergens's claim was a national law, the Equal Access Act (EAA), which was passed in 1984. The law's primary intent is to restrict the ability of public high schools to exclude faith-based religious extracurricular clubs. The act states, "It shall be unlawful for any public secondary school which receives Federal financial assistance . . . to deny equal access or a fair opportunity to, or discriminate against, any students who wish to conduct a meeting . . . on the basis of the religious, political, philosophical, or other content of the speech at such meetings."[3]

In 1981, prior to the act's passage, the U.S. Supreme Court had already affirmed these rights for students at public colleges and universities, but it had not yet done so for those in public high schools. As Mergens's case proceeded, it was far from certain that the Court would now affirm those same rights for high school students. The reason was the potential "impressionability of high school" students compared to those in college and beyond.[4] Would high school students be mature enough to distinguish between their

First Liberty Institute

▲ Liz Loverde, a sophomore at Wantagh High School in Long Island, New York, in 2014. Loverde successfully pressured her school to allow a Christian Bible study club, thus following in the footsteps of others, such as Bridget Mergens, in claiming rights under the Equal Access Act (EAA).

school's efforts to provide an open forum for voices and the possibility that the school itself endorsed the club members' beliefs?

In June 1990, five years after Bridget Mergens tried to start the Bible club, the Supreme Court ruled in her favor. The Court upheld high school students' rights to the same access for their faith-based extracurricular clubs as that granted to other student groups. It also upheld the constitutionality of the EAA. In her majority opinion in *Board of Education of Westside Community Schools v. Mergens*, Supreme Court justice Sandra Day O'Connor wrote, "There is a crucial difference between government and private speech endorsing religion, and, as Congress recognized in passing the Act, high school students are mature enough and are likely to understand that a school does not endorse or support student speech that it merely permits on a nondiscriminatory basis."[5]

To some, Mergens's efforts harkened back to the civil rights movement, in which African Americans claimed their own rights. The director of the Christian-based National Legal Foundation said so explicitly: "Just as officials in the 1950s shut the doors of the schoolhouse to black children, some school officials of the 1980s have attempted to keep out Christians who want to form a Bible club. Such arbitrary censorship is anti-religious discrimination, pure and simple."[6]

To others, including some of the members of the Supreme Court, the worry was more about the limits of Mergens's claims on her rights. Who else might make a claim based upon her efforts? Justice Anthony Kennedy raised a concern about the constitutionality of the EAA: that other students with other voices might also use the act to gain access for their student clubs, even if some of their issues of interest might make school administrators uncomfortable.[7] The free speech provisions of the EAA might also guarantee access for student groups with much more controversial agendas. It was this possibility that especially worried school administrators. Reflecting back upon his decision to deny Mergens's request and the Supreme Court's ruling, Omaha principal James Findley recounted, "I didn't have a concern about the five or six kids having a Bible study club. I was concerned about what and who it opens the doors to. I've had students say they'll start a Satanist club or a skinheads group."[8]

As it turned out, other groups of high school students *did* test the system, but perhaps not in the ways that Congress intended when it passed the EAA in the first place or in the ways that Principal Findley or members of the Supreme Court worried about. These groups were not Satanists or skinheads. One was a collection of young people in Boyd County, Kentucky, who wanted to start a GSA. In 2002, they circulated a petition declaring their intent. Driving the formation of GSAs was the desire not only to create solidarity between high school students with diverse sexual identities but also to provide a safe space for students who had not yet chosen to make public their own sexual identities, perhaps because of the potential for harassment by their fellow students.

School officials turned down the students' request to form the GSA. Of twenty-one student group applications, theirs was the only one denied. Requests from groups such as the Future Business Leaders of America and the Fellowship of Christian Athletes were approved.[9] The students then contacted the American Civil Liberties Union (ACLU) for help. One month after the ACLU sent a letter to the school board in which it referred to the EAA, the board reversed itself and approved the formation of the GSA.[10]

But that didn't fully settle the case. Back at Boyd County High, GSA club founders' fears of harassment turned out to be valid. According to testimony from the school's principal, at the first official meeting of the GSA, a crowd "directly confronted the GSA supporters 'with facial expressions, hand gestures . . . some very uncivil body language . . . people were using loud voices and angry voices.'"[11] Two days later, a group of students protesting outside the school "shouted at [GSA] students as they arrived, 'We don't want something like that in our school.'"[12]

In an emergency meeting held in December, the school board, following the recommendation of the district superintendent, decided to "ban all noncurricular clubs for the remainder of the 2002–03 school year."[13] After the decision, members of the GSA stopped using school facilities to meet, but other groups, including the school's drama and Bible clubs, continued to use the high school's facilities. The members of the GSA went to court.

Their case did not make it to the Supreme Court; it did not have to. In 2004, the ACLU announced a settlement with the Boyd County public schools and claimed victory: "The settlement requires that the district treat all student clubs equally and conduct an anti-harassment training for all district staff as well as all students in high school and middle school."[14]

Jeff Greenberg / Contributor

▲ Decades after the Mergens and Boyd County Supreme Court cases, students from Miami Coral Park Senior High's Gay Straight Alliance march with a banner at a pride festival in Miami Beach, Florida, in April 2017.

The GSA was not the first or the only case brought by student groups focused on challenging discrimination based on a student's sexual identity, but the efforts of these students highlight the ways in which individuals have used the political tools available to them to secure their own rights. In filing her lawsuit and pursuing her claims all the way to the Supreme Court, Bridget Mergens had help from the National Legal Foundation, a Christian public interest law firm.[15] The Boyd County High GSA had the help of the ACLU. While Mergens and the members of the Boyd County High GSA differed in the particular rights they asserted, they both staked their claims on the same federal law, the EAA. With help, they harnessed the power of the American judicial system to realize their goals.

Both groups' efforts were undertaken with knowledge of the complicated ways in which laws and policies are enacted in the United States and a strategic understanding of the political process. In this book, we will consider those dynamics in detail. We will also dive into the stories of many other individuals and groups who have sought to claim their rights and reshape the laws of the land. In a very deep sense, however, whether or not any of the others whose stories you will read "won" or "lost" is not the most important consideration. By adding their voices to the American conversation, they mattered.

The EAA is just one of many political instruments that individuals have used to claim their rights. Underpinning all of these instruments are the political ideals drawn from thinkers throughout history, expressed in the Declaration of Independence and affirmed as rights by the Framers of the Constitution of the United States. These rights form the basis for the story of this evolving thing we call American democracy, whether or not the Framers fully envisioned how others would use their ideas and the institutions that they created. These efforts are central to the subjects and approach of this chapter and of this book.

WHAT HAVE I **LEARNED?**

1. Why have high schools, colleges, and universities struggled with the expression of student voices in cases as diverse as those involving Christian Bible study clubs and gay-straight alliances (GSAs)?

2. How did Bridget Mergens and the members of the Boyd County High GSA make use of the same law, the Equal Access Act (EAA), to claim their rights?

3. What other rights might students in high schools, colleges, and universities claim?

Answer Key: 1. Students might reflect upon the rights of all students to have their voices made present in their educational institutions as well as on concerns of school officials that groups might form promoting unpopular, or even hateful, ideas; 2. Answers should focus on fundamental ideas such as freedom of expression; 3. Answers will vary and might focus on speech, safety, or many other areas.

democracy
a system of government where power is held and political decisions are made by the people in that society.

natural rights
rights that people have inherently that are not granted by any government.

social contract
an agreement in which people give to their governments the ability to rule over them to ensure an orderly and functioning society.

AMERICAN POLITICAL CULTURE IS BUILT ON A SET OF SHARED IDEAS

● **Define the key elements of American political culture.**

When they asserted their rights, Bridget Mergens and members of the Boyd County High GSA did so on the basis of a handful of ideas that form the foundation of the American Republic itself. Indeed, these ideas were affirmed in the Declaration of Independence in 1776, making them part of the country's basic DNA: "We hold these truths to be self-evident, that all men are created equal, that they are endowed by their Creator with certain unalienable Rights, that among these are Life, Liberty, and the pursuit of Happiness." These were revolutionary ideas, but they were not original ones. They weren't supposed to be.

In drafting the Declaration of Independence, Thomas Jefferson and his coauthors drew upon a set of ideas about liberty and government that were widely known in the colonies and Great Britain—ideas Jefferson knew needed to be persuasive and compelling enough to successfully launch a revolution. From the histories and philosophical works of ancient Greece and Rome, they borrowed the idea of **democracy** (from the Greek *demos*, meaning "people," and *kratos*, or "power"), whereby power is held by the people.

They borrowed from English Enlightenment philosopher John Locke, who had argued against the divine, or God-given, right of kings to rule with absolute power. Locke claimed that people are born with **natural rights** that kings cannot give or take away. A legitimate government, to Locke, is one that involves a **social contract**, in which people give to their governments the ability to rule over them to ensure an orderly and functioning society. If a government breaks that social contract by violating people's natural rights, then the people have the right to replace that unjust government with a just one.

From the French Enlightenment, Jefferson and his colleagues drew on the works of Baron de Montesquieu, who gave an institutional form to the ideas of natural rights and the social contract in proposing that power in government should be divided between different branches so that no one branch could become too powerful. Jefferson also drew upon Scottish Enlightenment thinkers such as David Hume. Given the historical tendency of leaders to abuse political power, Hume believed a just government should be carefully designed and the lessons of science and history carefully applied to its structure to keep the greedy and ambitious from using political power to their own advantage. In applying scientific principals from studies of the natural world to human political action and interaction, Hume and others like him made major contributions to the modern study of **political science**.

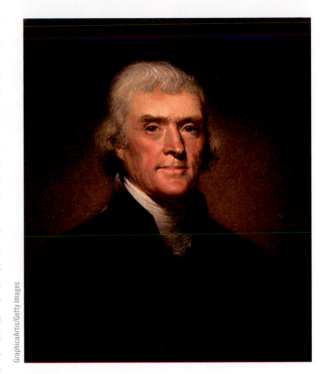

▲ Thomas Jefferson in an 1800 painting by Rembrandt Peale.

Later in the chapter we will see how those ideas gave rise to a revolution and helped form the basis for the institutions of modern government. Those ideas of liberty, equality, rights, happiness, and others also endure in other ways. Today they shape the shared set of beliefs, customs, traditions, and values that define the relationship of Americans to their government and to other American citizens. We call those shared beliefs **American political culture**.

EQUALITY IS ABOUT HAVING THE SAME RIGHTS OR STATUS

Central to all of this—and the first key idea expressed in the Declaration of Independence—is a commitment to equality, to having the same rights and status. This might involve **social equality**, in which no individuals have an inherently higher social status than others. Unlike Europe, with its nobility and royalty, America was founded on the idea that all individuals could reach the social status that they sought based on their own efforts. **Political equality** exists when members of a society possess the same rights under the laws of the nation. Finally, **economic equality** refers to a situation in which wealth is relatively evenly distributed across society. America does not have economic equality. In fact, differences in wealth and incomes are as stark today as they have ever been in the nation's history. Rather than emphasizing equality of economic *outcomes*, American political ideas tend to focus on ensuring equality of economic *opportunity*. (See Figure 1.1.)

These are two very different concepts. For example, think about American public education in high schools. Equality of opportunity would mean that all students have a right to attend equally good public high schools. Equality of outcomes, however, might point to their right to achieve the same graduation rates or test scores. We Americans weigh the differences between opportunity and outcomes all the time when we seek to resolve many important civil rights issues and make choices about domestic public policy options.

INALIENABLE RIGHTS EXIST ABOVE ANY GOVERNMENT POWERS

The thinking behind the Declaration of Independence and the government that was eventually based upon it is that some truths and some rights are *self-evident*. These are called **inalienable rights** in the sense that they exist before and above any government or its powers. Thomas Jefferson names "life,

political science
the systematic study of the ways in which ideas, individuals, and institutions shape political outcomes.

American political culture
a shared set of beliefs, customs, traditions, and values that define the relationship of Americans to their government and to other American citizens.

social equality
when no individual's social status is inherently higher than another's.

political equality
when members of a society possess the same rights under the laws of the nation.

economic equality
when wealth is relatively evenly distributed across society.

inalienable rights
rights that exist before and above any government or its power.

GraphicaArtis/Getty Images

Measuring Economic Equality

Economic inequality can be measured using the Gini coefficient, which measures the distribution of wealth across a population.

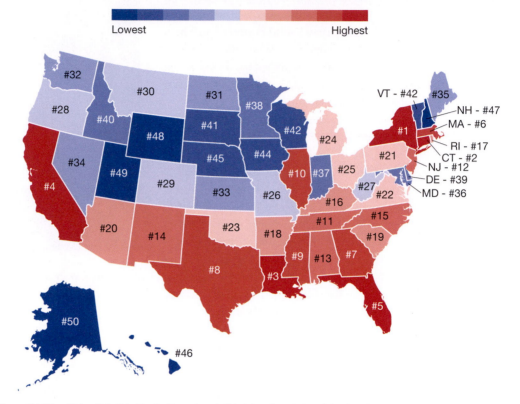

States with the Highest Levels of Income Inequality

Lowest   Highest

Source: Chris Kolmar, "States with the Highest Levels of Income Inequality," *Zippia,* https://www.zippia.com/advice/states-highest-lowest-income-inequality/.

liberty, and the pursuit of happiness" as among those inherent, self-evident rights. Since they—unlike *privileges* that a government might grant—may not rightly be taken away by a government, a just system of political rule must be constructed in such a way as to protect rights and their expression. The desire to safeguard individuals' rights led to the complex structure of American political institutions in the Constitution, which we will explore in the next chapter.

LIBERTY INVOLVES BOTH FREEDOM FROM INTERFERENCE AND FREEDOM TO PURSUE ONE'S DREAMS

Another foundational American ideal expressed in the Declaration is a commitment to **liberty**, to social, political, and economic freedoms. That liberty might involve freedom *from* interference by a government or a freedom *to* pursue one's dreams. The degree to which the government should focus on freedom *from* or freedom *to* remains a hotly debated topic in American politics. There is often also a tension between these two visions of liberty. In the case of Bridget Mergens's Bible study club, the tension between these two freedoms came into sharp relief. Mergens and her fellow students claimed the freedom *to* explore their faith in an extracurricular club. By allowing the group to meet, however, Omaha public school officials risked violating other students' freedoms *from* having a government endorse a particular religious faith, or endorse religious over nonreligious beliefs.

liberty
social, political, and economic freedoms.

MILLENNIALS AND THE AMERICAN DREAM

The state of the American dream in the twenty-first century is something that we can study empirically. Words are not the only ways to tell stories, nor are images and videos. Data can tell political stories as well. In this book, we will investigate data—numbers, statistics, and survey results—as well as the stories that political actors and reporters construct around the numbers. Make no mistake, data stories can be and are used for political purposes. In investigating data stories in this book, the goal is twofold: to help you become more capable and confident interpreters of data and to help you gain the skills to critically examine the narratives constructed around data.

We start with what at first glance seems like a very simple data story—one taken from the results of a Harvard University survey of eighteen- to twenty-nine-year-olds conducted in December 2015.[16]

In the 2015 Harvard survey, Americans between the ages of eighteen and twenty-nine were just about equally split between those who believed that the American dream was still alive (49 percent) and those who did not (48 percent).

....

WHAT Do You Think?

The authors of the survey report placed these results in context and went into much more detail about other factors. But let's assume that they did not. What conclusions might you draw from this figure alone? Does it reflect your experience? What other data from this survey would you want to know? If you could break out groups of young adult Americans based upon identities and characteristics, what would you examine?

As it turns out, in the Harvard survey, college graduates (58 percent) were more likely than those who had not graduated or ever enrolled (42 percent) to say the American dream was still alive. Young adult Americans in the survey who said that they were supporters of Democratic presidential candidate Bernie Sanders (56 percent) or Republican Party candidate Donald Trump (61 percent) reported that they felt the American dream was dead. What might these results mean for your understanding of the political attitudes of young adult Americans today?

Is the American Dream Alive or Dead for You?

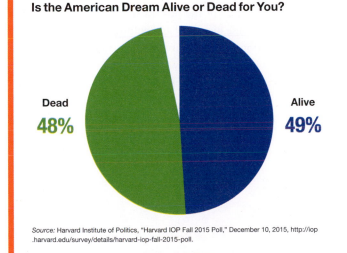

Dead **48%**   Alive **49%**

Source: Harvard Institute of Politics, "Harvard IOP Fall 2015 Poll," December 10, 2015, http://iop.harvard.edu/survey/details/harvard-iop-fall-2015-poll.

THE PURSUIT OF HAPPINESS IS AT THE CORE OF THE AMERICAN DREAM

When Thomas Jefferson wrote about "the pursuit of happiness," he was tapping into another core American political value: the belief that individuals should be able to achieve prosperity through hard work, sacrifice, and their own talents. The idea of the **American dream** has drawn immigrants to the nation's shores and borders since its founding, and it continues to do so today. Some observers, however, question whether the American dream remains alive and well in an era of such profound economic inequality.

AMERICAN POLITICAL CULTURE HAS MANY ROOTS

America's religious traditions have also helped shape American political culture in ways more significant than in many modern democratic governments. Some of the very first British colonies were founded by groups of individuals fleeing persecution for their religious beliefs and

American dream
the idea that individuals should be able to achieve prosperity through hard work, sacrifice, and their own talents.

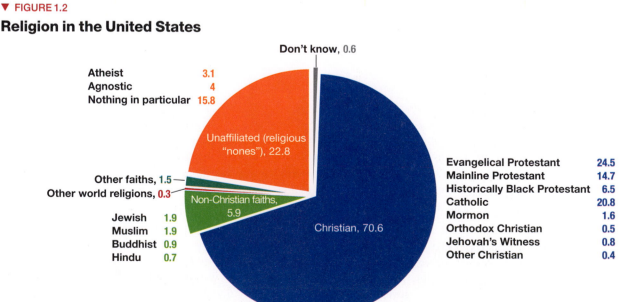

▲ Nan Dubin (left) of East Wallingford, Vermont, reads a prompt to Mahsen Bouchnak, originally from Syria, who immigrated to Vermont in January 2017 along with her two boys. Dubin has worked with the Bouchnaks and other refugee families since their arrival at the beginning of 2017. At its most basic level, the American dream promises hope and opportunity for all.

American exceptionalism
belief in the special character of the United States as a uniquely free nation based on its history and its commitment to democratic ideals and personal liberty.

hoping to practice their faiths without interference. While the diversity of religious faiths represented in American society continues to expand, America was, and is, a nation partly defined by religious faith and expression. In this book, we will continue to explore the theme of how a nation founded upon liberty, especially religious liberty, wrestles with decisions about if, or how, to place boundaries on religious expression.

Today, questions about the proper role of religion in the nation endure. What kinds of holiday displays are acceptable for a community to officially sponsor? Would a ban on immigration by members of specific religious faiths be constitutional? (See Figure 1.2 for the religious makeup of the United States today.)

AMERICAN EXCEPTIONALISM FLOWS FROM THE NATION'S HISTORICAL DEVELOPMENT

Finally, when Americans tell stories about themselves, their politics, and their histories, they often refer to the ways in which the nation is different because of the historical patterns of the nation's development. **American exceptionalism** refers to these historical and cultural differences, shaped in many ways by the voices of those who have contributed to the national chorus but also by the fact that America was an experiment, starting anew, without the legacy of the European monarchies to constrain its promise.[17] The idea of an exceptional America is not a new one. In 1630, Puritan leader John Winthrop delivered a sermon to a group of immigrants from Britain on board their ship as they waited to land in New England. In it he exhorted, "We must Consider that we shall be as a City upon a Hill, the eyes of all people are upon us."[18]

▼ FIGURE 1.2

Religion in the United States

Don't know, 0.6

Atheist 3.1
Agnostic 4
Nothing in particular 15.8

Unaffiliated (religious "nones"), 22.8

Other faiths, 1.5
Other world religions, 0.3

Jewish 1.9
Muslim 1.9
Buddhist 0.9
Hindu 0.7

Non-Christian faiths, 5.9

Christian, 70.6

Evangelical Protestant	24.5
Mainline Protestant	14.7
Historically Black Protestant	6.5
Catholic	20.8
Mormon	1.6
Orthodox Christian	0.5
Jehovah's Witness	0.8
Other Christian	0.4

Source: Pew Research Center, "Religious Landscape Study," 2017, http://www.pewforum.org/religious-landscape-study/.

WHAT HAVE I LEARNED?

1. The Declaration of Independence _____ the residents of the rebellious British colonies.

    a. granted fundamental political privileges to

    b. recognized the fundamental rights of

    c. granted colonial women the right to vote along with

    d. placed strict limits on the expression of rights of

2. The term *American exceptionalism* refers to _____.

    a. the fact that America is unique in its democratic form of government

    b. America's inability to protect individual rights

    c. the belief that America's unique history contributed to its special political culture and institutions

    d. All of the above

3. American society is characterized by _____.

    a. relative social equality and economic inequality

    b. relative economic equality and social inequality

    c. relative social equality and economic equality

    d. relative social inequality and economic inequality

4. What are some of the key components of American political culture?

Answers: 1. b; 2. c; 3. a; 4. Answers should include a discussion of inalienable rights, liberty, religious beliefs, and American exceptionalism.

POLITICS AND POLITICAL ACTION SET THE STAGE FOR REVOLUTION

- **Identify the political, social, and economic events and institutions that gave rise to the American Revolution and reflect upon what was and was not achieved.**

In April 1607, three British ships made their way up what would later become known as the James River in Virginia. After deciding on a spot far enough up the river to avoid Spanish warships, these individuals created the settlement of Jamestown, the first permanent British settlement in the modern-day United States of America.[19] Over the course of the next 170 years, the turbulent political, economic, and social experiences they faced would shape the conditions that led to their eventual separation from Great Britain and establish the foundations of a set of institutions that continue to shape American today.

COLONIAL SETTLEMENTS ESTABLISH A PRECEDENT FOR INDEPENDENCE

The colonists who established Jamestown did not set out on their own. They were backed, funded, and supported by the Virginia Company, chartered in 1606 to exploit the resources of North America for the benefit of Great Britain and the company's investors. They hoped to find gold, harvest forest products, and maybe find a valuable trade route.[20] In terms of the subsequent development of the thirteen British colonies and the free American states that later grew out of them, the initial political and economic structure of the colonies proved to be as important as any other factor. From the beginning, the British colonies in North America were used to doing things for themselves without much oversight or interference from the British government.

In 1619, the Virginia colony developed its own legislative assembly, the House of Burgesses, which was the first elected assembly in colonial America.[21] Each of the other thirteen colonies eventually did the same. These assemblies instilled in their colonies a tradition of self-governance and a resistance to being told what to do by Great Britain, especially by Parliament.

In addition, unlike France and Spain, Great Britain initially lacked a coherent colonial policy. Later, in the face of significant national debts incurred in part to protect its colonies from its European rivals, Great Britain tried to exert more centralized control over what it saw as ungrateful and entitled colonies and get them to pay their fair share of the costs of their own protection.[22] This move likely came too late, however; colonial governments were not about to give up the independence they had enjoyed for so long.

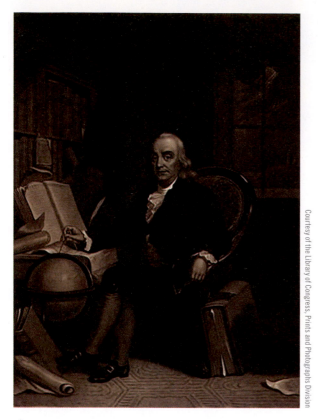

▲ Benjamin Franklin's skill in strategic politics as a representative of the would-be Republic abroad proved to be crucial to American independence.

A GLOBAL WAR FORCES CHANGE IN COLONIAL POLICY

The Treaty of Paris in 1763 ended the fourth major military conflict between two global powers, France and Great Britain, in less than seventy-five years. In Europe, this conflict was known as the **Seven Years' War**.[23] In the American colonies, it was known as the French and Indian War. It was a global war; fighting took place in North America, the Mediterranean Sea, the Indian Ocean, the West Indies, and the Philippines and involved most of the European powers of the time, including Great Britain, France, Austria, Prussia, Spain, and Sweden.

The North American part of the war began when members of the Ohio Company, a land speculation company established by a group of wealthy Virginians, pushed Virginia's claims on Native American lands in the Ohio River Valley into lands claimed by France. In 1754, a young officer named George Washington was sent to the territory to challenge French control and assert colonial claims. After an initial attack, Washington retreated to a hastily constructed fort, called Fort Necessity, in western Pennsylvania. Washington was later forced to surrender to the French but was allowed to withdraw with his surviving men.

Hoping to coordinate alliances with Native American peoples—and to keep them from allying with the French—Great Britain requested that its colonies meet at a conference in Albany, New York, in the summer of 1754. Seven colonies sent representatives there.[24] The so-called Albany Congress accomplished very little. However, one of its delegates, Benjamin Franklin, who later became America's first international celebrity, presented to the Congress a plan for closer coordination between the colonies. The **Albany Plan** called for a "Plan of Union," in which colonial legislatures would choose delegates to form an assembly under the leadership of a chief executive appointed by Great Britain.[25] This governing body would have power over dealings with Native American peoples and collective self-defense. And, in a premonition of an issue that would return again in debates over governance of the victorious United States, it would have the power to tax the colonies to pay for their collective defense.

Benjamin Franklin's proposal for a unified legislative body was not adopted by the colonial governments. It was not an idea whose time had come. Great Britain was better off dealing with its North American colonies individually rather than as a potentially powerful unified colonial legislature. For their part, many colonies did not want to give up their own sovereignty, especially when it involved land claims that might make a lucky few colonies (especially Virginia) grow even larger and more powerful than they already were at the expense of the small coastal colonies, such as Rhode Island and Delaware, whose boundaries were constricted by the ocean and those of neighboring colonies.

Benjamin Franklin may not have expected his plan to be adopted. He was a very savvy politician. But his plan did plant the seeds for an American union. Writing four years later, Franklin discussed the "impossibility" of an American union at that time, stating, "When I say such a union is impossible, I mean without the most grievous tyranny and oppression."[26] In the minds of many American revolutionaries, they would get just that.

ECONOMIC CONFLICTS GROW BETWEEN GREAT BRITAIN AND ITS COLONIES

After the Seven Years' War, Great Britain was the unquestioned European power in North America, in Canada, and in the modern United States east of the Mississippi River. With victory, however, came problems: Great Britain had to now confront increasingly assertive colonies. It had acquired a vast new territory that now had to be administered, defended, and paid for. But money was scarce. War had left Great Britain with a significant amount of debt. With bankruptcy a possibility, the British government fully expected its thirteen colonies to pay for their own costs to the British Crown so as not to make the debt problem even worse.[27] (See Figure 1.3.)

European Territorial Claims before and after the Seven Years' War

Following the Seven Years' War, Britain laid claim to much of the territory once held by the French, thus consolidating its power in the eastern portion of North America. Administering those colonies and finding ways to fund expansion were enormously difficult.

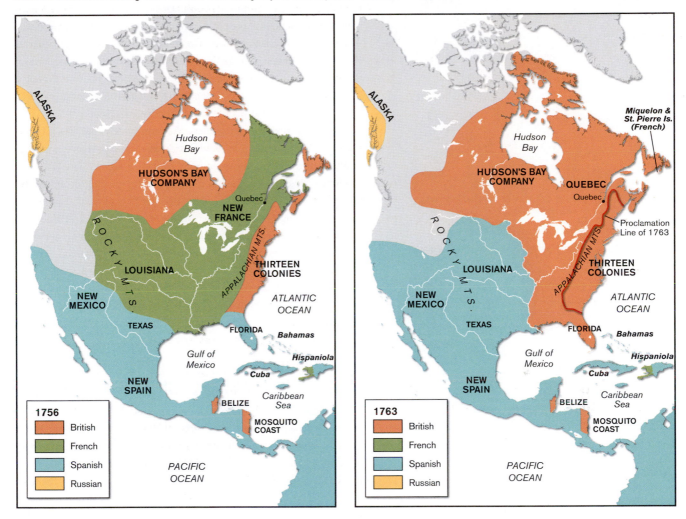

Beginning in 1763, a series of acts and proclamations began to enlarge the scope of Great Britain's involvement in colonial affairs, producing a backlash from colonists who felt that Great Britain was going too far. To make matters worse, these acts were instituted during an economic depression in the colonies. Colonial legislatures became increasingly resistant to having Parliament interfere in areas of economic life that the colonies, not Great Britain, had been in charge of for decades.

It was an environment full of misunderstanding and anxiety, vulnerable to the efforts of those who would capitalize on these fears to promote their own ideas about relations with Great Britain. This instability was made worse by the inability or refusal of Great Britain to fully understand what was happening in its thirteen North American colonies.

THE IDEA OF INDEPENDENCE IS GIVEN VOICE IN POLITICAL PROPAGANDA

In this uncertain political environment, there were a few who advocated resistance to Great Britain, some who remained loyal to Great Britain, and many more who were undecided and afraid of actions that might lead to a hopeless war against the greatest military power in the world. It was this last group of colonists, the undecided, who found themselves in the crosshairs of a radical few. Those few had a powerful, cheap, and flexible technology on their side. It was called the printing press, and the American radicals used it very well.

COMMON SENSE;

ADDRESSED TO THE

INHABITANTS

OF

AMERICA,

On the following interesting

SUBJECTS.

I. Of the Origin and Design of Government in general,
with concise Remarks on the English Constitution.

II. Of Monarchy and Hereditary Succession.

III. Thoughts on the present State of American Affairs.

IV. Of the present Ability of America, with some miscellaneous Reflections.

Man knows no Master save creating HEAVEN,
Or those whom choice and common good ordain.
THOMSON.

PHILADELPHIA;
Printed, and Sold, by R. BELL, in Third-Street.
MDCCLXXVI.

▲ The cover of Thomas Paine's pamphlet *Common Sense* (1776).

From the printing presses came inexpensive and easy-to-produce papers called pamphlets; the printers came to be called pamphleteers. Enough people had access to and the ability to read their products to make the pamphlet a revolutionary technological innovation.[28] The pamphleteers were engaged in **political propaganda**, "which is simply the attempt to control the actions of people indirectly by controlling their attitudes."[29] Their goal was to change public opinion—the distribution of people's attitudes and preferences on the issues of the day. American pamphleteers were not trying to show their intelligence or literary skill. They were trying to mobilize people in support of their cause. Words and ideas, as the pamphleteers knew well, could also constitute strategic political action.

Of all the American pamphlets, the most widely read was Thomas Paine's 1776 pamphlet *Common Sense*, which sold perhaps more than one hundred thousand copies in its first year alone. *Common Sense* ultimately "had more influence in focusing the spirit of revolt than the writings of all the intellectuals taken together."[30]

Calling King George III the "royal brute of England," Paine challenged the legitimacy of the British monarchy, refuted arguments in favor of reconciling differences with Great Britain, and announced that "the period of debate is closed."[31] He used the dreaded *I* word, *independence*, writing that independence from Great Britain was not only possible but sure to come to pass.[32] Drawing on the idea that the American colonists had a unique destiny in the world and in history, Paine called the colonists into action at just the time when many were ready to receive his message.

REVOLUTIONARIES TAKE ACTION, THEIR EYES ON INCREASING THE POWERS OF COLONIAL LEGISLATURES

Words alone, however powerful, were not enough to mobilize the colonists to make a final break from Great Britain. Colonial radicals began a planned strategy of resistance—one that involved propaganda, organization, and occasionally, violence. A common phrase associated with resistance to British tax policy was "No taxation without representation!" While it was used at the time, the phrase did not fully capture the struggle between colonial governments and Great Britain.

American radicals generally did not want to be represented in Parliament in Great Britain. Representatives would have been out of communication with the colonies during debates and consistently outvoted in Parliament even if some arrangement for their representation could be worked out. Instead, the colonists argued that the power of taxation should be held by colonial legislatures, not British Parliament. In many ways, colonial opposition to British policies was conservative. Its adherents wanted to go back to the way things had been prior to the Seven Years' War, when British colonial policy was more hands-off. Economic and political realities, however, made this an unrealistic goal.

THE SONS OF LIBERTY ATTEMPT TO MOBILIZE COLONISTS AROUND BRITISH TAX POLICIES. In 1765, in response to Great Britain's tax policies, a group of merchants and workingmen, including Sam Adams, formed the **Sons of Liberty**. It was a working-class organization, with a potentially much larger appeal to the general public than the revolutionary elites had. That potential made the Sons of Liberty both attractive and scary to the wealthy elites in the revolutionary movement. Their fear was that they might not be able to control the actions of the Sons of Liberty. Through rallies, sermons, protests, and heavy use of the newspapers, the Sons of Liberty tried to mobilize public opinion in support of resistance to Great Britain and its tax policies. They also resorted to violent protest. Acts of mob violence, including rioting and looting, in response to British policy only reinforced elite fear, causing "some conservative American political leaders . . . to worry more about the danger of mobs than they did about British policies."[33]

political propaganda
attempts to shape governmental actions and laws by changing people's beliefs and opinions.

Sons of Liberty
a group initially formed of merchants and workingmen in response to the Stamp Act that resisted Great Britain and its tax policies.

The group's violent actions backfired as a political strategy. Uncommitted colonists looked on the mob violence fearfully, wondering how bad things might get if the crisis were to deepen. In response, radicals changed their strategy. They planned and organized boycotts of British goods, pressuring fellow colonists to comply.

In October 1765, at the invitation of Massachusetts's colonial legislatures, nine of thirteen colonies sent representatives who met in New York to debate and prepare a colonial response to Britain's policies.[34] This so-called Stamp Act Congress (named after the Stamp Act, another British tax, that required the purchase of a stamp for nearly everything involved in trade) issued a Declaration of Rights and Grievances, which was, in

▲ Crispus Attucks and four others were shot and killed at the Boston Massacre.

many ways, quite mild. It affirmed colonial loyalty to the Crown. It did, however, protest against the imposition of taxes without colonial consent. Most importantly, the Stamp Act Congress was an early assembly of representatives across, not just within, the British colonies. In 1766, Great Britain repealed the Stamp Act, mostly due to the pressure of British merchants concerned about its effects on their profits. In fact, the Stamp Act had never been effectively enforced.

THE CRISIS ACCELERATES AS PROTESTS INTENSIFY.

Despite continuing tensions, the years following the repeal of the Stamp Act were relatively quiet politically, with radicals losing power and influence and moderates able to keep them in check. Beginning in 1770, however, radical responses to British policies—and British responses to these radical responses—began to shift power and support away from the moderates and into the radical camp.

The exact sequence of events leading up to the Boston Massacre in 1770 is not entirely clear, nor is the exact role of radicals in escalating the situation. It involved a confrontation between a mob of Bostonians and a small group of British soldiers, beginning with taunts and snowballs and ending in the deaths of five American colonials. One of those killed was Crispus Attucks, a young man of African and Native American descent. Sam Adams and other radicals quickly mobilized to use the press to rally support for their cause, describing "the blood of our fellow citizens running like water through King Street."[35]

THE BOSTON TEA PARTY ADDS FUEL TO THE REVOLUTIONARY FIRE.

In 1773, the Boston Sons of Liberty seized upon an even greater crisis to push away the possibility of reconciliation with Great Britain: the Boston Tea Party. It began over a corporate bailout of the East India Tea Company by the government of Great Britain. The British company was nearly bankrupt, and it had large stocks of unsold tea. Though corrupt and poorly managed, the East India Tea Company was no ordinary company. It ruled much of India with its own private army. It could count among its investors some of the wealthiest and most powerful men in Great Britain. It was—in modern terms—too big to fail.

It needed a bailout, and it got one with the Tea Act, passed by Great Britain in 1773. The act gave the East India Tea Company a tax-free monopoly on the tea trade to the colonies. New England merchants, some of whom were profiting handsomely by smuggling tea from Netherlands merchants into the colonies, were not pleased. The Tea Act cut out the middlemen in the colonial tea trade—the New England merchants—who saw "ruin staring them in the face."[36]

It was the fear of what Great Britain might do next as much as what it actually *had* done that drove many merchants into the radical camp. In November 1773, the *Dartmouth* entered Boston Harbor loaded with tea. Two other ships soon followed. With the merchants increasingly on their side, the Sons of Liberty provoked a crisis, dumping the tea from the ships into the harbor.

Not everyone in the American colonies cheered the actions of the radicals. That it was an act of lawlessness worried many. The violence that accompanied the protest seemed to some completely unjustifiable. The strategic actions of the Boston radicals placed the British government in a very difficult situation. It could not ignore the attack on British property and commerce. Asserting control, however, risked driving moderate colonials into the radical camp.

Parliament, with the support of King George III, clamped down. Hard. In a series of actions in 1774, known in the colonies as the **Intolerable Acts**, Britain sought to make an example of Massachusetts and its radicals. If Parliament and the Crown thought that this show of resolve—backed, if necessary, by force—would quiet the colonies, they were wrong. Writing many years after the Revolution, John Adams observed this:

> The colonies had grown up under constitutions of government so different, there was so great a variety of their religions, they were composed of so many different nations . . . that to unite them in the same principles in theory and the same system of action, was certainly a very difficult enterprise. . . . Thirteen clocks were made to strike together—a perfection of mechanism which no artist had ever before effected.[37]

The actions of the British government and the Boston radicals had both helped to synchronize these thirteen clocks.

THE INSTITUTION OF SLAVERY DENIED THE NATURAL RIGHTS OF AFRICAN AMERICANS

The first group of twenty Africans arrived in Jamestown, Virginia, in 1619 aboard a Dutch ship. Like the native peoples whose lands had been occupied by British settlers, the African peoples who followed this small group came from diverse cultures, nations, and kinship groups. Initially, some were given the status of indentured servants—people who still possessed the ability to pay off their "debts" through labor and achieve their freedom. Throughout the seventeenth and eighteenth centuries, whites arrived in numbers from Europe who also carried the status of indentured servitude. As the plantation economies of colonial America developed, however, African slaves and their descendants confronted legal systems designed more and more to strip African captives and their descendants of any legal or political rights or any hope of freedom under that legal order.

By the time Virginia's government fully codified the status of slaves in the eighteenth century, "no black, free or slave, could own arms, strike a white man, or employ a white servant. Any white person could apprehend any black to demand a certificate of freedom or a pass from the owner giving permission to be off the plantation."[38] Like the indigenous peoples, slaves and their descendants strove to maintain their ways of life, spiritual and cultural traditions, kinship networks, families, and dignity over the coming centuries.

As colonial America moved toward a revolution based on individual liberty, it was far from an equal society. To many Europeans, the prospect of individual advancement made America more equal than their class-stratified societies, with the exception of the almost feudal southern plantation societies.[39] In New England, working-class colonials had achieved a political status that few of their counterparts in Great Britain could. However, wealth was rapidly accumulating in the hands of a small number of colonial elites.[40]

The revolutionary philosophy of colonial America did not include African Americans—nor women, many religious minorities, or indigenous peoples—in the register of those capable of full citizenship and the rights associated with it. At times, slaves in Virginia and other slaveholding colonies organized and rose up against their oppression. In at least one uprising, slaves seized on the language of the American revolutionaries, shouting "Liberty!" while they rebelled.[41] Armed uprisings by slaves, however, were put down mercilessly with the goal of sending a message to any who would challenge the white order.[42]

The willingness of the majority of white colonial Americans to attack Great Britain for assaults on their liberty while allowing the enslavement of Africans did not go unnoticed by British officials and some white colonists. Thomas Hutchinson, governor of Massachusetts before the war, questioned how the American revolutionaries could "justify the depriving of more than a hundred thousand Africans of their rights to liberty, and the same *pursuit of happiness*, and in some degree to their lives, if these rights

Intolerable Acts
a term used in the American colonies to refer to a series of laws enacted by Great Britain in response to the Boston Tea Party.

are so absolutely inalienable."[43] Thomas Paine was one of only a relatively small number of white pamphleteers to point out the contradiction of calling for liberty in a society that allowed slavery. In a 1775 newspaper article, he wondered how the colonists could "complain so loudly of attempts to enslave them, while they hold so many hundred thousand in slavery."[44] This contradiction did not go unnoticed by slaves and free peoples of African descent either. Nor did some of these individuals ignore the potential social and political gains that might be made by pointing out the unfulfilled expression of liberty. In April 1773, a group of African Americans in Massachusetts petitioned the government for a redress of their grievances, drawing "a straight line between their own condition as chattel slaves and the conditions colonists were then objecting to as virtual slavery."[45] They asked that the same principles be applied to their own condition in colonial America.

"We expect great things," they wrote, "from men who have made such a noble stand against the designs of their *fellow men* to enslave them. . . . As the people of this province seem to be actuated by the principles of equity and justice, we cannot but expect your house will again take our deplorable case into serious consideration, and give us that ample relief which, *as men*, we have a natural right to."[46]

In 1776, Lemuel Haynes, a Massachusetts minister, wrote an unpublished pamphlet titled *Liberty Further Extended*. The son of an African father and a white mother, Haynes became a servant to a religious white farming family in the backcountry of Massachusetts. Haynes educated himself in Puritan theology and on the pamphlets of colonial America. He volunteered as a minuteman in Boston in 1774 and for the Continental Army in 1776. In his pamphlet, Haynes anchored his arguments about the injustice of slavery in the principle of natural rights and the Christian theology with which he and colonials were very familiar:

> Liberty is a Jewel which was handed Down to man from the cabinet of heaven, and is Coaeval with his Existence. And as it proceed from the Supreme Legislature of the univers, so it is he which hath a sole right to take away; therefore, he that would take away a mans Liberty assumes a prerogative that Belongs to another, and acts out of his own domain.[47]

▲ Lemuel Haynes, a Massachusetts minister, challenged slavery based on its violation of natural rights.

Interim Archives/Getty Images

REVOLUTIONARY WOMEN, THOUGH EXCLUDED, BUILT INSTITUTIONS OF THEIR OWN

In many ways, women in revolutionary America were legally and politically invisible. In spite of commonalities in their legal standing, however, *colonial women* as an all-encompassing term fails to capture significant differences in the status, economic class, and religious orientation of the women in question.[48] Women who were slaves, of African descent, or of Native American ancestry struggled against multiple forms of oppression. While sexual and physical abuse was a danger for all colonial women, those who were slaves or indentured servants faced a higher risk.[49] War only heightened these risks; during the conflict, sexual assault was sometimes practiced systematically. In 1776 in Staten Island, New York, and New Jersey, British troops repeatedly raped women in the area.[50]

White women, unless they had acquired property through widowhood, generally had no legal identity or ability to secure their personal and economic rights in a court of law. For those women who did not struggle against the destruction of their families, traditions, and ways of life—either as slaves or members of Native American communities—theirs was a "protective oppression," designed to keep them out of involvement in government and public life. Because of more restricted educational opportunities and, therefore, lower literacy rates than men, fewer women's voices were expressed in print. In spite of these challenges, however, many women did speak, write, and act against the restrictions on their own rights and liberties in colonial America.

A portrait of Esther de Berdt Reed by Charles Wilson Peale done sometime before 1780.

The Print Collector/Getty Images

Because of their general exclusion from public life, women had fewer opportunities to adopt leadership roles in revolutionary America. Religious organizations proved an important exception, as women could act as leaders in them without the same risk of social approbation they would face if acting in the male-dominated political space. Maintaining the boycotts of British goods in the years before revolution also "politicized women and the domestic arena," especially in the production of substitutes for those goods.[51] The replacement of British textiles, in particular, brought many colonial women together as **Daughters of Liberty** in spinning events. While these meetings still remained in the "acceptable" realm of home production in the view of the male-dominated white colonial society, they did provide an experience in collective organization—an act of public "joining" that was itself a departure from and challenge to traditional gendered roles.[52]

Efforts to support the Revolutionary War effort led Esther de Berdt Reed, Sarah Franklin Bache (daughter of Benjamin Franklin), and other colonial women to work to create a women's organization across, not just within, the United States. The Ladies Association was "the biggest domestic fundraising campaign of the war,"[53] in part because women and girls who were not wealthy could still participate.[54]

Reed's pamphlet, *The Sentiments of an American Woman*, published in June 1780, laid out the necessity for colonial women to organize to aid the revolutionary cause. The collection, accounting, and delivery of these donations required the development of an organizational and administrative structure. These fund-raising efforts were extremely successful, and this was perhaps the first truly national American women's organization. Though the members focused on activities considered acceptable for white women in colonial America, the act of organizing and institution building was itself revolutionary.

INDIGENOUS PEOPLES IN NORTH AMERICA CHALLENGED COLONIZATION

To the millions of indigenous peoples spread out across two continents, the arrival of the European colonists proved utterly destructive to their societies. Throughout this centuries-long process, however, indigenous peoples challenged this disruption, either outright through diplomacy or armed conflict or less visibly by trying to maintain centuries-old traditions in the face of constant threats to them.

The indigenous peoples, called Indians by the Europeans, were not passive inhabitants of a wild paradise. They had already shaped many North American ecologies and landscapes to suit their own diverse social and economic systems, often with significant environmental impact. The British colonists, in turn, attempted to reshape the landscapes of North America to suit their own purposes and lifestyles, which caused profound disruption of the traditional ways of life of the indigenous peoples.

The social, cultural, and linguistic diversity of the native peoples in North America was staggering. At the time of first contact with the European invaders, perhaps a quarter of "all human languages in the world were North American Indian."[55] Initially, British colonists depended on the adaptive technologies and agricultural advances of the native peoples for their own survival. As the British colonies grew in size and confidence, however, they began to assert their ideas about land ownership more aggressively, provoking resistance by native peoples who had not agreed to such terms. The violence that this clash led to was often horrific, including massacres of entire indigenous local communities and reprisals against individual British colonials.

By the time Thomas Jefferson sat down to draft the Declaration of Independence, the population of the indigenous peoples in the thirteen British colonies had been reduced to a fraction of its level before first contact with the Europeans. Diseases, against which indigenous peoples had little or no immunity, were the largest factor. Death from armed conflict also played a role. However, the disruption in the traditional ways of life of native peoples that arose from European settlement, including the cascading effects of losing their land—which upset agreements and boundaries between them and other native peoples—also had an effect. The impact of British colonization on traditional native ways of life was comprehensive and total. The habitats upon which the indigenous peoples depended were altered

Daughters of Liberty
a group of colonial-era women who participated in the boycotting of British goods.

and depleted. The traditional social and economic systems that had been developed before the British colonists arrived often broke down.

Indigenous peoples, however, did not sit idly by and allow this to happen. They resisted—at times militarily, and often quite successfully. Many indigenous peoples also practiced diplomacy among and between European powers and other native peoples. Sometimes this approach bore fruit, but sometimes it had disastrous outcomes, especially as the European powers were often quite willing to abandon their promises to their "allies" among the native peoples once European objectives had been met. Resistance for most indigenous peoples probably took personal, nonviolent, and largely unrecorded and unremembered forms as they tried to maintain the survival of their families and kinship networks, their spiritual traditions, and their economic and social structures in the presence of powerfully destabilizing forces.[56]

INDEPENDENCE BECOMES INSTITUTIONALIZED

By the time the delegates to the Second Continental Congress convened in Philadelphia in May 1775, the "war of pamphlets and protests was giving way to the war of rifles and cannon."[57] In April, British general Thomas Gage ordered troops to move on Lexington, Massachusetts—to arrest some radical leaders, including Sam Adams—and on Concord, Massachusetts—to seize some weapons. He failed to do both, and the battles of Lexington and Concord, though small, handed the radical pamphleteers the best ammunition they could hope for. They immediately published exaggerated reports of British atrocities against colonial citizens, especially women and children. Individual colonies began to organize or expand colonial militias and organize their manufacturers for war.

Though few could probably have imagined it that May, the **Second Continental Congress** remained the government of the United States until 1781, when a new American government, one designed by the Congress, took its place.[58] The Second Continental Congress was perpetually in crisis, trying to fight a war in the face of what seemed like unending military defeats and inadequate supplies, troops, and hard money. Its capital even had to be moved in the face of advancing British troops.

When the Second Continental Congress first assembled, the colonies were not yet united in the cause of war. A group of wealthy elites with personal, political, or financial ties to Great Britain opposed independence. A second group, the radicals, set their sights on armed conflict with Great Britain. A third group, the moderates, agreed that a show of force might be necessary but only to serve the ultimate end of a negotiated solution. There were other divisions, between slave and nonslaveholding states, large and small colonies, and urban and rural colonists. These divisions would become more important once independence had actually been achieved.

In the early months of 1776, events began to accelerate toward independence. *Common Sense* had given a clear voice to the cause, and British actions had given ammunition to the radicals. Individual colonies began to pass resolutions authorizing their delegates in Congress (often at the request of those delegates) to move for independence from Great Britain. On June 7, Richard Henry Lee of Virginia offered a motion in Congress declaring "that these united colonies are, and of right ought to be, free and independent states, that they are absolved from all allegiance to the British Crown, and that all political connection between them and the state of Great Britain is, and ought to be, totally dissolved."[59]

Congress was not quite ready to act on the Lee Resolution. The vote was postponed for three weeks to allow for more instructions to arrive from some of the colonies and to coerce reluctant colonies and their delegates on board. In the meantime, a committee was appointed to draft a basic structure for a government in the event of independence. A second committee was charged with trying to secure foreign aid. Another committee, consisting of Thomas Jefferson, John Adams, Benjamin Franklin, Roger Sherman, and Robert R. Livingston, was charged with writing a declaration, a justification, for American independence. On July 2, 1776, the Second Continental Congress approved the Lee Resolution, marking, perhaps, the actual date of America's formal declaration of independence from Great Britain. Two days later, on July 4, Congress approved Thomas Jefferson's revised Declaration of Independence, which justified its previous actions to the colonies and to the world, though the Congress had modified Jefferson's original draft.

Of all the changes that members of the Second Continental Congress made to Jefferson's first draft, none were more significant than the deletion of his charges against the king on the issue of slavery. The

Second Continental Congress
an assembly of delegates from the thirteen British colonies in America that drafted and approved the Declaration of Independence, conducted the Revolutionary War, and created the governmental structure that followed the war.

first section of the deleted charges accused the king of violating natural rights by allowing the slave trade to continue. Thomas Jefferson was a slave owner, one of the largest in Virginia. His lifestyle depended on the capture, sale, and oppression of other human beings. The second deleted section, in which Jefferson charged the king with trying to incite slave rebellions in the colonies, spoke directly to the fears of many southern plantation owners. British officials had recently made offers of freedom to colonial slaves who would join the British against the American revolutionaries. Many eventually did.

In the end, Jefferson's charges against the king on the issue of slavery were deleted, partly due to opposition from southern state delegates. The contradiction—of a new nation announcing its birth on the foundation of freedom while holding hundreds of thousands of people in slavery—remained.

THE AMERICAN REVOLUTION IS STILL UNDER CONSTRUCTION

From the start, the Revolutionary War went poorly for the Americans. Successive defeats, disease, and logistical problems all plagued the colonials and their general, George Washington. By adapting their tactics to suit their strengths—knowledge of the terrain and support among many of the locals—the colonials managed to use hit-and-run tactics to harass Britain and attack its long supply lines. With the help of Britain's rivals, especially France and its powerful navy, the Americans defeated Great Britain at the Battle of Yorktown in 1781. The Treaty of Paris, signed in 1783 and ratified by Congress in 1784, secured the independence of the United States of America.

Militarily and politically, the American Revolution wasn't technically a revolution. King George III was not overthrown; the British Empire remained intact. George would go on to become the longest-reigning British monarch until Queen Victoria in the nineteenth century. The conflict in America is more properly called a secession, in which a group of citizens break off from the larger government to form one of their own. In the backcountry, it was frequently a civil war, with members of the same communities fighting each other, often brutally.

It was, however, very much a revolution of ideas. Though imperfectly and incompletely, the idea of a government based upon natural rights and individual liberty had been given political and institutional form. Later American revolutionaries would undertake their own wars of ideas and political strategies to try to make the government live up to its promises. As part of their efforts, they would build, rebuild, and reshape the political institutions that protect and express Americans' natural rights in a representative democracy.

WHAT HAVE I **LEARNED**?

1. The Seven Years' War resulted in a change in British policy that involved _____.

   a. a large transfer of British land claims to France
   b. the decision to be more assertive toward colonists
   c. the immediate granting of independence to the colonies
   d. widespread religious persecution

2. The Albany Plan called for _____.

   a. closer cooperation between colonies
   b. independence from Great Britain
   c. new forms of taxation
   d. trade policy reform

3. Many colonial American elites worried about some of the actions of the Sons of Liberty because they _____.

   a. supported Great Britain and its policies
   b. failed to repeal the Stamp Act
   c. advocated for the rights of indigenous peoples
   d. threatened mob rule

4. Why was opposition to the Stamp Act on the part of residents of the British colonies in North America so strong?

5. What contradictions were inherent in colonialists' claims to independence on the basis of natural rights?

6. What political institutions did women in revolutionary America help build? Why does this matter?

THE STRUCTURE OF INSTITUTIONS AFFECTS HOW CITIZENS PARTICIPATE

- **Describe the core features of American political institutions.**

As we have seen in the stories that have already been mentioned, while the actions of people and their ideas matter to American government, the **political institutions** that structure how citizens may be involved matter as well. To a great extent, institutions determine how conflicts over political power are resolved, and they can also shape the ideas of people acting within them.

In devising a system of government, two basic questions need to be resolved: how much power that government will claim, and how political power will be distributed or withheld. Different forms of governments distribute power in very different ways. Totalitarian governments admit no limitations on their own power or competing centers of political power. Similarly, authoritarian governments suppress the voices of their citizens to maintain a grip on power; however, unlike totalitarian systems, authoritarian systems may have some economic or social institutions not under governmental control that may serve to moderate the government's power. Governments that admit no external challenge to their claims on power might be monarchies, ruled by royal figures; theocracies, ruled by religious elites; or oligarchies, ruled by a small group of powerful elites. At the other end of the spectrum of power is a **direct democracy**, in which citizens vote directly on public policies. (See Figure 1.4.)

The United States is none of these extremes. While the nation does have elements of direct democracy—in, for example, local votes to approve or reject public school budgets or property tax increases—the vast

political institutions
rules and structures that shape political action and representation.

direct democracy
a form of government in which citizens vote directly on policies.

▼ FIGURE 1.4

Types of Governments

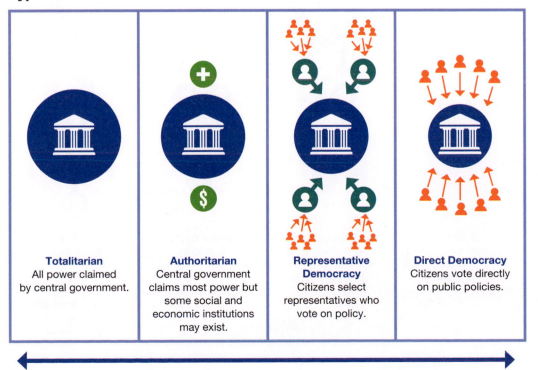

Totalitarian
All power claimed by central government.

Authoritarian
Central government claims most power but some social and economic institutions may exist.

Representative Democracy
Citizens select representatives who vote on policy.

Direct Democracy
Citizens vote directly on public policies.

Power concentrated in central government → Power concentrated in citizenry majority of conflicts over power in America are handled through a system of **representative democracy**, in which voters select representatives who then vote on matters of public policy. In doing so, voters in a representative democracy are confronted with a serious challenge: How can they be sure that their representatives are carrying out their wishes? This is a question that we will examine in some detail in this book.

The number of political institutions in America today is almost too long to list, composed of bodies at the local, state, and national levels. The most important institution in American political life, however, is the U.S. Constitution. This document forms the basis of the nation's government and, in turn, creates a host of political institutions through which conflicts over political power are resolved. It places textual limits on the power of the national government in order to protect Americans' fundamental rights. It also constitutes, or creates, a people with its first seven words: "We the People of the United States."

How does a society structure political institutions in such a way that the social contract is upheld? By ceding some of the expression of their natural rights to a government, Americans have tried to create institutions that ensure an orderly and prosperous society. In doing so, however, they run the risk of creating institutions that oppress instead of uplift. The United States of America is, institutionally and fundamentally, a **constitutional republic**. In it, Americans elect representatives to make most of the laws and policies in the nation, rather than voting on them directly, which would be unwieldy in a nation of more than 325 million people. In addition, and crucially, limits are placed on the power of government to infringe upon people's rights in a constituting document that is recognized as the highest and most supreme law of the nation.

The institutions and rules of a government not only structure the politics of a nation but also may serve to structure its **economy**, or the ways in which goods and services are produced and distributed within a society.

When comparing different economic systems, the key thing to focus on is how much power a government has to regulate the production and distribution of goods and services. In a **communist system**, a government acting on behalf of all workers in a society controls the means of production and

representative democracy
a political system in which voters select representatives who then vote on matters of public policy.

constitutional republic
a form of government in which people vote for elected representatives to make laws and policies and in which limits on the ability of that government to restrict individual rights are placed in a constituting document that is recognized as the highest law of the land.

economy
the systems and organizations through which a society produces and distributes goods and services.

communist system
a way of structuring economic activity in which a government exerts complete control over the production and distribution of goods and services.

▼ FIGURE 1.5

Types of Economic Systems

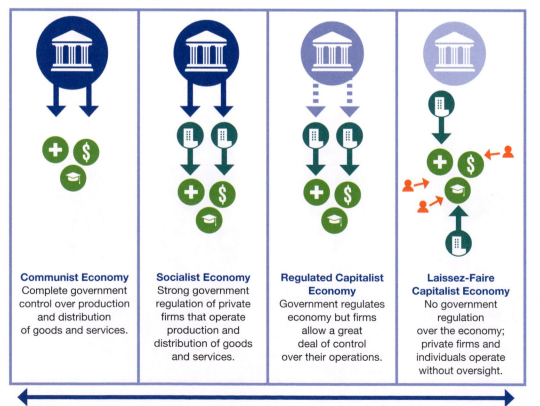

Communist Economy	Socialist Economy	Regulated Capitalist Economy	Laissez-Faire Capitalist Economy
Complete government control over production and distribution of goods and services.	Strong government regulation of private firms that operate production and distribution of goods and services.	Government regulates economy but firms allow a great deal of control over their operations.	No government regulation over the economy; private firms and individuals operate without oversight.

Stronger government control → Stronger private control

distribution. In a **socialist system**, private firms are allowed to operate but with significant intervention by the government, which may include governmental control of sectors of the economy, in the service of ensuring economic equality. In a **capitalist system**, private ownership of the means of production and distribution of a society's resources is emphasized and protected under the laws of that society. Capitalism emphasizes the efficiency of the marketplace in optimally allocating a society's resources. A completely unregulated capitalist system is called *laissez-faire* (from the French "let go," or "let be") and allows individuals and private firms to operate without regulation or oversight. No representative democracies currently practice laissez-faire capitalism. Instead, even nations like the United States that emphasize private economic action practice regulated capitalism, in which firms are allowed to control much of their own decision making but are also subject to governmental rules and regulations. (See Figure 1.5.)

WHAT HAVE I **LEARNED?**

1. American political decisions are made primarily through _____.

   a. majority rule

   b. the practice of direct democracy

   c. representatives who have been elected by the people to make laws and policies

   d. the executive office

2. In a republic, citizens _____.

   a. have little say in the formation of laws and policies

   b. vote directly on laws and policies

   c. elect representatives who then formulate laws and policies

   d. place their rights in the hands of unelected officials

3. What is the primary difference between capitalist and socialist economic systems?

   _____

Answer Key: 1. c; 2. c; 3. Answers should emphasize the role of government in regulating the markets.

DR. MARTIN LUTHER KING JR.'S "LETTER FROM BIRMINGHAM JAIL" LINKS THE CHALLENGE AGAINST RACIAL SEGREGATION TO CORE AMERICAN IDEALS

- Consider the ways in which the "Letter from Birmingham Jail" draws upon core American ideals.

As they led about forty protesters from the Sixteenth Street Baptist Church in Birmingham, Alabama, Reverend Martin Luther King Jr. and his close friend, Reverend Ralph David Abernathy, were dressed for jail. Wearing work shirts and jeans, carrying coats to ward off the cold and damp of Birmingham City Jail, King and Abernathy walked past hundreds of spectators, witnesses, and supporters. Some "sang freedom songs, some knelt in silence."[60] A few cried.

Despite the seriousness of the situation, the two leaders had tried to show calmness and strength. One evening prior to leaving for Birmingham, King had lightened the mood of all present when, looking at Abernathy and knowing well his friend's habits, he had said, "Let me be sure to get arrested with people who don't snore."[61] On the night before the march, King had told the planners and supporters gathered in Room 30 of the Gaston Motel in Birmingham, "I don't know what will happen. I don't know where the money will come from. But I have to make a faith act."[62]

Born in Atlanta in 1929, King received a doctorate in theology from Boston University and, like his father, joined the Christian clergy. After university, King moved back to the South, even though "there had been offers of jobs in safe northern universities."[63] Later he became one of the founders and the president of the Southern Christian Leadership Conference (SCLC), an organization devoted to challenging racial segregation and advocating for civil rights. In its founding statement, the conference's leaders pointed to the violence against those struggling for racial justice and announced that "we have no moral

socialist system
a way of structuring economic activity in which private firms are allowed to operate and make decisions over production and distribution, but with significant governmental involvement to ensure economic equality.

capitalist system
a way of structuring economic activity in which private firms are allowed to make most or all of the decisions involving the production and distribution of goods and services.

Birmingham, Ala. Public Library Archives

▲ Southern Christian Leadership Conference leaders march in Birmingham, Alabama, in April 1963. Fred Shuttlesworth (left) is not carrying a coat. The plan was for Shuttlesworth to join in the march to show solidarity but then break off to organize and raise funds for the conference. However, he was arrested with the others. Reverend Ralph Abernathy (center), with an extra layer of clothing and a coat in preparation for imprisonment, appears relaxed. Reverend Martin Luther King Jr. (right), also clothed in preparation for arrest, appears to be much more concerned and contemplative.

choice, before God, but to delve deeper into the struggle—and to do so with greater reliance on non-violence and with greater unity, coordination, sharing and Christian understanding."[64]

King, Abernathy, and other civil rights leaders faced a near-constant threat of violence for their opposition to racial segregation, as did many other women and men who took on the white racial order in the American South. King's own home in Montgomery, Alabama, had been bombed in 1956, though both King and his wife escaped harm. Prior to that act of racial violence, King had also been verbally threatened in an anonymous phone call—a clear attempt to intimidate him. It didn't work. King, as well as other leaders, members, and supporters of the SCLC, pressed ahead.

That they were marching in Birmingham in 1963 was no accident. The city was a bastion of segregation, and threats of violence to anyone who resisted were pervasive. The protests were designed as acts of civil disobedience in which one defied a law seen as unjust and accepted the consequences of that defiance, as King put it, "openly, lovingly."[65]

For breaking a prohibition on their marching or protesting, King, Abernathy, and about fifty others were arrested and taken to Birmingham City Jail. King was thrown into solitary confinement—"the hole," as it was called—with only a cot with metal slats to sleep on. "You will never know the meaning of utter darkness," he recalled, "until you have lain in such a dungeon."[66]

WHITE CLERGY MEMBERS URGE MODERATION

The morning after King's arrest, a copy of an article from the *Birmingham News* was "slipped in to" his cell.[67] Titled "White Clergymen Urge Local Negroes to Withdraw from Demonstrations," the letter, written by eight white members of the Protestant, Catholic, and Jewish clergies, admonished King and the other leaders of the SCLC to slow down, to stop protesting, to end the strategy of civil disobedience in Birmingham.[68]

Calling the demonstrations "unwise and untimely" and "directed and led in part by outsiders," the eight clergy members argued that "honest convictions in racial matters could properly be pursued in the courts." They "commend[ed] the [Birmingham] community as a whole and the local news media and law enforcement officials in particular, on the calm manner in which these demonstrations ha[d] been handled." (However, a photograph taken less than a month later and published in the *New York Times* showing a young African American man being attacked by a police dog under the direction of a Birmingham police officer led millions of Americans to question claims of police restraint.) In closing, the clergy members urged Birmingham's "Negro community to withdraw support from these demonstrations."

DR. KING'S LETTER AFFIRMS NATURAL RIGHTS FOR AFRICAN AMERICANS

Writing in the margins of the smuggled newspaper, Martin Luther King Jr. penned a response from jail to the clergymen's accusations and advice.[69] His notes were smuggled out of the jail, typed up, and eventually published by a group of Quakers as the "Letter from Birmingham Jail." Though it did not have the benefit of King's powerful speaking voice to increase its impact, it is one of the most important documents of the American civil rights movement.

THE POWER OF THE MEDIA

AP Photo/Bill Hudson

African American activists in the civil rights movement of the 1960s used a variety of strategies to bring about social change, including holding sit-ins in whites-only areas, such as lunch counters and on public transportation, and organizing marches and demonstrations across the South. The white clergy who urged "moderation" said that those types of protests were unwise and argued that protesters should pursue institutional avenues, such as the courts, for change.

This photograph of a student activist being attacked by a police dog in Birmingham, Alabama, appeared on the front page of the *New York Times* in 1963. President John F. Kennedy is reported to have viewed it and said it sickened him. He also is said to have registered that it would make the United States look bad across the world, as Birmingham was "a dangerous situation for our image abroad."[70] Shortly afterward, Kennedy delivered his own famous civil rights speech, vindicating Martin Luther King Jr.'s statements in the "Letter from Birmingham Jail."

WHAT Do You Think?

What role do you think images like this may have played in shaping American public opinion on civil rights? Might this role be similar or different in the era of cell phone cameras and YouTube?

In the letter, King begins by offering his reply as a sincere response to the white clergymen's concerns, calling them "men of genuine goodwill." Then he defends his presence in Birmingham professionally, as president of the Southern Christian Leadership Conference. However, he also lays out a much more fundamental basis for his involvement. He declares, "I am in Birmingham because injustice is here."

King defends his and his movement's tactics on the basis of natural rights, drawing a distinction between just and unjust laws: "A just law is a man-made code that squares with the moral law or the law of God. An unjust law is a code that is out of harmony with the natural law." Racial oppression, he asserts, in all of its legal manifestations, is unjust. Individuals, therefore, have the right to break these unjust laws, but, he adds, "One who breaks an unjust law must do so openly, lovingly."

In a single sentence, more than three hundred words long, King lists the grievances, the injustices, and the evidence that led to his and many others' revolutionary acts. In its use of language, logic, and the principles of natural rights, the "Letter from Birmingham Jail" knows no superior as an American revolutionary pamphlet. Politically, one of the most important passages in the letter pointed to the white moderate as a severe obstacle to justice: "I have almost reached the regrettable conclusion that the Negro's great stumbling block in the stride toward freedom is not the White citizens' 'Councilor' or the Ku Klux Klanner, but the white moderate who is more devoted to 'order' than justice; who prefers a negative peace which is the absence of tension to a positive peace which is the presence of justice."

Doyle Brunson, one of the greatest No-Limit Texas Hold'Em poker players of all time, said of his poker strategy, "I want to put my opponent to a decision for all his chips."[71] The radicals of the American Revolution meant to present the colonial moderates with exactly the same decision. Through their actions—and with help from British reactions to their strategies—the radicals took away the possibility of a comfortable, moderate, middle ground. By creating a crisis and a confrontation, King and his fellow protesters sought to force white moderates to make a choice, to decide if racial segregation and the oppression of African Americans was consistent with the ideals of the United States or not. In their own ways, Bridget Mergens and the members of the Boyd County High Gay-Straight Alliance did the same thing.

WHAT HAVE I LEARNED?

1. Civil disobedience focuses primarily on _____.

   a. efforts to change voting laws

   b. defying a law seen as unjust and accepting the consequences of that defiance

   c. destruction of public property

   d. using the nation's civil courts to make change

2. In his "Letter from Birmingham Jail," King was responding to _____.

   a. white supremacist groups, to persuade them to cease their violent attacks on black people

   b. the president of the United States, to urge him to step in and force southern states to pass laws barring segregation

   c. students in Birmingham, to inspire them to join in nonviolent protest

   d. white clergy members, in reaction to their urging King and others to pursue their response to injustice via the court system

3. How is the "Letter from Birmingham Jail" similar to the Declaration of Independence? How is it different?

Answer Key: 1. b; 2. d.; 3. Answers may focus on the similarities of the appeals to natural rights and a violation of the social contract and on the differences in time, place, and context.

CONCLUSION: THE AMERICAN EXPERIMENT CONTINUES, AND YOU ARE PART OF IT

A study of American government requires understanding the ideas upon which it is based. It requires an understanding of the ways in which political institutions promote, shape, or hinder the fulfillment of these fundamental ideas. It requires a study of the past and the present. However, and most importantly, a deep study of American government requires that you think, and perhaps act, as a strategic player in the political space, which is rarely, if ever, neat and clean.

Should you choose to act in American politics—should you choose to stake your own claims for your rights—you will want to be well informed, about both your own positions on critical issues and the positions of those with whom you disagree. You will want to have developed your skills in analyzing the words, images, and data that will serve as your tools along the way. And you will need to question. What is American political culture? Is there such a thing? How do the institutions of American government make "good government" more or less likely?

At the beginning of the chapter, I stated that this book would be centered on stories, and it is. But why? How is it useful to begin a book that teaches American government and politics with stories about a high school student trying to start a Christian Bible study club, a group of high school students trying to start a GSA, or the American Revolution and the drafting of the Declaration of Independence and Dr. Martin Luther King Jr. writing his "Letter from Birmingham Jail"? Why read the stories? Why not just skim the definitions for the "important" content? Because the stories and, most importantly, your engagement with them have the potential to capture what definitions and lists might not:

The understanding that American political institutions did not fall out of the sky; they were created through conscious action and contestation, sometimes based upon success, sometimes based upon failure, and sometimes based upon pure chance

The comprehension that in the world of American government and politics, there is rarely, if ever, an either/or solution to major problems but instead a complex interplay among ideals, actions, time, and place

The understanding that the development of American government and politics has always involved the experiences of individuals and groups whose lives were written out of conventional narratives

The realization that people matter, even if they do not succeed

The knowledge that your own voices matter—that your own opinions, thoughtfully constructed and respectfully offered, matter, even if these ideas and opinions may seem to be outside some perception of what you are supposed to think or what others tell you to think

As you read, engage with, and discuss the material in this book and in your courses, there are only two things of which I will try to convince you: People like you matter. And your stories matter as well, even if nobody ever retells them in a book.

The American experiment always was a complicated and incomplete thing. It still is. At its heart, it poses one difficult and basic question: Can a people design and maintain a government that uplifts and energizes its citizens rather than oppresses them? The answer to that question is not up to other people. It is up to you.

CHAPTER REVIEW

This chapter's main ideas are reflected in the Learning Objectives. By reviewing them here, you should be able to **remember** the key points, **know** the terms that are central to the topic, and **think** about the critical issues raised in each section.

1.1 Explain how diverse Americans have been able to use the same political tools to achieve their own distinct visions of good government.

REMEMBER
- The American political system is designed so that different individuals and groups of people, regardless of their points of view and backgrounds, are able to access the same political tools, such as federal and state laws and different forms of political action, in order to bring about change.

KNOW
- politics (p. 3)
- government (p. 3)

THINK
- Americans with very different political goals and perspectives have based their efforts on many of the same fundamental ideas. Why do you think this is possible?

1.2 Define the key elements of American political culture.

REMEMBER
- The American political system was founded on a set of shared ideas and values that together are called political culture.
- The most important aspects of American political culture are the commitments to equality, rights, liberty, the pursuit of happiness, and religious freedom, and the idea that America is unique in the ways it has developed.
- Those ideas and values define the relationship of Americans to their government and to each other.

KNOW
- American dream (p. 9)
- American exceptionalism (p. 10)
- American political culture (p. 7)
- democracy (p. 7)
- economic equality (p. 7)
- inalienable rights (p. 7)
- liberty (p. 8)
- natural rights (p. 7)
- political equality (p. 7)
- political science (p. 7)
- social contract (p. 7)
- social equality (p. 7)

THINK
- What are some of the key ideas that define American political culture?
- To what extent do your experiences inform you of the degree to which these ideas have been realized?

1.3 Identify the political, social, and economic events and institutions that gave rise to the American Revolution and reflect upon what was and was not achieved.

REMEMBER
- The Declaration of Independence was drafted primarily by Thomas Jefferson in connection with the Second Continental Congress in 1776.
- Jefferson and his colleagues in the Continental Congress made a series of strategic decisions in incorporating key ideas from history into a document that successfully laid out the justification for independence.
- Colonial economies depended upon slavery and slave labor. Slaves, the descendants of slaves, and native peoples were not extended rights under the Declaration of Independence.
- The Declaration was shaped by the politics and historical context of American colonies trying to assert themselves in the face of tyranny.
- The political, social, and economic ideas that circulated in political pamphlets, especially Paine's *Common Sense*, contributed greatly to the rationale for independence and revolution in the face of increasing British taxation.
- Women played a role in the economy and affairs of the colonies but were not extended full rights.

KNOW
- Albany Plan (p. 12)
- Daughters of Liberty (p. 18)
- Intolerable Acts (p. 16)
- political propaganda (p. 14)
- Second Continental Congress (p. 19)
- Seven Years' War (p. 12)
- Sons of Liberty (p. 14)

THINK
- What were the main ideas behind the Declaration of Independence?
- Do you think the ideals in the Declaration have been achieved in today's United States?

1.4 Describe the core features of American political institutions.

REMEMBER
- In the American model of representative democracy, the forms our political institutions take affect how people are represented.
- The institutional structure of the United States is that of a constitutional republic, in which the people elect representatives to make most of the laws and policies in the nation rather than voting on them directly.
- Institutions can both protect and restrict rights, and people may use and change them to protect their own rights or those of others.
- America's political institutions also structure the country's economy.

KNOW
- capitalist system (p. 23)
- communist system (p. 22)
- constitutional republic (p. 22)
- direct democracy (p. 21)
- economy (p. 22)
- political institutions (p. 21)
- representative democracy (p. 22)
- socialist system (p. 23)

THINK
- What form of government does America have?
- How are political decisions in America made?

1.5 Consider the ways in which the "Letter from Birmingham Jail" draws upon core American ideals.

REMEMBER
- Dr. Martin Luther King Jr.'s "Letter from Birmingham Jail" (1963), one of the most important documents of the civil rights movement, directly echoes the claims for rights made by Thomas Jefferson over 150 years prior.
- Even today, claims for natural rights—rights that cannot be denied by governments—must be made.

THINK
- In what ways is King's "Letter from Birmingham Jail" similar to the Declaration of Independence? In what ways do they differ?

Carl Juste/Miami Herald/TNS via Getty Images

CHAPTER 2

THE CONSTITUTION OF THE UNITED STATES

A New Vision of Representative Government

◀ Paulina Perez signs a giant banner printed with the preamble to the U.S. Constitution during a demonstration against a ruling by the Supreme Court in 2010 that allowed unlimited, though uncoordinated, campaign contributions by associations of individuals and corporations.

"**W**e the People of the United States. . . ." Perhaps no seven words are as important in American political history as these. Penned by Gouverneur Morris in Philadelphia, Pennsylvania, during the fateful summer of 1787, these words did more than begin a document. They sought to *constitute*, to create, a new nation. In the Declaration of Independence, Thomas Jefferson and the other members of the Second Continental Congress had announced to the colonies and to the world why they felt that separation from Great Britain was justified and necessary. Following the American Revolution, that goal was achieved . . . but then what?

In the years following the Revolution, the American states and the government that they had collectively agreed to form struggled against the realities of financial crises, the possibility of foreign invasion, and the threat of internal discord and even revolution. Against this backdrop, a group of delegates convened in Philadelphia in 1787 to create a new government—a new *kind* of government—although they were not united on a single vision.

The delegates to the Constitutional Convention drafted and then tried to sell to skeptical individuals in the thirteen American states a blueprint for a new government, though the delegates themselves were often divided about what this government should be, how it should be structured, and how much power it should have. In spite of all of these divisions and challenges, they produced a **constitution**, a document that simultaneously creates a people, sets out fundamental principles on which these people agree to be governed, and establishes the rules and institutions through which this governing will take place.

In this chapter, we will explore the stories of the events leading up to the Constitutional Convention, the political debates within the convention, and the debates surrounding the ratification process. We will focus primarily on one person: James Madison of Virginia. Though he was hardly the most powerful political figure of the time, Madison's efforts were instrumental in shaping the Constitution of the United States.

constitution
a document that defines and creates a people politically, sets out the fundamental principles of governance, and creates the rules and institutions through which a people choose to self-govern.

JAMES MADISON PLANS FOR A REPUBLIC THAT WILL LAST

- **Describe the ideas and historical context that shaped James Madison's thinking about republics.**

In the spring of 1786, James Madison Jr. settled into his home in Montpelier, Virginia, with two trunks full of books. As one of America's first political scientists, Madison's goal was to apply science to the study of government. The subject of his studies that spring was the unspringlike topic of death, specifically the death of governments. Kingdoms and empires had endured, sometimes for centuries, under the rule of monarchs and emperors. But **republics**, governments ruled by representatives of the people, without exception had eventually died. Madison wanted to know how a people could create a republic that lasted: one that could avoid being taken over by a small group of men or descending into civil war or anarchy, one that was strong enough to govern effectively but yet would not trample the rights of its citizens.

In 1786, America was in a precarious position. In the tumultuous years that followed independence, the young nation had been plagued by economic disruption, European military and economic powers,

republics
governments ruled by representatives of the people.

and the dangers of rebellion within the thirteen states. The country needed a clear path forward if it was to survive—a new American government. It needed someone who could sell such a plan to a skeptical public, too.[1] Madison poured himself into this project systematically, scientifically, and with a great deal of energy.

Though he was shy, often sick, and a quiet public speaker, Madison was well educated and he did his homework. In 1786, as the American government of the time came under increasingly harsh criticism and calls to fix or replace it grew louder, Madison's years of preparation allowed him to help shape the agenda of the debates taking place in his newly independent country and to get others to talk about his ideas, whether they agreed with him or not. In the spring of 1787, Madison, true to form, showed up in Philadelphia having done his homework. Together with a group of similarly practical men, he attempted to create a republic that would last, one that would be strong enough to govern but not so strong as to trample on the rights and liberties of its citizens. Madison and his compatriots sought practical, institutional solutions for the seemingly timeless tendency of political leaders to pursue power, prestige, and riches, even when this meant the downfall of their own republics. That Madison and his comrades were pragmatic politicians was no surprise; most of them had already been involved in the real-world politics of their own colonies and, later, states. Writing in 1923, Robert Livingston Schuyler captured this essential fact about those who shaped the new American Republic better than anyone since. "The Fathers," he declared, "were practical men."[2] Ideas and ideals are certainly part of America's constitutional heritage, but so are politics.

Madison's immediate concern in 1786 was to prepare for a conference set to take place in Annapolis, Maryland, in the fall. Officially, the Annapolis Convention had been called to address trade and navigation disputes between states. Unofficially, at least in the minds of Madison and those who shared his views, the hope was that the outcome of the convention might lead to significant changes in the fundamental structure of the government of the United States. Though Madison wanted to see major reforms, he was not optimistic about the prospect for real change. "Tho' my wishes are in favor of such an event," he wrote to Thomas Jefferson in August, "yet I despair so much of its accomplishment at the present crisis that I do not extend my views beyond a Commercial Reform. To speak the truth *I almost despair even of this.*"[3]

▲ An engraving of James Madison, American statesman and political theorist. His study of republics led him to investigate how to create a form of government led by people that was capable of enduring.

▲ Montpelier, Madison's residence in Orange County, Virginia, home to over one hundred slaves whose labor supported the plantation.

His lack of optimism turned out to be well founded. Only five of the thirteen states sent representatives to the convention; the other states either did not appoint anyone or did not do so in time to make it to the meeting. Despite the poor attendance, however, delegates to the convention kept the dialogue of reform moving by calling for a convention in Philadelphia the following spring to discuss how to make the American government more effective in dealing with issues of trade and other pressing needs of the nation.

Madison's research, preparation, intellect, and understated political skill played perhaps one of the most important roles in the creation of the Constitution of the United States. The American Republic that he helped shape was based on the premise that liberty is something with which people are born, something that cannot be given or taken away by governments. This concept was expressed powerfully in the Declaration of Independence in its timeless affirmation, "We hold these truths to be self-evident, that all men are created equal." As we have explored in Chapter 1, however, this American liberty was not originally meant for all.

Like Jefferson and George Washington—the most respected person in America during this period—Madison owned slaves. Though his own writings show that Madison struggled personally against the institution of slavery and that he realized how the practice had corrupted past republics, Madison's Virginia plantation had more than one hundred slaves. Under Virginia's laws of the time, Madison, or any other slave owner, could "correct" a slave for any offense. If that slave died under such a correction, the master would likely not be punished at all. He could take a child from his or her family and sell the child into an unknown future for profit.[4] As the delegates convened in Philadelphia, they had to struggle with these contradictions.

WHAT HAVE I LEARNED?

1. In a republic, citizens _____.
   a. vote on most laws
   b. select representatives to vote on laws
   c. interpret the Constitution
   d. are not allowed to vote

2. A constitution is _____.
   a. a trade agreement between countries
   b. a document that defines and creates a people politically, sets out the fundamental principles of governance, and creates the rules and institutions through which a people choose to self-govern
   c. a document granting citizenship to an individual
   d. a grant of sovereignty given to a new nation by other world nations

3. What was the main dilemma that James Madison faced in thinking about reforming American government?

4. What was the significance of the Annapolis Convention?

Answer Key: 1. b; 2. b; 3. Answers should include a discussion of the need to have a republic that was strong enough to last but not so strong as to trample on individual rights and liberties; 4. Answers should focus on the idea that the dialogue about reform of government advanced.

THE CONFEDERAL SYSTEM MADE COORDINATION BETWEEN THE STATES DIFFICULT

- Explain the challenges faced by the nation following the American Revolution in trying to form a government strong enough to rule effectively but not so strong as to oppress the rights of Americans.

The government that Madison and his like-minded colleagues hoped to change was the first government of the United States. It was a confederation: a union of thirteen sovereign states in which the states, not the union, were supreme. It had been created by the **Articles of Confederation and Perpetual Union**.

Articles of Confederation and Perpetual Union
a constituting document calling for the creation of a union of thirteen sovereign states in which the states, and not the union, were the centers of political power.

Adopted by the Second Continental Congress in 1777 and formally ratified in 1781, the articles created a union of sovereign states that depended on cooperation for its survival. While they had successfully guided the country through war and the accompanying economic and material devastation, the articles had few carrots or sticks to make member states work together to make and carry out national policy. By 1786, the American confederation was showing its limitations, at least in the minds of those who wanted a stronger union.

THE ARTICLES OF CONFEDERATION ATTEMPTED TO UNITE THE STATES WHILE PRESERVING THEIR AUTHORITY

When they created the Articles of Confederation, the delegates to the Second Continental Congress had debated two related issues. Both involved mistrust. Colonists in one state did not always trust the motives of the governments of the other states. They also did not trust any government that would rule over them from far away, whether it be that of Great Britain before the war or of the new American nation after victory had been achieved.

Though it may be difficult now to imagine a United States in which states were strong and the nation was weak, the idea that the states were the real centers of power was not at all unnatural for Americans at the time. Long after the Constitution was ratified, many Americans still referred to "these United States" instead of "the United States." Since their inception as business enterprises, plantations, or religious communities, the British colonies had been self-sufficient and left alone to govern themselves. Colonists often viewed members of other colonies with distrust. They also reacted strongly against Britain's tardy attempt to create a more centralized colonial policy in the decades before the American Revolution.[5]

During the debates over the Articles of Confederation, mistrust of other colonies crystallized in conflicts over land, representation, and sovereignty. Some colonies had land claims on parts of other colonies. Small coastal colonies, such as Delaware and Rhode Island, whose size was fixed by their location, viewed the western states' claims on Native American land with worry and suspicion. How big would Virginia, whose charter had land claims extending to the "South Sea," eventually become?[6] "The most acrimonious disagreements," according to one historian, "were over control of western lands."[7] The views of the indigenous peoples on questions of ownership did not factor into these calculations.

UNDER THE CONFEDERAL SYSTEM, STATES HAD SOVEREIGNTY AND EQUAL REPRESENTATION

Because of concerns over land rights, the Articles of Confederation provided states with protections against the possibility of any other state claiming disputed territory on its own, without the approval of the confederal government. In the face of the prospect of large, populous, and ever-growing neighbors, smaller states demanded, and received, equal representation in the new government. (See Figure 2.1.) Each state had one vote in the new Congress. This Confederation Congress was unicameral, meaning it had only one chamber. States selected their representatives to the legislature and could choose the number of representatives they sent, though each state's delegation had to agree on these decisions, and each state received only one vote. Finally, states and not the new union would be sovereign, a right that was firmly established in the document.[8]

Leading up to the Revolutionary War, the relationship between the colonies and Great Britain was one of mutual lack of understanding and mistrust. The colonies failed to see how they played a part in Britain's role in global politics and struggles against other empires. For its part, Great Britain failed to understand that what had been plantations, business enterprises, and religious outposts "had grown up and become states in the making."[9] This did not, however, mean naturally united colonies or, later, naturally united states. Each state had its own interests, and each worried that it might lose control over its future to other states or to a national government with its own agendas and desires.

The Original Thirteen Colonies and the Western Territories

These two maps show the original thirteen British colonies in 1775 and the American states and territories in 1790. Note the vast areas of land bordered by powerful states such as Virginia. Smaller coastal states feared the growth in size and power of these larger states.

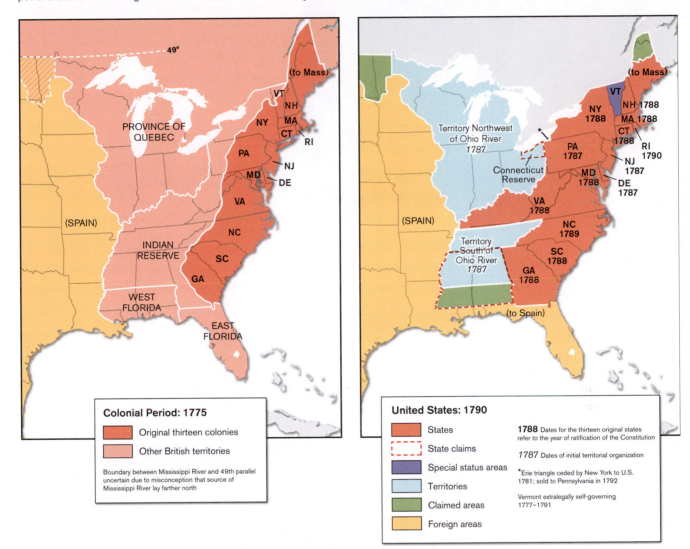

Colonial Period: 1775

- Original thirteen colonies
- Other British territories

Boundary between Mississippi River and 49th parallel uncertain due to misconception that source of Mississippi River lay farther north

United States: 1790

- States
- State claims
- Special status areas
- Territories
- Claimed areas
- Foreign areas

1788 Dates for the thirteen original states refer to the year of ratification of the Constitution

1787 Dates of initial territorial organization

*Erie triangle ceded by New York to U.S. 1781; sold to Pennsylvania in 1792

Vermont extralegally self-governing 1777–1791

THE CONFEDERAL GOVERNMENT WAS DESIGNED TO BE WEAK

The confederal government under the Articles of Confederation was intentionally made to be weak. Colonists were experiencing the tyranny of British rule, and they did not want to re-create it in a new American version. The confederal government could not tax its citizens, and it could not force states to carry out its policies. States could recall their representatives at will, and limits were placed on how long a representative could serve.[10] There was no independent judicial branch; one existed primarily to resolve differences between states but had no real way of enforcing these decisions. The president of the Confederation Congress was even less powerful than the delegates and was there mostly to keep order and count votes.

▲ A United States continental currency sixty-five-dollar banknote from 1779. The collapse in the value of the currency caused severe economic disruption and unrest in the years leading up to the Constitutional Convention.

The confederal government did have certain powers. Only it could declare war and conduct foreign policy, though it had to rely on states to pay for these activities. In practice, the confederal government continually faced the challenge of getting states to contribute to the national effort. Sometimes the states had good reason not to comply with these requests. During the war, colonies had been reluctant to send away scarce troops or supplies when they might be desperately needed close to home. Because of concerns over land rights, the Articles of Confederation provided states with protections against the possibility of any other state claiming disputed territory on its own, without the approval of the confederal government.

Lack of money was a constant problem, and the Continental Army was continually without adequate supplies and occasionally faced starvation. Due to the difficulties of collecting contributions from the states or getting loans from European governments, Congress made its own currency, called the continental, which was backed only by the promise of the government to make good on its debts, assuming it won and survived the war intact. The currency later collapsed, creating financial chaos, which only added to calls for reform.

▼ TABLE 2.1

The Confederal System: Key Features

Confederation government	Binding document	Sovereignty	Economy	Confederation Congress	Confederation judiciary	Confederation president
• Weak by design: no ability for government to tax, no enforcement of policies • States could recall representatives at will • Reliant on states for funding for things like war • Power to declare war, conduct foreign policy • Slavery permitted, not regulated	• Articles of Confederation • Protected states in land disputes • Amendment required all thirteen colonies' approval	• State are sovereign, not confederal government	• Currency = "the continental." • Not backed by gold	• Unicameral • One state = one vote • Delegates have term limits	• Not independent, little enforcement power • Focused on resolving conflicts between states	• Less power than delegates

THE PROSPECT OF CHANGES TO THE SYSTEMS OF SLAVERY AND REPRESENTATION SOWED UNREST

To ensure that the agreements made during their creation would hold, the Articles of Confederation placed a tall hurdle in the path of potential reformers: changing or amending the articles required the approval of all thirteen of the states. In spite of what many saw as problems with the articles, many Americans did not want to amend, much less replace, them.

Some in the southern states feared that slavery, which was allowed and unregulated under the confederal government, might be restricted or outlawed. Citizens of smaller states feared losing their equal representation in Congress and seeing it replaced by representation based on population, a change that would drastically weaken their position. And many worried that something worse than the problems with the articles might come out of a process of revising them. When a small group of people takes it upon themselves to overturn a political order, there is no guarantee that what they create will not be worse, maybe much worse, than what came before.

Politicians in many states were still mistrustful of the actions and motives of their counterparts in other states. Many were also still nervous about the idea of a strong national government. Since the American Revolution, the political landscape had altered and the balance of political power had shifted.[11] State legislative elections in 1786 and 1787 handed strong victories to nationalist candidates, who were in favor of a stronger national government. These nationalist-controlled legislatures would be selecting the delegates to the Philadelphia convention.

FEARS OF UNREST AND REBELLION WORRIED STATE GOVERNMENTS

Shays' Rebellion, named after Daniel Shays, one of its military leaders, was a grassroots popular uprising against the Massachusetts state government, one that, in the minds of many of its citizens, had grown too powerful, too distant, too much like that of Great Britain. Though the rebellion took place in Massachusetts, the conditions that caused it and the popular anger that fueled it were also present in other states. This crisis added to the sense of urgency in the American confederation, and it provided ammunition to those who tried to replace the structure of government under the articles. Some, like James Madison, wanted a stronger nation, a different kind of republic than had ever been tried before. Others sought a return to monarchy and the British Empire.

The roots of Shays' Rebellion were both economic and political. In the difficult economic times that followed the Revolutionary War, there was a shortage of "hard money," of gold and silver and money backed by gold and silver. What there was no shortage of was debt. Citizens and governments throughout the confederation found themselves unable to pay debts that had been incurred during the war or during the tough economic times that followed. Shopkeepers and cash-strapped state governments alike demanded that their customers and citizens pay debts and taxes in hard currency. Foreclosures—the taking of property to pay outstanding debts backed by that property—were widespread.

The first responses of citizens in Massachusetts and other states were political. Towns asked state governments to issue paper money to help citizens settle their debts. Local citizens petitioned their governments to take action to help them. Some towns in Massachusetts called for a new state constitutional convention. Much of the debt, however, was owed to wealthy elites, and those elites wanted to be paid back in real money, not paper promises. Some states were sympathetic to the people's demands. The government of Rhode Island issued paper money, and the state did not see widespread civil unrest, though many elites came to view the "paper money" politicians as dangerous and undependable. Rhode Islanders, for their part, refused to send delegates to the Constitutional Convention and continued to resist the push for a stronger national government.

The government of Massachusetts held the line, siding with the banking interests. Many of the state's citizens began to feel that they had successfully broken with an oppressive government in London only to replace it with one nearly as bad in Boston. When their attempts at political solutions failed, citizens—especially in the western part of the state—began to take the kind of action they had against King George III and the British Parliament. They rebelled.

REBELLION BEGAN

To each other, the members of Shays' Rebellion were "Regulators," a label used by the American rebels in the struggle against Great Britain.[12] Many were Revolutionary War veterans with sufficient military skills and popular support to provide a genuine challenge to the Massachusetts government. The Regulators organized themselves by town and family, and they made a point of trying not to antagonize the local population. Instead, they focused on the courts, as had been done before the Revolution, closing them down in the hopes of stalling the foreclosure process until a solution to the debt crisis could be achieved in the state legislature. Although many closures were committed by rebels carrying weapons, some of them "were peaceful, even jocular."[13]

The rebellion and Massachusetts's response to it began to follow a script similar to that of the American Revolution. Citizens took action. The government (this time of Massachusetts, not Great Britain) clamped down, which only made the population more radical. In October 1786, the Massachusetts legislature passed the Riot Act, which absolved sheriffs and other officials from prosecution for killing rioters. With fears of standing armies fresh in the minds of its members, the resistance grew and became more radical, though never as radical as it was portrayed in the Boston newspapers, which accused the Regulators of wanting to redistribute private property[14] or hoping to reunite with Great Britain.[15] Both claims were untrue but served to increase the level of fear and concern within and beyond the state's borders.

The Massachusetts state militia was unable to put down the rebellion. Many militia members, themselves Revolutionary War veterans, sided with the rebels. The government of the United States, the Confederation Congress, could not raise an army; its requests to the states for money were refused by every state except Virginia. The wealthy elites in Boston ultimately paid for an army on their own, loaning money to Massachusetts for the purposes of suppressing the rebellion.

Daniel Shays, a former captain in the Revolutionary War, joined the Regulators later than many but became a commander of its largest regiment, partly due to his notable service in the war. In January 1787, Shays' regiment and two others moved on the state armory at Springfield. Major General William Shepard, commanding the newly raised state militia and in possession of artillery that the Regulators lacked, defeated Shays and the rebels, who were forced to withdraw. Two rebel leaders were hanged, and most of the other rebels eventually returned to their farms and towns. Shays escaped to Vermont and was later pardoned, though he never returned to Massachusetts. With the help of the Boston newspapers, Daniel Shays became the personification of anarchy in the United States. In reality, most of the Regulators wanted only to keep their farms and keep their family and friends out of foreclosure or debtors' jail.

The Granger Collection, New York

▲ An engraving depicts the British colonial governor of North Carolina (center) suppressing a Regulators' revolt in 1771. Daniel Shays and other members of the rebellion in Massachusetts patterned their protests against the state government on the actions of the Revolutionary War Regulators.

FROM SHAYS' REBELLION CAME NEW OPPORTUNITY

After the Revolutionary War, George Washington had, as promised, stayed away from public life and retired to his slaveholding plantation in Mount Vernon. But upon receiving what turned out to be exaggerated reports of the strength of Shays' militia from one of his most trusted former generals, Washington grew fearful of what would become of the country. In a letter to James Madison in November 1786, Washington identified precisely what was needed to "check . . . these disorders": a strong and "energetic Constitution."[16]

IMAGE AS A POLITICAL TOOL

One skill in political science is the ability to *use* images for a political purpose—to highlight an issue, to advance an argument, or to challenges arguments that others are making. Another is the ability to *interpret* images so used—to understand what the creator is trying to accomplish, to look for cues in the images or ways in which they are presented, and to critique the creators' intent and arguments.

Consider these two depictions of Shays' Rebellion. Though they aim to depict the same broad set of events, they do so in very different ways. In the top image, the Regulators are seen calmly assembled on the steps of a Massachusetts courthouse.

The bottom image depicts violence and discord.

Recall the ways in which advocates for a stronger national government, such as James Madison, and those in favor of maintaining the Articles of Confederation disagreed with the most severe dangers facing the young nation. While these particular images were not used during the debates over amending or replacing the articles, they do point to differences between the two groups.

The Granger Collection, New York

WHAT Do You Think?

Which of these images corresponds better with the view of Shays' Rebellion held by those who wanted a stronger national government? Which might correspond better with the view of those who were wary of a strong national government? Can you think of images that you have seen of modern-day controversial events that try to shape the viewer's perception of those events?

The Granger Collection, New York

Madison may have sensed that Shays' Rebellion would be enough to lure Washington out of retirement and place his unequaled status among Americans behind the effort to create a new political order. Though initially reluctant to attend the Philadelphia conference, Washington eventually agreed; the Philadelphia convention would have the most famous and respected American there to give it legitimacy.

Rebellion was not the only worry among the new states. Great Britain had been defeated but hardly destroyed. The nation's troops had merely been pushed back into Canada, and that was only due to the help of Great Britain's other rivals, who themselves might not always be helpful to the young United States. As states sent their delegates to Philadelphia in the spring of 1787, the world powers were watching, expecting, and perhaps hoping for failure.

WHAT HAVE I LEARNED?

1. The Articles of Confederation produced a national government that was _____.

   a. supreme to the powers of the states

   b. dependent upon the state governments

   c. designed to ensure an efficient national government, just as in Great Britain

   d. similar in most ways to the government created by the Constitution

2. Key provisions in the Articles of Confederation that were designed to protect states against the power of other states included _____.

   a. a requirement that states could change their boundaries without approval

   b. a fully independent supreme court

   c. a unicameral legislature that gave each state one vote

   d. All of the above

3. What problems in the new nation did Shays' Rebellion highlight? How did people like James Madison capitalize on the crisis to pursue their political goals?

Answer Key: 1. b; 2. c; 3. Answers should discuss the inability of the national government to suppress the rebellion as well as how those in favor of a stronger national government highlighted this weakness.

DELEGATES REACH A COMPROMISE AT THE CONSTITUTIONAL CONVENTION

- **Describe the role that compromise over states' interests played in shaping the government during the Constitutional Convention.**

In May 1787, fifty-five delegates from twelve of the thirteen states began to arrive in Philadelphia. Rhode Island and its paper money men had refused to participate. Though it was by some reports a hot, humid summer, the windows of the Pennsylvania State House where delegates met were shut to ensure secrecy. This secrecy was partly to allow the delegates to say what they wanted, partly because none were sure how citizens in the various states would react to their deliberations. At the time, the meeting was called the Grand Convention or the Federal Convention, not the **Constitutional Convention** as it is called today. The delegates had not been sent to Philadelphia to write a new constitution, only to fix the Articles of Confederation as necessary. Writing a new constitution would have been thought of as a revolutionary act, which it was.

James Madison arrived eleven days early with his research in hand. Though he would become perhaps the most influential person at the convention, Madison was not the only delegate who shaped the final document. And he was certainly not the most famous person there. George Washington served as the president of the proceedings. Most delegates expected that he would be the leader of whatever government emerged, if the convention could agree on one. Benjamin Franklin, possibly the second-most famous person in America, was also present, but because of poor health, four prisoners from a city jail carried him through the streets of Philadelphia in a chair on his way to and from the convention. He remained a shrewd politician, however, and used his many skills at important moments in the debate.

Other delegates also guided and shaped the debates and outcomes. Alexander Hamilton, who had served as Washington's aide in the war, emerged as one of the leading proponents of a strong national government. James Wilson of Pennsylvania made important, often unheralded, intellectual contributions to the convention. Wilson served as an intellectual ally of Madison's during and after the convention. Also from Pennsylvania, Gouverneur Morris assembled the various resolutions passed by the convention into a whole document, adding his own literary style and crafting the declaration at its beginning, "We the People of the United States."

Constitutional Convention
a meeting held in Philadelphia in 1787 at which state delegates met to fix the Articles of Confederation that would result in the drafting of the U.S. Constitution.

Many important leaders from the Revolution could not or would not attend. Thomas Jefferson and John Adams, both future presidents and supporters of the Constitution, were out of the country in service of the American government. Others, like Samuel Adams and Patrick Henry, both vocal revolutionaries and opponents of a national constitution, were not selected as delegates or refused to go, sensing that the delegates planned to do much more than merely revise the Articles of Confederation. Their suspicions were correct. Samuel Adams was skeptical of what might emerge from the convention, wary of the dangers to liberty that a strong central government might pose and concerned that such a government could not adequately address the diverse needs of the states.[17] Patrick Henry became one of the most effective opponents to the document once it had been submitted to the states. "Here is a revolution as radical as that which separated us from Great Britain," he wrote.[18]

The Granger Collection, New York

▲ George Washington presiding at the Constitutional Convention at Philadelphia in 1787. Considerable measures were taken to ensure the secrecy of the proceedings at the convention.

The delegates who assembled in Philadelphia certainly did not represent a snapshot of the people living in the thirteen states. All were men. Most were well educated. None were slaves, former slaves, or Native Americans. Roughly one-third were slave owners. Not all were wealthy, but they were all elites. Unlike the revolutionaries who would soon lead France into chaos in the name of democracy, however, most of the Founders of the American Republic had previous practical political experience to guide them and temper their revolutionary ideals—Madison included. The solutions that the delegates came up with were pragmatic, political, and strategic, for better and for worse.

DELEGATES LOOK TO AMERICA'S STATE CONSTITUTIONS FOR MODELS, GOOD AND BAD

In the decade between the Declaration of Independence and the Philadelphia convention, individual states had drafted their own constitutions. They were often very different from each other. Pennsylvania's state constitution was the most democratic. All real power rested in a unicameral legislature whose legislators served one-year terms. To many elites, the Pennsylvania constitution represented nothing more than institutionalized mob rule,[19] sometimes at the expense of religious minorities. Massachusetts's constitution was much less democratic, with a much more powerful governor and property requirements to serve in the government. To the Regulators and those who sympathized with them, Massachusetts had replaced Great Britain's royal aristocracy with Boston's constitutional aristocracy. As they convened in Philadelphia, the delegates drew from the experiences of the various states as they tried to fashion a new form of government. Some worried about democracy, others about aristocracy. Most worried about failure.

DELEGATES DEBATE FORMS OF REPRESENTATION AND THE POWERS OF THE NATIONAL GOVERNMENT

By Friday, May 25, 1787, enough delegates had made it over the muddy Pennsylvania roads to begin the deliberations. Their first order of business was to unanimously select Washington as president of the convention. Madison, though not selected as the official reporter for the convention, took a seat up front and assumed the role informally. The other delegates were agreeable to this and made sure he got copies of their speeches to be entered into this unofficial record.[20] Much of what we know about what happened in Philadelphia comes from his notes.

The delegates adopted a set of rules to guide themselves, calling for absolute secrecy about their deliberations.[21] They knew that the enormous task of coming to an agreement would be made more difficult if the details of their discussions were leaked. It was said that a member of the convention was assigned to attend dinners with Franklin, who was fond of alcoholic beverages, to change the conversation if Franklin began to talk too loosely.[22] The delegates agreed not to record their individual votes so that they would not feel bound by previous votes if the same issues came up again, giving themselves the ability to compromise and change their positions as needed.

As the proceedings began, the Delaware delegation put the issue of how states were to be represented in the new government on the table—the most contentious issue of the convention and the one that determined so many other outcomes. No other question so dominated the convention during the early weeks and months of deliberations or threatened to tear it apart. How would states be represented in a new government? Would it be the same one state, one vote formula as under the Articles of Confederation? Or would states be represented on the basis of their population or wealth?

THE VIRGINIA PLAN OUTLINES A SYSTEM OF PROPORTIONAL REPRESENTATION FOR THE STATES

On the third day of the convention, the delegation from Virginia presented a set of proposals for the rest of the members to consider. The ideas behind what came to be known as the **Virginia Plan** were James Madison's. Madison had been building their foundations for more than a year and had coached the rest of the Virginia delegation in the days before their presentation.[23] The Virginia Plan was much more than a modification of the Articles of Confederation. Its proposals described a new, national form of government, although Madison and his allies used the less controversial word *federal* when presenting and defending it.

The Virginia Plan laid out the failures of the American confederation—weakness in national defense and the conduct of foreign policy, conflicts between states, and the failure to suppress internal rebellion—and stepped out an answer to those defects: The national government would be strong. Its constitution would be "paramount to the state constitutions."[24] It would consist of three branches: a legislative branch to make laws, an executive branch to carry the laws out, and a judicial branch to resolve disputes between the states and between the national government and the states. The national legislature would be bicameral, consisting of two houses. Members of the lower house would be elected directly by the people. The upper house would consist of representatives nominated by state legislatures and chosen by members of the lower house. The executive and some members of the judiciary would have the power to veto—or overturn—acts of the legislature, which could, in turn, override that veto. The supremacy of the national government would be unmistakable. It could make laws as needed to govern the country as a whole and use military force against states if necessary.

Many details were vague or literally left blank, such as the length of terms of members of Congress, the frequency of elections, and the number of votes needed to override a veto under his plan. The change in representation of states, however, was clear. The Virginia Plan proposed to overturn the one state, one vote structure of the Articles of Confederation. Instead there would be a system of proportional representation in which more populous states would have more members in both houses of the legislature. The answer to the question, "Proportional to what?" was left somewhat vague, however: Would population counts include slaves? The Virginia Plan was not clear.

Delegates from smaller states reacted immediately and strongly to the Virginia Plan's suggestion of proportional representation. They had successfully fought it off in the Second Continental Congress, when the articles were drafted, and they continued to fight against it. Under the Virginia Plan, Virginia would have sixteen votes to South Carolina's one, plus all there knew that Virginia's boundaries were far from settled. They seemed limitless. New Jersey's William Paterson vowed never to approve the plan, saying that New Jersey "would be swallowed up."[25]

For the next two weeks, however, the convention discussed the Virginia Plan and little else. Within days of its introduction, several provisions of the plan—a government of three branches and a bicameral legislature—had already been approved. Madison and his fellow nationalists had won the first victory in the strategic political struggle over the Constitution. They had set the agenda. They had forced the opposition to respond to their ideas.

THE NEW JERSEY PLAN MAINTAINS EQUAL VOTES IN THE LEGISLATURE

Two weeks later, Paterson presented the small states' response to the Virginia Plan. Known as the **New Jersey Plan**, it proposed to strengthen the power of the confederal government but make relatively few changes to the Articles of Confederation. There would be only one house in the legislature, just as

Virginia Plan
a plan of government calling for a strong national government with three branches of government and a bicameral legislature, with legislators elected using proportional representation.

New Jersey Plan
a plan of government that preserved many of the provisions in the Articles of Confederation, including the unicameral legislature with equal votes for each state, but strengthened the confederal government.

under the articles. Each state delegation (chosen by state legislatures) would still get one equal vote in that legislature. That legislature would get new powers, mostly over taxation and the economy, though it would still depend on the states for some revenue. The executive and judicial branches were much less well envisioned than under the Virginia Plan. Paterson correctly argued that his state's plan was consistent with the purpose of the meeting in Philadelphia; the original mandate of the convention had included only making some changes to the articles. However, delegates had already been debating almost nothing except the Virginia Plan, the framework of which centered on a strong national government and provisions that would essentially replace the current form of government.

After Paterson had presented his plan, Madison proceeded to "tear the New Jersey plan to pieces."[26] Madison argued that the New Jersey Plan would leave the nation with all the problems that had motivated the convention in the first place: tax collection across state borders would remain a disaster; rebellions such as the one Massachusetts had just barely put down would continue to plague the Republic.[27]

Madison and James Wilson grew frustrated over the less populous states' objections to the Virginia Plan. To these two men, neither the states nor the national government was or should be supreme; the people were supreme to both. How their numbers were apportioned was beside the point. To allow equal representation in Congress for states would allow the political divisions between and within states to infect national politics. Delegates from smaller states did not see it this way. To them, equal representation was not open for negotiation; it was essential to their sovereignty. At one point, Gunning Bedford from Delaware threatened that the small states might have to break off, form their own union, possibly even ally with a foreign power.[28] This was, in modern political terms, the "nuclear option" for the small states. There would be no going back if it were used. All knew it was a possibility, even if unlikely, but to have the idea raised so boldly and so publicly shocked the convention and highlighted for all present the stakes with which they were playing and the possible consequences should they fail to reach an agreement.

▲ A profile portrait of Irish-born American jurist William Paterson. Paterson presented what became known as the New Jersey Plan, which preserved most of the structure of the government as established under the Articles of Confederation.

THE GREAT COMPROMISE CALLS FOR A BICAMERAL LEGISLATURE WITH DIFFERENT METHODS OF REPRESENTATION IN EACH CHAMBER

With the issue of how states would be represented threatening to break apart the convention, the question was sent to a committee. While the young nation celebrated the Fourth of July, delegates to the convention were unsure if their work would succeed, or even continue. The stakes were very high. Elbridge Gerry of Massachusetts warned, "If we do nothing, it appears we must have war and confusion."[29] On July 5, the committee responded with a proposal to give something to each side. The new national legislature would be bicameral; it would have two chambers. Representation in the lower house would follow the Virginia Plan and representation in the upper house, the New Jersey Plan. Compromise having been put on the table, the mood of the convention began to shift. Bedford of Delaware—who had threatened the possibility that small states might seek an alliance with a foreign power—insisted that he had been misunderstood.[30]

On July 16, by a vote of 5–4, the delegates agreed to what would be called the **Great Compromise**.[31] Under this agreement, much like the committee's recommendations, the national legislature would be bicameral. States would be represented in the House of Representatives according to their populations. The people would directly elect these representatives. States would be represented equally in the upper chamber, the Senate. Two senators would be chosen from each state by their state legislatures. Not all of the small-state delegates were satisfied with the agreement; two left in protest. But the rest felt that having the Senate was protection enough, and they became much more cooperative in the weeks that followed. Delaware, for all its threats and opposition early in the convention, was the first state to later ratify the Constitution that was being hammered out in Philadelphia. (See Table 2.2.)

That the question of representation in Congress was settled first is important, as this shaped the political strategies of the delegates going forward. Having secured equal representation in the Senate, small

Great Compromise
an agreement for a plan of government that drew upon both the Virginia and New Jersey Plans; it settled issues of state representation by calling for a bicameral legislature with a House of Representatives apportioned proportionately and a Senate apportioned equally.

Legislative Structures under the Virginia Plan, New Jersey Plan, and Great Compromise

	Virginia Plan	New Jersey Plan	Great Compromise
Structure of Legislature	Bicameral (two chamber)	Unicameral (single chamber)	Bicameral (two chamber)
Apportionment	**Lower House** • Number of seats apportioned by state population • Members directly elected by citizens **Upper House** • Number of seats apportioned by state population • Members elected by lower house (from list supplied by state legislatures)	**Legislature** • Equal representation for states regardless of state population • Members appointed by the states	**House of Representatives** • States represented according to population • Members directly elected by citizens **Senate** • States represented equally (two senators per state) • Members appointed by state legislatures
Powers	• Legislature has strong powers	• Legislature has similar power as under the Articles of Confederation but can also levy taxes and regulate commerce	• Legislature has broad powers over commerce and the ability to make laws as necessary • House of Representatives has power to levy taxes

states offered less opposition to a strong national government. They were now less afraid of Congress, even seeing it as a defense against the power of their larger neighbors. Madison, who had wanted popular representation in both houses, began to push to strengthen the other two branches to act as a counter to the Congress that he had proposed but now mistrusted due to the equal state representation in the Senate.[32]

The Constitution did not fall out of the sky. It was the result of compromise. But it was also the result of adaptation to earlier compromises and to changes in the political landscape in which the delegates pursued their goals and those of the states that they had been chosen to represent.

WHAT HAVE I LEARNED?

1. Delegates to the Constitutional Convention were sent to Philadelphia with the charge of _____.

   a. amending the Articles of Confederation

   b. drafting a new constitution

   c. suppressing Shays' Rebellion

   d. creating a confederal system of government

2. According to the Virginia Plan, _____.

   a. there would be a unicameral legislature with members appointed by state legislatures, with equal representation for states regardless of population

   b. the bicameral legislature would have equal representation for all states, and all members would be directly elected

   c. there would be a bicameral legislature with members apportioned by state population; lower house seats would be directly elected, and upper house seats would be elected by members of the lower house

   d. members of the unicameral legislature would all be selected by state legislatures

3. Which aspects of the Virginia and New Jersey Plans were retained in the Great Compromise, and why?

Answers: 1. a; 2. c; 3. Answers should reference the bicameral legislature, proportional representation system in the lower chamber (House), and direct election of the lower house members, which was part of the Virginia Plan. From the New Jersey Plan, states would have equal representation in the upper house (Senate). The Great Compromise, in combining two systems of representation in Congress, balanced the preferences of small- and large-population states and allowed the convention to move forward.

DELEGATES WORK OUT DETAILS OF THE NEW GOVERNMENT

- Identify the institutions of government established by the Constitution and the distribution of political power among them.

With the bicameral legislature having resolved the first and largest issue of the convention—the distribution of representation between the states—the convention moved on to the structure of the rest of the government and the specific powers of each branch. In doing so, it confronted the second major issue of the convention: the question of national power. Many of the details of the new government were worked out in two committees over the rest of the summer and then presented to the full convention for approval. The Committee of Detail presented its recommendations on the structure of government and the relationships between the three branches. The Committee on Unfinished Parts took up issues that had not been resolved and generally tried to tie up loose ends in the structure of the new government.

THE LEGISLATIVE BRANCH IS MADE THE MOST POWERFUL

While representation in Congress had been settled, its powers still had to be worked out. To do so, delegates looked to the powers of the Confederation Congress under the Articles of Confederation as well as to state legislatures under the various state constitutions. As the **legislative branch** of government, Congress's purpose was to legislate—to make laws. Both houses had to work together to pass laws, but because of how congressional members were chosen, each house had a slightly different purpose. Members of the House of Representatives, who were elected directly by the people and had to run for reelection every two years, were meant to be more responsive to the people, to directly represent their constituents. Senators, who were chosen by state legislatures and served six-year terms, were there to check the passions of the people. Senators' terms were staggered in two-year shifts so that only about one-third of senators would be up for reelection in any given election year, making it more difficult for any swift change in mood among citizens to quickly affect national policy.

Congress, as expected, was made more powerful than the unicameral legislature under the Articles of Confederation, especially with regard to issues of money and the economy. Congress was given the power to borrow money, collect taxes, and "regulate Commerce with foreign Nations, and among the several states." This commerce clause has enabled Congress to become involved in large areas of the American economy, even within states. Debates over the power of and limits to the commerce clause continue today, especially between states and the federal government.

To preserve its flexibility, Congress was also given the ability "to make all Laws which shall be necessary and proper for carrying into Execution the foregoing Powers, and all the other Powers vested by this Constitution in the Government of the United States." The necessary and proper clause, combined with the commerce clause, paved the way for a dramatic expansion in Congress's power over national policy in the centuries following ratification.

THE EXECUTIVE BRANCH IS INITIALLY LESS THOROUGHLY PLANNED OUT

Neither the Virginia nor the New Jersey Plan had been very specific about the **executive branch** of government. Madison had not given it as much thought as he had Congress—at least until he decided he needed to build in more protections against equal state representation in the Senate. Initially there was not even a consensus over how many chief executives the country should have, much less over how powerful the branch should be. Alexander Hamilton, young, ambitious, self-made, and not trusted by many delegates, proposed a powerful president who would be elected for life. His plan made the Virginia Plan look moderate. Though it was not voted on, Hamilton's suggestion of an "American king"[33] followed him for the rest of his political career. Most delegates expected Washington would serve as an, if not *the*, executive of the country. Some wrote that confidence in Washington reduced anxiety about how powerful the executive would become.

In the end, the delegates settled on a single executive—a president—who would serve for four-year terms. As head of the executive branch, the president was there to "execute," or carry out, the laws that had been passed by Congress. The president was given some, but not unlimited, power over Congress

legislative branch
in a divided government, the institution responsible for making laws.

executive branch
the institution responsible for carrying out laws passed by the legislative branch.

with the ability to veto a piece of legislation that Congress had passed. Congress could, however, override the veto with a two-thirds vote in each of the two houses. The president was named commander in chief of the army and navy. Again, though, power was to be shared. Congress, not the president, was given the power to declare (and raise money for) war. Presidents were given power to oversee the people working in the executive branch and to obtain from them the information needed to govern the country, which has led to the growth of a large and influential federal bureaucracy. Finally, the president was given the power to make foreign policy, though, again, this responsibility was to be shared with the Senate.

More controversial than what powers the executive would have was how the president would be elected, raising once again the question of how states would be represented in the new government. In the end, delegates settled on a complicated compromise for electing the president, one that is still not fully understood by many Americans. Citizens would not vote directly for the president. Instead, an Electoral College consisting of electors awarded to states based on their representation in Congress would select the president. Each state received two electors (for their senators) plus one each for their members of the House of Representatives. States would decide how these electors were to be chosen, and successful candidates would need to win a majority of electors to become president. The system of the Electoral College continues to incite criticism and suggestions for reform. In the minds of the delegates, however, the complicated structure managed to avoid reigniting the disagreements between small and large states over representation.

The Granger Collection, New York

▲ Shown here arriving at Congress Hall in Philadelphia on March 4, 1793, for his second inauguration, George Washington chose to retire after his second term despite the fact that the Constitution would have permitted him to run for reelection for an unlimited number of terms.

judicial branch
the institution responsible for hearing and deciding cases via a system of federal courts.

THE JUDICIARY IS DESIGNED TO INTERPRET CONSTITUTIONAL CONFLICTS

The Virginia and New Jersey Plans were even less specific about the **judicial branch** of the government, the system of federal courts. Delegates decided on one Supreme Court to be the highest in the land and a system of lower federal courts whose structure and composition would be determined by Congress. Unlike the judiciary under the articles, the federal courts would have jurisdiction—the authority to hear and decide cases—over all disputes between states and the national government, between two or more states, and between citizens of different states. Combined with the supremacy clause of the Constitution, which declared that national treaties and laws "shall be the supreme law of the Land," the federal court emerged as superior to state courts.

Not included in the Constitution was an explicit description of the power of judicial review, which gives the judicial branch of government the authority to determine if a law, part of a law, or an act of government is or is not in violation of the highest law of the land and, if it *is* in conflict, it is thus invalid. In the United States, that supreme law is the Constitution, and the power of judicial review rests ultimately with the U.S. Supreme Court. While state supreme courts may exercise judicial review on state laws and actions, the supremacy clause of the Constitution ensures that the exercise of judicial review by the Supreme Court includes the authority to use that power over both national and state laws and actions.

In exercising this power, the Supreme Court does not claim to be above the executive or legislative branch. Instead, the Constitution and the people are above all three branches, and it is the role of the Court to act as the interpreter of conflict between the Constitution and governmental action. This power has been retained throughout history by shrewd political action and the conscious preservation of it by Supreme Court justices. We will examine the concept of judicial review, its foundations, and controversies surrounding its use in much more detail in our chapter on the judiciary.

The power of judicial review, combined with the supremacy clause, became crucial in later battles to protect civil liberties and secure civil rights, many of which were waged by citizens who because of their identity had been ignored by the original document or had their rights restricted by it. As with the other two branches, the judiciary was not to exist in isolation. Congress, not the Supreme Court, had the authority to create the lower federal courts. Congress would determine the number of Supreme Court justices, and the Senate had the power to confirm justices (with a majority vote), who first had to be nominated by the president.

SEPARATION OF POWERS ALLOWS FOR CHECKS AND BALANCES ON GOVERNMENT

In drawing up the powers of each of the three branches, the delegates tried to make sure that no one branch could become too powerful on its own. The idea of **separation of powers** was widely supported by delegates at the convention and well known to those who had studied the writings of Baron de Montesquieu. Under this system, branches are not meant to preside over their own spheres. Rather, a system of "separated institutions sharing power" was created.[34] Each branch, whose members tended to represent a different group of people, has to work with the other branches to make things happen, though not on every issue all the time (see Table 2.3). This was the central blueprint around which the national government was structured. Popularly known as the system of checks and balances, the idea of overlapping (but not perfectly overlapping) spheres of influence also applies to relations between the states and the federal government. Federalism, or the sharing of power over some aspects of governance between the states and the nation, is as central to American government as checks and balances, and it has been the source of much conflict and controversy throughout its history.

DELEGATES ADDRESS THE "UNFINISHED PARTS" BUT LEAVE THE PROBLEM OF SLAVERY BEHIND

At the beginning of September 1787, the Committee on Unfinished Parts[35] reported back to the convention on its efforts to address issues that had been left unresolved. Not all of these issues were ironed out, and the question of slavery threatened to break up the proceedings.

separation of powers a design of government that distributes powers across institutions to avoid making one branch too powerful on its own.

▼ TABLE 2.3

Separated Institutions Sharing Powers

	INSTITUTIONS		
	Executive Branch	Legislative Branch	Judicial Branch
Lawmaking Authority	• Executes laws • Has veto power • Nominates judges to the federal judiciary and key executive branch officials • Shapes legislative agenda	• Writes nation's laws • Has veto override • Senate confirms judicial nominees and key executive branch officials • Determines number of Supreme Court justices • Creates lower courts	• Interprets contested laws • Can declare both federal and state laws unconstitutional
National Security and Foreign Policy Responsibilities	• President acts as commander in chief of the military • Sets foreign policy agenda	• Declares war • Senate ratifies treaties with other nations	
Oversight Responsibilities	• Oversees federal bureaucracy	• Holds power of impeachment • Holds budgetary authority and power of oversight over executive branch agencies	• May declare laws or executive branch actions in conflict with the Constitution
Sovereignty	Sovereignty rests with the people. The Constitution is the supreme law of the nation.		

In an attempt to clear up commercial relationships between states, the delegates decided that "full faith and credit shall be given in each State to the public Acts, Records, and judicial Proceedings of every other State." The full faith and credit clause was designed to ensure that each state recognized contracts and other legal proceedings from other states. It has become an important constitutional element in the question of same-sex marriage and marriage equality in the United States (see Chapter 4). The structure of the Electoral College was finalized, as was the office of vice president of the United States, whose constitutional powers are quite limited but who plays an important role in presidential elections.

In important ways, however, the Constitution remained unfinished even after the delegates completed their deliberations in September. This was partly by design, partly due to political compromises made during the convention itself. By making provisions for changing the Constitution through a process of **amendment**, the Framers acknowledged that it would always be unfinished, that it would need to be adaptable if it were to endure. By *adaptable*, however, the delegates did not mean easily changed. They purposefully designed a system for amending the Constitution that made this very difficult to achieve. Once again, divisions over representation of states emerged, with small states arguing that states should have the power to approve amendments and the nationalists arguing that it should be left to the people to decide.

In the end, another complicated compromise emerged, with both the people—through official proposal in Congress—and the states—through the process of final ratification—being necessary to alter the Constitution. Amending the document is a two-stage process, with two possible routes to completion of each of the two stages needed for amendment. First, the amendment has to be officially proposed, which involves much more than someone just suggesting an idea. Proposal can happen in one of two ways, only the first of which has ever been used: (1) passage by a two-thirds vote in both the House and the Senate or (2) passage in a national convention called at the request of two-thirds of the states. After formal proposal, the proposed amendment must be ratified by one of two ways: by (1) a majority vote in three-fourths of the state legislatures or (2) acceptance by ratifying conventions in three-fourths of the states. The second method for ratification has been used only once.

Of the thousands of suggestions for amending the Constitution presented in Congress since its founding, only twenty-seven amendments have been formally ratified. The first ten of these, which make up the Bill of Rights, became part of the debate over ratification itself and are often thought of as part of the "original" Constitution. Two others—an amendment prohibiting the sale and consumption of alcoholic beverages and one repealing that prohibition—canceled each other out. Since the passage of the Bill of Rights, therefore, the Constitution has had only fifteen lasting changes. Though the Constitution has rarely been amended, some scholars argue that important decisions by the Supreme Court and major changes in how the American people view themselves have at critical times in history led to changes in government just as significant as formal amendments.[36]

THE FOUNDERS REACH A FATEFUL COMPROMISE ON SLAVERY. At the time of the convention, nearly one out of every six individuals living in the thirteen states was a slave. Most, but not all, lived in the southern states. Southern plantation owners, many of whom were politically powerful in their state legislatures and some of whom were delegates to the Philadelphia convention, had no intention of seeing their institution outlawed or heavily regulated. Plantation owners were not the only interests who benefited from slavery. The slave trade and the trade in goods made by slaves benefited some powerful shipping interests as well, especially in the Northeast. About one-third of the delegates to the convention, including Madison and Washington, were slave owners. A few others, however, saw the preservation of slavery as a moral failure and spoke out at the convention about the hypocrisy of trying to preserve liberty in a document that allowed slavery.

In spite of a few speeches on the floor of the convention, however, the question of slavery was not generally debated in terms of morality or of liberty but rather in terms of states' representation, the same issue that affected so many others at the convention: Would slaves count when it came time to tally a state's population? In the end, the question of slavery was settled on practical, political considerations.

The final document dealt with slavery in three ways. The word *slavery* never appears—a minor tactical victory for those who did not want the Constitution to appear to approve of it. On the question of

amendment
a constitutional provision for a process by which changes may be made to the original Constitution.

slavery and representation in Congress, the **Three-Fifths Compromise** ensured that a slave—called an "other person" in the Constitution—would count as three-fifths of a person for a state's representation.[37] Slaves could not vote or be represented, but their numbers would boost the influence of the slave states in which they were held; since slaves were counted among the population, slaveholding states would be allotted more members of Congress. In a second facet of the compromise, Congress would not be allowed to restrict the slave trade until 1808 at the earliest. Third, slaves who had successfully escaped would have to be returned to their owners, regardless of the laws of individual states.

Historians and political scientists have debated how the delegates could have agreed to preserve slavery when some observed that it went against the very idea of natural rights upon which the Constitution is based and at a time when some states were beginning to restrict or outlaw it on their own. There are several reasons, and they are not mutually exclusive.

The first reason is that slaves had not voted for their state legislators. Some delegates did oppose slavery, but slaves had no direct representation in the Constitutional Convention. While slaves were not represented, slave owners were, and their delegates used the threat of leaving the convention to secure their interests. Had the southern states pulled out, the Articles of Confederation, which contained no restrictions on slavery, would have remained the law of the land. Politics during the convention also played a large role. The question of slavery had been handed to the Committee of Detail, chaired by John Rutledge of South Carolina. Rutledge's committee proposed to give the slave states everything they demanded. In his notes, Madison commented on the political implications of this slave-state delegate being in charge of the committee that would set the agenda for debate on the issue of slavery.

Others have argued that the preservation of slavery was the result of a **logroll**, or a trading of votes, between the slave states and the northeastern commercial states. Northeastern states received the strong commercial policy they wanted in return for protections on slavery for the southern states. Evidence from the records of the convention supports the idea of a logroll.

Regardless of the reasons, the question of slavery was temporarily handled but fundamentally unsettled. Not until the country was literally torn apart in the Civil War eighty years later would the issue of slavery be ultimately decided. It would take nearly another century and a great deal of sacrifice and strategic political activity to make equality for African Americans a reality, or at least more of a reality, on the ground rather than just in words. Even today, the question of whether Americans are all truly equal in the Republic endures.

Library of Congress/Corbis/VCG via Getty Images

Three-Fifths Compromise
an agreement reached by delegates at the Constitutional Convention that ensured that a slave would count as three-fifths of a person for a state's representation.

logroll
an exchange of political favors, such as when legislators trade votes to support one another's proposed legislation.

▲ The members of the Liberian senate of 1893, made up mostly of freed African American slaves. The Republic of Liberia began as a settlement for freed slaves, similar to Madison's call to remove blacks from the regions populated by whites. But the motivation for the settlement was not always benign: white slaveholders thought that freed slaves in their midst would threaten slave societies in the South.

JAMES MADISON HOLDS CONTRADICTORY VIEWS ON SLAVERY

Although his views on slavery evolved over time, James Madison was never able to completely resolve the contradictions inherent in a Constitution and government that, although based on natural rights and liberties, permitted slavery. Some of his writings dating from the time of the drafting of the Constitution indicate that he understood that slaves were considered, contradictorily, as both property and as humans with rights under law.[38] Later in his life, Madison wrote out a plan for ending slavery that involved a "gradual" emancipation. Both master and slave would agree to the slave's freedom, compensation would be made to the master for his "loss," the slave would explicitly acknowledge preferring freedom to bondage, and all former slaves would be relocated to a region not "occupied by or allotted to a White population."[39]

Madison never did free his own slaves or provide for their freedom upon his death, as his colleague George Washington would do.

SLAVERY, POPULATION, AND THE BALANCE OF POWER BETWEEN SOUTHERN AND NORTHERN STATES

Basic to the use of data in political science is the idea of *counting*. It is far more consequential than it may sound at first. Counting is not a neutral thing. By assigning numbers to individuals or their actions, those who use numerical data to study political processes and outcomes can draw systematic conclusions about them. However, how we count people is also a political act, one with profound consequences. Today, for example, there is a strong debate about how we should count Americans in the national census conducted every ten years. Are the racial and ethnic categories used in the census forms sufficiently reflective of our diversity or of any one individual's identity? What about counting undocumented Americans? Doing so may help us better understand our changing population; however, asking individuals to reveal their undocumented status may put them at risk or in fear of being at risk on the basis of their undocumented status.

One of the most important divisions between the states during the Constitutional Convention was on the issue of slavery. In addition to being a moral issue, how slavery was handled during the proceedings, as all delegates knew, would have serious implications for the balance of political power in the federal government, especially in the House of Representatives. While states would be equally represented in the Senate, their representation in the House would depend upon their population. Did that population include slaves?

Figure 2-A shows the percentage of each state's population that was enslaved in 1790, three years after the drafting of the Constitution. The divisions between northern and southern states are striking. What might this mean for representation in the House?

▼ FIGURE 2-A

Percentage Slave Population by State

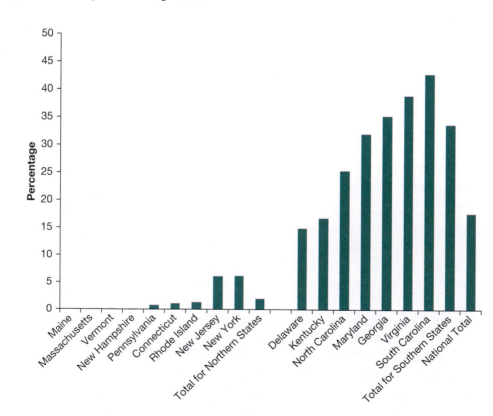

Figure 2-B presents the same data, but it does so in a way that breaks down the population—free, slave, and total—of each state and the two regions. Note the red bars, which represent the total population of the states and regions. Looked at this way, the balance of population between the northern and southern states is roughly equal, with just under two million individuals in each region. However, when one separates out the slave population (the green bars), the northern states have a population advantage of more than six hundred thousand people (the dark-blue bars). It was this math that drove much of the bargaining over slavery and representation in the convention.

WHAT Do You Think?

What information does Figure 2-B convey that Figure 2-A does not? Have you encountered different charts and tables that present the same or similar data in different ways, thus allowing you to draw different conclusions?

▼ FIGURE 2-B

Free and Slave Population Totals by State

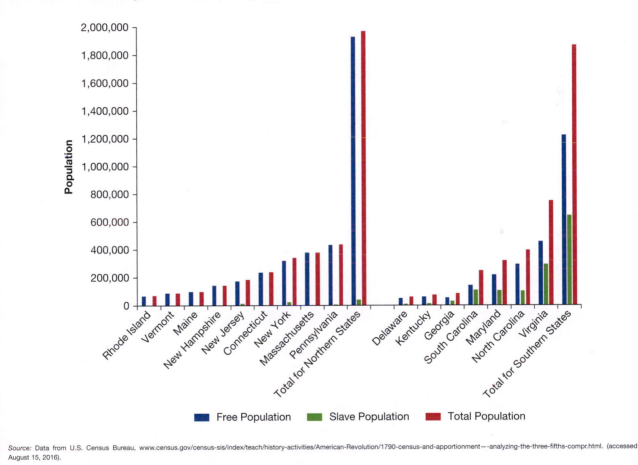

Source: Data from U.S. Census Bureau, www.census.gov/census-sis/index/teach/history-activities/American-Revolution/1790-census-and-apportionment—-analyzing-the-three-fifths-compr.html. (accessed August 15, 2016).

THE CONSTITUTION IS FINISHED BUT NOT YET MADE THE LAW OF THE LAND

By proposing a system of amendments, the Framers ensured that the Constitution would always be unfinished so that it could adapt over time. More immediately, however, the Constitution was unfinished because the states had yet to approve it. The document that emerged from Philadelphia was just a proposal. It carried no force until the states chose to adopt it. That would be determined by the battle over ratification.

A skillful move by Benjamin Franklin at the convention's conclusion required only that delegates sign their names as witnesses to their state's endorsement, which allowed some delegates to sign the Constitution even knowing that they would soon speak out against it. Franklin's move, and the departure over the summer of delegates who did not approve of the outcomes, made the delegates appear to be in greater agreement than they really were. In fact, many did have strong reservations, and three refused to sign.

The delegates also used a bit of trickery to get around another issue. The Articles of Confederation stipulated that amendments to the articles required the approval of all thirteen state delegations in Congress. This, members of the Constitutional Convention knew, was going to be very difficult. Rhode Island never sent any delegates, and many states were closely divided. So, the delegates declared that the Constitution would become the law of the land if ratifying conventions in nine out of thirteen states approved it, bypassing the state legislatures. Even with this somewhat unconventional ploy—breaking the spirit if not the law of the articles—it was still far from certain that the Constitution would be adopted.

WHAT HAVE I **LEARNED?**

1. The Framers of the Constitution intended for the three branches of government to _____.
   a. operate completely independently
   b. prevent any one branch from becoming too powerful
   c. preserve the ultimate authority of state governments
   d. preserve the system of government established under the Articles of Confederation

2. The Committee on Unfinished Parts addressed which of the following issues?
   a. Separation of powers and the system of representation in the legislature
   b. Slavery and ratification
   c. Full faith and credit, the amendment system, the Electoral College, and the office of the vice president
   d. Establishing judicial review

3. The process of amending the Constitution requires _____.
   a. either two-thirds of the members of Congress or three-fourths of the states to agree
   b. a unanimous vote in Congress
   c. the approval of all states
   d. a two-stage process involving proposal and ratification

4. Who do you think were the winners in the Constitutional Convention? Who were the losers?

Answer Key: 1. b; 2. c; 3. d; 4. Answers will vary. Students may focus on small states versus large states, slaves, or other individuals excluded from the political process.

FEDERALISTS AND ANTI-FEDERALISTS FIGHT OVER RATIFICATION

- **Compare and contrast the arguments put forth by the Federalists and anti-Federalists during the ratification debates.**

The fight between those in favor of the Constitution and those opposed to it was America's first national—and first *negative*—political campaign. Both sides issued dire premonitions of what might happen if the Constitution was or was not ratified. The debate was carried out through the printing presses, which had become widespread enough to allow both sides to carry their messages to the people. The supporters of the proposed Constitution scored the first tactical victory by claiming the name **Federalists** for their group. That was ironic because the proposed government was actually strongly national, whereas the term *federalist* generally meant more of a balance between the power of states and

Federalists
the name taken by supporters of the proposed Constitution; the Federalists called for a stronger national government.

the national government. That forced those arguing against the document to be tagged as **anti-Federalists** despite the fact that their position was in reality more federalist.

The anti-Federalists were therefore put in the difficult position of having to argue against a proposal, and basing their argument only on what was good about the Articles of Confederation was a tough sell. So they turned negative. They raised fears in the minds of Americans about what this potentially radical change in the government would bring. Mostly, they argued, it would trample on the rights of the people and the states in which they lived.

For their part, the Federalists pointed to the problems that plagued the government under the articles—inability to deal with foreign powers, economic challenges, and especially the threat of anarchy—and warned citizens that the only way to avoid these dangers was through the new Constitution. The Federalists had celebrity on their side in the figures of Washington and Franklin. The anti-Federalists, with the exception of a few misguided attempts to counter the celebrity endorsements of Washington and Franklin, stayed away from the issue of famous endorsements.

In some ways, the Federalists and anti-Federalists split along distinctions of class (see Table 2.4). Many wealthy merchants favored the strong economic policy that the Constitution would allow, and many wealthy southern plantation owners supported the agreements that had been struck. On the other side, a large number of anti-Federalists came from rural areas and mistrusted powerful elites in their states' capitals. To say that the Federalists were wealthy elites and the anti-Federalists small farmers and shopkeepers is, however, too strong a simplification. Many anti-Federalist leaders were educated elites;

▲ The fate of the Constitution was decided in the state ratifying conventions (nine states had to ratify for the Constitution to take effect), but it was the subject of intense debates everywhere—in homes, taverns, coffeehouses, and newspapers.

anti-Federalists
the name taken by those opposed to the proposed Constitution; the anti-Federalists favored stronger state governments.

▼ TABLE 2.4

Federalists and Anti-Federalists

Both Federalists and anti-Federalists were interested in a politically and economically secure nation, but they differed in how they thought that would best be achieved.

	Federalists	Anti-Federalists
View of proposed Constitution	Supporters	Opponents
Proponents of:	A strong national government	Stronger state government
Concerned about:	The tyranny of the majority	The tyranny of the minority
Proposed:	The idea of an extended republic to limit the problem of faction and help to resolve the tyranny of the majority	Strong restrictions on branches of government to help solve the problem of too-strong national government
Supporters included:	Wealthy merchants and southern plantation owners George Washington, Benjamin Franklin, Alexander Hamilton, James Madison, John Jay	People in rural areas, more farmers, and shopkeepers Fewer well-known supporters, but leadership included educated elites, Revolutionary War heroes, and convention delegates

some of the most prominent had been heroes in the Revolutionary War, delegates to the convention itself, or important members in state politics.

Though the Federalists tried to associate the threat of anarchy and Shays' Rebellion with their opponents, the anti-Federalists were just as concerned as their opponents with securing a stable future for the country. Instead, the divisions between the two sides represented fundamentally different visions for how to do so. Three main issues divided the anti-Federalists and the Federalists on a vision of this future: (1) the very possibility of creating a workable republic in such a large nation that would protect individual liberties against **tyranny** (the suppression of the rights of a people by those holding power), (2) the relative power of states and the nation, and (3) the lack of a bill of rights (a list of rights and liberties that people possess and that governments cannot take away) in the Constitution. Each of these issues was closely related to the others.

FEDERALISTS AND ANTI-FEDERALISTS DEBATE THE DANGERS OF POWER IN A LARGE REPUBLIC

As the debate over ratification got under way, the factions for and against the Constitution disagreed on the very possibility of a republic in a country as large as the United States. Many of the Enlightenment writers that Madison had drawn his ideas from had argued that republics had to be small to work properly, and all expected this one to grow even larger over time, making the challenges even worse. Anti-Federalists argued that the national government would grow more distant from the people over time and would eventually begin to oppress them. Congress having the power to tax would only make this danger greater, they claimed. Therefore, the anti-Federalists asserted, more restrictions needed to be placed on the national government and more power reserved for the states.

These challenges required more than a tactical shift on the part of the Federalists—they went positive. The Federalists made their case for the Constitution in a collection of eighty-five essays written primarily for the New York papers from the fall of 1787 to the spring of 1788. Published under the collective name *Publius*, **The Federalist Papers**, which were actually written by Alexander Hamilton, James Madison, and John Jay, are now considered some of the most important writings in American political history. They laid out the theory behind the Constitution (which itself does not directly speak to the reasons behind its own provisions), showing how a large republic could be constructed in a way that would prevent it from growing so self-interested and powerful that it would trample on the rights of states and their citizens.

Many of Madison's essays are now considered to be the most important in the collection. Two essays in particular, *Federalist* No. 10 and No. 51 (see Appendixes 4 and 5), tackle anti-Federalist critiques by laying out the reasons behind the proposed constitutional republic. From his research, Madison knew that in a republic one must not assume that people will always act in noble ways, putting their own needs behind what is best for the republic. Instead, a republic must be constructed to account for self-interest and selfish motives.[40]

A REPUBLIC MUST BE ABLE TO HANDLE THE PROBLEM OF FACTION. The danger was not only that people would act according to their self-interest but also that they might join forces with others who had the same motives. Collectively, this group of people, however large or small, could try to use the government to get what it wanted, trampling the rights of others in the process. Such a group of self-interested individuals would constitute what Madison called a **faction**, the most dangerous challenge to a republic.

Long before Karl Marx wrote about the inevitability of class conflict in capitalist societies, Madison made it clear in *Federalist* No. 10 that inequality of wealth is the primary driver of factionalization, asserting that "those who hold and those who are without property have ever formed distinct interests in society."[41] Madison included slave ownership as a source of faction, as slaves were considered a form of property during the discussions in the Constitutional Convention. However, this issue was not addressed in *Federalist* No. 10.

Madison saw several ways to solve the problem of faction. The first was tyranny—factions emerge under conditions of liberty, not tyranny—but tyranny was an unacceptable option. The second was

tyranny
the suppression of the rights of a people by those holding power.

The Federalist Papers
a series of eighty-five essays written by Alexander Hamilton, James Madison, and John Jay and published between 1787 and 1788 that lay out the theory behind the Constitution.

faction
a group of self-interested people who use the government to get what they want, trampling the rights of others in the process.

to create a totally unified, factionless society where everyone has "the same opinions, the same passions, and the same interests."[42] This second solution was unrealistic, especially in a large republic like the United States. Indeed, the American Republic has had factions since its origin. Political parties can be thought of as factions, as can interest groups. The question is how a republic can keep them in check.

The superior way to check their power, Madison argued in

Federalist poster circa 1800

Federalist No. 10, is through an **extended republic**: a republic so large and diverse, with so many factions vying for power, that no one faction is able to assert its will over all the others. Tactically, this was a clever argument. The anti-Federalists had claimed that the American Republic would be too large to govern effectively, whereas Madison argued that the only solution to the dangers of faction was precisely to have such a large republic. Madison, however, was no populist; his design for government placed brakes on popular passions, insulating representatives from the desires of their citizens.

FEDERALISTS AND ANTI-FEDERALISTS FEAR DIFFERENT FORMS OF TYRANNY. Federalists and anti-Federalists did not disagree in their mistrust of government and the harm that could be inflicted by a self-interested few. Rather, both sides acknowledged that tyranny could take two forms. In a **tyranny of the minority**, a small number of citizens trample on the rights of the rest of the larger population. In a **tyranny of the majority**, a large number of citizens use the power of their majority to trample on the rights of a smaller group. The two sides disagreed on which was the greater danger and, therefore, on how a republic should be structured.

The anti-Federalists focused more on the dangers of a tyranny of the minority. The Regulators had viewed the government of Massachusetts as becoming dangerously disconnected from the people and controlled by wealthy elites; the anti-Federalists feared the government of the United States would follow a similar path. While acknowledging the dangers of minority tyranny, Madison and the Federalists focused more on the dangers of majority rule and its necessary counters. A majority of people, if in control of all the levers of power, might use that power to oppress a minority of citizens. Slavery could be thought of as a tyranny of the majority, though in fact slaves outnumbered whites in many areas of the country.

Given Madison's earlier observations about property and the panic associated with Shays' Rebellion, one of the dangers the Federalists saw was a majority of poorer people using their power to redistribute wealth in a more equal way. In *Federalist* No. 10, Madison did not argue for direct democracy, in which citizens vote directly on policies, because he saw that form of government as too instable, with too few protections for personal security or private property.[43] Instead he argued for the delegation of power to representatives by the people and for power to be divided across government institutions. In *Federalist* No. 51, Madison laid out the blueprints of such a structure. Separation of powers is the guiding principle, with power divided and parsed between the states and nation, among the three branches of the national government, and within each branch.

▲ In this political cartoon, George Washington (shown in heaven) tells partisans to keep the pillars of federalism, republicanism, and democracy, warning party men to let all three stand to hold up peace and plenty, liberty and independence. At the left, a Democrat says, "This Pillar shall not stand / I am determin'd to support a just and necessary War," and at the right a Federalist claims, "This Pillar must come down / I am a friend of Peace."

extended republic
a republic so large and diverse, with so many factions vying for power, that no one faction is able to assert its will over all the others.

tyranny of the minority
when a small number of citizens trample on the rights of the larger population.

tyranny of the majority
when a large number of citizens use the power of their majority to trample on the rights of a smaller group.

FEDERALISTS AND ANTI-FEDERALISTS DEBATE WHERE POWER SHOULD BE CONCENTRATED

Debates over the relative power of the states and the nation were central to the political battles over ratification of the Constitution. The Federalists tried to convince American citizens that the proposed form of government was necessary to preserve their rights and liberties. The anti-Federalists argued against the proposed increase in national power and warned Americans of what might come to pass over time as the advantages given to the national government in the Constitution might allow it to infringe more and more on the authority of the states.

FEDERALISTS ARGUE FOR A STRONG NATIONAL GOVERNMENT. In their campaign to defend the proposed Constitution, the Federalists highlighted the problems and dangers of a government in which the states were strong and the nation was weak, pointing out failures of past republics as well as the problems experienced under the Articles of Confederation.[44] In *Federalist* No. 16, Hamilton argued that, for instance, if the national government in a confederacy were ever forced to use military might against one of its members, it would surely result in the "violent death of the confederacy."[45]

In his contributions to *The Federalist Papers*, Madison took a more moderate approach, emphasizing the balance between state and national power in the proposed Constitution. Across numerous papers, Madison argued that the Constitution divided the people's sovereignty in such a way as to preserve the integrity of both states and nation and to guard against the dangers of faction, with checks and balances built into both the legislative and executive branches.

ANTI-FEDERALISTS FEAR LOSING REPRESENTATION AT THE NATIONAL LEVEL. The anti-Federalists were not convinced by the arguments in *The Federalist Papers*. They feared what they saw as a radical increase in national power, not only in the proposed Constitution but in how the government might evolve over time. They feared the distant future as much as the immediate present. They were, in many ways, conservative, trying to preserve the power of the states as enjoyed under the Articles of Confederation. In American political history, there is no one work that encapsulates anti-Federalist thought in the same way that *The Federalist Papers* did for Federalists. There are no *Anti-Federalist Papers*; rather, as scholars have pointed out, "the Antifederalist literature is immense and heterogeneous, encompassing speeches, pamphlets, essays and letters."[46]

Many anti-Federalist concerns centered on how representation of the people's interests could be maintained as the country grew in size, population, and power. They "feared that, once elected and comfortable in their jobs, the representatives would not relinquish power," creating the possibility of a new, elected, American aristocracy.[47] This "democratic" aristocracy, an anti-Federalist essay warned, would be accompanied by an irresistible trend toward a large and complex national government, driven by the demands of a growing nation, ending in "despotism."[48]

The economic power of the national government to tax and regulate interstate commerce was one of the anti-Federalists' greatest worries, and it was only made worse by the necessary and proper clause of the proposed Constitution. In one anti-Federalist essay, the author argued that "this power, given [to] the federal legislature, directly annihilates all the powers of the state legislatures."[49]

A BILL OF RIGHTS IS A KEY ISSUE IN THE RATIFICATION DEBATES

Strategically, the most effective anti-Federalist charge against the Constitution was that it lacked a bill of rights—a list of rights and liberties with which people are born and which governments cannot take away. Many state constitutions already had them. Motions to include these statements were raised during the convention, but they did not pass. To Madison and other opponents of a bill of rights, such a statement was simply not necessary. In the republic that the delegates had fashioned, the people were already sovereign, and the government was already limited. There was no need to limit Congress's power over things that the Constitution gave it no control over in the first place. Some questioned if it was possible or even desirable to try to make a complete list of rights and liberties. What about the ones that were left out? Would Congress respect rights if they were not part of the official list?

Some, however, both during the convention and after, remained strongly in favor of a bill of rights. A bill of rights, they argued, was necessary to check the tendency of government to infringe on the rights and liberties of citizens over time. They pointed out that one should be concerned with what the government might become in the future, not just what it was in the present, as the prospect of tyranny loomed large in their minds. In addition, the anti-Federalists argued that a bill of rights served an important educational function in a republic.[50] It would serve to remind citizens of their natural rights and remind them to assert those rights when governments might, often slowly, try to take them away.

One proponent of including a bill of rights was anti-Federalist Mercy Otis Warren. Before and during the American Revolution, she had displayed her strong support for independence through her plays, pamphlets, and poems.[51] Publishing anonymously—and therefore assumed to be a man by many who read her essays—she corresponded with many revolutionary leaders, who were well aware of her contributions. Later, during the ratification debates, Warren warned that there was "no provision by a bill of rights to guard against dangerous encroachments of power in too many instances to be named."[52]

In the final days of the Constitutional Convention, two delegates proposed a clause that would guarantee liberty of the press. Their motion lost but by only one vote—a potential harbinger of future political realities of which, according to one political scientist, the nationalists should have taken heed.[53] As it turned out, the lack of a bill of rights proved to be the most effective argument that the anti-Federalists would make in the ratification campaign. Many Americans were suspicious of centralized power and wanted specific protections against it.

In February 1788, the Federalists won a narrow victory in Massachusetts, the sixth of nine states needed for ratification, but only after the proconstitutional forces agreed to propose a bill of rights once the original document had itself been ratified. Three months later, South Carolina also ratified, also contingent on a set of amendments that would be offered in the first national Congress. On June 21, 1788, with the help of some shrewd procedural tactics on the part of Federalists in the state convention, New Hampshire became the ninth state to ratify.[54] The Constitution of the United States would become the supreme law of the land the following year.

Even after New Hampshire, James Madison continued to worry. It was not North Carolina's reluctance or Rhode Island's rejection that worried him. If Virginia and New York failed to ratify, it might lead to deep divisions within the new country. Virginia ratified in June, and New York followed in July. North Carolina and, finally, Rhode Island ratified within a year. During the campaign, sensing the realities of the political landscape, Madison had shifted course and promised to introduce a bill of rights as proposed amendments during the first session of the new Congress once the Constitution had been ratified. Madison kept his word, and in 1791, ten of the amendments that he proposed became part of the Constitution.

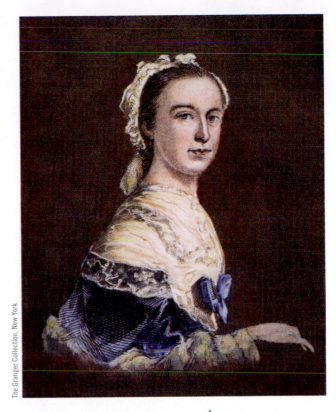

▲ A nineteenth-century steel engraving depicting Mercy Otis Warren.

1. The danger of faction, according to James Madison, _____.

   a. is best kept in check through the suppression of liberty

   b. cannot be avoided, only contained

   c. is best avoided in a homogenous political society

   d. was a problem only under the Articles of Confederation

2. James Madison's theory of the extended republic argued that _____.

   a. members of a republic should be wary of the growth of national power

   b. the greatest safeguard against faction is a people with closely similar ideas and goals

   c. competition between factions would serve as a safeguard against tyranny

   d. to guard against factions, significant restrictions need to be placed on citizens' liberties

3. What were some of the points of disagreement between Federalists and anti-Federalists?

Answer Key: 1. b; 2. c; 3. Answers may include support for or opposition to the Constitution, differing opinions on the dangers of national power, and/or the need for a bill of rights.

CONCLUSION: THE MOTIVES OF THE FRAMERS AND THE EFFECTS OF THE CONSTITUTION ARE STILL BEING DEBATED

While the delegates to the Constitutional Convention were debating and negotiating behind the closed windows of the Pennsylvania State House, many Americans wondered what they were really up to. And we still do.

To some scholars, constitutions give order to disorder. They make progress in a society possible, but only if the people place in them credible, enforceable restrictions on the power of those who would abuse such power.[55] The Constitution drew from the religious traditions and individual constitutions of the colonies. It is a document that creates—or constitutes—a people.[56] It sets out who those people are and why they are doing what they are doing.

To other scholars, American reverence for the Constitution is a dangerous thing. Faith in the Constitution as a symbol of liberty misdirects citizens from the fact that some persons, past and present, have been able to enrich themselves under its protections at the expense of others.[57] Inequality in all its forms has survived, and at times thrived, in the American Republic. Is the Constitution antidemocratic? Does it go against or restrain the will of the majority of the people? Yes, sometimes it is, and sometimes it does. The Constitution was intentionally designed to put brakes on popular desire to change public policy quickly. The result—incrementalism in public policy development whereby policy changes tend to be small and come slowly—has important implications for the United States.

James Madison's studies of the untimely deaths of republics helped to shape the longest-lived written national constitution in the history of human experience. That document did not ban slavery or the trade in slaves. It did not affirm or institutionalize the natural-born rights and liberties of women, Native Americans, slaves, former slaves, or many others. It did, however, affirm the rights of citizens to worship as they saw fit, to speak out and organize against tyranny, and to expect that their government would exist to protect and promote their rights and liberties. It created mechanisms to enforce these expectations, should those in power forget whom they were there to represent. And, intentionally or not, it provided a platform and a path for those ignored or oppressed by the original document to change it, to make it acknowledge their natural rights and liberties as well.

The Founders of the American Republic were practical, tactical, strategic men. Their compromises may have been necessary, but they had enormous consequences for people's lives. The document that emerged from the Pennsylvania State House was unfinished and imperfect. Would it allow for a remedy of its defects? Would it create, as Madison had hoped, a republic that would last? The answers to these questions cannot be found in studies of the motives of the Founders or even of the document itself. The answers have come not from words penned in quill and ink but from the efforts of political actors—sometimes generations later—using their own skills in strategic politics, developing their own ideas, and making their own compromises and mistakes. And having done their own homework.

CHAPTER REVIEW

This chapter's main ideas are reflected in the Learning Objectives. By reviewing them here, you should be able to **remember** the key points, **know** the terms that are central to the topic, and **think** about the critical issues raised in each section.

2.1 Describe the ideas and historical context that shaped James Madison's thinking about republics.

REMEMBER
- James Madison wanted to form a republic that would last. He and other delegates to the Constitutional Convention met and debated how best to strengthen their union and avoid significant political and economic problems.

KNOW
- constitution (p. 31)
- republics (p. 31)

THINK
- How did James Madison and other proponents of a stronger national government use the political events of the time to advance their own goals?

2.2 Explain the challenges faced by the nation following the American Revolution in trying to form a government strong enough to rule effectively but not so strong as to oppress the rights of Americans.

REMEMBER
- The Articles of Confederation seemed insufficient to hold together the new country, but delegates understood that amending them posed significant challenges.
- Large slave-holding states stood to gain much power, yet many feared a too-strong national government.
- Economic and political crises precipitated Shays' Rebellion, which in turn sparked the call for a stronger national constitution.

KNOW
- Articles of Confederation and Perpetual Union (p. 33)
- Shays' Rebellion (p. 37)

2.3 Describe the role that compromise over states' interests played in shaping the government during the Constitutional Convention.

REMEMBER
- The delegates to the Constitutional Convention were not charged with drafting a new Constitution but only with proposing possible changes to the Articles of Confederation.

KNOW
- Constitutional Convention (p. 40)
- New Jersey Plan (p. 42)
- Virginia Plan (p. 42)
- Great Compromise (p. 43)

THINK
- How did political divisions and compromises over them shape the debates during the Constitutional Convention?

2.4 Identify the institutions of government established by the Constitution and the distribution of political power among them.

REMEMBER
- The idea of separation of powers influenced the decision to create three separate but connected branches of the federal government.

KNOW
- amendment (p. 48)
- executive branch (p. 45)
- judicial branch (p. 46)
- legislative branch (p. 45)
- logroll (p. 49)
- separation of powers (p. 47)
- Three-Fifths Compromise (p. 49)

THINK
- Has the U.S. Constitution controlled the problem of faction in the twenty-first century? Why or why not?
- What factions do you see as especially powerful in America today?

2.5 Compare and contrast the arguments put forth by the Federalists and anti-Federalists during the ratification debates.

REMEMBER
- The proposed Constitution had to be ratified by nine of the thirteen states in order to replace the Articles of Confederation.
- Proponents and opponents of the Constitution tried to rally others to their side and convince individuals of their position.

KNOW
- anti-Federalists (p. 53)
- extended republic (p. 55)
- faction (p. 54)
- *The Federalist Papers* (p. 54)
- Federalists (p. 52)
- tyranny (p. 54)
- tyranny of the majority (p. 55)
- tyranny of the minority (p. 55)

THINK
- In what ways is the Constitution still under construction? What still needs to be accomplished?

Chip Somodevilla/Getty Images

CHAPTER 3

FEDERALISM

The Changing Boundaries between the Nation and the States

Angel Raich inhales vaporized marijuana in her home in Oakland, California. Her use is legal under the laws of her state but illegal under federal law, thus illustrating the tensions inherent in federalist systems of government.[1]

O n one fundamental issue the Constitution of the United States is absolutely clear: In its opening words, "We the People of the United States," it establishes that ultimate political authority rests with the people. We, and not the government, are sovereign and have supreme political authority.

What the Constitution is much less clear on are the precise mechanisms through which this supreme authority is vested in the government. Under the Articles of Confederation, the vast majority of the people's authority had been placed in state governments, which left the Confederation Congress constantly struggling to secure cooperation from these multiple governments. That changed with the ratification of the Constitution, but the issue was not settled once and for all. The new system of government divided the people's authority between two levels of government—the nation and the states—with some powers exercised by one level alone, some powers denied to both levels, and some powers shared by both levels. In doing so, a system of **federalism** was created.

The Constitution created much of the basic framework of this division but did not delineate the boundaries between the specific powers of the national government and those of the state governments. The process of setting these boundaries continues even today. Many of the most important and controversial issues in our representative democracy involve difficult questions of American federalism.

LEARNING OBJECTIVES

By reading this chapter, you will be able to do the following:

 3.1 Explain the tension in American federalism between state and federal laws highlighted by the issue of legalized marijuana.

3.2 Identify the elements of the U.S. Constitution that shape American federalism.

3.3 Describe the development of American federalism from the founding until the New Deal.

3.4 Examine the role that the New Deal played in fundamentally reshaping American federalism.

3.5 Discuss changes to American federalism in the modern era and how it might continue to evolve.

In this chapter, we will engage with the stories of Angel Raich and Diane Monson, who sought to secure access to medical marijuana, tracing the roots of their conflict back to the Great Depression and Roosevelt's New Deal. In doing so, we will explore the tensions inherent in American federalism, how it has changed over time, and where American federalism stands in the twenty-first century.

federalism
a structure of governance that places the people's authority in two or more levels of government.

THE FIGHT FOR ACCESS TO MEDICAL MARIJUANA REVEALS TENSIONS BETWEEN STATE AND FEDERAL LAW

- **Explain the tension in American federalism between state and federal laws highlighted by the issue of legalized marijuana.**

In 2002, Angel Raich and Diane Monson filed suit in a California federal court against the government of the United States. They argued that their use of medical marijuana, which was legal under the laws of California and eight other states at the time but illegal under federal law, was protected by the laws of their state and by the Constitution of the United States.

Both women were trying to cope with significant health issues, the treatment of which, they argued, was helped by the use of cannabis. Raich was struggling against an "inoperable brain tumor, seizures, endometriosis, scoliosis and a wasting disorder. She [weighed] only 97 pounds and said without pot she'd starve to death."[2] "I am not a criminal," Raich declared. "I do not deserve to be behind bars."[3] Monson used cannabis as part of her treatment for chronic back pain and spasms and grew her own plants to provide her medication: "Without cannabis, these spasms would be tortuous and unbearable no matter what other medications were available," she testified in federal court.[4]

Both were using marijuana under the supervision of their doctors and in compliance with a California state law, the Compassionate Use Act of 1996. This act made the use and cultivation of marijuana for medical purposes legal if undertaken under the supervision of a licensed physician and in accordance with state regulations. However, Raich and Monson feared that the federal government might restrict their future ability to obtain medical cannabis. The reason for their fears was the fact that the use, cultivation, or possession of marijuana was illegal under a federal law, the Controlled Substances Act (CSA) (1970).[5] Under that law, marijuana was classified as a Schedule I drug, among the most dangerous substances, such as heroin and LSD. Raich and Monson were caught between the laws of their state and those of the nation. As such, they found themselves front and center in one of the most enduring debates in American political life—that of federalism.

In August 2002, "county deputy sheriffs and agents from the federal Drug Enforcement Administration (DEA) came to Monson's home. After a thorough investigation, the county officials concluded that her cultivation and use of marijuana was entirely lawful as a matter of California law. Nevertheless, after a three-hour standoff, the federal agents seized and destroyed all six of her cannabis plants."[6] "As I stood by and watched," Monson later testified, "the DEA agents chopped down my medicinal plants. I was crying and my back began to tighten up; for the rest of the week I experienced debilitating back spasms. . . . We do not feel safe; we have had our civil rights and our rights under California law taken from us in our own back yard."[7]

IN *GONZALES V. RAICH,* THE SUPREME COURT SIDES WITH FEDERAL LAW

Facing a threat to their continued access to medical marijuana, the two women filed suit, and their case eventually made its way to the U.S. Supreme Court. In their case, Raich and Monson based their claims upon the laws of California and the Constitution of the United States. In restricting access to marijuana, they argued, the federal government was in violation of several amendments to the Constitution as well as of certain specific powers granted to Congress in the founding document.

In 2005, the Supreme Court decided to take up the case of Angel Raich and Diane Monson, weighing their rights against the authority of the federal government under the CSA and the commerce clause of the Constitution. For their part, representatives of the federal government and the DEA insisted that they were rightfully upholding federal law and federal authority. "Everything we're doing is according to the law," said Richard Meyer, a San Francisco–based DEA spokesman.[8] By enforcing federal law, however, the DEA agents were restricting actions that were legal under California state laws, which begs the central question, when it comes to pot and patients, does federal or state law rule?[9]

In his skeptical questioning of the women's attorneys, Justice Antonin Scalia, a conservative, challenged their assertion that growing and distributing cannabis—even if it stayed within California's borders—would not contribute to the nationally problematic underground market in marijuana. Justice Stephen Breyer, considered one of the liberal members of the Court, suggested that a better course of action for medical cannabis advocates was to change federal law itself, as California had done with the Compassionate Use Act, rather than using a state referendum to challenge federal policy.[10]

In its decision in *Gonzales v. Raich* (2005), by a 6–3 vote, the Court sided with the power of the federal government—and that of Congress under the commerce and supremacy clauses of the Constitution—and ruled against Raich and Monson.[11] The majority opinion explaining the Court's logic reached back more than sixty years, to a time in which the nation was battling its most severe financial crisis. In that case, an Ohio dairy and cattle farmer, Roscoe Filburn, happened to cultivate a small crop of winter wheat, some of which he used to feed his livestock and some of which he used to feed his family. Under federal laws of the time, Filburn was required to restrict his wheat acreage. Filburn, however, cultivated much more than was legally allowed by quota but, according to his testimony, only for use on his farm, not for sale.

Filburn argued that the federal government was exceeding its constitutional authority under the commerce clause (see below) since his activities were local, limited to his farm, and "their effects upon interstate commerce [were], at most, 'indirect.'"[12] The Supreme Court, in a unanimous decision in *Wickard v. Filburn,* disagreed. The Court found that even though the wheat never left the farm

▲ Plaintiff Diane Monson, shown at her California home, smokes marijuana from plants she grew herself to help alleviate back pain. In 2005, the Supreme Court ruled the federal government does have the authority to prohibit marijuana, despite state laws allowing it.

or the state, the quotas were a constitutional use of Congress's power under the commerce clause. According to one scholar of American federalism, "With such a definition of interstate commerce, nothing was local."[13]

If a product grown on a local farm for local consumption or marijuana grown at home for use in the home can be considered interstate commerce, then what *can't* be? In the debates over American federalism, defining the proper limits of the commerce clause remains a hotly contested issue.

Today, the landscape has changed from the time of *Gonzales v. Raich*. Almost all of the states have passed laws allowing the use of marijuana for certain medical conditions, though these laws vary considerably both in terms of the medical conditions covered and in the restrictions placed upon its use (see Figure 3.1). Others have decriminalized the possession of small amounts of marijuana, substituting civil fines for criminal penalties. In addition, nine states and the District of Columbia have legalized marijuana for recreational use. Federal law, however, has not changed, nor has the Supreme Court reversed its upholding of Congress's power to prohibit the growth, use, or possession of marijuana under the authority of the commerce clause.

This has put recent administrations in a very difficult spot. During President Barack Obama's second term in office, fully enforcing the CSA in the states had become impossible. In December 2015, in a federal suit brought by neighboring states against Colorado (one of the four states in which recreational use had been made legal at the time), Obama's solicitor general argued in a brief presented to the Supreme Court that it should not decide to hear the case. To some observers, the administration's

▼ **FIGURE 3.1**

Marijuana Legalization Today

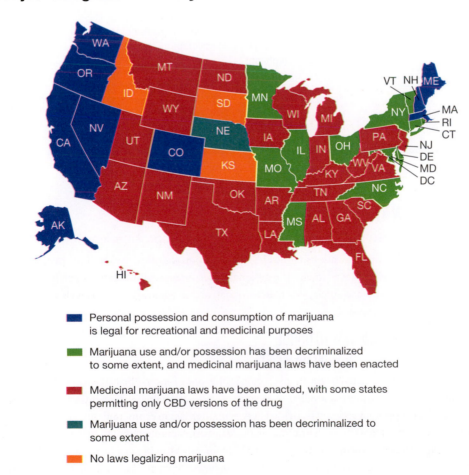

■ Personal possession and consumption of marijuana is legal for recreational and medicinal purposes

■ Marijuana use and/or possession has been decriminalized to some extent, and medicinal marijuana laws have been enacted

■ Medicinal marijuana laws have been enacted, with some states permitting only CBD versions of the drug

■ Marijuana use and/or possession has been decriminalized to some extent

■ No laws legalizing marijuana

Source: Map created with information from NORML.org, http://norml.org/. Accessed May 2, 2018.

position, though based on specific legal grounds, implied a position "that marijuana should be federally legalized—even for recreational use."[14] The Justice Department, under the president's direction, however, retained authority to prosecute the CSA, though it was to focus on drug trafficking and not on prosecuting "individuals who were in 'unambiguous compliance with existing state laws.'"[15]

With the election of Republican Donald Trump as president in 2016, many observers thought that federal policy might shift toward letting the states regulate medical and recreational marijuana use, possibly reclassifying or even removing marijuana from the list of controlled substances under federal law. By the spring of 2018, Attorney General Jeff Sessions remained staunchly opposed to legalized medical or recreational marijuana, helping to kill a congressional amendment that would prohibit the Justice Department from prosecuting marijuana businesses that were in compliance with their states' laws.[16]

What determines the boundaries between the nation and the states? The short answer is the Constitution. The long answer is nearly two and a half centuries of laws, court cases, and political action. The final answer is that there is no final answer; the boundaries between the nation and the states are not ever fully settled. To understand these dynamics more fully, we turn to the Constitution and its incomplete delineation of these boundaries.

WHAT HAVE I **LEARNED**?

1. The American federalist system _____.
   a. places the people's power in the national government
   b. places the people's power in the state governments
   c. divides power among national, state, and local governments
   d. divides power between national and state governments

2. What laws were in conflict in the case of Angel Raich and Diane Monson?

3. What deeper challenges to the placement of Americans' sovereignty does their case highlight?

_____

Answer Key: 1. d; 2. Answers should focus on the conflict between California law and those of the nation; 3. Answers should discuss the challenge of defining boundaries in the American federalist system.

THE CONSTITUTION DIVIDES POWER BETWEEN THE NATION AND THE STATES

- **Identify the elements of the U.S. Constitution that shape American federalism.**

One of the most important innovations of the U.S. Constitution was the division of the people's sovereignty between two levels of government: the national government and the states. Each level retained some exclusive powers and had some powers denied to it, and in some areas both levels were empowered to act on behalf of the people.

THERE IS MORE THAN ONE WAY TO DIVIDE POWER BETWEEN LEVELS OF GOVERNMENT

unitary systems
structures of governance that place the people's sovereignty in a national government, with subnational governments deriving their authority from it.

The American Republic created by the Constitution is only one of several possible ways of working out the relationship between different levels of government. The difference between these models is the way in which the people's sovereignty is divided between different governmental units (see Figure 3.2). In **unitary systems**, citizens place their power in one central government that then exercises authority over the subnational governments (such as states and provinces). Most policies are then actually carried out by these subnational governments that derive their power from the national government. Great Britain, France, and Japan are examples of democratic governments operating as unitary systems.

The Division of Power under Different Systems of Governance

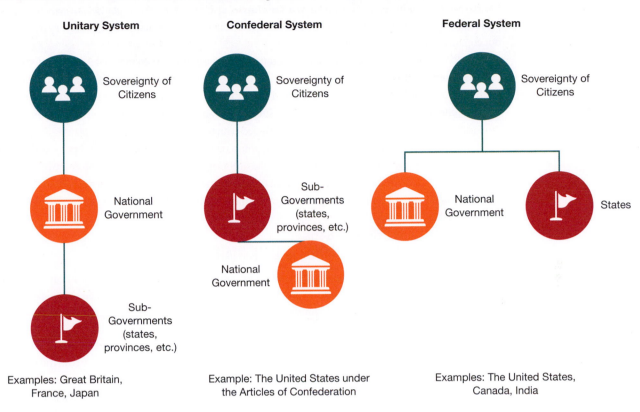

Examples: Great Britain, France, Japan

Example: The United States under the Articles of Confederation

Examples: The United States, Canada, India

At the opposite end of the spectrum are **confederal systems**. Here, citizens limit the authority of the national government, instead placing most of their sovereignty in the subnational governments, such as states, which then grant power and authority to the national government. In confederal systems, national governments are heavily dependent upon the states to carry out and pay for public policies. The United States under the Articles of Confederation was an example of a confederal system.

Finally, in **federal systems**, citizens divide their sovereignty between two or more levels of government, each of which may have exclusive authority to act in certain areas of policy, be denied from acting in an area of policy, or be required to share authority with another level in some areas. Key to a true federal system is the existence of constitutional protections for each level against encroachment on its powers by the other level(s). The United States, Canada, and India are examples of countries with federal systems.

The Constitution contains a set of provisions—the supremacy, necessary and proper, and commerce clauses—that shape the relative authority of the state and national governments. At the same time, however, it does not outline a perfectly clear vision of how the system of federalism would actually work.

THE SUPREMACY, NECESSARY AND PROPER, AND COMMERCE CLAUSES ARE THE KEYS TO AMERICAN FEDERALISM

One of the Constitution's most important statements about where the people's sovereignty is located is the **supremacy clause**, which reads, "This Constitution, and the Laws of the United States . . . shall be the supreme Law of the Land."[17] The supremacy clause is a powerful statement of national power. It means that the laws that Congress passes must be executed by the states, even if state constitutional provisions conflict with them. It means that states must abide by national treaties, and it also binds state courts to the Constitution.

confederal systems
structures of governance in which the subnational governments retain the majority of the granted authority.

federal systems
structures of governance that divide a people's sovereignty between two or more levels of government.

supremacy clause
a part of the Constitution that establishes the Constitution and the laws of the nation passed under its authority as the highest laws of the nation.

In another key clause, Congress is given the power to "make all Laws which shall be necessary and proper for carrying into Execution . . . Powers vested by this Constitution in the Government of the United States."[18] This **necessary and proper clause**, also called the elastic clause, is a critical source of power for the national government, granting Congress the authority to legislate as necessary for carrying out constitutionally granted powers.

In addition to these two clauses, there is a third that powerfully shapes modern American federalism: the **commerce clause**. In the language of the Constitution, this clause grants Congress the power to "regulate Commerce with foreign Nations, and among the several States, and with the Indian Tribes."[19]

Vagueness in the language regarding the specific powers of the national government has contributed to the growth of national power when combined with the necessary and proper clause. For example, under the authority of the commerce clause—in combination with the necessary and proper clause and the supremacy clause—Congress has claimed the authority to define nearly any productive activity as "Commerce . . . among the several States." Even though Diane Monson's homegrown marijuana was never sold or left her home state, the federal government claimed the authority to regulate it as interstate commerce.

THE CONSTITUTION DESCRIBES THE POWERS BELONGING TO THE NATION AND THE STATES

The word *federalism* does not appear in the Constitution. Nor is there any one section that clearly lays out how the Framers intended the people's sovereignty to be divided between the states and the national government. Instead, in various sections in the document, powers are given or denied to each level or allowed to be shared by both.

MOST POWERS OF THE NATIONAL GOVERNMENT ARE EXPLICIT. In general, the powers of the national government are explicitly listed and described by the Constitution. With a few exceptions, those of the state governments are assumed to encompass those powers not explicitly given to the national government. **Enumerated powers** refer to those powers granted to the national, or federal, government in the Constitution, and especially to Congress. These include the power to tax, coin money, declare war, raise and support an army and navy, make treaties, provide for the naturalization of American citizens, and "regulate Commerce with foreign Nations, and among the several States, and with Indian Tribes."[20] Most of the enumerated powers in the Constitution are granted to the legislative branch.

Implied powers are those not textually granted to the federal government but assumed to be given to it as a result of its need to make all laws "necessary and proper." For example, the Constitution does not give the national government the authority to create an air force (though the world had witnessed the first hot air balloon flight by the time of the drafting of the Constitution, so might have anticipated combat in the air). That authority, however, is assumed as part of its power to raise and support a military.

In addition to describing the enumerated and implied (or delegated) powers of the national government, the Constitution denies certain powers to it, especially if consent has not been given by the residents of the states, who usually act through their own state legislatures. The national government may not pass laws that violate the rights and liberties expressed in the Bill of Rights (or other later amendments). The national government may not admit new states to the Union, nor can it change state boundaries, without the consent of the state's citizens. It also cannot impose taxes on goods and services exported and imported between states.

THE POWERS OF STATE GOVERNMENTS ARE LESS EXPLICIT. The Constitution is much less specific on the powers allocated to the states. Much of the protection for state authority comes from the Tenth Amendment to the Constitution, which states, "The powers not delegated to the United States by the Constitution, nor prohibited by it to the States, are reserved to the States respectively, or to the people."

Called **reserved powers** because of the text of the Tenth Amendment, these are powers that were not given to the national government and are, therefore, reserved to the states. Among the most important of these are **police powers**, which state governments use to protect residents and provide for their safety, health, and general welfare. States are also authorized to conduct elections, including those for national office.[21] No amendments may be made to the Constitution without the consent of

Sidebar Glossary

necessary and proper clause
a part of the Constitution that grants the federal government the authority to pass laws required to carry out its enumerated powers; also called the elastic clause.

commerce clause
a part of the Constitution that grants Congress the authority to regulate business and commercial activity.

enumerated powers
powers explicitly granted to the government via the Constitution.

implied powers
powers not textually granted to a government but considered valid in order to carry out the enumerated powers.

reserved powers
powers reserved to the states if not textually granted to the federal government.

police powers
a category of reserved powers that includes the protection of people's health, safety, and welfare.

concurrent powers
powers granted to both states and the federal government in the Constitution.

three-fourths of the states, either by their legislatures or by ratification conventions in the states.[22] States are also empowered to establish local, town, county, and regional governmental bodies.

The Constitution also denies certain powers to state governments. States are prevented from entering into treaties or alliances with foreign powers—a real concern to the Framers, who saw the potential for European powers to divide the states for their own economic or political gain. States may not print their own money, tax imports or exports, or declare war.[23]

Finally, both the nation and the states are given the authority to act in certain areas of public policy. These **concurrent powers** allow national and state authority to overlap—an example of the concept of "separated institutions sharing power" discussed in Chapter 2.[24] The power to tax, already given to states under the Articles of Confederation, was extended to the new national government. Both levels are allowed to borrow money, though states have more restrictions on their own ability to go into debt than the federal government has. The nation and the states may both pass and enforce laws, create and operate a system of courts, and charter banks and corporations. (See Figure 3.3.)

RJ Sangosti/*The Denver Post* via Getty Images

▲ Graduates celebrate at the U.S. Air Force Academy in 2015. The Constitution gives the national government the implied power to create such an institution as the U.S. Air Force as part of its power to raise and support a military.

▼ FIGURE 3.3

Enumerated, Concurrent, and Reserved Powers in American Federalism

POWERS GRANTED

Federal
enumerated and implied powers
- tax citizens
- coin money
- declare war
- raise and support armed forces
- make treaties
- provide for the naturalization of citizens
- regulate interstate and foreign trade and trade with Indian tribes

Shared
concurrent powers
- levy taxes
- borrow money
- regulate interstate commerce
- regulate banks
- create and operate court systems
- determine voting qualifications

State
reserved powers
- tax citizens
- provide police and fire protection
- conduct elections
- amend the Constitution when 3/4 of states are in agreement
- establish local, town, county, and regional bodies
- regulate state commerce

POWERS DENIED

The federal government may not:
- violate rights and liberties outlined in the Bill of Rights
- admit new states without the consent of the territory's residents
- change state boundaries without consent of its residents
- impose taxes on goods and services exported and imported across state boundaries

States may not:
- enter into treaties with foreign governments
- print money
- tax imports or exports
- declare war

INTERPRETING GRAPHS AND CHARTS: AMERICANS' VIEWS OF FEDERAL, STATE, AND LOCAL GOVERNMENTS

The Pew Research Center is a nonpartisan organization that conducts and analyzes public opinion through surveys and other tools. In 2013, researchers asked individuals a series of questions about how *favorably* they viewed the federal government, their state governments, and their local governments. Those who answer these kinds of surveys are called *respondents*.

This was not the first time Pew researchers had asked the question. They had data going back to the 1990s. The researchers presented the collection of their findings over time with a **line graph** (sometimes called a line chart), which presents data as a set of points connected by lines.

These kinds of graphs can be useful in presenting trends over time. In this case, the line graph shows a widening gap between the favorability ratings that Americans who responded to the surveys (a group that changed with each survey) gave to the federal government, their state governments, and their local governments. According to these data, there appears to have been a notable decline in Americans' favorable views of the federal government in recent years.

One caution, though, when using and interpreting line charts comes from the lines themselves. When using solid lines to connect the actual data points (rather than broken lines or dots), readers may be more likely to interpret the findings as constant *trends* rather than as a series of discrete points. Consider the line associated with the federal government in the figure above. Was there really a trend toward favorability from 1997 to 2001 and then a different trend in more recent years, or were the years when more people gave favorable answers somehow different?

The researchers also found that differences in favorability views of government might be connected to the political party with which the individual answering the survey was affiliated, but not for every level of government.

Another way to present results of a survey is a **bar graph** (or bar chart), which represents data with rectangles of different sizes. The bars can be either horizontal or vertical.

These data came from one administration of the survey, in 2013. Note that differences in favorability ratings of the

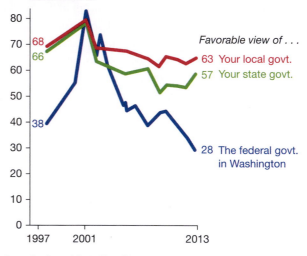

Widening Gap in Views of Federal, State and Local Governments

Favorable view of . . .

63 Your local govt.
57 Your state govt.
28 The federal govt. in Washington

68
66
38

1997   2001   2013

Source: Pew Research Center, "State Governments Viewed Favorably as Federal Rating Hits New Low," April 15, 2013, http://www.people-press.org/2013/04/15/state-govermnents-viewed-favorably-as-federal-rating-hits-new-low/.

federal government appear to be more strongly associated with, or *correlated* with, political party affiliations than views of state and local governments.

After studying these two presentations of data, consider and answer the following questions:

1. What do the numbers in the first figure, the line graph, represent?

2. What does the height of each bar in the second figure represent?

3. Which favorability rating of federal, state, and local government appears to be more connected to the political party that a respondent affiliates with?

4. Use the evidence presented in these two figures to construct an argument about what Americans think about federal, state, and local governments.

5. Pew Research is a respected organization, but let's say that it was not. Instead, consider how a research organization might shape the *surveys* to advance an argument. Discuss how the wording of the questions might shape the results presented (a topic to which we will return later in the book).

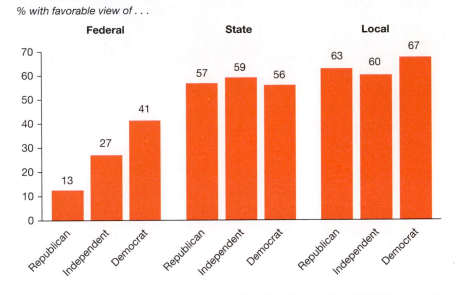

Less Partisan Views of State, Local Governments

% with favorable view of . . .

Source: Pew Research Center, "State Governments Viewed Favorably as Federal Rating Hits New Low," April 15, 2013, http://www.people-press.org/2013/04/15/state-govermnents-viewed-favorably-as-federal-rating-hits-new-low/.

REGIONAL AND LOCAL GOVERNMENTS HAVE NO EXPLICIT CONSTITUTIONAL POWERS. The Constitution does not describe the powers of the levels of government below the states—the cities, towns, counties, and districts. Generally, relationships between American states and their subgovernments are unitary, with the authority of the smaller units dependent upon and subordinate to the power and authority of the states. For example, state governments can change the boundaries of school districts or combine two school districts into a larger one if they choose to. If the relationship between these two levels of government were truly federal, this would not be possible without the consent of both the state and its school districts.

Therefore, while we often talk about three levels of government in the United States—national, state, and local—from the point of view of American federalism, there are only two—national and state. Dependence upon state authority is often a source of frustration for mayors, school board members, and other local officials, who have sometimes argued for something more like a three-level federalist system. Local officials are not powerless, however. According to political scientist Daniel Elazar, "The largest metropolitan centers, the so-called 'big city bloc,' do possess the political power needed to go directly to Washington."[25]

MEMBERS OF INDIGENOUS NATIONS HAVE A RELATIONSHIP WITH THE FEDERAL GOVERNMENT THAT IS DIFFERENT FROM AMERICAN FEDERALISM. As citizens both of the United States and their indigenous Native American nations, members of those nations have experienced a complicated and often tragic relationship between the federal government and their indigenous national governments, though one that is different from American federalism. The rules governing these relationships have been set down through centuries of treaties, laws, and Court decisions. We will consider one example of current debates involving members of indigenous nations in Chapter 4, when we examine the oil-pipeline protests near the Standing Rock Nation and what they tell us about civil liberties in the United States today.

line graph
a type of figure that presents data as a set of points connected by lines.

bar graph
a type of figure that represents data with rectangles of different sizes.

1. The necessary and proper clause _____.

   a. preserves necessary powers at the state level

   b. allows Congress to pass laws needed to carry out enumerated powers

   c. has since been ruled unconstitutional

   d. reserves unenumerated powers for the federal government

2. A key constitutional provision on which the Supreme Court based its decision in the case of Angel Raich and Diane Monson was _____.

   a. the commerce clause

   b. the Tenth Amendment

   c. separation of powers

   d. the Three-Fifths Compromise

3. What are reserved powers?

4. On what grounds did the Supreme Court rule against Angel Raich and Diane Monson in *Gonzales v. Raich*?

_____

Answer Key: 1. b; 2. a; 3. Answers should address the Tenth Amendment and discuss the lack of enumeration of most state powers; 4. Answers should focus on the history of interpretation of the commerce clause and cases such as *Wickard v. Filburn*.

FOR MUCH OF AMERICAN HISTORY, THE BOUNDARIES BETWEEN THE NATION AND THE STATES WERE SHARPER THAN THEY ARE TODAY

- **Describe the development of American federalism from the founding until the New Deal.**

Federalism is not one clean and unchanging concept, and there is no one set way to divide the people's sovereignty between levels of government. Defining the relative power of the two levels, as well as deciding how closely they will be intertwined, happens through the political process, and this has changed over the course of American history. In this section we will look at different types of federalism up through the early twentieth century and see how those relate to specific eras of American political history.

EARLY SUPREME COURT DECISIONS SHAPE THE DIVISION BETWEEN STATE AND NATIONAL POWER

The void left by the Framers of the Constitution in precisely defining the boundaries of American federalism was quickly filled by the Supreme Court—a role that it continues to pursue actively today. Perhaps the most important figure in shaping American federalism after the ratification of the Constitution was John Marshall, chief justice of the United States from 1801 to 1835 and the longest-serving chief justice in American history. During his tenure as chief justice, Marshall secured and issued several of the most important decisions in the area of American federalism.

MCCULLOCH V. MARYLAND RELIES ON THE NECESSARY AND PROPER CLAUSE TO ASSERT THE POWER OF CONGRESS. The first of these major decisions was in *McCulloch v. Maryland* (1819).[26] The case involved the Second Bank of the United States, a national bank chartered by Congress. Several states, including Maryland, passed laws to tax the state branches of the Second Bank for various reasons, such as to try to kill the branches, to defend their own state's banks, or just to raise money. The case centered on two questions: Did Congress have the authority to establish the bank in the first place? And did individual states have the authority to tax the bank's branches operating within their borders? Marshall, speaking for a unanimous

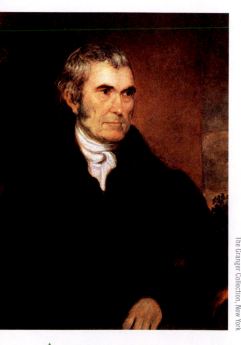

▲ Chief Justice John Marshall's decisions are widely held to be among the most important for shaping the powers and limits of federalism even today.

The Granger Collection, New York

Supreme Court, came down firmly on the side of the authority of the national government in both questions. Citing the necessary and proper clause of the Constitution, Marshall affirmed the right of Congress to establish the bank and denied the right of Maryland and other states to tax the bank's state branches.

GIBBONS V. OGDEN USES THE COMMERCE CLAUSE TO AFFIRM THE POWER OF CONGRESS TO REGULATE TRADE.

In *Gibbons v. Ogden* (1824), the Marshall Court weighed in on the powers of Congress under the commerce clause of the Constitution.[27] As with the *McCulloch* decision, in *Gibbons* the Court affirmed national power. Known as the "steamboat monopoly case," *Gibbons v. Ogden* arose from a battle between two powerful businessmen in the steamboat industry in New York and New Jersey. Aaron Ogden had been granted a monopoly by a New York state law that protected his routes within New York and between New York and New Jersey. Thomas Gibbons filed suit to block the monopoly.

Marshall's decision in the case reaffirmed national power but on a different constitutional principle. While *McCulloch* involved the necessary and proper clause, *Gibbons* focused on the power of Congress to regulate trade "among the several States" as part of its authority under the commerce clause. Marshall also cited the power of the national government under the supremacy clause of the Constitution. Marshall and the Court, again unanimously, struck down the steamboat monopoly between the two states and the part of the New York law that had made the monopoly possible. In doing so, Marshall affirmed the exclusive authority of Congress to regulate interstate commerce, defining commerce "among the several States" as including "the deep streams which penetrate our country in every direction [and] pass through the interior of almost every state in the Union."[28]

BARRON V. BALTIMORE RULES THAT THE DUE PROCESS CLAUSE APPLIES ONLY TO THE NATIONAL GOVERNMENT.

The third major federalism case decided by the Marshall Court was *Barron v. Baltimore* (1833).[29] *Barron* dealt with yet another part of the Constitution, in this case the portion of the Fifth Amendment's protections called the due process clause, which states, "No person shall . . . be deprived of life, liberty, or property, without due process of law; nor shall private property be taken for public use, without just compensation." John Barron, the owner of a wharf in Baltimore, sued the city for the cost to his business caused by sand that had accumulated in the waters off his wharf as a result of the city's development policies, thus depriving him of property without "just compensation." The Marshall Court issued another unanimous decision; however, in this case, it limited rather than expanded the power of the national government. The Court ruled that the Fifth Amendment's protections were aimed exclusively at restraining the power of the national government and were not intended to apply to the states.[30]

The Marshall Court affirmed national power, especially in relation to the necessary and proper clause and the commerce clause. However, Marshall handed down his decisions with an eye toward public opinion and tempered the expansion of national authority with an acknowledgment of state authority.

Lurking in the background during this time were the interconnected and unresolved problems of slavery, states' rights, and American federalism. The delegates to the Constitutional Convention had given in to the demands of the slave states to preserve their institution, in spite of the fact that slavery violated the essential principles of natural rights upon which the Constitution was based. In the nineteenth century, as the American Republic expanded to fill the continent, the question of slavery and its implications for the relationship between the nation and the states could no longer be ignored.

THE ERA OF DUAL FEDERALISM SEPARATES THE POWERS OF THE NATION AND THE STATES

For much of the history of the American Republic, the model of the relationship between states and the nation was one of **dual federalism**, which divided the people's sovereignty between the nation and the states. Dual federalism presumes a distinct, though not complete, separation between the two levels of authority, as if both operate side by side with relatively little interaction between the two.

dual federalism
a view of American federalism in which the states and the nation operate independently in their own areas of public policy.

▼ **FIGURE 3.4**

Dual Federalism

The state and federal levels of government operated under an arrangement of dual federalism for much of the history of the American Republic. In this model, federal and state governments have distinct powers and function independently of one another, addressing their own areas of policy.

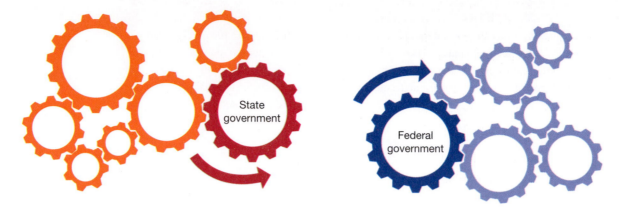

Dual federalism, according to an observer of American government in 1888, "is like a great factory wherein two sets of machinery are at work, their revolving wheels apparently intermixed, their bands crossing one another, yet each set doing its own work without touching or hampering the other."[31] (See Figure 3.4.)

The Supreme Court drew a similar image of two separate systems in the nineteenth century: "The government of the United States and the government of a state are distinct and independent of each other within their respective spheres of action, although existing and exercising their powers within the same territorial limits. Neither government can intrude within the jurisdiction, or authorize any interference therein by its judicial officers with the action of the other."[32] In fact, however, the division of authority between the nation and the states has never been this clean and neat. Even in areas of public policy that have been traditionally handled by the states, such as education, the federal government has been involved.[33] Driving much of the politics in the first half of the nineteenth century and heightening tensions between the states and the national government was the institution of slavery and the fears of southerners that it might be restricted or banned outright.

STATES' RIGHTS GROW DURING THE CIVIL WAR AND RECONSTRUCTION. The expansion of national power under the Marshall Court did not mean that this new balance of power would be permanent or go unchallenged. Efforts to assert the authority of states continued during the middle decades of the nineteenth century. As the original Federalist justices retired or passed away, many of their replacements held a stronger view of state authority. Increasingly, the question of federalism also became linked with the issues of slavery, **states' rights**, and the threat of secession. In the 1830s, South Carolina senator John Calhoun argued for the right of states to "nullify" federal laws that were in conflict with those of the states.

In December 1860, South Carolina seceded from the nation. Within six months, eleven southern states had followed to form the Confederate States of America. When the American Civil War finally ended in 1865, more than six hundred thousand soldiers had died and an unknown number of civilians had been killed.

The Civil War and the process of Reconstruction had settled the issues of secession and of legalized slavery; however, the question of how forcefully the national government would act to preserve the civil rights (the personal rights guaranteed to citizens or residents) of former slaves and their descendants was far from decided. As the government of the United States began to turn its attention to the expansion of the nation's empire toward the Pacific Ocean, the rights of African Americans received less and less consideration and protection.

states' rights
the idea that American states have the authority to self-govern, even when in conflict with national laws.

UNDER DUAL FEDERALISM, THE SUPREME COURT RESTRICTS AFRICAN AMERICANS' RIGHTS AFTER THE CIVIL WAR. Following the Civil War, the Supreme Court did not emerge as a defender of African American civil rights, a move that would have provided uniform protection for African Americans at the national level. Instead, it affirmed a vision of federalism that recognized state authority, even if that authority was used to restrict the rights of state citizens based only on their racial identity.

In the *Slaughterhouse Cases* (1873), the Supreme Court weighed in for the first time on the protections offered by the Fourteenth Amendment.[34] Like *Gibbons v. Ogden*, these cases involved a monopoly, this time of the slaughter of animals under a Louisiana state law. Butchers had challenged the monopoly as a violation of their rights under the Fourteenth Amendment, which prohibited the states from denying citizens "equal protection of the laws" (see Chapter 5). Ruling against the butchers, a closely divided Supreme Court drew a sharp distinction between the rights guaranteed under state and national citizenship.

Narrowly interpreting the equal protection clause of the Fourteenth Amendment to restrict discrimination only against African Americans (the butchers were white), the Court also placed limits on the privileges and immunities clause of the same amendment, stating that its protections apply only to national, not state, citizenship. In doing so, the Court upheld the authority of states to exercise their police powers.[35]

Plessy v. Ferguson (1896) was another landmark case in restricting the rights of African Americans following the Civil War and asserting states' rights. In this case, the Supreme Court upheld the constitutionality of legalized racial segregation (the separation of individuals based on their racial identity) and the ability of states to pass such laws.[36] *Plessy* was a test case, organized by the African American community in New Orleans to challenge Louisiana's segregation laws. Homer Plessy, "a light-skinned man who described himself as 'seven-eighths Caucasian,'" had been arrested and fined for violating a state law requiring separate railroad facilities for whites and African Americans.[37]

In the decision in *Plessy*, Justice Henry Billings Brown declared that Louisiana's law did not violate the Fourteenth Amendment. Arguing that "social prejudices cannot be overcome by legislation," Brown upheld Plessy's conviction and declared that "separate but equal" did not violate the Constitution. Justice John Marshall Harlan, the lone dissenter on the Court, countered, "Our Constitution is color-blind, and neither knows nor tolerates classes among citizens. In respect of civil rights, all citizens are equal before the law." Harlan, correctly, as it would turn out, saw *Plessy* as a dangerous and damaging ruling. Brown's majority opinion, however, set policy. The ruling that racial segregation could be constitutionally permissible endured for almost sixty years. We will explore the efforts—first in the states, later in the Supreme Court—of individuals to overturn this doctrine in detail in Chapter 5.

IN THE AGE OF INDUSTRY AND NATIONAL EXPANSION, COOPERATIVE FEDERALISM EMERGES. During the latter part of the nineteenth century and the early decades of the twentieth, the Supreme Court adopted a complex role toward the growing economy. On the one hand, important decisions during this time supported the ability of American businesses to pursue their interests without large amounts of regulation, especially by state and local governments. On the other hand, some decisions began to empower the national government to set broader regulatory rules. In many cases, states were happy to have the federal government take more of a leading role in regulating increasingly large and powerful corporations. As American corporations grew in size and power, states began to realize that they could not, on their own, "mobilize sufficient power to regulate wealthy railroads that could cut

Photo by © CORBIS/Corbis via Getty Images

▲ A young African American girl reads aloud during a lesson in a segregated elementary school in Washington, DC, March 1942. Schools remained explicitly segregated for nearly sixty years following the "separate but equal" ruling in *Plessy v. Ferguson* (1896).

Cooperative Federalism

Beginning in the late nineteenth century and extending into the early twentieth, state and federal governments forged a relationship of cooperative federalism in which they worked together to shape public policy. Notice that in cooperative federalism the gears are more closely interlinked, while they work more separately in the dual federalism system.

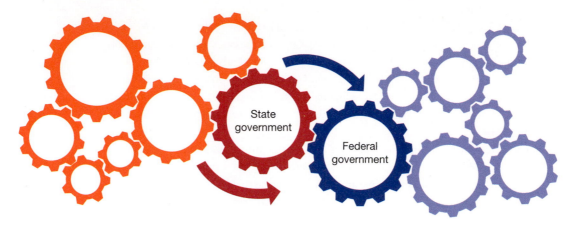

them off from the rest of the country in retaliation [for regulations], or deal with great industrial combines that could pull up and go elsewhere."[38]

Confronting the challenges and opportunities of economic growth together, the nation and the states began to forge what is called **cooperative federalism**, in which both levels work together in the same areas of public policy. Under this type of federalism, the two levels do not generally play the same roles. Instead, the national government tends to be "responsible for raising revenues and setting standards," while state and local governments remain "primarily responsible for administering the programs."[39] (See Figure 3.5.)

While both national and state governments began to build the foundations for cooperative federalism in the late nineteenth century, the dominant theme was one of not interfering with American business and the economy, at either the national or state level. Under this approach, government took little action to regulate or restrain private economic activity, even if it resulted in serious inequalities. In decisions that restricted the ability of the national government to regulate economic activity, the Supreme Court supported the philosophy of noninterference in the economy.[40]

While some of the seeds of the later growth in national power were planted during the era of big business, it would take a massive economic crisis, the inability of state governments to cope with the crisis, and the response of the national government to the crisis's challenges to fully realize this growth. To understand how major these changes would be, we need to understand the crisis itself: the Great Depression.

cooperative federalism
a vision of American federalism in which the states and the national government work together to shape public policy.

WHAT HAVE I **LEARNED**?

1. Confederal systems _____.
   a. place most of the people's authority within a strong centralized government
   b. divide authority between state and national governments
   c. lack a separation of powers between the branches
   d. place most of the people's authority within state governments

2. In *Plessy v. Ferguson*, the Supreme Court ruled that _____.

PRESIDENT FRANKLIN ROOSEVELT'S RESPONSE TO THE GREAT DEPRESSION RESHAPES AMERICAN FEDERALISM

- **Examine the role that the New Deal played in fundamentally reshaping American federalism.**

In the 1920s, plentiful rains across America's Great Plains region enticed many farmers to cultivate lands that their parents and grandparents had left untilled because they were too dry, too risky. But in the 1930s, droughts came and the newly plowed topsoil turned into dust, which was swept up into great dust storms that turned day into night.[41]

The boom times of the 1920s—wherein plentiful crops meant cheap and easy credit as well as the ability to borrow money to buy farmland or homes—dried up along with the land. So did the ability to speculate in stocks and bonds or to invest in the financial markets thousands of miles away.

But the debts taken on during the boom times remained. Prolonged deflation meant that money became scarce, loans were hard to come by or pay back, and prices fell. Faced with the simultaneous disasters of drought, falling prices, and unpayable debts, millions of farmers faced foreclosure. The collapse in farm prices was especially hard on tenant farmers, many of whom were racial and ethnic minorities and whose for-hire labor was no longer needed. In one of the largest migrations in American history, millions of displaced farmers and their families abandoned the "Dust Bowl" and headed West in search of whatever work they could find.

The hardship brought with massive dust clouds over American's heartland was only one of many in the nation. In October 1929, America's stock market crashed, a very visible signal of an industrial economy grinding to a halt. This signaled the start of the **Great Depression**, the most significant economic crisis in the nation's history. The nation's banking system nearly failed. Industrial production collapsed. Workers were laid off or had their wages cut. Foreclosures swept through cities, driving families into homelessness and hunger. The most vulnerable members of the American economy—children, women, and members of racial and ethnic minorities—often suffered the most.

The crisis of the Great Depression strained American federalism. During the boom times of the 1920s, states had increased their spending, especially to expand the highways for the nation's growing fleet of automobiles. To do so, states had borrowed large amounts of money. When the economic crisis took hold, many state governments themselves faced shortfalls and were unable to respond to their residents' needs. Local governments were similarly overwhelmed, unable to care for millions of unemployed workers. Faced with challenges they could not meet and citizens whose needs they could not assist, state and local governments appealed to the national government for help.

Great Depression
a period defined by the most significant economic crisis in American history.

Courtesy of the Library of Congress, Prints and Photographs Division

▲ A young Oklahoma mother stranded in California's Imperial Valley in 1937. She and her family were among the millions displaced during the Dust Bowl era and ensuing Great Depression. Those events precipitated major structural changes in the federalist system under President Franklin D. Roosevelt.

PRESIDENT ROOSEVELT GREATLY EXPANDS THE ROLE OF THE NATIONAL GOVERNMENT

At his inaugural address in 1933, President Franklin Delano Roosevelt made it clear that he was prepared to bring the full power of the executive branch to bear on the Great Depression. Should Congress not take proper action to assist, he said, "I shall ask Congress for . . . broad Executive power to wage a war against the emergency, as great as the power that would be given to me if we were in fact invaded by a foreign foe."[42]

Roosevelt meant what he said, and he would back up those promises and threats as one of the most powerful presidents in U.S. history. Within his first few months in office, Roosevelt secured the passage of fifteen major laws covering large areas of the nation's economy. Called the Hundred Days, this period in Roosevelt's administration resulted in the creation of a host of agencies; thousands of pages of regulations and rules; and a new, stronger role for the national government. It was part of the **New Deal**, Roosevelt's plan for tackling the Great Depression.

Roosevelt was able to use his uncanny sensibilities as a strategic political actor to exert a powerful influence on the country in a short amount of time. Roosevelt knew that state governments simply did not have the resources to handle the massive problems they faced. They were in no position to refuse the massive amount of federal aid that Roosevelt offered, even if accepting the aid meant trading away some state authority. This dynamic fundamentally changed the relationship between the states and the national government, dramatically strengthening the role of the national government in the economy. In terms of American federalism, it was a true revolution.

▲ Franklin Delano Roosevelt's inaugural address, March 4, 1933. In the address, President Roosevelt asserted, "This great Nation will endure as it has endured, will revive and will prosper. So, first of all, let me assert my firm belief that the only thing we have to fear is fear itself—nameless, unreasoning, unjustified terror which paralyzes needed efforts to convert retreat into advance."

Franklin D. Roosevelt Presidential Library & Museum

Roosevelt's first priority was the nation's crumbling banking system.[43] He officially closed the country's banks and introduced a series of bills to regulate the nation's economy and create a set of federal organizations to carry out and enforce these policies.[44] One of the most important, and controversial, results of the Hundred Days was the National Industrial Recovery Act (NIRA). Its purpose was to "drive prices up and put people back to work."[45] To do so, the act created an administrative agency, the National Recovery Administration (NRA), which became involved in regulating the American economy in ways few would have thought possible before the economic crisis hit. The primary tool of the NRA was a code (or set of rules) created by the NIRA governing prices, outputs, wages, working hours and conditions, management–labor relations, and the employment of children that American businesses pledged to follow.

The code was detailed. It "determined the precise components of macaroni; [it] determined what tailors could and could not sew. In the poultry industry the relevant line of code had banned customers from picking their own chickens."[46] The implementation of the code created political opposition both from business owners who were frustrated by their inability to raise prices and by workers and labor leaders who felt that the law's protections for workers' rights did not go far enough.[47] The complexity of the code also entangled government in the smallest of details of businesses, about which individual code inspectors often had little or no knowledge. Roosevelt was himself said to be nervous about wading so forcefully into workers' rights, but he later became more enthusiastic "in part because it strengthened workers' loyalty to the New Deal and the Democratic Party."[48]

THE SUPREME COURT PUSHES BACK AGAINST PRESIDENT ROOSEVELT'S NEW DEAL EXPANSIONS

New Deal
a set of policies passed during the administration of President Franklin Roosevelt to combat the Great Depression.

In 1934, Martin Schechter and his three brothers, operators of two kosher Jewish butcheries in New York, found themselves the target of the federal government's NRA regulators. The Schechter brothers' butcheries followed a set of practices that were "both a matter of religious observance and good business."[49]

One of the practices in which the Schechter brothers engaged was ensuring that their slaughtered chickens were "glatt kosher," meaning that the lungs of the carcasses were smooth and, therefore, free of tuberculosis, a very serious health issue in America at the time. As part of their observance of kosher practices, the Schechter brothers allowed customers to select and inspect poultry prior to sale. The Schechter brothers had followed those practices for years, earning them a loyal customer base.[50]

Those same practices placed the Schechter brothers at odds with the administration of President Franklin Delano Roosevelt. The brothers were charged with violating the NIRA federal code, including one charge that centered on the sale of "unfit chickens" not suitable for human consumption. All four brothers were indicted for violating the new laws, and all four were convicted and imprisoned. Instead of backing down, however, the Schechter brothers sued, and their case made it all the way to the Supreme Court. Their case, *Schechter Poultry Corp. v. United States* (1935), shook the foundations of Roosevelt's plan to fight the Great Depression.

The policy at the center of the battle was the code the NIRA created and the NRA was tasked to implement. The power of the NRA, its code inspectors, and the federal government seemed to the Schechter brothers and others overbearing and relentless. As they put it, "the NRA code did not make sense."[51] Their lawyers argued that the federal government overstepped its powers in granting Congress and the president authority over commerce that neither had possessed under the Constitution.

By the time the Schechter brothers' case made it to the Supreme Court, even members of Roosevelt's administration had begun to realize that such regulation could only produce political opposition without any larger political benefit. The "top-down culture of the NRA" began to take political fire,[52] and even the mainstream political establishment began to turn against it.

So did the Supreme Court.[53] In the early years of the New Deal, the Supreme Court was in no mood to allow the new president to expand federal authority in such an unprecedented way. In its opinion in *Schechter Poultry Corp. v. United States* (1935), the Supreme Court struck at the heart of Roosevelt's New Deal, arguing that his administration's policies had gone far beyond the authority granted by the Constitution and especially by the commerce clause. How, a majority of justices asked critically, could the butchery of chickens in New York City be considered "commerce . . . among the several States"?

In his arguments before the Supreme Court, Joseph Heller, the chief litigator on behalf of the Schechter brothers, argued that the federal government had exceeded its delegated, or implied, powers in its expansion of the commerce clause. In its regulation of the slaughter and sale of chickens in Brooklyn, the federal government, Heller asserted, had gone far beyond any reasonable interpretation of the word *among*. Almost all the chickens, he argued, had been purchased in New York, processed in New York, and sold in New York. Since no state boundary was crossed, the commerce clause could not have been violated.

In a unanimous opinion, the court sided with the Schechter brothers. Chief Justice Charles Evans Hughes argued that in enacting and enforcing the code, the NRA had exceeded its constitutional authority: "When the poultry had reached the defendants' slaughterhouses, the interstate commerce had ended."[54] Hughes wrote in his opinion that the actions of Congress and the Roosevelt administration consisted of "assertions of extra constitutional authority," a breach of the Tenth Amendment to the Constitution, which states that "the powers not delegated to the United States by the Constitution, nor prohibited to it by the States, are reserved to the States respective, or to the people."[55]

On both of these counts—exceeding the delegated power of the commerce clause and the excessive delegation of power to the president by Congress to formulate and enforce the code—the Supreme Court overturned the convictions of the Schechter brothers and, by implication, the NIRA and perhaps the entire New Deal. As Hughes put it, "the authority of the federal government may not be pushed

The Granger Collection, New York

▲ The Schechter brothers celebrate with their attorney, Joseph Heller (center), in his law offices in New York on May 27, 1935, upon learning of the Supreme Court's ruling in their favor in the case of *Schechter Poultry Corp. v. United States*. In this case, the National Industrial Recovery Act (NIRA) was determined to be unconstitutional.

to such an extreme as to destroy the distinction, which the commerce clause itself establishes, between commerce 'among the several States' and the internal concerns of a State."[56] The code-making and enforcing authority of the NRA, the Court found, violated the commerce clause and was therefore invalid. Without such authority, the NIRA was powerless.

The *Schechter* case was just the beginning. Justice Hughes was far from done, and "between 1933 and 1936, the Court overturned acts of Congress at ten times the traditional rate," actions that "created an atmosphere of crisis in Washington."[57]

PRESIDENT ROOSEVELT STRIKES BACK WITH A COURT-PACKING PLAN

The challenge to the president's authority would not go unanswered, however. In the months surrounding the Supreme Court's invalidation of the core of his New Deal, Roosevelt pushed ahead with his legislative agenda, called the Second New Deal. This period in Roosevelt's presidency saw passage of some of the most important New Deal programs.

The Social Security Act of 1935 created a set of programs to support vulnerable groups of Americans. It established unemployment insurance for American workers. It set up old-age insurance and elderly assistance programs, which were later supplemented with disability insurance. In addition, it established Aid to Dependent Children.[58] These programs were designed to be self-funding so as not to force the government to raise taxes and further depress the economy.

Passing more laws was not Roosevelt's only response to the Supreme Court's challenge to his power. Following his landslide reelection in 1936, in a move that alarmed even his closest advisers, Roosevelt decided to take on the Supreme Court directly. The president sought to use Congress's constitutional authority to increase the number of justices on the Court from nine to as many as fifteen, thus allowing him to appoint enough pro–New Deal justices to tip the balance of power decisively in his favor. Known as the "Court-packing plan," Roosevelt's gambit was constitutional but very bold and very risky.[59]

Roosevelt's bill died in the Democratic Congress. The Court-packing plan ultimately divided his own party, driving many conservative Democrats to side with Republicans in Congress, a split heightened over issues of civil rights for African Americans. Roosevelt eventually nominated replacements for most of the justices but only because his unprecedented four terms in office allowed him to outlast the tenure of most of them. Roosevelt would have a much friendlier Court in the later years of his presidency, but not because of Court-packing.

IN THE NEW DEAL, COOPERATIVE FEDERALISM REPLACES DUAL FEDERALISM

In the end, the Court did change its opinions, reversing in several key rulings its previous opposition to the constitutionality of Roosevelt's New Deal and similar state measures to regulate businesses and the economy. The New Deal survived, and it fundamentally altered the boundaries between the activities of the federal government and those of the states.

The expansion of national power under Roosevelt's New Deal—especially Congress's authority to regulate interstate commerce—permanently altered the relationship between the states and the nation. Cooperative federalism, in which both levels of government are involved in setting policy, firmly replaced earlier models of dual federalism and made the national government at least a coequal in many areas of public policy traditionally handled by the states.

▲ A cartoon from 1937 makes light of Franklin D. Roosevelt's Supreme Court–packing plan, which was challenged in regard to its constitutionality.

This change did not just happen. Nor was it necessarily inevitable. Roosevelt's popularity, political skill, and miscalculations all played a role. So did the decisions and the shifting opinions of the members of the Supreme Court. However, the revolution was also made possible by the severe economic crisis facing the nation and the inability of states to handle its fallout. States did not always fight Roosevelt's policies, desperate as they were for help in handling the impact of the Great Depression.

WHAT HAVE I **LEARNED?**

1. Roosevelt's Hundred Days refers to _____.
   a. the opening months of World War II
   b. President Roosevelt's political campaign
   c. a period of creation of bureaucratic agencies
   d. the Supreme Court's challenge to Roosevelt's policies

2. In writing the opinion in *Schechter Poultry Corp. v. United States*, Justice Hughes focused especially on _____.
   a. the Second Amendment
   b. the First Amendment

   c. the Tenth Amendment
   d. the Fourteenth Amendment

3. How did the New Deal change American federalism?

4. What role did the Supreme Court play in the expansion of cooperative federalism during the New Deal era?

Answer Key: 1. c; 2. c; 3. Answers should focus on the increasing power of the national government under cooperative federalism, especially under the commerce clause, and the creation of federal agencies to enact these policies; 4. Answers should include early attempts to roll back New Deal policies and later confirmation of their constitutionality in a consideration of Congress's power to regulate interstate commerce.

MODERN AMERICAN FEDERALISM REMAINS COOPERATIVE BUT FACES CHALLENGES

- **Discuss changes to American federalism in the modern era and how it might continue to evolve.**

During the second half of the twentieth century, the expansion of national involvement in the American economy initiated by Roosevelt continued and was in fact strengthened and expanded. Many federal agencies created during the New Deal stayed in place, and some grew larger. As the American economy recovered from the Great Depression and World War II, the conclusion of which left the United States as a global superpower, cooperative federalism remained the dominant model. The dual federalism of the nineteenth and early twentieth centuries was long gone—and, barring a major economic or social crisis, it is not coming back.

One of the primary tools that the federal government can use to achieve its policy objectives within the states is the **grant-in-aid**, money provided to states by the federal government in order to carry out a policy that the national government has decided is important. Though the use of grants-in-aid goes back to the early days of the Republic—especially in grants of land to support public education in the states and territories—they became a common tool in a variety of policy areas during and after the New Deal.

The main form of grant-in-aid during this period was the **categorical grant**, a grant provided to states or to local or regional governments for specific policy objectives and with certain conditions attached to receiving or spending the funds. (See the left-hand column of Figure 3.6.) These conditions might involve the requirement that the state, local, or regional authority provide matching funds in order to receive the federal monies. They might also include specific instructions on how the grant funds are to be used. Sometimes categorical grants are awarded based on formulas that allocate federal money according to factors such as population, income, and need.

grant-in-aid
federal money provided to states to implement public policy objectives.

categorical grant
a grant-in-aid provided to states with specific provisions on its use.

PRACTICING POLITICAL SCIENCE

READING AND STUDYING SUPREME COURT DECISIONS

In this book and in your course, you will at times be asked to interpret, analyze, and connect key U.S. Supreme Court cases. To do so, it will be important to become familiar with the format and components of Supreme Court decisions, as well as how to study them productively.

GENERAL Tips in Approaching Supreme Court Decisions

- Reading cases takes time, especially at first, because a legal decision is a specific kind of writing. Be sure to give yourself plenty of time.

- Become familiar with the most important facts of the case—who was involved, and how the case rose through the court system.

- What is the key issue? Or is there more than one central issue? In the cases that we will encounter, the fundamental issue always involves the Constitution. Therefore, be sure that you understand the particular clause or amendment that the Supreme Court is being asked to interpret.

- Try to gain a deeper understanding of the *context* of the case, which may include the larger political climate in which the case was decided.

- Generally, do not worry too much about details. Think about the big picture, especially the implications of the decision for constitutional law and public policy. Consider how the case sets a precedent to be applied in future cases.

- Be sure to practice comparing different cases. Sometimes one decision will build on others. Sometimes a decision may be overturned.

KEY Terms and Concepts in Reading Supreme Court Decisions

- Facts: Who were the parties involved? What happened to them?

- Issue: What constitutional dispute was the Court being asked to resolve?

- Holding: What did the Court decide? Who won?

- Precedent: What had been decided before in similar cases? In our legal system, even if the Court eventually overturns precedent, it does not do so lightly.

- Majority opinion: The decision and legal reasoning of the majority of justices. A majority opinion may be unanimous.

- Concurring opinion (concurrence): There may be no concurrences, or many. These are opinions written by justices who voted with the majority, but they have different or additional reasons for their decision.

- Dissenting opinion (dissent): There may be no dissents or several. These are opinions written by justices who voted with the minority. Though they do not carry the force of the Court, they may lay down the logic of the other side should the Court decide to reevaluate precedent in future cases.

Categorical grants-in-aid are an important source of national power. Though state, local, and regional governmental authorities are often not required to accept these funds, once they do, they accept the national regulation that goes along with taking the money. Once a state establishes a program based on the receipt of a categorical grant-in-aid, it depends on the continued provision of those funds by the national government, along with any attached strings, to avoid a potentially serious disruption of the provision of services to its citizens and residents.

In this way, categorical grants act as both a carrot—to encourage states to carry out national policy objectives—and a stick—to threaten states with the withholding of funds if they fail to carry out the federal government's policy objectives. According to critics of national power, categorical grants pose several problems for American federalism. They may act as "bribes to induce subnational governments to execute national policies" at the expense of their own authority.[60] Officials and citizens of wealthier states may feel that their taxes are being used to subsidize lower-spending state governments. The uncertainty surrounding the continued provision of the grants can make it harder for states to plan their own budgets. Finally, the administration of these programs requires a further expansion of the size of both national and state government.

Grants-in-Aid

Categorical Grant

Money provided by the national government to state, local, or regional governments that is tied to specific policy objectives and that carries certain conditions for receipt or expenditure.

- National government controls purse strings.
- Once a program is established, states depend upon national government for continuation of that program.
- Can mean that wealthier states "subsidize" poorer ones; but can also mean that inequalities between states are reduced and citizens in poorer states have access to benefits they might not otherwise have.
- Can make it harder for states to control their own budgets.
- Can lead to expansion in size of national and state government.

Block Grant

Money proved to state, local, or regional governments over which subnational governments have greater control.

- State, local, or regional governments have greater say in how funds are spent.
- Subnational governments given greater flexibility in long-term budget planning.
- States can have more authority in setting and enforcing welfare rules.
- Can mean that states decide what priorities to select for their population and are more "in touch" with their needs; but also can mean that federal oversight is reduced and the ability to compare outcomes across states is more limited.
- Can mean that localities with greater need lose out to localities with greater political clout in the allocation of funds.

Those who argue in favor of the use of categorical grants as a tool of national policymaking emphasize the degree to which the redistribution of monies between states can act to reduce inequality between the states. Also, these monies can help state, local, and regional governments improve the lives of their citizens in ways that might not be possible without the help of the federal government.[61]

PRESIDENT LYNDON JOHNSON'S GREAT SOCIETY EXPANDS COOPERATIVE FEDERALISM

The most significant expansion of national power through the use of categorical grants-in-aid in the post–New Deal era occurred during the presidency of Lyndon Baines Johnson. His Great Society program created a new set of administrative agencies aimed at improving social welfare in the United States. Social welfare involves the health, safety, education, and opportunities for citizens. Under the old system of dual federalism, social welfare policies were typically thought of as lying within the scope of the police powers of the states and, therefore, mostly under state control.

Although Roosevelt's policies had already involved the federal government in the provision of social welfare policy—for example, by addressing working conditions, unemployment relief, and income security—Johnson's policies expanded this role, aided by strong Democratic Party majorities in both the House and the Senate. Most of his initiatives were grants-in-aid to states and communities.

The Medicare program (1965) supplemented the Social Security program by providing health insurance coverage to individuals aged sixty-five and older. The Medicaid program (1965) provided health care assistance to individuals receiving other forms of aid as well as to those "who were medically indigent but not on welfare."[62] As with many Great Society programs, Medicaid was set up to be funded partly by the federal government and partly by the states. The Elementary and Secondary Education Act of 1965 (ESEA) "provided for the first time, general federal support for public elementary and secondary education."[63] Title I of the ESEA provided federal assistance to children from low-income families in both public and private schools.

Andrew Harrer/Bloomberg via Getty Images

▲ Pediatrician Lanre Falusi examines an infant patient in a Maryland community health clinic in 2015. With powerful lobbying efforts behind them, members of the American Medical Association pressured Congress to revamp physician reimbursement under Medicare.

WITH NEW FEDERALISM COMES DEVOLUTION AND ATTEMPTS TO ROLL BACK NATIONAL POWER

Some backlash followed on the heels of Johnson's Great Society programs and the expansion of national authority that they produced. When Richard Nixon was elected president in 1968, he promised to roll back the expansion of national authority and return at least some of the power to the states. He called his project "new federalism."

One of Nixon's main tools to try to reduce national authority was the **block grant**. Though they are still a type of grant-in-aid, block grants provide federal money for public policies in a way that tries to increase state, local, and regional authority in how that money is spent and decrease national authority in deciding which states, localities, or regions receive those funds. (Look back at the right-hand column in Figure 3.6 on p. 83.)

Efforts to restore more authority to the states continued under the presidency of Ronald Reagan, who, in his speech accepting the Republican Party's nomination in 1980, promised, "Everything that can be run more effectively by state and local government we shall turn over to state and local government, along with the funding sources to pay for it. We are going to put an end to the money merry-go-round where our money becomes Washington's money, to be spent by the states and cities exactly the way the federal bureaucrats tell them to."[64] As part of his program, Reagan reduced funding for several social welfare programs and increased the use of block grants for those that continued to be funded.

The goal of returning authority for federal programs back to the states is called **devolution**, in the sense that authority is devolved, or returned to, the states. Efforts at devolution involved trying to increase states' autonomy in economic and social policy by decentralizing control and administration of programs. One of the most important of these efforts focused on social welfare policies. Democratic president Bill Clinton signed into law the Personal Responsibility and Work Opportunity Reconciliation Act of 1996 (PRWORA). PRWORA replaced a Roosevelt-era aid program with Temporary Assistance for Needy Families (TANF), which placed time limits on receipt of welfare assistance and added work requirements. In addition, block grants and other changes to the administration of the program gave states more authority in setting and enforcing the rules of welfare programs.

Johnson's Great Society expanded the role of the national government and the vision of cooperative federalism that had been firmly established during Roosevelt's New Deal. The Republican administrations of Nixon and Reagan attempted to roll back some of the growth in national power that had occurred during and after the New Deal. Democratic president Clinton—confronted with firm Republican Party control in Congress—applied the principle of devolution to social welfare policy.

In terms of returning America to the dual federalism of its early history, however, none of the policies of the twentieth-century presidents even came close. At this point in American political history, there has been no going back to the stricter separation between state and national authority that operated prior to Roosevelt's revolution. However, as the United States confronts a new set of challenges in the twenty-first century, calls for a fundamental reexamination of American federalism have gained more and more attention.

block grant
a type of grant-in-aid that gives state officials more authority in the disbursement of federal funds.

devolution
a national policy goal of returning more authority to state or local governments.

STATE GOVERNMENTS HAVE
SEVERAL TOOLS TO PRESERVE THEIR INTERESTS

In spite of efforts to restrain the power of the national government during the periods of new federalism and devolution, the New Deal legacy of national involvement in state policy has not fundamentally changed, nor is it likely to. For states, opting out of the involvement of the federal government that comes with accepting federal funds would require opting out of the funds themselves and either replacing them or explaining to that state's citizens why certain services will no longer be provided. While individual states may do this in regard to individual programs, a national, wholesale withdrawal is almost unthinkable.

State and local governments, however, have not necessarily been passive players in cooperative federalism, and strategic political actors at the various levels have played a role in trying to shape the balance of power between the two levels of the American federalist system. That is likely to continue and may result in an increased use of tools to assert state power, even confrontationally. States have a handful of tools they can use to shape how they participate in cooperative federalism.

TAXATION. One area where states are beginning to try to set policy in the absence of a comprehensive federal policy is e-commerce taxation. When state residents are able to purchase items over the Internet from companies outside their states, state governments can lose out on sales tax revenue for those products. In many ways, the e-commerce giants, such as eBay and Amazon.com, present similar challenges to state governments as did the railroads of the nineteenth century, with individual states facing difficulties in regulating businesses that transcend state boundaries. In response, states are increasingly setting policies to collect tax revenues from products purchased online and are coordinating their policies with other state governments.

LOBBYING. Another tactic that state and local governments use is to try to influence the content of federal legislation as it is being written and voted on. **Intergovernmental lobbying**, which is often carried out by state or local governmental staff in Washington, involves attempts to influence the national policymaking process to protect state and local interests. In this way, these governments themselves become part of the national legislative process. Examples of intergovernmental lobbying organizations include the National Governors Association, the National Conference of State Legislatures, and the National League of Cities.

IMPLEMENTATION. Even when the federal government passes laws that govern state actions, the state governments are typically responsible for implementing these policies, giving them the opportunity to use the process of implementation "to enforce federal policies in a way that promotes their interests."[65] Although the federal government often has considerable power in crafting laws and creating administrative agencies, the fact that states actually carry out many of these policies provides an important source of state power. In *Federalist* No. 46, James Madison argued that states would have considerable power to resist the carrying out of an "unwarrantable measure of the federal government" by making it difficult, if not impossible, for those unpopular policies to actually be carried out.[66] In fact, according to one scholar of American federalism, "state governments have indeed succeeded tremendously in resisting, delaying, or altering the implementation of federal policies at the state level."[67]

CHALLENGES TO COOPERATION. While the modern system of cooperative federalism allows states opportunities to try to preserve their authority and influence over policymaking, the relationship between states and the national government is not always cooperative. At times, state governments have objected to federal regulations that, from the point of view of the states, are attempts to make the states pay for federal policies. Such unpaid, or underpaid, requirements are called **unfunded mandates** or, sometimes, underfunded mandates.

intergovernmental lobbying
efforts by state and local governments to act in Washington on behalf of their own interests.

unfunded mandates
federal regulations that must be followed by the states but whose costs must also be shouldered by the states.

AP Photo/Elaine Thompson.

▲ Adrienne Kosewicz, online business owner, shown in her home office in Seattle, Washington, in 2018. Kosewicz pays $3,600 a year for tax collection software to handle payments and reports to her home state. Her business sells toys through Amazon, which handles computation and collection.

From the point of view of Congress, there are strong incentives to make policies whose costs have to be carried by the states: "The legislator gets the credit for benefitting needy constituents, but the cost is paid by a lower governmental tier."[68] State, local, and regional governments have complained to Washington about the imposition of unfunded mandates in a variety of policy areas, including environmental policy, education policy, and the provision of health and social welfare benefits for low-income and disabled Americans. In March 2008, the governor of Montana complained, "We are putting up with the federal government on so many fronts, and nearly every month they come up with another harebrained scheme, an unfunded mandate to tell us that our life is going to be better if we'll just buckle under on some other kind of rule or regulation."[69]

One strategy that states use to try to reduce the impact of unfunded mandates is to pressure the federal government for waivers from certain provisions of a given law. Coordinated state pressure on the federal government can lead to exemptions from implementing—and paying for—certain unpopular provisions of a law.

As the American Republic enters the first decades of the twenty-first century, new state challenges to federal authority are emerging. One tool that many states have used to do this is the sovereignty resolution. Passed by state legislatures, **state sovereignty resolutions** affirm the sovereignty of states under the Tenth Amendment to the Constitution. Variations of these resolutions have been passed or considered in response to a variety of federal laws, including those covering education, immigration, and health care. They are often a result of state claims of unfunded mandates. They are typically only statements of protest, stopping short of actually nullifying a law but asserting the rights of states to do so in the future if necessary.

Though sovereignty resolutions are largely symbolic, the Tenth Amendment has become a more prominent tool in asserting state authority in recent decades, especially in the area of gun control, as several Supreme Court decisions have cited the amendment in the logic of their decisions. In 1995, in *United States v. Lopez*, the Court struck down a federal law banning the carrying of firearms near schools.[70] On March 10, 1992, Alfonso Lopez Jr. began yet another day of his senior year at Edison High School in San Antonio, Texas. However, this day he entered his high school with an unloaded .38 special revolver and five cartridges in his pocket. His task was to deliver the revolver and ammunition to another student in exchange for $44. Through anonymous sources, school authorities were made aware that Lopez was carrying an unloaded revolver and confronted him about these accusations. After admitting he was carrying a firearm and ammunition, Alfonso Lopez Jr. was charged with violating the Gun-Free School Zones Act of 1990.

Lopez subsequently moved to dismiss the charges, claiming that the Act of 1990 was unconstitutional, as Congress did not have the power to regulate public schools. However, the trial court denied the motion, claiming that the act was within the powers enumerated to Congress under Article I, Section 8, Clause 3 of the U.S. Constitution, as activities within elementary, middle, and high schools are components of interstate commerce. After being tried and convicted, Lopez appealed to the Fifth Circuit Court in hopes of reversing the decision by the trial court, as he and his representation felt that Congress had overstepped the enumerated powers granted in the commerce clause. The Fifth Circuit agreed, and the conviction was reversed.

The U.S. government was required to prove that the act was constitutional under the commerce clause and that the act dictated a significant portion of interstate commerce. The question presented to the Supreme Court was, "Is the 1990 Gun-Free School Zones Act, forbidding individuals from knowingly carrying a gun in a school zone, unconstitutional because it exceeds the power of Congress to legislate under the Commerce Clause?"[71] This issue of Congress overstepping the power of the commerce clause had not been reviewed by the Supreme Court since World War II, where the

state sovereignty resolutions
state legislative measures that affirm the sovereignty of states under the Tenth Amendment.

Court had held in the case of *Wickard v. Filburn* that the Agricultural Adjustment Act of 1938 was constitutional, dramatically increasing the economic legislative power of Congress. Also note that in *United States v. Darby* (1941), the Court upheld the Fair Labor Standards Act, claiming that "the power of Congress over interstate commerce is not confined to the regulation of commerce among the states. It extends to those activities intrastate. . . ."[72]

In a 5–4 decision, the Supreme Course upheld the ruling of the Fifth Circuit, claiming that "the possession of a gun in a local school zone is not an economic activity that might, through repetition elsewhere, have a substantial effect on interstate commerce. The law is a criminal statute that has nothing to do with 'commerce' or any sort of economic activity."[73] The majority opinion was delivered by Chief Justice William Rehnquist, with concurring opinions delivered by Justice Anthony Kennedy and Justice Clarence Thomas. The majority opinion was based on four key factors: whether the activity in question was an economic activity, whether the firearm had been transported in interstate commerce, whether there was a link between firearms and education, and whether there was a correlation between the activity and interstate commerce. Justice Stephen Breyer delivered the main dissenting opinion in which he concluded that gun violence could influence interstate commerce and education. He reasoned that a court should not examine a lone isolated case of regulation, but rather the overarching effect of firearms on school property. In 1997, in *Printz v. United States*, the Court again cited the Tenth Amendment when it struck down portions of a federal law that required local law enforcement officers to perform background checks on prospective handgun purchasers.[74]

Another tactic that states have occasionally used, and may continue to use in the future, is to pass a state law that is in direct violation of a federal law or policy, perhaps amending the state constitution to do so. During the election of 2012, several states passed laws or amendments to their constitutions that placed state policy in direct violation of federal policy. Three states—Montana, Alabama, and Wyoming—passed initiatives exempting state citizens from some of the provisions or penalties under President Barack Obama's health care overhaul, the Patient Protection and Affordable Care Act of 2010. And, as we have explored, more than half the states have now passed laws legalizing the medical or even recreational use of marijuana, in violation of federal law.

WHAT HAVE I **LEARNED?**

1. The term *devolution* refers to _____.
   a. returning powers over social welfare policy back to the states
   b. strengthening the role of the national government over police powers
   c. President Roosevelt's expansion of national power in response to the Great Depression
   d. limiting the powers of local governments

2. Categorical grants _____.
   a. are provided with specific provisions on their distribution
   b. allow state governments great flexibility in their use
   c. have been nullified, as they support a policy of "separate but equal"
   d. require state constitutional amendments to be accepted

3. An example of a way that state governments constitutionally try to assert their own authority is _____.
   a. nullification
   b. intergovernmental lobbying
   c. secession
   d. All of the above

4. How would you describe the current state of American federalism?

_____

Answer Key: 1. a; 2. a; 3. b; 4. Answers will vary and should be backed up with arguments. Some may focus on national power. Others may focus on cooperative federalism. Still others may point to increasing state resistance.

CONCLUSION: THE EVOLUTION OF FEDERALISM CONTINUES

Today, Angel Raich is "living very happily with her loving husband" and working as a consultant and advocate for individuals' right to use medical cannabis.[75] Raich, with the help of medical marijuana, has been able to maintain her health, pursue her goals, and express her voice as a political advocate.

However, the issue of the boundary between state and federal laws governing medical and recreational marijuana use remains far from settled. By 2018, almost all states had passed legislation legalizing at least some form of medical cannabis. Nine other states and Washington, DC, had also passed ballot initiatives legalizing the recreational use of marijuana.[76] However, the CSA still controlled federal law and policy.

According to the Office of National Drug Control Policy, "it is important to recognize that these state marijuana laws do not change the fact that using marijuana continues to be an offense under federal law. Nor do these state laws change the criteria or process for FDA [U.S. Food and Drug Administration] approval of safe and effective medications."[77] By federal law, any current user of marijuana, even if such use is legal under their own state laws, is violating the CSA and is subject to federal prosecution.

There is no possible—or practical—way that this situation can continue. By 2016, the CSA could not be effectively and totally enforced as federal law, since that would have entailed putting more than a million, perhaps millions, of state-law-abiding citizens in federal prison, not to mention the unimaginable political fallout from fully executing the law.[78] Officials with the federal government and the Obama administration were well aware of this situation. In a 2013 memorandum, the Department of Justice affirmed the legality and supremacy of the CSA but also acknowledged the impossibility of enforcing the law in the states in totality. It stated, "The Department is also committed to using its limited investigative and executorial resources to address the most significant threats in the most effective, consistent and rational way."[79] In the memorandum, the Justice Department declared that instead it would focus on preventing access to marijuana by youths, transport of marijuana from a state in which it is legal to states in which it is not, and the use of firearms in connection with the production or distribution of marijuana.

In the first two years of his administration, the Trump administration continued to express support for enforcement of the CSA. In a letter written on July 24, 2017, Attorney General Sessions responded to concerns expressed by the government of Washington State. In it, Attorney General Sessions stated: "Congress has determined that marijuana is a dangerous drug and that the illegal distribution and sale of marijuana is a crime. . . . The 'recreational licensed' marijuana market is also incompletely regulated. . . . Since legalization in 2012, Washington State marijuana has been found to have been destined for 43 different states."[80]

In the November 2018 elections, voters in Michigan approved the recreational use of marijuana, and those in two other states—Missouri and Utah—approved medical marijuana use. Voters in North Dakota, however, rejected a recreational marijuana ballot measure. The day after the election, Trump's attorney general, Jeff Sessions, announced his resignation after weeks of public criticism by the president. While it was far from clear what impact Sessions's resignation would have on federal marijuana policy, stock prices for Canadian marijuana company Tilray jumped 30 percent on the news.[81]

How to deal with the fact that an individual might be complying with the laws of her or his state but at the same time breaking federal law is a fundamental question of federalism that is still unanswered. American federalism has never been a well-defined thing. In the twenty-first century, it remains just as contested as it has been for most of the nation's history.

CHAPTER REVIEW

This chapter's main ideas are reflected in the Learning Objectives. By reviewing them here, you should be able to **remember** the key points, **know** the terms that are central to the topic, and **think** about the critical issues raised in each section.

3.1 Explain the tension in American federalism between state and federal laws highlighted by the issue of legalized marijuana.

REMEMBER
- The ultimate political authority in the American representative democracy rests with the people, but this authority is divided between two levels of government: the nation and the states.
- The use of medical marijuana in California was legal under the laws of the state but illegal under federal law.
- In *Gonzales v. Raich* (2005), the Supreme Court upheld the power of the federal government to set policy on the use and possession of marijuana and other controlled substances.

KNOW
- federalism (p. 63)

THINK
- Why do you think the Framers of the Constitution established the system of American federalism?

3.2 Identify the elements of the U.S. Constitution that shape American federalism.

REMEMBER
- The Constitution lays out much of the framework of American federalism but not in one clear, neatly defined section. Instead, multiple clauses and sections attempt to define its basic boundaries.

KNOW
- bar graph (p. 70)
- commerce clause (p. 68)
- concurrent powers (p. 69)
- confederal systems (p. 67)
- enumerated powers (p. 68)
- federal systems (p. 67)
- implied powers (p. 68)
- line graph (p. 70)
- necessary and proper clause (p. 68)
- police powers (p. 68)
- reserved powers (p. 68)
- supremacy clause (p. 67)
- unitary systems (p. 66)

THINK
- What do you think should be considered commerce "among the several States"? What should not?

3.3 Describe the development of American federalism from the founding until the New Deal.

REMEMBER
- For much of the nation's history, the states and the nation operated under dual federalism, in which each level tended to exercise influence over different areas of policy.
- The boundaries between the authority of national and state governments have changed over time. Many of these changes have come about as a result of Supreme Court decisions in interpreting the Constitution.
- The era of dual federalism also included the restriction of African Americans' rights, even after the abolition of slavery.

KNOW
- cooperative federalism (p. 76)
- dual federalism (p. 73)
- states' rights (p. 74)

THINK
- How much power do you think the Supreme Court should have in interpreting the boundaries between national and state powers?

3.4 Examine the role that the New Deal played in fundamentally reshaping American federalism.

REMEMBER
- The New Deal fundamentally reshaped American federalism, but the program was not without challenges, especially by the Supreme Court.

KNOW
- Great Depression (p. 77)
- New Deal (p. 78)

THINK
- Why has American federalism shifted toward more involvement by the national government in states' enactment of public policy?

3.5 Discuss changes to American federalism in the modern era and how it might continue to evolve.

REMEMBER
- After the New Deal, later administrations expanded upon the promises and programs of the New Deal. However, some presidents attempted to restrict the power of the federal government and turn over more administrative authority to the states. State and local governments continue to be active in asserting their governmental authority.

KNOW
- block grant (p. 84)
- categorical grant (p. 81)
- devolution (p. 84)
- grant-in-aid (p. 81)
- intergovernmental lobbying (p. 85)
- state sovereignty resolutions (p. 86)
- unfunded mandates (p. 85)

THINK
- Do you think American federalism might eventually return to a "dual federalism" model? Why or why not?
- How do you think the question of federal and state policy over medical and recreational marijuana will be resolved?

AP Photo/Ben Margot

CHAPTER 4

CIVIL LIBERTIES

Building and Defending Fences

▶ In March 2017, Keeli Little Leaf, from the Warm Springs tribe, protests in Portland, Oregon, in solidarity with the "Native Nations Rise" march on Washington, DC, against the construction of the Dakota Access Pipeline. Construction continues on the controversial pipeline, which will carry crude oil under Lake Oahe near the Standing Rock Sioux reservation reservoir.

The American Republic was founded upon the idea that people are born with certain fundamental rights and freedoms. In this representative democracy, citizens enter into a compact with their government: they willingly allow some restrictions upon their actions and expression of their rights in order to create a functioning political body, provided that government acts in such a way as to preserve and protect citizens' innate rights and liberties. This has always been an uneasy and shifting bargain. The scope of individual freedoms and the acceptable restrictions placed upon those freedoms is constantly in contestation.

The rights that citizens possess that are protected from unreasonable governmental restriction are referred to as **civil liberties**. In contrast, the term *civil rights* refers to the fundamental rights of individuals to be treated equally under the laws and policies of the government, regardless of their identities and experiences.

Civil liberties are often called **negative freedoms** because protecting them involves restricting—*not* allowing—government actions. The First Amendment to the Constitution begins, "Congress shall make no law. . . ." It is this affirmation of the *limits* on the proper powers of government that protects the fundamental freedoms of Americans. Most, but not all, the constitutional protections for American civil liberties reside in the **Bill of Rights**—the first ten amendments to the U.S. Constitution. In contrast, civil rights are often referred to as *positive freedoms* since their protection generally implies positive action, either on the part of citizens to exercise them or on the part of a government to secure them. We will explore civil rights and the challenges present in their protection and establishment in the next chapter.

The stories of this chapter—of the Standing Rock pipeline protests of 2016 and 2017, of Edie Windsor, of James Obergefell trying to secure marriage equality, and other brief ones along the way—are stories about struggles to define and protect fundamental liberties, stories about building fences, especially around the power of government to restrict their expression.

Two questions in particular emerge when thinking about the complexities involving the expression and protection of civil liberties: What exactly are the fundamental rights and freedoms that individuals possess? And, under what circumstances can a government legitimately restrict the expression of these rights and freedoms?

In their essence, questions about civil liberties are questions about boundaries between the rights and freedoms of individuals and governmental authority as well as between individuals as they claim their fundamental freedoms. One of the longest-running struggles in this area involves the tension between the need to have a safe and orderly society and the need to protect Americans' civil liberties. As we will explore in this chapter, the boundary lines between the rights and freedoms of individuals and the power of the U.S. government and its states are far from clear, fixed, or even agreed upon.

civil liberties
fundamental rights and freedoms of citizens, the protection of which involves restricting the power of a government.

negative freedoms
fundamental liberties of which protection is ensured by restricting governmental action and authority.

Bill of Rights
the first ten amendments to the U.S. Constitution that list a set of fundamental rights and freedoms that individuals possess and that government cannot infringe upon.

LEARNING OBJECTIVES

By reading this chapter, you will be able to do the following:

4.1 Define civil liberties and understand the key role they play in American political life.

4.2 Describe the civil liberties outlined in the Constitution, the amendments to it, and the process by which they were incorporated.

4.3 Explain the First Amendment protections granted to religion.

4.4 Outline the First Amendment protections concerning freedom of expression.

4.5 Summarize the civil liberties that are extended to those accused of crimes in the Bill of Rights.

4.6 Understand the role that the Ninth and Tenth Amendments play in shaping the protection of freedoms in the nation and across the states.

STANDING ROCK: WATER PROTECTORS CLAIM THEIR RIGHTS AND FREEDOMS IN NORTH DAKOTA

- Define civil liberties and understand the key role they play in American political life.

Shekóli. A single arrow may be snapped over one's knees with ease, but a bundle of arrows may not. This old adage is exemplified by the strength and fortitude shown by the gathering of water protectors in Hunkpapa territory north of the Standing Rock Sioux nation.[1]

In the letter quoted above, Ray Halbriter, chair of the Oneida nation of New York and publisher of *Indian Country Today*, was referring to protests aimed at stopping a $3.7 billion pipeline project designed to transport oil from the rich Bakken fields of North Dakota to Illinois, where it could then be sent along to major refineries and oil markets. Energy Transfer Partners (ETP), one of the largest owners and operators of oil and natural gas pipelines in the United States, was the parent company to the developers.[2]

Though the pipeline would run mostly through private land, whose owners had largely already ceded access, it would also be running under bodies of water. This brought federal agencies into the mix, especially the U.S. Army Corps of Engineers, who were tasked with studying its potential environmental and cultural impacts and risks.[3] By early 2016, all permits had been issued. Other federal agencies, however, including the Environmental Protection Agency (EPA) and the U.S. Department of the Interior, urged the Army Corps to undertake a more thorough environmental impact assessment.

The Dakota Access Pipeline's path would take it just north of the Standing Rock Reservation and under Lake Oahe, a body of water whose creation decades before had displaced members of the Standing Rock Nation when a portion of the Missouri River was dammed to produce electricity and control floods. "Out there, I lived down there with my grandmother and grandfather," said Verna Bailey when interviewed for the *New York Times*. "We had a community there. Now it's all gone."[4]

In April, a small group of people from the Standing Rock Reservation began gathering and camping near the banks of the Cannonball River on Army Corps land in protest and education. Each day, they would walk about a mile to a construction site. Through their exercise of their civil liberties of free speech, freedom of the press, and assembling in protest, the protesters aired their grievances with the federal government. They demanded tribal sovereignty, the preservation of sacred places, and water.

They worried about a potential leak into the waterways upon which they and other Americans downstream depended: "'We say "mni wiconi": Water is life,' said David Archambault II, the chairman of the Standing Rock Sioux. . . . 'We can't put it at risk, not for just us, but for everybody downstream. . . . We're looking out for our future, the children who are not even born yet. What is it they will need? It's water. When we start talking about water, we're talking about the future generations.'"[5]

ROBYN BECK/AFP/Getty Images

▲ Exercising their civil liberties, hundreds of Native American protesters and their supporters, who fear the Dakota Access Pipeline will pollute their water, force construction workers and security forces to retreat and work to stop in September 2016.

The Standing Rock protesters were few in number and off the national radar when they started out. In the summer and early fall of 2016, all of that began to change. Members of 280 indigenous nations joined the protests "in what activists [called] the largest, most diverse tribal action in at least a century."[6] They would later also be joined by nonindigenous supporters from across the country, #NoDAPL on Twitter, and Facebook campaigns to show solidarity. A group of military veterans announced in

November that up to 2,000 of their members would join Standing Rock to act as "human shields" and stand against, in their words, the "assault and intimidation at the hands of the militarized police force."[7]

Like others who had claimed their civil liberties before them, residents of Standing Rock and their supporters used not only protest as their tool. They also pursued legal action to stop construction until a thorough study of the pipeline's impact on sacred sites and potential environmental impacts was undertaken. In July 2016, the Standing Rock Nation sued the U.S. Army Corps of Engineers to halt the issuance of permits and order a stop to construction near the Standing Rock Reservation. They formed organizations, such as the Water Protector Legal Collective, to "provide legal advocacy, jail and court support, criminal defense, and civil and human rights to the Native peoples and their allies who gathered there."[8]

INTERACTION OF THE PROTESTERS WITH LAW ENFORCEMENT OFFICIALS BRINGS OTHER CIVIL LIBERTIES INTO QUESTION

As the Standing Rock protests grew in the summer and fall of 2016, tensions between the protesters and state, local, and federal law enforcement officers grew. In August, construction began on the disputed portion of the pipeline. Less than two weeks later, North Dakota governor Jack Dalrymple declared a state of emergency, citing public safety risks associated with the protests. In September, he mobilized about thirty National Guard members to a security checkpoint up the road.

Many local landowners and residents became nervous, viewing, according to an article in the *New York Times*, "the demonstrations with a mix of frustration and fear, reflecting the deep cultural divides and racial attitudes."[9] There were charges of violence on both sides. In July, a protester's hand was badly injured in an explosion, its source disputed. Protesters condemned private security contractors' use of dogs, claiming several of their number had been bitten.

Morton County sheriff Kyle Kirchmeier asserted that some protesters were believed to be readying pipe bombs. "Officers said that protesters had attacked them with firebombs, logs, feces and debris. . . . One woman who was being arrested, the authorities said, had pulled a gun out and fired at a police line."[10] Members of Standing Rock insisted that their protests were peaceful: "Weapons, drugs and alcohol are prohibited from the protest camp. Children march in daily demonstrations. The leaders believed the reports of pipe bombs were a misinterpretation of their calls for demonstrators to get out their wooden chanupa pipes—which have deep spiritual importance—and pass them through the crowd."[11] In November, law enforcement officials used water cannons on protesters in subzero weather, citing aggressive behavior by members of a crowd numbering in the hundreds. Sixteen protesters were arrested.

Not all relations between protesters and law enforcement officials were heated. Some members of local law enforcement knew members of the Standing Rock Nation. Some protesters tried to educate officers and others about their goals. Mekaski Horineck, whose father had marched with labor leader Cesar Chavez for agricultural workers' rights, told a group of police while he was sitting in a prayer circle, "This isn't just a native issue. We're here protecting the water, not only for our families and our children, but for your families and your children. For every ranch and farm living along the Missouri River."[12] While the original protest camp was on federal property, other protests and satellite camps were on private property, which local and state law enforcement officers noted in defending their actions.

It was largely this reality—protest and resistance on private property and law enforcement response to it—that linked the civil liberties of protest and speech to questions about other civil liberties, primarily those involving protections for those accused of crimes.

Protesters and supporters charged various officials and agencies of civil liberty violations throughout the legal processes for those arrested, from the collection of evidence to the imposition of bail.

▲ A protester is treated after being pepper-sprayed by private security contractors on land being graded for the Dakota Access Pipeline (DAPL), near Cannon Ball, North Dakota, September 3, 2016.

ROBYN BECK/AFP/Getty Images

EXAMINING HOW ISSUES MAY CUT ACROSS PARTY LINES

When we study critical issues in American politics, we often examine how opinions on those issues divide along lines of political party, and with good reason. They often do. Opinions on the Standing Rock protests followed this pattern. Many supporters—especially political leaders—were members of the Democratic Party. Critics of the protesters' actions were often Republicans. However, there were some, perhaps unexpected, points of agreement on issues relating to those that would emerge during the Standing Rock protests. One was what many felt was a counterproductive militarization of law enforcement, both in terms of tactics and in terms of military equipment often acquired as surplus from the wars in Afghanistan and Iraq.

For example, speaking in August 2014, Senator Rand Paul (R-KY) criticized the changes in local law enforcement techniques, equipment, and mentality as surplus weapons from America's wars in the Middle East found their way back home: "Washington has incentivized the militarization of local police precincts by using federal dollars to help municipal governments build what are essentially small armies—where police departments compete to acquire military gear that goes far beyond what most Americans think of as law enforcement."[13] In his efforts to scale back the provision of surplus military equipment to local law enforcement agencies, Paul, a Republican, was joined by Representative Hank Johnson of Georgia, a Democrat.

▲ U.S. Navy veteran John Gutekanst (left) from Athens, Ohio, waves an American flag as an activist approaches a heavily fortified police barricade with his hands up on a bridge near Oceti Sakowin Camp on the edge of the Standing Rock Sioux Reservation in December 2016 outside Cannon Ball, North Dakota.

WHAT Do You Think?

Why do you think there was some agreement across party lines in condemning the militarization of police forces in the United States?

According to a piece published by the American Civil Liberties Union in February of 2018, a county prosecutor "sought a search warrant for a NoDAPL Facebook group page."[14] It's original author or authors unclear, a Facebook post in 2016 quickly went viral: "The Morton County Sheriff's Department has been using Facebook check-ins to find out who is at Standing Rock in order to target them in attempts to disrupt the prayer camps. Water protectors are calling on EVERYONE to check in at SR to overwhelm and confuse them."[15] The goal of the social media campaign was partly to raise money and support, but also to confuse law enforcement. The Sheriff's Department categorically denied that it was using Facebook check-ins to monitor the protesters.

Critics challenged connections between law enforcement and private security firms hired by ETP, citing email communications allegedly "showing an alliance between the pipeline's private security firm, the FBI, the Bureau of Indian Affairs, North Dakota's U.S. attorney's office, and local law enforcement agencies."[16] There were sharp criticisms of what some saw as yet another example of the "militarization" of local law enforcement agencies. According to the American Civil Liberties Union, North Dakota received more than $3 million worth of surplus military equipment through a Department of Defense program that began in the 1990s.[17] "'We need our state and federal governments to bring justice and peace to our lands, not the force of armored vehicles,' said Dave Archambault II, the chairman of the Standing Rock Sioux tribe. 'We have repeatedly seen a disproportionate response from law enforcement to water protectors' nonviolent exercise of their constitutional rights.'"[18]

Arrested protesters claimed that their constitutional protections had been violated and that they were arrested only to later—sometimes weeks later—have the charges dropped, because, "although the protesters were on private property, no authority figure specifically requested that they leave.[19]

In the first weeks of his presidency, Donald Trump moved to speed up the pipeline's completion, with the Army formally approving construction of the last mile in February 2017. In a video broadcast in the Standing Rock camp, Linda Black Elk, a member of the protesters' "healer council," urged them to carry on after the camp was razed: "Pray for the water. Pray for the people. Pray for the water protectors. Pray for the tribe."[20]

The last group of protesters to hold out was forcibly removed under the evacuation order of North Dakota's new governor, Doug Burgum, two weeks later. Forty-six were arrested. In all, more than six hundred protesters had been arrested since the protests began. The governor and the North Dakota state legislature took further steps: "About an hour after the protest camp was cleared, Mr. Burgum signed into law four bills that had been passed largely as a result of the protests. They expand the scope of criminal trespassing laws, make it illegal to cover your face with a mask or hood while committing a crime, and increase the penalties for riot offenses."[21]

Where should the line between political expression and the need to maintain public order and safety be drawn? This remains one of the most important and contested issues in American civil liberties today. It has only grown more contested with technological advances that make it possible, for example, for the federal government to monitor every phone call, every email, every social media post that an individual makes.

By early 2017, the Standing Rock protest camps had been cleared. Construction continued, as did legal efforts by members of the Standing Rock Nation. But the underlying questions—about the policies themselves and law enforcement's responses to them—remained.

Civil liberties are not defined or defended in a vacuum. As we can see, these actions can draw in many other actors in the American political space, including the media, politicians, governmental agencies, law enforcement, the courts, and powerful interest groups. The protesters at Standing Rock were claiming their access to sacred places and to clean water. They used tools protected by the very first amendment to the U.S. Constitution: the freedom to speak, publish, and assemble in order to air their grievances with the government of the United States. However, other fundamental civil liberties also came into play as law enforcement's response to the actions of the protesters raised questions about the freedoms of Americans when being investigated, arrested, and tried for crimes. In the next section, we will look at the foundations for these protections: the Constitution and the Bill of Rights.

WHAT HAVE I **LEARNED?**

1. Civil liberties are called negative freedoms because they _____.
   a. are not good things
   b. reject elements of the Declaration of Independence
   c. place restrictions upon governmental action
   d. place restrictions upon individual action

2. The Bill of Rights is _____.
   a. a set of legal charges that can be made against the federal government for not protecting individuals' civil liberties
   b. the aggregate amount of taxes paid to the government to ensure that law enforcement has the necessary resources to uphold individuals' civil liberties

   c. the set of fundamental guarantees that ensure equal treatment and protection against discrimination
   d. the first ten amendments to the U.S. Constitution listing a set of fundamental rights and freedoms that individuals possess and that government cannot infringe upon

3. What kinds of tools did the Standing Rock protesters use to advance their civil liberties?

   _____

   Answer Key: 1. c; 2. d; 3. Answers may include references to protest (free speech and freedom of assembly) and reaching out via the media and other platforms (press freedoms).

▲ Federalist Alexander Hamilton, who opposed the inclusion of a bill of rights during the ratification debates.

THE BILL OF RIGHTS ESTABLISHES PROTECTIONS FOR AMERICANS' CIVIL LIBERTIES

- **Describe the civil liberties outlined in the Constitution, the amendments to it, and the process by which they were incorporated.**

One of the main concerns the delegates to the Constitutional Convention in 1787 brought with them was how they would secure the protection of individual rights. Following independence, most of the state governments had included some protections for individual rights in their own constitutions.[22] However, those protections varied considerably and often lacked key components that Americans today typically think of as fundamental rights, such as freedom of the press or religion. Well aware of the need to protect individual rights, the delegates agreed to place within the original document certain protections, such as a strict limit on the definition of treason as well as restrictions on punishments available for those convicted of it.[23] The delegates did not, however, include a bill of rights—a list of fundamental individual rights that a government cannot restrict or intrude upon except under specific circumstances.

THE BILL OF RIGHTS TAKES CENTER STAGE IN THE RATIFICATION DEBATES

During the ratification campaign following the Constitutional Convention, the anti-Federalists seized upon the lack of a bill of rights in the proposed document as a way to reject the proposed Constitution or to negotiate for a better outcome. Their motives for highlighting the issue were diverse. Some used the lack of a bill of rights as a tactical weapon, hoping to defeat the Constitution entirely. Some were opposed to the federal powers of taxation and regulation of commerce and wanted to see more protections for the rights of states in such a bill.[24] Others argued that such a list of fundamental rights was a necessary protection against the inevitable growth of centralized power in what was sure to become a large republic.

Against the anti-Federalists' charges, the Federalists offered several counterarguments. In *Federalist* No. 84, Alexander Hamilton argued first that a bill of rights was unnecessary. The proposed document, he noted, already contained provisions guaranteeing specific rights.[25] Second, Hamilton argued that including a bill of rights would be dangerous to individual liberty, not supportive of it. His central concern was that any list of individual rights would necessarily be incomplete. What about those rights not enumerated? Might the lack of their textual protections encourage a tyrant to deny them? As we will discuss later in the chapter, the question of protections for rights not specifically enumerated remains one of the most important topics in the study and application of American civil liberties today.

The anti-Federalists' strategy proved to be the winning one. On Monday, June 8, 1789, during the first session of Congress, James Madison introduced a draft of the Bill of Rights.[26] After reworking and revising his proposed list, Congress proposed twelve amendments to the Constitution and sent them to the states for ratification. Of these, ten were formally ratified on December 15, 1791.[27] The Bill of Rights had become part of the Constitution.

The list of rights was carefully crafted, covering a wide swath of issues.

The First Amendment prevents the legislative branch from passing laws restricting a variety of individual rights, including religion, speech, the press, and assembly. The next two amendments deal with powers generally under the authority of the executive branch involving firearms, state militias, and the quartering of soldiers in people's homes and on their property.

The Fourth through Eighth Amendments guarantee rights of Americans involved with the judicial system: those accused of, arrested for, tried for, and convicted of crimes as well as certain noncriminal

▼ TABLE 4.1

An Overview of Protections Contained within the Bill of Rights

Amendment	Protection
First Amendment	Restricts the lawmaking powers of Congress in the areas of religion, speech, the press, assembly, and petitioning the government
Second Amendment	The right to keep and bear arms
Third Amendment	No forced quartering of troops in homes
Fourth Amendment	Protects against unreasonable search and seizure and establishes the right to have warrants issued prior to arrest or search
Fifth Amendment	Right to a grand jury indictment in criminal cases, protection against double jeopardy and self-incrimination, the right to due process of law, and the right to just compensation when private property is taken for public use
Sixth Amendment	Protections during criminal prosecutions for a speedy and public trial by an impartial jury, the right to confront witnesses, the right to compel favorable witnesses to testify in one's defense, and the right to the assistance of defense counsel
Seventh Amendment	Right to a trial by jury in certain civil suits
Eighth Amendment	Protections against excessive bail, excessive fines, and cruel and unusual punishment
Ninth Amendment	Nonexclusion of rights not listed in the Constitution
Tenth Amendment	Powers not delegated to the federal government, nor prohibited by it to the states, are reserved to the states or to the people.

cases. The Ninth Amendment arose from concerns that any list of individual rights might be thought of as exhaustive. Therefore, it specifies that the list in the Bill of Rights does not presume or imply the protection of rights not enumerated. Finally, the Tenth Amendment declares that those powers not specifically delegated to the federal government are "reserved to the States" or, in a confounding addendum, "to the people." We will explore specific amendments in detail below. Table 4.1 summarizes the main provisions of the Bill of Rights.

THE BILL OF RIGHTS ESTABLISHES CIVIL LIBERTIES PROTECTIONS, AND SELECTIVE INCORPORATION APPLIES THEM TO THE STATES

The text of the Bill of Rights does not declare restrictions upon the actions of state governments. Instead, it acts to restrain the powers of the federal government—the perceived need for such protections being one of the main reasons anti-Federalists advocated for its inclusion. For example, the First Amendment begins, "Congress shall make no law," and not, "Congress and the Legislatures of the several States shall make no laws."

So, for much of the nation's history, the explicit protections contained within the Bill of Rights did not apply to state laws and actions, and the Supreme Court upheld this strict, textual reading of the Constitution. The foundation for extending the protections of the Bill of Rights to state laws and actions was laid down in the Fourteenth Amendment, ratified in 1868. The Fourteenth Amendment's guarantee against the deprivation by any state of "life, liberty, or property without due process of law"—called the **due process clause**—laid the constitutional foundations for the extensions of the protections within the Bill of Rights to the actions and laws of the states. This process, however, is still ongoing.[28]

In a process called **selective incorporation** because of its selective, piecemeal development, the Supreme Court has, over time, used the due process clause of the Fourteenth Amendment to expand the

due process clause
the clause in the Fourteenth Amendment that restricts state governments from denying their citizens the right to due process of law.

selective incorporation
the piecemeal process through which the Supreme Court has affirmed that almost all the protections within the Bill of Rights also apply to state governments.

▲ Benjamin Gitlow, right, running as a vice presidential candidate for the Workers Party in 1928.

Bettmann/Contributor

protections within the Bill of Rights to also cover state laws and actions. Initially, however, the Court refused to do so when given the chance. In *The Slaughterhouse Cases* (1873), the Supreme Court interpreted the Fourteenth Amendment's protections as applying only to African Americans and reaffirmed sharp distinctions between state and federal citizenship.[29] It was not until 1925 with *Gitlow v. New York* that the Court began to make use of the due process clause to incorporate protections contained within the Bill of Rights.[30]

In its decision in *Gitlow v. New York* (1925), the Supreme Court formally incorporated one of the amendments in the Bill of Rights—in this case the First Amendment—through the Fourteenth Amendment. In doing so, it signaled to the states that there were limits on their ability to restrict expression and that the freedoms of speech and the press constituted *fundamental freedoms* that were beyond the legitimate restriction by state actions in the absence of a compelling reason to do so.

Following the decision in *Gitlow*, over the next two decades the Supreme Court began to issue a series of decisions incorporating most of the First Amendment's protections for speech, the press, assembly, and religion. Several decades later, in another burst of activity, the Court incorporated the protections for those accused of, arrested for, tried for, and convicted of crimes under state laws. Most recently, in 2010, the Court incorporated the Second Amendment's affirmation of the right "to keep and bear arms" through the due process clause of the Fourteenth Amendment.[31] As of 2018, most but not all of the protections within the Bill of Rights had been incorporated (see Table 4.2). We will explore many of these cases in detail in this chapter as we consider specific amendments, the protections that they affirm, and the tensions and controversies arising from trying to delimit the boundaries of their promises.

THE RELATIONSHIP BETWEEN MEMBERS OF INDIGENOUS NATIONS AND THE BILL OF RIGHTS HAS EVOLVED OVER TIME

As citizens of two governments—their nations and the United States—indigenous Americans' civil liberties are defined by the laws of both their nations and the American nation. Through a long legal and judicial history—one that took place against an even longer backdrop of displacement, disenfranchisement, and use of force—most but not all of the protections of the Bill of Rights have been extended to indigenous Americans, placing limits on the actions of both the federal government and their own tribal governments as well.[32] Many indigenous nations also have their own tribal constitutions.

The Constitution of the Standing Rock Sioux Tribe, for example, includes a bill of rights that affirms many of the same fundamental liberties as the American Bill of Rights. Unlike the federal Constitution, however, that of the Standing Rock Sioux also orders its government to "recognize and promote the economic and educational opportunities of the Standing Rock Sioux Tribal members in a fair and impartial manner."[33]

The process of selective incorporation has cleared up one question about American civil liberties: Are state governments also restricted in their ability to infringe upon Americans' fundamental rights and freedoms? They are. Within the long list of protections contained within the Bill of Rights are many other questions, however, all revolving around where the boundaries of these protections lie. To investigate these issues, we will consider the amendments and the liberties affirmed within them in turn.

Selective Incorporation of the Bill of Rights

Amendment	Right Incorporated	Supreme Court Decision
First	Freedom from establishment of religion	*Everson v. Board of Education*, 330 U.S. 1 (1947)
	Freedom of religious expression	*Cantwell v. Connecticut*, 310 U.S. 296 (1940)
	Freedom of speech	*Gitlow v. New York*, 268 U.S. 652 (1925)
	Freedom of the press	*Near v. Minnesota ex rel. Olson*, 283 U.S. 697 (1931)
	Right to peaceably assemble	*De Jonge v. Oregon*, 299 U.S. 353 (1937)
Second	Right to keep and bear arms	*McDonald v. Chicago*, 561 U.S. 742 (2010)
Third	Right not to have soldiers quartered in homes	Not incorporated
Fourth	Protection against unreasonable searches and seizures	*Wolf v. Colorado*, 338 U.S. 25 (1949) (Illegally obtained evidence is still permissible in trial, however.)
	Warrant needed for search and seizure	*Mapp v. Ohio*, 367 U.S. 643 (1961) (Illegally obtained evidence cannot be used in trial.)
Fifth	Right to indictment by grand jury in cases involving a serious crime	Not incorporated
	Protection against double jeopardy	*Benton v. Maryland*, 395 U.S. 784 (1969)
	Protection against self-incrimination	*Malloy v. Hogan*, 378 U.S. 1 (1964)
	Right of just compensation for private property taken	*Chicago, Burlington, and Quincy Railroad v. City of Chicago*, 166 U.S. 226 (1897)
Sixth	Right to a speedy and public trial	*In re Oliver*, 333 U.S. 257 (1948); *Klopfer v. North Carolina*, 386 U.S. 213 (1967)
	Right to trial by an impartial jury	*Parker v. Gladden*, 385 U.S. 363 (1966)
	Right to confront witnesses	*Pointer v. Texas*, 380 U.S. 400 (1965)
	Right to compel witnesses to testify in the defendant's favor	*Washington v. Texas*, 388 U.S. 14 (1967)
	Right to counsel in cases involving capital punishment	*Powell v. Alabama*, 287 U.S. 45 (1932)
	Right to counsel in felony cases	*Gideon v. Wainwright*, 372 U.S. 335 (1963)
Seventh	Right to trial by jury in civil cases	Not incorporated
Eighth	Protection against excessive bail or fines	Not incorporated*
	Protection against cruel and unusual punishment	*Robinson v. California*, 370 U.S. 660 (1962)

*Some constitutional scholars disagree on whether this right has been formally incorporated. See *Schilb v. Kuebel*, 404 U.S. 357 (1971).

WHAT HAVE I LEARNED?

1. The Bill of Rights affirms the fundamental rights and freedoms of _____.

   a. the federal government

   b. the state governments

   c. both the federal and state governments

   d. individual citizens

2. At the Constitutional Convention, which of the following was not among the anti-Federalists' motives

(Continued)

(Continued)

for focusing on the issue of the lack of a bill of rights in the Constitution?

a. They were opposed to the taxation and regulation of commerce by the federal government.

b. They feared that without such a bill, there would not be enough protections against a large, centralized national government.

c. They claimed any attempt to draw up a bill of rights would be incomplete.

d. They saw the lack of a bill of rights as a strategic way to reject the proposed Constitution or to negotiate for a better outcome.

3. What were Alexander Hamilton's two main arguments against the need to include a bill of rights in the proposed Constitution?

4. What is the significance of the process of selective incorporation of the Bill of Rights?

Answer Key: 1. b; 2. c; 3. Answers should include Hamilton's argument that such a list was unnecessary, as the Constitution itself protected rights, and that he warned about the lack of protections for rights and freedoms not listed; 4. Answers should include the idea that selective incorporation affirms that state governments are also restricted in their ability to infringe upon Americans' fundamental rights and freedoms; however, questions remain about where the boundaries of these protections lie.

THE FIRST AMENDMENT'S FIRST TWO PROTECTIONS BOTH INVOLVE RELIGION

- **Explain the First Amendment protections granted to religion.**

The third suggested amendment in James Madison's list of seventeen ended up as the First Amendment to the Constitution. The First Amendment restricts the power of what most delegates to the Constitutional Convention thought would be the most powerful, and potentially the most dangerous, entity of the government: Congress, the legislative branch.

THE ESTABLISHMENT AND FREE EXERCISE CLAUSES ENSURE SEPARATION OF CHURCH AND STATE

The first two civil liberties affirmed and protected in the Bill of Rights involve religion. The First Amendment begins, "Congress shall make no law respecting an establishment of religion, or prohibiting the free exercise thereof." These two statements, or clauses, form the constitutional bases for protections of religious freedom and expression in America. The first is called the **establishment clause**, as it protects individuals from governmental establishment of, or support for, religion. The second statement is referred to as the **free exercise clause** because it guards the rights of individuals to exercise and express their religious beliefs.

Recall our discussion of Bridget Mergens in Chapter 1. Her case involved questions about the boundaries of establishment protections and those of free exercise. As with so many other areas of civil liberties, these clauses involve situations that are clear-cut as well as those that are not so easy to evaluate. For example, any attempt by the federal government or one of the states to declare an official religion would be a clear violation of the establishment clause. Similarly, any attempt to prohibit Americans' expressions of their religious faiths in their own homes, provided they did not violate others' fundamental rights and freedoms, would also be unconstitutional.

What about the more difficult cases, however? Consider a student who wants to say a prayer in her valedictory address at her public high school's graduation ceremonies. For the school to appear to condone her prayer implies a violation of the establishment clause. For it to restrict her right to say a prayer, however, implies a violation of the free exercise clause. How should this situation be handled? It is in difficult cases like this that the Supreme Court has had to decide what is and what is not constitutionally permissible.

COURTS HAVE TESTED THE ESTABLISHMENT CLAUSE OVER SCHOOL FUNDING FOR RELIGIOUS SCHOOLS. One of the most important Supreme Court decisions dealing with government support for or involvement with religion, and the one that incorporated the establishment clause, was

establishment clause
a First Amendment clause protecting individuals from governmental establishment of, or support for, religion.

free exercise clause
a First Amendment clause guarding the rights of individuals to exercise and express their religious beliefs.

Everson v. Board of Education (1947). The case considered a New Jersey law that authorized payment by local school boards of the costs of transportation to and from private schools, including Catholic ones. A New Jersey taxpayer filed suit claiming that the taxpayer support constituted impermissible government support for religion. In its decision, a divided Court ruled that the program, though "on the verge" of offering impermissible aid, was acceptable as it was a "general program to help parents get their children, regardless of their religion, safely and expeditiously to and from accredited schools."[34] In his opinion, however, Justice Hugo Black affirmed the principle of separation, stating, "In the words of Jefferson, the clause against establishment of religion by law was intended to erect 'a wall of separation between Church and State.'"[35]

In *Board of Education v. Allen* (1968), the Supreme Court again affirmed the principle that there could be some permissible forms of taxpayer support for private religious schools. Divided 6–3, the Court ruled in favor of a New York law that provided free textbooks to middle and high school students, including those in private religiously affiliated schools. In his dissenting opinion, Black critiqued the majority's reasoning and warned that it set a dangerous precedent: "It is true, of course, that the New York law does not, as yet, formally adopt or establish a state religion. But it takes a great stride in that direction. . . . And it nearly always is by insidious approaches that the citadels of liberty are most successfully attacked."[36]

COURTS HAVE ALSO TESTED THE ESTABLISHMENT CLAUSE OVER PRAYER IN SCHOOL. Perhaps no establishment clause issue has been more vexing to the Supreme Court than that of prayer in public schools. In 1962, in *Engle v. Vitale*, the Court ruled unconstitutional the voluntary reading in New York's public schools of the prayer, "Almighty God, we acknowledge our dependence upon Thee, and we beg Thy blessings upon us, our parents, our teachers and our Country."[37] Although the policy's supporters argued that the prayer was nondenominational and permitted students to remain silent or be excused from the classroom during the reading, the Court found that it violated the establishment clause. The next year, in *Abington School District v. Schempp*, the Court struck down a program that involved the reading of ten verses from the Bible and a recitation of the Lord's Prayer at the beginning of each day in Pennsylvania's public schools.[38] In his opinion, Justice Tom C. Clark quoted Madison's warnings about the dangers of enmeshing government and religion, even in seemingly small ways, noting that "it is proper to take alarm at the first experiment on our liberties."[39]

Supreme Court justices are not the only individuals who have had to try to balance the separation of government and religion against the need to protect the rights of individuals to express their own faiths. Administrators and teachers in the nation's public schools and universities have also had to navigate this complicated constitutional tension.

According to guidelines produced for public schools and districts by the U.S. Department of Education, students may not pray during instructional time but may do so (on their own volition) during noninstructional time, such as before school or during lunch. They may also, again on their own volition only, pray during "moments of silence" in schools, provided that the school makes it clear that such moments are not set aside to encourage prayer. Students may be excused from instruction "to remove a significant burden on their religious exercise . . . where doing so would not impose material burdens on other students," and they may participate in organized religious student groups and clubs under the same rules as the school sets for nonreligious groups. Students may express their religious beliefs in their homework and other assignments, but their work must be evaluated solely on its academic merits.

Anne Cusack/Los Angeles Times via Getty Images

▲ Students at Royal High School in Simi Valley, California—a public school—in prayer during a lunchtime meeting. As long as such meetings occur outside instructional time and are both initiated and led by students, they are constitutionally permissible.

Teachers and administrators may not encourage or discourage prayer in their official capacity but may participate in religious activities when not in their official capacity, such as a Bible study group with other teachers that meets outside instructional time. While schools may not offer organized prayers during assemblies and extracurricular events, individual students may—of their own volition, and assuming they have been chosen as speakers based on nonreligious criteria—express their own faith. Schools, however, are free to "make appropriate, neutral disclaimers to clarify that such speech (whether religious or nonreligious) is the speaker's and not the school's."[40] If all of this sounds complicated, that's because it is, for students, parents, school officials, and Supreme Court justices.

COURTS HAVE ADDRESSED THE BOUNDARIES OF THE ESTABLISHMENT OF RELIGION.

In trying to set guidelines for what is and is not permissible under the establishment clause, the Court has at different times employed various litmus tests for federal and state laws and actions. Proponents of a strict separationist approach to deciding the issue argue for a close textual reading of the establishment clause and say no forms of government support for religious institutions are permissible. However, given the history of religion in American political life and policy objectives—such as in helping students receive a good education—strict separation can be difficult to achieve in the real world. For example, in its decision in *Everson v. Board of Education*, in which it cited Jefferson's metaphor of a "wall of separation," the Court allowed taxpayer funds to be used for transporting students to and from religious schools.

One of the most important tools that the Court has used is the **Lemon test**, named after the Court decision in which it was formally laid out: *Lemon v. Kurtzman* (1971).[41] The case dealt with Rhode Island and Pennsylvania programs that supplemented the salaries of teachers and provided educational materials (though only the same ones used in the public schools) in religiously based private schools for the purpose of teaching nonreligious subjects. The Court struck down both programs as violating the establishment clause. In doing so, it set out a three-pronged test for permissible government involvement. First, the underlying statute must have a "secular legislative purpose." Second, its effect "must be one that neither advances nor inhibits religion." Third, it must not foster "excessive entanglement between government and religion."

The Lemon test has its critics. Many scholars, as well as some Supreme Court justices, have argued that the test is too subjective, requiring justices to ascertain the motives of the legislators who passed the laws in the first place. Others have argued that the test sets too high a wall of separation between church

Lemon test
a three-pronged test developed by the Supreme Court to determine whether a law or action by the federal or a state government violates the establishment clause.

▶ Mauro Morales, shown in front of his business sign in Rio Grande City, Texas, is one of three "Peyoteros," Texans licensed to sell peyote that grows near the border with Mexico to tens of thousands of Native American Church members across the United States The Supreme Court has decided that the use of peyote, a hallucinogen, is a constitutionally protected part of Native Americans' exercise of their First Amendment rights of free exercise of religion in spite of its classification as an illegal substance.

AP Photo/LM Otero

and state, one that is difficult to consistently apply. Since *Lemon*, the Court has been more willing to relax the standards of the test and instead has often followed a logic that emphasizes the principle of religious neutrality, examining the degree to which the law or policy in question provides benefits to a broad class of individuals and if the provision of public funds to religious institutions arises from individual choice without coercion on the part of the government.[42]

COURTS HAVE ADDRESSED THE BOUNDARIES OF THE FREEDOM OF RELIGIOUS EXPRESSION. Important cases concerning religious establishment have also often involved the second of the First Amendment's two guarantees on religious freedom: freedom of religious expression. While Americans are free to hold any religious beliefs, they are not always free to act on them. As is the case with the establishment clause, the Supreme Court has had to wrestle with the boundaries of free exercise.

The free exercise clause was incorporated through the due process clause of the Fourteenth Amendment in *Cantwell v. Connecticut* (1940). The case involved the distribution of religious materials and playing of religious messages on a phonograph by two members of the Jehovah's Witnesses in a predominantly Catholic neighborhood. The two men, Jesse Cantwell and his son, were arrested under a town ordinance that gave local government officials the authority to decide if such solicitation was legal or not. In its decision, the Supreme Court distinguished between "freedom to believe and freedom to act. The first [the Court noted] is absolute, but, in the nature of things, the second cannot be."[43] While the Court upheld the principle that the state might have a valid interest in restricting the actions involved in religious expression—to maintain safety and public order, for example—in this case the Cantwells' actions posed no threat other than being offensive to some. Their convictions were overturned.

More recently, in *Employment Division v. Smith* (1990), the Court adopted a **neutrality test** in deciding on conflicts between religious expression and legitimate state action. In that case, two individuals had been fired from their jobs as rehabilitation counselors for using the sacramental religious drug peyote in violation of Oregon state law. They were also denied unemployment benefits as a result of their termination. The two men argued that the use of peyote was within their First Amendment rights of free expression as members of the Native American Church.[44] In its opinion, the Court ruled that the state law banning the use and possession of peyote was not targeted toward individuals as a result of their beliefs but that it represented a valid, compelling state interest and was religiously neutral, even if it restricted the religious expression of individuals.

neutrality test
a Supreme Court test for examining questions of free expression that allows restrictions upon religious expression, provided that laws doing so not single out one faith, or faith over nonfaith.

WHAT HAVE I **LEARNED?**

1. With respect to religion, the establishment clause of the First Amendment protects Americans _____.
   a. from all prayer in school
   b. against the separation of church and state
   c. against federal government support of religion
   d. from the use of public funds for any religious purposes

2. Why is prayer in America's public schools such a contentious and constitutionally tricky issue?

3. What is the Lemon test used for? What are its three "prongs"?

Answer Key: 1. c. 2. Answers should include a discussion of the tension between establishment and free exercise; 3. Answers should include that it is used to determine if a violation of the establishment clause has occurred. Answers should also include: secular legislative purpose, does not advance or inhibit religion, and does not produce excessive government entanglement with respect to religion.

THE FIRST AMENDMENT ALSO PROTECTS EXPRESSION: SPEECH, PRESS, ASSEMBLY, AND PETITIONING THE GOVERNMENT

- Outline the First Amendment protections concerning freedom of expression.

Although they come after the two clauses about religion in the text, those parts of the First Amendment that deal with **freedom of expression** are often considered the most fundamental affirmations of Americans' rights and liberties. They involve the expression of political beliefs and opinions. The right to express one's thoughts, especially in being critical of those in power, is one of the cornerstones of American civil liberties. Thomas Jefferson's draft of the Declaration of Independence, Thomas Paine's *Common Sense*, the *Federalist Papers*, and anti-Federalist writings all involved or questioned the rights of individuals to speak, to publish, and to peaceably assemble without fear of retribution or imprisonment.

FREE EXPRESSION WAS CHALLENGED IN THE EARLY YEARS OF THE REPUBLIC

freedom of expression
a fundamental right affirmed in the First Amendment to speak, publish, and act in the political space.

Alien and Sedition Acts
four separate laws passed under the administration of President John Adams that, among other things, restricted the freedom of speech and the press.

Those who argued for the importance of freedom of expression had good reason to want to protect it. Shortly after the new nation was founded, it was confronted with the question of how far a government could go to restrict these rights. Like many other cases since, this one revolved around questions of national security. The situation involved laws known as the **Alien and Sedition Acts**, which were passed by Congress—controlled by the Federalist Party—and signed into law by Federalist president John Adams in 1798. Consisting of four separate acts, these laws attempted to suppress anti-Federalist opposition to the policies of the president and Congress. Among other provisions, the acts authorized severe restrictions on the rights of free speech and the free press. Any behavior that was judged by a federal court (usually controlled by Federalist Party judges) to be part of a conspiracy against the government of the United States, or any publication or speech that was deemed to be "false, scandalous, [or] malicious . . . against the government of the United States, or either house of the Congress of the United States, or the President of the United States," was punishable by fines and imprisonment.[45] Under the power of these acts, newspaper editors opposing Adams and the Federalists "were quickly indicted, and ten were brought to trial and convicted by juries under the influence of Federalist judges."[46]

A 1798 engraving depicting a fight in Congress over the Sedition Act of 1798.

COURTS HAVE ATTEMPTED TO BALANCE POLITICAL EXPRESSION AGAINST THE NEEDS OF NATIONAL SECURITY

One of the most difficult issues in the protection of political expression is balancing that fundamental right with the needs of national security. In 1917, Charles Schenck and Elizabeth Baer oversaw the printing and distribution of antiwar leaflets encouraging young men not to comply with the military draft. They were convicted under the Espionage Act of 1917, which made it a crime to interfere with military recruiting. In *Schenck v. United States* (1919), a unanimous Court ruled against the defendants, arguing that the restrictions on expression under the Espionage Act were permissible.

In its decision, the Court established the **clear and present danger test** to evaluate legitimate and illegitimate restrictions on political speech in which the context of that expression must be taken into account. The danger, so to speak, with the clear and present danger test is its subjectivity. If a government can restrict urgings not to comply with a draft, then the scope of restricted speech might be interpreted quite widely.

Several cases in the early twentieth century upheld the right of government to restrict such speech in the national interest. However, in a dissent in one of those cases, Supreme Court justice Oliver Wendell Holmes would go on to establish the idea that ideas should compete, as in a marketplace. He wrote, "The best test of truth is the power of the thought to get itself accepted in the competition of the market."[47] Holmes's words did not reflect the mind-set of the majority, but his language has been cited by justices in subsequent Courts as they wrestled with the need to balance free political expression with national security.

The modern standard for restrictions on political speech was set in 1969 in *Brandenburg v. Ohio*. At a Ku Klux Klan rally, Klan leader Clarence Brandenburg made a speech threatening that "if our President, our Congress, our Supreme Court, continues to suppress the white, Caucasian race, it's possible that there might have to be some vengeance taken."[48] The Supreme Court ruled for Brandenburg, establishing a two-pronged test of acceptable restrictions on such political speech: Speech that merits restriction must be "directed to inciting or producing imminent lawless action and [must be] likely to incite or produce such action."[49] The test that the Court developed placed a much higher standard on permissible restrictions of political speech, even allowing speech that advocates for the legitimacy of violent action, though it must not actually organize for it.

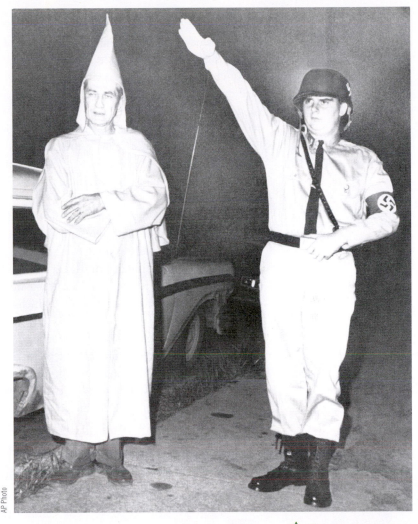

AP Photo

▲ Clarence Brandenburg (left), a Ku Klux Klan leader, with Richard Hanna, an admitted member of the American Nazi Party, in Cincinnati, Ohio, in August 1964. Brandenburg's case established a high standard of permissible speech, up to advocating for the legitimacy of violent action, but not organizing for it.

clear and present danger test
a Supreme Court tool to evaluate whether or not forms of political expression constitute such a threat to national security as to warrant restriction.

prior restraint
the suppression of material prior to publication on the grounds that it might endanger national security.

COURTS HAVE WEIGHED PRESS FREEDOMS AGAINST NATIONAL SECURITY

The tension between national security and limits on free expression also applies to the press. One of the goals of the Alien and Sedition Acts was to restrict the ability of the press to criticize the federal government. When such restriction happens before an article is published—as opposed to after the fact—it is known as **prior restraint**. The Alien and Sedition Acts were eventually repealed or expired, but the Supreme Court did not weigh in on the issue of prior restraint until the twentieth century.

The question of the permissibility of prior restraint during wartime came up during the Vietnam conflict and centered on attempts by the Nixon administration to prevent the *New York Times* and the *Washington Post* from publishing classified materials describing—often unflatteringly—high-level decision making on the part of U.S. officials in conducting the war. In *New York Times v. United States* (1971), the Supreme Court, in a highly divided opinion, ruled that the government did not demonstrate a sufficiently pressing interest to justify such prior restraint; this set a very high bar for the ability of government to prevent publication.[50]

SYMBOLIC SPEECH IS PROTECTED AS A FORM OF POLITICAL EXPRESSION

The Supreme Court has extended its protection of political expression to **symbolic speech**, such as images, signs, and symbols used as forms of political expression. In 1968, in *United States v. O'Brien*, the Court ruled against David Paul O'Brien and three other individuals in Boston who had burned their draft cards and encouraged others to do so as well in protest against the Vietnam War. In doing so, it set out a three-pronged test of acceptable restriction of symbolic speech under such circumstances: (1) the government must have a substantial interest in doing do, (2) the restriction must not be for the purposes of restricting speech, and (3) the "incidental restriction" of the First Amendment rights should be "no greater than is essential to the furtherance of that interest."[51] In this case, the Supreme Court held that the government's need to have young men register for the selective service passed such a test.

In a closely divided opinion, the Court ruled in *Morse v. Frederick* (2007) that school officials can restrict students' rights of expression if that conduct occurs on school grounds or under school supervision and if it violates or disrupts the mission of the school. The case involved a banner displayed by a group of students in Alaska during a school-supervised event featuring the carrying of the Olympic torch through Juneau. The banner read, "BONG HITS 4 JESUS," which school officials concluded promoted drug use, which was a violation of school rules and conduct.[52] The Court agreed.

The burning, alteration, or destruction of the American flag in protest has also received Supreme Court protection as a form of symbolic political expression. In *Texas v. Johnson* (1989), the Court overturned the conviction of a man who had burned the American flag in protest during the 1984 Republican National Convention. "The Government," the Court held, "may not prohibit the verbal or nonverbal expression of an idea merely because society finds the idea offensive or disagreeable, even where our flag is involved."[53]

symbolic speech
protected expression in the form of images, signs, and other symbols.

libel
expression in written form or similarly published media that defames a person's character.

slander
expression in spoken form that defames a person's character.

hate speech
speech that has no other purpose but to express hatred, particularly toward members of a group identified by racial or ethnic identity, gender, or sexual orientation.

Sipa via AP Images

▲ A man burns an American flag in Portland, Oregon, during a protest in January 2017 against the inauguration of President Donald J. Trump. The Supreme Court has made the symbolic act of flag burning a form of protected speech.

OTHER FORMS OF EXPRESSION HAVE MORE LIMITED PROTECTION

While political expression (in speech, writing, symbols, and of the press) has secured considerable protection, the Supreme Court has ruled that other types and forms of speech and publications do not have the same privilege, though it has often set a high bar for restrictions on them.

While political expression (in speech, writing, symbols, and of the press) has secured considerable protection, the Supreme Court has ruled that other types and forms of speech and publications do not have the same privilege, though it has often set a high bar for restrictions on them.

Expression that defames a person's character, whether in writing or similarly published media (**libel**) or in spoken form (**slander**), is not protected in the same way as political expression and may leave the actor responsible for such statements in legal trouble.[54] To win a case based on libel or slander in the United States, an aggrieved party must show that the statements or publications were made with the knowledge that they were untrue, which is rather difficult to prove. For public figures, the standard is even higher, though there is often an unclear line dividing those who qualify as public figures from those who do not.

Hate speech is another form of damaging expression upon which limits have been placed and for which the Court has struggled to define the proper boundaries. Hate speech is speech that has no other purpose but to express hatred, particularly toward members of a group identified by racial or ethnic identity, gender, or sexual orientation. One of the most charged forms of hate speech is the burning of crosses—sometimes even in people's yards—by white supremacist groups such as the Ku Klux Klan. In response to these acts, many communities have passed ordinances prohibiting such expression.

Another form of expression that receives weaker protection under the First Amendment is the issuance of **fighting words**—expression (spoken, written, or symbolic) that is likely to incite violence or disrupt the peace. In *Chaplinksy v. New Hampshire* (1942), the Court upheld restrictions on words that "by their very utterance, inflict injury or tend to incite an immediate breach of the peace," but it also affirmed that such restrictions must be narrowly targeted so as not to constitute an undue restriction of First Amendment rights.[55]

Finally, the Supreme Court has upheld restrictions on **obscenity and pornography**, though it has not always been clear just what constitutes an obscene statement or publication. In *Roth v. United States* (1957), the Court defined the standard for judging obscenity—and, therefore, constitutionally permissible restrictions on its expression—as "whether, to the average person, applying contemporary community standards, the dominant theme of the material, taken as a whole, appeals to prurient interest."[56] Marking the boundaries this way raises another challenge, however. What, exactly, are "contemporary community standards," and who gets to delimit them?

In *Miller v. California* (1973), the Supreme Court attempted to present a clearer definition of obscenity. It set out three criteria that all must be met for material to be considered obscene and, therefore, legitimately subject to restriction. First, the material must be "patently offensive." It must also be "utterly without redeeming social value." Finally, in determining the applicability of the first two parts of the test, "contemporary community standards" must be applied, meaning that different locales may have different standards.[57]

When one considers material published over the Internet, things become even more challenging. For example, how does one define community when considering online material? In 1997, the Court struck down provisions of the Communications Decency Act of 1996, which had been designed to protect minors from viewing obscene or pornographic material on the Internet. The Court held that the restrictions in the act were too vague and restrictive and that they carried the danger of having a "chilling effect on free speech."[58] Depictions of sexual material involving minors, however, have carried no similar First Amendment protections and are subject to full restriction and criminalization.

FREEDOM OF ASSEMBLY IS BROADLY PROTECTED

The final two rights within the First Amendment—the right to peaceably assemble and to petition the government—have received relatively little Supreme Court attention. When the Court has ruled on them, however, it has generally done so in a way similar to how it has treated political expression, regarding them as cornerstones of civil liberties and rights that should be broadly protected.

The right to peacefully assemble was incorporated in 1937 in *De Jonge v. Oregon*. In that case, the Court overturned an Oregon law under which a member of the Communist Party had been convicted and sentenced to seven years in prison for holding a public meeting. In his opinion, quoting an earlier case, Chief Justice Charles Evans Hughes noted, "The very idea of a government, republican in form, implies a right on the part of citizens to meet peaceably for consultation in respect to public affairs and to petition for a redress of grievances."[59]

As is probably clear by now, there has been a great deal of struggle, controversy, and Supreme Court action throughout American history with regard to freedom of religion, speech, the press, and assembly—and these all involve only the First Amendment.[60] In the Bill of Rights, there are many other liberties that are also addressed.

fighting words
expression (spoken, written, or symbolic) that is likely to incite violence or disrupt the peace.

obscenity and pornography
text, images, or video that depicts sexual activity in ways offensive to the broader community and that lacks any artistic merit.

1. Forms of political expression have generally received _____.
   a. scrutiny under the clear and present danger test
   b. little protection
   c. stronger protection than forms of commercial expression
   d. less protection than hate speech

2. Prior restraint enables the government to _____.
   a. arrest protesters who burn the American flag
   b. combat the distribution of pornography
   c. suppress a newspaper article

   d. sue individuals for questioning the character of a government official

3. What test has the Supreme Court used to evaluate legitimate and illegitimate restrictions upon the press in the area of national security?

4. What controversies surrounding freedom of speech do you observe in American society today?

Answer Key: 1. c; 2. c; 3. The clear and present danger test. 4. Answers might discuss current controversies over political expression, perhaps in issues involving racial, ethnic, or sexual identities.

THE CONSTITUTION ALSO PROTECTS INDIVIDUALS INVOLVED WITH THE CRIMINAL JUSTICE SYSTEM

- Summarize the civil liberties that are extended to those accused of crimes in the Bill of Rights.

As its defenders pointed out during the ratification debates, one area in which the proposed Constitution (prior to the adding of the Bill of Rights) did address civil liberties was in protecting the rights of the accused and convicted. Article I, which lays out the powers of Congress, prohibits that branch from passing laws—called *ex post facto* laws—that make illegal, and therefore punishable, conduct that was legal prior to the passage of a new law. It also prohibits bills of attainder, which are acts that punish individuals without a trial.[61]

Article I also establishes the right of an individual to demand a **writ of habeas corpus** upon his or her arrest or detention (except in the case of rebellion or invasion). Such a writ, if granted by a court, demands that authorities in charge of the person's detention establish the reasons for that detention. If the authorities fail to do so, the person is free to go. This has become one of the central issues in defining and debating the limits on presidential power as America engages in the war on terror in the twenty-first century (see Chapter 13).

All these protections, however, were not sufficient for many of the opponents of the proposed Constitution, who feared that the federal government would use its power to upend, violate, or ignore the actions of the courts within the states or of the individuals residing in the states. Ultimately, fully half of the ten amendments in the Bill of Rights set boundaries for federal governmental action in dealing with the breaking and enforcing of the laws. Central to the protections for those accused, tried, and/or convicted of a crime is the idea of **procedural justice**, in which the standard of fairness is applied to all participants equally.[62] Most but not all of these standards have since been applied to the actions of the states themselves through the process of incorporation.

THE FOURTH AMENDMENT PROTECTS AGAINST UNLAWFUL SEARCH, SEIZURE, WARRANTS, AND EVIDENCE

Under British rule, the American colonists had gained a vivid understanding of the potential dangers of allowing a government to stop or inspect individuals or to search citizens' homes without oversight or procedural protections for those who were targeted. Under what conditions can a government

writ of habeas corpus
a statement demanding that authorities in charge of a person's detention establish the reasons for that detention.

procedural justice
a judicial standard requiring that fairness be applied to all participants equally.

THE SECOND AMENDMENT, "PHILOSORAPTOR," AND INTERNET MEMES

Although firearms ownership by Americans has become a highly charged topic of debate in politics today, for most of its history the Supreme Court said very little about the issue. In 1939, the Court upheld restrictions on private ownership of certain types of weapons—sawed-off shotguns and machine guns—as a result of gangland violence during the era of Prohibition.[63] In his opinion in *United States v. Miller*, Justice James McReynolds stated that "in the absence of any evidence tending to show that possession or use of a 'shotgun having a barrel of less than eighteen inches in length' at this time has some reasonable relationship to the preservation or efficiency of a well regulated militia, we cannot say that the Second Amendment guarantees the right to keep and bear such an instrument."[64]

Not until 2008 did the Court rule directly on laws prohibiting personal possession of firearms generally, as opposed to specific types of them. In a 5–4 decision in *District of Columbia v. Heller*, the Court overturned a District of Columbia ban on handgun ownership for the purpose of self-defense within an individual's home.[65] As the *Heller* case involved Washington, DC, and not a state, it was decided based on the Second Amendment directly. Incorporation, however, happened two years later, in *McDonald v. Chicago*. In this case, the Court—again splitting 5–4—overturned a Chicago ban on handgun ownership.[66] The contemporary debate about the amendment continues, and of course has spread to the Internet.

In 2008, Sam Smith, a T-shirt designer, introduced to the world his image of "Philosoraptor," a dinosaur appearing to be engaged in deep contemplation. The image quickly became the subject of countless Internet memes, some of which alluded to debates over the Second Amendment.

Proponents of the right of Americans to carry firearms used the meme to challenge arguments that the Second Amendment referred to times past and does not apply in the twenty-first century.

Proponents of restrictions on firearms ownership used the same meme to challenge arguments that people, and not firearms, are the ultimate source of the problem of gun violence in America.

WHAT Do You Think?

Regardless of your own views on the Second Amendment and firearms ownership, how effective do you think the use of a meme such as "Philosoraptor" can be when trying to shape opinion on issues as hotly debated as gun ownership? Can the humor lead people to reflect, or might it undercut the seriousness of the underlying issues and debates? On what other issues have you encountered the use of memes to shape political opinion? Do you think they were successful?

Philosoraptor © LonelyDinosaur.com/CC BY-NC-SA, https://creativecommons.org/licenses/by-nc-sa/3.0/.

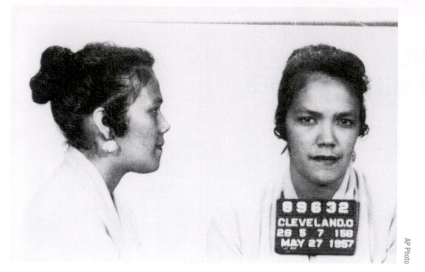

▲ Dollree Mapp at the time of her arrest in 1957. The case of *Mapp v. Ohio* extended Fourth Amendment protections to the states by establishing that evidence gathered via illegal search and seizure is inadmissible in criminal trials in a state court.

warrant
a writ issued by a judge authorizing some activity.

probable cause
reasonable belief that a crime has been committed or that there is evidence indicating so.

exclusionary rule
a rule governing the inadmissibility of evidence obtained without a proper warrant.

grand jury
a group of citizens who, based on the evidence presented to them, conclude whether or not a person is to be indicted and subsequently tried in a court of law.

double jeopardy
the prosecution of an individual more than once for the same crime.

legitimately search a person or persons? Even at the time of the adoption of the Bill of Rights, this was not an easy question to answer. With the development of modern technology, the question has only grown more complicated.

In *Katz v. United States* (1967), the Supreme Court established a standard for procedures for obtaining evidence of a crime and wrestled with the challenges that technology poses to setting such boundaries.[67] The case involved an individual, Katz, who had been convicted of operating a gambling operation based on evidence obtained from a police wiretap. While the Court found there was ample reason for a judge to issue a **warrant**—a writ issued by a judge authorizing some activity, such as tapping a phone line or searching an apartment—the officers had not done so in this case. The Court overturned Katz's conviction and established the need for officers to obtain a warrant from a judge based on **probable cause**, or reasonable suspicion that a crime has been committed or that there is evidence indicating so.

A closely related issue is whether or not evidence that has been obtained without following proper procedures can be used in a trial. The **exclusionary rule** governs the inadmissibility of evidence obtained without a proper warrant.

The case through which the Fourth Amendment's protections were extended to the states, *Mapp v. Ohio* (1961), dealt with just such an issue. While investigating a different crime (a recent bombing), police obtained in the dwelling of Dollree Mapp—without possessing a warrant—"certain lewd and lascivious books, pictures, and photographs," placing her in violation of an Ohio anti-obscenity law.[68] The Court threw out her conviction and declared, "All evidence obtained by searches and seizures in violation of the Federal Constitution is inadmissible in a criminal trial in a state court."

As it has wrestled with the trickier issues in interpreting the exclusionary rule, such as electronic communications and transportation, the Court has ruled that the Fourth Amendment's protections are not absolute. In 1989, the Court upheld the conviction of a suspected drug dealer whose luggage had been searched without a warrant based on his behavior—he had paid cash for his ticket, checked no bags, and appeared nervous, among other "tells." The Court found that the DEA agents conducting the search had "reasonable suspicion" of criminal activity "based on the totality of circumstances."[69]

The Court has also upheld the use of evidence connected with a crime (such as a weapon) that was not named in the warrant but that was discovered in plain sight while lawfully searching for a different type of evidence (the stolen property).[70] In 1996, the Court upheld the introduction of illegal drugs as evidence, though the drugs had been obtained as a result of a traffic stop in which the officers were found to have had "reasonable cause" to believe that a traffic violation had occurred.[71]

THE FIFTH AMENDMENT GUARANTEES THE ACCUSED CERTAIN PROCEDURES FOR THEIR DEFENSE

The Fifth Amendment also provides protections for those accused of crimes, especially in guaranteeing processes and procedures for their defense. Those suspected of having committed serious crimes must have an indictment handed down by a **grand jury**—a group of citizens who, based on the evidence presented to them, conclude whether or not the person is to be indicted and subsequently tried in a court of law. It also establishes protections against **double jeopardy**, which is the prosecution of an individual more than once for the same crime. However, while an individual cannot be acquitted of a crime and then convicted in a court in the same jurisdiction, individuals can be acquitted for an offense in a state court but then tried and convicted for the same incident in a federal court, but this time under federal charges.

Some of the most sweeping and important protections described in the Fifth Amendment involve the right not to have to testify or bear witness against oneself in a criminal case, either during the trial itself or during the introduction of testimony obtained prior to a criminal trial. These protections have been extended and strengthened by the Court over time.

One of the most important cases in delineating the protections of those accused of crimes was *Miranda v. Arizona* (1966). In that case, Ernesto Miranda had been convicted of kidnapping and rape, based partly on evidence obtained while he was being questioned by officers without an attorney present. During this questioning, he signed a confession. In its ruling, the Supreme Court overturned Miranda's conviction, declaring, "Prior to any questioning, the person must be warned that he has a right to remain silent, that any statement he does make may be used as evidence against him, and that he has a right to the presence of an attorney, either retained or appointed. The defendant may waive effectuation of these rights, provided the waiver is made voluntarily, knowingly and intelligently."[72] Police officers now routinely inform individuals suspected of criminal activity that they have the right not to speak and to have an attorney present during questioning; these rights are commonly referred to as **Miranda rights**.

THE SIXTH AMENDMENT GUARANTEES THE ACCUSED CERTAIN RIGHTS TO TRIALS AND REPRESENTATION

The Bill of Rights guarantees those accused of committing crimes the right to a speedy trial—a right that was extended to the states in 1963.[73] It also ensures the right to be tried in front of an impartial jury, which is more and more of a challenge given the instantaneous spread of news and opinion with modern technology. These protections, however, may not be of much use to a defendant if he or she does not have access to a qualified attorney during the complex legal process. While the Sixth Amendment guarantees the right to have counsel present at trial, for most of the nation's history that meant the right to hire an attorney only if you could afford one.

In 1932, the Court extended this right to include the provision of attorneys in federal capital murder cases that carried the possibility of the death penalty if conviction was reached.[74] In 1938, the Court extended these protections to all federal criminal cases.[75] It was not until 1963—in one of the most famous cases in Supreme Court history—that the Court extended the guarantee of counsel for those unable to afford it to state criminal cases. That decision, in *Gideon v. Wainwright*, involved the conviction for robbery of Clarence Gideon, who had resorted to defending himself in a Florida court when his request to the judge for an attorney was denied.[76] More recently, the Court has strengthened these protections to try to ensure that criminal defendants receive "effective" legal representation and not just legal representation.[77]

THE EIGHTH AMENDMENT GUARDS AGAINST CRUEL AND UNUSUAL PUNISHMENT

While a criminal defendant is awaiting a speedy trial before a jury, he or she may be able to post **bail**—an amount of money posted as a security to allow the charged individual to be freed while awaiting trial. Although the Eighth Amendment protects against "excessive bail," not every criminal defendant is entitled to bail at all. Those who are deemed to pose a sufficient risk of flight or further criminal activity may legitimately be denied the ability to post bail.

Much more contentious is the question of "cruel and unusual punishment," especially as it applies to the imposition of the death penalty. The death penalty was allowed at the time of ratification of the Constitution and the Bill of Rights, and the Fifth Amendment to the Constitution refers to

Miranda rights
the right not to speak and to have an attorney present during questioning; these rights must be given by police to individuals suspected of criminal activity.

bail
an amount of money posted as a security to allow the charged individual to be freed while awaiting trial.

AP Photo/Robert F. Bukaty

▲ A court-appointed "lawyer of the day" explains a legal implication to a person charged with a crime at Cumberland County Superior Court in Portland, Maine. In *Gideon v. Wainwright*, the Supreme Court extended the guarantee of counsel for those unable to afford it to state criminal cases.

circumstances in which individuals are "deprived of life." Proponents of its use argue that the death penalty can be an effective deterrent against the most heinous crimes. Opponents point to the potential for errors in conviction, discriminatory sentencing, and the movement away from its use in other democracies. While the Supreme Court has not declared the death penalty to be inherently in violation of the Eighth Amendment, it has imposed restrictions on its imposition.[78] For example, the Court has prohibited its use on convicted defendants with significant cognitive disabilities[79] and on juveniles.[80]

WHAT HAVE I **LEARNED?**

1. Central to the protections for those accused, tried, and/or convicted of a crime is the idea of _____.

   a. habeas corpus

   b. double jeopardy

   c. the exclusionary rule

   d. procedural justice

2. Miranda rights offer protections _____.

   a. for protest

   b. during arrest

   c. against being tried twice for the same incident

   d. in carrying out the death penalty

3. For what groups of individuals has the Supreme Court prohibited the use of the death penalty?

   _____

Answer Key: 1. d; 2. b; 3. Answers should include individuals with cognitive disabilities and juveniles.

THE NINTH AND TENTH AMENDMENTS HELP SHAPE FREEDOMS IN THE NATION AND ACROSS THE STATES

- Understand the role that the Ninth and Tenth Amendments play in shaping the protection of freedoms in the nation and across the states.

In 2009, Edith Windsor's wife, Thea C. Spyer, passed away from a progressive neurological disease. They had been married in Canada two years before, and their same-sex marriage had been recognized as valid by New York, their state of residence at the time of Spyer's passing.

Windsor and Spyer's marriage, however, was not considered legal under U.S. federal law. As such, after her wife's passing, Windsor was not entitled to the same federal tax provisions granted to surviving spouses in opposite-sex, federally recognized marriages. Therefore, Windsor had to pay more than $350,000 in federal estate taxes. With help, especially from the Lesbian, Gay, Bisexual, and Transgender (LGBT) Community Center in New York City, she sued the federal government, claiming her right to have her marriage recognized as legal under federal law and to "the equal protection principles that the Court has found in the Fifth Amendment's Due Process clause."[81]

THE DEFENSE OF MARRIAGE ACT RESTRICTS THE RIGHTS OF SAME-SEX COUPLES TO MARRY

At issue were a federal law and a right that Windsor claimed. The law was the Defense of Marriage Act (DOMA), passed by Congress during the presidency of Bill Clinton in 1996 by opponents of marriage equality. It was a reaction to an increasing belief that some states and state courts were likely to legalize same-sex marriages in the coming years. DOMA had two substantive sections. One section stated that for purposes of federal law, marriage meant a legal union between a man and a woman: "In determining the meaning of any Act of Congress, or of any ruling, regulation, or interpretation of the

various administrative bureaus and agencies of the United States, the word 'marriage' means only a legal union between one man and one woman as husband and wife, and the word 'spouse' refers only to a person of the opposite sex who is a husband or a wife."

Another section reaffirmed the power of the states to make their own decisions about marriage: "No State, territory, or possession of the United States, or Indian tribe, shall be required to give effect to any public act, record, or judicial proceeding of any other State, territory, possession, or tribe respecting a relationship between persons of the same sex that is treated as a marriage under the laws of such other State, territory, possession, or tribe, or a right or claim arising from such relationship." This section of DOMA tried to clarify, or delimit, the Constitution of the United States, specifically the **full faith and credit clause**, which states, "Full faith and credit shall be given in each state to the public acts, records, and judicial proceedings of every other state. And the Congress may by general laws prescribe the manner in which such acts, records, and proceedings shall be proved, and the effect thereof."[82]

Under the full faith and credit clause, a state is generally required to recognize and honor the public laws of other states unless those laws are contrary to the strong public policy of that state. Full faith and credit is why, for example, you only need a driver's license from one state. However, under DOMA, states were not required to give full faith and credit to same-sex marriages.

In a 5–4 decision in *United States v. Windsor* (2013), the Supreme Court ruled that the section of DOMA classifying only opposite-sex marriages as legal under federal law was unconstitutional.[83] In his majority opinion, Justice Anthony Kennedy decried the intent of DOMA, stating, "The history of DOMA's enactment and its own text demonstrate that interference with the equal dignity of same-sex marriages, a dignity conferred by the States in the exercise of their sovereign power, was more than an incidental effect of the federal statute. It was its essence."[84] In his dissent, one of several written by the members of the minority, Justice Samuel Alito, joined in part by Justice Clarence Thomas, challenged the foundations of the majority's logic, claiming, "Same-sex marriage presents a highly emotional and important question of public policy—but not a difficult question of constitutional law. The Constitution does not guarantee the right to enter into a same-sex marriage. Indeed, no provision of the Constitution speaks to the issue."[85] One of the most consequential results of the Court's decision in *Windsor* was the provision of the same rights to immigration procedures to same-sex married couples as those granted to opposite-sex married couples when one spouse is not an American citizen.

Two years after her landmark case, Windsor continued to work for LGBT causes and had turned her focus to transgender identity and at-risk youth. She stated, "I think we have a lot to do. A lot. There are a million things to still be done to make it equal. . . . First of all, I have a lot of feeling for trans people. They are making gorgeous progress, but it's a very painful progress. . . . We also have somewhere between 40 and 50% of kids living on the street who are gay. This is a whole chunk of us who also took the courage to come out but were thrown out of their homes and forced to live in the street.[86] After Windsor had made constitutional history, she stated, "Honey, you've got to be loud and proud."[87]

While the Supreme Court in *Windsor* had validated state-recognized same-sex marriages for *federal* purposes, it did not strike down the other substantive clause of DOMA, which allowed states to not give full faith and credit to same-sex marriage licenses from other states. Many Americans wondered when, or if, it ever would.

THE NINTH AMENDMENT AND PRIVACY, A RIGHT NOT ENUMERATED

While each of the first eight amendments in the Bill of Rights places literal, textual limits on the power of the federal government, the final two do not. Instead, the Ninth and Tenth Amendments more broadly structure the inclusion and exclusion of rights as well as powers of national and state governments.

▲ Thea Spyer (left) and Edith Windsor (right), whose same-sex marriage was legally recognized by the State of New York but not by the federal government. Following the passing of her wife, Windsor successfully fought to overturn a portion of a federal law that defined marriage as only between opposite-sex couples.

full faith and credit clause
a portion of the Constitution that generally requires states to honor licenses and judicial outcomes of other states.

One of the concerns raised by opponents of including a list of rights in the Constitution was that such a list would be necessarily incomplete. What about those rights assumed but not specified? Would future federal government officials recognize or try to restrict them? The Ninth Amendment was included to address these fears as well as general concerns by anti-Federalists about the future growth of federal governmental power. Its purpose was to put into writing one of the main worries about a bill of rights expressed during the ratification debates: that those fundamental rights and freedoms not textually listed might not be protected. The Ninth Amendment was ratified to make sure that American governments in the future would not be able to take advantage of the incompleteness of the listing of fundamental rights and freedoms to encroach on Americans' civil liberties.

▲ Tyron Garner (left) and John Lawrence greet supporters at Houston City Hall, where people had gathered to celebrate the landmark Supreme Court decision in the *Lawrence v. Texas* case on June 26, 2003. The court struck down a Texas sodomy law, a decision applauded by gay rights advocates as a historic ruling that overturned sodomy laws in thirteen states.

Part of Windsor's constitutional claims rested on a right not enumerated in the Bill of Rights: **privacy**. Because of this, Windsor was also resting her claim upon previous cases in American constitutional law. In its decisions in these cases, the Supreme Court had affirmed the right to privacy and applied it to several areas of Americans' private lives, such as birth control, abortion, and sexuality.

EARLY AFFIRMATION OF RIGHTS TO PRIVACY INVOLVED THE USE OF CONTRACEPTIVES.

The foundational case regarding privacy was *Griswold v. Connecticut* (1965).[88] In it, the Court overturned a Connecticut law that prohibited the provision of contraceptives and medical advice about contraceptive techniques to married couples. In striking down the law, Justice William O. Douglas cited affirmations of privacy in several amendments to the Constitution, including the First, which "has a penumbra where privacy is protected from governmental intrusion."[89]

EXPANSIONS OF PRIVACY RIGHTS INVOLVED SEXUAL CONDUCT BETWEEN CONSENTING ADULTS.

In later decades, the Supreme Court clarified that the right to privacy extended beyond the use of contraception. One area in which the Court affirmed privacy in the "penumbras" created by the Constitution's other protections was the right of consenting adults to express their sexuality. In 2003, in *Lawrence v. Texas*, the Court struck down a Texas law making same-sex sexual conduct illegal.[90] In his decision, Justice Kennedy stated, "Liberty presumes an autonomy of self that includes freedom of thought, belief, expression, and certain intimate conduct."[91]

PRIVACY RIGHTS ALSO INCLUDE A WOMAN'S DECISION TO TERMINATE A PREGNANCY.

In a series of decisions, the Court has also affirmed and upheld the right of a woman to terminate a pregnancy. In this area of privacy, the foundational case was *Roe v. Wade* (1973).[92] In that case, the Court struck down a Texas law that made abortion illegal. In affirming the right of a woman to obtain an abortion during the first three months of pregnancy, Justice Harry Blackmun drew on the Court's previous ruling in *Griswold*, stating, "This right of privacy, whether it be founded in the Fourteenth Amendment's concept of personal liberty and restrictions upon state action, as we feel it is, or . . . in the Ninth Amendment's reservation of rights to the people, is broad enough to encompass a woman's decision whether or not to terminate her pregnancy."[93]

In subsequent decisions, the Court has continued to uphold the fundamental right of a woman to have an abortion, but it has also allowed state legislatures to place certain limits upon this right. Examples of this are state laws requiring minors to obtain parental consent, assuming those laws do not place an "undue burden" on the woman, and certain restrictions upon late-term abortions.[94] Despite the

privacy

a right not enumerated in the Constitution but affirmed by Supreme Court decisions that covers individuals' decisions in their private lives, including decisions regarding reproductive rights and sexuality.

Court's rulings, the abortion issue remains a very contentious one in American politics. Since *Roe v. Wade*, trying to assess a nominee's future rulings on abortion has become a key factor in the Senate's application of its power of advice and consent in confirming justices to the Supreme Court and judges to the lower levels of the federal judiciary.

THE TENTH AMENDMENT IS INTENDED TO PROTECT STATE POWERS

The inclusion of the Tenth Amendment was a direct response to the fears and demands of the anti-Federalists during the ratification debates. Many of them wanted a direct statement of the limitation of national power to those powers textually listed, those enumerated in the original document. All other powers were to be reserved to the several states, which is why we call most state powers under the Constitution "reserved powers." As it has turned out, however, and as we have already explored in our discussion of the development of American federalism, the Tenth Amendment has not proven to be as strong a protector of state power as some might have thought. That is not to say that it is irrelevant, however. States and their legislatures are increasingly protesting the power of the federal government—especially when they feel that it is requiring them to enact policies without fully funding their implementation—using the Tenth Amendment as their constitutional justification for doing so.

Maddie McGarvey/For The Washington Post via Getty Images

▲ James Obergefell in 2015, two and a half months prior to the Supreme Court decision that would guarantee marriage equality for all Americans.

THE FINAL BLOW TO DOMA

While the Supreme Court's decision in *United States v. Windsor* required the federal government to recognize state-recognized same-sex marriages, striking down one of DOMA's two provisions against marriage equality, it had not required states to give full faith and credit to same-sex marriage licenses from other states. Nor had it legalized same-sex marriages generally. One person who would change that was James Obergefell. Though the actual Court decision bundled several cases together, Obergefell's was listed first, which placed his name on the decision. The facts of his case were, sadly, somewhat similar to those of Edith Windsor's.

In 2011, after a decades-long commitment to each other, Obergefell married John Arthur on the tarmac of a Maryland airport. The two men were residents of the state of Ohio, which did not recognize marriage equality, so they flew to Maryland, which did. Arthur was struggling with amyotrophic lateral sclerosis (ALS), a progressive neurological degenerative disease. ALS is often called Lou Gehrig's disease after the famous and widely respected baseball player who died from it in 1941. The disease has no known cure, though recently some medications have shown promise in slowing its progression.[95] The two men flew to Maryland in a medical transport plane, seeking to get married while they still could. In an interview for BuzzFeed News a few months before the Court's decision in his case, Obergefell described their ceremony: "We landed at Baltimore, sat on the tarmac for a little bit, said 'I do,' and 10 minutes later were in the air on the way home."[96] John Arthur passed away in 2013.

Obergefell and Arthur's state of residence did not recognize their marriage. According to the case decision, "Ohio law does not permit Obergefell to be listed as the surviving spouse on Arthur's death certificate. By statute they must remain strangers even in death, a state-imposed separation Obergefell deems 'hurtful for the rest of time.'"[97] Rather than accept Ohio's refusal to recognize their marriage, Obergefell sued. "This case," he said, "was another way to take care of him and to respect him and to respect our relationship."[98]

In 2015, in its decision in *Obergefell v. Hodges*, the Supreme Court, in yet another 5–4 vote, affirmed the legality of Obergefell and Arthur's marriage and guaranteed the right of all couples to marry. Citing many of the cases that we have discussed, constitutional protections of fundamental civil liberties, and the right to privacy, Justice Kennedy, in his majority opinion, affirmed that "the right to marry is a fundamental right inherent in the liberty of the person." The second major section of DOMA had been declared unconstitutional. More fundamentally, marriage equality had become the law of both the nation and the states.

Reflecting on his case in an interview with *USA Today* two months before the Court's decision, Obergefell recalled how he felt about having to fly, given his husband's serious medical issues, to another state just to get married: "All I thought was, 'This isn't right, I'm p—ed off.'"[99] In the same interview, on a much lighter note, he added, "I chuckle about law students and other people just having to learn how to pronounce Obergefell."[100]

WHAT HAVE I **LEARNED?**

1. The full faith and credit clause generally requires _____.

   a. individuals to comply with the laws only of the state in which they reside

   b. states to recognize and honor the public laws of other states unless those laws are contrary to the strong public policy of that state

   c. citizens to trust public officials to carry out federal and state laws

   d. states to ensure that their laws are in conformity with federal laws before passage

2. The right to privacy has been affirmed by the Supreme Court in cases having to do with _____.

   a. sexuality, contraception, and abortion

   b. free speech and freedom of religion

   c. firearms and the regulation of a militia

   d. Miranda rights, due process, and double jeopardy

3. How are the Ninth and Tenth Amendments different from the first eight?

_____

Answer Key: 1. b; 2. a; 3. Answers should include a discussion of rights not specified (Ninth) and powers reserved to the states (Tenth).

CONCLUSION: CIVIL LIBERTIES INVOLVE FENCES STILL UNDER CONSTRUCTION

The stories regarding civil liberties in the United States are stories about tensions—tensions between one individual's fundamental rights and freedoms and those of another and between individual freedoms and the evolving needs of a society. They are stories about courage and political action. They are controversial, as they should be. They are also evolving, as generations of activists, Supreme Court justices, and politicians have weighed in on the proper boundaries of American rights and freedoms. While initially the restrictions upon governmental action found in the Bill of Rights applied only to the federal government, through the process of selective incorporation, most now apply to state governments as well. Not all of the civil liberties enumerated in the Bill of Rights have received the same level of protection, however. Political speech and expression, for example, has been privileged as fundamental to the ability to secure all other rights and freedoms.

During the ratification debates, one of the most powerful arguments that the Federalists made against a bill of rights was that it would be necessarily incomplete, which might provide the federal government with an excuse to restrict those fundamental freedoms not enumerated. While the Ninth Amendment explicitly states that Americans possess fundamental freedoms not listed in the other amendments, protecting those freedoms has been left to the Supreme Court and to individuals willing to fight for them.

The protesters of Standing Rock, Edith Windsor, and Jim Obergefell may not have known where their actions would finally lead, but it is very likely that all knew the controversy that their actions would stir up and the risks being taken. Defining and defending civil liberties in American democracy has always been and will always be controversial and challenging; that is why it is so essential to the nation.

CHAPTER REVIEW

This chapter's main ideas are reflected in the Learning Objectives. By reviewing them here, you should be able to **remember** the key points, **know** the terms that are central to the topic, and **think** about the critical issues raised in each section.

4.1 Define civil liberties and understand the key role they play in American political life.

REMEMBER
- Protecting civil liberties involves placing restrictions upon the ability of government to limit them.

KNOW
- Bill of Rights (p. 93)
- civil liberties (p. 93)
- negative freedoms (p. 93)

THINK
- How do these tensions continue to be debated today?

4.2 Describe the civil liberties outlined in the Constitution, the amendments to it, and the process by which they were incorporated.

REMEMBER
- The Bill of Rights enumerates a list of fundamental freedoms that the federal government cannot infringe upon.
- The protections set out in the Bill of Rights as written applied to the actions of the federal government and not those of the state governments. A decades-long process, in which the Supreme Court played a key role, changed this.

KNOW
- due process clause (p. 99)
- selective incorporation (p. 99)

THINK
- What are the broad categories of fundamental liberties guaranteed by the Constitution and the Bill of Rights?
- Why was the process of selective incorporation important?

4.3 Explain the First Amendment protections granted to religion.

REMEMBER
- The first two clauses in the First Amendment to the Constitution both involve religion; they prevent the federal government from establishing religion and protect Americans' rights to exercise their religious freedoms.

KNOW
- establishment clause (p. 102)
- free exercise clause (p. 102)
- Lemon test (p. 104)
- neutrality test (p. 105)

- What are the tensions between the free exercise and establishment clauses of the First Amendment?

4.4 Outline the First Amendment protections concerning freedom of expression.

REMEMBER
- Political speech and expression are considered particularly important fundamental freedoms.
- Since the early years of the American Republic, the federal government has struggled with protecting these freedoms while also ensuring a secure and orderly society.

KNOW
- Alien and Sedition Acts (p. 106)
- clear and present danger test (p. 107)
- fighting words (p. 109)
- freedom of expression (p. 106)
- hate speech (p. 108)
- libel (p. 108)
- obscenity and pornography (p. 109)
- prior restraint (p. 107)
- slander (p. 108)
- symbolic speech (p. 108)

THINK
- How should government weigh the tensions between political expression and national security concerns?

4.5 Summarize the civil liberties that are extended to those accused of crimes in the Bill of Rights.

REMEMBER
- The Bill of Rights guarantees a set of protections for those accused of, investigated for, tried for, and convicted of crimes.

KNOW
- bail (p. 113)
- double jeopardy (p. 112)
- exclusionary rule (p. 112)
- grand jury (p. 112)
- Miranda rights (p. 113)
- probable cause (p. 112)
- procedural justice (p. 110)
- warrant (p. 112)
- writ of habeas corpus (p. 110)

THINK
- What are some of the protections for Americans involved in the criminal justice system?
- Do you think these protections are sufficient?

4.6 Understand the role that the Ninth and Tenth Amendments play in shaping the protection of freedoms in the nation and across the states.

REMEMBER
- The Ninth and Tenth Amendments more broadly structure the inclusion and exclusion of rights as well as powers of national and state governments.
- The Supreme Court, drawing upon the Ninth Amendment, which states that the Bill of Rights does not contain an exhaustive list of fundamental liberties, has affirmed a right of privacy in areas such as reproductive rights, sexuality, and marriage.

KNOW
- full faith and credit clause (p. 115)
- privacy (p. 116)

THINK
- What are the implications of the Supreme Court's identification of a right to privacy?

Alex Milan Tracy/Anadolu Agency/Getty Images

CHAPTER 5

CIVIL RIGHTS

How Equal Is Equal?[1]

▼ Judith Heumann, U.S. State Department special adviser for international disability rights (left), meets with German officials in Berlin to discuss a set of measures to improve inclusion of people with disabilities. A disabled American herself, Heumann has spent a lifetime advocating for the rights of people with disabilities in America and across the globe.

The preamble to the Declaration of Independence makes clear a central purpose of a representative government: to guard and protect the fundamental rights and freedoms of its citizens. However, it does not offer many specifics on the processes and structures needed to make this happen. The rules and institutions set out in the Constitution and later amendments to it have given detailed form to a federal government that would help to secure these rights. Even so, the institutions of American government do not run on autopilot. They require both the actions of those within the government to carry out their responsibilities and the actions of Americans to define, advocate for, and protect their **civil rights**—the fundamental rights of individuals to be treated equally under the laws and policies of governments, regardless of their identities and lived experiences.

Civil rights are not binary things. In a sense, one has them or not; however, in practice it is much more complicated than that. Recall the discussion of civil liberties from Chapter 4. As a rule, the protection of civil liberties requires that a government does not do certain things—does not pass laws that might restrict the expression of fundamental rights and freedoms. As with civil liberties, the Framers of the Constitution assumed that citizens possessed civil rights upon birth, though many Americans were excluded or ignored at that point in history. Unlike civil liberties, however, civil rights require positive action, both by individuals acting to secure them and by governments in taking action to ensure their expression. For this reason, civil rights are sometimes called **positive freedoms**.

The challenge with civil rights comes from deciding how vigorously a government should act to protect them. How much action does a government need to take? How strongly does government have to act? How equal is equal? There is no single answer to these questions. Americans have always disagreed on how strongly government should act to protect the civil rights of its citizens. In this chapter, we will examine the efforts of individuals such as Judith Heumann and other disability rights protesters, Thurgood Marshall and members of the National Association for the Advancement of Colored People (NAACP), American women, as well as many other people acting alone or in concert to achieve a broader, more robust, vision of Americans' civil rights.

civil rights
fundamental guarantees ensuring equal treatment and protecting against discrimination under the laws of a nation.

positive freedoms
fundamental rights and freedoms that require action by individuals to express and by governments to secure.

PROTESTERS ACT TO SECURE RIGHTS FOR AMERICANS WITH DISABILITIES

- **Understand that securing civil rights requires both actions by individuals and groups to claim them and actions by governments to secure and protect them.**

In January 2016, writing in celebration of the American holiday devoted to Dr. Martin Luther King Jr., Judith Heumann, a special adviser for international disability rights with the U.S. Department of State, posted an article to the State Department's official blog. In it, she looked both to the past and to the present:

A stable, prosperous democracy succeeds when individuals can fully participate in political and public life. As we celebrate MLK Day and reflect on past struggles fought by Americans determined to uphold their individual rights, Dr. King's message of inclusion lives on. Dr. King encouraged everyone to participate when he said, "It is not possible to be in favor of justice for some people and not be in favor of justice for all people."

While change takes time, we must take action to: establish disabled people's organizations; adopt and enforce strong laws; create and enforce standards that advance inclusion of disabled people; and remove barriers—physical and attitudinal in all areas of life.[2]

In writing about the struggles to secure rights and freedoms for persons with disabilities, Heumann knows what she is talking about. She has spent a lifetime advocating, protesting, and changing American laws that affect those with disabilities.

As a very young child in 1949, Heumann contracted polio, which required her to use a wheelchair for mobility for the rest of her life. In the 1950s, administrators at her local public elementary school in Brooklyn, New York, refused her attendance. They cited her inability to access the building since it had no ramps, which was pretty much universal at the time. They refused to relent even when her mother offered to carry her up and down the school's steps. "I was considered to be a fire hazard," Heumann recalled.[3] In spite of these obstacles—imposed not by her disability but by others' actions—Heumann earned two degrees, including a master of arts from the University of California at Berkeley in 1975. After graduation, she applied to become a teacher with the New York City schools but was rejected based on her disability. Instead of backing down, however, "she filed suit against them and won."[4]

But Heumann was far from done.

In the spring of 1977, a group of protesters gathered in San Francisco outside a regional office of the Federal Department of Housing, Education, and Welfare. They consisted of people with disabilities and their supporters, seeking to force the Carter administration to finally and fully implement Section 504 of the Rehabilitation Act of 1973, which stated, "No otherwise qualified handicapped individual in the United States . . . shall, solely on the basis of his handicap, be excluded from the participation in, be denied the benefits of, or be subjected to discrimination in any program or activity receiving Federal financial assistance." Though applying only to programs and activities receiving federal funding, effective implementation of Section 504 would put pressure on other firms and organizations to follow suit.

In his presidential campaign, President Jimmy Carter had promised to redress the lack of funding for and attention to the act under the Ford administration. However, in the view of many Americans with disabilities, President Carter was backtracking. Officials in the executive branch had not signed key regulations of the act, likely because of how much it would cost to do so. In particular, the protesters sought to put pressure on the secretary of health, education, and welfare (HEW), Joseph Califano Jr., who had just recently proposed greater flexibility in making buildings accessible, suggested that segregation of students with disabilities would be acceptable, and also suggested that individuals who were disabled and battling substance abuse could be legitimately denied access and services.

On April 5, the individuals who would come to be known as the "Section 504 protesters" moved into the federal building and occupied it, having announced their intentions beforehand. On the eve of the sit-in, one local reporter commented, "Thousands of handicapped Americans may risk being wheelchaired off to jail in a militant attempt to shut down government offices in 10 cities."[5] Judith Heumann was one of their leaders.

There were also sit-in protests at regional HEW offices in eight other cities as well as a sit-in protest in Washington, DC. The takeovers were extremely taxing and often dangerous. Protesters with significant physical disabilities and illnesses in particular risked their health, cut off from the medical support upon which they relied. In the nation's capital, the protesters were forced to give up after being denied food. Lack of supplies, strong and effective leadership, or community support all undermined the protest efforts, and the sit-ins ended. In San Francisco, however, the 504 protesters maintained their occupation for two weeks, finally securing Secretary Califano's signature on a new set of regulations banning many forms of discrimination against Americans with disabilities. Theirs remains the longest takeover of a federal building in American history.

The protests were called the "504 sit-ins" after the section of the law the protesters demanded be fully, immediately, and effectively implemented. According to one news account, "By the late '70s, Americans were used to seeing civil rights marches. But this one was something new: people in

▲ Left: Demonstrators converge on the offices of the Department of Health, Education, and Welfare in San Francisco in April 1977. They were part of a "504 sit-in" to urge that civil rights law for disabled Americans be fully implemented. In the center, a woman briefs the group in American Sign Language. Right: United Farm Workers president César Chávez (R) talks with Vice President Dolores Huerta during the grape pickers' strike in 1968. Leaders of a number of civil rights movements lent support to the 504 protesters, including Chávez and Jesse Jackson.

wheelchairs, people on portable respirators, deaf people, people with mental retardation. And most were fighting mad."[6]

In addition to the occupation, the 504 protesters held rallies, joined by activists from workers' and civil rights organizations. They issued a constant flow of press releases designed to gain support from the community and pressure local, state, and federal politicians to act to remove barriers to accessibility—in public spaces, transportation, and access to employment, educational and housing opportunities. They flew to Washington, DC, to testify at committee hearings.

The 504 protesters undertook strategic political action in the service of claiming their civil rights. They were also, however, challenging the perception that people with disabilities were weak and in need of hand-outs, attempting to rewrite themselves from "handicapped" (implying begging with a cap in hand) to "people with disabilities." They sought to show Americans and political figures that they were strong. "We want our rights now," Judith Heumann, then deputy director for the Council for Independent Living, stated in a press release. "We will wait no longer!! The Administration is forcing us to take to the streets and we will."[7]

The 504 protesters received telegrammed support from César Chávez, president of the United Farm Workers of America: "Greetings and best wishes in your struggle . . . Viva la Causa."[8] César Chávez, Dolores Huerta, and other leaders and members of the United Farm Workers had led and organized a years-long series of strikes and boycotts to call attention to the working conditions of American agricultural workers, a large percentage of whom were Latino and Latina. Leaders and members of civil rights movements for African Americans also supported the 504 protesters. The Reverend Jesse Jackson spoke in support; as did members of the Black Panthers, who helped to provide food and supplies during the takeover. In this way, the 504 protesters drew not only on the tactics and lessons from these other civil rights movements but also on their organization, logistics, and voices.

On April 28, the secretary of the Department of Health, Education, and Welfare endorsed a set of regulations contained within the law. The 504 protesters had succeeded in securing their immediate policy demands. Reflecting back on the time, Heumann recalled the personal risks that the activists were willing to take: "People weren't going to work, people were willing to risk arrest, people were risking their own health. Everybody was risking something. . . . Through the sit-in, we turned ourselves from being oppressed individuals into being empowered people. We demonstrated to the entire nation that disabled people could take control over our own lives and take leadership in the struggle for equality."[9]

THE AMERICANS WITH DISABILITIES ACT EXPANDS PROTECTIONS FOR PEOPLE WITH DISABILITIES

A later piece of legislation on which Heumann also worked tirelessly was the Americans with Disabilities Act (ADA), signed into law in 1990. Among its provisions, the ADA offered protections for Americans with disabilities against discrimination in the workplace and improved their access to public transportation, public services, and other areas of public and commercial life.[10] "The ADA was like the Emancipation Proclamation for disabled individuals," Heumann said in 2015, referring to the Civil War proclamation by President Abraham Lincoln that freed the slaves in the states that had rebelled.[11]

In her remarks on Martin Luther King Jr. Day in 2016, Heumann also referred to the words of Supreme Court justice Thurgood Marshall—the first African American appointed to the highest Court in the land—in an opinion that he wrote in 1985. The case involved the denial of a permit to build a facility to house and serve people with cognitive disabilities in Cleburne, Texas. The Court unanimously ruled against the city's actions, saying that the permit denial violated those individuals' constitutional rights.[12] In his opinion, Marshall directly connected the struggles to secure civil rights for Americans with disabilities to those of African Americans. The "mentally retarded," Marshall noted, "have been subject to a 'lengthy and tragic history' . . . of segregation and discrimination that can only be called grotesque."[13]

When he used the word *grotesque*, Marshall was not exaggerating. Throughout much of its history, the nation has discriminated against people with disabilities in restrictive, even violent ways. In addition to being excluded from the workplace, schools, transportation, and other forms of public and private life, Americans with disabilities—especially those with cognitive disabilities—have been forcibly institutionalized, and even sterilized.[14]

Many advocates for the rights of Americans with disabilities intentionally drew connections between their struggles and those of African Americans decades before. A 1999 position paper for the American Civil Liberties Union—which noted that "people with disabilities are the poorest, least employed, and least educated minority in America"—pointed to a long history of discrimination against Americans with disabilities.[15] "Finally," the report noted, "thanks in part to the inspiration provided by the civil rights struggles of the 1960's, disability rights advocates began to press for full legal equality and access to mainstream society. Through lobbying and litigation, laws were passed and rights established; public education and advocacy were used to promote reason and inclusiveness rather than fear and pity."[16] Heumann had helped to lead that charge.

WHAT HAVE I **LEARNED?**

1. Civil rights are called *positive freedoms* because _____.

   a. they are not protected in the Constitution

   b. they require governmental action to affirm their legitimacy

   c. they require individual and governmental action to secure them

   d. they can only be protected by the laws of a nation

2. What lessons might members of other groups who have experienced discrimination draw from the efforts to secure rights for people with disabilities?

3. What lessons might *you* draw from the efforts to secure rights for people with disabilities in securing your own rights?

CIVIL RIGHTS AMENDMENTS EMERGE FROM THE CIVIL WAR—BUT PROVIDE ONLY IMPERFECT PROTECTION

- Trace the history of racial segregation in America and the ratification of the Fourteenth Amendment to the Constitution, which laid the foundation for later struggles to secure civil rights.

Judith Heumann and the 504 protesters, Huerta and Chávez, Thurgood Marshall, and many others whom we've not yet met in this chapter claimed their civil rights. But on what basis did they do so? The short answer is the Constitution, or more precisely, amendments to it. The longer answer involves a longer story, and an often difficult and troubling part of American history. One, however, that also includes brave and strategic political action by many individuals.

As we explored in Chapter 2, neither the ratified Constitution of the United States nor the Bill of Rights abolished slavery. Three of the provisions of the original Constitution—though they did not mention slavery by name—served to protect it. Slaves were counted as three-fifths of a person for purposes of states' representation, Congress was forbidden from regulating the slave trade for two decades following ratification, and nonslave states were required to return escaped slaves to bondage. Many delegates and Americans at the time, however, knew and argued that slavery violated the foundations of the Republic itself. Many felt that these unresolved contradictions would eventually tear the nation apart. Slavery, however, endured.

THE SUPREME COURT DENIES CITIZENSHIP RIGHTS TO AFRICAN AMERICANS, HELPING TO SPARK A WAR THAT SPLITS THE NATION

The early and middle decades of the nineteenth century saw the young republic undergo many changes: rapid Westward expansion (often catastrophic to the indigenous peoples in those lands), a growing population, technological change, and economic growth. The question of slavery— unresolved during the Constitutional convention—however, remained. The slave states of the South and the free states of the North were becoming increasingly different economically and socially. But what about the West? Would these new states be slave or free? In a representative democracy, and a federalist one, it was more than a moral question. It would also be decisive in determining the balance of political power in the federal government.

In 1857, in *Dred Scott v. Sandford*, the Supreme Court ruled that Scott, former slaves, and the descendants of slaves were not citizens of the United States, even if they were residents of free states or territories. The natural rights proclaimed in the Declaration of Independence and protected in the Constitution, Justice Roger Taney wrote in his opinion, did not extend to individuals "whose ancestors were negroes of the African race," who, at the time of the founding, were considered an "inferior class of beings who had been subjugated by the dominant race, and, whether emancipated or not, yet remained subject to their authority, and had no rights or privileges but such as those who held the power and the Government might choose to grant them."[17] Natural rights, according to the Court, had been selectively bestowed.

Scott's inability to sue for his freedom or that of his family was not the only effect of Taney's majority opinion in *Dred Scott*. In addition, the Court—five of whose nine members were from the South— ruled that the Missouri Compromise, which was a plan that had been created by Congress in 1820 to maintain a balance of slave and nonslave states in the Senate, was unconstitutional. In practice, the balance between slave and nonslave states had already been upended. The Court's ruling in *Dred Scott*, though, threatened the constitutionality of any state laws against slavery, as slaves were considered property subject to the Constitution's protections. The Court's decision served to further polarize public opinion on the question of slavery and galvanize both proslavery and antislavery forces in the United States.

The threat that states might secede from the Union was not a new one. During the constitutional convention, a delegate from Delaware had raised it is an implicit threat against the American

Recorded according to Act of Congress, in the year 1857, by Frank Leslie, in the Clerk's Office of the District Court for the Southern District of New York. (Copyrighted June 23, 1857.)

No. 82.—VOL. IV.]   NEW YORK, SATURDAY, JUNE 27, 1857.   **[Price 6 Cents.**

Courtesy of the Library of Congress, Prints and Photographs Division

▲ A wood engraving depicting Dred Scott and his family on the front page of a newspaper in 1857. The Supreme Court ruled in *Dred Scott v. Sandford* that Scott could not sue for his freedom as he was not considered to be a citizen of the United States, even though he had resided in free territory for a time.

confederation during the Constitutional Convention, though in the context of state representation in Congress rather than over the regulation of slavery. To the southern states in the convention, however, the preservation of slavery in their states had been a precondition to their ratification of the Constitution.

SECESSION ENSUES, AND THEN CIVIL WAR

In December 1860, South Carolina made the long-simmering threat of secession a reality. Within six months, eleven southern states had seceded from the United States to form the Confederate States of America. In April they fired on a federal fort in Charleston Harbor. To reunite the Union, President Abraham Lincoln had to take what remained of the American Republic to war. Like many times before and since, leaders, soldiers, and citizens on both sides thought that the war would be over quickly. And like many times before and since, they were all wrong—tragically wrong.

When the American Civil War finally ended in 1865, more than six hundred thousand soldiers had died. An unknown number of civilians were killed as well. In some ways it was similar to other wars of the nineteenth century; disease and infection were just as deadly as bullets. In other ways, however, it was a "modern" war, foreshadowing the terrible devastation of the industrial wars of the twentieth century. Technology, modern transportation, and mass production of weapons led to massive casualties in the presence of traditional fighting techniques, such as mass charges of soldiers into prepared fighting positions. Toward the end of the war, some battlefields—with their trenches and emplaced gun works—looked like those of Europe would during World War I fifty years later. It was total war, and it did not end until the Union armies had literally destroyed the ability of the Confederacy to support and conduct war.

Historians continue to debate the relative roles of slavery, politics, and economics as causes of the Civil War. In many ways it is difficult to disentangle these causes from each other. Similarly, stories of the Reconstruction—the years after the Civil War when the rebellious southern states were brought back into the Union—have shifted in their focus over time.

During the war, President Lincoln signed the Emancipation Proclamation, which in 1863 declared that all slaves in the states under rebellion were "henceforward and forever free." However, it took the actions of Union troops and slaves themselves to make that proclamation a reality on the ground. Excluded from the proclamation were slaves in the border states still loyal to the Union and territories in the South already under federal control. This was a political move, designed to preserve the loyalty of the border states while also putting pressure on Europe not to come to the aid of the Confederacy.

As the war dragged on, African Americans were increasingly brought into the Union war effort. Although forced to serve in segregated units and often assigned to labor detachments, many of the nearly two hundred thousand African Americans who served in the Union Army used their experiences to gain education, advancement, and a claim of equal status as citizens in the victorious Union. African American combat units quickly gained a reputation for effectiveness and bravery under fire. "From the army," according to one historian, "would come many of the black political leaders of the Reconstruction, including at least forty-one delegates to state constitutional conventions, sixty legislators, three lieutenant governors, and four Congressmen."[18]

CONSTITUTIONAL AMENDMENTS ABOLISH SLAVERY AND AFFIRM VOTING AND CITIZENSHIP RIGHTS FOR AFRICAN AMERICANS DURING RECONSTRUCTION

At the conclusion of the war, southern states began to pass laws to preserve the predefeat status quo between whites and African Americans. Known as the black codes, these pieces of legislation attempted to restrict the economic and political rights of freedmen, to "make Negroes slaves in everything but name."[19] Some of these laws required former slaves to leave their former master's property to make new labor contracts but had them arrested for vagrancy when they did so—with punishment consisting of a return to servitude. Other laws restricted African Americans' rights in the courts or at the polls, prevented them from owning firearms, or made self-employment all but impossible through heavy taxes or obscure licensing requirements.

President Andrew Johnson, who succeeded Lincoln upon his assassination, pushed for quick readmission of the southern states with relatively little regard for the preservation of African American political rights. The Republican-controlled Congress, however, was more assertive. Some Republicans were staunch abolitionists based on moral grounds, while others also had strategic political calculations in mind. Making sure that African American men could vote—and, it was expected, vote Republican—was seen as a way to avoid an unbreakable and dominant political alliance of northern and southern Democrats.

Within five years of the conclusion of the Civil War, three amendments had been added to the Constitution, although not without considerable opposition. In 1865, the **Thirteenth Amendment** to the Constitution prohibited slavery within the United States. To ensure the power of the national government to make this provision a reality, and to prevent a Supreme Court from overturning antislavery laws as it had done in *Dred Scott*, Section 2 of the amendment stated that "Congress shall have the power to enforce this article by appropriate legislation." In 1868, the **Fourteenth Amendment** affirmed the citizenship of all persons "born or naturalized in the United States" and, for the first time in the history of the Constitution, placed explicit restrictions on the laws of states: "No State shall make or enforce any law which shall abridge the privileges and immunities of citizens of the United States; nor shall any State deprive any person of life, liberty, or property, without due process of law; nor deny to any person within its jurisdiction the equal protection of the laws."

The **equal protection clause** of the Fourteenth Amendment served as the constitutional basis for the assault on educational segregation in the courts and for the assertion of civil rights for Americans of many different identities in many different areas of public and private life. In addition to addressing issues of state debts and office holding for former Confederate leaders, the Fourteenth Amendment also overturned the three-fifths rule for representation in the original Constitution.

Faced with southern resistance to the Fourteenth Amendment—southern states rejected or ratified modified versions of it—the Republican Congress, having won major victories in the 1866 elections, passed

The Granger Collection, New York

▲ Members of Company E., 4th United States Colored Infantry in Washington, DC, in 1865. Many African American veterans followed their service in the Civil War with political activism after its conclusion.

Thirteenth Amendment
an amendment to the Constitution passed in 1865 prohibiting slavery within the United States.

Fourteenth Amendment
an amendment to the Constitution passed in 1868 affirming the citizenship of all persons born or naturalized in the United States and, for the first time in the history of the Constitution, placing explicit restrictions on the laws of states that sought to abridge the privileges and immunities of citizens of the United States.

equal protection clause
a clause of the Fourteenth Amendment that serves as the constitutional basis for the assault on educational segregation in the courts and for the assertion of civil rights for Americans of many different identities in many different areas of public and private life.

▲ A young African American man drinks from a segregated water fountain in Oklahoma City, Oklahoma, in 1939. Jim Crow laws persisted across the United States long after the civil rights acts of the late nineteenth century were passed.

The Granger Collection, New York

the First Reconstruction Act of 1867. This act disbanded southern governments, thus voiding their rejection of the Fourteenth Amendment, and replaced them with military rule. It gave freedmen the right to vote and took that right away from Confederate veterans, and it made ratification of the Fourteenth Amendment a necessary condition of readmission to the United States. The **Fifteenth Amendment**, ratified in 1870, went beyond threats against states for restricting voting rights and affirmed the voting rights of all freedmen, again giving Congress the power to make necessary laws: "The right of citizens of the United States to vote shall not be denied or abridged by the United States or by any State on account of race, color, or previous condition of servitude."

In addition to these Reconstruction amendments, Congress in this period passed several pieces of legislation aimed at securing the civil rights of African Americans. In 1865, Congress created the Freedmen's Bureau, which took steps to provide former slaves with the two things they desired most: land and education. This was not always done in the interests of freedmen, however. The bureau sometimes forced African Americans to work for whites.[20] "Free then, with a desire for land and a frenzy for schools," according to W. E. B. Du Bois, "the Negro lurched into the new day."[21] Throughout the South, former slaves organized for the purpose of building communities, churches, and especially schools, and they attempted to reconstruct families that had been sold into fragmentation. The Civil Rights Act of 1866 affirmed the legal and property rights of former slaves, while the Civil Rights Act of 1875 affirmed "the equality of all men before the law" and the duty of government to enforce that equality. The latter also acknowledged the rights of all to "the full and equal enjoyment of the accommodations, advantages, facilities, and privileges of inns, public conveyances on land or water, theaters, and other places of public amusement" regardless of race or "previous condition of servitude."

RACIAL OPPRESSION CONTINUES DESPITE NEW PROTECTIONS

These efforts did not go unopposed. As the Democratic Party gained political power in the southern states and the will of the Republican Party to make civil rights a reality on the ground faded, the early gains made by African Americans began to disappear. Southern states passed laws to preserve segregation and prevent African American men from exercising their Fifteenth Amendment right to vote. Known as **Jim Crow laws**, these efforts enforced segregation across all aspects of daily life, including transportation, entertainment, business, and education. While **legal segregation** (racial segregation by law) had been enforced in the North before the Civil War, by the time of Reconstruction it had largely disappeared there but remained deeply entrenched in the post–Civil War South. Selective enforcement of poll taxes, which required voters to pay a tax at the polling place, and literacy tests, which were used by registrars to determine whether voters were "qualified" to vote, combined to prevent African American men from voting.

Backing up the laws and statutes were violence and the persistent threat of violence against African Americans who tried to exercise their rights and against whites who tried to help them. The violence against African Americans, especially former soldiers, was often organized, sometimes random, and sometimes continued against a person's body after he or she had already died: "In Texas, one woman reported that it was a common sight to see the bodies of freedmen floating down a river."[22] Schools that educated former slaves were seen as especially dangerous to the white order. Many were burned; their white teachers were beaten and ostracized. Across the South, the Ku Klux Klan terrorized and murdered African American politicians and civic leaders. Thousands of African Americans were murdered,

Fifteenth Amendment
an amendment to the Constitution passed in 1870 affirming the voting rights of all freedmen.

Jim Crow laws
state and local laws passed after Reconstruction through the mid-1950s by which white southerners reasserted their dominance by denying African Americans basic social, economic, and civil rights, such as the right to vote.

legal segregation
the separation by law of individuals based upon their racial identities.

often to send a message that the racial order was not to be challenged. Terrorism in the postwar South was, as it has always been, a political weapon.

In a speech before the Republican Party National Convention in 1872, Frederick Douglass, a former slave, abolitionist leader, and noted orator, highlighted the incompleteness of efforts on behalf of African American civil rights and the dangers many continued to face. He declared, "You say you have emancipated us. You have; and I thank you for it. You say you have enfranchised us. You have; and I thank you for it. But what is your emancipation?—what is your enfranchisement? What does it all amount to, if the black man, after having been made free by the letter of your law, is unable to exercise that freedom, and, after having been freed from the slaveholder's lash, he is subject to the slaveholder's shot-gun?"[23]

OPPONENTS OF JIM CROW ATTEMPT TO USE THE JUDICIARY TO CHALLENGE IT, BUT FAIL

In the decades following the Civil War, the Supreme Court proved to be an enabler of racial oppression rather than a protector against it. In 1896, it upheld the constitutionality of legalized racial segregation, dealing a further blow to fading reconstructionist dreams.[24] *Plessy v. Ferguson* was a test case organized by the African American community in New Orleans to challenge Louisiana's Jim Crow laws.[25] Homer Plessy, "a light-skinned man who described himself as 'seven-eighths Caucasian,'"[26] had been arrested and fined for violating a state law requiring separate railroad facilities for whites and African Americans. In the racialized math of the time, his ancestry placed Plessy just over the legal boundary between white and African American in Louisiana. After losing in the state courts, he appealed his case to the Supreme Court.

In the decision in *Plessy*, Justice Henry Billings Brown declared that Louisiana's law did not violate the Fourteenth Amendment to the Constitution. Arguing that "social prejudices cannot be overcome by legislation," Brown upheld Plessy's conviction and declared that "**separate but equal**" did not violate the Constitution. Justice John Marshall Harlan, the lone dissenter on the Court, correctly, as it turned out, saw *Plessy* as a dangerous and damaging ruling, one that would "prove to be quite as pernicious as the decision made by this tribunal in the *Dred Scott* case." His charge, however, was only a dissent; Brown's majority opinion set policy. The doctrine of "separate but equal" remained constitutional for almost sixty years.

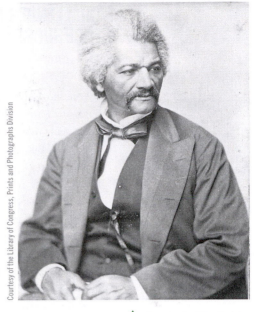

Courtesy of the Library of Congress, Prints and Photographs Division

▲ A portrait of Frederick Douglass in 1850. Douglass was a noted orator, writer, activist, staunch opponent of slavery, and supporter of women's suffrage.

....

Plessy v. Ferguson
a Supreme Court case in 1896 that upheld legal racial segregation.

separate but equal
the doctrine that racial segregation was constitutional so long as the facilities for blacks and whites were roughly equal.

WHAT HAVE I **LEARNED**?

1. *Dred Scott v. Sandford* (1857) negated _____.

   a. the Fourteenth Amendment

   b. equal protection of the laws

   c. the Missouri Compromise

   d. slavery

2. The Thirteenth Amendment _____.

   a. abolished slavery

   b. affirmed equal protection of the laws

   c. guaranteed the right of African American men to vote

   d. guaranteed the right of women to vote

3. In *Plessy v. Ferguson* (1896), the Supreme Court _____.

   a. overturned legal segregation

   b. upheld legal segregation

   c. overturned restrictions on voting

   d. upheld restrictions on voting

4. Why do you think the Court ruled the way it did in *Plessy*?

   _____

   Answer Key: 1. c; 2. a; 3. b; 4. Answers might mention public opinion or social prejudices.

CHALLENGES TO LEGAL SEGREGATION FACE SUCCESSES AND FAILURES

- **Explain efforts to end legal segregation, the strategies used, and their successes and failures.**

By the morning of December 9, 1952, hundreds of Americans—far more than the chamber could hold—had already lined up outside the Supreme Court of the United States. Those lucky enough to get seats would not give them up lightly; the better prepared had brought food, knowing someone else would take their place if they left. The line of people standing under the motto of the Supreme Court, "Equal Justice under Law," was integrated. African Americans and whites stood together for a chance to witness history. Though the line was integrated, the public schools of the District of Columbia where they were gathered were not. By law, African American and white children in the nation's capital and in the American South attended separate schools. On this day, those laws would be challenged.

In the audience was the president of Howard University, a predominantly African American university whose law school had trained a generation of civil rights lawyers, including the man who would lead his legal team in its attempt to challenge segregated education: Thurgood Marshall. Marshall was the chief litigator for the Legal Defense Fund of the National Association for the Advancement of Colored People (NAACP), and he and his team of lawyers were arguing five cases in front of the Court.[27] These five cases had been gathered together under the name of the first one on the list, *Brown v. Board of Education of Topeka*. Though differing in their details and pathways through the legal system, together the cases dealt with the same question—whether or not legal segregation, in this particular case the separation by law of African American and white children in the public schools based only upon their race, was constitutionally permissible.

It had been a long journey through the courts for Marshall and the NAACP. They had been waging a legal attack on segregation in the United States for decades. The individuals who had filed the lawsuits, those who helped organize them, and the lawyers who had prepared and argued the cases had often done so in the face of genuine personal danger. Some were threatened and assaulted. Many lost their jobs. Some had been shot at. In some cases their homes and churches had been burned.

THURGOOD MARSHALL AND THE NAACP DEVISE A STRATEGY TO END SCHOOL SEGREGATION

Marshall had shown up in Washington ten days before the trial began to coordinate his team and make sure that they were as prepared as they possibly could be. Their main concern was that the Supreme Court might agree that the African American children in the five cases had been treated unfairly, but only because their schools were not equal to the schools of the white children, not because they were segregated. It was not enough to have the Court declare that the educations of the African American children in the cases were unequal. That ruling would have forced the NAACP to try for remedies on a case-by-case basis, to sue to force thousands of school districts to equalize their educational facilities, with districts, counties, and states digging in their heels and trying to slow things down all along the way.

Marshall's legal team needed the Court to overturn its previous decisions—something that it is often hesitant to do—and declare that segregation itself was unequal. Merely showing that the educational facilities in the areas named in the cases were not equal for white and African American children might be a small tactical victory, but it would be a major strategic defeat. What Marshall and his team were trying to prove was that there was no possibility for equality in the presence of segregated education. They needed the Court to declare that segregation based on racial identity was *inherently* unequal and that it violated the Constitution of the United States.

The fact that Marshall and his team were fighting segregation in the courts—indeed, that they were fighting segregation at all—was not inevitable. Given the history of the Supreme Court with respect to the rights of African Americans, the NAACP's strategy was not promising. On several occasions in its history, including *Plessy*, the Court had issued rulings that severely restricted the rights of African Americans.

There were other possible strategies that would not have involved the courts. Marshall and his team could try to get new laws passed rather than over-turning existing ones by focusing their efforts on Congress or the state legislatures. Some voices within the NAACP and in many African American communities also felt that the scarce resources available would be better spent on economic devel-opment, on building communities and businesses, rather than on the courts or the legislatures. In the end, however, the NAACP decided to focus much of its resource base on attacking segregation through the courts, especially the Supreme Court, with the hope of making lasting social change. Thus, it adopted a judicial strategy.

The NAACP's choice to base much of its strategy on winning in the Supreme Court was a risky move. Even if its lawyers succeeded, they had to confront the fact that the judicial branch of the United States was not designed to be a strong instrument of public policy. Though no one branch was supposed to be too powerful on its own, the Founders generally regarded the judiciary as the weakest of the three, and had not given it powers to enforce its decisions. Justice Tom Clark, commenting on the decision in *Brown v. Board of Education*, cautioned that "we don't have money at the Court for an army and we can't take ads in the newspapers, and we don't want to go out on a picket line in our robes. We have to convince the nation by the force of our opinions."[28]

Charles Hamilton Houston oversaw the NAACP's early efforts in guiding educational seg-regation cases through the courts, a complicated and lengthy process even when things went well. Hamilton had been an officer in an African American artillery regiment in World War I and, as a law student, was the first African American editor of the *Harvard Law Review*. Later, as the dean of Howard Law School, he reorganized the school to make it a center of African American legal think-ing, training a new generation of civil rights lawyers. After Houston joined the NAACP in 1935, many of the cases brought by the organization focused on segregation in graduate schools. One rea-son for this was that "plaintiffs were more readily available in these cases than in cases involving elementary and secondary education, where becoming a plaintiff meant putting one's job or one's children at substantial risk."[29]

One important success in these graduate school cases came in 1938 in *Missouri ex rel Gaines v. Canada*.[30] Lloyd Gaines had applied for admission to Missouri's only, and all-white, law school. The state refused Gaines admission and instead offered him the choice of either accepting a scholar-ship to a law school in another state or applying to an all-black school in the state that would have to construct a law program for him as one did not exist. The Supreme Court in *Missouri* ruled that the scholarship option was unconstitutional and that Missouri had to provide an equal law school program for Gaines and other African American law school students. While the Court did not rule against segregated legal education within the state, it did take a close look at the equality of legal segregation in higher education. This case was followed by other, more sweeping, decisions in the coming decades.

Another important step during this time was the appointment of Thurgood Marshall as chief counsel for the desegregation cases. A star student of Houston's, Marshall was a skilled litigator and

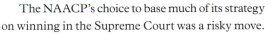

Bettmann/Contributor

▲ Thurgood Marshall (center), special counsel for the NAACP in *Brown v. Board of Education*, and two other members of his legal team in front of the Supreme Court following their landmark victory in 1954.

▲ Charles Hamilton Houston, lawyer, former dean of the Howard University School of Law, and an early leader in the NAACP's efforts to overturn legal segregation in the United States.

The Granger Collection, New York

adept at coordinating many different cases. Perhaps most importantly, Marshall was very thorough in his preparation, attending to all the details of the cases himself, knowing that much could be won or lost over what might seem at the time to be a small point. Marshall showed up early and prepared, just as James Madison had done at the Constitutional Convention nearly two centuries before.

Using what had been learned, Marshall and the NAACP won two important legal victories in 1950, one originating in Texas, the other in Oklahoma. *Sweatt v. Painter* was the Texas case.[31] Under pressure from Marshall, who threatened them with the possibility of Oklahoma beating them in the race to make legal history,[32] Texas's NAACP staff recruited Heman Sweatt, an African American applicant to the all-white University of Texas Law School. Trying to comply with the ruling in *Missouri*, Texas quickly put together an all-black law school and told Sweatt that he should apply there because of his race. Key to the NAACP's case in *Sweatt* was the sociological argument that Marshall put forward. It stated that one could not look only at the physical facilities when evaluating educational equality. Things like job networks, contacts, career support, and reputation could never be equal in segregated graduate schools. Intangibles mattered just as much as buildings and books. In its decision, the Supreme Court did not directly weigh in on "separate but equal"; however, it agreed that the intangible aspects of segregated education were destructive and impermissible, and it ordered the state to admit Sweatt to its larger, more established, all-white law school.

On the same day that the Supreme Court ruled in *Sweatt*, it handed down a similar decision on the Oklahoma case, *McLaurin v. Oklahoma State Regents for Higher Education*. Though admitted to the state's graduate school, George McLaurin "was made to sit at a desk by himself in an anteroom outside the regular classrooms where his course work was given. In the library, he was assigned a segregated desk in the mezzanine behind half a carload of newspapers. In the cafeteria, he was required to eat in a dingy alcove by himself and at a different hour from the whites."[33] Again, the Court refused to directly address "separate but equal," but it did rule that separate treatment within Oklahoma's graduate school violated McLaurin's civil rights. Removing legal restrictions on McLaurin's education might not overcome social prejudices.

Now armed with precedent and the sociological argument, Marshall and his team were ready to take on segregated elementary and secondary public education in the United States. In doing so, they sought to overturn *Plessy v. Ferguson*, "separate but equal," and Jim Crow itself.

THE SUPREME COURT RULES THAT "'SEPARATE BUT EQUAL' HAS NO PLACE"

Oliver Brown of Topeka, Kansas, was a railroad welder, a part-time minister, and a reluctant symbol for desegregation.[34] He had attempted to enroll one of his three daughters, Linda, in an all-white elementary school that was both closer to their house than the all-black school and that did not require Linda to walk among the busy and dangerous Rock Island railroad yards in order to get there. Brown's request was denied, so, with the help of the local NAACP, he and seven other parents sued. After losing in the state courts, they appealed all the way to the Supreme Court. The Kansas case was joined with four others, and they collectively bore the name ***Brown v. Board of Education***.

Arguing one of the five cases, Marshall got to the heart of the NAACP's arguments. All evidence, including evidence that had been accepted by the Court in earlier cases, had shown that black and white children were equal in their educational potential. Educational segregation, therefore, had no legitimate basis. Moreover, it violated the Fourteenth Amendment to the Constitution, which had been made part of the Constitution specifically to protect freed slaves from violations of the state legislatures.

Psychological evidence was a part of the NAACP's strategy. One piece of evidence introduced was a set of earlier research findings by psychologists Kenneth Clark and Mamie Clark. In those studies,

Brown v. Board of Education
a landmark 1954 Supreme Court ruling that overturned *Plessy v. Ferguson* and declared legal segregation in public education to be in conflict with the equal protection clause of the Fourteenth Amendment.

the Clarks presented young African American and white children with a set of brown and white dolls. A majority of children stated that they preferred the white dolls over the brown dolls, and many had negative comments about the brown dolls. After Marshall had presented his arguments, John W. Davis presented South Carolina's side. Davis highlighted the importance of local control in education: "Is it not a fact that the very strength and fiber of our federal system is local self-government in those matters for which local action is competent?"[35]

It was far from certain that Chief Justice Fred Vinson would rule in favor of the NAACP. He had already delayed the case once to ask for more evidence, and he had avoided taking on "separate but equal" in the two earlier law school cases. However, in one of those instances when chance plays a role in political development, Vinson passed away suddenly from a heart attack before a decision could be reached.

Bettmann/Contributor

▲ George McLaurin, the plaintiff in one of the two major graduate school cases, sits in a room apart from the main lecture room at the University of Oklahoma. Consider the sociological argument advanced by the NAACP in relation to this photograph. Thurgood Marshall and his team argued that intangible effects of segregation were damaging even when the physical facilities were identical.

Vinson's replacement as chief justice was California governor Earl Warren, chosen by President Dwight D. Eisenhower as much for his political skill and the fact that he was from California, which would be crucial in the next election, as for his judicial experience. Warren's own record on civil rights was not promising. As attorney general of California, he had supported the internment of Japanese Americans during World War II. He had never served as a judge—"not even," according to the press, "for five minutes in a police court."[36] Warren was, however, a skillful politician, and he used those skills to wrangle some of the most important votes in American constitutional history: those of the nine men on the U.S. Supreme Court.

On May 17, 1954, the last day of the Supreme Court's term, Warren read the Court's decision on *Brown*, years after the case first came before the Court: "Does segregation in public schools solely on the basis of race, even though the physical facilities and other 'tangible' factors may be equal, deprive the children of the minority groups of equal educational opportunities? We believe that it does."[37] Arguing that the premise of *Plessy*—that separation based on race caused no harm in those so separated—was flawed, Warren overturned the 1896 decision, saying, "We conclude that in the field of public education the doctrine of 'separate but equal' has no place. Separate educational facilities are inherently unequal. . . . We have now announced that such segregation is a denial of the equal protection of the laws." The Court was unanimous, a point that Warren inserted into his reading of the official decision.[38] It had to be; a deeply divided Court would not have had the legitimacy that it needed to take on segregation. The unanimous verdict, however, had taken Warren a long time and several compromises within the Court to achieve.

The reaction of the nation was strong and immediate, but not uniform. Many cheered the moral stance the Court had taken. "What the Justices have done," declared a Cincinnati newspaper, "is simply to act as the conscience of the American nation."[39] Many voices in the African American community were supportive but measured; history had shown that white support for their cause had not always been sustained. "As Charles [Hamilton] Houston had said years earlier, 'Nobody needs to explain to a Negro the difference between the law in books and the law in action.'"[40] In the South, there was discussion among moderates on how to make the required adjustments. The Court, after all, had not set a firm date for when "separate but equal" had to be abolished. But there was also anger. Mobs blocked schools and universities. South Carolina governor James F. Byrnes proclaimed, "Ending segregation [will] mark the beginning of the end of civilization in the South as we have known it."[41]

THE SOUTH RESISTS DESEGREGATION

Legal segregation began to disappear in the border states, with Washington, DC, the first of the five defendants in *Brown* to move to comply with the Supreme Court's ruling. Southern states, however, actively resisted. In 1956, Virginia's legislators passed a Resolution of Interposition, which

▲ The "doll study" research of Dr. Kenneth B. Clark (left) and his wife Dr. Mamie Clark (right) demonstrated the psychological harm of segregation and was used as evidence in *Brown v. Board of Education*.

argued that the state was "duty bound" to impose itself between children's education and the Supreme Court decision. Several other state legislatures also forbade their state officials from enforcing **desegregation**—the intentional reversal of segregated educational facilities based on children's race or ethnicity.

The Court's decision in *Brown* had intentionally avoided setting a strict timeline on achieving integration. In response to resistance to its efforts, the Court issued a follow-up decision the next year, in 1955. In what is now known as *Brown v. Board of Education of Topeka II*, the Warren Court urged compliance with *Brown I* "with all deliberate speed," a curious choice of words, hardly inflammatory, likely crafted out of political necessity. In addition, the Court dealt with questions of implementation, or making a policy a reality on the ground, by placing the federal district court judges in charge of actual desegregation efforts. Some southern district court judges were not sympathetic to the Court's ruling and tried to slow down compliance with it.[42] In general, in spite of the urging in the second *Brown* decision, compliance across the South was slow at best. Fears on the part of Supreme Court justices that their decision would not be obeyed proved to be well founded. In 1964, ten years after the Court's ruling in *Brown v. Board of Education*, 98 percent of African American children still attended completely segregated schools.

The decisions of the Supreme Court did not by themselves end the practice of segregation in the South. As was discussed in Chapter 2, the Constitution set up the American system of government to prevent one branch from having that kind of power. And, for a time, the Court found itself acting alone. According to law professor Gerald Rosenberg, "For ten years the Court spoke forcefully while Congress and the executive did little."[43] There were a few exceptions to this, however. In 1957, President Eisenhower sent federal troops to Little Rock, Arkansas, to enforce a Supreme Court order to segregate the schools against the will of the state's governor. The troops escorted nine African American students through an angry white mob. Also that year, Lyndon Johnson, senator and future president, sponsored the Civil Rights Act of 1957, the first piece of civil rights legislation to pass since Reconstruction. Its primary purpose was to put pressure on the states through the cost of litigation by supporting the lawsuits of African Americans who had been denied the right to vote. Though it did not effect significant policy change, it showed that civil rights legislation could make it past the southern Democrats in Congress.

CITIZENS ENGAGE IN NEW FORMS OF CIVIL DISOBEDIENCE AND PROTEST

Citizens themselves took increasingly strong action to end segregation in schools, workplaces, and the community. African American community leaders organized boycotts, in which people refused to buy services or products from an organization in order to force policy changes. Notable among these was the Montgomery bus boycott, which sought to put economic pressure on the city of Montgomery, Alabama, to end its policy of segregating bus passengers based on their race. At first, Montgomery community leaders tried to pressure the city into changing its policy, but this had no effect. In 1955, Claudette Colvin, an African American high school student, refused to move to the "Negro section" of a Montgomery bus. She was not sitting in the "white section," but in "no man's land," a vaguely defined buffer between the two sections that, according to segregationists, was created "to give the driver some discretion to keep the races out of each other's way."[44] Colvin refused to move and was handcuffed and placed under arrest. That year, other African American women in Montgomery were arrested for the same act of protest. Their case eventually resulted in the bus segregation law being declared unconstitutional.[45]

desegregation
the act of eliminating laws or practices that separate individuals based upon racial identity.

CAN THE SUPREME COURT EFFECT SOCIAL CHANGE?

Alexander Hamilton, in *Federalist* No. 78, argued that the Supreme Court had little power acting on its own "and must ultimately depend upon the aid of the executive arm even for the efficacy of its judgments." One scholar has collected data on the pace of integration in the South following *Brown v. Board* to make a similar argument: The Supreme Court cannot, acting on its own, produce social change on the ground. His data are displayed in the chart below.

It was not until 1970 that more than half of African American children in the South were attending integrated schools (and many of these were far from fully integrated). During this period, citizens took action through events such as the Montgomery bus boycott, in which African Americans in Montgomery, Alabama, refused to ride city buses in protest over segregated seating; the executive and legislative branches became more involved in the desegregation process; and the Court issued more related rulings. The data in the graph indicate that the decision of *Brown v. Board* did not immediately result in desegregation of schools in the South. To say that the Supreme Court is powerless, however, might be too strong a statement to make based on these data alone.

First, the branches were not designed to act alone, but in concert with (and sometimes in opposition to) each other. This is the principle of separation of powers discussed in Chapter 2. Second, *Brown* was only the first in a string of decisions on school desegregation handed down by the Court—decisions that became stronger and stronger during the time period covered in the graph.

WHaT Do You Think?

For ten years after *Brown*, southern public schools remained segregated. Considering all that you have read so far, why might this have been unsurprising? Do these data confirm that the Supreme Court cannot effect social change? Was the NAACP's decision to adopt a judicial strategy a wise one? Why or why not?

Percentage of African American Children Attending Integrated Schools in the South

Source: Data from Gerald N. Rosenberg, *The Hollow Hope* (Chicago: University of Chicago Press: 2008), 50–51, Table 2.1.

In December, Rosa Parks also refused to give up her bus seat and was later arrested. The decisions of Colvin and Parks were not taken lightly; they faced the prospect of criticism within their own communities and physical violence at the hands of whites. "When she [Rosa] was allowed to call home," one historian has noted, "her mother's first response was to groan and ask, 'Did they beat you?'"[46] Upon word of Parks's arrest, English professor Jo Ann Robinson and other community leaders organized a boycott, getting the word out with the help of African American

Mark Wilson/Getty Images

▲ By refusing to give up her seat on the bus, Rosa Parks became a civil rights icon. This one woman's civil disobedience has had a strong impact on political culture the world over and she is memorialized in countless ways, even today.

churches in the city. They printed flyers in secret in the middle of the night at Alabama State College, where Robinson taught. Dr. Martin Luther King Jr. was selected to lead the boycott. Addressing the community in a Montgomery church, King captured the simple, courageous reason behind the actions of the women of the city: "And you know, my friends, there comes a time when people get tired of being trampled over by the iron feet of oppression. . . . We are here—we are here because we are tired now."[47] After lasting for more than a year, the boycott ended with the Supreme Court's 1956 decision in the case of Colvin and three others that declared the bus law unconstitutional. Not only had they won in the Court, but it was a public victory—a citizens' victory.

There were many other acts of **civil disobedience** in the struggle against segregation. Individuals chose to disobey segregation laws despite the dangers they faced in order to point out the injustice inherent in those laws. In 1960, four African American college students sat down at a lunch counter reserved for whites at a Woolworth's in Greensboro, North Carolina, and requested service. They were denied. They returned the next day, and their numbers began to grow. College students, both African American and white, continued the sit-ins. Over the next months, with the organizational help of the Student Nonviolent Coordinating Committee (SNCC), similar protests occurred across the American South. Some protesters met with arrest, others with violence and intimidation.

In 1961, a group of African Americans and whites undertook another series of protests, these aimed at pressuring the administration of President John F. Kennedy to enforce Supreme Court decisions banning segregation in public facilities involved with interstate travel. These Freedom Riders also faced arrest and violence. In one case, a bus was firebombed, and many protesters were beaten with baseball bats and iron pipes.

The actions of these activists—and their often harsh treatment at the hands of local law enforcement, which was broadcast to Americans on their televisions—began to change public opinion toward the civil rights struggle. By voting in larger and larger numbers, African Americans also began to make their presence felt in Washington, DC. Close elections during the period highlighted to politicians the importance of securing the African American vote, which might tip an election in their favor.

Aware of changing political realities, Congress, under intense pressure from President Johnson, passed two major pieces of civil rights legislation, finally giving its support to efforts that had begun in the Supreme Court and on the streets. A version of the Civil Rights Act of 1964 had been part of President Kennedy's civil rights efforts prior to his assassination in 1963. The legislation that Congress passed in 1964 authorized the federal government to withhold grants from districts that did not integrate their schools. The act outlawed racial segregation in schools and public places and authorized the attorney general of the United States, and therefore the federal government, to sue individual school districts that failed to desegregate. In addition, the act outlawed employment discrimination based on race or ethnicity and also on religion, national origin, or gender. The provisions of the Civil Rights Act of 1964 proved to be as valuable to women and members of other minority groups in their efforts as the civil rights decisions in the Supreme Court. The Voting Rights Act of 1965 outlawed literacy tests for voters and authorized the Justice Department to send federal officers to register voters in uncooperative cities, counties, and states. The effects on African American voter registration were immediate and significant.

civil disobedience
the intentional refusal to obey a law in order to call attention to its injustice.

Major Milestones in American Civil Rights

The timeline below is by necessity incomplete, as it focuses primarily on the events covered in this chapter. Notice that the activities of one civil rights group overlap and inform the actions of others. Consider as well the other civil rights movements you know about. Where would those fall on this timeline?

1619 Slavery begins in the United States

Abolitionist movement begins (Prudence Crandall, Sarah and Angelina Grimké) **1830s**

1841 Frederick Douglass begins work as an abolitionist

Sojourner Truth begins work as an abolitionist **1844**

1848 Seneca Falls Convention (Lucretia Mott, Elizabeth Cady Stanton)

Dred Scott v. Sandford (denies citizenship rights to African Americans) **1857**

1861 Civil War begins

Civil War ends | Freedmen's Bureau **1865**
Thirteenth Amendment (prohibited slavery within the United States)

1866 Civil Rights Act of 1866 (affirmed legal and property rights of former slaves)
Woman's Rights Convention

Fourteenth Amendment (affirmed the citizenship of all persons **1868**
born or naturalized in the United States, equal protection clause)

1869 National Woman's Suffrage Association
American Women's Suffrage Association

Fifteenth Amendment (affirmed voting rights of all freedmen) **1870**

1875 Civil Rights Act of 1875 (affirmed the equality of all men before the law)

End of Reconstruction | Jim Crow laws begin **1877**

1896 *Plessy v. Ferguson* ("separate but equal")

Nineteenth Amendment (women's right to vote secured) **1920**

1954 *Brown v. Board of Education* (legal segregation of schools unconstitutional)

Claudette Colvin and Rosa Parks refuse to give up their seats **1955**
Martin Luther King Jr. joins Montgomery bus boycott

1956 Resolution of Interposition (Virginia)

Civil Rights Act of 1957 (supported the lawsuits of African Americans **1957**
who had been denied the right to vote)

1960 Lunch counter protests, SNCC helps organize

Freedom Riders **1961**

1962 National Farm Workers Association founded (César Chávez and Dolores Huerta)

March on Washington **1963**

1964 Civil Rights Act of 1964 (prohibited discrimination in employment based on
race, color, religion, national origin, or sex) | *Griffin v. Prince Edward County*

March on Selma **1965**

1966 Black Panthers founded

Dr. Martin Luther King Jr. assassinated **1968**

1969 *Alexander v. Holmes County Board of Education* (immediate desegregation)

Swann v. Charlotte-Mecklenburg Board of Education **1971**
(busing aimed at desegregation constitutional)

1972 Higher Education Act (Title IX)

Milliken v. Bradley (limits scope of action required by states to end **1974**
de facto segregation)

1977 Section 504 Protests

Regents of the University of California v. Bakke (affirmed goal **1978**
of increasing minority student enrollment)

1990 Americans with Disabilities Act

Gratz v. Bollinger and *Grutter v. Bollinger* (race may be considered **2003**
a factor in college admission as long as universities
can show it has a "compelling interest")

2016 *Fisher v. University of Texas* (upheld the constitutionality of considering
racial identity in college admissions)

THE COURT DELIVERS NEW RULES AIMED AT STRENGTHENING CIVIL RIGHTS

During this period, the Supreme Court also became more active in its rulings. In a series of decisions over the next decade and a half, the Court spoke with a firmer and firmer voice and began to take education policy into its own hands. When outright resistance failed, many southern states and districts tried more creative ways to get around the ruling in *Brown* without appearing to openly defy it.

One county in Virginia cut off all funding for the county's public schools; for four years, African American students received no public education. In place of the school funding, the county set up a foundation to provide funds for students to attend private schools, none of which accepted African American children. In 1964, the Court acted to put a stop to such end-around tactics. In *Griffin v. Prince Edward County*, the Court ordered Prince Edward County to reopen its public schools on an integrated basis. "The time for mere 'deliberate speed,'" Justice Hugo Black wrote in the opinion, "has run out."[48]

New Kent County, Virginia, adopted a "freedom of choice" plan, which, in theory, promoted desegregation by allowing students to choose between two high schools that prior to *Brown* had been strictly segregated by race. Three years after this plan was enacted, however, no African American children had been enrolled in the all-white high school. In *Green v. County School Board of New Kent County, Virginia*, the Court ruled that while New Kent County's plan was not unconstitutional, it was not enough. The district had an affirmative duty to comply; the burden of proof was on districts to show that they were desegregating in practice, on the ground. And the Court said that it would be watching.[49]

Two more decisions constituted the high-water mark for the Supreme Court's efforts in desegregation. In 1969, after Thurgood Marshall had joined the Court, Justice Black ruled in *Alexander v. Holmes County Board of Education* that "'all deliberate speed' for desegregation is no longer constitutionally permissible." Southern school districts were ordered to desegregate immediately.[50] In 1971, the Court ruled in *Swann v. Charlotte-Mecklenburg Board of Education* that busing—the use of transportation to desegregate public schools, even if it meant sending students to schools farther away from their homes—was constitutionally permissible.[51] Often unpopular with parents, busing efforts stirred up considerable political opposition in both the North and the South. Those in favor argued that such efforts were necessary given the deepness of the roots of segregation. Those opposed argued that the role of government in securing equal protection was only to strike down unjust laws, not to produce integration on the ground. The debate over civil rights had moved on from laws to policies, to how strongly government should act to contest segregation that exists even when there are no laws that support or maintain it.

The Granger Collection, New York

▲ A black student protests outside a Woolworth's in Greensboro, North Carolina, in 1960. A white counterdemonstrator follows him. The efforts of those involved in the lunch counter protests helped call attention to the injustices of segregation in the American South.

de jure segregation
the separation of individuals based on their characteristics, such as race, intentionally and by law.

de facto segregation
a separation of individuals based on identity that arises not by law but because of other factors, such as residential housing patterns.

THE COURT TESTS THE LIMITS OF EQUAL PROTECTION FOR AFRICAN AMERICANS

The southern segregation that Thurgood Marshall and the NAACP had challenged in the courts was written into law—sometimes even into state constitutions. In many cases, these laws did not just allow segregation, they required it. This type of segregation is called **de jure segregation**, meaning that it is written into law. The efforts of activists and citizens had largely eliminated racially based de jure segregation by the end of the 1960s. Attention now focused on **de facto segregation**, segregation based not on law but on private choices, sometimes-private acts of discrimination, or the lingering social consequences of legal segregation even after those laws were no longer on the books. Addressing de facto segregation has proven to be even more complicated than addressing de jure segregation.

The Supreme Court has been more cautious in addressing de facto segregation than legal segregation. In 1974, in *Milliken v. Bradley*, the Court considered a case of educational segregation that had been caused not by law but by residential housing patterns in and around Detroit, Michigan.[52]

The question in *Milliken* was of responsibility. How much action should be taken, and who should be required to take it, when there was no law to point to? In this case, the Court ruled that there was no requirement to try to desegregate the region's schools, since the district boundaries had not been drawn up to segregate them in the first place. The suburban districts did not have to participate in a plan that would move students across school district boundaries. Limits on busing or any other remedy that required action between school districts had been set.

Questions about how far the Court is willing to go to secure equality in the absence of discriminatory laws have arisen in other aspects of political and economic life as well. **Affirmative action**—a policy designed to address the consequences of previous discrimination by providing advantages to individuals based upon their identities—continues to be a subject of debate in American political life. The Court has issued a much less clear set of guidelines on the use of affirmative action than it has with legal segregation. Many of these cases have involved admissions practices at American colleges and universities that have sought to boost the enrollment of African Americans and members of other racial and ethnic minorities. Again, it boils down to what one means by "equal." To those who argue for less government intervention, "equal" only means removing any legal barriers to college admissions for members of racial and ethnic minorities. To those who argue for stronger government involvement, it means taking steps to ensure equality of representation that might selectively benefit certain individuals based on their identity, whether in schools or workplaces. In recent years, the Court has tried to navigate among these approaches, but it has not always done so in a clear-cut way.

A 1978 Supreme Court decision in *Regents of the University of California v. Bakke* concerned the use of quotas, or the setting aside of a number of school slots, contracts with the government, or job opportunities for groups who have suffered past discrimination.[53] In the case, Allan Bakke, who identified himself as white, had sued the regents of the University of California at Davis after having been denied admission to its medical school. Bakke argued that his academic record was superior to the group of sixteen minority applicants for whom seats had been set aside. He brought his suit under the Fourteenth Amendment, claiming that the quota system violated his rights under the equal protection clause of the Constitution. In its ruling, the Court agreed that the quota system had violated Bakke's rights and those of other white applicants and instructed the school to admit him. However, the Court also affirmed the worthiness of the goal of increasing minority student enrollment, leaving open the possibility for plans that did not involve strict quotas.

In the years after *Bakke*, the Court issued several rulings that attempted to define the limits of permissible affirmative action. In 2003, the Court issued two rulings on the same day that tried to clarify its position. In *Gratz v. Bollinger*, the Court considered the use of a points system in undergraduate admissions decisions.[54] Like Alan Bakke, Jennifer Gratz had been denied admission to a university, in this case the University of Michigan at Ann Arbor, and sued on the basis of discrimination. Rather than using a strict quota system, the university ranked applicants on a points system, much of which focused on academics. Some points, however, were awarded for having parents who attended the University of Michigan, being a state resident, having shown a commitment to public service, or having strong athletic ability. Forty of the 150 points were awarded on the basis of "other factors." One of these factors was membership in a traditionally underrepresented racial or ethnic group. The university argued that having a diverse student body was of educational benefit to the entire learning community. In *Gratz*, the Court ruled that the points system was unconstitutional, but it did not strike down the use of racial or ethnic identity as a consideration for admissions decisions.

In *Grutter v. Bollinger*, also decided in 2003, the Court affirmed the possibility of using racial and ethnic identity in admissions decisions.[55] Barbara Grutter had also sued the University of Michigan, though in this case, its law school. Unlike the admissions system at the undergraduate level, the law school did not use a points system, but it did include racial identity in a group of factors considered in the application decision. By a 5–4 vote, the Court ruled that the university

affirmative action
a policy designed to address the consequences of previous discrimination by providing advantages to individuals based upon their identities.

could use race as a factor as long as it could show that it had a "compelling interest" to do so. Ensuring a diverse student body, the Court concluded, does demonstrate such an interest. In June 2016, the Court, in a 4–3 ruling in *Fisher v. University of Texas at Austin*, upheld the constitutionality of considering racial identity in college admissions. President Barack Obama said of the decision, "We are not a country that guarantees equal outcomes, but we do strive to provide an equal shot to everybody."[56]

WHAT HAVE I **LEARNED**?

1. The NAACP decided to pursue a legal strategy to end desegregation because it thought _____.

   a. that would be less expensive than focusing on things such as community development

   b. Congress would move too quickly to pass laws

   c. legal remedies were more likely to be permanent

   d. None of the above

2. *Brown v. Board of Education* _____.

   a. put an end to Jim Crow laws, but only in the North

   b. made affirmative action in college admissions decisions constitutional

   c. effectively reversed the Thirteenth and Fourteen Amendments

   d. declared legal segregation in public education to be in conflict with the equal protection clause of the Fourteenth Amendment

3. The Civil Rights Act of 1964 _____.

   a. authorized the Justice Department to sue segregated school districts

   b. outlawed employment discrimination based on racial identity

   c. outlawed employment discrimination based on gender

   d. All of the above

4. Do you think the NAACP's decision to focus much of its energy and resources on using the judiciary to end legal segregation was the correct one?

_____

Answer Key: 1. c; 2. d; 3. d; 4. Answers should discuss the power of the federal judiciary in making broader social change as well as limitations on that power.

AMERICAN WOMEN WORK TO SECURE THEIR CIVIL RIGHTS

- **Trace the history of efforts to secure civil rights for American women.**

Though they constitute a slight majority of the American population, women have also struggled to secure their civil rights throughout the nation's history. Scholars often frame these efforts as having taken place in two waves. The first wave, the effort to secure the right to vote, was closely tied to the efforts of nineteenth-century American women to secure their rights in education and to end the practice of slavery. The second wave, which began in the middle of the twentieth century, extended the scope of civil rights protections to women's participation in the classroom and the workplace, their freedom from sexual harassment, and their control over their bodies and their sexuality.

WOMEN'S EARLY CIVIL RIGHTS EFFORTS FOCUS ON ENFRANCHISEMENT

abolitionist movement
a political struggle to end slavery and free all slaves.

Early efforts by women to secure their rights often focused on education, which was considered an acceptable political space for a nineteenth-century white woman to inhabit. Many early activists for women's rights were also active in the **abolitionist movement**—the movement to end the practice of slavery.

◀ An engraving depicting an attack on Prudence Crandall's school for "young ladies of color" in Connecticut in 1834. This, and previous threats against students and teachers, forced Crandall to close her school.

Prudence Crandall was a white educator whose political activism in the 1830s demonstrates the close link between education, opposition to slavery, and political activism on the part of early advocates for women's rights. In 1832, Crandall admitted Sarah Harris, an African American girl, to her school for ladies in Canterbury, Connecticut, so that Harris might herself become a teacher.[57] At a time when "progressive" white thinking on race generally involved plans to recolonize African Americans to the West Indies or Africa, the actions of Crandall and Harris were considered extraordinarily radical.

Rather than cave in to the strong community pressure that she was facing to expel Harris, Crandall closed her school. Two months later, she opened another school exclusively for African American girls and soon had seventeen students. Crandall was arrested and briefly jailed; her school was vandalized; "pupils and teachers . . . were stoned as they went for walks; manure was dropped in the well; local shopkeepers refused to sell food, and doctors denied their services."[58] With the help of some supportive community members and funds from abolitionists, the school remained open for a year and a half. However, after masked men attacked and vandalized the school using battering rams and attempted to burn it to the ground, Crandall feared for the physical safety of her students and closed her school for good in 1834.

The suppression of women's rights was often justified by claims that women needed to be protected from, and therefore shut out of, elements of public life. This "protection" had legal aspects. Rights of women were severely restricted in the public space, and married women had no legal identity outside their marriage. For the purposes of the courts, they did not exist. The restriction of women's rights was as much social as it was legal. Part of the effort to secure women's rights, therefore, involved redefining what was considered acceptable behavior for a woman. Taking action in the public space—by speaking out, organizing, and mobilizing public opinion—was as political in its challenge to the boundaries of acceptable behavior as was the act of actually changing laws.

The efforts of sisters Sarah and Angelina Grimké to organize and speak out against slavery in the 1830s challenged both the institution of slavery and the less visible institution of protection of women from public life. Daughters of a prominent South Carolina slaveholding family, the Grimké sisters set out in 1837 on an antislavery speaking tour in New England. In doing so, they helped to change public perception about a woman's proper role in public life. Their campaign drew much of its strength from their own Christianity—and drew much of its opposition from Christian churches. Their audiences included women and men, African Americans and whites. Their speeches highlighted the cruelty at the heart of the institution of slavery, and they expressed solidarity with women slaves. At a national convention of antislavery women in 1837, which the sisters had helped organize, Angelina presented a pamphlet that she had written, *An Appeal to the Women of the Nominally Free States*. She wrote,

And dear sisters, in a country where women are degraded and brutalized, and where their exposed persons bleed under the lash—where they are sold in the shambles of "negro brokers"—robbed of their hard earnings—torn from their husbands, and forcibly plundered of their virtue and their offspring; surely, in *such* a country, it is very natural that *women* should wish to know "the reason why"—especially when these outrages of blood and nameless horror are practiced in violation of the principles of our national Bill of Rights and the Preamble of our Constitution.[59]

A few of the male leaders of the abolitionist movement supported an active role for women as coparticipants along with their push for equal rights. Frederick Douglass published on the masthead of the newspaper that he edited, "Right is of no sex—Truth is of no color."[60] Others urged these advocates to drop their push for "a woman's rights," as it was called, fearful that the controversy might detract from the goal of abolition, but the proponents refused. However, the male-dominated abolitionist movement continued to prevent women from assuming public roles as leaders. Sometimes women were allowed to join antislavery conferences only as observers in segregated seating, without the right to speak or vote.

Shut out of prominent antislavery conventions in the mid-nineteenth century, abolitionist women organized their own. Lucretia Mott and Elizabeth Cady Stanton met at an antislavery convention in London in 1840 and on their way back to the United States began to plan a separate conference on women's rights. The conference met in a Methodist church in Seneca Falls, New York, over two days in July 1848. On the first day of what would come to be known as the Seneca Falls Convention, Stanton read a list of eleven resolutions, known as the Declaration of Sentiments. These resolutions derived their legitimacy from an appeal to higher law, just as the Declaration of Independence had done seventy-two years earlier and Dr. Martin Luther King Jr.'s "Letter from Birmingham Jail" would do 115 years later: "Resolved, That all laws which prevent woman from occupying such a station in society as her conscience shall dictate, or which place her in a position inferior to that of man, are contrary to the great precept of nature, and therefore of no force or authority. Resolved, That woman is man's equal—was intended to be so by the Creator, and the highest good of the race demands that she should be recognized as such."[61]

Support for the women's declaration was not universal. Only one-third of the delegates to the convention signed it. Some thought that it was too bold, especially in its call for suffrage (the right to vote) for women. The convention, however, had given energy to the movement. In the years following Seneca Falls, "a cascade of women's rights conventions . . . carried the movement into towns and villages throughout the Northeast and the Midwest."[62]

Unlike the efforts to secure the civil rights of African Americans, women's rights activists, especially in the first wave, pursued a mostly, though not solely, legislative strategy, attempting to change state and federal laws to guarantee they received equal protection in them. The legislative strategy was seen as necessary. Similar to the struggle for African American rights, the women's movement did not speak with a unified voice. Debates over goals and strategy led to sharp divisions within it. In the last national convention held before the Civil War, Stanton spoke out against marriage laws and in favor of new resolutions making it easier for a woman to obtain a divorce. Many reformers felt that she "had gone too far."[63]

These divisions continued after the Civil War, when giving the right to vote to freed African American men came onto the national agenda. Some women's rights activists wanted to include suffrage for women in the Fifteenth Amendment. Others feared that trying to obtain the right to vote for African Americans and women at the same time might stir up too much opposition. There was often a stated racial bias against African Americans on the part of white women's rights advocates, and far less attention was paid to the rights of African American women than either those of African American men or white women. According to one historian, the issue of suffrage was often portrayed as "a choice between black men and educated white women."[64]

Divisions within the women's rights movement crystallized in the formation of two separate organizations that agreed on the need for suffrage but disagreed over the importance of trying to secure a broader

CONSIDERING CONTRASTING OPINIONS AND ARGUMENTS

**Frances Ellen Watkins Harper on
Women's Rights, Racism, and American Society**

In an 1866 speech before the eleventh Woman's Rights Convention in New York, Frances Ellen Watkins Harper, a prominent African American activist and writer, challenged the most optimistic attendees, who argued that white women's suffrage would improve the situation of African Americans:

I do not believe that giving the woman the ballot is immediately going to cure all the ills of life. I do not believe that white women are dewdrops just exhaled from the skies. I think that like men they may be divided into three classes, the good, the bad, and the indifferent. The good would vote according to their convictions and principle; the bad, as dictated by prejudice or malice; and the indifferent will vote on the strongest side of the question, with the winning party.

You white women speak here of rights. I speak of wrongs. I, as a colored woman, have had in this country an education which has made me feel as if I were in the situation of Ishmael, my hand against every man, and every man's hand against me. Let me go to-morrow morning and take my seat in one of your street cars—I do not know that they will do it in New York, but they will in Philadelphia—and the conductor will put up his hand and stop the car there rather than let me ride. . . .

While there exists this brutal element in society which tramples upon the feeble and treads down the weak, I tell you that if there is any class of people who need to be lifted out of their airy nothings and selfishness, it is the white women of America.[65]

The Granger Collection, New York

▲ Frances E. W. Harper in a nineteenth-century engraving. Harper challenged the idea that the efforts of white women political activists would inevitably lead to gains for African American women.

WHAT Do You Think?

Harper's accusations were controversial in 1866, and they still are. They speak to divisions *between* Americans fighting for civil rights for different groups of excluded citizens. Today we are still confronted with this challenge. In struggles for civil rights in the twenty-first century, what are your perceptions about the solidarity between, or divisions among, different groups of civil rights advocates?

commitment to women's equality. In 1869, Stanton and Susan B. Anthony formed the National Woman Suffrage Association to try to secure civil rights for women beyond only the right to vote. Also in 1869, Lucy Stone helped to organize the American Woman Suffrage Association, which focused on suffrage, pursuing its goals at the level of state and territory.

Wyoming Territory granted women the right to vote in 1869. When Wyoming joined the Union in 1890, it became the first state to grant women the right to vote. By 1918, fifteen states had passed laws allowing women's suffrage. The right was secured at the national level in 1920 with the ratification of the **Nineteenth Amendment** to the Constitution, which had been drafted by Anthony and Stanton more than forty years earlier. The amendment stated, "The right of citizens of the United States to vote shall not

Nineteenth Amendment
a 1920 amendment to the Constitution that prevented states from denying the right to vote based on sex.

be denied or abridged by the United States or by any State on account of sex. Congress shall have power to enforce this article by appropriate legislation."

Though the constitutional right to vote came later for women than it did for African American men, women did not face the same kinds of tactics of resistance aimed to keep the legal right from becoming a practical right. As they began to exercise their right to vote, however, the broader vision of equality that many of the pioneers in the American women's movement hoped for was far from secured.

THE SECOND WAVE FOCUSES ON ONGOING INEQUALITIES

The second wave of the movement to secure the civil rights of women in the United States began in the 1960s. Like the first wave, much of the strategy involved changing laws. However, the focus went far beyond the voting booth and addressed inequalities at work and in the home as well as protection from violence and sexual harassment.

Crucial to these legislative and legal efforts was the Civil Rights Act of 1964. Title VII of the act prohibits discrimination in employment based on race, color, religion, national origin, or sex. While some scholars have argued that women were added to the act as an attempt to mobilize enough opposition to kill it, the southern congressman who introduced the amendment to add women to the legislation claimed that his motives were sincere.[66] Regardless of the truth, Title VII has proved to be an important element of equal rights for women and the basis for several rulings about gender discrimination by the Supreme Court.

One of the early leaders of this second wave was Betty Friedan. Her 1963 book, *The Feminine Mystique*, highlighted the ways in which American society assumed that domestic roles for women were "natural" and argued for a "dramatic reshaping of the cultural image of femininity that will permit women to reach maturity, identity, completeness of self, without conflict with sexual fulfillment."[67] Friedan also served as the first president of the National Organization for Women (NOW), a women's rights advocacy group that pushed for change in both the legislature and the Supreme Court. NOW initially organized largely to pressure the federal government to enforce the antidiscrimination provisions of Title VII. The organization's goals, however, became much more sweeping: "The purpose of NOW is to take action to bring women into full participation in the mainstream of American society now, exercising all the privileges and responsibilities thereof in truly equal partnership with men."[68]

In the 1960s and 1970s, women's rights activists secured several important pieces of legislation. They also lobbied to ensure that these laws were vigorously enforced—to make sure that equal meant equal in the workplaces and schools and not just in the laws. Through these pieces of legislation, women secured the legal right to receive equal pay for equal work in the same workplace and protections against discrimination based on gender, pregnancy, or childbirth. Many of these laws contain language that makes it illegal to retaliate against employees who file or participate in the filing of discrimination claims. The threat of retaliation can be a powerful disincentive for individuals to file discrimination claims, and, therefore, a powerful tool to preserve discrimination.

Protections against gender discrimination apply not just to workplaces but also to schools, states, and local governments. One of the most notable provisions is contained in a set of amendments to the Higher Education Act passed in 1972. Title IX of these amendments states, "No person in the United States shall, on the basis of sex, be excluded from participation in, or denied the benefits of, or subjected to discrimination under any educational program or activity receiving federal aid."[69] While its provisions apply equally to curriculum, health care, and residential life, Title IX has had a public impact on the provision of athletic programs and, more recently, on the efforts of students who are women and/or LGBT to overcome harassment based on sexual or gender identity.

Equal Rights Amendment
a proposed but not ratified amendment to the Constitution that sought to guarantee equality of rights based upon sex.

One of the most important elements of the legislative campaign for women's rights was an attempt to secure ratification of the **Equal Rights Amendment (ERA)** to the U.S. Constitution. The proposed amendment read, "Section 1: Equality of rights under the law shall not be denied or abridged by the United States or by any state on account of sex."

Activist Alice Paul had written the original version of the amendment in 1923, and it had been submitted to Congress for official acceptance (the first stage of the two-stage amendment process) every year since. Partly due to the help of NOW, the proposed amendment easily cleared the two-thirds vote requirement of the House of Representatives in 1971 and the Senate in 1972. Submitted to the states for ratification, the ERA got off to a quick and successful beginning, outpacing other recent amendments with its speed of state ratifications. By 1977, thirty-five of the needed thirty-eight states had ratified the ERA. No more states, however, would ratify. In spite of having its ratification deadline extended by Congress, the clock ran out on the ERA in 1982, and the amendment died.

Scholars continue to debate why the ERA failed. Part of the reason is that the Framers designed the amendment process in such a way that most proposals to amend it do fail. The Constitution was designed to be amendable, but the two-stage process for ratification is a very high hurdle. Other explanations have focused on the possibility that proponents did not mobilize as successfully at the state level as they had done in Congress during the first stage of the process. Additionally, the controversy surrounding the Supreme Court's decision on abortion in *Roe v. Wade* (see Chapter 4) may have mobilized opponents to the proposed amendment.[70] The fact that so many states ratified early on also allowed opponents to concentrate their resources on a smaller number of remaining states than if they had had to wage a counterstrategy in a larger number of states.[71]

Though the Equal Rights Amendment was not ratified, the debate over its ratification did help increase the visibility of women's rights issues and place them on the national agenda. And, as it turns out, the Fourteenth Amendment to the Constitution and Title VII of the Civil Rights Act of 1964 provided a sufficient basis for the Supreme Court to act in the absence of the Equal Rights Amendment.

Fred W. McDarrah/Getty Images

▲ Betty Friedan in a 1970 protest march commemorating the fiftieth anniversary of the ratification of the Nineteenth Amendment. Friedan was a writer, an activist in efforts to secure equal rights for American women, and the first president of the National Organization for Women.

THE SUPREME COURT USES DIFFERENT STANDARDS OF SCRUTINY ON GENDER DISCRIMINATION AND SEXUAL HARASSMENT

Although part of the strategy for women's rights advocates was to use the Supreme Court, as African American rights activists had done, they did so under a slightly different standard. Due to the nation's history of slavery, the Court has treated protection of civil rights based on race differently than protection for other groups. Historically, the Court has used three different standards to decide if a law or policy that treats people differently based on some aspect of their identity is allowable or not. Race has been considered a suspect classification for the purposes of this decision. It's not the people who are suspect, or their race. It's the treatment of people differently on the basis of race that is suspect. In cases involving racial identity, the Court applies a standard of **strict scrutiny** to any attempt to provide different or separate treatment. Under such scrutiny, a government has to show a "compelling interest" to justify the unequal treatment, a high standard that is difficult to meet.

At the other end of the spectrum is the **reasonableness standard**, in which differential treatment must be shown to be reasonable and not arbitrary. It is also called the rational basis standard as one merely has to show that there is a rational reason for the distinction.[72] This is a much lower bar legally. Under the application of the reasonableness standard, for example, government may tax people at different rates based on their incomes or impose a curfew on minors that does not apply to adults.

strict scrutiny
the most stringent judicial standard applied for deciding whether a law or policy is allowed to treat people differently.

Cases involving the rights of women have generally been considered by applying a standard in between these two extremes, one of **intermediate scrutiny**. While the Court has not yet placed gender on the same level as race in its critical view of justifications for differential treatment, it has placed gender on a higher standard than, for example, age or disability. In general, the Court has found most forms of differential treatment for men and women to be unconstitutional, except when such treatment can be justified as serving important objectives or necessities. This standard has evolved in recent years and continues to be a source of conflict and disagreement between the justices themselves.

Cases involving sexual harassment have generally been evaluated on the basis of the discrimination provisions of Title VII of the Civil Rights Act of 1964 rather than the Fourteenth Amendment. Though Title VII does not specifically mention sexual harassment, the Court has ruled in several recent cases that sexual, or gender-based, harassment does violate the act's antidiscrimination provisions. The Court has identified two types of harassment. *Quid pro quo* harassment occurs when employers request or demand sexual favors in return for advancement or employment. A *hostile working environment* involves actions, statements, or conditions that unreasonably interfere with the ability of employees to do their jobs. In cases of quid pro quo harassment, employers can be found liable for the behavior of their offending employees, even if that behavior was not known at the time it occurred. In cases involving hostile working environments, employers are generally held liable only if they knew about the offending behavior but did nothing to stop it. As with other forms of gender-based discrimination, the Court's treatment of sexual harassment is still evolving and is the source of considerable disagreements within the Court itself.

reasonableness standard
a more relaxed judicial standard in which differential treatment must be shown to be reasonable and not arbitrary.

intermediate scrutiny
a middle-ground standard for determining whether differential treatment is allowable.

WHAT HAVE I **LEARNED**?

1. Early activities by women to secure their civil rights were primarily focused on _____.

   a. enfranchisement

   b. segregation

   c. reproductive rights

   d. equal employment

2. The _____ prevented states or the nation from denying the right of suffrage to women.

   a. Fifteenth Amendment

   b. Equal Rights Amendment

   c. Nineteenth Amendment

   d. Civil Rights Act of 1964

3. The Equal Rights Amendment _____.

   a. guaranteed the right to vote regardless of gender

   b. was never ratified

   c. focused on reducing racial discrimination in the workplace

   d. All of the above

4. How has the Supreme Court treated gender equality differently than it has treated racial equality?

   _____

Answer Key: 1. a; 2. c; 3. b; 4. Answers should include a discussion of suspect classification, strict scrutiny, and the reasonableness standard.

AMERICANS CONFRONT OVERLAPPING FORMS OF DISCRIMINATION

- Evaluate the ways the diversity of Americans' identities shapes efforts to secure civil rights in the twenty-first century.

In 1851, Sojourner Truth, an orator, activist, and former slave, addressed a women's rights convention in Akron, Ohio. Her speech, only a few paragraphs long, drew from her own experiences as a person confronting more than one form of oppression:

I have plowed and reaped and husked and chopped and mowed, and can any man do more than that? I have heard much about the sexes being equal; I can carry as much as any man, and eat as much too, if I can get it. I am as strong as any man that is now. . . .

But the women are coming up bless be God and a few of the men are coming up with them. But man is in a tight place, the poor slave is on him, woman is coming on him, and he is surely between a hawk and a buzzard.[73]

Other African American women's rights activists had been hard at work in the decades before Truth's speech. For example, Maria W. Stewart, an African American essayist, activist, and orator from Boston, was the "first American woman to speak in public to a mixed audience of men and women, addressing a gathering at Boston's Franklin Hall in 1832."[74]

Truth's speech, however, has resonated throughout the history of civil rights and succinctly and eloquently captures the reality that many Americans have been confronting more than one form of inequality in their lived experiences. Scholars of identity and politics call the presence of multiple and overlapping identities and inequalities **intersectionality**.[75] This approach recognizes that multiple forms of oppression are not just additive; they interact with each other to present individuals with complex challenges to the assertion of their own rights.

This concept is more than the subject of academic study. Confronting inequalities based on both race and gender shaped the choices and strategies of early African American women activists. Some chose to focus their efforts primarily on abolition, confronting the very different expectations of "proper" behavior for white and African American women. Others focused their efforts within their own communities, challenging realities of poverty and poor education at the local level.[76] In the slave states, many African American women focused on keeping their families together and alive. This complex set of choices and challenges continues to present itself to Americans working to secure equal rights against multiple and overlapping forms of discrimination.

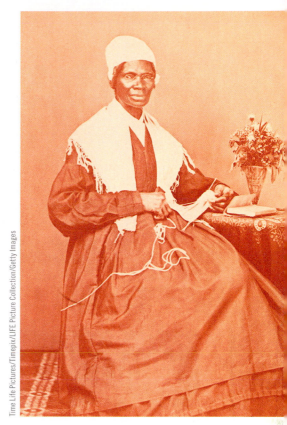

Time Life Pictures/Timepix/LIFE Picture Collection/Getty Images

▲ A portrait of Sojourner Truth. Her efforts to call attention to the multiple forms of oppression facing African American women in the nineteenth century highlighted what scholars now call challenges of intersectionality.

CIVIL RIGHTS CHALLENGES PERSIST FOR OTHER GROUPS AS WELL

In this chapter, we have focused on efforts to secure civil rights for Americans with disabilities, African Americans, and women. Throughout the nation's history, however, members of many other groups have acted to secure their own rights. Some of these struggles also go back to the early decades of the American Republic. To give proper attention to all of these efforts would require an entire book at least; therefore, we have focused on only some of them. The guiding principle of this necessary omission is that we cover many of these issues in other parts of this book.

As we explored in Chapter 4, the members of the Standing Rock nation, as well as individuals discussed in that chapter, based their right to protest and make their grievances known on civil liberties protected by the First Amendment to the Constitution. They also, however, did so in order to secure their civil rights. Similarly, the Supreme Court decision that established marriage equality, *Obergefell v. Hodges* (2015), did so based upon the Fourteenth Amendment's guarantee of equal protection of the laws.

Many Latinos and Latinas have employed and continue to employ tactics of protest, organization, education, and mobilization to challenge discrimination against members of their communities, especially on issues such as immigration and labor policy. As they are the fastest-growing group of Americans, issues of concern to Latino/a Americans are quickly becoming issues of concern to politicians and the major political parties, a subject to which we will return later in the book. Individuals and groups have also mobilized to secure the rights of gay, lesbian, transgender, and transsexual Americans.

In the United States in the twenty-first century, the concept of racial identity is becoming complicated as well. Multiracial Americans, or those with more than one distinctive racial heritage, have

intersectionality
the presence of multiple and overlapping identities and inequalities.

increasingly been carving out a space for themselves in discourse and policies involving race and ethnicity. In 2000, the U.S. Census allowed, for the first time, individuals to select more than one racial category. Slightly more than 2 percent chose to do so. By 2010, the number of Americans self-identifying as multiracial increased by 32 percent, to about nine million Americans. Where the most common combination in 2000 was "white and some other race," by 2010 the most common combination was "black and white." In addition, over the same ten-year period, the population of multiracial children increased by 50 percent, "making it the fastest growing youth group in the country."[77]

The increase in Americans who self-identify as multiracial is more than an issue of numbers. Traditional racial and ethnic identifications have been used as the basis for evaluating compliance with Title VII of the Civil Rights Act of 1964, the Voting Rights Act, and educational desegregation policies. Broadening the categories will impact all of these regulations, and some African American rights advocates have expressed concern that it might take away from gains in equality that have been achieved since the civil rights era.[78] Proponents of having multiracial classification argue that it more accurately reflects the changing realities of racial identity in the United States. Testifying before Congress, one parent of a multiracial child stated, "In my opinion, the most traumatic experience related to racial identification for the multiracial child occurs when he/she is asked to deny racial connectedness with one parent."[79]

WHAT HAVE I LEARNED?

1. How might intersectionality affect people's choices and strategies in pursuing their civil rights?

2. How might intersectionality be a challenge to securing equality?

Answer Key: 1. Answers should include the fact that members of different groups have faced different forms of discrimination and have adopted different tactics; 2. Answers should mention concerns that it might lead to increased political opposition.

CONCLUSION: HAVE AMERICANS' CIVIL RIGHTS BEEN SECURED?

The actions involved claiming and securing civil rights are not isolated things. In addition to confronting social, political, and economic inequalities, members and leaders of civil rights movements often draw support from others' efforts and learn from their successes and failures. Securing civil rights also speaks to the foundations of American democracy, forcing people to consider what full equality truly means. If they are to be successful, these efforts must involve strategic political action and use a variety of tools, including organization, protest, and the media. Equally fundamentally, securing civil rights is also about telling stories that resonate, stories that challenge the idea—often unspoken—that the exclusion of some Americans from full and equal participation in society is somehow natural, appropriate, or inevitable.

The struggle to achieve equality under the laws of the United States has never been simple or clear, and it has only grown more complex. Whatever future attempts to secure civil rights in the United States bring, however, this much is certain: Those attempts will require drawing upon the lessons of past struggles, well-planned action, and courage.

CHAPTER REVIEW

This chapter's main ideas are reflected in the Learning Objectives below. By reviewing them here, you should be able to **remember** the key points, **know** the terms that are central to the topic, and **think** about the critical issues raised in each section.

5.1 Understand that securing civil rights requires both actions by individuals and groups to claim them and actions by governments to secure and protect them.

REMEMBER
- Securing civil rights requires action, both on the part of individuals to advocate for their rights and on the part of government to secure and protect those rights.

KNOW
- civil rights (p. 123)
- positive freedoms (p. 123)

THINK
- How strongly should the American government act to secure civil rights?
- What actions did Judith Heumann take to secure civil rights for disabled people?

5.2 Trace the history of racial segregation in America and the ratification of the Fourteenth Amendment to the Constitution, which laid the foundation for later struggles to secure civil rights.

REMEMBER
- While the conclusion of the Civil War settled the question of secession and three amendments established a set of constitutional rights for African Americans, struggles to secure their rights continued, often under threats of economic and physical violence.

KNOW
- equal protection clause (p. 129)
- Fifteenth Amendment (p. 130)
- Fourteenth Amendment (p. 129)
- Jim Crow laws (p. 130)
- legal segregation (p. 130)
- *Plessy v. Ferguson* (p. 131)
- separate but equal (p. 131)
- Thirteenth Amendment (p. 129)

THINK
- What are the similarities and differences between the tactics and goals employed by individuals in trying to secure civil rights for Americans with disabilities, African Americans, and women?

5.3 Explain efforts to end legal segregation, the strategies used, and their successes and failures.

REMEMBER
- The NAACP's choice to focus its efforts on ending legal segregation was not preordained, nor was the strategy of using the courts instead of focusing on changing the laws in the states.

KNOW
- affirmative action (p. 141)
- *Brown v. Board of Education* (p. 134)
- civil disobedience (p. 138)
- de facto segregation (p. 140)
- de jure segregation (p. 140)
- desegregation (p. 136)

THINK
- What were the risks faced by Marshall and the NAACP in using the federal judiciary to end legal segregation?
- What role can the Supreme Court play in effecting change on the ground? What are some limitations on its ability to do so?
- The federal judiciary is only one of three branches and faces many challenges in changing public policy on the ground.

5.4 Trace the history of efforts to secure civil rights for American women.

REMEMBER	• Early efforts to secure civil rights for African Americans and those to secure civil rights for American women often overlapped, but with differences in their goals and tactics.

KNOW
- abolitionist movement (p. 142)
- Equal Rights Amendment (ERA) (p. 146)
- intermediate scrutiny (p. 148)
- Nineteenth Amendment (p. 145)
- reasonableness standard (p. 147)
- strict scrutiny (p. 147)

THINK
- How did advocates for gender equality overcome the failure to secure ratification of the Equal Rights Amendment?

5.5 Evaluate the ways the diversity of Americans' identities shapes efforts to secure civil rights in the twenty-first century.

REMEMBER
- Americans may face multiple forms of discrimination that may act to reinforce each other.

KNOW
- intersectionality (p. 149)

THINK
- In what ways do changes in the diversity and complexity of American society expand our understanding of efforts to secure civil rights?

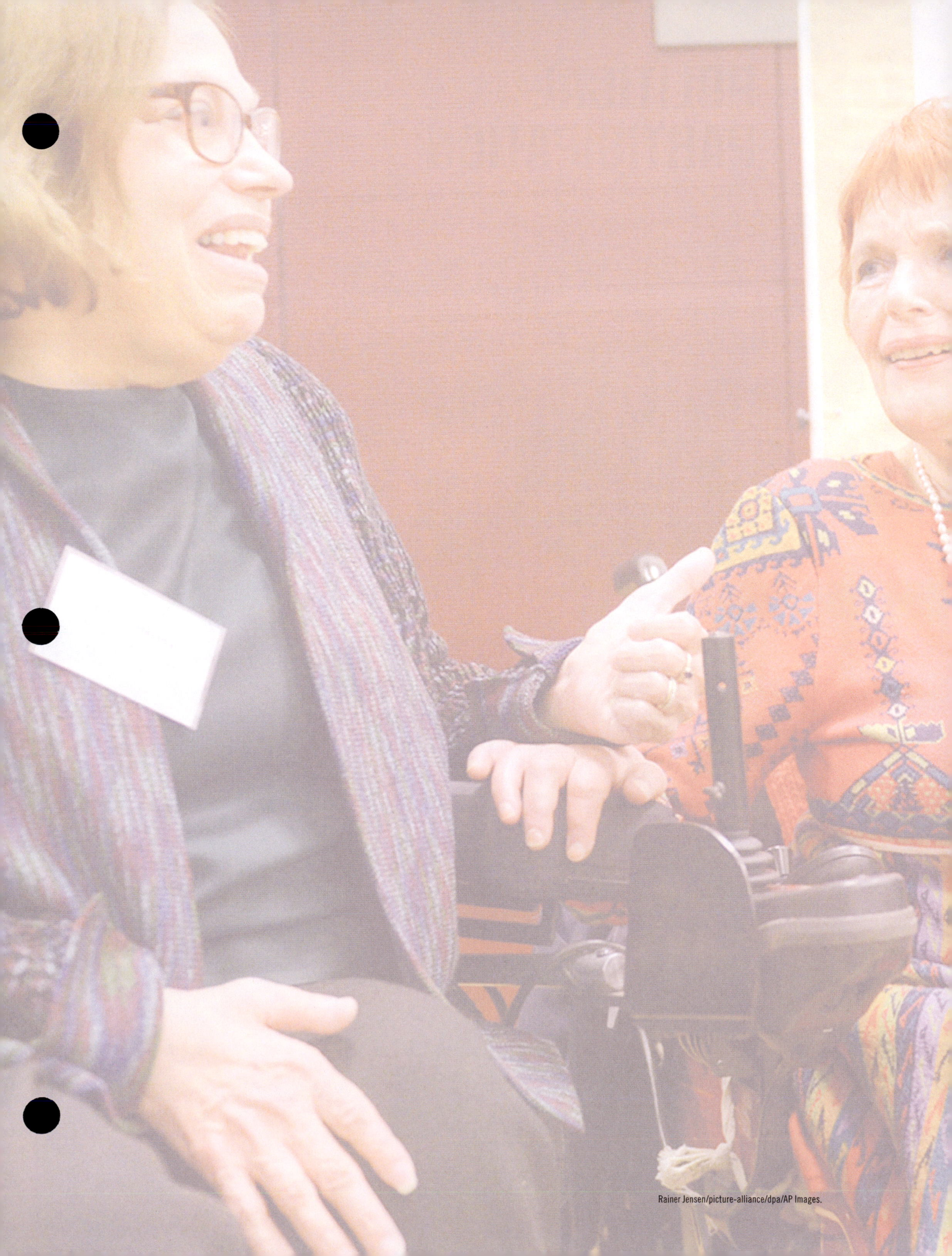

Rainer Jensen/picture-alliance/dpa/AP Images.

CHAPTER 6

POLITICAL PARTICIPATION

Carry That Weight[1]

Daniel Petty/The Denver Post via Getty Images

▲ Amanda Collins became an activist for campus carry legislation and a spokesperson for gun rights after being sexually assaulted on her campus. Here she urges the Nevada legislature to support a bill that would allow individuals with concealed carry permits to bring weapons onto state university and college campuses.

By its nature, representative democracy requires action. It cannot survive without it. Representatives act in the space of government to enact their constituents' concerns and preferences in the laws and policies of a nation. For their part, citizens must act to make their wishes known. They must find candidates they feel good about supporting and help those candidates achieve political office; they must also hold those representatives accountable after they are elected. In addition, individuals must rally others to their causes and speak as a member of a group rather than as a lone voice in the political wilderness. But how? What tools can people use to accomplish all of these weighty goals? That is where **political participation** comes in. Through its many avenues, people act to shape the laws and policies of the nation.

Political participation in a representative democracy can take many forms. One of them is voting in an election, which may seem kind of obvious. Participating as a voter is critical to the health of a representative democracy and acts, as James Madison noted, as a counterweight to the dangers of faction. As we will explore, however, many Americans do not vote. The decision to go to the polling place (or not) is often connected to a set of individual factors and lived experiences. Level of educational attainment, racial and ethnic identity, economic background, political beliefs, sex, and age play a big role in who votes. Institutional factors matter as well; some states make it easier to vote than others, some make it harder. Young adult Americans are one group that is consistently underrepresented at the voting booth, for reasons that are both individual and institutional.

But does this nonparticipation in the voting booth *have* to mean that young adult Americans are consistently underrepresented in American government? Not necessarily. While it is true that members of this generation vote at lower rates than members of older generations, they also participate in government through other

By reading this chapter, you will be able to do the following:

6.1 Consider the many forms of political participation that individuals may undertake and the ways in which participation on one issue may also involve actions on other issues.

6.2 Describe the traditional and nontraditional forms of political participation in American representative democracy.

6.3 Identify individual, legal, and election-specific factors affecting voter turnout.

6.4 Consider the ways in which acting in one space may lead others to act as well, including elected representatives.

6.5 Evaluate the ways in which political participation by young adult Americans may challenge traditional assumptions.

methods, such as volunteering, protesting, organizing, and other means made possible by modern communications technologies.

There is a universe of potential stories through which we might examine American political participation in the twenty-first century. In this chapter, we will engage primarily with difficult stories told by survivors of sexual violence on college campuses and their allies, and we will examine the different ways they have harnessed the American political process to make real change.

In doing so, we will consider the many forms that political participation may take as well as the factors that lead individuals to choose to, or choose not to, engage in them. Most fundamentally, we will also explore the *fluidity* of participation. One individual's acts in one political space may lead them to act in other spaces or on other issues. Acting may lead others to participate as well. It may place issues and challenges on the radar of national consciousness, and it may cause elected representatives to take notice.

TWO PERSPECTIVES ON CAMPUS CARRY OF FIREARMS IN RESPONSE TO SEXUAL VIOLENCE ON COLLEGE CAMPUSES

- **Consider the many forms of political participation that individuals may undertake and the ways in which participation on one issue may also involve actions on other issues.**

In March 2012, Amanda Collins offered her testimony before the Michigan State Senate. It was not the first time that Collins had testified, nor would it be the last. In her statement, Collins claimed

political participation
the different ways in which individuals take action to shape the laws and policies of a government.

the right for women to legally carry firearms on college and university campuses for their own protection. Collins stated, "My name is Amanda Collins. . . . I am going to share with you my experience of being denied my right to participate in my own self-defense, how my situation could have had a drastically different outcome, and why I have such strong convictions regarding this particular legislation."[2]

In her written remarks, Collins described her rape at gunpoint in a campus parking garage in 2007, while she was a student at the University of Nevada, Reno: "Heading towards my car I surveyed under and around my vehicle to make sure it was safe to approach. . . . I was confident I had just aced my exam and anxious to call my boyfriend who I knew would be my fiancé in a matter of days. . . . The terror I felt in those moments continued to haunt me for the next thirteen months, while my attacker remained at large, in ways that only other rape survivors can understand."[3]

The rapist was later arrested and convicted for his attack on Collins and two other women. He had raped and kidnapped another woman after his assault on Collins and raped and murdered another woman after that.

Collins's testimony was in support of a state bill that would allow individuals with concealed carry weapons (CCW) permits to carry their licensed firearms in areas in which they are typically prohibited, such as on college campuses. Collins had undergone the training, certification, and background checks necessary to obtain a CCW license. Her rapist had not. By law, Collins could not carry on campus.[4] She had been unarmed when she was assaulted. According to Collins,

I was raped less than 100 feet away from their campus police office, on the same floor where they park their cruisers. I was twenty-two-years-old when I faced my worst fear, defenseless. I never thought in my wildest dreams I would find myself in such a situation. Allowing law abiding adults to carry their permitted concealed weapons in all areas on campus can protect other potential victims from experiencing the loss and heartbreak that both my family and I have endured.

Jim Young/AFP/Getty Images

▲ Annette Harris (left) gets a "high five" after successfully completing the shooting portion of her concealed carry certification test at the Eagle Sports gun range in Oak Forest, Illinois, July 2017.

All I wanted was a chance to be able to defend myself and being able to carry that night would have given me that chance. I believe the choice to participate in one's own defense should be left to the individual. . . . I obeyed the law and left my firearm at home in order to avoid possible expulsion from school and losing my CCW permit. . . . I view concealed carry as, "the ultimate choice" for a woman. Women talk about not allowing the government to mandate what goes on inside their bodies, but then some women are willing to allow their self-protection to be arbitrated by a third party. I am not one of those women who is comfortable entrusting my protection to another person.[5]

Collins's political action did not stop with newspaper editorials and testimony before state legislatures. "After her assault," Collins "helped found the group, Women for Concealed Carry, which frames concealed carry as a victim's rights issue."[6] She is also featured on the website of a major national gun rights interest group, the National Rifle Association (NRA), on its page titled "NRA Women: Refuse to Be a Victim."

Other concealed carry advocacy groups have found ways to encourage young women to participate as well. As part of their Campus Leadership Program, members of the conservative Washington,

DC–based nonprofit Leadership Institute posted an instructional video on YouTube called "Strong Women Fight Back." In it, the video's creators give campus concealed carry proponents advice on how to host a self-defense or concealed carry activism event on campus, including suggestions to invite "other like-minded groups" to participate in the event and to "always have a camera ready" as "this project will be highly controversial."[7]

The efforts of Collins and other CCW activists have met with some success in recent years. In 2018, more than ten state legislatures were considering changing their laws to permit campus carry. Nevada assemblywoman Michele Fiore, who was sponsoring a campus carry bill in her state, argued, "The sexual assaults that are occurring would go down once these sexual predators get a bullet in their head."[8] Texas began allowing concealed carry on its college campuses in August 2016. Kansas, Arkansas, and Georgia have since followed suit. (See Figure 6.1.)

Advocating for CCW laws isn't the only possible avenue that politically motivated people can take toward solving the problem of sexual assault on campus. Indeed, some believe that carrying a concealed weapon could potentially do more to harm women than to help them, and there is some evidence to support that view. In a study reviewing survey data covering more than four thousand incidents of the use of firearms in self-defense in crimes in the nation between 2007 and 2011, two researchers from the Harvard School of Public Health challenged the effectiveness of self-defense gun use (SDGU). They concluded that "[c]ompared to other protective actions, the National Crime Victimization Surveys provide little evidence that SDGU is uniquely beneficial in reducing the likelihood of injury or property loss."[9]

▼ FIGURE 6.1

Campus Concealed Carry Policies by State

- ■ Concealed guns allowed by law
- ■ Concealed guns allowed by law, but schools limit locations/who carries
- ■ Concealed guns on campus prohibited by law
- ■ Schools decide weapons policy
- ■ Concealed guns allowed only in locked cars in parking lots

Source: "Guns on Campus: Laws for Public Colleges and Universities," Armed Campuses, www.armedcampuses.org. Courtesy of the Campaign to Keep Guns Off Campus (http://keepgunsoffcampus.org).

Others challenged the effectiveness of campus carry as a deterrent to campus sexual violence. Collins herself was subjected to intense questioning about this issue during her testimony in support of a proposed CCW measure in Colorado in 2013. State senator Evie Hudack (D-Westminster) told Collins that "chances are that if you would have had a gun, then he would have been able to get that from you and possibly use it against you." To Collins, these comments were extremely disturbing. She said, "I had a hard time falling asleep because I couldn't stop thinking about what she said to me."[10]

Researchers point to other factors in campus sexual violence that potentially make CCW a problematic solution. Most campus sexual assaults occur between individuals who know each other and in situations where access to a firearm might not be a realistic option once an assault has begun. According to John D. Foubert, Oklahoma State University professor and president of One in Four, an organization devoted to raising awareness of and combatting campus sexual violence, "If you have a rape situation, usually it starts with some sort of consensual behavior, and by the time it switches to nonconsensual, it would be nearly impossible to run for a gun."[11] There is also the concern that college students, "with high rates of binge drinking and other recklessness, would be particularly prone to gun accidents."[12] To some opponents of CCW, preventing sexual violence on campuses is more effectively carried out through campus awareness training and campus security personnel.

The debate over the effectiveness of campus carry takes place amid a much larger national debate about firearms in American society and regulations surrounding their use and ownership. In 2018, in response to school shootings such as one in a high school in Parkland, Florida, in February—in which seventeen students were killed—students in high schools and colleges across the nation rallied to protest for more state and federal restrictions on firearms. Others, though fewer in number, rallied in support of Americans' firearms rights under the Second Amendment to the Constitution. Politicians at the state and local level offered policies aimed at tackling the issue of school shootings, whether through firearms restrictions or in more effective screening of individuals with mental health issues when issuing licenses to own or carry firearms. The National Rifle Association filed a lawsuit to challenge legislation passed in Florida in response to the shootings that banned ownership of certain devices, called bump-stocks, used to increase the rate of fire for semiautomatic rifles.

One point of view shared by both CCW opponents and supporters, however, is that the American higher educational system is failing students on college campuses in its handling of sexual assault. Schools are failing to take adequate steps to prevent sexual violence in the first place, failing to adequately report incidents, and failing to handle the long-term consequences for those affected. According to Katherine Whitney, director of Women for Concealed Carry, "There seems to be kind of a dichotomy in this discussion where people assume either campus carry should be legalized or college campuses should take steps to reduce campus assault. . . . It should be both. We need colleges to acknowledge that campus assault happens, and we need administrators to do everything they can to prevent victimization."[13]

▲ Landen Gambill, a sophomore at the University of North Carolina at Chapel Hill, speaks to reporters at a campus rally in 2013. In addition to speaking out about university policy on handling campus sexual assault incidents, Gambill opposed the policy of allowing campus carry of firearms.

Travis Long/Raleigh News & Observer/MCT via Getty Images

In 2013, Landen Gambill, a student at the University of North Carolina at Chapel Hill, filed a federal civil rights complaint against her university over its handling of her sexual assault complaint. The university's adjudication process found her rapist guilty of harassment rather than sexual misconduct—a much less serious offense—and he was allowed to return to campus after a suspension.[14] Gambill later asserted that part of the university's decision to go with the lesser charge was based on the fact that she and her rapist had been in a relationship.

Gambill was threatened with expulsion for making public her experience, though she did so without naming her alleged rapist directly. She had chosen to have the university adjudicate her sexual assault complaint rather than filing a criminal or civil complaint in court, a decision she later regretted. As she told the crowd at a 2013 rally, "I have been treated with great injustice, but there are so many other survivors who have been treated just as poorly as I have and even worse. . . . I have so many heartbreaking stories. Stories of survivors who have been blamed, shamed, ignored, and silenced by this university. . . . I refuse to step back and watch survivors be called crazy sluts and liars."[15]

We will return to the efforts of Gambill and other survivors to use the legal system to force schools to change how they handle and adjudicate sexual assault complaints later in the chapter. Legal action, however, was not the only way in which Gambill chose to participate in the American political process. She also circulated a petition to multiple state legislatures arguing against allowing campus carry. For Gambill, the fact that her attacker repeatedly harassed and attacked her would have made her much less safe had he been allowed to carry a firearm on campus:

> Recently, lawmakers in thirteen states have introduced bills to overturn bans on guns in college campuses. They claim arming students is the key to curbing the epidemic of rape on campus.
>
> As a survivor, I know the opposite to be true. The rationale behind these bills rests on the myth that most people are raped by strangers; however, the vast majority of survivors of sexual assault, including myself, know their rapist. In fact, the presence of guns is proven to exacerbate violence against victims, not prevent it.
>
> If my rapist had a gun at school, I have no doubt I would be dead. That's why I started this petition asking legislators in these states not to allow guns on campuses and put survivors like me in even more danger.[16]

In this section, we have studied the political action taken by survivors of campus sexual violence, all acting in the political space to make college campuses safer. They advocated very different policy positions on the right of college students to carry a firearm. As we will explore, the right to carry is only one of the many issues associated with sexual safety on college campuses. Unfortunately, the testimonies of Amanda Collins and Landen Gambill will not be the last we will have to thoughtfully consider. Should campus carry be allowed or not? Will it reduce sexual assaults, or might it increase them or lead to a rise in gun-related deaths and accidental discharges? As these policies are so new, we cannot answer these questions with complete certainty, and this book will not attempt to do so. Instead, the goal will be to help provide students with the tools to critically examine the issues surrounding campus sexual assault policies and the ways in which those issues might be successfully addressed.

Ralph Barrera/Austin American-Statesman via AP

◀ Protesters at the University of Texas gather to oppose the passage of a new state law that in August 2016 expanded the rights of concealed handgun license holders to carry their weapons on public college campuses. Schools can, however, designate limited gun-free zones.

The efforts of these women and their supporters—all of which are examples of political participation—represent only a few of the many ways individuals undertake action to shape the laws and public policies of the nation. In this chapter, we will engage with the critical and difficult issue of political participation to end sexual violence on college campuses. In doing so, we will come to understand that political participation can and does extend far beyond the voting booth and that its many possible forms are often not separate and distinct things. One form of participation may lead an individual to act in other political spaces, or it may shape the actions of actors in other venues. We will also learn from strong individuals whose efforts to call attention to the crisis of sexual violence and make lasting political change are helping to carry the necessary weight of political participation in a representative democracy.

WHAT HAVE I LEARNED?

1. Those who argue against the effectiveness of campus carry as a sexual violence prevention tool on college campuses focus on _____.

   a. the fact that individual ownership of firearms off campus is currently illegal in most states

   b. a consensus that colleges and universities have already been successful in addressing the issue of sexual violence

   c. the inability of states to constitutionally set firearms use and ownership policies

   d. the possibility that it might actually endanger the lives of sexual assault victims

2. What forms of political participation did Amanda Collins and Landen Gambill use to advance their different beliefs about carrying a concealed weapon on campus?

3. What other forms of political participation might individuals employ to address the problem of campus sexual violence?

Answer Key: 1. d; 2. Answers might include newspaper editorials, speaking in public and to reporters, and testifying before state legislative bodies or using the legal system to force change; 3. Answers might include supporting candidates focusing on the issue in their campaigns, educating peers, or using social media to help organize for change.

POLITICAL PARTICIPATION CAN TAKE MANY FORMS

- **Describe the traditional and nontraditional forms of political participation in American representative democracy.**

While Americans often equate political participation with voting, and for good reason, casting a ballot is only one of many forms that political participation can take. While voting serves to choose elected representatives, other forms of participation may serve to influence the choices of those in office and the attitudes and actions of other citizens. Some believe these other forms may not have received enough attention from scholars of American politics. According to Sidney Verba, Kay Lehman Schlozman, and Henry E. Brady, "Studies of political participation traditionally have begun with—and too often ended with—the vote. Although voting is an important mode of citizen involvement in political life, it is but one of many political acts."[17]

In their foundational study of American political participation, Sidney Verba and Norman H. Nie sorted acts of political engagement into four categories: (1) voting, (2) supporting or participating in political campaigns, (3) contacting or pressuring politicians in office, and (4) acting outside the electoral process—for example, by volunteering or organizing in concert with fellow citizens.[18] The first two of these forms of participation take place within the electoral process; the second two take place after its outcomes have been determined or outside of it. (See Figure 6.2.) Within the electoral process, individuals may choose to vote. They may act to support candidates for office during the electoral process. Outside the electoral process, according to this framework, individuals may join with others to influence political outcomes and governmental policies, and they may choose to contact elected officials once in office.

Categories of Political Participation

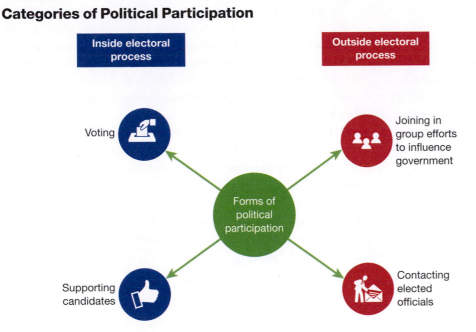

In the twenty-first century, individuals have many tools with which to initiate contact with their elected representatives. Apart from contacting them directly, individuals may testify at congressional hearings, organize petitions to state or federal lawmakers, or encourage and help others to do so. The key question, of course, is how much actual influence individuals have in voicing their individual preferences to elected officials in the presence of powerful groups with closer connections to the inside of the political process.

▼ FIGURE 6.3

Participation in Campaigns

Questions: Which if any did you do during the most recent election?

- Talk to other people to persuade them to vote for a particular party or candidate
- Show your support for a particular party or candidate by, for example, attending a meeting or putting up a poster, or in some other way

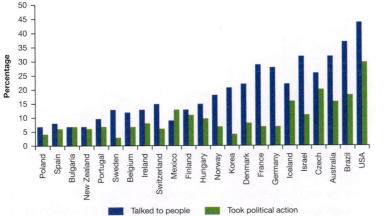

Source: Data from Steven Weldon and Russell Dalton, "Democratic Structures and Democratic Participation: The Limits of Consensualism Theory," *Elections and Democracy*, ed. Jacques Thomassen (New York: Oxford University Press, 2014), Table 7.1, "Levels of Political Participation."

▼ FIGURE 6.4

Americans' Participation in Elections outside the Voting Booth

Percent of respondents who reported having been involved in the following activities during the past year.

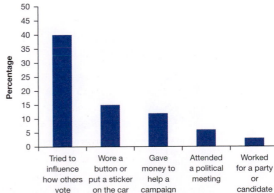

Source: American National Election Study, "Political Involvement and Participation in Politics," 2012, http://electionstudies.org/nesguide/gd-index.htm.

While Americans of voting age participate in elections at lower rates than members of other democratic societies, they remain highly active in participatory activities, such as volunteer work or interacting with members of their communities. These activities tend to involve interacting with others to influence votes.

Individuals might also join together to work cooperatively for a shared set of political goals. They may, for example, undertake volunteer work, help to organize members of their community, or work with members of their religious communities. They may use social media to reach out to others, encourage them to act on political issues, or learn more about key issues and ways to become involved in them. Individuals may join with others in organized interest groups, whose collective efforts may try to change policies from the inside or outside. They may join together by taking part in a social movement, which occurs when a group of people come together to make social and political change and place ideas and issues on the political agenda and make their voices heard. In doing so, however, individuals must consider the degree to which these efforts will lead to actual changes in governmental policies. We will turn to these questions in Chapter 10 with a focus on how insiders and outsiders mobilized to protect their interests in the aftermath of the 2008 financial crisis and growing economic inequality in the United States.

Most fundamentally, when participating in any of the diverse forms of political action, Americans express their commitment to **civic engagement**, which is working to make society better through political and nonpolitical action. While Americans participate at the voting booth at lower rates than individuals in other democracies, their rates of nonelectoral participation are equal to or higher than their counterparts in other nations.[19] (See Figures 6.3 and 6.4.)

AMERICANS' CIVIC ENGAGEMENT CAN BE FLUID

While it is useful to consider various forms of civic engagement as distinct things—especially since it helps us think about political involvement in ways that do not only include voting—in reality, the process is much more fluid than that. Consider the issue of sexual violence on college campuses, for example. Individuals may undertake any one of these various forms of participation and civic engagement. They may also undertake more than one form, either at the outset of their involvement

civic engagement
working to improve society through political and nonpolitical action.

▼ FIGURE 6.5

The Fluidity of Political Engagement: An Example

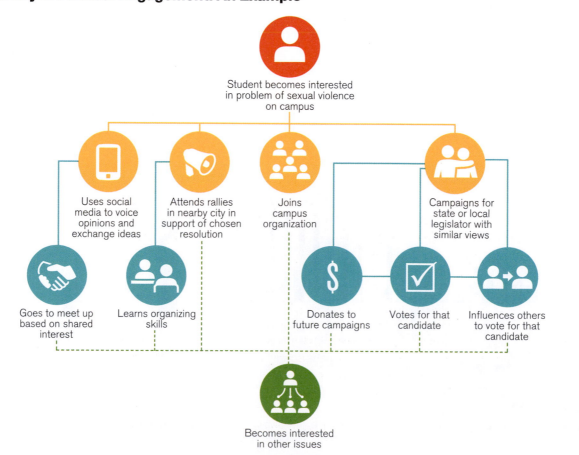

Student becomes interested in problem of sexual violence on campus

Uses social media to voice opinions and exchange ideas

Attends rallies in nearby city in support of chosen resolution

Joins campus organization

Campaigns for state or local legislator with similar views

Goes to meet up based on shared interest

Learns organizing skills

Donates to future campaigns

Votes for that candidate

Influences others to vote for that candidate

Becomes interested in other issues

or because of their experience with the political process along the way. Their involvement might encourage others to do so.

In considering all of this, we also need to think about the flip side: *not acting*. We will explore voting and nonvoting in more detail in the next section. However, it is important to note that individuals may choose to act in one space precisely because they have decided that acting in certain spaces will not lead to real change. Political scientists have wrestled with this issue, especially on the degree to which individuals may opt to act in one space as a result of feeling powerless in another venue *or* on the possibility that one form of participation may lead to a withdrawal from others or even a dissatisfaction with the democratic electoral process itself. While research debates continue, the idea that participation in protests constitute an "anti-politics" or "anti–formal politics" highlights the interconnectedness of avenues of political participation in ways that are not always neat and clear.[20]

WHAT HAVE I **LEARNED**?

1. Working to make society better through political and nonpolitical action is often called _____.

   a. direct political contact

   b. civic engagement

   c. protest

   d. political recruitment

2. What are some examples of forms of political participation outside the voting booth?

3. If you have participated in the political process within or outside the voting booth, how effective do you think it is in making political change?

_____

Answer Key: 1. b; 2. Answers might include volunteering, communicating with officials, or participating in protests or social movements; 3. Answers should focus on the degree to which students perceive that a given form of participation translates into changes in laws or policies.

THE DECISION TO VOTE OR NOT VOTE INVOLVES MANY FACTORS

- Identify individual, legal, and election-specific factors affecting voter turnout.

When Americans consider the concept of political participation, they often think about voting, and for many good reasons. Participation in the electoral process is an essential component of a representative democracy. Voting gives expression to individuals' voices and serves to hold elected representatives accountable for their promises and actions. It is foundational to what James Madison called the "Democratic Remedy" to the dangers of faction and the tyranny of the minority that we examined in Chapter 2.

The fact, however, is that large percentages of Americans do not vote. In 2016, a presidential election year, only an estimated 58 percent of eligible voters showed up at the polls, placing the United States near the bottom of democratic nations based on **voter turnout** (see the Practicing Political Science feature, page 164). Turnout in midterm elections is even lower. In 2014, roughly 36 percent of eligible voters cast ballots, continuing a trend of decline decades in the making and marking the lowest level of voter turnout since 1942, when the nation was involved in a global war.[21] The trend is unmistakable. Americans' relative lack of voting participation raises two immediate questions: Why? And, does it matter?

For Anthony Downs, writing in 1957, the decision not to vote might very well be a rational one, given the costs of voting in terms of an individual's time and intellectual effort and the infinitesimally small probability that any one vote will prove to be decisive, especially in national elections. According to Downs, "It may be rational for a [person] to delegate part or all of his political decision-making to others, no matter how important it is that [they] make correct decisions,"[22] a conclusion with which other political scientists have agreed. In the view of democratic theorists, however, should all potential voters make a rational calculation not to vote, then the mechanism of representation would be endangered.

voter turnout
the number of eligible voters who actually participate in an election versus the total number of eligible voters.

COMPARING AMERICAN VOTER TURNOUT WITH THAT OF OTHER NATIONS

Votes Cast in OECD Countries' Recent National Elections as a Percentage of Registered Voters and Voting Age Population

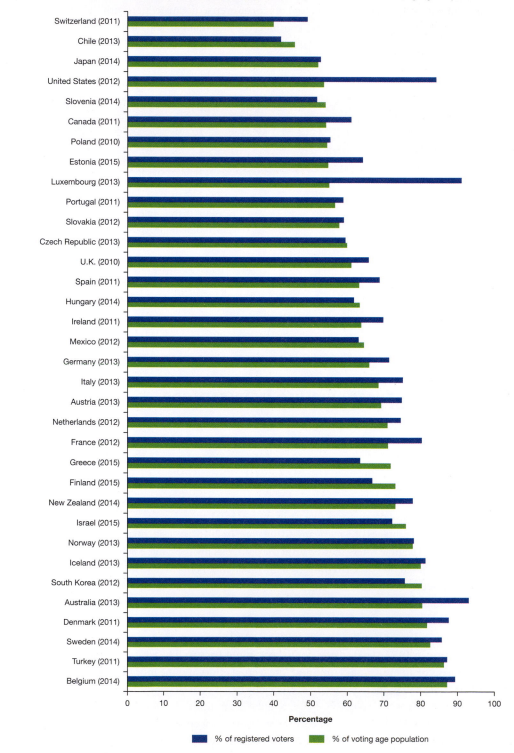

Percentage

■ % of registered voters   ■ % of voting age population

Source: Pew Research Center, "U.S. Voter Turnout Trails Most Developed Countries," August 2016, http://www.pewresearch.org/fact-tank/2016/08/02/u-s-voter-turnout-trails-most-developed-countries/.

n May 2015, the Pew Research Center published a graphic depicting voter turnout in national elections in member nations of the Organisation for Economic Co-operation and Development (OECD) since 2010. As is clear, voter turnout in the United States lagged behind that of almost all of its peer nations.[23]

Clearly, in terms of national voter turnout, the percentage of the voting-age population that voted in recent national elections (the green bars) in the United States is far below that of most other members of the OECD. What is going on? We will examine many of the contributors to this gap in this chapter. For now, however, notice the blue bars, which depict voter turnout as a percentage of registered voters. By that measure, voter turnout in the United States does not appear to be so different from the others and in fact leads most nations.

Voting age and *registered voters* are two very different terms. Large numbers of voting-age Americans are not voting eligible. Undocumented Americans as well as Americans convicted of felonies (in many states) are not allowed to vote. The numbers of individuals who are not allowed to vote because of a felony conviction—a large percentage of whom have been convicted for drug offenses—have grown dramatically in recent decades. In 2010, it was estimated that nearly six million Americans were denied the right to vote because of felony convictions.[24]

WHaT Do You Think?

Are you registered to vote? Are your friends and fellow students? If not, what are the barriers to registration that you or those close to you face in doing so? What policies might be enacted to make it easier for unregistered voting-age Americans to register for the vote?

INDIVIDUAL FACTORS SHAPE ELECTORAL PARTICIPATION

Many factors shape a person's decision of whether or not to vote. Some contributors to voter turnout are institutional, shaped by the laws and procedures surrounding the electoral process. Others depend upon the particulars of an election—for example, whether or not it takes place during a presidential election year. A third category of contributors centers on the potential voters themselves, their characteristics and lived experiences. Later in the book, we will examine how individual characteristics impact *how* people vote and *whom* they choose to support. Now we will consider how these characteristics shape *whether or not* people vote. Political scientists count a set of individual factors as among the most important determinants for voting: level of economic status, level of education, age, race or ethnicity, sex, and partisan attachment.

SOCIOECONOMIC STATUS AND EDUCATIONAL ATTAINMENT. Voting is costly. It takes time, commitment, and intellectual engagement. Not all voting-eligible Americans have the same resources with which to engage in the process of voting.[25] A key factor in voter turnout is an individual's **socioeconomic status (SES)**, which is a measure of an individual's wealth, income, occupation, and educational attainment.

A clear and consistent pattern in electoral participation is that Americans with higher levels of SES participate in electoral activities. There are several reasons for this, but the central idea is that individuals with higher incomes might have more money to donate to a political campaign. Also, certain occupations might be associated with networks in which political issues are more likely to be discussed and acted upon.

The most important contributor to the measure of an individual's SES, and one of the most important determinants of the decision to vote, is the level of educational attainment by a potential voter (Figure 6.6). Not only are higher levels of educational attainment associated with higher incomes, but they also reduce the "costs" of voting, in the sense of making it easier to navigate the issues involved in an election and the process of becoming a voter itself. While some recent research has challenged the conclusion that education attainment by itself *causes* increased political participation, the *correlation* between higher levels of educational attainment and an increased likelihood of voting is quite strong.[26]

socioeconomic status (SES)
a measure that captures an individual's wealth, income, occupation, and educational attainment.

Voting and Registration by Educational Attainment in the United States, 2014

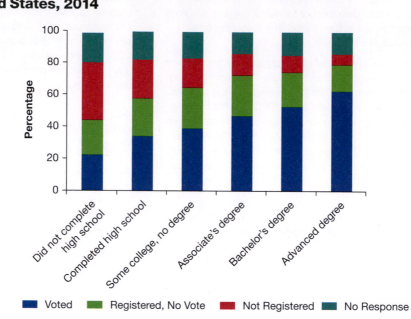

■ Voted ■ Registered, No Vote ■ Not Registered ■ No Response

Source: U.S. Census Bureau, "Voting and Registration," accessed February 16, 2016, http://thedataweb.rm.census.gov/TheDataWeb_HotReport2/voting/voting.hrml.

POLITICAL EFFICACY. Education also plays a role in shaping how individuals think about themselves as political actors and potential voters. The intellectual resources and skills that higher levels of education produce also increase an individual's sense of **political efficacy**, or one's confidence that she or he can make effective political change.

AGE. Another trend is also clear: Young adult voting-eligible Americans vote at lower rates than members of older generations (Figure 6.7).[27] Why? Again, like income and education, age is connected to many other factors. Older Americans are more likely to have higher levels of income and wealth. Another factor may be the challenges of learning about voter registration requirements, especially if the young adult voter is in college or has recently moved to a new state. For college students living in a different state, voter identification laws may add another hurdle to their decision to participate at the polling place. While a 1979 Supreme Court ruling affirmed the right of college students to vote in their states of school attendance,[28] state voting laws and local practices "often make students travel a rocky road."[29]

RACIAL AND ETHNIC IDENTITIES. The turnout of voting-age Americans is also highly correlated with racial and ethnic identity (Figure 6.8), which, again, is often connected to SES. While turnout rates between white and African American potential voters have narrowed in recent years, Latina and Latino American turnout rates lag far behind those of Americans with other racial and ethnic identities. While some Latino/a Americans are undocumented immigrants and therefore ineligible to vote, they are also as a group younger, and, as we have discussed, younger voting-eligible Americans vote in far fewer numbers than their older counterparts. As we will explore in Chapter 10, as Latino/a eligible voters grow older and grow in numbers, the political landscape is going to shift dramatically.

GENDER. Since the presidential election of 1980, women have voted at a slightly higher rate than men—typically a difference of a few percentage points.[30] Prior to 1980, voting-eligible men voted at higher rates than women. The differences between men's and women's modern voting patterns hold true

political efficacy
a person's belief that she or he can make effective political change.

Historical Patterns of Voter Turnout by Age

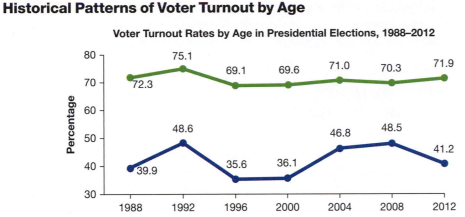

Voter Turnout Rates by Age in Presidential Elections, 1988–2012

Source: Pew Research Center, "Six Take-Aways from the Census Bureau's Voting Report," May 2013, http://www.pewresearch.org/fact-tank/2013/05/08/six-take-aways-from-the-census-bureaus-voting-report/.

Note: Date for those ages 25 to 64 not shown.

American Voter Turnout in Midterm Elections by Racial and Ethnic Identity

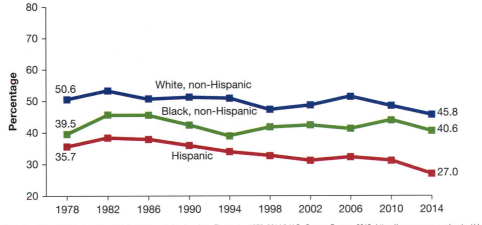

Source: Thom File, "Who Votes? Congressional Elections and the American Electorate: 1978–2014," U.S. Census Bureau, 2015, https://www.census.gov/content/dam/Census/library/publications/2015/demo/p20-577.pdf.

across racial and ethnic identities, with the largest percentage difference between black men and women, which was 9.5 percent in the 2016 presidential election. Differences in voter turnout in recent elections between men and women are also connected with age, as a higher percentage of women ages eighteen to seventy-four voted than men in the same age cohort, while men seventy-five and up voted at higher rates than women within the same age group.

PARTISAN ATTACHMENT. The degree to which an individual identifies with a political party also factors into not only the vote choices that individual makes but also the decision of whether to vote or not. Individuals with a stronger attachment to a political party are more likely to vote than those without one.[31] Efforts by members of American political parties to turn out the vote matter as well, and individuals with strong partisan attachment may find themselves more likely to be on the receiving end of party activities. **Political mobilization**, such as efforts to "get out the vote"

political mobilization
efforts by members of American political parties to turn out the vote and encourage their members to get others to do so.

(GOTV), can be decisive in an election. These efforts may be direct—recruitment, sponsorship of meetings, or requests for contributions—or indirect, such as in the building of social networks through which potential voters engage with their friends and associates.[32] We will discuss the role of political parties in mobilization, along with other critical roles that they play in the electoral process, in Chapter 9.

LEGAL AND INSTITUTIONAL FACTORS ENABLE AND CONSTRAIN VOTER TURNOUT

Other factors that affect voter turnout are not individual but rather systemic or institutional. Since the ratification of the Twenty-sixth Amendment to the Constitution in 1971, all American citizens eighteen years old or older have been guaranteed the right of **suffrage**. The practical exercise of this basic right, however, is complicated. As noted above, undocumented American immigrants are not granted the right of suffrage, and, in most states, otherwise eligible voters who have been convicted of felonies are also denied the right to vote in what is called **felon disenfranchisement**, though the time of their loss of this right varies according to state laws.

State **registration requirements** may also help or hinder the ability of voting-age Americans to participate in the electoral process. Voting actually involves two actions. The second is the casting of a ballot on an Election Day. But the first is the act of registering to vote. In some states, a voter may register on Election Day. In most states, however, would-be voters need to register prior to the election, often as many as thirty days before; otherwise they will not be allowed to vote.[33]

In addition, in order to register to vote, Americans need to show identification and/or proof of residency in their state. About 16 percent of states require a photo identification in order to vote. Others require another form of documentation of residency, and some accept a vouching of residency by another registered voter. Even in states that allow same-day registration, however, residency requirements may serve to disenfranchise certain Americans, such as the homeless, who may lack documentation such as utility bills that can serve to document state residency. (See Figure 6.9 for voter registration requirements by state.)

As state legislatures debate bills requiring identification at the polling place, college students are one, but not the only, group of voting-eligible Americans potentially disenfranchised by these current and proposed laws. Across the nation, state lawmakers continue to debate whether or not a college student should be able to use her or his ID as proof of residency in voter registration, especially if he or she attends a private college or university. When such policies were being debated in Texas, Natalie Butler, a graduate and former student government president of the University of Texas at Austin, spoke out against a state law that prohibited the use of school IDs as proof of residence. She especially noted the law's impact on participation in local elections, stating, "If we're going to make it even harder for students to impact city politics, that's a huge problem."[34]

The scheduling of national presidential and congressional elections, by tradition held on the first Tuesday after the first Monday of November, may also serve to discourage participation, as work schedules may make it more challenging for some Americans to make it to the polling place. Although states are increasingly allowing voters to cast **absentee ballots**, some reformers have proposed that national elections be held on weekends or that Election Day be declared a national holiday.

Finally, some advocates of electoral reform have focused on the process of registration itself, hoping to make it easier and less costly in terms of time and energy. In contrast to most modern representative democracies, in the United States the burden of registering to vote falls entirely on the potential voter, and there is no governmental action to register them automatically. The National Voter Registration Act of 1993, commonly called the **Motor Voter Law**, tried to make voter registration less difficult by allowing Americans to register to vote when applying for or renewing their driver's licenses and making it easier for

suffrage
the right to vote in political elections.

felon disenfranchisement
the denial of voting rights to Americans who have been convicted of felonies.

registration requirements
the set of rules that govern who can vote and how, when, and where they vote.

absentee ballots
votes completed and submitted by a voter prior to the day of an election.

Motor Voter Law
a law allowing Americans to register to vote when applying for or renewing their driver's licenses and making it easier for Americans with disabilities to register to vote.

Registration Requirements: Voter Identification and Forms of Registration by State

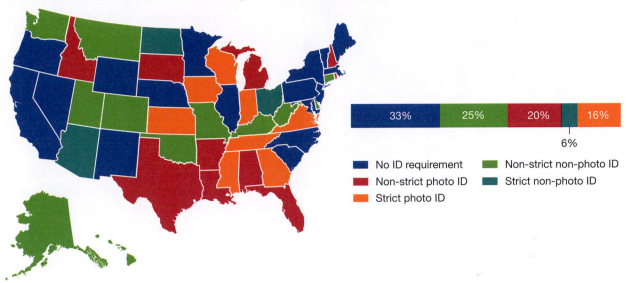

State Requirements for Photo Identification

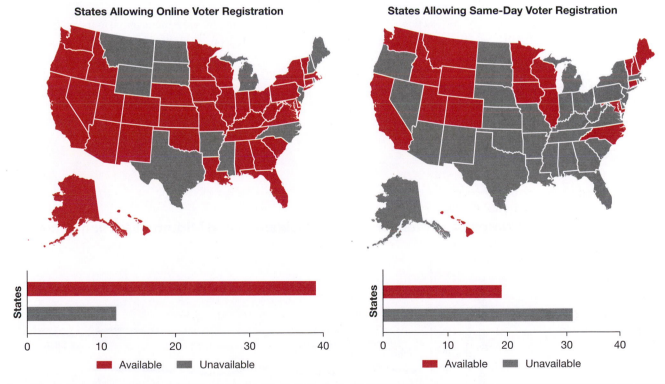

States Allowing Online Voter Registration

States Allowing Same-Day Voter Registration

Sources: "Voter Identification Laws by State," Ballotpedia, 2018, https://ballotpedia.org/Voter_identification_laws_by_state; "Same-Day Voter Registration," Ballotpedia, 2018, https://ballotpedia.org/Same-day_voter_registration; "Online Voter Registration," Ballotpedia, 2018, https://ballotpedia.org/Online_voter_registration.

Americans with disabilities to register to vote. As of 2018, thirty-eight states and the District of Columbia had established systems of online voter registration.[35] While effective online registration requires efforts to make the process secure and free from fraud, it offers the promise of increasing turnout.

ELECTION-SPECIFIC FACTORS ALSO AFFECT VOTER TURNOUT

Also contributing to the level of voter turnout in a given election are factors surrounding the election itself. If it is a presidential election year, then voters will turn out in higher numbers than if it is not (Figure 6.10). Media coverage and the use of media by candidates and their supporters in a given election may also impact voter turnout. As is the case with the effects of educational attainment on voter turnout, there remains a debate in political science about the effects of negative campaign advertisements on voter attitudes and behavior. One set of research advances the argument that negative campaign ads discourage voting while another argues that it may, in fact, encourage turnout. One possible answer to the lack of consensus may involve the methods that political scientists have used to study the effects of negative campaign ads. Studies using experimental settings have tended to find that ads discourage voting, while those that rely on studies of surveys have often concluded that negative campaigns may actually encourage voter turnout.[36] We will explore the use of surveys and the challenges of measuring what Americans think and know about politics in Chapter 7.

Finally, an "election" is not really one election. It is many. When Americans go to the polls, they are often confronted with a long list of choices that, depending on the election parameters, can include the president, members of Congress, state legislature positions, state judges, county supervisors, and members of a water resource board. **Ballot roll-off** refers to the fact that voters may often not complete the entire ballot; they may stop once they reach a set of races with which they are not familiar and for which they may not have traditional cues, such as partisan affiliation.

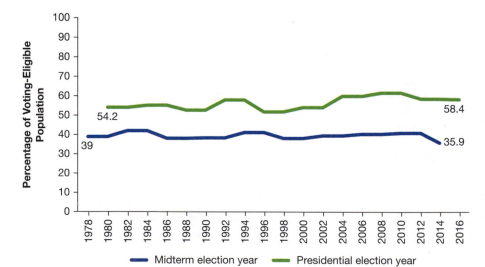

▲ Natalie Butler, former University of Texas student and advocate for the use of school IDs as acceptable proof of residency in voter registration.

Lizzie Chen/Carnegie-Knight News21.com

ballot roll-off

when voters do not cast votes for a set of races with which they are not familiar and for which they may not have traditional cues.

▼ FIGURE 6.10

Comparing Voter Turnout in Presidential and Midterm Election Years

Source: United States Elections Project, "Voter Turnout," accessed November 20, 2016, http://www.electproject.org/home/voter-turnout/voter-turnout-data.

WHAT HAVE I **LEARNED?**

1. One group of Americans with higher voter turnout rates includes _____.

   a. young adult Americans

   b. Latino/a Americans

   c. Americans with higher levels of educational attainment

   d. Americans who identify with the Democratic Party

2. Election-specific factors that affect voter turnout include _____.

   a. presidential or nonpresidential election years

   b. age

   c. level of education

   d. felon disenfranchisement

3. Why do you think Americans choose to vote or not vote?

   _____

Answer Key: 1. c; 2. a; 3. Answers might focus on demographic characteristics, election-specific factors, or thoughts about why people might feel that their voices do not matter.

ANOTHER RESPONSE TO CAMPUS SEXUAL VIOLENCE HIGHLIGHTS THE FLUIDITY OF PARTICIPATION

- **Consider the ways in which acting in one space may lead others to act as well, including elected representatives.**

At first, she chose to remain anonymous. One of three Columbia University undergraduates interviewed for a two-part article in the school's newspaper, Emma Sulkowicz shared her experiences without attribution as a survivor of a campus sexual assault in 2012. She also related her criticisms of what she saw as an inadequate, even traumatizing, university response to her reporting of the assault.[37] Later, partly out of frustration with this response, Sulkowicz went public. In an interview conducted with the *New York Times* in 2014, she recounted the assault and Columbia University's actions—or lack thereof. According to the article, "The accused, as is often the case in college, was someone she considered a friend, a man with whom she had had consensual sex twice the previous school year. The university's adjudication process, she said, left her feeling even more traumatized and unsafe. 'I've never felt more shoved under the rug in my life.'"[38]

Andrew Burton/Getty Images

▲ Columbia University senior Emma Sulkowicz carrying a mattress in protest of the university's response to her report of a sexual assault on campus during her sophomore year. Sulkowicz's protest was part of her senior thesis and was undertaken to pressure campus officials to reform school policies.

After conducting its adjudication process, the university found the accused man "not responsible." After receiving an email informing her of the school's decision, Sulkowicz recalled, "I didn't even cry at first. I don't know. Has anything ever happened to you that was just so bad that you felt like you became a shell of a human being?"[39]

A PERSONAL AND PUBLIC PROTEST CATALYZES CHANGE

Sulkowicz didn't remain numb for long, however. She took action to protest both the lack of attention paid to sexual assault incidents on college campuses and the mishandling of cases that were reported. For her senior thesis at Columbia University in 2015, Sulkowicz made her voice heard by

▲ Emma Sulkowicz with her installation piece, *Mattress Performance (Carry That Weight)*, in 2014.

combining protest and art. She created a performance art piece, *Mattress Performance (Carry That Weight)*, in which she chose to carry "a dorm bed mattress around with her wherever she goes. She'll carry it for as long as she attends the same school as her [alleged] rapist, which, as she told the *Columbia Spectator*, 'could potentially take a day . . . or it could go on until I graduate.'"[40]

Sulkowicz's protest sparked others to act. In October, as part of "Carry That Weight Day," students across the country demonstrated in support of Sulkowicz and other sexual violence survivors and in protest of how school administration officials were dealing with the crisis. Caroline DeCunzo, a student and protester at the University of Vermont, summed up one of the protesters' major goals: "I think that it's important for UVM to acknowledge that we have a sexual assault problem."[41]

In November 2014, "Columbia students carried twenty-eight mattresses around campus with messages of protest against rape and sexual assault, words of support for survivors, and demands for change to the University's sexual assault policy."[42] They called their action "Carry That Weight Day." In response, Columbia University officials announced that the students involved would be charged up to $1,500 for cleanup fees after the mattresses were dumped on the lawn of the university's president.

As part of her protest, Sulkowicz composed an installation piece in her studio on campus. In an interview for the *Washington Post*, Nato Thompson, chief curator at the New York–based arts organization Creative Time, said, "What's happening here is unique. . . . I can't think of another instance where a work of art has triggered a movement in this way."[43]

ELECTED OFFICIALS TAKE ACTION

Elected officials took notice of the efforts of Sulkowicz and other protesters during that year. In April 2014, at Columbia University, "student activists with red tape over their mouths tried to enter an event for prospective freshmen, to hand out letters encouraging the students to press university officials for details about resources available to victims of sexual assault. The next day, Senator Kirsten Gillibrand, Democrat of New York, visited Columbia to call for federal funding to improve handling of college sexual assault cases."[44]

In 2015, Senator Claire McCaskill (D-MO) introduced the Campus Accountability and Safety Act. She was joined by eleven other senators, including Gillibrand, in a bipartisan coalition. McCaskill had previously and successfully joined with other senators to address national policies on the handling of sexual assault claims in the United States Armed Forces. In a press release posted to her official website, McCaskill described the bill's intent: "With added input from survivors, students, colleges and universities, law enforcement and advocates, the bill would flip the current incentives of a broken system to provide real accountability and transparency from higher education institutions. The legislation would professionalize the response to and reporting of sexual assaults that occur on campuses to better protect and empower students, while also protecting the rights of accused students."[45]

The bill required colleges and universities to designate "confidential advisors" for student sexual violence survivors, enhance training of school personnel, make more transparent the extent of sexual violence incidents on campuses, increase coordination and uniformity of how sexual assault allegations

PRACTICING POLITICAL SCIENCE

THE USE OF IMAGES IN POLITICAL PROTEST AND MOBILIZATION

Public · Volunteering · Hosted by **Carrying the Weight Together** and **United Sta...** ★ Interested + Going ...

▲ A Facebook announcement for a 2015 protest by Carry the Weight Together calling for a national day of action.

In February 2015, the group Carry the Weight Together shared their event on Facebook: "Join us for the second national Day of Action to stand with students around the country to demand better policies to prevent and respond to gender-based violence on your campus! Hold a rally, speak out, protest, or collective carry on your campus and call on administrators to help #carrythatweight!" The image that they chose for the announcement was a simple graphic.

WHAT Do You Think?

The organizers of the protest chose a very stark and simple graphic to convey their goals and objectives. Do you think the image was effective? If you were to choose an image for organizing political action or a protest on an issue of importance to you, what images might you use?

on campuses are treated, and increase penalties for institutions that failed to uphold the new requirements.[46] Senator McCaskill's 2015 bill did not become law. As we explore in Chapter 12, the vast majority of bills introduced in Congress do not. However, she and others reintroduced it in 2017 as "The Bipartisan Campus Accountability and Safety Act." In addition to accountability measures, the current bill would establish new campus resources and support services, require minimum training for campus personnel, increase transparency in reporting of incidents of sexual violence, and stiffen penalties for schools that fail to comply with federal regulations.[47] As of the spring of 2018, the bill was under consideration in the Senate Health, Education, Labor, and Pensions Committee.

SURVIVORS ENGAGE THE POLITICAL PROCESS THROUGH TITLE IX

The actions of college students themselves helped to call lawmakers' attention to the issue of university treatment of sexual assaults. According to McCaskill, "students across the U.S. have filed complaints alleging that their universities have violated Title IX, which prohibits gender discrimination in education, by failing to prevent and respond to sexual assaults. Many administrators may be incorrectly telling female students that they're unlikely to obtain rape convictions in cases whether there's a dispute over whether sex was consensual."[48]

Sulkowicz was one of many students who had filed suit under Title IX and other federal regulations. In response to the increased focus on campus assault, many schools are now training faculty and staff on Title IX's provisions regarding sexual harassment.

Title IX refers to a section of the Educational Amendments of 1972, which modified a portion of the Civil Rights Act of 1964. Title IX states, "No person in the United States shall, on the basis of sex, be excluded from participation in, be denied the benefits of, or be subjected to discrimination under any education program or activity receiving Federal financial assistance."[49] While part of the impact of the provisions of the law increased gender equity in athletic programs in schools, it also provided a legal basis for preventing and adjudicating incidents of sexual harassment and violence in schools receiving federal funds, including colleges and universities.

In 2011, the U.S. Department of Education Office for Civil Rights issued a "Dear Colleague" letter clarifying the impact of Title IX on school policy. In it, Secretary Russlynn Ali clarified that compliance with Title IX requires schools to issue a notification of nondiscrimination, designate an employee to handle claims of sexual harassment or sexual violence, and institute procedures to investigate, adjudicate, and resolve incidents.[50] In response, colleges and universities have established procedures for compliance and have put in place training for faculty, administrators, and staff to identify incidents of sexual harassment and sexual violence, inform their students of the support procedures and institutions in place, and assist students who wish to inform teachers, teachers' assistants, or staff of an incident of sexual harassment or violence. In 2014, the Office issued a memorandum clarifying that transgender students are, under the protections of Title IX, to be treated "consistent with their gender identity" in single-sex classes and extracurricular activities.[51]

Title IX
a section of a 1972 federal law that prohibited discrimination on the basis of sex in any educational programs or activities.

▲ Senators Kirsten Gillibrand (D-NY), left, and Claire McCaskill (D-MO), right, led a bipartisan group of senators supporting the Campus Safety and Accountability Act aimed at curbing rape on campus. The proposed legislation came after a Senate subcommittee survey revealed that 41 percent of 236 American colleges had conducted no investigations of alleged assaults in the last five years.

Brooks Kraft LLC/Corbis via Getty Images

Landen Gambill, whose stance against campus carry we discussed earlier in the chapter, also based her legal action against the University of North Carolina at Chapel Hill on claims under Title IX. Returning to campus for her sophomore year "with a sense of dread," Gambill began to connect with other survivors who felt that the university administration mishandled their cases as well. She wrote, "I also learned that you can file a Title IX complaint with the government when schools mishandle reports of sexual violence. Later that semester, I got together with some fellow students and filed a complaint with the Department of Education's Office for Civil Rights. An assistant dean of students joined us in the complaint—she said the school had encouraged her to under-report cases of sexual assault to the government."[52]

To Gambill, however, speaking out is not the only way that survivors can act and make change. In an interview, she said, "I always try to be clear that those who speak out are not the only heroes: Many survivors are not able to speak up for legal reasons, or due to physical or emotional threats. Surviving in and of itself is heroic."[53]

THE DEBATE REACHES THE HIGHEST LEVELS OF GOVERNMENT

In September 2014, the issue of sexual assault on campuses received national attention when President Barack Obama and Vice President Joe Biden announced the formation of the It's On Us campaign, which urges men and women to commit to helping solve the problem of campus sexual assault. They addressed the topic in blunt and unequivocal terms. "Society still does not sufficiently value women," the president said.[54]

As the issue of sexual violence on college campuses began to take a more prominent place on the national political agenda, contrasting voices weighed in. In responding to accusations of gender-based violence, some male college students have argued that their rights have been violated by school sexual assault procedures on the basis of Title IX. Other groups have expressed concern that the due process rights of the accused have been undermined by some overreaching university sexual harassment and assault policies.[55]

In December 2014, Senator Gillibrand offered her testimony before the Senate Judiciary Committee in support of legislation to strengthen college and university requirements in preventing and addressing sexual violence. She stated, "Young women like Emma Sulkowicz, who was raped by a fellow student at Columbia University in 2012, reported her rape to police in 2014. . . . The detective responded by telling Emma that the encounter was consensual because she'd had previous consensual sex with this individual. The officer repeatedly stated that the perpetrator just 'got a little weird that night, right?' and told her that a defense attorney would rip her story apart."[56]

In 2015, the man accused in the assault of Emma Sulkowicz and two other women on campus filed a lawsuit against Columbia University trustees, administrators, and the professor who had supervised Sulkowicz's art installation, arguing that he had been "defamed and faced gender-based discrimination, and that Columbia was negligent and breached contracts."[57] Responding to the lawsuit, especially with regard to the professor involved, Sulkowicz replied, "If artists are not allowed to make art that reflect[s] on our experiences, then how are we to heal?"[58] Columbia University officials declined to comment.[59]

INDIVIDUALS ORGANIZE TO TEACH OTHERS HOW TO PERSONALLY INTERVENE IN CAMPUS SEXUAL ASSAULTS

In this chapter, we have examined many traditional and nontraditional forms of political participation through the lens of efforts to address sexual violence on college campuses. We have encountered stories of strong individuals choosing to testify, advocate, and mobilize in support of diverse policies in the hopes of addressing and eliminating this serious issue.

These individuals are not acting alone. On many college campuses, women and men are organizing to educate and promote a tactic called *bystander intervention*, in which individuals act to diffuse potentially abusive situations before they happen. One of the largest campus bystander intervention initiatives is Green Dot. The initiative's name refers to the replacement of a red dot on a map indicating where a campus sexual assault happened with a green dot indicating where an assault did *not* happen.

Green Dot's founder, psychologist Dorothy Edwards, recounted that her research-based strategy grew out of frustration with what was not working. On the initiative's website, she wrote, "Conference after conference we sat and listened to each other present on yet another clever poster campaign, another creative one-time-only mandatory program, and another date-rape skit. There seemed to be an unspoken agreement that we would resist the urge to cry out in the middle of the presentation, 'Are you frickin' kidding me? Isn't this the exact same thing I heard 10 years ago, just with a different slogan slapped on the front?'"[60]

Central to Green Dot's strategy, as well as those of other bystander intervention programs, are education and intervention. Students are trained to spot a potentially abusive situation—say at a college party—and then step in to diffuse it, often by distracting the potential assailant. According to Greg Liautaud, a junior at Connecticut College and a member of the men's hockey team when interviewed in 2016, "You step in like that and it kind of just ends the situation. It's not really about calling someone a bad person, it's just diffusing the situation."[61] For proponents of bystander intervention, one of its greatest strengths is that "rather than treating everyone as a potential rapist or rape victim, students are treated like allies who are empowered to step in."[62]

▲ Protesters in New York City in 2011, calling attention to the need to end the shaming of rape survivors and reframe policy debates to focus on the requirement for active consent.

While a friend, teammate, or fraternity brother seeing the potential for a sexual assault and offering to take a person out for mozzarella sticks to diffuse a potentially devastating situation might not seem like an act of political participation, it is. Bystander intervention by itself, however, will not end sexual violence on college campuses. Many sexual assaults happen when there are no observers present. Many, however, see it as a useful piece to an overall strategy of combating sexual harassment and violence, and some college and university training programs now include it in their materials.

WHAT HAVE I **LEARNED?**

1. Emma Sulkowicz's protest and senior project were designed to call attention to _____.
   a. the need for legal access to firearms on college campuses
   b. increased dialogue with those accused of sexual assault
   c. the handling of sexual assault claims by university officials
   d. bystander intervention to diffuse potentially violent situations

2. What role did Title IX play in the efforts of survivors to force change in their colleges and universities?

3. In what ways were the efforts of survivors to protest and call attention to campus policy on investigating sexual assaults connected to other forms of political action?

Answer Key: 1. c; 2. Answers might focus on the connection between gender equality in the law and efforts to reform college and university processes; 3. Answers might connect protests, testimony, filing lawsuits, and responses by elected officials to these actions.

ARE YOUNG ADULT AMERICANS REALLY DISCONNECTED FROM THE POLITICAL PROCESS?

- **Evaluate the ways in which political participation by young adult Americans may challenge traditional assumptions.**

As we explored earlier in this chapter, young voting-age Americans remain chronically underrepresented in elections. Voter turnout by young adult voters has been the lowest of any age group since at least 1971, the year the Twenty-sixth Amendment to the Constitution was ratified, guaranteeing suffrage for Americans ages eighteen to twenty-one. Results from the 2016 presidential election point to a continuation of this pattern, especially in key battleground states.[63] But why? "The bottom line," according to one political science professor, "is that people generally agree that the extent to which young adults feel they have a stake in the establishment is less than the older voter."[64]

We have explored legal and institutional barriers that work against young adult voting, including state voter registration requirements, especially for students enrolled in colleges and universities outside their home states. Dissatisfaction and disassociation from the political process also likely play a role. The new generation of young adult Americans, often called *millennials*, now constitute a massive group of potential voters—the nation's largest living generation. While the specific ages that qualify as being millennial often depend on who is describing the generation, as of 2016 there were more than 75 million Americans between the ages of eighteen and thirty-four.[65]

Currently, young adult Americans do not vote at rates comparable to those of members of older generations. Of course, as we have explored, members of this generation are likely to increase their levels of electoral participation as they age. However, young adult Americans constitute a potentially very powerful voting bloc should they choose to use that nascent power.[66] The big question, however, is how, or if, this bloc will use the power of its numbers to effect political change. The jury is still out on this.

Young adult Americans today constitute a complicated generation. They are, according to a 2014 study by the Pew Research Center, "America's most racially diverse generation," and "they are relatively unattached to organized politics and religion, linked by social media, burdened by debt, distrustful of people, in no rush to marry—and optimistic about the future."[67] Half of the millennials in the survey self-identified as "political independents," a pattern that is expected to hold true during the 2018 mid-term elections as well.[68]

Their patterns of political participation are also complicated. While it is true that young adult Americans vote in lower numbers than other generations, as we have seen, they do take part in many other forms of political participation. As we will explore later in this book, students and young adult Americans have often taken the lead in protests against the treatment of African American men by law enforcement officers in political movements such as Black Lives Matter. As we will also see, members of the millennial generation have also spearheaded protests against the persistent and growing income and wealth inequality in the nation through movements such as Occupy Wall Street and by supporting outsiders in the presidential election of 2016.

On his website, historian and student-organizing advocate Angus Johnston cataloged and documented 160 college and university student protests during the academic year 2014–2015 (Figure 6.11). His data also display the different forms of participation in which students were engaged and the issues they chose to address. Of the campus protests that Johnston documented, the majority were "focused on racism and police violence," with "about half" of the remainder "evenly split between two main themes: sexism/sexual assault and university governance/student rights."[69] Some of the points on the map highlighted Emma Sulkowicz's Columbia University protest and those of others in support of her efforts to bring attention to campus sexual violence. Another icon pointed to a walkout of Georgia high school students in support of a teacher who had been put on leave for bringing his Christian beliefs into the classroom. "I teach world history," the suspended teacher commented, "so there is a lot of talk about religion and really all I want is equality to talk about everything in America, including Christianity."[70]

▼ FIGURE 6.11

American Student Activism, 2014–2015

A screenshot from historian Angus Johnston's "American Student Protest Timeline, 2014–15," which is a snapshot in map form of student activism across the United States. The colored pinpoints correspond to different types of events: Red indicates activism targeting racism and police violence, blue corresponds to protests against sexual assault and sexism, green represent actions on tuition and funding, and yellow indicates activism regarding governance and student rights.

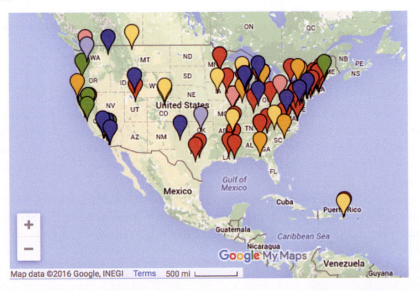

Source: Angus Johnston, "American Student Protest Timeline, 2014–15," Student Activism, December 4, 2014, https://studentactivism.net/2014/12/04/american-student-protest-timeline-2014-15/.

While the specific topics of these campus protests were as diverse as the women and men who led and participated in them, some observers of American politics took note of the disconnect between young adult Americans' lack of turnout at the polls and their efforts to mobilize and protest over social issues. "Young Americans are often characterized as politically apathetic and ignorant," noted Alia Wong in an essay for *The Atlantic* in 2014. "It's true that they vote at exceptionally low rates, but some say that's because they don't believe going to the polls makes much of a difference. . . . Sometimes students demonstrate precisely because they *don't* have political power."[71] According to researchers from Harvard University's Institute of Politics, "Although millennials may be souring on both political parties and Washington politics in general, our polling and other research also bear strong evidence that they care deeply about their country and are willing to work—with or without government—to improve the quality of life in their communities through public service programs and activities."[72]

For political scientist Russell J. Dalton, the burden is not on young adults to vote more but on members of other generations to come to grips with what political participation means to young people: "American youth thus have a different image of government and a different relationship to politics. . . . So the current challenge for American democracy is not to convince young people to act like their grandparents, but for us to understand their changing values and norms and respond in ways that integrate them into the political process—and potentially change the process to better match this new electorate."[73]

WHAT HAVE I LEARNED?

1. Factors that may contribute to lower voter turnout among young adult Americans as a whole include _____.

   a. dissatisfaction with the political process
   b. lower levels of educational attainment
   c. identification with a particular political party
   d. smaller numbers when compared with older generations

2. Why do you think young adult Americans choose to participate in the ways that they do?

Answer Key: 1. b; 2. Answers may focus on feeling disconnected from traditional forms of participation or feeling more connected to ways of participating outside the voting booth.

CONCLUSION: CARRYING THE WEIGHT OF SELF-GOVERNANCE

We know that young adult Americans continue to participate as voters at much lower rates than members of older generations. We also know, however, that something is happening among young adult Americans and the forms of political participation that they are choosing to engage in, though the impact of this engagement is not yet entirely clear. What is clear, however, is this: Many are speaking out with courage and determination.

Throughout this chapter and the stories in it, we have sustained one metaphor—that of "carrying." The decision to do so was intentional. Its use refers to the claim by Amanda Collins of the right to carry a licensed firearm to protect against sexual violence on campuses. It refers to Landen Gambill's activism to prevent campus carry. It refers to Emma Sulkowicz's protests and her art, in which she carried a mattress to call attention to how school administrators address campus sexual violence. It refers to the efforts of college students to act to diffuse potentially violent situations and educate their peers about the reality of campus sexual assault.

Most fundamentally, however, the idea of "carrying" highlights the difficult but necessary reality that all members of a representative democracy are tasked with carrying the weight of self-governance. In many ways that defy traditional notions of what it means to participate in the political process in a representative democracy, young adult Americans are carrying that weight. Even if their lived experiences, opinions, and political preferences have not yet been attended to by members of older generations in positions of political power, young adult Americans are speaking and acting, and they demand to be heard.

CHAPTER REVIEW

This chapter's main ideas are reflected in the Learning Objectives. By reviewing them here, you should be able to **remember** the key points, **know** the terms that are central to the topic, and **think** about the critical issues raised in each section.

6.1 Consider the many forms of political participation that individuals may undertake and the ways in which participation on one issue may also involve actions on other issues.

REMEMBER
- Individuals and groups undertake many different kinds of political activities to shape America's laws and public policies. One form of participation may lead an individual to act in other political spaces, or it may shape the actions of actors in other venues.

KNOW
- political participation (p. 155)

THINK
- In what ways have many young adult Americans tried to call attention to sexual violence on college and university campuses?

6.2 Describe the traditional and nontraditional forms of political participation in American representative democracy.

REMEMBER
- By participating politically, either in traditional or nontraditional ways, Americans express their commitment to civic engagement—to making society better.
- They vote at lower rates than individuals in other democracies, but their rates of nonelectoral participation are equal to or higher than those of their counterparts in other nations.
- Political scientists think of participation as taking place either inside or outside the electoral process, and for many it may be fluid.

KNOW
- civic engagement (p. 162)

THINK
- What forms can political participation take?
- How do Americans' patterns of political participation compare to those in other representative democracies?

6.3 Identify individual, legal, and election-specific factors affecting voter turnout.

REMEMBER
- Voting in elections is a core component of a representative democracy and is a mechanism by which elected officials may be held accountable to the people and by which the people's views may be heard.
- Political scientists have described how not voting may be considered a rational act: Voting is costly in terms of time and effort, and individual votes rarely matter.

- Voter turnout is affected by several factors, some of which are individual-level ones. Other factors that affect voter turnout are not individual but rather systemic or institutional.

- Members of American political parties engage in political mobilization to turn out the vote. Those efforts are often focused on reaching people with strong partisan attachment.

KNOW
- absentee ballots (p. 168)
- ballot roll-off (p. 170)
- felon disenfranchisement (p. 168)
- Motor Voter Law (p. 168)
- political efficacy (p. 166)
- political mobilization (p. 167)
- registration requirements (p. 168)
- socioeconomic status (SES) (p. 165)
- suffrage (p. 168)
- voter turnout (p. 163)

THINK
- What demographic factors shape an individual's decision to vote or not?

- What institutional, legal, and election-specific factors contribute to an individual's decision to vote or not?

6.4 Consider the ways in which acting in one space may lead others to act as well, including elected representatives.

REMEMBER
- As members of social movements, individuals may participate in political protests, attend political meetings, contact elected officials, or reach out to other citizens to educate them about the need to participate to make social and political change.

KNOW
- Title IX (p. 174)

THINK
- How might protest impact electoral politics?

6.5 Evaluate the ways in which political participation by young adult Americans may challenge traditional assumptions.

REMEMBER
- Young voting-age Americans remain chronically underrepresented in American elections, largely because they do not feel they have a stake in the political establishment. However, they do take part in many other forms of political participation.

THINK
- What are the patterns of political participation by young adult Americans? What effect do you think this participation has had or will have in the future?

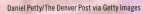
Daniel Petty/The Denver Post via Getty Images

CHAPTER 7

PUBLIC OPINION

How Are Americans' Voices
Measured, and Do They Matter?

▲ A protester holds up a sign during
a demonstration in Ferguson, Missouri.
Eighteen-year-old Michael Brown was killed
in a confrontation with a police officer,
sparking a series of protests that helped
lead to a nationwide conversation about
the treatment of blacks by law enforcement
officials and that seem to have influenced
the public's view of the issue.

Bilgin Sasmaz/Anadolu Agency/Getty Images

I n a representative government, citizens must have some knowledge of what their elected representatives are up to in order to keep watch on their activities, hold them accountable, and punish them at the voting booth if those representatives are no longer serving their interests. Conversely, elected representatives need to know what citizens' preferences are in order to appeal effectively to voters and to carry out their wishes once in office.

Nothing about that exchange of information can be taken for granted. Why? For starters, the act of conveying opinions to candidates or elected officials requires that people (as individuals and collectively) have preferences on issues in the first place and that these preferences are coherent and meaningful.

This is the central challenge of **public opinion**, the sum of individual attitudes about government, policies, and issues. Scholars debate the degree to which people have individually coherent and meaningful opinions about the issues with which government deals. When these individual bits of information become the collective thing that we call public opinion, they also wonder whether that produces anything meaningful or is just noise.

In this chapter, we will focus on American public opinion in one specific area: the treatment of young African American men by law enforcement officials and protests

aimed at calling attention to the issue. We will deal primarily with the difficult story of the shooting death of Michael Brown by a police officer in Ferguson, Missouri, and the events that followed. We will question whether or not these events have produced meaningful changes in American public opinion on the topic of police–community relations.

public opinion
the sum of individual attitudes about government, policies, and issues.

PUBLIC OPINION MAY BE MOVED BY IMPORTANT EVENTS LIKE FERGUSON

- **Understand how public opinion is fluid, often not unified, and shapable.**

On August 9, 2014, white law enforcement officer Darren Wilson killed Michael Brown, an unarmed eighteen-year-old African American man, during a police stop in Ferguson, Missouri. Some eyewitness accounts asserted that Brown had his hands raised in surrender when he was shot six times by Wilson.[1] His death sparked a massive public outcry. The day after Brown's death, protesters gathered in Ferguson. "Tension . . . flared off and on through the evening" as protesters cycled between peaceful prayer circles and candlelight vigils and more intense street demonstrations where they chanted "'We are Michael Brown' as wary police officers stood nearby with assault rifles."[2] By nightfall, there was violence: "After a candlelight vigil, people smash[ed] car windows, carr[ied] away armloads of looted goods from stores and burn[ed] down a Quick Trip."[3] By the time the first wave of violence ended, "more than two dozen businesses in Ferguson and neighboring Dellwood were damaged or looted."[4] The protests, some peaceful and some violent, continued for weeks.

Many of the protesters and other residents of Ferguson began to call for the arrest and prosecution of the officer who had shot Brown. Some chanted. One of their common refrains was "black life matters," a reference to the social movement #BlackLivesMatter, which began following the 2013 acquittal of George Zimmerman in the shooting death of Trayvon Martin in Florida. After Ferguson, however, Black Lives Matter became part of the national conversation in ways it had never been before. *Time* magazine included the protesters of Ferguson in its list of candidates for "Person of the Year."[5] The movement gained even more visibility in the public eye as numerous other unarmed African Americans were

▲ The Black Lives Matter movement grew after the death of Trayvon Martin, an unarmed black Florida teenager who was shot to death by a white neighborhood watch volunteer in 2012. The group continued protesting in Ferguson after Michael Brown's death.

killed by police officers during the year following. In Dayton, Ohio, police shot and killed twenty-one-year-old John Crawford inside a Walmart. Crawford was handling an air rifle, which officers thought was a firearm.[6] Roughly three weeks before Brown was killed, Eric Garner "died from a police chokehold in Staten Island, N.Y., after telling the arresting officers that he could not breathe."[7]

At the same time, the views of police officers involved were also shaping the public's perception of the events. In an interview with ABC News in the fall of 2014, Darren Wilson, who had announced his resignation from the Ferguson Police Department, argued that he had acted in self-defense in killing Brown: "I had to. If I don't, he [Brown] will kill me if he gets to me."[8] Ferguson police chief Thomas Jackson relayed to the public Wilson's suspicions that Brown and a friend were suspects in a convenience store robbery that had occurred shortly before the encounter.[9]

PUBLIC OPINION REFLECTS DIFFERENT FERGUSONS

After Michael Brown's death, deep divisions emerged, with Americans' views on the shooting split according to racial and ethnic identity. Ferguson, Missouri, was quickly becoming many Fergusons. A *New York Times* article stated that "where once there was only one Ferguson—an anonymous suburb of St. Louis—now there is another: a small city whose name has become known for civil unrest, racial division and police harassment."[10] It was not only the shooting that caused controversy. The different "Fergusons" did not exist only in the streets of the city. The opinions of the community's reactions were as divided as the opinions over the event itself. To some, the reactions represented a justifiable expression of inequalities and injustices too long ignored; to others, they were nothing more than violence and anarchy.

To many Americans, especially whites, the protesters' anger over the events in Ferguson came as a surprise. To large percentages of African Americans, however, the death of Brown was not unique—only another tragedy in a long history of tragedies when young African American men came face-to-face with the American law enforcement system. To individuals within African American communities across the country, the only surprising thing about the fallout from Ferguson was that the issue had not been more debated, more talked about. According to Representative John Conyers of Michigan, the dean of the Congressional Black Caucus, "There are virtually no African-American males—including congressmen, actors, athletes and office workers, who have not been stopped at one time or another for driving while black."[11]

Less than two weeks following Brown's death, the Pew Research Center published the results of a **public opinion survey**, which is a systematic attempt to make inferences about the opinions of large numbers of individuals by carefully sampling and asking questions of a small, randomly assigned sample of the larger population. Pew was looking at Americans' responses to what Ferguson and racial identity meant in the larger national conversation. To conduct the survey, researchers had contacted a random sample of one thousand American adults, half via landlines and half via cell phones. The divisions between African Americans and whites on what Ferguson meant were clear. A full 80 percent of blacks said that Brown's shooting raised "important issues about race." But only 37 percent of white respondents agreed. A full 47 percent of whites said that "race [was] getting more attention than it deserves" (see Figure 7.1). Clearly Americans were deeply split about whether Brown's death reflected important issues about the state of race in America. The idea that there were two Fergusons, one African American and one white, seemed to extend beyond the city limits and apply to the whole of the American public.

public opinion survey sampling a portion of the public in order to draw conclusions about the larger population's views on an issue.

Although public opinion was deeply divided especially along lines of racial identity, there were some, perhaps unexpected, complications to these divisions. For example, a 2012 survey by the Pew Research Center concluded that 48 percent of Americans agreed with the following statement: "Guns do more to protect people than place them at risk." In a similar survey in December 2014, the number of Americans agreeing with that statement had increased to 57 percent. Most strikingly, "the shift [in agreement] was even more substantial among African-Americans, going from 29 percent in early 2013 to 54 percent [in 2014] (though with a margin of error of almost 10 percent due to small sample size)."[12] Critics of the poll, however, questioned the wording of the survey items, suggesting that the pollsters may have shaped their findings by the way in which they posed the questions.

Reverend Kenn Blanchard, author of *Black Man with a Gun: Reloaded*, countered critiques of the Pew findings by claiming the emergence of "a generational shift in the black community, where all of the old heads say this [pro-gun] stuff is the devil [but] the new guys are, like, 'I don't think so.' . . . There's a racial divide, too, that the anti-gun people have been using to suggest that white people don't want black people to have firearms. But what I see are my white brothers, the old geezers, who are saying to the younger black generation, 'Here's a gun, I'll show you how to shoot it.'"[13] We will explore the issues in constructing and administering surveys later in the chapter.

As we will see in the chapter, in the years following Michael Brown's death, the national conversation about race in America may have changed. Of all the critical questions that arose from the events in Ferguson, these are the ones that we will explore: Did the events in Ferguson meaningfully shape American public opinion? If these events did have an impact on American public opinion, what effect did the resulting change in attitudes have on representation and the American political process? Did these changes endure, or did the national conversation go back to the way it was before, divided sharply by racial identity? Did leaders and government officials pay attention to these shifts in the opinion landscape?

▲ A political cartoon highlighting racial divisions in public opinion about the treatment of young African American men by law enforcement officials. The figure representing "Black America" is referring to the choking death of Eric Garner while in police custody in 2014. The figure representing "White America" is alleging that white Americans are not sufficiently aware of the underlying issues.

▼ FIGURE 7.1

Opinion about Ferguson Divided by Racial Identity

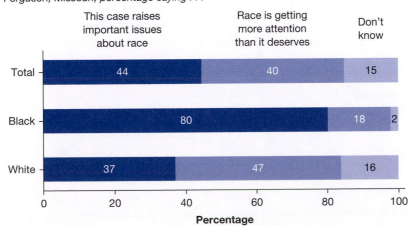

Thinking about the police shooting of an African American teen in Ferguson, Missouri, percentage saying . . .

	This case raises important issues about race	Race is getting more attention than it deserves	Don't know
Total	44	40	15
Black	80	18	2
White	37	47	16

Percentage

Note: Survey conducted August 14–17, 2014. Whites and blacks include only those who are not Hispanic. Figures may not add to 100% because of rounding.

Source: Pew Research Center, "Stark Racial Divisions in Reactions to Ferguson Police Shooting," August 18, 2014, www.people-press.org/2014/08/18/stark-racial-divisions-in-reactions-to-ferguson-police-shooting.

LOOKING FOR A "BREAK IN TREND" IN DATA AND DRAWING CONCLUSIONS OVER TIME

In public opinion polls conducted by the Pew Research Center and the *Washington Post* in 2009, 2011, and March 2014, the percentage of Americans who agreed that the nation had "made the changes needed to give blacks equal rights with whites" did not change much. In each poll, roughly half of Americans overall expressed the opinion that the nation had made these changes. Individual attitudes, however, diverged sharply by racial identity. Higher percentages of white Americans felt that the nation had made the necessary changes, but the vast majority of African American survey respondents (constituting a smaller part of the sample) felt that it had not.

Majority Says Nation Needs to Make Changes to Give Blacks Equal Rights

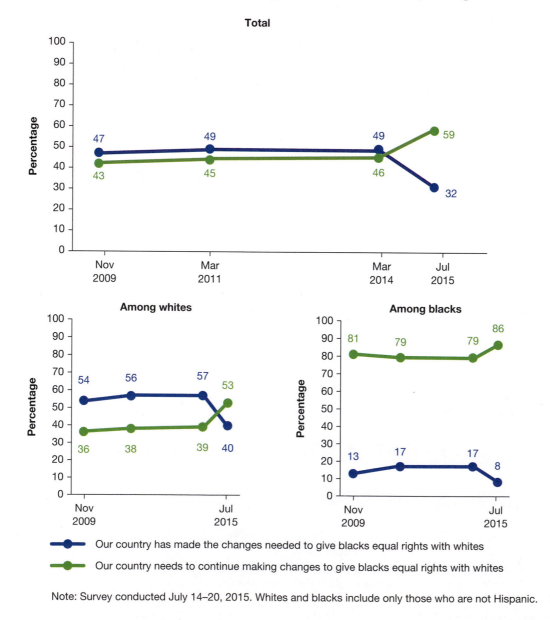

Note: Survey conducted July 14–20, 2015. Whites and blacks include only those who are not Hispanic.

Source: Pew Research Center, "Across Racial Lines, More Say Nation Needs to Make Changes to Achieve Racial Equality," August 5, 2015, www.people-press.org/2015/08/05/across-racial-lines-more-say-nation-needs-to-make-changes-to-achieve-racial-equality.

By the late summer of 2015, however, something appeared to have changed.[14] Between the polls conducted in March 2014, six months before Brown's shooting, and July 2015, nearly a year after, there appeared to be what political scientists call a "break in trend"—and a sharp one at that. In the 2015 survey, the percentages of Americans surveyed who felt that the nation had done enough to achieve equal rights appeared to have changed overall, and for both groups of Americans.

However, when drawing conclusions about the causes of this change in public opinion—including whether Ferguson caused this change—some caution is warranted. Other events between the 2014 and 2015 surveys may have contributed to the observed findings. A debate about the display of Confederate flags, for example, also made it onto the national political agenda during this time, as did more shootings and tragic events. We cannot, based on these data alone, confirm that Ferguson caused this change but only that there is a potentially meaningful correlation between the two. That said, this change in American public opinion, how quickly it happened, and how substantial it was are not things to be quickly dismissed.

WHAT Do You Think?

Do these results lead you to conclude that the shooting deaths in Ferguson and other cities and the protests in response actually changed American public opinion? What other evidence might you want to make a firmer conclusion?

WHAT HAVE I LEARNED?

1. Public opinion is _____.
   a. a set of facts known by only a subset of people
   b. the views of elites
   c. the sum of individual attitudes about government, policies, and issues
   d. views held by the masses as opposed to the elites

2. Public opinion surveys are _____.
   a. systematic attempts to make inferences about the opinions of large numbers of individuals by carefully sampling and asking questions of a small, randomly assigned sample of the larger population
   b. informal quizzes taken on social media sites such as Facebook
   c. individual responses to poll questions that have been simply multiplied by the size of the sampled population to arrive at the true opinion of a group

   d. groups of people hired to call random respondents to find out their views on important issues

3. Central to the concerns of protesters in Ferguson, Missouri, was _____.
   a. American immigration policy
   b. a state policy related to firearms ownership by individuals
   c. the treatment of African American men by law enforcement officials
   d. incarceration under the nation's drug laws

4. In what ways might the events in Ferguson have highlighted racial divisions in American public opinion?

Answer Key: 1. c; 2. a; 3. c; 4. Answers might include a discussion of racial divisions or the degree to which the events in Ferguson did or did not highlight the need for a broader national conversation on police–community relations.

PUBLIC OPINION IS THE SUM TOTAL OF INDIVIDUAL BELIEFS AND ATTITUDES

- Discuss differing theories about public opinion formation and expression and the degree to which it is meaningful.

One of the most important debates about American public opinion is whether or not there is such a thing. Of course, many Americans have thoughts and ideas about politics and policies, but many others do not have well-formed views on these topics. Some people might not care at all and wonder what all the fuss is about. And what do we really learn by asking Americans what they think? Recall the definition of public opinion presented previously: the sum of individual attitudes about government, policies, and issues. Public opinion, by definition, involves two components: an individual's own beliefs and attitudes as well as the accumulation of all of these individual preferences into something that we then call public opinion. Either of these two pieces—individual attitudes and the aggregation of individual attitudes—can make American public opinion difficult to understand. This is because individuals may not actually have meaningful preferences on any given issue, and, even if they do, the aggregation of these individual preferences might not yield meaningful and useful information.

These are more than just academic concerns. A representative democracy cannot function without meaningful public opinion. If our elected representatives do not know what we want, then how can they hope to represent us? Later in this book we will explore the role that constituents play in shaping the behavior of their elected senators and representatives. Inherent in the role of constituency, however, are two assumptions: that constituents have preferences and that they can meaningfully communicate those preferences to their members of Congress. In this chapter, we will consider both these assumptions.

THERE ARE COMPETING VIEWS ABOUT THE MEANING OF PUBLIC OPINION

Arguments about the meaning of public opinion in American political life fall into two general camps. One perspective holds that the average citizen either doesn't have or is unable to express meaningful opinions on the vast array of issues with which he or she is confronted. Maybe there are simply too many issues for any of us to have well-informed and meaningful opinions about all of them. Another perspective holds that even though individuals sometimes lack the information they need to form opinions, they can find ways to overcome or work around these challenges by, for example, making inferences based on their attitudes about other policies and questions, responding to messages from political parties, and/or relying on friends. Perhaps these shortcuts and cues help us arrive at an opinion. Aggregating individual opinions—even if they are individually unclear or inconsistent—can send a useful and impactful signal to elected representatives and government officials.

THE MINIMALIST PARADIGM HOLDS THAT MOST PEOPLE'S OPINIONS CONSIST OF STEREOTYPES AND NONATTITUDES. Proponents of what political scientists have called the **minimalist paradigm** emphasize how most people fall short of what we expect them to know, think about, and pay attention to in the complicated world of politics and policy.[15] Most people, according to this perspective, pay minimum attention to issues and have minimal information about them. Additionally, the opinions that they do have are minimally stable; they change over time or in response to attempts to control or shape them.

One of the earliest and most influential expressions of the minimalist argument was Walter Lippmann's *Public Opinion* (1922). A prominent journalist and political observer, Lippmann was concerned about how malleable (or flexible) and receptive Americans' attitudes appeared to be under the pressure of political propaganda leading up to the nation's involvement in World War I. If, in the mind of many observers of American public opinion, a nation could be led to a war most felt had nothing to do with American interests, then what couldn't the American people be talked into?

For Lippmann, a key concept was the **stereotype**, a preconceived, often oversimplified idea about something that people apply as a filter to the world. Stereotypes do not filter based upon a rational consideration of the issues but upon emotions, and in the world of politics they are easily manipulated by those who seek to shape American public opinion for their own political purposes.

Lippmann described a public that is dangerously unreflective and vulnerable to attempts to shape its opinions. To him, part of the reason why the Framers of the Constitution instituted so many checks and balances in the federal government, so many roadblocks to making major policy change, was mistrust of individuals' haphazard, shifting, and malleable stereotypes.

Inherent in the minimalist critique is the idea that not all Americans have the same amount of political information. A small number of individuals, the **elites**, may have well-informed and well-reasoned opinions, but the majority of individuals, the **masses**, do not. In an early study using large sample surveys, a group of researchers painted a grim picture of the majority of American voters. Most are not

minimalist paradigm
a theory of public opinion that emphasizes how most people fall short of what we expect them to know, think about, and pay attention to in the complicated world of politics and policy.

stereotype
a preconceived, often oversimplified idea about something that people apply as a filter to the world.

elites
a small number of individuals (who tend to have well-informed and well-reasoned opinions).

masses
the majority of individuals (who tend to be less informed).

politically involved and have only a limited awareness of political events.[16] Instead, voters often rely on their identification with a political party—an identification that itself might not be the result of careful, thoughtful, conscious deliberation.

In 1964, political scientist Philip Converse extended this critique to question whether masses can and do learn from elites, become more informed, and produce responses to surveys that are stable over time. Generally, Converse found, masses do not learn from elites.[17] Instead, most voters have **nonattitudes**. The opinions that most people express in, for example, a public opinion survey, might be vulnerable to the efforts of propagandists, as Lippmann feared, and, frankly, might just be random.

Concerns about a lack of coherent opinions in the American electorate and the challenges that this poses to American representative democracy have not gone away. Recently, two researchers found that significant percentages of Americans were not able to answer basic questions about American government, such as being able to name one or more branches of the federal government or name constitutional protections in the Bill of Rights.[18] At least as troubling was their finding that political knowledge was predictably and unequally distributed. Younger Americans, women, lower-income Americans, and members of racial and ethnic minorities consistently fared worse in their answers to such factual political knowledge questions. These gaps have remained consistent over the past few decades. Researchers with the Pew Research Center periodically administer a "News IQ" quiz to a random sample of Americans. The test contains questions regarding political figures, knowledge of current issues in domestic and international politics, and geography (see Figure 7.2). While

DeAgostini/Getty Images

▲ The Uncle Sam recruitment poster for the U.S. Army was originally published in 1916. The image was an effective piece of propaganda, and more than four million copies were printed in the years leading up to the United States' entry into World War I in 1919.

▼ FIGURE 7.2

A Sample Question from Pew's Political Knowledge Test

The News IQ Quiz

What is the name of this person?

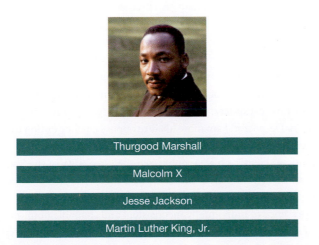

| Thurgood Marshall |
| Malcolm X |
| Jesse Jackson |
| Martin Luther King, Jr. |

Ninety-one percent of respondents to Pew's "News IQ" quiz were able to correctly identify this image of Dr. Martin Luther King Jr. Far fewer were able to identify images of 2014 Nobel Peace Prize winner Malala Yousafzai or Massachusetts senator Elizabeth Warren. Only about 33 percent knew there were three female Supreme Court justices.

Source: Pew Research Center, "The News IQ Quiz," accessed March 2017, www.pewresearch.org/quiz/the-news-iq-quiz.

the number of Americans who can correctly answer a question varies within and across these knowledge tests, significant numbers are unable to answer the questions correctly. To what extent does this information gap matter? Can Americans with unequal knowledge of, or access to, information about American politics express their desires with voices as impactful as those of informed Americans?

ANOTHER PERSPECTIVE SAYS THAT PEOPLE CAN OVERCOME INFORMATION GAPS. While more recent scholarship acknowledges the challenges posed by proponents of the minimalist paradigm, it also emphasizes the ways in which the public can still make sense of their opinions and transmit those opinions to their representatives, both collectively and individually. On the most basic point—that Americans often lack opinions on many issues in politics and policy—these scholars agree. Where they disagree is on the need for any one person to have an encyclopedic set of policy preferences so that she or he is able to offer an opinion. The aggregation of individuals' opinions, according to some scholars, can produce useful information even in the presence of noise at the individual level.

How do individuals answer survey questions? Do they act as file cabinets, carrying around preformed opinions and waiting to pull out the relevant opinion when prompted? Or do they construct at least some of their opinions when asked to do so—opinions that are based on their own understandings but also perhaps shaped by the survey and the context in which they answered the survey's questions? If that is how individual opinions might be "formed," then one might reasonably expect to see changes in answers to surveys over time and in different situations, since the administration of the survey will vary.

By incorporating findings from studies of cognition and political psychology, scholars have emphasized this more dynamic process and, though they acknowledge gaps in knowledge and understanding, present a more complex picture of the public's ability to make sense of the political world. For John Zaller, a basic concept in attitude construction is **consideration**, a combination of cognition and affect that contributes to any one answer to any one question or evaluation.[19] It's not as complicated a concept as it may seem. Basically, Zaller's theory says that our knowledge and our emotions both come into play when we form and express an opinion. We are not file cabinets, but we are also not the modeling clay that Lippmann worried about. We are something in between.[20]

Other research focuses on the ability of voters with low levels of specific political knowledge to make effective use of **cues and information shortcuts** to form meaningful opinions. These informational helpers may come from a variety of sources. Individuals' own personal experiences and interactions with government, accumulated over a lifetime, can help them make sense of an issue or problem. This "gut rationality" may not help on a political knowledge quiz, but it can assist people in making meaningful political choices.[21] In addition, individuals might rely on advice from friends and colleagues.[22]

Identification with a particular political party (called party identification) is another powerful informational shortcut that voters frequently use when evaluating candidates and forming opinions about specific issues.[23] If I identify as a Republican, I'm likely to be more favorable toward the Republican candidate than the Democratic candidate, even without knowing anything other than their party affiliations. Or if I identify as a Democrat, I am more likely to oppose a policy option that Republicans endorse than one Democrats endorse.

Finally, some political scientists have emphasized the possibility of the "wisdom of crowds,"[24] in which individuals, imperfectly informed, can come up with a meaningful assessment of a problem or situation. Benjamin Page and Robert Shapiro emphasized the possibility for a public to be collectively rational even in the presence of individually inconsistent and shapable opinions: "While we grant the rational ignorance of most individuals, and the possibility that their policy preferences are shallow and unstable, . . . public opinion as a collective phenomenon is nonetheless stable (though not immovable), meaningful, and indeed rational . . . : it is able to make distinctions; it is organized in coherent patterns; it is reasonable, based on the best available information; and it is adaptive to new information or changed circumstances, responding in similar ways to similar stimuli."[25]

nonattitudes
a term referring to the lack of stable and coherent opinions on political issues and candidates.

consideration
a combination of cognition and affect that contributes to any one answer to any one question or evaluation.

cues and information shortcuts
pieces of information individuals pick up that help them form political opinions.

1. According to political scientists who argue for the minimalist paradigm, _____.
   a. people's beliefs about political issues are mostly stable and coherent
   b. information generally passes from political elites to the masses
   c. most people fall short of what we expect them to know, think about, and pay attention to
   d. both cognition and affect contribute to respondents' answers on surveys

2. For political scientist John Zaller, individuals' opinions are shaped primarily by _____.

   a. facts
   b. political elites
   c. political propaganda
   d. knowledge and emotions

3. Do you think that Americans have meaningful opinions on the most important political issues today?

   _____

   Answer Key: 1. c; 2. d; 3. Answers may include a discussion of why or why not individuals have well-formed opinions.

PUBLIC OPINION IS TRANSMITTED AND MEASURED IN SEVERAL WAYS

- **Describe the issues involved in transmitting and measuring American public opinion and constructing the instruments used to do so.**

The act of representation in a republican form of government has two basic and crucial informational requirements. First, voters must have opinions and preferences that can be communicated to their elected representatives. Second, elected officials must respond to, or be forced to respond to, these expressed preferences. We have already considered the debates about whether or not Americans have meaningful opinions. The second part of the equation is just as important. How can Americans effectively communicate their preferences to their government? How do elected representatives learn about the preferences of their constituents? What tools can we use to make sure we are correctly gauging their responses?

CITIZENS' OPINIONS ARE TRANSMITTED TO PUBLIC OFFICIALS THROUGH DIRECT AND INDIRECT CHANNELS

One method that citizens use is to directly communicate with their elected officials through phone calls or emails. The challenge with direct communication as a tool of representation is that elected officials know that those who call or write do not represent their constituents as a whole but are only a motivated subset of people who are often unhappy about something. While direct communication can signal to an elected official the intense preferences of a small group of individuals, it does not convey a sense of the overall preferences of the citizens as a whole.

A tool that does give elected officials this broader knowledge is an election. While we may not often think about an election as a tool for measuring public opinion, that is precisely what it is. However, in this regard, elections have their own limitations. First, many eligible voters do not vote. The decision of whether or not to vote can be affected by efforts to mobilize potential voters, to get out the vote. In terms of measuring the preferences of constituents, the greater challenge with elections is that they tend to revolve around a small set of issues, albeit ones for which voters have intense preferences. For the majority of public policy issues with which elected officials will have to contend, elections are too broad a tool to reveal useful information.

Therefore, rather than waiting for individuals to contact them or trying to decipher the results of an election, public officials may go directly to the citizens to find out what they think and want. One

ANALYZING EDITORIAL CHOICES IN PRESENTING VISUAL INFORMATION

The *St. Louis Post-Dispatch* Changes Its Cover Photo

On the one-year anniversary of the death of Michael Brown, and over the space of a few hours, the editors and publishers of the *St. Louis Post-Dispatch* chose to replace the lead photograph for the next day's paper. The reason was another tragic event. The planned image was of a peaceful protest in which at least one thousand marchers commemorated the tragic events of one year prior and sought to keep public attention on the issue of the treatment of young African American men by law enforcement officials.

At night, however, police shot and critically wounded another young African American man, eighteen-year-old Tyrone Harris. St. Louis County police officials stated that prior to the shooting, two groups of men had been involved in a gunfight with each other and one had fired on four plain-clothed police officers in an unmarked car.

In his tweet, Lynden Steele, director of photography for the newspaper, contrasted the two images and the two headlines, highlighting yet another heartbreak. Notice the differences in tone and mood of the two images. In the first is an upside-down American flag. Officially, it is displayed as such only in times of distress. In this case the protesters used their First Amendment right to display the flag this way to signal the distress that they felt surrounding this issue. Notice the somber tone of the second image and the image itself—one of police officers surrounding a wounded young man—one with which Ferguson residents were well familiar.

Lynden Steele @manofsteele · Follow

News broke us in so many ways tonight. The two front pages for Monday in St. Louis. #Ferguson @stltoday

Lynden Steele/Twitter

RETWEETS **419**   LIKES **137**

1:26 AM - 10 Aug 2015

419   137

WHAT Do You Think?

The decision of the editors and publishers of the *St. Louis Post-Dispatch* to change their lead image highlights both the power of image in political storytelling and the speed with which coverage responds to events. To someone unfamiliar with the news article or the protest controversy, how do these two images frame the stories of the anniversary protests? As an editor of a newspaper, what might you consider when choosing a cover story image of protests in Ferguson or other cities?

---

tool sometimes used for this is the **focus group**, in which a small group of individuals is assembled for a directed conversation during which one hopes to uncover patterns of thinking about issues and individuals. Focus groups can be useful in understanding how individuals come to understand the political issues with which they are contending. However, by their nature, focus groups cannot paint a picture of the constituency as a whole and are therefore limited in their utility.

Another, deeper concern about focus groups and other tools for measuring public opinion comes from their origin in product marketing, in which companies use these tools to try to get a sense of which products will sell best and why. This textbook, in fact, as well as most others, involved the use of focus groups in its development. The challenge for representative democracy is whether or not we want our elected officials to think of their "products" like breakfast cereals. In one sense, we might. We want our

focus group
a small group of individuals assembled for a directed conversation during which one hopes to uncover patterns of thinking about issues and individuals.

elected representatives to care enough about our opinions to find out what they are. On the other hand, there is a danger that our elected representatives might be too concerned with taking the nation's pulse, too hesitant to make difficult decisions that might be unpopular but necessary. The Framers most certainly did not intend for elected representatives to consistently bend to the will of voters. That is part of the reason why they set up so many roadblocks to making major and sweeping changes to American public policy.

Even so, a candidate whose eyes are on the next election will use any tools that she or he has to gauge the opinions of the voters. The most effective of these is the **scientific poll**. With this tool, pollsters try to gain an understanding of a large group of individuals by obtaining the opinions of a carefully chosen small sample of the group, although they are aware of the limitations of the effort.

SCIENTIFIC POLLING IS BASED ON EFFORTS TO ACCURATELY SAMPLE REPRESENTATIVE POPULATIONS

A key question in considering how useful a scientific poll is involves its **validity**, the degree to which an instrument accurately measures what it is designed to. In theory, scientific polling is simple. Given the challenges and costs of having to ask everyone in a House district, a state, or the nation what he or she thinks, pollsters instead select a smaller representative subset of that constituency and ask its members what they think. That subgroup is called the **sample**. For some political polls, the sample population may be the entire voting-age population of the United States or of an individual state or congressional district. However, there are many other possible populations of interest in a survey, such as individuals with specific racial or ethnic identities or the student population of a college or university.

A key challenge in sampling is **random selection**. For the sample to be useful, it must represent the larger population as well as possible—with no systematic errors. Some errors in sampling are not a problem. If your **respondents**, or those individuals who respond to your survey, are more likely to choose blue over green socks, that is probably not an issue. If, however, a poll systematically oversamples or undersamples individuals based on characteristics that are relevant to what the poll is trying to measure—for example, support for a presidential candidate from the Democratic or Republican Party—then you have a problem. Pollsters are well aware of these challenges. Often, they use the technique of **weighting** to adjust the results of a survey. Weighting is done based on differences between the percentages of specific groups participating in the survey and what is known about the proportion of their representation in the larger population.

Unless one can survey every single person in a population, community, or nation, no researcher can ever know what the "true" opinion of that population is. The goal is to minimize the uncertainty as much as possible while also conducting a poll that does not cost vast sums of money or take an unacceptable amount of time to conduct. When pollsters present their results, they include a measure of the **sampling error** (or margin of error) in their surveys. In larger national polls, which typically aim for about 1,500 respondents, the sampling error is often plus or minus three points, meaning that they can assert that about 95 percent of the time, the true number—which is never known—lies within three points on either side of the measured number. In American politics, the number of citizens on either side of an issue might be closely divided. If, for example, an opinion survey with a margin of error of three points finds that one party's candidate for president has the support of 49 percent of Americans and the other party's candidate the support of 47 percent, then one could not confidently say that the first candidate would win in a national election. Increasing the size of the sample decreases the error, but it also increases the cost. In addition, the greater the variation in the population that one samples, the larger the sampling error.

PUBLIC OPINION SURVEY VALIDITY VARIES BY TYPE

In choosing how to administer a survey, a researcher has several options. The degree of confidence that one can place in the findings, however, depends critically upon the ways in which the sample is selected. One popular type of survey is a **straw poll**—an unofficial tally of opinion or support at

scientific poll
when pollsters try to gain an understanding of a large group of individuals by obtaining the opinions of a carefully chosen small sample of the group, although they are aware of the limitations of the effort.

validity
the degree to which a tool accurately measures what it is intended to.

sample
the subgroup of individuals from the larger population of whom one wants to measure the opinions.

random selection
how participants are selected from the population for inclusion in the study.

respondents
individuals who answer a survey.

weighting
a procedure in which the observed results of a survey are adjusted according to what is known about specific proportions in the larger population.

sampling error
error in a statistical analysis arising from the unrepresentativeness of the sample taken.

straw poll
an unofficial tally of opinion or support at a meeting or event.

▲ Two versions of straw polls are shown here. At left, a visitor to the 2015 Iowa State Fair casts a vote for presidential candidate Carly Fiorina with a kernel of corn. At right, attendees at the 2015 Conservative Political Action Conference (CPAC) vote in an electronic straw poll in National Harbor, Maryland.

a meeting or event, such as a political party meeting or caucus. While straw polls can be useful in exploring which individuals support a candidate and why, their target population is not randomly selected. The fact that people have chosen to attend the event at which the straw poll is conducted means that the sample was not randomly chosen and, therefore, cannot be relied upon to draw conclusions about general public opinion.

A **self-selected listener opinion poll (SLOP)**, in which respondents choose to respond to a survey prompt on their own, suffers from the same disadvantage. SLOPs are quite common. When individuals respond to a radio talk show host's requests to call in, or when a person fills out a quick survey after reading an article or watching a video on the Internet, he or she is participating in a SLOP. Because more involved and motivated individuals choose to participate—and these individuals do not represent a randomly selected subset of the overall population—one cannot confidently say that their opinions reflect the distribution of them in the larger population.

An **exit poll** is a survey conducted outside a polling place in which individuals are asked for whom or what they just voted and why. While there is much to be gained for a news organization that can call a race before other news outlets based on its exit poll results, there are risks as well. Individuals do not vote at random times, and an exit poll may unintentionally be sampling from a group that over- or underrepresents overall public opinion on an issue or candidate. Also, announcing the results of exit polls while polls are still open runs the risk of influencing an election. Learning that one candidate is supposedly winning may discourage another candidate's supporters from turning out to vote because they believe their votes will not matter. To avoid that problem, news networks have voluntarily committed to not releasing exit poll results until all of a state's polling places have closed. Exit polls can be useful, though, in understanding patterns of voting—for example, what issue was most on the minds of voters who voted for one candidate or another.

Because of the challenges posed by nonrandom selection, news organizations, media outlets, and research organizations rely primarily on the telephone when trying to gauge American public opinion. They may draw from lists of phone numbers or employ **random digit dialing** in which phone numbers are selected randomly by computer. That has the added advantage of potentially including unlisted numbers or those generally not in pollsters' (or marketers') databases, such as numbers for cell phones. Even with random digit dialing, however, there are always risks that a sample is not truly representative of the overall population. Are some of those one calls more likely to answer the survey than

self-selected listener opinion poll (SLOP)
a survey where respondents choose to respond to a survey prompt on their own.

exit poll
a survey conducted outside a polling place in which individuals are asked for whom or what they just voted for and why.

random digit dialing
when potential survey respondents are selected by computer-generated random numbers.

others? Might patterns of willingness or unwillingness to answer the survey bias the findings? Though pollsters are aware of and try to account for these issues, it is always a potential problem.

HOW PUBLIC OPINION SURVEYS ARE CONSTRUCTED AFFECTS THEIR VALIDITY

In addition to sample selection, pollsters must confront other issues that are important for informed consumers of public opinion surveys—such as the students reading this book—to note. We have explored the challenge that Americans may have nonattitudes on some issues, and there is also the risk that individuals may be unwilling to admit a lack of information or opinion and make up responses on the spot. In one survey of Americans, political scientist George Bishop asked respondents about their opinions of the Public Affairs Act of 1975. The trick was that the act never existed. In spite of this small fact, significant percentages of respondents offered an opinion on the piece of fictitious legislation, casting doubt on the reliability of results of surveys of Americans on specific public policies and policy proposals.[26] To try to prevent this, well-constructed survey questions should try to focus on issues with which their respondents will be familiar and have opinions about.

Even on issues for which respondents have actual preferences, other factors may shape the results of a public opinion survey. First, the **question order** might affect the results. Consider a question about whether or not individuals should be permitted to burn an American flag in protest. The same question might produce substantially different results if it were preceded by other questions that included the expressed opinions of other individuals.[27] Perhaps the flag-burning question was preceded by a question about the importance of patriotism, which might produce more opinions against allowing flag burning. Alternatively, the flag-burning question might have followed a question on the importance of free speech in American democracy, priming a different pattern of responses.

Similarly, the **question wording** might, intentionally or not, guide respondents to a specific answer. For example, in a 2003 Pew Research Center Survey about attitudes toward military action in Iraq, 68 percent of respondents said they favored action when asked if they would "favor or oppose taking military action in Iraq to end Saddam Hussein's rule." However, when asked if they would "favor or oppose taking military action in Iraq to end Saddam Hussein's rule even if it meant that U.S. forces might suffer thousands of casualties," only 43 percent of respondents favored military action.[28] Finally, the interviewers themselves may affect the results of a survey, especially one conducted in person. Political scientists have, for example, documented **race of interviewer effects**, in which the outcomes of surveys, even on questions asking only for political knowledge and information, may depend partly upon the racial identities of respondents and surveyors.[29]

INDIVIDUAL OPINIONS VARY ACCORDING TO DIRECTION, INTENSITY, STABILITY, AND SALIENCE

Political scientists and scholars of political psychology and mass communication not only need to think about the various techniques and types of instruments they can use to measure public opinion, but they also need language they can use to describe that individual's opinion, to break it down into distinct components. The first is the **direction** of the opinion, which is what we commonly focus on. Is the person for an issue, against it, or neutral? Does the person think favorably about a political candidate, unfavorably, or remain neutral? A second dimension of an opinion is the **intensity**, or strength of involvement and preference, with which an individual holds that opinion. Another component describes the **stability** of the opinion. Stable opinions tend not to change over time, in different contexts, or in response to differently worded survey questions. Some opinions, such as which political party one prefers, tend to be stable, while others, such as a preference over a specific water or transportation policy, tend to be much more variable over time and across different surveys—if the individuals have opinions at all. These two parts of an opinion are related. Intense opinions are more likely to be stable than those held with less intensity. Finally, there is the **salience** (or centrality) of an opinion in the sense that some strongly held opinions shape expressed opinions on other issues or candidate evaluations. For example, a strongly held belief about the need for an active and involved

question order
the ways in which earlier questions in a survey may shape answers to later questions.

question wording
the ways in which the phrasing of survey questions may shape answers.

race of interviewer effects
the potential impact of the racial identities of surveyors and respondents on the respondents' answers.

direction
the focus of an individual's opinion.

intensity
the strength of involvement and preference of an individual's opinion.

stability
the degree of change over time, in different contexts, or in response to differently worded survey questions of a particular opinion.

salience
the centrality of an individual's opinion in the sense of the opinion's ability to shape the individual's views on other issues or candidates.

government might shape a person's opinions about specific government policies. Salient opinions tend to be more intense and stable.

One area of representation in American government that continues to evoke intense, stable, and salient opinions is the equality of treatment of individuals by law enforcement officers and the relationship between that treatment and the racial and ethnic identity of those who interact with law enforcement and the criminal justice system. As residents of Ferguson and other communities in which young men of color had been killed by law enforcement officers reacted, protested, and expressed their anger, it quickly became clear that opinions about race and treatment by law enforcement officials were often highly intense and salient. These opinions, however, were sharply divided by race, ethnicity, age, and partisan affiliation.

POLLS ARE USED FOR COMMERCIAL, ACADEMIC, AND POLITICAL PURPOSES

Many different individuals and groups make use of public opinion polls. Media outlets work with major polling organizations when covering topics such as Americans' support or opposition to a candidate or policy proposal. Academic researchers rely on more in-depth polls to test theories about politics and public opinion. One tool that political scientists and other researchers may employ is the survey experiment, in which individuals are randomly assigned different surveys, perhaps with different question wording or framing. The goal here is not to try to measure the opinions of a larger population but to use the randomized experiments to better understand how people form opinions.

Polls also play key roles in political campaigns. The media may use tools such as exit polls to predict the outcomes of political races or to better understand why people voted one way or another in a given election. Candidates themselves may employ polls to better understand voters' interests and concerns or to gauge public support for themselves or their opponents as a campaign progresses. One controversial tool that candidates or those supporting them may employ is a push poll, which is not really a poll but a negative campaign tactic. Disguised as a survey, a **push poll** tries to present voters with negative or damaging portrayals of opposing candidates, sometimes with false or exaggerated information.

push poll
a negative campaign tactic disguised as a survey in which a candidate's opponent or opponents are portrayed in an unfavorable way.

WHAT HAVE I **LEARNED?**

1. The disadvantage in measuring public opinion that self-selected listener opinion (SLOP) polls and straw polls both share is that _____.
   a. they are too expensive to conduct nationally
   b. they tend to survey only conservative public opinion
   c. their respondents are not chosen randomly
   d. they tend to survey only liberal public opinion

2. Random selection of survey respondents is challenged by _____.
   a. the communications technology used to contact potential respondents
   b. the time of day in which a respondent is contacted
   c. the decisions of potential respondents to answer or not answer the survey
   d. All of the above

3. Individually salient opinions are important because they _____.
   a. are easily manipulated
   b. are based on issues constructed by the media
   c. tend to shape opinions on other issues
   d. often change depending on the particular survey

4. If you were to try to sample American public opinion on an issue that you care about, how might you go about trying to assemble a random sample? What challenges might you face?

5. What are four components of an individual opinion?

Answer Key: 1. c; 2. d; 3. c; 4. Answers will vary but should discuss the challenges of sampling from a given population; 5. Answers should include direction, intensity, stability, and salience (or centrality).

POLITICAL SOCIALIZATION AND POLITICAL IDEOLOGY SHAPE PUBLIC OPINION

- **Examine the contributors to individual attitudes and public opinion.**

For all of us, our lived experience contributes profoundly to what we believe and the political attitudes we hold. But there are several other key factors that shape our views, including our political ideology, the groups we belong to, and other influential groups and actors. Political scientists have long studied how those attitudes are formed in the first place, how they may be altered over time, and how they are influenced by others.

AP Photo/St. Louis Post-Dispatch, Robert Cohen

▲ In an exercise in civic education, students at Koch Elementary School in St. Louis, Missouri, participate in a vote on the lunch menu in November 2014.

POLITICAL SOCIALIZATION SHAPES INDIVIDUAL ATTITUDES

The formation and modification of opinions and attitudes toward politics, public policy, and political figures is a lifelong process. **Political socialization** refers to the variety of experiences and factors that shape our political values, attitudes, and behaviors.

FAMILIES, SCHOOLS, AND PEERS ARE EARLY SHAPERS OF INFORMATION AND OPINION. The first and most important contributor to the process of political socialization is the family, especially when it comes to shaping children's views about political figures and political authority.[30] **Party identification**—the degree to which an individual identifies with and supports a particular political party—is highly transmitted through families. Families provide, after all, the first source of political information for those who are seeking out information.[31]

Schools often intentionally play a role in political socialization through processes of **civic education** that aim to introduce students to politics and help them develop the ability to interpret and make sense of this knowledge.[32] Civic education can also transmit civic norms, such as the importance of being civically involved.[33] As spaces of learning and community, schools are also important for their ability to create a political climate, introduce students to opportunities for political participation, and introduce political learners to other students whose diverse lived experiences might reinforce or challenge the civic understandings that students bring into the classroom.[34] Families inform political learners first, then schools and educational experiences leave their mark. As such, an individual's civic education does not occur on a blank canvas but one that has already been at least partially painted by his or her upbringing.

PERSONAL EXPERIENCE AND FOCUSING EVENTS AFFECT INDIVIDUAL ATTITUDES OVER TIME. Individual political opinions are never set in stone. While families, schools, and peers play important but different roles in our political socialization, so do later experiences in life. Our interactions in daily life may also shape our opinions on both individual and national levels, especially when we experience **focusing events**, such as times of crisis.

We see this effect in several ways in the aftermath of Ferguson as individuals across the nation began to take a greater interest in politics and policy and became more informed and involved. One of the individuals attending a protest march at the end of August was forty-four-year-old Ian Buchanan. According to a reporter for the *St. Louis Post-Dispatch*, Buchanan, "a former principal in the St. Louis and Normandy school districts, drove to Ferguson from his home in Memphis, Tenn., to attend Saturday's march. 'I came here because I want to be part of the spirit of the movement,' he said. He spent part of the day talking to his former students about how to voice their concerns about injustice. 'The

political socialization the variety of experiences and factors that shape our political values, attitudes, and behaviors.

party identification the degree to which an individual identifies with and supports a particular political party.

civic education the transmission of information about the political world and civic norms to learners.

focusing events sudden and dramatic events that draw individuals' attention.

older generation usually wants to write off the younger generation, but to effect change, it comes from the young people,' Buchanan said."[35]

Sometimes the cumulative effect of a series of crises makes a difference at the national level in shifting public opinion. Commenting on the cluster of lethal shootings of young African American men in 2014, a sociologist at George Washington University claimed that while one single event might not move American public opinion, several might: "Once a critical mass of these incidents occur in real time it can certainly shift public opinion even among those . . . who might have thought the police could do no wrong."[36] Indeed, public opinion polls conducted in the weeks and months following the deaths of Michael Brown and Eric Garner found that a large majority of Americans, regardless of racial or ethnic identity or political party affiliation, expressed support for the use of body cameras by law enforcement officers to record their interactions with the public (see Figure 7.3).

American public opinion in the twenty-first century is more instantaneously shapable than has ever been previously possible. Social media allows, in theory, a national conversation between people of very different lived experiences and political attitudes.

PARTISAN IDENTIFICATION, INDIVIDUAL AND GROUP IDENTITIES, AND ELITE ATTITUDES INFORM OUR VIEWS

As we have seen, families, schools, and events (either over the course of a lifetime or focusing ones) play a major role in shaping public opinion. But other factors play important roles as well. How we identify politically, as well as how we define ourselves in terms of gender, race, or ethnicity, can form clear, consistent, and persistent patterns of similarity and division in American public opinion.

▼ FIGURE 7.3

Widespread Support for the Use of Body Cameras by Law Enforcement Officers

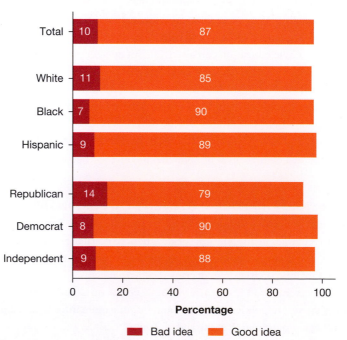

More police officers wearing body cameras to record interactions would be a . . . (%)

Notes: Survey conducted Dec. 3–7, 2014. "Don't know" responses not shown.
Whites and blacks include only non-Hispanics; Hispanics are of any race.

Source: Pew Research Center, "Sharp Racial Divisions in Reactions to Brown, Garner Decisions: Many Blacks Expect Police-Minority Relations to Worsen," December 8, 2014, www.people-press.org/2014/12/08/sharp-racial-divisions-in-reactions-to-brown-garner-decisions.

POLITICAL IDEOLOGY. One of the single most effective predictors of public opinion is an individual's identification with a political party. Partisan identification is closely connected to one's **political ideology**, which describes a person's beliefs about political goals, public policies, and acts to shape political choices. In the United States today, two political ideologies tend to dominate. **Liberalism**, in the modern usage of the term, refers to support for more robust governmental action to ensure equality of opportunity, particularly in regulation of the economy, as well as environmental regulation. **Conservatism** highlights a reduced role for the government and an emphasis on individual liberty, again, especially in economic matters.

While these two political ideologies do shape much of the landscape, there are others. **Socialism**, closely related to liberalism, emphasizes an even stronger role for the government in economic matters, including advocating for governmental control over entire sectors of the economy, such as health care. **Libertarianism**, on the other hand, shares an emphasis on individual liberty with conservatism but often takes it further, arguing that governmental involvement in the lives of Americans should be as minimal as possible.

These ideologies map onto partisan affiliation, with liberals, and some socialists, identifying with the Democratic Party, and conservatives and many libertarians identifying with the Republican Party. These mappings, however, are not always neat and clear. As we will explore in our discussion of political parties later in the book, tensions within political parties are often as consequential as debates between them.

Americans' response to Ferguson was no different. On the question of whether or not local law enforcement agencies could be trusted to administer the laws of the nation impartially and without regard to racial and ethnic identity, Americans were sharply divided according to the political parties to which they attached themselves. Similar divisions emerged in polls, showing that over two-thirds of Republicans thought that race was getting too much attention in the media coverage of Ferguson, whereas nearly 70 percent of Democrats thought that the shooting raised important issues about race in American society (see Figure 7.4).[37]

political ideology
a set of beliefs about the desired goals and outcomes of a process of governance.

liberalism
a political ideology that emphasizes more robust governmental action, especially to ensure equality.

conservatism
a political ideology that emphasizes a reduced role for government and emphasizes individual liberty.

socialism
a political ideology that emphasizes an even stronger role for government than liberalism, including government control and ownership of sectors of the economy.

libertarianism
a political ideology that emphasizes minimal governmental involvement in individual choices.

▼ **FIGURE 7.4**

Partisan Divisions in Public Opinion about Ferguson

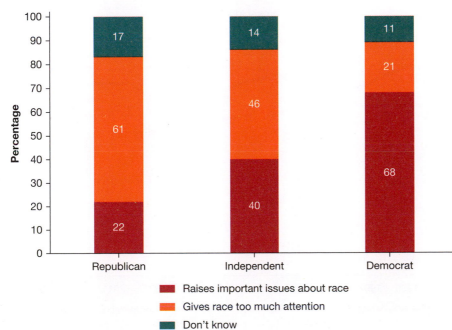

Percent saying police shooting of African-American teen . . .

Legend:
- Raises important issues about race
- Gives race too much attention
- Don't know

Source: Data from Pew Research Center, "Stark Racial Divisions in Reactions to Ferguson Police Shooting," August 18, 2014, www.people-press.org/files/2014/08/8-18-14-Ferguson-Release.pdf.

An ongoing debate among political scientists who study American political parties and elections has been about the sources of political polarization in Congress. Members of Congress are increasingly voting with members of their own party. Why? It is not clear if this trend represents an increasingly polarized environment among political elites, political masses, or both, or if some other factor or factors are at play.[38]

GENDER. American public opinion is also often divided along gender lines. On many issues, such as comparative levels of spending on social welfare programs versus national defense, polls have consistently found differences between men and women. These differences in opinion are translated into differences in support for American political parties. **Gender gap** refers to the fact that American women are more likely to identify with and vote for Democratic Party candidates than men, who are more likely to vote for Republican Party candidates (see Figure 7.5).

RACIAL AND ETHNIC IDENTITY. American public opinion is also often divided on the basis of racial and ethnic identity. Members of American racial and ethnic minorities emphasize the importance of social justice and equality of opportunity more than white Americans,[39] patterns that are correlated with the fact that racial and ethnic minorities are more likely to experience economic challenges and poverty.[40] In addition, scholars of race and gender in American politics have found evidence to support the notion of **linked fate**, in which individuals accept "the belief that [their own] life chances are inextricably tied to the group as a whole."[41] In the days following the shooting in Ferguson, public opinion surveys revealed sharp racial divisions on the event. African Americans overwhelmingly felt that Brown's shooting raised important racial issues and that the police response to the shooting was inappropriate or insufficient. They also expressed a lack of confidence in the subsequent investigations into the shooting (see Figure 7.6).[42]

To say that any community (as defined by the sum of their common experiences) would be united would be far too simplistic. Bernie Frazier, an African American speaker and career strategist from Ferguson, told the *New York Times*, "I've had moments where I feel violated by the protesters. To be honest, I feel violated by the media. I read a headline that said, 'Ferguson under siege.' I saw an article that described Ferguson as 'impoverished.' I've just stopped reading comments online. I'm done."[43]

gender gap

a term that refers to the fact that American women are more likely to identify with and vote for Democratic Party candidates than men, who are more likely to vote for Republican Party candidates.

linked fate

a theory of group identification that describes ways in which individuals tie their own life chances to those of members of a group who share their lived experiences.

▼ FIGURE 7.5

The Gender Gap in American Politics

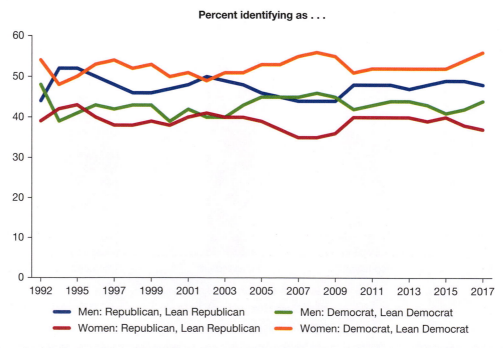

Source: Data from Pew Research Center, "Party Identification Trends, 1992–2017," March 20, 2018, http://www.people-press.org/2018/03/20/party-identification-trends-1992-2017/.

Racial and Ethnic Divisions in Opinions of Authorities' Handling of the Ferguson Investigation

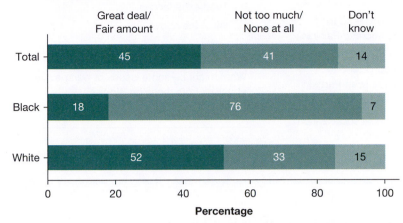

How much confidence in shooting investigations?

Notes: Survey conducted August 14–17, 2014. Whites and blacks include only those who are not Hispanic. Figures may not add to 100% because of rounding.

Source: Pew Research Center, "Stark Racial Divisions in Reactions to Ferguson Police Shooting," August 18, 2014, www.people-press.org/files/2014/08/8-18-14-Ferguson-Release.pdf.

GOVERNMENT AND MEDIA INFLUENCE PUBLIC OPINION

To many of the protesters in Ferguson, the treatment of young African American men by the American political and legal system had been a critical issue for a very long time. One of the many tasks of the president is to act as a "communicator in chief"—to focus attention on specific issues and events and to make sense of tragedies and challenges. In this role, President Barack Obama addressed the shooting of Brown in a speech at the White House, saying, "In too many communities around the country, a gulf of mistrust exists between local residents and law enforcement. . . . In too many communities, too many young men of color are left behind and seen only as objects of fear."[44]

Advancements in technology have also affected public opinion. In the next chapter, we will explore the ways that social media and online information are revolutionizing the role of the media in American political life. In the interconnected, live, and unfiltered world of social media, Ferguson made this point very clear. Following the death of Brown and the decision of the grand jury not to indict Wilson, social media lit up. According to the *Washington Post*, "'Black Twitter' . . . emerged as a powerful forum for activism and debate regarding Ferguson, helping sway public opinion by challenging racially biased interpretations of Brown's killing."[45]

WHAT HAVE I **LEARNED?**

1. Political socialization refers to _____.
   a. the fundamentally political nature of all society
   b. individuals' preferences for certain social groups
   c. the degree to which individuals were born into families that discussed politics
   d. the variety of experiences and factors that shape individual political values, attitudes, and behaviors

2. The gender gap in American politics refers to the fact that _____.
   a. Republican Party voters outnumber Democratic Party voters

(Continued)

(Continued)

b. the number of women representatives and senators has been decreasing in recent decades

c. women voters in American elections tend to support candidates from the Democratic Party in state and national elections

d. women voters in American elections tend to support candidates from the Republican Party in state and national elections

3. Contributors to the processes of political socialization include _____.

a. families

b. schools

c. lived experiences

d. All of the above

4. When you reflect upon the events of Ferguson, what divisions in American public opinion do you observe? What might be some issues or perspectives not apparent from these divisions?

_____

Answer Key: 1. d; 2. c; 3. d; 4. Answers will vary. Students might focus on ideas such as linked fate or differences in opinion about police–community relations.

FERGUSON AND THE EFFECTS OF PUBLIC OPINION ON DEMOCRATIC REPRESENTATION

- **Evaluate the power of individuals, events, and people's interpretations of events to make lasting change in American politics.**

Did Ferguson matter? Did the shooting, the protests following the shooting, other tragic events, and the national coverage of the controversy actually change the national conversation in a way that affected American public policy?

In 2015, on the one-year anniversary of Michael Brown's death, the city of Ferguson was once again witness to protest and then violence. On August 9, a group of demonstrators made their way to West Florissant Avenue in Ferguson, Missouri, shouting, "Hands up, don't shoot!"[46] By 2015, the word *Ferguson* had taken on meanings beyond what many of its residents might have previously

▶ Protesters prepared to march in downtown St. Louis on August 10, 2015, to mark the one-year anniversary of Michael Brown's death. The police response to the march was markedly different from previous protests and was much more measured and low key.

REUTERS/Rick Wilking

imagined. News reports noted, "A peaceful day of protest and remembrance dissolved into chaos late Sunday after shots were fired and one person was hit by gunfire."[47] In that sense, the two Fergusons, the peaceful daytime and troubled nighttime Fergusons, had not changed in the year since Brown's tragic death.

Certain behaviors and attitudes had changed, however. For one, even though there was some violence at the protest, the police response was different. As reported by the *New York Times*, "No police officers in riot gear emerged Friday night when protesters arrived, a tactic that has drawn criticism. Rather, a small handful of officers calmly walked out and spoke with demonstrators. Many of the Ferguson police on the scene wore white polo shirts rather than their regular uniforms," an effort to deescalate potential tensions by projecting a less military-style profile.[48] Second, there was clear evidence that Black Lives Matter had registered their policy concerns on the national stage. Political leaders and candidates for the 2016 presidential election were paying attention to the protests. They began to talk about Ferguson and what it meant for the nation going forward. During the first Democratic Party presidential candidate debate in October 2015, one of the invited members of the public asked, "My question for the candidates is, do black lives matter, or do all lives matter?" Senator Bernie Sanders (I-VT) immediately replied, "Black lives matter," and the crowd applauded.[49] When pressed by a moderator, former Maryland governor Martin O'Malley "expressed solidarity with the phrase."[50] Both Sanders and O'Malley had been confronted with public disruptions on the campaign trail challenging them to be more outspoken in their support for criminal justice reform.[51] Following the debate, members of Black Lives Matter were encouraged by the attention and conversation but wanted more specifics about how each candidate would make the words a reality.

Members of Congress were paying attention as well. In January 2015, as reported by the *St. Louis Post-Dispatch*, "On the eve of the Martin Luther King holiday, leading black members of Congress squeezed into a packed Ferguson church to deliver a specific message: We've got your backs . . . There, they vowed to push for criminal justice reform."[52] The article quoted Representative André Carson (D-IN), who said, "We're not here to tell you what to do . . . [but] just to let you know you've got some firepower in Washington, D.C. Ferguson is a clarion call. Ferguson is the new Selma."[53] In August, the *St. Louis Post-Dispatch* reported that "prominent Ferguson protesters announced on Friday Campaign Zero, a policy platform to end killings by the police in the United States, and a website to help voters keep track of where political candidates stand on police brutality."[54] Political science professor Terry Jones, an expert on urban politics and policies interviewed for the article, said, "This is an effort to put some policy meat on the protest bones and say, 'We're not simply for or against that, but here's what our policies would look like.' . . . It's an appropriate evolutionary step. Anyone who says 'I don't think the world is right as it is' should be prepared to answer the question, 'Well, what do you want to do about it?'"[55]

In August 2016, during the team's first preseason game of the National Football League against the Green Bay Packers, San Francisco 49ers' quarterback Colin Kaepernick had his own answer, and it would not go down without controversy.[56] He refused to stand during the pregame rendition of the national anthem in protest of racism, especially in police–community relations. "I am not going to stand up to show pride in a flag for a country that oppresses black people and people of color," Kaepernick later told a reporter. "To me, this is bigger than football and it would be selfish to look the other way. There are bodies in the street and people [police officers] getting paid leave and getting away with murder."[57] Kaepernick added that he had not told his team ahead of time what he planned on doing, and he fully expected that there would be repercussions, though the NFL later issued a statement saying that players in the NFL are encouraged, but not required, to stand during the anthem. "If they take football away, my endorsements from me," Kaepernick, a biracial American and #BlackLivesMatter supporter, added, "I know that I stood up for what is right."[58]

Rather than continuing to sit on the bench during the anthem, Kaepernick decided that he would kneel instead to show respect for the flag and military while protesting. During the 2016 season, other NFL players, athletes in other men's and women's professional sports, and even high school

▶ NFL quarterback Colin Kaepernick (center) kneels with fellow players during the national anthem in a regular-season game against the Seattle Seahawks, 2016, in protest against police violence.

Steve Dykes / Stringer

students began to protest in similar ways.[59] Protests expanded and continued into the 2017 NFL season. The level of tension only grew, and so did the politics. While Kaepernick remained unsigned by any NFL team, President Donald Trump, in a series of tweets and public statements, did not mince words: "Wouldn't you love to see one of these NFL owners, when somebody disrespects our flag, to say, 'Get that son of a bitch off the field right now, he's fired!' You know, some owner is going to do that."[60] Players, and some NFL owners, sharply criticized the president's stance. At a game between the 49ers and the Indianapolis Colts, Vice President Mike Pence left the game after several 49ers players kneeled during the anthem.

In 2017, Kaepernick filed a lawsuit against the NFL, arguing that the league had colluded to prevent teams, even those who had experienced injuries to their starting quarterbacks, to even bring him in for a workout. NFL commissioner Roger Goodell countered that the decisions were up to individual teams and not the league as a whole.[61] In May 2018, NFL team owners unanimously approved a policy that required players to stand for the anthem if on the field during it. Players were given the option to remain in the locker rooms during the anthem if they chose, and teams could be fined if any of their players failed to show respect for the national anthem.[62]

At about the same time, public opinion researchers with the Pew Research Center released the results of a survey asking Americans the degree to which they felt that racism was a "big problem" in American society. While, unsurprisingly, racial divisions continued, what was especially notable was the sharp increase in divisions based on political partisanship, perhaps reflecting the degree to which the issue, the NFL protests, and President Trump's comments highlighted deep divides in American public opinion. (See Figure 7.7.)

While the political rhetoric surrounding national anthem protests continued to ratchet up, another tragic event shook the nation. Once again, the question of police–community interactions was at the forefront. Several protests in Charlottesville, Virginia, in the spring and summer of 2017 ultimately ended in tragedy. The initial focal points were statues of Confederate States of America (CSA) generals Robert E. Lee and Thomas "Stonewall" Jackson. Just as the NFL protests galvanized and polarized American public opinion, so did the question of removing or keeping in place statues from military and political leaders from the Confederate South. While the Charlottesville City Council had voted to remove the statues, others vowed to protest. Following protests in May, and again in July—in

Wide Partisan Gap in Views of Racism as a "Big Problem" Grows Even Wider

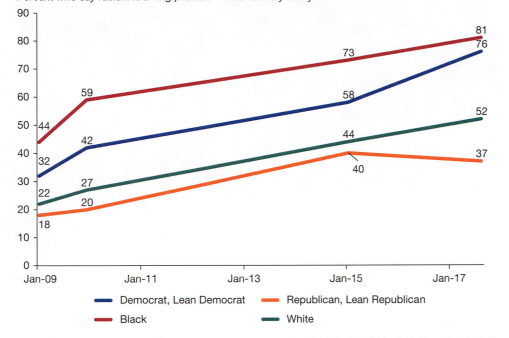

Percent who say racism is a "big problem" in our society today . . .

Source: Data from Pew Research Center, "Wide Partisan Gap in Views of Racism as 'Big Problem' Grows Even Wider; Racial Divisions Persist," August 29, 2017, http://www.pewresearch.org/fact-tank/2017/08/29/views-of-racism-as-a-major-problem-increase-sharply-especially-among-democrats/ft_17-08-29_racismproblem_2/.

which members of the white supremacist group the Ku Klux Klan (KKK) participated—the city prepared for more protests and counter-protests.

On August 11, 2017, a group calling themselves "Unite the Right" prepared to protest the removal of statues, having obtained a permit to do so. While lawyers debated whether the event would or should proceed, its location was moved at the last minute. Early on August 12, with one school resource officer—according to an independent study of the events—trying to maintain order in one area of the protests and counter protests, James Fields drove his vehicle into a crowd of counterprotesters, killing one of them, thirty-two-year-old Heather Heyer, and injuring nineteen others. The authors of the study concluded that "the City of Charlottesville protected neither free expression nor public safety on August 12 . . . which has led to a deep distrust of government within this community."[63] Speaking before an event for military veterans, President Donald Trump "blamed the unrest 'on many sides,'" prompting members of his own administration to issue clarifications condemning the murder of Heather Heyer.[64]

A Marist College Institute for Public Opinion conducted immediately following the Charlottesville murder found that a majority of Americans were not satisfied with the president's response, including a plurality of whites. "Not surprisingly," according to Center director Dr. Lee M. Miringoff, "African Americans and Latinos do not feel the president has their back, but of note, many whites are not in the president's corner either."[65] As we have explored, tracing the causal effects of any one event, even one as tragic and focusing as Ferguson, on American public opinion is difficult to do. However, there is one other way in which events may serve to shape public opinion. They may serve as lenses through which future events are viewed and interpreted. For many Americans, it was not possible to try to come to terms with Charlottesville without placing it in the larger context of the question of not just two Fergusons, but two Americas.

► People gather in front of the White House on August 13, 2017, in Washington, DC, for a vigil in response to the death of a counterprotester in the August 12 "Unite the Right" rally that turned violent in Charlottesville, Virginia.

ZACH GIBSON/AFP/Getty Images

WHAT HAVE I **LEARNED?**

1. On the one-year anniversary of Michael Brown's death, Ferguson police responded to protests by _____.

   a. banning further demonstrations

   b. keeping a lower profile

   c. trying to intimidate the crowd

   d. refusing to keep order

2. In the years even further on, what appeared to have changed? What may not have changed?

3. What do the results of public opinion surveys tell us about these potential changes?

Answer Key: 1. b; 2. Answers might emphasize the fact that the underlying issue had not gone away but that attitudes had changed and people now felt the need to pay more attention to the concerns raised by the protesters; 3. Answers should focus on an apparent break in trend, in both black and white opinion.

CONCLUSION: HOW MEANINGFUL IS PUBLIC OPINION?

Political scientist John Kingdon once asked, "But what makes an idea's time come?"[66] That is a very good question and one to which individuals must attend if they are trying to shape laws and policies to get their voices heard. In terms of public opinion, we might rephrase Professor Kingdon's question as this: But what makes a change of public opinion's time come? And, we might add, does it even matter if public opinion changes at all?

Reflecting upon Ferguson, other protests inspired by Black Lives Matter, and more recent tragic events, one thing has appeared to have changed, and that is the list of issues on the national political agenda. To that list has been added the treatment of African Americans, especially young African

American men, by the American law enforcement system: "'I live in one of the poorest zip codes in Missouri,' said Ferguson protester Tory Russell in a conference call with reporters, adding that fellow African Americans in the area experience high rates of mortality and murder. 'I never heard any of my elected officials declare those things a state of emergency,' said Mr. Russell, who started the group Hands Up United after Mr. Brown's death to seek justice in Ferguson and beyond."[67]

In this chapter, we have explored debates over the coherence and impact of what we call American public opinion by focusing mostly on one tragic event. While the ultimate effects of the tragedy—as well as the protests and efforts at political mobilization that followed—are not yet certain, at the very least the nation's political conversation has been altered.

In October 2014, "Lesley McSpadden, Mr. Brown's mother, made one of her regular visits to the place where her son was killed. . . . She comes to the memorial all the time, she said, even though visits to the site of her son's death deepen her pain. . . . Gazing down at the memorial, Ms. McSpadden pondered the question of how long it should stay in place. 'Forever,' she said."[68]

CHAPTER REVIEW

This chapter's main ideas are reflected in the Learning Objectives below. By reviewing them here, you should be able to **remember** the key points, **know** the terms that are central to the topic, and **think** about the critical issues raised in each section.

7.1 Understand how public opinion is fluid, often not unified, and shapable.

REMEMBER
- Public opinion is characterized as the aggregation of individual beliefs and attitudes.
- Public opinion is not fixed or static.

KNOW
- public opinion (p. 183)
- public opinion survey (p. 184)

THINK
- What about American public opinion did the events after Ferguson reveal?

7.2 Discuss differing theories about public opinion formation and expression and the degree to which it is meaningful.

REMEMBER
- Representative democracy depends upon individuals having meaningful preferences on issues. Only when constituents are able to convey meaningful opinions can they be adequately represented by public officials.

KNOW
- consideration (p. 190)
- cues and information shortcuts (p. 190)
- elites (p. 188)
- masses (p. 188)
- minimalist paradigm (p. 188)
- nonattitudes (p. 189)
- stereotype (p. 188)

THINK
- What are some of the challenges in identifying what we can meaningfully conclude from measures of public opinion?
- What are some contrasting perspectives on the coherence of mass public opinion?

7.3 Describe the issues involved in transmitting and measuring American public opinion and constructing the instruments used to do so.

REMEMBER
- Americans need to be able to communicate their preferences to government, and their representatives need mechanisms that allow them to learn what those preferences are.

KNOW
- direction (p. 195)
- exit poll (p. 194)
- focus group (p. 192)
- intensity (p. 195)
- push poll (p. 196)
- question order (p. 195)
- question wording (p. 195)

- race of interviewer effects (p. 195)
- random digit dialing (p. 194)
- random selection (p. 193)
- respondents (p. 193)
- salience (p. 195)
- sample (p. 193)
- sampling error (p. 193)

- scientific poll (p. 193)
- self-selected listener opinion poll (SLOP) (p. 194)
- stability (p. 195)
- straw poll (p. 193)
- validity (p. 193)
- weighting (p. 193)

THINK
- In what ways do most people have meaningful opinions? Does this matter? How much do we have to know in order to meaningfully participate in American politics?
- Are public opinion poll results trustworthy? Why or why not?

7.4 Examine the contributors to individual attitudes and public opinion.

REMEMBER
- Forming and changing political opinions and attitudes is a lifelong process. The process by which our experiences and other personal factors shape our attitudes toward political issues and public policies is called political socialization. There are many sources of political socialization.
- Party identification and political ideology are important contributors to public opinion.

KNOW
- civic education (p. 197)
- conservatism (p. 199)
- focusing events (p. 197)
- gender gap (p. 200)

- liberalism (p. 199)
- libertarianism (p. 199)
- linked fate (p. 200)
- party identification (p. 197)

- political ideology (p. 199)
- political socialization (p. 197)
- socialism (p. 199)

THINK
- How much do you think your fellow students' opinions about important issues in American government are really open to listening, to reflection, and reevaluation? What about your own?
- How has social media changed how you learn about, interpret, and derive conclusions about American politics today?

7.5 Evaluate the power of individuals, events, and people's interpretations of events to make lasting change in American politics.

REMEMBER
- Important events can shape public opinion. Individuals may filter their interpretation of these events through lenses such as partisan identification, gender, or racial or ethnic identity. How the media portray these events may also play a role in opinion formation and change.

THINK
- In your experience, can focusing events, including tragic ones, change the national conversation?
- If you were to write a letter to a member of Congress, another public official, or a celebrity, what would you tell them that they need to pay more attention to? Why?

CHAPTER 8

THE MEDIA

Truth, Power, and American Democracy

Jaap Arriens/NurPhoto via Getty Images

▼ Fake Donald Trump tweets are shown in a Twitter timeline in February 2017. In China, a site that generates fake tweets that look as if they were generated by U.S. president Donald Trump is being used to mock the president.

140   ⚡ Tweet

View 11 new Tweets

· 4m

p @realDonaldTrump · Now

porting FAKE NEWS again. So ot nice!

VORITES
839

2017 · Details

essives · 4m

e our recap and find out what's on the agenda for next
→ socsde.ms/ZUF

f · 9m

september nog met roken telegraaf.nl/r/27512366

Donald J. Trump
@realDonaldTrump

45th President of the United S
America

📍 Washington, DC
📅 Joined March 2009

⚡ Tweet to Donald J.

👤 58 Followers you know

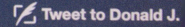

Americans' political knowledge is sometimes learned directly through experiences like going to a school board meeting, talking with a political candidate, or attending a rally or protest. More often, however, it is mediated, filtered through the news outlets that inform us of political issues. Collectively, this group of news providers is called the **news media**, a broad term that includes newspapers, magazines, radio, television, Internet sources, blogs, and social media postings, all in service of informing or persuading. The word *media* is plural, as it refers to a universe of venues and outlets. As we will explore, the way those news sources are produced, who their audiences are, and what technological capabilities they possess all shape the presentation, reception, effect, and even the definition of the news itself.

The American news media is in a period of radical flux. Technology-driven change, partisan politics, ownership, trustworthiness, bias, and objectivity are front and center in debates about the current, or proper, role of the American news media in our political lives. Americans are simultaneously witnessing a major decline in daily newspaper readership, the rise of social media, and increasingly divisive language in political talk shows. What do these changes in the media landscape mean for political representation and participation in the twenty-first century?

We will explore that question and others through the prism of two stories: the controversy surrounding media coverage of accusations of Russian involvement in the presidential election of 2016 and a fake radio-broadcasted invasion from Mars in 1938. Why these two stories, separated by nearly 80 years? Because they are united by two enduring questions: How effective are the news media in shaping Americans' views? Can we trust our news media sources? These are not separate questions, in fact. At their core, both point directly to Americans' role not only as receivers of the news media but as shapers of the media that they choose as their sources. This issue returns us to questions raised in our study of public opinion: How shapable are Americans' attitudes and preferences? Are we filing cabinets with a set of predetermined and firm attitudes and opinions? Or are we pieces of clay, vulnerable to outside forces to shape as they see fit? If there was a proper test of these questions, 2016 provided it. The answers, though, are still unsettled.

....

news media
the variety of sources providing information and covering events, including newspapers, television, radio, the Internet, and social media.

LEARNING OBJECTIVES

By reading this chapter, you will be able to do the following:

8.1 Describe both who the news media are and the major questions of truth, power, and trust at stake in the media today.

8.2 Trace the historical development of the American news media.

8.3 Understand the issue of bias in the American media.

8.4 Discuss changes in the regulation of media ownership and media content.

8.5 Explain the different perspectives on the power of the media to shape political understanding and behaviors.

CAN A FOREIGN GOVERNMENT CHANGE A PRESIDENTIAL ELECTION? HOW POWERFUL ARE THE MEDIA?

• **Describe both who the news media are and the major questions of truth, power, and trust at stake in the media today.**

"Weaponized information."[1]

These were the words that Hillary Clinton used to describe what she thought contributed to her loss to Republican Donald Trump in the 2016 presidential election. Interviewed before a live audience at a May 2017 conference, Clinton and her interviewers talked about how domestic or foreign political actors might use the media, especially social media, to influence or undermine a political candidate. They returned time and again to the idea that under certain conditions, news stories could be made powerful enough to become political weapons—vastly more destructive than in earlier campaign cycles.

The specific weapons Clinton was talking about were the release late in the campaign of a series of emails, without authorization and allegedly stolen, from the Democratic National Committee (DNC).

 Hillary Clinton speaks at a conference in March 2017, where she leveled charges that the Russians had weaponized news stories against her, costing her the 2016 election.

Some of the most incendiary emails involved alleged exchanges among Clinton's campaign chairman, John Podesta; his aides; Clinton family members; and influential donors. In those unflattering emails, Podesta and others talked about the perception of Secretary Clinton's close ties to Wall Street, reactions to the controversy surrounding Clinton's use of a private email server to conduct official business while serving as secretary of state (which would later come under Federal Bureau of Investigation [FBI] review without charges), and plans to attack the policy positions and record of Senator Bernie Sanders, the other remaining Democratic nominee.

It is common for the staff involved in such a high-stakes political campaign to think of every angle, plan for every possibility. That is what they are hired to do. However, Hillary Clinton believed that the steady leak of those emails through the website WikiLeaks might have helped to shape the narrative of her presidential campaign and damage her political image.

Many speculated about who was behind the leaked emails and the news stories they generated. Clinton pointed directly to the Russian government, saying, "If you look at Facebook, the vast majority of the news items posted were fake. They were connected to, as we now know, the 1,000 Russian agents who were involved in delivering these messages."[2] Secretary Clinton noted, "I take responsibility for every decision I made, but that's not why I lost. So I think it's important that we learn the real lessons from this last campaign because the forces that we are up against are not just interested in influencing our election and our politics, they're going after our economy and they're going after our unity as a nation."[3]

Indeed, a January 2017 intelligence community assessment involving members of the Central Intelligence Agency (CIA), the FBI, and the National Security Agency (NSA) concluded that "Russian President Vladimir Putin ordered an influence campaign in 2016 aimed at the US presidential election. Russia's goals were to undermine public faith in the US democratic process, denigrate Secretary Clinton, and harm her electability and potential presidency."[4]

Not everyone agreed, most especially President Donald Trump, who challenged the certainty of these conclusions. In a tweet from January 2017, President Trump asserted, "Julian Assange [the founder of WikiLeaks] said 'a 14 year old could have hacked Podesta'[;] why was DNC [the Democratic National Committee] so careless? Also said Russians did not give him the info!"[5] The presidential election of 2016 was a very close one, decided by perhaps 80,000 votes in a few key battleground states, so the idea that Russia might have used the American media to tip the election was not a welcome one and potentially undermining for a new administration. It should be noted, too, that Clinton was not the only candidate facing negative press. Candidate Trump was hardly the darling of most mainstream newspaper and television outlets and faced plenty of negative coverage of his own: "He was subject to not just relentless partisan attacks but also to overwhelmingly negative media coverage, much of it due to his own endless gaffes and scandals."[6]

Donald J. Trump ✔
@realDonaldTrump

Follow ∨

Now that Russian collusion, after one year of intense study, has proven to be a total hoax on the American public, the Democrats and their lapdogs, the Fake News Mainstream Media, are taking out the old Ronald Reagan playbook and screaming mental stability and intelligence.....

4:19 AM - 6 Jan 2018

33,729 Retweets **145,043** Likes

💬 37K   ↻ 34K   ♡ 145K   ✉

 President Donald Trump took to Twitter to protest what he saw as unfair media coverage. The question of how much power the media have to influence the publics' beliefs and opinions is the subject of much debate.

In February 2018, President Trump's director of national intelligence, Dan Coats, contradicted Trump's denial of Russian intervention and warned senators that Russia intended to build on the efforts of 2016 in the upcoming midterm elections. "There should be no doubt that Russia perceives its past efforts as successful and views the 2018 U.S. midterm elections as a potential target for Russian influence operations," Director Coats stated.[7] The CIA director and the FBI director concurred with the dire assessment.[8]

Investigations and debates into the source of the email hacking are ongoing, and legislators, lawyers, and historians will ultimately draw their final conclusions. Our focus in this chapter, however, is not on the intent of Russian agents but more broadly on the capability of media in general: Do the media really have the power to determine the outcome of an event as important as the election of 2016?

That question speaks very much to how fair and just media sources are in their coverage and the power they wield as organizations. But it also speaks to Americans' potential vulnerability to the media's power, especially in the era of new media. As a first step in our investigation of those questions, it is useful to study the development of the American media; we will learn that the role of the American media in politics is the one story that is not really new.

Truth, trust, and power. These are the issues with which consumers of the American news media have always had to contend. Technology may have changed the medium, but the same questions endure.

WHAT HAVE I **LEARNED?**

1. By "weaponized information," Hillary Clinton meant _____.

   a. a type of information that requires security clearances before journalists can gain access

   b. that media sources were able to transform news stories into politically damaging information

   c. untrue media reports of military activity

   d. information published on Russian state news sites that was unfavorable to her

2. What concerns did Secretary Clinton and President Trump express about Russian interference in the 2016 elections?

3. How powerful do you think the various forms of news media are? Is one more influential than the others?

Answer Key: 1. b; 2. Answers might focus on the power of a foreign country to use the media to undermine the legitimacy of the electoral process, the current administration, and other institutions; 3. Answers might involve a discussion of the media's power in shaping political knowledge and attitudes and a defense of why a particular form is more powerful than the others if stated.

THE EVOLUTION OF AMERICAN MEDIA SHOWS THAT ISSUES OF POWER AND TRUSTWORTHINESS ARE NOT NEW

- Trace the historical development of the American news media.

The news media have played an important role in shaping American political culture and Americans' attitudes toward their political leaders and institutions from before the country's founding to today. Throughout this history, the connection between the nation's media and American politics has also been shaped in important ways by technological change, politics, and the tension between the rights of a free press and other demands, especially the desire to preserve national security.

EARLY NEWSPAPERS AND PAMPHLETS SHAPE A NEW NATION

The pamphlet, a loosely stitched booklet made on a hand-cranked printing press, was the first type of media to shape American attitudes, mobilizing support for the cause of independence from Great Britain. While printing had become cheaper and more widespread in the years leading up to the Revolutionary War, publishing was far from easy. The British colonial administration recognized the pamphlet for what it was, a potentially powerful and revolutionary tool. According to Patrick Novotny, the British seized some printer's presses, "while still others hid their presses or fled their homes with their families, taking their presses with them. Others closed their shops before the British could."[9]

The number of weekly and then daily newspapers grew in the years following the Revolutionary War, and the newspaper took its place as the primary source for information about American politics. First published in 1783, the *Pennsylvania Evening Post, and Daily Advertiser* was the nation's first daily newspaper; its young salesmen were instructed to shout out to passersby, "All the news for two coppers."[10] Like the pamphlets, early newspapers were a form of print media. Like the pamphlets as well, early newspapers were hand printed, one sheet at a time, which made them expensive and restricted their access, even to those who could read them.

Four years later, the nation's second daily newspaper, the *Pennsylvania Packet, and Daily Advertiser*, published just blocks away from where the *Evening Post* had started out, was the first to print the full text of the proposed Constitution of the United States. The delegates to the Constitutional Convention had been very careful to prevent any leaks during the proceedings, thus starving the weeklies and dailies of raw materials for their stories. With the publication of the proposed Constitution, which spurred a flood of editorials for and against the document, newspapers took their place at the center of American political life in the late 1780s.

FREEDOM OF THE PRESS BECOMES ENSHRINED IN THE CONSTITUTION THROUGH THE BILL OF RIGHTS

With memories of British colonial suppression of freedoms of speech and of the press fresh in their minds, the delegates to the Constitutional Convention were well aware of the need to preserve and protect these freedoms. On August 20, 1787, Charles Pinckney from South Carolina proposed the inclusion of the guarantee, "The liberty of the Press shall be inviolably preserved."[11] While a guarantee of freedom of the press did not end up in the original Constitution, Pinckney's proposal signaled support for including specific rights and liberties in a constituting document. As the ratification debates began, the argument to include such a list—a Bill of Rights—became one of the most convincing arguments that the anti-Federalists presented.

While the Bill of Rights was not part of the original document, a promise to introduce a set of amendments during the session of Congress in 1789 proved crucial to securing the ratification of the Constitution. Included in the first of the ten ratified amendments was language very close to Pinckney's initial proposal: "Congress shall make no law . . . abridging the freedom of speech, or of the press." This provided the foundation for press freedoms.

The press also played a pivotal role in the ratification debates themselves, as proponents and opponents of the document made their cases through the nation's newspapers, often writing under pseudonyms. *The Federalist Papers*, the classic statement of the theory behind the Constitution, authored by Alexander Hamilton, James Madison, and John Jay, first appeared as a series of essays written under the pseudonym "Publius" in the New York newspapers. For their part, the anti-Federalists produced essays warning of the dangers to liberty presented by the proposed Constitution.

THE MEDIA GO "MASS" WITH THE PENNY PRESSES IN THE EIGHTEENTH AND NINETEENTH CENTURIES

In the late eighteenth and early nineteenth centuries, however, the dailies and weeklies reached only a relatively small part of the population, in no small part because they were expensive and often available only through an annual subscription, which required putting down a large sum of money all at once rather than for each issue. Political and financial elites were the main consumers, not the mass public. Much of the space in newspapers was taken up by advertisements, and the stories' content was often overtly political, a fact that was hardly hidden or a point of controversy. Political parties and candidates often supported the presses financially in addition to providing them with essays, stories, and content.[12] By taking political positions and supporting candidates and parties, these papers were acting as a **partisan press**. The nation's first political parties were backed by a partisan press. James Madison and Thomas Jefferson supported the founding of the *National Gazette* in 1791 in response to the partisan coverage presented by the *Federalist Gazette* of the United States.

As the cost to produce and, therefore, buy a newspaper fell during the 1830s, readership grew rapidly. The **penny press**, so labeled because an individual paper cost one penny, could be purchased on the street from newsboys hawking their products. Within just a few months of its introduction as the nation's first penny press, the *New York Sun* was the city's top-selling paper; by 1834, the *Sun* "was selling 15,000 copies a day."[13] The penny press was truly an example of the **mass media**—sources of information and

partisan press
media outlets or organizations that promote a particular political ideology or support a political party.

penny press
nineteenth-century American newspapers that sold for only one cent each, thus increasing the size of the audience that could afford to purchase them.

mass media
sources of information that appeal to a wide audience, including newspapers, radio, television, and Internet outlets.

entertainment (including newspapers, television and radio broadcasts, and Internet content) designed to reach large audiences.

Its content was sometimes overtly political; however, the penny papers depended far less on political parties for funding or support. They had a new boss: the public. Instead of relying on parties, candidates, or politicians for their content, the penny papers had to make their own. To do so, they hired reporters to dig up the kinds of stories that would lure readers and advertisers. Newspapers depended on sales and on providing an audience for the advertisers, so they often focused on dramatic stories of crime, riots, and scandalous behavior.[14] **Yellow journalism**, the use of sensational headlines, cartoons and graphics, and emotional language, had a very commercial reason behind its emergence. It worked, boosting sales and profits.

Sensationalism was not confined to stories of crime, misdeeds, and moral failures. In skilled hands, bold headlines, enticing leads, and emotional language could also be put to political purposes. William Randolph Hearst, publisher of the *New York Journal*, harnessed yellow journalism to advocate war with Spain in the late 1890s. While the Spanish-American War had many causes, Hearst's efforts helped to shape public opinion about the prospect for war. This example of the potential power of the press to influence public opinion raised the specter of a malleable American public at the mercy of presses and publishers with their own political agendas.

World History Archive / Alamy Stock Photo

▲ A newsboy carrying inexpensive newspapers called *penny press* runs along a train platform selling papers to passengers. As the cost of printing decreased with technological advances in the process, the price of newspapers also decreased, and readership dramatically increased.

yellow journalism
an approach to reporting employed in the nineteenth century that relied on sensational headlines and emotional language to persuade readers and sell newspapers.

wire service
an organization that gathers and reports on news and then sells the stories to other outlets.

investigative journalism
an approach to newsgathering in which reporters dig into stories, often looking for instances of corruption or failures to uphold the interests of citizens.

JOURNALISTS BECOME INVESTIGATORS AND ACTIVISTS IN THE NINETEENTH CENTURY

A faster and cheaper printing press was not the only technological development that shaped the newspaper in the nineteenth century. The telegraph allowed news to travel instantaneously over distances that might have taken days or weeks otherwise. The papers benefited tremendously from the technology and helped to finance and spread it. In 1846, New York newspapers combined their efforts to fund a pony express route to more quickly deliver news of the Mexican War, thus creating the Associated Press.[15] Though the technology they were originally funding ran on four legs, the Associated Press took advantage of the telegraph to create a **wire service**, an organization that gathers the news and offers it for sale to other media outlets. The nineteenth century also witnessed a new approach to news coverage, **investigative journalism**, in which journalists actively dug up and dug into stories rather than simply conveying the speeches and opinions of political leaders. During the Progressive Era, an important group of investigative reporters became known as *muckrakers*; the name was a reference to a tool used to collect manure. Muckrakers used their investigative tactics to bring to light corruption and scandal and also to shape public opinion in support of business or governmental reforms.[16]

THE TWENTIETH CENTURY BRINGS RADIO AND TV NEWS DIRECTLY INTO AMERICANS' HOMES

Technological advances during the twentieth century brought political figures into Americans' lives and homes in a direct way, first providing their voices with the advent and widespread adoption of radio and

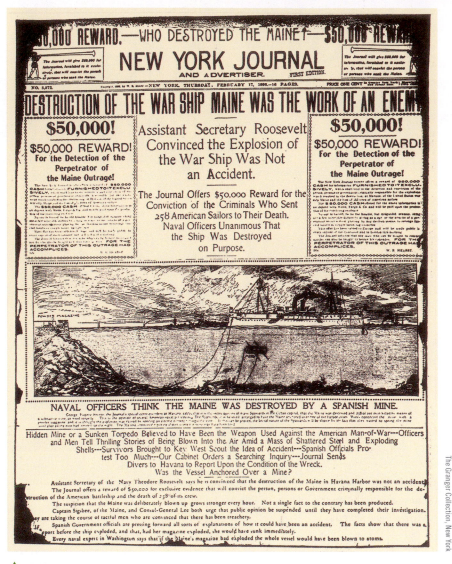

The Granger Collection, New York

▲ An example of yellow journalism, the sensationalistic coverage by Hearst of the destruction of the USS *Maine* contributed to public support for the decision to declare war on Spain.

then adding their faces and actions with television. Radio and television, which are examples of **broadcast media**, offered political news to citizens directly and immediately. Its consumption was often a shared experience, with only one radio or television set in the home or in the neighborhood, and the news could be consumed while doing other things, such as driving, doing chores, working, or eating a meal. These forms of media were also truly "mass" in the sense of a shared media experience by their consumers. In breaking down geographic barriers, the broadcast media were truly national in scope.

As an instrument of conveying political news, radio really came into its own in the 1930s, and no public official was more adept in its use than President Franklin Delano Roosevelt. Beginning in March 1933, Roosevelt began broadcasting speeches to the American public; these speeches became known as "fireside chats," a term coined by a bureau chief with CBS News, even though there was no fireplace.[17] The broadcasts were designed to calm anxious Americans during the depths of the Great Depression, present Roosevelt's Depression-fighting policies, and later guide citizens through the travails of World War II.

Today, the nation's radios crackle with political commentary from the other side of the debate. Many of these shows lean Republican, such as *The Rush Limbaugh Show*, but there are liberal examples as well. These talk radio broadcasts have been criticized for their efforts to "provoke emotional responses (e.g., anger, fear, moral indignation) from the audience through the use of overgeneralizations, sensationalism, misleading or patently inaccurate information, ad hominem attacks, and belittling ridicule of opponents."[18]

If the 1930s signaled the emergence of radio as a powerful new force in political news, the late 1950s did the same for television. Television's version of Roosevelt was also a president: John F. Kennedy. Even though most American homes had a television by the 1950s (see Figure 8.1 in the next section), newspapers remained the primary source of news and coverage of political events. In September 1960, candidates Kennedy and Richard Nixon participated in the first televised presidential debates in American history. While experts and radio listeners did not declare a clear winner, Kennedy's image on television came across as robust and energetic, while Nixon, who had been fighting the flu, appeared pallid and sweaty. In 1961, Kennedy, having won the presidency, gave the first live televised news conference.

As television news broadcasts lengthened and more and more Americans relied upon the major networks for their news and coverage of political events, television news anchors became trusted figures in relaying, describing, and interpreting these events. As the Vietnam War progressed, American casualties mounted, and protests against American involvement spread and grew, trusted television journalist Walter Cronkite questioned if the war had become unwinnable. It was widely reported that President Lyndon Johnson observed, "If I've lost Cronkite, I've lost Middle America."[19] Though this response may be apocryphal, the idea that a trusted news anchor could so strongly affect American public opinion in an area as vital as foreign policy speaks to the power that many attributed to television news anchors during the heyday of network news.

The 1990s witnessed the rise of a new outlet for television and television news, and its emergence as a major player came about during wartime. First broadcasting in 1980, CNN, the Cable News Network, presented Americans with twenty-four-hour coverage of the news. CNN's coverage of the Persian Gulf War, however, placed it squarely on the news media map. In 1991, CNN broadcast video coverage of the bombing of Baghdad by American and coalition forces during the Persian Gulf War live, in real time, and unconstrained by the set news broadcast schedule typically employed by the major broadcast networks.

The American political news media had broken the clock. They had gone 24/7, and America tuned in. Later that decade, in 1996, Australian media entrepreneur Rupert Murdoch launched Fox News, which provided a self-consciously conservative interpretation of the nation's news and political events. Americans who felt that network news coverage was too liberal tuned in.

Cable television news changed more than just the schedule of coverage; it changed the form itself. Operating under looser regulatory constraints than the broadcast networks and in a time when those constraints were being relaxed (see next section), television news became more avowedly partisan, less "objective." To some, this overt partisanship seemed like a new and dangerous thing. In fact, it was not new—questions of the objectivity of network news had long been a common source of commentary and conversation. Cable television news coverage became more like what newspapers had been during much of the nation's history: unapologetically partisan.

NEW MEDIA HAVE REINVENTED THE MEDIA LANDSCAPE

Developed and deployed though a collaboration between the Defense Advanced Research Projects Agency (DARPA) and research universities, the Internet revolutionized the media landscape in the late twentieth and early twenty-first centuries. The adoption of broadband reception, the Internet, and other communications technologies enabled Americans to receive and send text, sound, and video at increasingly fast speed and in increasingly large volume. Broadband and wireless technology has followed an accelerating pattern of adoption of new technologies not entirely different from that of radio and television (see Figure 8.1).

These new forms of media communication have revolutionized far more than the speed of delivery, or even the content, of political news available to consumers of the news and politics. In the era of 24/7 news coverage and the merging of entertainment and social media, individuals can be journalists, citizens can be editors and commentators, and members of the media can be and are often pressured to be celebrities. Throughout much of the nation's history, most Americans had a limited number of choices in their news media outlets—generally, one or two daily newspapers, several radio stations, and a few major television broadcast networks. The rise of cable television expanded the number of options, then the Internet increased these options even further.

Courtesy of the Library of Congress, Prints and Photographs Division

▲ President Franklin Delano Roosevelt at a fireside chat in 1936. Roosevelt's broadcasts to the nation during times of crisis helped calm a worried population and enabled him to successfully pitch his policies.

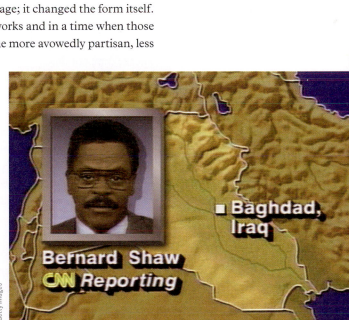

CNN via Getty Images

▲ A screenshot of CNN correspondent Bernard Shaw reporting on the bombing of Baghdad, Iraq, via satellite phone on the first night of the Gulf War, January 16, 1991. The network's strategy for round-the-clock news coverage established a new pattern for how the news was covered.

Patterns of Adoption of Communications Technologies

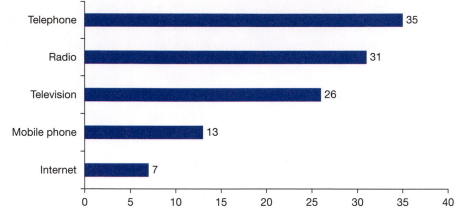

Number of years until used by 25 percent of Americans

Telephone	35
Radio	31
Television	26
Mobile phone	13
Internet	7

Source: Data from "Happy Birthday, World Wide Web," *The Economist*, March 12, 2014, www.economist.com/blogs/graphicdetail/2014/03/daily-chart-7?%3Ffsrc%3Dscn%2F=tw%2Fdc.

The rise of **social media** put these trends into hyperdrive. However, the story was not only about the rise of new media outlets but also about the need for old media outlets, such as broadcast television, to stay relevant. One strategy was to create a greater presence of traditional network broadcast journalists in other venues and highlight their visibility, even celebrity, in order to reach larger audiences in an age of intense competition.

Much of the news content transmitted through social media is generated in traditional ways—previously produced stories, videos, and commentaries linked to on Facebook, posted on YouTube, or tweeted to members of one's social network. Other content, however, is generated by **citizen journalists**, nonprofessionals who cover events, say, through filming them on their cell phones or by providing their own commentaries and analysis. The Internet and modern communications technologies did not create the idea of citizen journalism, but they did provide the ability to capture, report on, and transmit citizen-generated news content more quickly and cheaply than has ever been possible. While citizen journalists operate in a variety of contexts, one of the most extreme is combat and military operations abroad. Some scholars of the news media point to the benefits of its democratization, but others worry because citizen journalists lack the ability to fact-check that large news organizations possess.

The term *new media* is used to refer to all of the various digital platforms through which individuals receive, share, and produce content. In one sense, the new media are examples of mass media. They often reach large audiences and in many cases do so with startling speed. In another sense, however, there are also aspects to the new media that are very old. They often do not have mass appeal but cater to a group of individuals with shared perspectives, similar to many cable news channels but even more so. They shatter geographic boundaries, like the mass media, but create their own form of fragmentation, providing an opportunity for individuals to self-select into narrow political and informational enclaves. This type of journalism is known as **niche journalism**.

One of the most important developments in the Internet age has been the rise of social media outlets, such as Facebook and Twitter. These interactive media environments allow individuals to create or share text, image, and video as well as comment on the content and forward it to other members of their own personal networks. We have already discussed the effects of new technologies in supporting citizen journalism and addressed concerns about the ability to verify such reports for accuracy. For politicians, however, there is another concern. As they are often acting and speaking amid a sea of cell phone cameras, they must always be aware that any spontaneous, off-the-cuff

social media
forms of electronic communication that enable users to create and share content or to participate in social networking.

citizen journalists
nonprofessionals who cover or document news and events or offer their own analyses of them.

niche journalism
media that cater to fragmented and specialized audiences.

DRAWING CONCLUSIONS FROM DATA: DO THE MEDIA MAKE US SMART (OR NOT SO SMART)? OR DO WE MAKE THEM LOOK GOOD (OR NOT SO GOOD)?

In 2007, the Pew Research Center reported the findings of a study of Americans' political knowledge and media usage.[20] Part of the study was a political knowledge quiz in which the roughly 1,500 respondents were asked to identify individuals and answer questions about American government. Based on how well they did answering these questions, researchers divided the respondents into three groups: high knowledge, moderate knowledge, and low knowledge.

Another part of the survey asked respondents to identify which sources of political news they regularly consumed, including print, radio, television, cable, and Internet sources. The sources themselves were then "scored" based on how knowledgeable their regular consumers were. While no one technology emerged as being more or less consumed by more or less knowledgeable individuals, there were some considerable differences between specific sources.

The Daily Show and *The Colbert Report*, along with newspaper websites, had the most knowledgeable consumers. The conservative Rush Limbaugh radio show and *O'Reilly Factor* also had relatively knowledgeable consumers. Fox News Channel and the network morning shows had the least knowledgeable consumers.

WHAT Do You Think?

What conclusions can we draw from these data? This is where it is important to be careful. It may be that *The Daily Show* is very educational, making its consumers more informed. On the other hand, it may be that it attracts more informed consumers, as much of the show's humor is not that funny without some background information. Or it may be a combination of these two causes. What more information might be useful in making stronger conclusions?

Knowledge Levels by News Source

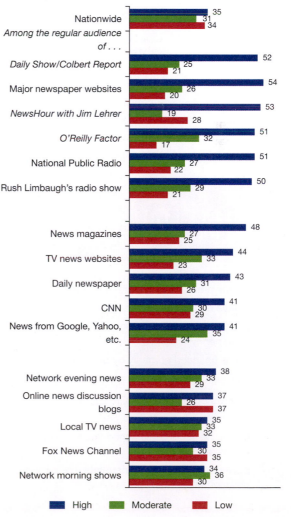

Percentage of Survey Respondents Who Can Identify . . .

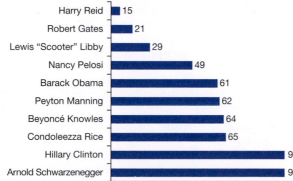

Percentage of Survey Respondents Who Can Recall the Name of . . .

Source: Pew Research Center, "What Americans Know: 1989–2007," April 2007, http://www.people-press.org/files/legacy-pdf/319.pdf.

Source: Pew Research Center, "What Americans Know: 1989–2007" April 2007, http://www.people-press.org/files/legacy-pdf/319.pdf.

▼ FIGURE 8.2

Generational Differences in Primary Sources for Political News

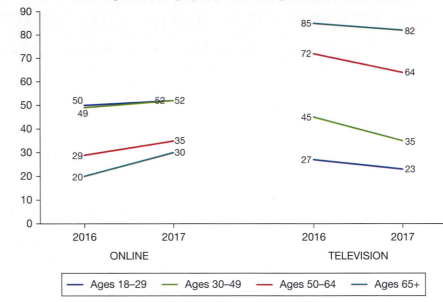

Percentage of each age group who *often* gets news on each platform

Legend: Ages 18–29, Ages 30–49, Ages 50–64, Ages 65+

Source: Jeffrey Gottfried and Elisa Shearer, "Americans' Online News Use Is Closing in on TV News Use," Pew Research Center, September 7, 2017, http://www.pewresearch.org/fact-tank/2017/09/07/americans-online-news-use-vs-tv-news-use/.

remarks might find their way onto YouTube or Facebook within minutes. While the use of social media as the primary source of political news has grown tremendously in recent years, these trends are very much divided by generational differences (see Figure 8.2). Skillful political actors can take advantage of the power of social media to advance their own goals and policy objectives. Enter President Donald Trump.

WHAT HAVE I **LEARNED**?

1. The penny press was important because _____.
   a. it gave equal time to all political viewpoints
   b. it focused only on economic issues, hence the word *penny*
   c. it was financed primarily by political parties
   d. it brought the news to a much larger audience

2. Cable news outlets such as CNN _____.
   a. are strictly nonpartisan
   b. follow the same basic schedule as broadcast television news outlets
   c. have more regulatory constraints than broadcast news outlets
   d. have fewer regulatory constraints than broadcast news outlets

3. In what ways did radio and television change Americans' reception of the news?

4. How have the new media changed coverage of political news?

Answer Key: 1. d; 2. d; 3. Answers might include a discussion of the role that these media played in standardizing coverage and bringing it directly into Americans' homes; 4. Answers might include the speed and immediacy of coverage but also the pressure new media has put on broadcast media outlets to compete and survive in the new media landscape.

QUESTIONS OF BIAS CHALLENGE AMERICANS' TRUST IN THE MEDIA'S OBJECTIVITY

- **Understand the issue of bias in the American media.**

In 2017, President Donald Trump declared war.

It was not on Russia but on the media covering the story about his administration's alleged ties with that nation—CNN in particular. In a series of tweets that escalated to the boiling point that summer, the president accused CNN, MSNBC, the *New York Times*, and other mainstream media outlets of broadcasting "fake news" with the goal of undermining his presidency.

In February, President Trump took on the *New York Times* and the rest of the mainstream American media directly, using his Twitter account:

The president's accusation was based upon allegations that the *New York Times* had run an inaccurate and poorly sourced story about his ties to the Russian government.[21]

The term **fake news** is thrown about frequently today, but what does it really mean? To some, it means the intentional use of the media to support a political party, something that would have been hardly surprising to editors of nineteenth-century newspapers. To others, it means the intentional presentation of material that the news agency knows to be untrue, or at least unverified. To others, it means the intentional use of the mass media to change political outcomes to intentionally deceive the public. In reality, it can be all of these. The challenge for consumers of the American media is to determine fact from fiction. It is not an easy task, especially in a new media environment so politically charged and one that moves at warp speed.

In June 2017, Project Veritas released what it claimed was undercover footage from an interview with a supervising producer of CNN. In it, the producer allegedly claimed that the 24/7 coverage of President Trump's possible ties with Russia was all about ratings: "Trump is good for business right now."[22] Asked if the Russia story was "bullsh*t," the producer was recorded as saying, "Could be bullsh*t. I mean it's mostly bullsh*t. Like we don't have any big giant proof."[23] In another video, widely watched CNN political commentator Van Jones was recorded as saying, "The Russia thing is just a big nothing burger."[24] Later that month, three journalists resigned from CNN "after the cable news network was forced to retract and apologize for a story on its website involving a close ally of President Trump."[25]

For its part, CNN countered that Sean Spicer, President Trump's press secretary at the time, misrepresented the story. Jake Tapper from CNN reinforced the conclusions of members of the intelligence community that asserted Russian influence in the 2016 elections.[26] In the end, however, all of it—from President Trump's tweets to CNN's round-the-clock coverage of the controversy—was, in spite of their starkly partisan differences, driven by the same objective: attracting an audience. In the twenty-first century, according to the fictitious character Rachel Berry in Fox's show *Glee*, "Fame is the most important thing in our culture now." The war of words, messages, and images in the service of attracting an audience dominates.

Donald J. Trump ✔
@realDonaldTrump

Follow

After being forced to apologize for its bad and inaccurate coverage of me after winning the election, the FAKE NEWS @nytimes is still lost!

5:39 AM - 4 Feb 2017

17,437 **Retweets** 102,728 **Likes**

💬 25K   ⇄ 17K   ♡ 103K   ✉

President Donald J. Trump/Twitter

▲ Using his Twitter account, President Trump took on the *New York Times* and the rest of the mainstream American media directly.

fake news
a term that may refer to the intentional presentation of news in favor of a political party or the intentional presentation of unverified or inaccurate news.

THE NEWS CAN FUNCTION AS ENTERTAINMENT

Commercial demands upon mainstream news providers have changed the approach with which many network executives treat not just their anchors and reporters but the news divisions themselves. According to one communications scholar, "Once upon a time, news was a money loser, but was kept separate from the other divisions of the networks so that the journalists in their employ could operate without much attention to the bottom line. No more."[27] In the run-up to the election of 2016 and in its aftermath, the cable channels CNN, Fox News, and MSNBC saw substantial increases in viewership as audiences became glued to coverage of the debates and the developments in the early months of the Trump administration.

▲ Presidential candidate Hillary Clinton appears with DJ tWitch on *The Ellen DeGeneres Show*. Reaching audiences through talk shows has long been a way for candidates to gain exposure to viewers who might not otherwise be tuned in to political news.

The pressure of attracting an audience in a marketplace with so many easily accessible alternatives has led many news outlets to focus on **infotainment**, a merging of information and entertainment in a way designed to attract viewers and gain market share. This dynamic includes pressures to provide **soft news**—stories that focus on celebrities, personalities, and entertaining events rather than on events of local, national, or international political or economic significance.

Scholars continue to debate the effects of soft news on Americans' political knowledge and understanding. Candidate appearances on talk shows might engage viewers who otherwise would not have been exposed to their candidacy or the campaign in general,[28] an engagement that can increase the likelihood that voters will select candidates who more closely resemble citizens' political preferences.[29]

Soft news can act to engage individuals with foreign policy issues.[30] On the other hand, scholars have found that viewership of political comedy shows such as *The Daily Show* with Trevor Noah may decrease individuals' support for and engagement with political institutions, exposing them to political issues but increasing cynicism in the process.[31] There are also concerns that soft news may decrease the amount of knowledge about public affairs—knowledge that is necessary for effective democratic governance.[32]

BIAS AND THE PERCEPTION OF BIAS ARE A PROBLEM IN MEDIA COVERAGE

A perennial critique of the American news media is that it is biased. Typically, the charge, especially against the nation's largest newspapers and mainstream television news outlets, is that a **partisan bias** is demonstrated and a liberal one at that. Many studies and critiques of journalists have focused on the fact that a majority of them self-identify as liberal.[33] So are the media politically biased? This is actually a very complicated question.[34] Journalists are more likely to self-identify as liberal than members of the general population, but they also tend to have higher levels of educational attainment, which may contribute to these patterns. However, journalists also operate under norms and professional expectations that reward objectivity. Finally, the perception that the media are politically biased might itself be partly shaped by certain media outlets that run stories on the "biased media," thereby encouraging their readers, listeners, or viewers to believe a bias exists.[35] Perhaps unsurprisingly, an individual's view on whether or not the news media are politically biased breaks down differently depending upon that person's own political viewpoints. The percentages of Americans who feel that there is a "great deal" of political bias in the news have risen recently (see Figure 8.3). In addition, perceptions that the news media keep political leaders in check have divided sharply along partisan lines in the Trump era (Figure 8.4).

infotainment
a merging of information and entertainment in a way designed to attract viewers and gain market share.

soft news
stories that focus on celebrity and personality rather than political or economic issues.

partisan bias
the slanting of political news coverage in support of a particular political party or ideology.

Do Americans Think the News Media Are Biased?

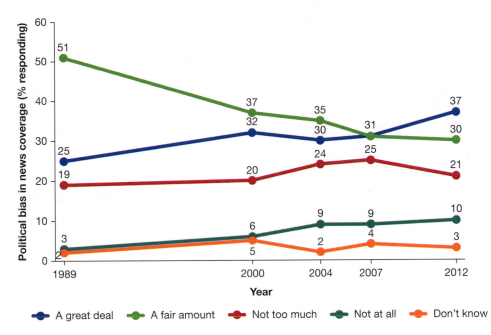

Source: Pew Research Center, "Perceptions of Bias, News Knowledge," February 7, 2012, www.people-press.org/2012/02/07/section-3-perceptions-of-bias-news-knowledge/?src=prc-number.

▼ FIGURE 8.4

Partisanship and the Media's Watchdog Role

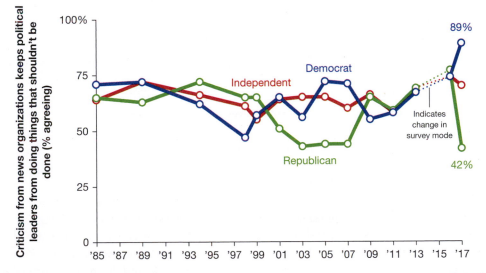

Source: Pew Research Center, "Americans' Attitudes about the News Media Deeply Divided along Partisan Lines," May 10, 2017, http://www.journalism.org/2017/05/10/americans-attitudes-about-the-news-media-deeply-divided-along-partisan-lines/.

Concerns about bias in the media have been accompanied by a lack of trust in the news sources. Confidence in television news, in particular, has fallen dramatically (see Figure 8.5).

To the reader of a penny press publication in the nineteenth century, the idea that a particular news outlet pursued a partisan agenda would probably not have been all that surprising; it was an accepted part of the format. Factors other than the political orientation of the journalists, editors, or publishers of a specific media outlet may also shape coverage in important ways. Most mainstream news outlets employ the **beat system**, in which reporters are assigned to specific types of news, policies, and events.

beat system
the practice of assigning reporters to specific types of news, policies, and events.

The Decline in Confidence in Television News

The percentage of Americans expressing a "great deal" or "quite a lot" of confidence in television news has declined dramatically over the past twenty years.

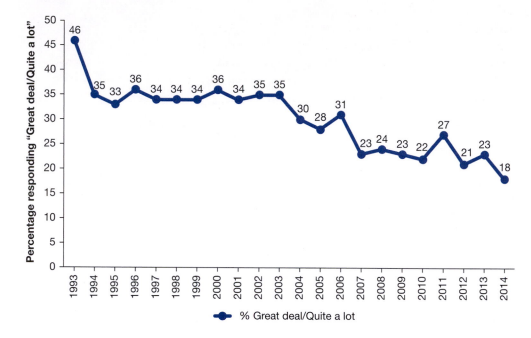

Source: Frank Newport, "Brian Williams Situation Plays Out in Context of Already Low Trust in Mass Media," Gallup, February 11, 2015, www.gallup.com/opinion/polling-matters/181544/brian-williams-situation-plays-context-already-low-trust-mass-media.aspx?g_source=trust%20media&g_medium=search&g_campaign=tiles.

From the standpoint of efficiency and expertise, the beat system makes a lot of sense. Journalists can be more informed reporters if they become familiar with the lay of the land in a specific area. The worry is that certain beats are either not covered or not covered in much detail. The president, the Department of Defense, and the State Department, for example, receive much attention under this system; the Department of Transportation, not so much.

When thinking about bias in news coverage, one cannot ignore one of the most important potential sources of the problem: us. The news media—even outlets that are operated as nonprofit entities—need to attract an audience. They need us to consume their products, and they may shape their coverage accordingly. This creates the possibility of **commercial bias** in which some news outlets might pursue inflammatory, sensational coverage to secure their niche of the marketplace, while others might choose to play it safe for fear of upsetting their audience.

Commercial bias may shape not just how stories are covered but also which stories are covered. Stories, for example, about government regulation or public policies are often far from the compelling narratives that will attract a large audience, unless, of course, a major disaster or event shines a spotlight on some underlying problem. In a competitive marketplace, news, including political news, is based on providing compelling narratives—stories that we want to read, hear, watch, and retweet. It is easy, and often useful, to critique the American news media for failing to report on the "important stories." However, one might also ask if we would tune in to the "Federal Bureaucracy Channel" with any regularity.

CONTEMPORARY PRESSURES AFFECT HOW THE MEDIA COVER CAMPAIGNS AND ELECTIONS

The drive to attract an audience also shapes how media outlets cover political campaigns and elections, and it affects how candidates try to present themselves. When covering political campaigns, news outlets may focus on the drama of the race rather than on the policy differences between candidates, a tendency often called the **horse race phenomenon**.

commercial bias

the shaping of the content and focus of news based upon the desire to capture news consumers.

horse race phenomenon

coverage of political campaigns that focuses more on the drama of the campaign than on policy issues.

Scandals also sell, as we have explored, tempting media outlets to focus on them and often crowding out discussions of policy, a pattern that political scientist Larry Sabato has called a "feeding frenzy."[36] A recent report by the Media Research Center showed that in one month's time, of all news coverage of President Trump, a full 55 percent was devoted solely to the Russia investigation, with the remainder devoted to a range of other issues.[37]

Candidates and politicians are not bystanders in the coverage of politics; they actively try to shape the news agenda and the content of the stories covered. They and members of their staff try to get their message out and shape its reception. The goal is to control the message, sometimes seemingly obsessively, by focusing on one message per news cycle, per day. Allowing or restricting access by journalists is also a strategic decision, made according to what strategy seems best able to "spin" a story in the desired way.

WHAT HAVE I LEARNED?

1. The merging of information and entertainment in a way designed to attract viewers and gain market share is called _____.
   a. social media
   b. soft news
   c. investigative journalism
   d. infotainment

2. What are some of the potential sources of bias in news media coverage?

3. Do you think the news media are biased?

Answer Key: 1. d; 2. Answers might cover the structure of news organizations themselves, commercial pressures, and the horse race phenomenon; 3. Answers should include evidence and examples to back up the specific argument and might distinguish between different types of media in the analysis.

MEDIA OWNERSHIP AND CONTENT ARE SUBJECT TO REGULATION

- Discuss changes in the regulation of media ownership and media content.

Although the media serve, in part, to try to exercise control over elected officials and government employees, the media are themselves subject to regulation and control by the government. While the challenges to effective and fair regulation have often been specific to certain times, places, and technologies, the desire for elected officials to shape the landscape of media coverage has been present for a long time. These efforts have focused primarily on regulating two things: media ownership and media content.

REGULATION AFFECTS WHO OWNS THE MEDIA AND HOW WE CONSUME IT

With the technological revolutions of radio and television in the twentieth century came demands from both citizens and content providers themselves for the federal government to regulate the broadcast media. The business logic behind these regulations was based upon the fact that the nation's radio and television frequencies were finite, like rivers, canals, and grazing lands.[38] Demands to use them, however, were not. From the point of view of publishers and broadcasters, regulations were necessary to prevent "overgrazing." Radio stations, for instance, all too often were wandering onto the electronic lands of others, given the technological reality that "the physical capacity of the available channels, or wave lengths, [were] already far exceeded by the number of stations actually in operation."[39] There were also calls to regulate the morality of the content of the material that beamed directly into Americans' homes. And there were calls to regulate the political content of radio and television broadcasts to ensure that multiple political viewpoints were all represented.

REGULATION AFFECTS MEDIA TECHNOLOGIES AND OWNERSHIP

The Radio Act of 1927 established the Federal Radio Commission and required broadcasters to obtain a license to broadcast on specific frequencies in an attempt to try to bring order to "the utter confusion within the broadcasting band."[40] The Communications Act of 1934 expanded the federal role in governing the nation's broadcast media, creating the Federal Communications Commission (FCC) to oversee its implementation. National defense was cited as one of the reasons that the FCC was needed as a matter of public policy.

In the latter half of the twentieth century, spiking demand from content providers and marketplace competition as well as changes in the ways news stories were created and distributed forced government once again to rethink the rules governing telecommunications. New legislation was needed to help overcome what was an increasingly messy traffic jam in the nation's telecommunications systems. The Telecommunications Act of 1996 was passed by Congress in order "to let anyone enter any communications business—to let any communications business compete in any market against any other."[41] The act essentially brought deregulation to media ownership, setting in motion a process that led to massive consolidation of media ownership (see Figure 8.6). While deregulation might have been expected to increase the diversity of the nation's major news outlets, it had the opposite effect. It led to increasing consolidation as news firms tried to maximize their profits in the face of declining sales on things like printed classified advertisements, long a mainstay of traditional newspaper revenue, made obsolete by the Internet.

The concentration of ownership of major media outlets is not only due to relaxation of regulations. There is also a logic to it. Media outlets largely fund their operations through advertising revenue. Advertisers, for their part, want to reach as many consumers as possible. Therefore, media outlets try to expand their reach as far as they can, whether by attracting the largest audiences possible or by purchasing smaller content providers. This has consequences for the content of media coverage as well. Providers may shape their coverage to attract as wide an audience as possible.

The twenty-first century has also witnessed a marked decline in consumption of printed newspapers (see Figure 8.7). Does that mean overall consumption of news has declined? The story is more complicated than that. Traditional papers have gone online, sometimes for free and with advertisements, sometimes behind firewalls that require registration and/or a subscription fee. Nontraditional Internet news sources often get their stories from a process called **aggregating**. In this process they still rely on the basic reporting that newspaper journalists do, but then they disseminate and comment on the original coverage.

> **aggregating**
> a process through which Internet and other news providers relay the news as reported by journalists and other sources.

▼ FIGURE 8.6

Consolidation of Media Ownership

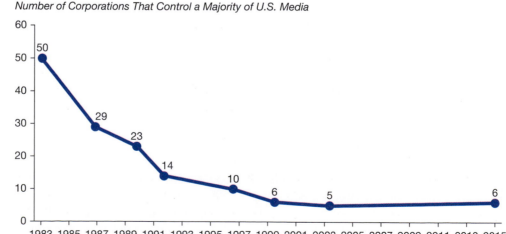

Number of Corporations That Control a Majority of U.S. Media

Source: Modified from Ben H. Bagdikian, *The New Media Monopoly* (Boston: Beacon Press, 2004). Available online at www.corporations.org/media.

▼ FIGURE 8.7

Changes in American Political News Consumption

The results of a 2013 survey by the Pew Research Center show that for the first time, more than half of Americans cited the Internet as one of their major sources for national and international news.

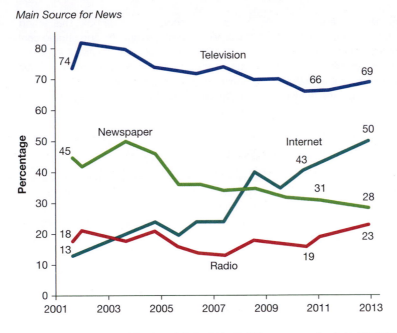

Main Source for News

Source: Andrea Caumot, "12 Trends Shaping Digital News," Pew Research Center, October 16, 2013, www.pewresearch.org/fact-tank/2013/10/16/12-trends-shaping-digital-news.

During this era of proliferation of media outlets and the federal government's relaxation of many of the regulations first introduced during the days of radio and later television, the question of "Who owns the grazing lands?" has not gone away. In fact, with the issue of net neutrality, it is still here, only in a somewhat different form. **Net neutrality** is the idea that Internet service providers should treat all data and content providers equally and not discriminate based upon content or bandwidth demands. However, some feel that companies that provide the highways of the Internet and broadband age should be able to charge more to content providers whose "livestock" chew up more bandwidth. Critics who support net neutrality say that allowing firms to price-discriminate based on bandwidth use will stifle the expression of multiple and diverse views.

Pro–net neutrality laws that had been advanced by the Obama administration appeared to be targets for opponents to net neutrality within the Trump administration. Under Obama, in June 2016, the DC Circuit Court of Appeals upheld the FCC's net neutrality rules, but several major telecommunications companies promised to appeal the decision. In 2017, President Trump nominated a series of anti–net neutrality commissioners to the FCC's board, signaling relaxed enforcement of those rules. In June 2018, the Senate voted to repeal net neutrality; however, the House had not yet scheduled a vote.

REGULATION ALSO AFFECTS CONTENT

While the federal government plays only a small role in providing media content—with exceptions such as the Corporation for Public Broadcasting, created by Congress in 1967—it has played an important role in regulating its content. The Communications Act of 1934 led to the establishment of several rules designed to shape news media content to serve the public at large. One of these, the **equal time rule**, requires licensees to guarantee political candidates equal time to present their views and opinions.

net neutrality
the idea that Internet service providers should not be allowed to discriminate based upon content or bandwidth demands.

equal time rule
a regulation that requires American radio and television broadcast networks to provide equal time for political candidates to present their views on issues.

EVALUATING ARGUMENTS: IN DEFENSE OF DEREGULATION

In a 2003 article, Wayne Crews from the politically conservative Cato Institute argued in favor of the trend toward deregulation and against concerns over the consolidation of news media that it has led to. His arguments focused on the free flow of information and the limiting effects of governmental efforts to shape the media landscape:

Absent government censorship, there is no fundamental scarcity of information. More information can always be created, and in a free society, nobody can silence anybody else. The most that big media can do is refuse to share their megaphones and soapboxes, which is not a violation of anybody's rights. Real suppression requires governmental censorship, or the actual prohibition of the airing of alternative views.

Ironically, opponents of deregulation feel entitled to commandeer someone else's resources, to limit the size of someone else's soapbox. This action is the true violation of free speech and should concern the public. This effective constraint imposed upon another's property is regarded as acceptable, however, and even laudatory, as long as it is called a "media ownership rule" and has the support of enough politicians.[42]

WHAT Do You Think?

Crews's article advocates a particular political position: reduced governmental influence on media ownership. Do you find the argument convincing? Why or why not? These comments also raise other fundamental questions. For example, how should American representative democracy balance the First Amendment's protections for free speech and press against the goal of ensuring equal access to political information? Can you think of other areas in American politics in which tensions like these are present?

One of the more controversial aspects of the equal time provision was an implicit—and perhaps unintended—incentive for broadcasters to avoid presenting the platforms of candidates at all for fear of running afoul of the law. According to media and politics scholar Doris Graber, the equal time provision may have acted to restrict rather than expand political information, as a station may choose not to cover candidates at all, especially those in local races, wherein many candidates are vying for office. "This keeps many viable candidates off the air and has led to widespread dissatisfaction with the equal time rule and demands to abandon it."[43]

The rise of social media has also challenged the ability to ensure equal coverage. Political candidates who are also celebrities, for example, can obtain disproportionate attention based on their celebrity status alone. In the 2016 presidential campaign, Republican candidate Donald Trump used his large following on Twitter to obtain coverage without having to purchase as much airtime as other candidates.

The **fairness doctrine**, introduced in 1949, expanded regulations for American political news coverage beyond just the provision of time for candidates to the content of the coverage itself. It required "that every licensee devote a reasonable portion of broadcast time to the discussion and consideration of controversial issues of public importance" and that broadcasters "affirmatively endeavor to make . . . facilities available for the expression of contrasting viewpoints held by responsible elements with respect to the controversial issues presented."[44] Again, scholars and broadcasters have questioned the unintended consequences of the fairness doctrine. In trying to avoid the appearance of being unfair, political news media providers might decide to play it safe, "to shy away from programs dealing with controversial public issues to avoid demands to air opposing views, in place of regular revenue-producing programs."[45] The fairness doctrine had ceased to be rigorously enforced and was largely repealed in the 1980s. In 2011, the FCC formally scrapped it. However, debates about its potential reinstatement (and how the Supreme Court would rule on such an action in the age of the Internet) continue.

fairness doctrine
a federal rule that expanded regulations for American political news coverage beyond just the provision of time for candidates to the content of the coverage itself.

WHAT HAVE I LEARNED?

1. The primary motivation behind the Radio Act of 1927 and the Communications Act of 1934 was to ensure that _____.
   a. all political viewpoints were equally represented
   b. broadcasters could not encroach on others' channels
   c. Americans of different racial and ethnic backgrounds were included in news coverage
   d. the federal government would receive revenue from broadcasters

2. The primary effect of the Telecommunications Act of 1996 was _____.
   a. a consolidation of ownership of media outlets
   b. the prevention of many cable television outlets from entering the marketplace

   c. to ensure equal treatment of outlets in access to bandwidth
   d. All of the above

3. What challenges has technological change presented to the relevance and enforcement of the equal time rule and the fairness doctrine?

4. How strongly do you think the news media should be regulated? In what ways?

Answer Key: 1. b; 2. a; 3. Answers should discuss the challenges presented by cable television and the Internet to rules originally designed to cover the activities of broadcast media outlets; 4. Arguments should include reasons why the media in general, or certain aspects of coverage, should or should not be subject to regulation, citing specific examples.

THE POWER OF THE MEDIA TO AFFECT THE PUBLIC IS TESTED

- **Explain the different perspectives on the power of the media to shape political understanding and behaviors.**

It was fake news, intentionally so.

On Sunday, October 30, 1938, the night before Halloween, Orson Welles, who would later gain notoriety for directing movies, served up a bit of mischief to American audiences. Welles was that night directing a radio adaptation of the H. G. Wells 1897 science fiction piece *The War of the Worlds*, which centered on an invasion of England by Martians, for the CBS radio program *Mercury Theatre on the Air.*

It was a play, on radio, meant to entertain. The problem was that many Americans did not realize that fact at the time, and it caused a panic.[46]

Welles and his collaborators had decided to set their adaptation not in England but in Grover's Mill, New Jersey. During the process of creating the teleplay, a secretary who had transcribed the original novel was reported to have remarked, "Those old Martians are just a lot of nonsense! It's all too silly!"[47] Welles, with little more than twenty-four hours before the broadcast, was worried that his play would be far from good theater.

So he made a choice: He would make it seem real, drawing on the horrific commentary and screams that accompanied the true coverage of the explosion of the airship *Hindenburg* the year before. Welles also decided to mimic the real "news flash" interruptions of Americans' regular comedy or music broadcasts, tapping into the fears of an already very worried nation who had become used to those kinds of announcements. At the time, the lingering gray clouds of the Great Depression seemed like they would never go away and the ominous storm clouds of the rise of Hitler's Nazi Party cast a shadow across the globe. Reporters would often break into the entertaining radio broadcasts of that dominant medium of the day. With those trappings of "real news" in place, the broadcast went live.

During the play's climax, a fake announcer recounted, "Now the whole field's caught fire. (Explosion) The woods . . . the barns . . . the gas tanks of automobiles . . . it's spreading everywhere. It's coming this way. About twenty yards to my right . . . (CRASH OF MICROPHONE . . . THEN DEAD SILENCE . . .)."[48] Six seconds of complete silence followed.

"War" Victim

Caroline Cantlon, WPA actress, listening to this radio in West 49th St., heard announcement of "smoke in Times Square." Running to street, she fell, broke her arm.

"I Didn't Know", Orson Welles, after broadcast expresses amazement at public reaction. He adapted H. G. Wells' "War of the Worlds" for radio and played principal role. Left: a machine conceived for another H. G. Wells story. Dramatic description of landing of weird "machine from Mars" started last night's panic.
—Story on page 2.

NY Daily News Archive via Getty

▲ A respected newspaper's coverage of the "fake news" broadcast of "The War of the Worlds."

Another announcer followed: "Ladies and gentlemen, due to circumstances beyond our control, we are unable to continue our broadcast from Grover's Mill. Evidently, there's some difficulty with our field transmission."[49]

As theater, it was genius. To many listeners, the absurdities of the scenario were obvious, so it was nothing more than captivating entertainment. To an unknown number of Americans, however, it seemed real: "All they knew was that something horrible was happening on the Eastern Seaboard—and that, perhaps, it was coming their way."[50] At the conclusion of the broadcast, Orson Welles stepped out of his persona as a fake Princeton University professor and assured his audience, "This is Orson Welles, ladies and gentlemen, out of character to assure you that THE WAR OF THE WORLDS has no further significance than the holiday offering it was meant to be."[51]

Some Americans missed Welles's disclaimer. The aftermath was intense. Stories of frightened Americans were everywhere in other forms of the media, especially the newspaper on Halloween day. Welles received sharp criticism but was not accused or tried of any crime. Others have asserted that the panic over the broadcast was deliberately overblown by competitor newspapers "to attack their newfangled rival, the radio."[52] Perhaps it was not a "War of the Worlds" but a battle between two media outlets—newspapers and radio—for legitimacy.

In the aftermath of "The War of the Worlds," one thing was clear: the power of the news media—whether or not they could convince Americans that they were under attack by Martians—was not fake. In the sections that follow, we will further explore the debates about the media's power to influence individual and group behavior.

SCHOLARS HAVE DIFFERED ON THE MEDIA'S EFFECTS

When it comes to democratic representation, none of the topics that we have explored in this chapter matter unless one thing is true: that the media can actually shape individuals' political knowledge and understanding. Why regulate the media, for instance, unless you presume it can affect people's political beliefs and understanding?

But just how much power does the media have? Are they major players in the national political drama or just commentators on it? As with so much else about the American news media, the answers to these questions are evolving. Scholars' views of **media effects**—the power of the news media in shaping individuals' political knowledge, understanding, and preferences—have evolved along with the media itself.

In the early decades of the twentieth century, many observers of American political life considered the media a powerful and potentially dangerous force. The effectiveness of World War I propaganda posters and efforts, which helped mobilize the nation in support of intervention in a European conflict about which many Americans were ambivalent, seemed to indicate that the public was like political Play-Doh: shapable and malleable. In this view, media were thought to have a direct effect on a public.

This model of the direct effects of the media began to fall out of favor in later decades as scholars, employing empirical techniques and focusing primarily on the effects of the media in vote choices, found important but limited effects of the media on political outcomes. Though playing an important role in citizen information about candidates and their policy positions, the media were found to be only one factor in an individual's ultimate choice about which candidates to vote for in a given election.[53]

The current view of most scholars of the relationship between the media and American politics lies somewhere between those of the direct- and limited-effects models. The model of subtle effects focuses not so much on how the media may or may not change—for example, the partisan affiliation or vote

media effects

the power of the news media in shaping individuals' political knowledge, preferences, and political behavior.

choice of a given individual—but on the ways in which the media may shape the overall conversation taking place in the public sphere.

How the media place a story in a larger context—the textual or visual cues that they present along with a particular story—may cause individuals to focus on particular considerations when consuming a media product, an effect known as **framing**. According to political scientists James Druckman and Kjersten Nelson, "for example, if a speaker describes a hate-group rally in terms of free speech, then the audience will subsequently base their opinions about the rally on free speech considerations and, perhaps, support the right to rally. In contrast, if the speaker uses a public-safety frame, the audience will base their opinions on public-safety considerations and oppose the rally."[54] Similarly, a particular media source's coverage of a candidate or issue may highlight specific contextual details in providing the coverage, thereby **priming** individuals to draw on those details when forming opinions.

The power of the media to select which stories are covered cannot be understated. In the choice of coverage, the media may exert an **agenda-setting** role by highlighting which issues are worthy of coverage and, as a consequence, worthy of the public's attention. The question of agenda setting gets to the very purpose of the role of the media in a representative democracy. According to political scientist Harold Lasswell, the media perform three important and interconnected functions: to survey and report on political events and outcomes, to interpret those events and outcomes to the public, and to educate citizens.[55] To these three, media and politics scholar Doris Graber has added a fourth function: to deliberately manipulate the political process.[56]

Lasswell's assertion that the media survey and report on the political world is often what we think about when we consider the media's role in American representative democracy—hard-hitting journalists asking hard-hitting questions and acting as a watchdog for, or perhaps more accurately, a watchtower over, American politics. The role of watchdog is well entrenched in Americans' understanding of the role of journalists, editors, and anchors. Objective, aggressive interviews designed to get to the truth are very much a part of the ideal of the American news media. The tricky questions, however, are these: On what issues does the watchtower shine its light? Corruption? Scandal? Infrastructure? Cats? Who controls its aim and focus? To whom does the watchtower's controller answer? Corporate interests, powerful politicians, fellow journalists, or the American consumer? They are important questions with no easy answers. A watchtower cannot, by design, focus on the entire ocean—only a very small part of it at one time. Who decides where the light is to shine, and what are the consequences of those decisions?

The challenge of interpreting the dynamics behind these findings illustrates an important concept in empirical political science research: that correlation does not, by itself, establish causation. As you consume stories that show a relationship between variables, be careful not to assume that this relationship demonstrates that one factor is causing another.

AMERICANS MAY BE SEPARATED BY A DIGITAL DIVIDE

At first glance, the proliferation of news sources in the twenty-first century might provide scholars of the news media with a source of optimism. Perhaps, through infotainment, the diversity of perspectives on cable stations, and the spread of social media, Americans who were previously disconnected from the political process might be brought into it and prompted to think about issues and to connect friends and family in their own social networks to American politics. Again, it may not be that simple; the story might not be so neat and inspiring. All Americans do not make use of the new technologies and outlets in the same way. According to the work of political scientist Markus Prior, the new technologies and media avenues may be dividing Americans, making them more partisan.[57] We call those gaps the **digital divide**.

Americans with the skills to navigate this media landscape that contains many options and unclear editorial standards may benefit tremendously, but those who cannot, or choose not to, may be left behind. The Internet, according to Prior, "has widened gaps in news exposure, political knowledge, and turnout between those who like news and those who prefer entertainment."[58] Older, low-income, rural, Spanish-speaking, and disabled Americans are among those less likely to make use of the Internet, as are those with lower levels of educational attainment.[59]

framing
influencing people's interpretations of news, events, or issues through the presentation of the context.

priming
shaping individuals' interpretations of news or events by highlighting certain details or contexts.

agenda-setting
the media's ability to highlight certain issues and bring them to the attention of the public.

digital divide
divisions in society that are driven by access to and knowledge about technologies; these gaps often fall along the lines of partisanship, class, race, and ethnicity.

1. Commercial bias refers to _____.
   a. the increase of commercials in television news
   b. the role that journalists play in trying to push a certain political perspective
   c. the ways in which the media shape their coverage to attract an audience
   d. All of the above

2. How have scholars' views of the power of the media changed over time?

3. Why are scholars worried about an increasing digital divide?

Answer Key: 1. c; 2. Answers should include a discussion of the direct-effects, limited-effects, and subtle-effects models; 3. Answers should include the connection between access to news sources and individuals' identities and lived experiences.

CONCLUSION: DEBATES ABOUT THE POWER OF THE MEDIA CONTINUE

By 2018, "The War of the Worlds" had long since passed into American history. The war of words, however, raged on. Secretary Clinton continued to argue that Russian interference, especially through the social media, helped to tilt the election in Trump's favor. In a series of tweets in January 2018, Donald Trump challenged Clinton and the Democratic Party, arguing that "Russian collusion, after one year of intense study, has proven to be a total hoax on the American public. . . ." With warnings by President Trump's own intelligence officials that the 2018 midterms could once again, in their assessment, be swayed by Russian interference, the issue was not going away.

How powerful are American media sources in the twenty-first century?

Amid all of the controversy surrounding allegations of Russian intervention in the presidential election of 2016, for us, no one question is as important as this one. The challenges of filtering the truth of the images, issues, and arguments with which they are bombarded is a major task for Americans. This is as true today in the multilayered media environment of the twenty-first century as it was for listeners tuning in to hear about a Martian invasion in 1938 and for pamphlet readers at the start of the nation. Because so much of our knowledge about the political world comes indirectly from the media and not from direct interaction with politicians, policymakers, or the political process, Americans are tasked with the challenge of needing to be very savvy about the media they consume. Why are we being bombarded with one set of specific issues and not others? What issues are being ignored, and why?

CHAPTER REVIEW

This chapter's main ideas are reflected in the Learning Objectives. By reviewing them here, you should be able to **remember** the key points, **know** the terms that are central to the topic, and **think** about the critical issues raised in each section.

8.1 Describe both who the news media are and the major questions of truth, power, and trust at stake in the media today.

REMEMBER
- The news media include newspapers, magazines, radio, television, Internet sources, blogs, and social media postings, all in service of informing or persuading.
- The media landscape is transforming today, with major changes in technology, partisanship, and consolidation.

| **KNOW** | • news media (p. 211) |
| **THINK** | • How have the sources of Americans' political news changed in the twenty-first century? What do these changes mean? |

8.2 Trace the historical development of the American news media.

REMEMBER
- Since the founding, there has been tension between the constitutional rights to freedom of speech and of the press and constraints on those rights.
- For much of the history of the American media, the press has been partisan—funded by and disseminating the point of view of particular political factions.

KNOW
- broadcast media (p. 216)
- citizen journalists (p. 218)
- investigative journalism (p. 215)
- mass media (p. 214)
- niche journalism (p. 218)
- partisan press (p. 214)
- penny press (p. 214)
- social media (p. 218)
- wire service (p. 215)
- yellow journalism (p. 215)

THINK
- How did changes in the eighteenth and nineteenth centuries drive changes in the news media?
- How have new media transformed the news landscape?
- How has the media's approach to political partisanship changed over time?

8.3 Understand the issue of bias in the American media.

REMEMBER
- Newer technologies, such as the Internet, broadband, and social media, have not only increased the pace and volume of news content but have also blurred the lines between information, entertainment, citizens, and journalists. Americans increasingly perceive the media as politically biased and less trustworthy.
- Scholars' views of the power of the media to shape political understanding and behaviors have changed over time.

KNOW
- beat system (p. 223)
- commercial bias (p. 224)
- fake news (p. 221)
- horse race phenomenon (p. 224)
- infotainment (p. 222)
- partisan bias (p. 222)
- soft news (p. 222)

THINK
- Are the media biased? Can we trust them?

8.4 Discuss changes in the regulation of media ownership and media content.

REMEMBER
- Some efforts to regulate the news media have focused on ownership; others have focused on its content.
- The equal time rule and fairness doctrine sought to ensure a level playing field for political candidates; however, recent regulatory and technological changes have reduced their impact and raised questions about their relevance.

KNOW
- aggregating (p. 226)
- equal time rule (p. 227)
- fairness doctrine (p. 228)
- net neutrality (p. 227)

THINK
- How strongly should the media be regulated? Should some outlets be subject to more regulation than others?

8.5 Explain the different perspectives on the power of the media to shape political understanding and behaviors.

REMEMBER
- Scholars' views of media effects have changed over time along with the media itself. Today most believe that the effects are subtle.

KNOW
- agenda-setting (p. 231)
- digital divide (p. 231)
- framing (p. 231)
- media effects (p. 230)
- priming (p. 231)

THINK
- How has the need to attract an audience shaped the coverage of political news?
- What are possible sources of bias in coverage of political news? Which of these do you think are the most significant?
- Can the media shape Americans' political understandings?
- How powerful are the media? Do they shape your own attitudes and understandings? If so, how?

new Tweets

aldTrump · Now

g FAKE NEWS again. So
!

Donald J. Trum
@realDonaldTrump

45th President of the Unit
America

📍 Washington, DC

📅 Joined March 2009

Tweet to Donal

p and find out what's on the agenda for next
.ms/ZUF

58 Followers you know

r nog met roken telegraaf.nl/r/27512366

CHAPTER 9

POLITICAL PARTIES

The Insurgents versus the Establishment

▶ A supporter of then-candidate Donald Trump poses in her homemade shirt at one of Trump's campaign rallies in Dallas, Texas, in September 2015. Her sentiment toward both the Democratic and Republican parties was echoed by many people in the electorate during the 2016 election cycle. The increasing numbers of Americans who identify as independents have profoundly affected both Republican and Democratic parties.

In a representative democracy, elections involve a lot of uncertainty—not just in which candidates might win an election but also in how citizens figure out which candidates to support. How can voters be sure they are selecting individuals who will advocate for their interests, act on issues they care about, and govern effectively? Given the wide variety of governmental policies, it is extremely challenging for even the most attentive voters to know all the details of what a candidate stands for or hopes to accomplish once in office.

Enter the **political party**. By organizing and supporting candidates running for office, parties provide labels to those candidates—shortcuts for voters, really—that cut through the noise and signal to voters that this is a candidate who deserves their support. Once in office, those candidates work with the support of other party members to advance a set of policies.

Party leaders face another challenge: creating an attractive and consistent message that gets their candidates elected and maintains party cohesion. American political parties have often been successful in doing this, but not always. Once in a while, a party finds itself challenged not by another party but by members within its own ranks who have felt that their voices are being ignored by party leaders.

In 2016, both of America's dominant parties, the Democrats and the Republicans, found themselves confronting just such a situation. Two candidates, Senator Bernie Sanders of Vermont and entrepreneur and television celebrity Donald Trump—as far apart on the traditional American political spectrum as one could diagram—emerged as major forces in their respective parties. Sanders and Trump, regardless of how far they would make it in their respective campaigns, changed the national conversation. Despite their differences, both men were outsiders and insurgents, and a lot of Americans responded to their campaigns.

By reading this chapter, you will be able to do the following:

 9.1 Reflect on the ways in which the presidential campaigns of Bernie Sanders and Donald Trump challenged their parties' establishment.

 9.2 Identify the roles the political parties play in supporting and nominating candidates for office.

9.3 Evaluate the changing role of parties as labels for citizens to learn about candidates and their positions on issues.

 9.4 Reflect on the implications of the presidential election of 2016 for the Democratic and Republican parties.

 9.5 Examine the role of parties in government and the traditional dominance of two major political parties in national elections.

So much conventional wisdom turned on its head, so many experts in American politics forced to admit that they had gotten it wrong, and so many of the established leaders in America's dominant political parties left scrambling to figure out what was going on and what to do about it: This was the presidential election of 2016.

This election may very well be studied by future political scientists as one of the more important in the nation's history. How did this all come to pass? And what will it mean for the future of America's political parties? Was it all just a circus? Or could it result in a reshaping of party politics or even the fragmentation of one or both of America's major political parties? Even in 2018, we do not yet know the answers to these questions with certainty. However, trying to get a bead on the election of 2016 provides a chance to do much more than analyze one presidential election. It also offers the chance to better understand the role that parties play in American representative democracy and the challenges that they face.

TWO PRESIDENTIAL CANDIDATES SHAKE UP THE FIELD . . . AND CONVENTIONAL WISDOM ABOUT THE POWER AND COHESION OF THEIR PARTIES

● **Reflect on the ways in which the presidential campaigns of Bernie Sanders and Donald Trump challenged their parties' establishment.**

American presidential elections are often filled with drama. However, traditionally, most of the drama is between the parties or between candidates trying to stake their claim as the best person to represent the goals of their party. To put it mildly, 2016 was different. Two of the leading candidates

political party
an organized group of candidates, officeholders, voters, and activists who work together to elect candidates to political office.

in the election, Republican multimillionaire Donald Trump and Vermont senator Bernie Sanders, an independent running as a Democrat, in different times would probably have been regarded as too extreme to pose a legitimate threat to party status quo. Trump's highly unconventional and controversial campaign in particular upended many widely accepted political rules and challenged the belief that political party leaders are powerful.

In 2016, Trump and Sanders advanced far in the electoral process due to voters' profound disgust with "politics as usual." Both made statements or adopted policy positions that were on the fringes of party platforms or far out of touch with the mainstream. And,

▲ During his campaign, Donald Trump's unconventional, populist-style political rallies drew substantial crowds. More than 20,000 tickets were distributed in advance of this event in Texas in 2015.

unlike many presidential contenders, neither of them concentrated on courting the best-known activists and leaders in their parties—the so-called party establishment or party elites, who are the most powerful insiders in party politics. In fact, their campaigns seemed at times to go out of their way to alienate those elites.

Other presidential candidates have run similar campaigns. The emphasis on criticizing elites and the establishment has a long tradition and has taken many forms, some of which are generally referred to as **populism**. America has witnessed several powerful populist movements in its history, many of which tied their critique of the establishment to perceptions of racial, ethnic, or cultural superiority or to strong anti-immigrant views, a charge frequently leveled against Trump. What made Trump and Sanders more noteworthy was that their criticisms struck such a deep chord with so many voters; each kept winning state nomination contests long after many political observers were certain they would fade.

BERNIE SANDERS CHALLENGES FELLOW DEMOCRATS TO FOCUS MORE ON INCOME INEQUALITY

To many Democratic and Republican stalwarts, the presidential campaigns of Sanders and Trump represented the opposite of what parties should present to voters—an umbrella of interests, linked by a shared goal, forming a larger, unified system.

Sanders didn't even belong to the Democratic Party when he announced he was running for that party's nomination. Instead, he described himself as an "independent socialist," strongly in favor of the idea that government and society should meet the needs of the public, even if that means rich people can't earn as much as they normally would. He was known for criticizing so-called corporate welfare—government benefits, such as special provisions in the tax code, provided to businesses in the hopes of enabling them to succeed and keep workers on their payrolls. As public resentment rose toward financial companies in 2011 and gave rise to the Occupy Wall Street movement, Sanders endorsed the movement's widespread demonstrations. Though Sanders was not the first, or only, candidate to call attention to wealth inequality in the country in the twenty-first century, his message that the playing field was unacceptably tilted toward the top 1 percent of Americans resonated with many voters, especially young adults struggling with student loan debt or seeking to stake their claim on the American dream.

Many Democrats also supported the Occupy Wall Street protests. Yet some of them, unlike Sanders, nonetheless accepted generous campaign donations from the same Wall Street companies and employees that were the targets of the Occupy movement. Sanders often made an issue of how much his main Democratic opponent, Hillary Clinton, received from such firms—more than $15 million as of early 2016, according to the nonpartisan watchdog group Center for Responsive Politics.[1]

populism
a political movement that challenges the political establishment.

In 2010, President Barack Obama proposed extending tax cuts that were set to expire and that would mostly benefit the wealthiest Americans. Some Democrats joined the president in supporting the extension. But Sanders was upset with the idea—so upset that he spoke against it on the floor of the Senate for more than eight hours without once taking a break. He said the cuts would make already-rich people even richer and called for a proposal that "better reflects the needs of the middle class and working families of our country and to me, most importantly, the children of our country."[2]

The speech catapulted Sanders into the national spotlight. His stances made him popular with many liberals, especially young ones. They agreed with his calls to substantially raise taxes on the wealthy, expand the reach of health care beyond Obama's Patient Protection and Affordable Care Act (better known as Obamacare), and make college education free. Sanders said his campaign involved creating a "political revolution" that could serve "millions of Americans, working people who have given up on the political process."[3]

But Clinton and many others in the mainstream of the Democratic Party said Sanders's proposals were unrealistic. They were concerned those ideas might lead many voters to think that the Democratic Party wanted to raise everyone's taxes and have the federal government run everything. That perception, they worried, could drive away people who otherwise might support Democrats in other races. Clinton criticized Sanders for wanting the United States to resemble Denmark, a country that offers its citizens free health care and free tuition—but where taxes are more than 26 percent of the country's gross domestic product, compared to less than 10 percent in the United States.[4] Many Americans, especially young American voters, disagreed. "I really like Bernie Sanders for his consistency, authenticity and relative independence from corporate interests," said Anton Terrell, a twenty-three-year-old recent college graduate in Austin, Texas, summing up why many liberal millennial voters positively regarded Sanders.[5]

▲ A supporter of Bernie Sanders voices his displeasure with the Democratic National Committee (DNC) at a rally in June 2016. Some Sanders supporters, like Sanders himself, were not Democrats, or at least were highly critical of the Democratic party, and felt that the primary was "rigged" in Clinton's favor.

DONALD TRUMP CHALLENGES FELLOW REPUBLICANS ON POLICY AND WITH CONTROVERSIAL REMARKS

Like Sanders, Trump was very much an outsider in his party. Unlike Sanders and most other presidential candidates, though, he had never held elected office. That disturbed some in the GOP ("Grand Old Party" or Republican Party), as they believed those seeking the nation's highest legislative post should have at least some prior political experience. As well, between 1987 and 2012, Trump had switched political parties seven times, registering for periods of time as a Democrat, a Republican, or as an independent until he became a Republican again in 2012.[6] That made conservative Republicans question whether Trump would remain faithful to the party. Many Republicans also viewed his claim that he would use his business acumen to cut deals to benefit the U.S. economy as directly contradicting their philosophy of limited government; the conservative magazine *National Review* devoted an entire issue to arguing why its readers shouldn't support Trump for that reason.[7]

On the campaign trail, Trump did little to assure the Republican Party that he would toe their line. Trump's extreme statements on immigration caused a further uproar. He called for building a massive wall on the U.S.-Mexican border to keep out those coming into the country illegally and for a ban on allowing Muslims to enter the United States. His positions enraged Hispanics and Muslims, and a number of Republicans said he had gone too far. Part of Trump's campaign theme, "Make America Great Again," involved replacing "stupid" decision makers with smart ones. His blaming of all politicians—not just Democratic ones—for what he called their inability to solve problems irked the GOP's establishment, which he bluntly described as ineffectual. He accused them of being too beholden to what he said were the party's narrow interests and unresponsive to the public's massive hostility toward government. "People are angry . . . I just know it can be turned around. It can be turned around quickly," Trump said.[8]

Trump could afford to alienate the Republican establishment because of his celebrity and his ability to command significant news media attention without buying advertisements. Unlike other Republicans, he feuded with Fox News, whose audience consisted largely of hard-core GOP loyalists. One study estimated that he had essentially been given $2 billion in free media coverage in newspapers, television, and other journalistic sources. That was two and a half times more than Democratic Party candidate Hillary Clinton and many times greater than that of any of his Republican rivals.[9] Trump made frequent use of Twitter, regularly condemning his opponents with tweets that drew even more media attention.

Many of Trump's supporters cared little about any of the criticisms leveled against him. He tapped into their deep frustration with politics and, in turn, the parties. They said they agreed with Trump's call to upend the entire system and described him as refreshingly authentic and blunt—qualities they said mattered more to them than his sometimes-vague policy stances. "He disrupts a broken political process and beats establishment candidates who've long ignored their interests," a lawyer in a poor, rural North Carolina town wrote in explaining Trump's widespread appeal there.[10]

SANDERS AND TRUMP SHARE IN A BASIC CHALLENGE TO THEIR PARTIES' ESTABLISHMENT

Trump and Sanders had completely different styles and messages, but they shared some things in common. One was a refusal to rely on large outside campaign contributions, which gave them an image among their supporters that they "couldn't be bought." Another trait they shared was a message of economic pessimism. Both drew strong support from voters who were found to be the most anxious about where the economy was headed.[11] In particular, both actively criticized their parties' mainstream beliefs on trade with other countries. They accused the parties of supporting trade deals that had led to thousands of American jobs being outsourced to foreign competitors. Trade is an issue that splits Americans less along lines of party than those of economic class, especially in states with a lot of factories and blue-collar industrial workers. The senior ranks of the Democratic Party and especially the Republican Party tend to strongly support trade deals as being essential to the U.S. economy because they open up new markets for goods and services. They argue that the creation of jobs by those new markets more than offsets the losses in manufacturing to other countries and that companies are unlikely to bring back jobs that have moved overseas.[12]

In a normal presidential election campaign, Sanders and Trump might have made a splash, but neither would probably have had a real chance at securing the nomination, especially Trump, with his incendiary statements. However, 2016 was not such a year. "We have something happening that makes the Republican Party probably the biggest political story in the world," Trump said early in 2016. "Millions of people are coming into [sic] vote. . . . Democrats are coming in, independents are coming in, and—very, very important—people who have never voted before. It's an incredible thing."[13] While Trump's opponents repeatedly questioned his interpretations of polls, Trump stood by his claims that he was sparking a revolution in Republican Party politics. For his part, Sanders emphasized the resonance of his message of ensuring economic opportunities for Americans by taking on Wall Street and promising to enact legislation providing free college education.

To the astonishment of both Republican and Democratic loyalists in their respective parties, Trump would eventually go on to win the general election and become the forty-fifth president of the United States. Americans asked for a disrupter, and they got one. Everything political insiders thought parties had the power to do—choose candidates, influence their messaging during the election cycle, and win voters—seemed to be coming apart. Bernie Sanders, though losing the Democratic Party nomination to Hillary Clinton, continued to advocate for his policies as a U.S. senator. In 2018, Sanders proposed a plan to guarantee a 15-dollar-an-hour job (or training for one) for every American who wants one.[14]

WHAT HAVE I LEARNED?

1. In the 2016 presidential campaigns, Donald Trump and Bernie Sanders agreed on _____.

    a. the need to restrict immigration

    b. a more robust role for the American military in world affairs

    c. a dissatisfaction with political insiders and elites

    d. the need for a more robust national social welfare policy

2. What concerns did Trump and Sanders *both* try to highlight in their respective campaigns?

3. How were their campaigns different?

PARTIES ACT TO IDENTIFY, SUPPORT, AND NOMINATE CANDIDATES FOR ELECTED OFFICE

- **Identify the roles the political parties play in supporting and nominating candidates for office.**

The Constitution of the United States does not mention political parties. In fact, many of the Framers and early leaders of the young Republic feared the potential consequences from parties grown too powerful. The parties have "baneful effects," President George Washington warned in 1796, because they are rooted "in the strongest passions of the human mind," causing splits that lead to political conflict and stagnation.[15] Parties are, after all, factions, with all of the dangers that a group of like-minded citizens can inflict upon others that factions entail.

Political parties, however, have long been central to democracy and serve several functions. A healthy party serves as a credible check on the opposition, promoting ideas and candidates that differ from the other party's so that voters can choose how they want to be represented. In 1950, a committee composed of members of the American Political Science Association reflected upon the importance of parties for most Americans, noting that "the most valuable opportunity to influence the course of public affairs is the choice they are able to make between the parties in the principal elections."[16]

In developing what is now called the **responsible party model**, the report's authors called for changes in the organization and function of America's political parties. They highlighted the need for parties to present their members with clear positions to which the parties are strongly committed (allowing for reasoned and lively debate between their members), party cohesion both in the party in power and in the party in opposition, an ability to resist pressures from interest groups, and the deliverance to their members of the promises that they make. Party members, for their part, should also act strongly to hold their party leadership accountable in fulfilling those promises.[17]

Political scientist V. O. Key Jr. identified three primary roles that political parties play in American representative democracy:[18]

1. As organizations, political parties recruit, nominate, and support candidates for political office.

2. In the electorate, parties act as labels that are provided to candidates and officeholders and that voters can use as shortcuts in identifying candidates closer to their own political ideologies and advocating similar policy positions.

3. In government, a party enacts the policy positions of its members and acts as an opposition to the majority party when it is in the minority.

responsible party model
a proposal for party reform that emphasized cohesive party positions that present voters with a clear set of choices and allow members' voices to be effectively incorporated into party positions on issues.

In this chapter, we will consider all three of these roles, and the challenges to their successful fulfillment in the twenty-first century. We begin with the first, through an exploration of the role of parties in finding, supporting, and nominating candidates for office.

PARTIES UNITE PEOPLE AS ORGANIZATIONS

A political party seeks to unite people under a shared banner of social, economic, and ideological goals. It finds and supports candidates to run for federal, state, and local offices, which includes mobilizing voters and potential voters to support its candidates. Parties raise money to fund campaigns and provide other forms of help to try to get their candidates elected. If those candidates win, the parties then try to make sure the politicians stay in office. The parties also come up with themes and principles that they want their candidates to follow in appealing for votes.

POLITICAL PARTIES ARE DECENTRALIZED. When some people think of political parties, they think of big shots in Washington, DC, commanding the armies of supporters below them. The reality is that parties are decentralized. They're basically a large collection of state organizations that, in turn, are loose collections of local groups. This is because the system of federalism dictates that power should not just be concentrated at the top. As reporter Jonathan Rauch explained it, "state parties play a key role. They recruit and cultivate political talent, building a farm team of candidates for higher office. They coordinate campaigns up and down the ballot, connecting politicians to each other and discouraging rogue behavior. They build networks of volunteers, connecting leaders with the party base. They gather voter data and make it available to all candidates, building a library of knowledge about the electorate."[19] (See Figure 9.1.)

Today, however, many state party organizations are struggling, in part because of the ability of non-party groups to legally raise and spend large amounts of money on behalf of political causes. This has overshadowed not just state parties but the federal ones as well. Another problem facing state parties is the complexity of the campaign finance system. Its rules restrict the ability of the state parties to raise and spend money and to coordinate campaigns so that candidates of the same party can pool their expenses.

PARTY LEADERS ARE ADVISERS, NOT RULERS. The president generally chooses the chair of his or her national party. The national party chair raises money and serves as a prominent spokesperson on television and other media. But the national party organization's power over the state and local parties is advisory; it can't tell them what to do. In fact, the state parties can put pressure on national parties. In 2014, for example, Republican Party officials at the state level began dropping party platforms and policies opposing same-sex marriage; the national committee leadership later followed their lead. One of the sharpest divisions between the Democratic and Republican Party 2018 platforms was on climate change, with Democrats highlighting the need to address it and Republicans skeptical of the science behind it.

Each state has a central committee made up of people from that state's counties and legislative districts who run for office and are elected to terms just like regular politicians. They help shape the national party's governance, or how it manages its money and runs its operations.

PARTIES SHAPE ELECTIONS BY RECRUITING AND SUPPORTING CANDIDATES

One way a party tries to shape elections is through **recruitment**, which is considered one of its central tasks. The parties seek candidates who best reflect the party's philosophy and who can attract the voters the parties seek to mobilize. Party officials often recruit by finding people who can appeal to specific groups with high concentrations of voters, such as African Americans or Latinos. The parties also look for people who can contrast sharply with their opponents.

In recruiting, parties also try to discourage prospective candidates within their own ranks who aren't seen as having a good chance of winning. They fear that those candidates could end up drawing votes away from their preferred choice.

Parties play a key role in national, state, and local political campaigns. While we often talk about one candidate's "campaign," in fact there are several phases to a campaign, each with its own dynamics. First, candidates have to decide to run, which often involves the help of party leaders and activists.

recruitment
the process through which political parties identify potential candidates.

The Organization of Missouri's Republican Party

A sample party organization chart from the Missouri Republican Party.

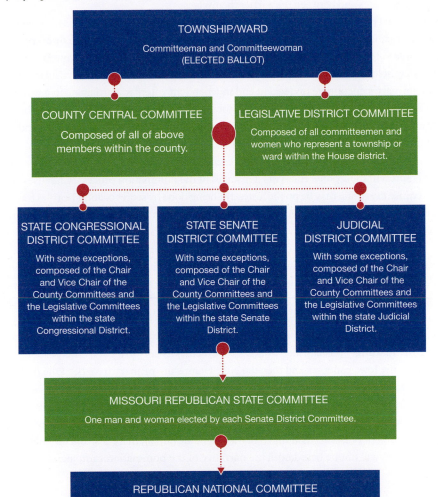

TOWNSHIP/WARD
Committeeman and Committeewoman
(ELECTED BALLOT)

COUNTY CENTRAL COMMITTEE
Composed of all of above members within the county.

LEGISLATIVE DISTRICT COMMITTEE
Composed of all committeemen and women who represent a township or ward within the House district.

STATE CONGRESSIONAL DISTRICT COMMITTEE
With some exceptions, composed of the Chair and Vice Chair of the County Committees and the Legislative Committees within the state Congressional District.

STATE SENATE DISTRICT COMMITTEE
With some exceptions, composed of the Chair and Vice Chair of the County Committees and the Legislative Committees within the state Senate District.

JUDICIAL DISTRICT COMMITTEE
With some exceptions, composed of the Chair and Vice Chair of the County Committees and the Legislative Committees within the state Judicial District.

MISSOURI REPUBLICAN STATE COMMITTEE
One man and woman elected by each Senate District Committee.

REPUBLICAN NATIONAL COMMITTEE
Our State Committee Chair, elected by the MRSC, and a National Committeeman and Committeewoman, both elected at our State Convention, represent Missouri at the RNC.

Source: Missouri Republican Party, "Republican Party Organizational Structure," accessed August 15, 2016, https://www.missouri.gop/wp-content/uploads/2015/07/Org-Flowchart-Transparent-e1438705456327.png.

Second, parties establish a process through which they will nominate their chosen candidates. Finally, parties act to support their nominees in the elections themselves. We will examine the decision to run for national office as well as the dynamics of presidential and congressional campaigns later in this chapter. Here, the focus will be on the process of nomination.

PARTIES SELECT CANDIDATES THROUGH THE NOMINATION PROCESS. In Chapter 10, we will study presidential and congressional campaigns and elections in detail. For now, we will focus on the roles political parties play in the nomination process for presidential candidates.

After recruiting and supporting candidates, parties shape the process of **nomination**, in which a party officially selects one candidate to run for one office against the nominees from other parties. In some races and in some states, the electoral process may pit members of the same party against each other in the general election.

Once the official presidential campaign process kicks off, declared candidates vie with others in their own party for that party's nomination. Beginning early in the election year, candidates seek to

nomination
the formal process through which parties choose their candidates for political office.

get the support of party **delegates**, whose votes they will later need to secure the party's nomination. While many of the rules governing the nomination process are set by federal and state laws, most of the details about *how* things actually work are hammered out by the parties themselves. There remain key differences across states and between the parties themselves.

Most states hold **presidential primary elections** wherein a state's voters choose delegates who support a particular candidate (see Figure 9.2). In some states, these elections may be **open primaries**, in which all eligible voters may vote in a party's primary election, regardless of that voter's partisan affiliation. Others may hold **closed primaries**—open only to registered voters from a particular political party. While open primaries encourage undecided and independent voters to participate in a way that closed primaries do not, they also open up the possibility for strategic voting. Feeling confident in the chances of the presumed nominee in their own party, voters may then use their votes to sabotage the candidate in the opposing party whom they see as the biggest threat to their own preferred candidate.

Some states hold caucuses wherein eligible voters gather to discuss candidates and issues and to select delegates to represent their preferences in later stages of the nomination process. Caucuses differ from primaries because the voting may be public instead of being done by secret ballot. The rules for taking part in a **caucus** are also more complicated, as they involve more than simply marking a ballot to record the selection of a candidate. Because of their complexity, caucuses tend to draw fewer participants than primaries and attract those who are more committed to a candidate or cause.[20]

The schedule of primary elections and caucuses also matters to the ultimate outcomes of the nomination process. Party leaders in a state have a strong incentive to hold their primary election as early as possible in order to garner media attention as well as candidate attention. A win in an early state helps party candidates establish momentum, and issues that are important to specific states may translate later into policy attention should one of the party's candidates win the presidency. To take advantage of this, states try to engage in a process of **front-loading**—pushing their primaries or caucuses as early in the season as possible.

By tradition, the Iowa caucuses and then the New Hampshire primary have been the first two on the schedule. While neither state's nomination process results in a large number of delegates awarded, their early position creates a problem of perception and demographics, the grouping of individuals based on shared characteristics such as ancestry, race, ethnicity, and gender. Since both states have larger white, non-Hispanic voting populations than much of the rest of the nation, there is a concern that the diversity of American voices will not be heard until the narrative of the nomination campaign has already been established.

▼ FIGURE 9.2

Presidential Primary Systems by State, 2016

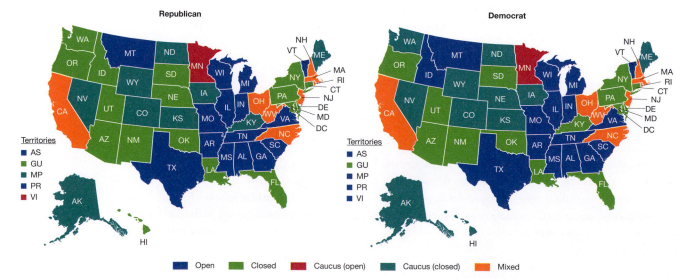

Source: Information about the 2016 primary calendar is from 2016 Election Central, "2016 Primary Schedule," accessed January 15, 2016, www.uspresidentialelectionnews.com/2016-presidential-primary-schedule-calendar.

USING MAPS TO EXPLORE THE CONSEQUENCES OF PRIMARY AND CAUCUS SCHEDULES

Geographical representations of data can be useful tools in exploring important topics in political science. We have discussed the fact that the schedule of state caucuses and primaries can and does have important political consequences. One of the issues with this scheduling involves the degree to which voters in states that participate early in the cycle may be advantaged in selecting eventual nominees. Figure 9A displays the month of a state's primary or caucus in the 2016 presidential elections.

Keeping Figure 9-A in mind, consider Figure 9-B, which displays counties in which racial or ethnic minorities constituted a majority of voters in 2014. While the data are county based, focus on the patterns between states,

connecting these population patterns to the data presented in Figure 9-A.

WHAT Do You Think?

One of the criticisms of the current caucus and primary schedule is that it disadvantages members of racial and ethnic minorities by bringing states with larger minority populations into the nomination process later in the process, when many campaign narratives have already been constructed or reconstructed. Do you think these data support that argument? What other data might you want to investigate this issue further?

▼ **FIGURE 9-A**

Frontloading: Presidential Primary and Caucus Scheduling by State, 2016

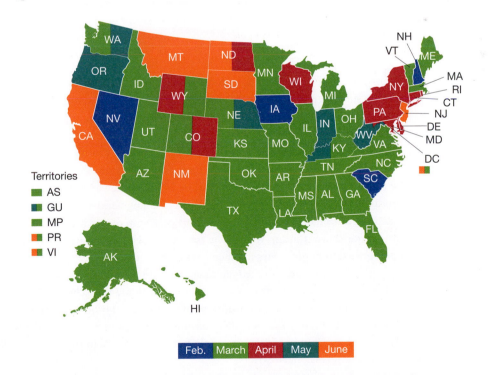

Source: Data from "Presidential Primaries and Caucuses by Month (2016)," FrontloadingHQ, January 31, 2016, http://frontloading.blogspot.com/p/2016-presidential-primary-calendar.html.

Note: In states where Democrats and Republicans hold primaries and caucuses in different months, the timing of the Democratic elections is shown on the left and the timing of the Republican elections is shown on the right.

(Continued)

(Continued)

The Distribution of Counties in Which Racial and Ethnic Minorities Constitute a Majority of the Population

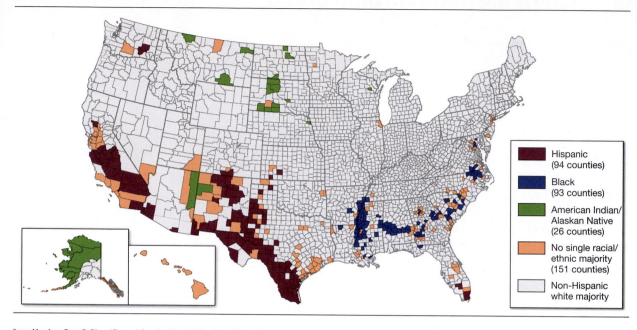

Hispanic (94 counties)

Black (93 counties)

American Indian/ Alaskan Native (26 counties)

No single racial/ ethnic majority (151 counties)

Non-Hispanic white majority

Source: Map from Drew DeSilver, "Share of Counties Where Whites Are a Minority Has Doubled since 1980," Pew Research Center, July 1, 2015, http://www.pewresearch.org/fact-tank/2015/07/01/share-of-counties-where-whites-are-a-minority-has-doubled-since-1980/.

The final phase of the nomination process takes place in the **national conventions** held by the parties in the summer of the presidential election year. During the conventions, delegates vote to select the party's nominee. For much of American history, national conventions were sources of high drama, with many rounds of delegate voting required to select a nominee; in recent decades, the final outcome is already known or expected. In modern conventions, the drama comes from the selection of the vice-presidential nominee—typically done by the presumptive presidential nominee.

The two major political parties have differed in how they award delegates based on primary elections and caucus results. The rules continue to change and evolve, but the Democratic Party has tended to award delegates through a proportional system in which delegates are divided based upon total vote share, though with a few twists and wrinkles. One of these is the existence of **superdelegates**. Superdelegates are members of the Democratic Party—usually elected officials or party activists—who are not pledged to any certain candidate based on the outcomes of their state's primary or caucus. They can support any candidate they choose. The Republican Party, on the other hand, has tended toward more of a winner-take-all (or winner-take-most) system of awarding delegates, in which a state's committed delegates are awarded either to the winning candidate statewide or, more commonly, split between winners in the state overall and winners in the individual congressional districts.

Questions about what parties do and how they should go about it both involve another consideration: how effective parties are in going about their activities. In 2008, four political scientists argued in an influential book titled *The Party Decides* that party leaders serve as powerful gatekeepers. The parties—whom the political scientists defined not just as senior party officials but the organized advocacy and interest groups that make them up—"scrutinize and winnow the field before voters get

national convention
a meeting where delegates officially select their party's nominee for the presidency.

superdelegates
members of the Democratic Party—usually leaders or members of note—who are not pledged to any certain candidate based on the outcomes of their state's primary or caucus.

▲ Parties typically select their nominees for president at their national conventions amid much fanfare but without much drama. In 2016, both the Republican National Convention in Cleveland, Ohio (left), and the Democratic National Convention in Philadelphia, Pennsylvania (right), had more drama than usual. At the Republican Convention, some Republican Party leaders refused to endorse Trump, and Sanders's supporters disrupted the proceedings in Philadelphia at several points. Eventually, however, both Donald Trump and Hillary Clinton received their party's nod.

involved, attempt to build coalitions behind a single preferred candidate, and sway voters to ratify their choice."[21]

In the complicated relationship between candidates and their parties, politicians rely on their parties to help them get elected or stave off challengers, but in doing so they grant power to party leaders. According to political scientist John Aldrich, things get really interesting when candidates no longer feel that the parties and party leadership are serving their goals and may "turn elsewhere to seek the means to win."[22] Does the party decide, steering the nomination process toward selecting the most "electable" candidates in the general election, or can voters in primaries and caucuses impose their will should they feel that party leaders are not responding to the issues that voters want addressed? If there ever was a presidential election to put this question to the test, it was 2016.

▼ FIGURE 9.3

Who Are the Democratic Party's Superdelegates?

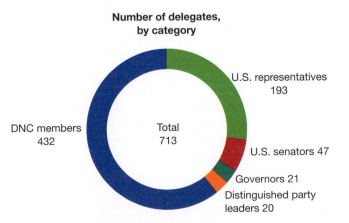

Number of delegates, by category

DNC members 432

Total 713

U.S. representatives 193

U.S. senators 47

Governors 21

Distinguished party leaders 20

A breakdown of Democratic Party superdelegates, by position.

Source: "Who Are the Democratic Superdelegates," Pew Research Center, May 2016, http://www.pewresearch.org/fact-tank/2016/05/05/who-are-the-democratic-superdelegates/.

Notes: Four vacant Democratic National Convention (DNC) positions not shown. Twelve governors, senators, and representatives are also DNC members; they are categorized by elective office only.

1. The responsible party model encourages parties to _____.

   a. present voters with clear and distinguishable messages

   b. place more authority in party leaders

   c. adopt an array of different policy positions and let members choose which ones

   d. attend to the preferences of interest groups

2. Party delegates _____.

   a. focus on recruiting potential candidates

   b. vote to determine a candidate's nomination

   c. determine whether a state will have a caucus or a primary

   d. vote in state primary elections

3. How do state caucuses and primaries differ?

   _____

Answer Key: 1. a; 2. b; 3. Answers should focus both on the different mechanics of the processes and on the differences between participants.

PARTIES PROVIDE LABELS TO CANDIDATES TO ASSIST VOTERS IN MAKING THEIR CHOICES

- Evaluate the changing role of parties as labels for citizens to learn about candidates and their positions on issues.

Recall our discussion of the informational challenges that individuals face in forming and expressing opinions on the multitude of issues with which they are confronted. Given that we cannot know and form opinions about every issue, we sometimes rely on informational shortcuts to sift through them. It is the same with candidates. How can a voter know where every candidate stands on all the issues of concern to them? The answer is that voters cannot. The solution, again, is informational shortcuts, only in the case of candidates, through the use of *labels*. Parties provide candidates with political labels that act as informational shortcuts for voters.

PARTY IDENTIFICATION HELPS CANDIDATES CONNECT WITH VOTERS

Parties shape American politics not only through their organizational capabilities but also through their ability to connect with voters. In their efforts to do this, parties rely on a variety of methods. One is party identification, or the degree to which voters are connected to a particular party. One of the most important things that parties do is signal that they will advance the agendas associated with a particular set of political beliefs, which is key to their role in providing candidates with labels and voters with cues and shortcuts.

In Chapter 7, we also discussed the concept of political ideology, which refers to a person's beliefs about political goals and public policies and acts to shape individual electoral choices. In the United States today, two political ideologies, liberalism and conservativism, have long dominated, whereas socialism and libertarianism have fewer adherents. Recall, too, that these ideologies map onto partisan affiliation, with liberals and some socialists identifying with the Democratic Party and conservatives and many libertarians with the Republican Party.

Divisions between socialists and Democrats and between libertarians and Republicans, however, can cause severe frictions *within* the two major parties, which is very much a driver of the central stories of this chapter.

It is important to remember, though, that political ideology and party identification are not the same thing. Parties do try to appeal to potential members by focusing on issues, policies, and solutions that might appeal to individuals with particular ideologies. Individuals' political beliefs, including partisan party identification, however, have many contributors and sources, including family, education, and life experiences.

Political Ideology: How Democrats and Republicans Differ

Democrat		Republican
Pro-choice	Abortion	Pro-life
Maintain race-based preferences	Affirmative action	Abolish race-based preferences
Protect the rights of the accused	Crime	Punish offenders more strictly
Increase regulation and worker protection	Business	Ease regulation and keep government out of business
Ban	Death penalty	Maintain
Decrease or maintain	Defense spending	Increase
More regulation	Gun control	Protect gun ownership
Maintain or expand the Affordable Care Act	Health care	Repeal the Affordable Care Act
Amnesty for undocumented immigrants, allow undocumented people to obtain driver's licenses	Immigration	Prevent amnesty, no driver's licenses, create a national ID card, add border fences
Increase	Minimum wage	Lower or eliminate
Legalize	Same-sex marriage	Ban
End	School vouchers	Expand
Increase taxes, especially for wealthy	Taxes	Cut taxes, especially for businesses

Liberalism (left side label) — *Conservativism* (right side label)

AMERICANS' IDENTIFICATION WITH EITHER OF THE TWO MAJOR POLITICAL PARTIES IS CHANGING

Since the 1980s, more people have identified themselves as Democrats than as Republicans. These mappings, however, are not always neat and clear. Tensions *within* political parties are often as consequential as debates *between* them. One frustration for both parties is that increasingly larger numbers of people consistently have not identified with either party.[23] Instead, the percentage of Americans self-identifying as independent has grown sharply (see Figure 9.5). Why? A big part of it is Americans' deep frustration with the inability of the federal government to enact policies. Note, though, that when those who "lean" Democrat or Republican are included in the party identification numbers for the two parties, the observed decline in party support does not look as strong. As we explored in Chapter 7, the wording of the questions asked in public opinion surveys can act to shape our interpretation of the "facts on the ground."

Voters have shown less inclination in recent decades to back candidates of different parties in a single election, a practice known as **split-ticket voting**. From 1964 until 1988, as many as one-third of House elections featured a candidate of one party winning even though a presidential candidate of the other party got the most votes in that House candidate's district. Once people identify a group to which they belong, "they are much more likely to vote for their party and less likely to split a ticket," according to political scientist Matthew Levendusky. "They are more likely to become devoted cheerleaders."[24] In 2016, despite deep divisions in the Republican Party establishment, every state that went for Trump elected a Republican senator. On the other side of the aisle, every state that went in Clinton's favor elected a Democrat to the Senate.

The resonance of the campaigns of Trump and Sanders occurred in part because Americans have become less attached to political parties in recent years. At the same time, the country has grown increasingly more polarized by political ideology. More conservatives hold strongly conservative views than in the past, and more liberals strongly liberal views. The party organizations have shouldered much of the blame for creating and fostering an environment in which the two sides seem forever locked in combat. Despite this ongoing battle, the parties haven't become any stronger. According to journalist Jonathan Rauch, "Here is the reigning political paradox of our era: Partisanship is strong, but parties are weak."[25]

split-ticket voting
when a voter chooses a candidate from one party for one office and a candidate from a different party for another position on the ballot.

Americans' Party Identification over Time

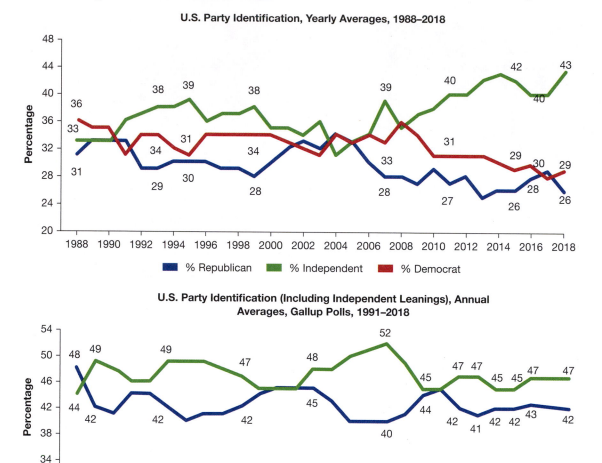

U.S. Party Identification, Yearly Averages, 1988–2018

U.S. Party Identification (Including Independent Leanings), Annual
Averages, Gallup Polls, 1991–2018

Sources: Data from "Party Affiliation," Gallup, www.gallup.com/poll/15370/party-affiliation.aspx; Jeffrey M. Jones, "Americans' Identification as Independents Back Up in 2017," Gallup, http://news.gallup.com/poll/225056/americans-identification-independents-back-2017.aspx. Copyright © 2016 Gallup, Inc. All rights reserved. The content is used with permission; however, Gallup retains all rights of republication.

Note: Gallup began regularly measuring independents' party learnings in 1991.

WHAT HAVE I LEARNED?

1. The political ideology of liberalism in America emphasizes _____.

   a. traditional Libertarian Party values

   b. minimal governmental intervention in individual choices

   c. more robust government action to secure economic equality

   d. less robust government action to secure economic equality

2. How has party identification by the American electorate changed in recent decades?

3. Do you feel strongly identified with a political party? If so, why?

Answer Key: 1. c; 2. Answers should emphasize the fact that while most Americans still identify as either Democratic or Republican, the percentage of those who identify as independents has risen; 3. Answers should include issues of concern that a party emphasizes or reasons why the student does not identify with a party, such as issues that are not being addressed by one party or identification with part of one party's issues and part of another.

THE PRESIDENTIAL ELECTION OF 2016
THROWS CONVENTIONAL WISDOM OUT THE WINDOW

- Reflect on the implications of the presidential election of 2016 for the Democratic and Republican parties.

As the presidential nomination season of 2016 progressed, both Bernie Sanders and Donald Trump surprised political scientists, political pundits, and their own party leaders with their success, although, in Sanders's case, Hillary Clinton was still seen as the almost inevitable nominee for the Democratic Party. On the Republican side, several mainstream candidates, such as former Florida governor Jeb Bush, Florida senator Marco Rubio, and New Jersey governor Chris Christie, all vied for their party's endorsement, along with more than a dozen other candidates. "Successful political parties unite interests under a broadly shared policy agenda," social scientist Joel Kotkin observed.[26] Under Clinton, Kotkin said, Democrats "share basic positions on many core issues and a unifying belief in federal power as the favored instrument for change. In contrast, the Republican Party consists of interest groups that so broadly dislike each other that they share little common ground."[27]

SANDERS'S SUPPORTERS CRY "FOUL!"

During the primary and caucus season of 2016, many Sanders supporters argued that the party's superdelegate system provided Hillary Clinton with an unfair advantage. Even though Sanders actually won the vote in some state primaries and caucuses, the party's rules for how delegates are allocated neutralized his victory, handing Clinton the nomination. The Democratic Party had developed a specific set of rules precisely because it wanted to be able to pick presidential nominees strategically. Party members believed that long-term party members would have an interest in backing the strongest possible candidates and that giving those officials the power to switch their votes could avoid messy fights over the nomination.[28]

Sanders alienated many in the Democratic Party establishment over a controversy involving access to computerized voter data. Employees working for Sanders were accused of improperly obtaining information from Clinton's data files after a firewall between the two campaigns' information was inadvertently dropped. The Democratic National Committee (DNC) retaliated by cutting off the Sanders campaign's access to the committee's own voter file information, leading the senator's supporters to accuse the party of blatantly favoring Clinton, even though Sanders himself apologized to Clinton at a debate over the incident. His campaign later filed a lawsuit against the committee.[29]

Louise Wateridge/Pacific Press/LightRocket via Getty Images

▲ Democratic presidential candidates Hillary Clinton and Bernie Sanders at a CNN debate in 2016. Clinton's "insider" status within the Democratic party was a significant factor in her ultimately securing the nomination.

The Sanders campaign also argued with the DNC about the number and timing of debates during the primary season. Underdog candidates always vastly prefer as many debates as possible because it gives them great visibility without having to spend any campaign dollars. The committee had scheduled some debates on Saturday nights, when the senator said fewer people would be watching. In one instance, an Iowa debate ran at the same time as a big University of Iowa football game. The party said that was a coincidence, but Sanders said it was done deliberately to draw attention away from the debate.[30]

A POLITICAL CARTOON DEPICTS BERNIE SANDERS'S CAMPAIGN

I n June 2016, Hillary Clinton secured the magic number of 2,383 pledged delegates to the Democratic Party's national convention in July. It was not a primary or caucus that carried her over the hurdle, but commitments by previously uncommitted superdelegates (composed of members of Congress, governors, and other party leaders). During the early months of 2016, many supporters of Bernie Sanders criticized the fact that a large number of superdelegates had already pledged to support Clinton, even while the nomination campaign was just getting under way. Activists with MoveOn.org started a petition to require that superdelegates wait to pledge until after results of the caucuses and primaries were in. Following Clinton's nomination, however, MoveOn.org poured its energies into defeating Donald Trump in the general election.

In May, prior to the official nomination, political cartoonist Mike Keefe created the image above right.

Consider the image, noting that, in political cartoons, even the smallest details are chosen to convey a point or argument. What do you think the cartoonist meant with the image of the bull's-eye? What do you think the speeding car is meant to represent here?

WHƏT Do You Think?

What themes do you think Keefe is trying to portray with this image? What do you make of the portrayal of Bernie Sanders and Hillary Clinton in this image? Which of the two candidates do you think is pictured in a more positive way? In a more negative way?

In the early voting states, Sanders did better than Clinton at caucuses than in primaries. That is because caucuses tend to favor candidates who have extremely enthusiastic supporters, which Bernie Sanders often had. In caucuses, participants get to make speeches to try to persuade others to support their candidates, and there are sometimes multiple rounds of voting, neither of which occurs in a primary, where a voter casts a private ballot alone.

The Democratic Party provided Clinton with other advantages over Sanders. The most obvious was that she actually belonged to the party; he did not. That gave her a broad network of prominent supporters who coalesced ahead of primary voting to warn of what they saw as the danger of a Sanders candidacy affecting other races in which Democrats were running. "Here in the heartland, we like our politicians in the mainstream, and [Sanders] is not—he's a socialist," said Democratic Missouri governor Jay Nixon two months before his state's primary. "He's entitled to his positions, and it's a big-tent party. But as far as having him at the top of the ticket, it would be a meltdown all the way down the ballot."[31]

Sanders's message, however, had gotten through. Sanders succeeded in forcing Clinton to take positions similar to his on trade and jobs. For example, when she first declared her candidacy, Clinton vowed to be "president for the struggling, the striving and the successful."[32] But after losing the Michigan primary, she said, "I don't want to be the president for those who are already successful—they don't need me. I want to be the president for the struggling and the striving."[33] She also expressed a greater willingness to raise taxes on the wealthy to keep Social Security from going broke.[34] After her loss to Sanders in the Michigan primary, Clinton won primaries in other states, such as Ohio and Missouri, where trade and job losses to foreign countries were big concerns.

DONALD TRUMP'S CAMPAIGN BENEFITS IN UNEXPECTED WAYS FROM REPUBLICAN RULES

In his campaign, Donald Trump took positions that were so extreme—and made statements considered so outrageous and off-putting—that fewer than usual Republican Party loyalists were willing to join him, even though his stances and pugnacious style attracted public support. Few senior party officials took Trump seriously in the early months after he announced his candidacy. But as he gained strength in the polls and began winning primaries, those party officials were caught in a difficult bind. Many of them were appalled by Trump, yet the Republican National Committee (RNC) had created the rules that enabled Trump to prevail in the early primaries. RNC chair Reince Priebus insisted that the party would support whoever emerged as its nominee, boasting in January that he was "100 percent" confident of that fact.[35]

▲ The field of contenders for the Republican presidential ticket in 2016 was extensive. In an early debate in October 2015, ten of the top candidates participated in a prime-time event (another group debated earlier). Shown from left to right are, former Pennsylvania senator Rick Santorum, former New York governor George Pataki, Kentucky senator Rand Paul, former Arkansas governor Mike Huckabee, Florida senator Marco Rubio, Texas senator Ted Cruz, retired neurosurgeon Ben Carson, real estate magnate Donald Trump, former Florida governor Jeb Bush, Wisconsin governor Scott Walker, former CEO Carly Fiorina, Ohio governor John Kasich, and New Jersey governor Chris Christie.

Trump's candidacy exposed the Republican Party's weaknesses in several ways. Republicans could not, as they had in some past elections, unify around a consensus candidate. Several candidates who were popular with the party's establishment all plunged into the race, including Jeb Bush and Marco Rubio. None of the consensus mainstream candidates succeeded in captivating broad swaths of voters, however, and all eventually dropped out.

Part of the reason for this was that the RNC, in drawing up the rules for 2016, ended up providing Trump with significant institutional advantages. The RNC had come under criticism within the party for the primary process in 2012, which dragged on for months before Mitt Romney emerged as the nominee. Thus, for 2016, it moved up its schedule with the hope that a front-runner could emerge more quickly. The result was that many states that year voted in March, a month or two earlier than they had in 2012.

Another change intended to help cement an early front-runner was that a majority of the Republican delegates at stake were awarded by states' congressional districts—the winner of each district received two delegates, the runner-up received one, and none of the other finishers received any. In making those changes, the RNC was trying to placate both the party's establishment, which wanted a shorter calendar, and its conservative activists, who had advocated for proportional delegate selection. But it did not anticipate that Trump would get more votes than candidates from either of those groups. As journalist Trip Gabriel put it, "It's right in line with what the folks designing these rules wanted. It's just not the candidate they preferred."[36]

Trump's campaign rallies, in which several demonstrators were attacked and Trump offered to pay his supporters' legal fees, made party officials even more uneasy, leading the RNC chair to issue a public call for calm. By March, some prominent Republicans said it was impossible for them to support Trump. "If our party is no longer working for the things we believe in . . . then people of good conscience should stop supporting that party until it is reformed," said Republican senator Ben Sasse of Nebraska.[37] The result was that many Republican officials switched their endorsements to Texas senator Ted Cruz, a man many of them loathed for his disdain for working with colleagues in his party and for likening the Republican establishment to a "cartel," or drug mafia. Cruz also picked up some of the delegates from other candidates who had abandoned their campaigns. In Louisiana, for example, Trump beat Cruz by four percentage points, but Cruz picked up several of Marco Rubio's delegates.[38]

Cruz and Trump became locked in a race filled with a nastiness never before seen in modern presidential politics. Trump repeatedly referred to Cruz as "Lyin' Ted." When the supermarket tabloid *National Enquirer* subsequently alleged that Cruz had had multiple extramarital affairs, the Texas senator blamed "Trump and his henchmen" for spreading a story he said was "garbage" and "complete and utter lies."[39] As the bickering raged, the Republican Party's image nosedived. A CNN poll in late March found the party's unfavorable rating at its highest level since the partial government shutdown in 2013, when it had notched its worst ratings in polling dating back to 1992. Just 34 percent of adults said they had a positive view of the party, with 61 percent saying they had a negative one. Even among registered Republicans, the favorability rating plunged from 73 percent in January to 66 percent.[40]

The RNC had anticipated acrimony among the large field of candidates. In 2015, the committee asked all of them to sign a formal public pledge that they would support the party's eventual nominee. Initially, the candidates agreed during several debates—even those laden with personal attacks—that they would stick to it. But at a town hall meeting in March 2016, Cruz backed away from the pledge, followed by Ohio governor John Kasich and Trump.[41] Trump's campaign accused senior party officials and the news media of conspiring against Trump. "The press is printing the narrative that the Republican establishment is setting," said Barry Bennett, a senior adviser to Trump's campaign.[42]

BOTH MAJOR PARTIES CONTINUE TO WRESTLE WITH INSURGENCIES

After having finally endorsed and supported nominee Hillary Clinton during the summer's Democratic Party Convention, Bernie Sanders continued to campaign on her behalf. Some observers, however, wondered if Sanders could have beaten Donald Trump in the general election, drawing out voters who might have ended up staying home on the day of the general election. Donald Trump's candidacy, though ultimately successful, struggled against opposition from the Republican Party establishment. For example, former Republican presidents George H. W. Bush and George W. Bush refused to endorse Trump.

In the weeks leading up to the general election, the situation continued to heat up for both candidates. In October, a 2005 taped conversation between Donald Trump and a reporter from *Access Hollywood* emerged, recording statements in which Trump made derogatory, hostile, and demeaning comments about women. Eleven days before the general election, FBI director James Comey sent a letter to Congress alerting members that he was reviewing possible new evidence related to the investigation into Secretary Clinton's use of a private email server while she was in office. Two days before the election, Director Comey announced that the reopened inquiry was being closed.

In the end, Donald Trump defeated Hillary Clinton in the only vote that matters for the presidency: the Electoral College (Chapter 10). While Secretary Clinton won the popular vote, Trump defeated Clinton in the Electoral College and claimed the presidency. To many observers' surprise, Trump managed to breach what had been called the "blue wall" of solidly Democratic states, including Pennsylvania, Michigan, and Wisconsin. In the days following Donald Trump's win, protests erupted around the nation, some of them turning violent. A few posts on Facebook and Twitter called for his assassination.

While political scientists will no doubt be talking about the election of 2016 for years, one of the main questions will be this: What impact will the candidacies of Bernie Sanders and Donald Trump have on their respective political parties? Sanders attempted to push the Democratic Party to embrace the need to address economic inequality, issues that nominee Clinton began to address more frequently as her campaign progressed.

Donald Trump's populist rhetoric had alienated many Republican leaders. According to an RNC official, "Donald Trump has done to the Republican Party what the killer comet did to the dinosaurs."[43] In terms of conventional wisdom, Trump's extreme statements should have doomed his candidacy. Yet they did not. When the dust had settled on the presidential election of 2016, the Republican Party emerged in control of the White House, Congress, and the majority of state governorships and legislatures. What that would mean for Trump's ability to enact *his* policies, however, was far from certain.

1. One institutional structure that advantaged Hillary Clinton in the Democratic nomination process was _____.

    a. having a party convention

    b. superdelegates

    c. nonvoting delegates

    d. having caucuses within the same month

2. How did Republican Party rules end up advantaging the candidacy of Donald Trump?

3. Do you feel that the parties' establishment treated either Bernie Sanders or Donald Trump unfairly in the nomination process? If so, why?

Answer Key: 1. b; 2. Answers should focus on efforts to secure an earlier consensus on a nominee or on the allocation of delegates in state primaries and caucuses; 3. Answers should include specific reasons why a party did or did not treat either Sanders or Trump fairly.

POLITICAL POLARIZATION, GRIDLOCK, AND TWO-PARTY DOMINANCE ARE THE DEFINING FEATURES OF PARTIES IN GOVERNMENT TODAY

- Examine the role of parties in government and the traditional dominance of two major political parties in national elections.

If they have been successful in mobilizing citizens to vote for the candidates they have selected and supported, a party's members take office and begin the process of governing. At the national level, during presidential nomination conventions, party members write, argue over, and agree on a **party platform**, which seeks to define the party's general stance on issues and the policies that its members will pursue in governing. These platforms are then voted on at the conventions. Because it is not a binding document, and because it covers dozens and dozens of often-arcane issues, some people question the usefulness of a platform.

Former House Speaker John Boehner, an Ohio Republican, once said the platform should be no more than one page because "that way, Americans could actually read it."[44] Because of the difficulty in getting large groups of people, even those with similar beliefs, to agree on something, the platforms can be the source of great controversy. In 2012, Democrats initially took out a sentence in their party's platform about helping individuals reach their "God-given potential." But that removal would have removed any references to God in the platform, and Democrats feared it would lead Republicans to depict them as out of touch with religious Americans. The sentence was added back.[45]

By May 2016, with Donald Trump closing in on enough delegates to secure the Republican nomination outright, there was less talk about what a Trump platform might look like than about his battles with the party establishment, which were partly because of his refusal to present detailed policy positions on many issues. According to a *Los Angeles Times* reporter, "One cannot even agree with Trump in his 'policies,' because that is like committing to the blob in a lava lamp."[46] As Bernie Sanders continued to perform well in the Democratic primaries and caucuses, however—though the delegate math was turning against him—many observers looked ahead to a Sanders-influenced Democratic Party platform in the summer conventions with Hillary Clinton as the presumptive nominee.

POLARIZATION LEADS TO GRIDLOCK IN AMERICAN GOVERNANCE

Although Americans often say they want politicians to compromise, some experts have found that in reality, they generally prefer the other side to accede to their wishes. That's because consistency has been shown to be very important to people, no matter what their ideology. The parties reflect those attitudes. As one scholar of political beliefs stated, "Few people march under a banner that says, 'We may be right, we may be wrong, let's compromise!' You know, that's not good politics."[47]

....

party platform
a set of positions and policy objectives that members of a political party agree to.

In general, the parties try to make their case to the public by offering sharp contrasts to each other. Both the Republican and Democratic national committees make daily assertions and put out dozens of news releases, videos, tweets, and other social media presentations that seek to further a single larger point: The other side is wrong. In this sense, both parties have a partisan agenda—they are less interested in fostering cooperation than they are in criticizing their opponents.

All members of a political party do not hold the same beliefs. Each party contains factions within it that try to pressure the party to adopt its positions. Labor unions are one important faction within the Democratic Party; they push the party to raise the minimum wage and pass other bills aimed at improving working conditions. In the Republican Party, the House Freedom Caucus has become an influential faction within the last decade. It is not a formal party but a loosely organized collection of groups that demands steep cuts in government spending, extremely limited regulation of private companies, and more accountability from government employees.

The pressures that parties face to point out sharp differences between their positions and those of the opposition have led to increasing **political polarization**. Polarization isn't the result of a flaw in our constitutional system, but the Constitution's separation of powers has made it worse. In Washington, increased polarization has led to **gridlock**, which occurs when parties are unable to find any common ground to work together, an increasingly common occurrence over the last few decades. When separation of powers is combined with extreme positions, the result is deadlock, according to political scientist Jane Mansbridge. "Deadlock was less of a problem in the early days of the republic, when today's interdependence in commerce, law and order could not even have been imagined, and the national legislature did not have to pass many laws. Today that deadlock is a disaster."[48]

An ongoing debate among political scientists who study American political parties and elections has been about the sources of partisan polarization in Congress. Members of Congress are increasingly voting with members of their own party. Why? It is not clear if this trend represents an increasingly polarized environment among political elites, political masses, or both, or if some other factor or factors are at play.[49]

WHILE THE LANDSCAPE OF PARTIES IN GOVERNMENT HAS CHANGED, IT HAS HISTORICALLY BEEN DOMINATED BY TWO MAJOR PARTIES

For about the past 150 years, most politicians have belonged to either the Democratic or Republican party. Since then, control of government has shifted back and forth between the parties in periods of **realignment**, which occur when public support shifts substantially from one party to the other. Periods of realignment may be ushered in by **critical elections** (or critical eras) in which, according to political scientist Aldrich, a short event or era leads to a "new period of relative stability."[50] While political scientists continue to debate the boundaries of major eras in party control and how decisive a particular election was in signaling a change in those boundaries, they often draw on the underlying idea to which Aldrich was referring—periods of stability punctuated by periods of rapid change. They call the more or less stable eras **party systems**. Political scientists often divide American political history into six party systems (see Figure 9.6).

America's first president, George Washington, was not a member of a political party and indeed had warned the nation about the dangers partisanship posed to the young Republic. However, during his tenure, Washington's administration split into two factions: those like Treasury secretary Alexander Hamilton and Vice President John Adams, supporting a strong federal government, and those like Secretary of State Thomas Jefferson and James Madison, who believed that individual states should be given more authority over their own affairs. As these individuals tried to gain support for their policies in Congress and in the state legislatures, they coalesced into two parties: the Democratic-Republicans (Jefferson and Madison) and the Federalists (Adams and Hamilton), signaling the first party system.

The Democratic-Republican Party had largely dissolved by 1824, with many of its members moving to form what became known as the Whig Party. This era also saw the decline of the Federalist Party. Due to the granting of suffrage to large numbers of white men who had previously been excluded because of their lack of wealth or property, this era saw the rise of the Democratic Party and the election of Andrew Jackson as president in 1828 and the rise of the second party system. The Democratic Party remained the

---

political polarization
a sharp ideological distance between political parties.

gridlock
an inability to compromise and enact legislation that is driven by political polarization.

realignment
a major shift in allegiance to the political parties that is often driven by changes in the issues that unite or divide voters.

critical election
a major national election that signals a change either in the balance of power between two major parties or the emergence of a new party system.

party systems
periods of stability of the composition of political parties and the issues around which they coalesce, brought on by shorter periods of intense change.

American Party Systems

1790–1828

FIRST PARTY SYSTEM
- Hamilton and Adams's Federalist Party: strong federal government
- Jefferson and Madison's Democratic-Republicans: more power to states

1828–1856

SECOND PARTY SYSTEM
- Demise of the Democratic-Republican Party, replaced largely by the Whig Party
- Decline of the Federalist Party; rise of the Democratic Party

1856–1892

THIRD PARTY SYSTEM
- Disputes about slavery precipitate realignment. Party identification becomes regionally divided
- "Free Soil" Democrats join Whigs, together form Republican Party: opposed to slavery

1892–1932

FOURTH PARTY SYSTEM
- Democrats and Republicans dominate with some third-party challenges
- Electorate divided by urban/rural splits and other policy issues

1932–1968

FIFTH PARTY SYSTEM
- Depression-era Democratic Party focuses on strong federal government
- Republican Party fights for smaller federal role

1968–present

SIXTH PARTY SYSTEM
- Democratic and Republican parties remain divided about role of government but also reorient on the issue of civil rights

dominant party in Congress for the next three decades. The politics of national campaigns evolved into how we now think about them, featuring broad appeals to voters and strengthening party organizations.

The unresolved issue of slavery led to a major realignment, with members of both parties divided among themselves. This led to the forming of two new parties. "Free Soil" Democrats joined with Whigs in arguing that slavery should be kept out of the rapidly expanding southwestern territories in the United States. They stressed a belief in the potential of the individual and argued against slavery on moral grounds.[51] The antislavery Whigs and Democrats formed the Republican Party. After the Civil War, the United States entered the third party system and the ongoing period of two-party dominance by the Democratic and Republicans. Party identification became sharply regional, with Republicans dominating the Northeast and Democrats the South. Support for the parties was divided in the midwestern states.

During the fourth party system, Democrats and Republicans continued to dominate national politics, though not without occasional challenges by third parties. Slavery had ended, but the two parties were divided by the politics of Reconstruction and differences of opinion about how strongly the federal government should act to secure civil rights. In addition, divisions between urban and rural voters as well as debates over immigration and federal policy in an era of massive industrialization shaped politics and party success and failure.

In 1932, the Great Depression ushered in another major change in the party system (the fifth). The election of Franklin Roosevelt in 1932 and in three subsequent elections led to a period of Democratic Party dominance. Between 1930 and 1994, the Democrats lost their majority in the House just twice, in 1946 and 1952, and they quickly regained control two years later both times.[52] The Democratic Party emphasized a commitment to a strong federal government in the service of social welfare policies. Republicans emphasized a smaller role for the federal government and less involvement in and regulation of the economy.

The sixth party system is the one that many political scientists argue has defined party politics for the past fifty years. The Democratic Party has remained focused on a vigorous federal government in the service of securing civil rights and support for affirmative action and a woman's right to choose. Republicans have remained focused on a smaller federal government, advocating conservative views on social issues, lower taxes, and fewer restrictions on American businesses. What changed were the coalitions of voters supporting the parties, especially with regard to the geography of partisan support in the nation. Much of this had been driven by the realignment of large numbers of southern white voters from the Democratic Party to the Republican Party during the civil rights era.

Sharp, but numerically close, divisions on these issues and support for party positions on them has led to repeated changes in party control of the national government in recent years (see Figure 9.7). These changes have contributed to gridlock and significant policy shifts. As we will explore in Chapter 13, they have also contributed to the sharp and similarly close divide between justices of the U.S. Supreme Court.

The sixth party system has been one of the longest in the nation's history. However, it is unclear how much longer it will last. The Democratic and Republican parties are trying to stay relevant in an age of intense and increasing polarization. That polarization has led some voters to become engaged not just because they support their party but out of an intense dislike of the other side.

It remains to be seen what this means for the parties. Robert Reich, an economist and liberal activist who served as secretary of labor under President Bill Clinton, predicted that an antiestablishment "People's Party" made up of disaffected Democrats and Republicans could take root as soon as 2020.[53] Others say such a shift could occur but that it's also possible the parties could absorb elements that are currently in the other party.

If voters and observers were looking for a clear signal of a change in the U.S. party system in the 2018 midterm elections, they did not get it. Control of the House flipped to the Democratic Party; however, an incumbent president's party losing seats in or control of one or more legislative chambers in a midterm election is the historical norm. Battles for ideological dominance within each party continued, with all looking ahead to 2020.

▼ FIGURE 9.7

Changes in Party Control, 2000–2018

Election	Presidency	House	Senate
2000	Republican George W. Bush	Republican	Democrat
2002		Republican	Republican
2004	Republican George W. Bush	Republican	Republican
2006		Democrat	Democrat
2008	Democrat Barack Obama	Democrat	Democrat
2010		Republican	Democrat
2012	Democrat Barack Obama	Republican	Democrat
2014		Republican	Republican
2016	Republican Donald Trump	Republican	Republican
2018		Democrat	Republican

In the cases of both the Democratic and Republican Parties, many experts agree that they are institutions formed in a different era; they now must deal with a host of obstacles to maintain the social conditions that help parties thrive. And the landscape is changing dramatically. As we will explore in the next chapter, America is in the midst of a massive demographic shift, with Latino and Latina voters rapidly growing as a share of the electorate. How well the major parties do in communicating their messages to Latino and Latina voters in the coming decades will, in no small part, determine their strength and relevance in American national politics.

AMERICA'S ELECTORAL SYSTEM LEADS TO TWO-PARTY DOMINANCE

There is no law requiring that American national politics be dominated by two major political parties. Other countries have none, one, two, or many political parties dominating national politics, with the existence of more than two being the norm. (See Figure 9.8.) With a few very important exceptions, a two-party system has been dominant for most of America's political history. Why?

Scholars usually point to institutional explanations for America's two-party dominance, specifically the ways in which candidates are elected to national office, especially Congress. The U.S. method of voting—a **single-member plurality system** in which voters have a single vote for one candidate and the candidate with the most votes wins—encourages this. Other countries have **proportional representation systems** in which the rules discourage a two-party system. Although there are many differences between nations in the details, proportional representation systems award party representation in legislative bodies based upon percentage of votes overall.

In the American winner-take-all single-member plurality system, the candidate who gets the most votes in a state or congressional district wins the election. In presidential elections, with the exceptions of Maine and Nebraska, the candidate who wins the popular vote in a state wins all of that state's electoral votes. As a result of their use of proportional representation systems, other nations witness larger numbers of major parties than the United States (Figure 9.8).

The winner-take-all system allows the largest politically cohesive groups—the Democrats or Republicans—to elect almost every office in a jurisdiction. Proponents of the system say this promotes stability; if people are happy with the job that a representative from one of those parties is doing, they can keep voting for that representative's party even after he or she leaves office.

Critics say it doesn't do much to help people who are stuck in an area in which one party dominates, such as Republicans in cities and Democrats in rural states. They say that this can be a significant barrier

single-member plurality system
a structure of electoral representation in which a candidate and the party that he or she represents must win the most votes in a state or district in order to be represented in government.

proportional representation system
a structure of electoral representation in which parties are represented in government according to their candidates' overall share of the vote.

▼ FIGURE 9.8

Differences across Countries in the Number of Major Political Parties

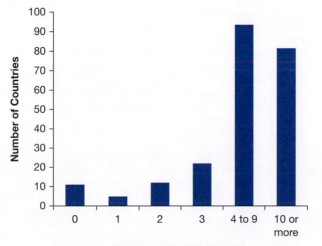

Source: Data from *CIA World Factbook*, "Political Parties and Leaders," accessed June 15, 2016, https://www.cia.gov/library/publications/the-world-factbook/fields/2118.html.

to encouraging greater numbers of people, including minority groups and young people, to take part in politics. Instead, candidates can run divisive campaigns aimed at turning out only the most partisan voters, since the winner-take-all system provides little incentive to reach out to opponents.

MINOR PARTIES MAY CHALLENGE THE TWO MAJOR PARTIES

third party (minor party)
a political party operating over a limited period of time in competition with two other major parties.

The Democratic and Republican parties have occasionally had some competition. Candidates from a **third party (minor party)** usually focus on a single issue that they don't think the major parties are emphasizing enough. "What happens is, third parties act as a gadfly," said Sean Wilentz, director of the American Studies program at Princeton University. "There'll be an issue that's being neglected or that is being purposely excluded from national debate because neither party wants to face the political criticism that it would bring."[54] (See Table 9.1.)

▼ TABLE 9.1

Third Parties Compared: A Selection

Party	Platform
Constitution Party: "The sole purpose of government, as stated in the Declaration of Independence, is to secure our inalienable rights given us by our Creator. When Government grows beyond this scope, it is usurpation, and liberty is compromised."	Pro: life, states' rights, Second Amendment, limited government Against: illegal immigration and amnesty, influence of the United Nations and other globalist organizations on the United States, undeclared wars, free trade
Green Party: "An independent political party that is connected to American social movements, and is part of a global Green movement."	Democracy, social justice, ecological sustainability, economic justice and sustainability
Libertarian Party: "Minimum government, maximum freedom."	Personal liberty, economic liberty, securing liberty
Peace and Freedom Party: "California's feminist socialist political party."	Doubling the minimum wage and indexing it to the cost of living; global disarmament of nuclear, chemical, and biological weapons; defending and extending liberties guaranteed in the Bill of Rights; full and free high-quality public education from pre-K to graduate school; lifelong learning and retraining; cancellation of student debt; free high-quality health care; restoring and protecting the environment
Prohibition Party: "Charactered leadership driven by hope for a return to traditional values."	Loyalty to the Constitution and especially the Bill of Rights, U.S. sovereignty, no relations with countries that do not practice humanitarian treatment of all people and no aid to unfriendly nations, no wars without consent of Congress, legislation to nullify judicial decisions based on foreign or international law, nine-year term limits to Supreme Court justices, lawyers not allowed to hold legislative or executive branch office, abolition of Federal Reserve system, all-volunteer army
Reform Party: "A moderate, centrist and populist party that sits in the center of the political spectrum."	Fiscal responsibility and accountability; fair taxation without special interest exceptions; an "America first" position on job creation; affordable, accessible health care based on decision making between doctors and patients; reforms at the federal level to enforce the highest ethical standards and effective oversight; protection of natural resources while addressing needs for economic development; energy independence; border security; upholding of Constitution to define scope of government and rights of citizens; no stance on abortion or gay marriage
Socialist Party USA: "Strives to establish a radical democracy that places people's lives under their own control—a non-racist, classless, feminist socialist society . . . where working people own and control the means of production and distribution through democratically-controlled public agencies, cooperatives, or other collective groups."	Global transformation from capitalism to democratic socialism, opposition to U.S. imperialism, workers' rights to organize and collectively own means of production and distribution, human rights for all, opportunities for all to participate in arts and cultural activities, free movement across borders, repeal of the USA PATRIOT Act, public ownership of natural resources, animal rights

Sources: Quotes and other information are from the party websites: Constitution Party, http://www.constitutionparty.com/; Green Party, http://www.gp.org/; Libertarian Party, http://www.lp.org/; Peace and Freedom Party, http://www.peaceandfreedom.org/home/; Prohibition Party, http://www.prohibitionparty.org/; Reform Party, http://reformparty.org/; Socialist Party, http://socialistparty-usa.net/.

Third-party candidates do sometimes make fairly big splashes. In the 2000 election, consumer activist Ralph Nader captivated many liberals when he ran for president under the Green Party banner. He won 2.74 percent of the popular vote—just enough, many Democrats continue to believe, to deny the presidency to Al Gore.[55] The tendency among some voters to conclude that a vote for a third-party candidate essentially is a vote helping someone they oppose has made it difficult for third-party candidates to win national elections. Even so, increasing numbers of Americans support the idea of more viable and competitive third parties (see Figure 9.9).

The Democratic and Republican parties have worked to discourage third-party candidacies. One way is to prevent those candidates from taking part in presidential debates. Another is having local officials set stringent requirements for candidates to collect a certain number of signatures before they can appear on a ballot, which can be difficult for many third-party hopefuls.

During the general election in 2016, as the Clinton and Trump campaigns both struggled against heavily negative perceptions, third-party challengers emerged, drawing votes from both. Gary Johnson, candidate for the Libertarian Party; Jill Stein, the Green Party candidate; and Evan McMullin, an independent candidate, all vied to establish their respective parties as credible challengers to the Democratic and Republican parties. Many observers originally expected third-party presidential candidates to do well, Johnson and Stein in particular; ultimately, none presented a serious challenge to Hillary Clinton or Donald Trump.[56]

Third parties have had better luck in local government races. This is because of election rules that help them compete in those races, such as ranked choice voting, which allows voters to rank the candidates in order of preference instead of voting for a single candidate. Proponents of the idea say that it provides voters with more choices and prevents having to hold runoff elections. They point to Cambridge, Massachusetts, a city outside Boston where Harvard is located. Cambridge has used the system since 1941 to elect its city council and school board members, and proponents say it has resulted in greater representation by minority groups and women and has increased voter turnout.[57] Critics of the approach, however, say that the system can be confusing for voters. And they claim it actually discriminates against minorities, non-English speakers, and people without much education. When the city of San Francisco used the system in 2011, turnout was the lowest it had been in thirty-six years.[58]

▼ FIGURE 9.9

Americans' Opinions of the Need for Third Parties in the United States

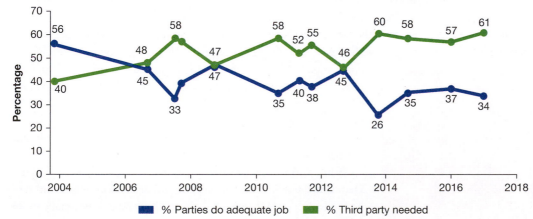

In your view, do the Republican and Democratic parties do an adequate job of representing the American people, or do they do such a poor job that a third major party is needed?

■ % Parties do adequate job   ■ % Third party needed

Sources: Justin McCarthy, "Majority in U.S. Maintain Need for Third Major Party," Gallup, September 25, 2015, http://www.gallup.com/poll/185891/majority-maintain-need-third-major-party.aspx; Lydia Saad, "Perceived Need for Third Major Party Remains High in U.S.," Gallup, September 27, 2017, http://news.gallup.com/poll/219953/perceived-need-third-major-party-remains-high.aspx. Copyright © 2015 Gallup, Inc. All rights reserved. The content is used with permission; however, Gallup retains all rights of republication.

1. The primary reason for two-party dominance in American political history is _____.

    a. the Constitution of the United States

    b. U.S. Supreme Court decisions

    c. the method of electing individuals to national office

    d. lack of public support for a strong third party

2. Party realignment signals _____.

    a. the inability of parties to work together once in office

    b. stable periods of party positions and membership

    c. the aligning of the two major parties in agreement on issues

    d. a major shift in the composition of a party allegiance

3. If *you* were to start a third major party, what might your platform include?

_____

Answer Key: 1. c; 2. d; 3. Answers should focus on specific issues that either or both Democrats and Republicans are not emphasizing sufficiently or on one or more issues that cut across the two parties' positions.

CONCLUSION: HOW WILL THE PARTIES RESPOND?

There is a somewhat obscure 1950s science fiction movie called *Attack of the Crab Monsters*. Thanks to, I think, radiation, giant mutant crabs on an island evolve, eat people, and absorb their unfortunate victims' voices, personalities, and knowledge to grow stronger, more powerful, and more dangerous. The mutant crabs use the voices and identities they've stolen to lure other unsuspecting humans to their doom. In the "words" of one of the crab monsters, impersonating a human and trying to lure a group of people into the caves, "It is almost exhilarating! Will you come?"[59]

This is what the two dominant political parties in American political history have always tried to do with insurgents—without the eating-people part, of course. An internal revolution is often a signal that the party has to adapt, to bring the voices of those insurgents back into the fold, to keep the party viable, relevant, and strong. Or, if that fails, to put an end to the insurgency, once and for all.

One might imagine a story—a science fiction one, based on an alternate timeline—that begins something like this: "Once in office, President Donald Trump settled all of his differences with the Republican establishment, and he and the Party moved forward in unity and harmony." Not in ours. The American political reality in our 2018 is far different. Trump remains at war with many Republican establishment leaders, under investigation, tweeting like always, running toward and not away from conflicts. Bernie Sanders continues to push the Democratic Party to move left on social and economic issues, promoting European-style socialist policies, trying to rally Americans, especially young adult Americans, to his causes.

In June 2018, officials from the Democratic National Committee moved forward with a rules change that would force presidential candidates to identify as Democrats. While Sanders could still receive the nomination in 2020 if he chooses to seek it, under the proposed changes he would have to do so as a Democrat, not an independent. The move angered many Sanders supporters. "I really don't get the motivation for the resolution at all," a senior adviser to Sanders's 2016 presidential bid stated. "Thousands, if not millions of [his] votes were young people and independents he brought into the Democratic Party."[60]

While Vermont senator Bernie Sanders was not at the center of the Democrats' political story in the 2018 midterm elections, he did easily win reelection. Moreover, many of the candidates, especially those referring to themselves as "Democratic Socialists," campaigned on issues that Sanders had been highlighting, such as free college tuition. For his part, President Trump pointed to the electoral success that

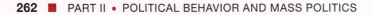

many Republicans who supported him achieved, especially in Senate races, as proof that he was pulling the party toward his presidency and policies.

In this chapter, we have explored the challenge that Bernie Sanders and Donald Trump presented to their own parties' establishment. That turned out to be very true; however, the story of the struggles of both major parties to respond to their insurgencies is not over. As both parties look ahead to 2020, they are also looking within.

CHAPTER REVIEW

This chapter's main ideas are reflected in the Learning Objectives. By reviewing them here, you should be able to **remember** the key points, **know** the terms that are central to the topic, and **think** about the critical issues raised in each section.

9.1 Reflect on the ways in which the presidential campaigns of Bernie Sanders and Donald Trump challenged their parties' establishment.

REMEMBER
- Political parties help citizens figure out which candidates to vote for, send cues about policy positions, and help translate platforms into policy.
- In the election of 2016, Trump and Sanders both challenged their parties' leadership and platforms, claiming to be speaking for citizens whose interests weren't actually being represented by their parties.

KNOW
- political party (p. 237)
- populism (p. 238)

THINK
- Do you feel that the Democratic Party or the Republican Party establishments are currently doing a good job of incorporating citizens' concerns and preferences?

9.2 Identify the roles the political parties play in supporting and nominating candidates for office.

REMEMBER
- Ideally, political parties provide clear positions on issues the parties are strongly committed to, demonstrate internal cohesion both while in power and when in opposition, and have the ability to resist interest group pressure.
- Parties recruit candidates to run for offices at all levels, selecting people who reflect the ideals of the party and who would make strong challengers for office.
- In conjunction with federal and state laws, state parties establish the rules by which their candidates are nominated for the presidency, including what type of primary election process that state will have and when it will be held.
- Parties shape the nomination process by setting rules for how candidates are picked and selecting candidates to run on their tickets.
- Political scientists have argued that parties often play a deciding role in candidate selection.
- Candidates for the presidency must seek the support of delegates who will later vote for their nomination.

KNOW
- caucus (p. 244)
- closed primary (p. 244)
- delegates (p. 244)
- front-loading (p. 244)
- national convention (p. 246)
- nomination (p. 243)
- open primary (p. 244)
- presidential primary elections (p. 244)
- recruitment (p. 242)
- responsible party model (p. 241)
- superdelegates (p. 246)

THINK
- Do you think parties are helpful or harmful to American democracy?
- Do you think parties are attending to the issues of concern to most Americans?

9.3 Evaluate the changing role of parties as labels for citizens to learn about candidates and their positions on issues.

REMEMBER
- Parties are reflected in the electorate by citizens who express solidarity with their views.
- In government, elected officials work to enact their parties' policies.
- Parties signal to voters their support for a particular set of political beliefs. Consistent party ideology provides candidates with labels and voters with cues and shortcuts.
- Fewer Americans are identifying with the Republican and Democratic parties, which has consequences for voting behavior.
- Once in office, parties advocate for issues that align with their platform; the party out of power does what it can to resist policy changes at odds with its views. Pressure to maintain contrasts between the parties has led to increased polarization. Inability to compromise has led to gridlock.
- There is increasing partisanship in the U.S. electorate, and parties are more polarized than ever.
- At the same time, parties themselves are becoming weaker and less able to enact their preferred policies.

KNOW
- split-ticket voting (p. 249)

THINK
- Do you identify with one of the two major American political parties?
- If you have voted, have you ever split-ticket voted? Why?

9.4 Reflect on the implications of the presidential election of 2016 for the Democratic and Republican parties.

REMEMBER
- Both the Democratic and Republican races for the presidency in 2016 presented a major challenge to the idea that the parties, and not voters themselves, ultimately decide who the candidate will be.
- Trump's candidacy exposed important weaknesses within the Republican Party in terms of its cohesion, problems that were further complicated by some of the rules the party implemented prior to the election that gave Trump certain institutional advantages.

THINK
- What was so unusual about the presidential candidacies of Sanders and Trump?
- Do you feel that the Democratic Party or the Republican Party establishments were fair to either Bernie Sanders or Donald Trump?

9.5 Examine the role of parties in government and the traditional dominance of two major political parties in national elections.

REMEMBER
- Coherent party systems exist during periods of stability between episodes of realignment. Major parties are then identified with a clear set of issues and compete for voter support based on stable distinctions.
- Scholars generally have divided American political history into six party systems.
- Unlike most countries in the world, the United States has for most of its history had just two major parties. For the last 150 years, those have been the Democratic and Republican parties.
- The United States uses a single-member plurality system (or winner-take-all system), which typically means that the largest politically cohesive groups—the Democrats or Republicans—are able to elect every office in a jurisdiction.
- Competition for the two main parties in the United States has sometimes come from third (or minor) parties, which tend to focus on a single issue their members think the other parties are not emphasizing enough. The major parties generally try to squelch their efforts.
- Third parties tend to have more success at the local level, where different electoral rules give them more space.

- critical election (p. 256)
- gridlock (p. 256)
- party platform (p. 255)

- party systems (p. 256)
- political polarization (p. 256)
- proportional representation system (p. 259)

- realignment (p. 256)
- single-member plurality system (p. 259)
- third party (minor party) (p. 260)

- Why have American party systems been relatively stable throughout the nation's history? What has led to change?

- Do you think a new major third party might emerge in the near future? If so, what might its core beliefs be?

CHAPTER 10

CAMPAIGNS AND ELECTIONS

Candidates and Voters in an Era of Demographic Change

▲ Fabiola Vejar (right) registers Stephanie Cardenas to vote in front of a Latino supermarket in Las Vegas, Nevada, in June 2016. Vejar, eighteen, who was covered by the Deferred Action for Childhood Arrivals (DACA) program, could not vote, so instead she volunteered with the organization Mi Familia Vota, encouraging others to be heard at the ballot box. "I don't have that voice," she says, "but there's other people . . . who feel the way I do. They should vote."

AP Photo/John Locher

National **elections** are the tools with which the American political system chooses its representatives— its presidents and members of Congress. National **campaigns** are the tools that would-be representatives use to connect to American voters. Candidates use them to introduce themselves and to convince voters that they—and not any of their opponents—are the best choice for making the people's wishes known in Washington and enacting these wishes in legislation and policies.

As we will explore, however, campaigns and elections are both composed of many moving parts. The rules governing them, the people who choose to run, and the composition of the electorate all may shift over time, sometimes with profound and long-lasting consequences. Candidates, even those who have been in elected office for years, need to be aware and adaptable, ready to change message or strategy if necessary. American political campaigns are no place for dinosaurs . . . not in the long run.

In this chapter, we will focus on the stories of presidential candidates in the election of 2016 and on congressional candidates in the elections of 2016 and 2018. We will highlight their efforts to capture the votes of Latina and Latino voters. Candidates sought to mobilize these voters to turn out in the elections and to convince members of these

LEARNING OBJECTIVES

By reading this chapter, you will be able to do the following:

 10.1 Explain why changes in the constituency lead candidates to reach out to new groups of voters.

 10.2 Understand the rules and institutions that structure national elections.

10.3 Identify the stages of presidential elections.

 10.4 Explore the role that incumbency plays in candidates' campaign decisions.

10.5 Identify the structure of and issues involved in congressional elections.

communities that they were the ones best suited to make the Latino voice heard in the national government. This is not always an easy task. Even the term that candidates, political scientists, and others use to describe these voters is up for discussion and contestation. Some sources refer to them as Latino or Latino/a, others as Hispanic.[1] As we will also explore, however, energizing and capturing the votes of those Americans who identify as Latino/a or Hispanic is going to be one of the major stories in American national elections in the coming decades.

PRESIDENTIAL CANDIDATES ADDRESS LATINO VOTERS IN 2016

- **Explain why changes in the constituency lead candidates to reach out to new groups of voters.**

As the 2016 presidential election kicked into high gear, one reality was becoming impossible to ignore: the American Latino vote, especially the young adult Latino vote, was going to be critical. Latinos have become the fastest-growing ethnic group in the United States, a trend that is very likely to continue for decades. Should these potential voters speak with a coordinated voice and cast ballots in an election, this could fundamentally reshape American national elections, and candidates ignore this possibility at tremendous political risk. However, in 2016, the group's nascent electoral power was far from fully realized, in large part because their presence at the polls was not guaranteed.

Candidates and leaders within both major parties took notice of the seemingly inevitable demographic ascendency of Latinos in American national politics and tried to convince these potential voters that if they were elected they would truly represent the diverse interests of members of Latino American communities. However, as the 2016 presidential campaign unfolded, many leading candidates in both parties were struggling with these attempts to connect.

REPUBLICAN HOPEFULS ADOPT VERY DIFFERENT APPROACHES

On the Republican side, two of the would-be presidential nominees highlighted their Latino ancestry and the fact that none of the likely Democratic Party nominees shared that ancestry. Both Republican Party hopefuls were U.S. senators of Cuban American descent—two of only three Latino Americans

elections
the political system through which American voters choose their representatives.

campaigns
the political process that would-be representatives use to connect to American voters in hopes of winning office.

serving in the Senate at the time.[2] During the nomination campaign, Ted Cruz of Texas and Marco Rubio of Florida both sought to portray their candidacies as the one best able to represent Latino voters and siphon support from the eventual Democratic Party nominee in the fall. Both also focused on the issues many Latino voters said they cared about.

When announcing his candidacy for the Republican Party's nomination in Miami in April 2015, Rubio alluded to his ancestry and family history. He took a subtle jab at his opponent, Republican governor Jeb Bush, the son of one former president and the brother of another, when he stated, "I live in an exceptional country where the son of a bartender and a maid can have the same dreams and the same future as those who come from power and privilege."[3] Cruz and his supporters also tried to highlight the benefits for the Republican Party's prospects should it nominate a Hispanic candidate. "Ted has a history of connecting with Hispanic voters. In his run for Texas Senator he garnered 40 percent of the Hispanic vote," proclaimed a web page run by powerful backers. "To win a swing state like Florida, Ted would need to receive 66 percent of the Cuban vote. Considering Ted himself is of Cuban descent, winning key swing states with large Hispanic populations is feasible."[4]

As Cruz and Rubio reached out to Latino voters, however, they faced two challenges. The first was the diversity of lived experiences of individuals captured by the term used to describe them. As Cuban Americans, Cruz and Rubio share ancestry with only one of many nationalities of origin of Americans who self-describe as Hispanic or Latino. This diversity of origin is accompanied by a diversity of views and policy preferences, with many Latino voters expressing connections to their nation of ancestry rather than to an umbrella term like *Hispanic*. For example, Maria Herrera, a retired housekeeper in Las Vegas interviewed for the *Washington Post* in 2016, expressed "no affinity for Marco Rubio even as he aims to make history as the first Hispanic president of the United States. As she explained: 'He's Cuban. I'm Mexican. . . . I would never vote for him just because he's Latino.'"[5]

Another challenge involved the issues at play in politics in 2016. To many critics, some within the Republican Party itself, solutions were to be found in policies, not the identities of candidates. In the words of J. C. Watts, an African American and former member of Congress (R-OK), "Where are our solutions to deal with incarceration reform, unemployment, the trouble blacks and Hispanics have getting home mortgages? Republicans who ignore Ferguson and Baltimore and Black Lives Matter are refusing to hear the depths of what people are experiencing."[6] College senior Jessica Carrera summed up the feelings of many young Latinos when she stated, "Certain candidates in the Republican party just don't embody any of the qualities that I want to see in the future president. . . . They're just so closed off to the possibility that immigrants can have a positive effect on the country."[7]

During a series of Republican Party debates, Cruz and Rubio both tried to portray the other as "a major flip-flopper on immigration."[8] Political advertisements made in support of two of Rubio's opponents—Cruz and Jeb Bush— "cast him [Rubio] as cozy with President Obama and Democratic Sen[ator] Chuck Schumer" in devising a failed 2013 effort to pass immigration reform in Congress.[9] For his part, Rubio took on Cruz as well. In an appearance on ABC's *This Week*, Rubio said of Cruz, "When it comes to Ted, he has changed his position on immigration all over the place."[10]

For their part, members and candidates from the Democratic Party tried to convince voters that neither of the two Republican hopefuls could best represent Latino voters, arguments based on both policy and politics. On the public policy side, to those leveling the charges the core issue was clear. It was about their

▲ Republican candidates Marco Rubio (left) and Ted Cruz take part in debates at the Reagan Library in Simi Valley, California.

Justin Sullivan/Getty Images

positions and statements on immigration policy and criticisms that neither would be a strong advocate for immigration reform. Democratic Party activist attacks on Rubio and Cruz, however, were also about political strategy. Should either win the Republican Party nomination, the thinking went, he might draw Latino voters, who traditionally have tended to vote Democrat, away from that political party and away from that party's presidential nominee.

Of the leading Republican candidates for that party's nomination, Rubio and Cruz were not the only ones singled out for their policy proposals and statements on American immigration policy. Another hopeful, not considered a serious contender by experts at first but continuing to defy conventional wisdom as the campaign progressed, was Donald Trump. Mr. Trump made inflammatory statements about immigration policy and the need to build a border wall with Mexico to prevent the arrival of undocumented individuals.

Candidate Trump also took aim at two policies of the Obama administration: Deferred Action for Childhood Arrivals (DACA) and Deferred Action for Parents of Americans and Lawful Permanent Residents. Both policies, created by Obama executive orders, aimed to defer deportation of undocumented Americans, either students who met certain conditions or undocumented parents of American citizens or legal permanent residents. "We will immediately terminate President Obama's two illegal executive amnesties," Trump promised during a campaign rally in Arizona, "in which he defied federal law and the constitution to give amnesty to approximately 5 million illegal immigrants."[11]

▲ Supporters of then–Republican presidential candidate Donald Trump show their support for his call to "build a wall" to staunch illegal immigration and put an end to sanctuary cities.

Andrew Renneisen/Getty Images

DEMOCRATIC HOPEFULS FACE THEIR OWN CHALLENGES

On the other side of the political aisle, however, things were not going entirely smoothly either. In December 2015, Democratic Party front-runner Hillary Clinton posted to her official campaign website, "7 Things Hillary Clinton Has in Common with Your Abuela [Grandmother]."[12] The post led with a picture of Clinton and her husband, former president Bill Clinton, with their new granddaughter. Its goal was to reach out to Latino voters and potential voters and to connect Clinton's goals, experiences, and policy positions to issues of concern to them.

In the post, Clinton highlighted the fact that "she isn't afraid to talk about the importance of *el respeto*" [respect].[13] She also voiced her concerns for children throughout the nation, saying, "You shouldn't have to be the granddaughter of a former president to live up to your God-given potential in America. You should be able to be the granddaughter of a factory worker or the grandson of a truck-driver—and every day as your president, I'm going to get up trying to figure out what more I can do to make sure every person, and particularly every child, has a chance to do just that."[14]

Clinton's efforts to reach out to Latino voters did not go completely as planned; some "criticized the list as pandering to Hispanics, while others pushed back against Clinton's economic privileges and advantages."[15] Some Twitter followers and political commentators called these efforts "Hispandering"[16] and said they were not backed up by a stronger call for a basic, and substantial, overhaul of American immigration policy.

In his ultimately unsuccessful efforts to capture the Democratic Party's nomination, Vermont senator Bernie Sanders often tried to connect with Latino voters by emphasizing his main point of economic inequality in the United States. In a Spanish-language television advertisement for the Univision network, Sanders's campaign highlighted the challenges of a farmworker in Florida: "'*Voy a luchar mientras*,' she [said] in Spanish: 'I will always fight.'"[17] As the campaign progressed, however, some observers questioned Sanders's efforts to connect with Latino and African American voters through his focus on "curbing financial inequality and confronting climate change."[18]

DEMOGRAPHIC CHANGES IN THE AMERICAN ELECTORATE WILL IMPACT FUTURE POLITICAL CAMPAIGNS

While both parties' candidates faced their own challenges in convincing Latino voters that they were best qualified to represent the diverse interests of these communities, they realized that this was a

▲ Left: A 2015 photo from Hillary Clinton's official campaign website in which she tries to reach out to Latino voters. Right: Tweets to #NotMyAbuela in which these Latina posters sharply criticized Hillary Clinton's strategy.

political effort that had to be made. It was a battle for votes that had to be won, both in this election and those that would follow. The reason for this is math.

In the future, American political campaigns will be increasingly influenced by changes in **demographics**, which are groupings of individuals based on shared characteristics. The composition of the American electorate will be changing over the next several decades. Candidates, parties, and political activists are already very familiar with what is coming down the pike in terms of this future composition of the nation. The ways in which American parties and candidates respond to these changes will, to a very large degree, determine their electoral successes and failures and, perhaps, their very survival in their current form.

Driving all of this is the growth in the number of Latino Americans via immigration, birth rates, and generational change. By 2043, according to analysts with the U.S. Census Bureau, America will be a plural nation, with members of no single traditional racial or ethnic group constituting an absolute majority of the population. This will mark the first time in the nation's history that white non-Hispanics will not have constituted a majority of Americans and eligible voters.[19]

The force behind these changes is the massive growth of the population of Hispanic Americans. By 2060, Hispanics are projected to make up over 30 percent of the nation's population—nearly doubling the percentage of just a few decades prior. In contrast, the percentage of white, non-Hispanic Americans in the nation's population is projected to decline from more than 60 percent in 2013 to roughly 43 percent (see Figure 10.1).

While the math may be very clear, the political changes due to this shift in demographics are not. The political consequences will be profound if—and this is a big *if*—eligible voters from Latino communities exercise the power of their collective numbers by voting and by mobilizing other potential voters within their communities. That big *if* is very much part of the political calculi of candidates and political parties. In the coming decades, in the political battles between America's two major political parties—or any hopeful third party—much of the fight will center on capturing and energizing Latino votes.

COULD A GROWING LATINO VOTE ALTER THE PARTY LANDSCAPE?

In Chapter 9, we discussed the issue of party realignments in American political history. The future demographic changes in the American electorate might have the potential to produce a major shift in

demographics
the grouping of individuals based on shared characteristics, such as ancestry, race, ethnicity, and gender.

Projected Changes in the Racial and Ethnic Makeup of the United States

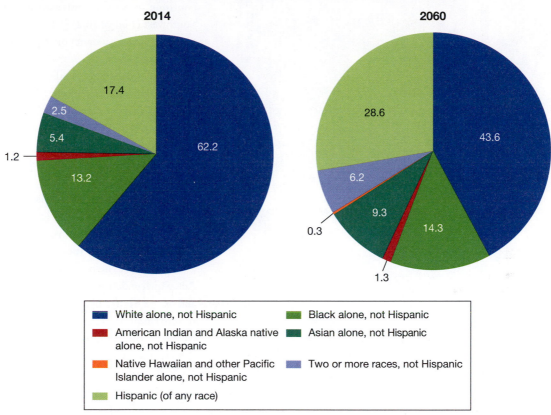

2014

17.4
2.5
5.4
1.2
13.2
62.2

2060

28.6
43.6
6.2
0.3
9.3
14.3
1.3

	White alone, not Hispanic		Black alone, not Hispanic
	American Indian and Alaska native alone, not Hispanic		Asian alone, not Hispanic
	Native Hawaiian and other Pacific Islander alone, not Hispanic		Two or more races, not Hispanic
	Hispanic (of any race)		

Source: Data from Jonathan Vespa, David M. Armstrong, and Lauren Medina, "Demographic Turning Points for the United States: Population Estimates and Projections for 2020 to 2060," *U.S. Census Bureau*, March 2018, https://www.census.gov/content/dam/Census/library/publications/2018/demo/P25_1144.pdf.

the party system, depending upon the participation rates of Latino voters as well as their support for one political party or another. Consider Texas, for example. In 2016, the state had thirty-eight electoral votes, second only to California's fifty-five (we will explore what electoral votes are later in the chapter). Traditionally a safe Republican state in modern presidential elections, Texas is undergoing a profound demographic change. By 2020, Hispanic Texans are expected to outnumber whites; by 2042, they are expected to make up a majority of the state's population.[20] Should these changes tip the state to the Democratic Party in future presidential elections, it would be very difficult for any Republican candidate to secure the presidency.

Republican Party officials are well aware of these challenges. In a 2012 report by the Republican National Committee's Growth and Opportunity Project, often referred to as the "autopsy report," party officials and strategists concluded, "The nation's demographic changes add to the urgency of recognizing how precarious our position has become. America is changing demographically, and unless Republicans are able to grow our appeal the way GOP [Republican Party] governors have done, the changes tilt the playing field even more in the Democratic direction."[21] In the 2012 presidential election, the Republican nominee lost to President Barack Obama after capturing only 27 percent of Hispanic votes. In 2004, in contrast, George W. Bush won 40 percent of the Hispanic vote in his successful reelection campaign.[22]

As Marco Rubio, Ted Cruz, Donald Trump, Hillary Clinton, Bernie Sanders, and other candidates sought the presidential nomination in 2016, they all realized that the Latino vote had the potential to impact the outcomes of their nomination campaigns. In that year, 27.3 million Latinos were eligible

voters—a national record. However, the growth in this demographic has been, and is likely to continue to be, concentrated in the West and Southwest (Figure 10.2).[23] This uneven distribution has had significant consequences, as we will explore later.

The candidates' calculations and strategies were also informed by another fact: Latino voters, in spite of their growing *potential* electoral power, were not voting, at least not in comparison to white and African American voters. According to Kate Linthicum of the *Los Angeles Times*, "for all the talk of the growing Latino electorate and the pivotal role it is expected to play in coming elections, there is another historical reality: Latinos, along with Asian Americans, remain dramatically underrepresented in most U.S. elections. Half a century after the passage of the Voting Rights Act, which ended legal barriers to voting for blacks across the South, blacks and whites now vote at roughly equal rates, especially in presidential elections. But Latinos and Asians lag far behind in all races, even when noncitizen immigrants are accounted for."[24]

The reasons for the comparative lack of turnout by Latino voters are complicated. Part of the answer is age. Latino Americans tend to be younger than members of other racial and ethnic groups, and young voting-eligible Americans, as we discussed in Chapter 6, vote at lower rates than older ones. In addition, the fact that Latino voters tend to cluster in states such as California and Texas—states that tend to lean heavily to either the Democratic or Republican Party—has led to an unintentional, but rational, neglect. Since neither is a swing state, these two states get relatively less attention than those that are seen to be "in play" during an election. "Organizations and political parties aren't focused enough on this segment of the population," says Marcela Ruiz, the deputy director of California Rural Legal Assistance.[25] As the percentage of Latino voters grows in **swing states**—states such as Nevada, where no one political party tends to dominate national elections—that will almost certainly change.

In this chapter, we will explore American national campaigns and elections through the lens of candidates and political parties confronting, successfully or not, a profound coming change in the composition of the nation's electorate. In doing so, we will learn about the nuts and bolts of presidential and congressional campaigns and elections. We will also gain a deeper understanding of the ways in which the electoral process does, or does not, respond to the diversity of voices within the electorate. Once again, the stories are about people, how their choices matter, and what all of this means for American representative democracy.

▲ Top: Voters cast their ballots at the House of Mercy in Los Angeles in November 2012. Latino voters made up almost 25 percent of all registered voters in California during that election cycle. Bottom: A chalkboard sign at a mock caucus event in Des Moines, Iowa, held by LULAC, the League of United Latin American Citizens.

swing states
states where no one political party tends to dominate national elections.

Distribution of the Latino Population in the United States in 2016

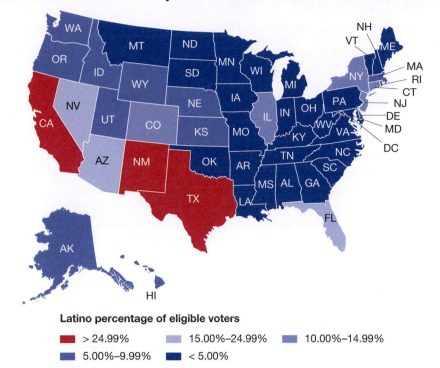

Latino percentage of eligible voters

- ▮ > 24.99%
- ▮ 15.00%–24.99%
- ▮ 10.00%–14.99%
- ▮ 5.00%–9.99%
- ▮ < 5.00%

Source: Pew Research Center, "Mapping the Latino Electorate by State," January 19, 2016, http://www.pewhispanic.org/interactives/mapping-the-latino-electorate-by-state/.

WHAT HAVE I **LEARNED?**

1. Projections of the future composition of the American electorate in the twenty-first century predicted that by 2060, _____.

   a. white, non-Hispanic voters will remain a majority but by a smaller margin

   b. the percentage of African Americans will nearly double

   c. the percentage of Hispanic voters will nearly double

   d. Asian Americans will constitute nearly 20 percent of the American population

2. The Deferred Action for Childhood Arrivals (DACA) _____.

   a. was part of an executive order issued by President Obama

   b. guaranteed free college tuition for undocumented Americans

   c. was part of President Trump's immigration reforms

   d. came about as a result of a Supreme Court decision

3. What are some challenges that Ted Cruz and Marco Rubio faced in reaching out to Latino voters?

4. What are some of the reasons for relative underrepresentation of Latino Americans at the national polls?

Answer Key: 1. c; 2. a; 3. Answers may mention the diversity of the experiences and ancestry of Latino voters as well as Republican Party stances on issues such as immigration, which remain problematic to many Latinos; 4. Answers should include characteristics such as undocumented status, the fact that they are younger as a group, or the fact that many live in states that tend to receive less candidate attention.

NATIONAL ELECTIONS SERVE TO HOLD OFFICIALS ACCOUNTABLE, BUT REGULATING THEM IS NOT ALWAYS EASY

● **Understand the rules and institutions that structure national elections.**

As we explored in Chapter 9, political parties ordinarily do strongly affect the outcomes of elections. In this chapter, we look more closely at the electoral process that brings candidates to office. National elections are the tools with which the American political system chooses its presidents and members of Congress. National campaigns are the tools that would-be representatives use to connect to American voters.

Campaigns and elections are both composed of many moving parts. The rules governing them, the people who choose to run, and the composition of the electorate all may shift over time, sometimes with profound and long-lasting consequences. Candidates, even those who have been in elected office for years, need to be aware and adaptable, ready to change message or strategy if necessary.

The Framers of the Constitution did not want the system they created to be *too* democratic; they feared the potential mischief of faction and the dangers of tyranny of the majority. Therefore, they built in roadblocks to slow down the transmission of the "passions of the people" into public policy. Senators, for example, were originally chosen by state legislatures rather than by the people.

Another safeguard against faction is the system of American federalism, which divides sovereignty between the nation and the states. The Constitution requires that "The Times, Places and Manner of holding Elections for Senators and Representatives, shall be prescribed in each State by the Legislature thereof."[26] The effects of this clause have been consequential. For example, prior to ratification of the Nineteenth Amendment, women could vote in some states but not others. And today its language ensures that states can devise their own voting technologies, whether electronic or paper based, and have different policies on whether or not those convicted of felonies are allowed to vote.[27]

American elections are also notable for the fact that they occur on fixed and predictable schedules. Unlike in parliamentary systems, in which the chief national executive has the choice of when to "call" an election (subject to specific rules and constraints), in the United States, voters weigh in on their president every four years, regardless of what is happening in the nation or world, through economic depressions and even war. They pass their judgments on members of the House of Representatives every two years, as well as on the one-third of senators whose "class" is up for reelection in that cycle (though retirements, resignations, or other reasons may change the numbers a bit in any given senatorial election).

Compared to other democracies in the world, Americans get to exercise their right to vote with a frequency that is rather unique. If one includes local, county, state, and national officials, Americans, in the aggregate, have the chance to decide how more than half a million governmental posts are filled. As we explored in Chapter 6, however, many Americans do not vote, sometimes because they choose not to do so and in some cases because they are shut out of the process. The latter may occur because of immigration status, small but significant barriers to registering as voters (e.g., inability to make it to the polling place during a workday), residing out of state as a college or university student, or previous involvement with the criminal justice system.

Scott Olson/Getty Images

▲ Protesters outside Republican Party headquarters in Chicago, Illinois, hold signs calling for immigration reform and a new focus on domestic policies such as education, which is one of the most important issues to many Latino voters.

ELECTIONS HELP HOLD ELECTED OFFICIALS ACCOUNTABLE

In a representative democracy, elections serve other important purposes besides selecting individuals for a specific office or position in government. Elections are the key way Americans can keep their elected officials in line. Voters achieve this by using the threat of voting an **incumbent** out of office and voting in a **challenger** if they decide the incumbent's performance has not been in line with their goals and policy preferences. This reflecting back on an incumbent's past performance in an election is called **retrospective voting**.[28] Elections also serve as a signal—a way of transmitting information to elected officials about voters' preferences and priorities.

Elections help define or change the national agenda, especially when candidates respond to the growing electoral and political power of voters whose agenda-setting preferences may not have been well addressed in the past. For instance, trying to assess the top issues for Latino voters, one of the fastest-growing demographic groups in the United States, is not always an easy task. It is a diverse group, and many surveys are not conducted in Spanish. However, a 2014 Pew Research Center survey concluded that the top five issues for Latino registered voters were—in order of perceived importance—education, jobs and the economy, health care, immigration, and conflicts in the Middle East.[29]

Elections also confer legitimacy on the laws and public policies enacted. Finally, participation in the electoral system may serve to remind Americans of their rights and liberties and the need to protect those rights; thus, they are educative.

ELECTIONS ARE EXPENSIVE

In the 2016 presidential campaign, roughly $1.5 billion in total was spent in support of each of the campaigns of Democratic candidate Hillary Clinton and Republican candidate Donald Trump and the other minor-party candidates, a figure that includes candidate spending, national party spending, and money spent by others in support of their respective campaigns.[30]

incumbent
a current officeholder.

challenger
a candidate for office who does not currently hold office.

retrospective voting
voting based on reflecting back on an incumbent's past performance in an election.

▼ FIGURE 10.3

Comparing the Cost of Presidential Campaigns, American Gross Domestic Product (GDP), and Gold

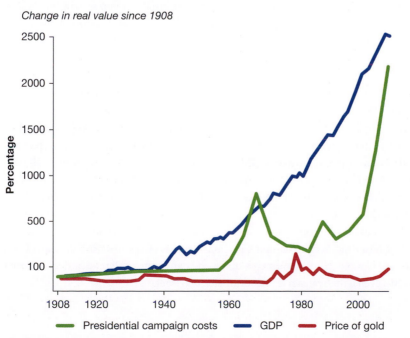

Change in real value since 1908

Legend: Presidential campaign costs — GDP — Price of gold

Source: Dave Gilson, "The Crazy Cost of Becoming President, from Lincoln to Obama," *Mother Jones*, February 20, 2012, http://www.motherjones.com/mojo/2012/02/historic-price-cost-presidential-elections.

Adding in total candidate and outside spending on the other national elections that year, the total spent was about $6.8 billion. According to CBS News, "that's more than what consumers spend on cereal ($6 billion), pet grooming ($5.4 billion) and legal marijuana ($5.4 billion)."[31]

CANDIDATES BUY ADVERTISEMENTS AND TRY TO MOBILIZE VOTERS. What do candidates get for all of this money? Where does it go? First and foremost, money buys media time on television and radio, in print, and in social media outlets. Some campaign advertisements focus on the candidate's qualities and creating a positive image. Others focus on policy differences between the candidate and his or her opponents. **Negative campaign advertisements** attack an opponent or opponents and try to raise doubts in voters' minds about them. While negative campaigning is pervasive and often uncomfortable, not all scholars agree that it is a bad thing. Political scientist John Geer has argued that negative campaign ads may actually "increase the quality of information available to voters as they make choices in elections."[32]

Money also allows a candidate to hire campaign staff, help manage the campaign message, coordinate a campaign and media strategy, arrange public appearances, and conduct public opinion polls. Efforts to mobilize voters or potential voters, called **get out the vote (GOTV)** efforts, also cost money. Finally, having a sizable war chest, especially early in a campaign, might discourage potential challengers from entering a race in the first place. In this way, money is also a strategic weapon. For all of these reasons, the cost of winning the presidency has only gone up.

CAN CAMPAIGN CONTRIBUTIONS BE EFFECTIVELY REGULATED? Given the power of money, several sources, including activists, the Supreme Court, and the federal government, have long struggled to control the dangers of campaign finance. In the 1970s, following the Watergate scandal, Congress passed the Federal Election Campaign Act, which created the Federal Election Commission (FEC), a bureaucratic entity charged with overseeing and implementing national campaign finance laws. The act also set rules for the disclosure of the source of campaign funds, placed limits on campaign contributions, and instituted a system for public financing of presidential elections. In 1976, in *Buckley v. Valeo*, the Supreme Court upheld the constitutionality of restrictions on campaign contributions by individuals, though not on monies spent independently, monies spent by the candidates themselves, or the total amount of contributions.[33]

When it comes to money and elections, however, controlling the influence of money has often been like handling a balloon—squeeze it in one place and it seems to pop up somewhere else. In 2002, in an effort to more effectively control the balloon, Congress passed the Bipartisan Campaign Reform Act (BCRA), which placed stricter limits on campaign contributions. Since then, however, the Supreme Court has limited these regulations. In *Citizens United v. Federal Election Commission* (2010), in a divided 5–4 decision, the Court struck down portions of the BCRA, ruling that independent, uncoordinated political contributions by corporations during political campaigns is protected by the First Amendment.[34]

The "new world" of campaign finance in the United States is thorny. Although limits on individual campaign donations remain in place, groups of individuals may contribute, but the rules are complicated. **Political action committees (PACs)** are groups of at least fifty individuals who seek to raise money to elect and defeat candidates. PACs may contribute higher dollar amounts than individuals, though, again, there are limits. In the wake of the Court's decision in *Citizens United*, certain types of PACs called **super PACs** are allowed to spend unlimited amounts on a political campaign; however, that spending must not be coordinated with that campaign. These contributions raise a tricky issue. Even if there is no contact between a super PAC and members of a campaign, if the super PAC, for example, runs a series of campaign advertisements that work, candidates will take notice. Information will still change hands, even if this transfer is uncoordinated and legal.

negative campaign advertisements
campaign ads that attack an opponent or opponents and try to raise doubts in voters' minds about them.

get out the vote (GOTV)
efforts to mobilize voters or potential voters.

political action committees (PACs)
organizations that raise money to support chosen candidates and defeat others.

super PACs
political action committees permitted to spend unlimited amounts of money in a campaign, though these actions must not be coordinated with that campaign.

WHAT HAVE I **LEARNED?**

1. The term *retrospective voting* refers to _____.
   a. successful candidates reflecting back on campaign promises when voting in Congress
   b. when voters reflect back upon an incumbent's performance
   c. incumbents drawing upon their previous experience in other offices
   d. when voters look to challengers' past statements on issues

2. A super PAC _____.
   a. can spend unlimited amounts of money but must not coordinate with a campaign
   b. has strict limits placed on its allowable contributions

   c. can spend unlimited amounts of money in coordination with a campaign
   d. can no longer make campaign contributions

3. In a debate about the degree to which contributions to political campaigns should be restricted or regulated, what might some arguments be for each side?

4. Have negative campaign advertisements ever affected your thoughts on an election?

Answer Key: 1. b; 2. d; 3. Answers for restrictions may focus on wealth inequality or factions. Answers against might focus on free speech and the First Amendment; 4. Answers might include examples where negative advertisements did or did not influence the student's opinions about candidates or issues or enthusiasm for a political race.

PRESIDENTIAL ELECTIONS HAVE MANY STAGES AND MOVING PARTS

- **Identify the stages of presidential elections.**

Presidential elections have two official campaign phases: the nomination campaign, in which candidates try to secure the nomination of their political party, and the general election campaign, in which successful nominees compete for the presidency. While the ways in which parties structure their nomination processes have changed, the general trend in modern campaigns has been one of increasing openness, of taking some of the power away from party elites and placing it in the hands of party activists and average Americans. This is not to say that party leaders do not matter, however. They still have more power to shape the nomination than the average American voter.

CANDIDATES LAY THE FOUNDATIONS FOR THEIR CAMPAIGNS LONG BEFORE FORMAL NOMINATION

Nomination campaigns begin long before the actual events through which the nominees are picked. Presidential hopefuls may work on laying the foundations for their bids years before the official process begins. They begin raising money and set up an **exploratory committee**, which is subject to different federal campaign finance rules than a campaign committee. An exploratory committee allows a potential candidate to "test the waters," to travel around the country in order to conduct public opinion polls, make outreach phone calls, and raise money to pay for all of this. In addition, a candidate's announcement that he or she has formed an exploratory committee may gain a bit of a bump in media coverage.

If a candidate decides to press ahead, his or her campaign will become official, a status that can be triggered through a potential candidate's statements and fund-raising or other activities.

exploratory committee a group that helps determine whether a potential candidate should run for office and that helps lay the groundwork for the campaign.

Marco Rubio ✔ @marcorubio · 13 Apr 2015
I'm **running for President** of the United States.

Become a Day One Supporter at tinyurl.com/ofl2kk8

VISIT MARCORUBIO.COM

GIF

↩ ⟲ 619 ♥ 746 •••

@marcorubio, Twitter

▲ Senator Marco Rubio announces his bid for the American presidency in a tweet.

CANDIDATES TRY TO SECURE THEIR PARTY'S NOMINATION

Once the official campaign process kicks off, declared candidates vie with others in their own party for that party's nomination. Beginning early in the election year, candidates seek to get the support of party delegates, whose votes they will later need to secure the party's nomination (Chapter 9). While many of the rules governing the nomination process are set by federal and state laws, most of the details about *how* things actually work are hammered out by the parties themselves. Key differences exist across states and between the parties themselves. As we discussed earlier in the chapter, most states hold presidential primary elections in which a state's voters choose delegates who support a particular candidate. The concluding phase of the nomination process takes place in the national conventions held by the parties late in the summer of the presidential election year.

NOMINEES COMPETE IN THE GENERAL ELECTION

Once selected by their parties, the nominees then proceed to the general election campaign. At this point, candidates need to pivot from speaking mainly to their base of core supporters and begin to try to appeal to independent and undecided voters. This can be a trap. Voters who participate during the nomination campaigns trend toward the wings of their parties, and there are not often enough of them to win a general election.

Maintaining the energy of core party voters while also appealing to the undecided middle is a challenge. If core partisan voters think their nominee has moved too far to the center and abandoned core party goals, they will not help mobilize undecided voters to join their nominee's side. On the other hand, if a candidate has survived the nomination campaign by appealing primarily to the extremes of the party, then he or she may be seen as too far left or too far right to be the best person for governing the nation in the views of independents and undecided voters.

THE RULES OF THE ELECTORAL COLLEGE DECIDE THE PRESIDENCY

The dynamics of the **Electoral College** system presents another significant challenge. Technically speaking, American voters do not vote for the president. Instead, they vote for a slate of electors pledged to vote for a nominee in the presidential election. These electors are chosen by party leaders within their respective states in a system called the Electoral College. It is their vote that actually chooses the president. Established in the original Constitution and modified since the founding, its roots lie partly in the Framers' mistrust of direct democracy but also in concerns of convention delegates from less populous states, who feared that elected presidents would always be Virginians since theirs was the most populous and powerful state at the time.

Presidential candidates need to clear 270 Electoral College votes to win. Each of the fifty states is allocated one electoral vote for each of its two senators and one for each of its members of the House of Representatives, guaranteeing each state at least three electoral votes. Adding the three electoral votes allocated to the District of Columbia brings the total to 538. In all but two states, Maine and Nebraska, electoral votes are awarded in a winner-take-all system. In those states, the nominee who wins the popular vote in the state receives two electoral votes, plus one electoral vote for winning.

Electors are chosen from party leaders and loyal activists. Although they have pledged to vote for their party's candidate, there is a risk that they may become **faithless electors**, changing their minds

Electoral College
a slate of individuals apportioned to states who are pledged to vote for a presidential candidate.

faithless electors
members of the electoral college who do not cast their vote for the pledged candidate.

between the general election and the electors' vote. Though there have been faithless electors in American presidential electoral history—including in 2016—none have changed the outcome of an election.

This system has significant consequences. It shapes candidate strategies. Given that all but two states award their electoral votes in a block, candidates tend to focus their campaigns on states with a large number of electoral votes and those whose electoral votes seem to be in play, largely ignoring other states.

Theoretically, it is possible to become president by winning in only the eleven most populous states. Given the fact that, at least for now, California tends to go Democrat and Texas Republican, that outcome remains unlikely. More significantly, a presidential candidate can win the presidency without actually winning the popular vote. That can happen when a third-party candidate poses a serious challenge, preventing a candidate from winning a majority of the popular vote even if he or she wins a plurality of it, as was the case in President Bill Clinton's victory in 1992, or when a candidate wins a majority of the popular vote but loses in the Electoral College, which happened in 2000 when George W. Bush defeated Al Gore, and again in 2016 when Donald Trump defeated Hillary Clinton (see Figure 10.4).

▲ Donald Trump's 2016 electoral victory is announced against the backdrop of the Empire State Building in Manhattan.

▼ FIGURE 10.4

Electoral College Results (Pledged Electors), 2016

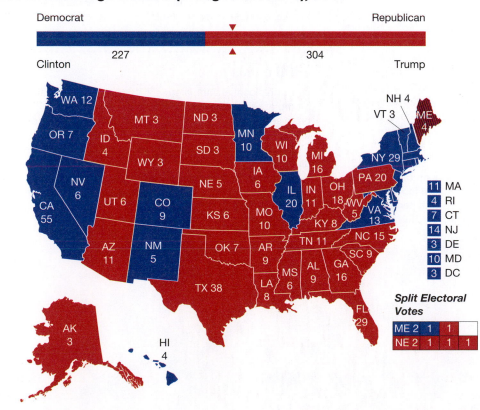

Source: Data from National Archives and Records Administration, "U.S. Electoral College," accessed March 30, 2018, https://www.archives.gov/federal-register/electoral-college/2016/election-results.html.

Note: Trump won enough states and one district in Maine to gain a total of 306 electoral votes. But because two faithless electors did not cast their ballots for him in Texas, his total is 304. In total, seven pledged electors defected, five pledged to Hillary Clinton and two to Donald Trump.

"MY STORY | DULCE CANDY" AND SELF-PRESENTATION IN THE TWENTY-FIRST CENTURY

Websites like YouTube and social media outlets are increasingly important in political campaigns and national elections. They are used not only by candidates but also by individuals trying to add their voices to national conversations. A useful skill in analyzing these posts, tweets, images, and videos is to consider the ways in which individuals combine image and text to present themselves, to tell their own stories, and to add their perspectives to debates.

During the early weeks of the 2016 presidential primary and caucus season, Fox News cohosted a Republican Party debate. One of the questioners selected—from a group of influential YouTube video creators—was Dulce Candy Tejeda Ruiz, who had served with the army in Iraq as a mechanic. While in service, she began to create and post videos featuring cosmetics tips. By the time of the Republican Party debate in January 2016, she had become a successful social media entrepreneur. Though candidate Trump declined to attend the debate, his opponents did get Dulce Candy's question. "There are many immigrants who contribute positively to the American economy," she asked, "but some of the comments in the campaign make us question our place in this country. If America does not seem like a welcoming place for immigrant entrepreneurs, will the American economy suffer?"[35]

In 2013, Dulce Candy had stated that she came to America as an undocumented immigrant from Mexico with her mother and three sisters when she was six years old. In the opinion of a commentator from the highly conservative website Breitbart.com, the decision to include her as a questioner "was likely intended to hit Donald Trump" on the issue of immigration, given his highly controversial proposals and, to many, inflammatory statements.[36]

In a video posted to her YouTube account, titled "My Story | Dulce Candy," entrepreneur, author, and former member of the U.S. Army Dulce Candy shared with her audience her goals for her growing and very successful business:

My success is OUR success and together, we can achieve our dreams, and make the world a more creative and loving place. Beauty and Fashion are our forms of expression, but the true beauty lies from within. Your beauty inspires me everyday, so I thank each and every one of you from the bottom of my heart! And a big thank you to YouTube for creating this amazing video about me. I'm humbled Always remember, happiness is now! xo, Dulce[37]

Included in the video were photographs from her service with the Army in Iraq.[38]

In an interview conducted after the 2015 Hispanicize event, at which Dulce received the first Latinovator award, she directly related her service in Iraq—during which she and her fellow soldiers came under attack with rocket-propelled grenades—to her entrepreneurship. She stated, "You're restricted from wearing makeup and expressing your individuality. For 15 months, I had to blend in like everyone else."[39]

Another video posted to her YouTube account presents a very different image, one that focuses on her business, expertise, and entrepreneurship.

WHAT Do You Think?

In his presidential campaign in 2016, candidate Donald Trump assailed American immigration policy and promised if elected to build a wall across the entirety of the U.S-Mexico border, which was to be paid for by Mexico. In justifying the policy proposal, Trump portrayed undocumented immigrants as dangerous to American democracy and security. In what ways does Dulce Candy's use of image challenge these accusations? If you were to present counterstereotypical images of an issue of importance to you, what might they be?

Courtesy of Dulce Candy Ruiz

Snaps Studio

1. In presidential elections, nominees must win _____.
   a. a majority of state elections
   b. the majority of the national popular vote
   c. a majority of congressional districts
   d. a majority of electoral votes

2. American federalism affects presidential elections by _____.
   a. producing different rules over the methods of voting
   b. allowing states to choose their number of electors
   c. producing different nomination processes in the major parties
   d. standardizing how states deal with faithless electors

3. How might the timing of state caucuses and primaries structure the ways in which the diversity of Americans' lived experiences is made present in the nomination process?

4. What are some of the potential problems raised by the Electoral College?

Answer Key: 1. d; 2. a; 3. Students may want to focus on the demographic makeup of Iowa and New Hampshire and how that might shape opinions of candidates before voters in more diverse states have had a chance to weigh in; 4. Answers may include the possibility of winning the popular vote but failing to secure the presidency or how the system alters presidential campaign strategies.

A FIRST-TIMER RUNS FOR CONGRESS, WINS, AND THEN TURNS TOWARD REELECTION

- **Explore the role that incumbency plays in candidates' campaign decisions.**

In 2015 in California, a newcomer threw his hat into the ring to run for election to the House of Representatives for the first time. His name was Salud Carbajal. According to an article in the *Santa Barbara Independent*,

> Born in Mexico, Carbajal moved with his family when he was five years old to Bagdad, a small copper mining town in western Arizona. His father worked the mines while his mother, who suffered from arthritis, stayed home with their eight children. When Carbajal was in sixth grade, the copper mine closed and the family moved to Oxnard [California], where Carbajal spent his junior high and high school years while his father worked in the fields.

> In Oxnard, the Carbajals lived in the projects of an economically depressed neighborhood. . . . "The police were there constantly," Carbajal said over lunch [in 2008] at El Zarape, a Westside Mexican eatery not far from his West Islay Street home. "It was a tough neighborhood."[40]

NEWCOMERS CHOOSE THE RIGHT TIME TO JUMP IN

Salud Carbajal was running as a Democrat, seeking to represent the voters of California's Twenty-Fourth District, a congressional district just north along the coast from Los Angeles that includes the counties of Santa Barbara and San Luis Obispo. As is the case with so many congressional districts in the state and in the American Southwest, the composition of voters in the district was changing. By 2016, just below 35 percent of the population of the district was Latino.[41]

When he announced his decision to run in April 2015, Carbajal presented to voters his reasons for standing for national office:

> Our region has been well represented by Congresswoman Capps for the past 17 years and I am privileged to have had the opportunity to work collaboratively with her to improve our local communities.

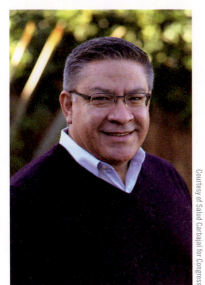

▲ An image of candidate Salud Carbajal from his campaign website. The description reads, "Salud Carbajal tiene un historial efectivo y comprobado en unir personas para trabajar juntos en fortalecer nuestra comunidad." (In English, "Salud Carbajal has an effective and proven track record in bringing people to work together to strengthen our community.")

Courtesy of Salud Carbajal for Congress

Following her recent announcement that she would not run for reelection, I have decided to run for Congress to be an effective voice in Washington for the issues that people care about on the Central Coast—creating jobs, educational opportunity for all, preserving essential safety net services, improving our infrastructure and protecting the environment.

I have a proven track record of working in a bipartisan way to get results on these issues in my service as County Supervisor and want to bring the same effective and collaborative approach to Congress.[42]

While Carbajal's announcement described to potential voters his policy objectives, politically, one of the most telling parts of his statement was this: "Our region has been well represented by Congresswoman Capps for the past 17 years." Carbajal was giving respect to Democratic congresswoman Lois Capps, who was retiring from Congress. Her retirement probably was one of the key factors in Carbajal's decision to run for Congress for the first time.

The decision to stand for national legislative office, though a monumental one, is only the first step in the long journey toward election to Congress. For first-timers such as Carbajal, this initial decision is made knowing that each new step along the way is just another in a very steep climb. The odds are usually stacked against them.

Due to the retirement of Capps, there was no incumbent, no sitting member of the House running for reelection in the Twenty-Fourth District. The election was an **open seat election**, with no incumbent defending her or his seat. That, as we will soon explore, is extremely important. In congressional elections, the most important determinant of who will win is incumbency. Stated simply, incumbents usually win, and those with serious aspirations to enter Congress are often, and wisely, very wary of challenging an incumbent representative or senator. Losing looks bad; serious contenders do not like to lose.

In terms of political experience, Carbajal was no rookie. He announced his bid while serving as a member of the Santa Barbara County Board of Supervisors. In terms of Congress, however, Carbajal was an outsider. His victory was far from assured. He faced other qualified candidates, including the Democratic mayor of Santa Barbara, Helene Schneider, and Katcho Achadjian, a Republican state assemblyman.

The dynamics of the 2016 race were profoundly shaped by Capps's decision to retire. When incumbents run for reelection, they are often opposed by, frankly, amateurs, or those candidates who only want to make a statement but expect to lose. In open seat elections, the serious potential challengers like Carbajal often take their shot. Capps's decision may have been partly affected by the changing makeup of the Twenty-Fourth District, changes brought about by shifting demographics and a redistricting following the 2010 census (Table 10.1).

CANDIDATES MUST NAVIGATE THE ELECTORAL RULES

Unlike how the majority of states do things, Carbajal was running under California's **top-two primary system** (also called a nonpartisan blanket primary), in which statewide and federal candidates, regardless of party, compete in the primary elections and are listed on the same ballot.[43] The top two vote-getters then move on to the general election. In some forms of blanket primaries, such as the one used in Louisiana, there is only a second round of voting if no one candidate receives a majority of votes in the first round. In California's top-two system, in contrast, the top two vote-getters in the first round face off in the general election.

The result is that two potential nominees from the same political party might very well face off against each other in the general election, especially in a congressional district whose voters are predominantly Democrat or Republican.

California's system stands in contrast to how most states conduct their congressional primary elections; in most states, voters choose potential nominees within a party. As we have discussed in the

open seat election
an election in which no incumbent is seeking reelection.

top-two primary system
an electoral system in which candidates, regardless of party, compete in the primary elections, with the top two vote-getters, regardless of party, advancing to the general election.

The Difference Redistricting Makes: California's Twenty-Fourth District before and after Redistricting

	111th Congress (2009–2010)	113th Congress (2013–2014)
Population	681,622	526,519
Gender	49.5% Male 50.5% Female	50.2% Male 49.8% Female
Race and Ethnicity	75.9% White 28.8% Hispanic 6.3% Asian 1.7% Black	79.6% White 34.7% Hispanic 4.6% Asian 2.0% Black
Median Household Income	$79,562	$56,943
High School Diploma	88.2%	83.4%
Bachelor's Degree or Higher	33.70%	31.70%

Source: Data from U.S. Census Bureau, "2010 Census Data and Resources," accessed August 3, 2018, https://www.census.gov/rdo/data/2010_census.html.

context of presidential nominations, the structure of a party's nomination process can and does lead to strategic voting choices.

For Salud Carbajal, California's primary system meant that if he moved on from the primary, he might well have faced a fellow Democrat, given the fact that California's Twenty-Fourth District tends to lean slightly Democratic. In 2016, however, there were a lot of "probables" that no longer seemed as close to certain. A Republican Party surge in the national elections, especially the surge of a Republican presidential nominee, could have meant a Democrat running in California's Twenty-Fourth District might face additional headwinds. This phenomenon—when a presidential nominee's popularity surges, energizing support for his or her party and its policies—is called the **coattail effect**.

Carbajal and his opponents were not only confronting the changes to California's electoral system; they also had to deal with the fact that the boundaries defining the people they were trying to represent had also shifted. In elections to the House of Representatives, as we will discuss shortly, the boundaries of the House districts are not set in stone.

Drawing these lines is often—and for very practical reasons—a contested and political process. After the 2010 census and the redrawing of district boundaries that followed, the boundaries that defined California's Twenty-Fourth District had changed. The *Los Angeles Times* reported that "Capps' district, once derided as the 'ribbon of shame' because of its blatantly gerrymandered boundaries, was redrawn into a politically balanced 'swing district' that could be won by a candidate of either major party. Registration [in late 2015 was] nearly even—37 percent Democratic, 34 percent Republican—with more than 23 percent of voters unaffiliated" with either major party.[44]

In the 2014 general election, Capps won a narrow victory, defeating her Republican Party opponent by a hardly comfortable margin of 52 to 48 percent, down considerably from her ten-point victory in the election before that. This slimmer margin can partly be attributed to redistricting. After the 2010 census, Capps's congressional district lost "heavily Democratic Oxnard while adding the conservative interiors of Santa Barbara and San Luis Obispo counties."[45] Latino voters then comprised 34 percent of the Twenty-Fourth District's eligible voters. According to an April 2015 analysis by *Politico*, "Republicans view the seat as a potential pickup opportunity in the 2016 election cycle."[46] According to a political scientist from Claremont McKenna College, "The Capps seat leans Democratic, but could be within reach for Republicans if everything goes right for them."[47]

coattail effect
a phenomenon that occurs when a presidential candidate's increasing popularity results in increased support for congressional candidates of the same party.

CANDIDATES RAISE MONEY AND SECURE ENDORSEMENTS

In what was playing out as a potentially hotly contested election, Carbajal and his opponents, Democrat and Republican alike, had a lot of work to do. The battle for votes would be fought in the shadow of two other contests: the battle for money and the battle for endorsements from influential politicians, business leaders, community activists, and other key players in California politics.

By both measures, as 2015 turned into 2016, Carbajal's campaign was doing very well. Mayor Schneider received support from "women's groups,"[48] but Carbajal picked up an early and key endorsement from retiring incumbent Capps. After that, House minority leader and former House majority leader Nancy Pelosi added her endorsement to his campaign, "a rare pick in a contested Democratic primary."[49] In an interview with *The Hill*, former state assemblyman Pedro Nava said, "It's shaping up as though Carbajal is essentially the institutional Democratic candidate."[50] Pelosi's endorsement, though extremely helpful, did not come without its own risks, however. It exposed Carbajal to charges that he was running as part of the establishment—an establishment that many voters felt was in need of change.

By December 2015, Carbajal was also doing very well in the fund-raising battle. His campaign hit the $1 million mark, far outpacing his rivals from either party. "I continue to be amazed by the tremendous support I have received in the past few months and am grateful to the many individual [sic] who have contributed to our campaign," said Carbajal. "We are building a movement for a stronger middle class and the broad support we have received demonstrates the momentum that we are building."[51] (See Figure 10.5.) Momentum, or "Big Mo" as political scientist Larry Bartels describes it in his book, *Presidential Primaries and the Dynamics of Public Choice*, may be the most important and hard-to-obtain resource that a candidate for national office can hope to have.[52] At the beginning of 2016, Carbajal appeared to have it.

He did, and his "Big Mo" continued. In the November 2016 congressional elections, Salud Carbajal won, becoming California's Twenty-Fourth House District representative to Congress. Carbajal secured the seat, winning roughly 53 percent of the vote to Fareed's nearly 47 percent. Once in office,

▼ **FIGURE 10.5**

Reported Donations to Candidates in California's Twenty-Fourth District House Race as of June 2016

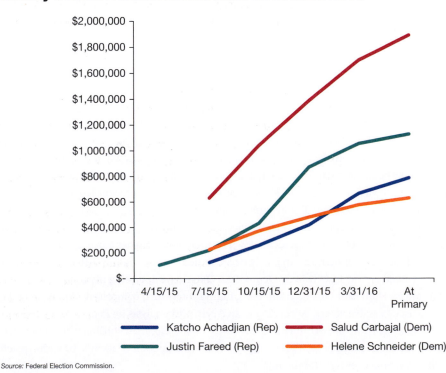

Source: Federal Election Commission.

though, there would be rules to learn (Chapter 12), policies to promote and advocate, and money to raise. For a new member of Congress, especially in the House, there is no time for looking back. There are constituents to serve, interest groups to deal with, and money for reelection to be secured.

THE FIRST DAY ON THE JOB BEGINS THE NEXT CAMPAIGN

Arriving in the nation's capital in 2017, Representative Carbajal noted his sense of excitement for the opportunities ahead but the need to focus on issues and policy: "The excitement is waning now a little bit. It just feels like, let's get on with it."[53] He also got a very quick reminder of the powerful interests that would be lined up to attempt to shape his actions and votes. His congressional office, "a work in progress," with unpacked boxes adorning it, was already the site of much activity: "The corridor outside Carbajal's second-floor office in the Cannon House Office Building was jammed with well-wishers during a two-hour reception, while representatives from the likes of PG&E [a California utility], the National Education Association and various labor unions signed in and distributed business cards."[54] Several months later, as Carbajal settled in to work in the House, it was time to hit the campaign trail again.

In the run-up to the 2018 elections, Carbajal faced off against a familiar opponent. Justin Fareed ran as the leading Republican to try to flip the seat to his party. This time, though, Fareed and the Republican Party tried a long and true strategy to unseat a sitting member of Congress. They called Carbajal an insider, a member of the establishment, part of the problem in Washington, DC. "I have been dismayed at the lack of leadership for the Central Coast," Fareed stated in a news release announcing his candidacy in 2017. "Rep. Carbajal has voted with Nancy Pelosi [D-CA and House minority leader] more than 97% of the time and has been rewarded with hundreds of thousands of dollars from special interest groups that care more about their agenda than the people in our diverse communities."[55] Salud Carbajal won his 2018 reelection bid, again defeating Justin Fareed. Representative Carbajal, along with other successful candidates, may very well be already thinking about 2020.

Sam Goldman / Noozhawk

▲ Democrat incumbent Representative Salud Carbajal (right) and Republican challenger Justin Fareed face one another at a 2016 debate in Santa Barbara during the primary race for California's Twenty-Fourth Congressional District.

WHAT HAVE I **LEARNED?**

1. The structure of California's congressional primary system in 2016 guaranteed that _____.
   a. the top two vote-getters, regardless of party, advanced to the general election in November
   b. every California House election was an open seat election
   c. incumbents' prospects for reelection were secure
   d. the general election featured one Republican and one Democrat

2. As California's Twenty-Fourth District race got into full gear in 2016, candidates struggled to secure many things to help them get elected. What were these things? Which of them do you think are most important?

3. Why are open seat elections often different from elections that are not?

Answer Key: 1. a; 2. Answers might mention money, endorsements, or momentum; 3. Answers should include a discussion of the presence of more high-quality challengers.

THE DETAILS OF CONGRESSIONAL ELECTIONS DIFFER BY STATE, BUT MANY OF THE RULES ARE THE SAME

- Identify the structure of and issues involved in congressional elections.

The most important difference between legislative and presidential elections is defining whom the legislative candidate hopes to represent. States differ on where the bar is set for congressional nominees in the general elections. In most states, a candidate needs a **plurality** of votes in the primaries or general election, meaning that the candidate receives more votes than any other candidate. In other states, a candidate needs a **majority** of votes (more than 50 percent), which may lead to a **runoff election** between the two with the highest total if no one candidate scores a majority.

IN CONGRESSIONAL ELECTIONS, CONSTITUENCY IS KEY

At the most basic level, the rules governing the division of voters into **constituencies**—bodies of voters in a given area who elect a representative or senator—are laid out in the Constitution. However, the process of this division, especially for the House of Representatives, is often controversial. Even the Supreme Court has had to weigh in on the process in the past. The ways in which incumbent members of Congress use their incumbency to enhance their chances of getting reelected have significant effects on the behavior of all candidates in an election. Finally, every election is unique. Local, state, and national conditions during a given election matter as well, and there are always unanticipated events that can powerfully shape a given candidate's electoral chances.

SENATORS REPRESENT THEIR ENTIRE STATES. The size of the Senate depends only on the number of states in the Union, since two senators represent each state. Since the admission of Hawaii as the fiftieth state in 1959, therefore, the Senate has been composed of one hundred members, each representing the entire state from which they were elected. Because the Senate was divided into three "classes" in order to stagger the elections of senators, no two senate seats from the same state will be up for grabs in the same election unless a retirement or other event has opened up one of the seats.

Like many other aspects of the basic structure of the federal government, the guarantee of equal state representation in the Senate came about as a result of conflicts and bargaining between less populous and more populous states as well as between slaveholding and nonslaveholding states during the Constitutional Convention. The result of equal *state* representation is that individual *voters* are unequally represented in the Senate. The 585,501 citizens of Wyoming get two senators, and so do the 39.25 million citizens of California.

MEMBERS OF THE HOUSE REPRESENT THEIR DISTRICTS. In spite of the potential repercussions of equal state representation in the Senate, determining one's potential constituents is a very simple matter for that chamber. When it comes to the House of Representatives, however, things are a bit more complicated—and political.

POPULATION DETERMINES THE NUMBER OF SEATS IN THE HOUSE FOR EACH STATE. While initially the size of the House was allowed to grow with the population, it is now fixed at 435 members.[56] The size of a state's representation in the House depends upon its population. The process of determining the number of representatives for each state is called **apportionment**; through this process, the number of representatives is allocated based on the results of the census that is conducted every ten years. As part of the process of apportionment, each state is divided into one or more congressional districts, with one seat in the House representing each district and each state guaranteed one representative, no matter how small its population (see Figure 10.6).

Given the fact that the size of the House is capped, changes in population can produce "winners and losers" among the states following each census. Trends in population growth and distribution in recent decades have produced a clear pattern of gains in House seats for states in the South and the West and losses for states in the Northeast and Midwest.

plurality
when a candidate receives more votes than any other candidate.

majority
when a candidate receives more than 50 percent of the vote.

runoff election
an election that is held between the two candidates with the highest total votes if no one candidate scores a majority.

constituencies
bodies of voters in a given area who elect a representative or senator.

apportionment
the process of determining the number of representatives for each state using census data; states are divided into congressional districts that have at least one representative each.

Apportionment Gains and Losses after the 2010 Census

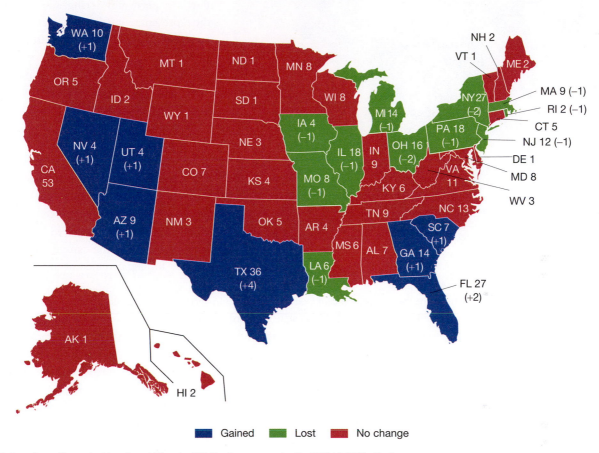

Gained   Lost   No change

Source: U.S. Census Bureau, "Congressional Apportionment," November 2011, https://www.census.gov/prod/cen2010/briefs/c2010br-08.pdf.

Note: Numbers to the right of the state names show the total number of representatives allocated to the state. Numbers below show the change as either a gain (+) or a loss (–).

REDISTRICTING AND GERRYMANDERING SHAPE CONSTITUENCIES AND ELECTIONS IN HOUSE RACES

While the process of apportionment has important consequences for the representation of states in the House, it also has important consequences for the boundaries of constituency. Following each census, states enter into the process of **redistricting** in which they redraw the electoral district boundaries. Seven states have only one representative; therefore, their district boundaries are the same as the boundaries of the state. Some states have undertaken redistricting *between* censuses, especially when a political party gains control over the state's legislative and executive branches, though many states have constitutional or legislative prohibitions against this practice.

The stakes involved in redistricting are high, and the process is often very political and controversial. In most states, the legislature appoints the members of a commission to draw the district boundaries. In others, a bipartisan or nonpartisan commission handles the process to try to make it less political, though the state legislatures typically still have to approve these plans.

The intentional use of redistricting to benefit a specific interest or group of voters is referred to as **gerrymandering**. The term comes from state legislative districts that were oddly drawn in 1812 under Massachusetts governor Elbridge Gerry to benefit his Democratic-Republican Party. Federalists complained that one district looked like a monster or a salamander, and the term created by the fusion of salamander with the governor's last name stuck. There are three types of gerrymandering: partisan, racial and ethnic, and incumbent.

redistricting
states' redrawing of the electoral district boundaries following each census.

gerrymandering
the intentional use of redistricting to benefit a specific interest or group of voters.

▲ Texas state representative Gabi Canales (D-Alice), left, holds a Texas flag as Representative Jose Menendez (D-San Antonio), center, and Representative Mark Homer (D-Paris), right, stand arm in arm during a news conference at a hotel in Ardmore, Oklahoma, in May 2013.

PARTISAN GERRYMANDERING INVOLVES STRATEGIC CALCULATIONS.

Partisan gerrymandering aims to increase the representation of one political party at the expense of another. The idea is to concentrate the opposing party's supporters in a small number of districts, which that party will win easily. The party in control then tries to maximize the number of districts that its candidates will win comfortably but not by huge margins. By doing so, the party in charge of redistricting is able to "waste" many of the votes of its opposition, since there is no more of an advantage—in terms of the number of House seats a party has—to winning 90 percent of the votes in any one district than there is to winning 55 percent. Redistricting can put incumbents at risk by changing the composition of their constituencies or by forcing two incumbents to run for the same seat.

One of the most heated recent examples of partisan gerrymandering occurred in Texas following the 2002 elections, which placed the Texas state government firmly in the hands of the Republican Party for the first time in 130 years. It was a between-censuses redistricting, as the state had just completed redistricting following the 2000 census, which also had its own share of drama and controversy. At the urging of House majority leader Tom Delay and Texas governor Rick Perry, the Republicans attempted to use their control of the legislature and the governorship to "thoroughly dismantle several House Democrat's districts," either by changing the makeup of their constituencies or by placing them in the same congressional districts.[57]

Democrats in the Texas state legislature resisted, twice fleeing the state "en masse (once to Oklahoma once to New Mexico) to prevent action by denying legislative quorums while avoiding arrest under a Texas statue aimed at preventing just this tactic."[58] The Texas Democrats' strategy of holing up in hotel rooms across the state's borders delayed but did not ultimately defeat the Republicans' partisan gerrymander. As political scientist Gary Jacobson observed, "Only one targeted Democrat . . . managed to survive" the redistricting and win reelection in 2004.[59] Delay was later admonished by the House Ethics Committee for attempting to use federal law enforcement resources to track down the elusive Texas Democrats.[60]

RACIAL AND ETHNIC GERRYMANDERING AIMS TO INCREASE MINORITY REPRESENTATION.

A second form of gerrymandering aims to increase the likelihood of electing members of racial and ethnic minorities as representatives by concentrating voters of minority ethnicity within specific congressional districts. Racial and ethnic gerrymandering results in **majority-minority districts** in which voters of *minority* ethnicity constitute an electoral *majority* within the electoral district. Racial and ethnic gerrymandering has led to some oddly shaped congressional districts—some of the most notable of which were drawn after the 1990 census. The Twelfth Congressional District in North Carolina, for example, "stitched together African American communities in several of the state's larger cities, using Interstate 85 . . . as the thread."[61]

INCUMBENT GERRYMANDERING IS FAR LESS COMMON.

The third form of strategic redistricting is incumbent gerrymandering, wherein district lines are drawn to protect the reelection prospects of an incumbent representative. It is often less compelling for a party in power in state government to undertake incumbent gerrymandering, as it does not necessarily improve the prospects of the party overall. In addition, ambitious members of a state legislature may themselves be eyeing a seat in the House, giving them a strong incentive to ensure their party's victory in their home district but few incentives to protect the electoral fortunes of a potential rival.

majority-minority district
a district in which voters of a minority ethnicity constitute an electoral majority within that electoral district.

THE REPRESENTATIONAL CONSEQUENCES OF THE GREAT COMPROMISE

As we explored in Chapter 2, one of the most contentious battles in the Constitutional Convention, especially during the early weeks, was over changing the "one state, one vote" structure of state representation in the Confederal Congress (under the Articles of Confederation). Less populous states, such as New Jersey, Delaware, and Connecticut, were not about to consent to the formation of a new congress in which states received votes based on their populations. The Great Compromise settled this question, with the House of Representatives apportioning seats based on population and the Senate allotting seats equally, two to each state.

While the compromise avoided what many feared was a fight that would tear the Constitutional Convention, and perhaps the young nation, apart, it did so with representational consequences. Although each state is guaranteed at least one representative in the House, there are variations between states in the number of representatives per resident, which range from about six hundred thousand residents per representative to nearly a million, with an average of about 710,000 residents per representative.

These variations, however, are very small in comparison to those in the Senate, where each resident of each state is represented by two senators regardless of the state's population. Given the sizable differences between state populations, the number of state residents per senator varies dramatically.

The bar chart below presents the number of constituents per senator by state. As they come from the most populous state in the Union, each of California's two senators must represent more than sixty-five times the number of citizens

(Continued)

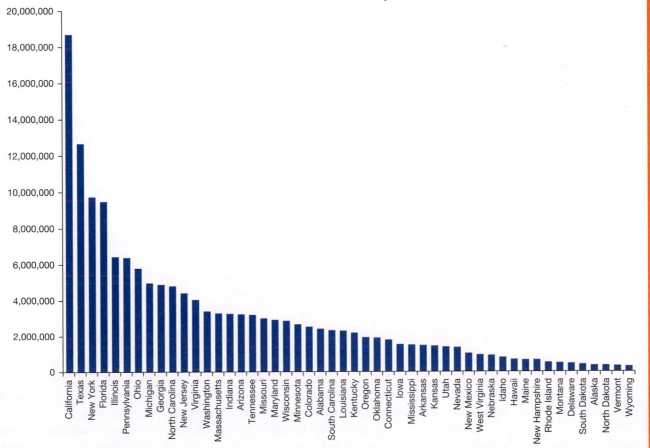

Number of U.S. Residents per Senator

Source: Data from "2012–2020 Federal Representation by People per House Seat, Senate Seat, and Electors," The Green Papers, January 5, 2011, http://www.thegreenpapers.com/Census10/FedRep .phtml?sort=Sena#table.

(Continued)

as a senator from Wyoming, the nation's least populous state.[62] This means California's senators are spread much more thinly when trying to address the concerns of individual constituents. There is also evidence that the least populous states benefit more from congressional spending than they would if the Constitution did not guarantee them equal representation in the Senate.[63]

WHaT Do You Think?

Say that you are a researcher exploring whether or not citizens from less populous states receive better senatorial representation than those from the most populous states. How might you define *better*? What evidence would you look for to form your hypothesis?

THE SUPREME COURT CONTINUES TO WEIGH IN ON GERRYMANDERING. In recent decades, the Supreme Court has become more active in ruling on congressional district boundaries, the drawing of which had generally been left up to the states and the political process. Affirming the "one person, one vote" rule of representation, the Court in two cases ruled that **malapportionment**—where the population is distributed in uneven numbers between legislative districts—is unconstitutional as it violates the equal protection clause of the Fourteenth Amendment.[64]

While the Court has highlighted potential problems with partisan gerrymandering in several recent cases, it has not gone so far as to declare the practice inherently unconstitutional. The Court has held that voters in these districts are still represented but by members from different political parties. *Davis v. Bandemer* (1986) involved an Indiana redistricting plan. The Court upheld the plan, ruling that the partisan gerrymander did not violate the Fourteenth Amendment's equal protection clause.[65] *Vieth v. Jubelirer* (2004) involved a Pennsylvania partisan gerrymander. In this case, the Court overturned the Republican-controlled gerrymander, but it did so on the grounds that the plan created districts with unequal numbers of voters, not because it was an attempt to favor one political party.[66] In 2006, in *League of United Latin American Citizens v. Perry*, the Court upheld most of the Texas redistricting plan from 2003 but required that one district's lines be redrawn to protect the voting rights of Hispanic Americans.[67]

In 2018, the Supreme Court declined to consider two partisan gerrymandering cases, both on narrower procedural grounds. In doing so, the Court gave no indication of how it might rule on similar cases in the future.[68] With Brett Kavanaugh replacing the retired Justice Anthony Kennedy in 2018 (see Chapter 15), a more conservative Court will be approaching any partisan gerrymandering cases presented to it going forward.

The Court has also weighed in on the proper role of racial and ethnic considerations in drawing district boundaries. In *Thornburg v. Gingles* (1986), the Court overturned a state's legislative district boundaries on the basis that they diluted the electoral power of African American voters and violated their voting rights.[69] In *Shaw v. Reno* (1993), the Court rejected a North Carolina reapportionment plan designed to produce majority-minority districts because it resulted in a bizarrely shaped district and used race to such a degree in drawing these boundaries that it could "only be understood as an effort to segregate voters into separate districts on the basis of race"[70] (Figure 10.7). Since *Shaw v. Reno*, states are allowed to use race as a consideration but not as the predominant factor in drawing district boundaries.

CONGRESSIONAL INCUMBENTS HAVE SIGNIFICANT INSTITUTIONAL ADVANTAGES

Incumbents have many resources at their disposal. Knowing this, potential challengers often wait until there is no incumbent defending a seat. Making full use of the resources available to them, incumbent representatives and senators possess many advantages over any candidate who might challenge them. This **incumbency advantage** has only grown stronger in recent decades.

The vast majority of congressional incumbents who seek reelection succeed. Incumbent senators and members of the house have reelection rates of 80 to 90 percent.[71] Given the fact that incumbents enjoy such an advantage, "nearly everything pertaining to candidates and campaigns for Congress is profoundly influenced by whether a candidate is already an incumbent, is challenging an incumbent, or is pursuing an open seat."[72]

malapportionment
the uneven distribution of the population between legislative districts.

incumbency advantage
institutional advantages held by those already in office who are trying to fend off challengers in an election.

North Carolina's Twelfth Congressional District: The "I-85 District"

The Twelfth Congressional District in North Carolina was put in place for the 1992 elections and was one of the primary districts at issue in *Shaw v. Reno*. It was designed with the aid of computer technology to merge predominantly African American communities. The narrow parts of the district followed Interstate I-85. According to the Redistricting Task Force for the National Conference of State Legislatures, "the laboratory that made this birth possible was the computer technology that became available for the 1990s redistricting cycle. The progeny won no Beautiful Baby contests. A *Wall Street Journal* editorial described the 12th as 'political pornography.' Known as the 'I-85 district,' the 12th stretched 160 miles across the central Piedmont region of the State, for part of its length no wider than the freeway right-of-way."

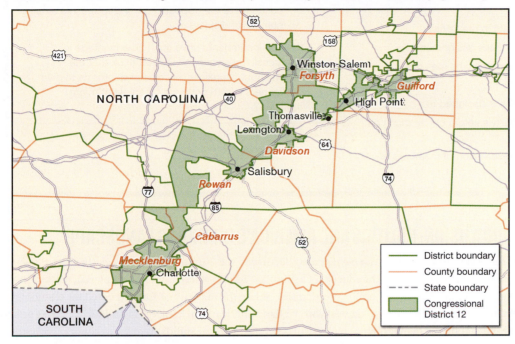

Political scientist David Mayhew explained the strategic logic of incumbents and how they use their institutional advantages to maximize their chances of reelection. For Mayhew, legislators are "single-minded seekers of re-election" who make the most of their institutional advantages.[73] These advantages include using their franking privileges, the free use of the mail for communication with constituents, to advertise their campaigns. Incumbents usually enjoy higher levels of name recognition than their challengers, which is increased by more media coverage than that available to any potential challengers. In media coverage and public events, incumbents claim credit for what they have done in Washington and announce their positions on key pieces of legislation of interest to their constituents.[74] Finally, incumbents perform casework for individual constituents, especially in helping them deal with the federal and state bureaucracy.

If incumbents are usually in no danger, then why do they spend so much time and energy trying to secure reelection? Another strategic explanation involves decisions made by potential challengers. Not all challengers are equally credible, and incumbents maximize their resources to try to ensure that they will not face qualified challengers. Knowing the odds, credible challengers often wait for their chance to run in an open seat election in which there is no incumbent to face.

What makes for a high-quality challenger? Successful challengers are skillful with the media and public events. They also are knowledgeable about the issues and where their constituents stand on those issues. But they need two things above all else: experience and money. Experience is usually gained by moving up through the layers of local and state politics to become professional, polished, and respected. Money buys more than airtime, advertising, and campaign events—it also buys information, by, for instance, hiring pollsters to help them better understand their constituents' preferences. Money can help scare off potential opponents and signal to other potential donors that this is a campaign with a legitimate shot at success. Most challengers lack the financial resources to wage effective campaigns.[75]

WHAT HAVE I LEARNED?

1. Apportionment refers to _____.
   a. the allocation of seats in the House of Representatives
   b. the allocation of seats in the Senate
   c. congressional committee assignments
   d. the number of candidates who may run in a congressional election

2. Partisan gerrymandering is designed to _____.
   a. spread your own party's voters out as much as possible
   b. encourage the representation of members of minority groups

   c. protect incumbents in the House of Representatives
   d. concentrate the opposing party's voters in a small number of districts

3. Why do incumbents have such an advantage in congressional elections? Do you think that the nation should consider any electoral reforms to give challengers a better chance? If so, what might these be?

   _____

   Answer Key: 1. a; 2. a; 3. Answers should describe specific characteristics of theories of the incumbency advantage.

CONCLUSION: POLITICS AND AMERICA'S CHANGING LANDSCAPE

While the Latino vote may not have proved decisive in the 2016 presidential race, there were several lessons to be learned. First, the concept of a singular "Latino vote," as we have explored, masks a great deal of complexity within Latino communities. While the majority of Latinos voted for Clinton, for example, Trump appeared to do well with Cuban Americans, helping him win Florida. In addition, the inevitability of demographic change will continue to press candidates to try to connect with these growing communities.

The 2018 midterm elections resulted in an increasing diversity across many identities in the Congress that would convene in January (Chapter 12). Texas, for example, elected its first two Latina congresswomen, Sylvia Garcia and Veronica Escobar, both Democrats. Alexandria Ocasio-Cortez (D-NY) became the youngest woman ever elected to serve in the House of Representatives.

Exit poll data collected on voting day indicated perhaps record-breaking Latino turnout, with immigration as one of the key issues mentioned by nearly all voters. While detailed turnout analyses were yet to come, these are early indications that Latinos could represent the highest percentage of total turnout ever for this group of voters in a midterm election.[76] As the election took place, an asylum-seeking group of Central American and Mexican individuals was making its way to the U.S. border, and President Trump vowed that they would not be allowed to cross.

The combination of the geographical distribution of Americans of diverse identities, the division of partisan support between urban and rural areas of the nation, and the structure of Congress established as a result of the Great Compromise in the Constitutional Convention are likely to act as powerful forces in shaping congressional political outcomes going forward.

In the 2018 midterms—as part of their successful effort to reclaim the House of Representatives—Democrats "flipped" the last remaining "purely urban" House district in Republican hands, one covering Staten Island and parts of Brooklyn, New York. Urbanization and demographic change benefit the Democrats in coming House elections. Republicans, however, benefit from the mapping of conservative and rural voters onto a larger number of less populated states, giving

Republicans an advantage in their efforts to hold on to the Senate. Both of these mappings, and the underlying political and demographic trends, advantage the political parties going forward, but in different chambers, raising the likelihood of a divided Congress going forward. Finally, both Republicans and Democrats also made key pickups in state gubernatorial races, which may very well be an important factor in the state redistricting battles that will surely follow the 2020 census.

CHAPTER REVIEW

This chapter's main ideas are reflected in the Learning Objectives below. By reviewing them here, you should be able to **remember** the key points, **know** the terms that are central to the topic, and **think** about the critical issues raised in each section.

10.1 Explain why changes in the constituency lead candidates to reach out to new groups of voters.

REMEMBER
- The continuing growth of the American Latino voting-age population presents the political parties and their candidates with significant opportunities and challenges as they try to reach out to voters in these communities.
- During the 2016 presidential campaign, candidates in both major parties tried to convince Latino voters that their candidacies were worth supporting, though all faced challenges in doing so.

KNOW
- campaigns (p. 267)
- elections (p. 267)
- swing states (p. 272)
- demographics (p. 270)

THINK
- What challenges did the leading candidates for nomination in the 2016 presidential elections face in reaching out to Latino voters?
- How were these political challenges shaped by the parties that the candidates sought to represent?
- What effects do you think the expected massive growth in the percentage of Latinos of voting age will have on national electoral outcomes?
- What might limit the impact of this demographic change?
- Do you think the diversity of Americans' lived experiences is represented in national electoral outcomes? Why or why not?

10.2 Understand the rules and institutions that structure national elections.

REMEMBER
- American national elections are somewhat unique among democratic nations in that they occur on fixed and regular schedules.
- In national campaigns, money can be used to purchase advertising, mobilize voters and supporters, and discourage potential challengers from entering a race.
- Certain federal efforts to control or restrain campaign finance have been found to be constitutionally permissible, while others have been modified or rejected.

KNOW
- challenger (p. 275)
- negative campaign advertisements (p. 276)
- retrospective voting (p. 275)
- get out the vote (GOTV) (p. 276)
- super PACs (p. 276)
- political action committees (PACs) (p. 276)
- incumbent (p. 275)

THINK
- How much does money matter in American national elections?
- Should campaign contributions be limited? Why or why not?

10.3 Identify the stages of presidential elections.

REMEMBER
- The presidential campaign involves two formal stages: the nomination campaign and the general elections.
- Prior to the formal campaign, would-be presidential candidates lay the groundwork for their eventual campaigns.
- Political parties have constructed different systems and sets of rules for selecting their nominees.
- In the general election, the system of the Electoral College determines the winner, with states being awarded electoral votes according to their representation in Congress.

KNOW
- Electoral College (p. 278)
- exploratory committee (p. 277)
- faithless electors (p. 278)

THINK
- Why did the Framers mistrust direct democracy? What do you think have been the implications of this mistrust?
- What challenges do presidential candidates face from the different groups of voters who turn out in the nomination phase of the campaigns as opposed to the general elections?

10.4 Explore the role that incumbency plays in candidates' campaign decisions.

REMEMBER
- Salud Carbajal entered the race for the House of Representatives in California's Twenty-Fourth Congressional District.
- Carbajal's decision to do so was likely influenced by the fact that he would not be facing an incumbent.
- Carbajal, who faced a recently redrawn district and a new congressional electoral system, sought to convince voters that he was the candidate best suited to represent his constituents' interests.

KNOW
- coattail effect (p. 283)
- open seat election (p. 282)
- top-two primary system (p. 282)

THINK
- How was California's top-two primary system different from that of most other states? What do you think are some advantages and disadvantages of this system?

10.5 Identify the structure of and issues involved in congressional elections.

REMEMBER
- Congressional newcomers face many challenges in seeking election against entrenched incumbents, which often drives credible challengers to wait for an open seat election.
- The rules of congressional elections vary by state, and these differences can affect candidate strategies.
- The redrawing of congressional district lines, typically done following a census, can be a very political process in state politics and can have significant electoral consequences.
- In some cases, the process of redistricting is designed to benefit certain groups of voters, such as those of minority racial or ethnic identity.

KNOW
- apportionment (p. 286)
- constituencies (p. 286)
- gerrymandering (p. 287)
- incumbency advantage (p. 290)
- majority (p. 286)
- majority-minority district (p. 288)
- malapportionment (p. 290)
- plurality (p. 286)
- redistricting (p. 287)
- runoff election (p. 286)

THINK
- In what ways do the differences of constituency shape the strategies of congressional candidates as opposed to presidential candidates?
- Why do incumbents have such an advantage in congressional elections?

CHAPTER 11

INTEREST GROUPS AND SOCIAL MOVEMENTS

Collective Action, Power, and Representation

▼ A decade after the financial crisis of 2008, tensions still exist between interests representing Wall Street and the financial industry and the social movements representing people who want financial reforms to benefit those who are not wealthy. Here, demonstrators hold a sign while marching outside the Federal Reserve Bank of New York during a Fed Up protest in March 2018.

EMPLOYEES ONLY

FED UP

When we think of the people who represent the interests of citizens in government, we tend to think of the leaders those citizens have elected. Elected officials, however, are not the only people who try to represent American interests. The people themselves come together to shape policy or to call attention to issues as well. They form **voluntary associations**—groups and communities who join with each other in pursuit of collective interests and common goals.

In this chapter, we will dive into two related stories: the first is of lobbyists acting on behalf of America's banks and financial firms following the financial collapse of 2007–2008 and the other of a group of protesters who came together a few years later under the name Occupy Wall Street (OWS) to call attention to the issue of income inequality. Both groups were acting on behalf of someone and representing that someone's interests. However, the financial firms and their representatives in Washington acted as **interest groups**, voluntary associations of people who come together with an agreed-upon set of political and policy objectives and who attempt to pull the levers of political power in service of these defined goals. By contrast, OWS attempted to spark a social movement. **Social movements** (sometimes referred to as political movements) are associations of individuals who also come together to change things or keep things from changing, but they often do so by calling attention to a set of injustices in order to get policymakers to act. They also work to educate the public about a set of issues.

As we will explore, members of interest groups and social movements often resort to different tactics to achieve their goals. They do so because they have to. Their choices depend upon a rational determination of what will work to achieve their objectives and of what tools they can bring to bear. Though there are important distinctions between an interest group and a social movement, they are often connected. A social movement, for example, may spawn one, or many, interest groups over the course of its development and expression. For example, the National Association for the Advancement

of Colored People (NAACP), in its efforts to end legal segregation (Chapter 5), was acting as an interest group but also as part of a larger social movement in the struggle for civil rights. What typically distinguishes these types of associations are questions of power and tactics.

There is, however, always a danger inherent with both interest groups and social movements: faction. How can one be sure that a group or movement does not trample on the rights of others? As the stories you will explore show, some voices do get heard more clearly than others.

LEARNING OBJECTIVES

By reading this chapter, you will be able to do the following:

 11.1 Explore financial firms' response to the 2008 housing crisis to understand how interest group members try to wield the levers of political power to shape policy.

 11.2 Summarize the challenges associated with interest group activity.

 11.3 Discuss the types of interest groups in the American political landscape and the different tactics they use.

 11.4 Explore the efforts of Occupy Wall Street to understand the challenges individuals face and the strategies they employ to make social and political changes.

11.5 Analyze the tactics social movements use to advocate on their members' behalf and contrast them with those of interest groups.

voluntary associations
groups and communities who join with each other in pursuit of collective interests and common goals.

interest groups
voluntary associations of people who come together with an agreed-upon set of political and policy objectives and who attempt to pull the levers of political power in service of these defined goals.

social movements
voluntary associations of individuals who come together to change things or keep things from changing, but they often do so by calling attention to a set of injustices or wrongs in order to get policymakers to act and to educate the public about the issue.

A HOUSING BUBBLE BURSTS, AND INTEREST GROUPS POP OUT

- Explore financial firms' response to the 2008 housing crisis to understand how interest group members try to wield the levers of political power to shape policy.

WALL STREET RESPONDS TO A NATIONAL FINANCIAL CRISIS

In the early 2000s, a small number of individuals grew unimaginably rich selling what had once been a very ordinary product: the home mortgage, a type of loan issued by a financial firm to cover the

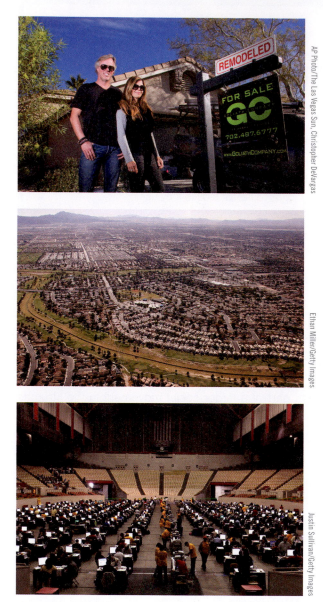

Scenes from the financial crisis: the attraction of flipping houses proved irresistible to many Americans; mountains of bad loans resulted in sprawling developments full of abandoned homes; borrowers seeking help to avoid foreclosure or sell their house filled stadiums.

purchase of a home. They did so by turning the humble home loan into a financial monster that nearly wiped out the global economy. How that happened, and what happened in the aftermath, give us important insight into the power of interest groups.

FINANCIAL ENGINEERING SOWS THE SEEDS FOR A MAJOR CRISIS

In the economic boom years of the 2000s, lenders started to issue loans to people who would not have qualified for them under older rules and with terms that were very dicey. Even Americans with very low incomes enjoyed much easier access to home loans, envisioning them as springboards for sending their children to college and moving their families a few rungs up the economic ladder. Banks at the time issued these subprime mortgages with full confidence that the government would cover for them if things went south.

As lenders got busy lending, prominent banks and investment firms also started creating remarkable new investment products based on those risky mortgages. Local banks would sell their subprime and other mortgages to larger financial firms, who would then chop the loans into little bits (the process is really complicated) and reconstitute them into financial products called mortgage-backed securities (MBSs). By the time they were sufficiently chopped, those MBSs couldn't be traced back to the assets that secured them in the first place, so their real value was unclear, and the relationship between the borrower and the holder of the loan was by that point totally disconnected. While MBSs had been invented decades prior, during the housing boom of the early 2000s firms began to find ever more creative, lucrative, and riskier variations on them, and investors gobbled them up. MBSs ultimately became so complex that the banks themselves did not fully understand the risks they posed. What they *did* know was that there was a lot of money to be made from buying and selling these new financial Frankenfoods. Banks started to take bigger and bigger risks and issue more and more loans. Between 2000 and 2005, those risks seemed to be paying off for investors, who got very, very rich.

For all of this to keep going, however, home prices had to keep going up, and homeowners had to keep making their payments. That was not to be the case. In 2006, home sales peaked and prices began to decline; foreclosure rates began to spike as the people who were least likely to be able to repay their loans *did not* repay those loans. The market began to crash. The housing bubble was popping.

By 2007, one of the main lenders, Freddie Mac, announced that it was going to stop buying the riskiest subprime mortgages and MBSs, sending shock waves through the markets. Other banks that had issued those loans started failing. Some analysts started to suspect that the party was about to end. Others saw less cause for concern. Ben Bernanke, then chair of the Federal Reserve, reassured a congressional committee in March 2007 that things would not get out of hand, saying, "At this juncture . . . the impact on the broader economy and financial markets of the problems in the subprime market seems likely to be contained."[1]

Bernanke was wrong. By late 2008, a total of nine major U.S. banks were teetering on the brink of ruin, and nearly $20 trillion of Americans' wealth had been vaporized (Figure 11.1).[2] The Wall Street bankers and investment firms behind the mess plunged into a panic as global markets imploded.

THE LOBBYISTS' PRESSURE PLAY BEGINS

Powerful interest groups stepped in immediately. Wall Street insiders and the interest groups acting on their behalf quickly realized that it was time to scramble for seats on whatever financial lifeboat

The Crash of the American Housing Market

Foreclosures and Housing Prices

Source: Ben Beachy, "A Financial Crisis Manual: Causes, Consequences, and Lessons of the Financial Crisis," Global Development and Environment Institute Working Paper No. 12-06, Tufts University, December 2012, http://www.ase.tufts.edu/gdae/Pubs/wp/12-06BeachyFinancialCrisis.pdf, Figure 2.

the U.S. government might launch. Henry ("Hank") Paulson, then Treasury secretary, recounted the steps he took when things began breaking badly: "I immediately started making phone calls to see how Wall Street was responding: Dick Fuld at Lehman, Stan O'Neal at Merrill Lynch, Steve Schwarzman at Blackstone, and Lloyd Blankfein at Goldman Sachs. All these CEOs were on edge."[3] The financial firms wanted a bailout—a big one. Appearing on the Sunday morning political news talk shows that month, Paulson warned the public "of an economic doomsday if Congress [did not] immediately okay a colossal Wall Street bailout."[4]

Privately, behind closed doors in Washington, DC, Paulson and Bernanke together spoke to members of Congress "in such apocalyptic terms that lawmakers were struck dumb with horror."[5] They argued that the only way to stop the collapse was with taxpayer money—$700 billion, to be exact— and it needed to be delivered *immediately.* Such a transaction would transfer these riskiest loans out of the hands of the suddenly imperiled financial giants and place them firmly in the hands of American taxpayers.

Under fire from skeptical members of Congress who objected both to the price tag and the time frame, Paulson and his supporters pointed to Paulson's previous experience on and connections to Wall Street as a plus. There was no place for amateurs, they argued, in safeguarding Americans' interests. Paulson had firsthand insight into how things worked in the industry and the kinds of personal connections necessary to make things happen as he ran this enormous, unprecedented, one-man ATM. Prior to leading the Department of the Treasury, Paulson had served as chair and chief executive officer of the investment-banking titan Goldman Sachs & Co. Indeed, he had led Goldman during "the Gold Rush that brought the global financial system to the brink of collapse."[6]

As the Senate considered how, or whether, to bail out financial firms and homeowners, lobbyists from America's financial firms were hard at work. Representatives of major banks spent days on Capitol Hill in private conversation with members of Congress and their staffs, and their efforts appeared to pay off.[7] The Bush administration's originally more limited plans to bail out the financial firms evolved in short order into a situation where Wall Street was effectively dictating the terms. The "Securities Industry and Financial Markets Association, Wall Street's main trade and lobbying group, [was by then holding] conference calls to discuss 'your firms' views and priorities related to Treasury's proposal,' according to an e-mail message sent to members."[8]

▲ House Speaker Nancy Pelosi of California (center right) and House Democratic leaders meet with Treasury secretary Henry Paulson (center left) and Federal Reserve chair Ben Bernanke (second from left) in Pelosi's office on Capitol Hill to discuss the financial crisis.

COUNTERPRESSURE ARISES FROM OUTSIDE GROUPS

At the same time, opposition to a Wall Street bailout was emerging from other groups, and some wondered just how well Americans' interests were being represented by Paulson and other financial insiders. Messages from Americans to their members of Congress were clear and came in heavy volume. "The phone calls into the district office are about 75 percent saying: Don't do this. They think this is about Wall Street" and not about helping average homeowners, reported a Republican member of the House.[9] In addition to average Americans, organized interest groups joined the chorus of voices expressing concerns about the possible effects of the proposals on struggling Americans. Groups representing farmers, senior citizens, and undocumented Americans as well as civil rights advocates began to put pressure on Washington to advocate for *their* members' interests.[10]

As the congressional negotiations reached a critical point in September 2008, calls to include help for average homeowners grew louder. "We will not simply hand over a $700 billion blank check to Wall Street and hope of a better outcome. Democrats will act responsibly to insulate Main Street from Wall Street," House Speaker Nancy Pelosi (D-CA) promised.[11] The Speaker's promise was made, no doubt, partly because "rank-and-file members were getting an earful from their constituents—and showing signs of a populist revolt."[12]

THE BAILOUT BEGINS

In October 2008, the Senate passed a bailout bill. Included in the bill were tax breaks for consumers to purchase energy-efficient appliances, $500 million in tax breaks for film producers, breaks for rum producers and Alaskan fishermen, and a "$10 million credit to help employers defray the costs of storing the bicycles of their employees who commute to work."[13] The strategy, which was designed to peel off enough of the no votes in the House so that the bill could proceed to the Senate, worked. The bailout bill ultimately made it to President George W. Bush's desk, wherein it became law. Along the way, however, the tab had grown to $850 billion, inflated by lawmakers' efforts to extract concessions for their constituents and for interest groups important to their electoral fortunes. One of the small, but noted, additions to the bailout bill—no doubt a result of members of Congress acting on requests from their constituents and interest group actions—was an elimination of a tax on "wooden archery arrows used by kids."[14]

Wall Street breathed a sigh of relief; the stock market stabilized.

In the aftermath of the financial crisis and the Wall Street bailout, many Americans clamored for financial reforms to make sure that what many saw as a taxpayer-backed reward for excessive risk-taking by financial firms would not be repeated. In May 2009, President Barack Obama urged Congress to act on legislation that would provide for more oversight over the riskiest of Wall Street's complex financial instruments, called swaps and derivatives. As the *New York Times* noted, however, lobbyists were already on the move to curtail reforms that would limit their group's interests: "Hinting at a lobbying campaign to come . . . the chief executive of the International Swaps and Derivatives Association, a trade group, said his organization 'looked forward to working with policy makers to ensure these reforms help preserve the widespread availability of swaps and other important risk management tools.'"[15]

To some, preserving the availability to freely market with insufficient oversight the very securities whose collapse had nearly brought the global financial system to a dead stop seemed worrisome. A study published in 2011 by the National Bureau of Economic Research concluded that those firms involved in the greatest risk-taking leading up to the crisis were among the most active in lobbying for the bailout program Congress passed and benefited the most from it.[16]

Congressional action on financial reform once again brought interest groups into the mix. According to a Politico report in 2010, "Wall Street has dramatically expanded its influence on Capitol Hill over the past year, using a lobbying army that includes nearly 1,500 former federal employees and 73 former members of Congress who have been deployed during debate on financial reform legislation. . . . 'Wall Street hires former members of Congress and their staff for a reason,' said Public Citizen Congress Watch Director David Arkush, 'These people are influential because they have personal relationships with current members and staff. It's hard to say no to your friends.'"[17]

WHAT HAVE I LEARNED?

1. Mortgage-backed securities (MBSs) contributed to the 2008 financial crisis because _____.

   a. they allowed fewer Americans to buy homes in the years leading up to it

   b. they prevented financial firms from entering the mortgage market

   c. many financial firms had made increasingly riskier bets using them

   d. excessive regulation of them harmed financial firms

2. Why were many ordinary Americans unhappy with the government's response to the financial crisis?

3. What other groups of Americans might have had an interest in the government's response to the crisis?

Answer Key: 1. c; 2. Answers might indicate that many Americans felt it was unfair to use taxpayer money to bail out financial firms in crisis due to their own mistakes and greed; 3. Answers might include homeowners or individuals threatened with unemployment as the crisis unfolded.

AMERICANS FACE CHALLENGES IN ACTING COLLECTIVELY IN A REPRESENTATIVE DEMOCRACY

- Summarize the challenges associated with interest group activity.

As we have seen with our story about the Wall Street bailout, groups of people acting on behalf of different interests engaged in efforts to get the policies they preferred adopted and to make their points of view heard. Their efforts require massive coordination, however. How do such groups form in the first place? On what basis might they make their claims? Regardless of their differences, members of voluntary associations do share some common traits. Their rights to organize and press their claims upon government are protected in the Constitution, specifically in the First Amendment's restrictions on Congress's ability to impinge upon free expression: "Congress shall make no law . . . abridging the freedom of speech . . . or the right of the people peaceably to assemble, and to petition the Government for a redress of grievances."

In exercising these fundamental rights, people create what James Madison described in *Federalist* No. 10 as a faction: a group of individuals, large or small, who come together to get what they want out of the political process. Madison recognized that factions were potentially dangerous. Their actions risk trampling upon the rights of others or damaging the political community as a whole. Yet, paradoxically, the freedoms protected under the Constitution virtually guarantee the formation of factions. We can eliminate faction at its source, Madison argued, but only by preventing individuals from coming together, speaking, writing, and pressing their government to address their concerns. While effective, such restrictions upon liberty go against the very principles of a representative democracy. If you have freedom, Madison concluded, you will have faction. The challenge is not how to eliminate it but how to make sure that no one faction can do too much damage.

Madison developed a theory as to how the effects of faction would be moderated in an extended republic. He believed many factions would compete with each other in the large political space of the American Republic, making any one faction less of a danger to the nation as a whole. Given that so many competing factions would all fight to achieve their goals in a system that allowed each a voice, the most dangerous consequences of their inevitable formation could be contained.

But . . . can they *really* be contained? In the history of the American Republic, and, for certain, with regard to the financial crisis of the twenty-first century and the federal government's response to it, no question has been more important or more controversial.

THEORIES OF INTEREST GROUP FORMATION FOCUS ON THE CHALLENGES OF FACTION

In Frenchman Alexis de Tocqueville's *Democracy in America,* his book recounting his observations while traveling the country from 1831 to 1832, Tocqueville famously called America a "nation of joiners," so struck was he by the passion with which Americans made use of the "powerful instrument" of association.[18] His idea of a nation of joiners is a compelling one, provoking us to address some key questions. Who joins? What does it mean to join? What do people get from joining? And, most crucially, are the opportunities to join—and the results of doing so—equally effective for all Americans?[19]

One of the primary and enduring causes of faction is inequality of wealth. James Madison wrote, "The most common and durable source of factions, has been the various and unequal distribution of property. Those who hold, and those who are without property, have ever formed distinct interests in society."[20] Nearly two centuries later, political scientist Robert Dahl confronted the same basic problem: "How does a 'democratic' system work amid an inequality of resources?"[21] Drawing upon Madison's theory of the extended republic, Dahl explored the theory of **pluralism**, in which the distribution of political power—unequal as it may be—among many competing groups serves to keep any one of them in check. Such a widely contested and competitive political space also gives groups that might otherwise be excluded an entry into the political process, helping to ensure the representation of the interests of the less powerful—although not their success.

Not all of Dahl's contemporaries agreed with his pluralist framework or its optimistic conclusion that democratic societies can function effectively despite the presence of inequality of resources and wealth. The debate continues today. In contrast to pluralist perspectives, **elitist theory** focuses on the advantages that certain interests have in the political process based on the unequal distribution of economic and political power. For C. Wright Mills, writing in 1956, a **power elite** composed of the top echelons of people in the business world, government, and military could "look down upon . . . and by their decisions mightily affect, the everyday worlds of ordinary men and women."[22] To Mills, the nation's defense industry and its allies in government posed the greatest danger. Many Americans in the twenty-first century would add the nation's financial firms to a list of power elites.

In his study, Mills also noted that the exercise of power may be seen not only in those actions that are taken but also in inaction or in preventing actions to which the elites are opposed. A few years later, E. E. Schattschneider explored the ways in which elites used power to shut down opposition, including preventing organization from happening in the first place, preventing ideas from being discussed at all, and exercising power to keep certain ideas off the **policy agenda**, which is the set of issues to which policymakers attend.[23] These debates were not settled in the 1960s, and they still have not been. While some scholars point to the dominance of business- and corporate-focused interest groups in campaign contributions (as we will see below), others point out that elite-oriented interest groups are often competing against each other.

pluralism
a theory of governmental influence that views the distribution of political power among many competing groups as serving to keep any one of them in check.

elitist theory
a theory of governmental influence that focuses on the advantages that certain interests have in the political process based on the unequal distribution of economic and political power.

power elite
a group composed of the top echelons of people in the business world, government, and military.

policy agenda
the set of issues to which government officials, voters, and the public attend.

▼ FIGURE 11.2

How Americans Join

Where Do People Volunteer?

Participation Rates by State

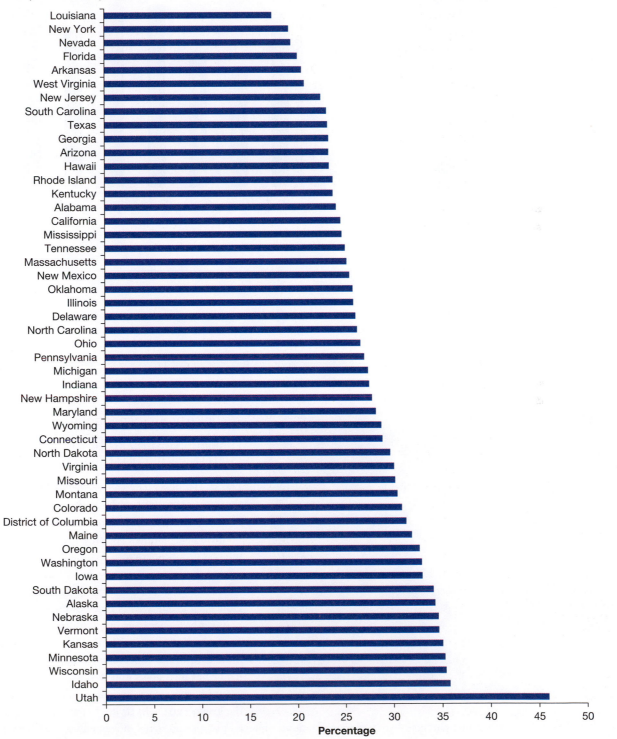

(Continued)

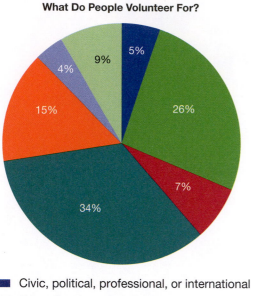

What Do People Volunteer For?

- 5%
- 26%
- 7%
- 34%
- 15%
- 4%
- 9%

Who Volunteers?

■ Civic, political, professional, or international
■ Educational or youth service
■ Hospital or other health
■ Religious
■ Social or community service
■ Sport, hobby, cultural or arts
■ Other

Source: Data from Corporation for National and Community Service, "National–Volunteer Activities," accessed June 11, 2018, https://data.nationalservice.gov/National-Service/National-Volunteer-Activities/pz9s-gsz3.

THEORIES OF INTEREST GROUP FORMATION ALSO EXPLORE THE CHALLENGES OF COLLECTIVE ACTION

David Truman's *The Governmental Process* is one of the most important early works that systematically examines the dynamics of interest groups in American political life.[24] While exploring the pluralist theory of interest group operation, Truman's study also highlighted the fact that interest groups can wield a considerable amount of power in American political life. How each group wields that power—and how much power it has—depends upon organization within the group itself. Interest groups, after all, are not monolithic entities but collections of individuals, each with his or her own goals and desires. Successful interest groups harness those energies and direct them toward the group's goals. In trying to do so, however, leaders and members of voluntary associations—interest groups and social movements alike—have to overcome challenges to successful organization and coordination.

In getting organized and acting for the interests of their members, advocates for American financial firms and (as we shall see) the members of OWS both had to contend with one similar basic challenge, that of **collective action**—getting individuals to contribute their energy, time, or money to a larger group goal. However, the members of these two voluntary associations did not necessarily solve

▲ A businessman, likely someone Mills would have characterized as a member of the power elite, walks by the Bank of New York in Midtown Manhattan, which is home to many of the world's banks, in April 2009.

Jeff Hutchens/Getty Images

this problem in the same way. Differences in size, wealth, and political power all shape the strategies available to the leaders of voluntary associations as they try to overcome the challenges of collective action.

Economist Mancur Olson developed one of the most influential theories of the logic of interest group participation, or, more precisely, the logic of choosing *not* to participate. According to Olson, "rational, self-interested individuals will not act to achieve their common or group interests . . . unless there is coercion to force them to do so, or unless some separate incentive, distinct from the achievement of the common or group interest, is offered to the members of the group individually on the condition that they help bear the costs or burdens involved in the achievement of group objectives."[25]

A key concept in this framework is the **collective good** (also called a public good), which is some benefit or desirable outcome that individuals can enjoy or profit from even if they do not help achieve or secure it.[26] The problem with collective goods comes from the fact that people can enjoy their benefits without contributing to their provision. Since, in this framework, individuals are completely rational with how they allocate their

Mike Baldwin/CartoonStock.com

▲ A political cartoon illustrating the concept of free riding. The character who is hitchhiking is taking advantage of the character creating the wheel.

time, energy, and resources, there is no incentive for them to help out, as they know they will receive the benefits of others' efforts. A strong national defense, clean air, or a really nice fireworks display may all be thought of as examples of collective goods. Those individuals who enjoy collective goods without help to secure them are called **free riders**, and they pose a serious challenge to the efforts of any voluntary association to work toward collective goals. Note that free riders are acting rationally in this framework. Based upon a pure cost-benefit logic, individuals should "free ride" and devote their energies elsewhere, knowing that others will make up for their inaction.

In the absence of some way to force individuals to contribute, therefore, public goods will be underprovided. Taxes, laws, and other forms of coercion are tools that governments use to overcome the challenges of public goods provision.[27] Voluntary associations of individuals, however, do not generally have the coercive power of government behind them, yet people still join and contribute, even at great personal cost and risk. Why? One explanation, which Olson discussed, is that a given group might be small and homogenous enough that the payoffs for individual participation and the collective risks of nonparticipation are obviously clear and compelling.

Other explanations for how interest groups can overcome the challenges of collective action focus on the incentives such groups offer to individuals to join or contribute.[28] These inducements may include **selective benefits**, which are made available only to those who join or contribute to the group. One set of selective benefits is **material rewards**, which may include discounts on goods and services, access to group publications and information, special offers, travel opportunities, or a host of other tangible benefits available only to members and contributors. AARP (formerly known as the American Association of Retired Persons) is widely known for the material benefits it provides its members. Professional associations or trade unions may provide their members with the credentials needed to operate in their profession, as is the case for state bar associations and regulation of the practice of law, or achieve for their members higher wages or better benefits, as may be the case for trade unions.

collective action
political action that occurs when individuals contribute their energy, time, or money to a larger group goal.

collective good
also called a public good; some benefit or desirable outcome that individuals can enjoy or profit from even if they do not help achieve or secure it.

free riders
individuals who enjoy collective goods without helping to secure them.

selective benefits
goods that are made available only to those who join or contribute to a group.

material rewards
a type of tangible benefit made available to members and contributors of a group.

Other rewards that may be available only as a result of participation are **social benefits**, which might allow members to network with other individuals with similar interests and goals. Social benefits may come in the form of personal relationships and the benefits individuals attach to forming such relationships for their own sake, or they may take the form of job opportunities and other avenues for personal advancement. A third set of selective benefits arises from the satisfaction of working with others to achieve a common goal or purpose. For this reason, these inducements are referred to as **purposive benefits**.

WHAT HAVE I **LEARNED?**

1. James Madison formulated the theory of _____, whereby many factions would compete with each other in the large political space of the American Republic.

   a. the extended republic

   b. elitist politics

   c. representative democracy

   d. social movements

2. Collective action is _____.

   a. when individuals contribute their time and energy to an effort

   b. rarely successful

   c. when opposing sides agree on a middle ground

   d. easier when the group has diverse goals

3. What kinds of things do interest groups do to overcome the challenges of collective action?

   _____

   Answer Key: 1. a; 2. a; 3. Answers should include concepts such as selective, material, social, and purposive benefits.

INTEREST GROUPS VARY BY TYPE AND TACTIC

- Discuss the types of interest groups in the American political landscape and the different tactics they use.

While representatives from Wall Street firms mobilized in force during and after the financial crisis, they were not the only ones acting. Other interest groups advocated as well, although many of their members were less connected to the corridors of political power than the titans of the American financial services industry. AARP, for example, argued that in the wake of the crisis, "the social safety net needs to be strengthened and extended. Workers should not have to worry about losing their health and pension benefits when they lose a job."[29] In this section, we will explore the landscape of interest groups in the United States and the varied tactics they use to advance their members' goals.

Americans with a wide variety of political goals join, hire, or support interest groups in order to make their wishes known. Interest groups are often categorized and analyzed according to the broader goals they set out to achieve and for which they are advocating. Though scholars differ on specific classification schemes, the central idea is to examine what kinds of benefits the groups are seeking.

Economic interest groups, as their name implies, advocate on behalf of the economic interests of their members. These groups form the largest category of interest groups and are responsible for the largest amount of campaign donations. Within the category of economic interest groups, the largest and generally most influential subcategory is business groups, which advocate for the policies that favor their particular firms or industries. Labor groups, such as trade unions, advocate on behalf of the workers they represent. Finally, farm groups have a long historical tradition of acting in American politics on behalf of farmers.

In contrast, **public interest groups** act on behalf of the collective interests of a broad group of individuals—many of whom may not be members or contributors to the organization. Groups

social benefits
rewards in the form of new connections or access to networks that members of a group receive through their participation.

purposive benefits
rewards in the form of satisfaction from working with others to achieve a common goal or purpose.

economic interest groups
groups that organize to advocate on behalf of the economic interests of their members.

public interest groups
groups that act on behalf of the collective interests of a broad group of individuals, many of whom may not be members or contributors to the organization.

2016 CAMPAIGN CONTRIBUTIONS BY ECONOMIC SECTOR

The OpenSecrets.org project by the independent nonprofit Center for Responsive Politics collects, analyzes, and shares data on money, lobbying, politics, and elections. The center focuses a considerable amount of its efforts on tracking reportable campaign contributions. The figure that follows presents the total amounts of campaign contributions in the 2016 election cycle reported to the Federal Election Commission (FEC), broken down by sector of the economy. It includes contributions from individuals (of $200 or more) and PACs as well as contributions given to super PACs and other groups.

As is clear in the figure, the finance/insurance/real estate sector accounted for the single largest group of contributions. Contributions were dominated by economic sectors; however, interest groups and individuals within

the labor sector as well as those representing single-issue groups also made significant campaign contributions. Note also that the relative allocation of sector donations to Democratic and Republican candidates varied considerably.

WHAT Do You Think?

Why might these groups and individuals have allocated their contributions across the two major political parties in the way that they did? What strategic choices might have been involved in these decisions? What other campaign contribution data would you like to analyze in order to assess the landscape of interest group involvement in American campaigns and elections?

Reportable Campaign Contributions by Economic Sector, 2016

Rank	Sector	Amount	To Candidates/Parties	Dems	Repubs
1	Finance, Insurance, Real Estate	$1,113,153,986	$605,868,478	46.00%	53.80%
2	Other	$750,993,365	$640,705,722	59.30%	40.30%
3	Ideology, Single-Issue	$591,281,521	$375,843,951	62.50%	37.30%
4	Miscellaneous Business	$488,166,461	$345,358,362	45.50%	54.10%
5	Communications and Electronics	$323,490,793	$208,774,756	70.60%	29.00%
6	Health	$280,567,527	$204,229,964	51.80%	47.90%
7	Lawyers and Lobbyists	$258,024,696	$242,876,443	70.70%	29.00%
8	Labor	$217,046,189	$67,341,173	87.90%	12.00%
9	Energy and Natural Resources	$172,056,686	$114,641,434	22.90%	77.00%
10	Construction	$130,003,469	$87,354,036	31.10%	68.60%
11	Agribusiness	$116,049,429	$85,126,680	26.40%	73.00%
12	Transportation	$92,771,145	$75,053,758	30.40%	69.40%
13	Defense	$29,712,984	$28,130,772	39.40%	60.30%

Source: Center for Responsive Politics, "Totals by Sector," OpenSecrets.org, accessed June 11, 2018, https://www.opensecrets.org/overview/sectors.php?cycle=2016.

Note: Percentages may not add up to 100 percent, as money can be given to third-party candidates and party committees.

▲ This political cartoon depicts the perception that Wall Street's contributions to the federal government give its "elite" members undue political influence. The title "Occupy D.C." is a reference to the Occupy Wall Street (OWS) movement.

advocating in the areas of civil rights, civil liberties, social welfare, education, or the environment are all examples of public interest groups. Many of these associations focus on one specific area of public policy and are, therefore, often called single-issue groups. A key subcategory of public interest groups advocates for their members with regard to issues of identity and lived experiences. The actions of the National Association for the Advancement of Colored People (NAACP) in challenging legal segregation, of the National Organization for Women (NOW) on behalf of gender equality, and of groups acting to secure marriage equality are all examples of public interest groups whose efforts you may be familiar with.

Finally, **governmental interest groups** act on behalf of state, regional, local, or even foreign governments to keep their members apprised of policy discussions; weigh in on the regulatory process; and generally act on behalf of the relevant government, especially during the appropriations process in Congress, which we will explore in detail in the next chapter.

"INSIDE" INTEREST GROUPS LOBBY TO INFLUENCE POLICYMAKING

All interest groups share the same ultimate goal: to influence public policy on the ground. To do so, they may try to influence any one stage of the policymaking process at the federal, state, or local level.

When one pictures organized interest group activity, one of the first things that often comes to mind is the act of **lobbying**, or interacting with government officials to advance a group's goals in the area of public policy. Lobbying in America is as old as the Republic itself. The stereotypical idea of lobbying is often of powerful interest group members contacting members of Congress and pressuring them to act on the group's behalf. Though that may be part of the story, lobbying is actually a much more complex and nuanced process. In the first place, interest group members lobby all three branches of the federal government, not just Congress, though the tactics they use may vary depending on which branch is being lobbied. Second, even when they do approach Congress, lobbyists' tactics are varied and complicated and often focus as much on providing information to representatives, senators, and congressional staff members as they do on pushing for a specific position directly.

Rather than being a single effort, lobbying is most accurately thought of as an ongoing process, in which a lobbyist "seldom does only one specific thing at one specific time . . . but multiple things over a period of time."[30] It may involve efforts to shape policy across all three branches; legislative lobbying seeks to influence how legislation is written, executive branch lobbying focuses on how these laws are implemented, and judicial lobbying centers on how the laws are interpreted.

TODAY'S LOBBYISTS ARE PROFESSIONALS. The First Amendment to the Constitution guarantees the right of any citizen to lobby—"to petition the Government for a redress of grievances." Modern lobbying, however, is very much a professional undertaking. It involves large numbers of people and a lot of money. The Center for Responsive Politics calculated that in 2017, more than 11,542 paid lobbyists spent a total of $3.37 billion lobbying Congress and federal agencies.[31] As these figures are based only on registered lobbyist activities, however, they understate the actual numbers of total activity, both in the number of lobbyists and in the amount of money they spent (see Figure 11.3).

Successful lobbyists must be able to provide a service to their clients, the people and firms that hire and pay them. To do so effectively, lobbyists need solid, useful knowledge about the particular policy

governmental interest groups
organizations that act to secure the interests of local, state, or foreign governments in the political process.

lobbying
interacting with government officials to advance a group's goals in the area of public policy.

Lobbying by the Numbers

Total Lobbying Spending (in billions of U.S. dollars)	
1998	$1.45
1999	$1.44
2000	$1.57
2001	$1.63
2002	$1.83
2003	$2.06
2004	$2.19
2005	$2.44
2006	$2.63
2007	$2.87
2008	$3.30
2009	$3.50
2010	$3.52
2011	$3.33
2012	$3.31
2013	$3.24
2014	$3.25
2015	$3.22
2016	$3.15
2017	$3.37

Number of Lobbyists	
1998	10,405
1999	12,926
2000	12,541
2001	11,826
2002	12,118
2003	12,919
2004	13,168
2005	14,074
2006	14,482
2007	14,827
2008	14,157
2009	13,751
2010	12,932
2011	12,622
2012	12,185
2013	12,116
2014	11,824
2015	11,520
2016	11,175
2017	11,529

Source: Center for Responsive Politics, "Lobbying Database," OpenSecrets.org, accessed May 5, 2018, https://www.opensecrets.org/lobby.

area and the ability to be heard by those in government. For this reason, former government officials are often in high demand by lobbying firms. And government agencies themselves may recruit individuals from lobbying firms and the private sector for their experience and expertise. The movement of individuals between government and lobbying positions is called the **revolving door phenomenon**. Those who argue that the revolving door is a good thing point to benefits that agencies receive from the experience of former lobbyists and argue that effective lobbying depends on the kind of knowledge and experience that former government officials can bring to the table. Others, however, have raised concerns about the degree to which those groups capable of paying high prices for well-connected lobbyists tilt public policy in favor of the wealthy and powerful.

Members of interest groups know that their organizations are not all created equally with regard to their wealth, political clout, and access to powerful governmental officials. As such, they may modify their particular lobbying strategies to make the best use of the resources and advantages they have. Consideration of whether or not all these strategies are equally effective, however, also raises questions about the degree to which Americans are fairly and competently represented . . . or represented at all.

LOBBYISTS INFLUENCE LEGISLATION IN CONGRESS. Because it writes the nation's laws, Congress is a natural target for lobbyists, who employ several strategies in their efforts to influence legislation. One method, and the one that many people think of when they think of the term *lobbying*, is when

revolving door phenomenon the movement of individuals between government and lobbying positions.

Where Do "Revolving Door" People Go after Working for the Government?

One of the databases maintained and published by the Center for Responsive Politics is "The Revolving Door," a door, the website's editors note, "that shuttles former federal employees into jobs as lobbyists, consultants and strategists just as the door pulls former hired guns into government careers."

Profiling what many call "revolving door people," the table shows the top organizations hiring people who have come from government, excluding lobbying firms themselves.

Organization	Number of "Revolving Door" Employees
U.S. Chamber of Commerce	123
National Association of Manufacturers	59
Goldman Sachs	49
Pharmaceutical Research & Manufacturers of America	48
Lockheed Martin	47
General Electric	47
Boeing Co.	45
Center for American Progress	43
AT&T Inc.	40
Citigroup Management Corp.	37
American Petroleum Institute	37
Biotechnology Industry Organization	36
National Federation of Independent Business	36
Fannie Mae	33
American Medical Association	33
George Washington University	32
Raytheon	32
Mortgage Bankers Association	32
Microsoft Corp.	32
National Association of Broadcasters	31

Of the top twenty firms listed, note that four are financial firms or organizations involved in the mortgage industry (Goldman Sachs, Citigroup, Fannie Mae, and the Mortgage Bankers Association).

Source: Center for Responsive Politics, "Top Lobbying Firms," OpenSecrets.org, accessed June 11, 2018, http://www.opensecrets.org/revolving/top.php?display=F.

inside lobbying
when lobbyists contact members of Congress or their staff directly to advocate for their group's position.

lobbyists contact members of Congress or their staff directly to advocate for their group's position. This kind of direct contact is an example of **inside lobbying**, and it takes many forms, which is not surprising given how complex the legislative process is.

In addition to direct contact with representatives, senators, and congressional staff members, lobbyists may prepare research reports and briefs, work to shape the legislative agenda by bringing more attention to their issues of interest, or help coordinate a legislative strategy on an issue.[32] These efforts may focus on the content of a piece of legislation and also on the levels of funding for agencies and programs though the appropriations process. Lobbyists may try to influence the total amount of funding available to an agency, spending priorities within that agency, earmarks for specific projects, or riders to appropriations bills, which may specify how money *cannot* be spent and are often a powerful weapon in shaping the implementation of the laws that Congress passes.[33] Successful inside lobbying often depends on personal relationships, access to decision makers, and financial resources—something not all interest groups possess. Much of the power of inside lobbying, however, also relies on the provision of useful and timely information, such as research that might save a congressional staff valuable time, specific language or wording that may shape or find its way into a bill, or studies that convincingly portray the group's position as one that a member's constituents care about and agree with. Testifying at committee or subcommittee hearings and providing members of Congress with research reports and summaries are two common ways interest groups use information to try to advance their positions.

LOBBYISTS INFLUENCE EXECUTIVE BRANCH IMPLEMENTATION. From the point of view of interest groups and their lobbyists, winning or losing the battle in Congress is only part of the war. As it is tasked with executing the laws that Congress writes—shaping legislation through the process of implementation—the executive branch also finds itself the target of lobbying efforts. Congress cannot account for every detail within the policy areas covered by its laws. Some flexibility needs to be built in to allow for effective implementation, and legislators eyeing reelection may prefer not to specify certain provisions in too much detail. In trying to influence the appropriations process in Congress, members of organized interest groups try to shape the implementation of the laws by the executive branch. In some cases, they do so directly by lobbying the president (or, more realistically, members of his or her executive staff) or members of the federal bureaucracy.

Federal law requires executive branch agencies to notify the public and solicit its input when establishing rules and procedures, an opening into which organized interests happily step.[34] The detailed nature of most proposed legislation provides an advantage to interest groups armed with data and knowledge of the minutiae of the legislation and the affected policy.[35] Interest groups may work to increase the prominence of their goals in the executive branch agenda, and they may also use the courts to challenge federal rules to which they are opposed.

Closely connected to the idea of the revolving door is the risk of **agency capture** (also called regulatory capture), in which those agencies tasked with regulating businesses, industries, or other interest groups are populated by individuals with close ties to the very firms they are supposed to regulate. This can result in ineffective oversight or regulatory actions that favor the firms over the general interests of society or those not so strongly represented.[36]

LOBBYISTS INFLUENCE JUDICIAL ACTIONS.

Interest groups and their lobbyists may also try to shape how the nation's laws are interpreted by targeting the federal judiciary. As the thought of a lobbyist badgering an individual member of the Supreme Court about a group's position seems somehow unseemly and, depending on the justice, might actually backfire, groups generally use other methods to try to shape the activities of the federal judiciary, especially the Supreme Court.

Interest groups may try to influence judicial appointments, either through the presidential nomination or Senate confirmation process. Given the importance of the federal judiciary and its influence over a host of issues, interest groups often have a very strong desire to shape the appointment process. In the heated weeks leading up to the confirmation of Brett Kavanaugh as Supreme Court justice, senators were on the receiving end of hundreds of thousands of dollars of interest group pressure, especially moderate Republicans who had expressed concerns about the sexual assault allegations against him.

The Supreme Court has two decisions to make on each case that comes before it: whether or not to hear the case and how to rule should it decide to hear it. Interest groups may try to influence each of these decisions, typically by filing amicus curiae briefs, which describe a group's position and the arguments for it. As one scholar put it, "although they were originally envisioned as a 'friend of the Court' and neutral toward the parties, amici are now more appropriately viewed as friends of the participants to the litigation."[37] There is evidence that a high number of amici can increase the chances that justices will hear a case,[38] though some scholars have pointed out that this does not necessarily mean that interest groups have any particular advantage when it comes time for the Court to rule on the merits of the case.[39]

Interest groups may sponsor litigation, guiding a case through the judiciary, but this is an expensive and time-consuming task, even when it goes well. In the 1950s, the Legal Defense Fund of the NAACP undertook a lengthy, expensive, and risky strategy in trying to use the federal judiciary to bring an end to legal segregation in the United States. To do so, the group had to find individuals willing to bring suits in court, which could, and did, subject many of them to physical and economic violence. The litigators and staff of the Legal Defense Fund also had to conduct the research and legal analysis that formed the bases of these lawsuits, which was also a personally risky undertaking.

LOBBYING ACTIVITIES ARE REGULATED.

Given the potential influence of lobbyists on shaping public policy, it is not surprising that attempts have been made over the years to regulate their activities. This is not, however, a simple task. First, the Constitution protects the fundamental rights of interest groups to act on their members' behalf, which includes lobbying activities. Second, there are incentives for members of Congress not to overregulate these activities, since representatives and senators may benefit from the information and campaign support that interest groups provide. Most recent efforts to regulate lobbying have focused on making the process more transparent.

INTEREST GROUPS EXERT INFLUENCE THROUGH WEBS AND NETWORKS.

One of the classic, and worrisome, depictions of the connections between interest groups and government is the **iron triangle** (see Figure 11.4). As the term suggests, the iron triangle consists of three parts—interest groups, Congress, and the bureaucracy—each of which works with the other two to achieve their shared policy goals, even if achieving those goals runs counter to the general interests of society or specific groups within it. In doing so, the members of the triangle act as factions, each helping the other two members and receiving benefits from doing so.

Interest groups provide electoral support to members of Congress, who use their influence, especially on committees and subcommittees, to advance legislation favorable to the interest groups and reduce oversight of interest group activities. These same interest groups lobby on behalf of the relevant

agency capture
when agencies tasked with regulating businesses, industries, or other interest groups are populated by individuals with close ties to the very firms they are supposed to regulate.

iron triangle
the coordinated (and mutually beneficial) activities of interest groups, Congress, and the bureaucracy to achieve shared policy goals, sometimes against the general interests of society or specific groups within it.

The Iron Triangle

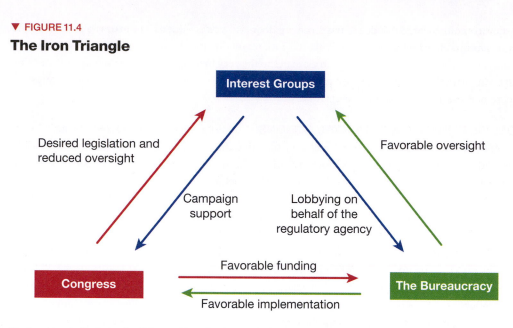

The iron triangle illustrates the linkage of benefits that each of the three members provide to the other two. While all members help each other, it is their common interest in the overall policy goal that drives individual decisions.

bureaucratic agencies to secure the agencies' desired funding and policy goals. In return, the agencies conduct their job of regulation in ways favorable to interest group objectives. Finally, members of Congress determine funding levels and pass legislation desired by the bureaucratic agencies, which, in turn, implement the laws passed by Congress in ways desired by those members of Congress.

Due to the growth in the number of interest groups and an increasingly fluid and complex policy landscape in recent decades, political scientists have employed the concept of the **issue network** to describe the webs of influence among interest groups, policymakers, and policy advocates. In contrast to iron triangles, issue networks are often temporary, arising to address a specific policy problem. Any one issue may give rise to competing issue networks, each of which advocates on a different side of the issue. In this way, issue networks are closer to the idea of pluralism than iron triangles.

INTEREST GROUPS ARE INVOLVED IN ELECTION-RELATED ACTIVITIES. Interest groups are often heavily involved in the electoral process. First, and perhaps foremost, their participation revolves around the targeted distribution of financial resources. Money is a powerful strategic tool, as it can fund media coverage, a solid ground campaign, and research. Money can also act as a weapon to discourage others from even running for election. Campaigns are often won or lost long before the actual vote. If a candidate can signal to potential opponents that they will be facing a formidable and well-funded foe, then savvy would-be competitors may very well wait until conditions are more favorable for a realistic run; no serious potential challenger wants to wage a hopeless campaign. Serious challengers are smart and patient; they wait if they have to.

How and under what conditions interest groups contribute to political campaigns is often determined by the status under which they file with the Internal Revenue Service (IRS). Those classified, for example, as 501(c)(3) organizations, whose contributions are tax deductible, face defined rules on the amounts that they may contribute and on the activities toward which those funds may be deployed. Political action committees (PACs) may spend more money on campaigns than individuals and may solicit funds from their members to do so, but they also operate with limits. Following an important Supreme Court decision in 2010, American politics has seen the emergence and rapid rise of the so-called super PAC, which is allowed to raise and spend money without financial limits but only in ways that are uncoordinated with a campaign itself.[40]

Efforts to regulate interest group spending on campaigns and elections are ongoing and not always successful. In addition to financial contributions and spending, interest groups also try to influence

issue network
the webs of influence among interest groups, policymakers, and policy advocates.

electoral outcomes by mobilizing voters through get out the vote (GOTV) campaigns and by recruiting and endorsing candidates.

GRASSROOTS LOBBYING AND POLITICAL PROTESTERS ACT FROM "OUTSIDE" TO INFLUENCE POLICY

Interest groups that attempt to represent less powerful constituencies often have to use a different set of tactics than those available to the better-funded and better-connected groups. They also aim to change public policy, but they often face different challenges and have to adjust accordingly. Their members generally consist of a diverse group of previously immobilized and possibly unorganized individuals. Problems associated with collective action and the dangers of free riding are often of more concern to such groups.

These less powerful groups may engage in **outside (grassroots) lobbying**, which focuses on reaching constituents and mobilizing them to pressure their representatives rather than pressuring the representatives directly. A group may decide that outside lobbying is its best course of action, or it may have no other choice and have to use this tactic "out of desperation when an 'inside' strategy has failed."[41] Using outside lobbying tactics is also referred to as grassroots lobbying.

In some cases, when grassroots support does not really exist, or would not exist if it hadn't been "purchased" by a lobbying firm, an interest group will present the facade of grassroots support. This is referred to as **Astroturf lobbying**; the term alludes to the fact that the "grassroots" drawn upon are made out of fake grass and thus do not reflect genuine public support. While Astroturf lobbying is widely criticized, the lines between genuine grassroots support and Astroturf lobbying may not always be entirely clear. As political scientist Ken Kollman has questioned, "if two interest groups mobilize the same number of people to contact Congress, but one of them relies on volunteers and its own members and the other pays a consulting house to generate telephone calls and letters, who is to say which is real and which is artificial?"[42] Astroturf lobbying can be effective, and according to political scientist Kenneth Goldstein, its increasing use may be contributing to a new wave of citizen participation that would not exist if not for the fact that "interest groups and lobbying firms inside the beltway are increasingly utilizing new and sophisticated techniques to water the grass roots outside the beltway."[43]

INTEREST GROUPS FACE CHALLENGES IN REPRESENTATION

Writing in the 1960s, Grant McConnell pointed out that corporations and private interest groups do not rule themselves democratically and that there are far fewer protections provided within them than those afforded to citizens.[44] McConnell's critique of the exercise of power within interest groups also raises questions about representation within social movements themselves—even those that attempt to speak for the less powerful.

In recent decades, political scientists have come back to the questions of power and representation raised by scholars such as Robert Dahl, C. Wright Mills, and E. E. Schattschneider. They have done so often empirically, using the tools of quantitative analysis to get a better understanding of the dynamics of representation among and within interest groups. In general, in spite of a proliferation of groups and movements devoted to the less well-represented members of society, such as minorities, women, and the elderly, much of the evidence points to a continuation of overrepresentation of the elite, powerful, and wealthy.

Exploring data involving nearly seven thousand interest groups, political scientist Kay Lehman Schlozman concluded that in spite of the growth of public interest groups since the 1960s, business and commerce interest groups still account for the majority of associations, a fact that she attributes to their staying power in the face of all the pressures on a group to maintain its membership and influence.[45] Political scientist Dara Strolovitch concluded that even in interest groups devoted to representing more marginalized members of American society, the relatively better-advantaged members within those groups receive more attention and political effort.[46]

outside (grassroots) lobbying
a type of lobbying that focuses on reaching constituents and mobilizing them to pressure their representatives rather than pressuring the representatives directly.

Astroturf lobbying
when a group presents the facade of grassroots support that does not exist on its own or would not exist without the "purchase" of support by the lobbying firm itself.

OCCUPY WALL STREET ILLUSTRATES THE STRUGGLES, SUCCESSES, AND FAILURES OF SOCIAL MOVEMENTS

- **Explore the efforts of Occupy Wall Street to understand the challenges individuals face and the strategies they employ to make social and political changes.**

In September 2011, almost three years after the financial collapse, about a thousand people gathered in New York's Zuccotti Park, just blocks from Wall Street and the New York Stock Exchange in lower Manhattan, to protest against the concentration of wealth at the very top of American society and what they saw as a deep and structural lack of fairness, made far worse by the bailout of Wall Street. This disparate and evolving group of protesters became known as Occupy Wall Street, or OWS; the movement's message, one fueled by disillusionment and frustration, eventually spread around the globe via strategic use of social media.

Many observers attribute the origins of OWS to a blog entry posted in July 2011 by the Canadian activist group Adbusters.[47] The founder of Adbusters, Kalle Lasn, told the press that "his group originally proposed one demand—to separate money from politics." According to an article in *the Christian Science Monitor*, "when asked . . . why it was such a slow burn for people to finally protest the financial crisis, Mr. Lasn said that it took some time for people to realize that President Obama," who was by then president, "was not handling the meltdown effectively, going so far as to call him a 'gutless wonder.'"[48]

REUTERS/Eduardo Munoz

▲ An Occupy Wall Street (OWS) activist takes part in a protest at Zuccotti Park on July 11, 2012, advocating for the right to form a social movement.

At that first protest in Zuccotti Park, about eighty individuals were arrested, mostly on charges of blocking traffic, a relatively minor offense. However, in some cases, arrests were accompanied by charges

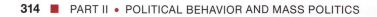

DEPICTING INCOME INEQUALITY IN THE UNITED STATES

Using data on wealth and income concentrations in the United States compiled by academic researchers, individuals with Occupy Wall Street created the following image, which found its way into major media outlets and onto T-shirts and posters.

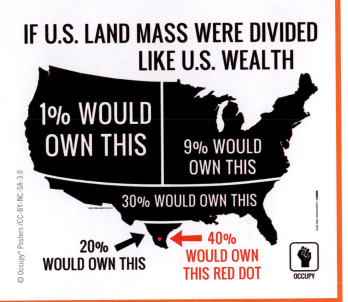

WHAT Do You Think?

How effective do you think this image is in conveying the inequality of wealth in the United States? Though the figure is based on actual data, the creator acknowledges, "I drew the lines in a somewhat impressionistic manner."[49] Does that use of creative license detract at all from the image's power? What other images might one manipulate in a similar way to communicate the central point?

of police brutality. Videos that seemed to support those charges went viral on platforms like YouTube. A few weeks later, OWS protesters marched across the Brooklyn Bridge, again leading to many arrests, hundreds this time. By this point, however, people were more aware of the movement's existence.

Those who joined OWS did so for a variety of reasons; they were not united by self-interest, as the Wall Street financial firms had been. However, their message that a small faction of the wealthiest Americans was working against the interests of everyone else caught on. According to reporter John Ennis, "'WE ARE THE 99 PERCENT' became the rallying cry of a generation. The simplicity and inclusivity of that message was worthy of the advertising gurus on Madison Avenue."[50] Early efforts of OWS barely received a mention in the nation's press. What coverage they did get was condescending and dismissive. Though protesters were generally united behind a message of income inequality, OWS as a whole struggled to further define what that message was, a common challenge for those who would start a social movement. It is a particular challenge to successfully mobilize Americans to respond to political and economic inequalities, since this depends upon communicating to them an understanding of the messy details of the workings of government. "What do you say about a financial crisis where the villains are obscure and the solutions are obscure?" wondered one critic.[51] While the media may have had a hard time figuring out what OWS was all about, the movement's members felt it was clear that something had gone wrong in the nation. The rich were getting richer, and everyone else seemed to be getting left behind. Change was needed, and Americans needed to be woken up. As Rachel Pletz, a participant in the Zuccotti Park protests who helped to organize similar efforts in Philadelphia, put it, "This is about solidarity. This is about getting people together and figuring it out. We just know something's wrong."[52]

OWS protesters did find a way to make strategic use of social media and other creative protest methods to coordinate and communicate and ultimately got attention from some high-profile celebrity activists, who also helped spread word of the cause. The OWS movement quickly went national, even international. In the first week of October, "smaller-scale protests spread . . . to Los Angeles, Chicago, Boston, Denver, Washington, Albuquerque, Portland, Maine, and several other cities. An 'Occupy Toronto' protest [was] planned in Canada."[53]

The communication tactics used by OWS were also different. As loudspeakers were prohibited in Zuccotti Park, OWS members invented a very low-tech way of communicating. Referred to as "the people's mic," it involved relaying messages through the crowd person by person: "This is how it works:

AP Photo/Bebeto Matthews

▲ John Hector, one of the relatively few people of color among Occupy Wall Street (OWS) protesters, wraps himself in a blanket against cold temperatures at the group's protest in Zuccotti Park in November 2011. "My concern is the economic situation and particularly police brutality and stop-and-frisk policies in Black and Latino communities," said Hector.

Someone screams 'mic-check' to grab everyone's attention and get the people's mic started. The speaker will then say something, for instance, 'Thank you for your patience tonight,' which the crown repeats. This goes on until the speaker is finished."[54] This was more than just a novel way to communicate; it embodied the ethos of the movement. According to Sheila Nichols, a protester in Los Angeles, "[The] people's mic forces people to be participatory, to listen, to understand that we're in it together. . . . And it's an active experience that forces people to be a part of something that's a whole."[55]

As the protests gained momentum, some critics claimed that not only did the movement fail to represent the diverse interests of its members, but also that it was actively discriminatory, especially toward the American Jewish community. In October 2011, the Republican National Committee issued a memo that "included three videos showing anti-Semitic outbursts by purported Wall Street protestors," though a spokesperson for the Anti-Defamation League countered that these outbursts were "isolated incidents."[56]

The movement was also criticized for failing to sufficiently empower members from traditionally marginalized groups or address their concerns. An article in the *New York Times* in late October 2011, for example, described a sense of alienation felt by a group of organizers from the South Bronx, an area with a high concentration of low-income individuals and those of minority ethnicity. "'Nobody looked like us,' said Rodrigo Venegas, thirty-one. 'It was white, liberal, young people who for the first time in their life are feeling a small percentage of what black and brown communities have been feeling for hundreds of years.'"[57]

Other members of minority groups concluded that a unity of voices—based not on identity but a shared struggle against those in power—might make the social movement stronger. One journalist's account is telling: "Frank Diamond, a 26-year-old-Haitian-American from Jamaica, Queens, who was holding an 'Occupy the Hood' sign at a recent rally, said that many working-class blacks who had originally watched the protests from a distance, were starting to realize they should join. 'It takes a wave to realize that the boat you have been riding is too small,' he said. 'We need to be represented here too. This is about us, too.'"[58]

On September 29, 2011, the NYC General Assembly adopted a declaration of the goals of the movement. One of many participation-based assemblies across the globe, the New York assembly operated on consensus, trying to invite as many voices as was practical into the conversation. The declaration stated that "as we gather together in solidarity to express a feeling of mass injustice, we must not lose sight of what brought us together. We write so that all people who feel wronged by the corporate forces of the world can know that we are your allies."[59] In spite of the theme of solidarity, the list of grievances in the declaration included charges against such disparate entities as Wall Street and home foreclosures, national agriculture policy, labor conditions, health care, money in politics, the death penalty, and American foreign policy.

By November 2011, New York City authorities began to clamp down, stripping the demonstrators in Zuccotti Park of their generators and fuel just as a snowstorm and cold wave "blanketed their tents and tarps with sleet and ice, and left at least one protestor hospitalized for hypothermia."[60] Less than two weeks later, Mayor Michael Bloomberg and city authorities evicted the protesters from Zuccotti Park.

Reporter Michelle Nichols described the removal: "Wearing helmets and wielding batons, New York police evicted Occupy Wall Street . . . two months after they set up camp and sparked a national movement against economic inequality. Hundreds of police dismantled the sea of tents, tarps, and outdoor furniture, mattresses and protests signs at Zuccotti Park, arresting 147 people, including about a dozen who had chained themselves to each other and to trees."[61] Other cities removed protesters as well.

By the spring of 2012, the tents had mostly disappeared from New York, Boston, Los Angeles, and other cities. Protests continued, but without the same level of media coverage. Some debated what had been accomplished. A letter to the editor of the *New York Times* framed the question not in terms of what OWS should do but what America should do, asking, "What will they do now? That question misses the point. Whether the 99 percenters retake Zuccotti Park in New York isn't the issue. The question we should be asking ourselves is, What will we do now? The American democracy—our system of capitalism and free markets, the electoral system and tax policies—has been distorted by moneyed interests. Our challenge is to revive America as a land of equal opportunity."[62]

Other observers had a very different set of suggestions for the movement's leaders. According to one reporter, "many pundits suggest that it's time for the activists to hire political consultants and assemble a list of demands—in short, to become much more involved in electoral politics."[63] It was time, in other words, for OWS to stop trying to form a social movement and become an interest group.

WHAT HAVE I **LEARNED?**

1. Which of the following issues do you think might by closest to Occupy Wall Street's *primary* agenda?

   a. Health care

   b. Immigration

   c. Education

   d. Student loan debt

2. Financial industry insiders headed straight to Washington, DC, when the economy looked like it was about to collapse. Occupy Wall Street headed to Zuccotti Park in lower Manhattan as it mobilized to protest. Why?

3. Do you think Occupy Wall Street achieved its goals? Why or why not?

Answer Key: 1. d; 2. Answers might include a realistic assessment of the tactics most suited to the groups' different resources; 3. Answers should discuss how one should measure the success or failure of a nascent social movement and give specific examples, such as how OWS did or did not change policy or the national conversation.

SOCIAL MOVEMENTS EMPLOY DIFFERENT TACTICS FROM INTEREST GROUPS TO MAKE CHANGE AND EDUCATE

- Analyze the tactics social movements use to advocate on their members' behalf and contrast them with those of interest groups.

American political history teaches us that social movements can achieve major policy changes over time: the civil rights movement and the struggle for the rights of women; African Americans; disabled Americans; and lesbian, gay, bisexual, and transgender (LGBT) Americans are all widely acknowledged as social movements that have had significant impact. Though their specific goals were different, those groups often employed similar tactics.

They used **protest**, a public demonstration designed to call attention to the need for action or change. As part of these protests, some members engaged in civil disobedience, the intentional breaking of a law for the purpose of calling attention to an injustice. Protest and civil disobedience can be powerful and effective tactics, especially in altering the political agenda—placing an injustice front and center on the national stage and forcing people to confront it. Both of these tactics are risky, however, not only for the individuals involved but also for the movement itself.

protest
a public demonstration designed to call attention to the need for action or change.

In leading or joining an act of protest or civil disobedience, individuals may endanger their freedom, jobs, physical safety, or even their lives. For the movement itself, there is a chance that these activities may alienate rather than mobilize—that they may further isolate the movement from those whom its members hope to convince of the importance of the cause. There is also the risk that the protesters will be ignored. The story of OWS illustrates the power and effectiveness of protest and civil disobedience but also the challenges such movements face.

THE SUCCESS OF SOCIAL MOVEMENTS IS DIFFICULT TO MEASURE

As we have explored, small, homogenous, and economically powerful interest groups have many advantages in overcoming the challenges of collective action. When broad, diverse, voluntary associations of individuals come together to create a social movement, they lack many of the advantages of the more powerful groups. According to Olson, there is a logic to the idea that social movements should not come together at all. Yet some do. Why?

This is not an easy question to answer, either for scholars or for participants in the social movements themselves.[64] Part of the problem lies in the inherent differences in observing success and failure between interest groups and social movements.[65] When an interest group tries to influence legislation in Congress, for example, it is much easier to see if its efforts pay off or if they do not. However, what does it mean for a social movement to succeed, and how would we know if it did or did not? Those social movements that fail are difficult to study, like the proverbial tree that falls in the forest with nobody there to observe. To dive a bit deeper into this question, we have to incorporate insights from both political science and sociology, which is a close relative of political science but focuses more on social processes than on political institutions, processes, and outcomes.

For social movements, success or failure may be best determined not by the final public policy outcomes or by laws that were or were not passed but by the fact that the movement came together at all—that it managed to overcome the problems of collective action and engaged others in its efforts to challenge the political dynamics, that it persuaded the uninvolved to become involved, to mobilize, infuriate, and educate. These efforts do not go unopposed, whether by governments, other powerful political players, or the inertia of a public confronted with a new cause or call to combat an injustice.[66] For sociologist Edwin Amenta, some answers, and a better framing of the question itself, may lie in the uneven power relationships that define interest groups and social movements. He argued, "Asking why social movements fail is a little like asking why children do not have backyards full of ponies. Most social movements fail most of the time because they embody a recipe for failure: they combine ambitious goals with severe power deficits."[67] By some accounts, and not without cause, it is not even clear if OWS created a social movement at all. By the three-year anniversary of the first Zuccotti Park protests, the movement seemed to be over. In comparison to widely acknowledged twenty-first century movements such as Black Lives Matter, OWS did not appear to have the same staying power or to have built the necessary infrastructure to sustain it over the long haul.

However, in our exploration of political parties, we studied the insurgent candidacy of Senator Bernie Sanders, I-VT, who most certainly highlighted American economic inequality in his campaign.

▲ Lucas Brinson takes on the role of a human microphone, relaying information throughout the Occupy Wall Street encampment in New York's Zuccotti Park days before police cleared out protesters in mid-November 2011.

AP Photo/Bebeto Matthews

The efforts of Sanders and others to call attention to this issue illustrate one of the primary tools that social movements have: changing the conversation in an effort to influence the political agenda.

Trying to determine whether or not a social movement has been successful by focusing only on what laws were or were not passed might miss this key contribution.[68] The policy agenda is a shifting and evolving thing; nothing is ever settled, and those who wish to influence political outcomes can never let their guard down.[69] The outcome of any one social movement may teach the members of future movements important lessons about what has worked and what has not. The activities of individuals involved with the civil rights movement, for example, served as lessons to members of future movements, such as those for Americans with disabilities, that sought to call attention to other forms of injustice.[70]

WHAT HAVE I LEARNED?

1. In contrast to interest groups, members of social movements _____.
   a. generally have more access to political insiders
   b. can contribute more money to political campaigns
   c. focus more on calling public attention to issues
   d. avoid the dangers of faction

2. What social movements do you think are the most impactful in American politics today?

3. What do you think a social movement needs most to succeed?

Answer Key: 1. c; 2. Answers will vary but should be accompanied with specific reasons why one or more is viewed as impactful; 3. Answers will vary but might include a focused message, gaining national attention or changing public policy.

CONCLUSION: ORGANIZING IN AMERICAN POLITICAL LIFE

Separated in space only by city blocks and in time by only three years, the activities of powerful and well-connected American financial firms in 2008 and the protests of OWS in 2011 might seem as far apart as the citizens they tried to represent. In many ways, they were. The tactics used in these two situations were, to be sure, very different. Insiders—the CEOs of financial institutions and their well-paid lobbyists—worked the levers of the American political system to ensure the survival of the firms they represented. Outsiders—students, opponents of the American capitalist system, advocates for economic equality, and many others without a well-defined agenda—tried to come together and use tools of protest and action to bring about social change.

These two groups, as different as they were, shared more in common than even they may have realized. Their leaders and members had to assess where they stood strategically in the real world of American economic and political power, and they had to adjust their strategies accordingly. They had to motivate and coerce members to join and contribute. Most fundamentally, they had to decide exactly whose interests they were trying to represent.

The stories of the financial bailout and OWS are united by two strong and interconnected threads: power and inequality. Even within a social movement that hopes to represent the interests of outsiders, the disconnected, and the less powerful, there is no guarantee that all voices within that movement will be heard. When one compares the activities of interest groups and social movements, the challenges are even greater. The concentration of wealth at the very top of the economic strata is as great as it has ever been in the nation's history.

From these two stories, one could draw a simple, neat conclusion: One faction ended up tipping the balance of power in its favor, and the other failed—end of story. However, the complex ways in which social movements have been involved in the American political space are better thought of as seeds. Political seeds—sometimes derided, attacked, or ignored from their beginnings—need two key ingredients: their own potential and the soil upon which that potential falls. Whether or not OWS had a consistent, clear, salable message and what effect that message had on the political process in 2011 or in the years since is not the main concern in this view. What matters is whether or not the efforts of OWS sowed the seeds for a true challenge to the power structure of the American political system in the twenty-first century. And did these efforts fall upon a receptive and fertile soil? Did the political dynamics of Americans' confrontation with the inevitable challenge of faction—and the inevitable contribution of economic inequality to the formation of faction in republican forms of government—change? The verdict is still out.

CHAPTER REVIEW

This chapter's main ideas are reflected in the Learning Objectives below. By reviewing them here, you should be able to **remember** the key points, **know** the terms that are central to the topic, and **think** about the critical issues raised in each section.

11.1 Explore financial firms' response to the 2008 housing crisis to understand how interest group members try to wield the levers of political power to shape policy.

REMEMBER
- In the wake of the financial crisis of 2008, interest groups, especially those representing American financial firms, acted to advocate for the goals shared by their members.

KNOW
- interest groups (p. 297)
- social movements (p. 297)
- voluntary associations (p. 297)

THINK
- Why did many Americans criticize the federal government's response to the financial crisis?
- Do you agree with these criticisms?

11.2 Summarize the challenges associated with interest group activity.

REMEMBER
- The Constitution of the United States ensures the ability of Americans to form voluntary associations and make their wishes known.
- Political scientists have offered a variety of explanations for why Americans choose to join or not join voluntary associations in political life.
- When acting collectively, there are often rational incentives for individuals to allow others to carry the burdens of doing so.

KNOW
- collective action (p. 305)
- collective good (p. 305)
- elitist theory (p. 302)
- free riders (p. 305)
- material rewards (p. 305)
- pluralism (p. 302)
- policy agenda (p. 302)
- power elite (p. 302)
- purposive benefits (p. 306)
- selective benefits (p. 305)
- social benefits (p. 306)

THINK
- What are major challenges to successful collective action?
- How do interest groups and social movements attempt to overcome these challenges?

11.3 Discuss the types of interest groups in the American political landscape and the different tactics they use.

REMEMBER
- Interest groups may form to advocate for a variety of goals, including those focused on business and the economy, public issues, and the interests of governmental units.
- Interest groups lobby all levels of government.

- When lobbying the federal government, interest groups act to influence the actions of the legislative, executive, and judicial branches.
- Interest groups also act to influence campaigns and elections.

KNOW
- agency capture (p. 311)
- Astroturf lobbying (p. 313)
- economic interest groups (p. 306)
- governmental interest groups (p. 308)
- inside lobbying (p. 310)
- iron triangle (p. 311)
- issue network (p. 312)
- lobbying (p. 308)
- outside (grassroots) lobbying (p. 313)
- public interest groups (p. 306)
- revolving door phenomenon (p. 309)

THINK
- What have you learned about the different tactics employed by interest groups acting on the "inside" versus those acting on the "outside"?

11.4 Explore the efforts of Occupy Wall Street to understand the challenges individuals face and the strategies they employ to make social and political changes.

REMEMBER
- In the presence of increasing economic inequality in the years following the financial bailout, members of Occupy Wall Street attempted to create a social movement in order to call attention to economic inequality in the United States.

THINK
- Did Occupy Wall Street create a new social movement?
- Were its tactics successful?

11.5 Analyze the tactics social movements use to advocate on their members' behalf and contrast them with those of interest groups.

REMEMBER
- Members of social movements often employ tactics such as protest and civil disobedience to make political change and to educate others.
- It is often more difficult to determine whether a social movement succeeded or failed than it is to evaluate the success of activities of a given interest group.

KNOW
- protest (p. 317)

THINK
- Why do you think some social movements succeed and others fail?
- How open do you think the American political process is?

CHAPTER 12

CONGRESS

Representation, Organization, and Legislation

▼ A group of future women candidates take a selfie at the conclusion of their final training session of a program run by Emerge Virginia in 2017. The organization, part of the larger Emerge America organization, trains women from all walks of life who want to run for office at a local, state, or national level. Many women currently in Congress got their start in local and state races, but few benefited from programs like this one that provided them with knowledge and skills about fund-raising, speech giving, how to be a good candidate, where they should run, and more.

Andrew Innerarity/For The Washington Post via Getty Images

Congress is in some ways a story of division. Members are divided into two chambers: the House and the Senate. They are increasingly divided along lines of political partisanship. They sort themselves into various committees and subcommittees to do the actual work of their institution. In spite of those divisions, however, all members of U.S. Congress are united in one thing. They are there to **represent**, to stand for, the interests of the voters who sent them there.[1]

Americans cannot all fit into the Capitol—at least not without computer-generated graphics. Therefore, Americans elect people to make the laws, raise and spend the nation's money, and watch over other institutions in the federal government, along with a host of activities that shape American public policy in a profound way.

The stories we tell in this chapter are focused primarily on one particular group in Congress: women. We will look back on what has been accomplished and ahead to what still needs to be done to achieve more equal representation for women in Congress. We will also learn that their experience as legislators is, like their colleagues', shaped by the institution itself. The ways that their stories are both similar to and different from those of other members of Congress allows us to get at the heart of what representation means in American democracy.

By reading this chapter, you will be able to do the following:

 12.1 Understand how questions of representation involve political and institutional considerations as well as questions of identity.

 12.2 Describe how the Constitution created Congress, including its structure and powers.

 12.3 Describe the rules, institutions, and processes that Congress itself has created to carry out its constitutional role.

 12.4 Explain the steps of the legislative process and how it can diverge from traditional "textbook" descriptions.

 12.5 Understand the factors that influence an individual's decision to run, and the resources and skills that successful candidates need.

12.6 Connect the issues surrounding the representation of women in Congress to the challenges involving representation of other individuals in America.

represent
to "stand for" the interests of voters in government.

THE ELECTIONS OF 2018 HIGHLIGHT THE CONNECTIONS AMONG PARTISANSHIP, INSTITUTIONS, AND IDENTITIES IN CONGRESS

- **Understand how questions of representation involve political and institutional considerations as well as questions of identity.**

As the midterm congressional elections of 2018 approached, there were so many stories.

It was not a presidential election year; 2016 had provided all of that drama. However, there would be state and local elections: governorships, state legislative bodies, school budget requests, state judgeships, county board supervisors, and many others all up for grabs. But the American national press was largely focused on the 2018 elections for the U.S. House of Representatives and the U.S. Senate. For good reason.

Would the Republicans retain a majority in both the House of Representatives and the Senate? Would the Democratic Party manage to take control over one, or even both, chambers?

Clearly, a Democratic-controlled House, Senate, or both would limit President Donald Trump's ability to pursue his agenda in a time of sharply divided partisan politics. However, as the congressional elections of 2018 were under way, there was another word thrown into the mix: *impeachment*. Not a term to be thrown out lightly when discussing an American president, but one that was most certainly being mentioned, even by members of Congress. It was highly unlikely that the Senate, even with a slight Democratic majority, would expect that President Trump would be removed from office. However, an impeachment battle, even if won, distracts a president in ways that former president William Jefferson Clinton knows well.

Negotiations with North Korea, and a hard-line approach to America's economic relationship with trading partners, also dominated the news. President Trump's policies on immigration, and his tweets on those, also took center stage. The American economy was doing well, and President Trump counted on jobs to keep Republican control of at least one chamber of Congress.

IN 2018, WOMEN RAN IN HISTORIC NUMBERS

There was another story unfolding in 2018, closely connected to the question of partisan divides in the American electorate and in Congress. Some writers and political analysts were using a phrase that had not been widely used for decades to describe the election: "The year of the woman."

A record number of women had declared their candidacies in federal, state, and local elections. More than three hundred women were running for the House of Representatives alone, and "36,000 women—nearly 40 times the number from the last election cycle," had contacted a women's electoral interest group stating that they wanted to "run or work on campaigns."[2] According to Representative Anna Eshoo (D-CA), "this is not just a curiosity. It's not an interesting number or statistic. It's historic."[3]

It was not just the number of women candidates that was notable. It was also their diversity of identities and experiences: "It includes more women of color than previous electoral years, as well as a number of immigrants. There are more female veterans in the mix than we've seen before, and they're representing both sides of the aisle."[4]

While it was still unclear in the summer and fall how many women would win, because of the results of the spring primaries and caucuses, there were likely to be some changes.

Texas was poised to elect its first two Latinas to the House of Representatives, given that both nominees were running in districts that heavily favored their political party (Democratic). Pennsylvania was guaranteed to change the fact that it had no women serving in the House or the Senate, never having elected a woman senator. In Pennsylvania's fifth district, both of the two candidates who secured their major party's nomination were women. Barring unexpected events, the PA-5th would likely be represented by a woman, and a first-time candidate.

The Democratic nominee was attorney Mary Gay Scanlon, who had devoted much of her career to being an advocate for children, especially those at risk, and to securing and improving educational

▼ **FIGURE 12.1**

Women Candidates for Congressional Office, 2000–2018

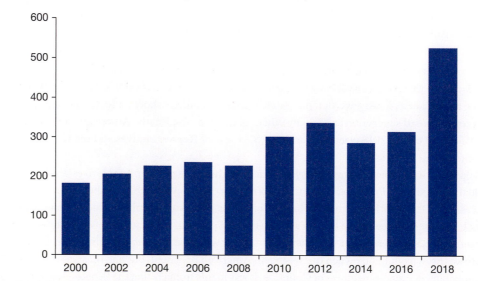

Source: "Record Numbers of Women Running for Office May Not Mean Big Gains in Congress," Bloomberg, May 7, 2018, https://www.bloomberg.com/graphics/2018-women-candidates/.

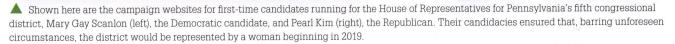

▲ Shown here are the campaign websites for first-time candidates running for the House of Representatives for Pennsylvania's fifth congressional district, Mary Gay Scanlon (left), the Democratic candidate, and Pearl Kim (right), the Republican. Their candidacies ensured that, barring unforeseen circumstances, the district would be represented by a woman beginning in 2019.

opportunities. Asked why she was running, Scanlon replied, "It has to do with the work I've been doing forever representing women and kids and public schools and immigrants and folks in the criminal justice system. And just all of that work feels like it's under attack with this administration, particularly the Department of Justice and the Department of Education. So, I am running to continue doing that work, just in a new forum."[5]

On the Republican side was Pearl Kim, a first-generation American of South Korean descent. Also an attorney, Kim had served as a prosecutor, focusing on human trafficking and sexual violence, and secured Pennsylvania's first conviction under an older human trafficking law. When interviewed, Kim discussed her own reasons for bringing her experience on fighting human trafficking and sexual violence to Congress: "I have a personal passion for human trafficking. And when we are dealing with human trafficking I think you intersect naturally with immigration, with labor, and on the far end of that spectrum you are dealing with public safety you are dealing with foreign affairs and terrorism."[6]

Both candidates were seeking to fill the open seat of Pat Meehan (R), who had retired "after one of his female staffers accused him of sexually harassing her."[7]

There is a common phrase in American electoral parlance: "All politics are local." Well, they are and they aren't. Of course, candidates for and members of Congress must face the political landscapes of their districts or states. However, the national political landscape—especially the sharply divided partisan politics of 2018—was connected in important ways to the decisions of women to run, their chances of winning, and what it would mean for the nation if large numbers of them did.

In 2018, a sizable majority of women candidates were Democrats. Many first-time candidates in their party stated that their motivation to run came from their reaction to the policies and antiwomen statements of Republican president Donald Trump. These motivations were also connected to the #MeToo movement that arose in response to seemingly never-ending revelations of accusations of sexual harassment and rape by famous men in politics, business, and entertainment.[8]

A "blue wave," in which the party made electoral gains in Congress (and other races), would help their chances and have a direct impact on how many women would be in Congress when it convened in 2019. It would also affect their chances to influence public policy. As we will see, having a majority in Congress means more than having the most votes; it is also key to holding power in the institutional structures that define how Congress works.

Should voters reject the politics of the Democratic Party—which many saw as moving farther left— then the electoral chances of women candidates overall would be challenged, and the legislative power of those women who did win, diminished.

But 2018 was not the first election year to be called "the year of the woman." That would be 1992, when also a record number of women ran for and won seats in Congress, along with other state and local races. Later in the chapter, we will look back to 1992 to explore why individual women candidates chose to run and what obstacles they had to overcome to represent their districts or states.

To understand what the congressional elections of 2018 may or may not mean for national politics, however, we need to explore the institution that the candidates hoped to join or rejoin. We start with the Constitution, which set the broad structure and power of Congress, only to leave it up to its members to figure out how they would go about their work.

WHAT HAVE I LEARNED?

1. Representation in Congress means _____.
   a. advancing one's personal agenda
   b. running first for a seat in the House and then advancing to the Senate
   c. the act of "standing for" one's constituents in government
   d. voting according to the majority view

2. What reason did women *not* give for deciding to run for Congress in 2018?
   a. They wanted to challenge the numerical imbalance between men and women

   b. They wanted to respond to Donald Trump's election
   c. They were inspired by the #MeToo movement
   d. The large number of incumbents running would guarantee party stability

3. What do you think it means for members of Congress to represent the voters' interests?

Answer Key: 1. c; 2. d; 3. Answers might include various aspects of congressional activity and/or speaking for the people.

THE CONSTITUTION DEFINES CONGRESS'S SHAPE AND POWERS

- **Describe how the Constitution created Congress, including its structure and powers.**

The U.S. Congress is called the *first branch* of government for good reason: The Constitution deals with its powers and procedures first, in more detail, and at greater length than it does those of the executive and judicial branches.

THE HOUSE AND SENATE SERVE DIFFERENT ROLES

The Great Compromise that emerged from the Constitutional Convention in 1787 called for the creation of a bicameral legislature composed of two chambers, the House of Representatives and the Senate. While both the House and the Senate are involved in the legislative process, the Framers of the Constitution saw their roles differently.

These differences were designed partly to add checks and balances *within* Congress and not just between Congress and the other branches. In *The Federalist Papers*, James Madison emphasized the dangers of faction, in which a group of individuals could damage the rights and liberties of others or the interests of the Republic itself. Federalism and the separation of powers between the three branches were two ways in which the Framers tried to contain the dangers of faction. Separating legislative authority within Congress itself was another.

THE HOUSE OF REPRESENTATIVES IS DESIGNED FOR GREATER ACCOUNTABILITY.

Members of the House of Representatives are meant to be close to the people and their wishes. At the Constitutional Convention, delegates agreed upon two-year terms for each representative, believing this would keep them close and accountable to the people while also giving them enough time to become competent in their work and familiar with all the relevant laws and issues.

Today, 435 representatives serve in the House, each directly elected by eligible voters in state districts that have been apportioned by population. The Constitution requires that representatives be at least twenty-five years old, a resident of their state, and a citizen of the United States for seven years.[9]

The Constitution did not include property ownership or affiliation in a particular religion as restrictions, because the Framers believed that the requirements for legislative service in the House should be "open to merit of every description."[10] While the Constitution did not explicitly bar women from holding office, the states did, excluding all but a few from participating in public life. Slaves and indigenous peoples were barred—often brutally—from public service, one of many restrictions upon their natural rights and liberties.

THE SENATE IS DESIGNED FOR GREATER STABILITY.

Senators, in contrast, are meant to be more insulated from the whims of the public, adding stability to the legislative branch. Elected for six-year terms, the classes of senators are staggered so that about only one-third are up for reelection in a given cycle.

Today, one hundred senators serve in the Senate, two for each state. Senatorial candidates have to be older than representatives—at least thirty years old—and citizens for at least nine years, and they must live in the state they seek to represent. Missing from the Constitution was any mention of **term limits**—limitations on how many terms a given representative or senator could serve—and today the idea is often debated.

CONGRESS HAS THREE KEY POWERS: LAWMAKING, BUDGETING, AND OVERSIGHT

The powers of Congress fall into three broad areas: those related to its role as the main lawmaking body, those related to its position at the center of the budgeting process, and those it exerts when exercising oversight of the federal bureaucracy and other public officials.

term limits
formal limits on the number of times an elected official may serve in a given office.

▼ FIGURE 12.2

Key Stats on the 115th Congress

	House	Senate
Political party	237 Republicans, 197 Democrats*	51 Republicans, 47 Democrats, 2 Independents
Average age	57.8	61.8
Most frequently listed occupation	Public service, politics	Law
Percentage holding bachelor's degree	94.1	100
Average length of service in office (years)	9.4	10.1
Percentage of "freshmen" members	13.8	13
Religious majority	241 Protestant members	58 Protestant members
Gender	89 women	23 women
African American	48	3
Hispanic/Latino American	41	5
Asian/Pacific Islander American	15	3
American Indian	2	0
Foreign born	18	5
Military service	78	18

Source: Jennifer Manning, "Membership of the 115th Congress: A Profile," *Congressional Research Service*, May 15, 2018. https://www.senate.gov/CRSpubs/b8f6293e-c235-40fd-b895-6474d0f8e809.pdf

Note: *some senate vacancies at time of writing.

The House of Representatives and the Senate Compared

	House of Representatives	Senate
Requirements for Membership	At least twenty-five years old	At least thirty years old
	Seven years of citizenship	Nine years of citizenship
	Resident of the state	Resident of the state
Service	Two-year terms, with unlimited number of terms	Six-year terms, divided into three classes, with unlimited number of terms
Constituency	District, apportioned to states by population	Entire state
Organization	More governed by rules, more institutionally structured, more power to individual leadership positions	Less governed by rules, more power to individual members, more informal
Goals	To be closer to voters' preferences	To be more insulated from voters' preferences

LEGISLATIVE AUTHORITY IS KEY TO CONGRESSIONAL POWER. The most important power of Congress is its legislative authority—the ability to pass laws in areas of national policy. The body of law that Congress creates is called statutory law as it is written down in the **statutes** that Congress passes.

Among legislative bodies in the world's democracies, the U.S. Congress is the most active and independent in terms of its ability to make national policy. The list of the enumerated powers of Congress is substantial; Congress is authorized to legislate in economic policy, national security, foreign policy, and other policy areas (see Table 12.2).

THE BUDGETING PROCESS IS ANOTHER KEY POWER OF CONGRESS. The second major role of Congress involves its central position in setting a federal budget. Creating a bureaucratic agency requires two steps: First, congressional action authorizes the department or agency. Second, through the process of **appropriation**, Congress funds the agency's activities. Many of the rules governing the budgetary process were first set out in the Congressional Budget Act of 1974.[11] The Budget Act created the Congressional Budget Office (CBO), whose role is to provide information and estimates of the likely budgetary consequences of funding the agencies and programs created by Congress. The Budget Act also established the process of reconciliation, whereby congressional committees work out how federal spending will align with the overall congressional budget. Reconciliation bills are passed using a more streamlined process than other bills in Congress. This can make them harder to stop.

One controversial way in which members of Congress have been involved in the budgetary process has been through **earmarks**, through which members direct monies to projects within their districts or states. Popular with constituents, earmarks have been criticized for putting particular interests ahead of those of the nation's voters as a whole. In 2011, the House of Representatives, led by Republicans, instituted a ban on earmarks.

CONGRESS ALSO HAS THE POWER OF OVERSIGHT. The third major role of Congress in national policymaking is that of **oversight**; Congress uses its authority to ensure that laws are implemented in the way that Congress intended when it passed them. Given the growth in the size and complexity of the federal government, this is not an easy task.

Congress has oversight responsibilities over the federal bureaucracy as well as over other branches of government and elected and appointed officials. Congressional committees and subcommittees may

statutes
written laws established by a legislative body.

appropriation
the process through which congressional committees allocate funds to executive branch agencies, bureaus, and departments.

earmarks
additions to a piece of legislation that direct specific funds to projects within districts or states.

oversight
efforts by Congress to ensure that executive branch agencies, bureaus, and cabinet departments, as well as their officials, are acting legally and in accordance with congressional goals.

Legislative Powers of Congress in the Constitution

The Constitution grants Congress the power to legislate in the following areas.

Enumerated Powers			
	Both Chambers	House	Senate
Economic Policy	Create and collect taxes, coin money, borrow money, regulate the value of currency, borrow money, and regulate commerce.	All bills to raise revenue must be generated in the House.	In practice, the Senate has become a coequal partner in setting national revenue policy.
Foreign Policy	Regulate trade with other nations.		Ratify treaties entered into by a president.
National Security	Declare war, raise and support armies and a naval force and make rules for their governance and regulation, call up the military, define and punish piracies and felonies committed on the high seas.		
Other Powers Involving the Executive Branch		Impeach the president, vice president, and other executive branch officers.	Confirm presidential nominations of executive branch officers, try members of the executive branch impeached by the House.
Powers Involving the Judicial Branch	Create levels of the judicial branch below the Supreme Court, establish the number of Supreme Court justices.	Impeach members of the federal judiciary.	Confirm by majority vote presidential nominees to the federal judiciary, try members of the federal judiciary who have been impeached.
Via Necessary and Proper Clause			
	"To make all Laws which shall be necessary and proper for carrying into Execution the foregoing Powers, and all other Powers vested by this Constitution in the Government of the United States."		
Via Subsequent Amendments			
	Individual amendments (such as the Thirteenth, Fourteenth, and Fifteenth) grant Congress "the power to enforce, by appropriate legislation," those amendments.		

conduct hearings and investigations into the actions of executive agencies to try to ensure that funds appropriated for programs are being spent efficiently and in accordance with the law's intent and that agents are not abusing their powers. While many committee hearings are routine, some may be called in the event of a perceived breakdown or failure by an executive branch agency.

Starting in 2017, congressional committees began investigating many aspects of the 2016 presidential election, including accusations of Russian interference into the elections, communications between current and former officials in the administration of President Donald Trump with that nation, and alleged efforts of members of the prior administration of President Barack Obama to shape the narrative of the investigation into the use of an unsecured server by former secretary of state Hillary Clinton.

The calling of hearings in response to a visible crisis is called **fire alarm oversight**, with oversight being triggered only by an alarm call. This kind of oversight is different from **police patrol oversight**, in which Congress continually monitors the actions of a bureaucracy. Because of the difficulty in continuously monitoring the immense federal bureaucracy, fire alarm oversight is more commonly used than police patrol oversight.[12]

fire alarm oversight
a term that describes congressional oversight procedures primarily in response to problems or complaints.

police patrol oversight
a term that describes congressional oversight as a process of constant monitoring rather than responding to specific crises.

OTHER CONGRESSIONAL POWERS INVOLVE ADVICE AND CONSENT, SENATORIAL COURTESY, AND IMPEACHMENT. In implementing the idea of checks and balances, the Constitution gave each of the branches shared authority over some aspects of governance, which allows a kind of oversight of one branch over the other two. As discussed earlier, Congress is given the authority to declare war and the Senate to ratify treaties, thus forcing the executive and legislative branches to work together in important aspects of foreign and national security policy.

Using its power of advice and consent, the Senate confirms presidential nominees to the federal courts by a simple majority. The norm of **senatorial courtesy** generally allows senators to nominate lower-level federal judges to serve in their states with the expectation that they will be confirmed without significant opposition. Also with respect to the judiciary, both the House and Senate have a role in the nation's court system, as they have the power "to constitute Tribunals inferior to [below] the Supreme Court"[13] and set the number of justices on the Supreme Court.

In addition to the confirmation of presidential nominees to the federal judiciary, the Senate exercises the same role of advice and consent in the confirmation of most presidential nominees to important posts in the federal bureaucracy.

Congress is also given the authority to remove federal officials—including the president, vice president, government officials, and federal judges—through the process of **impeachment**. The House of Representatives votes to impeach if a majority of its members feel that an official has committed "Treason, Bribery, or other high Crimes and Misdemeanors."[14] The vagueness of this language has resulted in debates about just what constitutes an impeachable offense.

If a majority of the members of the House votes to impeach, the trial takes place in the Senate, with a two-thirds majority needed to convict.[15] Impeachment is a power that has been used rarely. Two presidents have faced successful House resolutions to impeach, but neither was removed from office. Andrew Johnson—impeached during the Reconstruction era following the Civil War—survived by a single vote in the Senate. Bill Clinton—charged with lying during and obstructing an investigation into his relationship with intern Monica Lewinsky—was acquitted by a vote of 55–45.

These fundamental structural features, grounded in the Constitution, are the framework within which all members of Congress operate once they are in Congress. However, as we will explore in the next section, the Constitution left many details undefined, especially relating to *how* all of this is to actually happen. Congress itself has filled in these blanks.

senatorial courtesy
a traditional norm in which presidents consult with senators from the states when considering potential nominees to the lower levels of the federal judiciary.

impeachment
a legislative process for removing elected and appointed officials.

WHAT HAVE I **LEARNED?**

1. In the Constitution, the Senate was designed to _____.
   a. be more responsive to the people's desires and preferences than the House of Representatives
   b. act as the slower-moving, more deliberative legislative chamber
   c. reflect proportionately the actual population totals of each state
   d. be responsible for generating bills to raise revenue

2. The Constitution gives Congress the power to _____.
   a. rule on the constitutionality of laws
   b. create lower levels of the federal judiciary
   c. execute the nation's laws
   d. All of the above

3. Legislative authority refers to the power to _____.
   a. pass laws
   b. implement policy
   c. rule on the constitutionality of laws
   d. run for office

4. What tools does the Constitution give Congress to oversee or keep watch on the other two branches of government?

_____

Answer Key: 1. b; 2. b; 3. a; 4. Answers should consider processes of congressional oversight as well as control over funds.

CONGRESS IS ORGANIZED AROUND FORMAL AND INFORMAL RULES

- Describe the rules, institutions, and processes that Congress itself has created to carry out its constitutional role.

The congressional elections of 2018 offered the chance for a significant number of newcomers to join the institution, and likely a very diverse group of newcomers, including, perhaps, the largest number of women serving in the nation's history. But what would they do once they got there? To be effective, they would quickly have to learn how the institution actually works. Members of Congress must be very familiar with the organizational structure of Congress if they are to succeed in advancing their agenda. Groups may form around a shared set of lived experiences, a shared set of policy goals, or a shared desire to reform how Congress works. In addition, members gain power and influence as their congressional careers develop and they establish seniority within the institution.

While rules and procedures may seem like a dry subject of study, they matter a great deal to what legislation does or does not emerge from Congress. Battles over organization or congressional procedure are often just as heated and consequential as battles over specific policies.

The Constitution is much more specific on what Congress does than on how it is supposed to do it. With a few exceptions, the Constitution does not describe most of the day-to-day processes and procedures of Congress. These rules and details have been created by the chambers themselves; important modifications have been made over time. Congress includes both formal and informal organizational features. Formally, political parties, party leaders, and the committee system shape much of what happens in the House and Senate. Congressional staff and the congressional bureaucracy are involved as well. Informally, norms and traditional ways of doing things also play a role.

POLITICAL PARTIES SHAPE HOW CONGRESS IS STRUCTURED

Much of the formal structure of Congress revolves around the role of political parties and party leaders. The majority party, which is the party with the most members in each chamber, and the minority party, which has the second-highest number of members, each control important leadership positions and organize congressional behavior—both to advocate for their preferred policies and to help individual members in their reelection efforts.

In contrast to most modern representative assemblies, party leaders in the U.S. Congress often struggle to make sure that their own members act and vote in support of party positions, especially when a member's constituent preferences clash with those of the member's political party. Leaders, however, are not powerless and have a variety of carrots and sticks with which to steer their members in the desired direction. Party leaders work through party caucuses (Democratic Party) and party conferences (Republican Party), in which members of a party meet, set up goals, choose leaders, assign members to committees, and try to present a unified voice to the American electorate through the media.

Alex Wong/Getty Images

▼ U.S. House majority leader Kevin McCarthy (R-CA) (left), House majority whip Steve Scalise (R-LA) (center), and Speaker of the House Paul Ryan (R-WI) appear at a news conference in May 2018 on Capitol Hill. Ryan's announcement that he would not seek re-election in 2018 left the role of the Speaker up for grabs should Republicans hold on to their majority in the House. Many speculated that both McCarthy and Scalise were contenders for the role.

PARTY LEADERS PLAY AN IMPORTANT ROLE IN THE HOUSE OF REPRESEN-TATIVES. Larger than the Senate since the founding of Congress, the House of Representatives is, by necessity, more formally structured than the Senate, with rank-and-file House members being individually less powerful than their Senate colleagues. The **Speaker of the House**—the only House leadership position described in the Constitution—wields a considerable amount of power, though that power has changed over time in response to demands on the House and strategic political action on the part of its members.

Speaker of the House
the leader of the House of Representatives, chosen by an election of its members.

At the beginning of each new Congress (every two years), members of the House elect the Speaker, who has almost always been a member of the majority party. A long history of successful service in the House is usually a prerequisite. Increasingly, the ability to raise money for other members of one's party is considered in selecting a Speaker. These leadership political action committees (PACs) "are designed for two things: to make money and to make friends," and representatives use that money to assist fellow party members' campaigns.[16] The Speaker is second in the line of succession (behind the vice president) to the presidency in the event of death, resignation, removal from office, or inability to conduct the office's duties. In Congress, the Speaker has considerable power over the House agenda and committee assignments.

Assisting the Speaker are the **House majority leader**, the majority **whip** (and other members of the whip system), and various caucus and conference chairs and vice chairs. Members of the whip system collect information about how individual members are planning to vote, corralling their support on key votes and setting party strategy in Congress. The term comes from British hunting; the "whipper-in" tried to keep the hounds in some sort of a coherent group. The **House minority leader** has far less structural influence in the House than the Speaker but works to coordinate minority party activity, opposition to the majority party, and overall strategy. House minority party leadership also includes its own whips and whip systems.

PARTY LEADERS ALSO SHAPE ACTION IN THE SENATE. Constitutionally, the official leader of the Senate is the vice president of the United States, though she or he can cast a vote only in the event of a tie. The president pro tempore presides over the chamber's proceedings when the vice president is not present (which is almost all the time) but wields no real power. Typically, junior senators fill in to oversee the day-to-day proceedings.

The most powerful position in the Senate is the **Senate majority leader**, who is chosen from the majority party by its members in caucus or conference. Although individual senators retain more power than their colleagues in the House, the Senate majority leader is not as powerful as the Speaker; however, she or he plays a key role in shaping the legislative agenda. The Senate minority leader—chosen by the minority party members—acts as the leader of the opposition in the Senate. Assisting both party leaders are party whips, leadership committees, and party caucuses and conferences. (See Figure 12.3.)

House majority leader
the head of the party with the most seats in the House of Representatives, chosen by the party's members.

whip
an individual in the House or Senate, chosen by his or her party members, whose job is to ensure party unity and discipline.

House minority leader
the head of the party with the second-highest number of seats in Congress, chosen by the party's members.

Senate majority leader
a chosen senator who speaks for the majority party and helps to shape the Senate agenda.

▼ FIGURE 12.3

The Structure of Leadership in Congress

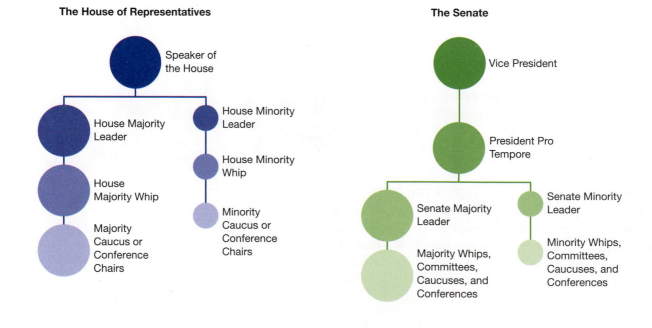

The House of Representatives

- Speaker of the House
  - House Majority Leader
    - House Majority Whip
      - Majority Caucus or Conference Chairs
  - House Minority Leader
    - House Minority Whip
      - Minority Caucus or Conference Chairs

The Senate

- Vice President
  - President Pro Tempore
    - Senate Majority Leader
      - Majority Whips, Committees, Caucuses, and Conferences
    - Senate Minority Leader
      - Minority Whips, Committees, Caucuses, and Conferences

THE WORK OF CONGRESS IS DONE THROUGH THE COMMITTEE SYSTEM

The work that Congress deals with is considerable and complex. There is no way any one member could be directly involved in each piece of legislation. To divide the workload, both the House and the Senate have established the committee system, a system of committees and subcommittees that do most of the work of Congress.

PARTY LEADERS AND SENIORITY SHAPE COMMITTEE MEMBERSHIP AND LEADERSHIP. Committee membership is determined and negotiated by party leaders and generally reflects the ratio of party membership in each chamber. Seniority, or the length of consecutive service on the committee, plays a major role in determining **committee chairs**. These chairs have considerable influence over committee processes, especially in setting the committee's agenda. Because of the differences in the size of the chambers, House committees tend to have more members than Senate committees, while individual senators tend to serve on more committees than their colleagues in the House.

New representatives and senators often try to get appointed to committees that deal with issues of interest to their constituents or that provide benefits to their districts and states. That has the added advantage of helping their prospects for reelection along the way. Requests for committee membership, though, may also be driven by genuine policy interests on the part of members of Congress.[17]

DIFFERENT TYPES OF COMMITTEES PERFORM DIFFERENT ROLES. Congress has four types of committees: standing, joint, conference, and select. Standing committees are where most of the work of Congress gets done. They are so named because they continue across Congresses, and members tend to serve on them for multiple terms, developing expertise and working to bring benefits to their districts and states. Standing committees consider legislation and exercise oversight of bureaucratic agencies, usually recommending funding levels for them. They are divided by policy areas, with a given committee having jurisdiction over its area of specialization. (See Table 12.3.) Standing committees are divided into subcommittees, which specialize even further, usually considering parts of legislation under instructions from their parent committees.

Joint committees contain members of both the House and the Senate. In general, they do not have a great deal of power but are used to focus public attention on an issue, gather information for Congress, or help party leaders speed things along in the legislative process.

The conference committee is a temporary joint committee that resolves differences between the House and Senate versions of a bill, which is required by the Constitution before a president can sign the bill into law. Party leaders determine conference committee membership, though members who have been centrally involved in a bill are usually included.

The fourth type of committee is the select or special committee. These temporary bodies are usually called upon to investigate an issue, sometimes in response to a crisis or a scandal. Select committees may be given the authority to report legislation, but their role is usually informational only.

CONGRESSIONAL STAFF AND THE CONGRESSIONAL BUREAUCRACY HELP MEMBERS REPRESENT THEIR CONSTITUENTS

The third component of the formal organization of Congress consists of the people and institutions developed to help members represent their constituents. Congressional staff assist representatives and senators in providing casework and give members information about policies, legislation, and constituent preferences. Staff often work closely with members in drafting bills. As the size of the American Republic and the complexity of issues before Congress have both grown, so has the size of the congressional staff.

Congress has also developed bureaucratic organizations to assist its members' efforts. These nonpartisan institutions provide members with estimates of the likely impact of laws on the national budget and keep them informed about how well agencies are performing the tasks Congress intended of them. For instance, the Government Accountability Office (GAO) keeps track of agencies created and funded by Congress.

committee chairs
leaders of the subunits of congressional committees who have authority over the committee's agenda.

Standing Committees in the 115th Congress

House of Representatives	Joint	Senate
Agriculture	Security and Cooperation in Europe	Agriculture, Nutrition, and Forestry
Appropriations	The Library	Appropriations
Armed Services	Printing	Armed Services
Budget	Taxation	Banking, Housing, and Urban Affairs
Education and Workforce	Economic	Budget
Energy and Commerce		Commerce, Science, and Transportation
Ethics		Energy and Natural Resources
Financial Services		Environment and Public Works
Foreign Affairs		Finance
Homeland Security		Foreign Relations
House Administration		Health, Education, Labor, and Pensions
Judiciary		Homeland Security and Governmental Affairs
Natural Resources		Indian Affairs
Oversight and Government Reform		Judiciary
Rules		Rules and Administration
Science, Space, and Technology		Small Business and Entrepreneurship
Small Business		Veterans' Affairs
Transportation and Infrastructure		
Veterans' Affairs		
Ways and Means		

Source: "Congressional Committees," GovTrack, accessed August 7, 2018, https://www.govtrack.us/congress/committees/.

Note: Does not include select committees.

NORMS ARE INFORMAL CONTRIBUTORS TO CONGRESSIONAL ORGANIZATION

norms
unwritten expectations of how members are supposed to act that help members balance representing their constituents and contributing to the smooth functioning of the House and Senate.

In addition to the formal structures, less formal processes also play a role in congressional action. **Norms** are unwritten expectations of how members are supposed to act and help members balance representing their constituents and contributing to the smooth functioning of the House and Senate. Members are expected to be respectful toward their colleagues, to reciprocate help from other members, and to specialize in one or more policy areas to assist the overall level of information and expertise in Congress. Animosity between members of the two political parties has challenged the role of norms in constraining member behavior in recent years.

WHAT HAVE I **LEARNED?**

1. Two of the most important organizational features of Congress are _____.
   a. justices and clerks
   b. agencies and departments
   c. political parties and committees
   d. states and local governments

2. One of the most important powers of the Senate majority leader and the Speaker of the House is the ability to _____.
   a. interpret the laws
   b. veto legislation
   c. shape the legislative agenda
   d. confirm presidential nominees

3. An example of a joint committee is _____.
   a. a conference committee
   b. a Senate subcommittee
   c. a House subcommittee
   d. None of the above

4. Why is seniority so important to Senate and House leadership?

_____

THE LEGISLATIVE PROCESS IS COMPLEX BY DESIGN

- **Explain the steps of the legislative process and how it can diverge from traditional "textbook" descriptions.**

By design, the legislative process is complicated and multistepped, with each stage offering another chance to kill a prospective law. Having seen the passions of the people sweep through state legislatures and sometimes trample on minority rights, the Framers of the Constitution intentionally placed many hurdles in the path of legislation.

What's more, the modern legislative process rarely follows the traditional, linear "textbook" way that it is described, especially when it comes to major legislation. Political scientist Barbara Sinclair used the term **unorthodox lawmaking** to describe the realities of the modern legislative process: whereas "the route to enactment used to be linear and predictable; now it is flexible and varied."[18] This reality does not mean that legislators are bypassing constitutional provisions, only that the process is much more fluid, complex, and political than any flowchart can adequately describe (see Figure 12.4).

THE FIRST STEP IS BILL INTRODUCTION

The first stage of the legislative process is the formal introduction of a **bill**, a draft of a proposed law, into either the House or the Senate. Any member may introduce a bill, but only members of Congress may do so. Even here we see evidence of unorthodox lawmaking, as other actors often play a role in shaping a bill or encouraging a member to introduce it. For instance, the president, for all of her or his tremendous power, cannot literally walk into the House of Representatives and place a bill into "the hopper" for consideration; only a member of the House can do that. However, presidents can encourage, cajole, and press members of either chamber to get a major piece of legislation on the legislative agenda, whether through discussions with party leaders or though appeals to the American public.

Once introduced, a particular bill must wind its way through the originating chamber and then proceed to the other chamber to begin the process anew. Formally, only the House may introduce revenue bills. In practice, however, both chambers often act simultaneously on similar policies, with frequent communication between party leaders in each chamber. In addition, the Senate (along with the president) has become a coequal partner in the overall revenue and spending process.

unorthodox lawmaking
a term that refers to ways in which legislative activity, especially on major bills, is often more fluid than described in a traditional textbook.

bill
a draft of a proposed law.

▼ FIGURE 12.4

The Legislative Process

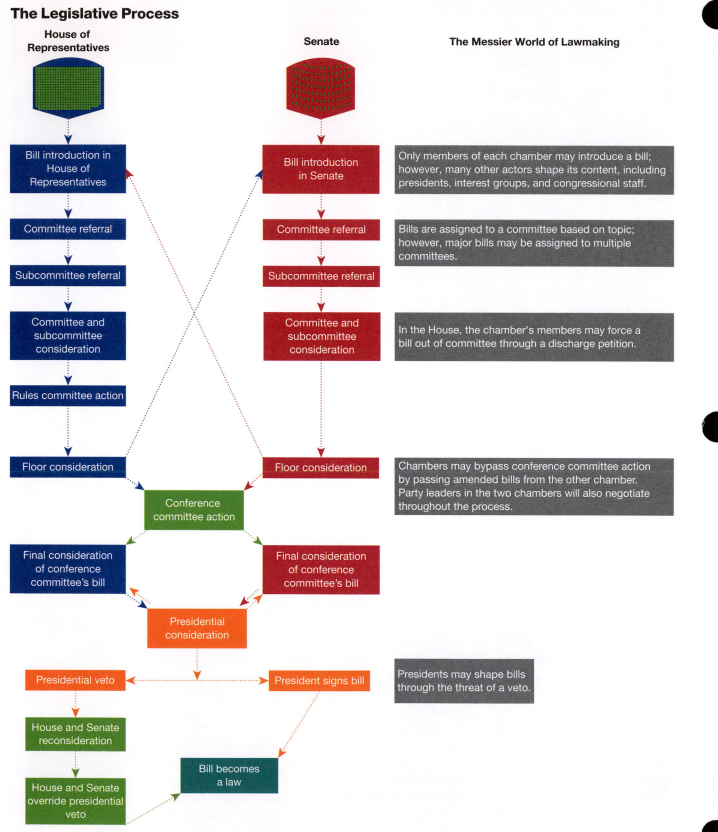

House of Representatives

Senate

The Messier World of Lawmaking

Bill introduction in House of Representatives

Bill introduction in Senate

Only members of each chamber may introduce a bill; however, many other actors shape its content, including presidents, interest groups, and congressional staff.

Committee referral

Committee referral

Bills are assigned to a committee based on topic; however, major bills may be assigned to multiple committees.

Subcommittee referral

Subcommittee referral

Committee and subcommittee consideration

Committee and subcommittee consideration

In the House, the chamber's members may force a bill out of committee through a discharge petition.

Rules committee action

Floor consideration

Floor consideration

Chambers may bypass conference committee action by passing amended bills from the other chamber. Party leaders in the two chambers will also negotiate throughout the process.

Conference committee action

Final consideration of conference committee's bill

Final consideration of conference committee's bill

Presidential consideration

Presidential veto

President signs bill

Presidents may shape bills through the threat of a veto.

House and Senate reconsideration

Bill becomes a law

House and Senate override presidential veto

The vast majority of bills introduced never become law, and members realize these odds. According to Sinclair, "members may introduce legislation for a variety of reasons, ranging from placating a pesky interest group in their home state or district to publicizing a little recognized problem or an innovative approach to an acknowledged problem. Members may not expect certain of their bills to pass and, sometimes, may not even want them to."[19]

REFERRAL TO COMMITTEE INVOLVES POLITICAL STRATEGY

Because committees are so important to the ultimate success or failure of a bill, assignment to committee involves strategic political calculations. In the textbook model, a bill simply goes to the committee that has jurisdiction over that policy area. In practice, committees sometimes fight for bill assignments that would expand or protect their jurisdiction.

Bills may be assigned to more than one committee—a process called multiple referral—especially if the bill is large and complex. The rules governing multiple referral have changed over time, and the practice is more common in the House than the Senate. While multiple referral can be useful in that "multiple perspectives are brought to bear on complex problems," having more than one committee involved often increases the chances that a bill will get hung up in the legislative process and expire.[20]

BILLS ARE ALTERED—AND DIE—DUE TO COMMITTEE AND SUBCOMMITTEE ACTION. Once referred to one or more committees, legislation is usually sent to one or more subcommittees—more narrowly focused groups of legislators operating under the guidance of the parent committee of which they are a part. Committees and subcommittees hold hearings to gather information about a bill or issue. Outside experts may be brought in to testify. The **markup** session allows committee members to make changes to a bill before the committee reports it to the floor. The committee report follows the bill from committee to floor. It acts as a history of the bill and offers guidance to administrative agencies and (if necessary) courts about the committee's intent regarding the bill. Sometimes early cost estimates of the bill's provisions are included in the conference report.

Congressional committees are the graveyards of most bills. In committee, bills can die from a committee's refusal to report the bill to the full chamber, changes made to them to make them impassable on the House or Senate floor, or simple neglect. The committee may reject the bill by vote, or it may table the bill with no further action. In the House, a member may file a discharge petition to free a bill from an unfriendly committee and move it to the House floor for a vote if this is agreed to by a majority of representatives. Discharge efforts are rarely successfully used, but they can serve to "pressure a committee and the majority party leadership to bring to the floor measures that they would rather not consider."[21] Often the mere threat of using a procedural maneuver can shape legislative outcomes by signaling to other members that they may face opposition from members of the minority party.

VOTING TAKES PLACE DURING FLOOR CONSIDERATION. Once they have successfully passed out of committee, bills proceed to consideration on the floors of the House and Senate.

RULES AND INSTITUTIONS SHAPE CONSIDERATION IN THE HOUSE. An important difference between the House and the Senate is the role of the House **Committee on Rules** in the legislative process, which has no equally powerful analogue in the Senate. A majority of the House Rules Committee's members are chosen by the Speaker. This committee determines when a bill will be subject to debate and vote on the House floor, how long the debate will last, and whether amendments will be allowed on the floor. These special rules can play a major role in whether the bill passes the House or not.

Open rules allow all relevant amendments, while closed rules prohibit amendments other than those reported by committee. Most bills are considered under rules that fall in between these extremes, with modified open or modified closed rules. The rules about amendments are important because adding amendments to a bill is yet one more way to kill a piece of legislation. Killer amendments are designed to do just that by peeling away support for a bill by adding unpalatable or indefensible language or provisions. Closed rules can occasionally be used to kill a bill as well, if there are only enough members who would support a bill if key amendments were added, which is not allowed under closed rules.

markup
the process during which a bill is revised prior to a final vote in Congress.

Committee on Rules (House)
a powerful committee that determines when a bill will be subject to debate and vote on the House floor, how long the debate will last, and whether amendments will be allowed on the floor.

Tom Williams/CQ Roll Call

If the House approves the rules governing a bill, then floor debate on the bill begins under those rules. A vote to accept or reject the rules reported out of the Rules Committee can be just as consequential to the fate of a piece of legislation as an actual vote on a bill—though in ways that are less visibly clear to most American voters. If allowed, amendments may be offered and, perhaps, amendments to amendments. The time allowed for debate and who controls that time will also have been set by the Rules Committee.

A **roll-call vote** is a vote in which each member of the chamber debating a bill indicates "yea," "nay," or "present." In the House, most votes are electronic. Many interest groups keep track of key votes on issues relevant to them, scoring individual members on how friendly or unfriendly their votes have been to the members of that interest group.

▲ Senator Tammy Duckworth, D-IL, heads into the Capitol building for a vote in April 2018, bringing her newborn daughter, Maile Pearl, along with her. Earlier that week, the Senate had passed a resolution to allow children younger than one year old onto the Senate floor during votes, a change that facilitated Duckworth's participation.

INDIVIDUAL SENATORS PLAY A STRONGER ROLE IN SENATE CONSIDERATION.

In the Senate, individual senators have more ability to shape outcomes on the floor than their House colleagues. Party leadership still matters, however, and the Senate majority leaders schedule the agenda. While the House was first to adopt more formal procedures for bill consideration, the Senate has also become more formalized—though not to the same degree as the House. In the Senate, most procedures are governed by unanimous consent, in which all senators agree to let a motion proceed to a vote. A simple unanimous consent request may be used on noncontroversial measures. A more complex unanimous consent agreement will be worked out between the parties on major legislation to govern the length of debate and the rules governing amendments.

If an individual senator objects to a bill or part of a bill, that senator may place a hold on the legislation and communicate to the majority leader her or his reservations about the bill. In their ability to place holds, offer amendments, and debate issues on the floor, individual senators have the ability to consume Congress's scarcest resource: time. As Sinclair reported, "a single dissatisfied senator, even if she is junior and a minority party member, can cause a great deal of trouble."[22] While the majority leader does not have to honor the hold request, a hold indicates the possibility of a filibuster on the bill.

A **filibuster** is the use of the power of individual senators to continue to debate issues in order to delay a motion or vote on the floor.[23] Only a successful vote of **cloture**, which requires three-fifths of senators (sixty), can shut down debate and end a filibuster, allowing the Senate to move on to a vote. Therefore, a determined minority party, provided they have at least forty-one seats and are able to maintain party unity, can delay or kill legislation through the use of the filibuster.

The filibuster has a long and controversial history in the Senate. In 1917, under the urging of President Woodrow Wilson, the Senate adopted the rule of cloture. At the time, ending a filibuster required a two-thirds majority; it was changed to three-fifths in 1975. The placing of holds and threats of a filibuster are increasingly common in a closely split but deeply divided Senate. Because of the increased use of the filibuster threat, votes of cloture have become much more numerous as well. Senators have not only threatened to filibuster a bill they object to; they have also at times held up an unrelated vote or confirmation of a presidential nominee in order to extract concessions on something else, a process referred to as hostage taking.[24]

Changes to Senate rules lowered the cloture threshold to a simple majority for executive branch nominees and lower-level federal judges (by the Democratic-controlled Senate in 2013) and for Supreme Court nominees (by the Republican-controlled Senate in 2017). The ability to filibuster most bills in the

roll-call vote
a recorded vote on a bill.

filibuster
a tactic through which an individual senator may postpone action on a piece of legislation.

cloture
a procedure through which senators can end debate on a bill and proceed to action, provided three-fifths of senators agree to it.

Senate, however, remained. During debates over the budget bill in the spring of 2017, President Trump called for the elimination of the filibuster entirely in a set of Twitter posts. "Either elect more Republican Senators in 2018 or change the rules now to 51%," he tweeted. "Our country needs a good 'shutdown' in September to fix this mess!"[25] In a rare bipartisan response to his comments, "sixty-one senators signed a letter circulated by Senators Chris Coons, Democrat of Delaware, and Susan Collins, Republican of Maine, backing the 60-vote threshold on legislation."[26]

THE HOUSE AND SENATE RESOLVE DIFFERENCES BETWEEN THEIR BILLS

The next step in the legislative process is to resolve differences between House and Senate versions of a bill prior to presidential action. The formal structure for reconciling differences between two versions of a bill is the conference committee. Traditionally bipartisan, the Speaker of the House chooses that chamber's members. Because the Senate operates under unanimous consent, leaders from both parties choose its members to conference. Key players on a bill's progress through Congress are usually included as well.

When the differences are over spending amounts, negotiation is usually more straightforward. When they involve major policy differences—especially if one party controls the House and another the Senate—negotiations may be much more difficult. Because the process of sending a bill to conference from the Senate requires several procedural votes, which are subject to filibuster threat, the modern Congress often bypasses conference, though it still has to produce identical language.

On minor bills, or when the differences are small, one chamber may avoid going to conference by simply accepting the other chamber's version of the bill. This especially happens late in a session when time is scarce and can be used by the political opposition as a weapon.[27] Party leaders may also negotiate informally behind the scenes, with the results of these negotiations offered as amendments. The strategy of ping-ponging (also called amendment exchange) is also designed to avoid having to go to conference. House and Senate versions are amended and sent back and forth between the two chambers until the process has produced a single text.

BILLS GO BACK TO THE FLOOR FOR RECONSIDERATION

Once differences between the two versions have been resolved, the single bill goes back to each chamber for reconsideration, without the possibility of amendment. By this point, on major bills, party leaders have already engaged in lengthy negotiations with their counterparts in the other chamber to avoid any surprises.

THE PRESIDENT TAKES ACTION

Following successful passage in each chamber, the bill goes to the president for action. The president then has three choices for each bill that lands on her or his desk. The president may sign it, in which case the bill becomes a law. She or he may **veto** it, sending it back to Congress with the objections noted. Bills that are vetoed can still become law if two-thirds of both chambers vote to override the president's veto. Veto overrides are not common and signal a deep disconnect between a president and Congress.

As with a filibuster in the Senate, the power of a presidential veto lies as much with the *threat* of its use as with the actual veto. Veto bargaining is a negotiation tactic used by presidents to shape the legislation before it lands on his or her desk by using the threat of an eventual veto to gain desired concessions or amendments.[28] The president's third option is to do nothing, though what happens next depends on how much time is left in that session of Congress. If the president does nothing and there are ten or more days left in session (Sundays excluded), the bill becomes law anyway. This quiet veto does not change the outcome, but it might signal to American voters presidential displeasure with all or part of the law. If Congress has adjourned that year's session during the ten-day period and the president has not signed it, then the law is vetoed, an outcome that is called a pocket veto. A controversial tactic for Congress to avoid a pocket veto is to leave one or more members behind while everyone else goes home.

veto
the power of a president to reject a bill passed by Congress, sending it back to the originating branch with objections noted.

1. Most bills are _____.

    a. defeated on the floors of the House and the Senate

    b. defeated in committee

    c. passed by the House but defeated in the Senate

    d. vetoed by the president

2. The term *unorthodox lawmaking* refers to the ways in which _____.

    a. bills representing excluded groups of Americans are introduced into Congress

    b. interest groups use campaign contributions to influence the legislative process

    c. there are possibly illegal ways of passing laws

    d. standard processes of lawmaking are more fluid than those presented in textbooks

3. The threat of a filibuster is used to force members of the _____.

    a. House of Representatives to reconsider or revise a bill

    b. Senate to reconsider or revise a bill

    c. federal judiciary to reconsider cases before it

    d. state legislatures to sign off on a proposed bill

4. Why might referral to a particular committee be an effective use of political power?

_____

Answer Key: 1. b; 2. d; 3. b; 4. Answers should include the role of committee chairs and committee makeup in determining the fate of a bill.

GETTING TO CONGRESS INVOLVES PERSONAL, PROFESSIONAL, ELECTORAL, AND FINANCIAL FACTORS

- **Understand the factors that influence an individual's decision to run, and the resources and skills that successful candidates need.**

The 115th Congress, which began in January 2017 and will be replaced in 2019, is the most diverse in the nation's history.[29] Despite those gains, women represent only a fraction of Congress even though they make up just over half of the voting-eligible population. Members of other historically under-represented groups have also made numerical gains within the institution, but, again not in numbers proportionate to the population.

Getting elected, however, is only one of several steps. Would-be members must first decide to run. They must win, learn to navigate the institution, rise up the ranks of power, and get reelected.

Why do candidates choose to run for office in the first place? How are their chances affected by the structure of congressional elections? How have the rules and organization of Congress itself shaped how much power they have within the institution? To explore these questions, we jump back in time to 1992, when a record number of women ran for and won seats in Congress.

That year, many of these women began their journeys as congressional representatives, joining the lone two women senators then on the Hill.[30] Many thought it was about time. In the run-up to the elections, Dianne Feinstein, then a candidate for a Senate seat for California, famously remarked, "Two percent may be good for fat in milk, but it's bad for women in the U.S. Senate."[31] Their collective electoral success meant that 1992 would go down as "the year of the woman," with a record fifty-three women in total elected to Congress.[32] As these new senators embarked on their new jobs, each had to learn the spoken and unspoken rules that governed the U.S. Congress, figure out how to make their voices heard, and find mentors to show them the way.

Like all members of Congress, the pathways that ultimately led the women who ran for office in 1992 to Congress were as diverse as they were and involved factors like their personal motivations, their professional experience, the way congressional elections work, and whether they had

AP Photo/Greg Gibson, File

◀ Senate Judiciary Committee members Joseph R. Biden, D-DE (presiding), and Senator Ted Kennedy, D-MA (right), ask pointed and skeptical questions of Anita Hill during the Clarence Thomas confirmation hearings, 1991.

basic supports like money and staff. So, how did this particular group get to Washington? And why did they run?

A SINGULAR EVENT GALVANIZES A NEW FIELD OF CANDIDATES

For many of the women who ran in that fateful election, one moment in congressional history crystalized their commitment to bringing about change in Congress: the Senate confirmation hearings of Clarence Thomas to the U.S. Supreme Court.

Federal judicial confirmations are often very politically charged, since appointments have profound and long-lasting consequences. Given Thomas's conservative views, the confirmation proceedings were bound to be heated. However, an unusual point of controversy emerged during Thomas's hearings. Thomas's former aide, Professor Anita Hill, asserted that Thomas had sexually harassed her while the two were serving in the federal government.

Though many women were concerned about the specific charges of sexual harassment, it was the skepticism displayed by the members of the all-white, male Senate Judiciary Committee to Hill's testimony—dismissive and condescending in the eyes of many—that galvanized women around the country by "symbolizing the lack of representation for women and their interests on Capitol Hill."[33] In response, "many voters decided that if given the chance they would vote for a woman candidate, in part because she was a woman. . . . [P]arty and grassroots organizations redoubled their efforts to find and fund women candidates. And . . . a number of women decided that they would put themselves on the line and run for local, state, and national office."[34]

Across the country in Washington State, Patty Murray, then a state legislator, "watched in disbelief as the committee members questioned Hill's veracity about Thomas' sexual advances and innuendo. Murray found herself asking 'Who's saying what I would say if I were there?'"[35] That evening, at a neighborhood party, as others expressed similar frustration, Murray announced, "You know what? I'm going to run for the Senate."[36]

POLITICAL AMBITION LAUNCHES CAREERS

Murray exemplifies a characteristic that, according to political scientists Linda Fowler and Robert McClure, sets declared candidates apart from "the unseen candidates—the men and women who

PRACTICING POLITICAL SCIENCE

GENDER AND METAPHORS OF POWER IN IMAGE

Paul Hosefros/The New York Times/Redux

AP Photo/Joe Rosenthal

Barbara Boxer, Nita Lowey, Eleanor Holmes Norton, Pat Schroeder, Jolene Unsoeld, and the late Patsy Mink, the Democratic women members of the House of Representatives in 1991, march to the U.S. Senate to voice their concerns about the treatment of Anita Hill and her charges of sexual harassment during the Clarence Thomas confirmation hearings. The American press called their action "the women's Iwo Jima," conjuring up the iconic images of American servicemen during World War II. In the second photo, we see that image.

For Boxer, "that was an angle tailored by the media. We wanted to try to help the senators rethink their position, and we felt that they might appreciate hearing our perspective. . . . All we were asking was that the Senate take a serious look at Anita Hill's charges."[37]

WHAT Do You Think?

Why do you think a war metaphor was used to portray the efforts of the congresswomen? In what ways might a traditionally male-gendered metaphor shape readers' perceptions of their efforts?

Think about candidates running for Congress. Have you encountered images and portrayals of those you might choose as your representative or senator? How did those depictions reflect your own views of these individuals or your own goals for congressional action? How might they have not?

could have run for Congress but chose not to." That is, she had **political ambition**.[38] Only those with the strongest personal desire to act in politics decide to face the long odds against success, especially if such a bid would mean facing a well-resourced incumbent. Where does political ambition come from? The answers are not always neatly categorized by gender, racial or ethnic identity, or any one simple category. As Murray's example shows, political ambition is as unique to a potential candidate as it is to the constituents she or he hopes to represent.

The decision to stand for national legislative office, though a monumental one, is only the first step in the long journey toward membership in the U.S. Congress. The next step is to actually get elected. For first-timers, this involves a very steep climb. The odds are stacked against them. In this process, the first thing a candidate has to assess is whose votes she or he is trying to win.

CONSTITUENCY, INCUMBENCY, AND OTHER ELECTORAL FACTORS LAY THE GROUNDWORK

political ambition
a personal desire to enter politics.

The Constitution sets the framework for the boundaries of constituency. Would-be senators hope to represent the voters of their states. Hopeful candidates for the House strive to secure the votes of the constituents in their congressional districts, the boundaries of which can and do change in response to fluctuations in state population and the often intensely political process of redistricting, as we explored in Chapter 10.

As we have also explored, the power of incumbency—running for reelection as opposed to running for the first time—strongly affects the outcomes of congressional elections. Congressional incumbents possess so many advantages, such as media coverage, a record of providing beneficial service and legislation to a state or district, and name recognition, that qualified challengers often rationally wait until they can run in an open seat election after an incumbent has retired or moved on to another office.

In the 1992 elections, there was an important crack in the normal power of incumbency. For a variety of reasons, there were a record high number of open congressional seats and potential challengers who had been waiting for their chance pounced. The advantages that incumbent candidates would normally have enjoyed were gone. According to government professor Clyde Wilcox, "For experienced women politicians who lived in the open districts, 1992 was likely to be their best shot for many years at a House seat."[39]

Moreover, the end of the Cold War focused voters' attention away from issues of national security and onto issues of domestic policy, issues on which a number of women candidates had strong track records. Finally, with Democrat Bill Clinton's presidential victory that year, the electoral strength of the Democratic Party helped other Democratic candidates. Of the twenty-four women elected to the House for the first time in 1992, twenty were Democrats. All five of the newly elected or successfully reelected women in the Senate were Democrats as well.

▲ Senator Patty Murray (D-WA) is the ranking member of the Senate Health, Education, Labor and Pensions Committee; a member of the powerful Senate Appropriations Committee; and sits on the committees for the Budget and for Veterans' Affairs. She has risen the ranks of Congress since her first election in 1992.

EXPERIENCE AND MONEY LEGITIMIZE CANDIDATES

When challengers do decide to stand for office, they need many things; however, above all else, they need experience and money. Experience is hard earned, usually gained by moving up through the layers of local and state politics and becoming professional, polished, and respected. Congressional elections are usually no place for amateurs, who often lack the knowledge, political organization, and well-honed political skills prerequisite to success in the high-stakes enterprise of a national campaign.

Looking back on her successful campaign for the U.S. Senate in 1992, Senator Dianne Feinstein, D-CA, advised congressional hopefuls, especially young women, to "earn your spurs" by starting locally on the school board or town council and building a coherent portfolio that reflects a set of consistent policies "so that people will turn to you."[40] Money is inseparable from congressional elections. It buys media spots, funds a ground campaign, and acts to scare off potential opponents. The pressures of fund-raising in the modern Congress are relentless.

The opportunity presented in 1992 would not have translated into electoral success without a slate of experienced and well-funded candidates. Women candidates were able to recruit individuals and organizations who were willing to contribute money and time to their political campaigns and to organize and mobilize voters on their behalf.

For Carol Moseley Braun, who had previously served in the Illinois House of Representatives, the Thomas confirmation hearings were most certainly a contributor to her decision to run for the Senate in 1992. However, her path to the chamber was also paved by the hard-earned experience of Chicago politics—as tough a venue as there is in American government. In the primary, Moseley Braun would defeat the incumbent Democrat from Illinois who had voted to confirm Clarence Thomas and then also beat the Republican challenger in the general election.

For candidates like Moseley Braun and Murray, the Thomas confirmation hearings and the increased national attention on issues of concern to American women voters brought money to the table. Organizations called political action committees (PACs), which raise and spend money on behalf of candidates, contributed large amounts of money to their campaigns that year. In particular, PACs that were focused on financing and advising women candidates played a major role. Patty Murray's

▲ Carol Moseley Braun greets constituents in her hometown of Chicago, Illinois.

campaign received critical early support from one of the largest, EMILY's List, a pro-choice Democratic women's PAC. As political scientist Candice Nelson put it, "Early money enables candidates to do the things necessary to establish credibility: hire a pollster, develop a campaign plan, and be prepared for challenges to her credibility when they occur."[41] EMILY's List was founded in 1985, and by 1992, it was the largest of all PACs in the election.[42] The group's membership grew from three thousand before the Thomas-Hill hearings to twenty-four thousand after the election.[43]

Just as in 1992, the 2018 election campaigns saw a significant jump in contributions by women toward congressional campaigns. According to the nonpartisan Center for Responsive Politics in October 2017, the "number of female donors to federal candidates and committees has skyrocketed by roughly 284 percent," compared to a similar point in the 2015–2016 election cycle, all the more noteworthy given that 2018 is not a presidential election year.[44]

All congressional candidates are driven to run for office to advance and advocate a set of policy goals—to change the congressional conversation. Each has a set of issues they want to focus on. Having succeeded in winning office, the next step is for them to figure out how to translate those goals into actual laws in order to make their voices, and those of their constituents, heard in Congress.

WHAT HAVE I **LEARNED**?

1. The term *political ambition* refers to _____.
   a. the need for potential candidates to have the commitment necessary to overcome the long odds faced by a challenger running against an incumbent
   b. a willingness on the part of first-time candidates to skirt campaign fund-raising laws
   c. a desire to use a seat in Congress as a springboard to the presidency
   d. the willingness of congressional incumbents to use their advantages to prevent credible challengers

2. _____ tend(s) to attract more first-time challengers in congressional elections.
   a. Open seat elections
   b. Elections held in the same years as presidential elections
   c. Long-time incumbents
   d. A strong economy

3. What were some of the reasons why a record number of women candidates decided to run for Congress in 1992?

4. What qualities do successful first-time candidates for Congress generally need?

Answer Key: 1. a; 2. a; 3. Answers should include the fallout from the Thomas confirmation hearings, the number of open seat elections, and campaign support from outside groups; 4. Answers should include experience and money and may discuss the challenges of running against incumbents.

MEMBERS REPRESENT CONSTITUENTS BY HOW THEY ACT AND WHO THEY ARE

- Connect the issues surrounding the representation of women in Congress to the challenges involving representation of other individuals in America.

The most difficult question in the study of Congress is what may seem to be the simplest: What does it mean to represent one's constituents in Congress? Political theorist Hannah Pitkin has written about the multiple meanings of representation in Congress, noting for starters that "representation means . . . *re-presentation*, a making present again."[45] What are constituents asking their representatives to "make present" in Washington that was not there before? Part of the answer lies in *acting*—in the sense of what representatives do. In a representative democracy, citizens choose representatives to act on their behalf—to vote on the floor and in committee, to sponsor legislation, to negotiate, and to lead. Another part of the answer lies in *being*—in the sense of who the representatives are.

When voters select representatives, they are choosing people who may or may not reflect and share their policy preferences, identities, interests, and lived experiences. They ask that their representatives transmit information about them—the constituents—to the other members of Congress by adding their voices to the debates and deliberations within the institution. In doing so, according to political scientist Richard Fenno, voters are in a sense asking their representatives to take on sometimes competing roles, which he used the term *home style* to denote. Voters want their political representatives to be effective in Washington, which takes them away from home. However, voters also want their members to come home, to present themselves and explain to voters what they have been up to and what they are going to accomplish.[46] More time at home connects representatives and senators to their constituents, while effective representation necessarily involves spending time operating in the intricate machinery of Congress.

ACTING IN CONGRESS INVOLVES VISIBLE AND INVISIBLE LEGISLATIVE WORK

Passing laws—the legislative function—is Congress's most important task, and voting on the House and Senate floor is the most public legislative act members undertake. However, the process of legislation involves many stages and many less visible acts, such as committee work, bill sponsorship, and negotiation, which can pose a challenge to constituents trying to keep tabs on their elected representatives.

LEGISLATORS' VOTING DECISIONS ARE AFFECTED BY CONSTITUENTS' INTERESTS AND POLITICAL PARTIES. When approaching a vote in Congress, members have several factors to consider.[47] First, they must always at least consider their constituents' interests. Though a senator or representative may ultimately decide to vote against the wishes of those who sent her or him to Washington, no member can ignore voters repeatedly without facing a constituent backlash. If, however, a senator or representative has earned a level of trust from constituents through long and successful service to them, then she or he may be more willing to act against constituent interests if it feels like the right course of action.[48]

A member's political party also influences how that member will vote. Members may seek input from their colleagues, especially if those colleagues are policy specialists and are known to have a particular expertise relevant to a bill. Input from a member's congressional staff may play a role, as may signals from interest groups, especially if individuals within the interest groups can convince the representative that his or her constituents agree with the group's position. Finally, the president may try to convince representatives to vote a certain way, especially if they are in the same political party.

REPRESENTATIVES' ACTIONS ARE SHAPED BY LEVEL OF CONSTITUENT KNOWLEDGE. Elections are the primary tool that voters have to shape the actions of their elected representatives. Voters can pressure candidates to make certain promises during campaigns in exchange for their vote and also threaten backlash in the future if those promises are not kept.[49] Both of these mechanisms, however, require some basic level of information on the part of constituents and representatives. Constituents must have policy preferences to begin with and must communicate those

preferences to their representatives. They must also have some basic level of information about the actions of their representatives in Congress to know whether to reward or punish those representatives in the next election.

Unfortunately, a long tradition of research in political science has shown that on most issues, the majority of constituents are poorly informed, uninterested, or lack any coherent policy preferences. Some constituents are far better informed than others, especially if they have formed themselves into an interest group for the purpose of influencing congressional action. This inequality of information runs the risk of tilting Congress in the direction of acting only in the interests of its most informed and involved constituents to the detriment of the majority of uninformed ones.

▲ Vocal constituents like Patty Smith, above, help shape the behavior of their representatives in Congress. Here, Smith poses a question to Senator Jeff Flake (R-AZ) at a town hall event in April 2017 in Mesa, Arizona. Republican lawmakers across the country have been confronted with angry voters in similar settings. Flake eventually decided not to run for reelection in 2018.

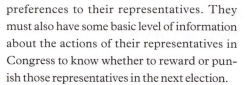

Political scientist R. Douglas Arnold's research explored the ways in which Congress might pass laws that benefit the many even if they impose costs on a well-informed and involved few. But this is not easy.[50] First, representatives must shield themselves as much as possible from the backlash of powerful interests, with as few easily traceable votes as possible. Their leaders must frame failure to act as an unacceptable alternative, making it easier for members to explain individually costly votes.

In addition, there must be a real threat that voters who are not currently paying attention might become aware of and involved in an issue in the future. Interest groups may perform the role of "auditing" on behalf of less informed and less aware voters.[51] Congressional challengers may also play a role, bringing up issues in a campaign that incumbents incorporate into their own agendas.[52] Even the most secure incumbents worry about an issue that might cause their constituents alarm or concern. Successfully worrying about what might happen is part of what has kept them in office in the first place.

KEY ASPECTS OF LAWMAKING HAPPEN OUTSIDE THE PUBLIC EYE. There is another challenge to the ability of constituents to control or influence representatives' actions. While votes on the floor or in committee can usually be traced to a particular member, much of the actual work on legislation happens outside the public eye. The choices that representatives make in allocating their time and energy can have important consequences for the fate of legislation, whether these choices determine how much effort to undertake to steer a bill through the constitutional obstacle course that is Congress or how much energy to devote to blocking a bill's progress.[53] The challenge for constituents is that these individual choices are difficult to observe and, therefore, reward or punish.

Yet members do act, even when the reelectoral math does not add up. Why? Sometimes the decision to act comes from personal motivations and experiences. Senators Feinstein and Moseley Braun both were involved in one of the most important pieces of legislation taken up by the 103rd Congress: a comprehensive effort to reduce crime and reshape criminal justice policy. Following their elections in 1992, both joined the powerful Senate Judiciary Committee and used their experience and qualifications to translate their influence into legislation. According to one article, in the Senate, "Moseley-Braun . . . highlighted racial concerns while Feinstein led a successful floor fight to add an assault weapons ban to the Senate crime bill."[54] Feinstein had personally witnessed the assassinations of San Francisco mayor George Moscone and supervisor Harvey Milk, becoming acting mayor in the aftermath of their shooting deaths. Moseley Braun summed up her colleague's efforts: "I'd say that the assault weapons ban is a testimony to her hard work and just doggedness, because at a time when I and every other member of the Committee had concluded that this was a symbolic thing and there was no way we were going to get the votes, Dianne went out and worked and got the votes."[55]

**PARTISAN POLARIZATION STRONGLY AFFECTS VOTING AND COOPER-
ATION.** Representatives do not act in a vacuum. Their behavior is influenced both by the rules and procedures in Congress and by political parties. Political scientists, congressional observers, and some members themselves have become increasingly concerned about trends in partisan polarization in which members of parties vote and act strongly with their own party and become less likely to cross the aisle and cooperate with each other. While scholars disagree about the causes of polarization in Congress, voting records on the House and Senate floor show a clear trend toward intraparty cohesion (see Figure 12.5).[56]

▼ FIGURE 12.5

Visualizing Partisan Polarization

In 2015 a group of researchers mapped the networks of members of the House of Representatives from 1949 to 2011, identifying points of agreement between members on significant issues based on political party. Democratic members are identified in blue and Republicans in red. Each dot represents an individual. The connections represent points of agreement above a specific threshold. Note that over time, the dots have increasingly separated into red and blue groups and are increasingly tightly clustered.

Source: Clio Andris et al., "The Rise of Partisanship and Super-Cooperators in the U.S. House of Representatives," *PloS One* 10, no. 4 (2015), http://journals.plos.org/plosone/article?id=10.1371/journal.pone.0123507.

REUTERS/Jonathan Ernst

▲ Senator Barbara Mikulski, D-MD (right), was well known for her mentoring of other women in the Senate. Here, Mikulski plays host to fellow women senators, including new senator-elect Joni Ernst, R-IA (left), at a meeting at the U.S. Capitol in Washington on November 13, 2014. Also pictured are Senator Patty Murray, D-WA (second from left); Senator Jeanne Shaheen, D-NH; and Senator Kirsten Gillibrand, D-NY.

Intense partisanship can lead to more than ill feelings between members. It may contribute to gridlock, a situation in which Congress's ability to legislate is slowed or stopped by its inability to overcome divisions, especially those based on partisanship. Gridlock is made more likely in a period of divided government, which occurs when control of the presidency and one or both chambers of Congress are split between the two major parties.

MENTORSHIP IS ANOTHER FORM OF REPRESENTATION. One important, but not frequently discussed, way that legislators can represent their own constituents—as well as those in other states and districts—is to act as mentors to newly elected colleagues. Mentorship builds the kinds of personal connections that a legislator needs to advance the interests of her or his constituents and also helps build a more effective legislative body.

After successfully defending her Senate seat in 1992, Barbara Mikulski took it upon herself to mentor her four new women colleagues, a practice she continued up to her retirement in 2017.

DESCRIPTIVE REPRESENTATION IS ABOUT WHO MEMBERS ARE

Many of the Framers and supporters of the U.S. Constitution expected that Congress would be a reflection or "portrait" of the people in the Republic, though the definition of who had the right to be a represented person was highly restrictive.

Several issues and challenges arise when attempting to view Congress as a portrait of America. The first is that no single member can represent each of his or her constituents' diverse identities, experiences, and interests. Even if somehow possible, this might not be desirable in the extreme. Constituents, for example, might want their legislators to be more knowledgeable about, experienced in, and motivated to act in the messy space of politics than the average American voter.

DESCRIPTIVE REPRESENTATION INVOLVES WHO MEMBERS ARE. Instead, when scholars and observers talk about making Congress a more accurate reflection of America, they are referring to increasing **descriptive representation**: Members of Congress "mirror some of the more frequent experiences and outward manifestations of belonging to the group."[57] Usually the goal of increasing descriptive representation in Congress is to selectively increase the membership of a particular group or groups who because of other historical and contextual factors remain underrepresented in proportion to their share of the population.[58]

Looking at the modern Congress, it is clear that the members do not come close to presenting a mirror of the American electorate. While Congress has grown more descriptively representative in recent years, women, lower-income Americans, members of racial and ethnic minorities, members of certain religious faiths, and lesbian, gay, bisexual, and transgender (LGBT) Americans remain underrepresented in proportion to their percentage of the American voting-age population.

As a whole, members of Congress tend to be older, whiter, wealthier, and more educated than the American electorate. The lack of descriptive representation raises a complicated set of related questions: Does it matter? Is it necessary for a member of Congress to share the lived experiences of the constituents whom she or he hopes to represent? Can a man represent a woman? Can a wealthy person represent a lower-income person?

Some scholars have argued that there may be benefits to having a descriptively representative legislature apart from what it actually does in Congress. Seeing a diversity of faces in Congress may, in the eyes of the American electorate, confer greater legitimacy to the institution and the policies that it passes.

descriptive representation
the degree to which a body of representatives in a legislature does or does not reflect the diversity of that nation's identities and lived experiences.

Other scholars have pointed out that legislators who do not descriptively represent a particular group of constituents still need to pay attention to their concerns.

Another challenge to descriptive representation is that any given legislator may share key attributes with some of her or his constituents but not others. Does a wealthy African American legislator from an urban district reflect her constituents? In terms of racial and ethnic identity, quite possibly. In terms of income and wealth, perhaps not so much. Similarly, does a white legislator from a midwestern agricultural district with little experience in farming describe his constituents? Again, in some ways, probably, but maybe not in others.

PRACTICING POLITICAL SCIENCE

REPRESENTING REPRESENTATION

The U.S. Congress remains descriptively unrepresentative. Women and members of most minority groups remain underrepresented in Congress in proportion to their numbers in the American voting-age population.

There has been improvement in recent elections, however. Telling the story of this improvement in pictures and graphs is subject to the way in which these data are presented. As with all data stories told with graphs, how one draws the *scale* of the chart, the vertical or *y*-axis here, can convey very different impressions using the same data. Consider this graph of the percentages of women in the Senate over the past twenty-five Congresses (fifty years). In this chart, the gains made by women in recent elections look quite impressive. Notice, however, that the *y*-axis (the vertical one) does not go from zero to one hundred—the actual number of senators—but from one to twenty-five.

Women Senators in the U.S. Congress

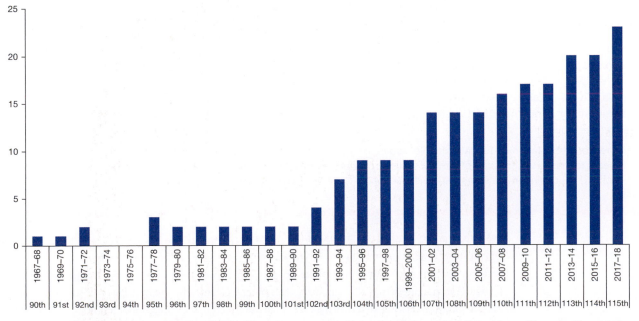

Source: Jennifer E. Manning and Ida A. Brudnick, "Women in Congress, 1917–2018: Service Dates and Committee Assignments by Member, and Lists by State and Congress," Congressional Research Service, May 17, 2018, https://www.senate.gov/CRSpubs/bee42bd4-0624-492c-a3b0-a5436cb9e9a2.pdf.

(Continued)

Women Senators Scaled by the Full Senate Numbers

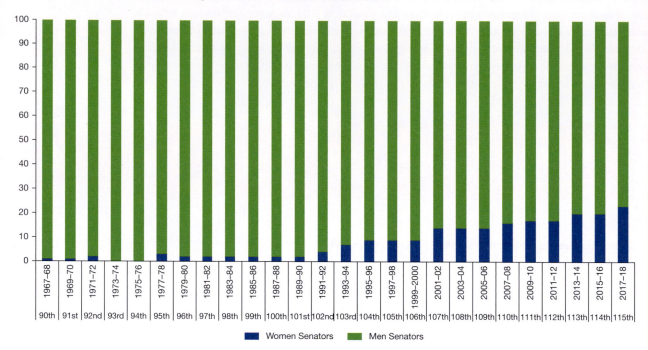

Source: Jennifer E. Manning and Ida A. Brudnick, "Women in Congress, 1917–2018: Service Dates and Committee Assignments by Member, and Lists by State and Congress," Congressional Research Service, May 17, 2018, https://www.senate.gov/CRSpubs/bee42bd4-0624-492c-a3b0-a5436cb9e9a2.pdf.

Consider the same data but with the scale of the *y*-axis showing the full range of the number of senators that might be categorized on the basis of gender, from zero to one hundred.

This presentation of the same data in the second graph tells a very different story. With the full scale changed from zero to one hundred, recent gains in the descriptive representation of women in the Senate do not look so impressive. The tactic of cutting off, or truncating, the scale of a graph can be used to either present a pessimistic or an optimistic portrait, depending on the data storyteller's objective.

In the first presentation of the data, the election of 1992 appears to mark the beginning of a major wave of change, which it did. Looking at the same data in the second figure, however, tells a somewhat different story; there were gains, to be sure, but much less revolutionary ones.

When reading a graph and the story it's telling, pay attention to the ways in which different presentations of the same set of data—in this case the scale—can portray very different narratives depending on which one the data storyteller wishes to present. The presentation of data can be just as political as that of word stories.

WHaT Do You Think?

Knowing that both figures represent the same data, might one still draw different conclusions? How might a strategic "data storyteller" make use of scale in graphs to argue different points?

RACIAL AND ETHNIC GERRYMANDERING INCREASES DESCRIPTIVE REPRES-ENTATION. States have redrawn congressional districts to try to improve the electoral chances of legislators of racial and ethnic minority identities and therefore the descriptive representation of Congress along these characteristics. There is, however, a potential contradiction in the logic of such racial and ethnic gerrymandering. Recall that in the case of partisan gerrymandering, the logic is to isolate the opposing party into a small number of districts, conceding those districts to the opposing party but diluting their votes in a larger number of other districts, thus "wasting" the opposing party's votes. In the case of racial and ethnic gerrymandering, the tactic is the same, but the goal is different: to concentrate minority voters in a small number of districts in order to help their overall representation in Congress.

Not all scholars agree that creating these majority-minority districts increases the overall representation of minorities in Congress. Political scientist Carol Swain has argued that while creating such districts increases the probability of electing African Americans within those districts, it does not necessarily improve the representation of African Americans overall.[59] Perhaps, Swain argued, it is better to have a larger number of legislators who have to consider the views of their African American constituents than to have a small number of descriptively representative legislators who lack enough votes to advocate for their positions.

If the creation of majority-minority districts dilutes the degree to which members have to attend to their minority constituents' interests, then that risk might need to be counterbalanced by having members who have a close connection to specific issues and are willing to undertake the work of making those voices present by, for example, introducing or sponsoring legislation.

ESSENTIALISM PROBLEMATIZES A FOCUS ON IDENTITY. Thinking about constituents in terms of specific characteristics poses another challenge, that of **essentialism**, which political theorist Jane Mansbridge defined as "the assumption that members of certain groups have an essential identity that all members of that group share and of which no others can partake."[60] Essentialism risks masking the complexity of views *within* members of that group, sidelining policy disagreements between them in the name of some shared "women's interest" or "African American interest." Second, it also risks cordoning off members' efforts into a few predefined acceptable issues: the idea that women should talk only about "women's issues" or that black people should talk only about "black issues."

SUBSTANTIVE REPRESENTATION CONNECTS HOW MEMBERS ACT AND WHO THEY ARE

Both the acts that members of Congress undertake and the degree to which they share the lived experiences of their constituents shape representation. It is the connection between acting and reflecting that holds the promise of sorting out some of the contradictions and challenges in each. While it very well may be important for American voters to feel that their Congress is a legitimate portrait of the nation, what really matters is, according to Hanna Pitkin, "the nature of the activity itself, what goes on during representation, the substance of the content of acting for others."[61] Pitkin calls this **substantive representation**.

Substantive representation is important because it holds the promise of linking constituents' lived experiences not just to the actions of their own legislators but to the actions of the institution itself, to the way that the institution works. It has the potential to improve the way that Congress deliberates by expanding the congressional agenda and by facilitating representation across geographical and partisan boundaries.

DELIBERATION MAY BE IMPROVED BY SUBSTANTIVE REPRESENTATION. As imagined by those who designed it, Congress is supposed to be much more than just a place to count predecided votes and hear preformed arguments. It is also supposed to be a place for **legislative deliberation**, the considered argument and discussion of the issues. Deliberation is discussion of "which policies are good for the polity as a whole, which policies are good for representatives' constituents, and when the interests of various groups within the policy and constituency conflict."[62]

Deliberation is itself a complicated thing. For viewpoints to be discussed, they must first capture the attention of a large enough number of legislators. Second, deliberation is personal, as often are its politics. Individual relationships between members who share interests and experiences can make for a more effective deliberative body. When this occurs, members who share common experiences can work with colleagues in the other party, thereby helping to counter trends in partisan polarization.

In any given session of Congress, there are only so many issues that can be dealt with and discussed, the list of which constitutes the legislative agenda. Why some issues seem to rocket toward the top of the agenda and others languish at the bottom or are ignored is sometimes easily explained—for example, in times of national crisis, some concerns are seen as more urgent than others. However, the setting of the

essentialism
the risks posed by linking individuals' lived experiences to policy preferences, whether by identifying those individuals by those policies or by excluding them from advocating different policy objectives.

substantive representation
the degree to which elected representatives or senators represent the interests and policy preferences of their constituents.

legislative deliberation
the considered argument and discussion of the issues by congressional representatives.

congressional agenda is often unpredictable.[63] By bringing unconsidered issues to Congress's table and making them salient, legislators who share common lived experiences with underrepresented constituents may enlarge the institution's agenda. In doing so, members are acting (in political theorist Jane Mansbridge's analysis) as surrogate representatives—they are representing people who may not live in their district or state but with whom they share common concerns.[64]

Presenting information to one's legislative colleagues is an important part of representation. After the 2000 election, a reporter asked Senator Kay Bailey Hutchinson, R-TX, "Why can't a male senator do everything a woman senator can do?" Hutchinson's reply was, "Sometimes, from our experience there are issues that men just haven't thought about. . . . Most of the time our colleagues are supportive once we've made the case."[65] Research supports Senator Hutchinson's assertion. For example, a 2017 study by the Rutgers University Center for American Women and Politics found—based on interviews with 83 of the 108 women in the 114th Congress—that women members were more likely to attend to issues of concern to women, "placing issues related to women's lives on the congressional agenda."[66] It is important to note that women members' approaches to representation did not mean that their policy solutions had to be the same. Women Republicans and Democrats often promoted different solutions to the same salient issues. The authors also reported that women members felt that their approach to bipartisanship benefited the institution overall.

In 1993, Carol Moseley Braun, D-IL—the only African American senator serving at the time—brought to the chamber's attention the larger implications of an issue that might have seemed trivial to many members, if it was on their radar at all. Senator Jesse Helms, R-NC, had offered as an amendment a renewal of the patent for the design of the symbol of the United Daughters of the Confederacy, which included the Confederate flag—an image many African Americans find problematic. Had Moseley Braun been focused only on her reelectoral prospects, this was probably not a battle that needed to be fought. Yet Moseley Braun successfully killed the amendment and in doing so signaled to her own constituents as well as to African American voters across the nation that she intended to voice their shared concerns in the Senate.

Rarely, however, can one legislator reshape the congressional agenda on his or her own. It requires enough members to join in advocating minority positions. And, as we have seen, the importance of committee action suggests that effective substantive representation requires enough members with shared experiences to make present these voices not just on the floor but behind closed doors in committees. Equally important is going beyond just getting a "woman's issue" or an "African American issue" on the congressional agenda by having enough voices to reveal the conflicts and tensions *within* members of these groups and presenting the full range of opinion on the issues.

WHAT HAVE I LEARNED?

1. Representation in Congress _____.
   a. has both descriptive and substantive elements
   b. involves both acting on behalf of constituents and understanding their concerns
   c. is affected by racial and ethnic gerrymandering
   d. All of the above

2. When members of Congress consider how to vote on a bill, they take into consideration _____.
   a. constituent interests
   b. their own reelectoral considerations
   c. information from staffers and fellow members of Congress
   d. All of the above

3. The difference between descriptive and substantive representation is _____.
   a. that descriptive representation focuses more on what members of Congress do than who they are
   b. that descriptive representation focuses on making present the lived experiences of members
   c. that descriptive representation focuses on creating a portrait of America in Congress
   d. All of the above

4. What do you think it means to truly represent one's constituents in Congress?

Answer Key: 1. d; 2. d; 3. c; 4. Answers should focus on the relationship between descriptive and substantive representation.

CONCLUSION: REPRESENTATION REMAINS COMPLEX, BUT THE LANDSCAPE CONTINUES TO CHANGE

Today, representation in Congress involves the same issues it always has: standing for constituents, bringing voices and energy to its deliberations and outcomes, and operating within an institution intentionally designed by the Framers of the Constitution to place brakes on the pace of political change.

By the time the results of the congressional election of 2018 were in, some things were clear, others very much in the air.

The 2018 midterm elections resulted in a set of firsts and records for American congresswomen. With several congressional races around the nation not yet fully counted—or headed for a runoff, a recount, or a legal challenge—a record-setting 118 women had won their House or Senate races, though not without several women incumbents losing their reelection bids.[67]

Included in the winners were the nation's first Latina congresswomen, Veronica Escobar (D-TX) and Sylvia Garcia (D-TX), its first Muslim congresswomen, Rashida Tlaib (D-MI) and Ilhan Omar (D-MN), and its first Native American congresswomen, Deb Haaland (D-NM) and Sharice Davids (D-KS).[68] Women Democrats far outnumbered women Republicans in gaining or defending seats, continuing the sharp gendered split between the two parties in Congress. A key consequence of the gendered partisan divide will be for chamber leadership in the Congress that convenes in January 2019.

In the House of Representatives, which shifted to Democratic control, the increase in the number of women and, crucially, the increasing seniority of women incumbents will result in increased representation of women in key leadership positions. Nancy Pelosi (D-CA) has been considered the likely, but not certain, front-runner for Speaker of the House. Maxine Waters (D-CA) is a front-runner to chair the House Financial Services Committee, a position that Waters indicated she would use to vigorously investigate President Trump's business dealings and potential ties to Russia. In the Senate, Republicans maintained control, ensuring that many of the seniormost women in the chamber would not be chosen to serve as committee chairs, as the Democratic Party remained the minority party.

The Framers of the Constitution did not intend for Congress to be purely and perfectly representative. They mistrusted the ability of *citizens* to avoid the dangers of faction. In recent decades, however, Congress has come to more accurately reflect the American electorate, though it is still far from being perfectly descriptive. These gains have not come about by chance; they are mostly due to the strategic actions of citizens to reshape Congress to better portray the diversity of the nation.

Representation and lawmaking in Congress are complicated, messy, and often uncomfortable. Though the legislative branch is the first branch of government—and viewed as the most powerful by the Framers—it is still only one of three. Over the course of American history, strategic political actors in the other two branches—the executive and judicial—have also tried to shape the power of their institutions, to present their own views of representation in the United States, and to stand for the people.

CHAPTER REVIEW

This chapter's main ideas are reflected in the Learning Objectives below. By reviewing them here, you should be able to **remember** the key points, **know** the terms that are central to the topic, and **think** about the critical issues raised in each section.

12.1 Understand how questions of representation involve political and institutional considerations as well as questions of identity.

REMEMBER
- The congressional elections of 2018 were importantly shaped by sharp partisan divides.
- One of the key issues in the elections was a record number of women running.
- Women congressional candidates were primarily running as Democrats.

KNOW
- represent (p. 323)

THINK
- Why do you think much larger numbers of women were running for Congress as Democrats than as Republicans?

12.2 Describe how the Constitution created Congress, including its structure and powers.

REMEMBER
- Congress is a bicameral legislature: the House of Representatives and the Senate are divided to establish a set of checks and balances within Congress.
- Members of the House are meant to be closer to the people. Senators are meant to be more insulated from the public to ensure greater stability.
- The House and Senate have legislative authority as well as budgetary and oversight powers.

KNOW
- appropriation (p. 328)
- earmarks (p. 328)
- fire alarm oversight (p. 329)
- impeachment (p. 330)
- oversight (p. 328)
- police patrol oversight (p. 329)
- senatorial courtesy (p. 330)
- statutes (p. 328)
- term limits (p. 327)

THINK
- What were the intended differences that the Framers devised in separating legislative representation between the House and the Senate?

12.3 Describe the rules, institutions, and processes that Congress itself has created to carry out its constitutional role.

REMEMBER
- Political parties exert a good deal of influence in Congress, especially over key leadership positions.
- Congressional committees do most of the work of Congress.
- Norms and traditional ways of doing things also play a role—albeit a more informal one—in the smooth functioning of Congress.

KNOW
- committee chairs (p. 333)
- House majority leader (p. 332)
- House minority leader (p. 332)
- norms (p. 334)
- Senate majority leader (p. 332)
- Speaker of the House (p. 331)
- whip (p. 332)

THINK
- How do the rules of congressional organization shape its outcomes?

12.4 Explain the steps of the legislative process and how it can diverge from traditional "textbook" descriptions.

REMEMBER
- Before they can become law, bills must be passed by both the House and Senate and then approved by the president.
- Actors other than members of Congress may play a role in influencing whether a bill gets introduced.
- Most bills are never passed.

KNOW
- bill (p. 335)
- cloture (p. 338)
- Committee on Rules (House) (p. 337)
- filibuster (p. 338)
- markup (p. 337)
- roll-call vote (p. 338)
- unorthodox lawmaking (p. 335)
- veto (p. 339)

THINK
- What are the stages of getting bills passed in Congress? How do they often differ from "textbook" descriptions of the processes?

12.5 Understand the factors that influence an individual's decision to run, and the resources and skills that successful candidates need.

REMEMBER
- Factors that contribute to a decision to run for election include election-specific ones: adequate funding resources and personal ambition.
- Factors that contribute to winning a seat in Congress include incumbency, understanding one's constituency, experience, and money.

KNOW
- political ambition (p. 342)

THINK
- What are the obstacles that first-time candidates for Congress face? What are the political strategies they employ?

12.6 Connect the issues surrounding the representation of women in Congress to the challenges involving representation of other individuals in America.

REMEMBER
- When taking action in Congress, members must consider the preferences of their constituents, their party, and other influencers.
- Representation in Congress may be descriptive or substantive.

KNOW
- descriptive representation (p. 348)
- essentialism (p. 351)
- legislative deliberation (p. 351)
- substantive representation (p. 351)

THINK
- What does it mean for representatives and senators to "stand for" the interests of their constituents?
- Are Americans descriptively represented in Congress? Do you think the answer to this question matters?
- What lessons might we learn from the efforts of women in Congress that could be germane to the struggles of other underrepresented groups to secure substantive representation?

CHAPTER 13

THE AMERICAN PRESIDENCY

Institutions, Individuals, and Power

▼ The powers of the American presidency are great, but their boundaries have long been contested. Many recent presidents have pushed what some consider to the limits of executive authority. President Donald Trump, with his own unique approach to the office, finds himself embroiled in conflicts of power that are both foreign and domestic, political and personal.

As, arguably, the most powerful officeholder in the world, the American president stands alone—and not just at a podium or a press conference but also in comparison to leaders of other democratic nations. The job is unique; no other democratic nation selects, empowers, or limits its top elected leader in quite the same way. However, the American president does not *operate* alone, which is as the Framers of the Constitution intended. The president sits atop a massive collection of organizations, agencies, and bureaus. In the American political system, the president acts as the head of the executive branch of government, which is charged with executing, or putting into effect, the laws of the nation. These many organizations and suborganizations can provide a president with unparalleled information and an ability to shape American public policy on the ground. However, these same organizations can act as a brake on presidential power if they choose to do so.

The American president must also contend with a Congress whose members have their own political goals, even if the majority of those members are from the president's own political party. If the majority of one or both chambers in Congress is not from the president's party, then things get even tougher. And then there are the American people, to whom a president speaks directly. With the American people on his or her side, a president can be very powerful, especially when dealing with

members of Congress. Without this support, presidents are vulnerable.

In this chapter, we will explore the constitutional, institutional, and informal sources of both presidential power and limitations on that power. We will also explore what it means for one *person* to hold the office and to, at times, push the boundaries of those limits. Throughout, we will consider one critical question: In American representative democracy, how much power should any one person have, even if he or she is the elected president?

LEARNING OBJECTIVES

By reading this chapter, you will be able to do the following:

13.1 Consider the American president as one individual acting with and against many institutions and other political actors.

 13.2 Describe the powers of presidency as defined in the Constitution and the constitutional limitations placed on those powers.

 13.3 Discuss institutional and informal sources of and influences on presidential power.

 13.4 Understand how presidents have tested the limits of executive power during wartime and other crises.

13.5 Evaluate the tools that presidents use to further expand their power.

ONE PRESIDENT'S WARS: A WEEK IN THE ADMINISTRATION OF DONALD TRUMP

- **Consider the American president as one individual acting with and against many institutions and other political actors.**

The week of April 9–15, 2018, was like any other week in the administration of President Donald Trump, which is to say it was a week unlike any other week in his administration. Conflict within, conflict without, a new major story seemingly every day, and one person at the center of it all.

PRESIDENT TRUMP FIGHTS WARS ABROAD

Hanging in the balance was a potential American and allied military strike on Syria, a nation consumed in a cauldron of civil war, insurgency, and the intervention of global powers. On April 9, 2018, Nikki Haley, then U.S. ambassador to the United Nations in the administration of Donald Trump, joined other members of the UN Security Council (UNSC) to attempt to reach an accord to send a team of chemical weapons inspectors to Syria. The call for inspectors was in response to an alleged chemical weapons attack in Douma, a suburb of Damascus, that was reported to have killed more than forty civilians, many of them children. According to U.S. officials, the Syrian government of Bashar al-Assad was responsible for the attack. An immediate and robust set of inspections, the American administration argued, was the only way to stave off military action.

Syria and its allies, notably Russia, denied that an attack had taken place or that the government was involved.[1] Russian officials issued dire warnings about the military consequences of a U.S. and allied strike on the Assad regime in response to these allegations. Russia's ambassador to Lebanon stated that Russia would respond to any attack by targeting not only the missiles themselves but the ships or bases from which they were launched: "If there is a strike by the Americans then . . . the missiles will be downed and even the sources from which the missiles were fired," he warned.[2]

This was not the first time that the Assad regime had been accused of using chemical weapons against its own citizens, nor that an American president had used or threatened to use military force in response to the use or alleged use of chemical weapons by the Syrian government. President Trump had ordered a missile attack on a Syrian air base almost exactly a year before. In 2013, President Barack Obama had threatened military strikes in response to an attack; however, they were called off in response to a Russian-led diplomatic effort to secure inspections.

What would President Trump do? That was the question on so many minds. As commander in chief of American forces (see below), President Trump sat at the top of the chain of command of the most powerful military in the world. But would he employ it? If so, how? When?

True to form, President Trump took to Twitter. Portending a potentially massive military response, the president tweeted, "Russia vows to shoot down any and all missiles fired at Syria. Get ready Russia, because they will be coming, nice and new and 'smart!' You shouldn't be partners with a Gas Killing Animal who kills his people and enjoys it!"[3]

TRUMP FIGHTS WARS AT HOME

During the week of April 9–15, Syria was only one of Donald Trump's wars. They seemed to be too numerous to count. At various times the president had battled with Congress, with Hillary Clinton and the Democratic Party, with members of his own party and individuals in federal agencies technically under his control, with members of his cabinet, and with the American media.

Constant conflict and combat defined Trump's successful presidential campaign, and it seemed destined to define his presidency as well. According to a December 2017 article in the *New York Times*, Trump, fueled by cable news and Diet Cokes, was taking on his job as president just as he did his candidacy during his campaign, as a constant battle with many fronts:

> As he ends his first year in office, Mr. Trump is redefining what it means to be president. He sees the highest office in the land much as he did the night of his stunning victory over Hillary Clinton—as a prize he must fight to protect every waking moment, and Twitter is his Excalibur. Despite all his bluster, he views himself less as a titan dominating the world stage than a maligned outsider engaged in a struggle to be taken seriously, according to interviews with 60 advisers, associates, friends and members of Congress.[4]

For his part, Trump denounced reports of his diet of cable news and sodas as offered by "people with fake sources—you know, fake reporters, fake sources."[5]

Members of his own party openly questioned the wisdom of the president's leadership style. "The problem he's going to face," according to Senator Lindsey Graham [R-SC], "is there's a difference between running for the office and being president. You've got to find that sweet spot between being a fighter and being president."[6]

As Nikki Haley prepared to represent the president in the United Nations Security Council, there were new faces and missing faces on his national security and foreign policy team, not exactly an unsurprising development given the high rate of turnover in the Trump administration. That very day, Monday April 9, 2018, was the first day of work for John Bolton, Trump's new and controversial choice for national security adviser, one of the few top posts in a president's formal administration that does not require Senate confirmation. Bolton was himself no stranger to controversy. His previous hard-line statements suggesting preemptive strikes on North Korea and Iran worried many observers.[7]

There was no secretary of state to advise and represent President Trump that week. Having recently dismissed former secretary of state Rex Tillerson via a tweet, Trump nominated CIA director Mike

Executive Branch Turnover: Major Offices

Turnover in the Trump White House is higher than in past administrations. In his first year in office, there was 34 percent turnover, compared to 9 percent in the Obama administration and 6 percent in the George W. Bush administration.[8]

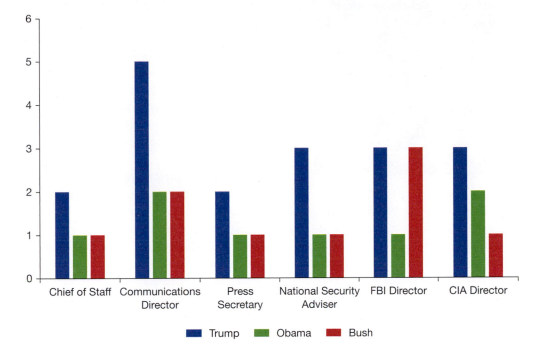

Source: Data from Manuela Tobias, "Comparing Unprecedented Trump White House Turnover with Bush, Obama," Politifact, March 15, 2018, http://www.politifact.com/truth-o-meter/article/2018/mar/15/trump-white-house-turnover/.

Pompeo for the post.[9] Pompeo faced a tough confirmation process, with key Republicans such as Rand Paul (R-KY) expressing their concerns or opposition to Pompeo's confirmation, in Senator Paul's case based upon his concerns for the nominee's stated "defense of torture and support for the NSA's [National Security Administration's] government spying programs."[10]

Pompeo was not the first of Trump's cabinet appointment to have a rough go of it in the Senate. Betsy DeVos—Trump's choice for secretary of education and a staunch proponent of school choice and school vouchers—was confirmed only with Vice President Mike Pence casting a tie-breaking vote in the Senate, a constitutional power not often needed or used.

Trump's authority to authorize strikes without prior congressional approval came under question by members of the legislative branch. President Trump's secretary of defense, Jim Mattis, would later say he had urged the president to obtain congressional approval for strikes before authorizing them, but that Trump overruled him.[11]

And all of these conflicts took place under the shadow of ongoing investigations led by special counsel Robert S. Mueller III—former head of the FBI—into likely Russian interference in the election of 2016 and the possibility that Trump or his campaign played a role in colluding with the Russian government. In addition to covering Trump's many other battles in the week of April 9–13, major American media outlets focused on accusations by adult-film star Stormy Daniels that she and Trump had previously had an affair.[12]

On April 11, the UNSC once again tried to forge an agreement between the United States and its allies and Russia and its allies. It failed. On Friday the thirteenth, America and key allies launched missile and guided munitions strikes on alleged chemical weapons facilities in Syria. The administration claimed it was a success. Russia and Iran—with their own military presence in Syria in support of the regime of Bashar al-Assad—claimed that Syrian air defenses, provided by Russia, succeeded in taking out most of the missiles. Two weeks later, Russian officials claimed to have captured an American cruise missiles intact. No Russian military personnel were reported to have been killed or wounded in the strikes, and a wider war was avoided for the time.

▲ Donald Trump announces that he has launched missile strikes on Syria in retaliation for an apparent chemical attack by the regime of Bashar al-Assad on a rebel town on April 13, 2018.

Mike Theiler/Pool via Bloomberg

IS PRESIDENT TRUMP AT WAR WITH CONVENTIONAL WISDOM?

As we will explore in this chapter and in the next—when we turn to the executive branch bureaucracy—a president sits atop a vast machinery of vast machineries—departments, agencies, bureaus, and staff. When operating smoothly and in concert with a president's objectives, they represent an awesome source of policymaking power. When not, they are a powerful parking brake. By all accounts, President Trump was at war with much of his own machinery. Yet he still appeared to be obtaining at least some of his objectives. How?

As we will also explore, part of the alchemy of presidential power is his or her relationship with the American people, which can serve as a potent counterweight to an entrenched establishment if the people are on the president's side. Yet President Trump's approval ratings that week were low, though not drastically out of line with those of other presidents at similar points in their administrations (see below). Finally, there is presidential personality, a vague, hard-to-pin-down thing that, deep down, most believe matters. Could it be that President Trump's powerful personality, trumps, so to speak, *everything* else? If so, it would most certainly enter his name as one of the most study-worthy presidents in American history.

To argue that Donald Trump's presidential style is unique is an understatement, to put it mildly. What matters for our analysis, however, is the question of how much it really matters. How much can one president, one person, do, for better or worse? In the case of Donald Trump, it is still too soon to know for sure what his legacy will be.

In this chapter, we will explore the American presidency, its awesome power, and the limits on the use of that power. Though our stories will highlight the choices that presidents make in their efforts in the realm of national security, we will discover that institutions, rules, and the American public all act to constrain and bound these decisions. For their part, individual presidents have pushed and tested these boundaries in securing their vision of what it means to make Americans safe and prosperous. We start with the Constitution of the United States, and the new and unique office that it created.

WHAT HAVE I LEARNED?

1. The executive branch of government is charged with _____.

    a. hiring and firing members of the other branches of government

    b. putting the nation's laws into effect

    c. interpreting the nation's laws

    d. creating legislation

2. What are the different kinds of "wars" that face the president on a day-to-day basis?

3. What might be the effect of high levels of staff turnover in the Trump White House?

Answer Key: 1. b; 2. Answers should range from handling international conflicts and wars to managing relationships with allies to overseeing administrators within the White House to carrying out policy goals to hiring and firing cabinet members and other staff; 3. Answers might include difficulties the president could have in administering the office and achieving policy goals as well as the tradeoff of having the "right" person in the right position.

THE CONSTITUTION OUTLINES THE POWERS OF THE AMERICAN PRESIDENCY AND PLACES LIMITS ON THOSE POWERS

- Describe the powers of presidency as defined in the Constitution and the constitutional limitations placed on those powers.

James Madison had given more thought to creating a new type of republic than any of the other delegates to the Constitutional Convention. Even so, even he hadn't fully specified the details for what would become the executive office. Like so many other details involving the office, the agreement that there would be one president was worked out later in the convention. Some provisions, especially the method of electing presidents, were sources of intense conflict. One reason was that the job the delegates ended up creating had no real precedent, though delegates looked to the constitutions of the individual states and other sources for its formation.

Delegates to the convention were in general agreement that the new government would have to be more powerful than that under the Articles of Confederation. That confederal government had been in perpetual financial crisis, often unable to coerce individual states to contribute sufficient funds to allow it to operate effectively. While the Framers of the Constitution knew that the executive needed to be powerful enough to lead, they also feared that the office might become too powerful. They were in no mood to recreate the tyranny of the British monarchy with an elected one on American shores.

The most prominent advocate for a strong and single executive was James Madison's ally, James Wilson of Pennsylvania, whom George Washington considered "one of the strongest men in the convention."[13] According to presidential scholar Clinton Rossiter, "persistent voices were raised against almost every arrangement that eventually appeared in Article II [which describes the presidency], and Wilson and his colleagues were able to score their final success only after a series of debates, decisions, reconsiderations, references to committees, and private maneuvers that still leave the historian befuddled."[14]

DELEGATES SETTLE QUESTIONS OF SELECTION, QUALIFICATIONS FOR OFFICE, AND LENGTH OF TERMS

Once they settled on a single president, the most contentious issue facing the delegates was how this person was going to be selected. The factionalized debate between less populous and more populous states that had resulted in the bicameral Congress reared its head once again. Less populous states feared that direct popular election of the president would see their states' interests swallowed up by their more populous neighbors. Most delegates assumed that voters would pick candidates from their own states. Many delegates also mistrusted Americans' ability to responsibly directly elect a president. In the end, the delegates agreed to a method of presidential selection that did not involve direct popular election. Instead, electors, chosen by state legislatures and apportioned to states based on congressional representation, were to choose the president.

Universal History Archive/Getty Images

▲ A portrait of George Washington, the first president of the United States, circa 1796. That Washington was so respected a figure may have calmed fears that the executive office would be overly powerful.

Delegates also settled on a term of four years with the possibility of reelection. No limits were placed on the number of times a person could be elected president. The nation's first president, George Washington (1789–1797), chose not to seek a third term, however, establishing a precedent that held until Franklin Roosevelt (1933–1945) was elected four times.[15] Ratified largely in response to Roosevelt's multiple terms, the Twenty-Second Amendment (1951) prohibited future presidents from being elected more than twice, and allowed election only once if that person had assumed the office (due to a death, resignation, or impeachment) more than two years prior to the end of a partial term.

Delegates set out a number of conditions for eligibility for the office of the presidency. A candidate had to be "a natural born Citizen, or a Citizen of the United States at the time of the Adoption of this Constitution," be thirty-five years old or older, and have been a resident of the United States for at least fourteen years.[16] The Constitution did not explicitly prohibit women from holding the office; however, at the time of ratification, women were generally denied the right to vote or hold political office within their states.[17]

THE PRESIDENT IS GRANTED CONSIDERABLE POWERS

One of the main reasons that the method of selecting the president caused so much debate was that as the summer of 1787 progressed, the office grew in power and scope. The expectation that Washington, trusted and admired throughout the nation, would be the first president may have allayed delegates' concerns about the powerful office they were creating. Although the convention settled on the simple title of president of the United States, Washington was said to have preferred "His High Mightiness, the President of the United States and Protector of their Liberties."[18]

When the delegates hammered out the framework of the American presidency, they created an institution that had never been seen on a national scale. In some ways, there is still no exact equivalent to its scope and complexity in modern democracies. The powers placed in the president's hands are three-fold. Expressed (or enumerated) powers are those given to the president explicitly in the Constitution. Implied powers, though not laid out in the text, are assumed as part of the president's expressed powers, as they are necessary to carry out the expressed powers. Delegated powers are those that Congress grants to the president in order to execute, or carry out, the laws that Congress has passed (hence the name the *executive branch*). In wielding these three types of powers, the American president assumes a variety of roles.[19]

AS CHIEF EXECUTIVE, THE PRESIDENT CARRIES OUT THE NATION'S LAWS. As the head of the executive branch, the president is responsible for carrying out the laws of the nation. He or she oversees what has become a large and complex system of agencies and bureaucracies in order to do so. The Constitution, however, does not offer many specifics as to what it means to execute the laws. Article II, which is devoted to the presidency, begins, "The executive Power shall be vested in a President of the United States of America."[20] When taking the oath of office, the president promises to "faithfully execute the Office of the President of the United States" and is later instructed to "take Care that the Laws be faithfully executed."[21] Other than that, the Constitution does not give much detail on *how* the president is supposed to run the federal government.

Presidents *are* given some help, however. They are authorized to "require the Opinion, in writing, of the principal Office in each of the executive Departments, upon any Subject relating to the Duties of their respective Offices."[22] Though not mentioned by name, the president's cabinet has evolved into a powerful source of information and a point of contact with the nation's sprawling federal bureaucracy. It also provides a way to reward individuals and members of important interest groups for past (and future) support through their appointment to positions within the cabinet.

Modern presidents have the authority to appoint individuals to thousands of administrative positions, from their closest advisers and heads of large agencies to lower-level administrative staff. Roughly one thousand of these appointments require Senate confirmation. Presidents also nominate individuals to serve as judges in the federal judiciary; each nomination also requires Senate confirmation. A president may make a **recess appointment** without Senate confirmation while Congress is not in session,

recess appointment occurs when Congress is not in session and the president appoints a person to fill a position that would normally require the advice and consent of the Senate. Unless the person is formally confirmed when the Senate reconvenes, the position ends at the conclusion of the next session of Congress.

but the term of the recess appointment ends at the conclusion of that congressional session unless that person is formally confirmed.

AS CHIEF DIPLOMAT, THE PRESIDENT GUIDES FOREIGN POLICY.

The president is also responsible for guiding U.S. foreign policy and interacting with the heads of other nations. The president is authorized "to make Treaties," to "appoint Ambassadors," and to "receive Ambassadors and other public Ministers."[23] This diplomatic power is partly symbolic and ceremonial; events like state dinners and parties showcase the power and prestige of the office.

The diplomatic power of the president helps to shape national foreign policy. While Congress, particularly the Senate, plays a major role in foreign affairs, the fact that the president is one person—and not 100 or 435, as is the case for the Senate and House—gives him or her an advantage over Congress in the ability to act quickly and decisively on the international stage. As one presidential scholar put it, "secrecy, dispatch, unity, continuity, and access to information—the ingredients of successful diplomacy—are properties of his office, and Congress . . . possesses none of them."[24]

AS COMMANDER IN CHIEF, THE PRESIDENT IS RESPONSIBLE FOR THE NATION'S SECURITY.

Perhaps the most fateful role that the Constitution creates for the president is his or her authority as "Commander in Chief of the Army and Navy of the United States, and of the Militia of the several States."[25] The president is at the top of the entire military chain of command, including the strategic nuclear forces of the nation, an awesome responsibility.

Originally, the constitutional war-making power of the presidency was a limited one; it was designed so the president could efficiently lead the American armed forces during a time of war and to allow for quick response to threats when Congress was not in session. Therefore, the president was also given a role in national war making, though the Commander-in-chief clause remained "the forgotten clause" of the Constitution for the early decades of the nation's history.[26]

In the twentieth Century, Congress attempted to reassert its role in setting American military policy. The **War Powers Resolution of 1973**, passed despite Richard Nixon's veto, has been one of the most enduring and controversial legacies of his presidency.[27] Initially intended by its sponsors to reassert congressional authority over the introduction of American armed forces into combat, the resolution is credited by some scholars as being "the high-water mark of congressional reassertion in national security affairs."[28] Passed during the weakening of Nixon's authority as the Watergate investigations unfolded, the resolution was the product of widespread public and congressional dissatisfaction with the prosecution and expansion of the Vietnam conflict as well as unilateral presidential actions carried out by Lyndon Johnson and Nixon.

Drawing on Congress's authority under the necessary and proper clause of the Constitution, the resolution's purpose was to recenter war-making authority.[29] Under the terms of the War Powers Resolution, a president may only introduce armed forces into conflict or likely conflict if one of the three following conditions is present:

1. "a declaration of war [by Congress],"

2. "a specific statutory authorization [by Congress]," or

3. "a national emergency created by an attack on the United States, its territories or possessions, or its armed forces"[30]

Handout/Getty Images

▲ After months of saber rattling, some diplomacy: Here, North Korean leader Kim Jong-un (left) shakes hands with President Donald Trump during their historic summit in Singapore in June 2018. Trump hoped that the historic meeting would bring an end to decades of hostility and the threat of North Korea's nuclear program.

War Powers Resolution of 1973 a law passed over a presidential veto that restricts the power of the president in committing the nation's armed forces into combat or situations of likely combat.

Once introduced, the president is required within forty-eight hours to notify Congress of "the circumstances necessitating the introduction of United States Armed Forces; . . . the constitutional and legislative authority under which such introduction took place; and . . . the estimated scope and duration of the hostilities or involvement."[31] Unless Congress has declared war, passed specific authorization, extended the notification deadline, or is physically unable to meet, the president must withdraw those forces within sixty days, with a thirty-day extension allowed if necessary to withdraw those forces safely.[32]

The last war officially declared by Congress was World War II in 1941. Since that time, American armed forces have been stationed in more than one hundred countries, though many of these are allies or military partners. Presidents have often held that the War Powers Resolution unconstitutionally restricts their war power, though they have also routinely pursued congressional authorization of the use of military force consistent with the resolution.[33] Some critics of the resolution argue that it actually makes the president more powerful, since he or she may feel less constrained during those sixty or ninety days than he or she would if the resolution did not exist.

PRESIDENTS USE THE STATE OF THE UNION ADDRESS TO ADVANCE THEIR GOALS.

In devising a system where power was to be shared between the three branches, the Framers gave the president a limited and mostly negative role in the legislative process. However, this role has since been extended quite far.

The president is directed to "from time to time give Congress Information of the State of the Union."[34] For much of the nation's history, presidents sent written reports to Congress without actually addressing the legislative branch in person. Today, no president would pass on the opportunity provided by the **State of the Union address** to speak live on television before Congress, members of the Supreme Court, the military, and most importantly, the entire nation. In the address, a president highlights the administration's achievements during the previous year. He or she also encourages or cajoles Congress to pass key pieces of his or her legislative agenda. The real audience, however, is the American people, and presidents use the address to try to mobilize support and pressure members of Congress to act.

The president is also expected to "recommend to their [Congress's] Consideration such Measures as he shall judge necessary and expedient."[35] While, as we saw in Chapter 12, only members of Congress can formally introduce bills, presidents work with party leaders in both chambers to shape the legislative agenda. Finally, the president is given the power to veto legislation, although this veto is subject to a potential override by a two-thirds vote in both chambers. Individual presidents have varied considerably in the use (and successful use) of the veto. Overrides are rare; marshaling the required two-thirds vote in both chambers is usually very difficult to do. The mere threat of a presidential veto is often enough to shape a piece of legislation more to a president's liking.[36] Vetoes are more likely during periods of divided government, when one or both chambers of Congress are under the control of a party other than that of the president.

PRESIDENTS HAVE THE POWER TO ISSUE PARDONS.

Another power the Constitution carves out for the president is the ability to issue a **presidential pardon**. The "Power to grant Reprieves and Pardons for Offenses against the United States, except in Cases of Impeachment," allows the president to release individuals convicted of federal crimes from all legal consequences and restore their benefits of citizenship.[37] Presidents often grant pardons in the final days and weeks of office. In cases where it appears that pardoned individuals have close personal or professional ties to the president, this practice can be quite controversial.

THE POWERS OF THE PRESIDENCY ARE ALSO CONSTITUTIONALLY LIMITED

The Framers also placed limitations on the power of the office, primarily by granting specific powers to Congress and the federal judiciary (see Table 13.1).[38] In most circumstances, the judicial branch

Powers and Limits to Powers of the President

Enumerated, Implied, and Delegated Powers	Limits to Powers
The president may:	*Congress may:*
Execute the nation's laws	Investigate or impeach the president
Submit the annual federal budget	Pass the budget
Appoint and seek the advice of cabinet departments	Confirm, delay, or block nominations
Shape foreign policy by enacting treaties, appointing ambassadors, and conducting diplomacy	Ratify treaties
Provide information and make policy recommendations to Congress; veto congressional legislation	Override vetoes
Act as commander in chief of the armed forces	Declare war and fund the armed forces
Deliver pardons but may not pardon individuals who have been impeached	Not override a pardon (and neither can the judiciary)

has little involvement with presidential actions and responsibilities. Congress, however, is a different story. Presidents cannot accomplish most of their objectives without at the very least a lack of opposition by Congress, as the Constitution places in Congress's hands several negative checks on presidential action. Presidents need majority support in Congress to pass the laws, create and fund the programs, and confirm the presidential appointments that are necessary to fully realize their policy objectives. The president must obtain from the Senate majority approval to confirm appointments to the federal judiciary as well as to many executive branch offices. Ratification of a treaty requires a two-thirds vote in the Senate.[39] With a two-thirds vote in each chamber, Congress can override a presidential veto, though veto overrides are relatively uncommon given the high vote hurdle needed to succeed.

Congress has the power to impeach the president (as well as "the Vice President and all civil Officers of the United States") for the vaguely defined transgressions of "Treason, Bribery, or other high Crimes and Misdemeanors."[40] A majority vote in the House is needed to pass articles of impeachment. Once an officeholder is impeached, the trial takes place in the Senate. The chief justice of the United States presides over a presidential impeachment and a two-thirds vote is necessary to convict.[41]

Only two presidents have been impeached, and none have been removed from office. Andrew Johnson barely survived a Senate vote over political battles following the Civil War in 1868, and Bill Clinton avoided conviction over charges of perjury and obstruction of justice during an investigation into his involvement with a White House intern, Monica Lewinsky, in 1998. President Richard Nixon would almost certainly have been impeached and convicted for his role in covering up a break-in at the Democratic Party national headquarters (the so-called Watergate affair) in 1972. He resigned from office in 1974 before a House vote took place, however, and received a pardon from his successor, President Gerald R. Ford, later that year.

1. Which of the following is *not* among the conditions to qualify for the office of the presidency?

   a. Natural-born citizen

   b. Forty years old or older

   c. Resident of the United States for at least the last fourteen years

   d. Political experience

2. The War Powers Resolution _____.

   a. was passed over a presidential veto

   b. attempted to restrict congressional power in war-making activities

   c. has never been formally subject to judicial review

   d. All of the above

3. Removing a president through the process of impeachment requires _____.

   a. Supreme Court action

   b. the consent of state legislatures

   c. a national vote

   d. both House and Senate action

4. In what ways are the powers of the presidency constitutionally limited?

   _____

   Answer Key: 1. d; 2. a; 3. d; 4. Answers should include the power of Congress to check the president via impeachment, wield the "power of the purse," control the nomination process, ratify treaties, override vetoes, and declare war.

INSTITUTIONS AND OTHER INFORMAL SOURCES OF POWER SHAPE THE MODERN EXECUTIVE BRANCH

- **Discuss institutional and informal sources of and influences on presidential power.**

While the American presidency must feel at times like the loneliest job in the world, no president truly acts alone. Instead, the president operates at the center of multiple organizations and institutions. Like many aspects of the presidency, the size and complexity of the presidential establishment is both a source of presidential power and a constraint on it. The machinery of the presidential establishment allows the president to act in many areas of domestic and foreign policy and provides him or her with large amounts of information, which is an important commodity in dealing with other nations, Congress, and the many actors in American politics. However, the size and complexity of the executive branch establishment—especially the federal bureaucracy—can act as a powerful brake on presidential initiatives, particularly since most lower-level federal bureaucrats keep their jobs long after any one president has come and gone.

THE VICE PRESIDENCY PLAYS A LIMITED BUT IMPORTANT ROLE

While the Constitution's vague language created an ambiguous but ultimately powerful presidency, it also created a very weak second in command: the office of the vice president. Delegates to the Constitutional Convention were not even sure that the nation needed a vice president. The ultimate inclusion of the position was probably driven by the need to soothe tensions between more populous and less populous states over the presidential election process.[42]

Constitutionally, the vice president has two jobs. He or she is "President of the Senate, but shall have no Vote, unless they be equally divided."[43] Rarely does the vice president actually preside over the Senate. Instead, the president pro tempore of the Senate usually presides officially, but junior senators routinely fill in for this role. The logic behind the vice president's leadership role in the Senate was to ensure that no state lost its equal Senate representation by virtue of having one of its two senators serving as president of the chamber.

Second, the vice president assumes the office of the presidency should a serving president vacate the office due to death, resignation, or impeachment. The Twenty-Fifth Amendment (1967) established the modern rules of succession and also established a process for replacing a vice president who leaves office during his or her term. In this process, the president nominates a replacement, and approval is required "by a majority vote of both Houses of Congress."

In addition to addressing succession, the Twenty-Fifth Amendment also established a procedure through which the vice president may temporarily assume the role of acting president in the event "that the President is unable to discharge the powers and duties of his office." During his presidency, George W. Bush twice notified Congress that he would temporarily be unable to fulfill his duties as he underwent sedation for colonoscopies, making Vice President Dick Cheney acting president for about two hours each time.

Although the office of the vice presidency is officially weak, any vice president knows that he or she is a heartbeat away from perhaps the most powerful position in the world. Reflecting on his role as the nation's first vice president, John Adams noted, "I am Vice President. In this I am nothing, but I may be everything."[44] In calling for the abolition of the institution of the vice presidency, one scholar argued, "The Vice President has only one serious thing to do: that is, to wait around for the President to die. This is hardly the basis for a cordial and enduring friendship."[45] In the nation's history, eight vice presidents have assumed the office of the presidency upon the death of the serving president and one upon the president's resignation.

Historically, most vice presidents have had little impact on national policy, but it has recently become more common for vice presidents to have a larger role in White House deliberations. Other than being ready to take over, the main job of the vice president is to help the president get elected. Vice presidential nominees have often been selected to "balance the ticket" with respect to geographical representation, connections to important blocks of voters, or experience.

▲ Vice President Mike Pence (right, front) departs a news conference in the White House Rose Garden in June 2018, followed by Secretary of State Mike Pompeo (center) and national security adviser John Bolton (left). Pence's strong ties to religious conservatives as well as the industrial Midwest (he is a former governor of Indiana) made him a good counterbalance to Trump.

AP Photo/Andrew Harnik

THE CABINET AND THE EXECUTIVE BRANCH BUREAUCRACY HELP ADVISE THE PRESIDENT

The president's cabinet consists of the heads of the fifteen major executive branch departments, the vice president, and the heads of other agencies that the president wishes to assign cabinet-level status. In addition to leading their agencies, cabinet department heads, most of whom are called secretaries, advise the president and act as the link between the president and their own bureaucracies. Unlike the majority of people who work for the federal bureaucracy, heads of the executive branch departments typically come and go with each new administration. (See Figure 13.2.)

In choosing cabinet members, presidents have to juggle several considerations. Presidents need capable, experienced, and strong appointees to provide useful information and to effectively run their departments. However, assertive cabinet secretaries, who often have their own bases of power, can challenge the president or drag their heels if they disagree with a policy objective. Presidents must also consider politics and public opinion in their choices. Cabinet department heads with ties to important interest groups—teachers or members of the business community, for example—can help a president to be informed of the concerns of those groups as policy is shaped. Cabinet appointments can also signal to a diverse constituency of Americans and those who represent them that the president will advance their interests.

THE EXECUTIVE OFFICE OF THE PRESIDENT ASSISTS THE PRESIDENT WITH POLICY

Established in 1939 upon the recommendation of a presidential commission that concluded "the president needs help," the **Executive Office of the President** (EOP) is a collection of agencies and offices that assist the president in both an advisory and policymaking capacity.[46] The White House chief of staff oversees the EOP and is usually a close, trusted, and politically skilled associate of the president.

Executive Office of the President
a collection of offices within the White House organization designed primarily to provide information to the president.

The Organization of the Executive Cabinet and Executive Office

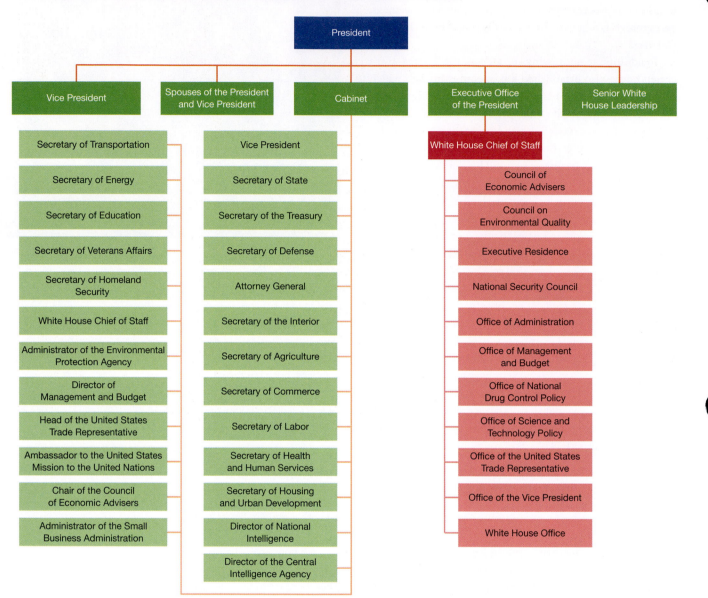

Source: "The Cabinet," WhiteHouse.gov, accessed June 18, 2018, https://www.whitehouse.gov/the-trump-administration/the-cabinet/.

The chief of staff often acts as a protector of the president's scarcest resource: time. Most individuals who work for the various agencies within the EOP are appointed by a president and not expected to serve past that administration, though some of the larger offices do have permanent staff members.

The Office of Management and Budget advises and assists the president in crafting the national budget and studies various plans and initiatives designed to increase the efficiency of executive branch departments. The National Security Council advises the president on issues of national security, the military, and foreign policy.

The White House Office (part of the EOP) has grown into an important bureaucracy itself, and its most important members share offices near the president's. The hundreds of staff members in this office are there to support the president in achieving his or her policy objectives. They achieve this by effectively communicating the president's vision to the American people, building support for goals and polices, and playing the complicated and high-stakes game of Washington politics. In choosing the members of the White House staff, presidents value political skill and loyalty. Many times staff members are individuals who were involved in the campaign or with the president in previous roles. Directors and deputy directors of communication ensure that the president's message is delivered to the American people. The White House press secretary acts as the president's spokesperson to members of the media and conducts daily press briefings, partly to inform but also partly to shape the national conversation in a way that helps the president achieve his or her policy goals.

THE FIRST SPOUSE CAN HELP THE PRESIDENT CONNECT

The wife or husband of a president occupies no formal role in an administration but is in a unique position to act as an adviser to the president and as a public and personal link between the president and the American people.

Edith Bolling Galt Wilson, President Woodrow Wilson's wife, was probably the most powerful first lady. She helped to organize and run the White House after her husband suffered a serious stroke in 1919, becoming, to some, an acting president. Eleanor Roosevelt spoke and wrote frequently about public policy and had a successful and influential career in public life following Franklin Roosevelt's death in 1945. Modern first spouses often choose one or more policy areas and use their influence and visibility to call attention to issues in those areas and promote solutions.

Keystone-France/Gamma-Keystone via Getty Images

▲ Marian Anderson, renowned opera singer, receives the Spingarn Medal from first lady Eleanor Roosevelt in Richmond, Virginia, in July 1939. Eleanor Roosevelt's efforts to overcome racial discrimination in the United States were among her most important achievements on behalf of her husband's administration.

POLITICAL PARTIES INFLUENCE THE EXECUTIVE OFFICE

The role that the president plays as "chief of party" is not mentioned in the Constitution. The Framers worried privately and publicly about the dangers of faction—of which political parties were viewed as a particularly dangerous example. Parties, however, are nearly as old as the Republic; divisions between President Washington's closest advisers gave rise to the nation's first political parties.

Modern presidents serve as the unofficial, but real, leaders of their own political parties. They often choose the official leadership of their party, or at least have a major say in it. Presidents must contend with partisan politics in Congress, especially if they serve during a period of divided government and the opposing political party is controlling one or both chambers of Congress. Periods of divided government are often associated with legislative gridlock in which Congress's ability to pass laws is diminished or grinds to a halt completely.[47]

Presidents expect to have to battle and negotiate with members of the opposing party in Congress. However, support from their own party members can never be taken for granted either. Even with Republican control of both chambers of Congress, President Trump has found it far from easy to achieve his policy objectives. Presidents and members of Congress serve different constituencies. The American people demand that their presidents keep them safe and prosperous. Demands on senators and representatives are often more local and address the unique characteristics and needs of their states or districts. No member of Congress can ignore the wishes of her or his constituents without risk, even if the president requests it. Skillful presidents are fully aware of these tensions and—working with party leaders in Congress—often try to accommodate individual defections by members of their own party with the expectation that loyalty will be shown on less locally contentious votes somewhere down the line.

THE MEDIA AND THE RISKS OF THE PHOTO OP

In the photo (right), President George W. Bush delivers a speech aboard the aircraft carrier USS *Abraham Lincoln* on May 1, 2003. The president's speech declared an end to major combat operations in Iraq. Behind him is a banner reading "Mission Accomplished." Administration officials insisted that the banner referred to the specific deployment of the carrier and its crew. As violence within Iraq and attacks on American forces increased in the months following Bush's speech, critics of the war and the Bush administration pointed to the photo opportunity as an indication of the president's unwarranted optimism and lack of candor with the American people about the challenges of a war that would go on for eight more years, claiming more than four thousand American lives and likely resulting in more than one hundred thousand Iraqi deaths.[48]

STEPHEN JAFFE/AFP/Getty Images

WHAT Do You Think?

What do this photograph and the controversy surrounding it illustrate about the use of the media by presidents trying to win public support for their programs and goals? How might presidents benefit from these major photo opportunities? What might the dangers be?

THE PRESIDENT TRIES TO USE THE MEDIA TO SHAPE PUBLIC OPINION

As the power of the American presidency has evolved, so has the president's relationship to the nation's citizens. Public opinion—the distribution of people's preferences and evaluations of policies and individual political actors—has come to play an important role in expanding or constraining the power of individual presidents. When expertly harnessed, public opinion is a powerful tool in battles with Congress, the judiciary, or too-independent members of a president's own political party. If it is poorly mobilized or understood, however, the unfortunate president, in the words of one scholar, "will find himself exposed to all those enemies who multiply like mosquitoes in a [New] Jersey August. The various institutions and centers of power that check the President are inept and often useless without public opinion—and with it are often wondrously armed."[49]

Modern communications technologies and ease of travel have significantly contributed to connecting the president to the American public. But long before the Internet, television, and even radio, individual presidents recognized and tried to harness the latent power of public opinion. Andrew Jackson, who drew on his public support in battles with Congress and the judiciary, commented, "The President must be accountable at the bar of public opinion for every act of his administration."[50] Modern presidents attempt to make full use of communications technologies and public appearances in order to mobilize American public opinion in support of their own goals and policies. Political scientist Samuel Kernell used the term **going public** to describe "a strategy whereby a president promotes himself and his policies in Washington by appealing directly to the American public for support."[51]

going public
a strategy through which presidents reach out directly to the American people with the hope that the people will, in turn, put pressure upon their representatives and senators to press for a president's policy goals.

Perhaps no president in American history is as tied to public opinion as President Donald Trump. Without question, his use of social media has been more powerful and effective than that of any other candidate, or president. The question, though, is this: Does the immediacy of connection outweigh the risk of poorly timed or, perhaps, not politically savvy tweets?

AMERICANS' EVALUATIONS OF PRESIDENTIAL PERFORMANCE CAN AFFECT THE PRESIDENT'S POLICY AGENDA

Since Franklin Roosevelt's presidency, pollsters have periodically taken the national pulse on Americans' views of how well their presidents are doing. These presidential approval ratings provide more than just a snapshot of the public's views. A president with high approval ratings is in a more powerful position in relation to Congress than one with low or sinking ratings. Sometimes unanticipated events—and the president's response to them—can produce dramatic changes in presidential approval. A national economic or military crisis, if handled successfully in the eyes of the American public, can produce a surge in presidential approval. In the months after the 9/11 attacks, President

▼ FIGURE 13.3

Presidential Approval Ratings in Comparison

President Trump's second-year approval ratings, though on the low end compared to those of other presidents, were not significantly different.

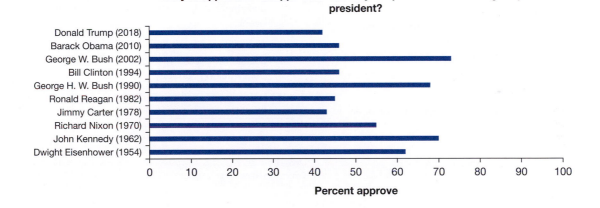

Do you approve or disapprove of the way the president is handling his job as president?

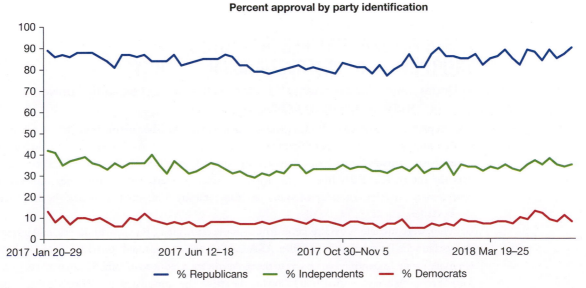

Percent approval by party identification

— % Republicans   — % Independents   — % Democrats

Source: "Presidential Approval Ratings—Donald Trump," Gallup, accessed June 18, 2018, http://news.gallup.com/poll/203198/presidential-approval-ratings-donald-trump.aspx.

Bush's approval rating rose to 90 percent, the highest ever recorded, but it later declined as the public became increasingly skeptical of his handling of the war in Iraq and of the nation's economy.

Some patterns of presidential approval are more predictable. A president—especially after a convincing first-term victory—ordinarily enjoys a period of strong public approval, called a honeymoon period. For this reason, presidents often try to secure major legislative victories early in their first terms to capture public support and build momentum for future battles with Congress. Presidential approval, however, usually declines over time as the American public begins to assign blame to the president for things that are not going well, whether this is deserved or not. There is also typically some recovery in presidential approval as the term draws to a close.[52]

WHAT HAVE I LEARNED?

1. The office of the vice presidency was created to _____.

   a. act as an important check on presidential power and main adviser to the president

   b. function as an apprenticeship for the office of the presidency

   c. serve as the nonvoting president of the Senate except during tie votes, and to assume the presidency if the serving president vacates the office

   d. serve as the chief of state, whereas the president is the head of government

2. In choosing cabinet members, presidents consider _____.

   a. their qualifications

   b. politics and interest group support

   c. public opinion

   d. All of the above

3. The president's executive office _____.

   a. drafts legislation based on the policies the president favors

   b. acts primarily as a group of administrative assistants, helping schedule diplomatic and other events

   c. serves as the president's cabinet

   d. assists the president in both an advisory and policymaking capacity

4. In what ways does the president play a role as the unofficial leader of his or her political party?

   _____

Answer Key: 1. c; 2. d; 3. d; 4. Answers should mention that the president helps choose the official leadership of his or her party and manages partisan politics in Congress to overcome gridlock.

PRESIDENTS HAVE PUSHED THE LIMITS OF THEIR POWER TO PRESERVE NATIONAL SECURITY

- Understand how presidents have tested the limits of executive power during wartime and other crises.

On a September morning in 2011, a group of men had just finished eating breakfast in a remote desert in the country of Yemen. One of them was Anwar al-Awlaki, an American citizen who was, to counterterrorism officials, "a rock star propagandist for al-Qaeda's arm in Yemen who recruited followers over the Internet."[53] Patrolling the Yemeni skies that day were American drones launched from an airstrip in Saudi Arabia and remotely piloted from far away. Noticing the drones, the men "scrambled to get to their trucks."[54]

They were too late. Two Predator drones marked the men's trucks with lasers, and larger Reaper drones launched three Hellfire missiles. Al-Awlaki's vehicle "was totally torn up into pieces," according to reports from unidentified witnesses to the strike, the men reduced to "small human parts."[55]

For more than a year and a half following the strike, the administration of President Barack Obama remained officially silent on the targets. Under pressure from members of Congress, including some key Democrats, Attorney General Eric Holder formally acknowledged in May 2013 that the 2011 strike had targeted an American citizen: al-Awlaki. According to the *New York Times*, "for what was apparently the first time since the Civil War, the United States government had carried out the deliberate killing of an American citizen as a wartime enemy and without a trial."[56] Al-Awlaki's name had been placed at the top of the Central Intelligence Agency (CIA) list of individuals to be captured if possible or killed if not. Many of the details about how individuals made this list were secret, but reporters learned that the target list was vetted and approved in secret by the National Security Council and others on the administration's legal team.[57]

It was the "secret" part of the administration's decision to target al-Awlaki that made many uncomfortable. In a public speech in 2012, Obama's top counterterrorism adviser, John Brennan, reassured his audience that individuals, including Americans, were targeted for killing only if capture was not a realistic option and only after careful and thorough review.[58]

Some of the details surrounding why and how Anwar al-Awlaki was targeted are known: Born in New Mexico in 1971 but later raised in Yemen, al-Awlaki returned to the United States for undergraduate and graduate education. He was serving as imam of a mosque near Washington, DC, in 2001 at the time of the 9/11 attacks. In the weeks following, al-Awlaki presented a moderate face to Americans trying to understand what had happened and to many Muslim Americans worried about a backlash against members of their faith. However, according to the *New York Times*, "nine years later, from his hide-out in Yemen, [he] declared war on the United States," his primary weapon being the Internet.[59] His "website became a favorite for English-speaking Muslims who were curious about jihad."[60] With his command of the English language and ability to draw on American social and cultural references in his posts and videos, al-Awlaki became a very effective "recruiter and propagandist."[61]

By al-Awlaki's own account, it was U.S. intervention in countries like Iraq, Afghanistan, Pakistan, and Yemen that drove him to follow "the religious obligation to defend his faith."[62] Interviews with others who knew him cited al-Awlaki's eighteen months in a Yemeni prison—much of it in solitary confinement—as the driving force behind his radicalization. He blamed the United States for allowing his detention, and there is some evidence that this was the case. The *New York Times* reported that "John D. Negroponte, then director of national intelligence, told Yemeni officials that the United States did not object to his detention."[63]

Expanding on the comments of other administration officials, in a May 22, 2013, memo informing congressional leaders of the administration's 2011 decision to target and kill al-Awlaki, Attorney General Holder laid out the administration's case for why such measures had been necessary. He based the justification not on al-Awlaki's inflammatory rhetoric but on intelligence that al-Awlaki had moved from the role of terrorist propagandist to one of senior leadership in al-Qaeda in the Arabian Peninsula (AQAP). Holder said the decision to target and kill al-Awlaki had been taken only after an extensive review process and only after the conclusion that he could not feasibly be captured alive and brought to a court for a hearing.[64]

In its justification for the targeted killing of al-Awlaki, the Obama administration argued that it was left with no other options to protect national security. Al-Awlaki had, in the estimation of officials, become a clear and present danger to the United States. As one anonymous counterterrorism official in the Obama administration told the *New York Times*, "American citizenship doesn't give you carte blanche to wage war against your own country."[65]

The targeted killing of al-Awlaki and other American citizens in the war on terror is a hotly debated issue in the nation's politics. When President Obama ordered the targeted killing of Anwar al-Awlaki, he

▲ American citizen and Muslim cleric Anwar al-Awlaki poses for a photo at Dar Al-Hijrah mosque in October 2001 in Falls Church, Virginia. Ten years later, al-Awlaki was killed in a targeted drone strike by the United States in Yemen.

did so with the conviction that he was acting within his constitutional powers as the commander in chief of the United States. Some questioned whether this was in fact true.

What is not up for debate, however, is that Obama was neither the first American president to challenge the boundaries of war-making authority in the name of national security nor the last. President Donald Trump ordered missile strikes in Syria without Congress's consent early in his term and again in April 2018.[66] More than a century and a half before, another president—albeit in very different times—had also pushed the boundaries of executive authority, this time to try to restore a nation torn apart by a civil war.

ABRAHAM LINCOLN SUSPENDS HABEAS CORPUS DURING THE CIVIL WAR

In April 1861, at the outset of the Civil War, a mob attacked a group of Union soldiers in Baltimore, Maryland, en route to Washington, DC.[67] Someone fired a pistol into the group of soldiers, and the soldiers—frightened and disorganized—fired upon the mob.[68] Four Union soldiers and twelve civilians died in the violence.

Four days later, John Merryman, a prominent and well-to-do Marylander and member of a Southern secessionist group operating in that state, oversaw and led the burning of at least six railroad bridges and the toppling of some telegraph lines that formed one of the key military links between Washington, DC, and the Union states of the North. Merryman claimed he was acting on orders from a former U.S. Army captain. According to witnesses, "barking orders, repeatedly citing his 'authority,' Merryman proclaimed his intention to stop Northern troops from invading Maryland. . . . 'We'll stop them from coming down and stealing our slaves.'"[69]

President Abraham Lincoln (1861–1865) knew that keeping the border states from joining the South was key to any hope of winning the war and reconstituting the Union, and Maryland was one of the most important of these states (see Figure 13.4). If Maryland was lost, then the Union's capital in Washington, DC, would be nearly impossible to defend, as it would be cut off from supplies and

▼ FIGURE 13.4

The United States at the Start of the Civil War

The map in Figure 13.4 shows Union states to the north and Confederate states to the south. Lincoln knew that ensuring the border states (shown in yellow) did not secede was key to winning the war. Maryland, where John Merryman was jailed for treason, was one of the most important of these states: If it joined the Confederacy, the Union's capital in Washington, DC, would be nearly impossible to defend.

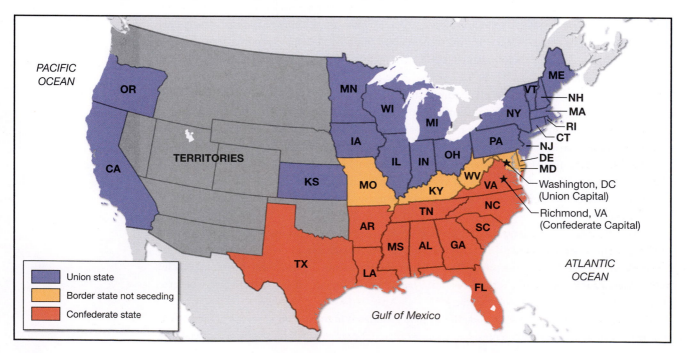

reinforcements by land. Lincoln used the full force of his presidency to ensure the border states remained in the Union: He called up state militias, blockaded Southern ports, expanded the army and the navy, spent $2 million from the U.S. Treasury, "closed the Post Office, . . . suspended the writ of habeas corpus in certain localities, [and] caused the arrest and detention of persons who were 'represented to him as being engaged in treasonable practices.'"[70] Calling up the state militias was within his executive authority. All of his other actions, including suspending habeas corpus, were "without any statutory authorization."[71]

On the morning of May 25, 1861, federal troops roused Merryman from his bed and took him to Fort McHenry in Baltimore Harbor, where he was imprisoned. As he was from a prominent family and had powerful political connections in Maryland, Merryman's detention did not go unnoticed. Within hours of his internment at the federal fort, Merryman's lawyers arrived and prepared a petition for his release. Supreme Court chief justice Robert Brooke Taney received Merryman's petition and issued a writ of habeas corpus on his behalf. Taney noted that Merryman had been "imprisoned by the commanding officer, without warrant from any lawful authority . . . upon charges of treason and rebellion, without proof and without giving the names of the witnesses, or specifying the acts which, in the judgment of the military officer, constituted these crimes."[72]

Taney called on the Union general in charge of the fort to produce "the body of John Merryman"[73] so the charges against him could be examined. Habeas corpus—from the Latin "you [shall] have the body"—defines a procedure

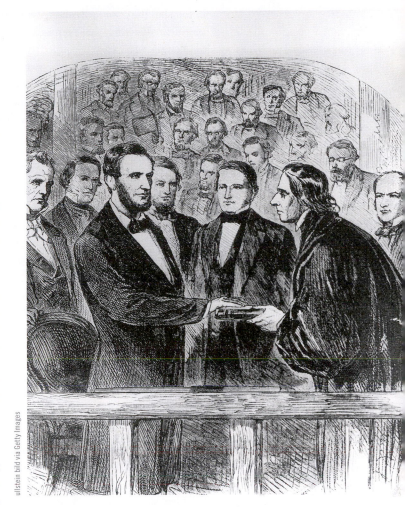

▲ Abraham Lincoln (left), shown here with Chief Justice Roger Brooke Taney at Lincoln's inauguration on March 4, 1861. *Ex parte Merryman* pitted the two men against one another in a watershed case that tested the limits of executive power.

through which a person can challenge what they see as unlawful detention. If Taney's writ of habeas corpus in the case of Merryman was honored, either an arrest warrant would be issued for Merryman or Merryman would be free to go.

The Union commander refused to honor the writ. Instead, he sent an aide, who showed up in Taney's courtroom without Merryman. It became clear to Justice Taney that Merryman was being held under the authority of President Lincoln and was not to be released, not even upon Taney's direct demand. According to Baltimore mayor George William Brown, "a more important question could hardly have occurred. Where did the president acquire such a power? Was it true that a citizen held his liberty subject to the arbitrary will of any man? In what part of the Constitution could such a power be found?"[74]

Taney pushed back, threatening to arrest the fort's commander if his orders were not followed, and directed the aide to have the commander produce Merryman by noon the next day, Tuesday, May 28. Taney's demand was again refused, and Merryman remained imprisoned, without a trial or an arrest warrant, under the authority of the president of the United States.

On Tuesday morning, having been twice rebuffed, Taney prepared to confront the president. He wrote and swiftly delivered an opinion, *Ex parte Merryman* (1861), in which he challenged the president's authority to suspend writs of habeas corpus, even in times of war and rebellion.[75] "The President, under the Constitution and laws of the United States," Taney declared, "cannot suspend the privilege of the writ of *habeas corpus*, nor authorize any military officer to do so."[76]

In his opinion, Taney acknowledged that the Constitution does grant the federal government the power to suspend the writ of habeas corpus during times of rebellion or invasion.[77] However, Taney noted, Article I gives that power to Congress, not the executive branch. And, Taney continued, the judicial branch has the power to issue arrest warrants, not the president or the military under his command. The president, therefore, "has exercised a power which he does not possess under the Constitution."[78]

For his part, Lincoln justified to members of Congress and the Union "these actions of dubious constitutionality by reference to the 'war powers' granted to the executive."[79] In other words, he argued that the war powers granted to the presidency were sufficient grounds for his actions. Congress retroactively approved most of Lincoln's actions taken that year. However, it did not approve the suspension of habeas corpus (with some limits) until 1863, after the president had issued a broader suspension of the privilege the year before.[80]

Such drastic unilateral presidential action in times of war and national crisis led political scientist Edward Corwin to conclude that "the Constitution is an easily dispensable factor of our war effort—perhaps one might say 'expendable' factor," transforming it, during wartime, "from a *Constitution of Rights* into a *Constitution of Powers*."[81]

Taney expected to be impeached or even arrested over his confrontation with Lincoln, and Lincoln is said to have contemplated it. In the end, however, the president simply ignored Taney, prosecuting the war with whatever means he saw necessary to restore the Union. Lincoln continued to defend his suspension of habeas corpus and other measures as valid uses of the constitutional power of the government "when in cases of Rebellion or Invasion the public Safety may require it."[82]

Lincoln believed that the powers he had to assume during the war would no longer be necessary once the crisis of the Civil War was successfully resolved. In this prediction, he proved to be correct. Presidential power did recede in the decades following the Union victory, and Congress once again assumed its position as the strongest of the three branches. But not forever. As America again confronted wars, major crises, and other extraordinary circumstances, other presidents have also tested the limits of executive branch power or impacted the office through their actions.

When President Obama ordered the targeted killing of Anwar al-Awlaki, he did so with the conviction that he was acting within his constitutional powers as the commander in chief of the United States. Some questioned whether this was in fact true. As we explored earlier, there have been several instances where presidents have asserted presidential war-making authority, testing the limits of the president's proper powers. As we also discussed previously, the Framers originally viewed the war powers of the president as more limited than Congress's powers.

Since George Washington was inaugurated as the nation's first president in 1789, the institution of the American presidency has undergone a major transformation, one that would likely seem remarkable to the Framers of the Constitution. The office has grown in power, prestige, and complexity, "not smoothly but with great leaps, periods of dormancy, and occasional setbacks."[83] These changes have been affected by the actions, choices, and strategic behavior of the individuals who have held the nation's highest office. Most significantly, individual presidents have, whether out of opportunity or necessity, seized upon crises and key turning points in American political development to redefine the boundaries of their power and influence.

WHAT HAVE I **LEARNED?**

1. Obama administration officials conceded that for the first time since the Civil War, the United States government had _____.

   a. carried out the deliberate killing of an American citizen as a wartime enemy and without a trial

   b. found an American citizen guilty of treason and revoked his citizenship

   c. found a foreign national guilty of being a terrorist and sentenced him to life in prison in the United States

   d. None of the above

2. Justice Taney issued a writ of habeas corpus on behalf of John Merryman, but Abraham Lincoln intervened, suspending all writs. Lincoln did so because _____.

a. he believed Merryman and others had committed acts of treason against the government of the United States and were a direct threat to national security

b. he wanted to protect Merryman from charges of treason

c. he believed Taney was overstepping his role as chief justice of the Supreme Court

d. he saw it as way to appeal to Union voters and ensure his reelection

3. What justifications did the Obama administration offer for its action against al-Awlaki? What criticisms did it receive?

4. What were Justice Taney's reasons for issuing *Ex parte Merryman*?

Answer Key: 1. a; 2. a; 3. Answers might include a discussion of how the administration argued that al-Awlaki had become a member of the organization's leadership as well as concerns that he was an American citizen who was targeted and killed without trial; 4. Answers should include Taney's argument that the right to suspend writs of habeas corpus in times of war or insurrection rests with Congress.

THE PRESIDENT HAS SEVERAL TOOLS FOR UNILATERAL ACTION

- **Evaluate the tools that presidents use to further expand their power.**

Scholars' views of the American presidency and the power of the office have, like the institution itself, changed over time and in response to the individual presidents and the times in which they have governed. Increasingly, political scientists have focused on a unilateral model of presidential action in which presidents attempt to influence both domestic and foreign policy with few or no constraints by Congress or the judiciary. It is, in other words, when presidents try to act alone. Individual presidents have often tried to defend the power of their office or even push the boundaries of that power, but the scope and frequency of unilateral presidential action in recent administrations has raised questions about the degree to which powers truly remain separated between the three branches of the U.S. government.

Presidents attempt to exercise independent control over information through the assertion of **executive privilege**, in which they try to shield from Congress, the judiciary, and, ultimately the public the details of debates, discussions, memos, and emails surrounding presidential decisions and actions. Since the administration of George Washington, presidents have asserted that their ability to control information is essential to their effectiveness.[84] During the investigation of President Nixon and his role in the Watergate affair, Nixon refused to hand over to a special prosecutor audio recordings of his conversations with senior aides as well as other documents relating to the investigation, citing the power of executive privilege. In *United States v. Nixon* (1974), the Supreme Court affirmed the power of executive privilege, finding that "a President and those who assist him must be free to explore alternatives in the process of shaping policies and making decisions, and to do so in a way many would be unwilling to express except privately."[85] However, the Court also demanded that the president hand over the recordings and documents, balancing the need for executive privilege with the need for the rule of law in criminal investigations.

In the area of foreign policy, presidents may sign **executive agreements** with foreign nations without Senate ratification, which is needed for treaties. Though they are not binding upon future presidents in the way that treaties are, executive agreements can give a president a way to shape foreign policy that bypasses the Senate's role of advice and consent. Their details are often kept secret from the public and Congress for reasons of national security.

In the president's role in the legislative process, the use of **signing statements** has gained increased attention recently. When a president signs a bill into law, he or she may add written comments that convey instructions to the various agencies that will actually carry out the law or that offer the president's interpretation of the law. Sometimes signing statements are far from controversial; they may be offered to try to build a public record of support for an issue, to call attention to an issue, or to offer a slightly different interpretation of a law that a president otherwise supports. However, if the president either interprets the law differently from the way Congress intended or instructs agencies to execute it selectively or differently, then concerns can be raised that the president is taking the lawmaking authority intended for Congress for himself or herself.

executive privilege
a right claimed by presidents to keep confidential certain conversations, records, and transcripts from outside scrutiny, especially that of Congress.

executive agreements
agreements between a president and another nation that do not have the same durability in the American system as a treaty but may carry important foreign policy consequences.

signing statements
text written by a president while signing a bill into law, usually consisting of political statements or reasons for signing the bill but possibly also including the president's interpretation of the law itself.

Executive Orders, Washington to Trump

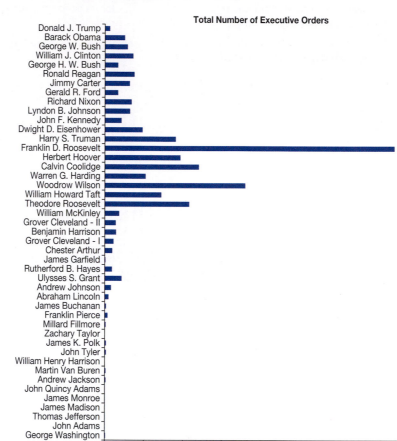

Source: Data for executive orders are from Gerhard Peters, "Executive Orders," in *The American Presidency Project*, ed. John T. Woolley and Gerhard Peters (Santa Barbara: University of California, 1999–2016), http://www.presidency.ucsb.edu/data/orders.php#orderlist.

Note: Data for the Trump administration are current through June 2018.

Executive orders are policy directives issued by presidents to the executive branch bureaucracy that do not require congressional approval. Most executive orders are issued under congressional authorization and constitute a set of instructions given by the president to the executive branch agencies informing them of how they are supposed to go about implementing a law or policy. Often they deal with routine administrative procedures. Presidents have also used executive orders, however, to make major changes in public policy (see Figure 13.5).[86]

In 1942, President Roosevelt issued Executive Order 9066, which authorized the secretary of war to declare certain areas in the United States as "military areas . . . from which any or all persons may be excluded, and with respect to which the right of any person to enter, remain in, or leave shall be subject to whatever restrictions the Secretary of War or the appropriate Military Commander may impose in his discretion."[87] Issued for the declared purpose of "protection against espionage and against sabotage to national-defense material," Roosevelt's executive order led to the internment of more than 130,000 individuals, most of whom were Japanese Americans. In *Korematsu v. United States* (1944), the Supreme Court upheld Roosevelt's authority. In a dissent, however, one justice commented about the internment: "I need hardly labor the conclusion that Constitutional rights have been violated."[88]

The Supreme Court, however, has not always upheld presidential use of the executive order, even during wartime. In *Youngstown Sheet & Tube Co. v. Sawyer* (1952), the Court rejected the authority of President Harry S. Truman (1945–1953) to order the seizure of most of the nation's steel mills to avert a strike by steel workers while the nation was at war in Korea.[89] The Court concluded that the president's

executive orders

directions made by a president to the executive branch departments that often contain nothing more than instructions to be carried out by agencies, bureaus, and departments but may at times be considered acts of presidential lawmaking.

power did not extend to labor disputes and that he lacked legislative authorization for his actions.

While you have read primarily about unilateral presidential action in the area of national security, questions about its exercise extend to many other political fields. As political scientist William Howell has examined, presidents may act first and alone across a wide variety of policy areas, often by issuing directives to the vast federal bureaucracy without waiting for Congress to clarify the laws that it has passed (see Chapter 12). In doing so, "the president moves policy first and thereby places upon Congress and the courts the burden of revising a new political landscape."[90] Acting first and acting alone may force the other two branches to react.

PRESIDENTIAL CHARACTER AFFECTS THE SUCCESS OF A PRESIDENCY

Some political scientists have looked to the character and personality of individual presidents to explain their relative effectiveness in office. That individual presidents—their characters, skills, successes, and failures—have all contributed to the development of the American presidency is a point on which most would agree. For scholars of the presidency, however, the challenge is to figure out just how these traits matter to presidential performance. Some scholars have classified presidents based on personal and psychological characteristics as a way of gaining insight into behavior inside the Oval Office.[91] Successfully predicting presidential behavior based on assessments of character is, however, a difficult thing to do. Separating the person of the president from the times and context in which that president governed is never easy. In addition, sudden, unexpected events can thrust a president into situations that none could have imagined or predicted.

Presidential scholar Richard Neustadt painted a strategic, but constrained, portrait of the source of presidential power. For Neustadt, the power of an individual president is not automatic but must be developed, especially through skillful political action.[92] Neustadt wrote that presidential power is the power of information, of presenting a credible threat to known and potential political enemies, and, finally, of convincing allies and opponents that supporting the president is in their own self-interest. According to him, "the essence of a President's persuasive task is to convince such men that what the White House wants of them is what they ought to do for their sake and on their own authority."[93]

In times of crisis, especially economic or military crises, no single actor in the American political system is able to react to the demands of the situation as quickly and decisively as the president: "Under crisis conditions the political system undergoes a drastic change. The White House becomes a command post, Congress and interest groups assume minor roles, the public becomes acutely aware of the threat and looks fervently to the president for authoritative guidance."[94] As we explored in Chapter 3, President Roosevelt's response to the Great Depression fundamentally altered American federalism and increased the power of the national government and the executive branch. It has been in times of military crises and threats to national security, however, when the nation has witnessed the starkest increase in presidential authority and the transformation of the character, scope, and reach of the American president.

Arguing in favor of a single executive in *Federalist* No. 74, Alexander Hamilton saw the potential of and need for presidential power in wartime. He wrote, "Of all the cares or concerns of government, the direction of war most peculiarly demands those qualities which distinguish the exercise of power by a single hand."[95] Writing in 1888, noted observer of American political life James Bryce confirmed the transformative power of war and conflict on the American presidency, saying, "In quiet times the power of the President is not great. . . . In troublous times it is otherwise, for immense responsibility is then thrown on one who is both the commander-in-chief and the head of the civil executive."[96] The ability to act first and act alone is a tool unique to the president. Its power is only magnified during times of threat and crisis.

▲ Following President Roosevelt's Executive Order 9066, two soldiers escort a Japanese American couple during their evacuation from Bainbridge Island, Washington, to a relocation center in 1942. More than 130,000 individuals were interned as a result of the order.

THE PROBLEM OF SMALL NUMBERS IN THE STUDY OF THE PRESIDENCY

How much do the personal characteristics of an individual president matter to his or her performance in office? Can we say anything systematic about the relationship between character and performance?

Originally published in 1972, James David Barber's *The Presidential Character: Predicting Performance in the White House* applied understandings from psychology to try to predict how presidents would behave—and how successful they would be—by categorizing them into four types based on two separate personality traits: (1) how active or passive they were, in the sense of the energy and innovation they bought to the office, and (2) how positively or negatively they approached their duties, in the sense of the enjoyment they displayed in managing the ship of state.

Based on these determinations, George Washington, for example, was a passive-negative president in that he reluctantly led the nation and preferred stability over dramatic change. Thomas Jefferson, on the other hand, was an active-positive president who actively engaged in the give-and-take of politics in the service of a grand vision for the young nation.

Though it has been highly influential in political science, Barber's approach has not escaped criticism. Some have argued that the many institutional and political limitations on presidential action overwhelm the ability to define a president's actions. Others have critiqued the validity of the two underlying measures themselves.

There is another challenge in drawing systematic conclusions about individual presidents that goes beyond the issue of character. The reality is that there have not been that many presidents; thus, the question is one of sample size. To demonstrate empirical relationships with confidence, we need a certain number of observations to better ensure that the patterns we observe are indeed representative of the group under study.

....

WHaT Do You Think?

How might political scientists get around the problem of the limited number of presidents in making social scientific claims about executive branch politics? One option might be to look at executives across nations, giving us more observations. The problem here is that other systems are typically very different from that of the United States. Another approach might be to look at state governors. The challenge here, though, is that the American federalist system defines very different roles for state and federal executives. This is not to say that such an approach might not be useful—only that we should be careful in using it. What might we learn from examining the behavior of state governors that could translate into a better understanding of the American presidency?

WHAT HAVE I LEARNED?

1. Which of the following are *not* among the tools of unilateral action that presidents have at their disposal?

   a. Signing statements

   b. Executive agreements

   c. Executive orders

   d. Executive judicial confirmations

2. What are the challenges of evaluating the role individual character plays in the president's success?

3. Why have some scholars argued that presidential power is enhanced during times of crisis?

Answer Key: 1. d; 2. Answers should mention that it is hard to separate the president's personal traits from the times and context in which he or she governed; 3. Answers should include a president's ability to act much more quickly than Congress, the public's turning to the president for leadership, and the ability to mobilize the executive branch.

CONCLUSION: THE PARADOXES OF THE PRESIDENCY CONTINUE

Facing a Democrat-controlled House of Representatives in 2019, President Donald Trump will likely have more battles on his hands. Maxine Waters (D-CA), considered a likely candidate to chair the House Financial Services Committee, vowed to bring its investigative powers to bear on his financial dealings and possible ties with Russia. Other House members called for impeachment proceedings against the President, though some Democratic leaders cautioned against such an approach. For his part, and in his own controversial and combative style, the president warned in a tweet that he would unleash the investigatory power of the Senate against Democrats and the Russian-collusion probe in retaliation.

The power of the American presidency is not easily defined, nor are its roots and sources easily traced or separated. Many factors—constitutional provisions, institutional and political contexts, individual personality and skill, and responses to crises—have all played a role in its development. As scholars have observed, the office of the presidency is full of paradoxes.[97] The Framers wanted a strong and decisive office, yet they were wary of creating an elected monarch. Americans often look to their presidents for leadership above the fray of partisan politics, yet the position is, by design, political and embedded in a system of checks and balances. Americans look to their presidents for leadership yet expect them to follow the will of the people.

The modern presidency is a massively powerful office. As Americans are confronted with a global war on terror in the twenty-first century—a war that features undefined boundaries and no specific nation with which to conclude a peace treaty—the question of the proper limits of presidential power remains as vital as it did in 1861 when Abraham Lincoln expanded his authority to reconstitute a nation divided.

Want a better grade?

Get the tools you need to sharpen your study skills. **SAGE edge** offers a robust online environment featuring an impressive array of free tools and resources. Access practice quizzes, eFlashcards, video, and multimedia at **edge.sagepub.com/abernathy2e**.

SAGE edge™ for CQ Press

CHAPTER REVIEW

This chapter's main ideas are reflected in the Learning Objectives. By reviewing them here, you should be able to **remember** the key points, **know** the terms that are central to the topic, and **think** about the critical issues raised in each section.

13.1 Consider the American president as one individual acting with and against many institutions and other political actors.

REMEMBER
- No president truly acts alone. The president operates at the center of multiple organizations and institutions within the executive branch.

THINK
- How much power do you think a president truly has?
- How much of this power do you think is due to the individual person and how much to the office and institutions?

13.2 Describe the powers of presidency as defined in the Constitution and the constitutional limitations placed on those powers.

REMEMBER
- The Framers called for a single executive, the president, with enough power to lead successfully but not so much power to make him or her susceptible to tyranny.
- As set out in the Constitution, the president serves a four-year term with the possibility of reelection. Candidates must be natural-born citizens, at least thirty-five years old, and a resident of the nation for fourteen years.
- The office of the presidency is granted a set of expressed, implied, and delegated powers.
- Executive power is constitutionally limited by powers granted to Congress and the judiciary.

KNOW	• presidential pardon (p. 364)	• State of the Union address	• War Powers Resolution of
	• recess appointment (p. 362)	(p. 364)	1973 (p. 363)

<table>
<tr><td>THINK</td><td>• What are the powers of the American president as laid out in the Constitution?</td></tr>
</table>

THINK
- What are the powers of the American president as laid out in the Constitution?
- What are the tensions between the president and Congress in making war as established in the Constitution?
- How have those tensions been resolved or changed?

13.3 Discuss institutional and informal sources of and influences on presidential power.

REMEMBER
- The institutions of the presidency can enhance or limit presidential power.
- The size and scale of the executive branch make it possible for the president to act on multiple fronts, but at the same time they can act as a brake on presidential initiatives.
- The president's cabinet and executive office act as sources of information for the president and also can communicate to the citizens a president's commitment to representing all Americans and their interests.
- Public opinion has come to play an important role in expanding or constraining the power of individual presidents. However, a president's approval ratings tend to decline over time.

KNOW
- Executive Office of the President (p. 367)
- going public (p. 370)

THINK
- What are the functions of the president's cabinet and executive office?
- What role does the president play with respect to his or her party?
- How and why does the president try to shape public opinion?

13.4 Understand how presidents have tested the limits of executive power during wartime and other crises.

REMEMBER
- The Constitution provides that the U.S. government has certain powers to suspend rights during times of rebellion or invasion. The text granting that power is within Article I, which is devoted to the structure and powers of Congress, not the executive branch. However, presidents have sometimes pointed to the "war powers" granted to the executive as justification for their actions.
- President Lincoln suspended habeas corpus during the Civil War on the grounds that the crisis necessitated it.

THINK
- How is the war on terror different—or not—from previous American crises in terms of presidential authority?
- Is the modern president too powerful? Not powerful enough?
- What was the controversy surrounding President Lincoln's use of executive authority during the Civil War?
- On what basis did Lincoln defend his use of executive authority?

13.5 Evaluate the tools that presidents use to further expand their power.

REMEMBER
- Presidents sometimes attempt to exercise a degree of unilateral authority through the assertion of executive privilege, signing statements, and executive orders.

KNOW
- executive agreements (p. 377)
- executive privilege (p. 377)
- signing statements (p. 377)
- executive orders (p. 378)

THINK
- Do individual presidents matter? How?
- What are the constraints on their ability to reshape the office?

Alex Wong/Getty Images

CHAPTER 14

THE FEDERAL BUREAUCRACY

Putting the Nation's Laws into Effect

▼ As Hurricane Harvey slammed into Houston, Texas, in late August 2017, people came out to help their neighbors navigate the streets after some areas were inundated with flooding. The preparation in advance of the storm and the response afterward from local and state officials and the Federal Emergency Management Agency (FEMA), combined with the efforts of everyday people, likely saved many lives.

Joe Raedle/Staff

To most Americans, the word bureaucracy refers to something that must be dealt with when necessary, complained about at times, and perhaps feared when confronted with its seemingly faceless exercise of power. Bureaucracy, however, simply describes an organization designed to carry out specific tasks according to a prescribed set of rules and procedures. In this chapter, you will learn about the federal bureaucracy—what it is, how it is structured, and how it works. Formally, the federal bureaucracy is part of the executive branch of the national government, charged with executing, or putting into action, the laws that Congress has written. However, the federal bureaucracy is actually a powerful player in the American political scene in its own right, though one that rarely makes the news unless something goes wrong. Whether you realize it or not, this is the part of the federal government that actually impacts your life in a more personal way than the actions of the president, Congress, or the judiciary typically do.

Americans often have contradictory views of bureaucracy, and make many demands of it. At times, they complain that bureaucracy is too powerful, capable of making their lives more difficult or expensive—or even that it is corrupt. At other times, they complain that it is powerless to help them, incompetent, wasteful, and inefficient. As you will see, these enduring tensions have spurred periods of reform and change since the nation's founding, in turn shaping the modern bureaucracy.

In this chapter, we will examine the American federal bureaucracy through the lenses of recent natural disasters and the responses to them—three hurricanes

that impacted the Caribbean, the Gulf of Mexico region, and the United States mainland in 2017 as well as one extraordinarily destructive hurricane whose effects along the Gulf Coast are still being felt fourteen years after its impact in 2005. The impacts, levels of response, and evaluations of the bureaucratic response to each of these was as unique as each storm and the main challenges it presented.

In considering the federal bureaucracy in the light of these natural disasters, you will gain a deeper understanding of its complexity, how it has changed over time, and efforts to make it more efficient and successful given the myriad tasks Americans place upon it.

FEDERAL BUREAUCRATIC ACTION CONSISTS OF MANY ACTORS AND EVOLVES OVER TIME

- **Understand how federal bureaucratic action involves many different agencies and evolves over time, often in response to lessons learned from past actions.**

When we think about the term **federal bureaucracy**, we may be inclined to think of it as one thing. It is not. As we will explore, it is a machinery constructed from many smaller units, each with its own objectives and administrative structures. We may also be inclined to see federal bureaucratic action as static in time. As we will see, it is not that either. Bureaucracies evolve and learn, unfortunately sometimes because of failure and political pressure applied in response to that failure. To begin to explore these issues, we examine a series of twenty-first-century disasters, hurricanes specifically. We start with three Atlantic Ocean hurricanes that came ashore in different places in the same year, 2017.

federal bureaucracy
the organizations and suborganizations within the executive branch that are tasked with putting the laws of the nation into effect.

HURRICANES HARVEY, IRMA, AND MARIA TEST THE FEDERAL RESPONSE

The first of the 2017 Atlantic monsters was Hurricane Harvey. It would become the costliest tropical cyclone in U.S. history. Making U.S. landfall at Rockport, Texas, as a 200-mile-wide but slow-moving Category 4 storm (with 5 being the most dangerous), Harvey's main impact was not wind but rain, torrential rain. In places over a large part of South Texas, it dropped almost unimaginable amounts, as much as 60 inches in the areas worst hit.

Houston was especially inundated. The flooding was so severe that, according to a NASA scientist (NASA is a federal agency and part of the bureaucracy), the weight of the water pushed the earth and bedrock in West Houston and nearby areas down by 2 centimeters.[1]

To some experts and observers, it could have been far worse. A combination of good advance preparation and community spirit helped. Warnings went out to residents ahead of time, low-lying roads were barricaded, and—as the devastation became clear for all to observe—"thousands of ordinary folks walked out into the rain, some with just a scant idea of how they might be of assistance."[2] Officials and staff for FEMA (Federal Emergency Management Agency) had prepositioned supplies in Texas. In addition to members of other agencies and the National Guard, more than 31,000 people delivered millions of meals and millions of liters of water.[3]

However, in the aftermath of the storm, some asked what could have been done better. Two reservoirs constructed by the Army Corps of Engineers (yet another part of the federal bureaucracy) in the 1940s to protect Houston residents had proved insufficient to handle the storm waters, as Houstonians had built homes and businesses far beyond the land they were designed to protect. Thousands of homes outside the two reservoirs flooded. Some blamed Congress for not directing the Corps to plan for a larger area of population density to protect and for not funding the Corps accordingly.[4]

While the recovery efforts continued from Harvey, Irma landed, and with force.

With Irma, unlike Harvey's rains, the main damage was the wind and the "storm surge," the ocean water pushed landward by the power of the storm and the differences in pressure between it and the surrounding ocean water.

At the peak of its power, Irma was a Category 5 hurricane. It devastated the Virgin Islands, the Caribbean, and then also Key West, Florida. In the United States, at least ninety people lost their lives. In the West Indies and the Caribbean Islands, Irma was just as destructive. On the American mainland, from Key West to South Carolina, Irma and its storm surge wreaked havoc.

On the U.S. mainland, five million Floridians lost power. Federal and state officials struggled to reach them. "Basically, every house in the Keys was impacted some way," reported a FEMA administrator. The federal response was equally massive. FEMA deployed thousands of people and transferred even more meals and liters of water than it had when Harvey impacted Texas.[5]

And then there was Maria.

That hurricane did not wreak the kind of destruction Harvey and Irma had on the U.S. mainland. Both had caused devastation and loss of lives as they made their way to the United States across the islands and nations of the Caribbean and the Atlantic basin.

Instead, Maria wreaked most of its havoc on Puerto Rico, a U.S. territory though not a state. For Maria, the consequences were devastating, destroying the entire infrastructure of Puerto Rico.

Much of Puerto Rico remained without power, food distribution, and clean water for months.[6] Many questioned President Donald Trump's employment of the United States' power in relief efforts, through its federal bureaucracy, in repairing the damage that Maria brought. President Trump cited the difficulties of reaching the island territory: "It's very tough because it's an island. . . . In Texas and Florida and we will also see on Puerto Rico, but the difference is this is an island sitting in the middle of an ocean, and it's a big ocean."[7]

In June 2018, eight months after Maria made landfall, Puerto Rico was still struggling to recover. It was not even clear how many people had lost their lives in the storm the year before. The official

▲ *Left:* Yamiles Vazquez poses with her baby Joy on a section of her family's damaged property three weeks after Hurricane Maria hit Puerto Rico in October 2017. Despite multiple visits from FEMA, at that time the town had yet to receive any FEMA aid. The area, which is about 40 miles south of San Juan, was without running water or grid power for months. Puerto Rico experienced widespread damage to most of its electrical, gas, and water grid as well as agriculture. *Right:* Nine months after Maria made landfall, at the annual National Puerto Rican Day Parade in New York City, people paid tribute to those who died in the hurricane with signs saying "Remember Our Dead"/"Recordamos Nuestros Muertos." Independent researchers say the death toll in Puerto Rico was vastly greater—as many as 4,645—than the official estimates of sixty-four.

government toll was sixty-four. Researchers from Harvard University, however, calculated it to be much, much larger—as many as 4,645—once deaths due to effects such as delayed medical care were taken into account.[8] That month, protesters gathered in New York City to demand that an *international* bureaucratic organization, the United Nations, investigate the official conclusions of the Puerto Rican government. "They took their shoes off as a symbol of the people who died as a result of the storm but who were not immediately counted."[9] In bureaucratic politics, the act of counting is itself an act of political power.

The 2018 Atlantic hurricane season officially began on June 1, a date established by a federal bureaucracy in the 1960s, largely based on the time when hurricane reconnaissance aircraft began to patrol the ocean in the absence of the widespread weather satellite coverage now employed. Prior to each hurricane season, the National Hurricane Center publishes a list, for different ocean basins and regions, of names to be given to storms as they reach significant status as a tropical storm and/or hurricane (with the World Meteorological Organization controlling the actual procedure). The names are applied alphabetically, reused in six-year cycles until a name gets retired and replaced if that storm resulted in significant death or destruction.

Should there be named storms in 2018, and there very likely will be—as each Atlantic season has, on average, six named hurricanes, two of them major—the names Harvey, Irma, and Maria will not be among them.[10] They have all been retired.

There was another notable storm whose name will not be included if the list of named storms reaches K. Not only did that storm produce devastation that still shapes New Orleans, the Gulf Coast, and many lives fourteen years after its impact, but it resulted in one of the deepest questionings of the actions of federal bureaucracies in preparation for and responses to natural disasters in the twenty-first century.

Its name was Katrina.[11]

KATRINA PROVIDES UNCOMFORTABLE LESSONS ABOUT THE FEDERAL RESPONSE

Max Mayfield saw it coming, and he tried to warn as many people as he could. As director of the National Hurricane Center, based in Miami, Florida, Mayfield and the scientists on his team sounded the alarm on August 26, 2005, that a potentially catastrophic hurricane would make

The effects of Hurricane Katrina were felt far beyond New Orleans. New Orleans residents, including five-year-old Donte Percy, were evacuated first to the Superdome and then ultimately to places like this shelter for refugees in Houston, Texas.

landfall on the coast of Louisiana, southeast of New Orleans. In predicting the point of impact for the hurricane's eye, they were off by a mere eighteen miles. As one reporter noted, "In the business of hurricane prediction, that's laser-beam accuracy."[12]

Two days prior to landfall, "Mayfield was so worried about Hurricane Katrina that he called the governors of Louisiana and Mississippi and the mayor of New Orleans. On Sunday, he even talked about the force of Katrina during a video conference call to President George W. Bush. . . . 'I just wanted to be able to go to sleep that night knowing that I did all I could do.'"[13]

As the storm approached shore, officials warned that it could make landfall with winds in excess of 130 miles per hour, pushing ahead of it a storm surge of devastating intensity and volume. New Orleans mayor C. Ray Nagin cautioned residents to leave the city, saying, "This is the real deal. Board up your homes, make sure you have enough medicine, make sure the car has enough gas. Do all things you normally do for a hurricane but treat this one differently because it is pointed towards New Orleans."[14]

Of all the concerns, the most worrisome was the city's system of levees and pumps, designed by the Army Corps of Engineers to keep the water at bay. With much of the city below sea level, a failure in any one section of the system would cause New Orleans "to fill up like a bathtub."[15] By the morning of Sunday, August 28, New Orleans was under evacuation orders. The roads were packed. Inbound lanes of the main highways were redirected to handle outbound traffic. Many residents, however, could not or would not leave. In a press conference, Nagin had acknowledged that the Superdome would be needed to temporarily house the one hundred thousand or more of the city's residents who lacked the transportation needed to leave the city, a disproportionate number of whom were elderly, poor, or African American.[16] When the Superdome opened to receive those unable to evacuate, "people on walkers, some with oxygen tanks, began checking in."[17]

On the morning of August 29, Hurricane Katrina's eyewall made its first Gulf Coast landfall at Plaquemines Parish, Louisiana. Initially, New Orleans and its mayor were hopeful that a disaster had been avoided. The city had been spared the storm's strongest winds and storm surge. Within hours, however, it became clear that the levee system was failing. Water overtopped the levees in some areas. In others, leaks developed and the pumps designed to protect the city from the water entering it began to fail. The "bathtub" that included many of the city's poorest neighborhoods began to fill up.

More than one thousand residents of Louisiana died in the storm and the flooding that followed, many of them its most vulnerable. A study of the bodies recovered following the storm concluded that "64 percent of the people who died were elderly."[18] Immediately after the scope of the devastation became clear, calls went out for donations to private relief agencies, such as the American Red Cross and the Salvation Army. Money—rather than food, blankets, or other goods—was the main request, which allowed these organizations to respond more quickly and effectively as they saw needs arise. Then, in the days, weeks, and months that followed, Gulf Coast residents looked to the Federal Emergency Management Agency (FEMA) to step in and lead recovery efforts. However, as refugees from New Orleans evacuated to nearby states following the storm, they shared not only stories of loss and devastation but plenty of criticism for how public officials had handled the disaster. Some of the sharpest words came from those who sheltered at the Superdome. One woman, Maia Brisco, told reporters the stadium was "a total hell hole."[19]

In the aftermath of Hurricane Katrina, the performance of local, state, and federal officials in predicting, preparing for, and responding to the storm came under intense scrutiny. Figuring prominently in this process was the federal bureaucracy, which is really a small universe of organizations operating across the country. Within this vast system are departments, agencies, and bureaus, which themselves are often divided and subdivided into smaller organizational units. The National Hurricane Center, for example, and Max Mayfield and the members of his team, are part of the National Weather Service, which is part of the National Oceanic and Atmospheric Administration, which, in turn, is part of the Department of Commerce.

As the nation was confronted with scenes of devastation and loss in Katrina's wake, parts of the federal bureaucracy, such as the National Hurricane Center, were singled out for praise. Others, however, such as the Army Corps of Engineers and FEMA, received sharp criticism. How could some parts of the vast machinery of the federal government have gotten things right while others seemed to have gotten them so wrong? As Congress, the White House, and the American people asked this very question, it was concluded that the answers were complicated, just like the vast bureaucracy responsible for preparing for and responding to disasters such as Hurricane Katrina.

DID THE BUREAUCRACY LEARN FROM KATRINA?

As the affected areas began to clean up and rebuild from the triple monsters in late 2017, two questions were commonly posed: Had the federal and state agencies learned from Katrina? Did they put this dearly paid-for education into practice on the ground?

The year 2017 was not the first time these questions had been asked since Katrina laid waste to New Orleans and the Gulf Coast in 2005. In 2012, Hurricane Sandy spread destruction from the Caribbean to the East Coast of the United States, from Florida to Maine. More than 140 people died as a direct result of Sandy. In the United States, the devastation was worst in New Jersey and New York, mostly due to flooding. While some praised the response to Sandy by the administration of President Barack Obama, others critiqued it.

By some accounts, government had learned and adapted. Enabled by legislation passed in Katrina's wake, President Obama was able to quickly instruct FEMA to coordinate and streamline its rescue response across all responders.[20] Three months after Sandy's landfall, however, when a blast of arctic air hit the Northeast, some critics pointed to families having to rely on space heaters to stave off the cold while still awaiting repairs and rebuilding. The bureaucratic apparatus might have been more responsive in preparation, but in terms of rebuilding, it seemed to be too slow yet again.

In the aftermath of the hurricanes of 2017, there were similarly mixed reviews. Once again, for example, the National Hurricane Center received widespread praise for its work. Though not perfect—a very difficult thing to achieve with hurricanes—the Hurricane Center developed, and disseminated, shocking predictions of likely rainfall totals associated with Harvey.[21] They were right. Rebuilding efforts in Puerto Rico in the wake of Maria undertaken by federal and territorial agencies, on the other hand, continue to come under sharp criticism.

Differences in evaluations of bureaucratic performance, however, also depend upon competing political demands on the bureaucracy and on Americans' views of its proper role in American public life. And they are shaped by politics. In March 2018, during the administration of President Donald Trump, the agency tasked as a watchdog over FEMA (the Department of Homeland Security's Office of Inspector General) removed from its website twelve reports, many positive, of the handling of natural disasters—including Hurricane Sandy—under the administration of President Obama. A former FEMA administrator from the Obama administration called the removal "curious."[22]

Those who have argued for a reduced role for government in American public policy have highlighted the successes of the private sector in responding to the challenges of rebuilding: "In particular, hurricane-damaged areas should encourage the private sector to play a large role in both disaster response and long-term recover. Firms like Walmart and Home Depot were crucial to both processes during Katrina and were again at the forefront [in the 2017] hurricane season."[23]

Can bureaucracies learn and adapt? To gain any traction on this critical question, we need to start with two others: Which bureaucracy? Learn what, precisely? We begin by trying to tease out what this thing we call "bureaucracy" is.

WHAT HAVE I LEARNED?

1. The American federal bureaucracy is _____.

   a. a specialized part of the executive branch, carrying out the orders of the president

   b. the organizations and suborganizations of people who put into effect national public policy through the use of specialization, division of labor, and standardization of administrative processes

   c. the organizations based at the state level with powers equal to the legislative, judicial, and executive branches

   d. the branch of government primarily responsible for making the nation's laws

2. What were some of the criticisms leveled at the federal bureaucracy following Hurricane Katrina?

3. What are some of the challenges associated with assessing bureaucratic performance?

Answer Key: 1. b; 2. Answers might include criticism of FEMA for its response or of the Army Corps of Engineers for the failed levee system; 3. Answers might include political pressure, competing demands on bureaucratic agencies, or the fact that many bureaucracies are often involved in solving problems.

THEORIES OF BUREAUCRATIC ORGANIZATION FOCUS ON RULES, PEOPLE, AND TASKS

- **Describe the key characteristics of bureaucratic organization and the theories that explain why that organization happens.**

Americans' ambivalence about the federal bureaucracy may be partly due to the fact that—unlike Congress, the president, or the Supreme Court—Americans actually have contact with it in their personal or professional lives.

Any American-made product you consume involved federal agencies making sure that the factory was safe for its employees, that it did not discriminate in hiring, that it dealt with labor issues and complaints fairly, and that it did not degrade the environment. For anything you purchase manufactured by a foreign country, the bureaucracy acted to ensure that the country of origin was following rules of fair trade and labor practices promised in trade agreements. Driving much of this bureaucratic involvement in daily life are the demands of Americans themselves—for safe products, fair labor practices, and environmentally conscious factories. Ensuring that these demands are met involves the federal bureaucracy in many areas of the nation's economy and private life. The vast majority of the federal bureaucracy lies within the executive branch of the federal government, which is tasked with executing, or carrying out, federal laws.

In addition to the federal bureaucracy, there is another category of public bureaucracies: **state and local bureaucracies**. These agencies are also involved in the lives of Americans: they made the rules that governed the construction of the house in which the citizen lives; determine the property taxes that he or she pays; provide the school, police station, and firehouse down the street; and supply the water in the glass next to the alarm clock (the time on which is actually regulated by a federal bureaucratic agency, believe it or not).[24]

What's more, the same products regulated by public bureaucracies—federal, state, and local—have been produced by another category of bureaucratic organizations: **private bureaucracies**. While

state and local bureaucracies
public organizations below the federal level designed to carry out specific tasks according to a prescribed set of rules and procedures.

private bureaucracies
privately owned corporations and companies that carry out specific tasks according to a prescribed set of rules and procedures.

corporations and companies are not usually called bureaucracies, they in fact are. They share some, though not all, of the characteristics of public bureaucracies. A common critique of public bureaucracies is that they should try to operate more like the makers of consumer products and less like the government, a topic to which we will return later in the chapter. In short, bureaucratic organization is everywhere. It is an elaborate system, but not necessarily a mysterious one.

Before we begin to untangle the complex constellation of federal administrative organizations, we need to consider how bureaucracies operate. The term *bureaucracy* describes an organization or a set of organizations, but it also describes a way of organizing, a way of distributing power. Scholars have offered a variety of theoretical approaches to explaining bureaucratic organization, none of which have to be mutually exclusive. Three approaches, in particular, highlight different aspects of bureaucratic organization: rules, people, and tasks.

WEBER'S THEORY FOCUSES ON RULES

Max Weber (pronounced VAY-ber), a German sociologist, was among the first to define the boundaries and characteristics of bureaucratic organization. Weber saw bureaucracy as a large and complex machine. Each individual in this machine—a bureaucrat—was "only a single cog in an ever-moving mechanism."[25] For Weber, bureaucratic power rested upon what he called "rational-legal authority," in which citizens accept the authority of organizations, or, more precisely, the rules and organizational structures that define that authority and place limits upon it. Once firmly established, Weber concluded, "bureaucracy is among those social structures which are hardest to destroy."[26]

The Weberian bureaucracy is characterized by four main organizational traits. First, bureaucrats have defined tasks and rules governing how these tasks should be carried out, creating a clear division of labor within the organization. The sets of rules governing the behavior of bureaucrats are commonly referred to as **standard operating procedures**. Second, authority in bureaucracy is hierarchical, with "a clearly established system of super- and sub-ordination in which there is a supervision of the lower offices by the higher ones."[27] Third, individual jobs within the organization are specialized, with workers increasingly selected for specific jobs based on their technical competence. Finally, the modern bureaucracy is characterized by impersonal relationships. Weber's ideal of a bureaucracy was, by design, divorced from politics and personal relationships, its effective functioning made more likely if "it succeeds in eliminating from official business love, hatred, and all purely personal, irrational, and emotional elements which escape calculation."[28]

BARNARD'S THEORY FOCUSES ON PEOPLE

Chester Barnard drew on decades of experience with the American Telephone and Telegraph Company in the early twentieth century to outline a theory of the bureaucracy in which people—and not just rules and procedures—mattered to the life of a bureaucracy. For Barnard, the essence of a bureaucracy is that it involves "conscious coordination" of the activities of individuals in pursuit of a joint objective.[29]

Whenever people undertake action in pursuit of a common goal, however, they are taking a risk that others involved might not do what they are supposed to do. Political scientists often describe these risks in terms of the **principal-agent problem**. The "principal" in this model is the actor who asks the agent to carry out a task. The challenge in doing so is twofold. First, the agent may have his or her own goals, which may not be the same as the principal's. Second, the agent may have information that the principal lacks, which opens up the opportunity for the agent to behave in a way that is not in the interests of the principal.

Ken James/Bloomberg via Getty Images

▲ An employee performs the first inspection of fresh potatoes at the Campbell Soup Co. plant in Sacramento, California. Campbell produces up to ten million cans of soup every day. Every can is impacted by the rules and regulations that are administered by federal, state, and local bureaucracies. These regulations cover everything from the soup's production to its distribution, sale, and consumption.

standard operating procedures
the sets of rules governing the behavior of bureaucrats.

principal-agent problem
the challenge that arises when one actor, the principal, tasks another, the agent, to carry out the principal's wishes in the presence of uncertainty and unequal information.

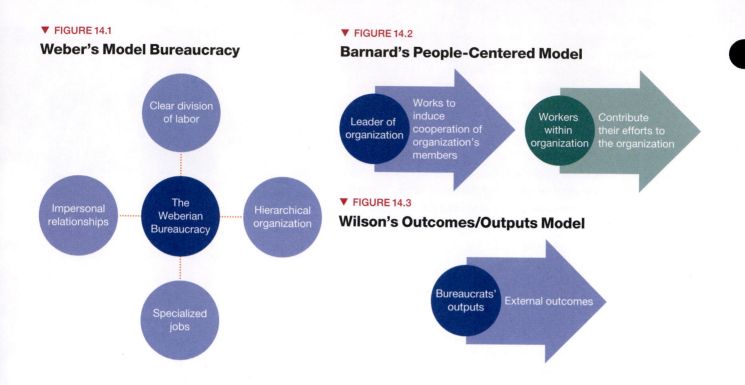

▼ FIGURE 14.1
Weber's Model Bureaucracy

- Clear division of labor
- Impersonal relationships
- The Weberian Bureaucracy
- Hierarchical organization
- Specialized jobs

▼ FIGURE 14.2
Barnard's People-Centered Model

Leader of organization — Works to induce cooperation of organization's members — Workers within organization — Contribute their efforts to the organization

▼ FIGURE 14.3
Wilson's Outcomes/Outputs Model

Bureaucrats' outputs — External outcomes

Principal-agent relationships are everywhere. An example from politics is that when voters (the principals) elect members of Congress (the agents), the voters run the risk that their elected representatives will not faithfully carry out their wishes, especially during the parts of the legislative process that are harder to observe and happen out of public view.

According to Barnard, bureaucratic leadership is central to the success of a bureaucracy. The job of the leader is to secure the cooperation of those within the organization.[30] In this effort, **incentives**—those inducements that the leaders of a bureaucracy can offer to their employees— are key to successful performance. Incentives do not always have to involve money. Power, prestige, a sense of accomplishment, and a shared vision of important work can also act as incentives for successful bureaucratic performance. As we will examine later, however, incentives can act the other way, sending bureaucrats off in directions that Congress, the president, or the American people did not intend for them to go.

WILSON'S THEORY FOCUSES ON TASKS

For political scientist James Q. Wilson, rules and procedures mattered, as did individuals. However, his analysis added a third element of bureaucratic organization: tasks, or what different bureaucrats in their organizations actually do. Wilson wrote that "people matter, but organization matters also, and tasks matter most of all."[31] Of special concern in Wilson's analysis was the ability or inability to observe two consequences of bureaucratic action: outputs and outcomes. Outputs are what bureaucratic operators do; outcomes are what changes in the world as a result of their actions. When either outputs or outcomes are difficult to observe with any certainty, problems arise. When both are difficult to discern, "effective management is almost impossible."[32]

Consider the nation's public schools.[33] When a teacher closes the classroom door, that teacher's outputs are largely unseen except by the students. Sure, the principal can observe the teacher, but both know that the observation day is likely not a typical class. More problematically, especially as America is testing its students like never before, it is very difficult and expensive to try to measure a teacher's outcomes, or what a teacher is adding to the mind of one particular student.[34] In order to be effectively managed, both outputs and outcomes must be "visible."

incentives
inducements that leaders of a bureaucracy can offer to their employees to spur successful performance.

1. According to Max Weber, one of the key characteristics of bureaucratic organization is ＿＿＿.

    a. its highly political nature

    b. a set of standard operating procedures

    c. the highly personal nature of relationships within it

    d. the ability to vote bureaucrats out of office

2. In a people-centered model of bureaucracy, one of the most important elements is ＿＿＿.

    a. strict control of employees based on rules and procedure

    b. using incentives to encourage better performance

    c. weak leadership

    d. routine weekly meetings

3. What is the principal agent problem?

＿＿＿＿＿＿＿＿＿＿＿＿＿＿＿＿＿＿＿＿

Answer Key: 1. b; 2. b; 3. Answers should discuss the challenges principals face in holding their agents accountable, especially in the presence of unequal levels of information.

THE BUREAUCRACY HAS DEVELOPED IN RESPONSE TO DEMANDS AND CRISES

- **Outline the historical development of the American federal bureaucracy.**

In the early years of its history, the American bureaucracy was tiny, reflecting the reality that the autonomous and mostly agrarian society did not place many demands on the young national government. From its beginnings as a small set of departments employing few people, the bureaucracy has grown enormously and today has nearly three million civilian employees working across the country.

This growth has not been steady and gradual, but—like the power of the national government itself—has experienced periods of relatively little growth and periods of intense expansion. The increase in the nation's population and boundaries, the complexity of tasks performed by the federal government, and greater demands for services by citizens have all contributed to this process. In addition, responses to crises—economic, social, and military—have produced some of the most dramatic expansions in the size, scope, and complexity of the federal bureaucracy.

THE FOUNDERS WERE SKEPTICAL OF, AND UNCLEAR ABOUT, THE ROLE OF THE BUREAUCRACY

Although the delegates to the Constitutional Convention wrestled a great deal with the issue of the power and independence of the chief executive, they spent very little time discussing the administrative apparatus itself, and the "Constitution is virtually silent on the subject."[35] Much of the constitutional basis for the bureaucracy lies in Article II, which lays out the functions and processes of the executive branch of government. In it, the president is authorized to "require the Opinion, in writing, of the principal Officer in each of the executive Departments, upon any Subject relating to the Duties of their respective Offices."[36] This section forms the basis for the executive branch departments, special organizations created by acts of Congress to assist the president in executing the laws of the nation. The heads of these departments are referred to as secretaries. Those secretaries form the president's cabinet, along with the vice president and the heads of other offices given cabinet-level status.

DELEGATES AIMED TO AVOID TYRANNY BUT PRESERVE EFFICIENCY. The delegates to the Constitutional Convention brought with them a deep mistrust of administrative power that was born out of experiences under British colonial rule: many of the charges against King George III in the

Declaration of Independence focused on administrative abuses. The delegates were in no mood to create a homegrown swarm of officers.

On the other hand, the delegates also held the general belief, gained from hard experience, that placing administrative responsibilities entirely in the hands of the legislature would be slow and inefficient. The Continental Congress had done just that, with numerous committees handling the business of fighting a revolution. This arrangement worked poorly, and individual members of the Congress were constantly overworked and overburdened.

Trying to steer a course between executive tyranny and legislative inefficiency, the delegates agreed to place in the hands of the president the authority to nominate executive branch officials rather than having a council of officers selected by Congress, which had been discussed in the convention. The Senate, though, retained the role of advice and consent in approving presidential nominees by a majority vote.[37] In addition, Congress retained the ability to impeach (in the House) and try (in the Senate) "all civil Officers of the United States" for "Treason, Bribery, or Other high Crimes and Misdemeanors."[38]

HOW OFFICERS WOULD BE REMOVED REMAINED UNSETTLED.

Having settled on how executive branch offers would be selected, the most contentious question facing the delegates was how these people were to be removed. Did the president have the authority to remove officers at will, was it Congress's job, or should there be a role for both the president and the Congress? Or were these people to serve for life with no possibility for removal? On this question—other than setting out the rarely used process of impeachment—the Constitution remained silent.

Only weeks after the first national Congress assembled, the issue of the removal of officers came before it in what has become known as the Decision of 1789. Following what became "the first major constitutional debate" in the young Republic,[39] Congress left the power of removal in the hands of the president. The question, however, reemerged with the Tenure of Office Act (1867), which—largely because of the tense politics following the Civil War—restricted the president's authority of removal. Only in 1926, in the case of *Myers v. United States*, which held the Tenure of Office Act unconstitutional, was the question settled. Presidents retained the authority to remove officials in the executive branch, a necessary ability in their role of ensuring that laws are faithfully executed.[40]

WASHINGTON FORMED THE FIRST ADMINISTRATION AND THE FIRST CABINET DEPARTMENTS.

President George Washington's cabinet included just four men and three official departments. Secretary of State Thomas Jefferson oversaw the Department of State, handling the young nation's dealings with foreign nations as well as publishing laws and overseeing the hiring of civil officials. The Department of War (later incorporated into the Department of Defense) oversaw the nation's small military with less than one hundred civilian employees. Alexander Hamilton used his position as secretary of the Treasury to advance his goal of expanding the role of the federal government in the nation's economic affairs. Finally, Washington's attorney general (later made the head of the Department of Justice) acted as a legal adviser to the president and members of his cabinet. In the centuries since, Congress has created new departments and reorganized others. (See Figure 14.4.)

In forming his first cabinet, Washington tried to reassure members of the experimental nation that his government was competent and representative of all thirteen states. He knew this task would not be easy. A week after his inauguration, the president wrote to a friend, "I anticipate that one of the most difficult and delicate parts of the duty of my Office will be that which relates to nominations for appointments."[41] Three of the members of his small cabinet represented diverse and powerful states: Massachusetts, New York, and Virginia.[42]

Washington was right to be worried. Within the first three years of his administration, "open warfare had broken out" between two powerful members of his cabinet: Alexander Hamilton and Thomas Jefferson.[43] With very different visions of the role of the federal government—especially in the nation's economic life—these men participated in some of the first **turf wars** in the history of the federal bureaucracy, in which each tried to take duties and responsibilities away from the other's department or keep his opponent from doing so.

turf wars
when bureaucrats compete to take duties and responsibilities away from one another's departments or keep their opponents from doing so.

Executive Branch Departments: Year of Establishment and Primary Tasks

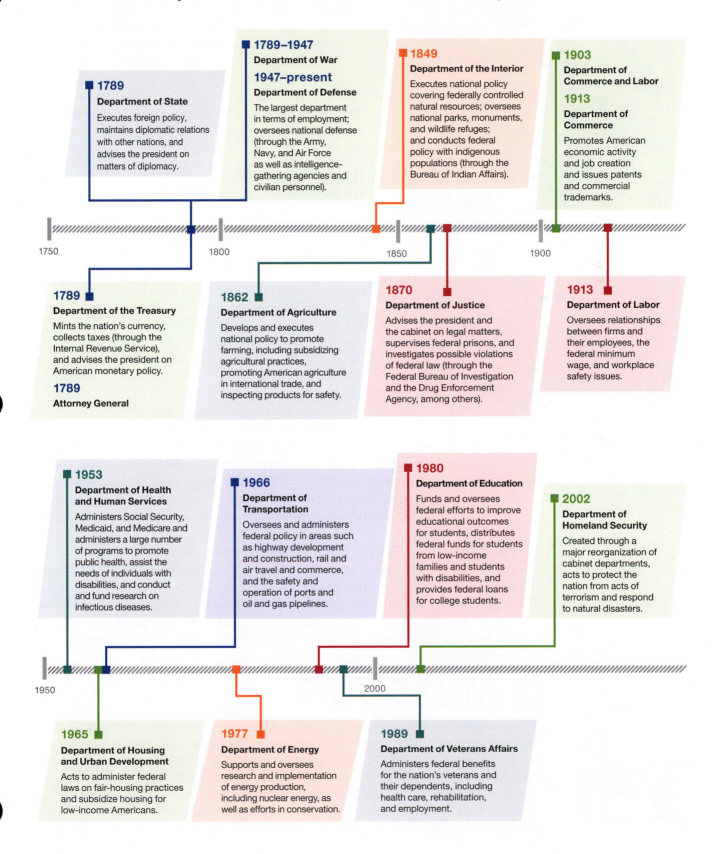

1789–1947
Department of War

1947–present
Department of Defense

The largest department in terms of employment; oversees national defense (through the Army, Navy, and Air Force as well as intelligence-gathering agencies and civilian personnel).

1789
Department of State

Executes foreign policy, maintains diplomatic relations with other nations, and advises the president on matters of diplomacy.

1849
Department of the Interior

Executes national policy covering federally controlled natural resources; oversees national parks, monuments, and wildlife refuges; and conducts federal policy with indigenous populations (through the Bureau of Indian Affairs).

1903
Department of Commerce and Labor

1913
Department of Commerce

Promotes American economic activity and job creation and issues patents and commercial trademarks.

1789
Department of the Treasury

Mints the nation's currency, collects taxes (through the Internal Revenue Service), and advises the president on American monetary policy.

1789
Attorney General

1862
Department of Agriculture

Develops and executes national policy to promote farming, including subsidizing agricultural practices, promoting American agriculture in international trade, and inspecting products for safety.

1870
Department of Justice

Advises the president and the cabinet on legal matters, supervises federal prisons, and investigates possible violations of federal law (through the Federal Bureau of Investigation and the Drug Enforcement Agency, among others).

1913
Department of Labor

Oversees relationships between firms and their employees, the federal minimum wage, and workplace safety issues.

1750 • 1800 • 1850 • 1900

1953
Department of Health and Human Services

Administers Social Security, Medicaid, and Medicare and administers a large number of programs to promote public health, assist the needs of individuals with disabilities, and conduct and fund research on infectious diseases.

1966
Department of Transportation

Oversees and administers federal policy in areas such as highway development and construction, rail and air travel and commerce, and the safety and operation of ports and oil and gas pipelines.

1980
Department of Education

Funds and oversees federal efforts to improve educational outcomes for students, distributes federal funds for students from low-income families and students with disabilities, and provides federal loans for college students.

2002
Department of Homeland Security

Created through a major reorganization of cabinet departments, acts to protect the nation from acts of terrorism and respond to natural disasters.

1950 • 2000

1965
Department of Housing and Urban Development

Acts to administer federal laws on fair-housing practices and subsidize housing for low-income Americans.

1977
Department of Energy

Supports and oversees research and implementation of energy production, including nuclear energy, as well as efforts in conservation.

1989
Department of Veterans Affairs

Administers federal benefits for the nation's veterans and their dependents, including health care, rehabilitation, and employment.

In choosing men to fill out his administration, Washington's primary consideration was what he referred to as "fitness of character," by which he meant integrity, a man's standing in the community, and qualities that would ensure the nation's confidence. Washington's priorities ensured that members of the upper social classes tended to be the ones to fill these positions.[44] Technical competence, except in a few positions, such as those involving legal matters, was not the primary consideration. Washington also viewed his cabinet as very much subordinate to his leadership, sometimes calling on his cabinet secretaries to take dictation.

THE JACKSONIAN ERA SAW THE RISE OF POLITICAL PATRONAGE

In the early decades of the nineteenth century, most of the growth of the federal bureaucracy was a result of the geographic expansion of the nation; one particular issue that needed to be addressed was delivery of the mail across the growing territory. The bureaucratic reforms of President Andrew Jackson (1829–1837) sought to separate the person from the office. In his inaugural address, Jackson railed against the sense of "ownership" of important (and sometimes well-paying) administrative positions on the part of the officeholders, who in some cases unofficially handed the positions down to their heirs, as had been done officially in Britain and other European countries.

As part of his reforms, Jackson employed what is called **political patronage**—filling administrative positions as a reward for support rather than based solely on merit. His use of patronage is commonly referred to as the **spoils system**; the name indicates that part of the "spoils" of a successful election is the ability to clean house of one's opponents and install supporters in their place. Although politics—specifically removing political opponents and installing supporters—played a role in Jackson's reforms, so did a desire to separate the man from the office he held in order to undercut individual power bases as a challenge to Jackson's power and authority.

Ironically, one of the consequences of patronage was to make the federal bureaucracy in some ways closer to what Weber described: impartial, neutral, driven by standard operating procedures and technical expertise. If, after elections, a nation is constantly shuffling people in and out of important administrative positions—people who often have little expertise in the operations of those agencies and departments—then it becomes necessary to standardize procedures. Otherwise, little would get done, or at least done well. Thus, through their overtly political practices, Jackson and his supporters laid the foundations for the modern federal bureaucracy.

POST–CIVIL WAR, THE BUREAUCRACY GREW ALONG WITH THE NATION'S TERRITORIES

As America emerged from the devastation of the Civil War, the nation found itself engaged in relentless expansion of both the nation's boundaries in the West and of agriculture and industry. To cope with the demands placed upon the federal government as a result of this expansion, the bureaucracy grew in size and also in the scope of its involvement with the nation's economy.

As large corporations such as the railroads outgrew the ability of individual states to control and regulate them, demands by the public for a more active federal role in supervising businesses and commerce led to the creation of independent regulatory agencies, which exist outside the major cabinet

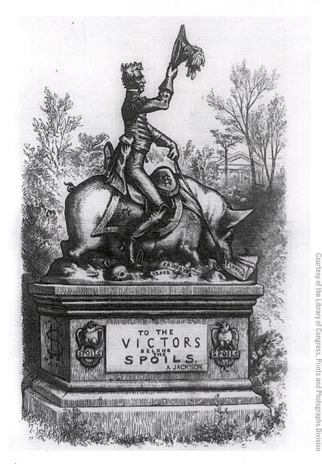

▲ "In Memoriam—Our Civil Service as It Was," a cartoon by Thomas Nast, 1877. Nast's depiction highlights the end of the spoils system under civil service reforms.

Courtesy of the Library of Congress, Prints and Photographs Division

political patronage
filling administrative positions as a reward for support rather than based solely on merit.

spoils system
the practice of cleaning house of one's opponents and installing supporters in their place following a successful election.

departments and whose job is to monitor and regulate specific sectors of the economy. Congress created the first, the Interstate Commerce Commission, in 1887 in order to monitor price setting and other practices by the railroads.

In addition to calls for regulation, the federal bureaucracy found itself confronted with the demands of organized interests, such as farmers, who sought to use the power of the federal government to advance and promote their own endeavors. The result was the development of **clientele agencies**, which, as their name implies, act to serve and promote the interests of their clients. The Department of Agriculture (1862) served the interests of farmers—one of the most powerful clientele groups of the time—by, for example, collecting and distributing data about advancements in agricultural practices.[45]

The development and expansion of the federal bureaucracy happened relatively late in the life of the American democracy, especially when compared to European democracies of the period. For most of these nations, a well-developed bureaucracy existed before they became democracies, having developed under the rule of monarchs. For political scientist Stephen Skowronek, the fact that the American bureaucracy had to develop in the shadow of two other, already established, sets of political institutions—the court system and political parties—resulted in a federal bureaucracy that was more fragmented and decentralized than its European counterparts.[46]

Political scientist Theda Skocpol looked to the same period in state development to explain why America never developed the kind of comprehensive social welfare state as Europe, even though America introduced some of the earliest social welfare policies in the world with its system of pensions for Civil War veterans and their survivors. For Skocpol, the well-developed system of federal courts was hostile to large-scale government intervention on behalf of citizens, and American political parties did not want to give up the power they gained by providing benefits in return for political patronage.[47]

Both of these studies highlight the idea of American exceptionalism, in which scholars have examined how the unique histories, paths, and development of American political institutions may have led to uniqueness in the nation's representative government itself. In doing so, scholars have also stressed the importance of **path dependence**, in which a set of political choices at one time produces a set of outcomes that shapes the possibilities for future politics and public policies.

clientele agencies
organizations that act to serve and promote the interests of their clients.

path dependence
the way in which a set of political outcomes shapes future possibilities for political action.

BUREAUCRATIC EXPANSION IN THE PROGRESSIVE ERA FOCUSED ON LABOR AND ELIMINATING PATRONAGE

The Progressive Era (roughly from 1890 to 1920) is known for the continued expansion of the role of the federal bureaucracy in the nation's economic life and for attempts to take politics out of the bureaucracy itself. Congress created the Department of Commerce and Labor in 1903 to oversee and regulate workplaces, the rights of employees, and working conditions, which had become the focus of reform-minded journalists called muckrakers.[48] In

North Wind Picture Archives via AP Images

A NAUSEATING JOB, BUT IT MUST BE DONE

▲ A political cartoon depicting President Theodore Roosevelt as a muckraker taking on the meatpacking industry. Muckrakers focused on a variety of abuses in private industry, including working conditions.

1913, the department was split in two, with the Department of Commerce focusing on economic growth and the Department of Labor on employee–employer relations and workplace conditions.

The Progressive Era also witnessed attempts to reform the bureaucracy, especially in trying to alleviate the effects of the patronage system of appointment. The model that these reformers used was one of science and business. Their target was what they saw as a corrupt, inefficient, and too-political bureaucracy. Under President Chester A. Arthur (1881–1885), Congress passed the Civil Service Reform Act of 1883, commonly known as the Pendleton Act in reference to its primary Senate sponsor. The Pendleton Act created the first U.S. Civil Service Commission. Its three members, appointed by Arthur, were active reformers. Their task was to draw up and enforce rules on hiring, promotion, and tenure of office within the civil service.

Under these new rules, members of the **federal civil service** were hired and promoted on the basis of the **merit system**, in which competitive testing results, educational attainment, and other qualifications formed the basis for hiring and promotion rather than politics and personal connections. In the early years after the act's passage, only a small percentage of federal bureaucrats were covered by its content; by 2016, more than 90 percent were.

TWENTIETH-CENTURY CRISES EXPANDED CLIENTELE AGENCIES AND THE MILITARY BUREAUCRACY

As we discussed in Chapter 3, President Franklin Roosevelt's "New Deal" efforts to combat the crisis of the Great Depression resulted in an unprecedented expansion of the size of the federal bureaucracy as well as an equally startling expansion of the role of government and the bureaucracy in the American economy. Roosevelt created a host of bureaucratic agencies (despite challenges from the Supreme Court) that were primarily clientele agencies, acting on behalf of specific groups of citizens, such as the unemployed. Their purpose was to increase the provision of social services to affected Americans, including senior citizens, low-income and unemployed Americans, and individuals with disabilities.

Roosevelt and the nation faced a second struggle during his administration. As president, Roosevelt was commander in chief during most of his nation's involvement in World War II. Roosevelt and his administration oversaw a massive expansion of the military, the creation of new agencies to prosecute the war, and significant federal intervention in the American economy in order to support and supply the war effort.

That expanded bureaucracy remained in place after the war. America and its former ally, the Soviet Union, entered a decades-long period of competition for global supremacy known as the Cold War. While no full-scale global war broke out, the United States, and the Soviet Union aimed thousands of nuclear weapons at each other and engaged in smaller military confrontations across the globe, supporting opposing sides without directly engaging each other's militaries on a large scale.

To fight the Cold War, the federal bureaucracy saw the creation of new agencies. President Harry S. Truman (1945–1953) signed into law the National Security Act of 1947, which created the National Security Council to advise the president on security matters and the Central Intelligence Agency (CIA) to advise the president on intelligence matters and help coordinate intelligence-gathering activities.[49] Not a formal cabinet department, the CIA is an example of an **independent executive agency**. These agencies resemble cabinet departments in many ways, such as having their top administrators appointed by and reporting to the president, but they exist outside the cabinet structure and usually have a narrower focus of mission.

IN THE MID-TWENTIETH CENTURY, THE SOCIAL SAFETY NET GREW

Postwar economic prosperity allowed the nation to fund a large expansion in the national bureaucracy in the areas of defense and the provision of social services. Under the umbrella of the Great Society, President Lyndon B. Johnson (1963–1969) proposed a series of expansions to the social safety net with the goal of securing opportunity for more Americans. Health care, education, housing, transit, job training, and urban renewal all became targets for Johnson's programs, and an increase in the size and budgets of federal departments and agencies made it possible to carry these projects out. The Department of Housing and Urban Development was created in 1965 and the Department of Transportation in 1966. Efforts to secure civil rights for Americans and battle discrimination based on sex and race led to the passage of the Civil Rights Act of 1964.[50] The act created the Equal Employment Opportunity Commission, which today acts to enforce prohibitions on discrimination in the workplace based on racial identity, sex, religious preference, national origin, age, or disability.

federal civil service
the permanent professional branches of government concerned with administrative functions, excluding the armed forces and political appointments.

merit system
a system of hiring and promotion based on competitive testing results, education, and other qualifications rather than politics and personal connections.

independent executive agency
an agency similar to a cabinet department but existing outside the cabinet structure and usually having a narrower focus of mission.

 Surrounded by members of his cabinet, President Donald Trump speaks before signing an executive order titled "Comprehensive Plan for Reorganizing the Executive Branch in the Oval Office of the White House" in March 2017. From left are Veterans Affairs secretary David Shulkin, Budget director Mick Mulvaney, Small Business Administration administrator Linda McMahon, Interior secretary Ryan Zinke, UN ambassador Nikki Haley, Housing and Urban Development secretary Ben Carson, Vice President Mike Pence, Energy secretary Rick Perry, Transportation secretary Elaine Chao, Commerce secretary Wilbur Ross, Defense secretary James Mattis, and Attorney General Jeff Sessions.

Jabin Botsford/The Washington Post via Getty Images

THE LATE TWENTIETH CENTURY BROUGHT REFORM AND SCALING BACK

When he was elected president of the United States in 1980, Ronald Reagan (1981–1989) promised to reduce the size of the federal government as well as its impact on the daily lives of Americans. As discussed in Chapter 3, efforts at devolution attempted to return power over implementing public policy back to the individual states. Efforts at deregulation aimed to reduce government oversight of and involvement with specific industries, notably transportation, banking, and utilities. Though Reagan, his Republican successor George H. W. Bush (1989–1993), and his Democratic successor Bill Clinton (1993–2001) all promised some form of bureaucratic reform or improvement, the federal bureaucracy did not undergo a major restructuring during the period. One area in which the federal bureaucracy did see a significant reduction, however, was in defense; this was a result of the end of the Cold War with the collapse of the Soviet Union in 1991 and a reprioritizing of American military goals and strategy. After being elected in 2016, President Donald Trump promised to shrink the American federal bureaucracy and its power over the American economy. According to an article published by *Fortune* magazine, on this he has made progress: "According to the American Action Fund, his actions have reduced regulatory costs by $70 billion."[51]

WHAT HAVE I LEARNED?

1. Reasons for the growth of the federal bureaucracy include _____.

    a. growth in the nation's population

    b. demands for services

    c. the complexity of tasks performed by government

    d. All of the above

2. The cabinet includes _____.

    a. the heads of executive branch departments

    b. members of key congressional committees

    c. federal justices

    d. All of the above

3. The spoils system refers to _____.

    a. ruining the chances of one's electoral competition

    b. rewarding political supporters with political appointments

    c. restrictions on campaign contributions

    d. firing bureaucrats for incompetence

4. What is the theory of path dependence?

_____

Answer Key: 1. d; 2. a; 3. b; 4. Answers should describe the ways in which a set of political outcomes shapes future possibilities for political action.

THE GROWTH OF THE FEDERAL BUREAUCRACY

One of the common concerns about the federal bureaucracy has been its dramatic increase in size, number of regulations, and spending, especially over the last century. This growth has led to charges that the federal government is becoming too powerful, too involved in Americans' lives. Critics often imply that more power—and more money—should be found at the state and local level.

Consider Figure 14-A, which plots the real (inflation-adjusted) per capita federal expenditures from 1947 to 2004 (with and without defense spending included).[52]

Based on the chart above, one might plausibly tell a story about the massive growth in the influence of the federal government in the past fifty years. For example, in the early 1950s, real per capita federal spending was about $2,000. By the early 1980s, it had grown to $6,000 per person, three times as much, even when adjusted for inflation. When reading and interpreting graphs, however, it is often useful to also consider data that are not presented when making an argument—data that might complicate or counter the argument being made. Consider a similar chart that plots spending by state and local governments during roughly the same period.

Adding Figure 14-B leads to a more complex story. The past fifty years have witnessed increased spending across all levels of the American bureaucracy—federal, state, and local. Again, note that real per capita expenditures by state and local bureaucracies nearly tripled in the same time period (from the early 1950s to the early 1980s), rising from about $1,000 per person to nearly $3,000 per person. While the amounts were smaller than federal spending, the rate of growth was nearly the same.

WHaT Do You Think?

How might these additional data affect your evaluations about the development of bureaucracy in the United

▼ FIGURE 14-A

Real per Capita Federal Expenditures, 1947–2004

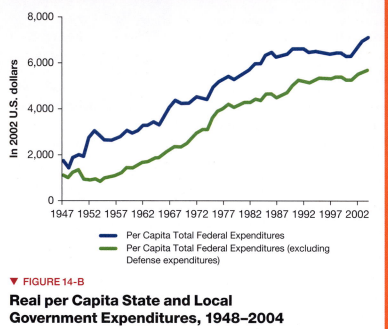

Per Capita Total Federal Expenditures

Per Capita Total Federal Expenditures (excluding Defense expenditures)

▼ FIGURE 14-B

Real per Capita State and Local Government Expenditures, 1948–2004

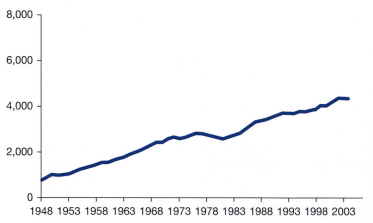

States? What other data or graphs might you want to have in order to fully evaluate the growth in the federal bureaucracy?

A FUNCTIONING BUREAUCRACY DEPENDS UPON EFFECTIVE ORGANIZATION

- Describe the structure of the federal bureaucracy, including executive branch agencies, cabinet departments, and regulatory bodies.

Today, bureaucratic tasks have become increasingly technical and specialized. The organization of authority within the federal bureaucracy and the tasks that agencies undertake matter, not just because they are complex but because both can affect how well a bureaucracy functions and how easy it can be to reform one that has gone astray. The individual parts of the federal bureaucracy are people, not bits of a machine, and they have their own priorities and competencies. Politics, competition, and even faction are as present in bureaucratic action as they are in any other endeavor in which individuals work to achieve goals.

THE FEDERAL BUREAUCRACY IS A WEB OF ORGANIZATIONS

The American federal bureaucracy is not one structure but a complex web of organizations. As the head of the executive branch, the president is tasked to ensure that the bureaucracy faithfully executes the laws of the nation. She or he appoints (with Senate confirmation) people to the top levels of the bureaucracy and directs and advises the departments, bureaus, and agencies on how they should go about putting the laws into effect. The requirements of this task, however, are by no means only technical. They are also political. When the American people feel that the federal bureaucracy has failed, the president acts as a lightning rod for their outrage. Less than a month after Katrina, a second hurricane bore down on Texas. With the lessons of Katrina firmly in mind, President George W. Bush flew to his home state to signal to the nation that his administration was prepared and engaged. Briefings held with then–Texas governor Rick Perry, the heads of federal agencies, and Pentagon officials showed that, according to White House press secretary Scott McClellan, "[Bush] is the president, and he has indicated [that] it is his responsibility when it comes to the federal government's role in these hurricanes."[53]

Cabinet departments serve as the primary administrative units in the federal bureaucracy. Congress has the authority to establish and fund the departments, each of which is responsible for a major area of public policy. They are typically divided into subunits based on the policy in which they specialize. The division of tasks among departments does not always follow a clear logic; historical development, politics, and competition among the divisions of the federal bureaucracy over the authority to perform a specific task—and spend the funds Congress has allocated to do so—have all shaped the division of labor among departments. There are currently fifteen cabinet departments.

There is considerable diversity in the size and budgets of the cabinet departments. Sizable budgets do not always mean large numbers of employees. For example, the Department of Health and Human Services (which issues payments for Social Security and Medicare) and the Department of the Treasury (which makes interest payments on the national debt) both have relatively large budgets for the number of employees in them. Prestige also varies among the departments, including one of its most visible markers: face time with the president.

Cabinet departments are headed by cabinet secretaries (or by the attorney general in the case of the Justice Department), who are nominated by the president and confirmed by a majority vote in the Senate. Cabinet secretaries formally work under the president; however, they also depend on Congress for appropriation of funds and for legislation that sets out specific goals and objectives for their departments. In addition, cabinet secretaries often have to contend with pressure from those affected by the actions of their departments, such as citizens or organized interest groups.

Independent executive agencies like NASA (the National Aeronautics and Space Administration) and FEMA function similarly to departments in many ways but are usually narrower in focus and retain more independence in carrying out their goals.

Independent regulatory agencies act to oversee and regulate governmental function, especially in economic affairs. Created by Congress to have enough independence to protect them from political partisanship, they are typically headed by appointed boards with fixed and staggered terms of service, making it more difficult to remove their leadership.

Government corporations act as businesses within the federal government, charging fees for their services but still subject to governmental control and possible financial subsidization. The earliest government corporation was the Federal Deposit Insurance Corporation (FDIC), established as part of the New Deal to avoid a repeat of the bank runs in the Great Depression by insuring deposits in the nation's banks.

Private contractors are not officially a part of the federal bureaucracy, but the government increasingly relies on them to provide goods and services in support of federal activity. The U.S. military, for example, relies on contractors for logistical support. Proponents of contracting argue

cabinet departments
federal executive departments created and funded by Congress.

independent regulatory agencies
organizations that exist outside the major cabinet departments and whose job is to monitor and regulate specific sectors of the economy.

government corporations
organizations that act as businesses within the federal government, charging fees for their services but still subject to governmental control and possible financial subsidization.

private contractors
nongovernmental workers hired by the federal bureaucracy to provide goods and services in support of federal activity.

that it allows the military and federal agencies to focus on their core missions. Opponents worry about a lack of careful oversight of contractor activities.

BUREAUCRATIC AUTHORITY IS HIERARCHICAL

Formally, authority across the federal bureaucracy is structured like a pyramid (Figure 14.5).[54] At the top are the **executive political appointees**, such as cabinet secretaries and deputy secretaries, who serve at the pleasure of the president and are subject to presidential removal. Of the roughly 6,500 political appointees in the executive branch, about 1,500 require Senate confirmation. Compared to the vast majority of federal bureaucrats, these individuals are short-timers. They do not expect to transition from one administration to the next. Presidents must juggle several considerations in selecting who will lead their departments and agencies. Experience and competence are certainly important, but so are political calculi and a desire to signal to important constituencies a willingness to work with them. The American people also expect a commitment to representing the wide diversity of their interests, experiences, and backgrounds.

Below this top level are the members of the **Senior Executive Service**. These individuals—most of whom are drawn from the lower ranks of the federal bureaucracy—enjoy slightly more job security than high-level appointees and are paid and treated more like vice presidents of businesses than political figures. They are expected to use their authority to achieve concrete results.

The vast majority of employees occupy the bottom of the pyramid. They are the career civil servants, whose job ranks are clearly defined according to the General Service levels. Entrance into and advancement within the federal civil service is governed by the merit system, which relies on competitive examinations, educational qualifications, and performance reviews. Career civil servants enjoy considerable protections from termination, especially for political reasons. This job security is by design, though it presents presidents with a significant challenge. The federal bureaucracy is not a power station in which a president flips a switch and makes things happen automatically. Instead, it is a complex hierarchy of people, most of whom will still have their jobs long after the president and political appointees have moved on.

THE CORE TASKS OF THE BUREAUCRACY ARE IMPLEMENTATION, RULEMAKING, ADVISING, AND REPRESENTATION

The primary function of the federal bureaucracy is **implementation** of, or putting into action, the laws that Congress has passed. Implementation is rarely, if ever, a straightforward process.[55] New

executive political appointees
employees at high levels in the federal bureaucracy who serve at the pleasure of the president and are subject to presidential removal.

Senior Executive Service
federal employees with higher-level supervisory and administrative responsibilities who are paid and treated more like vice presidents of businesses than political figures.

implementation
the bureaucracy's role in putting into action the laws that Congress has passed.

▼ FIGURE 14.5

The Hierarchy of Labor in the Federal Bureaucracy

The structure of the federal bureaucracy, including the civil service system, is in many ways similar to that described by Max Weber: hierarchical and organized, with clear divisions between the levels. This structure was intentional, designed to insulate the majority of federal bureaucrats from the ebb and flow of party control of the executive branch.

policies are not enacted in isolation; they are introduced into a universe of existing policies, sometimes with competing demands.[56]

The technical knowledge required of many federal bureaucrats in order to successfully implement public policies also acts as a brake on the ability of a president or her or his political appointees to shape bureaucrats' actions. High-level executive branch officials may lack the technical expertise necessary to evaluate or challenge the actions of their subordinates. In addition, many front-line bureaucrats interact directly with citizens in an environment that makes it difficult to observe and control their behavior effectively. Law enforcement officers, teachers, and social workers are all examples of what are called street-level bureaucrats.[57] Because of their close contact with citizens, street-level bureaucrats may conclude that they need to "bend the rules" to do their jobs as they see them.

When Congress passes laws, it often only sets general goals and targets, leaving many of the details up to the bureaucratic agencies themselves. The complexity involved with implementing policies, the technical and specialized knowledge often required to do so, and the flexibility needed to handle unforeseen circumstances all argue for giving bureaucrats the authority to flesh out parts of the laws in action. By doing so, however, Congress opens up a space for **bureaucratic discretion**, in which the bureaucrats have some power to decide how a law is implemented and, at times, what Congress actually meant when it passed a given law. In addition, those affected by legislation cannot go about planning how they are going to respond to a law or set of regulations until they actually know the details of it. How much will it cost to comply? What changes must be made in order to do so? The answers to these important questions more often than not come from the bureaucracy rather than Congress, the president, or the courts.

The process through which the federal bureaucracy fills in critical details of a law is called **rulemaking**. By law, agencies must follow a specific set of steps. The first is to announce a proposed set of rules and allow interested parties to weigh in; this process is called notice and comment. Agencies may have to notify the president or Congress about the anticipated impact of a proposed rule or set of rules. Finally, the adopted rules must be published in the Federal Register, which is published annually and typically runs more than seventy thousand pages. These rules matter; "they carry the same weight as congressional legislation, presidential executive orders, and judicial decisions."[58]

Part of the Framers' purpose in establishing the president's cabinet advisors and other executive branch officials was for them to share their expertise and knowledge with the president, Congress, and increasingly, clientele groups and the public. At times the bureaucracy also acts somewhat like a court. It may settle disputes between parties that arise over the implementation of federal laws and presidential executive orders or determine which individuals or groups are covered under a regulation or program—a role called **bureaucratic adjudication**.

Finally, and perhaps surprisingly, bureaucrats can act as representatives of the American public, especially if they have the ability to act on behalf of their clients in the way that street-level bureaucrats often do.[59] While cabinet secretaries are increasingly representative of the diversity of the American people, they still do not present a complete portrait of the nation. Members of the civil service, in contrast, do represent the nation's diversity in many ways, save perhaps educational attainment (as it factors into the hiring and promotion process). In this view, having a "representative bureaucracy"—a civil service that truly reflects the diversity of the American people—may also act to legitimize its actions.[60]

One area in which federal employees are restricted from acting is the political process. Concerns about political patronage in President Roosevelt's New Deal programs led to the passage in 1939 of what is commonly known as the Hatch Act, which restricted the actions of federal workers in the political realm, with exceptions for the highest-level political appointees. Federal workers were prohibited from participating in political campaigns, coercing other employees to participate, raising funds for a campaign, or holding all but a few elective offices. The Federal Employees Political Activities Act of 1993 relaxed some of the restrictions of the Hatch Act, allowing most federal employees to run in nonpartisan elections and contribute to and participate in fund-raising for political campaigns, as long as they do not use their official authority to do so.

bureaucratic discretion
the power to decide how a law is implemented and, at times, what Congress actually meant when it passed a given law.

rulemaking
the process through which the federal bureaucracy fills in critical details of a law.

bureaucratic adjudication
when the federal bureaucracy settles disputes between parties that arise over the implementation of federal laws and presidential executive orders or determines which individuals or groups are covered under a regulation or program.

WHAT HAVE I LEARNED?

1. Independent executive agencies are different from cabinet departments because _____.

    a. cabinet departments are responsible for fewer tasks

    b. independent executive agencies are narrower in their focus

    c. independent agencies charge fees for their services

    d. cabinet heads are hired to lobby the government

2. The top of the federal bureaucratic organizational structure consists of _____.

    a. executive political appointees

    b. career civil servants

    c. members of the Senior Executive Service

    d. private contractors

3. A process through which many details of laws are filled in is _____.

    a. rulemaking

    b. appropriation

    c. bureaucratic discretion

    d. bureaucratic adjudication

4. In what ways can bureaucrats act as quasi-legislators?

    _____

THE BUREAUCRACY IS CONSTRAINED BY OVERSIGHT AND REFORM

- **Describe the tools of bureaucratic control, oversight, and reform.**

While complaints about the bureaucracy are as old as the institution itself, recent decades have seen a renewed focus on highlighting its failures and offering reforms to fix them. One set of critiques focuses on the inefficiency of large and complex bureaucracies. The term *red tape*, derived from "the narrow ribbons used at one time in England and America to tie up packets of legal and government documents," conjures up images of bureaucrats mindlessly following rules and standard operating procedures, whether or not it actually helps get things done.[61] Another line of critique emphasizes the tendencies of federal departments, bureaus, and agencies to be budget maximizers—that is, to seek to expand their level of appropriations beyond that necessary for the efficient provision of their services.[62]

Still another accusation points to problems that arise when bureaucracies stray from their established goals and devote their energies and efforts to nonessential tasks, an outcome known as **bureaucratic drift**. Worries about straying from the intended mission may apply to individual bureaucrats as well. Individuals may not do their jobs effectively or responsibly, a failing commonly referred to as shirking. Or they may actively work against the stated mission of their agency, substituting their own evaluations of a proper course of action, which is referred to as sabotage.[63] From the point of view of the bureaucrat, sabotage may be for very good reasons—for example, bending the rules to help out a client confronted with a rigid set of rules and procedures.

Another concern, especially for bureaucrats in regulatory agencies, is that individuals may undermine effective regulation if their own interests are more closely aligned with the targets of regulation than the mission of the agency, a problem known as agency capture. If regulators have close ties to the industry being regulated—either through previous employment or, perhaps, expected future employment—then there may be temptations to "look the other way," instruct their subordinates to do so, or conduct their jobs in such a way as to benefit a few preferred clients.[64]

bureaucratic drift
when bureaucracies stray from their established goals and devote their energies and efforts to peripheral tasks.

SEPARATION OF POWERS MAKES OVERSEEING THE BUREAUCRACY DIFFICULT

The system of separation of powers that the Framers designed poses a special challenge to controlling the bureaucracy. As authority over the federal bureaucracy is divided between different branches, federal agencies and bureaus often have to answer to more than one overseer. According to political scientist Joel Aberbach, "since usually no one set of institutional actors has clear control and signals often conflict, it is difficult to hold the bureaucracy . . . reasonably to account."[65]

THE PRESIDENT IS AT THE TOP OF THE FEDERAL BUREAUCRACY.
As head of the executive branch, the president formally controls most of the federal bureaucracy.[66] He or she has the authority to appoint and remove individuals at the top layers of the bureaucracy. Presidents can also shape bureaucratic priorities in the annual budgets that they present to Congress and, with congressional approval, by reorganizing agencies. As discussed in Chapter 13, executive orders carry the force of law and typically instruct departments, agencies, and bureaus on how they are to go about implementing policy.

Presidents, however, often confront restrictions in their control over the day-to-day functions of the bureaucracy. Bureaucratic discretion and the bureaucracy's size and complexity all conspire against achieving quick results.

CONGRESS CREATES AND FUNDS THE FEDERAL BUREAUCRACY.
Congress plays a key role in controlling and guiding the bureaucracy. The Senate has power over confirmation for the higher levels of the federal service. Congress as a whole can pass legislation creating or terminating agencies and programs and, through the process of appropriation, has control over the resources that departments, bureaus, and agencies receive to carry out their tasks. Congressional committees, especially the House and Senate appropriations committees, are key players in these processes.

While legislation can be a proactive way to shape bureaucratic behavior by setting goals, priorities, and the overall organizational structure, Congress also has the ability to influence what happens when agencies are up and running through the process of oversight. Congress has established its own bureaucracies to keep tabs on executive branch implementation. The Government Accountability Office (GAO) is an example of this type of agency. Its work can have real bite. One GAO report investigating what had happened after Hurricane Katrina stated, "No one was designated in advance to lead the overall federal response in anticipation of the event despite clear warnings from the National Hurricane Center."[67]

When deciding how to oversee the federal bureaucracy, Congress has a choice. By doing field investigations, conducting hearings, or requiring information from the agencies, Congress may exercise police patrol oversight, analogous to a law enforcement official surveying the neighborhood to make sure all is well. The problem with police patrol oversight is that it is expensive, especially in terms of Congress's scarcest resource: time. Therefore, Congress often chooses instead to exercise fire alarm oversight, bringing the machinery of investigation and correction into action only when individuals or interest groups—some formally authorized to acquire information or bring suit in court—sound the alarm that part of the federal bureaucracy has gone astray.[68]

THE JUDICIARY, THE MEDIA, AND PUBLIC OPINION ALSO INFLUENCE THE BUREAUCRACY.
Decisions by the federal judiciary can significantly impact bureaucratic behavior. Judicial control is typically negative—not in the sense that it is bad, but in the sense that judicial decisions on, for example,

▲ A political cartoon depicting octopus-shaped red tape from Washington, DC, gripping the states with its tentacles.

▲ Senators Jon Tester (D-MT), Jack Reed (D-RI), and Patrick Leahy (D-VT) talk before a Senate Appropriations Committee markup in the Dirksen Building in June 2018.

civil liberties and civil rights, restrict and constrain the scope of accepted bureaucratic action. One part of the federal bureaucracy may also find its actions constrained by other departments, agencies, and bureaus. Bureaucratic jurisdiction—the authority to act in a certain policy area—is often not clearly or cleanly defined. **Interagency rivalry** occurs when two or more agencies are charged with a similar mandate, an outcome that becomes more likely in times of budget cuts and competition for scarce or dwindling appropriations. Clientele groups and businesses affected by federal rules, whether proposed or formalized, will lobby parts of the federal bureaucracy as well as Congress to get a more favorable outcome according to their perceived interests.

As a rule, the media infrequently cover the workings of the federal bureaucracy. Most Americans are understandably not well informed of the day-to-day workings of the vast bureaucracy, and there are no doubt numerous agencies many Americans don't know even exist. Crises are exceptions to public inattention. When the machinery of government is involved in a major crisis or catastrophe that becomes highly publicized—and especially when it appears that it has failed—the federal bureaucracy might find itself center stage, with a full and angry audience in attendance. Such was the case after Katrina. A year after its landfall on the Gulf Cost, thousands of residents were still waiting for federal help, and public opinion had turned against President Bush on his handling of the disaster. A national poll found that only 31 percent of Americans approved of his management of the storm, and 56 percent did not "believe that the country [was] ready for another disaster."[69]

REFORM EFFORTS INVOLVE DEVOLUTION, DEREGULATION, REINVENTION, AND PRIVATIZATION

In addition to calls for oversight of bureaucracies and the agencies in which they operate, pushes have been made—especially in recent decades—to shrink, overhaul, or eliminate parts of the federal bureaucracy. Ronald Reagan's petitions to roll back the growth in the size and power of the bureaucracy in his successful presidential bid in 1980 focused public attention on these efforts. As discussed in Chapter 3, devolution aimed to transfer power over public policy back to the states and shrink the size of the federal government by allowing states to have more authority to determine how taxpayer dollars should be spent. Proponents of **deregulation** argued that the personnel rules of the civil service, along with excessive red tape, made it difficult to attract "talented energetic potential candidates" to the federal service and restrained their energies once hired.[70] As a result of deregulation efforts beginning in the 1970s, certain federal agencies saw their authority curtailed or were abolished entirely, particularly in the areas of transportation, commerce, and the provision of utilities.

Another set of reforms sought to make the federal bureaucracy work more efficiently—more like the private sector. The National Performance Review, conducted under the administration of President Clinton, collected detailed data on bureaucratic efficiency and proposed measures to streamline bureaucratic operations as part of an effort to "reinvent government."[71]

Other reform proposals advocate placing control over the provision of certain functions in the hands of the private sector and not the federal bureaucracy. Proponents of **privatization** argue that many tasks currently handled by the federal service can be more efficiently and more cheaply addressed by private organizations and businesses. Opponents of privatization argue that reducing or eliminating governmental oversight over the provision of these services might lead to waste or fraud or might undermine the larger policy goals of the national government.

Political scientist James Q. Wilson pointed out that there might be valid reasons for the fact that public bureaucracies often act differently and less efficiently than private bureaucracies. By their very nature, public bureaucracies operate under a different set of constraints. Congress, and not the marketplace, sets the goals for, budgets of, and allocation of resources within the federal service. In addition, the American public often

interagency rivalry
when two or more agencies are charged with a similar mandate, an outcome that becomes more likely in times of budget cuts and competition for scarce or dwindling appropriations.

deregulation
the reduction or elimination of government power in a particular industry, usually in order to create more competition within the industry.

privatization
shifting control over the provision of certain governmental functions from the federal bureaucracy to the private sector.

demands a higher standard of fairness in the actions of its public bureaucracies than it does of private ones. Public schools, for example, generally face more binding constraints over admission and expulsion of students than do the nation's private schools.[72]

Following Katrina, investigators and members of Congress questioned both the government's reliance on private contractors in relief efforts and governmental interference with private sector efforts. According to a local official in Louisiana, FEMA had blocked private relief efforts as well: "We had Wal-Mart deliver three trailer trucks of water. FEMA turned them back. They said we didn't need them."[73] As it became clear that the effects from Katrina would be felt for years, many private organizations and individuals stepped up to help. Habitat for Humanity dispatched thousands of volunteers to the Gulf Coast to rebuild housing for low-income residents. Mary Gray founded MinnesotaHelpers, a "Mississippi-to-Minnesota arts pipeline" to provide opportunities for Gulf Coast artists to display and sell their work, as they had few such venues in their own devastated communities.[74]

▲ Trucks from Walmart with relief supplies for residents of the Gulf Coast. FEMA was widely criticized for hampering private efforts at assistance.

Not all private responses were viewed so positively, however. Some were accused of running scams to take advantage of the federal dollars that flowed into devastated areas, prompting the government to establish the Hurricane Katrina Fraud Task Force to "thwart and prosecute hurricane-related fraud."[75] Some initiatives, though not illegal, seemed to take advantage of the disaster. In January 2006, a local tour bus company planned to operate a "Hurricane Katrina Tour—America's Worst Catastrophe!" to offer tourists the chance to see the aftermath of the storm from air-conditioned buses, though the company promised a portion of the $35 ticket price would benefit recovery efforts.[76]

In the aftermath of Maria in 2017, the question of the proper role of private bureaucracies in hurricane recovery efforts came into public focus. Whitefish Energy, "a little-known energy firm based in Montana," secured a $300 million contract to restore power to Puerto Rico.[77] Some lawmakers questioned how and why such a small firm beat out larger utilities. In a press briefing, White House press secretary Sarah Sanders answered, "This is a contract that was determined by the local authorities, not something the federal government played a role in."[78]

WHAT HAVE I **LEARNED?**

1. Red tape refers to _____.

   a. overly burdensome rules and regulations

   b. going over the budget set by Congress

   c. rules set by the Republican Party

   d. the publication of federal rules

2. Agency capture happens when _____.

   a. Congress folds one agency into another

   b. civil servants are fired

   c. an agency has close ties to the group it regulates

   d. an agency undertakes a different mission than it is tasked to

3. Proponents of privatization argue that the private sector can more efficiently carry out tasks than the government. Can you think of some tasks that the private sector carries out better than government? Do you think there are tasks that should not be left up to private firms to carry out?

Answer Key: 1. a; 2. c; 3. Answers should raise questions about whether potential gains in efficiency might come at the cost of waste, fraud, or undermining larger governmental goals.

ANALYZING CONGRESSIONAL TESTIMONY

In her prepared testimony before the Select Bipartisan Committee to Investigate the Preparation for and Response to Hurricane Katrina in December 2005, New Orleans resident Leah Hodges raised troubling concerns about how she and other individuals who sought refuge had been treated.[79] While not all of the witnesses testifying felt that African Americans were treated differently because of their race, Hodges's assessment of the connection between racial identity and equality of treatment echoed the accusations of many others. Hodges testified,

> I come from a family of musicians. Before Hurricane Katrina, we were planning a musical family reunion. I had taken time off from pursuing my law degree to care for my sick granddad. I was also in the process of working with community leaders on setting up music and art workshops for youths. The manual I was writing for the workshops was severely damaged in the flood. I intend to finish it. . . . But I have also started a new project, which is all about my experience as a detainee at the Highway 10 causeway.

> My family was ordered to evacuate our home. We were directed to evacuation points. . . . We were then lured to the so-called evacuation points. This was several days after the hurricane had struck. The city was flooded. Soldiers had showed up with M16s and military weapons. They had declared New Orleans and Jefferson Parish a war zone.

> We were just three miles from an airport, but we were detained there for several days. Many of those who were there when we arrived had already been there several days. On any given day there were at least ten thousand people in the camp. On my last day there, I would estimate there were still three thousand detainees. By that time, nearly all the white

▲ New Orleans citizens and evacuees (from left) Terrol Williams, Doreen Keeler, Patricia Thompson, Leah Hodges, and "Mama D" Dyan French testify before Congress in December 2005.

> people had been selected to evacuate first. They were put on buses and shipped out, leaving the remaining population 95 percent black.

> People died in the camp. We saw the bodies lying there.

> They were all about detention, as if it were Iraq, like we were foreigners and they were fighting a war. They implemented war-like conditions. They treated us worse than prisoners of war. Even prisoners of war have rights under the Geneva Convention.

WHAT Do You Think?

Some of the harshest criticism about the response to Hurricane Katrina involved accusations of differential treatment of African Americans. Can you think of other examples where a federal, state, or local agency has been accused of racial and ethnic bias? Have you or people close to you experienced this?

CONCLUSION: WHAT DOES A "GOOD" BUREAUCRACY LOOK LIKE?

Americans place many demands upon their federal bureaucracy, and it usually only makes the news when something has gone wrong. As we have explored, the federal bureaucracy is not a unified thing, nor is it static. Departments, agencies, and bureaus can learn and adapt; however, they often do not do so quickly—relying on Congress to give them much of the ability to do so—nor efficiently. Equally fundamentally, bureaucracies can adapt and change. However, this change may be slow, given challenges of coordination and the inertia inherent in a large and complex organization. Competing demands on any given department, agency, or bureau can slow the processes of change down further.

Americans want the primary instrument of national policy implementation to be effective and strong. When they feel that it is not—such as was the case with Hurricane Katrina—they demand change. However, Americans do not want the federal bureaucracy to be too strong. When they feel that it has become too powerful, they worry. Both the separation of powers and the realities of American federalism shape the behaviors of the federal departments, agencies, and bureaus. These organizations are not smoothly running machines but a constellation of teams operating in an often political space; they have multiple constraints on their behavior and also must contend with multiple interests and groups trying to shape that behavior. Such is the complex nature of the American federal bureaucracy.

CHAPTER REVIEW

This chapter's main ideas are reflected in the Learning Objectives. By reviewing them here, you should be able to **remember** the key points, **know** the terms that are central to the topic, and **think** about the critical issues raised in each section.

14.1 Understand how federal bureaucratic action involves many different agencies and evolves over time, often in response to lessons learned from past actions.

REMEMBER
- The federal bureaucracy consists of organizations and suborganizations within the executive branch that are tasked with putting the laws of the nation into effect.
- Bureaucracies change over time, sometimes as a result of significant failures.

KNOW
- federal bureaucracy (p. 385)

THINK
- Can bureaucracies learn and adapt? What do the examples of Hurricanes Katrina, Sandy, Harvey, Irma, and Maria tell us about that?

14.2 Describe the key characteristics of bureaucratic organization and the theories that explain why that organization happens.

REMEMBER
- Most of the federal bureaucracy lies within the executive branch. State and local bureaucracies also make rules that impact people's daily lives.
- Private bureaucracies are companies and corporations that also operate like federal, state, and local bureaucracies.
- Various theories of bureaucracies exist to explain how and why they are organized the way they are.

KNOW
- incentives (p. 392)
- principal-agent problem (p. 391)
- private bureaucracies (p. 390)
- standard operating procedures (p. 391)
- state and local bureaucracies (p. 390)

THINK
- What are the main ways the three models of bureaucratic organization differ?

14.3 Outline the historical development of the American federal bureaucracy.

REMEMBER
- The federal bureaucracy has grown exponentially over time, as has the complexity of the tasks it must perform and the demands for services placed upon it by the American people.
- The Constitution calls for executive branch departments to assist the president in executing the laws of the nation. To control the power of the executive, Congress was given the power to approve nominees and impeach executive officers.

KNOW
- clientele agencies (p. 397)
- federal civil service (p. 398)
- independent executive agency (p. 398)
- merit system (p. 398)
- path dependence (p. 397)
- political patronage (p. 396)
- spoils system (p. 396)
- turf wars (p. 394)

THINK
- How would you characterize the major developments over time in the federal bureaucracy?

14.4 Describe the structure of the federal bureaucracy, including executive branch agencies, cabinet departments, and regulatory bodies.

REMEMBER
- The federal bureaucracy is a complex web of organizations and organizations within organizations, headed by the president.
- Congress has the authority to establish and fund the departments, each of which is responsible for a major area of public policy.
- Independent regulatory agencies act to oversee and regulate governmental function, especially in economic affairs.
- The bureaucracy is a hierarchy, with executive political appointees at the top and Senior Executive Service employees with supervisory and administrative responsibilities in the middle. Career civil servants make up the bulk of the employees.
- Implementing the laws passed by Congress is one of the bureaucracy's core tasks.

KNOW
- bureaucratic adjudication (p. 403)
- bureaucratic discretion (p. 403)
- cabinet departments (p. 401)
- executive political appointees (p. 402)
- government corporations (p. 401)
- implementation (p. 402)
- independent regulatory agencies (p. 401)
- private contractors (p. 401)
- rulemaking (p. 403)
- Senior Executive Service (p. 402)

THINK
- Why is the federal bureaucracy organized the way it is?

14.5 Describe the tools of bureaucratic control, oversight, and reform.

REMEMBER
- Perceived inefficiency, bureaucratic drift, agency capture, and interagency rivalry are common complaints and problems of the federal bureaucracy.
- Control over the bureaucracy is challenging given that responsibility and power are shared across the executive, legislative, and judicial branches of government.
- Efforts to reform the bureaucracy include devolving responsibilities to the states, deregulation, and privatizing government responsibilities to increase competitiveness.

KNOW
- bureaucratic drift (p. 404)
- deregulation (p. 406)
- interagency rivalry (p. 406)
- privatization (p. 406)

THINK
- What are some of the major problems that the bureaucracy encounters? What mechanisms exist to help solve them?

Joe Raedle / Staff

CHAPTER 15

THE FEDERAL JUDICIARY

Politics, Power, and the "Least Dangerous" Branch[1]

▲ Supreme Court Justice Sonia Sotomayor (left) joins family and friends before a game between the Boston Red Sox and New York Yankees at Yankee Stadium in August 2017 in the Bronx borough of New York City. Sotomayor has said that her experience growing up in New York as the child of Puerto Rican immigrants has informed her judicial decision making. Because they are appointed to lifetime terms, Supreme Court justices are very influential, and their appointment can be a challenging political process.

Rich Schultz/Getty Images

hat is the federal judiciary? As with many questions you are asked to consider in this book, there are both simple answers and deeper ones. In this chapter, we will deal with both. The definition is simple. The **federal judiciary** is one of the three branches of the nation's government. Its role is to interpret and apply the laws of the nation. Sitting atop the federal judiciary is the U.S. **Supreme Court**, which was established in the Constitution and serves as the highest court in the nation.

On a deeper level, however, more difficult questions arise. First, how different is the federal judiciary from the other two branches—or, more precisely, how *political* is it? How political should it be? Also, how *powerful* is it? As we have explored, both Congress and the president have at their disposal powerful levers to shape national public policy. Congress writes the laws; it has the power to tax and to fund. The president is the commander in chief of the armed forces and is tasked with carrying out the laws of the nation. What power does the federal judiciary have other than the authority to apply the law to the cases brought before it?

These questions are very much interconnected. The power of the federal judiciary affects how it engages as a political actor. Conversely, the degree to which the federal judiciary chooses to involve itself in political controversies has and will continue to impact its legitimacy with the American public.

By reading this chapter, you will be able to do the following:

 15.1 Explore the role of politics in modern Supreme Court nomination proceedings.

 15.2 Describe the structure and powers of the federal judiciary as laid out in the Constitution.

 15.3 Explain John Marshall's development of judicial review in the Supreme Court decision in *Marbury v. Madison*.

 15.4 Describe the structure of the American legal system and the federal judiciary.

15.5 Compare theories of judicial decision making as well as arguments for or against judicial restraint and activism in constitutional review.

In this chapter, you will engage with the stories of recent Supreme Court confirmations as well as John Marshall's establishment of judicial review. They are presented as "trials," though none of the individuals were actually *on* trial. Their institution, however, was, and it still is.

federal judiciary
the branch of the federal government that interprets and applies the laws of the nation.

Supreme Court
the highest level of the federal judiciary, which was established in the Constitution and serves as the highest court in the nation.

THE POLITICS OF SUPREME COURT CONFIRMATIONS PLACE NOMINEES ON "TRIAL"

• **Explore the role of politics in modern Supreme Court nomination proceedings.**

The power to confirm presidential nominees to the Supreme Court and other levels of the federal judiciary—granted to the Senate in the Constitution—is a weighty one. In the modern era, Supreme Court confirmations have often resembled elections more than formal affairs, with nominees choosing their answers to Senators' questions carefully. Sometimes, the nominees themselves must have felt they were on trial as the Senate weighed their candidacies. Whether or not this is a good thing is the subject of much debate, and it revolves around the "proper" role of the judiciary in American political life, a topic we will explore in detail in this chapter. The stakes are high, and—short of impeachment—there is no way that the American people can remove these justices from office if they don't like how they are performing their duties.

SONYA SOTOMAYOR'S "TRIAL" HIGHLIGHTS THE ROLE OF LIVED EXPERIENCE IN JUDICIAL DECISION MAKING

In May 2009, President Barack Obama was presented with his first opportunity to nominate an individual to the U.S. Supreme Court. The retiring justice, David H. Souter, ordinarily sided with the liberal bloc of justices in his decisions, so Obama's appointment, likely a liberal, would probably not shift the ideological balance of the Court. In the intensely partisan world of the modern federal government, that lessened, if only a bit, the tensions surrounding the nomination. Even so, observers and insiders expected an intensely political battle, as justices on the Supreme Court are appointed for life.

Although the nomination of a liberal justice was expected, there were other hopes pinned on the president's selection. With only one woman, one African American, and no Latino justices on the bench, many urged the president to use the opportunity to expand the diversity of the Court. On Obama's short list was Sonia Sotomayor, the daughter of Puerto Rican immigrants, a graduate of Yale Law School, a former prosecutor and litigator, and a sitting judge with the U.S. Court of Appeals for the Second Circuit. She was, however, according to the *Washington Post*, the "riskiest choice" of the likely nominees, largely because of public remarks she had made on the importance of identity and personal history in approaching judicial decision making.[2]

When Sotomayor's nomination became official, both sides swung into campaign mode, each accusing the other of violating norms of propriety in handling a Supreme Court nomination. Although she was not *literally* on trial as the confirmation proceedings in the Senate began, Sotomayor may very well have felt like she was—and with good reason.

Republicans in the Senate painted Sotomayor as a justice who was "willing to expand constitutional rights beyond the text of the constitution."[3] Given the president's popularity at the time, and with the Senate under Democratic control, defeating Sotomayor was unlikely. Still, Republicans hoped to use the confirmation proceedings to "galvanize a movement demoralized by Republican electoral defeats."[4] Remarks made by Sotomayor at a public lecture in 2001 received particular scrutiny from Republicans during the confirmation proceedings. Sotomayor had highlighted the role that her Latina identity and life experiences played in her judicial career—a perspective that, to her, helped her make just decisions, especially in cases involving equality and discrimination. Addressing the attendees, Sotomayor said the following:

> Who am I? I am a "Newyorkrican." For those of you on the West Coast who do not know what the term means: I am a born and bred New Yorker of Puerto Rican–born parents who came to the states during World War II. . . .
>
> No one person, judge or nominee will speak in a female or people of color voice. . . . Yet, because I accept the proposition that, as Judge Resnik describes it, "to judge is an exercise of power" and because as, another former law school classmate, Professor Martha Minow of Harvard Law School, states "there is no objective stance but only a series of perspectives—no neutrality, no escape from choice in judging," I further accept that our experiences as women and people of color affect our decisions. The aspiration to impartiality is just that—it's an aspiration because it denies the fact that we are by our experiences making different choices than others. . . .
>
> Justice O'Connor has often been cited as saying that a wise old man and a wise old woman will reach the same conclusions in deciding cases . . . I am also not so sure that I agree with the statement. First, as Professor Martha Minow has noted, there can never be a universal definition of wise. Second, I would hope that a wise Latina woman with the richness of her experiences would more often than not reach a better conclusion than a white male who hasn't lived that life.[5]

President Obama urged quick action on the nomination, but the press raised the specter of failed confirmations of the past, wondering if a similar ideological showdown was looming.[6] A leading Republican senator summed up his party's planned line of questioning: "Do I want a judge that objectively applies the law to the facts?"[7]

The Senate Judiciary Committee began its proceedings on the nomination in mid-July. Sotomayor rehearsed her testimony and her answers to expected questions in the week before the hearings. Addressing her critics, Sotomayor affirmed her judicial legacy, stating that in her seventeen years on the bench, she had "applied the law to the facts at hand."[8]

In the end, the vote in the Senate Judiciary Committee was without much drama or surprise. In a 13–6 vote, with one Republican joining the unanimous Democrats, the committee approved her nomination and sent it to the full Senate, wherein an expected filibuster-proof confirmation vote was all but certain. On August 9, the Senate confirmed Sotomayor's appointment to the Supreme Court by a vote of 68–31. Like other supporters gathered at a "vote watch" party nearby, law student Lucy Flores was jubilant, but she offered words of caution for those who might think Sotomayor's confirmation marked an end, rather than just a step forward. "It shouldn't be a historic moment," she said. "Everyone of all races and all backgrounds should be able to get to where she is based on their ability and their desire."[9]

On Saturday, August 8, Sotomayor took the judicial oath of office, promising to "administer justice without respect to persons, and do equal right to the poor and the rich" as the nation's newest member of the Supreme Court. As a member of the Court, Sotomayor would be carrying the hopes and aspirations of many Americans on her shoulders. She would also be joining an institution that itself carries the burdens of adjudicating Americans' claims upon their rights and defining and protecting the Constitution that established a nation.

ROBERT BORK'S "TRIAL" HIGHLIGHTS THE ROLE OF POLITICS IN CONFIRMATIONS

Lurking in the background of Sotomayor's confirmation proceedings was a nomination that failed, that of Robert Bork. In the summer of 1987, even before President Ronald Reagan named his selection to fill a pending vacant seat in the Supreme Court, the atmosphere had become politically charged. Reagan's nominee had the potential to tilt the closely divided Court away from its liberal-moderate majority. It was also a chance for the president, struggling to enact his programs in the face of a Democratic-controlled Congress, to help cement his legacy in American political history.

President Reagan chose Robert H. Bork, then serving on the Court of Appeals for the District of Columbia. While none questioned Bork's powerful intellect or his legal and professional qualifications, his rulings and statements in many cases involving highly charged social issues, such as abortion, sexuality, civil rights, and rights of the accused, sparked serious concern among liberals, especially since cases in many of these areas were awaiting Supreme Court action.

As the Senate Judiciary Committee scheduled its confirmation hearings for September, its chair, Senator Joe Biden, promised civil rights leaders that "he would lead the battle against Judge Bork in the Senate."[10] A senior administration official promised that President Reagan "would 'use all his resources' to push the Bork nomination."[11] Both sides prepared their arguments "like a championship fight," according to a lobbyist helping Bork to prepare.[12]

At the core of the controversy was Bork's view of constitutional interpretation. Bork believed that a justice should focus on the language and intent of the Constitution rather than supplying his or her own interpretation of the document—or, more significantly, inventing his or her own constitutional rights and liberties. Many, including key Democrats, were uncomfortable with the potential implications of Bork's approach. He had previously argued that the Supreme Court's decision in *Roe v. Wade* (1973), which recognized a woman's right to an abortion, was unconstitutional.[13] The death penalty, he argued, as referred to in the original text of the Constitution, was not.[14]

After twelve days of testimony by 110 witnesses, the Senate Judiciary Committee voted 9–5 against confirmation, spelling certain defeat for the nomination in the Democratic-controlled Senate. Republican senators called on the president to withdraw the nomination in order to preserve his

▲ President Ronald Reagan with Judge Robert Bork in 1987.

dwindling political capital. There were also calls for Bork to withdraw on his own volition. Bork refused, not because he thought there was a chance of a successful outcome but in protest over what he saw as an overtly political process of confirmation to the Supreme Court. He would later write, "Federal judges are not appointed to decide cases according to the latest opinion polls. They are appointed to decide cases impartially according to the law. But when judicial nominees are assessed and treated like political candidates the effect will be to chill the climate in which judicial deliberations take place, to erode public confidence in the impartiality of our judges, and to endanger the independence of the judiciary."[15] In the end, the Senate voted 58–42 against Bork's confirmation, the largest margin of defeat for a Supreme Court nominee in American history.[16]

ONE NOMINEE GETS HIS TRIAL, THE OTHER DOES NOT: MERRICK GARLAND AND NEIL GORSUCH

Fast forward nearly thirty years to February 2016: Justice Antonin Scalia had passed away suddenly and unexpectedly, presenting President Barack Obama with the possibility of a third Supreme Court nomination during his tenure. While Sonia Sotomayor's confirmation had been somewhat contested, his second, that of Elena Kagan, had gone relatively smoothly. In March 2016, with ten months left in office, Obama nominated Judge Merrick Garland to fill Scalia's seat. Republicans, with a majority in the Senate, refused even to consider the president's nominee, arguing that the nomination should be made by the next president, a gamble that a Republican might win the White House. As Scalia was one of the staunchest conservatives on the Court, Republicans knew that his replacement would have the potential to shift the ideological balance of the Court for years if not decades.

Both Donald Trump's win in the presidential election of 2016 and the continuing Republican control of the Senate ensured that Garland would not get his "trial." As a candidate, Trump had presented his own list of possible Supreme Court nominees. In 2017, he secured the nomination of Neil Gorsuch to the bench after Senate Republicans changed the chamber's rules to prevent a filibuster (Chapter 12). Replacing a very conservative justice, Antonin Scalia, Gorsuch's confirmation did not shift the Court's balance of political power. In fact, three Democrats voted for his confirmation.

In June 2018, Justice Anthony Kennedy announced his retirement. Though nominated by a Republican president (Ronald Reagan), Kennedy proved to be a moderate, centrist justice. Many of Kennedy's votes proved decisive in a closely divided Court, which issued a host of 5–4 decisions on politically and socially contentious issues during

The Asahi Shimbun via Getty Images

▲ U.S. Supreme Court associate justice Anthony Kennedy (R) administers the judicial oath to Judge Neil Gorsuch as his wife, Marie Louise Gorsuch, holds a Bible and President Donald Trump looks on during a ceremony in the Rose Garden at the White House in April 2017. Gorsuch's appointment was viewed as a major political victory for Republicans.

Kennedy's tenure. With the potential to move the Court in a more conservative direction, President Trump's choice for his replacement was sure to draw intense scrutiny.

While considerable attention was paid to President Trump's successful Supreme Court nomination, much less was paid to the president's successes in the appellate and district court confirmation process—perhaps as, or more, important for the shape of the federal courts in the years to come. As of January 2018—one year into office—President Trump had secured twenty-three confirmations for these lower federal courts, six of them replacing Democratic-appointed judges. Twelve of these were at the appellate level, the second-highest first-year total for a president since 1912, when the previous appellate system was reorganized into its modern form.[17] Ignoring the ratings of the American Bar Association, which was highly unusual, Trump nominated strong conservatives. Of the twenty-three successful nominees, only nine had prior judicial experience; the rest had backgrounds in litigation, private or public.[18]

The process of becoming a Supreme Court justice, just like judicial decision making itself, is grounded in the Constitution but is also profoundly shaped by the political environment and individuals' experiences and their approaches to judicial interpretation. We explore each of those aspects throughout the rest of the chapter.

WHAT HAVE I LEARNED?

1. The federal judiciary _____.
   a. exerts day-to-day oversight over the federal bureaucracy
   b. interprets and applies federal laws
   c. writes the nation's laws
   d. works with state judiciaries to interpret federal laws

2. What were the objections some raised to Sotomayor's nomination to the Supreme Court? How did others respond?

3. Imagine that you were nominated to serve on the Supreme Court. Do you think that any of your own life experiences might inform your own decisions? If so, on any specific issues?

_____

Answer Key: 1. b; 2. Answers should discuss concerns about whether Sotomayor would apply the facts to the cases before her as well as her assertion that embracing her heritage would allow her to make more just decisions; 3. Answers should include specific references to the ways in which lived experiences might inform judicial decisions; answers might focus on a particular topic or question in American constitutional law.

THE CONSTITUTION CASTS THE JUDICIARY AS THE WEAKEST BRANCH

- **Describe the structure and powers of the federal judiciary as laid out in the Constitution.**

The delegates to the Constitutional Convention spent much less time debating the structure and powers of the federal judiciary than they did hammering out the design of the legislative and executive branches. They were in general agreement that the judicial branch would be the weakest of the three, lacking an equivalent to Congress's power of the purse and the president's power as commander in chief. Second, the delegates agreed that the judiciary should retain a degree of independence from the other two branches—especially in the processes of appointment and removal of judges—though the specific details were not worked out until the summer of 1787.[19] That federal judges should have tenure with "good Behavior" was generally agreed upon, as was the need to protect their salaries from efforts to reduce them by an unhappy or vengeful Congress.[20] Both of these protections made it into the final document.[21] The question of appointment, however, remained unresolved until late in the convention, with the delegates finally approving a process through which the president would nominate federal judges and the Senate through its role of advice and consent would confirm the nominations.[22]

Finally, a diverse group of delegates agreed that the judiciary should have the power to strike down laws that were in violation of the Constitution. Unfortunately, the federal "courts were not *expressly* given the power to rule on constitutionality," an instance of "carelessness" that would have a profound impact on the court.[23]

THE CONSTITUTION GRANTS THE FEDERAL JUDICIARY SUPREMACY OVER LOWER STATE COURTS

This issue of constitutionality and the judiciary is not the only instance in which the text of the Constitution is less than thorough. Only the highest level of the federal judiciary—the Supreme Court—is actually described in the document, while the establishment of lower federal courts was left in the hands of Congress: "The judicial Power of the United States, shall be vested in one supreme Court, and in such inferior Courts as the Congress may from time to time ordain and establish."[24]

On one point the Constitution was clear: the federal judiciary, and the Supreme Court in particular, was to be the highest judicial power in the land: "The judicial power shall extend to all Cases, in Law and Equity, arising under this Constitution, the laws of the United States, and Treaties made, or which shall be made, under their Authority."[25] This judicial power, when combined with the supremacy clause of the Constitution, which declared the "Constitution, and the Laws of the United States" to be "the supreme Law of the Land; and [instructed that] the Judges in every State shall be bound thereby," established the federal judiciary as supreme to those of the states.[26]

In defining the scope of the power of the federal judiciary, the Constitution also (briefly) describes one of the most fundamental characteristics of any court: its jurisdiction, or its authority to hear and decide on specific cases.[27] Although there are many types and classifications of jurisdiction, the two most relevant to the study of the American judicial system are original and appellate jurisdiction. If a court has **original jurisdiction** in a case, then that court acts as the originating court, with the authority to hear the case first and to establish the facts pertaining to it. Courts with original jurisdiction are commonly referred to as trial courts. If a court has **appellate jurisdiction** over a case, then it possesses the authority to review the decision of a lower court and, if it so decides, to revise that decision. Courts operating under appellate jurisdiction generally focus on the lower courts' actions and procedures without finding facts on their own.

DURING RATIFICATION, CONCERNS ABOUT JUDICIAL ABUSE OF POWER ARE ADDRESSED

During the ratification debates, those who opposed the Constitution, the anti-Federalists, raised concerns about potential abuses of power by the proposed federal judiciary. Where the courts were concerned, anti-Federalists feared the growth in power of the national government and an associated subjugation of the rights of states and individuals by an increasingly powerful federal judiciary. In granting the power to overturn legislation to the Supreme Court, anti-Federalists argued that the nation would run the risk of unconstrained justices imposing their own views of what is constitutional and what is not.

In *Federalist* No. 78, Alexander Hamilton sought to reassure skeptical anti-Federalists and others that the planned federal judiciary would not trample upon their rights and liberties because it would neither want to nor be able to. In the first place, Hamilton argued, members of the federal judiciary—because of the process of their selection and their lifetime tenure—would stand apart from politics and the dangers that politics might pose to liberties and be able to "secure a steady, upright, and impartial administration of the laws."[28] Second, the federal judiciary was weak—indeed, it would be "the least dangerous" branch.[29] Compared to the powers of the executive branch's sword and the legislature's purse, Hamilton reassured, the federal judiciary—exercising only the power of judgment and located outside the arena of political struggle—was not to be feared. He argued that it was in fact the judiciary that needed protection from encroachment on its limited powers by the other two branches.

CONGRESS FILLS IN THE BLANKS WITH THE JUDICIARY ACT OF 1789

Taking up its constitutional authority to establish "inferior Courts" in the federal judiciary, the first Congress passed the Judiciary Act of 1789 to flesh out "the nature and the organization" of the court system.[30] Only the chief justice of the United States is mentioned in the Constitution; the document does not specify the number of justices in the Court, instead leaving that decision to Congress. The Judiciary Act added five associate judges to the Supreme Court, bringing the total number of justices to six, and it instructed that the Court was to meet in session twice a year in February and August. (Although the number of justices has varied throughout the nation's history, it has been set at nine since 1869.) The act also established two lower tiers to the federal judiciary, as only the Supreme Court had been set out in the Constitution, though changes have been made to their organization since.

original jurisdiction
the authority of a court to act as the first court to hear a case, which includes the finding of facts in the case.

appellate jurisdiction
the authority of a court to hear and review decisions made by lower courts in that system.

DIFFERENT VISUALS, DIFFERENT STORIES: THE PRESENTATION OF THE SUPREME COURT

Periodically, members of the Supreme Court pose for a "class photo," which is posted on the Court's official website (left).

While several of the justices appear to be relaxed, the presentation in this image is a formal, ceremonial one, robes and all. Unlike members of Congress or the president, justices have an official "costume." While there is no requirement for justices to wear robes, some scholars have argued that the ceremony surrounding the Court and its proceedings adds to its legitimacy in the view of the American public.

Compare the 2017 image to a picture taken during the "class photo" shoot in 2006, in which Justice Clarence Thomas, a staunch conservative, interacts with Justice Stephen Breyer, one of the Court's liberal justices (right).

While Breyer and Thomas are far apart ideologically, the second photo presents an image of camaraderie and fellowship between the two justices—a friendship of two people, not two members of a hallowed institution or two political opponents.

WHAT Do You Think?

Why might the federal judiciary be the only institution that employs a uniform dress code when its officials are presented to the public? How important are the robes, rituals, and formality of the Supreme Court in maintaining its legitimacy in the view of the American public?

Members of the U.S. Supreme Court pose for a group photograph in June 2017. In the front row, from left, are Associate Justice Ruth Bader Ginsburg, Associate Justice Anthony M. Kennedy, Chief Justice of the United States John G. Roberts, Associate Justice Clarence Thomas, and Associate Justice Stephen Breyer. Standing, from left, are Associate Justice Elena Kagan, Associate Justice Samuel Alito Jr., Associate Justice Sonia Sotomayor, and Associate Justice Neil Gorsuch.

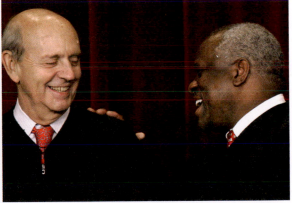

Supreme Court justices Stephen Breyer (left) and Clarence Thomas.

The Judiciary Act of 1789 also created the office of attorney general "to prosecute and conduct all suits in the Supreme Court in which the United States shall be concerned, and to give his advice and opinion upon questions of law when required to by the president of the United States."[31] Today, the office of the solicitor general represents the president in the Supreme Court, while the attorney general is head of the Justice Department. Finally, the act gave the Supreme Court the power to review and reverse actions of the state courts if it found them to be in conflict with the Constitution—a power tied to both the Constitution's description of the scope of judicial power and the supremacy clause.

WHAT HAVE I **LEARNED?**

1. The combination of language in Article III, which describes the federal judiciary, and the supremacy clause of the Constitution _____.

   a. sets the federal judiciary as superior to the state judiciaries in all cases in the nation

   b. sets the state judiciaries as superior to the federal judiciary in all cases in the nation

   c. leaves the question of supremacy unresolved

   d. establishes the Constitution as supreme with the federal judiciary superior in constitutional matters, federal laws, and treaties

2. What concerned anti-Federalists about the proposed federal judiciary?

3. What was Alexander Hamilton's response to these concerns in *Federalist* No. 78?

4. Do you agree more with the Federalist or the anti-Federalist arguments about the federal judiciary? Why?

THE "TRIAL" OF JOHN MARSHALL ESTABLISHES THE PRINCIPLE OF JUDICIAL REVIEW

- Explain John Marshall's development of judicial review in the Supreme Court decision in *Marbury v. Madison*.

In 2017, perhaps no issue in American government was more important than the confirmations of Supreme Court justices. In April 2017, after Republicans in the Senate had changed the institution's rules to prevent a filibuster of a Supreme Court nominee, Neil Gorsuch joined the bench. As a replacement for the deceased, and highly conservative, Antonin Scalia, that appointment did not cause as much concern as future ones might. If President Trump, however, is able to replace a more liberal or moderate justice, it might have consequences for American policy for decades. But why? Aren't justices supposed to be insulated from politics? That is a very important question, to which we will now turn.

THE ELECTION OF 1800 GIVES RISE TO A FEDERALIST JUDICIAL STRATEGY

The election of 1800 was one of the nastiest in American history. The seeds of faction that had been planted during George Washington's presidency came into full bloom in the late 1790s as political parties took root. President John Adams, once Washington's vice president and now seeking his own second term in office, had allied with Alexander Hamilton, who had been Washington's secretary of the treasury, under the banner of the Federalists. In Hamilton, Adams saw a partner who would help him promote a strong national government, especially in the area of economic policy and banking.[32]

They squared off against Thomas Jefferson and the Republican Party.[33] They mistrusted the Federalists' motives and the reach of Hamilton's economic policies. As each side sought support for its views in Congress and in the state legislatures, America's first political parties increasingly gained power, like new planets pulling more and more supporters into their political gravity. Throughout the election, Republicans accused Adams and the Federalists of trying to bring a British-style monarchy to America. For their part, the Federalists accused Jefferson and his fellow Republicans of being too close to France and pointed to the chaos that had unfolded in that country in the wake of the French Revolution. Both campaigns were bitter, partisan, and personal right up to the election.

And then there was a tie: Jefferson, the Republican, had unexpectedly tied for votes, in the electoral system of the time, not with John Adams but with Aaron Burr.

The decision about who would become president would move from the Electoral College to the House of Representatives.

Months of post-election discord followed, with accusations of voting irregularities flying and partisan rancor so intense that some feared a civil war would break out. Thomas Jefferson was finally elected president of the United States by the House on the thirty-sixth ballot. Jefferson, in his inaugural address, sought to calm tensions throughout the nation. "We are all republicans," he said. "We are all federalists."[34] Nonetheless, the Federalist Party paid dearly. It had been soundly defeated in both the presidential election and the congressional elections. Its days in power were numbered.

Trying to preserve their influence within the national government, the Federalists turned to the federal judiciary, the one branch where they might endure, given that the Constitution grants federal judges lifetime job security.[35] In the waning weeks of Adams's administration, the Federalists in the legislature and the executive branches made several changes to the federal judiciary to cement their power.[36]

With the Judiciary Act of 1801, Federalists in Congress changed the Supreme Court's schedule, reduced the size of the Court from six to five justices, and reorganized the lower federal courts in such a way as to create sixteen vacancies that were promptly filled by Adams's administration. The reduction in the size of the Supreme Court could not force a justice out; that would have been unconstitutional. What it did do was ensure that incoming president Jefferson would not be able to fill the next vacancy with someone the Federalists presumed would be a Republican.

Just before leaving office, Adams set about filling the vacancies created by the Judiciary Act of 1801. He also set about building up the administration of the nation's new capital in Washington, DC (the seat of government had been recently relocated from Philadelphia in 1800). There were many good jobs to fill there, including justices of the peace.[37] One candidate for one of these new jobs was a Mr. William Marbury.

Less than two weeks before Adams signed the Judiciary Act of 1801 into law, the Senate confirmed the president's appointment of his secretary of state, John Marshall, to be the new chief justice of the United States.[38] Marshall was a Federalist and an experienced politician. For the last weeks of the Adams administration, Marshall was also both chief justice and secretary of state. He had a lot on his plate—as it turned out, perhaps too much. In the scramble to complete the paperwork before the Republicans took the reins of government, some of the commissions Adams had signed, including one for William Marbury, had not been delivered and were still sitting on Secretary of State Marshall's desk when Adams's term expired at midnight.

Upon assuming office, President Jefferson did deliver the commissions to some of those hastily approved appointees after he took office. But William Marbury and several others did not receive theirs. Marbury, along with three other men, brought suit against Jefferson's secretary of state, James Madison, requesting that the Court issue a writ of mandamus ("we command") ordering Madison to deliver their commissions as justices of the peace.[39] The men argued that all of the required steps in their appointments had been properly taken: President Adams had nominated them, the Senate had confirmed their nominations, and the commissions had been signed and affixed with the presidential seal. Marshall's failure to deliver the commissions, they insisted, constituted nothing more than a serious breach of etiquette and tradition.

CHIEF JUSTICE JOHN MARSHALL CONFRONTS POLITICS AND THE POWER OF THE SUPREME COURT

As he contemplated how the Court would respond to the demands of Marbury and his fellow would-be justices, Marshall confronted two powerful and related sets of questions about the role of the federal judiciary in the life of the American Republic—the same two questions with which we began this chapter:

Bettmann / Contributor

CARICATURE OF JEFFERSON.

▲ A political cartoon criticizing Thomas Jefferson during the presidential campaign of 1800. The American eagle attempts to snatch the Constitution from Jefferson, who is trying to burn it on the "Altar of Gallic Despotism"—an allusion to Jefferson's supposed sympathies with the French revolutionaries.

▲ The election of 1800 had far-reaching implications. John Adams lost the election, and the Federalist Party unraveled. In addition, friendships and political alliances were fractured. Here, Alexander Hamilton and Aaron Burr, Thomas Jefferson's vice president, prepare to duel in July 1804. Hamilton was killed in the duel.

How powerful is the federal judiciary? And how political is it? In *Marbury v. Madison* (1803), the Court found itself involved in an intense partisan battle between the defeated Federalists and the victorious Republicans.[40] That Congress and the executive were highly political branches was obvious to everyone, especially after the election of 1800. The judiciary, however, was supposed to be different. It was constrained and defined by law, not politics. How should such an institution handle its role in the larger political life of the nation?

Chief Justice Marshall could not ignore either of these considerations; both had to be addressed. If his Court waded into the political battle of the time forcefully—ordering Jefferson's administration to deliver the commissions—he risked being rebuffed by the president or even impeached by the Republican-controlled Congress. Marshall *could* choose not to enter the battle. He could deny Marbury's petition, thus preventing a confrontation with Jefferson and his Republicans. However, to do so might send a message that the judiciary was weak in the face of powerful political forces, which could deal a blow to its power, prestige, and independence.[41] Marshall was in a bind and he knew it. In the decision that he ultimately delivered, Marshall noted the "peculiar delicacy of this case."[42] The way in which Marshall dealt with this dilemma continues to shape the role of the Supreme Court in American political life to this day. The two questions with which he wrestled, however, have not gone away: How political is the federal judiciary? How powerful is it?

MARBURY V. MADISON LEADS TO THE ESTABLISHMENT OF JUDICIAL REVIEW

Because of the changes to the Supreme Court's schedule brought about by the Judiciary Act of 1801, Marbury and his associates had to wait for nearly two years before the Court heard their request to issue a writ of mandamus to Secretary of State Madison. Both of Chief Justice Marshall's apparent options in the case seemed likely to diminish the power of his judiciary. Either he could order Jefferson's administration to deliver the commissions and risk being refused or ignored, or he could decide not to challenge the president and risk looking weak and timid.

Marshall chose neither option. Instead, in a tactically brilliant move, he broke the decision before him into three separate questions. First, the chief justice asked if the men were entitled to their commissions. To this first question, Marshall, in his opinion, answered "yes." The presidential signing of such commissions is the last formal act, and that had been done. Delivery of the commissions, Marshall noted, "is a practice directed by convenience, but not by law."[43] Once this part of the decision was established, Marshall considered whether or not a legal remedy involving the courts was available to Marbury and his fellow plaintiffs. To this second question, Marshall also answered in the affirmative, arguing that "the individual who considers himself [so] injured has a right to resort to the laws of the country for a remedy."[44]

So far, it seemed that Marshall was going to take on Jefferson's administration with all of the risks that such a strategy entailed. But he did not. Instead, Marshall presented a third question for his Court to consider: Were Marbury and the other plaintiffs entitled to the remedy that they sought—the writs of mandamus? To this question, Marshall answered no. The power to issue these kinds of writs in this particular instance, he declared, had been improperly given to the Court by a section of the Judiciary Act of 1789.[45] Though the reasoning is a bit technical, Marshall argued that when Congress had granted the Court the authority "to issue writs of mandamus to public officers," it was attempting to expand the scope of the original jurisdiction of the Court, which Congress cannot do. Only the Constitution can. Therefore, the Court did not have the power to give Marbury the remedy he sought.

In stating the inability of his Court to legitimately provide the sought-after remedy, Marshall also found that the part of the Judiciary Act that tried to give his Court such power was in violation of the

judicial review
the authority of the highest court in a political system to determine if a law is or is not in conflict with a government's highest law, which in the United States is the Constitution.

Bettmann / Contributor

Constitution and, therefore, invalid: "A law repugnant to the Constitution is void, and . . . courts, as well as other departments, are bound by that instrument."[46]

It proved to be a bold, strategic move. Madison did not have to deliver the commissions. Marshall, however, had just asserted what the Constitution had failed to lay out in its brief treatment of the third branch: The Supreme Court had the power of **judicial review**, which is the authority of a court to review laws and actions of other branches and levels of government to decide if they are in conflict with the highest law of the land—in this case, the Constitution—and, if they are, to declare those laws or actions invalid.

In establishing the precedent for judicial review over federal laws, Marshall expanded the Court's responsibility in **constitutional interpretation**, in which the judiciary reviews laws and actions in light of the meaning of the Constitution. In exercising judicial review, according to Marshall's logic, the Court does not place itself above the other two branches; it is coequal to them, and the Constitution is supreme to all three.

President Jefferson had been a student and practitioner of the law, and he clearly understood the implications of Marshall's decision. Jefferson argued that Marshall had set a dangerous precedent. In a letter to Abigail Adams in 1804, Jefferson worried, "But the opinion which gives to the judges the right to decide what laws are constitutional, and what not, not only for themselves in their own sphere of action, but for the legislature and executive also, in their spheres, would make the judiciary a despotic branch."[47]

Under the decades-long tenure of Marshall, the Supreme Court used the tool of judicial review to weigh in on the constitutionality of several state laws, declaring some invalid. Marshall, however, never again used the power of judicial review to strike down an act of Congress. It would be more than fifty years before the Court took such an action again, in its infamous decision in *Dred Scott v. Sandford* (1857). In this case, Justice Roger Taney and his Court overturned the Missouri Compromise, deepening national divisions over the future of slavery[48]

In the end, William Marbury and his fellow job seekers never received their commissions, and the power of judicial review and the role of the Court in constitutional interpretation remain highly debated issues to this day. Before we can explore the implications of this claimed authority, however, it is necessary to examine the structure and operation of the American judicial system.

The Granger Collection, New York

▲ Judicial nominee William Marbury, whose suit against James Madison in *Marbury v. Madison* established judicial review of federal law.

constitutional interpretation
the process of applying the Constitution in assessing whether or not a law, part of a law, or an action by a governmental official is or is not in conflict with the Constitution.

WHAT HAVE I **LEARNED?**

1. Facing defeat after the election of 1800, the losing Federalist Party chose to _____.

   a. accept its losses

   b. impeach the incoming president

   c. use judicial appointments to secure its future power

   d. use the Supreme Court to overturn the election

2. Judicial review refers to _____.

   a. congressional review of justices' behavior

   b. the authority to review laws and actions to determine if they are in conflict with the Constitution

   c. review of the decisions of lower federal courts

   d. executive branch oversight of the federal judiciary

3. What was John Marshall's strategy in his decision in *Marbury v. Madison*?

   Answer Key: 1. c.; 2. b; 3. Answers should include his creation of judicial review over federal laws without directly confronting the power of President Jefferson.

▲ Abigail Adams, wife of President John Adams and correspondent to Thomas Jefferson. Their conversations via letters outline Jefferson's fear that Marshall's decision could make the judicial branch "despotic."

adversarial system
a legal structure in which two opposing sides present their case in the most persuasive way possible.

plaintiff
a person or group who brings a case in court.

defendant
a person or group against whom a case is brought in court.

criminal law
a category of law covering actions determined to harm the community itself.

plea bargaining
a legal process in which the plaintiff and defendant agree to an outcome prior to the handing out of a verdict.

civil law
a category of law covering cases involving private rights and relationships between individuals and groups.

THE AMERICAN LEGAL SYSTEM IS DEFINED BY FEDERALISM

- Describe the structure of the American legal system and the federal judiciary.

Each of the two levels in the federalist system—the nation and the states—operates its own system of courts, with a single federal judiciary for the nation and separate state judiciaries in each of the fifty states. While the structure of American federalism defines the basic organization of the nation's legal system, the dual systems of federal and state courts share in common the tradition of the **adversarial system** of justice, in which the opposing parties present their sides of a case in the most persuasive way possible. In this system, a **plaintiff** is the party bringing a complaint and the **defendant** is the party accused of wrongdoing.[49]

CASES ARE DIVIDED INTO CRIMINAL AND CIVIL TYPES

Whether or not a specific court has jurisdiction over a specific case may depend on whether that court is a state or a federal court, the details of the case, or where that court lies within the overall structure of the federal or state court system. Both state and federal courts have jurisdiction over two categories of law, criminal and civil (see Figure 15.1).[50] **Criminal law** covers actions determined to harm the community itself, such as committing an act of violence against another person.[51] In a criminal case, the state or federal government acts as the plaintiff and tries to prove the guilt of the defendant, the party accused of a crime. Although many acts (such as murder or assault) are considered to be criminal offenses in all of the states, some acts (such as gambling or recreational use of marijuana) are legal in some states but not in others. As of 2018, for example, an adult in several states could lawfully use marijuana recreationally according to state law (subject to certain restrictions) but in doing so be in violation of federal law, presenting a tricky issue for American federalism.[52] States may also vary in the punishments handed out for those convicted of similar crimes.

In 1992, an all-white California jury found four white Los Angeles police officers not guilty of assaulting Rodney King, an African American man, during a traffic stop and arrest, much of which was captured on videotape by a witness. That verdict was quickly followed by rioting and heightened racial tensions throughout the city. The next year, a federal jury found two of the officers guilty of violating King's civil rights through the application of excessive force or a refusal to stop the exercise of excessive force during the original incident.

Being convicted under a criminal statute leads to some form of punishment, such as fines, imprisonment, or, in some cases, the death penalty.[53] Most criminal cases are resolved through the process of **plea bargaining**. In this process, a defendant in a criminal case agrees to plead guilty to a lesser charge than the one brought by the prosecutors in order to reduce his or her punishment. Plea bargaining is also used in civil cases. As is the case with defendants during the arrest and trial phases, those ultimately convicted of crimes have constitutional protections, specifically against the Eighth Amendment's protection against the imposition of "cruel and unusual punishments." Whether or not the death penalty—or specific methods of instituting it—constitutes a violation of the Eighth Amendment's protections continues to be debated today.

Noncriminal law, commonly referred to as **civil law**, covers cases involving private rights and relationships between individuals and groups. In a civil case, the plaintiff is the party who argues that she or he has been wronged and the defendant is the party accused of violating a person's rights or breaking an agreement. While in criminal cases, a government (state or federal) is always the

The Granger Collection, New York

Comparing Criminal and Civil Law

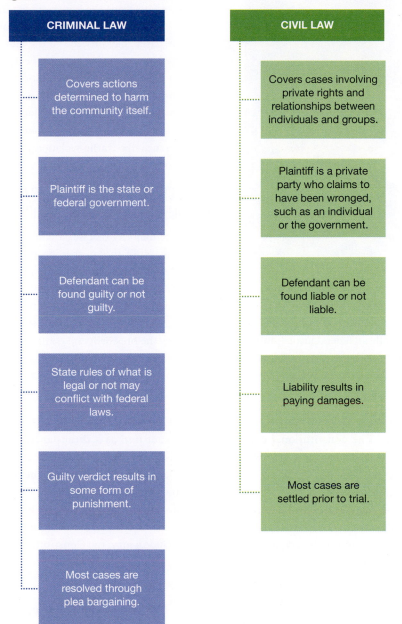

CRIMINAL LAW	CIVIL LAW
Covers actions determined to harm the community itself.	Covers cases involving private rights and relationships between individuals and groups.
Plaintiff is the state or federal government.	Plaintiff is a private party who claims to have been wronged, such as an individual or the government.
Defendant can be found guilty or not guilty.	Defendant can be found liable or not liable.
State rules of what is legal or not may conflict with federal laws.	Liability results in paying damages.
Guilty verdict results in some form of punishment.	Most cases are settled prior to trial.
Most cases are resolved through plea bargaining.	

plaintiff, in civil cases the plaintiff may be a government or an individual. A jury or a judge might decide civil cases, though most are settled without a formal verdict either before the case goes to trial or during the proceedings.

STATE COURTS HANDLE THE MAJORITY OF CASES IN THE UNITED STATES

While our focus is on the federal judiciary, it is important to note that state courts handle the vast majority of court cases in the United States. While states may vary in how their judicial systems are structured and organized—including how judges are selected—the state court systems share a few common traits. State judicial systems handle both criminal and civil cases. Each state has a system of trial courts that does most of the work of the state's judiciary, handles cases arising under that state's laws, and possesses original jurisdiction. More than half of the states have an intermediate

KTLA

Charlie Steiner

▲ Video taken by a bystander captured the beating of black motorist Rodney King by Los Angeles police officers in March 1991. The following year, a jury found four white Los Angeles police officers not guilty of assault, but a federal jury found two of the officers guilty of violating King's civil rights.

system of appellate courts that operate with appellate jurisdiction. Each state has at least one state supreme court, which acts as the highest court in that state's system and as the final level of appeal.[54] A select group of cases may proceed to the federal judiciary from the highest state court of appeals. These types of cases generally involve a question arising under the Constitution, such as a claim that an individual's constitutional rights have been violated. States also operate systems of specialized courts that typically handle issues like traffic violations, family disputes, and small claims.

MOST OF THE IMPACTFUL CASES ARE HANDLED BY THE FEDERAL JUDICIARY

While the majority of cases are handled by the state courts, many of the most impactful happen at the federal level. The federal judiciary includes two types of courts. The term *constitutional courts* refers to the Supreme Court and the lower levels of the federal judiciary that the Constitution authorized Congress to create in Article III. Legislative courts are specialized courts created by Congress under its authority in Article I to handle matters such as tax and trade law. While all federal justices must be nominated by the president and confirmed by a majority vote in the Senate, justices in the legislative courts, unlike those in the constitutional courts, serve for fixed terms. Our focus in this chapter will be on the constitutional court system rather than on the specialized legislative courts.

THE FEDERAL DISTRICT COURTS SERVE AS THE BOTTOM LEVEL OF THE FEDERAL JUDICIARY. The constitutional court system is structured as a three-layered pyramid (see Figure 15.2). At the bottom are the nation's **federal district courts**. Congress created the district courts in the Judiciary Act of 1789. In most federal cases, district courts act as the trial courts and possess original jurisdiction. As of 2018, there were ninety-four district courts in the United States, and each state had at least one. District court boundaries do not cut across state lines. The district courts handle most of the work of the federal courts, and their cases are heard by a single federal judge. Cases heard in a district court may or may not include a jury; the Constitution guarantees the right to a jury trial in all federal criminal cases (Sixth Amendment) and in some civil cases (Seventh Amendment).

THE APPELLATE COURTS SIT IN THE MIDDLE. The **federal courts of appeals** occupy the middle level of the constitutional courts. There are thirteen courts of appeals; eleven have jurisdiction over regionally based "circuits," one has jurisdiction over the District of Columbia (which handles appeals involving federal agencies), and the thirteenth handles cases arising under international trade and patent law. The courts of appeals exercise appellate jurisdiction only, reviewing decisions made by the federal district courts and certain specialized federal courts (see Figure 15.3). The federal appellate courts have, as their name implies, appellate jurisdiction only and are staffed with justices specifically appointed to that level of the federal judiciary.

THE SUPREME COURT SITS AT THE TOP. At the top of the federal judicial system is the U.S. Supreme Court, which, as the Constitution established, is the highest court in the nation. Part of the Court's intended purpose was to resolve differences between the states, which had not effectively been provided for in the government created by the Articles of Confederation. The Court also acts to resolve differing interpretations of the law in the lower federal courts. Each justice has a small number of clerks to assist in selecting, researching, and issuing decisions in Court cases. The Court meets in session

federal district courts
the lowest level of the federal judiciary; these courts usually possess original jurisdiction in cases that originate at the federal level.

federal courts of appeals
the middle level of the federal judiciary; these courts review and hear appeals from the federal district courts.

The Modern Court System

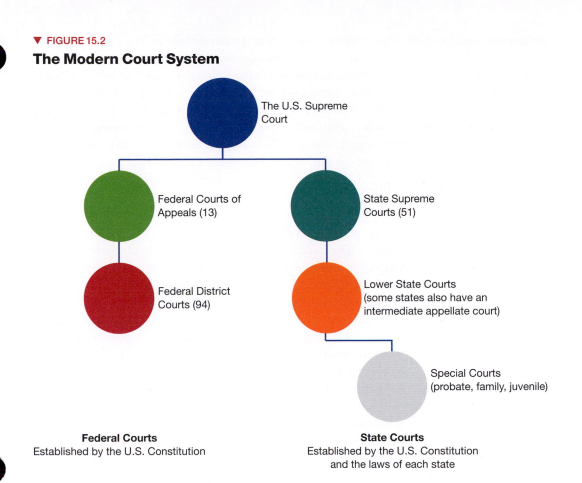

The U.S. Supreme Court

Federal Courts of Appeals (13)

State Supreme Courts (51)

Federal District Courts (94)

Lower State Courts (some states also have an intermediate appellate court)

Special Courts (probate, family, juvenile)

Federal Courts
Established by the U.S. Constitution

State Courts
Established by the U.S. Constitution and the laws of each state

▼ FIGURE 15.3

Map of the District and Appellate Courts

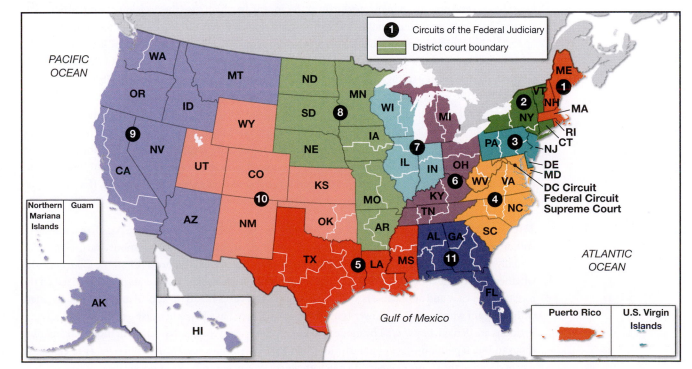

Source: U.S. Courts, "Geographic Boundaries of United States Courts of Appeals and United States District Courts," accessed August 9, 2018, www.uscourts.gov/uscourts/images/CircuitMap.pdf.

roughly nine months out of the year, beginning on the first Monday in October. Those cases still on the docket (the schedule of cases to be heard) when a term ends continue to the next term's docket.

Cases in which the Supreme Court exercises original jurisdiction are few and are described in Article III of the Constitution: "In all Cases affecting Ambassadors, other public Ministers and Consuls, and those in which a State shall be a Party, the supreme Court shall have original jurisdiction."[55] In all other cases in which the federal judiciary has jurisdiction, the Court possesses appellate jurisdiction only. In addition to having appellate jurisdiction over all federal cases, the Court possesses appellate jurisdiction over certain state cases, especially those involving a federal issue.

CASES INVOLVING FEDERAL QUESTIONS PROCEED THROUGH THE FEDERAL JUDICIARY

Those cases that begin in the federal judiciary—in which the federal courts have original jurisdiction—must fall into one of three categories. The first category is cases in which the federal government is a party in a dispute. Second, the federal judiciary possesses original jurisdiction in civil suits involving parties from two different states in which the amount of money in question is more than $75,000. Finally—and, for our purposes, most importantly—the federal judiciary possesses original jurisdiction in cases that involve a federal question, such as a case in which a party files a claim of violations of rights under the Constitution, a dispute involving a federal treaty, or a case involving a federal law. Cases involving federal questions may be either criminal or civil cases. State cases that proceed to the Supreme Court also involve federal questions. Many of the most important federal cases in American history—and most of the cases that we consider in this book—are those involving charges of violations of constitutional rights and liberties.

As the courts of original jurisdiction in most federal cases, the federal district courts act as the trial courts, finding facts and delivering opinions on the case. Litigants who lose in a district court have an option to appeal the decision to the appellate courts, in which case the case moves up to the next level.[56] Most federal cases, however, go no farther than the district courts.

Appellate courts possess appellate jurisdiction only and review cases on appeal. Rather than finding facts, the appellate courts focus on how the decision of the district court was rendered and if that decision was appropriate in the context of the law. With cases typically heard by three-judge panels, an appellate court has several options. It may refuse to hear the appeal, in which case the decision of the district court (or specialized federal court) holds. Litigants whose appeal is refused by the appellate court may still appeal to the Supreme Court, though their odds of receiving a hearing by the Court are very small.

If it decides to hear a case, an appeals court may choose to affirm the judgment of the lower court, confirming that court's ruling. It may reverse the decision; if this is the case, it is typically based on questions of how the lower court proceeded or applied the law. Finally, it may remand the case back to the lower court for reconsideration, again often because the appellate court judges had questions about procedure or application of the law. These options are not mutually exclusive for any one case. The court could affirm part of a lower court's decision in a particular case, reverse part of it, and remand yet another part, though this is far from a common outcome. The side that loses in an appellate court has the right to appeal to the Supreme Court, but there is no guarantee that its case will be heard. If not, the decision of the appellate court stands, though it applies only to that circuit.[57]

THE SUPREME COURT DECIDES WHETHER TO TAKE CASES ON APPEAL. In exercising its authority of appellate jurisdiction, the Supreme Court is confronted with two questions, the first of which actually determines the outcome of roughly 99 percent of the appeals before it. First, the Court decides whether or not to hear the case. Second, if it does decide to hear the case, it issues its decision based on the merits of the case and applicable law. The vast majority of cases heard on appeal in the Court originate with a litigant who has lost in a lower court filing a petition to have his or her case heard. Almost all such petitions are denied, however. The modern Court receives, on average, between eight thousand and nine thousand such petitions a year but hears less than 1 percent of these cases, or about seventy to eighty. In recent decades, the Court has gained a much greater degree of control over its docket.

A petitioner who wishes to have the Court accept his or her case files an argument with the Court in a written **brief**, which presents the arguments for the appeal. Not everyone can file a legitimate brief before the Court. In addition to certain other technical requirements about the facts and merits of a case, a petitioner must demonstrate that he or she has **standing**, which involves demonstrating an actual or imminent harm from a law or action in question. As we will discuss later in the chapter, the need to establish standing acts as a limitation on the power of the Court to shape national public policy. The opposing party in a case may also file a brief with the Court laying out her or his arguments.[58] As the Constitution offers little guidance on which cases the Court does or does not take, justices have adopted the custom of the rule of four, which simply means that it will generally hear a case if four or more justices vote to do so. If it decides to hear a case, the Court issues a **writ of certiorari** (from the Latin "to be more informed") to the lower court for the records of the case, a process that is commonly referred to as certiorari, or "granting cert." As discussed earlier, very few petitions for cert are granted. In its own rules, the Court makes it clear that the hurdle for having a case heard on appeal is high: "Review on a writ of certiorari is not a matter of right, but of judicial discretion. A petition of a writ of certiorari will be granted only for compelling reasons."[59] The most important factor in the decision to grant or deny cert is if there is confusion about or alternate interpretations of a law or previous ruling among or between lower-level federal courts or state supreme courts. Cases presenting a federal question are also more likely to be heard. The Court does not, however, act as the corrector of all lower court mistakes in finding fact or applying the law when these errors do not present or affect important federal concerns.

Interested parties who are not plaintiffs or defendants may also try to signal to the Court their interest in the decision to grant cert or on the merits of the case should cert be granted. Plaintiffs and defendants are not the only parties that may file briefs. An interested party (such as an interest group) may also submit its opinions to the Court in what is called an amicus curiae brief (from the Latin, "friend of the court").[60] The volume, authorship, and content of these briefs can act as a signal to the Court about how the public or interest groups view an issue.[61] An especially important filer of amici curiae briefs is the **solicitor general**, who is appointed by the president to represent the federal government in the Court. An indication to the Court that the government (or the president, specifically) is interested in a case can be a powerful signal both on the question of whether or not the Court should hear a particular case and on its ruling should it decide to do so.

The preferences of the justices may also play a role in the decision to grant cert. After all, the final decision rests on the votes of the justices themselves. While scholars continue to debate the role that justices' political or policy preferences play in their decisions (which we will examine later in the chapter), a justice who supports a particular view on an issue before the Court must consider how the other justices are likely to vote on the merits of the case. Justices are well aware that the outcome of a Supreme Court case can set a **precedent**, or a judicial decision that acts as a basis for deciding similar cases in the future. An individual justice may be more or less likely to grant cert if there is a perceived likelihood that the outcome might be a precedent that the justice desires or wishes to avoid.

ONCE CASES ARE TAKEN UP, THE SUPREME COURT CONSIDERS AND DECIDES THEM.
If the Supreme Court decides to grant cert to a case, it requests briefs from both sides laying out their full arguments. Court clerks will assist the justices in reviewing these briefs. The case is then scheduled for **oral argument** before the assembled justices, during which each side gets a fixed amount of time (typically half an hour) to present. In exceptional circumstances, filers of amicus curiae briefs

Mark Wilson/Getty Images

▲ Senate Judiciary Committee chairman Chuck Grassley (R-IA) (second from right) greets Justice Department nominees (left to right) Noel Francisco, to be solicitor general; Makan Delrahim, to be an assistant attorney general in the Antitrust Division; and Steven Engel, to be an assistant attorney general in the Office of Legal Counsel, prior to their Senate Judiciary Committee confirmation hearing in May 2017.

brief
a legal document presented by plaintiffs, defendants, and, at times, other interested parties outlining their arguments in a case.

standing
the legal ability to bring a case in court.

writ of certiorari
the process through which most cases reach the Supreme Court; after four justices concur that the Court should hear the case, a writ of certiorari is issued to the lower court to request the relevant case records.

solicitor general
a presidential appointee who represents the federal government in the Supreme Court.

may also be given time during oral arguments, but this is not common. During this phase, the justices are not passive but frequently interrupt and question the lawyers as they present, though some justices tend to interrupt and question more than others. Cameras are not allowed in the courtroom during oral arguments, though sketch artists and audio recordings are.

Scholars debate how influential oral arguments are in shaping justices' rulings in a case.[62] This process, however, is often of intense interest to members of the public, who analyze the content of justices' questions for clues as to how those justices will ultimately vote. As most of what follows the oral argument phase happens in secret, court watchers have few other means to try to divine the Court's decisions ahead of time. After oral argument, the case proceeds to judicial conference, in which the justices meet and vote in secret; not even their clerks are present. The process can go on for months (on and off, of course), and individual justices can and do change their votes during this phase.

Finally, the Court issues its decision. The majority opinion consists of the ruling—and the logic behind it—of the majority of justices in the case. When it acts under appellate jurisdiction (which is most of the time), the Court has the same options as other appellate courts. It may affirm, reverse, or remand back to the lower court the case (or certain rulings within a case).[63] The decision and the majority opinion are binding and serve to guide lower courts and future courts in handling similar cases. If the chief justice is in the majority, then he or she selects the author of the majority opinion. If not, the most senior member of the majority does so. The power to choose the author of an opinion can be a useful strategic tool, as even justices who vote together may have differences in their interpretations of certain points brought up in the case. If there is no majority, which typically occurs when many justices disagree on the logic behind a ruling, then a plurality opinion will be written that expresses the views of the largest number of justices who voted together.

A justice voting with the majority may also write a concurring opinion (often called a concurrence) explaining the reasoning behind his or her particular vote. More than one justice may collaborate on a concurrence. Concurrences are more common when a justice has some differences in logic or reasoning with the other members of the majority but not enough to cause that justice to side against them. A justice who voted with the minority may write a dissenting opinion, called a dissent, also alone or with other justices. These opinions do not carry the weight of the Court behind them (since the justice writing the dissent was on the losing side). However, if a future court should revisit a precedent with a thought to perhaps overturning it, a dissent may provide a useful record and analysis of why at least one justice thought the Court got it wrong the first time. (See Figure 15.4.)

APPOINTMENT TO THE FEDERAL JUDICIARY IS OFTEN POLITICAL

While individual states vary in how they select their judges, all federal judges must be nominated by the president and confirmed by a majority vote in the Senate. As federal judges are appointed for life—assuming "good behavior"—successfully placing individuals on the federal bench is one of the most important things a president can do. Trying to preserve the influence of their defeated party after the election of 1800 was what drove John Adams and the Federalists to try to pack the federal judiciary with as many of their people as possible.

While most district court nominees are approved, the confirmations of appellate and Supreme Court judges have become increasingly affected by partisan political battles in recent years, though there have been many other periods in American history where this has also been the case. Part of the reason that things tend to run more smoothly at the district court level is the custom of senatorial courtesy, in which presidents (and the high-ranking members of the Justice Department who do much of the actual work of identifying candidates) consult with senators from the state in which the vacant district judgeship is located, especially if those senators are from the president's political party.

The higher two levels of the federal judiciary often witness more direct presidential involvement in the nomination process, and these nominations are more likely to be caught up in partisan battles. While most Supreme Court nominees are confirmed, their confirmation hearings can and have often involved intense scrutiny of the nominee. In addition, recent confirmation votes in the Senate have tended to

precedent
a judicial decision that guides future courts in handling similar cases.

oral arguments
presentations made by plaintiffs and attorneys before the Supreme Court.

How Cases Move through the Court System

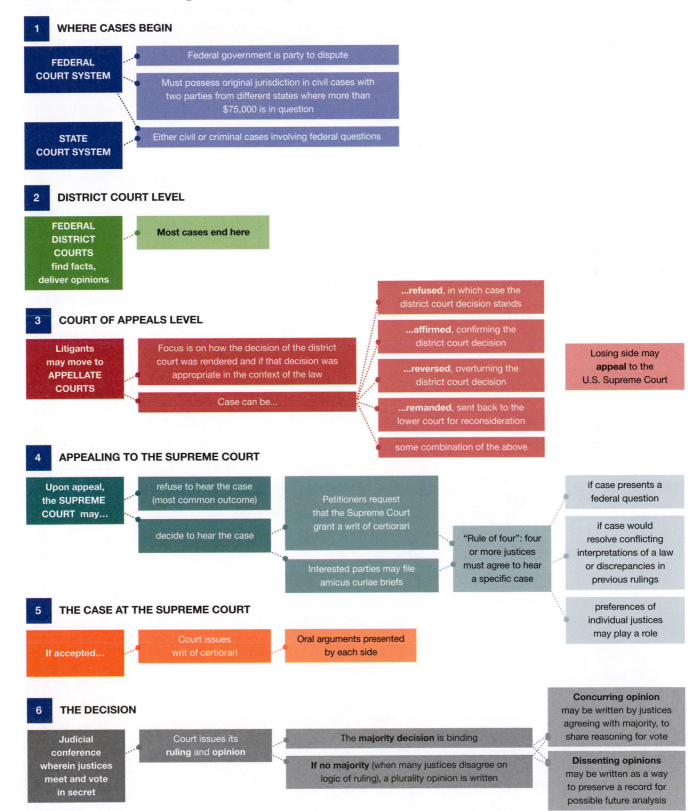

1 WHERE CASES BEGIN

FEDERAL COURT SYSTEM
- Federal government is party to dispute
- Must possess original jurisdiction in civil cases with two parties from different states where more than $75,000 is in question

STATE COURT SYSTEM
- Either civil or criminal cases involving federal questions

2 DISTRICT COURT LEVEL

FEDERAL DISTRICT COURTS find facts, deliver opinions
- **Most cases end here**

3 COURT OF APPEALS LEVEL

Litigants may move to APPELLATE COURTS
- Focus is on how the decision of the district court was rendered and if that decision was appropriate in the context of the law
- Case can be...
  - ...**refused**, in which case the district court decision stands
  - ...**affirmed**, confirming the district court decision
  - ...**reversed**, overturning the district court decision
  - ...**remanded**, sent back to the lower court for reconsideration
  - some combination of the above

Losing side may **appeal** to the U.S. Supreme Court

4 APPEALING TO THE SUPREME COURT

Upon appeal, the SUPREME COURT may...
- refuse to hear the case (most common outcome)
- decide to hear the case
  - Petitioners request that the Supreme Court grant a writ of certiorari
  - Interested parties may file amicus curiae briefs
    - "Rule of four": four or more justices must agree to hear a specific case
      - if case presents a federal question
      - if case would resolve conflicting interpretations of a law or discrepancies in previous rulings
      - preferences of individual justices may play a role

5 THE CASE AT THE SUPREME COURT

If accepted...
- Court issues writ of certiorari
- Oral arguments presented by each side

6 THE DECISION

Judicial conference wherein justices meet and vote in secret
- Court issues its **ruling** and **opinion**
  - The **majority decision** is binding
  - **If no majority** (when many justices disagree on logic of ruling), a plurality opinion is written
    - **Concurring opinion** may be written by justices agreeing with majority, to share reasoning for vote
    - **Dissenting opinions** may be written as a way to preserve a record for possible future analysis

be closer than those in decades prior. As with other presidential nominees subject to Senate approval, federal judicial nominees have sometimes found their paths blocked by a filibuster or the threat of one. That obstacle began to go away in 2013 when a Democrat-controlled Senate changed the chamber's rules to prevent effective filibusters of federal district and appellate court judges. In 2017, a Republican-controlled Senate did the same for Supreme Court nominees.

PRESIDENTS BALANCE LEGAL AND POLITICAL CONSIDERATIONS IN MAKING SUPREME COURT NOMINATIONS. Unlike presidents and members of Congress, the Constitution places no requirements on the necessary qualifications to serve in the federal judiciary; judges do not even have to be lawyers. When vacancies occur in the Supreme Court, presidents are presented with an important, though challenging, opportunity to help shape policy for years to come. When the position of chief justice is vacant, a president may nominate a sitting member of the Court for that position and fill the newly vacant position of associate justice (which is how it usually happens), or the president may nominate an individual from outside the Court to the position of chief justice directly.

Because they are such high-profile appointments, nominees to the Court have to be weighed especially carefully. When choosing Court nominees, presidents have to balance both legal and political considerations. Experience, ethical integrity, and legal accomplishment are extremely important factors and can help smooth the confirmation process. Modern Court nominees will have typically already served in the federal judiciary or a similarly high-level position.

Presidents may also strive to nominate individuals who share their judicial philosophies and approaches to constitutional interpretation. Once confirmation occurs, however, presidents have no control over the behavior of their nominees. More than one president has successfully nominated an individual only to be surprised by some of that justice's later decisions. Political calculations come into play as well. Nominees who are considered outspoken on contentious political issues are likely to face careful scrutiny and intense questioning by senators concerned about these stances. As the Court, like Congress, still does not descriptively represent the American people, presidents may also consider nominating those with diverse backgrounds to the Court to make it more closely resemble a portrait of the nation.

WHAT HAVE I **LEARNED?**

1. The number of levels in the federal judiciary (aside from some smaller specialized courts) is _____.

   a. one

   b. two

   c. three

   d. four

2. The American court system is based on _____.

   a. the assumption that plaintiffs are guilty until proven innocent

   b. the notion that criminal law is more important than civil law

   c. an adversarial system of justice

   d. an informal system of rules

3. What considerations do Supreme Court justices take into account when deciding whether or not to grant cert?

4. What factors do presidents typically consider in making Supreme Court nominations?

Answer Key: 1. c; 2. c; 3. Answers should include whether or not the case involves a federal issue, the filing of briefs, conflict in the lower courts, and individual strategic considerations of justices; 4. Answers should cover both legal considerations (i.e., experience, ethical integrity, judicial philosophy or approach, and legal accomplishments) and political considerations (i.e., how likely it is that the candidate can get through confirmation).

JUDICIAL REVIEW RAISES QUESTIONS OF CONSTITUTIONAL INTERPRETATION AND JUDICIAL DECISION MAKING

- **Compare theories of judicial decision making as well as arguments for or against judicial restraint and activism in constitutional review.**

Since its inception, the federal judiciary itself has been on trial—in the court of constitutional law, political science, and American public opinion. The chief defendant in this long and sometimes contentious history has been the Supreme Court, and the primary behavior in question has been the use of judicial review. Four main problems lie at the heart of the issue.

The first, and potentially biggest, concern about judicial review arises from the fact that Supreme Court justices are not elected by the people but are appointed for life terms, removable only through the process of impeachment. In striking down state or federal laws, a small group of unelected justices can overturn acts passed by representatives who *were* elected. Alexander Bickel described the **countermajoritarian difficulty** in the exercise of judicial review: the worry that in striking down legislation, the Court "exercises control, not in behalf of the prevailing majority, but against it."[64]

This is precisely what President Thomas Jefferson warned about when he feared the judiciary would become a too powerful.[65]

Second, there is the concern that Americans may become less vigilant about who they elect, knowing that if they do a poor job in choosing their representatives, the Supreme Court will be there to bail them out. In modern terms, this is called the problem of moral hazard. The term comes from the concept of unwanted incentives created by having insurance. When a person is insured against bad outcomes from his or her own actions, then the person may take less care in avoiding those outcomes. By acting as a safety valve against poor, factious, or tyrannical legislation, the Court might actually make unwanted legislative outcomes more, not less, likely.

Third, the power of judicial review lies as much in its power to affirm as in its power to negate. In upholding the constitutionality of laws, the Supreme Court also exercises power over the legislative process by adding legitimacy in the minds of the American public to those laws passed by Congress.[66] In doing so, the Court risks validating laws that trample on the rights of minorities, thereby giving its stamp of approval to tyranny of the majority.

Finally, there exists the challenge inherent in interpreting and applying the Constitution to a variety of specific cases and circumstances across time and by individuals with their own opinions on what is or is not in accordance with the document, its language, and its intent. As James Thayer cautioned in an 1893 article, "much which will seem unconstitutional to one man, or body of men, may reasonably not seem so to another; [and] the constitution often admits of different interpretations."[67] To fully consider this issue, however, it is first necessary to explore in more detail how justices go about interpreting the Constitution and applying this highest law of the land to the cases brought before them.

JUSTICES TAKE SEVERAL APPROACHES TO CONSTITUTIONAL INTERPRETATION

Trying to figure out why justices vote the way they do on any specific case is very difficult, given all the factors that likely contribute to an individual justice's vote. However, political scientists have identified several models that describe different approaches to judicial decision making. While a justice may emphasize one approach more than others, these models are best thought of as elements in the overall process and not as exclusive approaches that a given justice will use only. Justices themselves likely combine several considerations when approaching a case, especially difficult ones involving constitutional interpretation.

THE LEGAL MODEL EMPHASIZES FACTS AND PREVIOUS DECISIONS. The legal model focuses on applying the law to the facts of the case. In this model, justices rely on

countermajoritarian difficulty
the concern that judicial review empowers the Supreme Court to overturn the will of the majority of citizens who have acted through their elected officials.

precedent—a previous decision on a similar case that serves as a basis for future decisions. When a justice follows precedent, he or she is said to be employing the doctrine of **stare decisis** (from the Latin "to stand by things decided").[68] All justices—even the ones who emphasize their own capacity to interpret the Constitution—are bound by and employ the legal model to some extent in their decisions. There is good reason for this. It is, after all, how the legal system operates; similar cases are supposed to be decided in similar ways. To do otherwise would bring an unacceptable lack of uniformity to the legal system. There is also, however, a more strategic concern. A Supreme Court that is constantly ignoring its own precedents would likely not retain much legitimacy and authority in the eyes of the American people. While all justices employ the legal model, especially when deciding criminal cases, when it comes to those cases with significant implications for public policy—when the constitutionality of laws is at stake—other models may factor into judicial decision making as well.

Some justices applying the legal model look to the written text of the Constitution and the intent of the Framers of the document for guidance rather than to their own interpretation of the document's intent. Proponents of original understanding (or originalism) argue that the process of constitutional amendment, not Supreme Court decisions, should be the primary way to make major changes in the fundamental law of the nation.

THE ATTITUDINAL MODEL EMPHASIZES POLICY PREFERENCES. The attitudinal model describes a process through which the political and policy preferences of individual justices shape their votes on cases rather than a neutral weighing of the facts and the law.[69] This model describes an overtly political approach to judicial decision making, one very far from Alexander Hamilton's reassurances about the nonpolitical federal judiciary in *Federalist* No. 78. Much of the research in this area has focused on explaining and predicting the votes of justices based on what we know about their political ideologies.[70] For scholars who emphasize the role of the individual attitudes and political ideologies of justices, the countermajoritarian difficulty can be especially worrisome. Not only can unelected justices strike down the will of the majority, but they may do so to advance their own political and policy agendas.

THE STRATEGIC MODEL EMPHASIZES STRATEGIC CALCULATION Finally, the strategic model portrays individual justices as strategic political actors who, according to political scientist Walter Murphy, try to make the best use of their "resources, official and personal, to achieve a particular set of policy objectives."[71] Strategic justices do more than just vote according to their individual preferences. They consider the likely behaviors of their fellow justices; understand the national political context and the system of shared powers in which their branch of government operates; and, when deciding how to act, "compute in terms of costs and revenues whether a particular choice is worth the price which is required to attain it."[72] Strategic considerations may shape whether or not a justice votes to grant cert,[73] how justices vote on cases before them, and how justices craft their opinions.[74] (See Figure 15.5.)

JUSTICES EXERCISE DEGREES OF JUDICIAL RESTRAINT AND JUDICIAL ACTIVISM

Related to the question of how justices make their decisions is the issue of how willing or reluctant they are to exercise the authority of judicial review. How eager, in other words, should the Court be to overturn the actions of the other two branches of government?

Proponents of **judicial restraint** argue that the Court should use this power rarely and whenever possible defer to the judgment of the legislative and executive branches on decisions that those branches have made. These proponents offer several justifications for their caution. First, they point to the dangers of the countermajoritarian difficulty and the potential antidemocratic consequences

stare decicis
a doctrine of constitutional interpretation based upon following earlier decisions in similar cases.

judicial restraint
a philosophy of constitutional interpretation that asserts justices should be cautious in overturning laws.

Theoretical Models of Constitutional Interpretation

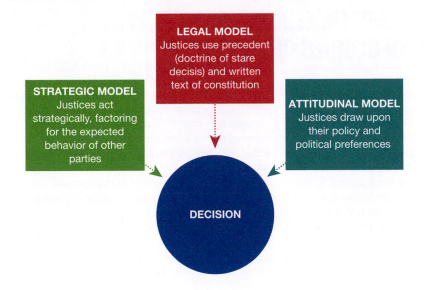

of unelected justices overturning the actions of elected representatives. In addition, the Supreme Court's voice in declaring a law to be unconstitutional is more authoritative when used sparingly, sending a clear signal in those times when it is employed. Finally, justices are legal and constitutional specialists; they are not policy specialists, nor are they clerks. The public policies that may be impacted by the use of judicial review may involve complex technical questions, the details of which justices may not fully understand.

Proponents of **judicial activism**, on the other hand, argue that justices should be willing to step in and overturn laws when they see a need to do so. Sometimes the other two branches may make mistakes or, worse, trample on individual rights and liberties. The very power that fuels concerns about the countermajoritarian difficulty—that the Court can strike down the will of the majority— also gives it the power to protect the rights of minorities. Proponents of activism point to times when the other two branches act in ways damaging to rights and liberties; they also point to the fact that these branches often do not act at all. Free from the need to be concerned about the popularity of their actions, Supreme Court justices can place on the agenda issues that Congress and the president are unwilling to tackle.

Judicial activism and restraint are not inherently linked to political liberalism or conservatism. During the 1960s, an activist and liberal Court used the power of judicial review to strike down state laws restricting the civil rights of Americans in areas such as education and voting. In the 1930s, however, the strongest opposition to President Franklin Roosevelt's efforts to employ the power of the federal government in his New Deal came from an activist, conservative Supreme Court willing to use the power of judicial review to oppose the reforms enacted by the president and members of his Democratic Party.

THE SUPREME COURT ACTS AS NATIONAL POLICYMAKER

No one branch of the federal government operates in a vacuum, and the federal judiciary, including the Supreme Court, is no exception. When the Court attempts to influence public policy, it does so in the face of multiple constraints on its independent use of authority, but its unique role within the system of shared powers offers it opportunities to shape policy in a way that the other two branches cannot.

judicial activism
a philosophy of constitutional interpretation that asserts justices should wield the power of judicial review when needed.

ANALYZING DATA ACROSS TIME: JUDICIAL REVIEW AND THE POLITICAL IDEOLOGIES OF JUSTICES

What role do the political ideologies of Supreme Court justices play in the willingness of justices to overturn federal or state laws? This is a very complex question that political scientists continue to debate. Part of the issue is actually measuring the political ideologies of justices, as they are not required to wear a label or announce to the world their personal politics. Many presidents are unhappily surprised to find that a justice they nominated has a different judicial philosophy than expected once the justice is on the Court and serving a lifetime term.

Using data from the Supreme Court Database—created and shared by a group of scholars—we can begin to explore this question. Figure 15-A displays the total number of cases in which the Court declared unconstitutional an act of Congress or a state or territorial law (or state constitutional provision) during a specific time in the Court's history: 1953–1968. These years cover the Warren Court, in which Earl Warren served as the chief justice. The Warren Court is often considered to be one of the most liberal Courts in the nation's history. The blue bars indicate a use of judicial review to overturn a law or provision in a liberal direction as defined by the scholars, and the green bars indicate a use that overturned a law in a conservative direction. The largest group of these decisions involved questions of civil rights, followed by First Amendment concerns.

▼ FIGURE 15-A

Liberal and Conservative Uses of Judicial Review in the Warren Court, 1953–1968

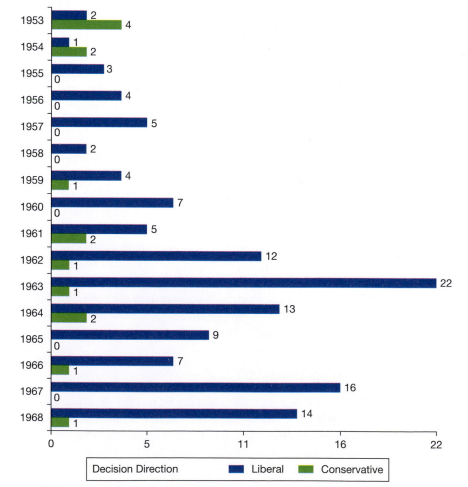

Decision Direction ■ Liberal ■ Conservative

Source: Data from Harold Spaeth et al., "2018 Supreme Court Database," accessed August 11, 2018, http://supremecourtdatabase.org.

Liberal and Conservative Uses of Judicial Review in the Hughes Court, 1929–1940

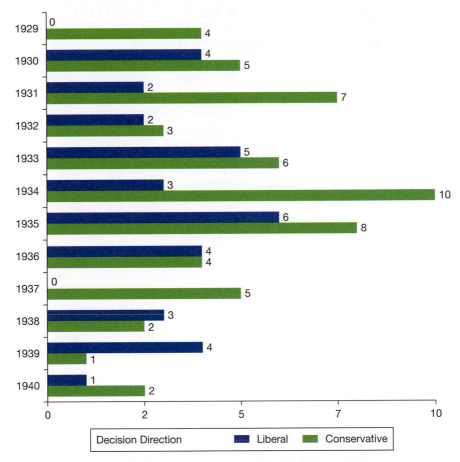

Source: Data from Harold Spaeth et al., "2018 Supreme Court Database," accessed August 11, 2018, http://supremecourtdatabase.org.

Based on Figure 15-A, one might infer that liberal justices are more likely to overturn federal or state laws than conservative justices, since nearly 90 percent of the decisions are in a liberal direction and the Court was considered to be composed of a majority of liberal justices.

However, it is important to remember that these data are from only one Supreme Court era. Figure 15-B presents a similar analysis; however, these data are from the tenure of Chief Justice Charles Evans Hughes when the Court was considered to be a very conservative one.[75] In contrast to the Warren Court, the majority of uses of judicial review to overturn federal or state laws in the Hughes Court era were conservative and focused primarily on economic activity and taxation policy. In terms of federal laws, many of these uses of judicial review focused on challenging President Roosevelt's New Deal, which we discussed in Chapter 3.

The data from Figure 15-B present a more complex picture of the connection between judicial ideology and the willingness of justices to overturn federal or state laws, especially before Roosevelt began a series of appointments (some of whom served on the Warren Court) in 1937. These data challenge the assertion that liberal justices are *necessarily* more likely to exercise judicial review to overturn federal or state laws than conservative ones. However, they do support the idea that the political ideologies of the justices *can* affect patterns of the use of judicial review. This important issue is one scholars will continue to examine.

• •

WHaT Do You Think?

To what extent do you think justices should or should not bring their own political views into the use of judicial review? What responsibility should the Senate exercise in trying to ascertain the politics of Supreme Court nominees during the confirmation proceedings?

THERE ARE LIMITATIONS ON THE POWER OF THE SUPREME COURT. One constraint on the power of the Court is the legal process itself. A Court, no matter how activist, cannot simply declare unconstitutional a law that it does not like. It can only rule on a specific case that has been properly filed and brought before it. Only plaintiffs who can demonstrate standing can bring suit in court, which requires that they demonstrate that they have been wronged by a law or action and that the law in question covers the interests the plaintiff alleges to have been violated or denied. Even when everything works efficiently, the process of moving a case through the federal judiciary takes time. When a case begins in a state judiciary, the process can take even longer.

The legislative and executive branches may also act as a check on the power of the federal judiciary. We have discussed the role of the president in nominating justices and that of the Senate in confirming them. We have also examined the role of Congress in setting the size of the Supreme Court and establishing other federal courts. Congress and the states may collectively amend the Constitution, the results of which are not subject to judicial review. In addition, the Court lacks the tools for implementing public policy and often must turn to the other two branches to add force to its rulings. When a Court goes against the will of the president or Congress, the other branches may be less than supportive in implementing the decisions or even might ignore or defy the Court entirely. Even when the other two branches do not openly defy the Supreme Court, their lack of support of its rulings can limit the Court's power in setting national policy.

Finally, although justices are appointed for life and do not need to worry about being reelected, they do operate in the American political system in which public opinion plays an important role. Political scientists continue to debate the degree to which Supreme Court justices attend to public opinion in crafting specific decisions; however, scholars agree that it is not something that can completely be ignored.[76] President Washington ensured that the first Court "contained judges from Massachusetts, New York, Pennsylvania, Virginia, Maryland, and South Carolina" to demonstrate to the experimental nation his commitment to ensuring representation from all parts of the country.[77]

Since the time of John Marshall, justices have had to attend to the fact that their power in exercising judicial review is tied to Americans' views of the legitimacy of their branch of government. It is no accident that of all the branches, only the federal judiciary, and the Supreme Court in particular, chooses to retain its costumes, secrecy, and traditional ways of doing things, as out of time as they may seem. The drama of the Court adds to its legitimacy in the view of the American people, and all justices—whatever their own political beliefs—know that they play a key role in preserving the story of the Court and its power.

ONE POWER THE SUPREME COURT HAS IS AGENDA SETTING. While the Supreme Court and the rest of the federal judiciary cannot act as all-powerful, unilateral makers of public policy, their particular position in the nation and the federal government does give them a unique role in American politics: that of setting the national agenda. Because they do not face elections like members of the other two branches, Supreme Court justices are able to bring up in the national conversation issues that need to be discussed. They can act in front of public opinion—perhaps not *too* far but far enough to force debate on the national stage. Recent Court rulings on marriage equality may be perfect examples of this power. In exercising this power, the Court may not necessarily be acting against the wishes of elected representatives, or at least of all of them. A member of Congress or a president who may be afraid to weigh in on an important and

▼ Missionary Samuel Worcester was arrested for residing within the limits of the Cherokee Nation without a license, thus violating a Georgia state law. The Marshall Court declared Georgia's law unconstitutional, but Georgia continued to enforce it regardless.

New Echota Historical Site

controversial issue out of fear of the backlash from public opinion can point to a Court decision and tell the American people they now have to act. Providing political cover for elected representatives who wish to act on an issue may be one of the most important powers of the unelected branch of government.

WHAT HAVE I **LEARNED?**

1. The term *countermajoritarian difficulty* refers to _____.
   a. the ability to impeach Supreme Court justices
   b. the fact that justices are not elected by the people
   c. congressional oversight of the Supreme Court
   d. presidential nominations of justices

2. What are some of the limitations on the power of the Supreme Court?

3. What are arguments made in support of judicial restraint? Of judicial activism?

Answer Key: 1. b; 2. Answers should include the fact that the Court decides only on cases before it, executive and legislative checks on its functioning, and the fact that it has few tools with which to implement public policy; 3. For restraint, answers should focus on the countermajoritarian difficulty, the fact that justices may not have policy expertise, and the risk of its overuse; for activism, answers should focus on the fact that Congress may not act in areas that it needs to and the danger of tyranny of the majority.

CONCLUSION: THE TRIAL OF THE SUPREME COURT CONTINUES

When moderate swing justice Anthony Kennedy announced his retirement in June 2018, it was known that the confirmation process for his replacement would be contentious. It proved to be far more than that. In the weeks leading up to the Senate confirmation vote and the midterm elections, Christine Blasey Ford, a California university psychology professor, and several other women alleged that the president's nominee, Judge Brett Kavanaugh, had sexually assaulted them decades prior. Kavanaugh's final vote was delayed a week for an additional FBI investigation into the allegations, though critics asserted that it was not thorough enough. In the end, Kavanaugh secured the confirmation by a 50–48 vote, the narrowest margin in more than a century.

In this chapter, we have explored two important and closely related questions: How political is the Court? And how powerful is it? In *Federalist* No. 78, Alexander Hamilton—a proponent of a strong national government—tried to reassure a skeptical confederation during the ratification debates that the Court was neither political nor powerful. History has proven Hamilton correct and incorrect on both counts.

The justices of the Supreme Court and the federal judiciary are not political in the ways that presidents, representatives, and senators are, in no small part because they do not have to worry about reelection. They must consider the facts of the case and the letter of the law when ruling on cases. Justices are, however, political people, and their personal views on issues may affect their decisions on impactful cases. They must always be strategic in understanding the role their institution plays in the system of separation of powers and in Americans' views on the legitimacy of the institution.

Theirs is a power that must be nurtured, cultivated, and protected, as John Marshall and subsequent members of the federal judiciary have had to learn. Compared to the legislative and executive branches, the power of the federal judiciary in national policymaking is much less imposing. It cannot write laws; it has no army. It has only the power of its decisions and the willingness of the people and the members of the other two branches to acquiesce to its decisions. It is not powerless; it is just different. How dangerous—or promising—this difference is continues to be a central subject of debate in American politics.

CHAPTER REVIEW

This chapter's main ideas are reflected in the Learning Objectives. By reviewing them here, you should be able to **remember** the key points, **know** the terms that are central to the topic, and **think** about the critical issues raised in each section.

15.1 Explore the role of politics in modern Supreme Court nomination proceedings.

REMEMBER
- Recent Supreme Court confirmation proceedings reveal the importance of the decision for political parties.
- Questions about how much justices should incorporate their own experiences and outlooks into their decisions have played a key role in confirmation debates.

KNOW
- federal judiciary (p. 413)
- Supreme Court (p. 413)

THINK
- What role do politics play in Supreme Court confirmation proceedings?
- How political should this process be?

15.2 Describe the structure and powers of the federal judiciary as laid out in the Constitution.

REMEMBER
- The Constitution contains less detail about the judiciary than about the legislative or executive branches, but it is clear that the Framers intended it to be the weakest of the three and also relatively independent of the other two.
- Article III does not expressly give the judiciary the power to strike down laws that it views as being in violation of the Constitution.

KNOW
- appellate jurisdiction (p. 418)
- original jurisdiction (p. 418)

THINK
- Do you think that the arguments for and against the proposed federal judiciary during the ratification debates are still relevant in the twenty-first century? Why or why not?

15.3 Explain John Marshall's development of judicial review in the Supreme Court decision in *Marbury v. Madison*.

REMEMBER
- In part of his ruling in *Marbury v. Madison*, Marshall found that part of the law that Marbury was basing his claim on, the Judiciary Act of 1789, was unconstitutional and thus unenforceable.
- Marshall, therefore, asserted that the Supreme Court had the power of judicial review over federal laws.

KNOW
- constitutional interpretation (p. 423)
- judicial review (p. 423)

THINK
- Was Chief Justice John Marshall acting politically? Can politics be kept out of the federal judiciary? Should it?

15.4 Describe the structure of the American legal system and the federal judiciary.

REMEMBER
- All courts in the American system are based on the adversarial system, with plaintiffs and defendants arguing their opposing sides of the case in the most persuasive way possible.
- Criminal law covers actions determined to harm the community itself, whereas civil law covers cases involving private rights and relationships between individuals and groups.
- The federal judiciary is composed of constitutional courts and specialized legislative courts. The constitutional courts are organized into three levels: federal district courts, the federal court of appeals, and the Supreme Court.

KNOW
- adversarial system (p. 424)
- brief (p. 429)
- civil law (p. 424)
- criminal law (p. 424)
- defendant (p. 424)
- federal courts of appeals (p. 426)
- federal district courts (p. 426)
- oral arguments (p. 429)
- plaintiff (p. 424)
- plea bargaining (p. 424)
- precedent (p. 429)
- solicitor general (p. 429)
- standing (p. 429)
- writ of certiorari (p. 429)

THINK
- What do you think are some of the most important constitutional questions today?

15.5 Compare theories of judicial decision making as well as arguments for or against judicial restraint and activism in constitutional review.

REMEMBER
- Judicial review raises a series of questions concerning the scope of powers of an unelected group of justices; citizen neglect of civic responsivity; the potential of validating laws that trample on the rights of minorities; and challenges of interpretation and application of the Constitution.
- There are three main models of constitutional interpretation: legal, attitudinal, and strategic.
- Justices may diverge in their approach to decision making, showing either judicial restraint or judicial activism.

KNOW
- countermajoritarian difficulty (p. 433)
- judicial activism (p. 435)
- judicial restraint (p. 434)
- stare decisis (p. 434)

THINK
- What approach or approaches to constitutional interpretation do you think justices should follow?

APPENDIX 1
Articles of Confederation

To all to whom these Presents shall come, we the undersigned Delegates of the States affixed to our Names send greeting.

Articles of Confederation and perpetual Union between the states of New Hampshire, Massachusetts-bay Rhode Island and Providence Plantations, Connecticut, New York, New Jersey, Pennsylvania, Delaware, Maryland, Virginia, North Carolina, South Carolina and Georgia.

ARTICLE I

The Stile of this Confederacy shall be "The United States of America".

ARTICLE II

Each state retains its sovereignty, freedom, and independence, and every power, jurisdiction, and right, which is not by this Confederation expressly delegated to the United States, in Congress assembled.

ARTICLE III

The said States hereby severally enter into a firm league of friendship with each other, for their common defense, the security of their liberties, and their mutual and general welfare, binding themselves to assist each other, against all force offered to, or attacks made upon them, or any of them, on account of religion, sovereignty, trade, or any other pretense whatever.

ARTICLE IV

The better to secure and perpetuate mutual friendship and intercourse among the people of the different States in this Union, the free inhabitants of each of these States, paupers, vagabonds, and fugitives from justice excepted, shall be entitled to all privileges and immunities of free citizens in the several States; and the people of each State shall free ingress and regress to and from any other State, and shall enjoy therein all the privileges of trade and commerce, subject to the same duties, impositions, and restrictions as the inhabitants thereof respectively, provided that such restrictions shall not extend so far as to prevent the removal of property imported into any State, to any other State, of which the owner is an inhabitant; provided also that no imposition, duties or restriction shall be laid by any State, on the property of the United States, or either of them.

If any person guilty of, or charged with, treason, felony, or other high misdemeanor in any State, shall flee from justice, and be found in any of the United States, he shall, upon demand of the Governor or executive power of the State from which he fled, be delivered up and removed to the State having jurisdiction of his offense.

Full faith and credit shall be given in each of these States to the records, acts, and judicial proceedings of the courts and magistrates of every other State.

ARTICLE V

For the most convenient management of the general interests of the United States, delegates shall be annually appointed in such manner as the legislatures of each State shall direct, to meet in Congress on the first Monday in November, in every year, with a power reserved to each State to recall its delegates, or any of them, at any time within the year, and to send others in their stead for the remainder of the year.

No State shall be represented in Congress by less than two, nor more than seven members; and no person shall be capable of being a delegate for more than three years in any term of six years; nor shall any person, being a delegate, be capable of holding any office under the United States, for which he, or another for his benefit, receives any salary, fees or emolument of any kind.

Each State shall maintain its own delegates in a meeting of the States, and while they act as members of the committee of the States.

In determining questions in the United States in Congress assembled, each State shall have one vote.

Freedom of speech and debate in Congress shall not be impeached or questioned in any court or place out of Congress, and the members of Congress shall be protected in their persons from arrests or imprisonments, during the time of their going to and from, and attendance on Congress, except for treason, felony, or breach of the peace.

ARTICLE VI

No State, without the consent of the United States in Congress assembled, shall send any embassy to, or receive any embassy from, or enter into any conference, agreement, alliance or treaty with any King, Prince or State; nor shall any person holding any office of profit or trust under the United States, or any of them, accept any present, emolument, office or title of any kind whatever from any King, Prince or foreign State; nor shall the United States in Congress assembled, or any of them, grant any title of nobility.

No two or more States shall enter into any treaty, confederation or alliance whatever between them, without the consent of the United States in Congress assembled, specifying accurately the purposes for which the same is to be entered into, and how long it shall continue.

No State shall lay any imposts or duties, which may interfere with any stipulations in treaties, entered into by the United States in Congress assembled, with any King, Prince or State, in pursuance of any treaties already proposed by Congress, to the courts of France and Spain.

No vessel of war shall be kept up in time of peace by any State, except such number only, as shall be deemed necessary by the United States in Congress assembled, for the defense of such State, or its trade; nor shall any body of forces be kept up by any State in time of peace, except such number only, as in the judgement of the United States in Congress assembled, shall be deemed requisite to garrison the forts necessary for the defense of such State; but every State shall always keep up a well-regulated and disciplined militia, sufficiently armed and accoutered, and shall provide and constantly have ready for use, in public stores, a due number of filed pieces and tents, and a proper quantity of arms, ammunition and camp equipage.

No State shall engage in any war without the consent of the United States in Congress assembled, unless such State be actually invaded by enemies, or shall have received certain advice of a resolution being formed by some nation of Indians to invade such State, and the danger is so imminent as not to admit of a delay till the United States in Congress assembled can be consulted; nor shall any State grant commissions to any ships or vessels of war, nor letters of marque or reprisal, except it be after a declaration of war by the United States in Congress assembled, and then only against the Kingdom or State and the subjects thereof, against which war has been so declared, and under such regulations as shall be established by the United States in Congress assembled, unless such State be infested by pirates, in which case vessels of war may be fitted out for that occasion, and kept so long as the danger shall continue, or until the United States in Congress assembled shall determine otherwise.

ARTICLE VII

When land forces are raised by any State for the common defense, all officers of or under the rank of colonel, shall be appointed by the legislature of each State respectively, by whom such forces shall be raised, or in such manner as such State shall direct, and all vacancies shall be filled up by the State which first made the appointment.

ARTICLE VIII

All charges of war, and all other expenses that shall be incurred for the common defense or general welfare, and allowed by the United States in Congress assembled, shall be defrayed out of a common treasury, which shall be supplied by the several States in proportion to the value of all land within each State, granted or surveyed for any person, as such land and the buildings and improvements thereon shall be estimated according to such mode as the United States in Congress assembled, shall from time to time direct and appoint.

The taxes for paying that proportion shall be laid and levied by the authority and direction of the legislatures of the several States within the time agreed upon by the United States in Congress assembled.

ARTICLE IX

The United States in Congress assembled, shall have the sole and exclusive right and power of determining on peace and war, except in the cases mentioned in the sixth article—of sending and receiving ambassadors—entering into treaties and alliances, provided that no treaty of commerce shall be made whereby the legislative power of the respective States shall be restrained from imposing such imposts and duties on foreigners, as their own people are subjected to, or from prohibiting the exportation or importation of any species of goods or commodities whatsoever—of establishing rules for deciding in all cases, what captures on land or water shall be legal, and in what manner prizes taken by land or naval forces in the service of the United States shall be divided or appropriated—of granting letters of marque and reprisal in times of peace—appointing courts for the trial of piracies and felonies committed on the high seas and establishing courts for receiving and determining finally appeals in all cases of captures, provided that no member of Congress shall be appointed a judge of any of the said courts.

The United States in Congress assembled shall also be the last resort on appeal in all disputes and differences now subsisting or that hereafter may arise between two or more States concerning boundary, jurisdiction or any other causes whatever; which authority shall always be exercised in the manner following. Whenever the legislative or executive authority or lawful agent of any State in controversy with another shall present a petition to Congress stating the matter in question and praying for a hearing, notice thereof shall be given by order of Congress to the legislative or executive authority of the other State in controversy, and a day assigned for the appearance of the parties by their lawful agents, who shall then be directed to appoint by joint consent, commissioners or judges to constitute a court for hearing and determining the matter in question: but if they cannot agree, Congress shall name three persons out of each of the United States, and from the list of such persons each party shall alternately strike out one, the petitioners beginning, until the number shall be reduced to thirteen; and from that number not less than seven, nor more than nine names as Congress shall direct, shall in the presence of Congress be drawn out by lot, and the persons whose names shall be so drawn or any five of them, shall be commissioners or judges, to hear and finally determine the controversy, so always as a major part of the judges who shall hear the cause shall agree in the determination: and if either party shall neglect to attend at the day appointed, without showing reasons, which Congress shall judge sufficient, or being present shall refuse to strike, the Congress shall proceed to nominate three persons out of each State, and the secretary of Congress shall strike in behalf of such party absent or refusing; and the judgement and sentence of the court to be appointed, in the manner before prescribed, shall be final and conclusive; and if any of the parties shall refuse to submit to the authority of such court, or to appear or defend their claim or cause, the court shall nevertheless proceed to pronounce sentence, or judgement, which shall in like manner be final and decisive, the judgement or sentence and other proceedings being in either case transmitted to Congress, and lodged among the acts of Congress for the security of the parties concerned: provided that every commissioner, before he sits in judgement, shall take an oath to be administered by one of the judges of the supreme or superior court of the State, where the cause shall be tried, 'well and truly to hear and determine the matter in question, according to the best of his judgement, without favor, affection or hope of reward': provided also, that no State shall be deprived of territory for the benefit of the United States.

All controversies concerning the private right of soil claimed under different grants of two or more States, whose jurisdictions as they may respect such lands, and the States which passed such grants are adjusted, the said grants or either of them being at the same time claimed to have originated antecedent to such settlement of jurisdiction, shall on the petition of either party to the Congress of the United States, be finally determined as near as may be in the same manner as is before prescribed for deciding disputes respecting territorial jurisdiction between different States.

The United States in Congress assembled shall also have the sole and exclusive right and power of regulating the alloy and value of coin struck by their own authority, or by that of the respective States—fixing the standards of weights and measures throughout the United States—regulating the trade and managing all affairs with the Indians, not members of any of the States, provided that the legislative right of any State within its own limits be not infringed or violated—establishing or regulating post offices from one State to another, throughout all the United States, and exacting such postage on the papers passing through the same as may be requisite to defray the expenses of the said office—appointing all officers of the land forces, in the service of the United States, excepting regimental officers—appointing all the officers of the naval forces, and commissioning all officers whatever in the service of the United States—making rules for the government and regulation of the said land and naval forces, and directing their operations.

The United States in Congress assembled shall have authority to appoint a committee, to sit in the recess of Congress, to be denominated 'A Committee of the States', and to consist of one delegate from each State; and to appoint such other committees and civil officers as may be necessary for managing the general affairs of the United States under their direction—to appoint one of their members to preside, provided that no person be allowed to serve in the office of president more than one year in any term of three years; to ascertain the necessary sums of money to be raised for the service of the United States, and to appropriate and apply the same for defraying the public expenses—to borrow money, or emit bills on the credit of the United States, transmitting every half-year to the respective States an account of the sums of money so borrowed or emitted—to build and equip a navy—to agree upon the number of land forces, and to make requisitions from each State for its quota, in proportion to the number of white inhabitants in such State; which requisition shall be binding, and thereupon the legislature of each State shall appoint the regimental officers, raise the men and cloath, arm and equip them in a solid-like manner, at the expense of the United States; and the officers and men so cloathed, armed and equipped shall march to the place appointed, and within the time agreed on by the United States in Congress assembled. But if the United States in Congress assembled shall, on consideration of circumstances judge proper that any State should not raise men, or should raise a smaller number of men than the quota thereof, such extra number shall be raised, officered, cloathed, armed and equipped in the same manner as the quota of each State, unless the legislature of such State shall judge that such extra number cannot be safely spread out in the same, in which case they shall raise, officer, cloath, arm and equip as many of such extra number as they judge can be safely spared. And the officers and men so cloathed, armed, and equipped, shall march to the place appointed, and within the time agreed on by the United States in Congress assembled.

The United States in Congress assembled shall never engage in a war, nor grant letters of marque or reprisal in time of peace, nor enter into any treaties or alliances, nor coin money, nor regulate the value thereof, nor ascertain the sums and expenses necessary for the defense and welfare of the United States, or any of them, nor emit bills, nor borrow money on the credit of the United States, nor appropriate money, nor agree upon the number of vessels of war, to be built or purchased, or the number of land or sea forces to be raised, nor appoint a commander in chief of the army or navy, unless nine States assent to the same: nor shall a question on any other point, except for adjourning from day to day be determined, unless by the votes of the majority of the United States in Congress assembled.

The Congress of the United States shall have power to adjourn to any time within the year, and to any place within the United States, so that no period of adjournment be for a longer duration than the space of six months, and shall publish the journal of their proceedings monthly, except such parts thereof relating to treaties, alliances or military operations, as in their judgement require secrecy; and the yeas and nays of the delegates of each State on any question shall be entered on the journal, when it is desired by any delegates of a State, or any of them, at his or their request shall be furnished with a transcript of the said journal, except such parts as are above excepted, to lay before the legislatures of the several States.

ARTICLE X

The Committee of the States, or any nine of them, shall be authorized to execute, in the recess of Congress, such of the powers of Congress as the United States in Congress assembled, by the consent of the nine States, shall from time to time think expedient to vest them with; provided that no power be delegated to the said Committee, for the exercise of which, by the Articles of Confederation, the voice of nine States in the Congress of the United States assembled be requisite.

ARTICLE XI

Canada acceding to this confederation, and adjoining in the measures of the United States, shall be admitted into, and entitled to all the advantages of this Union; but no other colony shall be admitted into the same, unless such admission be agreed to by nine States.

ARTICLE XII

All bills of credit emitted, monies borrowed, and debts contracted by, or under the authority of Congress, before the assembling of the United States, in pursuance of the present confederation, shall be deemed and considered as a charge against the United States, for payment and satisfaction whereof the said United States, and the public faith are hereby solemnly pledged.

ARTICLE XIII

Every State shall abide by the determination of the United States in Congress assembled, on all questions which by this confederation are submitted to them. And the Articles of this Confederation shall be inviolably observed by every State, and the Union shall be perpetual; nor shall any alteration at any time hereafter be made in any of them; unless such alteration be agreed to in a Congress of the United States, and be afterwards confirmed by the legislatures of every State.

And Whereas it hath pleased the Great Governor of the World to incline the hearts of the legislatures we respectively represent in Congress, to approve of, and to authorize us to ratify the said Articles of Confederation and perpetual Union. Know Ye that we the undersigned delegates, by virtue of the power and authority to us given for that purpose, do by these presents, in the name and in behalf of our respective constituents, fully and entirely ratify and confirm each and every of the said Articles of Confederation and perpetual Union, and all and singular the matters and things therein contained: And we do further solemnly plight and engage the faith of our respective constituents, that they shall abide by the determinations of the United States in Congress assembled, on all questions, which by the said Confederation are submitted to them. And that the Articles thereof shall be inviolably observed by the States we respectively represent, and that the Union shall be perpetual.

In Witness whereof we have hereunto set our hands in Congress. Done at Philadelphia in the State of Pennsylvania the ninth day of July in the Year of our Lord One Thousand Seven Hundred and Seventy-Eight, and in the Third Year of the independence of America.

Agreed to by Congress 15 November 1777

In force after ratification by Maryland, 1 March 1781

APPENDIX 2

Declaration of Independence

On June 11, 1776, the responsibility to "prepare a decla-ration" of independence was assigned by the Continental Congress, meeting in Philadelphia, to five members: John Adams, Benjamin Franklin, Thomas Jefferson, Robert Livingston, and Roger Sherman. Impressed by his talents as a writer, the committee asked Jefferson to compose a draft. After modifying Jefferson's draft, the committee turned it over to Congress on June 28. On July 2, Congress voted to declare independence; on the evening of July 4, it approved the Declaration of Independence.

In Congress, July 4, 1776,

The Unanimous Declaration of the Thirteen United States of America,

When in the Course of human events, it becomes necessary for one people to dissolve the political bands which have connected them with another, and to assume among the Powers of the earth, the separate and equal station to which the Laws of Nature and of Nature's God entitle them, a decent respect to the opinions of mankind requires that they should declare the causes which impel them to the separation.

We hold these truths to be self-evident, that all men are created equal, that they are endowed by their Creator with certain unalienable Rights, that among these are Life, Liberty and the pursuit of Happiness. That to secure these rights, Governments are instituted among Men, deriving their just powers from the consent of the governed. That whenever any form of Government becomes destructive of these ends, it is the Right of the People to alter or to abolish it, and to institute new Government, laying its foundation on such principles and organizing its powers in such form, as to them shall seem most likely to effect their Safety and Happiness. Prudence, indeed, will dictate that Government long established should not be changed for light and transient causes; and accordingly all experience hath shown, that mankind are more disposed to suffer, while evils are sufferable, than to right themselves by abolishing the forms to which they are accustomed. But when a long train of abuses and usurpations, pursuing invariably the same Object evinces a design to reduce them under absolute Despotism, it is their right, it is their duty, to throw off such Government, and to provide new Guards for their future security. Such has been the patient sufferance of these Colonies; and such is now the necessity which constrains them to alter their former Systems of Government. The history of the present King of Great Britain is a history of repeated injuries and usurpations, all having in direct object the establishment of an absolute Tyranny over these States. To prove this, let Facts be submitted to a candid world.

He has refused his Assent to Laws, the most wholesome and necessary for the public good.

He has forbidden his Governors to pass Laws of immediate and pressing importance, unless suspended in their operation till his Assent should be obtained; and when so suspended, he has utterly neglected to attend to them.

He has refused to pass other Laws for the accommodation of large districts of people, unless those people would relinquish the right of Representation in the Legislature, a right inestimable to them and formidable to tyrants only.

He has called together legislative bodies at places unusual, uncomfortable, and distant from the depository of their Public Records, for the sole purpose of fatiguing them into compliance with his measures.

He has dissolved Representative Houses repeatedly, for opposing with manly firmness his invasions on the rights of the people.

He has refused for a long time, after such dissolutions, to cause others to be elected; whereby the Legislative Powers, incapable of Annihilation, have returned to the People at large for their exercise; the State remaining in the mean time exposed to all the dangers of invasion from without, and convulsions within.

He has endeavored to prevent the population of these States; for that purpose obstructing the Laws of Naturalization of Foreigners; refusing to pass others to encourage their migration hither, and raising the conditions of new Appropriations of Lands.

He has obstructed the Administration of Justice, by refusing his Assent to Laws for establishing Judiciary Powers.

He has made Judges dependent on his Will alone, for the tenure of their offices, and the amount and payment of their salaries.

He has erected a multitude of New Offices, and sent hither swarms of Officers to harass our People, and eat out their substance.

He has kept among us, in times of peace, Standing Armies without the Consent of our legislature.

He has affected to render the Military independent of and superior to the Civil Power.

He has combined with others to subject us to a jurisdiction foreign to our constitution, and unacknowledged by our laws; giving his Assent to their acts of pretended legislation:

For quartering large bodies of armed troops among us:

For protecting them, by a mock Trial, from Punishment for any Murders which they should commit on the Inhabitants of these States:

For cutting off our Trade with all parts of the world:

For imposing taxes on us without our Consent:

For depriving us in many cases, of the benefits of Trial by Jury:

For transporting us beyond Seas to be tried for pretended offences:

For abolishing the free System of English Laws in a neighbouring Province, establishing therein an Arbitrary government, and enlarging its Boundaries so as to render it at once an example and fit instrument for introducing the same absolute rule into these Colonies:

For taking away our Charters, abolishing our most valuable Laws, and altering fundamentally the Forms of our Governments:

For suspending our own Legislature, and declaring themselves invested with Power to legislate for us in all cases whatsoever.

He has abdicated Government here, by declaring us out of his Protection and waging War against us.

He has plundered our seas, ravaged our Coasts, burnt our towns, and destroyed the lives of our people.

He is at this time transporting large armies of foreign mercenaries to compleat the works of death, desolation and tyranny, already begun with circumstances of Cruelty & perfidy scarcely parallel in the most barbarous ages, and totally unworthy the Head of a civilized nation.

He has constrained our fellow Citizens taken Captive on the high Seas to bear Arms against their Country, to become the executioners of their friends and Brethren, or to fall themselves by their Hands.

He has excited domestic insurrections amongst us, and has endeavoured to bring on the inhabitants of our frontiers, the merciless Indian Savages, whose known rule of warfare, is an undistinguished destruction of all ages, sexes and conditions.

In every stage of these Oppressions We have Petitioned for Redress in the most humble terms: Our repeated Petitions have been answered only by repeated injury. A Prince, whose character is thus marked by every act which may define a Tyrant, is unfit to be the ruler of a free People.

Nor have We been wanting in attention to our British brethren. We have warned them from time to time of attempts by their legislature to extend an unwarrantable jurisdiction over us. We have reminded them of the circumstances of our emigration and settlement here. We have appealed to their native justice and magnanimity, and we have conjured them by the ties of our common kindred to disavow these usurpations, which would inevitably interrupt our connections and correspondence. They too have been deaf to the voice of justice and of consanguinity. We must, therefore, acquiesce in the necessity, which denounces our Separation, and hold them, as we hold the rest of mankind, Enemies in War, in Peace Friends.

We, therefore, the Representatives of the United States of America, in General Congress, Assembled, appealing to the Supreme Judge of the world for the rectitude of our intentions, do, in the Name, and by Authority of the good People of these Colonies, solemnly publish and declare, That these United Colonies are, and of Right ought to be Free and Independent States; that they are Absolved from all Allegiance to the British Crown, and that all political connection between them and the State of Great Britain, is and ought to be totally dissolved; and that as Free and Independent States, they have full Power to levy War, conclude Peace, contract Alliances, establish Commerce, and to do all other Acts and Things which Independent States may of right do. And for the support of this Declaration, with a firm reliance on the Protection of Divine Providence, we mutually pledge to each other our Lives, our Fortunes and our sacred Honor.

John Hancock.

New Hampshire:
Josiah Bartlett,
William Whipple,
Matthew Thornton.

Massachusetts-Bay:
Samuel Adams,
John Adams,
Robert Treat Paine,
Elbridge Gerry.

Rhode Island:
Stephen Hopkins,
William Ellery.

Connecticut:
Roger Sherman,

Samuel Huntington,
William Williams,
Oliver Wolcott.

New York:
William Floyd,
Philip Livingston,
Francis Lewis,
Lewis Morris.

Pennsylvania:
Robert Morris,
Benjamin Harris,
Benjamin Franklin,
John Morton,
George Clymer,

James Smith,

George Taylor,

James Wilson,

George Ross.

Delaware:

Caesar Rodney,

George Read,

Thomas McKean.

Georgia:

Button Gwinnett,

Lyman Hall,

George Walton.

Maryland:

Samuel Chase,

William Paca,

Thomas Stone,

Charles Carroll of Carrollton.

Virginia:

George Wythe,

Richard Henry Lee,

Thomas Jefferson,

Benjamin Harrison,

Thomas Nelson Jr.,

Francis Lightfoot Lee,

Carter Braxton.

North Carolina:

William Hooper,

Joseph Hewes,

John Penn.

South Carolina:

Edward Rutledge,

Thomas Heyward Jr.,

Thomas Lynch Jr.,

Arthur Middleton.

New Jersey:

Richard Stockton,

John Witherspoon,

Francis Hopkinson,

John Hart,

Abraham Clark.

APPENDIX 3

Constitution of the United States

The U.S. Constitution was written at a convention that Congress called on February 21, 1787, for the purpose of recommending amendments to the Articles of Confederation. Every state but Rhode Island sent delegates to Philadelphia, where the convention met that summer. The delegates decided to write an entirely new constitution, completing their labors on September 17. Nine states (the number the Constitution itself stipulated as sufficient) ratified by June 21, 1788.

The Framers of the Constitution included only six paragraphs on the Supreme Court. Article III, Section 1, created the Supreme Court and the federal system of courts. It provided that "[t]he judicial power of the United States, shall be vested in one supreme Court," and whatever inferior courts Congress "from time to time" saw fit to establish. Article III, Section 2, delineated the types of cases and controversies that should be considered by a federal—rather than a state—court. But beyond this, the Constitution left many of the particulars of the Supreme Court and the federal court system for Congress to decide in later years in judiciary acts.

We the People of the United States, in Order to form a more perfect Union, establish Justice, insure domestic Tranquility, provide for the common defence, promote the general Welfare, and secure the Blessings of Liberty to ourselves and our Posterity, do ordain and establish this Constitution for the United States of America.

ARTICLE I

Section 1. All legislative Powers herein granted shall be vested in a Congress of the United States, which shall consist of a Senate and House of Representatives.

Section 2. The House of Representatives shall be composed of Members chosen every second Year by the People of the several States, and the Electors in each State shall have the Qualifications requisite for Electors of the most numerous Branch of the State Legislature.

No Person shall be a Representative who shall not have attained to the age of twenty five Years, and been seven Years a Citizen of the United States, and who shall not, when elected, be an Inhabitant of that State in which he shall be chosen.

*Representatives and direct Taxes shall be apportioned among the several States which may be included within this Union, according to their respective Numbers, which shall be determined by adding to the whole Number of free Persons, including those bound to Service for a Term of Years, and excluding Indians not taxed, three fifths of all other Persons.[*1] The actual Enumeration shall be made within three Years after the first Meeting of the Congress of the United States, and within every subsequent Term of ten Years, in such Manner as they shall by Law direct. The Number of Representatives shall not exceed one for every thirty Thousand, but each State shall have at Least one Representative; and until such enumeration shall be made, the State of New Hampshire shall be entitled to chuse three, Massachusetts eight, Rhode-Island and Providence Plantations one, Connecticut five, New-York six, New Jersey four, Pennsylvania eight, Delaware one, Maryland six, Virginia ten, North Carolina five, South Carolina five, and Georgia three.

When vacancies happen in the Representation from any State, the Executive Authority thereof shall issue Writs of Election to fill such Vacancies.

The House of Representatives shall chuse their Speaker and other Officers; and shall have the sole Power of Impeachment.

Section 3. The Senate of the United States shall be composed of two Senators from each State, *chosen by the Legislature thereof,[*2] for six Years; and each Senator shall have one Vote.

Immediately after they shall be assembled in Consequence of the first Election, they shall be divided as equally as may be into three Classes. The Seats of the Senators of the first Class shall be vacated at the Expiration of the second Year, of the second Class at the Expiration of the fourth Year, and of the third Class at the Expiration of the sixth Year, so that one third may be chosen every second Year; *and if Vacancies happen by Resignation, or otherwise, during the Recess of the Legislature of any State, the Executive thereof may make temporary Appointments until the next Meeting of the Legislature, which shall then fill such Vacancies.[*3]

No Person shall be a Senator who shall not have attained to the Age of thirty Years, and been nine Years a Citizen of the

United States, and who shall not, when elected, be an Inhabitant of that State for which he shall be chosen.

The Vice President of the United States shall be President of the Senate, but shall have no Vote, unless they be equally divided.

The Senate shall chuse their other Officers, and also a President pro tempore, in the Absence of the Vice President, or when he shall exercise the Office of President of the United States.

The Senate shall have the sole Power to try all Impeachments. When sitting for that Purpose, they shall be on Oath or Affirmation. When the President of the United States is tried, the Chief Justice shall preside: And no Person shall be convicted without the Concurrence of two thirds of the Members present.

Judgment in Cases of Impeachment shall not extend further than to removal from Office, and disqualification to hold and enjoy any Office of honor, Trust or Profit under the United States: but the Party convicted shall nevertheless be liable and subject to Indictment, Trial, Judgment and Punishment, according to Law.

Section 4. The Times, Places and Manner of holding Elections for Senators and Representatives, shall be prescribed in each State by the Legislature thereof; but the Congress may at any time by Law make or alter such Regulations, except as to the Places of chusing Senators.

The Congress shall assemble at least once in every Year, and such Meeting shall ★be on the first Monday in December★,[4] unless they shall by Law appoint a different Day.

Section 5. Each House shall be the Judge of the Elections, Returns and Qualifications of its own Members, and a Majority of each shall constitute a Quorum to do Business; but a smaller Number may adjourn from day to day, and may be authorized to compel the Attendance of absent Members, in such Manner, and under such Penalties as each House may provide.

Each House may determine the Rules of its Proceedings, punish its Members for disorderly Behaviour, and, with the Concurrence of two thirds, expel a Member.

Each House shall keep a Journal of its Proceedings, and from time to time publish the same, excepting such Parts as may in their Judgment require Secrecy; and the Yeas and Nays of the Members of either House on any question shall, at the Desire of one fifth of those Present, be entered on the Journal.

Neither House, during the Session of Congress, shall, without the Consent of the other, adjourn for more than three days, nor to any other Place than that in which the two Houses shall be sitting.

Section 6. The Senators and Representatives shall receive a Compensation for their Services, to be ascertained by Law, and paid out of the Treasury of the United States. They shall in all Cases, except Treason, Felony and Breach of the Peace, be privileged from Arrest during their Attendance at the Session of their respective Houses, and in going to and returning from the same; and for any Speech or Debate in either House, they shall not be questioned in any other Place.

No Senator or Representative shall, during the Time for which he was elected, be appointed to any civil Office under the Authority of the United States, which shall have been created, or the Emoluments whereof shall have been encreased during such time; and no Person holding any Office under the United States, shall be a Member of either House during his Continuance in Office.

Section 7. All Bills for raising Revenue shall originate in the House of Representatives; but the Senate may propose or concur with Amendments as on other Bills.

Every Bill which shall have passed the House of Representatives and the Senate, shall, before it become a Law, be presented to the President of the United States; If he approve he shall sign it, but if not he shall return it, with his Objections to that House in which it shall have originated, who shall enter the Objections at large on their Journal, and proceed to reconsider it. If after such Reconsideration two thirds of that House shall agree to pass the Bill, it shall be sent, together with the Objections, to the other House, by which it shall likewise be reconsidered, and if approved by two thirds of that House, it shall become a Law. But in all such Cases the Votes of both Houses shall be determined by yeas and Nays, and the Names of the Persons voting for and against the Bill shall be entered on the Journal of each House respectively. If any Bill shall not be returned by the President within ten Days (Sundays excepted) after it shall have been presented to him, the Same shall be a Law, in like Manner as if he had signed it, unless the Congress by their Adjournment prevent its Return, in which Case it shall not be a Law.

Every Order, Resolution, or Vote to which the Concurrence of the Senate and House of Representatives may be necessary (except on a question of Adjournment) shall be presented to the President of the United States; and before the Same shall take Effect, shall be approved by him, or being disapproved by him, shall be repassed by two thirds of the Senate and House of Representatives, according to the Rules and Limitations prescribed in the Case of a Bill.

Section 8. The Congress shall have Power To lay and collect Taxes, Duties, Imposts and Excises, to pay the Debts and provide for the common Defence and general Welfare of the United States; but all Duties, Imposts and Excises shall be uniform throughout the United States;

To borrow Money on the credit of the United States;

To regulate Commerce with foreign Nations, and among the several States, and with the Indian Tribes;

To establish an uniform Rule of Naturalization, and uniform Laws on the subject of Bankruptcies throughout the United States;

To coin Money, regulate the Value thereof, and of foreign Coin, and fix the Standard of Weights and Measures;

To provide for the Punishment of counterfeiting the Securities and current Coin of the United States;

To establish Post Offices and post Roads;

To promote the Progress of Science and useful Arts, by securing for limited Times to Authors and Inventors the exclusive Right to their respective Writings and Discoveries;

To constitute Tribunals inferior to the supreme Court;

To define and punish Piracies and Felonies committed on the high Seas, and Offences against the Law of Nations;

To declare War, grant Letters of Marque and Reprisal, and make Rules concerning Captures on Land and Water;

To raise and support Armies, but no Appropriation of Money to that Use shall be for a longer Term than two Years;

To provide and maintain a Navy;

To make Rules for the Government and Regulation of the land and naval Forces;

To provide for calling forth the Militia to execute the Laws of the Union, suppress Insurrections and repel Invasions;

To provide for organizing, arming, and disciplining, the Militia, and for governing such Part of them as may be employed in the Service of the United States, reserving to the States respectively, the Appointment of the Officers, and the Authority of training the Militia according to the discipline prescribed by Congress;

To exercise exclusive Legislation in all Cases whatsoever, over such District (not exceeding ten Miles square) as may, by Cession of particular States, and the Acceptance of Congress, become the Seat of the Government of the United States, and to exercise like Authority over all Places purchased by the Consent of the Legislature of the State in which the Same shall be, for the Erection of Forts, Magazines, Arsenals, dock-Yards, and other needful Buildings;—And

To make all Laws which shall be necessary and proper for carrying into Execution the foregoing Powers, and all other Powers vested by this Constitution in the Government of the United States, or in any Department or Officer thereof.

Section 9. The Migration or Importation of such Persons as any of the States now existing shall think proper to admit, shall not be prohibited by the Congress prior to the Year one thousand eight hundred and eight, but a Tax or duty may be imposed on such Importation, not exceeding ten dollars for each Person.

The Privilege of the Writ of Habeas Corpus shall not be suspended, unless when in Cases of Rebellion or Invasion the public Safety may require it.

No Bill of Attainder or ex post facto Law shall be passed.

No Capitation, or other direct, Tax shall be laid, unless in Proportion to the Census or Enumeration herein before directed to be taken.[5]

No Tax or Duty shall be laid on Articles exported from any State.

No Preference shall be given by any Regulation of Commerce or Revenue to the Ports of one State over those of another; nor shall Vessels bound to, or from, one State, be obliged to enter, clear, or pay Duties in another.

No Money shall be drawn from the Treasury, but in Consequence of Appropriations made by Law; and a regular Statement and Account of the Receipts and Expenditures of all public Money shall be published from time to time.

No Title of Nobility shall be granted by the United States: And no Person holding any Office of Profit or Trust under them, shall, without the Consent of the Congress, accept of any present, Emolument, Office, or Title, of any kind whatever, from any King, Prince, or foreign State.

Section 10. No State shall enter into any Treaty, Alliance, or Confederation; grant Letters of Marque and Reprisal; coin Money; emit Bills of Credit; make any Thing but gold and silver Coin a Tender in Payment of Debts; pass any Bill of Attainder, ex post facto Law, or Law impairing the Obligation of Contracts, or grant any Title of Nobility.

No State shall, without the Consent of the Congress, lay any Imposts or Duties on Imports or Exports, except what may be absolutely necessary for executing its inspection Laws: and the net Produce of all Duties and Imposts, laid by any State on Imports or Exports, shall be for the Use of the Treasury of the United States; and all such Laws shall be subject to the Revision and Controul of the Congress.

No State shall, without the Consent of Congress, lay any Duty of Tonnage, keep Troops, or Ships of War in time of Peace, enter into any Agreement or Compact with another State, or with a foreign Power, or engage in War, unless actually invaded, or in such imminent Danger as will not admit of delay.

ARTICLE II

Section 1. The executive Power shall be vested in a President of the United States of America. He shall hold his Office during the Term of four Years, and, together with the Vice President, chosen for the same Term, be elected, as follows:

Each State shall appoint, in such Manner as the Legislature thereof may direct, a Number of Electors, equal to the whole Number of Senators and Representatives to which the State may be entitled in the Congress: but no Senator or Representative, or Person holding an Office of Trust or Profit under the United States, shall be appointed an Elector.

*The Electors shall meet in their respective States, and vote by Ballot for two Persons, of whom one at least shall not be an Inhabitant of the same State with themselves. And they shall make a List of all the Persons voted for, and of the Number of Votes for each; which List they shall sign and certify, and transmit sealed to the Seat of the Government of the United States, directed to the President of the Senate. The President of the Senate shall, in the Presence of the Senate and House of Representatives, open all the Certificates, and the Votes shall then be counted. The Person having the greatest Number of Votes shall be the President, if such Number be a Majority of the whole Number of Electors appointed; and if there be more than one who have such Majority, and have an equal Number of Votes, then the House of Representatives shall immediately chuse by Ballot one of them for President; and if no Person have a Majority, then from the five highest on the list the said House shall in like Manner chuse the President. But in chusing the President, the Votes shall be taken by States, the Representation from each State having one Vote; A quorum for this Purpose shall consist of a Member or Members from two thirds of the States, and a Majority of all the States shall be necessary to a Choice. In every Case, after the Choice of the President, the Person having the greatest Number of Votes of the Electors shall be the Vice President. But if there should remain two or more who have equal Votes, the Senate shall chuse from them by Ballot the Vice President.*6

The Congress may determine the Time of chusing the Electors, and the Day on which they shall give their Votes; which Day shall be the same throughout the United States.

No Person except a natural born Citizen, or a Citizen of the United States, at the time of the Adoption of this Constitution, shall be eligible to the Office of President; neither shall any Person be eligible to that Office who shall not have attained to the Age of thirty five Years, and been fourteen Years a Resident within the United States.

In Case of the Removal of the President from Office, or of his Death, Resignation, or Inability to discharge the Powers and Duties of the said Office,[7] the Same shall devolve on the Vice President, and the Congress may by Law provide for the Case of Removal, Death, Resignation or Inability, both of the President and Vice President, declaring what Officer shall then act as President, and such Officer shall act accordingly, until the Disability be removed, or a President shall be elected.

The President shall, at stated Times, receive for his Services, a Compensation, which shall neither be encreased nor diminished during the Period for which he shall have been elected, and he shall not receive within that Period any other Emolument from the United States, or any of them.

Before he enter on the Execution of his Office, he shall take the following Oath or Affirmation:—"I do solemnly swear (or affirm) that I will faithfully execute the Office of President of the United States, and will to the best of my Ability, preserve, protect and defend the Constitution of the United States."

Section 2. The President shall be Commander in Chief of the Army and Navy of the United States, and of the Militia of the several States, when called into the actual Service of the United States; he may require the Opinion, in writing, of the principal Officer in each of the executive Departments, upon any Subject relating to the Duties of their respective Offices, and he shall have Power to grant Reprieves and Pardons for Offences against the United States, except in Cases of Impeachment.

He shall have Power, by and with the Advice and Consent of the Senate, to make Treaties, provided two thirds of the Senators present concur; and he shall nominate, and by and with the Advice and Consent of the Senate, shall appoint Ambassadors, other public Ministers and Consuls, Judges of the supreme Court, and all other Officers of the United States, whose Appointments are not herein otherwise provided for, and which shall be established by Law: but the Congress may by Law vest the Appointment of such inferior Officers, as they think proper, in the President alone, in the Courts of Law, or in the Heads of Departments.

The President shall have Power to fill up all Vacancies that may happen during the Recess of the Senate, by granting Commissions which shall expire at the End of their next Session.

Section 3. He shall from time to time give to the Congress Information of the State of the Union, and recommend to their Consideration such Measures as he shall judge necessary and expedient; he may, on extraordinary Occasions, convene both Houses, or either of them, and in Case of Disagreement between them, with Respect to the Time of Adjournment, he may adjourn them to such Time as he shall think proper; he shall receive Ambassadors and other public Ministers; he shall take Care that the Laws be faithfully executed, and shall Commission all the Officers of the United States.

Section 4. The President, Vice President and all civil Officers of the United States, shall be removed from Office on Impeachment for, and Conviction of, Treason, Bribery, or other high Crimes and Misdemeanors.

ARTICLE III

Section 1. The judicial Power of the United States, shall be vested in one supreme Court, and in such inferior Courts as the Congress may from time to time ordain and establish. The Judges, both of the supreme and inferior Courts, shall hold their Offices during good Behaviour, and shall, at stated Times, receive for their Services, a Compensation, which shall not be diminished during their Continuance in Office.

Section 2. The judicial Power shall extend to all Cases, in Law and Equity, arising under this Constitution, the Laws of the United States, and Treaties made, or which shall be made, under their Authority; — to all Cases affecting Ambassadors, other public Ministers and Consuls; — to all Cases of admiralty and maritime Jurisdiction; — to Controversies to which the United States shall be a Party; — to Controversies between two or more States; — between a State and Citizens of another State;[8] — between Citizens of different States; — between Citizens of the same State claiming Lands under Grants of different States, and between a State, or the Citizens thereof, and foreign States, Citizens or Subjects.[8]

In all Cases affecting Ambassadors, other public Ministers and Consuls, and those in which a State shall be Party, the supreme Court shall have original Jurisdiction. In all the other Cases before mentioned, the supreme Court shall have appellate Jurisdiction, both as to Law and Fact, with such Exceptions, and under such Regulations as the Congress shall make.

The Trial of all Crimes, except in Cases of Impeachment, shall be by Jury; and such Trial shall be held in the State where the said Crimes shall have been committed; but when not committed within any State, the Trial shall be at such Place or Places as the Congress may by Law have directed.

Section 3. Treason against the United States, shall consist only in levying War against them, or in adhering to their Enemies, giving them Aid and Comfort. No Person shall be convicted of Treason unless on the Testimony of two Witnesses to the same overt Act, or on Confession in open Court.

The Congress shall have Power to declare the Punishment of Treason, but no Attainder of Treason shall work Corruption of Blood, or Forfeiture except during the Life of the Person attainted.

ARTICLE IV

Section 1. Full Faith and Credit shall be given in each State to the public Acts, Records, and judicial Proceedings of every other State. And the Congress may by general Laws prescribe the Manner in which such Acts, Records and Proceedings shall be proved, and the Effect thereof.

Section 2. The Citizens of each State shall be entitled to all Privileges and Immunities of Citizens in the several States.

A Person charged in any State with Treason, Felony, or other Crime, who shall flee from Justice, and be found in another State, shall on Demand of the executive Authority of the State from which he fled, be delivered up, to be removed to the State having Jurisdiction of the Crime.

No Person held to Service or Labour in one State, under the Laws thereof, escaping into another, shall, in Consequence of any Law or Regulation therein, be discharged from such Service or Labour, but shall be delivered up on Claim of the Party to whom such Service or Labour may be due.[9]

Section 3. New States may be admitted by the Congress into this Union; but no new State shall be formed or erected within the Jurisdiction of any other State; nor any State be formed by the Junction of two or more States, or Parts of States, without the Consent of the Legislatures of the States concerned as well as of the Congress.

The Congress shall have Power to dispose of and make all needful Rules and Regulations respecting the Territory or other Property belonging to the United States; and nothing in this Constitution shall be so construed as to Prejudice any Claims of the United States, or of any particular State.

Section 4. The United States shall guarantee to every State in this Union a Republican Form of Government, and shall protect each of them against Invasion; and on Application of the Legislature, or of the Executive (when the Legislature cannot be convened) against domestic Violence.

ARTICLE V

The Congress, whenever two thirds of both Houses shall deem it necessary, shall propose Amendments to this Constitution, or, on the Application of the Legislatures of two thirds of the several States, shall call a Convention for proposing Amendments, which, in either Case, shall be valid to all Intents and Purposes, as Part of this Constitution, when ratified by the Legislatures of three fourths of the several States, or by Conventions in three fourths thereof, as the one or the other Mode of Ratification may be proposed by the Congress; Provided *that no Amendment which may be made prior to the Year One thousand eight hundred and eight shall in any Manner affect the first and fourth Clauses in the Ninth Section of the first Article; and*[10] that no State, without its Consent, shall be deprived of its equal Suffrage in the Senate.

ARTICLE VI

All Debts contracted and Engagements entered into, before the Adoption of this Constitution, shall be as valid against the United States under this Constitution, as under the Confederation.

This Constitution, and the Laws of the United States which shall be made in Pursuance thereof; and all Treaties made, or which shall be made, under the Authority of the United States, shall be the supreme Law of the Land; and the Judges in every State shall be bound thereby, any Thing in the Constitution or Laws of any State to the Contrary notwithstanding.

The Senators and Representatives before mentioned, and the Members of the several State Legislatures, and all executive and judicial Officers, both of the United States and of the several States, shall be bound by Oath or Affirmation, to support this Constitution; but no religious Test shall ever be required as a Qualification to any Office or public Trust under the United States.

ARTICLE VII

The Ratification of the Conventions of nine States, shall be sufficient for the Establishment of this Constitution between the States so ratifying the Same.

Done in Convention by the Unanimous Consent of the States present the Seventeenth Day of September in the Year of our Lord one thousand seven hundred and Eighty seven and of the Independence of the United States of America the Twelfth. IN WITNESS whereof We have hereunto subscribed our Names,

George Washington, President and deputy from Virginia, and thirty-eight other delegates.

[The language of the original Constitution, not including the amendments, was adopted by a convention of the states on September 17, 1787, and was subsequently ratified by the states on the following dates: Delaware, December 7, 1787; Pennsylvania, December 12, 1787; New Jersey, December 18, 1787; Georgia, January 2, 1788; Connecticut, January 9, 1788; Massachusetts, February 6, 1788; Maryland, April 28, 1788; South Carolina, May 23, 1788; New Hampshire, June 21, 1788.

Ratification was completed on June 21, 1788.

The Constitution subsequently was ratified by Virginia, June 25, 1788; New York, July 26, 1788; North Carolina, November 21, 1789; Rhode Island, May 29, 1790; and Vermont, January 10, 1791.]

AMENDMENTS

AMENDMENT I

[First ten amendments ratified December 15, 1791.]

Congress shall make no law respecting an establishment of religion, or prohibiting the free exercise thereof; or abridging the freedom of speech, or of the press; or the right of the people peaceably to assemble, and to petition the Government for a redress of grievances.

AMENDMENT II

A well regulated Militia, being necessary to the security of a free State, the right of the people to keep and bear Arms, shall not be infringed.

AMENDMENT III

No Soldier shall, in time of peace be quartered in any house, without the consent of the Owner, nor in time of war, but in a manner to be prescribed by law.

AMENDMENT IV

The right of the people to be secure in their persons, houses, papers, and effects, against unreasonable searches and seizures, shall not be violated, and no Warrants shall issue, but upon probable cause, supported by Oath or affirmation, and particularly describing the place to be searched, and the persons or things to be seized.

AMENDMENT V

No person shall be held to answer for a capital, or otherwise infamous crime, unless on a presentment or indictment of a Grand Jury, except in cases arising in the land or naval forces, or in the Militia, when in actual service in time of War or public danger; nor shall any person be subject for the same offence to be twice put in jeopardy of life or limb; nor shall be compelled in any criminal case to be a witness against himself, nor be deprived of life, liberty, or property, without due process of law; nor shall private property be taken for public use, without just compensation.

AMENDMENT VI

In all criminal prosecutions, the accused shall enjoy the right to a speedy and public trial, by an impartial jury of the State and district wherein the crime shall have been committed, which district shall have been previously ascertained by law, and to be informed of the nature and cause of the accusation; to be confronted with the witnesses against him; to have compulsory process for obtaining witnesses in his favor, and to have the Assistance of Counsel for his defence.

AMENDMENT VII

In Suits at common law, where the value in controversy shall exceed twenty dollars, the right of trial by jury shall be preserved, and no fact tried by a jury, shall be otherwise re-examined in any Court of the United States, than according to the rules of the common law.

AMENDMENT VIII

Excessive bail shall not be required, nor excessive fines imposed, nor cruel and unusual punishments inflicted.

AMENDMENT IX

The enumeration in the Constitution, of certain rights, shall not be construed to deny or disparage others retained by the people.

AMENDMENT X

The powers not delegated to the United States by the Constitution, nor prohibited by it to the States, are reserved to the States respectively, or to the people.

AMENDMENT XI [RATIFIED FEBRUARY 7, 1795]

The Judicial power of the United States shall not be construed to extend to any suit in law or equity, commenced or prosecuted against one of the United States by Citizens of another State, or by Citizens or Subjects of any Foreign State.

AMENDMENT XII [RATIFIED JUNE 15, 1804]

The Electors shall meet in their respective states and vote by ballot for President and Vice-President, one of whom, at least, shall not be an inhabitant of the same state with themselves; they shall name in their ballots the person voted for as President, and in distinct ballots the person voted for as Vice-President, and they shall make distinct lists of all persons voted for as President, and of all persons voted for as Vice-President, and of the number of votes for each, which lists they shall sign and certify, and transmit sealed to the seat of the government of the United States, directed to the President of the Senate; — The President of the Senate shall, in the presence of the Senate and House of Representatives, open all the certificates and the votes shall then be counted; — The person having the greatest number of votes for President, shall be the President, if such number be a majority of the whole number of Electors appointed; and if no person have such majority, then from the persons having the highest numbers not exceeding three on the list of those voted for as President, the House of Representatives shall choose immediately, by ballot, the President. But in choosing the President, the votes shall be taken by states, the representation from each state having one vote; a quorum for this purpose shall consist of a member or members from two-thirds of the states, and a majority of all the states shall be necessary to a choice. *And if the House of Representatives shall not choose a President whenever the right of choice shall devolve upon them, before the fourth day of March next following, then the Vice-President shall act as President, as in the case of the death or other constitutional disability of the President. —*[11] The person having the greatest number of votes as Vice-President, shall be the Vice-President, if such number be a majority of the whole number of Electors appointed, and if no person have a majority, then from the two highest numbers on the list, the Senate shall choose the Vice-President; a quorum for the purpose shall consist of two-thirds of the whole number of Senators, and a majority of the whole number shall be necessary to a choice. But no person constitutionally ineligible to the office of President shall be eligible to that of Vice-President of the United States.

AMENDMENT XIII [RATIFIED DECEMBER 6, 1865]

Section 1. Neither slavery nor involuntary servitude, except as a punishment for crime whereof the party shall have been duly convicted, shall exist within the United States, or any place subject to their jurisdiction.

Section 2. Congress shall have power to enforce this article by appropriate legislation.

AMENDMENT XIV [RATIFIED JULY 9, 1868]

Section 1. All persons born or naturalized in the United States, and subject to the jurisdiction thereof, are citizens of the United States and of the State wherein they reside. No State shall make or enforce any law which shall abridge the privileges or immunities of citizens of the United States; nor shall any State deprive any person of life, liberty, or property, without due process of law; nor deny to any person within its jurisdiction the equal protection of the laws.

Section 2. Representatives shall be apportioned among the several States according to their respective numbers, counting the whole number of persons in each State, excluding Indians not taxed. But when the right to vote at any election for the choice of electors for President and Vice President of the United States, Representatives in Congress, the Executive and Judicial officers of a State, or the members of the Legislature thereof, is denied to any of the male inhabitants of such State, being twenty-one years of age,[12] and citizens of the United States, or in any way abridged, except for participation in rebellion, or other crime, the basis of representation therein shall be reduced in the proportion which the number of such male citizens shall bear to the whole number of male citizens twenty-one years of age in such State.

Section 3. No person shall be a Senator or Representative in Congress, or elector of President and Vice President, or hold any Office, civil or military, under the United States, or under any State, who, having previously taken an oath, as a member of Congress, or as an officer of the United States, or as a member of any State legislature, or as an executive or judicial officer of any State, to support the Constitution of the United States, shall have engaged in insurrection or rebellion against the same, or given aid or comfort to the enemies thereof. But Congress may by a vote of two-thirds of each House, remove such disability.

Section 4. The validity of the public debt of the United States, authorized by law, including debts incurred for payment of pensions and bounties for services in suppressing insurrection or rebellion, shall not be questioned. But neither the United States nor any State shall assume or pay any debt or obligation incurred in aid of insurrection or rebellion against the United States, or any claim for the loss or emancipation of any slave; but all such debts, obligations and claims shall be held illegal and void.

Section 5. The Congress shall have power to enforce, by appropriate legislation, the provisions of this article.

AMENDMENT XV [RATIFIED FEBRUARY 3, 1870]

Section 1. The right of citizens of the United States to vote shall not be denied or abridged by the United States or by any State on account of race, color, or previous condition of servitude.

Section 2. The Congress shall have power to enforce this article by appropriate legislation.

AMENDMENT XVI [RATIFIED FEBRUARY 3, 1913]

The Congress shall have power to lay and collect taxes on incomes, from whatever source derived, without apportionment among the several States, and without regard to any census or enumeration.

AMENDMENT XVII [RATIFIED APRIL 8, 1913]

The Senate of the United States shall be composed of two Senators from each State, elected by the people thereof, for six years; and each Senator shall have one vote. The electors in each State shall have the qualifications requisite for electors of the most numerous branch of the State legislatures.

When vacancies happen in the representation of any State in the Senate, the executive authority of such State shall issue writs of election to fill such vacancies: *Provided,* That the legislature of any State may empower the executive thereof to make temporary appointments until the people fill the vacancies by election as the legislature may direct.

This amendment shall not be so construed as to affect the election or term of any Senator chosen before it becomes valid as part of the Constitution.

AMENDMENT XVIII [RATIFIED JANUARY 16, 1919]

Section 1. After one year from the ratification of this article the manufacture, sale, or transportation of intoxicating liquors within, the importation thereof into, or the exportation thereof from the United States and all territory subject to the jurisdiction thereof for beverage purposes is hereby prohibited.

Section 2. The Congress and the several States shall have concurrent power to enforce this article by appropriate legislation.

Section 3. This article shall be inoperative unless it shall have been ratified as an amendment to the Constitution by the legislatures of the several States, as provided in the Constitution, within seven years from the date of the submission hereof to the States by the Congress.[13]

AMENDMENT XIX [RATIFIED AUGUST 18, 1920]

The right of citizens of the United States to vote shall not be denied or abridged by the United States or by any State on account of sex.

Congress shall have power to enforce this article by appropriate legislation.

AMENDMENT XX [RATIFIED JANUARY 23, 1933]

Section 1. The terms of the President and Vice President shall end at noon on the 20th day of January, and the terms of Senators and Representatives at noon on the 3d day of January, of the years in which such terms would have ended if this article had not been ratified; and the terms of their successors shall then begin.

Section 2. The Congress shall assemble at least once in every year, and such meeting shall begin at noon on the 3d day of January, unless they shall by law appoint a different day.

Section 3.[14] If, at the time fixed for the beginning of the term of the President, the President elect shall have died, the Vice President elect shall become President. If a President shall not have been chosen before the time fixed for the beginning of his term, or if the President elect shall have failed to qualify, then the Vice President elect shall act as President until a President shall have qualified; and the Congress may by law provide for the case wherein neither a President elect nor a Vice President elect shall have qualified, declaring who shall then act as President, or the manner in which one who is to act shall be selected, and such person shall act accordingly until a President or Vice President shall have qualified.

Section 4. The Congress may by law provide for the case of the death of any of the persons from whom the House of Representatives may choose a President whenever the right of choice shall have devolved upon them, and for the case of the death of any of the persons from whom the Senate may choose a Vice President whenever the right of choice shall have devolved upon them.

Section 5. Sections 1 and 2 shall take effect on the 15th day of October following the ratification of this article.

Section 6. This article shall be inoperative unless it shall have been ratified as an amendment to the Constitution by the legislatures of three-fourths of the several States within seven years from the date of its submission.

AMENDMENT XXI [RATIFIED DECEMBER 5, 1933]

Section 1. The eighteenth article of amendment to the Constitution of the United States is hereby repealed.

Section 2. The transportation or importation into any State, Territory, or possession of the United States for delivery or use therein of intoxicating liquors, in violation of the laws thereof, is hereby prohibited.

Section 3. This article shall be inoperative unless it shall have been ratified as an amendment to the Constitution by conventions in the several States, as provided in the Constitution, within seven years from the date of the submission hereof to the States by the Congress.

AMENDMENT XXII [RATIFIED FEBRUARY 27, 1951]

Section 1. No person shall be elected to the office of the President more than twice, and no person who has held the office of President, or acted as President, for more than two years of a term to which some other person was elected President shall be elected to the office of the President more than once. But this Article shall not apply to any person holding the office of President when this Article was proposed by the Congress, and shall not prevent any person who may be holding the office of President, or acting as President, during the term within which this Article becomes operative from holding the office of President or acting as President during the remainder of such term.

Section 2. This article shall be inoperative unless it shall have been ratified as an amendment to the Constitution by the legislatures of three-fourths of the several States within seven years from the date of its submission to the States by the Congress.

AMENDMENT XXIII [RATIFIED MARCH 29, 1961]

Section 1. The District constituting the seat of Government of the United States shall appoint in such manner as the Congress may direct:

A number of electors of President and Vice President equal to the whole number of Senators and Representatives in Congress to which the District would be entitled if it were a State, but in no event more than the least populous State; they shall be in addition to those appointed by the States, but they shall be considered, for the purposes of the election of President and Vice President, to be electors appointed by a State; and they shall meet in the District and perform such duties as provided by the twelfth article of amendment.

Section 2. The Congress shall have power to enforce this article by appropriate legislation.

AMENDMENT XXIV [RATIFIED JANUARY 23, 1964]

Section 1. The right of citizens of the United States to vote in any primary or other election for President or Vice President, for electors for President or Vice President, or for Senator or Representative in Congress, shall not be denied or abridged by the United States or any State by reason of failure to pay any poll tax or other tax.

Section 2. The Congress shall have power to enforce this article by appropriate legislation.

AMENDMENT XXV [RATIFIED FEBRUARY 10, 1967]

Section 1. In case of the removal of the President from office or of his death or resignation, the Vice President shall become President.

Section 2. Whenever there is a vacancy in the office of the Vice President, the President shall nominate a Vice President who shall take office upon confirmation by a majority vote of both Houses of Congress.

Section 3. Whenever the President transmits to the President pro tempore of the Senate and the Speaker of the House of Representatives his written declaration that he is unable to discharge the powers and duties of his office, and until he transmits to them a written declaration to the contrary, such powers and duties shall be discharged by the Vice President as Acting President.

Section 4. Whenever the Vice President and a majority of either the principal officers of the executive departments or of such other body as Congress may by law provide, transmit to the President pro tempore of the Senate and the Speaker of the House of Representatives their written declaration that the President is unable to discharge the powers and duties of his office, the Vice President shall immediately assume the powers and duties of the office as Acting President.

Thereafter, when the President transmits to the President pro tempore of the Senate and the Speaker of the House of Representatives his written declaration that no inability exists, he shall resume the powers and duties of his office unless the Vice President and a majority of either the principal officers of the executive departments or of such other body as Congress may by law provide, transmit within four days to the President pro tempore of the Senate and the Speaker of the House of Representatives their written declaration that the President is unable to discharge the powers and duties of his office. Thereupon Congress shall decide the issue, assembling within forty-eight hours for that purpose if not in session. If the Congress, within twenty-one days after receipt of the latter written declaration, or, if Congress is not in session, within twenty-one days after Congress is required to assemble, determines by two-thirds vote of both Houses that the President is unable to discharge the powers and duties of his office, the Vice President shall continue to discharge the same as Acting President; otherwise, the President shall resume the powers and duties of his office.

AMENDMENT XXVI [RATIFIED JULY 1, 1971]

Section 1. The right of citizens of the United States, who are eighteen years of age or older, to vote shall not be denied or abridged by the United States or by any State on account of age.

Section 2. The Congress shall have power to enforce this article by appropriate legislation.

AMENDMENT XXVII [RATIFIED MAY 7, 1992]

No law varying the compensation for the services of the Senators and Representatives shall take effect, until an election of Representatives shall have intervened.

Source: U.S. Congress, House, Committee on the Judiciary, *The Constitution of the United States of America, as Amended*, 100th Cong., 1st sess., 1987, H Doc 100–94.

NOTES

1. The material between the asterisks was changed by Section 2 of the Fourteenth Amendment.
2. The material between the asterisks was changed by the first paragraph of the Seventeenth Amendment.
3. The material between the asterisks was changed by the second paragraph of the Seventeenth Amendment.
4. The material between the asterisks was changed by Section 2 of the Twentieth Amendment.
5. The Sixteenth Amendment gave Congress the power to tax incomes.
6. The material between the asterisks was superseded by the Twelfth Amendment.
7. This provision was affected by the Twenty-fifth Amendment.
8. These clauses were affected by the Eleventh Amendment.
9. This paragraph was superseded by the Thirteenth Amendment.
10. The material between the asterisks is now obsolete.
11. The material between the asterisks was superseded by Section 3 of the Twentieth Amendment.
12. See the Nineteenth and Twenty-sixth Amendments.
13. This amendment was repealed by Section 1 of the Twenty-first Amendment.
14. See the Twenty-fifth Amendment.

APPENDIX 4

Federalist No. 10

The Same Subject Continued: The Union as a Safeguard Against Domestic Faction and Insurrection.

From the New York Packet

Friday, November 23, 1787.

Author: James Madison

To the People of the State of New York:

AMONG the numerous advantages promised by a well constructed Union, none deserves to be more accurately developed than its tendency to break and control the violence of faction. The friend of popular governments never finds himself so much alarmed for their character and fate, as when he contemplates their propensity to this dangerous vice. He will not fail, therefore, to set a due value on any plan which, without violating the principles to which he is attached, provides a proper cure for it. The instability, injustice, and confusion introduced into the public councils, have, in truth, been the mortal diseases under which popular governments have everywhere perished; as they continue to be the favorite and fruitful topics from which the adversaries to liberty derive their most specious declamations. The valuable improvements made by the American constitutions on the popular models, both ancient and modern, cannot certainly be too much admired; but it would be an unwarrantable partiality, to contend that they have as effectually obviated the danger on this side, as was wished and expected. Complaints are everywhere heard from our most considerate and virtuous citizens, equally the friends of public and private faith, and of public and personal liberty, that our governments are too unstable, that the public good is disregarded in the conflicts of rival parties, and that measures are too often decided, not according to the rules of justice and the rights of the minor party, but by the superior force of an interested and overbearing majority. However anxiously we may wish that these complaints had no foundation, the evidence, of known facts will not permit us to deny that they are in some degree true. It will be found, indeed, on a candid review of our situation, that some of the distresses under which we labor have been erroneously charged on the operation of our governments; but it will be found, at the same time, that other causes will not alone account for many of our heaviest misfortunes; and, particularly, for that prevailing and increasing distrust of public engagements, and alarm for private rights, which are echoed from one end of the continent to the other. These must be chiefly, if not wholly, effects of the unsteadiness and injustice with which a factious spirit has tainted our public administrations.

By a faction, I understand a number of citizens, whether amounting to a majority or a minority of the whole, who are united and actuated by some common impulse of passion, or of interest, adversed to the rights of other citizens, or to the permanent and aggregate interests of the community.

There are two methods of curing the mischiefs of faction: the one, by removing its causes; the other, by controlling its effects.

There are again two methods of removing the causes of faction: the one, by destroying the liberty which is essential to its existence; the other, by giving to every citizen the same opinions, the same passions, and the same interests.

It could never be more truly said than of the first remedy, that it was worse than the disease. Liberty is to faction what air is to fire, an aliment without which it instantly expires. But it could not be less folly to abolish liberty, which is essential to political life, because it nourishes faction, than it would be to wish the annihilation of air, which is essential to animal life, because it imparts to fire its destructive agency.

The second expedient is as impracticable as the first would be unwise. As long as the reason of man continues fallible, and he is at liberty to exercise it, different opinions will be formed. As long as the connection subsists between his reason and his self-love, his opinions and his passions will have a reciprocal influence on each other; and the former will be objects to which the latter will attach themselves. The diversity in the faculties of men, from which the rights of property originate, is not less an insuperable obstacle to a uniformity of interests. The protection of these faculties is the first object of government. From the protection of different and unequal faculties of acquiring property, the possession of different degrees and kinds of property immediately results; and from the influence of these on the sentiments and views of the respective proprietors, ensues a division of the society into different interests and parties.

The latent causes of faction are thus sown in the nature of man; and we see them everywhere brought into different degrees of activity, according to the different circumstances of civil society. A zeal for different opinions concerning religion, concerning government, and many other points, as well of speculation as of practice; an attachment to different leaders ambitiously contending for pre-eminence and power; or to persons of other descriptions whose fortunes have been interesting to the human passions, have, in turn, divided mankind into parties, inflamed them with mutual animosity, and rendered them much more disposed to vex and oppress each other than to co-operate for their common good. So strong is this propensity of mankind to fall into mutual animosities, that where no substantial occasion presents itself, the most frivolous and fanciful distinctions have been sufficient to kindle their unfriendly passions and excite their most violent conflicts. But the most common and durable source of factions has been the various and unequal distribution of property. Those who hold and those who are without property have ever formed distinct interests in society. Those who are creditors, and those who are debtors, fall under a like discrimination. A landed interest, a manufacturing interest, a mercantile interest, a moneyed interest, with many lesser interests, grow up of necessity in civilized nations, and divide them into different classes, actuated by different sentiments and views. The regulation of these various and interfering interests forms the principal task of modern legislation, and involves the spirit of party and faction in the necessary and ordinary operations of the government.

No man is allowed to be a judge in his own cause, because his interest would certainly bias his judgment, and, not improbably, corrupt his integrity. With equal, nay with greater reason, a body of men are unfit to be both judges and parties at the same time; yet what are many of the most important acts of legislation, but so many judicial determinations, not indeed concerning the rights of single persons, but concerning the rights of large bodies of citizens? And what are the different classes of legislators but advocates and parties to the causes which they determine? Is a law proposed concerning private debts? It is a question to which the creditors are parties on one side and the debtors on the other. Justice ought to hold the balance between them. Yet the parties are, and must be, themselves the judges; and the most numerous party, or, in other words, the most powerful faction must be expected to prevail. Shall domestic manufactures be encouraged, and in what degree, by restrictions on foreign manufactures? are questions which would be differently decided by the landed and the manufacturing classes, and probably by neither with a sole regard to justice and the public good. The apportionment of taxes on the various descriptions of property is an act which seems to require the most exact impartiality; yet there is, perhaps, no legislative act in which greater opportunity and temptation are given to a predominant party to trample on the rules of justice. Every shilling with which they overburden the inferior number, is a shilling saved to their own pockets.

It is in vain to say that enlightened statesmen will be able to adjust these clashing interests, and render them all subservient to the public good. Enlightened statesmen will not always be at the helm. Nor, in many cases, can such an adjustment be made at all without taking into view indirect and remote considerations, which will rarely prevail over the immediate interest which one party may find in disregarding the rights of another or the good of the whole.

The inference to which we are brought is, that the CAUSES of faction cannot be removed, and that relief is only to be sought in the means of controlling its EFFECTS.

If a faction consists of less than a majority, relief is supplied by the republican principle, which enables the majority to defeat its sinister views by regular vote. It may clog the administration, it may convulse the society; but it will be unable to execute and mask its violence under the forms of the Constitution. When a majority is included in a faction, the form of popular government, on the other hand, enables it to sacrifice to its ruling passion or interest both the public good and the rights of other citizens. To secure the public good and private rights against the danger of such a faction, and at the same time to preserve the spirit and the form of popular government, is then the great object to which our inquiries are directed. Let me add that it is the great desideratum by which this form of government can be rescued from the opprobrium under which it has so long labored, and be recommended to the esteem and adoption of mankind.

By what means is this object attainable? Evidently by one of two only. Either the existence of the same passion or interest in a majority at the same time must be prevented, or the majority, having such coexistent passion or interest, must be rendered, by their number and local situation, unable to concert and carry into effect schemes of oppression. If the impulse and the opportunity be suffered to coincide, we well know that neither moral nor religious motives can be relied on as an adequate control. They are not found to be such on the injustice and violence of individuals, and lose their efficacy in proportion to the number combined together, that is, in proportion as their efficacy becomes needful.

From this view of the subject it may be concluded that a pure democracy, by which I mean a society consisting of a small number of citizens, who assemble and administer the government in person, can admit of no cure for the mischiefs of faction. A common passion or interest will, in almost every case, be felt by a majority of the whole; a communication and concert result from the form of government itself; and there is nothing to check the inducements to sacrifice the weaker party or an obnoxious individual. Hence it is that such democracies have ever been spectacles of turbulence and contention; have ever been found incompatible with personal security or the rights of property; and have in general been as short in their lives as they have been violent in their deaths. Theoretic politicians, who have patronized this species of government, have erroneously supposed that by reducing mankind to a perfect equality in their political rights, they would, at the same time, be perfectly equalized and assimilated in their possessions, their opinions, and their passions.

A republic, by which I mean a government in which the scheme of representation takes place, opens a different prospect, and promises the cure for which we are seeking. Let us examine the points in which it varies from pure democracy, and we shall comprehend both the nature of the cure and the efficacy which it must derive from the Union.

The two great points of difference between a democracy and a republic are: first, the delegation of the government, in the latter, to a small number of citizens elected by the rest; secondly, the greater number of citizens, and greater sphere of country, over which the latter may be extended.

The effect of the first difference is, on the one hand, to refine and enlarge the public views, by passing them through the medium of a chosen body of citizens, whose wisdom may best discern the true interest of their country, and whose patriotism and love of justice will be least likely to sacrifice it to temporary or partial considerations. Under such a regulation, it may well happen that the public voice, pronounced by the representatives of the people, will be more consonant to the public good than if pronounced by the people themselves, convened for the purpose. On the other hand, the effect may be inverted. Men of factious tempers, of local prejudices, or of sinister designs, may, by intrigue, by corruption, or by other means, first obtain the suffrages, and then betray the interests, of the people. The question resulting is, whether small or extensive republics are more favorable to the election of proper guardians of the public weal; and it is clearly decided in favor of the latter by two obvious considerations:

In the first place, it is to be remarked that, however small the republic may be, the representatives must be raised to a certain number, in order to guard against the cabals of a few; and that, however large it may be, they must be limited to a certain number, in order to guard against the confusion of a multitude. Hence, the number of representatives in the two cases not being in proportion to that of the two constituents, and being proportionally greater in the small republic, it follows that, if the proportion of fit characters be not less in the large than in the small republic, the former will present a greater option, and consequently a greater probability of a fit choice.

In the next place, as each representative will be chosen by a greater number of citizens in the large than in the small republic, it will be more difficult for unworthy candidates to practice with success the vicious arts by which elections are too often carried; and the suffrages of the people being more free, will be more likely to centre in men who possess the most attractive merit and the most diffusive and established characters.

It must be confessed that in this, as in most other cases, there is a mean, on both sides of which inconveniences will be found to lie. By enlarging too much the number of electors, you render the representatives too little acquainted with all their local circumstances and lesser interests; as by reducing it too much, you render him unduly attached to these, and too little fit to comprehend and pursue great and national objects. The federal Constitution forms a happy combination in this respect; the great and aggregate interests being referred to the national, the local and particular to the State legislatures.

The other point of difference is, the greater number of citizens and extent of territory which may be brought within the compass of republican than of democratic government; and it is this circumstance principally which renders factious combinations less to be dreaded in the former than in the latter. The smaller the society, the fewer probably will be the distinct parties and interests composing it; the fewer the distinct parties and interests, the more frequently will a majority be found of the same party; and the smaller the number of individuals composing a majority, and the smaller the compass within which they are placed, the more easily will they concert and execute their plans of oppression. Extend the sphere, and you take in a greater variety of parties and interests; you make it less probable that a majority of the whole will have a common motive to invade the rights of other citizens; or if such a common motive exists, it will be more difficult for all who feel it to discover their own strength, and to act in unison with each other. Besides other impediments, it may be remarked that, where there is a consciousness of unjust or dishonorable purposes, communication is always checked by distrust in proportion to the number whose concurrence is necessary.

Hence, it clearly appears, that the same advantage which a republic has over a democracy, in controlling the effects of faction, is enjoyed by a large over a small republic,—is enjoyed by the Union over the States composing it. Does the advantage consist in the substitution of representatives whose enlightened views and virtuous sentiments render them superior to local prejudices and schemes of injustice? It will not be denied that the representation of the Union will be most likely to possess these requisite endowments. Does it consist in the greater security afforded by a greater variety of parties, against the event of any one party being able to outnumber and oppress the rest? In an equal degree does the increased variety of parties comprised within the Union, increase this security. Does it, in fine, consist in the greater obstacles opposed to the concert and accomplishment of the secret wishes of an unjust and interested majority? Here, again, the extent of the Union gives it the most palpable advantage.

The influence of factious leaders may kindle a flame within their particular States, but will be unable to spread a general conflagration through the other States. A religious sect may degenerate into a political faction in a part of the Confederacy; but the variety of sects dispersed over the entire face of it must secure the national councils against any danger from that source. A rage for paper money, for an abolition of debts, for an equal division of property, or for any other improper or wicked project, will be less apt to pervade the whole body of the Union than a particular member of it; in the same proportion as such a malady is more likely to taint a particular county or district, than an entire State.

In the extent and proper structure of the Union, therefore, we behold a republican remedy for the diseases most incident to republican government. And according to the degree of pleasure and pride we feel in being republicans, ought to be our zeal in cherishing the spirit and supporting the character of Federalists.

PUBLIUS.

APPENDIX 5

Federalist No. 51

The Structure of the Government Must Furnish the Proper Checks and Balances Between the Different Departments

From the New York Packet.

Friday, February 8, 1788.

Author: James Madison

To the People of the State of New York:

TO WHAT expedient, then, shall we finally resort, for maintaining in practice the necessary partition of power among the several departments, as laid down in the Constitution? The only answer that can be given is, that as all these exterior provisions are found to be inadequate, the defect must be supplied, by so contriving the interior structure of the government as that its several constituent parts may, by their mutual relations, be the means of keeping each other in their proper places. Without presuming to undertake a full development of this important idea, I will hazard a few general observations, which may perhaps place it in a clearer light, and enable us to form a more correct judgment of the principles and structure of the government planned by the convention.

In order to lay a due foundation for that separate and distinct exercise of the different powers of government, which to a certain extent is admitted on all hands to be essential to the preservation of liberty, it is evident that each department should have a will of its own; and consequently should be so constituted that the members of each should have as little agency as possible in the appointment of the members of the others. Were this principle rigorously adhered to, it would require that all the appointments for the supreme executive, legislative, and judiciary magistracies should be drawn from the same fountain of authority, the people, through channels having no communication whatever with one another. Perhaps such a plan of constructing the several departments would be less difficult in practice than it may in contemplation appear. Some difficulties, however, and some additional expense would attend the execution of it. Some deviations, therefore, from the principle must be admitted. In the constitution of the judiciary department in particular, it might be inexpedient to insist rigorously on the principle: first, because peculiar qualifications being essential in the members, the primary consideration ought to be to select that mode of choice which best secures these qualifications; secondly, because the permanent tenure by which

the appointments are held in that department, must soon destroy all sense of dependence on the authority conferring them.

It is equally evident, that the members of each department should be as little dependent as possible on those of the others, for the emoluments annexed to their offices. Were the executive magistrate, or the judges, not independent of the legislature in this particular, their independence in every other would be merely nominal. But the great security against a gradual concentration of the several powers in the same department, consists in giving to those who administer each department the necessary constitutional means and personal motives to resist encroachments of the others. The provision for defense must in this, as in all other cases, be made commensurate to the danger of attack. Ambition must be made to counteract ambition. The interest of the man must be connected with the constitutional rights of the place. It may be a reflection on human nature, that such devices should be necessary to control the abuses of government. But what is government itself, but the greatest of all reflections on human nature? If men were angels, no government would be necessary. If angels were to govern men, neither external nor internal controls on government would be necessary. In framing a government which is to be administered by men over men, the great difficulty lies in this: you must first enable the government to control the governed; and in the next place oblige it to control itself.

A dependence on the people is, no doubt, the primary control on the government; but experience has taught mankind the necessity of auxiliary precautions. This policy of supplying, by opposite and rival interests, the defect of better motives, might be traced through the whole system of human affairs, private as well as public. We see it particularly displayed in all the subordinate distributions of power, where the constant aim is to divide and arrange the several offices in such a manner as that each may be a check on the other that the private interest of every individual may be a sentinel over the public rights. These inventions of prudence cannot be less requisite in the distribution of the supreme powers of the State. But it is not possible to give to each department an equal power of self-defense. In republican government, the legislative authority necessarily predominates. The remedy for this inconveniency is to divide the legislature into different branches; and to render them, by different modes of election and different principles of action, as little connected with each other as the nature of their common functions and their common dependence on the society will admit. It may even be necessary to guard against dangerous encroachments by still further precautions. As the weight of the legislative authority requires that it should be thus divided, the weakness of the executive may require, on the other hand, that it should be fortified.

An absolute negative on the legislature appears, at first view, to be the natural defense with which the executive magistrate should be armed. But perhaps it would be neither altogether safe nor alone sufficient. On ordinary occasions it might not be exerted with the requisite firmness, and on extraordinary occasions it might be perfidiously abused. May not this defect of an absolute negative be supplied by some qualified connection between this weaker department and the weaker branch of the stronger department, by which the latter may be led to support the constitutional rights of the former, without being too much detached from the rights of its own department? If the principles on which these observations are founded be just, as I persuade myself they are, and they be applied as a criterion to the several State constitutions, and to the federal Constitution it will be found that if the latter does not perfectly correspond with them, the former are infinitely less able to bear such a test.

There are, moreover, two considerations particularly applicable to the federal system of America, which place that system in a very interesting point of view. First. In a single republic, all the power surrendered by the people is submitted to the administration of a single government; and the usurpations are guarded against by a division of the government into distinct and separate departments. In the compound republic of America, the power surrendered by the people is first divided between two distinct governments, and then the portion allotted to each subdivided among distinct and separate departments. Hence a double security arises to the rights of the people. The different governments will control each other, at the same time that each will be controlled by itself. Second. It is of great importance in a republic not only to guard the society against the oppression of its rulers, but to guard one part of the society against the injustice of the other part. Different interests necessarily exist in different classes of citizens. If a majority be united by a common interest, the rights of the minority will be insecure.

There are but two methods of providing against this evil: the one by creating a will in the community independent of the majority that is, of the society itself; the other, by comprehending in the society so many separate descriptions of citizens as will render an unjust combination of a majority of the whole very improbable, if not impracticable. The first method prevails in all governments possessing an hereditary or self-appointed authority. This, at best, is but a precarious security; because a power independent of the society may as well espouse the unjust views of the major, as the rightful interests of the minor party, and may possibly be turned against both parties. The second method will be exemplified in the federal republic of the United States. Whilst all authority in it will be derived from and dependent on the society, the society itself will be broken into so many parts, interests, and classes of citizens, that the rights of individuals, or of the minority, will be in little danger from interested combinations of the majority.

In a free government the security for civil rights must be the same as that for religious rights. It consists in the one case in the multiplicity of interests, and in the other in the multiplicity of sects. The degree of security in both cases will depend on the number of interests and sects; and this may be presumed to depend on the extent of country and number of people comprehended under the same government. This view of the subject must particularly recommend a proper federal system to all the sincere and considerate friends of republican government, since it shows that in exact proportion as the territory of the Union may be formed into more circumscribed Confederacies, or States oppressive combinations of a majority will be facilitated: the best security, under the republican forms, for the rights of every class of citizens, will be diminished: and consequently the stability and independence of some member of the government, the only other security, must be proportionately increased. Justice is the end of government. It is the end of civil society. It ever has been and ever will be pursued until it be obtained, or until liberty be lost in the pursuit. In a society under the forms of which the stronger faction can readily unite and oppress the weaker, anarchy may as truly be said to reign as in a state of nature, where the weaker individual is not secured against the violence of the stronger; and as, in the latter state, even the stronger individuals are prompted, by the uncertainty of their condition, to submit to a government which may protect the weak as well as themselves; so, in the former state, will the more powerful factions or parties be gradually induced, by a like motive, to wish for a government which will protect all parties, the weaker as well as the more powerful.

It can be little doubted that if the State of Rhode Island was separated from the Confederacy and left to itself, the insecurity of rights under the popular form of government within such narrow limits would be displayed by such reiterated oppressions of factious majorities that some power altogether independent of the people would soon be called for by the voice of the very factions whose misrule had proved the necessity of it. In the extended republic of the United States, and among the great variety of interests, parties, and sects which it embraces, a coalition of a majority of the whole society could seldom take place on any other principles than those of justice and the general good; whilst there being thus less danger to a minor from the will of a major party, there must be less pretext, also, to provide for the security of the former, by introducing into the government a will not dependent on the latter, or, in other words, a will independent of the society itself. It is no less certain than it is important, notwithstanding the contrary opinions which have been entertained, that the larger the society, provided it lie within a practical sphere, the more duly capable it will be of self-government. And happily for the REPUBLICAN CAUSE, the practicable sphere may be carried to a very great extent, by a judicious modification and mixture of the FEDERAL PRINCIPLE.

PUBLIUS.

APPENDIX 6

Political Party Affiliations in Congress and the Presidency, 1789–2017

Year	Congress	House		Senate		President
		Majority party	Principal minority party	Majority party	Principal minority party	
1789–1791	1st	AD-38	Op-26	AD-17	Op-9	F (Washington)
1791–1793	2nd	F-37	DR-33	F-16	DR-13	F (Washington)
1793–1795	3rd	DR-57	F-48	F-17	DR-13	F (Washington)
1795–1797	4th	F-54	DR-52	F-19	DR-13	F (Washington)
1797–1799	5th	F-58	DR-48	F-20	DR-12	F (John Adams)
1799–1801	6th	F-64	DR-42	F-19	DR-13	F (John Adams)
1801–1803	7th	DR-69	F-36	DR-18	F-13	DR (Jefferson)
1803–1805	8th	DR-102	F-39	DR-25	F-9	DR (Jefferson)
1805–1807	9th	DR-116	F-25	DR-27	F-7	DR (Jefferson)
1807–1809	10th	DR-118	F-24	DR-28	F-6	DR (Jefferson)
1809–1811	11th	DR-94	F-48	DR-28	F-6	DR (Madison)
1811–1813	12th	DR-108	F-36	DR-30	F-6	DR (Madison)
1813–1815	13th	DR-112	F-68	DR-27	F-9	DR (Madison)
1815–1817	14th	DR-117	F-65	DR-25	F-11	DR (Madison)
1817–1819	15th	DR-141	F-42	DR-34	F-10	DR (Monroe)
1819–1821	16th	DR-156	F-27	DR-35	F-7	DR (Monroe)
1821–1823	17th	DR-158	F-25	DR-44	F-4	DR (Monroe)
1823–1825	18th	DR-187	F-26	DR-44	F-4	DR (Monroe)
1825–1827	19th	AD-105	J-97	AD-26	J-20	DR (John Q. Adams)
1827–1829	20th	J-119	AD-94	J-28	AD-20	DR (John Q. Adams)
1829–1831	21st	D-139	NR-74	D-26	NR-22	DR (Jackson)
1831–1833	22nd	D-141	NR-58	D-25	NR-21	D (Jackson)
1833–1835	23rd	D-147	AM-53	D-20	NR-20	D (Jackson)
1835–1837	24th	D-145	W-98	D-27	W-25	D (Jackson)
1837–1839	25th	D-108	W-107	D-30	W-18	D (Van Buren)
1839–1841	26th	D-124	W-118	D-28	W-22	D (Van Buren)
1841–1843	27th	W-133	D-102	W-28	D-22	W (W. Harrison)

Year	Congress	House Majority party	House Principal minority party	Senate Majority party	Senate Principal minority party	President
						W (Tyler)
1843–1845	28th	D-142	W-79	W-28	D-25	W (Tyler)
1845–1847	29th	D-143	W-77	D-31	W-25	D (Polk)
1847–1849	30th	W-115	D-108	D-36	W-21	D (Polk)
1849–1851	31st	D-112	W-109	D-35	W-25	W (Taylor)
						W (Fillmore)
1851–1853	32nd	D-140	W-88	D-35	W-24	W (Fillmore)
1853–1855	33rd	D-159	W-71	D-38	W-22	D (Pierce)
1855–1857	34th	R-108	D-83	D-42	R-15	D (Pierce)
1857–1859	35th	D-131	R-92	D-35	R-20	D (Buchanan)
1859–1861	36th	R-113	D-101	D-38	R-26	D (Buchanan)
1861–1863	37th	R-106	D-42	R-31	D-11	R (Lincoln)
1863–1865	38th	R-103	D-80	R-39	D-12	R (Lincoln)
1865–1867[1]	39th	U-145	D-46	U-42	D-10	U (Lincoln)
						U (A. Johnson)
1867–1869	40th	R-143	D-49	R-42	D-11	R (A. Johnson)
1869–1871	41st	R-170	D-73	R-61	D-11	R (Grant)
1871–1873	42nd	R-139	D-104	R-57	D-17	R (Grant)
1873–1875	43rd	R-203	D-88	R-54	D-19	R (Grant)
1875–1877	44th	D-181	R-107	R-46	D-29	R (Grant)
1877–1879	45th	D-156	R-137	R-39	D-36	R (Hayes)
1879–1881	46th	D-150	R-128	D-43	R-33	R (Hayes)
1881–1883	47th	R-152	D-130	R-37	D-37	R (Garfield)
						R (Arthur)
1883–1885	48th	D-200	R-119	R-40	D-36	R (Arthur)
1885–1887	49th	D-182	R-140	R-41	D-34	D (Cleveland)
1887–1889	50th	D-170	R-151	R-39	D-37	D (Cleveland)
1889–1891	51st	R-173	D-159	R-37	D-37	R (B. Harrison)
1891–1893	52nd	D-231	R-88	R-47	D-39	R (B. Harrison)
1893–1895	53rd	D-220	R-126	D-44	R-38	D (Cleveland)
1895–1897	54th	R-246	D-104	R-43	D-39	D (Cleveland)
1897–1899	55th	R-206	D-134	R-46	D-34	R (McKinley)
1899–1901	56th	R-185	D-163	R-53	D-26	R (McKinley)
1901–1903	57th	R-198	D-153	R-56	D-29	R (McKinley)

(Continued)

(Continued)

		House		Senate		
Year	Congress	Majority party	Principal minority party	Majority party	Principal minority party	President
						R (T. Roosevelt)
1903–1905	58th	R-207	D-178	R-58	D-32	R (T. Roosevelt)
1905–1907	59th	R-250	D-136	R-58	D-32	R (T. Roosevelt)
1907–1909	60th	R-222	D-164	R-61	D-29	R (T. Roosevelt)
1909–1911	61st	R-219	D-172	R-59	D-32	R (Taft)
1911–1913	62nd	D-228	R-162	R-49	D-42	R (Taft)
1913–1915	63rd	D-290	R-127	D-51	R-44	D (Wilson)
1915–1917	64th	D-231	R-193	D-56	R-39	D (Wilson)
1917–1919	65th	D-216	R-210	D-53	R-42	D (Wilson)
1919–1921	66th	R-237	D-191	R-48	D-47	D (Wilson)
1921–1923	67th	R-300	D-132	R-59	D-37	R (Harding)
1923–1925	68th	R-225	D-207	R-51	D-43	R (Coolidge)
1925–1927	69th	R-247	D-183	R-54	D-40	R (Coolidge)
1927–1929	70th	R-237	D-195	R-48	D-47	R (Coolidge)
1929–1931	71st	R-267	D-163	R-56	D-39	R (Hoover)
1931–1933	72nd	D-216	R-218	R-48	D-47	R (Hoover)
1933–1935	73rd	D-313	R-117	D-59	R-36	D (F. Roosevelt)
1935–1937	74th	D-322	R-103	D-69	R-25	D (F. Roosevelt)
1937–1939	75th	D-333	R-89	D-75	R-17	D (F. Roosevelt)
1939–1941	76th	D-262	R-169	D-69	R-23	D (F. Roosevelt)
1941–1943	77th	D-267	R-162	D-66	R-28	D (F. Roosevelt)
1943–1945	78th	D-222	R-209	D-57	R-38	D (F. Roosevelt)
1945–1947	79th	D-243	R-190	D-56	R-38	D (F. Roosevelt)
						D (Truman)
1947–1949	80th	R-246	D-188	R-51	D-45	D (Truman)
1949–1951	81st	D-263	R-171	D-54	R-42	D (Truman)
1951–1953	82nd	D-234	R-199	D-48	R-47	D (Truman)
1953–1955	83rd	R-221	D-213	R-48	D-46	R (Eisenhower)
1955–1957	84th	D-234	R-201	D-48	R-47	R (Eisenhower)
1957–1959	85th	D-233	R-200	D-49	R-47	R (Eisenhower)
1959–1961	86th	D-283	R-153	D-64	R-34	R (Eisenhower)
1961–1963	87th	D-262	R-175	D-64	R-36	D (Kennedy)
1963–1965	88th	D-258	R-176	D-67	R-33	D (Kennedy)

		House		Senate		
Year	Congress	Majority party	Principal minority party	Majority party	Principal minority party	President
						D (L. Johnson)
1965–1967	89th	D-295	R-140	D-68	R-32	D (L. Johnson)
1967–1969	90th	D-248	R-187	D-64	R-36	D (L. Johnson)
1969–1971	91st	D-243	R-192	D-58	R-42	R (Nixon)
1971–1973	92nd	D-255	R-180	D-54	R-44	R (Nixon)
1973–1975	93rd	D-242	R-192	D-56	R-42	R (Nixon)
						R (Ford)
1975–1977	94th	D-291	R-144	D-60	R-37	R (Ford)
1977–1979	95th	D-292	R-143	D-61	R-38	D (Carter)
1979–1981	96th	D-277	R-158	D-58	R-41	D (Carter)
1981–1983	97th	D-242	R-192	R-53	D-46	R (Reagan)
1983–1985	98th	D-269	R-166	R-54	D-46	R (Reagan)
1985–1987	99th	D-253	R-182	R-53	D-47	R (Reagan)
1987–1989	100th	D-258	R-177	D-55	R-45	R (Reagan)
1989–1991	101st	D-260	R-175	D-55	R-45	R (G. H. W. Bush)
1991–1993	102nd	D-267	R-167	D-56	R-44	R (G. H. W. Bush)
1993–1995	103rd	D-258	R-176	D-57	R-43	D (Clinton)
1995–1997	104th	R-230	D-204	R-52	D-48	D (Clinton)
1997–1999	105th	R-226	D-207	R-55	D-45	D (Clinton)
1999–2001	106th	R-223	D-211	R-55	D-45	D (Clinton)
2001–2003	107th	R-221	D-212	D-50	R-50	R (G. W. Bush)
2003–2005	108th	R-229	D-204	R-51	D-48	R (G. W. Bush)
2005–2007	109th	R-232	D-202	R-55	D-44	R (G. W. Bush)
2007–2009	110th	D-233	R-202	D-49	R-49	R (G. W. Bush)
2009–2011	111th	D-256	R-178	D-55	R-41	D (Obama)
2011–2013	112th	D-193	R-242	D-51	R-47	D (Obama)
2013–2015	113th	R-234	D-200	D-53	R-45	D (Obama)
2015–2017	114th	R-247	D-188	R-54	D-44	D (Obama)
2017–2019	115th	R-241	D-194	R-52	D-46	R (Trump)
2019–[2]	116th	D-225	R-201	R-51	D-44	R (Trump)

Sources: For data through the 33rd Congress, see U.S. Bureau of the Census, *Historical Statistics of the United States, Colonial Times to 1970* (Washington, DC: Government Printing Office, 1975), 1083–84. For data after the 33rd Congress, see U.S. Congress, Joint Committee on Printing, *Official Congressional Directory* (Washington, DC: Government Printing Office, 2008), 553–54. For 2008–2016 election data, see "Election Statistics, 1920 to Present," U.S. House of Representatives, Office of the Clerk, accessed August 14, 2018, http://history.house.gov/Institution/Election-Statistics/Election-Statistics/. Data for 2008–2016 reflect the immediate results of the elections. Data for 2018 election data (at time of press) from "Live Election Results (House and Senate)," *ABC News*, accessed November 9, 2018, https://abcnews.go.com/Politics/fullpage/midterm-election-map-2018-live-results-58723598.

Notes: Figures are for the beginning of the first session of each Congress. Key to abbreviations: AD—Administration; AM—Anti-Masonic; D—Democratic; DR—Democratic-Republican; F—Federalist; J—Jacksonian; NR—National Republican; Op—Opposition; R—Republican; U—Unionist; W—Whig.

1. The Republican Party ran under the Union Party banner in 1864.

2. Results as of November 9, 2018, pending recounts, runoffs, and challenges.

APPENDIX 7

Summary of Presidential Elections, 1789–2016

Year	No. of states	Candidates		Electoral vote		Popular vote	
1789[a]	10	Fed. George Washington		Fed. 69		—[b]	
1792[a]	15	Fed. George Washington		Fed. 132		—[b]	
1796[a]	16	Dem.-Rep. Thomas Jefferson	Fed. John Adams	Dem.-Rep. 68	Fed. 71	—[b]	
1800[a]	16	Dem.-Rep. Thomas Jefferson Aaron Burr	Fed. John Adams Charles Cotesworth Pinckney	Dem.-Rep. 73	Fed. 65	—[b]	
1804	17	Dem.-Rep. Thomas Jefferson George Clinton	Fed. Charles Cotesworth Pinckney Rufus King	Dem.-Rep. 162	Fed. 14	—[b]	
1808	17	Dem.-Rep. James Madison George Clinton	Fed. Charles Cotesworth Pinckney Rufus King	Dem.-Rep. 122	Fed. 47	—[b]	
1812	18	Dem.-Rep. James Madison Elbridge Gerry	Fed. George Clinton Jared Ingersoll	Dem.-Rep. 128	Fed. 89	—[b]	
1816	19	Dem.-Rep. James Monroe Daniel D. Tompkins	Fed. Rufus King John Howard	Dem.-Rep. 183	Fed. 34	—[b]	
1820	24	Dem.-Rep. James Monroe Daniel D. Tompkins	—[c]	Dem.-Rep. 231	—[b]	—[b]	
1824[d]	24	Dem.-Rep. Andrew Jackson John C. Calhoun	Dem.-Rep John Q. Adams Nathan Sanford	Dem.-Rep. 99	Dem.-Rep. 84	Dem.-Rep 151,271 41.3%	Dem.-Rep 113,122 30.9%
1828	24	Dem.-Rep. Andrew Jackson John C. Calhoun	Nat.-Rep. John Q. Adams Richard Rush	Dem.-Rep. 178	Nat.-Rep. 83	Dem.-Rep. 642,553 56.0%	Nat.-Rep. 500,897 43.6%
1832[e]	24	Dem. Andrew Jackson Martin Van Buren	Nat.-Rep. Henry Clay John Sergeant	Dem. 219	Nat.-Rep. 49 54.2%	Dem. 701,780	Nat.-Rep. 484,205 37.4%
1836[f]	26	Dem. Martin Van Buren Richard M. Johnson	Whig William H. Harrison Francis Granger	Dem. 170	Whig 73	Dem. 764,176 50.8%	Whig 550,816 36.6%

		Dem.	Rep.	Dem.	Rep.	Dem.	Rep.
1840	26	Dem. Martin Van Buren Richard M. Johnson	Whig William H. Harrison John Tyler	Dem. 60	Whig 234	Dem. 1,128,854 46.8%	Whig 1,275,390 52.9%
1844	26	Dem. James Polk George M. Dallas	Whig Henry Clay Theodore Frelinghuysen	Dem. 170	Whig 105	Dem. 1,339,494 49.5%	Whig 1,300,004 48.1%
1848	30	Dem. Lewis Cass William O. Butler	Whig Zachary Taylor Millard Fillmore	Dem. 127	Whig 163	Dem. 1,233,460 42.5%	Whig 1,361,393 47.3%
1852	31	Dem. Franklin Pierce William R. King	Whig Winfield Scott William A. Graham	Dem. 254	Whig 42	Dem. 1,607,510 50.8%	Whig 1,386,942 43.9%

		Candidates		Electoral vote		Popular vote	
Year	No. of states	Dem.	Rep.	Dem.	Rep.	Dem.	Rep.
1856[g]	31	James Buchanan John C. Breckinridge	John C. Frémont William L. Dayton	174	114	1,836,072 45.3%	1,342,345 33.1%
1860[h]	33	Stephen A. Douglas Herschel V. Johnson	Abraham Lincoln Hannibal Hamlin	12	180	1,380,202 29.5%	1,865,908 39.8%
1864[i]	36	George B. McClellan George H. Pendleton	Abraham Lincoln Andrew Johnson	21	212	1,812,807 45.0%	2,218,388 55.0%
1868[j]	37	Horatio Seymour Francis P. Blair Jr.	Ulysses S. Grant Schuyler Colfax	80	214	2,708,744 47.3%	3,013,650 52.7%
1872[k]	37	Horace Greeley Benjamin Gratz Brown	Ulysses S. Grant Henry Wilson		286	2,834,761 43.8%	3,598,235 55.6%
1876	38	Samuel J. Tilden Thomas A. Hendricks	Rutherford B. Hayes William A. Wheeler	184	185	4,288,546 51.0%	4,034,311 47.9%
1880	38	Winfield S. Hancock William H. English	James A. Garfield Chester A. Arthur	155	214	4,444,260 48.2%	4,446,158 48.3%
1884	38	Grover Cleveland Thomas A. Hendricks	James G. Blaine John A. Logan	219	182	4,874,621 48.5%	4,848,936 48.2%
1888	38	Grover Cleveland Allen G. Thurman	Benjamin Harrison Levi P. Morton	168	233	5,534,488 48.6%	5,443,892 47.8%
1892[l]	44	Grover Cleveland Adlai E. Stevenson	Benjamin Harrison Whitelaw Reid	277	145	5,551,883 46.1%	5,179,244 43.0%
1896	45	William J. Bryan Arthur Sewall	William McKinley Garret A. Hobart	176	271	6,511,495 46.7%	7,108,480 51.0%
1900	45	William J. Bryan Adlai E. Stevenson	William McKinley Theodore Roosevelt	155	292	6,358,345 45.5%	7,218,039 51.7%
1904	45	Alton B. Parker Henry G. Davis	Theodore Roosevelt Charles W. Fairbanks	140	336	5,028,898 37.6%	7,626,593 56.4%

(Continued)

(Continued)

Year	No. of states	Candidates Dem.	Candidates Rep.	Electoral vote Dem.	Electoral vote Rep.	Popular vote Dem.	Popular vote Rep.
1908	46	William J. Bryan John W. Kern	William H. Taft James S. Sherman	162	321	6,406, 801 43.0%	7,676,258 51.6%
1912[m]	48	Woodrow Wilson Thomas R. Marshall	William H. Taft James S. Sherman	435	8	6,293,152 41.8%	3,486,333 23.2%
1916	48	Woodrow Wilson Thomas R. Marshall	Charles E. Hughes Charles W. Fairbanks	277	254	9,126,300 49.2%	8,546,789 46.1%
1920	48	James M. Cox Franklin D. Roosevelt	Warren G. Harding Calvin Coolidge	127	404	9,140,884 34.2%	16,133,314 60.3%
1924[n]	48	John W. Davis Charles W. Bryant	Calvin Coolidge Charles G. Dawes	136	382	8,386,169 28.8%	15,717,553 54.1%
1928	48	Alfred E. Smith Joseph T. Robinson	Herbert C. Hoover Charles Curtis	87	444	15,000,185 40.8%	21,411,991 58.2%
1932	48	Franklin D. Roosevelt John N. Garner	Herbert C. Hoover Charles Curtis	472	59	22,825,016 57.4%	15,758,397 39.6%
1936	48	Franklin D. Roosevelt John N. Garner	Alfred M. Landon Frank Knox	523	8	27,747,636 60.8%	16,679,543 36.5%
1940	48	Franklin D. Roosevelt Henry A. Wallace	Wendell L. Willkie Charles L. McNary	449	82	27,263,448 54.7%	22,336,260 44.8%
1944	48	Franklin D. Roosevelt Harry S. Truman	Thomas E. Dewey John W. Bricker	432	99	25,611,936 53.4%	22,013,372 45.9%
1948[o]	48	Harry S. Truman Alben W. Barkley	Thomas E. Dewey Earl Warren	303	189	24,105,587 49.5%	21,970,017 45.1%
1952	48	Adlai E. Stevenson II John J. Sparkman	Dwight D. Eisenhower Richard M. Nixon	89	442	27,314,649 44.4%	33,936,137 55.1%
1956[p]	48	Adlai E. Stevenson II Estes Kefauver	Dwight D. Eisenhower Richard M. Nixon	73	457	26,030,172 42.0%	35,585,245 57.4%
1960[q]	50	John F. Kennedy Lyndon B. Johnson	Richard M. Nixon Henry Cabot Lodge	303	219	34,221,344 49.7%	34,106,671 49.5%
1964	50*	Lyndon B. Johnson Hubert H. Humphrey	Barry Goldwater William E. Miller	486	52	43,126,584 61.1%	27,177,838 38.5%
1968[r]	50*	Hubert H. Humphrey Edmund S. Muskie	Richard M. Nixon Spiro T. Agnew	191	301	31,274,503 42.7%	31,785,148 43.4%
1972[s]	50*	George McGovern Sargent Shriver	Richard M. Nixon Spiro T. Agnew	17	520	29,171,791 37.5%	47,170,179 60.7%

Year	No. of states	Candidates		Electoral vote		Popular vote	
		Dem.	Rep.	Dem.	Rep.	Dem.	Rep.
1976[t]	50*	Jimmy Carter Walter F. Mondale	Gerald R. Ford Robert Dole	297	240	40,830,763 50.1%	39,147,793 48.0%
1980	50*	Jimmy Carter Walter F. Mondale	Ronald Reagan George H. W. Bush	49	489	35,483,883 41.0%	43,904,153 50.7%
1984	50*	Walter F. Mondale Geraldine Ferraro	Ronald Reagan George H. W. Bush	13	525	37,577,185 40.6%	54,455,075 58.8%
1988[u]	50*	Michael S. Dukakis Lloyd Bentsen	George H. W. Bush Dan Quayle	111	426	41,809,074 45.6%	48,886,097 53.4%
1992	50*	William J. Clinton Albert Gore	George H. W. Bush Dan Quayle	370	168	44,909,326 43.0%	39,103,882 37.4%
1996	50*	William J. Clinton Albert Gore	Robert J. Dole Jack F. Kemp	379	159	47,402,357 49.2%	39,198,755 40.7%
2000	50*	Albert Gore Joseph I. Lieberman	George W. Bush Richard B. Cheney	266	271	50,992,335 48.4%	50,455,156 47.9%
2004	50*	John Kerry John Edwards	George W. Bush Richard B. Cheney	252	286	59,026,013 47.3%	62,025,554 50.7%
2008	50*	Barack Obama Joe Biden	John McCain Sarah Palin	365	173	69,498,516 52.9%	59,948,323 45.7%
2012	50*	Barack Obama Joe Biden	Mitt Romney Paul Ryan	332	206	65,915,796 51.0%	60,933,500 47.2%
2016	50*	Hillary Clinton Tim Kaine	Donald Trump Mike Pence	227	304	65,853,510 48.2%	62,984,824 46.1%

Sources: Harold W. Stanley and Richard G. Niemi, *Vital Statistics on American Politics, 2007–2008* (Washington, DC: CQ Press, 2008), 26–30; *CQ Press Guide to U.S. Elections*, 5th ed. (Washington, DC: CQ Press, 2006), 715–19. For 2008–2016 presidential race data, see "Find Election Results and Analysis," CQ Press Voting and Elections Collection, accessed August 14, 2018, http://library.cqpress.com/elections/advsearch/election-results.php. The database is searchable.

Notes: Dem.-Rep.—Democratic-Republican; Fed.—Federalist; Nat.-Rep.—National-Republican; Dem.—Democratic; Rep.—Republican.

a. Elections from 1789 through 1800 were held under rules that did not allow separate voting for president and vice president.

b. Popular vote returns are not shown before 1824 because consistent, reliable data are not available.

c. 1820: One electoral vote was cast for John Adams and Richard Stockton, who were not candidates.

d. 1824: All four candidates represented Democratic-Republican factions. William H. Crawford received 41 electoral votes and Henry Clay received 37 votes. Because no candidate received a majority, the election was decided (in Adams's favor) by the House of Representatives.

e. 1832: Two electoral votes were not cast.

f. 1836: Other Whig candidates receiving electoral votes were Hugh L. White, who received 26 votes, and Daniel Webster, who received 14 votes.

g. 1856: Millard Fillmore, Whig-American, received 8 electoral votes.

h. 1860: John C. Breckinridge, southern Democrat, received 72 electoral votes. John Bell, Constitutional Union, received 39 electoral votes.

i. 1864: Eighty-one electoral votes were not cast.

j. 1868: Twenty-three electoral votes were not cast.

k. 1872: Horace Greeley, Democrat, died after the election. In the Electoral College, Democratic electoral votes went to Thomas Hendricks, 42 votes; Benjamin Gratz Brown, 18 votes; Charles J. Jenkins, 2 votes; and David Davis, 1 vote. Seventeen electoral votes were not cast.

l. 1892: James B. Weaver, People's Party, received 22 electoral votes.

m. 1912: Theodore Roosevelt, Progressive Party, received 88 electoral votes.

n. 1924: Robert M. La Follette, Progressive Party, received 13 electoral votes.

o. 1948: J. Strom Thurmond, States' Rights Party, received 39 electoral votes.

p. 1956: Walter B. Jones, Democrat, received 1 electoral vote.

q. 1960: Harry Flood Byrd, Democrat, received 15 electoral votes.

r. 1968: George C. Wallace, American Independent Party, received 46 electoral votes.

s. 1972: John Hospers, Libertarian Party, received 1 electoral vote.

t. 1976: Ronald Reagan, Republican, received 1 electoral vote.

u. 1988: Lloyd Bentsen, the Democratic vice presidential nominee, received 1 electoral vote for president.

* Fifty states plus the District of Columbia.

GLOSSARY

abolitionist movement: a political struggle to end slavery and free all slaves.

absentee ballots: votes completed and submitted by a voter prior to the day of an election.

achievement gap: the persistent differences in school performance of students of majority ethnicity and higher incomes versus those of minority ethnicity and lower incomes.

adversarial system: a legal structure in which two opposing sides present their case in the most persuasive way possible.

affirmative action: a policy designed to address the consequences of previous discrimination by providing advantages to individuals based upon their identities.

agency capture: when agencies tasked with regulating businesses, industries, or other interest groups are populated by individuals with close ties to the very firms they are supposed to regulate.

agenda-setting: the media's ability to highlight certain issues and bring them to the attention of the public.

aggregating: a process through which Internet and other news providers relay the news as reported by journalists and other sources.

Albany Plan: a proposal for a union of British colonies in North America in which colonial legislatures would choose delegates to form an assembly under the leadership of a chief executive appointed by Great Britain.

Alien and Sedition Acts: four separate laws passed under the administration of President John Adams that, among other things, restricted the freedom of speech and the press.

amendment: a constitutional provision for a process by which changes may be made to the Constitution.

American dream: the idea that individuals should be able to achieve prosperity through hard work, sacrifice, and their own talents.

American exceptionalism: belief in the special character of the United States as a uniquely free nation based on its history and its commitment to democratic ideals and personal liberty.

American political culture: a shared set of beliefs, customs, traditions, and values that define the relationship of Americans to their government and to other American citizens.

anti-Federalists: the name taken by those opposed to the proposed Constitution; the anti-Federalists favored stronger state governments.

appellate jurisdiction: the authority of a court to hear and review decisions made by lower courts in that system.

apportionment: the process of determining the number of representatives for each state using census data; states are divided into congressional districts that have at least one representative each.

appropriation: the process through which congressional committees allocate funds to executive branch agencies, bureaus, and departments.

Arab Spring: a series of protests taking place across North Africa and the Middle East beginning in early 2010 that led to democratic reforms in some nations and civil war and chaos in others.

Articles of Confederation and Perpetual Union: a constituting document calling for the creation of a union of thirteen sovereign states in which the states, and not the union, were the centers of political power.

Astroturf lobbying: when a group presents the facade of grassroots support that does not exist on its own or would not exist without the "purchase" of support by the lobbying firm itself.

bail: an amount of money posted as a security to allow the charged individual to be freed while awaiting trial.

ballot roll-off: when voters do not cast votes for a set of races with which they are not familiar and for which they may not have traditional cues.

bar graph: a type of figure that represents data with rectangles of different sizes.

beat system: the practice of assigning reporters to specific types of news, policies, and events.

bill: a draft of a proposed law.

Bill of Rights: the first ten amendments to the U.S. Constitution that list a set of fundamental rights and freedoms that individuals possess and that government cannot infringe upon.

bipolarity: a distribution of power in the international system where two states exert most of the power and influence.

block grant: a type of grant-in-aid that gives state officials more authority in the disbursement of federal funds.

brief: a legal document presented by plaintiffs, defendants, and, at times, other interested parties outlining their arguments in a case.

broadcast media: outlets for news and other content that rely on mass communications technology to bring stories directly into people's homes; these media sources are subject to stricter content regulations than cable television outlets and alternative sources of information.

Brown v. Board of Education: a landmark 1954 Supreme Court ruling that overturned *Plessy v. Ferguson* and declared legal segregation in public education to be in conflict with the equal protection clause of the Fourteenth Amendment.

budget deficit: when the federal government takes in less money than it spends.

budget resolution: a step in the budgeting process in which Congress provides broad outlines for federal spending.

budget surplus: when the federal government takes in more money than it spends.

bureaucratic adjudication: when the federal bureaucracy settles disputes between parties that arise over the implementation of federal laws and presidential executive orders or determines which individuals or groups are covered under a regulation or program.

bureaucratic discretion: the power to decide how a law is implemented and, at times, what Congress actually meant when it passed a given law.

bureaucratic drift: when bureaucracies stray from their established goals and devote their energies and efforts to peripheral tasks.

business cycle: the fluctuation of economic activity around a long-term trend, with periods of expansion and contraction.

cabinet departments: federal executive departments created and funded by Congress.

campaigns: the political process that would-be representatives use to connect to American voters in hopes of winning office.

capitalist system: a way of structuring economic activity in which private firms are allowed to make most or all of the decisions involving the production and distribution of goods and services.

categorical grant: a grant-in-aid provided to states with specific provisions on its use.

caucus: a process through which a state's eligible voters gather to discuss candidates and issues and select delegates to represent their preferences in later stages of the nomination process.

Central Intelligence Agency (CIA): the federal agency charged with collecting intelligence around the world to protect national security.

challenger: a candidate for office who does not currently hold office.

charter schools: public schools that are funded only by taxpayer money and subject to many of the same regulations as traditional public schools but are accountable primarily to their founding document (their charter) and have greater curricular and professional autonomy.

citizen journalists: nonprofessionals who cover or document news and events or offer their own analyses of them.

civic education: the transmission of information about the political world and civic norms to learners.

civic engagement: working to improve society through political and nonpolitical action.

civil disobedience: the intentional refusal to obey a law in order to call attention to its injustice.

civil law: a category of law covering cases involving private rights and relationships between individuals and groups.

civil liberties: fundamental rights and freedoms of citizens, the protection of which involves restricting the power of a government.

civil rights: fundamental guarantees ensuring equal treatment and protecting against discrimination under the laws of a nation.

clear and present danger test: a Supreme Court tool to evaluate whether or not forms of political expression constitute such a threat to national security as to warrant restriction.

clientele agencies: organizations that act to serve and promote the interests of their clients.

closed primary: a primary election in which only registered voters from a particular political party may vote.

cloture: a procedure through which senators can end debate on a bill and proceed to action, provided three-fifths of senators agree to it.

coattail effect: a phenomenon that occurs when a presidential candidate's increasing popularity results in increased support for congressional candidates of the same party.

Cold War: the period between 1945 and 1991 that was characterized by conflict between the United States and its allies and the Soviet Union and its allies but did not result in full global war.

collective action: political action that occurs when individuals contribute their energy, time, or money to a larger group goal.

collective good: also called a public good; some benefit or desirable outcome that individuals can enjoy or profit from even if they do not help achieve or secure it.

command-and-control economy: a type of economic policy in which government dictates much of a nation's economic activity, including the amount of production and prices for goods.

commerce clause: a part of the Constitution that grants Congress the authority to regulate business and commercial activity.

commercial bias: the shaping of the content and focus of news based upon the desire to capture news consumers.

committee chairs: leaders of the subunits of congressional committees who have authority over the committee's agenda.

Committee on Rules (House): a powerful committee that determines when a bill will be subject to debate and vote on the House floor, how long the debate will last, and whether amendments will be allowed on the floor.

communist system: a way of structuring economic activity in which a government exerts complete control over the production and distribution of goods and services.

concurrent powers: powers granted to both states and the federal government in the Constitution.

confederal systems: structures of governance in which the subnational governments retain the majority of the granted authority.

Congressional Budget Office (CBO): the federal agency tasked with producing independent analyses of budgetary and economic issues to support the congressional budget process.

conservatism: a political ideology that emphasizes a reduced role for government and emphasizes individual liberty.

consideration: a combination of cognition and affect that contributes to any one answer to any one question or evaluation.

constituencies: bodies of voters in a given area who elect a representative or senator.

constitution: a document that defines and creates a people politically, sets out the fundamental principles of governance, and creates the rules and institutions through which a people choose to self-govern.

Constitutional Convention: a meeting held in Philadelphia in 1787 at which state delegates met to fix the Articles of Confederation that would result in the drafting of the U.S. Constitution.

constitutional interpretation: the process of applying the Constitution in assessing whether or not a law, part of a law, or an action by a governmental official is or is not in conflict with the Constitution.

constitutional republic: a form of government in which people vote for elected representatives to make laws and policies and in which limits on the ability of that government to restrict individual rights are placed in a constituting document that is recognized as the highest law of the land.

consumer price index (CPI): an economic measure that is used to assess price changes associated with the cost of living.

containment: a Cold War foreign policy strategy designed to restrict expansion of Soviet ideological and military influence, using military force if necessary.

cooperative federalism: a vision of American federalism in which the states and the national government work together to shape public policy.

countermajoritarian difficulty: the concern that judicial review empowers the Supreme Court to overturn the will of the majority of citizens who have acted through their elected officials.

criminal law: a category of law covering actions determined to harm the community itself.

critical election: a major national election that signals a change either in the balance of power between two major parties or the emergence of a new party system.

cues and information shortcuts: pieces of information individuals pick up that help them form political opinions.

Daughters of Liberty: a group of colonial-era women who participated in the boycotting of British goods.

de facto segregation: a separation of individuals based on identity that arises not by law but because of other factors, such as residential housing patterns.

defendant: a person or group against whom a case is brought in court.

deflation: when a cascading series of defaults arises because there is not enough money to pay off outstanding debt.

de jure segregation: the separation of individuals based on their characteristics, such as race, intentionally and by law.

delegates: people who act as voters' representatives at a convention to select their party's presidential nominee.

democracy: a system of government where power is held and political decisions are made by the people in that society.

demographics: the grouping of individuals based on shared characteristics, such as ancestry, race, ethnicity, and gender.

Department of Defense: the executive branch department responsible for formulating and enacting American defense policy and managing the U.S. Armed Forces.

Department of Homeland Security: the executive branch department responsible for overseeing and implementing policies enacted to respond to national disasters, secure transit points to and within the United States, and protect the nation's borders.

Department of State: the cabinet department primarily responsible for diplomatic relationships with other nations.

deregulation: the reduction or elimination of government power in a particular industry, usually in order to create more competition within the industry.

descriptive representation: the degree to which a body of representatives in a legislature does or does not reflect the diversity of that nation's identities and lived experiences.

desegregation: the act of eliminating laws or practices that separate individuals based upon racial identity.

deservingness: the idea of who is rightfully owed a certain benefit.

devolution: a national policy goal of returning more authority to state or local governments.

digital divide: divisions in society that are driven by access to and knowledge about technologies; these gaps often fall along the lines of partisanship, class, race, and ethnicity.

direct democracy: a form of government in which citizens vote directly on policies.

direction: the focus of an individual's opinion.

director of national intelligence: the head of all the intelligence agencies in the United States.

discretionary spending: spending for programs and policies at the discretion of Congress and the president.

domestic policy: policy designed to improve the social welfare of citizens.

double jeopardy: the prosecution of an individual more than once for the same crime.

dual federalism: a view of American federalism in which the states and the nation operate independently in their own areas of public policy.

due process clause: the clause in the Fourteenth Amendment that restricts state governments from denying their citizens the right to due process of law.

earmarks: additions to a piece of legislation that direct specific funds to projects within districts or states.

economic equality: when wealth is relatively evenly distributed across society.

economic interest groups: groups that organize to advocate on behalf of the economic interests of their members.

economic policy: the efforts of government to regulate and support the economy in order to protect and expand citizens' financial well-being and economic prospects and to support businesses in the global financial system.

economic recession: a period of decline in economic activity, typically defined by two consecutive quarters of negative GDP growth.

economy: the systems and organizations through which a society produces and distributes goods and services.

elections: the political system through which American voters choose their representatives.

Electoral College: a slate of individuals apportioned to states who are pledged to vote for a presidential candidate.

elites: a small number of individuals (who tend to have well-informed and well-reasoned opinions).

elitist theory: a theory of governmental influence that focuses on the advantages that certain interests have in the political process based on the unequal distribution of economic and political power.

entitlement programs: programs wherein one receives a set of benefits regardless of income provided one meets certain categorical requirements, such as age or a minimum number of years of payroll contributions.

enumerated powers: powers explicitly granted to the government via the Constitution.

equal protection clause: a clause of the Fourteenth Amendment that serves as the constitutional basis for the assault on educational segregation in the courts and for the assertion of civil rights for Americans of many different identities in many different areas of public and private life.

Equal Rights Amendment: a proposed but not ratified amendment to the Constitution that sought to guarantee equality of rights based upon sex.

equal time rule: a regulation that requires American radio and television broadcast networks to provide equal time for political candidates to present their views on issues.

essentialism: the risks posed by linking individuals' lived experiences to policy preferences, whether by identifying those individuals by those policies or by excluding them from advocating different policy objectives.

establishment clause: a First Amendment clause protecting individuals from governmental establishment of, or support for, religion.

European Union (EU): an association of European countries formed in the 1990s for the purpose of achieving political and economic integration.

exclusionary rule: a rule governing the inadmissibility of evidence obtained without a proper warrant.

executive agreements: agreements between a president and another nation that do not have the same durability in the American system as a treaty but may carry important foreign policy consequences.

executive branch: the institution responsible for carrying out laws passed by the legislative branch.

Executive Office of the President: a collection of offices within the White House organization designed primarily to provide information to the president.

executive orders: directions made by presidents to the executive branch departments that often contain nothing more than instructions to be carried out by agencies, bureaus, and departments but may at times be considered acts of presidential lawmaking.

executive political appointees: employees at high levels in the federal bureaucracy who serve at the pleasure of the president and are subject to presidential removal.

executive privilege: a right claimed by presidents to keep confidential certain conversations, records, and transcripts from outside scrutiny, especially that of Congress.

exit poll: a survey conducted outside a polling place in which individuals are asked who or what they just voted for and why.

exploratory committee: a group that helps determine whether a potential candidate should run for office and that helps lay the groundwork for the campaign.

extended republic: a republic so large and diverse, with so many factions vying for power, that no one faction is able to assert its will over all the others.

faction: a group of self-interested people who use the government to get what they want, trampling the rights of others in the process.

fairness doctrine: a federal rule that expanded regulations for American political news coverage beyond just the provision of time for candidates to the content of the coverage itself.

faithless electors: members of the Electoral College who do not cast their vote for the pledged candidate.

fake news: a term that may refer to the intentional presentation of news in favor of a political party or the intentional presentation of unverified or inaccurate news.

federal bureaucracy: the organizations and suborganizations within the executive branch that are tasked with putting the laws of the nation into effect.

Federal Bureau of Investigation (FBI): the federal agency charged with carrying out investigations for the attorney general and with safeguarding national security within the United States.

federal civil service: the permanent professional branches of government concerned with administrative functions, excluding the armed forces and political appointments.

federal courts of appeals: the middle level of the federal judiciary; these courts review and hear appeals from the federal district courts.

federal district courts: the lowest level of the federal judiciary; these courts usually possess original jurisdiction in cases that originate at the federal level.

federalism: a structure of governance that places the people's authority in two or more levels of government.

The Federalist Papers: a series of eighty-five essays written by Alexander Hamilton, James Madison, and John Jay and published between 1787 and 1788 that lay out the theory behind the Constitution.

Federalists: the name taken by supporters of the proposed Constitution; the Federalists called for a stronger national government.

federal judiciary: the branch of the federal government that interprets and applies the laws of the nation.

Federal Reserve System: the central bank of the United States.

federal systems: structures of governance that divide a people's sovereignty between two or more levels of government.

felon disenfranchisement: the denial of voting rights to Americans who have been convicted of felonies.

Fifteenth Amendment: an amendment to the Constitution passed in 1870 affirming the voting rights of all freedmen.

fighting words: expression (spoken, written, or symbolic) that is likely to incite violence or disrupt the peace.

filibuster: a tactic through which an individual senator may postpone action on a piece of legislation.

fire alarm oversight: a term that describes congressional oversight procedures primarily in response to problems or complaints.

fiscal policy: a set of activities through which government tries to lower unemployment, support economic activity, and stabilize the economy by using policies of taxation and spending.

focus group: a small group of individuals assembled for a directed conversation during which one hopes to uncover patterns of thinking about issues and individuals.

focusing events: sudden and dramatic events that draw individuals' attention.

foreign policy: the ways in which political actors in a nation engage others at home and abroad to advance their nation's interests, protect and secure national security, and support their own economies.

Fourteenth Amendment: an amendment to the Constitution passed in 1868 affirming the citizenship of all persons born or naturalized in the United States and, for the first time in the history of the Constitution, placing explicit restrictions on the laws of states that sought to abridge the privileges and immunities of citizens of the United States.

framing: influencing people's interpretations of news, events, or issues through the presentation of the context.

freedom of expression: a fundamental right affirmed in the First Amendment to speak, publish, and act in the political space.

free exercise clause: a First Amendment clause guarding the rights of individuals to exercise and express their religious beliefs.

free riders: individuals who enjoy collective goods without helping to secure them.

free trade: a trade policy characterized by few restrictions on the flow of goods and services across national borders.

front-loading: when a state pushes its primary or caucus to a date as early in the season as possible to become more instrumental in the nomination process.

full faith and credit clause: a portion of the Constitution that generally requires states to honor licenses and judicial outcomes of other states.

gender gap: a term that refers to the fact that American women are more likely to identify with and vote for Democratic Party candidates than men, who are more likely to vote for Republican Party candidates.

gerrymandering: the intentional use of redistricting to benefit a specific interest or group of voters.

get out the vote (GOTV): efforts to mobilize voters or potential voters.

going public: a strategy through which presidents reach out directly to the American people with the hope that the people will, in turn, put pressure upon their representatives and senators to press for a president's policy goals.

government: a system of rules and institutions that defines and shapes the contours of public action.

governmental interest groups: organizations that act to secure the interests of local, state, or foreign governments in the political process.

government corporations: organizations that act as businesses within the federal government, charging fees for their services but still subject to governmental control and possible financial subsidization.

grand jury: a group of citizens who, based on the evidence presented to them, conclude whether or not a person is to be indicted and subsequently tried in a court of law.

grant-in-aid: federal money provided to states to implement public policy objectives.

Great Compromise: an agreement for a plan of government that drew upon both the Virginia and New Jersey Plans; it settled issues of state representation by calling for a bicameral legislature with a House of Representatives apportioned proportionately and a Senate apportioned equally.

Great Depression: a period defined by the most significant economic crisis in American history.

gridlock: an inability to compromise and enact legislation that is driven by political polarization.

gross domestic product (GDP): a measure of the total value of goods and services produced by a nation's economic activity.

hate speech: speech that has no other purpose but to express hatred, particularly toward members of a group identified by racial or ethnic identity, gender, or sexual orientation.

horse race phenomenon: coverage of political campaigns that focuses more on the drama of the campaign than on policy issues.

House majority leader: the head of the party with the most seats in the House of Representatives, chosen by the party's members.

House minority leader: the head of the party with the second-highest number of seats in the House of Representatives, chosen by the party's members.

hyperinflation: extremely rapid or out-of-control inflation brought on by excessive printing of money and loss of faith in a currency.

impeachment: a legislative process for removing elected and appointed officials.

implementation: the bureaucracy's role in putting into action the laws that Congress has passed.

implied powers: powers not textually granted to a government but considered valid in order to carry out the enumerated powers.

inalienable rights: rights that exist before and above any government or its power.

incentives: inducements that leaders of a bureaucracy can offer to their employees to spur successful performance.

income-based repayment: a type of loan repayment plan in which individual student debtors could have their loan payments reduced and eventually forgiven based on their incomes and ability to pay off these significant debts.

incumbency advantage: institutional advantages held by those already in office who are trying to fend off challengers in an election.

incumbent: a current officeholder.

independent executive agency: an agency similar to a cabinet department but existing outside the cabinet structure and usually having a narrower focus of mission.

independent regulatory agencies: organizations that exist outside the major cabinet departments and whose job is to monitor and regulate specific sectors of the economy.

inflation: the rise in the prices of goods and services purchased by individuals.

infotainment: a merging of information and entertainment in a way designed to attract viewers and gain market share.

inside lobbying: when lobbyists contact members of Congress or their staff directly to advocate for their group's position.

intelligence community: the collective name for all the intelligence agencies in the United States and their members.

intensity: the strength of involvement and preference of an individual's opinion.

interagency rivalry: when two or more agencies are charged with a similar mandate, an outcome that becomes more likely in times of budget cuts and competition for scarce or dwindling appropriations.

interest groups: voluntary associations of people who come together with an agreed-upon set of political and policy objectives and who attempt to pull the levers of political power in service of these defined goals.

interest rates: the rates paid to borrow money.

intergovernmental lobbying: efforts by state and local governments to act in Washington on behalf of their own interests.

intermediate scrutiny: a middle-ground standard for determining whether differential treatment is allowable.

internationalism: an approach to international affairs that emphasizes close contact and cooperation between nations.

intersectionality: the presence of multiple and overlapping identities and inequalities.

Intolerable Acts: a term used in the American colonies to refer to a series of laws enacted by Great Britain in response to the Boston Tea Party.

investigative journalism: an approach to newsgathering in which reporters dig into stories, often looking for instances of corruption or failures to uphold the interests of citizens.

iron triangle: the coordinated (and mutually beneficial) activities of interest groups, Congress, and the bureaucracy to achieve shared policy goals, sometimes against the general interests of society or specific groups within it.

isolationism: a foreign policy orientation in which a nation attempts to stay out of foreign entanglements.

issue network: the webs of influence among interest groups, policymakers, and policy advocates.

Jim Crow laws: state and local laws passed after Reconstruction through the mid-1950s by which white southerners reasserted their dominance by denying African Americans basic social, economic, and civil rights, such as the right to vote.

Joint Chiefs of Staff: an advisory body reporting to the president on military operations.

judicial activism: a philosophy of constitutional interpretation that asserts justices should wield the power of judicial review when needed.

judicial branch: the institution responsible for hearing and deciding cases via a system of federal courts.

judicial restraint: a philosophy of constitutional interpretation that asserts justices should be cautious in overturning laws.

judicial review: the authority of the highest court in a political system to determine if a law is or is not in conflict with a government's highest law, which in the United States is the Constitution.

laissez-faire economy: a type of economic policy in which governments intrude as little as possible in the economic transactions between citizens and businesses.

legal segregation: the separation by law of individuals based upon their racial identities.

legislative branch: in a divided government, the institution responsible for making laws.

legislative deliberation: the considered argument and discussion of the issues by congressional representatives.

Lemon test: a three-pronged test developed by the Supreme Court to determine whether a law or action by the federal or a state government violates the establishment clause.

libel: expression in written form or similarly published media that defames a person's character.

liberalism: a political ideology that emphasizes more robust governmental action, especially to ensure equality.

libertarianism: a political ideology that emphasizes minimal governmental involvement in individual choices.

liberty: social, political, and economic freedoms.

line graph: a type of figure that presents data as a set of points connected by lines.

linked fate: a theory of group identification that describes ways in which individuals tie their own life chances to those of members of a group who share their lived experiences.

lobbying: interacting with government officials to advance a group's goals in the area of public policy.

logroll: an exchange of political favors, such as when legislators trade votes to support one another's proposed legislation.

magnet schools: public schools designed to attract students due to their focus or excellence; they may have admissions procedures.

majority: when a candidate receives more than 50 percent of the vote.

majority-minority district: a district in which voters of a minority ethnicity constitute an electoral majority within that electoral district.

malapportionment: the uneven distribution of the population between legislative districts.

markup: a process during which a bill is revised prior to a final vote in Congress.

Marshall Plan: a Cold War policy wherein loans and aid were made available to the nations of Western Europe; it also established organizations of economic cooperation.

masses: the majority of individuals (who tend to be less informed).

mass media: sources of information that appeal to a wide audience, including newspapers, radio, television, and Internet outlets.

material rewards: a type of tangible benefit made available to members and contributors of a group.

media effects: the power of the news media in shaping individuals' political knowledge, preferences, and political behavior.

merit system: a system of hiring and promotion based on competitive testing results, education, and other qualifications rather than politics and personal connections.

minimalist paradigm: a theory of public opinion that emphasizes how most people fall short of what we expect them to know, think about, and pay attention to in the complicated world of politics and policy.

Miranda rights: the right not to speak and to have an attorney present during questioning; these rights must be given by police to individuals suspected of criminal activity.

mixed economy: a type of economic policy in which many economic decisions are left to individuals and businesses but the federal government also plays a role in shaping these decisions.

monetary policy: a set of economic policy tools designed to regulate the amount of money in the economy (in circulation and in the deposits).

Monroe Doctrine: a policy that asserted American interests in and primacy over actions in the Western hemisphere.

Motor Voter Law: a law allowing Americans to register to vote when applying for or renewing their driver's licenses and making it easier for Americans with disabilities to register to vote.

national convention: a meeting where delegates officially select their party's nominee for the presidency.

national debt: the sum of all previously incurred annual federal deficits.

National Security Council: an advisory body that provides the president with intelligence, analysis, and advice on critical matters of national security.

natural rights: rights that people have inherently that are not granted by any government.

necessary and proper clause: a part of the Constitution that grants the federal government the authority to pass laws required to carry out its enumerated powers; also called the elastic clause.

need-based assistance: social welfare programs whose benefits are allocated to individuals demonstrating specific needs.

negative campaign advertisements: campaign ads that attack an opponent or opponents and try to raise doubts in voters' minds about them.

negative freedoms: fundamental liberties of which protection is ensured by restricting governmental action and authority.

net neutrality: the idea that Internet service providers should not be allowed to discriminate based upon content or bandwidth demands.

neutrality test: a Supreme Court test for examining questions of free expression that allows restrictions upon religious expression, provided that laws doing so not single out one faith, or faith over nonfaith.

New Deal: a set of policies passed during the administration of President Franklin Roosevelt to combat the Great Depression.

New Jersey Plan: a plan of government that preserved many of the provisions in the Articles of Confederation, including the unicameral legislature with equal votes for each state, but strengthened the confederal government.

news media: the variety of sources providing information and covering events, including newspapers, television, radio, the Internet, and social media.

niche journalism: media that cater to fragmented and specialized audiences.

Nineteenth Amendment: a 1920 amendment to the Constitution that prevented states from denying the right to vote based on sex.

nomination: the formal process through which parties choose their candidates for political office.

nonattitudes: a term referring to the lack of stable and coherent opinions on political issues and candidates.

norms: unwritten expectations of how members are supposed to act that help members balance representing their constituents and contributing to the smooth functioning of the House and Senate.

North American Free Trade Agreement (NAFTA): a regional trade agreement made between the United States, Canada, and Mexico designed to increase trade between the nations.

North Atlantic Treaty Alliance (NATO): an alliance created during the Cold War that requires America and all other members to come to the military aid of each other in case of attack.

obscenity and pornography: text, images, or video that depicts sexual activity in ways offensive to the broader community and that lacks any artistic merit.

Office of Management and Budget (OMB): the executive branch office whose purpose is to assist the president in setting national spending priorities.

open primary: a primary election in which all eligible voters may vote, regardless of their partisan affiliation.

open seat election: an election in which no incumbent is seeking reelection.

oral arguments: presentations made by plaintiffs and attorneys before the Supreme Court.

original jurisdiction: the authority of a court to act as the first court to hear a case, which includes the finding of facts in the case.

outside (grassroots) lobbying: a type of lobbying that focuses on reaching constituents and mobilizing them to pressure their representatives rather than pressuring the representatives directly.

oversight: efforts by Congress to ensure that executive branch agencies, bureaus, and cabinet departments, as well as their officials, are acting legally and in accordance with congressional goals.

partisan bias: the slanting of political news coverage in support of a particular political party or ideology.

partisan press: media outlets or organizations that promote a particular political ideology or support a political party.

party identification: the degree to which an individual identifies with and supports a particular political party.

party platform: a set of positions and policy objectives that members of a political party agree to.

party systems: periods of stability of the composition of political parties and the issues around which they coalesce, brought on by shorter periods of intense change.

path dependence: the way in which a set of political outcomes shapes future possibilities for political action.

penny press: nineteenth-century American newspapers that sold for only one cent each, thus increasing the size of the audience that could afford to purchase them.

plaintiff: a person or group who brings a case in court.

plea bargaining: a legal process in which the plaintiff and defendant agree to an outcome prior to the handing out of a verdict.

Plessy v. Ferguson: a Supreme Court case in 1896 that upheld legal racial segregation.

pluralism: a theory of governmental influence that views the distribution of political power among many competing groups as serving to keep any one of them in check.

plurality: when a candidate receives more votes than any other candidate.

police patrol oversight: a term that describes congressional oversight as a process of constant monitoring rather than responding to specific crises.

police powers: a category of reserved powers that includes the protection of people's health, safety, and welfare.

policy agenda: the set of issues to which government officials, voters, and the public attend.

policy diffusion: the process through which states emulate and adopt policies enacted by other states.

policy entrepreneurs: individuals in government, academic institutions, think tanks, interest groups, and other venues who try to shape the political agenda and get their solutions implemented.

policy feedback: the idea that policies, once enacted, open up and close off future policy options, especially because of the effects of policy on politics and political actors.

political action committees (PACs): organizations that raise money to support chosen candidates and defeat others.

political ambition: a personal desire to enter politics.

political efficacy: a person's belief that she or he can make effective political change.

political equality: when members of a society possess the same rights under the laws of the nation.

political ideology: a set of beliefs about the desired goals and outcomes of a process of governance.

political institutions: rules and structures that shape political action and representation.

political mobilization: efforts by members of American political parties to turn out the vote and encourage their members to get others to do so.

political participation: the different ways in which individuals take action to shape the laws and policies of a government.

political party: an organized group of candidates, officeholders, voters, and activists who work together to elect candidates to political office.

political patronage: filling administrative positions as a reward for support rather than based solely on merit.

political polarization: a sharp ideological distance between political parties.

political propaganda: attempts to shape governmental actions and laws by changing people's beliefs and opinions.

political science: the systematic study of the ways in which ideas, individuals, and institutions shape political outcomes.

political socialization: the variety of experiences and factors that shape our political values, attitudes, and behaviors.

politics: the process of influencing the actions of officials and the policies of a nation, state, locality, or community.

populism: a political movement that challenges the political establishment.

positive freedoms: fundamental rights and freedoms that require action by individuals to express and by governments to secure.

power elite: a group composed of the top echelons of people in the business world, government, and military.

precedent: a judicial decision that guides future courts in handling similar cases.

preemptive war: a type of war in which a state uses its military might to challenge adversaries before they launch attacks or harbor those who might do so.

presidential pardon: the presidential authority to forgive an individual and set aside punishment for a crime.

presidential primary elections: elections in which a state's voters choose delegates who support a particular candidate for nomination.

priming: shaping individuals' interpretations of news or events by highlighting certain details or contexts.

principal-agent problem: the challenge that arises when one actor, the principal, tasks another, the agent, to carry out the principal's wishes in the presence of uncertainty and unequal information.

prior restraint: the suppression of material prior to publication on the grounds that it might endanger national security.

privacy: a right not enumerated in the Constitution but affirmed by Supreme Court decisions that covers individuals' decisions in their private lives, including decisions regarding reproductive rights and sexuality.

private bureaucracies: privately owned corporations and companies that carry out specific tasks according to a prescribed set of rules and procedures.

private contractors: nongovernmental workers hired by the federal bureaucracy to provide goods and services in support of federal activity.

private market: an exchange of goods or services in which the quality is determined by the willingness of private individuals to consume it, thus setting its price.

privatization: shifting control over the provision of certain governmental functions from the federal bureaucracy to the private sector.

probable cause: reasonable belief that a crime has been committed or that there is evidence indicating so.

procedural justice: a judicial standard requiring that fairness be applied to all participants equally.

proportional representation system: a structure of electoral representation in which parties are represented in government according to their candidates' overall share of the vote.

protectionism: restricting access by foreign producers to American markets in order to benefit specific domestic agricultural, industrial, and service providers.

protest: a public demonstration designed to call attention to the need for action or change.

proxy wars: wars in which major powers support different sides but do not directly go to war with each other.

public interest groups: groups that act on behalf of the collective interests of a broad group of individuals, many of whom may not be members or contributors to the organization.

public opinion: the sum of individual attitudes about government, policies, and issues.

public opinion survey: sampling a portion of the public in order to draw conclusions about the larger population's views on an issue.

public policy: the intentional use of governmental power to secure the health, welfare, opportunities, and national security of citizens.

purposive benefits: rewards in the form of satisfaction from working with others to achieve a common goal or purpose.

push poll: a negative campaign tactic disguised as a survey in which a candidate's opponent or opponents are portrayed in an unfavorable way.

question order: the ways in which earlier questions in a survey may shape answers to later questions.

question wording: the ways in which the phrasing of survey questions may shape answers.

race of interviewer effects: the potential impact of the racial identities of surveyors and respondents on the respondents' answers.

random digit dialing: when potential survey respondents are selected by computer-generated random numbers.

random selection: how participants are selected from the population for inclusion in the study.

Reagan Doctrine: a foreign policy agenda under President Ronald Reagan offering American assistance, including military training and weaponry, to anticommunist groups.

realignment: a major shift in allegiance to the political parties that is often driven by changes in the issues that unite or divide voters.

reasonableness standard: a more relaxed judicial standard in which differential treatment must be shown to be reasonable and not arbitrary.

recess appointment: occurs when Congress is not in session and the president appoints a person to fill a position that would normally require the advice and consent of the Senate. Unless the person is formally confirmed when the Senate reconvenes, the position ends at the conclusion of the next session of Congress.

recruitment: the process through which political parties identify potential candidates.

redistricting: states' redrawing of the electoral district boundaries following each census.

registration requirements: the set of rules that govern who can vote and how, when, and where they vote.

represent: to "stand for" the interests of voters in government.

representative democracy: a political system in which voters select representatives who then vote on matters of public policy.

republics: governments ruled by representatives of the people.

reserved powers: powers reserved to the states if not textually granted to the federal government.

respondents: individuals who answer a survey.

responsible party model: a proposal for party reform that emphasized cohesive party positions that present voters with a clear set of choices and allow members' voices to be effectively incorporated into party positions on issues.

retrospective voting: voting based on reflecting back on an incumbent's past performance in an election.

revolving door phenomenon: the movement of individuals between government and lobbying positions.

roll-call vote: a recorded vote on a bill.

Roosevelt Corollary: a policy that asserted that the United States was the guarantor of political, military, and economic stability in Latin America and the Caribbean.

rulemaking: the process through which the federal bureaucracy fills in critical details of a law.

runoff election: an election that is held between the two candidates with the highest total votes if no one candidate scores a majority.

salience: the centrality of an individual's opinion in the sense of the opinion's ability to shape the individual's views on other issues or candidates.

sample: the subgroup of individuals from the larger population of whom one wants to measure the opinions.

sampling error: error in a statistical analysis arising from the unrepresentativeness of the sample taken.

school choice: a type of reform that allows parents and guardians to choose their students' schools and produces competition between the schools themselves to attract students.

scientific poll: when pollsters try to gain an understanding of a large group of individuals by obtaining the opinions of a carefully chosen small sample of the group, although they are aware of the limitations of the effort.

Second Continental Congress: an assembly of delegates from the thirteen British colonies in America that drafted and approved the Declaration of Independence, conducted the Revolutionary War, and created the governmental structure that followed the war.

secretary of defense: the head of the Department of Defense.

secretary of state: the head of the Department of State.

selective benefits: goods that are made available only to those who join or contribute to a group.

selective incorporation: the piecemeal process through which the Supreme Court has affirmed that almost all the protections within the Bill of Rights also apply to state governments.

self-selected listener opinion poll (SLOP): a survey where respondents choose to respond to a survey prompt on their own.

Senate majority leader: a chosen senator who speaks for the majority party and helps to shape the Senate agenda

senatorial courtesy: a traditional norm in which presidents consult with senators from the states when considering potential nominees to the lower levels of the federal judiciary.

Senior Executive Service (SES): federal employees with higher-level supervisory and administrative responsibilities who are paid and treated more like vice presidents of businesses than political figures.

separate but equal: the doctrine that racial segregation was constitutional so long as the facilities for blacks and whites were roughly equal.

separation of powers: a design of government that distributes powers across institutions to avoid making one branch too powerful on its own.

Seven Years' War: a war principally between France and Great Britain and other European nations that was fought across the globe.

Shays' Rebellion: a grassroots popular uprising against the government of Massachusetts that led to calls for reform, or replacement, of the Articles of Confederation.

signing statements: text written by a president while signing a bill into law, usually consisting of political statements or reasons for signing the bill but possibly also including the president's interpretation of the law itself.

single-member plurality system: a structure of electoral representation in which a candidate and the party that he or she represents must win the most votes in a state or district in order to be represented in government.

slander: expression in spoken form that defames a person's character.

social benefits: rewards in the form of new connections or access to networks that members of a group receive through their participation.

social contract: an agreement in which people give to their governments the ability to rule over them to ensure an orderly and functioning society.

social equality: when no individual's social status is inherently higher than another's.

social insurance programs: programs such as Social Security that are financed by payroll taxes paid by individuals and that do not have income-based requirements to receive their benefits.

socialism: a political ideology that emphasizes an even stronger role for government than liberalism, including government control and ownership of sectors of the economy.

socialist system: a way of structuring economic activity in which private firms are allowed to operate and make decisions over production and distribution, but with significant governmental involvement to ensure economic equality.

social media: forms of electronic communication that enable users to create and share content or to participate in social networking.

social movements: voluntary associations of individuals who come together to change things or keep things from changing, but they often do so by calling attention to a set of injustices or wrongs in order to get policymakers to act and to educate the public about the issue.

social welfare policies: governmental efforts designed to improve or protect the health, safety, education, and opportunities for citizens and residents.

socioeconomic status (SES): a measure that captures an individual's wealth, income, occupation, and educational attainment.

soft news: stories that focus on celebrity and personality rather than political or economic issues.

soft power: the advancement of a nation's interests by exporting its values and culture abroad.

solicitor general: a presidential appointee who represents the federal government in the Supreme Court.

Sons of Liberty: a group initially formed of merchants and workingmen in response to the Stamp Act that resisted Great Britain and its tax policies.

Speaker of the House: the leader of the House of Representatives, chosen by an election of its members.

split-ticket voting: when a voter chooses a candidate from one party for one office and a candidate from a different party for another position on the ballot.

spoils system: the practice of cleaning house of one's opponents and installing supporters in their place following a successful election.

stability: the degree of change over time, in different contexts, or in response to differently worded survey questions of a particular opinion.

standard operating procedures: the sets of rules governing the behavior of bureaucrats.

standards-based reforms: reforms that set specific state or nationwide student achievement goals, rewards for success, and, most notably, consequences for failure.

standing: the legal ability to bring a case in court.

stare decicis: a doctrine of constitutional interpretation based upon following earlier decisions in similar cases.

state and local bureaucracies: public organizations below the federal level designed to carry out specific tasks according to a prescribed set of rules and procedures.

State of the Union address: an annual speech before Congress in which the president highlights the administration's achievements and presses a legislative agenda.

state sovereignty resolutions: state legislative measures that affirm the sovereignty of states under the Tenth Amendment.

states' rights: the idea that American states have the authority to self-govern, even when in conflict with national laws.

statutes: written laws established by a legislative body.

stereotype: a preconceived, often oversimplified idea about something that people apply as a filter to the world.

straw poll: an unofficial tally of opinion or support at a meeting or event.

strict scrutiny: the most stringent judicial standard applied for deciding whether a law or policy is allowed to treat people differently.

substantive representation: the degree to which elected representatives or senators represent the interests and policy preferences of their constituents.

suffrage: the right to vote in political elections.

superdelegates: members of the Democratic Party—usually leaders or members of note—who are not pledged to any certain candidate based on the outcomes of their state's primary or caucus.

super PACs: political action committees permitted to spend unlimited amounts of money in a campaign, though these actions must not be coordinated with that campaign.

superpower: an extremely powerful state that is capable of influencing international events and the actions of other less powerful states.

supremacy clause: a part of the Constitution that establishes the Constitution and the laws of the nation passed under its authority as the highest laws of the nation.

Supreme Court: the highest level of the federal judiciary, which was established in the Constitution and serves as the highest court in the nation.

swing states: states where no one political party tends to dominate national elections.

symbolic speech: protected expression in the form of images, signs, and other symbols.

term limits: formal limits on the number of times an elected official may serve in a given office.

terrorism: the use of violence as a means to achieve political ends.

third party (minor party): a political party operating over a limited period of time in competition with two other major parties.

Thirteenth Amendment: an amendment to the Constitution passed in 1865 prohibiting slavery within the United States.

Three-Fifths Compromise: an agreement reached by delegates at the Constitutional Convention that ensured that a slave would count as three-fifths of a person for a state's representation.

Title IX: a section of a 1972 federal law that prohibited discrimination on the basis of sex in any educational programs and activities.

top-two primary system: an electoral system in which candidates, regardless of party, compete in the primary elections, with the top two vote-getters, regardless of party, advancing to the general election.

Trans-Pacific Partnership (TPP): a regional trade agreement struck between twelve nations in the Pacific Rim, including Mexico, Australia, and East Asian and South American nations.

turf wars: when bureaucrats compete to take duties and responsibilities away from one another's departments or keep their opponents from doing so.

tyranny: the suppression of the rights of a people by those holding power.

tyranny of the majority: when a large number of citizens use the power of their majority to trample on the rights of a smaller group.

tyranny of the minority: when a small number of citizens trample on the rights of the larger population.

unemployment rate: the percentage of the total labor force that is unemployed.

unfunded mandates: federal regulations that must be followed by the states but whose costs must also be shouldered by the states.

unipolarity: a distribution of power in the international system where one state exerts most of the power and influence.

unitary systems: structures of governance that place the people's sovereignty in a national government, with subnational governments deriving their authority from it.

United Nations: an international organization formed in 1945 to promote international dialogue and cooperation.

unorthodox lawmaking: a term that refers to ways in which legislative activity, especially on major bills, is often more fluid than described in a traditional textbook.

validity: the degree to which a tool accurately measures what it is intended to.

veto: the power of a president to reject a bill passed by Congress, sending it back to the originating branch with objections noted.

Virginia Plan: a plan of government calling for a strong national government with three branches of government and a bicameral legislature, with legislators elected using proportional representation.

voluntary associations: groups and communities who join with each other in pursuit of collective interests and common goals.

voter turnout: the number of eligible voters who actually participate in an election versus the total number of eligible voters.

voucher program: an educational policy that distributes public funds to parents and guardians, allowing them to send their students to private and alternative schools.

War Powers Resolution of 1973: a law passed over a presidential veto that restricts the power of the president in committing the nation's armed forces into combat or situations of likely combat.

warrant: a writ issued by a judge authorizing some activity.

weighting: a procedure in which the observed results of a survey are adjusted according to what is known about specific proportions in the larger population.

whip: an individual in the House or Senate, chosen by his or her party members, whose job is to ensure party unity and discipline.

wire service: an organization that gathers and reports on news and then sells the stories to other outlets.

writ of certiorari: the process through which most cases reach the Supreme Court; after four justices concur that the Court should hear the case, a writ of certiorari is issued to the lower court to request the relevant case records.

writ of habeas corpus: a statement demanding that authorities in charge of a person's detention establish the reasons for that detention.

yellow journalism: an approach to reporting employed in the nineteenth century that relied on sensational headlines and emotional language to persuade readers and sell newspapers.

NOTES

CHAPTER 1

1. Tony Mauro, "Bible Club vs. School Lands in High Court," *USA Today*, January 8, 1990.
2. Ibid.
3. 98 Stat. 1302, 20 U.S.C. §§ 4071–4074. Cornell University Law School, Legal Information Institute, https://www.law.cornell.edu/uscode/text/20/4071.
4. Nat Hentoff, "A Bible Study Club in a Public School?" *Washington Post*, March 14, 1989.
5. *Board of Education of Westside Community Schools v. Mergens by and through Mergens*, 496 U.S. 226 (1990).
6. Robert K. Skolrood, "Don't Bar Bible Clubs from Schools," *USA Today*, January 10, 1990.
7. *Board of Education of Westside Community Schools v. Mergens*.
8. Ruth Marcus, "Schools Brace for Fallout from Bible-Club Ruling: Some Officials Fear Disruptive Groups Will Enter through Door Opened by Court to Religion," *Washington Post*, June 11, 1990.
9. *Boyd County High School Gay Straight Alliance v. Board of Education of Boyd County, KY*, 258 F. Supp. 2d 667 (E.D. Ky. 2003).
10. Ibid. The ACLU had sent the letter in September before the meeting in which the decision to deny was taken.
11. Ibid.
12. Ibid.
13. Ibid.
14. American Civil Liberties Union, "ACLU Wins Settlement for Kentucky School's Gay-Straight Alliance," February 3, 2014, https://www.aclu.org/news/aclu-wins-settlement-kentucky-schools-gay-straight-alliance.
15. National Legal Foundation, "Welcome," www.nlf.net.
16. Philip Bump, "48 Percent of Millennials Think the American Dream Is Dead. Here's Why," *Washington Post*, December 10, 2015, https://www.washingtonpost.com/news/the-fix/wp/2015/12/10/48-percent-of-millennials-think-the-american-dream-is-dead-heres-why. The authors obtained their data from Harvard Institute of Politics, "Harvard IOP Fall 2015 Poll: Trump, Carson Lead Republican Primary; Sanders Edging Clinton among Democrats, Harvard IOP Poll Finds," December 10, 2015, http://iop.harvard.edu/survey/details/harvard-iop-fall-2015-poll.
17. Samuel Huntington, *American Politics: The Promise of Disharmony* (Cambridge, MA: Harvard University Press, 1983); John Kingdon, *America the Unusual* (New York: St. Martin's Press, 1999).
18. John Winthrop, "A Model of Christian Charity," 1630, The Winthrop Society, http://winthropsociety.com/doc_charity.php.
19. Paraphrasing Eric Foner, *Give Me Liberty! An American History* (New York: W. W. Norton, 2006), 36.
20. George Brown Tindall and David E. Shi, *America: A Narrative History*, brief 2nd ed. (New York: W. W. Norton, 1989), 16.
21. Foner, *Give Me Liberty!*, 43.
22. Charles M. Andrews, *The Colonial Background of the American Revolution* (New Haven, CT: Yale University Press, 1924), 42–44.
23. Global war began in 1756, while conflict in the colonies started two years earlier. Other major European powers became involved in various theaters in the war.
24. The colonies that sent representatives were Connecticut, Maryland, Massachusetts, New Hampshire, New York, Pennsylvania, and Rhode Island.
25. Eleven of the thirteen colonies were included in Franklin's proposed plan; Georgia and Delaware were not. Virginia and Massachusetts would each have had seven of the forty-eight total seats, being the largest and wealthiest colonies.
26. Richard Hofstadter, William Miller, and Daniel Aaron, *The American Republic*, vol. 1 (Upper Saddle River, NJ: Prentice Hall, 1970), 144.
27. Merrill Jensen, *The Founding of a Nation* (Indianapolis: Hackett, 2004), 4–5.
28. Literacy rates varied significantly by gender and race.
29. Philip Davidson, *Propaganda and the American Revolution, 1763–1783* (Chapel Hill: University of North Carolina Press, 1941), xiii.
30. Andrews, *The Colonial Background of the American Revolution*, 64–65.
31. Thomas Paine, *Common Sense* (New York: Buccaneer Books, 1976), 63, 69.
32. Eric Foner, *Tom Paine and Revolutionary America* (New York: Oxford University Press, 1976), 74.
33. Jensen, *The Founding of a Nation*, 99.
34. New Hampshire, Virginia, North Carolina, and Georgia did not send delegates. Support in several of these colonies was strong, but royal governors prevented them from sending delegates.
35. "Newspaper Account of the Boston Massacre," in *English Historical Documents*, ed. Merrill Jensen, vol. IX, *American Colonial Documents to 1776* (New York: Oxford University Press, 1955), 749.
36. Andrews, *The Colonial Background of the American Revolution*, 157.

37. "John Adams to Hezekiah Niles," in *The Works of John Adams*, ed. C. F. Adams, vol. X (Boston, 1850–56), 283, cited in Jensen, *The Founding of a Nation*, 33.

38. Foner, *Give Me Liberty!*, 53.

39. Jackson Turner Main, *The Social Structure of Revolutionary America* (Princeton, NJ: Princeton University Press, 1965), 221–27.

40. Ibid., 221.

41. Ibid., 123.

42. Sylvia R. Frey, *Water from the Rock: Black Resistance in a Revolutionary Age* (Princeton, NJ: Princeton University Press, 1991), 17.

43. Thomas Hutchinson, *Strictures upon the Declaration of the Congress at Philadelphia* (London, 1776), 9–10, quoted in Sylvia R. Frey, "Liberty, Equality, and Slavery: The Paradox of the American Revolution," in *The American Revolution: Its Character and Limits*, ed. Jack P. Greene (New York: New York University Press, 1987), 230.

44. Foner, *Give Me Liberty!*, 73.

45. Thomas J. Davis, "Emancipation Rhetoric, Natural Rights, and Revolutionary New England: A Note on Four Black Petitions in Massachusetts, 1773–1777," *New England Quarterly* 62, no. 2 (June 1989): 248–63.

46. Herbert Aptheker, ed., *Documentary History of the Negro People in the United States*, vol. 1 (New York: International Publishers), 7–8, cited in Davis, "Emancipation Rhetoric, Natural Rights, and Revolutionary New England," 255–56.

47. Ruth Bogin, "'Liberty Further Extended': A 1776 Antislavery Manuscript by Lemuel Haynes," *William and Mary Quarterly* 40, no. 1 (January 1983): 94.

48. Elaine F. Crane, "Dependence in the Era of Independence: The Role of Women in a Republican Society," in *The American Revolution: Its Character and Limits*, ed. Jack P. Greene (New York: New York University Press, 1987).

49. Joan R. Gunderson, *To Be Useful to the World: Women in Revolutionary America*, rev. ed. (Chapel Hill: University of North Carolina Press, 2006), 23.

50. Mary Beth Norton, *Liberty's Daughters: The Revolutionary Experience of American Women, 1750–1800* (Boston: Little, Brown, 1980), 22.

51. Sara M. Evans, *Born for Liberty: A History of Women in America* (New York: Free Press, 1989), 48.

52. Carol Berkin, *Revolutionary Mothers: Women in the Struggle for America's Independence* (New York: Alfred A. Knopf, 2005), 21.

53. Ibid., 44.

54. Ibid., 46.

55. Russell Shorto, *The Island at the Center of the World: The Epic Story of Dutch Manhattan and the Forgotten Colony That Shaped America* (New York: Doubleday, 2004), 50.

56. See, for example, Gail D. MacLeitch, *Imperial Entanglements: Iroquois Change and Persistence on the Frontiers of Empire* (Philadelphia: University of Pennsylvania Press, 2011); Karim M. Tiro, *The People of Standing Stone: The Oneida Nation from the Revolution through the Era of Removal* (Amherst: University of Massachusetts Press, 2011).

57. Hofstadter et al., *The American Republic*, 167.

58. The Articles of Confederation and Perpetual Union (see Chapter 2).

59. "The Virginia Resolutions for Independence," in Jensen, *English Historical Documents*, 867–68.

60. Jonathan S. Bass, *Blessed Are the Peacemakers: Martin Luther King, Jr., Eight White Religious Leaders, and the "Letter from Birmingham Jail"* (Baton Rouge: Louisiana State University Press, 2001), 112.

61. Taylor Branch, *Parting the Waters: America in the King Years, 1954–63* (New York: Simon & Schuster, 1988), 706.

62. Ibid., 729.

63. Godfrey Hodgson, *Martin Luther King* (Ann Arbor: University of Michigan Press, 2009), 3.

64. Montgomery Improvement Association, "Bus Protesters Call Southern Negro Leaders Conference on Transportation and Nonviolent Integration," January 7, 1957, The Martin Luther King Papers Project, Montgomery, Alabama, http://mlk-kpp01.stanford.edu/primarydocuments/Vol4/7-Jan-1957_MIAConference.pdf.

65. Martin Luther King Jr., "Letter from Birmingham Jail," http://okra.stanford.edu/transcription/document_images/undecided/630416-019.pdf.

66. Clayborne Carson, ed., *The Autobiography of Martin Luther King, Jr.* (New York: Warner Books, 1998), 184.

67. Ibid., 187.

68. "White Clergymen Urge Local Negroes to Withdraw from Demonstrations," *Birmingham News*, April 13, 1963, Birmingham Public Library Digital Collections, http://bplonline.cdmhost.com/cdm/singleitem/collection/p4017coll2/id/746/rec/8.

69. Parts of the letter were also written on paper later smuggled in or provided to King by his attorneys.

70. Quoted from Jonathan Rieder, "The Day President Kennedy Embraced Civil Rights—and the Story behind It," *The Atlantic*, June 11, 2013, http://www.theatlantic.com/national/archive/2013/06/the-day-president-kennedy-embraced-civil-rights-and-the-story-behind-it/276749/.

71. Doyle "Texas Dolly" Brunson, *Doyle Brunson's Super Strategy*, 3rd ed. (New York: Cardoza, 2002), 442.

CHAPTER 2

1. Madison's two papers were titled "Notes of Ancient and Modern Confederacies," written in the spring of 1786, and "Vices of the Political System of the United States," written in the spring of 1787.

2. Robert Livingston Schuyler, *The Constitution of the United States: An Historical Survey of Its Formation* (New York, 1923), 90.

3. "Letter from James Madison to Thomas Jefferson, May 12, 1786," in *The Papers of James Madison*, ed. Robert

A. Rutland and William M. E. Rachal, vol. 9, 9 April 1786–24 May 1787 (Chicago: University of Chicago Press, 1975), 97.

4. William Waller Hening, "Virginia Laws for Blacks—17C & 18C," in *Laws of Virginia, 1619–1792* (1823), I–III. For more on Madison's ambivalence toward slavery, see William Lee Miller, *The Business of May Next: James Madison and the Founding* (Charlottesville: University Press of Virginia, 1992), 177–84.

5. Charles M. Andrews, *The Colonial Background of the American Revolution* (New Haven, CT: Yale University Press, 1924), 26.

6. Merrill Jensen, *The Articles of Confederation: An Interpretation of the Social-Constitutional History of the American Revolution, 1774–1781* (Madison: University of Wisconsin Press, 1948), 150.

7. Robert W. Hoffert, *A Politics of Tensions: The Articles of Confederation and American Political Ideals* (Niwot: University Press of Colorado, 1992), 86.

8. Article 2.

9. Andrews, *The Colonial Background of the American Revolution*, 44.

10. This idea of term limits is one that we continue to debate today. For a discussion of challenges of coordination under the Articles of Confederation, see Keith L. Dougherty, *Collective Action under the Articles of Confederation* (New York: Cambridge University Press, 2001).

11. Jensen, *The Articles of Confederation*, 240.

12. "We do Each one of us, acknowledge our Selves to be Inlisted . . . in colo Hazeltons Regiment of Regulators … for Suppressing of tyrannical government in the Massachusetts State." "Report of the Commissioners, April 27, 1787," in David P. Szatmary, *Shays' Rebellion: The Making of an Agrarian Insurrection* (Amherst: University of Massachusetts Press, 1980), 63.

13. James MacGregor Burns, *The Vineyard of Liberty* (New York: Alfred A. Knopf, 1982), 14.

14. Szatmary, *Shays' Rebellion*.

15. Louise B. Dunbar, "A Study of 'Monarchical' Tendencies in the United States from 1776 to 1801," in Rutland and Rachal, *The Papers of James Madison*, 162.

16. "Letter from George Washington to James Madison, November 5, 1786," in Rutland and Rachal, *The Papers of James Madison*, 162.

17. Ira Stoll, *Samuel Adams: A Life* (New York: Free Press, 2008), 229–30.

18. Patrick Henry, "Virginia Ratifying Convention, June 4 and 5, 1788," in *The Essential Antifederalist*, 2nd ed., ed. W. B. Allen and Gordon Lloyd (New York: Rowman & Littlefield, 2002), 130.

19. Gordon S. Wood, "The Origins of the Constitution," in *This Constitution: A Bicentennial Chronicle* (American Political Science Association, 1987), available online at www.apsanet.org/imgtest/OriginsofConst.pdf.

20. Max Farrand, ed., *The Records of the Federal Convention of 1787*, vol. I (New Haven, CT: Yale University Press, 1911), xi.

21. "Notes of James Madison, May 29, 1787," in Farrand, *Records of the Federal Convention*, 15.

22. Catherine Drinker Bowen, *Miracle at Philadelphia: The Story of the Constitutional Convention, May to September 1787* (Boston: Little, Brown, 1966), 22.

23. Though Madison would state that the entire Virginia delegation was responsible for it. See Bowen, *Miracle at Philadelphia*.

24. Ibid., 18.

25. "Notes of James Madison, June 9, 1787," in Farrand, *Records of the Federal Convention*, 179.

26. Bowen, *Miracle at Philadelphia*, 116.

27. Ibid., 285.

28. Ibid., 492.

29. "Notes of Robert Yates, July 2, 1787," in Farrand, *Records of the Federal Convention*, 519.

30. "Notes of James Madison, May 29, 1787," in Farrand, *Records of the Federal Convention*, 531.

31. It is also known as the Connecticut Compromise, after Roger Sherman, a Connecticut delegate, member of the committee, and author of the proposal. One state delegation was split.

32. For an analysis of Madison's strategic shift, see Miller, *The Business of May Next*, 78–80.

33. Bowen, *Miracle at Philadelphia*, 115.

34. Richard E. Neustadt, *Presidential Power and the Modern Presidents: The Politics of Leadership from Roosevelt to Reagan* (New York: Free Press, 1990), 29.

35. Also called the Committee of Eleven.

36. Bruce Ackerman, *We the People: Foundations* (Cambridge, MA: Harvard University Press, 1991).

37. Native Americans not paying taxes would not count at all.

38. James Madison, *Federalist* No. 54, in *The Federalist Papers*, ed. George W. Carey and James McClellan (Indianapolis: Liberty Fund, 2001), 283.

39. James Madison, "James Madison to Robert I. Evans, June 15, 1819," Library of Congress, June 15, 1819, https://www.loc.gov/item/mjm018592.

40. Madison, *Federalist* No. 51, 269.

41. Madison, *Federalist* No. 10, 44.

42. Ibid., 43.

43. Ibid., 46.

44. Alexander Hamilton, *Federalist* No. 9, in Carey and McClellan, *The Federalist Papers*, 41.

45. Alexander Hamilton, *Federalist* No. 16, 76–77.

46. W. B. Allen and Gordon Lloyd, *The Essential Antifederalist*, 2nd ed. (New York: Rowman & Littlefield, 2002), xxiii.

47. Ibid., xxiii.

48. "Centinel Letter I, October 5, 1787," in Allen and Lloyd, *The Essential Antifederalist*, 102–3. See also Herbert J. Storing, *What the Antifederalists Were For* (Chicago: University of Chicago Press, 1981), 57.

49. "Brutus Essay V, December 13, 1787," in Allen and Lloyd, *The Essential Antifederalist*, 119.

50. See Storing, *What the Antifederalists Were For*.

51. See Kate Davies, Catharine Macaulay, and Mercy Otis Warren, *The Revolutionary Atlantic and the Politics of Gender* (New York: Oxford University Press, 2005).

52. Mercy Otis Warren, *Observations on the New Constitution, and on the Federal and State Conventions, by a Columbian Patriot* (Washington, DC: Library of Congress, 1788).

53. William H. Riker, *The Strategy of Rhetoric: Campaigning for the American Constitution* (New Haven, CT: Yale University Press, 1996).

54. Ibid., 211.

55. Douglass C. North and Barry R. Weingast, "Constitutions and Commitment: The Evolution of Institutions Governing Public Choice in Seventeenth-Century England," *Journal of Economic History* 49, no. 4 (December 1989): 803–32.

56. Donald S. Lutz, "From Covenant to Constitution in American Political Thought," in *Covenant, Polity, and Constitutionalism*, ed. Daniel Elezar and John Kincaid (Lanham, MD: University Press of America, 1983).

57. Edward S. Corwin, "The Constitution as an Instrument and as a Symbol," *American Political Science Review* 30, no. 6 (December 1936): 1071–85. See also Edward S. Corwin, *The "Higher Law" Background of American Constitutional Law* (Ithaca, NY: Great Seal Books, 1928).

CHAPTER 3

1. Joel Roberts, "Dying Woman Loses Medical Marijuana Case," CBSNews.com, March 14, 2007, www.cbsnews.com/news/dying-woman-loses-medical-marijuana-case.

2. Dan Reed, "Medicinal Pot Users Renew Legal Challenge," *San Jose Mercury News*, October 10, 2002, available from Lexis-Nexis Academic.

3. Brian Anderson, "Women File Suit for Continued Access to Marijuana," *Contra Costa Times*, October 10, 2002, available from Lexis-Nexis Academic.

4. "Declaration of Diane Monson in Support of Motion for Preliminary Injunction," *Raich v. Ashcroft*, 248 F. supp 2d 918 (ND Cal. 2003).

5. Comprehensive Drug Abuse and Control Act of 1970, 84 Stat. 1236.

6. *Gonzales v. Raich*, 545 U.S. 1 (2005).

7. "Declaration of Diane Monson."

8. Anderson, "Women File Suit for Continued Access to Marijuana."

9. Richard Willing, "Medical-Pot Fight Goes to Justices," *USA Today*, November 26, 2004, available from Lexis-Nexis Academic.

10. Richard Willing, "Justices Doubtful about Medical Marijuana," *USA Today*, November 30, 2004, available from Lexis-Nexis Academic.

11. *Gonzales v. Raich*.

12. *Wickard v. Filburn*, 317 U.S. 111 (1942).

13. Paul E. Peterson, *The Price of Federalism* (Washington, DC: Brookings Institution, 1995), 12.

14. Reagan Ali and M. David, "Obama Effectively Tells Supreme Court to Legalize Marijuana," *Counter Current News*, January 17, 2016, http://countercurrentnews.com/2016/01/obama-tells-supreme-court-to-legalize.

15. Ariane de Vogue, "Obama Admin Weighs in on Legalized Marijuana at the Supreme Court," CNN.com, December 16, 2015, www.cnn.com/2015/12/16/politics/supreme-court-marijuana-colorado-obama.

16. Editorial, "Trump and Sessions Are Ignoring Voters' Overwhelming Support for Medical Marijuana, Will Congress Listen?," *Los Angeles Times*, September 9, 2017, www.latimes.com/opinion/editorials/la-ed-medical-marijuana-20170909-story.html.

17. U.S. Constitution, art. VI.

18. U.S. Constitution, art. I, sec. 8.

19. Ibid.

20. Ibid.

21. U.S. Constitution, art. I, sec. 2, 4; art. II, sec. 1.

22. U.S. Constitution, art. V.

23. U.S. Constitution, art. I, sec. 10.

24. Richard E. Neustadt, *Presidential Power and the Modern Presidents: The Politics of Leadership from Roosevelt to Reagan* (New York: Free Press, 1990), 29.

25. Daniel J. Elazar, *American Federalism: A View from the States* (New York: Thomas Y. Crowell, 1972), 190.

26. *McCulloch v. Maryland*, 17 U.S. (4 Wheat.) 316 (1819).

27. *Gibbons v. Ogden*, 22 U.S. (9 Wheat.) 11 (1824).

28. Ibid.

29. *Barron v. Mayor and City Council of Baltimore*, 32 U.S. 243 (1833).

30. This interpretation would change during the process of incorporation, which began in the twentieth century (see Chapter 4).

31. James Bryce, *The American Commonwealth*, vol. I (New York: Macmillan, 1888), 432.

32. *Tarble's Case*, 80 Wall. 397 (1871).

33. The Northwest Ordinance of 1787, for example, stated, "Religion, morality, and knowledge, being necessary to good government and the happiness of mankind, schools and the means of education shall forever be encouraged" (Henry Steele Commager, ed., *Documents of American History*, 8th ed. [New York: Appleton-Century-Crofts, 1968], 131).

34. *Slaughterhouse Cases*, 83 U.S. (16 Wall.) 36 (1873).

35. Ronald M. Labbé and Jonathan Lurie, *The Slaughterhouse Cases: Regulation, Reconstruction, and the Fourteenth Amendment* (Lawrence: University Press of Kansas, 2003), 211.

36. *Plessy v. Ferguson*, 163 U.S. 537 (1896).

37. Mark V. Tushnet, *The NAACP's Legal Strategy against Segregated Education, 1925–1950* (Chapel Hill: University of North Carolina Press, 1987), 21.

38. Elazar, *American Federalism*, 33.

39. Ibid., 47–48.

40. See *United States v. E.C. Knight Company*, 156 U.S. 1 (1895); *Hammer v. Dagenhart*, 247 U.S. 251 (1918).

41. National Drought Mitigation Center, "Drought in the Dust Bowl Years," http://drought.unl.edu/DroughtBasics/DustBowl/DroughtintheDustBowlYears.aspx.

42. Ibid., 15.

43. Arthur M. Schlesinger Jr., *The Age of Roosevelt*, vol. II, *The Coming of the New Deal* (Boston: Houghton Mifflin Company, 1958), 4.

44. See the Banking Act of 1933, the Securities Act of 1933, and the Securities Exchange Act of 1934.

45. Amity Shlaes, *The Forgotten Man: A New History of the Great Depression* (New York: HarperCollins, 2007), 150.

46. Ibid., 151.

47. Schlesinger, *The Age of Roosevelt*, 121.

48. Alan Brinkley, *Franklin Delano Roosevelt* (New York: Oxford University Press, 2010), 52.

49. Steven Horwitz, "The Story of the Schechter Brothers," George Mason University History News Network, http://historynewsnetwork.org/blog/57574.

50. The brothers were charged with violating the Code of Fair Competition for the Live Poultry Industry of the Metropolitan Area in and about the City of New York.

51. Ibid., 220.

52. Ibid., 227.

53. See also *Panama Refining Co. v. Ryan*, 293 U.S. 388 (1935).

54. Ibid.

55. Ibid.

56. Ibid.

57. Jeff Shesol, *Supreme Power: Franklin Roosevelt vs. the Supreme Court* (New York: W. W. Norton, 2010), 2–3.

58. Pub. L. 74-271, 49 Stat 620–648 (1935). The programs were collectively called Old-Age, Survivors, and Disability Insurance (OASDI), commonly referred to as Social Security. Aid to Dependent Children was later renamed Aid to Families with Dependent Children (AFDC), which was abolished in 1996 and replaced with Temporary Assistance to Needy Families (TANF).

59. Shesol, *Supreme Power*, 3–4.

60. Joseph F. Zimmerman, *Contemporary American Federalism: The Growth of National Power* (New York: Praeger, 1992), 118.

61. Ibid., 118–19.

62. Lawrence D. Brown, James W. Fossett, and Kenneth T. Palmer, *The Changing Politics of Federal Grants* (Washington, DC: Brookings Institution, 1984), 7.

63. Ibid., 8.

64. "Acceptance Speeches: Reagan: 'Time to Recapture Our Destiny,'" in *CQ Almanac 1980*, 36th ed. (Washington, DC: Congressional Quarterly, 1981), available at http://library.cqpress.com/cqalmanac/cqal80-860-25879-1173673.

65. John D. Nugent, *Safeguarding Federalism: How States Protect Their Interests in National Policymaking* (Norman: University of Oklahoma Press, 2009), 6.

66. James Madison, *Federalist* No. 46, in *The Federalist Papers*, ed. George W. Carey and James McClellan (Indianapolis: Liberty Fund, 2001), 246.

67. Nugent, *Safeguarding Federalism*, 56.

68. Peterson, *Price of Federalism*, 45.

69. Bryan Schweitzer, "Montana Governor on 'REAL ID' Act" by Melissa Block (host), National Public Radio's *All Things Considered*, March 7, 2008, quoted in Nugent, *Safeguarding Federalism*, 66.

70. *United States v. Lopez*, 514 US 549 (1995).

71. Ibid.

72. Ibid.

73. Ibid.

74. *Printz v. United States*, 521 US 898 (1997).

75. "Angel McClary Raich," angeljustice.org, http://angeljustice.org/angel/Angel_Raichs_Bio.html.

76. Alaska, California, Colorado, Maine, Massachusetts, Nevada, New Hampshire, Oregon, and Washington.

77. Office of National Drug Control Policy, "Marijuana Resource Center: State Laws Related to Marijuana," https://www.whitehouse.gov/ondcp/state-laws-related-to-marijuana.

78. "Number of Legal Medical Marijuana Patients (as of March 1, 2016)," ProCon.org, March 3, 2016, http://medicalmarijuana.procon.org/view.resource.php?resourceID=005889.

79. James M. Cole, "Memorandum for All United States Attorneys," U.S. Department of Justice, August 29, 2013, https://www.justice.gov/iso/opa/resources/3052013829132756857467.pdf.

80. Jefferson B. Sessions III, Office of the Attorney General, letter to "The Honorable Jay Inslee, Governor, The State of Washington," July 24, 2017, https://s3.amazonaws.com/big.assets.huffingtonpost.com/LtrfromSessions.pdf.

81. Thomas Franck, "Marijuana Stock Tilray up 30% after Cannabis Foe Jeff Sessions Resigns under Pressure," *CNBC.com*, November 8, 2018, https://www.cnbc.com/2018/11/07/pot-stock-tilray-up-22percent-after-jeff-sessions-quits-as-attorney-general.html.

CHAPTER 4

1. Ray Halbritter, "Letter from the Publisher," *Indian Country Today*, Fall 2016, https://ictmn.lughstudio.com/wp-content/uploads/2016/10/DAPL-Magazine-2016_PREVIEW_r1.pdf.

2. "Corporate Overview," Energy Transfer, accessed March 12, 2018, http://www.energytransfer.com/company_overview.aspx.

3. Jack Healy, "Occupying the Prairie: Tension on the Plains as Tribes Move to Block a Pipeline," *New York Times*, August 23, 2016, https://www.nytimes.com/2016/08/24/us/occupying-the-prairie-tensions-rise-as-tribes-move-to-block-a-pipeline.html.

4. Jack Healy, "'I Want to Win Someday': Tribes Make Stand against Pipeline," *New York Times*, September 8, 2016, https://www.nytimes.com/2016/09/09/us/dakota-access-pipeline-protests.html.

5. Jack Healy, "From 280 Tribes, a Protest on the Plains Speaks Out against an Oil Pipeline," *New York Times*, September 12, 2016, https://www.nytimes.com/interactive/2016/09/12/us/12tribes.html.

6. Ibid.

7. Christopher Mele, "Veterans to Serve as 'Human Shields' for Dakota Pipeline Protesters," *New York Times*,

November 29, 2016, https://www.nytimes.com/2016/11/29/us/veterans-to-serve-as-human-shields-for-pipeline-protesters.html.

8. Water Protector Legal Collective, "Mission Statement," accessed March 12, 2018, https://waterprotectorlegal.org.

9. Jack Healy, "Neighbors Say South Dakota Pipeline Protests Disrupt Lives and Livelihoods," *New York Times*, September 13, 2016, https://www.nytimes.com/2016/09/14/us/north-dakota-pipeline-protests.html.

10. Sue Skalicky and Monica Davey, "Tension between Police and Standing Rock Protesters Reaches Boiling Point," *New York Times*, October 29, 2016, https://www.nytimes.com/2016/10/29/us/dakota-access-pipeline-protest.html.

11. Healy, "Occupying the Prairie."

12. Jack Healy, "The View from Two Sides of the Standing Rock Front Lines," *New York Times*, November 1, 2016, https://www.nytimes.com/2016/11/02/us/standing-rock-front-lines.html.

13. Lauren Carroll, "Rand Paul Says Federal Program Incentivizes Police Militarization," *Tampa Bay Times*, August 21, 2014, available from Lexis-Nexis Academic.

14. Jenna Bitar, "6 Ways Government Is Going after Environmental Activists," ACLU.org, February 6, 2018, https://www.aclu.org/blog/free-speech/rights-protesters/6-ways-government-going-after-environmental-activists.

15. Katie Rogers, "Why Your Facebook Friends Are Checking In to Standing Rock," *New York Times*, November 1, 2016, https://www.nytimes.com/2016/11/01/us/why-your-facebook-friends-are-checking-into-standing-rock.html.

16. Bitar, "6 Ways Government Is Going After Environmental Activists."

17. "Stand with Standing Rock: Protect Protesters' Rights," ALCU.org, accessed March 13, 2018, https://www.aclu.org/issues/free-speech/rights-protesters/stand-standing-rock.

18. Skalicky and Davey, "Tension between Police and Standing Rock Protesters Reaches Boiling Point."

19. Erin Mundahl, "As North Dakota Continues to Try Standing Rock Protesters, Dismissed Cases Pile Up," InsideSources.com, May 29, 2017, http://www.insidesources.com/nd-dismissed-cases-standing-rock/.

20. Jack Healy, "Army Approves Construction of Dakota Access Pipeline," *New York Times*, February 7, 2017, https://www.nytimes.com/2017/02/07/us/army-approves-construction-of-dakota-access-pipeline.html.

21. Mitch Smith, "Standing Rock Protest Camp, Once Home to Thousands, Is Razed," *New York Times*, February 23, 2017, https://www.nytimes.com/2017/02/23/us/standing-rock-protest-dakota-access-pipeline.html.

22. Catherine Drinker Bowen, *Miracle at Philadelphia: The Story of the Constitutional Convention, May to September 1787* (Boston: Little, Brown, 1966), 244.

23. U.S. Constitution, art. III, sec. 3.

24. Irving Brant, *The Bill of Rights: Its Origin and Meaning* (New York: Bobbs-Merrill, 1965), 39.

25. Alexander Hamilton, *Federalist* No. 84, in *The Federalist*, ed. George W. Carey and James McClellan (Indianapolis: Liberty Fund, 2001), 447.

26. *Annals of Congress*, House of Representatives, 1st Cong., 1st sess. (June 8, 1789), 440–41, available at http://memory.loc.gov/ammem/amlaw/lwac.html.

27. Two of the proposed twelve did not receive enough votes to secure ratification. The first involved apportionment of seats in the House of Representatives; the second restricted Congress's ability to raise its own pay. This latter amendment was ratified, but not until 1992 (the Twenty-Seventh Amendment). Amendments are typically proposed including a date of expiry, but this was not the case for the two unratified, originally proposed amendments.

28. The Fifth Amendment to the Constitution includes a similar clause asserting that "No person … shall be deprived of life, liberty, or property, without due process of law," but the Supreme Court had interpreted the Fifth Amendment as restricting the power of only the federal government.

29. *The Slaughterhouse Cases*, 83 U.S. 36 (1873). The Court also placed limits on the privileges and immunities clause of the same amendment, stating that its protections apply only to national, not state, citizenship.

30. *Gitlow v. New York*. In *Chicago, Burlington & Quincy Railroad Company v. Chicago*, 166 U.S. 226 (1897), the Supreme Court had already applied the Fifth Amendment's due process clause to state actions in its reasoning, though ruling against the plaintiffs.

31. *McDonald v. Chicago*, 561 U.S. 742 (2010).

32. James A. Poore III, "The Constitution of the United States Applies to Indian Tribes," 59 Mont. L. Rev. (1998), available at http://scholarship.law.umt.edu/mlr/vol59/iss1/4.

33. *The Constitution of the Standing Rock Sioux Tribe*, enacted in 1959 and since amended, http://indianaffairs.nd.gov/image/cache/standing_rock_constitution.pdf.

34. *Everson v. Board of Education*, 330 U.S. 1 (1947). The justices were closely divided, 5–4.

35. *Everson v. Board of Education*.

36. *Board of Education v. Allen*, 392 U.S. 236 (1968). The Court has been similarly divided over the issue of tax relief for tuition reimbursement. See *Committee for Public Education v. Nyquist*, 413 U.S. 756 (1973), *and Mueller v. Allen*, 463 U.S. 388 (1983). In *Zobrest v. Catalina Foothills School District*, 509 U.S. 1 (1993), the Court, again divided 5–4, ruled in favor of using taxpayer funds to provide a student in a Catholic high school with a sign language interpreter.

37. *Engle v. Vitale*, 370 U.S. 421 (1962).

38. *Abington School District v. Schempp*, 374 U.S. 203 (1963). The Pennsylvania case was considered with a similar program in Maryland.

39. James Madison, "A Memorial and Remonstrance," in *The Constitution and Religion: Leading Supreme Court Cases on Church and State*, ed. Robert S. Alley (Amherst, MA: Prometheus Books, 1999), 30, quoted in *Abington School District v. Schempp.*

40. U.S. Department of Education, "Guidance on Constitutionally Protected Prayer in Public Elementary and Secondary Schools," February 7, 2003, http://www2.ed.gov/policy/gen/guid/religionandschools/prayer_guidance.html.

41. *Lemon v. Kurtzman*, 403 U.S. 602 (1971). In establishing the test, the Court drew on the logic of *Board of Education v. Allen* (1968) and other cases.

42. *Mueller v. Allen*, 463 U.S. 388 (1983); *Witters v. Washington Dept. of Services for the Blind*, 474 U.S. 481 (1986); *Zobrest v. Catalina Foothills School Dist.*, 509 U.S. 1 (1993).

43. *Cantwell v. Connecticut*, 310 U.S. 296 (1940).

44. *Employment Division Dept. of Human Resources of Oregon v. Smith*, 494 U.S. 872 (1990).

45. "The Sedition Act (1798)," in *Documents of American History*, 8th ed., ed. Henry Steele Commager (New York: Appleton-Century-Crofts, 1968), 177–78.

46. Paul E. Peterson, *The Price of Federalism* (Washington, DC: Brookings Institution, 1995), 8.

47. Ibid.

48. *Brandenburg v. Ohio*, 395 U.S. 444 (1969).

49. Ibid.

50. *New York Times v. United States*, 403 U.S. 713 (1971).

51. *United States v. O'Brien*, 391 U.S. 367 (1968).

52. *Morse v. Frederick*, 551 U.S. 393 (2007).

53. *Texas v. Johnson*, 491 U.S. 397 (1989). See also *Spence v. Washington*, 418 U.S. 405 (1974).

54. The definitions of legal terms in this section are informed by Bryan A. Garner, ed., *Black's Law Dictionary*, 8th ed. (St. Paul, MN: Thomson/West, 2004).

55. *Chaplinksy v. State of New Hampshire*, 315 U.S. 586 (1942).

56. *Roth v. United States*, 354 U.S. 476 (1957).

57. *Miller v. California*, 413 U.S. 15 (1973).

58. *Reno v. American Civil Liberties Union et al.*, 521 U.S. 844 (1997).

59. *De Jonge v. Oregon*, 299 U.S. 353 (1937). See also *Edwards v. South Carolina*, 372 U.S. 229 (1963).

60. Noting, however, that the process of incorporating these rights has involved the Fourteenth Amendment as well.

61. U.S. Constitution, art. I, sec. 9.

62. John Rawls, *A Theory of Justice* (Cambridge, MA: Belknap Press of Harvard University Press, 1999).

63. National Firearms Act (1934).

64. *United States v. Miller*, 307 U.S. 174 (1939).

65. *District of Columbia v. Heller*, 554 U.S. 570 (2008).

66. *McDonald v. Chicago*. A similar law in Oak Park, a suburb of Chicago, was also overturned.

67. *Katz v. United States*, 389 U.S. 347 (1967).

68. *Mapp v. Ohio*, 367 U.S. 643 (1961).

69. United States v. Sokolow, 490 U.S. 1 (1989).

70. *Horton v. California*, 496 U.S. 128 (1990).

71. *Whren v. United States*, 517 U.S. 806 (1996).

72. *Miranda v. Arizona*, 384 U.S. 436 (1966). Miranda was retried without the illegally obtained evidence but was convicted based on other evidence, including identification by the victim and the testimony of his girlfriend.

73. *Kloppfer v. North Carolina*, 386 U.S. 213 (1967).

74. *Powell v. Alabama*, 287 U.S. 45 (1932).

75. *Johnson v. Zerbst*, 304 U.S. 458 (1938).

76. *Gideon v. Wainwright*, 372 U.S. 335 (1963).

77. *Wiggins v. Smith*, 539 U.S. 510 (2003).

78. The Court's decision in *Furman v. Georgia*, 408 U.S. 238 (1972), invalidated the use of the death penalty according to the state laws at the time, finding them arbitrary and discriminatory. Rewritten death penalty statutes were held constitutional in *Gregg v. Georgia*, 428 U.S. 153 (1976).

79. *Atkins v. Virginia*, 536 U.S. 304 (2002).

80. *Roper v. Simmons*, 543 U.S. 551 (2005).

81. *United States v. Windsor*, 570 U.S. __ (2013).

82. U.S. Constitution, art. IV, sec. 1.

83. *United States v. Windsor.*

84. Ibid.

85. Ibid.

86. Justin Jones, "The Godmother of Gay Marriage: Edie Windsor's Passionate Life," *Daily Beast*, March 18, 2015, http://www.thedailybeast.com/articles/2015/03/18/the-godmother-of-gay-marriage-edie-windsor-s-passionate-life.html.

87. Ibid.

88. *Griswold v. Connecticut*, 381 U.S. 479 (1965).

89. Ibid.

90. *Lawrence v. Texas*, 539 U.S. 558 (2003). In its ruling, the Court overturned *Bowers v. Hardwick*, 478 U.S. 186 (1986).

91. *Lawrence v. Texas.*

92. *Roe v. Wade*, 410 U.S. 113 (1973).

93. Ibid.

94. See *Webster v. Reproductive Health Services*, 492 U.S. 490 (1989); *Planned Parenthood v. Casey*, 505 U.S. 833 (1992); *Stenberg v. Carhart*, 530 U.S. 914 (2000); *Gonzales v. Carhart*, 550 U.S. 124 (2007).

95. "What Is ALS?," ALS Association, accessed March 12, 2016, http://www.alsa.org/about-als/what-is-als.html.

96. Chris Geidner, "Two Years after His Husband's Death, Jim Obergefell Is Still Fighting for the Right to Be Married," BuzzFeed.com, March 22, 2015, *http://www.buzzfeed.com/chrisgeidner/his-husband-died-in-2013-but-jim-obergefell-is-still-fighting#.ldrnVM0Ag.*

97. *Obergefell v. Hodges*, 576 U.S. __ (2015).

98. Geidner, "Two Years after His Husband's Death."

99. Richard Wolf, "Grieving Widower Takes Lead in Major Gay Marriage Case," *USA Today*, April 10, 2015, http://www.usatoday.com/story/news/nation/2015/04/10/supreme-court-gay-marriage-obergefell/25512405/.

100. Ibid.

CHAPTER 5

1. Harriet Hartman and Moshe Hartman, "How Equal Is Equal? A Comparison of Gender Equality among Israeli and American Jews," *Contemporary Jewry* 14, no. 1 (1993): 48–72.

2. Judith Heumann, "Justice for All: Advancing Dr. King's Call," *DIPNOTE, U.S Department of State Official Blog,* January 18, 2016, https://blogs.state.gov/stories/2016/01/18/justice-all-advancing-dr-king-s-call.

3. Team Celebration, "Judith E. Heumann—Woman of Action," A Celebration of Women, July 24, 2012, http://acelebrationofwomen.org/2012/07/judith-e-heumann-woman-of-action/.

4. Ibid.

5. Jack Anderson and Les Whitten, "Sit-Ins Planned by Handicapped," March 27, 1977, *Progress Bulletin from Pomona (California)*.

6. "A Look Back at 'Section 504,'" Minnesota Governor's Council on Developmental Disabilities, April 28, 2002, http://mn.gov/mnddc/ada-legacy/npr-504.html. The article was drawn from the transcript of "Disability Rights, Part II," National Public Radio, April 28, 2002, http://www.npr.org/templates/story/story.php?storyId=1142485.

7. HolLynn D'Lil, *Becoming Real in 24 Days* (HolLynn D'Lil, 2015), 16.

8. Cesar Chavez, telegram to Judy Heuman [sic], April 2, 1977 (D'Lil, 16).

9. Michael Irvin, "The 25 Day Siege That Brought Us 504," Independent Living Institute, accessed March 17, 2016, http://www.independentliving.org/docs4/ervin1986.html.

10. Lanny E. Perkins, Esq. and Sara D. Perkins, Esq., "ADA Update," Multiple Sclerosis Foundation, accessed March 16, 2016, http://msfocus.org/article-details.aspx?articleID=340.

11. Ginger Adams Otis, "Trailblazing Advocate Judy Heumann Says There's More Work to Do 25 Years after Americans with Disabilities Act Was Signed into Law," *New York Daily News*, July 25, 2015, http://www.nydailynews.com/news/national/ada-advocate-judy-heumann-work-article-1.2304397.

12. *City of Cleburne, Texas v. Cleburne Living Center, Inc.,* 473 U.S. 432 (1985).

13. *University of California Regents v. Bakke,* 438 U.S. 265, 438 U.S. 303 (1978), quoted in *City of Cleburne, Texas v. Cleburne Living Center, Inc.*

14. David Pfeiffer, "Eugenics and Disability Discrimination," *Disability and Society* 9, no. 4 (1994): 481–99.

15. American Civil Liberties Union, "Disability Rights—ACLU Position/Briefing Paper," no. 21 (Winter 1999), https://www.aclu.org/disability-rights-aclu-positionbriefing-paper.

16. Ibid.

17. *Dred Scott v. Sandford,* 60 U.S. 393 (1857).

18. Eric Foner, *Give Me Liberty! An American History* (New York: W. W. Norton, 2006), 4.

19. W. E. B. Du Bois, *Black Reconstruction in America, 1860–1880* (New York: Anthem, 1992), 167.

20. Ibid., 9.

21. Du Bois, *Black Reconstruction in America,* 123.

22. Richard Wormser, *The Rise and Fall of Jim Crow* (New York: St. Martin's Press, 2003), 11.

23. Francis Curtis, *The Republican Party: A History of Its Fifty Years' Existence and a Record of Its Measures and Leaders,* vol. II (New York: Knickerbocker Press, 1904), 51.

24. *Plessy v. Ferguson,* 163 U.S. 737 (1896).

25. *Plessy* did not deal with education. In 1899, the Supreme Court approved segregated educational facilities in *Cumming v. Board of Education,* 175 U.S. 528 (1899).

26. Mark V. Tushnet, *The NAACP's Legal Strategy against Segregated Education, 1925–1950* (Chapel Hill: University of North Carolina Press, 1987), 21. The section on the NAACP's strategic decision-making processes draws heavily on Tushnet's analysis and Richard Kluger's historical account.

27. The four states were Kansas (*Brown v. Board of Education,* 98 F. Supp. 797 [D. Kan. 1951]); South Carolina (*Briggs v. Elliot,* 103 F. Supp. 920 [E.D.S.C. 1952]); Delaware (*Gebhart v. Belton,* 33 Del. 145, 91 A.2d. 137 [1952]); and Virginia (*Davis v. County School Board of Prince Edward County, Virginia,* 103 F. Supp. 337 [E.D. Va. 1952]). The Washington, DC, case was *Bolling v. Sharpe,* 347 U.S. 497 (1954). As the District of Columbia is not a state, the case was tried under the due process clause of the Fifth Amendment. Thurgood Marshall argued the South Carolina case before the Supreme Court. His legal team divided the oral arguments.

28. Richard Kluger, *Simple Justice: The History of* Brown v. Board of Education *and Black America's Struggle for Equality* (New York: Vintage Books, 1977), 706.

29. Tushnet, *The NAACP's Legal Strategy,* 36.

30. *State of Missouri ex rel Gaines v. Canada,* 305 U.S. 337 (1938).

31. Sweatt v. Painter, 339 U.S. 629 (1950); *McLaurin v. Oklahoma State Regents for Higher Education,* 339 U.S. 637 (1950).

32. Tushnet, *The NAACP's Legal Strategy,* 125.

33. Kluger, *Simple Justice,* 268.

34. Ibid., 395.

35. Quoted in Kluger, *Simple Justice,* 574.

36. Ibid., 664.

37. *Brown v. Board of Education of Topeka,* 347 U.S. 483 (1954).

38. It was said that Justice Felix Frankfurter told Justice Stanley Reed, who was most likely to dissent, that "a dissent is written for the future, but that there was no future for segregation" (Jack Greenberg, *Crusaders in the Courts: How a Dedicated Band of Lawyers Fought for the Civil Rights Revolution* [New York: Basic Books, 1994], 198).

39. Quoted in Jennifer Hochschild, *The New American Dilemma: Liberal Democracy and School Desegregation* (New Haven, CT: Yale University Press, 1984), 15.

40. Juan Williams, *Eyes on the Prize: America's Civil Rights Years, 1954–1965* (New York: Viking Penguin, 1987), 35.

41. Ibid., 34.

42. *Brown v. Board of Education of Topeka.*

43. Gerald N. Rosenberg, *The Hollow Hope: Can Courts Bring About Social Change?* (Chicago: University of Chicago Press, 1991), 49.

44. Taylor Branch, *Parting the Waters: American in the King Years, 1954–63* (New York: Simon & Schuster, 1988), 129.

45. *Gayle v. Browder*, 352 U.S. 903 (1956).

46. Branch, *Parting the Waters*, 129.

47. Ibid., 139–40.

48. *Griffin v. Prince Edward County*, 375 U.S. 391 (1964).

49. *Green v. County School Board of New Kent County, Virginia*, 391 U.S. 430 (1968).

50. *Alexander v. Holmes County Board of Education*, 396 U.S. 19 (1969).

51. *Swann v. Charlotte-Mecklenburg Board of Education*, 401 U.S. 1 (1971).

52. *Milliken v. Bradley*, 418 U.S. 717 (1974).

53. *Regents of the University of California v. Bakke*, 438 U.S. 265 (1978).

54. *Gratz v. Bollinger*, 539 U.S. 244 (2003).

55. *Gunner v. Bollinger*, 539 U.S. 306 (2003).

56. Adam Liptak, "Supreme Court Upholds Affirmative Action Program at University of Texas," *New York Times*, June 23, 2016, http://www.nytimes.com/2016/06/24/us/politics/supreme-court-affirmative-action-university-of-texas.html?_r=0.

57. See Eleanor Flexner, *Century of Struggle: The Woman's Rights Movement in the United States* (Cambridge, MA: Belknap Press, 1959); Edwin W. Small and Miriam R. Small, "Prudence Crandall: Champion of Negro Education," *New England Quarterly* 17, no. 4 (December 1944): 506–29.

58. Flexner, *Century of Struggle*, 39.

59. Angelina Grimké, "An Appeal to the Women of the Nominally Free States," in Kathryn Kish Sklar, *Women's Rights Emerges within the Antislavery Movement: A Brief History with Documents* (Binghamton: State University of New York, 2000), 101–2.

60. Sklar, *Women's Rights Emerges*, 58.

61. *Woman's Rights Conventions, Seneca Falls & Rochester, 1848* (New York: Arno, 1969), 4.

62. Sklar, Women's Rights Emerges, 1.

63. Frances Ellen Watkins Harper, "We Are All Bound Up Together," in *Proceedings of the Eleventh Women's Rights Convention* (New York: Robert J. Johnston, 1866). Read more at BlackPast.org, http://www.blackpast.org/1866-frances-ellen-watkins-harper-we-are-all-bound-together-0#sthash.rrwYWPvy.dpuf.

64. McMillen, *Seneca Falls*, 167.

65. Sally G. McMillen, *Seneca Falls and the Origins of the Women's Rights Movement* (New York: Oxford University Press, 2008), 119.

66. See Jo Freeman, "How 'Sex' Got into Title VII: Persistent Opportunism as a Maker of Public Policy," *Law and Inequality: A Journal of Theory and Practice* 9, no. 2 (March 1991): 163–84; Rosalind Rosenberg, *Divided Lives: American Women in the Twentieth Century* (New York: Hill and Wang, 2008), 187–88.

67. Betty Friedan, *The Feminine Mystique* (New York: Dell, 1963), 351.

68. National Organization for Women, "National Organization for Women (N.O.W.) Statement of Purpose, 1966," accessed August 11, 2016, http://coursesa.matrix.msu.edu/~hst306/documents/nowstate.html.

69. Title IX of the Education Amendments of 1972, vol. 20, U.S.C. sec. 1681.

70. Jane J. Mansbridge, *Why We Lost the ERA* (Chicago: University of Chicago Press, 1986).

71. Mark R. Daniels and Robert E. Darcy, "As Time Goes By: The Arrested Diffusion of the Equal Rights Amendment," *Publius* 15, no. 4 (Autumn 1985): 51–60.

72. The distinction originally appeared in a footnote to Justice Harlan Fiske Stone's opinion in *United States v. Carolene Products Co.* 304 U.S. 144 (1938).

73. In Sklar, *Women's Rights Emerges*, 179–80. Many versions of Truth's speech have been presented. Some were heavily edited by newspapers of the time, which sometimes changed her words to fit racial stereotypes of the period. See Carla Peterson, *"Doers of the Word": African American Women Speakers and Writers in the North (1830–1880)* (New York: Oxford University Press, 1995), 47–55.

74. Sklar, *Women's Rights Emerges*, 10. See also Marilyn Richardson, ed., Maria W. Stewart, *America's First Black Woman Political Writer: Essays and Speeches* (Bloomington: Indiana University Press, 1987).

75. Kimberlé Crenshaw, "Demarginalizing the Intersection of Race and Sex: A Black Feminist Critique of Antidiscrimination Doctrine, Feminist Theory, and Antiracist Politics," *University of Chicago Legal Forum* 1989, no. 1, http://chicagounbound.uchicago.edu/cgi/viewcontent.cgi?article=1052&context=uclf.

76. See Shirley J. Yee, *Black Women Abolitionists: A Study in Activism, 1828–1860* (Knoxville: University of Tennessee Press, 1992).

77. Susan Saulny, "Census Data Presents Rise in Multiracial Population of Youths," *New York Times*, March 24, 2011, http://www.nytimes.com/2011/03/25/us/25race.html.

78. Molefi Kete Asante, "Racing to Leave the Race: Black Postmodernists Off-Track," *Black Scholar* 23 (Summer/Fall 1993): 50–51.

79. Marvin C. Arnold, "Testimony before the Subcommittee on Census, Statistics, and Postal Personnel of the House Committee on Post Office and Civil Service 103-7," June 30, 1993, 162.

CHAPTER 6

1. From a protest and art installation titled *Mattress Performance (Carry That Weight)* by Columbia University student Emma Sulkowicz.

2. "Statement by Amanda Collins," Michigan State Senate, Senate Committee on Natural Resources, Environment and Great Lakes, March 22, 2012, http://senate.michigan.gov/committees/files/2012-SCT-NAT_-03-22-1-02.PDF.

3. Ibid.

4. Nevada CCW permit holders were allowed to carry on university campuses but only after having received written permission from the Nevada System of Higher Education, which generally denies such requests (Brian Vasek, "Rethinking the Nevada Campus Protection Act: Future Challenges & Reaching a Legislative Compromise," *Nevada Law Journal* 15, no. 1 [2014]: 389–430).

5. "Statement by Amanda Collins."

6. Crimesider Staff, "Women with Guns: Is It a Solution to Rape on Campus?," CBS News, February 24, 2015, http://www.cbsnews.com/news/women-with-guns-is-the-push-for-concealed-carry-legislation-a-solution-to-rape-on-campus/.

7. Leadership Institute, "CLP Activism: Strong Women," YouTube, January 16, 2015, https://www.youtube.com/watch?v=iFsdZGRWUWc.

8. Alan Schwarz, "A Bid for Guns on Campus to Deter Rape," *New York Times*, February 19, 2015, https://www.nytimes.com/2015/02/19/us/in-bid-to-allow-guns-on-campus-weapons-are-linked-to-fighting-sexual-assault.html.

9. David Hemenway and Sara J. Solnick, "The Epidemiology of Self-Defense Gun Use: Evidence from the National Crime Victimization Surveys 2007–2011," *Preventative Medicine: Special Issue on the Epidemiology and Prevention of Gun Violence* 79 (October 2015): 22–27.

10. Ryan Parker, "Colorado Senator's Comments to Rape Victim Drawing Criticism," *San Jose Mercury News*, March 5, 2013, available from Lexis-Nexis Academic.

11. Schwarz, "A Bid for Guns on Campuses to Deter Rape."

12. Alan Schwarz, "Advocates Push Guns as Tactic to Fight Rape on Campus," *International New York Times*, February 19, 2015, available from Lexis-Nexis Academic.

13. Crimesider Staff, "Women with Guns."

14. Landen Gambill, "Returning to College, Where I Was Raped," *Refinery* 29, October 23, 2014, http://www.refinery29.com/campus-rape-survivor.

15. Dave Dewitt, "Sexual Assault Case Splits Campus, Prompts Federal Investigation," WUNC, March 7, 2013, http://wunc.org/post/sexual-assault-case-splits-campus-prompts-federal-investigation#stream/0.

16. Landen Gambill, "Don't Vote to Allow Guns on College Campuses," Change.org, accessed May 13, 2016, https://www.change.org/p/arizona-state-house-don-t-vote-to-allow-guns-on-college-campuses.

17. Sidney Verba, Kay Lehman Schlozman, and Henry E. Brady, *Voice and Equality: Civic Voluntarism in American Politics* (Cambridge, MA: Harvard University Press, 1995), 42.

18. Sidney Verba and Norman H. Nie, *Participation in America: Political Democracy and Social Equality* (New York: Harper & Row, 1972), 46–48.

19. Russell J. Dalton, "The Myth of the Disengaged American," *Comparative Study of Electoral Systems (CSES)*, 2005, http://www.cses.org/resources/results/POP_Oct2005_1.htm.

20. Clare Saunders, "Anti-politics in Action? Measurement Dilemmas in the Study of Unconventional Political Participation," *Political Research Quarterly* 67, no. 3 (2014): 574–88.

21. Jose A. DelReal, "Voter Turnout in 2014 Was the Lowest Since WWII," *Washington Post*, November 10, 2014, https://www.washingtonpost.com/news/post-politics/wp/2014/11/10/voter-turnout-in-2014-was-the-lowest-since-wwii/.

22. Anthony Downs, *An Economic Theory of Democracy* (New York: HarperCollins: 1957), 233.

23. Drew DeSilver, "U.S. Voter Turnout Trails Most Developed Countries," Pew Research Center, May 6, 2015, http://www.pewresearch.org/facttank/2015/05/06/u-s-voter-turnout-trails-mostdeveloped-countries/.

24. Christopher Uggen and Sarah Shannon, "State-Level Estimates of Felon Disenfranchisement in the United States, 2010," Sentencing Project, July 2012, http://sentencingproject.org/doc/publications/fd_State_Level_Estimates_of_Felon_Disen_2010.pdf.

25. Raymond E. Wolfinger and Steven J. Rosenstone, *Who Votes?* (New Haven, CT: Yale University Press, 1980).

26. See Alexander K. Mayer, "Does Education Increase Political Participation?" *Journal of Politics* 73, no. 3 (August 3, 2011): 633–45.

27. See Eric Plutzer, "Becoming a Habitual Voter: Inertia, Resources, and Growth in Young Adulthood," *American Political Science Review* 96, no. 1 (March 2002): 41–56.

28. *Symm v. United States*, 439 U.S. 1105 (1979).

29. Laura Fitzpatrick, "College Students Still Face Voting Stumbling Blocks," *Time*, October 14, 2008, http://content.time.com/time/nation/article/0,8599,1849906,00.html.

30. Rutgers, Eagleton Institute of Politics, Center for American Women and Politics, "Fact Sheet: Gender Differences in Voter Turnout," July 2017, http://www.cawp.rutgers.edu/sites/default/files/resources/genderdiff.pdf.

31. Angus Campbell et al., *The American Voter*, Midway Reprint (Chicago: University of Chicago Press, 1960).

32. Steven J. Rosenstone and John Mark Hansen, *Mobilization, Participation, and Democracy in America* (New York: Macmillan, 1993).

33. "Voter Registration Deadlines for the General Election by State," USA.gov, accessed February 17, 2016, https://www.usa.gov/voter-registration-deadlines.

34. Jack Fitzpatrick, "College Students Face New Voting Barriers," Minnpost, August 16, 2012, https://www

.minnpost.com/politics-policy/2012/08/college-students-face-new-voting-barriers.

35. National Conference of State Legislatures, "Online Voter Registration," December 6, 2017, http://www.ncsl.org/research/elections-and-campaigns/electronic-or-online-voter-registration.aspx; "Online Voter Registration," Ballotpedia, 2018, https://ballotpedia.org/Online_voter_registration.

36. Paul S. Martin, "Inside the Black Box of Negative Campaign Effects: Three Reasons Why Negative Campaigns Mobilize," *Political Psychology* 25, no. 4 (2004): 545–62.

37. BWOG Staff, "'Accessible, Prompt, and Equitable?' An Examination of Sexual Assault at Columbia," BWOG: Columbia Student News, January 23, 2014, http://bwog.com/2014/01/23/accessible-prompt-and-equitable-an-examination-of-sexual-assault-at-columbia/.

38. Richard Perez-Pena and Kate Taylor, "Fight against Sex Assaults Holds Colleges to Account," *New York Times*, May 4, 2014, available from Lexis-Nexis Academic.

39. Ibid.

40. Lucia Peters, "Columbia Student Emma Sulkowicz's 'Mattress Performance/Carry That Weight' Performance Art Piece Tackles Campus Sexual Assault Culture Head-On," Bustle, September 3, 2014, http://www.bustle.com/articles/38346-columbia-student-emma-sulkowiczs-mattress-performancecarry-that-weight-performance-art-piece-tackles-campus-sexual-assault-culture.

41. Laura Krantz, "UVM Students Raise Awareness of Sexual Assault on Campus," *Brattleboro Reformer* (Vermont), October 31, 2014, available from Lexis-Nexis Academic.

42. Feminist Newswire, "Columbia University Fined Student Activists for the Carry That Weight Day of Action," Feminist Majority Foundation, November 10, 2014, https://feminist.org/blog/index.php/2014/11/10/columbia-university-fined-student-activists-for-the-carry-that-weight-day-of-action/.

43. Sarah Kaplan, "No Longer Just a Mattress, but a Symbol," *Washington Post*, November 29, 2014; available from Lexis-Nexis Academic.

44. Perez-Pena and Taylor, "Fight against Sex Assaults Holds Colleges to Account."

45. Office of United States Senator Claire McCaskill, Press Release, "Expanded Bipartisan Coalition Introduces Legislation to Prevent Sexual Assaults on College and University Campuses," February 26, 2015, http://www.mccaskill.senate.gov/media-center/news-releases/expanded-bipartisan-coalition-introduces-legislation-to-prevent-sexual-assaults-on-college-and-university-campuses.

46. Office of United States Senator Claire McCaskill, "The Bipartisan Campus Accountability and Safety Act," accessed February 20, 2016, http://www.mccaskill.senate.gov/imo/media/doc/CampusAccountabilityAndSafetyAct.pdf.

47. Claire McCaskill, "Bipartisan Coalition of Senators Renew Legislation to Combat Sexual Assault on College

& University Campuses," April 6, 2017, https://www.mccaskill.senate.gov/media-center/news-releases/bipartisan-coalition-of-senators-renew-legislation-to-combat-sexual-assault-on-college-and-university-campuses.

48. John Lauerman, "Campus Sexual Assault Hearings Planned by Senator McCaskill," Bloomberg Business, April 22, 2014, http://www.bloomberg.com/news/articles/2014-04-22/campus-sexual-assault-hearings-planned-by-senator-mccaskill.

49. Title IX of the Education Amendments of 1972 (Title IX), 20 U.S.C. §§ 1681 *et seq.*

50. Russlynn Ali, Assistant Secretary for Civil Rights, "'Dear Colleague' Memo," April 4, 2011, https://www2.ed.gov/about/offices/list/ocr/letters/colleague-201104.pdf.

51. Catherine E. Lhamon, Assistant Secretary for Civil Rights, Memorandum, December 1, 2014, https://www2.ed.gov/about/offices/list/ocr/docs/faqs-title-ix-single-sex-201412.pdf.

52. Gambill, "Returning to College, Where I Was Raped."

53. Ibid.

54. Roberta Smith, "In a Mattress, a Fulcrum of Art and Political Protest," *New York Times*, September 22, 2014, available from Lexis-Nexis Academic.

55. Ariel Kaminer, "New Factor in Campus Sexual Assault Cases: Counsel for the Accused," *New York Times*, November 19, 2014, https://www.nytimes.com/2014/11/20/nyregion/new-factor-in-campus-sexual-assault-cases-counsel-for-the-accused.html.

56. "Gillibrand Testimony before Senate Judiciary at Hearing to Examine Role of Law Enforcement in Campus Sexual Assault Cases," Plus Media Solutions, December 10, 2014, available from Lexis-Nexis Academic.

57. Jessica Glenza, "Columbia University Student at Center of Alleged Rape Calls Lawsuit 'Ridiculous,'" *The Guardian*, April 24, 2015, available from Lexis-Nexis Academic.

58. Ibid.

59. Ibid.

60. Dorothy Edwards, "Origin of Green Dot Etc.," Greendot.etcetra, accessed May 15, 2016, https://www.livethegreendot.com/gd_origins.html.

61. Tyler Kingkade, "This Is Why Every College Is Talking about Bystander Intervention," *Huffington Post*, February 8, 2016, http://www.huffingtonpost.com/entry/colleges-bystander-intervention_us_56abc134e4b0010e80ea021d.

62. Ibid.

63. Collin Brennan and Kristi Cook, "Why College Students Aren't Voting (and Why It Matters)," *USA Today*, September 25, 2015, http://college.usatoday.com/2015/09/25/why-college-students-arent-voting/.

64. Ibid.

65. Richard Fry, "Millennials Overtake Baby Boomers as America's Largest Generation," Pew Research Center, April 25, 2016, http://www.pewresearch.org/fact-tank/2016/04/25/millennials-overtake-baby-boomers.

66. Hollie Russon Gilman and Elizabeth Stokes, "The Civic and Political Participation of Millennials," New America, 2014, https://www.newamerica.org/downloads/The_Civic_and_Political_Participation_of_Millennials.pdf.

67. Pew Research Center, "Millennials in Adulthood: Detached from Institutions, Networked with Friends," March 7, 2014, http://www.pewsocialtrends.org/2014/03/07/millennials-in-adulthood/.

68. Ibid.

69. Alia Wong, "The Renaissance of Student Activism," *The Atlantic*, May 21, 2015, http://www.theatlantic.com/education/archive/2015/05/the-renaissance-of-student-activism/393749/.

70. Mike Paluska, "Hundreds of Students Protest for Embattled History Teacher," CBS46.com, September 9, 2014, http://www.cbs46.com/story/26491159/hundreds-of-students-protest-for-embattled-history-teacher.

71. Wong, "The Renaissance of Student Activism."

72. Harvard University, Institute of Politics, "Survey of Young Americans' Attitudes toward Politics and Public Service: 26th Edition," October 29, 2014, http://www.iop.harvard.edu/sites/default/files_new/fall%20poll%2014%20-%20exec%20summ%20final.pdf.

73. Russell J. Dalton, *The Good Citizen: How a Younger Generation Is Reshaping American Politics* (Washington, DC: CQ Press, 2008), 171.

CHAPTER 7

1. "Police-Community Reform and the Two Fergusons," Editorial, *St. Louis Post-Dispatch*, December 3, 2014, www.stltoday.com/news/opinion/columns/the-platform/editorial-police-community-reform-and-the-two-fergusons/article_c486f098-588a-5951-af85-036d74bd6999.html.

2. Leah Thorsen, "Shooting of Teen by Ferguson Police Officer Spurs Angry Backlash," *St. Louis Post-Dispatch*, August 10, 2014, available from Lexis-Nexis Academic.

3. "Ferguson Timeline," *St. Louis Post-Dispatch*, August 2, 2015, available from Lexis-Nexis Academic.

4. Tim Barker, "Ferguson-Area Businesses Cope with Aftermath of Weekend Riot," *St. Louis Post-Dispatch*, August 12, 2014, available from Lexis-Nexis Academic.

5. Joe Holleman and Kevin Johnson, "Ferguson Notes Ferguson Police Shooting," *St. Louis Post-Dispatch*, November 22, 2014, available from Lexis-Nexis Academic.

6. Amanda Paulson, "In Ferguson's Wake, Outcries Arise about Police Shootings in Other Cities," *Christian Science Monitor*, August 19, 2014, available from Lexis-Nexis Academic.

7. "When Does a Moment Become a Movement?," *Washington Post*, August 24, 2014, available from Lexis-Nexis Academic.

8. Christine Byers, "Darren Wilson Resigns from Ferguson Police Department: 'It Is My Hope That My Resignation Will Allow the Community to Heal,'" *St. Louis Post-Dispatch*, November 30, 2014, available from Lexis-Nexis Academic.

9. Frances Robles and Michael S. Schmidt, "Shooting Accounts Differ as Holder Schedules Visit," *New York Times*, August 20, 2014, available from Lexis-Nexis Academic.

10. Julie Bosman, "Bruised and Weary, Ferguson Struggles to Heal," *New York Times*, October 7, 2014, available from Lexis-Nexis Academic.

11. "Police-Community Reforms and the Two Fergusons."

12. Patrick Jonsson, "How Current Events Might Play into America's Shift in Favor of Gun Rights," *Christian Science Monitor*, December 11, 2014, available from Lexis-Nexis Academic.

13. Ibid.

14. Pew Research Center, "Across Racial Lines, More Say Nation Needs to Make Changes to Achieve Racial Equality," August 5, 2015, www.people-press.org/2015/08/05/across-racial-lines-more-say-nation-needs-to-make-changes-to-achieve-racial-equality; Scott Clement, "A Year after Ferguson, 6 in 10 Americans Say Changes Are Needed to Give Blacks and Whites Equal Rights," *Washington Post*, August 5, 2015, https://www.washingtonpost.com/news/the-fix/wp/2015/08/05/what-changed-since-ferguson-americans-are-far-more-worried-about-black-rights.

15. See Paul M. Sniderman, Richard A. Brody, and Philip E. Tetlock, *Reasoning and Choice: Explorations in Political Psychology* (New York: Cambridge University Press, 1991).

16. Angus Campbell et al., *The American Voter* (Chicago: University of Chicago Press, 1960), 151.

17. Philip E. Converse, "The Nature of Belief Systems in Mass Publics," in *Ideology and Discontent*, ed. David E Apter (London: Free Press of Glencoe, 1964), 212.

18. Michael Delli Carpini and Scott Keeter, *What Americans Know about Politics and Why It Matters* (New Haven, CT: Yale University Press, 1996).

19. John Zaller, *The Nature and Origins of Mass Opinion* (New York: Cambridge University Press, 1992).

20. While Zaller also maintains the traditional distinction between elite and mass opinion, his work emphasizes the ability of masses to draw on political elites in the process of constructing opinions.

21. Samuel L. Popkin, *The Reasoning Voter: Communication and Persuasion in Political Campaigns* (Chicago: University of Chicago Press, 1991), 212.

22. Arthur Lupia and Mathew D. McCubbins, *The Democratic Dilemma: Can Citizens Learn What They Need to Know?* (New York: Cambridge University Press, 1998).

23. Wendy M. Rahn, "The Role of Partisan Stereotypes in Information Processing about Political Candidates," *American Journal of Political Science* 37, no. 2 (1993): 472–96.

24. See James Surowiecki, *The Wisdom of Crowds* (New York: Doubleday, 2004).

25. Benjamin I. Page and Robert Y. Shapiro, *The Rational Public: Fifty Years of Trends in Americans' Policy Preferences* (Chicago: University of Chicago Press, 1992), 14.

26. Robert D. Behn, "What Right Do Public Managers Have to Lead?" *Public Administration Review* 58, no. 3 (1998): 209–24.

27. James M. Druckman, "The Implications of Framing Effects for Citizen Competence," *Political Behavior* 23, no. 3 (Sep. 2001): 225–56.

28. Pew Research Center, "Questionnaire Design," accessed July 31, 2018, www.pewresearch.org/methodology/u-s-survey-research/questionnaire-design.

29. Darren W. Davis and Brian D. Silver, "Stereotype Threat and Race of Interviewer Effects in a Survey on Political Knowledge," *American Journal of Political Science* 47, no. 1 (2003): 33–45.

30. Bosman, "Bruised and Weary"; Fred I. Greenstein, "The Benevolent Leader: Children's Images of Political Authority," *American Political Science Review* 54, no. 4 (1960): 934–43; David Easton and Robert D. Hess, "The Child's Political World," *Midwest Journal of Political Science* 6, no. 3 (1962): 229–46. For a more qualified view of the effectiveness of parent–child transmission of political attitudes and values, see M. Kent Jennings and Richard G. Niemi, "The Transmission of Political Values from Parent to Child," *American Political Science Review* 62, no. 1 (1968): 169–84.

31. Christopher H. Achen, "Parental Socialization and Rational Party Identification," *Political Behavior* 24, no. 2 (2002): 151–70.

32. See Kenneth P. Langton and M. Kent Jennings, "Political Socialization and the High School Civics Curriculum in the United States," *American Political Science Review* 62, no. 3 (1968): 852–67.

33. David E. Campbell, *Why We Vote: How Schools and Communities Shape Our Civic Life* (Princeton, NJ: Princeton University Press, 2006).

34. Lee H. Ehman, "The American School in the Political Socialization Process," *Review of Educational Research* 50, no. 1 (1980): 99–119.

35. Lisa Brown, "Hundreds of Protesters March to Ferguson Police Department," *St. Louis Post-Dispatch*, August 21, 2014, available from Lexis-Nexis Academic.

36. David Hunn, "No Charges for Wilson, Arson, Rioting Erupt in Ferguson Decision: Federal Inquiries Continue," *St. Louis Post-Dispatch*, November 25, 2014, available from Lexis-Nexis Academic.

37. Pew Research Center, "Stark Racial Divisions in Reactions to Ferguson Police Shooting," August 18, 2014, www.people-press.org/files/2014/08/8-18-14-Ferguson-Release.pdf.

38. See for example, Morris P. Fiorina, *Culture War? The Myth of a Polarized America* (New York: Longman/Pearson, 2011).

39. Michael Dawson, *Black Visions: The Roots of Contemporary African American Political Ideologies* (Chicago: University of Chicago Press, 2001).

40. Dennis Chong and Dukhong Kim, "The Experiences and Effects of Economic Status among Racial and Ethnic Minorities," *American Political Science Review* 100, no. 3 (2006): 335–51.

41. Evelyn M. Simien, "Race, Gender, and Linked Fate," *Journal of Black Studies* 35, no. 5 (2005): 529.

42. Pew Research Center, "Stark Racial Divisions."

43. Bosman, "Bruised and Weary."

44. Julie Hirschfeld Davis, "Calling for Calm in Ferguson, Obama Cites Need for Improved Race Relations," *New York Times*, August 19, 2014, available from Lexis-Nexis Academic.

45. "When Does a Moment Become a Movement?"

46. Mitch Smith, "A Year on, Ferguson Killing Is Recalled," *New York Times*, August 8, 2015, http://www.nytimes.com/2015/08/09/us/a-year-on-ferguson-killing-is-recalled.html?_r=0.

47. "1 Person Shot, Crowd Scatters as Gunshots Ring Out Late Sunday in Ferguson," *St. Louis Post-Dispatch*, August 10, 2015, available from Lexis-Nexis Academic.

48. Mitch Smith, "A Year on, Ferguson Killing Is Recalled," *New York Times*, August 8, 2015, www.nytimes.com/2015/08/09/us/a-year-on-ferguson-killing-is-recalled.html?_r=0.

49. Zeeshan Aleem, "The First Democratic Debate Proved That Black Lives Matter Is Making a Difference," Policy.Mic, October 14, 2015, http://mic.com/articles/126730/the-first-democratic-debate-proved-that-black-lives-matter-is-making-a-difference.

50. Ibid.

51. Ibid.

52. Lilly Fowler, "Members of the Congressional Black Caucus Arrive in Ferguson to Pledge Their Support," *St. Louis Post-Dispatch*, January 19, 2015, available from Lexis-Nexis Academic.

53. Ibid.

54. Jeremy Kohler, "Prominent Ferguson Protesters Publish Anti-Police Violence Policy Platform," *St. Louis Post-Dispatch*, August 22, 2015, available from Lexis-Nexis Academic.

55. Ibid.

56. It was not until the third week of the preseason, when a photo showed him sitting during the anthem, that his protests garnered significant attention.

57. "Colin Kaepernick Protests Anthem over Treatment of Minorities," ESPN.com News Services, August 27, 2016, http://theundefeated.com/features/colin-kaepernick-protests-anthem-over-treatment-of-minorities/.

58. Ibid.

59. Adam Stiles, "Everything You Need to Know about NFL Protests during the National Anthem," SBNation.com, October 19, 2017, https://www.sbnation.com/2017/9/29/16380080/donald-trump-nfl-colin-kaepernick-protests-national-anthem.

60. Ibid.

61. Jason Le Canfora, "Colin Kaepernick's Grievance against NFL Moving Forward, Dates to Be Determined,"

CBSSports.com, February 6, 2018, https://www
.cbssports.com/nfl/news/colin-kaepernicks-grievance-
against-nfl-moving-forward-dates-to-be-determined/.

62. Kevin Seifert and Dan Grazino, "New Policy Requires
On-field Players, Personnel to Stand for Anthem," ESPN
.com, May 24, 2018, http://www.espn.com/nfl/story/_/
id/23582533/nfl-owners-approve-new-national-anthem-
policy.

63. "Final Report: Independent Review of the 2017 Protest
Events in Charlottesville, Virginia," Hunton & Williams
LLP, accessed July 31, 2018, https://www.huntonak
.com/images/content/3/4/v4/34613/final-report-ada-
compliant-ready.pdf, p. 6; see also Laurel Wamsley,
"What Went Wrong in Charlottesville? Almost
Everything, Says Report," National Public Radio,
December 1, 2017, https://www.npr.org/sections/thetwo-
way/2017/12/01/567824446/charlottesville-made-major-
mistakes-in-handling-protest-review-finds.

64. Glenn Thrush and Rebecca R. Ruiz, "White House
Acts to Stem Fallout from Trump's First Charlottesville
Remarks," *New York Times*, August 13, 2017, https://
www.nytimes.com/2017/08/13/us/charlottesville-protests-
white-nationalists-trump.html.

65. Marist Poll, "8/17: Trump's Response to Charlottesville
Weak, Says Majority," August 17, 2017, http://maristpoll
.marist.edu/817-trumps-response-to-charlottesville-
weak-says-majority-two-thirds-call-fatal-car-rampage-
an-act-of-domestic-terrorism/.

66. John W. Kingdon, *Agendas, Alternatives, and Public
Policies*, 2nd ed. (New York: Longman, 2003), 1.

67. Mark Trumbull, "How Differently Do Blacks and
Whites View Ferguson? Here Are the Numbers,"
Christian Science Monitor, November 21, 2014, available
from Lexis-Nexis Academic.

68. Bosman, "Bruised and Weary."

CHAPTER 8

1. Eric Johnson (@Heyheygj), "Full Transcript: Hillary
Clinton at Code 2017," Recode, May 31, 2017, https://
www.recode.net/2017/5/31/15722218/hillary-clinton-
code-conference-transcript-donald-trump-2016-russia-
walt-mossberg-kara-swisher.

2. Ibid.

3. Ibid.

4. Office of the Director of National Intelligence,
"Assessing Russian Activities and Intentions in Recent
US Elections," January 6, 2017, ICA 2017-01D, ii.

5. President Donald J. Trump (@realDonaldTrump),
"Julian Assange said 'a 14 year old could have
hacked Podesta,'" Twitter, January 4, 2017,
4:22 a.m., https://twitter.com/realdonaldtrump/
status/816620855958601730?lang=en.

6. David French, "A Beginner's Guide to the Trump/Russia
Controversy," *National Review*, March 31, 2017, www
.nationalreview.com/article/446339/donald-trump-russia-
2016-election-controversy-explained.

7. Natasha Bertrand, "Trump's Top Intelligence Officials
Contradict Him on Russian Meddling," *The Atlantic*,
February 13, 2018, https://www.theatlantic.com/politics/
archive/2018/02/the-intelligence-community-warns-
congress-russia-will-interfere-in-2018-elections/553256/.

8. Ibid.

9. Patrick Novotny, *The Press in American Politics, 1787–
2012* (Denver, CO: Praeger, 2014), 1.

10. Ibid., 2.

11. Max Farrand, ed., *The Records of the Federal Convention
of 1787*, vol. II (New Haven, CT: Yale University Press,
1911), 334.

12. Michael Schudson, *Discovering the News: A Social History
of American Newspapers* (New York: Basic Books, 1978),
15–16.

13. Ibid., 18.

14. John D. Stevens, *Sensationalism and the New York Press*
(New York: Columbia University Press, 1991).

15. Associated Press, "AP's History," accessed July 31, 2018,
www.ap.org/company/history/ap-history.

16. David Protess, *The Journalism of Outrage: Investigative
Reporting and Agenda Building in America* (New York:
Guilford Press, 1991).

17. Novotny, *The Press in American Politics*, 96.

18. Jeffrey M. Berry and Sarah Sobieraj, *The Outrage
Industry: Political Opinion Media and the New Incivility*
(New York: Oxford University Press, 2014), 7.

19. Jules Witcover, "Brian Williams' Fib: Embellished
Stories May Be the Norm in Politics, but They're a
Career-Killer in Journalism," *Baltimore Sun*, February
10, 2015, http://www.pressreader.com/usa/baltimore-
sun/20150210/281762742683097.

20. Pew Research Center, "What Americans Know:
1989–2007," April 15, 2007, www.people-press.org/files/
legacy-pdf/319.pdf.

21. James Carson, "What Is Fake News? Its Origins and
How It Grew in 2016," *The Telegraph*, March 16, 2017,
www.telegraph.co.uk/technology/0/fake-news-origins-
grew-2016.

22. Project Veritas, "American Pravda: CNN Producer Says
Russia Narrative 'Bullsh★t,'" YouTube, June 26, 2017,
https://www.youtube.com/watch?v=jdP8TiKY8dE.

23. Ibid.

24. Project Veritas, "Van Jones: Russia Is 'Nothing Burger'—
American Pravda: CNN Part 2," YouTube, June 28,
2017, https://www.youtube.com/watch?v=l2G360HrSAs.

25. Michael M. Grynbaum, "3 CNN Journalists Resign
after Retracted Story on Trump Ally," *New York Times*,
June 26, 2017, https://www.nytimes.com/2017/06/26/
business/3-cnn-journalists-resign-after-retracted-story-
on-trump-ally.html.

26. Jake Tapper, "Trump: 'I Think It Was Russia' behind
Election Hacks," CNN.com, January 11, 2017, www
.cnn.com/videos/politics/2017/01/11/jake-tapper-defends-
donald-trump-intelligence-report-fake-news-sot.cnn.

27. Gloria Goodale, "Brian Williams Suspended: How Big
a Blow Was Dealt to Network News?," *Christian Science*

Monitor, February 10, 2015, available from Lexis-Nexis Academic.

28. Michael Parkin, "Taking Late Night Comedy Seriously: How Candidate Appearances on Late Night Television Can Engage Voters," *Political Research Quarterly* 63, no. 1 (2010): 3–15.

29. Matthew A. Baum and Angela S. Jamison, "The *Oprah* Effect: How Soft News Helps Inattentive Citizens Vote Consistently," *Journal of Politics* 68, no. 4 (2006): 946–59.

30. Matthew A. Baum, "Sex, Lies, and War: How Soft News Brings Foreign Policy to the Inattentive Public," *American Political Science Review* 96, no. 1 (2002): 91–109.

31. Jody Baumgartner and Jonathan S. Morris, "The *Daily Show* Effect: Candidate Evaluations, Efficacy, and American Youth," *American Politics Research* 34, no. 3 (2006): 341–67.

32. Thomas E. Patterson, "Doing Well and Doing Good," Faculty Research Working Paper Series, RWP01-001 (Cambridge, MA: Harvard University, John F. Kennedy School of Government, 2000).

33. See, for example, Bernard Goldberg, *Bias: A CBS Insider Exposes How the Media Distort the News* (New York: Perennial, 2002).

34. See, for example, William Schneider and I. A. Lewis, "Views on the News," *Public Opinion* 8, no. 4 (1985): 6–13.

35. D. Domke et al., "The Politics of Conservative Elites and the 'Liberal Media' Argument," *Journal of Communication* 49, no. 4 (1999): 35–58.

36. Larry J. Sabato, *Feeding Frenzy: How Attack Journalism Has Transformed American Politics* (New York: Free Press, 1991).

37. Amber Athey, "Study: Broadcast Networks Obsessed with Russia," *Daily Caller*, June 27, 2017. http://dailycaller.com/2017/06/27/study-broadcast-networks-obsessed-with-russia.

38. Garrett Hardin, "The Tragedy of the Commons," *Science* 162, no. 3859 (1968): 1243–48.

39. *Annual Report of the Federal Radio Commission to the Congress of the United States for the Fiscal Year Ended June 30, 1927* (Washington, DC: Government Printing Office, 1927), 1.

40. Ibid.

41. Federal Communications Commission, "Telecommunications Act of 1996," accessed July 31, 2018, https://transition.fcc.gov/telecom.html.

42. Clyde Wayne Crews Jr., "Counterpoint: A Defense of Media Monopoly," *Communications Lawyer* (Fall 2003): 13–14.

43. Doris A. Graber, *Mass Media and American Politics*, 8th ed. (Washington, DC: CQ Press, 2010), 52.

44. "Applicability of the Fairness Doctrine in the Handling of Controversial Issues of Public Importance," 29 Fed. Reg. 10426 (1964), quoted in Kathleen Ann Ruane, "Fairness Doctrine: History and Constitutional Issues,"

(Washington, DC: Congressional Research Service, 2011), 2.

45. Graber, *Mass Media and American Politics*, 53.

46. This section also draws heavily on "American Experience: War of the Worlds," dir. Cathleen O'Connell, telescript and story by Michelle Ferrrari and A. Brad Schwartz, WBGH, aired October 29, 2013.

47. John Gosling, *Waging the War of the Worlds: A History of the 1938 Radio Broadcast and Resulting Panic* (Jefferson, NC: McFarland, 2009), 34.

48. Howard Koch, "The War of the Worlds," original script for radio, reprinted in A. Brad Schwartz, *Broadcast Hysteria: Orson Welles's* War of the Worlds *and the Art of Fake News* (New York: Hill and Wang, 2015), 202.

49. Ibid., 202–3.

50. A. Brad Schwartz, *Broadcast Hysteria: Orson Welles's* War of the Worlds *and the Art of Fake News* (New York: Hill and Wang, 2015), 77.

51. Koch, "War of the Worlds," 218.

52. Schwartz, *Broadcast Hysteria*, 103.

53. Bernard R. Berelson, Paul F. Lazarsfeld, and William N. McPhee, *Voting: A Study of Opinion Formation in a Presidential Campaign* (Chicago: University of Chicago Press, 1954).

54. James N. Druckman and Kjersten R. Nelson, "Framing and Deliberation: How Citizens' Conversations Limit Elite Influence," *American Journal of Political Science* 47, no. 4 (2003): 730. See also Thomas E. Nelson, Rosalee A. Clawson, and Zoe M. Oxley, "Media Framing of a Civil Liberties Conflict and Its Effect on Tolerance," *American Political Science Review* 91, no. 3 (1997): 567–83.

55. Harold Lasswell, "The Structure and Function of Communication in Society," in *Mass Communications*, ed. Wilbur Schram (Urbana: University of Illinois Press, 1969), 103, as discussed in Graber, *Mass Media and American Politics*, 5.

56. Graber, *Mass Media and American Politics*, 5.

57. Markus Prior, *Post-Broadcast Democracy: How Media Choice Increases Inequality in Political Involvement and Polarizes Elections* (New York: Cambridge University Press, 2007).

58. Prior, *Post-Broadcast Democracy*, 142.

59. Andrea Caumont, "Who's Not Online? 5 Factors Tied to the Digital Divide," Pew Research Center, November 8, 2013, www.pewresearch.org/fact-tank/2013/11/08/whos-not-online-5-factors-tied-to-the-digital-divide.

CHAPTER 9

1. Center for Responsive Politics, "Hillary Clinton (D): Top Industries, Federal Election Data," February 22, 2016, http://www.opensecrets.org/pres16/indus.php?id=N00000019&cycle= 2016&type=f&src=o.

2. Michael Barone and Chuck McCutcheon, *The Almanac of American Politics 2014* (Chicago: University of Chicago Press, 2013), 1704–5.

3. "Transcript of the Democratic Presidential Debate in Milwaukee," *New York Times*, February 11, 2016, http://www.nytimes.com/2016/02/12/us/politics/transcript-of-the-democratic-presidential-debate-in-milwaukee.html?_r=0.

4. Eliza Gray, "Why Democrats Love Denmark," *Time*, October 14, 2015, http://time.com/4073063/why-democrats-love-denmark/.

5. Chuck McCutcheon, "Young Voters," *CQ Researcher*, October 2, 2015, http://library.cqpress.com/cqresearcher/document.php? id=cqresrre2015100203.

6. Joshua Gillin, "Bush Says Trump Was a Democrat Longer Than a Republican 'in the Last Decade,'" PolitiFact, August 24, 2015, www.politifact.com/florida/statements/2015/aug/24/jeb-bush/bush-says-trump-was-democrat-longer-republican-las.

7. Ibid.

8. "'This Week' Transcript: Gov. John Kasich," *ABC News*, December 27, 2015, http://abcnews.go.com/Politics/week-transcript-gov-john-kasich/story?id=35959367.

9. Nicholas Confessore and Karen Yourish, "Measuring Donald Trump's Mammoth Advantage in Free Media," *New York Times*, March 15, 2016, www.nytimes.com/2016/03/16/upshot/measuring-donald-trumps-mammoth-advantage-in-free-media.html.

10. Michael Cooper Jr., "A Message from Trump's America," *U.S. News & World Report*, March 9, 2016, www.usnews.com/news/the-report/articles/2016-03-09/a-message-from-trumps-america.

11. Lee Drutman, "Sanders and Trump Really Are the Candidates of Economic Pessimism," Vox.com, April 1, 2016, http://www.vox.com/polyarchy/2016/4/1/11340264/sanders-trump-economic-pessimism.

12. Jim Tankersley, "Five Myths about Trade," *Washington Post*, April 8, 2016, https://www.washingtonpost.com/opinions/five-myths-about-trade/2016/04/08/97cc317c-fcf0-11e5-80e4-c381214de1a3_story.html.

13. Julia Glum, "Is Donald Trump Expanding the Republican Party? White Voters May Not Determine 2016 Election," *International Business Times*, March 16, 2016, http://www.ibtimes.com/donald-trump-expanding-republican-party-white-voters-may-not-determine-2016-election-2336070.

14. Jeff Stein, "Bernie Sanders to Announce Plan to Guarantee Every American a Job," *Washington Post*, April 23, 2018, https://www.washingtonpost.com/news/wonk/wp/2018/04/23/bernie-sanders-to-unveil-plan-to-guarantee-every-american-a-job/?noredirect=on&utm_term=.460cbaca7f32.

15. "Washington's Farewell Address," Digital History, (1796) 2016, http://www.digitalhistory.uh.edu/disp_textbook.cfm?smtID=3&psid=160.

16. American Political Science Association, "A Report of the Committee on Political Parties: Toward a More Responsible Two-Party System," *American Political Science Review* 44, no. 3 (September 1950): part 2, supplement.

17. Austin Ranney, "Toward a More Responsible Two-Party System: A Commentary," *American Political Science Review* 45, no. 2 (1951): 488–99.

18. V. O. Key Jr., *Politics, Parties, and Pressure Groups*, 5th ed. (New York: Cromwell, 1964).

19. Jonathan Rauch, "The Secret to Saner Elections? Stronger State Parties," *Los Angeles Times*, March 22, 2016, http://www.latimes.com/opinion/op-ed/la-oe-0322-rauch-state-parties-20160322-story.html.

20. Drew DeSilver, "So Far, Turnout in This Year's Primaries Rivals 2008 Record," Pew Research Center, March 8, 2016, www.pewresearch.org/fact-tank/2016/03/08/so-far-turnout-in-this-years-primaries-rivals-2008-record.

21. Marty Cohen et al., *The Party Decides: Presidential Nominations before and after Reform* (Chicago: University of Chicago Press, 2008), 3.

22. John H. Aldrich, *Why Parties? The Origin and Transformation of Political Parties in America* (Chicago: University of Chicago Press, 1995), 26.

23. Jeffrey M. Jones, "Democratic, Republican Identification Near Historical Lows," Gallup, January 11, 2016, www.gallup.com/poll/188096/democratic-republican-identification-near-historical-lows.aspx?g_source=Politics&g_medium=lead&g_campaign=tiles.

24. Tom Price, "Polarization in America," *CQ Researcher*, February 28, 2014, http://library.cqpress.com/cqresearcher/document.php? id=cqresrre2014022800.

25. Rauch, "The Secret to Saner Elections?"

26. Joel Kotkin, "Farewell, Grand Old Party," *Orange County Register*, March 20, 2016, http://www.ocregister.com/articles/party-708782-trump-voters.html.

27. Ibid.

28. D. Stephen Voss, "Will Superdelegates Pick the Democratic Nominee? Here's Everything You Need to Know," *Washington Post*, February 26, 2016, https://www.washingtonpost.com/news/monkey-cage/wp/2016/02/26/will-superdelegates-pick-the-democratic-nominee-heres-everything-you-need-to-know.

29. Nolan D. McCaskill, "Sanders' Camp Serves DNC with Lawsuit over Voter Data," *Politico*, March 24, 2016, http://www.politico.com/blogs/2016-dem-primary-live-updates-and-results/2016/03/bernie-sanders-dnc-lawsuit-221216.

30. John Wagner, "Sanders Says DNC's Timing of Saturday Night's Debate Was Meant to 'Protect' Clinton," *Washington Post,* December 20, 2015, https://www.washingtonpost.com/news/post-politics/wp/2015/12/20/sanders-says-dncs-timing-of-saturday-nights-debate-was-meant-to-protect-clinton/.

31. Jonathan Martin, "Alarmed Clinton Supporters Begin Focusing on Sanders's Socialist Edge," *New York Times*, January 19, 2016, http://www.nytimes.com/2016/01/20/us/politics/alarmed-hillary-clinton-supporters-begin-focusing-on-bernie-sanders-socialist-edge.html.

32. Amy Chozick, "After Michigan Loss, Hillary Clinton Sharpens Message on Jobs and Trade," *New York Times*,

March 9, 2016, http://www.nytimes.com/2016/03/10/us/politics/after-michigan-loss-hillary-clinton-retools-message-on-jobs-and-trade.html?_r=0.

33. Ibid.

34. Dylan Scott, "Clinton Is Moving Left on Social Security," *National Journal*, August 13, 2015, http://www.govexec.com/management/2015/08/clinton-moving-left-social-security/119093/.

35. Eliza Collins, "Priebus '100 Percent' Confident He Can Rally GOP behind Cruz or Trump," Politico, January 8, 2016, http://www.politico.com/story/2016/01/reince-priebus-ted-cruz-trump-217489.

36. Trip Gabriel, "Donald Trump Finds Ally in Delegate System, Much to GOP's Chagrin," *New York Times*, February 29, 2016, http://www.nytimes.com/2016/03/01/us/politics/donald-trump-delegates.html.

37. Senator Ben Sasse, "An Open Letter to Trump Supporters," Facebook, February 28, 2016, https://www.facebook.com/sassefornebraska/posts/561073597391141.

38. Reid Epstein, "Ted Cruz Gains in Louisiana after Loss There to Donald Trump," *Wall Street Journal*, March 24, 2016, http://www.wsj.com/articles/ted-cruz-gains-in-louisiana-after-loss-there-to-donald-trump-1458861959.

39. David Weigel, "Cruz: *National Enquirer* Story Is 'Garbage' from 'Donald Trump and His Henchmen,'" *Washington Post*, March 25, 2016, http://www.washingtonpost.com/news/post-politics/wp/2016/03/25/cruz-national-enquirer-story-is-garbage-from-donald-trump-and-his-henchmen/.

40. Jennifer Agriesta, "CNN/ORC Poll: Clinton Tops Trump on Presidential Traits," CNN.com, March 24, 2016, http://www.cnn.com/2016/03/24/politics/hillary-clinton-donald-trump-cnn-poll-2016-election/index.html.

41. Dan Balz, "How the GOP Loyalty Pledge Completely Fell Apart," *Washington Post*, March 30, 2016, https://www.washingtonpost.com/politics/the-gops-patina-of-cohesion-has-been-shattered-by-the-candidates/2016/03/30/850de0c6-f69c-11e5-a3ce-f06b5ba21f33_story.html.

42. Robert Costa, "Internal Memo Reveals Trump Campaign's Mounting Fury with Its Critics," *Washington Post*, April 4, 2016, https://www.washingtonpost.com/news/post-politics/wp/2016/04/04/internal-memo-reveals-trump-campaigns-mounting-fury-with-its-critics/.

43. Alex Isenstadt, "Republicans Prep for Long, Ugly Nomination Fight," *Politico*, March 15, 2016, http://www.politico.com/story/2016/03/republicans-nomination-trump-cruz-220757.

44. Marc Fisher, "GOP Platform through the Years Shows Party's Shift from Moderate to Conservative," *Washington Post*, August 28, 2012, https://www.washingtonpost.com/politics/gop-platform-through-the-years-shows-partys-shift-from-moderate-to-conservative/2012/08/28/09094512-ed70-11e1-b09d-07d971dee30a_story.html.

45. Mark Landler, "Pushed by Obama, Democrats Alter Platform over Jerusalem," *New York Times*, September 5, 2012, http://www.nytimes.com/2012/09/06/us/politics/pushed-by-obama-democrats-alter-platform-over-jerusalem.html.

46. Jonah Goldberg, "The Republican Aristocracy Is Already Bending Its Knee to King Trump," *Los Angeles Times*, May 10, 2016, http://www.latimes.com/opinion/op-ed/la-oe-0510-goldberg-trump-party-20160510-column.html.

47. Steve Inskeep and Shankar Vedantam, "Why Compromise Is a Bad Word in Politics," National Public Radio, March 13, 2012, http://www.npr.org/2012/03/13/148499310/why-compromise-is-terrible-politics.

48. Jane Mansbridge, "Three Reasons Political Polarization Is Here to Stay," *Washington Post*, March 11, 2016, https://www.washingtonpost.com/news/in-theory/wp/2016/03/11/three-reasons-political-polarization-is-here-to-stay/.

49. See, for example, Morris P. Fiorina, *Culture War? The Myth of a Polarized America* (New York: Longman/Pearson, 2011).

50. Aldrich, *Why Parties?*, 261. See also V. O. Key Jr., "A Theory of Critical Elections," *Journal of Politics* 17, no. 1 (February 1955): 3–18.

51. Amy Kittelstrom, "Ignorance, Racism and Rage," *Salon,* April 9, 2016, www.salon.com/2016/04/09/ignorance_racism_and_rage_the_gops_transformation_to_the_party_of_stupid_started_long_before_donald_trump/?utm_source=twitter&utm_medium=socialflow.

52. Ibid., 1002.

53. Robert Reich, "Robert Reich Sees the Future: Why America's Two-Party System May Collapse," Alternet.org, March 22, 2016, www.alternet.org/election-2016/robert-reich-sees-futurewhy-americas-two-party-system-may-collapse.

54. Kristina Nwazota, "Third Parties in the U.S. Political Process," *PBS NewsHour*, July 26, 2004, www.pbs.org/newshour/updates/politics-july-dec04-third_parties.

55. "2000 Presidential Election Results," U.S.ElectionAtlas.org, accessed July 31, 2018, http://uselectionatlas.org/RESULTS/national.php?year=2000.

56. Christopher J. Devine and Kyle C. Kopko, "5 Things You Need to Know about How Third-Party Candidates Did in 2016," *Washington Post*, November 15, 2016, https://www.washingtonpost.com/news/monkey-cage/wp/2016/11/15/5-things-you-need-to-know-about-how-third-party-candidates-did-in-2016.

57. "Spotlight: Cambridge," FairVote.org, accessed July 31, 2018, http://www.fairvote.org/spotlight_cambridge.

58. "Closer Look: Criticism Mounting over Ranked-Choice Voting," *CBS News*, November 11, 2011, http://sanfrancisco.cbslocal.com/2011/11/16/closer-look-criticism-mounting-over-ranked-choice-voting/.

59. Channel3YouTube, "Attack of the Crab Monsters" (roughly 39:24 into the film), YouTube, March 8, 2015, https://www.youtube.com/watch?v=-RA12RHnYIA.

60. David Siders, "DNC Rule Change Angers Sanders Supporters," *Politico*, June 8, 2018, https://www.politico.com/story/2018/06/08/dnc-rule-change-sanders-supporters-634998.

CHAPTER 10

1. In this chapter, we will generally use the term *Latino*, though with occasional references to *Hispanic* when quoting others or referring to census data and other official categorizations.

2. The third senator of Latino heritage is Bob Menendez (D-NJ), also of Cuban descent.

3. Ashley Parker and Alan Rappeport, "Marco Rubio Announces 2016 Presidential Bid," *New York Times*, April 13, 2015, http://www.nytimes.com/2015/04/14/us/politics/marco-rubio-2016-presidential-campaign.html?_r=0.

4. Theodore Schleifer, "Cruz Allies Tout His Latino Background as General Election Benefit," CNN.com, January 26, 2016, http://www.cnn.com/2016/01/26/politics/cruz-latino-general-election-2016/.

5. Mary Jordan, "'He's Cuban. I'm Mexican.': Can Rubio and Cruz Connect with Latino Voters?," *Washington Post*, January 10, 2016, https://www.washingtonpost.com/politics/2016/01/10/32d20f8e-b4bc-11e5-a842-0feb51d1d124_story.html.

6. Marc Fisher, "The GOP's Identity-Politics Crisis: Holding Race-Card Aces but Loath to Play Them," *Washington Post*, November 19, 2016, https://www.washingtonpost.com/politics/the-gops-identity-politics-crisis-a-diverse-field-but-an-aversion-to-tout-it/2015/11/29/48c6f040-8fad-11e5-ae1f-af46b7df8483_story.html.

7. Esther Yu-Hsi Lee, "Young Latinos Are Set to Change American Elections," ThinkProgress.org, January 22, 2016, http://thinkprogress.org/immigration/2016/01/22/3741434/latino-voters-millennials/.

8. Amanda Sakuma, "The Rubio-Cruz Immigration War Heats Up," MSNBC, January 15, 2016, http://www.msnbc.com/msnbc/the-rubio-cruz-immigration-war-heats.

9. Ibid.

10. Eric Bradner, "Rubio Hits Cruz on Immigration, Snowden," CNN.com, January 10, 2016, http://www.cnn.com/2016/01/10/politics/marco-rubio-ted-cruz-immigration-edward-snowden/.

11. "Full Text: Donald Trump Immigration Speech in Arizona," *Politico*, August 31, 2016, https://www.politico.com/story/2016/08/donald-trump-immigration-address-transcript-227614.

12. Paola Luisi, "7 Things Hillary Clinton Has in Common with Your Abuela," HillaryClinton.com, accessed December 21, 2015, https://www.hillaryclinton.com/feed/8-ways-hillary-clinton-just-your-abuela/?utm_medium=social&utm_source=fb&utm_campaign=20151222feed_abuela.

13. Ibid.

14. Ibid.

15. Jane C. Timm, "Clinton's 'Abuela' Pitch to Latinos Prompts Twitter Backlash," *NBC News,* December 23, 2015, http://www.nbcnews.com/politics/2016-election/clinton-s-abuela-pitch-latinos-prompts-twitter-backlash-n485166.

16. Ben Norton, "'Not My Abuela': Twitter Explodes in Outrage over Hillary Clinton's 'Hispandering,'" Salon.com, December 23, 2015, http://www.salon.com/2015/12/23/not_my_abuela_twitter_explodes_in_outrage_over_hillary_clintons_hispandering/.

17. Priscilla Alvarez, "The Sanders-Clinton Battle for Latino Voters," *The Atlantic*, March 11, 2016, https://www.theatlantic.com/politics/archive/2016/03/sanders-clinton-latino-voters/473271/.

18. Steven W. Thrasher, "Bernie Sanders Isn't Winning Minority Votes—and It's His Own Fault," *The Guardian*, May 3, 2016, https://www.theguardian.com/commentisfree/2016/may/03/bernie-sanders-failure-diversity-hispanic-black-voters.

19. Stephanie Ewert, "U.S. Population Trends: 2000 to 2060," U.S. Census Bureau, October 15, 2015, http://www.ncsl.org/Portals/1/Documents/nalfo/USDemographics.pdf.

20. Joshua Fletcher, "Hispanics to Outnumber Whites in Texas by 2020, State Says," MySanAntonio.com, July 9, 2015, http://www.mysanantonio.com/news/local/article/Hispanics-to-outnumber-whites-in-Texas-by-the-end-6375597.php.

21. Republican National Committee, "Growth and Opportunity Project," accessed June 23, 2016, http://goproject.gop.com/rnc_growth_opportunity_book_2013.pdf.

22. Nate Cohn, "Hispanic Voters Are Important for Republicans, but Not Indispensable," *New York Times*, November 20, 2014, http://www.nytimes.com/2014/11/21/upshot/hispanic-voters-are-important-for-republicans-but-not-indispensable.html?_r=0.

23. Pew Research Center, "Mapping the Latino Electorate by State," January 19, 2016, http://www.pewhispanic.org/interactives/mapping-the-latino-electorate-by-state/.

24. Kate Linthicum, "The Latino Vote Is Growing—but It Could Be Much Bigger," *Los Angeles Times*, September 10, 2015, http://www.latimes.com/nation/politics/la-na-latino-voters-20150910-story.html.

25. Ibid.

26. U.S. Constitution, art. I, sec. 4.

27. The power of states to restrict the rights of convicted felons to vote, which is called felony (or felon)

disenfranchisement, is rooted in the Fourteenth Amendment's vague phrase, "or other crime."

28. Morris P. Fiorina, *Retrospective Voting in American National Elections* (New Haven, CT: Yale University Press, 1981).

29. Mark Hugo Lopez, Ana Gonzalez-Barrera, and Jens Manuel Krogstad, "Chapter 4: Top Issues in This Year's Election for Hispanic Voters," Pew Research Center, October 29, 2014, www.pewhispanic.org/2014/10/29/chapter-4-top-issues-in-this-years-election-for-hispanic-voters.

30. Center for Responsive Politics, "2016 Presidential Race," accessed July 31, 2018, OpenSecrets.org, https://www.opensecrets.org/pres16.

31. Jonathan Berr, "Election 2016's Price Tag: $6.8 Billion," CBSNews.com, November 8, 2016, www.cbsnews.com/news/election-2016s-price-tag-6-8-billion.

32. John G. Geer, *In Defense of Negativity: Attack Ads in Presidential Campaigns* (Chicago: University of Chicago Press, 2006), 13.

33. *Buckley v. Valeo*, 424 U.S. 1 (1976).

34. *Citizens United v. Federal Election Commission*, 558 U.S.__ (2010).

35. Team Fix, "7th Republican Debate Transcript, Annotated: Who Said What and What It Meant," *Washington Post*, January 28, 2016, https://www.washingtonpost.com/news/the-fix/wp/2016/01/28/7th-republican-debate-transcript-annotated-who-said-what-and-what-it-meant/.

36. Neil Munro, "Fox, Google Pick 1994 Illegal Immigrant to Ask Question in Iowa GOP Debate," Breitbart.com, January 27, 2016, http://www.breitbart.com/2016-presidential-race/2016/01/27/fox-google-pick-1994-illegal-immigrant-to-ask-question-in-iowa-gop-debate/.

37. Dulce Candy, "My Story | Dulce Candy," YouTube, November 11, 2015, https://www.youtube.com/watch?v=CR2fIM5TJpE.

38. "Digital Exclusive: The Dulce Candy Interview," Latino USA, November 17, 2015, http://latinousa.org/2015/11/17/digital-exclusive-the-dulce-candy-interview/.

39. Carmen Sesin, "'Hispanicize 2015' Showcases Latino Ventures, Talent," *NBC News*, March 18, 2015, http://www.nbcnews.com/news/latino/hispanicize-2015-event-showcases-latino-ventures-talent-n325646.

40. Chris Meagher, "Can Salud Carbajal Really Be Everything to Everyone?," *Santa Barbara Independent*, March 27, 2008, http://www.independent.com/news/2008/mar/27/can-salud-carbajal-really-be-everything-everyone/.

41. "California's 24th Congressional District," Ballotpedia, accessed January 26, 2016, https://ballotpedia.org/California%27s_24th_Congressional_District#2016.

42. Oscar Flores, "Candidates Already Announce Bids for Capps' Seat," KEYT-KCOY-KKFX, April 8, 2015, http://www.keyt.com/news/local-politicians-announce-bid-for-congressional-district-seat/32264312.

43. California's primary nomination system does not apply to candidates for the U.S. presidency and some local offices. The system that California uses is often called a "jungle primary"; however, that term is less precise.

44. Jean Merl, "No-Incumbent Races Draw Crowd; Two of the Three Such California House Seats Favor Democrats," *Los Angeles Times*, October 25, 2015, available from Lexis-Nexis Academic.

45. "Analysis of California's Congressional Districts (January Edition)," Races and Redistricting, January 11, 2012, http://racesandredistricting.blogspot.com/2011/12/analysis-of-californias-congressional.html.

46. Cristina Marcos, "Lois Capps's Daughter Won't Run for Her Mother's Seat," The Hill.com, April 28, 2015, available from Lexis-Nexis Academic.

47. Merl, "No-Incumbent Races Draw Crowd."

48. Ben Kamisar, "Pelosi Backs Ally's Pick for Successor," The Hill.com, October 7, 2015, available from Lexis-Nexis Academic.

49. Ibid.

50. Ibid.

51. "Salud Carbajal Brings in More Than $407,000 in Third Quarter," *A-Town Daily News*, October 8, 2015, http://atowndailynews.com/salud-carbajal-brings-in-more-than-407000-in-third-quarter/37321/.

52. Professor Bartels attributes the term to a comment made by George H. W. Bush in 1980 (Larry M. Bartels, *Presidential Primaries and the Dynamics of Public Choice* [Princeton, NJ: Princeton University Press, 1988], 27.

53. U.S. Congressman Salud Carbajal, "Here's What the First Day of Congress Was Like for the Five Democrats Who Joined California's House Delegation Today," January 3, 2017, https://carbajal.house.gov/news/documentsingle.aspx?DocumentID=35.

54. Michael Doyle, "1st Vote Doesn't Go So Great for Newly Sworn In Congressman," McClatchy.com, January 3, 2017, http://www.mcclatchydc.com/news/politics-government/congress/article124367754.html.

55. Matt Van Slyke, "Republican Justin Fareed to make third run for Congress," KSBY.com, September 27, 2017, http://www.ksby.com/story/36469948/republican-justin-fareed-to-make-third-run-for-congress.

56. The size of the House was fixed at 435 members by the Reapportionment Act of 1929. The number rose to 437 for a time after the admission of Alaska and Hawaii as states, but it has stayed at 435 since the apportionment following the 1960 census. Washington, DC, has three nonvoting delegates in the House.

57. Gary C. Jacobson, *The Politics of Congressional Elections*, 7th ed. (New York: Pearson Longman, 2009), 12.

58. Ibid., 12.

59. Ibid., 12.

60. Ibid., 23 (footnotes).

61. Ibid., 13.

62. California's voting-age population was twenty-eight million in 2010 and Wyoming's was 428,000, according to the 2010 census. United States Census Bureau,

Statistical Abstract of the United States: 2012, accessed May 4, 2013, http://www.census.gov/compendia/statab/.

63. Frances E. Lee, "Representation and Public Policy: The Consequences of Senate Apportionment for the Geographic Distribution of Federal Funds," *Journal of Politics* 60, no. 1 (February 1998): 34–62.

64. *Wesberry v. Sanders*, 376 U.S. 1 (1964); *Reynolds v. Sims*, 377 U.S. 533 (1964).

65. *Davis v. Bandemer*, 478 U.S. 109 (1986).

66. *Vieth v. Jubelirer*, 541 U.S. 267 (2004).

67. *League of United Latin American Citizens v. Perry*, 548 U.S. 399 (2006). The Court ruled that the proposed Texas Twenty-Fifth District violated the rights of Hispanic Americans protected under provisions of the Voting Rights Act of 1965.

68. Adam Liptak, "Supreme Court Avoids an Answer on Partisan Gerrymandering," *The New York Times*, June 18, 2018, https://www.nytimes.com/2018/06/18/us/politics/supreme-court-wisconsin-maryland-gerrymander-vote.html.

69. *Thornburg v. Gingles*, 478 U.S. 30 (1986); the Voting Rights Act of 1965.

70. *Shaw v. Reno*, 509 U.S. 630 (1993).

71. Gary C. Jacobson, *The Politics of Congressional Elections*, 8th ed. (New York: Pearson, 2012), 27.

72. Ibid., 27–28.

73. David R. Mayhew, *Congress: The Electoral Connection* (New Haven, CT: Yale University Press), 5. See also David R. Mayhew, "Congressional Elections: The Case of the Vanishing Marginals," *Polity* 6, no. 3 (Spring 1974): 295–317.

74. Mayhew, *Congress*, 49–77.

75. Alan I. Abramowitz, Brad Alexander, and Matthew Gunning, "Incumbency, Redistricting, and the Decline of Competition in U.S. House Elections," *Journal of Politics* 68, no. 1 (February 2006): 82.

76. Gary Langer and Benjamin Siu, "Election 2018 Exit Poll Analysis: Voter Turnout Soars, Democrats Take Back the House, ABC News Projects," *ABC News*, November 7, 2018, https://abcnews.go.com/Politics/election-2018-exit-poll-analysis-56-percent-country/story?id=59006586.

CHAPTER 11

1. Chairman Ben S. Bernanke, "The Economic Outlook," testimony before the Joint Economic Committee, United States Congress, March 28, 2007, www.federalreserve.gov/newsevents/testimony/bernanke20070328a.htm.

2. U.S. Department of the Treasury, "The Financial Crisis Response in Charts," April 2012, www.treasury.gov/resource-center/data-chart-center/Documents/20120413_FinancialCrisisResponse.pdf.

3. Henry M. Paulson Jr., *On the Edge: Inside the Race to Stop the Collapse of the Global Financial System* (New York: Business Plus, 2010), 63.

4. Helen Kennedy, "Economy Is Headin' for Cliff! OK Bailout Soon or Else, Says Treasury Chief," *New York Daily News*, September 22, 2008, available from Lexis-Nexis Academic.

5. Ibid.

6. Kevin G. Hall, "Is It Safe to Trust a Wall Street Veteran with a Wall Street Bailout?," *McClatchy Newspapers*, September 21, 2008, available from Lexis-Nexis Academic.

7. Jeffrey H. Birnbaum, "Vital Part of Housing Bill Is Brainchild of Banks," *Washington Post*, June 25, 2008, www.washingtonpost.com/wp-dyn/content/article/2008/06/24/AR2008062401389.html.

8. Jenny Anderson, Vikas Bajaj, and Leslie Wayne, "Big Financiers Start to Lobby for Wider Aid," *New York Times*, September 21, 2008, www.nytimes.com/2008/09/22/business/22lobby.html?_r=0.

9. Jerry Zremski, "Bailout Plan Hit by Backlash; Congress Expresses Outrage; Reflects Taxpayers' Mood amid Call for Quick Action," *Buffalo News* (New York), September 24, 2008, available from Lexis-Nexis Academic.

10. Tony Pugh, "Groups Say Bailout Doesn't Do Enough for Struggling Homeowners," Knight Ridder Washington Bureau, September 23, 2008, available from Lexis-Nexis Academic.

11. Helen Kennedy, "Dems Balk at Bailout. Press Help for Homeowners, Exec Pay Cuts as Part of Deal," *New York Daily News*, September 23, 2008, available from LexisNexis Academic.

12. Ibid.

13. Juan Gonzalez, "Bailout Dish Has Heaping Side of Pork," *New York Daily News*, October 3, 2008, available from Lexis-Nexis Academic.

14. Kenneth Stier, "Tax Break for Arrows? Why It's Part of the Bailout," CNBC.com, October 2, 2008, https://www.cnbc.com/id/26995651.

15. Stephen Labaton and Jackie Calmes, "Obama Proposes a First Overhaul of Finance Rules," *New York Times*, May 14, 2009, available from Lexis-Nexis Academic.

16. Deniz Igan, Prachi Mishra, and Thierry Tressel, "A Fistful of Dollars: Lobbying and the Financial Crisis," National Bureau of Economic Research Working Paper 17076, May 2001, http://www.nber.org/papers/w17076.

17. Ibid.

18. Alexis de Tocqueville, *Democracy in America*, trans. George Lawrence, ed. J. P. Mayer (New York: Harper Perennial Modern Classics, 1966), 9.

19. For a historical treatment of these ideas, see Arthur M. Schlesinger, "Biography of a Nation of Joiners," *American Historical Review* 50, no. 1 (October 1944): 1–25.

20. James Madison, *Federalist No. 54*, in *The Federalist Papers*, ed. George W. Carey and James McClellan (Indianapolis: Liberty Fund, 2001), 44.

21. Robert A. Dahl, *Who Governs? Democracy and Power in an American City* (New Haven, CT: Yale University Press, 1961), 3.

22. C. Wright Mills, *The Power Elite* (New York: Oxford University Press, 1956), 4–5.

23. E. E. Schattschneider, *The Semisovereign People: A Realist's View of Democracy in America* (Hinsdale, IL: Dryden Press, 1960), 32.

24. David B. Truman, *The Governmental Process: Political Interests and Public Opinion* (New York: Alfred A.

Knopf, 1962), 5. Truman used the term *pressure groups* to describe the phenomenon.

25. Mancur Olson, *The Logic of Collective Action: Public Goods and the Theory of Groups* (Cambridge, MA: Harvard University Press, 1965), 2. Italics are the author's.

26. Paul Samuelson, "The Pure Theory of Public Expenditure," *The Review of Economics and Statistics* 36, no. 4 (November 1954): 387–89. Technically, the characteristic is called *nonexcludability*. Public goods also exhibit the characteristic of *nonrivalry*, referring to the fact that the consumption of the good by one individual does not reduce its availability to others.

27. Olson, *The Logic of Collective Action*, 14–15.

28. David C. King and Jack L. Walker, "The Provision of Benefits by Interest Groups in the United States," *Journal of Politics* 54, no. 2 (May 1992): 394–426.

29. Sandy Mackenzie, "The Impact of the Financial Crisis on Older Americans," *Insight on the Issues, AARP Public Policy Institute* 19 (December 2008): 11.

30. Anthony J. Nownes, *Total Lobbying: What Lobbyists Want (and How They Try to Get it)* (New York: Cambridge University Press, 2006), 6.

31. Center for Responsive Politics, "Lobbying Database," OpenSecrets.org, 2017, https://www.opensecrets.org/lobby. Their figures were calculated from data obtained from the Senate Office of Public Records.

32. Kay Lehman Schlozman and John T. Tierney, *Organized Interests and American Democracy* (New York: Harper & Row, 1986), 148–57.

33. Joseph White, "Making Connections to the Appropriations Process," in *The Interest Group Connection: Electioneering, Lobbying, and Policymaking in Washington*, 2nd ed., ed. Paul S. Herrnson, Ronald G. Shaiko, and Clyde Wilcox (Washington, DC: CQ Press, 2005), 164–88.

34. Administrative Procedure Act (APA), Pub. L.79–404, 60 Stat. 237. The act was passed in 1946.

35. Scott R. Furlong, "Exploring Interest Group Participation in Executive Policymaking," in Herrnson et al., *The Interest Group Connection*, 282–97.

36. Marver Bernstein, *Regulating Business by Independent Commission* (Princeton, NJ: Princeton University Press, 1955).

37. Karen O'Connor, "Lobbying the Justices or Lobbying for Justice? The Role of Organized Interests in the Judicial Process," in Herrnson et al., *The Interest Group Connection*, 331.

38. Gregory A. Caldeira and John R. Wright, "Organized Interests and Agenda Setting in the U.S. Supreme Court," *American Political Science Review* 82, no. 4 (December 1988): 1109–27.

39. Lee Epstein and C. K. Rowland, "Debunking the Myth of Interest Group Invincibility in the Courts," *American Political Science Review* 85, no. 1 (March 1991): 205–17.

40. *Citizens United v. Federal Election Commission*, 558 U.S. __ (2010).

41. Norman J. Ornstein and Shirley Elder, *Interest Groups, Lobbying, and Policymaking* (Washington, DC: CQ Press, 1978), 88.

42. Ken Kollman, *Outside Lobbying: Public Opinion and Interest Group Strategies* (Princeton, NJ: Princeton University Press, 1998), 80.

43. Kenneth M. Goldstein, *Interest Groups, Lobbying, and Participation in America* (New York: Cambridge University Press, 1999), 125.

44. Grant McConnell, *Private Power and American Democracy* (New York: Alfred A. Knopf, 1966), 5.

45. Kay Lehman Schlozman, "What Accent the Heavenly Chorus? Political Equality and the American Pressure System," *Journal of Politics* 46, no. 4 (November 1984): 1006–32.

46. Dara Z. Strolovitch, *Affirmative Advocacy: Race, Class, and Gender in Interest Group Politics* (Chicago: University of Chicago Press, 2007).

47. Maud Dillingham, "Top 5 Targets of Occupy Wall Street," *Christian Science Monitor*, October 24, 2011, available from Lexis-Nexis Academic.

48. Ibid.

49. Occupy*Posters, Tumblr, accessed July 3, 2016, http://owsposters.tumblr.com/post/11944143747/if-us-land-mass-were-distributed-like-us.

50. John Wellington Ennis, "Three Years Later, What Has Come of Occupy Wall Street?," *Huffington Post*, September 17, 2014, www.huffingtonpost.com/john-wellington-ennis/three-years-later-what-ha_b_5833682.html.

51. James C. McKinley Jr., "At the Protests, the Message Lacks a Melody," *New York Times*, October 19, 2011, available from Lexis-Nexis Academic.

52. Harold Brubaker, "'Occupy Wall Street' Protest Movement Seeks a Philadelphia Foothold," *Philadelphia Inquirer*, October 2, 2011, available from Lexis-Nexis Academic.

53. Brad Knickerbocker, "Occupy Wall Street Protest 'about People Claiming Some Autonomy,'" *Christian Science Monitor*, October 2, 2011, available from Lexis-Nexis Academic.

54. Carrie Kahn, "Battle Cry: Occupy's Messaging Tactics Catch On," National Public Radio, December 6, 2011, http://www.npr.org/2011/12/06/142999617/battle-cry-occupys-messaging-tactics-catch-on.

55. Ibid.

56. Jonathan Easley, "GOP: Dems Mum on Anti-Semitism from Occupy Wall Street Protestors," The Hill.com, October 20, 2011, available from Lexis-Nexis Academic.

57. Alice Speri, "Struggling to Make 'the 99%' More Representative of Reality," *New York Times*, October 29, 2011, available from Lexis-Nexis Academic.

58. Ibid.

59. NYC General Assembly, #Occupy Wall Street, "Declaration of the Occupation of New York City," September 29, 2011, accessed December 4, 2014, http://www.nycga.net/resources/documents/declaration/.

60. Cara Buckley and Colin Moynihan, "A Protest Reaches a Crossroads," *New York Times*, November 6, 2011, available from Lexis-Nexis Academic.

61. Michelle Nichols, "Wall Street Demonstrators Evicted by New York Police," *Reuters*, November 16, 2011, available from Lexis-Nexis Academic.

62. "Occupy Wall Street: The Next Chapter," letter to the editor, *New York Times*, November 17, 2011, available from Lexis-Nexis Academic.

63. Gloria Goodale, "Occupy Wall Street: Time to Become More Overtly Political?," *Christian Science Monitor*, November 16, 2011, available from Lexis-Nexis Academic.

64. See, for example, Dennis Chong, *Collective Action and the Civil Rights Movement* (Chicago: University of Chicago Press, 1991).

65. This section draws upon Ken Kollman, *The American Political System* (New York: W. W. Norton, 2012), 378–79.

66. Christian Davenport, "How Social Movements Die—the Blog Entry (Book on the Way)," University of Notre Dame, Center for the Study of Social Movements, Mobilizing Ideas, December 2, 2013, https://mobilizingideas.wordpress.com/2013/12/02/how-social-movements-die-the-blog-entry-book-on-the-way.

67. Edwin Amenta, "Failure Is Not an Option," University of Notre Dame, Center for the Study of Social Movements, Mobilizing Ideas, December 2, 2013, https://mobilizingideas.wordpress.com/2013/12/02/failure-is-not-an-option.

68. Erik W. Johnson, "Social Movement Size, Organizational Diversity and the Making of Federal Law," *Social Forces* 86, no. 3 (2008): 967–93.

69. John W. Kingdon, *Agendas, Alternatives, and Public Policies*, updated 2nd ed. (Boston: Longman, 2011).

70. David S. Meyer and Steven A. Boutcher, "Signals and Spillover: *Brown v. Board of Education* and Other Social Movements," *Perspectives on Politics* 5, no. 1 (2007): 81–93.

CHAPTER 12

1. Hanna Fenichel Pitkin, *The Concept of Representation* (Berkeley: University of California Press, 1972).

2. Julie Kohler and Felicia Wong, "Why 2018 Might Not Be the Year of the Woman, *The Nation*, April 27, 2018, https://www.thenation.com/article/why-2018-might-not-be-the-year-of-the-woman/.

3. Heather Caygle, "Record-Breaking Number of Women Run for Office," *Politico*, March 8, 2018, https://www.politico.com/story/2018/03/08/women-rule-midterms-443267.

4. Margaret Talbot, "The Women Running in the Midterms during the Trump Era," *The New Yorker*, April 18, 2018, https://www.newyorker.com/news/news-desk/2018-midterm-elections-women-candidates-trump.

5. Holly Otterbein, "Meet Mary Gay Scanlon, the Education Advocate and Ballard Lawyer Running for Congress | #PA5," *The Inquirer*, May 9, 2018, http://www.philly.com/philly/columnists/clout/congress-mary-gay-scanlon-pennsylvania-fifth-district-20180509.html.

6. Paul Englkemier, "Former Senior Deputy Attorney General Considers Run for PA-7," PoliticsPA, February 13, 2018, http://www.politicspa.com/former-senior-deputy-attorney-general-considers-run-for-pa-7/86457/.

7. Amanda Terkel, "Pennsylvania's Congressional Delegation Will No Longer Be All Men," *HuffPost*, May 31, 2018, https://www.huffingtonpost.com/entry/pennsylvania-congress-men_us_5afc3659e4b06a3fb50c85d4.

8. Caygle, "Record-Breaking Number of Women Run for Office."

9. Although they are required by the Constitution only to live in the states that they represent, members of the House are, by custom, expected to maintain a residence in their electoral district.

10. James Madison, *Federalist* No. 52, in *The Federalist Papers*, ed. George W. Carey and James McClellan (Indianapolis: Liberty Fund, 2001), 273.

11. Also referred to as The Congressional Budget Control and Impoundment Act of 1974, P.L. 93-344.

12. Mathew McCubbins and Thomas Schwartz, "Congressional Oversight Overlooked: Police Patrols versus Fire Alarms," *American Journal of Political Science* 28 (1984): 165–79.

13. U.S. Constitution, art. I, sec. 8.

14. U.S. Constitution, art. II, sec. 4.

15. If the president is being tried for impeachment, the chief justice of the Supreme Court presides (U.S. Constitution, art. 1, sec. 3).

16. "Leadership PACs," OpenSecrets.org, accessed August 7, 2018, www.opensecrets.org/industries/indus.php?ind=Q03.

17. Richard F. Fenno Jr., *Congressmen in Committees* (Boston: Little, Brown, 1973).

18. Barbara Sinclair. *Unorthodox Lawmaking: New Legislative Processes in the U.S. Congress*, 2nd ed. (Washington, DC: CQ Press, 2000), 33.

19. Ibid., 3.

20. Ibid., 14.

21. Ibid., 15.

22. Ibid., 52.

23. The term *filibuster* has also been generally used to describe several other delaying tactics in the Senate.

24. Sinclair, *Unorthodox Lawmaking*, 43.

25. Carl Hulse, "Trump Gets a Win He Wasn't Counting On: He Saved the Filibuster," *New York Times*, May 3, 2017, https://www.nytimes.com/2017/05/03/us/politics/trump-filibuster.html?rref=collection%2Ftimestopic%2FFilibusters%20and%20Debate%20Curbs&action=click&contentCollection=timestopics&region=stream&module=stream_unit&version=latest&contentPlacement=2&pgtype=collection&_r=0.

26. Ibid.

27. Sinclair, *Unorthodox Lawmaking*, 58.

28. See Charles M. Cameron, *Veto Bargaining: Presidents and the Politics of Negative Power* (New York: Cambridge University Press, 2000).

29. "114th United States Congress," Ballotpedia, accessed August 7, 2018, https://ballotpedia.org/114th_United_States_Congress.

30. There had been a total of four women serving in the Senate at some point during the 102nd Congress. Jocelyn Burdick, D-ND, had served as an interim appointee before retiring in December 1992, and the success of Dianne Feinstein, D-CA, in the election on November 3, 1992, enabled her to serve out the remainder of the term of interim appointee John F. Seymour, R-CA. The numbers for the House of Representatives do not include nonvoting delegates.

31. Chris Chrystal, "Democratic Women Battle for 2 California Senate Seats," UPI, May 31, 1992, www.upi.com/Archives/1992/05/31/Democratic-women-battle-for-2-California-Senate-seats/6261707284800.

32. Debra L. Dodson et al., *Voices, Views, Votes: The Impact of Women in the 103rd Congress* (New Brunswick, NJ: Rutgers, Eagleton Institute of Politics, Center for American Women and Politics, 1995), 2.

33. Clara Bingham, "Queens of the Hill: Will the Newly Empowered Women Lawmakers Clean Up Congress?" *Washington Monthly*, January–February 2007, www.washingtonmonthly.com/features/2007/0701.bingham.html.

34. Michael X. Delli Carpini and Ester R. Fuchs, "The Year of the Woman? Candidates, Voters, and the 1992 Election," *Political Science Quarterly* 108, no. 1 (1993): 34–35.

35. Barbara Mikulski et al., *Nine and Counting: The Women of the Senate* (New York: Perennial, 2001), 48–49.

36. "The Year of the Woman. Then and Now: Women in U.S. Politics in 1992 and 2008," International Museum of Women, Global Fund for Women, http://exhibitions.globalfundforwomen.org/exhibitions/women-power-and-politics/elections/year-woman.

37. Mikulski et al., *Nine and Counting*, 47.

38. Linda L. Fowler and Robert D. McClure, *Political Ambition: Who Decides to Run for Congress* (New Haven, CT: Yale University Press, 1989), xii. See also Jennifer L. Lawless, *Becoming a Candidate: Political Ambition and the Decision to Run for Office* (New York: Cambridge University Press, 2012).

39. Clyde Wilcox, "Why Was 1992 the 'Year of the Woman?' Explaining Women's Gains in 1992," in *The Year of the Woman: Myths and Realities*, ed. Elizabeth Adell Cook et al. (Boulder, CO: Westview Press, 1994), 5.

40. Barbara Mikulski et al., *Nine and Counting*, 44.

41. Candice J. Nelson, "Women's PACs in the Year of the Woman," in *The Year of the Woman: Myths and Realities*, ed. Elizabeth Adell Cook et al. (Boulder, CO: Westview Press, 1994), 183.

42. Debra L. Dodson, "Whatever Happened to the 'Year of the Woman'?" *Public Perspective* (August/September, 1996), 5.

43. Jean R. Schoedel and Bruce Snyder, "Patty Murray: The Mom in Tennis Shoes Goes to the Senate," in *The Year of the Woman: Myths and Realities*, ed. Elizabeth Adell Cook et al. (Boulder, CO: Westview Press, 1994), 60–61.

44. Kate Ackley, "Women—and the Power of the Purse—Will Be Key in 2018," Roll Call, October 26, 2017, https://www.rollcall.com/news/politics/99810-2.

45. Pitkin, *The Concept of Representation*, 8.

46. Richard F. Fenno Jr., *Home Style: House Members in Their Districts* (New York: HarperCollins, 1978).

47. John W. Kingdon, *Congressmen's Voting Decisions*, 3rd ed. (Ann Arbor: University of Michigan Press, 1989).

48. Fenno, *Home Style*.

49. Jane Mansbridge calls the former *promissory representation* and the latter *anticipatory representation*. Jane Mansbridge, "Rethinking Representation," *American Political Science Review* 97, no. 4 (November 2003): 515–28.

50. R. Douglas Arnold, *The Logic of Congressional Action* (New Haven, CT: Yale University Press, 1990).

51. Ibid.

52. Tracy Sulkin, *Issue Politics in Congress* (New York: Cambridge University Press, 2005).

53. Richard L. Hall, *Participation in Congress* (New Haven, CT: Yale University Press, 1996).

54. "1994 Committee Supplement: Senate Judiciary," *CQ Weekly*, March 5, 1994, http://library.cqpress.com/cqweekly/wr103403788.

55. Dodson et al., *Voices, Views, Votes*, 13.

56. See Morris P. Fiorina, Samuel J. Abrams, and Jeremy C. Pope, *Culture War? The Myth of a Polarized America*, 3rd ed. (New York: Longman, 2011); Alan I. Abramowitz, *The Disappearing Center: Engaged Citizens, Polarization, and American Democracy* (New Haven, CT: Yale University Press, 2010).

57. Jane Mansbridge, "Should Blacks Represent Blacks and Women Represent Women? A Contingent 'Yes,'" *Journal of Politics* 61, no. 3 (August 1999): 628.

58. Ibid., 632.

59. Carol M. Swain, *Black Faces, Black Interests: The Representation of African Americans in Congress* (Cambridge, MA: Harvard University Press, 1995), 5.

60. Mansbridge, "Should Blacks Represent Blacks?," 637.

61. Pitkin, *The Concept of Representation*, 114.

62. Mansbridge, "Should Blacks Represent Blacks?," 634.

63. John W. Kingdon, *Agendas, Alternatives, and Public Policies*, 2nd ed. (New York: Longman, 2003).

64. Mansbridge, "Rethinking Representation," 522.

65. Mikulski et al., *Nine and Counting*, 197.

66. Kelly Dittmar, Kira Sanbonmatsu, Susan J. Carroll, Debbie Walsh, and Catherine Wineinger, *Representation Matters: Women in the U.S. Congress* (New Brunswick, NJ: Rutgers, Eagleton Institute of Politics, Center for American Women and Politics, 2017), 5.

67. As of November 9, 2018, the Arizona Senate race between Kyrsten Sinema (D) and Martha McSally (R) had not been called. As both candidates are women, however, the only question will be which party a new woman senator will represent.

68. Kayla Epstein and Eugene Scott, "The Historic Firsts of the 2018 Midterms," *The Washington Post*, November 7, 2018, https://www.washingtonpost.com/politics/2018/11/07/historic-firsts-midterms/?noredirect=on.

CHAPTER 13

1. Ben Hubbard, "Dozens Suffocate in Syria as Government Is Accused of Chemical Attack," *New York Times*, April 8, 2018, https://www.nytimes.com/2018/04/08/world/middleeast/syria-chemical-attack-ghouta.html.

2. Tom Embury-Dennis, "Russia Will Shoot Down US Missiles Fired at Syria and Retaliate against Launch Sites, Says Ambassador," Independent.co.uk, April 11, 2018, https://www.independent.co.uk/news/world/middle-east/russia-us-missiles-syria-launch-sites-lebanon-zasypkin-putin-a8298941.html.

3. President Donald J. Trump (@realDonaldTrump), "Russia vows to shoot down any and all missiles fired at Syria," Twitter, April 11, 2018, 3:57 a.m., https://twitter.com/realDonaldTrump/status/984022625440747520?ref_src=twsrc%5Etfw&ref_url=https%3A%2F%2Fwww.vox.com%2Fworld%2F2018%2F4%2F11%2F17223606%2Fsyria-gas-attack-donald-trump-twitter&tfw_site=voxdotcom.

4. Maggie Haberman, Glenn Thrush, and Peter Baker, "Inside Trump's Hour-by-Hour Battle for Self-Preservation," *New York Times*, December 9, 2017, https://www.nytimes.com/2017/12/09/us/politics/donald-trump-president.html.

5. Ibid.

6. Ibid.

7. Gregory Krieg, "John Bolton on: Bombing Iran, North Korea, Russia and the Iraq War," CNN, March 23, 2018, https://www.cnn.com/2018/03/23/politics/what-john-bolton-said-iraq-iran-north-korea/index.html.

8. Kathryn Dunn Tenpas, "Why Is Trump's Staff Turnover Higher Than the 5 Most Recent Presidents?" Brookings, January 19, 2018, https://www.brookings.edu/research/why-is-trumps-staff-turnover-higher-than-the-5-most-recent-presidents/.

9. Peter Baker, Gardiner Harris, and Mark Landler, "Trump Fires Rex Tillerson and Will Replace Him with C.I.A. Chief Pompeo," *New York Times*, March 13, 2018, https://www.nytimes.com/2018/03/13/us/politics/trump-tillerson-pompeo.html.

10. Russell Berman, "The Humbling of Mike Pompeo," *The Atlantic*, April 17, 2018, https://www.theatlantic.com/politics/archive/2018/04/pompeo-trump-secretary-state-cia-senate-confirmation/558242/.

11. Helene Cooper, "Mattis Wanted Congressional Approval before Striking Syria. He Was Overruled," *New York Times*, April 17, 2018, https://www.nytimes.com/2018/04/17/us/politics/jim-mattis-trump-syria-attack.html.

12. Mark Berman, "Stormy Daniels Is Now Denying Her Affair with Trump. Here's How She's Confirmed It Before," *Washington Post*, January 31, 2017, https://www.washingtonpost.com/news/post-nation/wp/2018/01/31/stormy-daniels-is-now-denying-her-affair-with-trump-heres-how-shes-confirmed-it-before/?noredirect=on.

13. Max Farrand, *The Framing of the Constitution of the United States* (New Haven, CT: Yale University Press, 1913), 21.

14. Clinton Rossiter, *The American Presidency*, 2nd ed. (Baltimore, MD: Johns Hopkins University Press, 1987), 62.

15. Ulysses S. Grant unsuccessfully sought a third term in 1880.

16. U.S. Constitution, art. II., sec. 1.

17. In some states, widows with property were allowed to participate in public and political life.

18. Farrand, *The Framing of the Constitution of the United States*, 169.

19. Many of these titles are described in Clinton Rossiter, *The American Presidency*, 2nd ed. (Baltimore: Johns Hopkins University Press, 1987).

20. U.S. Constitution, art. II, sec. 1.

21. U.S. Constitution, art. II, sec. 1; art. II, sec. 3.

22. U.S. Constitution, art. II, sec. 2.

23. U.S. Constitution, art. II, sec. 2, 3.

24. Rossiter, *The American Presidency*, 12.

25. U.S. Constitution, art. II, sec. 2.

26. Edward S. Corwin, *Presidential Power and the Constitution: Essays* (Ithaca, NY: Cornell University Press, 1976), 163.

27. Pub. L. No. 93-148, 87 Stat. 555 (November 7, 1973). Codified in 50 U.S.C. 33, Sections 1541–48 (1973). It is also called the War Powers Act, which was the title of the version of the joint resolution passed in the Senate.

28. Louis Fisher and David Gray Adler, "The War Powers Resolution: Time to Say Goodbye," *Political Science Quarterly* 113, no. 1 (1998): 1.

29. War Powers Resolution, Section 2(a).

30. War Powers Resolution, Section 2(c).

31. War Powers Resolution, Section 4(a). The president must notify both the Speaker of the House and the president of the Senate pro tempore.

32. Congress authorized military operations in Afghanistan in Authorization for Use of Military Force, Pub. L. 107-40 (2001), and in Iraq in Authorization for Use of Military Force against Iraq Resolution of 2002, Pub. L. 107-243 (2002).

33. See Fisher and Adler, "The War Powers Resolution."

34. U.S. Constitution, art. II, sec. 3.

35. Ibid.

36. Charles M. Cameron, *Veto Bargaining: Presidents and the Politics of Negative Power* (New York: Cambridge University Press, 2000).

37. U.S. 37. U.S. Constitution, art. II, sec. 2.

38. U.S. Constitution, art. I, 3.

39. U.S. Constitution, art. II, sec. 2.

40. U.S. Constitution, art. II, sec. 4.

41. The chief justice presides only when presidents are impeached. Otherwise, the presiding office of the Senate would chair the proceedings.

42. Farrand, *The Framing of the Constitution of the United States*, 169.

43. U.S. Constitution, art. I, sec. 3.

44. Rossiter, *The American Presidency*, 123.

45. Arthur M. Schlesinger Jr., "Is the Vice Presidency Necessary?," *The Atlantic*, May 1, 1974, http://www.theatlantic.com/magazine/archive/1974/05/is-the-vice-presidency-necessary/305732/.

46. The *Report of the President's Committee on Administrative Management* (1937), also known as the Brownlow Committee Report. The Reorganization Act of 1939 provided the legislative authorization for President Roosevelt's reorganization of the executive branch.

47. For a challenge to the argument that divided government necessarily leads to legislative gridlock, see David R. Mayhew, *Divided We Govern: Party Control, Lawmaking, and Investigations, 1946–1990* (New Haven, CT: Yale University Press, 1991).

48. Following the April 2018 air strikes on Syria, President Trump tweeted "Mission Accomplished!" (Adrienne LaFrance, "'Mission Accomplished' and the meme presidency," *The Atlantic*, April 14, 2018, https://www.theatlantic.com/politics/archive/2018/04/mission-accomplished-and-the-meme-presidency/558047/).

49. Rossiter, *The American Presidency*, 54, 56.

50. J. D. Richardson, ed., *Messages and Papers of the Presidents* (New York, 1879), 3, quoted in Benjamin I. Page and Mark P. Petracca, *The American Presidency* (New York: McGraw-Hill, 1983), 118.

51. Samuel Kernell, *Going Public: New Strategies of Presidential Leadership* (Washington, DC: CQ Press, 2007), 1–2.

52. James A. Stimson, "Public Support for American Presidents: A Cyclical Model," *Public Opinion Quarterly* 40, no. 1 (1976): 1–21.

53. Dina Temple-Rastan, "Kill and Tell: Inside the President's Terrorist Hunt," *Washington Post*, June 17, 2012, B01, available from Lexis-Nexis Academic.

54. Mark Mazzetti, Charlie Savage, and Scott Shane, "A U.S. Citizen in America's Cross Hairs," *New York Times*, March 10, 2013, A1, available from Lexis-Nexis Academic.

55. "Details of Al-Awlaki's Death," *Yemen Times*, October 3, 2011, available from Lexis-Nexis Academic.

56. Ibid.

57. Scott Shane, "Judging a Long, Deadly Reach," *New York Times*, October 1, 2011, A1, available from Lexis-Nexis Academic.

58. Charlie Savage, "Top U.S. Security Official Says 'Rigorous Standards' Used for Drone Strikes," *New York Times*, May 1, 2012, A8, available from Lexis-Nexis Academic.

59. Scott Shane and Souad Mekhennet, "From Condemning Terror to Preaching Jihad," *New York Times*, May 9, 2010, A1, available from Lexis-Nexis Academic.

60. Scott Shane and Mark Mazzetti, "A Newly Religious Immigrant Is Linked to a Militant Yemeni-American Cleric," *New York Times*, May 7, 2010, A13, available from Lexis-Nexis Academic.

61. Anthony Shadid and David D. Kirkpatrick, "As the West Celebrates a Cleric's Death, the Mideast Shrugs," *New York Times*, October 2, 2011, A14, available from Lexis-Nexis Academic.

62. Shane and Mekhennet, "From Condemning Terror to Preaching Jihad."

63. Ibid.

64. Charlie Savage, "Secret U.S. Memo Made Legal Case to Kill a Citizen," *New York Times*, October 9, 2011, A1, available from Lexis-Nexis Academic.

65. Scott Shane, "A Legal Debate as C.I.A. Stalks a U.S. Jihadist," *New York Times*, May 10, 2010, A1, available from Lexis-Nexis Academic.

66. Charlie Savage, "Trump Had Power to Attack Syria without Congress, Justice Dept. Memo Says," *New York Times*, June 1, 2018, https://www.nytimes.com/2018/06/01/us/politics/trump-war-powers-syria-congress.html.

67. "Startling from Baltimore: The Northern Troops Mobbed and Fired Upon," *New York Times*, April 19, 1861, available from ProQuest Historical Newspapers.

68. "Testimony of William Lynch, September 9, 1861," quoted in Jonathan W. White, *Abraham Lincoln and Treason in the Civil War: The Trials of John Merryman* (Baton Rouge: Louisiana State University Press, 2011), 13.

69. Brian McGinty, *The Body of John Merryman: Abraham Lincoln and the Suspension of Habeas Corpus* (Cambridge, MA: Harvard University Press, 2011), 67.

70. Edward S. Corwin, *Presidential Power and the Constitution: Essays* (Ithaca, NY: Cornell University Press, 1976), 130.

71. Ibid.

72. *Ex parte Merryman*, 17 Fed. Cases 146 (1861).

73. See McGinty, *The Body of John Merryman*.

74. George William Brown, *Baltimore and the Nineteenth of April 1861: A Study of the War* (Baltimore: Johns Hopkins University Press, 1887), 88.

75. *Ex parte Merryman*. The legal term *ex parte* refers to a decision that affects one party only or a suit that is brought by or on behalf of one individual. Justice Taney, in standard practice at the time, also served as a circuit court judge, with Baltimore included in his circuit. Scholars continue to debate whether Taney was properly acting as chief justice of the Supreme Court (which the *Merryman* opinion so identifies him as) or in his role as circuit judge when he issued the opinion.

76. Brown, *Baltimore and the Nineteenth of April 1861*, 89.

77. U.S. Constitution, art. I, sec. 9.

78. *Ex parte Merryman*.

79. Page and Petracca, *The American Presidency*, 51.

80. Habeas Corpus Suspension Act of March 3, 1863, 12 Stat 755 (1863).

81. Corwin, *Presidential Power and the Constitution*, 112, 158.

82. U.S. Constitution, art. I, sec. 9.

83. Page and Petracca, *The American Presidency*, 40.

84. See, for example, Mark J. Rozell, "The Law: Executive Privilege: Definition and Standards of Application," *Presidential Studies Quarterly* 29, no. 4 (1999): 918–30.

85. *United States v. Nixon*, 418 U.S. 683 (1974).

86. Kenneth R. Mayer, *With the Stroke of a Pen: Executive Orders and Presidential Power* (Princeton, NJ: Princeton University Press, 2001).

87. Executive Order 9066, 7 Federal Register 1407 (February 19, 1942).

88. *Korematsu v. United States*, 323 U.S. 214 (1944).

89. *Youngstown Sheet & Tube Co. v. Sawyer*, 343 U.S. 579 (1952). The president's order was Executive Order No. 10340, 16 Federal Register 3503 (April 8, 1952).

90. William G. Howell, *Power without Persuasion: The Politics of Direct Presidential Action* (Princeton, NJ: Princeton University Press, 2003), 14.

91. See James David Barber, *The Presidential Character: Predicting Performance in the White House*, 4th ed. (Englewood Cliffs, NJ: Prentice Hall, 1992).

92. Richard E. Neustadt, *Presidential Power and the Modern Presidents: The Politics of Leadership from Roosevelt to Reagan* (New York: Free Press, 1990), 163.

93. Ibid., 30.

94. Lester G. Seligman, "On Models of the Presidency," *Presidential Studies Quarterly* 10, no. 3 (1980): 356.

95. Alexander Hamilton, *Federalist No. 74*, in *The Federalist Papers*, ed. George W. Carey and James McClellan (Indianapolis, IN: Liberty Fund, 2001), 385.

96. James Bryce, *The American Commonwealth*, vol. 1 (New York: Macmillan, 1888), 83–84.

97. Thomas E. Cronin and Michael A. Genovese, *The Paradoxes of the American Presidency*, 2nd ed. (New York: Oxford University Press, 2004).

CHAPTER 14

1. "Crushing Weight of Harvey's Floodwaters Pushed Houston Down, GPS Data Reveals," ABC13.com, September 13, 2017, http://abc13.com/science/crushing-weight-of-harvey-flood-pushed-houston-down/2413363/.

2. Mike Tolson and Cindy George, "Harvey's Heartbreaking Losses: Collective Human Damage Tells a Story of Its Own," *Houston Chronicle*, September 15, 2017, http://www.houstonchronicle.com/news/houston-texas/houston/article/Harvey-s-heartbreaking-losses-12201961.php.

3. Eric Levenson, "3 Storms, 3 Responses: Comparing Harvey, Irma, and Maria," CNN, September 27, 2017, http://www.cnn.com/2017/09/26/us/response-harvey-irma-maria/index.html.

4. Cassandra Pollock, "The Brief: Harvey-Flooded Houston Homeowners Left in the Lurch," *Texas Tribune*, October 12, 2017, https://www.texastribune.org/2017/10/12/brief-oct-12/.

5. Levenson, "3 Storms, 3 Responses."

6. Ed Morales, "Puerto Rico in the Dark," *New York Times*, November 4, 2017, https://www.nytimes.com/2017/11/04/opinion/sunday/puerto-rico-hurricane-maria.html.

7. Levenson, "3 Storms, 3 Responses."

8. Jeffrey C. Mays, "Protesters Demand Audit of Hurricane Maria Death Toll in Puerto Rico," *New York Times*, June 2, 2018, https://www.nytimes.com/2018/06/02/nyregion/protesters-puerto-rico-hurricane-maria.html.

9. Ibid.

10. Based on season averages between 1966 and 2009. "Tropical Cyclone Climatology," National Hurricane Center, accessed June 16, 2018, https://www.nhc.noaa.gov/climo/.

11. Katrina was not the only "K" name to have been retired; "Klaus" and "Keith" had been retired since the modern naming system rules were put into place.

12. Tamara Lush, "For Forecasting Chief, No Joy in Being Right," *St. Petersburg Times*, August 30, 2005, 3A, available from Lexis-Nexis Academic.

13. Ibid.

14. Deana Poole and Pat Beall, "New Orleans Emptying: Katrina on Path to Bring Disaster," *Palm Beach Post*, August 28, 2005, 1A, available from Lexis-Nexis Academic.

15. Donald F. Kettl, *The Next Government of the United States: Why Our Institutions Fail Us and How to Fix Them* (New York: W. W. Norton, 2009), 18.

16. Poole and Beall, "New Orleans Emptying."

17. John Ashton, "Thousands Flee as Hurricane Nears U.S. Coast," *Birmingham Post*, August 29, 2005, 9, available from Lexis-Nexis Academic.

18. Tina Hesman, "Most People Killed by Katrina Were Elderly, Researcher Finds," *St. Louis Post-Dispatch*, February 17, 2006, A5, available from Lexis-Nexis Academic.

19. Bryan Dean and Ryan McNeill, "Facing the Future: Hurricane Survivors Express Thanks to State," *The Oklahoman*, September 5, 2005, 1A, available from Lexis-Nexis Academic.

20. Sarah Ladislaw, "Hurricane Sandy: Evaluating the Response One Year Later," *Center for Strategic and International Studies*, November 4, 2013, https://www.csis.org/analysis/hurricane-sandy-evaluating-response-one-year-later.

21. Jason Samenow, "Forecasts for Harvey Were Excellent but Show Where Predictions Can Improve," *Washington Post*, August 28, 2017, https://www.washingtonpost.com/news/capital-weather-gang/wp/2017/08/28/forecasts-for-harvey-were-excellent-but-show-where-predictions-can-improve/?noredirect=on&utm_term=.250fcf8536c5.

22. Ledyard King, "Mostly Positive FEMA Reports under Obama Removed," *USA Today*, March 10, 2018, https://www.usatoday.com/story/news/politics/2018/03/09/government-watchdog-removes-fem/411369002/.

23. Steven Horwitz, "Recovery Lessons from Katrina, Harvey, Irma, and Maria," *Fort Worth Star Telegram*, October 3, 2017, http://www.star-telegram.com/opinion/opn-columns-blogs/other-voices/article176821186.html.

24. The United States Department of Transportation. The Uniform Time Act of 1966 (15 U.S.C. §§ 260-64) established the system of uniform Daylight Saving Time.

States are allowed to opt out of the national daylight savings program. If they do participate, they must change the time according to a federally set schedule.

25. Max Weber, "The Permanent Character of the Bureaucratic Machine," in *From Max Weber: Essays in Sociology*, ed. H. H. Gerth and C. Wright Mills (1991 [1948]), 229.

26. Max Weber, *Economy and Society: An Outline of Interpretive Sociology*, trans. and ed. Guenther Roth and Claus Wittich (Berkeley: University of California Press, 1978), 987. The work was first published in Germany, posthumously, in 1922.

27. Ibid., 957–58.

28. Ibid., 975.

29. Chester I. Barnard, *The Functions of the Executive* (Cambridge, MA: Harvard University Press, 1968 [1938]), 72.

30. Ibid., 82.

31. James Q. Wilson, *Bureaucracy: What Government Agencies Do and Why They Do It* (New York: Basic Books, 1989), 173.

32. Wilson calls this category of bureaucracies "coping organizations" (Wilson, *Bureaucracy*, 175).

33. Public education is largely governed by the states, not the federal government; however, the illustration applies to the actions of federal bureaucrats as well.

34. See Scott F. Abernathy, *No Child Left Behind and the Public Schools* (Ann Arbor: University of Michigan Press, 2007), 25–45.

35. James Q. Wilson, "The Rise of the Bureaucratic State," *The Public Interest* 41 (Fall 1975): 77.

36. U.S. Constitution, art. II, sec. 2.

37. Roughly 1,350 of 6,500 presidentially nominated officials require Senate confirmation.

38. U.S. Constitution, art. II, sec. 2, 4.

39. Leonard D. White, *The Federalists: A Study in Administrative History* (New York: Macmillan, 1948), 20.

40. *Myers v. United States*, 272 U.S. 52 (1926).

41. George Washington to Edward Rutledge, March 21, 1789, quoted in White, *The Federalists*, 258.

42. White, *The Federalists*, 259.

43. Ibid., 222.

44. David H. Rosenbloom, *Federal Service and the Constitution: The Development of the Public Employment Relationship* (Ithaca, NY: Cornell University Press, 1971), 35. See also Brian J. Cook, *Bureaucracy and Self-Government: Reconsidering the Role of Public Administration in American Politics* (Baltimore: Johns Hopkins University Press, 1996), 45.

45. The Department of Agriculture was given full cabinet status in 1889.

46. Stephen Skowronek, *Building a New American State: The Expansion of National Administrative Capacities, 1877–1920* (New York: Cambridge University Press, 1982).

47. Theda Skocpol, *Protecting Soldiers and Mothers: The Political Origins of Social Policy in the United States* (Cambridge, MA: Belknap Press, 1992). Professor Skocpol also examined the gendered aspects of American social welfare policy and how the degree to which recipients were seen as "deserving" shaped the policies themselves.

48. In *The Jungle* (1906), Upton Sinclair described unhealthy and dangerous working conditions in the meatpacking industry, which helped secure the passage of the Pure Food and Drug Act and the Meat Inspection Act.

49. The National Security Act of 1947 also reorganized the cabinet structure of the departments and agencies involved in defense.

50. Public Law 88-352 (78 Stat. 241).

51. Thomas Binion, "Here's What Trump Has Done Right in His First 6 Months," *Fortune*, July 20, 2017, http://www.motherteresa.org/07_family/volunteering/v_cal.html.

52. Thomas A. Garrett and Russell M. Rhine, "On the Size and Growth of Government," *Federal Reserve Bank of St. Louis Review* 88, no. 1 (January/February 2006): 13–30.

53. Richard W. Stevenson, "After Katrina's Lesson, Bush Is Heading to Texas," *New York Times*, September 23, 2005, A1, available from Lexis-Nexis Academic.

54. The U.S. Armed Forces, which is part of the executive branch, has a different organizational structure, though the secretary of defense and deputy and assistant secretaries are political appointees.

55. For a foundational study of the challenges of implementation, see Jeffrey L. Pressman and Aaron Wildavsky, *Implementation: How Great Expectations in Washington Are Dashed in Oakland; or, Why It's Amazing That Federal Programs Work at All, This Being a Saga of the Economic Development Administration as Told by Two Sympathetic Observers Who Seek to Build Morals on a Foundation of Ruined Hopes*, 3rd ed. (Berkeley: University of California Press, 1984).

56. Ibid., 4.

57. Michael Lipsky, *Street-Level Bureaucracy: Dilemmas of the Individual in Public Services* (New York: Russell Sage Foundation, 1980).

58. Cornelius M. Kerwin, *Rulemaking: How Government Agencies Write Laws and Make Policy* (Washington, DC: CQ Press, 1994), 4.

59. Kenneth J. Meier, "Representative Bureaucracy: A Theoretical and Empirical Exposition," in *Research in Public Administration*, ed. James Perry (Greenwich, CT: JAI Press, 1993).

60. Sally Coleman Selden, *The Promise of Representative Bureaucracy: Diversity and Responsiveness in a Government Agency* (Armonk, NY: ME Sharpe, 1997).

61. Charles T. Goodsell, *The Case for Bureaucracy: A Public Administration Polemic*, 2nd ed. (Chatham, NJ: Chatham House, 1985), 63.

62. William A. Niskanen, "The Peculiar Economics of Bureaucracy," *American Economic Review* 58, no. 2 (May 1968): 293–305.

63. John Brehm and Scott Gates, *Working, Shirking, and Sabotage: Bureaucratic Responses to a Democratic Public* (Ann Arbor: University of Michigan Press, 1997).

64. For a classic study of the challenges posed by outside pressures on bureaucrats and how bureaucratic agencies deal with them, see Herbert Kaufman, *The Forest Ranger: A Study in Administrative Behavior* (Washington, DC: Resources for the Future, 1960).

65. Joel D. Aberbach, *Keeping a Watchful Eye: The Politics of Congressional Oversight* (Washington, DC: Brookings Institution, 1990), 4.

66. The legislative and judicial branches also contain bureaucratic organizations, though these are few in number and small in size compared to the departments, agencies, and bureaus in the executive branch.

67. U.S. Government Accountability Office, "Preliminary Observations on Hurricane Response," GAO-06-365R, February 1, 2006, http://www.gao.gov/assets/100/94002.pdf.

68. Mathew D. McCubbins and Thomas Schwartz, "Congressional Oversight Overlooked: Police Patrols versus Fire Alarms," *American Journal of Political Science* 28, no. 1 (February 1984): 165–79.

69. William Douglas and Steven Thomas, "On Katrina Anniversary, Bush Returns to Gulf Coast," Knight Ridder Washington Bureau, August 28, 2006, available from Lexis-Nexis Academic.

70. John J. DiIulio Jr., Gerald Garvey, and Donald F. Kettl, *Improving Government Performance: An Owner's Manual* (Washington, DC: Brookings Institution, 1993), 64.

71. David Osborne and Ted Gaebler, *Reinventing Government: How the Entrepreneurial Spirit Is Transforming the Public Sector* (New York: Plume/Penguin Books, 1993), xix.

72. Wilson, *Bureaucracy*, 134–36.

73. Brad Delong, "Katrina Reveals the Presidential Flaws," *Financial Times*, September 7, 2005, 13, available from Lexis-Nexis Academic.

74. Anthony Lonetree, "From the Wreckage of Katrina to the Walls of Local Art Centers: Artwork That Survived or Was Influenced by the Hurricane Makes Its Way Here from Mississippi in Yet Another Step in the Long Recovery," *Star Tribune*, January 11, 2006, 1B, available from Lexis-Nexis Academic.

75. David Hench, "Katrina Response Brings Out the Best, Worst in People," *Portland Press Herald* (Maine), September 15, 2005, available from Lexis-Nexis Academic.

76. "See Katrina's Trail," *Gold Coast Bulletin*, December 17, 2005, 96, available from Lexis-Nexis Academic.

77. Donna Borak, Martin Savidge, and Greg Wallace, "How Whitefish Landed Puerto Rico's $300 Million Power Contract," CNN.com, October 29, 2017, http://money.cnn.com/2017/10/27/news/economy/puerto-rico-whitefish-montana-deal/index.html.

78. Ibid.

79. Leah Hodges, written testimony, Select Bipartisan Committee to Investigate the Preparation for and Response to Hurricane Katrina, December 6, 2005.

CHAPTER 15

1. The title refers to Alexander Hamilton's characterization in *Federalist* No. 78 of the federal judiciary as "least dangerous to the political rights of the Constitution." Alexander Hamilton, *Federalist* No. 78, in *The Federalist Papers*, ed. George W. Carey and James McClellan (Indianapolis: Liberty Fund, 2001), 402. Alexander M. Bickel also chose the phrase in the title of his critique of judicial power, *The Least Dangerous Branch: The Supreme Court at the Bar of Politics* (Indianapolis: Bobbs-Merrill Educational, 1962).

2. Robert Barnes and Michael A. Fletcher, "Riskiest Choice on Obama's List Embodies His Criteria; President and Judge Cite Her Life Experience," *Washington Post*, May 27, 2009, available from Lexis-Nexis Academic.

3. Charlie Savage, "Conservatives Map Strategies on Court Fight," *New York Times*, May 17, 2009, available from Lexis-Nexis Academic.

4. Ibid.

5. Sonia Sotomayor, "A Latina Judge's Voice," *Berkeley La Raza Law Journal* 13, no. 1 (Spring 2002): 87–93.

6. David S. Broder, "After Bork—and Obama; Confirmation Fights Still Echo," *Washington Post*, June 4, 2009, available from Lexis-Nexis Academic.

7. "GOP Senator Sums Up Sotomayor Issue," *Washington Post*, June 7, 2009, available from Lexis-Nexis Academic.

8. Peter Baker and Neil A. Lewis, "Judge Focuses on Rule of Law at the Hearings," *New York Times*, July 14, 2009, available from Lexis-Nexis Academic.

9. N. C. Aizenman, "For Latinos, Confirmation Is an Emotional Moment," *Washington Post*, August 7, 2009, available from Lexis-Nexis Academic.

10. Martha A. Miles and Caroline Rand Herron, "The Nation: Bork Opponents: N.A.A.C.P., N.E.A., and Biden, Too," *New York Times*, July 12, 1987, available from Lexis-Nexis Academic.

11. David Hoffman, "Confirm Bork, Reagan Urges," *Washington Post*, July 30, 1987, available from Lexis-Nexis Academic.

12. Edward Walsh and Al Kamen, "Ideological Stakes High in Bork Fight: On Eve of Hearings, Both Sides Seem Eager to Keep Calm," *Washington Post*, September 13, 1987, available from Lexis-Nexis Academic.

13. *Roe v. Wade*, 410 U.S. 113 (1973).

14. Ruth Marcus, "Bork on 'Judicial Imperialism': Judges Accused of Inventing Constitutional Rights to Fit Their Views," *Washington Post*, July 2, 1987, available from Lexis-Nexis Academic.

15. Robert H. Bork, *The Tempting of America: The Political Seduction of the Law* (New York: Free Press, 1990), 313–14.

16. Edward Walsh and Ruth Marcus, "Bork Rejected for High Court: Senate's 58-to-42 Vote Sets Record for Margin of Defeat," *Washington Post*, October 24, 1987, available from Lexis-Nexis Academic.

17. Kyle Kim, "Trump Appointing Judges at a Rapid Pace," *Los Angeles Times*, January 19, 2019, http://www.latimes.com/projects/la-na-pol-trump-federal-judiciary/.

18. Ibid.

19. Forrest McDonald, *Novus Ordo Seclorum: The Intellectual Origins of the Constitution* (Lawrence: University Press of Kansas, 1985), 253.

20. The delegates did debate the need to raise judges' salaries to keep up with changes in the cost of living, but they ultimately left the issue of pay raises out of the document.

21. U.S. Constitution, art. III, sec. 1.

22. U.S. Constitution, art. II, sec. 2.

23. McDonald, *Novus Ordo Seclorum*, 254–55.

24. U.S. Constitution, art. III, sec. 1.

25. U.S. Constitution, art. II, sec. 1.

26. U.S. Constitution, art. VI.

27. The term *jurisdiction* is also applied in other contexts, such as the authority of a specific law enforcement agency to investigate a case. However, we will focus only on the jurisdiction of courts in this chapter.

28. Hamilton, *Federalist* No. 78, in Carey and McClellan, *The Federalist Papers*, 402.

29. Ibid.

30. "The Judiciary Act of 1789," in *Documents of American History*, 6th ed., ed. Henry Steele Commager (New York: Appleton-Century-Crofts, 1958), 153.

31. Ibid., 155.

32. John Adams and Alexander Hamilton were not always in complete agreement. Adams and other Federalists sometimes expressed misgivings about Hamilton's ardent nationalism.

33. Jefferson's party is often referred to as the Democratic-Republican Party, though it was more commonly called the Republican Party at the time. "Jeffersonian Republicans" is also a commonly used label today.

34. "Thomas Jefferson, First Inaugural Address, 4 March 1801," in *Basic Writings of Thomas Jefferson*, ed. Philip S. Foner (New York: Wiley, 1944), 333.

35. U.S. Constitution, art. III, sec. 1.

36. Kathryn Turner, "Federalist Policy and the Judiciary Act of 1801," *William and Mary Quarterly* 22, no. 1 (January 1965): 32. Turner noted that as many of the provisions in the Judiciary Act of 1801 had been introduced prior to the election, there were other reasons for these provisions, particularly a desire to strengthen the power of the national government. The electoral results, however, "gave a driving urgency to the fight for its passage" (p. 32).

37. David Loth, *Chief Justice: John Marshall and the Growth of the Republic* (New York: W. W. Norton, 1949), 176.

38. Oliver Ellsworth, the former chief justice, had retired shortly before.

39. The four plaintiffs were William Marbury, Dennis Ramsay, Robert Townsend Hope, and William Harper.

40. *Marbury v. Madison*, 5 U.S. 137 (1803).

41. For fans of the television and film series *Star Trek*, Marshall's dilemma might be seen as one of America's first political Kobayashi Maru scenarios. In *Star Trek* lore, Captain James T. Kirk defeated the no-win training scenario only by cheating, something that several historians and scholars have accused Marshall of doing in his interpretation and reading of the Constitution and Judiciary Act of 1789.

42. *Marbury v. Madison*.

43. Ibid.

44. Ibid.

45. Section 13 of the Judiciary Act of 1789.

46. *Marbury v. Madison*.

47. "Thomas Jefferson to Abigail Adams, Monticello, VA, 11 September 1804," in Foner, *Basic Writings of Thomas Jefferson*, 670.

48. *Dred Scott v. Sandford*, 60 U.S. 393 (1857).

49. For cases heard on appeal, the petitioner is the party that lost in the lower court and the respondent is the other party in the case.

50. Another category of law, called procedural law, refers to proceedings and rules through which laws are enforced, such as how law enforcement officials interact with those accused of crimes.

51. Many of the definitions of legal terms in this chapter are informed by Bryan A. Garner, ed., *Black's Law Dictionary*, 8th ed. (St. Paul, MN: Thomson/West, 2004).

52. The relevant federal law is the Controlled Substances Act (1970). Under that act, marijuana, along with heroin, ecstasy, and other substances, is classified as a controlled substance having a high potential for abuse and no accepted medical use.

53. As of August 2018, thirty-one states had the death penalty (Death Penalty Information Center, "States with and without the Death Penalty," accessed August 11, 2018, www.deathpenaltyinfo.org/states-and-without-death-penalty). The U.S. government also has the authority to impose the death penalty for conviction under certain federal laws. In addition, the military retains the death penalty for conviction of certain offenses under the Uniform Code of Military Justice, though it has not been carried out since 1961.

54. Two states, Texas and Oklahoma, have separate state supreme courts for criminal and civil cases.

55. U.S. Constitution, art. III, sec. 2.

56. A small set of cases may bypass the appellate courts in this process, such as those involving voting rights and aspects of the 1964 Civil Rights Act.

57. The Supreme Court automatically hears a small set of cases on appeal—those involving voting rights and congressional redistricting. Unless overturned by the Supreme Court, appellate court decisions are binding, but only within the jurisdiction of that specific court of appeals. Such jurisdictions (excepting the DC and federal circuits) are geographically determined.

58. The opposition files a "brief in opposition to a petition for a writ of certiorari." Briefs in opposition are mandatory only in capital cases (U.S. Supreme Court, *Rules of the Supreme Court of the United States*, Rule 15, accessed August 11, 2018, www.supremecourt.gov/ctrules/2013RulesoftheCourt.pdf).

59. U.S. Supreme Court, *Rules of the Supreme Court*, Rule 10.

60. Only attorneys admitted to the Bar of the Court may file amicus curiae briefs (U.S. Supreme Court, *Rules of the U.S. Supreme Court*, Rule 37).

61. Gregory A. Caldiera and John R. Wright, "Amici Curiae before the Supreme Court: Who Participates, When, and How Much?," *Journal of Politics* 52, no. 3 (August 1990): 782–806.

62. See, for example, Timothy R. Johnson, Paul J. Wahlbeck, and James F. Spriggs Jr., "The Influence of Oral Arguments on the U.S. Supreme Court," *American Political Science Review* 100, no. 1 (February 2006): 99–113.

63. Another option for the Court is to send it back to the lower court under the status of review being improvidently granted. In such a case, the Court has decided that after review, it now chooses not to give a full hearing to the case. If so, the lower ruling stands, but the Court has not officially weighed in on that ruling.

64. Bickel, *The Least Dangerous Branch*, 17.

65. For historical perspectives on the countermajoritarian difficulty, see Sylvia Snowiss, *Judicial Review and the Law of the Constitution* (New Haven, CT: Yale University Press, 1990). Also see Barry Friedman, "The History of the Countermajoritarian Difficulty, Part One: The Road to Judicial Supremacy," *New York University Law Review* 73, no. 2 (May 1998): 333–433.

66. Bickel, *The Least Dangerous Branch*, 29–33.

67. James B. Thayer, "The Origin and Scope of the American Doctrine of Constitutional Law," *Harvard Law Review* 7, no. 3 (October 25, 1893): 144.

68. Jack Knight and Lee Epstein, "The Norm of Stare Decisis," *American Journal of Political Science* 40, no. 4 (November 1996): 1018–35. For an analysis that challenges the use of stare decisis, especially when crafting dissenting opinions, see Jeffrey A. Segal and Harold J. Spaeth, "The Influence of Stare Decisis on the Votes of United States Supreme Court Justices," *American Journal of Political Science* 40, no. 4 (November 1996): 971–1003.

69. Glendon A. Schubert, *The Judicial Mind: The Attitudes and Ideologies of Supreme Court Justices*, 1946–63 (Evanston, IL: Northwestern University Press, 1965).

70. Jeffrey A. Segal and Albert D. Cover, "Ideological Values and the Votes of U.S. Supreme Court Justices," *American Political Science Review* 83, no. 2 (June 1989): 557–65.

71. Walter F. Murphy, *Elements of Judicial Strategy* (Chicago: University of Chicago Press, 1964), 3–4.

72. Ibid., 35–36.

73. Charles M. Cameron et al., "Strategic Auditing in a Political Hierarchy: An Informational Model of the Supreme Court's *Certiorari* Decisions," *American Political Science Review* 94, no. 1 (March 2000): 101–16.

74. James F. Spriggs II, Forrest Maltzman, and Paul J. Wahlbeck, "Bargaining on the U.S. Supreme Court: Justices' Responses to Majority Opinion Drafts," *Journal of Politics* 61, no. 2 (May 1999): 485–506.

75. The cases listed under the year 1929 were decided in 1930 following Hughes's confirmation as chief justice in February 1930.

76. Kevin T. McGuire and James A. Stimson, "The Least Dangerous Branch Revisited: New Evidence on Supreme Court Responsiveness to Public Preferences," *Journal of Politics* 66, no. 4 (November 2004): 1018–35.

77. Leonard D. White, *The Federalists: A Study in Administrative History* (New York: Macmillan, 1948), 259–60.

INDEX

Figures and tables are indicated by f and t after the page number.

AARP (American Association of Retired Persons), 306
Aberbach, Joel, 405
Abernathy, Ralph David, 23–24, 24f
Abington School District v. Schempp (1963), 103
Abolitionist movement, 142–143
Absentee ballots, 168
ADA (Americans with Disabilities Act), 126
Adams, Abigail, 423, 424f
Adams, John, 16, 41, 367, 420–421
Adams, Samuel, 41
Adbusters, 314
Adversarial system, 424
Affirmative action, 141–142
African Americans
   Black Lives Matter, 203
   civil rights amendments and, 127–131
   Hurricane Katrina and, 408, 408f
   Jim Crow laws, 130–131
   Ku Klux Klan and, 107, 107f, 130–131
   Montgomery bus boycott, 136–138
   NFL protests and, 203–204, 204f
   separate but equal, 75
   voting, 166, 167f
   See also Ferguson shooting; Racial and ethnic minorities;
      Segregation; Slavery
Age and generational differences
   news media selection and, 220, 220f
   volunteerism and, 304f
   voting and, 166, 167f
Agencies. *See* Federal bureaucracy
Agency capture, 311
Agenda-setting, 231, 438–439
Aggregating news, 226–227
Aid to Dependent Children, 80
Al-Awlaki, Anwar, 372–374, 373f, 376
Albany Congress, 12
Albany Plan, 12
Aldrich, John, 247
Alexander v. Holmes County Board of Education (1969), 140
Ali, Russlynn, 174
Alien and Sedition Acts, 106, 107
Alito, Samuel, 115
Amendments, 48, 337. *See also specific constitutional
   amendments*
Amenta, Edwin, 318
American Association of Retired Persons (AARP), 306
American dream, 9, 9b

American exceptionalism, 10
American political culture, 7–10
American Revolution
   background of, 11–13
   indigenous peoples and, 18–19
   pamphlets shaping opinions, 13–14
   Second Continental Congress and, 19–20
   slavery and, 16–17
   Sons of Liberty and, 14–16
   women's voice in, 17–18
Americans with Disabilities Act (ADA), 126
American Women Suffrage Association, 145
Amicus curiae briefs, 311, 429
Annapolis Convention, 32–33. *See also*
      Constitutional Convention
Anthony, Susan B., 145
Anti-Federalists, 52–57, 53t, 418
An Appeal to the Women of the Nominally Free States
   (Grimké), 143–144
Appellate jurisdiction, 418
Apportionment, 286–290, 287f
Appropriations, 328
Approval ratings, 371–372, 371f
Archambault, David, II, 94, 96
Army Corps of Engineers, 386
Arthur, Chester A., 397–398
Arthur, John, 117
Article I of the Constitution, 426
Article II of the Constitution, 362–365, 365t, 393
Article III of the Constitution, 426, 428
Articles of Confederation and Perpetual Union, 33–39
Articles of the constitution. *See* Constitution
   of the United States
Associated Press, 215
Astroturf lobbying, 313
Attitudinal model of judicial decision making, 434, 435f
Attorney general, 418–419
Attorneys, right to, 113, 113f
Attucks, Crispus, 15
Authoritarian governments, 21, 21f
Autopsy report (Growth and Opportunity Project), 271

Bache, Sarah Franklin, 18
Baer, Elizabeth, 106–107
Bail, 113
Bailey, Verna, 94
Bakke, Allan, 141

Ballot roll-off, 170
Bank bailout, 297–301, 298–300f
Banking, 78–80
Barber, James David, 380
Bar graphs, 70, 71, 71f, 349–350, 349–350f
Barnard, Chester, 391–392, 392f
Barron v. Baltimore (1833), 73
BCRA (Bipartisan Campaign Reform Act), 276
Beat system, 223–224
Bedford, Gunning, 43
Bennett, Kaitlin, 154f
Bernanke, Ben, 298, 299, 300f
Biden, Joe, 174, 341f, 415
Big Mo (momentum), 284
Bill of Rights
   about, 98–99, 99t
   civil liberties protection, 93, 98–100, 101t
   defined, 93
   Eighth Amendment, 99t, 101t, 113–114, 424
   Fourth Amendment, 99t, 101t, 110–112
   indigenous peoples and, 100
   Ninth Amendment, 99, 99t, 114–117
   ratification of Constitution and, 56–57, 98–99
   selective incorporation of, 99–100, 101f
   Sixth Amendment, 99t, 101t, 113
   Third Amendment, 99t, 101t
   See also Fifth Amendment; First Amendment; Second
      Amendment; Tenth Amendment
Bills, legislative, 335
Bills of attainder, 110
Bipartisan Campaign Reform Act (BCRA), 276
Bipartisan Campus Accountability and Safety Act, 173
Bishop, George, 195
Black, Hugo, 103, 139–140
Black codes, 129
Black Elk, Linda, 97
Black Lives Matter, 203
Black Man with a Gun: Reloaded (Blanchard), 185
Blackmun, Harry, 116
Blanchard, Kenn, 185
Block grants, 83f, 84
Board of Education of Westside Community Schools v. Mergens
   (1990), 4–5
Board of Education v. Allen (1968), 103
Body cameras, 198, 198f
Bolton, John, 358
Bork, Robert, 415–416, 415f
Boston Massacre, 15, 15f
Boston Tea Party, 15–16
Bouchnak, Mahsen, 10f
Boxer, Barbara, 342
Boyd County High, 4–5
Brady, Henry E., 160
Brandenburg v. Ohio (1969), 107
Brennan, John, 373
Breyer, Stephen, 64, 87
Briefs, 429

Brinson, Lucas, 318f
Broadcast media, 216–217
Brown, George William, 375
Brown, Henry Billings, 75, 131
Brown, Michael, 183–184, 202–203, 202f, 207. *See also*
   Ferguson shooting
Brown v. Board of Education (1954), 132–136
Brown v. Board of Education of Topeka II (1955), 136
Brunson, Doyle, 25
Bryce, James, 379
Buchanan, Ian, 197–198
Buckley v. Valeo (1976), 276
Budgeting, 328
Burden of proof, 147–148
Bureaucracy. *See* Federal bureaucracy
Bureaucratic adjudication, 403
Bureaucratic discretion, 403
Bureaucratic drift, 404
Bureaucratic jurisdiction, 406
Bush, George H. W., 399
Bush, George W., 367, 370, 371–372, 401
Bush, Jeb, 268
Busing, 140
Butler, Natalie, 168, 170f
Bystander intervention, 175–176

Cabinet, 358–359, 367, 368f. *See also specific departments*
Cabinet departments, 401
Cabinet secretaries, 401
Cable television, 217
Calhoun, John, 74
Califano, Joseph, Jr., 124
California, House of Representatives 24th district,
   281–285, 282–285f
Cambridge, Massachusetts, 261
Campaign contributions, 276, 307, 343–344
Campaigns
   advertising for, 276
   defined, 267
   demographics of, 270
   incumbency and, 281–285, 282–285f, 290–291, 343
   interest groups and, 312–313
   media portrayal, 224–225
   negative ads, 170
   phases of, 242–243
   political participation and, 160, 161f
   social media for, 280
   See also Elections; Presidential election of 2016; Voters and
      voting process
Campbell soup, 391f
Campus Accountability and Safety Act, 172–173
Campus carry, 154f, 155–160, 157f
Canales, Gabi, 288f
Candy, Dulce, 280
Cantwell v. Connecticut (1940), 105
Capitalist system, 22f, 23
Capps, Lois, 282, 283

Carbajal, Salud, 281–285, 282–285f
Cardenas, Stephanie, 266f
Carrera, Jessica, 268
Carry That Weight performance art, 171–172, 172–173f
Carson, André, 203
Carter, Jimmy, 124
Categorical grants, 81–83, 83f
Caucuses, 244, 252
CBO (Congressional Budget Office), 328
CCW (concealed carry weapons), 155–160, 157f
Center for Responsive Politics, 307
Central Intelligence Agency (CIA), 398
Certiorari, writs of, 429
Challengers, 275, 291
Chaplinksy v. New Hampshire (1942), 109
Charlottesville protests, 204–205
Charts, 70, 70–71f, 349–350, 349–350f
Chávez, César, 125, 125f
Checks and balances. *See* Separation of powers
Cheney, Dick, 367
Chief of staff, 367–368
CIA (Central Intelligence Agency), 398
Citizen journalists, 218
Citizenship, 127, 129
Citizens United v. Federal Election Commission (2010), 276
Civic education, 197, 197f
Civic engagement, 161–162f, 162–163
Civil disobedience, 136–138, 317–318
Civil law, 424–425, 425f
Civil liberties
　　about, 93, 118–119
　　civil rights compared, 123
　　criminal justice system and, 110–114
　　defined, 93
　　Standing Rock and, 97
　　See also Bill of Rights; *specific amendments*
Civil rights
　　civil disobedience to obtain, 136–138, 317–318
　　civil liberties compared, 123
　　Civil War's aftermath of segregation, 128–131
　　court strengthening of, 139–142
　　defined, 93, 123
　　de jure and de facto segregation and, 140–142
　　disability rights, 123–126, 123f, 125f
　　first wave for women, 142–146
Fourteenth Amendment, 99–100, 129–130
　　intersectionality of inequality, 148–150
　　Letter from Birmingham Jail, 23–25
　　milestones in, 139f
　　racial discrimination and, 127–131
　　second wave for women, 146–147
Civil Rights Act of 1866, 130
Civil Rights Act of 1875, 130
Civil Rights Act of 1957, 136
Civil Rights Act of 1964, 138, 146, 148, 398
Civil service, 398, 402
Civil Service Reform Act (Pendleton Act), 397–398

Civil War, 74, 128–129, 129f, 374–375f, 374–376.
　　See also Lincoln, Abraham
Clark, John, 133
Clark, Kenneth, 134–135, 136f
Clark, Mamie, 134–135, 136f
Clark, Tom C., 103
Clear and present danger test, 107
Clientele agencies, 397, 398
Clinton, Bill, 84, 330, 365, 399
Clinton, Hillary
　　Democratic Party favoritism of, 251–252, 251f
　　donations from Wall Street, 238
　　Latinos/Latinas and, 269, 270f
　　media use and, 211–212, 212f, 222f
　　on Sanders, 239
　　See also Presidential election of 2016
Closed primaries, 244, 244f
Closed rules, 337
Cloture, 338
CNN, 217, 217f, 221, 222
Coattail effect, 283
Cohen, Marty, 246–247
Cold War, 398
Collective action, 304–305
Collective good, 305
Collins, Amanda, 155–156, 156f, 158
Colonies, 33–39, 35f, 36t. *See also* American Revolution
Columbia University, 171–172, 175
Colvin, Claudette, 136
Commander in chief, 363–364
Commerce clause, 45, 64–65, 68, 73
Commercial bias, 224
Committee chairs, 333
Committee of Detail, 45
Committee on Rules, 337–338
Committee on Unfinished Parts, 45, 47–51, 50–51f
Committee system in Congress, 333, 334t, 337, 339
Common Sense (Paine), 14, 14f
Communications Act of 1934, 226, 227–228
Communications Decency Act, 109
Communist system, 22–23, 22f
Company E, 129f
Compassionate Use Act, 63–64
Comprehensive Plan for Reorganizing the Executive Branch
　　in the Oval Office of the White House, 399f
Concealed carry weapons (CCW), 155–160, 157f
Concurrent powers, 69, 69f
Concurring opinions, 430
Confederal system, 33–39, 35f, 36t, 67, 67f
Confederate flag, 352
Confederate States of America, 74, 128
Confederation Congress, 34
Conference committees, 333, 339
Congress
　　cabinet departments and, 401
　　committee system, 333, 334t, 337, 339
　　Constitution and, 326–330, 327f, 328–329t

descriptive representation and, 348–351
factors influencing campaigns and elections, 340–344, 341–344f
federal bureaucracy and, 405
legislative process, 335–339, 336f
lobbying, 309–310
partisanship and, 323–324
party systems and, 256–258, 257f
powers of, 327–330, 329t, 363–364, 365t
presidency and, 369
representation issue, 345–352, 346–350f
rules and processes of, 331–334, 332f, 334t
substantive representation and, 351–352
visible and invisible work of, 345–348
See also House of Representatives; Senate; Women in Congress
Congressional Budget Act, 328
Congressional Budget Office (CBO), 328
Congressional elections
constituencies and, 286–291, 287–289f, 291f
1992 elections, 340–344
2018 midterm election, 323, 353
See also Women in Congress
Conservativism, 199
Consideration, 190
Constituencies, 286–291, 287–289f, 291f, 345–346
Constitutional Convention
Committee on Unfinished Parts, 47–51, 50–51f
confederal system and, 33–39, 35f, 36t, 66, 67f
executive branch, 45–46, 361–365
federal bureaucracy and, 393–394
future impacts of, 58–59
judicial branch, 46–47, 417–419
legislative branch, 45
Madison's preparation for, 31–33
news media printing draft from, 214
ratification, 52–57, 53t
slavery and, 48–51, 50–51f, 127
state representation debates, 40–44, 44t, 48–51, 50–51f, 289–290, 326
See also Constitution of the United States
Constitutional courts, 426
Constitutional interpretation, 423
Constitutional republics, 22
Constitution of the United States
about, 22
amendment of, 48
Article I, 110, 426
Article II, 362–365, 365t, 393
Article III, 426, 428
commerce clause, 45, 64–65, 68, 73
concurrent powers, 69, 69f
Congress defined in, 326–330, 327f, 328–329t
due process clause, 73, 99–100
enumerated versus implied powers, 68, 69f
equal protection clause, 129–130
establishment clause, 102–105
federalism and, 66–71, 67f, 69f
full faith and credit clause, 48, 115
importance of, 31
necessary and proper clause, 45, 68, 72–73
presidency and, 361–365, 361f, 365t
presidential term limits, 362
ratification, 52–57, 53t, 418
reserved powers, 68, 69f
selective incorporation to states, 99–100, 101t
slavery and, 127
states ratifying, 57
supremacy clause, 67
voting issues, 168
See also Bill of Rights; Constitutional Convention; Federalism; *specific Amendments*
Constitution Party, 260t
Constitutions, 31, 41, 100
Continental Army, 36
Continental currency, 36, 36f
Contraceptives, 116
Controlled Substances Act (CSA), 64, 88
Converse, Philip, 189
Conyers, John, 184
Cooperative federalism, 75–76, 76f, 80–81, 83
Corporate welfare, 238
Corporation for Public Broadcasting, 227
Corwin, Edward, 376
Countermajoritarian difficulty, 433, 435
Counting, 50–51, 50–51f, 387
Court opinions, 82
Court-packing plan, 80, 80f
Courts of appeals, 427, 427f
Crandell, Prudence, 143, 143f
Crawford, John, 184
Crews, Wayne, 228
Criminal justice system, 110–114
Criminal law, 424, 425f
Critical elections, 256
Cronkite, Walter, 217
Cross burning, 109
Cruel and unusual punishment, 113–114
Cruz, Ted, 253–254, 268, 268f
CSA (Controlled Substances Act), 64, 88
Cues and information shortcuts, 190

DACA (Deferred Action for Childhood Arrivals), 269
Dahl, Robert, 302
Dakota Access Pipeline protests, 94–96f, 94–97
Dalton, Russell J., 178
Daughters of Liberty, 18
Davis, John W., 135
Davis v. Bandemer (1986), 290
Deadlock, 256, 348
"Dear Colleague" letter, 174
Death penalty, 113–114, 424
Decision of 1789, 394
Declaration of Independence, 6–10, 19–20, 33

Declaration of Rights and Grievances, 15
Declaration of Sentiments, 144–145
DeCunzo, Caroline, 172
De facto segregation, 140–142
Defendants, 424
Defense of Marriage Act (DOMA), 114–117
Deferred Action for Childhood Arrivals (DACA), 269
Deferred Actions for Parents of Americans and Lawful
    Permanent Residents, 269
De Jonge v. Oregon (1937), 109
De jure segregation, 140
Delegated powers, 362
Delegates, 243–244, 246
Democracy, defined, 6, 7
Democracy in America (Tocqueville), 302
Democratic National Convention, 211–212, 262
Democratic National Convention (DNC), 251
Democratic Party
    delegates, 246, 251, 252
    history of, 256–258
    political ideology and, 199, 248, 249f
    See also Presidential election of 2016
Democratic-Republican Party, 256
Demographics, 270
Department of Agriculture, 397
Department of Commerce, 397
Department of Education, U.S., 174
Department of Housing and Urban Development, 398
Department of Justice, 88
Department of Labor, 397
Department of Transportation, 398
Deregulation, 406
Descriptive representation, 348–351
Desegregation, 136
Devolution, 84, 406
DeVos, Betsy, 359
Diamond, Frank, 316
Digital divide, 231
Diplomacy, president and, 363
Direct democracy, 21, 21f
Direction of opinions, 195
Disability rights, 123–126, 123f, 125f
Discrimination
    disability rights and, 123–126, 123f, 125f
    intersectionality of inequality, 148–150
    workplace protections, 146
    See also Racial and ethnic minorities; Segregation
Dissenting opinions, 430
District courts, 426, 427
District of Columbia v. Heller (2008), 111
DNC (Democratic National Convention), 251
Doll studies, 134–135, 136f
DOMA (Defense of Marriage Act), 114–117
Double jeopardy, 112
Douglas, William O., 116
Douglass, Frederick, 131, 131f, 144
Downs, Anthony, 163

Dred Scott v. Sanford (1857), 127, 128f, 423
Druckman, James, 231
Dual federalism, 73–74, 74f
Dubin, Nan, 10f
Du Bois, W. E. B., 130
Duckworth, Tammy, 338f
Due process clause, 73, 99–100
Dust Bowl era, 77, 77f

EAA (Equal Access Act), 4–6
Earmarks, 328
East India Tea Company, 15–16
E-commerce taxation, 85, 86f
Economic equality, 8f
Economic interest groups, 306
Economic opportunity, 7
Economic systems, 22–23, 22f
Economy, 22, 37
Education
    faith-based religious extracurricular clubs, 4–5
    prayer in schools, 103–104, 103f
    racism and, 140
    taxpayer support of private schools, 103
    voting participation and level of, 165, 166f
    See also Civil rights
Educational Amendments of 1972, 173–174
Edwards, Dorothy, 175
1800 election, 420, 422f
Eighth Amendment, 99t, 101t, 113–114, 424
Eisenhower, Dwight D., 135, 136
Elastic clause. *See* Necessary and proper clause
Elazar, Daniel, 71
Elections
    congressional, 286–291, 287–289f, 291f
    cost of, 275–276, 275f
    critical elections, 256
    defined, 267
    1800 election, 420–421, 422f
    political participation and, 160, 161f
    primary elections, 244, 244f, 252, 282–283
    public opinion transmitted by, 191, 275
    rules and institutions affecting, 274–275f, 274–276
    stages of, 277–279, 278–279f
    See also Campaigns; Congressional elections; Presidential
        election of 2016; 2018 midterm election; Voters and
        voting process
Electoral College, 46, 254, 278–279, 279f
Elementary and Secondary Education Act (ESEA), 83
Elites, 188–189
Elitist theory, 302
Emancipation Proclamation, 128
Emerge Virginia, 322f
EMILY's List, 344
Employment Division v. Smith (1990), 105
Energy Transfer Partners (ETP), 94
Enfranchisement. *See* Voters and voting process
Engle v. Vitale (1962), 103

Enumerated powers, 68, 69f
Environmental issues. *See* Standing Rock
EOP (Executive Office of the President), 367–369
Equal Access Act (EAA), 4–6
Equal Employment Opportunity Commission, 398
Equality, 7, 8f
Equal protection clause, 129–130
Equal Rights Amendment (ERA), 146–147
Equal time rule, 227–228
Ernst, Joni, 348f
ESEA (Elementary and Secondary Education Act), 83
Eshoo, Anna, 324
Espionage Act of 1917, 106–107
Essentialism, 351
Establishment clause, 102–105
ETP (Energy Transfer Partners), 94
Everson v. Board of Education (1947), 103, 104
Exclusionary rule, 112
Executive agreements, 377
Executive branch, 45–46, 310, 394, 395f. *See also* Federal
    bureaucracy; Presidency; Presidential election of 2016
Executive Office of the President (EOP), 367–369
Executive Order 9066, 378, 379f
Executive orders, 378–379, 378f, 399f
Executive political appointees, 402
Executive privilege, 377
Exit polls, 194
Ex parte Merryman (1861), 375–376
Exploratory committees, 279
Ex post facto laws, 110
Expressed powers, 362
Extended republics, 55

Factions, 54–55, 256, 274, 326
Fairness doctrine, 228
Faith-based religious extracurricular clubs, 4–5
Faithless electors, 278–279
Fake news, 221, 229–230, 230f
Falusi, Lanre, 84f
Fareed, Justin, 284–285, 284–285f
FCC (Federal Communications Commission), 226
FDIC (Federal Deposit Insurance Corporation), 401
FEC (Federal Election Commission), 276
Federal bureaucracy
    after Civil War, 396–397
    characteristics of, 390–391
    Constitutional Convention and, 393–394
    control and oversight tools, 404–407
    core tasks of, 402–403
    defined, 385
    evolution of actors in, 385–390, 387–388f
    growth of, 400, 400f
    under Jackson, 396
    in Progressive Era, 397–398
    structure of, 400–402, 402f
    theories of, 391–392, 392f
    in twentieth century, 398–399

Federal civil service, 398, 402
Federal Communications Commission (FCC), 226
Federal Convention. *See* Constitutional Convention
Federal courts of appeals, 427, 427f
Federal Department of Housing, Education and Welfare
    (HEW), 124
Federal Deposit Insurance Corporation (FDIC), 401
Federal district courts, 426, 427
Federal Election Campaign Act, 276
Federal Election Commission (FEC), 276
Federal Emergency Management Agency
    (FEMA), 386, 389, 407, 407f
Federal Employees Political Activities Act, 403
Federalism
    beginnings, 62f
    Constitutional division and, 66–71, 67f, 69f
    cooperative federalism, 75–76, 76f, 80–81, 83
    defined, 63
    dual federalism, 73–74, 74f
    elections and, 274
    grants-in-aid and, 81–84, 83f
    Great Depression and, 77–81
    historical perspective, 72–77, 74f, 76f
    judicial branch and, 424–430
    medical marijuana and, 62f, 63–66, 65f
    modern structure of, 81–87, 83f
    new federalism, 84
Federalist Gazette, 214
The Federalist Papers (Hamilton, Madison & Jay)
    about, 54–56
    factions, 326
    influence of, 214
    No. 10, 54–55, 301–302
    No. 16, 56
    No. 46, 85
    No. 51, 55
    No. 74, 379
    No. 78, 137, 418, 434
    No. 84, 98
Federalist Party, 256
Federalists, 52–57, 53t
Federal judiciary, 413. *See also* Judicial branch;
    Supreme Court
Federal Radio Commission, 226
Federal Register, 403
Federal systems, 67, 67f
Fed Up protest, 296f
Feinstein, Dianne, 340, 343, 346
Felon disenfranchisement, 168
FEMA (Federal Emergency Management Agency),
    386, 389, 407, 407f
The Feminine Mystique (Friedan), 146
Fenno, Richard, 346
Ferguson shooting
    about, 183–187, 184–186f
    as focusing event, 197–198
    impact of, 182f, 202–205, 202f, 204–206f, 206–207

partisan identification and, 199, 199f
public opinion and, 184–185, 185–186f
race and ethnic identity predicting response to, 200, 201f
Fields, James, 205
Fifteenth Amendment, 130
Fifth Amendment
about, 98, 99t
criminal justice system and, 112–113
due process clause, 73
selective incorporation of, 101t
Fighting words, 109
Filburn, Roscoe, 64
Filibusters, 338–339, 432
Findley, James, 4, 5
Fiore, Michele, 157
Fire alarm oversight, 329, 405
Firearms ownership. *See* Second Amendment
Fireside chats, 216
First Amendment
about, 98, 99t
establishment clause, 102–105
freedom of assembly, 109
freedom of expression, 105, 106–109
freedom of the press, 106, 107, 214
free exercise clause, 102, 105
interest groups and, 303
lobbying and, 308
selective incorporation of, 101t
First Reconstruction Act of 1867, 130
First spouse, 369, 369f
First wave of civil rights for women, 142–146
Fisher v. University of Texas at Austin (2016), 142
Fitness of character, 396
504 sit-ins, 124–125, 125f
Flag burning, 108, 108f
Flores, Lucy, 415
Focus groups, 192–193
Focusing events, 197–198
Ford, Gerald R., 365
Foreign policy, 363, 398
Foubert, John D., 158
Fourteenth Amendment, 99–100, 129–130
Fourth Amendment, 99t, 101t, 110–112
Fox News, 217, 222
Framing in media, 231
Franklin, Benjamin, 12, 12f, 40–42, 52
Frazier, Bernie, 200
Freedmen's Bureau, 130
Freedom of assembly, 109
Freedom of choice plans, 140
Freedom of expression, 105, 106–109
Freedom of the press, 106, 107, 214
Freedom Riders, 138
Freedoms. *See* Bill of Rights; Civil liberties
Free exercise clause, 102, 105
Free riders, 305, 305f
Free Soil Democrats, 257

Free speech, 106–109
French and Indian War, 12
Friedan, Betty, 146, 147f
Friend of the Court briefs, 311
Front-loading, 244–245, 245f
Full faith and credit clause, 48, 115

Gaines, Lloyd, 133
Gambill, Landen, 158–159, 158f, 174
GAO (Government Accountability Office), 405
Garland, Merrick, 416
Garner, Eric, 184, 185f
Garner, Tyron, 116f
Gay-Straight Alliance (GSA), 5, 5f
Gender, voting and, 166–167. *See also* Women;
Women in Congress
Gender discrimination and sexual harassment, 146–148
Gender gap in party affiliation, 200, 200f
Generational differences. *See* Age and generational
differences
George III, King, 20
Gerry, Elbridge, 43, 287
Gerrymandering, 287–290, 291f, 350–351
Get out the vote (GOTV), 167–168, 276
Gibbons v. Ogden (1824), 73
Gideon v. Wainwright (1963), 113, 113f
Gillibrand, Kirsten, 172, 174f, 175, 348f
Gitlow, Benjamin, 100f
Gitlow v. New York (1925), 100
Going public, 370
Gonzalez v. Raich (2005), 64
GOP. *See* Republican Party
Gorsuch, Neil, 416, 416f, 420
GOTV (get out the vote), 167–168, 276
Government, defined, 3
Government Accountability Office (GAO), 405
The Governmental Process (Truman), 304
Government corporations, 401
Government interest groups, 308
Graham, Lindsey, 358
Grand Convention. *See* Constitutional Convention
Grand juries, 112
Grants-in-aid, 81–84, 83f
Graphs, 70–71, 70–71f, 349–350, 349–350f
Grassroots lobbying, 313
Gratz, Jennifer, 141
Gratz v. Bollinger (2003), 141
Great Britain, 11–16, 13f, 20, 34
Great Compromise on state representation, 43–44, 44t,
289–290, 326
Great Depression, 77–81
Great Society program, 83
Green Dots, 175
Green Party, 260t
Green v. County School Board of New Kent County, Virginia
(1968), 140
Gridlock, 256, 348

Griffin v. Prince Edward County (1964), 139
Grimké, Angelina, 143–144
Grimké, Sarah, 143–144
Griswold v. Connecticut (1965), 116
Growth and Opportunity Project (autopsy report), 271
Grutter, Barbara, 141–142
Grutter v. Bollinger (2003), 141–142
GSA (Gay-Straight Alliance), 5, 5f
Gun control, 86–87, 111, 111f, 155–160, 157f
Gun-Free School Zones Act, 86–87
Gutekanst, John, 96f
Gut rationality, 190

Habeas corpus, writs of, 375–376
Halbriter, Ray, 94
Haley, Nikki, 357, 358
Hamilton, Alexander
    Constitutional Convention attendance, 40, 45
    1800 election, 420–421
    image of, 98f
    role under Washington, 394
    See also The Federalist Papers (Hamilton, Madison & Jay)
Hard money versus paper money, 37
Harlan, John Marshall, 75, 131
Harper, Frances Ellen Watkins, 145, 145f
Harris, Sarah, 143
Harris, Tyrone, 192f
Hatch Act, 403
Hate speech, 108–109
Haynes, Lemuel, 17, 17f
Hearst, Randolph, 215
Hector, John, 316f
Heller, Joseph, 79
Henry, Patrick, 41
Herrera, Maria, 268
Heumann, Judith, 122f, 123–126
HEW (Federal Department of Housing, Education
    and Welfare), 124
Heyer, Heather, 205
Higher Education Act, 146
Hill, Anita, 341–342
Hispanics. *See* Latinos/Latinas
Hodges, Leah, 408, 408f
Holmes, Oliver Wendell, 107
Homer, Mark, 288f
Home style, 346
Horineck, Mekaski, 95
Horse race phenomenon, 224–225
Hostile working environment, 148
House Freedom Caucus, 256
House majority leaders, 332
House minority leaders, 332
House of Burgesses, 11
House of Representatives
    California's 24th district, 281–285, 282–285f
    Committee on Rules, 337–338
    constituencies, 286–290, 287f

Constitution and, 327
Senate compared to, 328t
Speaker of the House, 331–332
state representation debates, 43, 289–290
statistics on, 327f
See also Congress
Housing crisis of 2008, 297–301, 298–300f
Houston, Charles Hamilton, 133, 134f
Howell, William, 379
Hudack, Evie, 158
Hughes, Charles Evans, 79–80, 109
Hughes Court, 437, 437f
Hume, David, 7
Hundred Days, 78
Hurricane Harvey, 384f, 386
Hurricane Irma, 386
Hurricane Katrina, 387–390, 388f, 405, 407, 408
Hurricane Maria, 386–387, 387f, 407
Hurricane Sandy, 389
Hutchinson, Bailey, 352
Hutchinson, Thomas, 16–17

I-85 district, 290, 291f
Ideology. *See* Political ideology
Images as political tools, 39, 39f
Immigration, 268–269, 269, 269f
Impeachment, 323, 330, 365
Implementation, 402–403
Implied powers, 68, 362
Incumbency advantage, 282, 290–291, 343
Incumbent gerrymandering, 288
Incumbents, 275
Indentured servitude, 16
Independent executive agencies, 398
Independent regulatory agencies, 401
Independents, 249, 250f
Indians. *See* Indigenous peoples
Indigenous peoples, 18–19, 71, 100, 104f
Infotainment, 222
Inside lobbying, 309–310
Intensity of opinions, 195–196
Interagency rivalry, 406
Interest groups
    challenges of, 301–306, 303–305f
    defined, 297
    housing crisis of 2008 and, 297–301, 298–300f
    iron triangle of influence, 311–312, 312f
    lobbying, 308–313, 309–310f, 312f
    tactics compared to social movements, 317–319
    types of, 306–308
    See also Constituencies; Social movements
Intergovernmental lobbying, 85
Intermediate scrutiny, 148
Internet, 217, 218f
Internment of Japanese Americans, 378–379, 379f
Intersectionality of inequality, 148–150
Interstate Commerce Commission, 397

Intolerable Acts, 16
Introduction of bills, 335
Investigative journalism, 215
Iowa caucuses, 244
Iron triangle of influence, 311–312, 312f
Issue networks, 312
It's On Us campaign, 174

Jackson, Andrew, 370, 396
Jamestown, 11
Jay, John, 54–56
Jefferson, Thomas
    Constitutional Convention attendance, 41
    correspondence with Madison, 32
    1800 election, 420–421
    inalienable rights, 7–8
    on judicial review, 423
    news media and, 214
    personality of, 380
    picture, 7f
    pursuit of happiness and, 9
    role under Washington, 394
    slavery and, 19–20
    See also Declaration of Independence
Jim Crow laws, 130–131
Johnson, Andrew, 129, 330, 365
Johnson, Lyndon, 83, 217, 398
Johnston, Angus, 177
Joint committees, 333
Judicial activism, 435
Judicial branch
    beginnings, 46–47
    Constitutional Convention and, 417–419
    criminal versus civil cases, 424–425, 425f
    defined, 46
    federal bureaucracy and, 405–406
    federal courts, 426–430, 427f
    federalism and, 424–430
    jurisdiction, 46, 418
    lobbying, 311
    politics of appointments to, 430–432
    process of cases, 431f
    senatorial courtesy, 330, 430
    state courts and, 425–426
    See also Supreme Court; specific court cases
Judicial restraint, 434–435
Judicial review, 46–47, 420–423, 433, 436–437, 436–437f
Judiciary Act of 1789, 418–419, 422–423
Judiciary Act of 1801, 421
Juries, right to, 113
Jurisdiction, 46, 418, 428
Just versus unjust laws, 25

Kaepernick, Colin, 203–204, 204f
Katz v. United States (1967), 112
Kavanaugh, Brett, 290, 311, 439
Kennedy, Anthony, 5, 115, 116, 118, 416

Kennedy, John F., 216
Kennedy, Ted, 341f
Kernell, Samuel, 370
Key, V. O., Jr., 241
Killer amendments, 337
Kim, Pearl, 325, 325f
Kim Jon-un, 363f
King, Martin Luther, Jr., 23–25, 24f, 138
King, Rodney, 424, 426f
Kingdon, John, 206
Kirchmeier, Kyle, 95
Kollman, Ken, 313
Korematsu v. United States (1944), 378
Kosewicz, Adrienne, 86f
Kotkin, Joel, 251
Ku Klux Klan, 107, 107f, 130–131

Labor unions, 256
Ladies Association, 18
Laissez-faire capitalist system, 22f, 23
Lake Oahe, 94
Land rights, 36
Lasn, Kalle, 314
Lasswell, Harold, 231
Latinos/Latinas
    civil rights and, 149
    election of 2016 and, 267–272, 268–273f
    election of 2018 and, 292, 353
    increase in numbers of, 270, 271f, 273f
    voting and, 166, 275
    See also Racial and ethnic minorities
Law enforcement, 96, 196, 198, 198f
Lawmaking. See Congress; Legislative branch; specific laws
Lawrence, John, 116f
Lawrence v. Texas (2003), 116, 116f
Lawyers, right to, 113, 113f
Leadership Institute, 157
League of United Latin American Citizens v. Perry (2006), 290
Lee, Richard Henry, 19
Lee Resolution, 19
Legal Defense Fund of the NAACP, 311
Legal model of judicial decision making, 433–434, 435f
Legal segregation, 130–131
Legislative branch, 45. See also Congress; House of
    Representatives; Senate; specific laws
Legislative courts, 426
Legislative deliberation, 351–352
Legislative process, 335–339, 336f, 377
Lemon test, 104–105
Lemon v. Kurtzman (1971), 104–105
Lesbian, gay, bisexual, and transgender rights, 115, 146, 348
"Letter from Birmingham Jail," 23–25
Levendusky, Matthew, 249
LGBT rights, 115, 146, 348
Liautaud, Greg, 175
Libel, 108
Liberalism, 199

Liberian senate, 49f
Libertarianism, 199
Libertarian Party, 260t
Liberty, 16–17, 33
Liberty Further Extended (Haynes), 17
Lincoln, Abraham, 128, 374–375f, 374–376
Line graphs, 70, 70f, 71
Linked fate, 200
Linthicum, Kate, 272
Lippmann, Walter, 188
Little Leaf, Keeli, 92f
Lobbying, 85, 308–313, 309–310f, 312f.
    See also Interest groups
Local governments, constitutional powers of, 71
Locke, John, 7
Logrolls, 49
Lopez, Alfonso, Jr., 86–87
Loverde, Liz, 4f
Lowey, Nita, 342
Lunch counter protests, 138, 140f

Madison, James
    about, 31–33, 32f
    Bill of Rights and, 98
    correspondence with Washington, 32, 38–39
    on factions, 54–56, 326
    judicial review and, 421–423
    news media and, 214
    preparation for Constitutional Convention by, 31–33
    residence of, 32f
    slavery and, 33, 49
    state representation debates and, 40–44
    wealth inequality, 302
Majority-minority districts, 288, 291f
Majority of votes, 286
Majority opinions, 430
Malapportionment, 290
Mandamus, writs of, 421, 422
Mansbridge, Jane, 256, 351
Mapp, Dollree, 112, 112f
Mapp v. Ohio (1961), 112
Marbury, William, 421–423, 423f
Marbury v. Madison (1803), 421–423
Marijuana, 62f, 63–66, 65f, 88
Markup of bills, 337
Marriage, same-sex, 114–117, 438–439
Marshall, John, 72, 72f, 421–423
Marshall, Thurgood, 126, 132–136, 133f
Martin, Trayvon, 184f
Maryland, 374–375, 374f
Massachusetts, 37–39, 261
Masses versus elites, 188–189
Mass media, 214–215, 217, 218f
Material rewards, 305
Mattis, Jim, 359
Mattress Performance (Carry That Weight), 171–172, 172–173f
Mayfield, Max, 387–388

Mayhew, David, 291
MBSs (mortgage-backed securities), 298
McCarthy, Kevin, 331f
McCaskill, Claire, 172, 173, 174f
McConnell, Grant, 313
McCulloch v. Maryland (1819), 72–73
McDonald v. Chicago (2010), 111
McLaurin, George, 134, 135f
McLaurin v. Oklahoma State Regents for Higher
    Education (1950), 134
McReynolds, James, 111
McSpadden, Lesley, 207
Media. *See* News media; Social media
Media effects, 230–231
Medicaid, 83
Medical marijuana, 62f, 63–66, 65f, 88
Medicare, 83
Menendez, Jose, 288f
Mentorship, 348
Mergens, Bridget, 4–5, 6, 8
Merit system, 398
Merryman, Ex parte (1861), 375–376
Merryman, John, 374–376
Mikulski, Barbara, 348, 348f
Militarization of law enforcement, 96
Military, 363–364
Millennial voters, 176–178, 177f
Miller v. California (1973), 109
Milliken v. Bradley (1974), 140–141
Mills, C. Wright, 302
Minimalist paradigm, 188
Mink, Patsy, 342
Minorities. *See* African Americans; Latinos/Latinas;
    Racial and ethnic minorities
Miranda rights, 113
Miranda v. Arizona (1966), 113
Miringoff, Lee M., 205
Missouri Compromise, 127
Missouri ex rel Gaines v. Canada (1938), 133
Momentum (Big Mo), 284
Monson, Diane, 63, 64f
Montesquieu, Baron de, 7
Montgomery bus boycott, 136–138
Montpelier, 32f
Morales, Mauro, 104f
Moral hazard problem, 433
Morris, Gouverneur, 31, 40
Morse v. Frederick (2007), 108
Mortgage-backed securities (MBSs), 298
Moseley Braun, Carol, 343, 344f, 346, 352
Motor Voter Law, 168–169
Mott, Lucretia, 144
MoveOn.org, 252
MSNBC, 221, 222
Muckrakers, 215, 397f
Mueller, Robert S., III, 359
Multiple referral, 337

Multiracial Americans, 149–150
Murdoch, Rupert, 217
Murphy, Walter, 434
Murray, Patty, 341–344, 343f, 348f
Myers v. United States (1926), 394
"My Story | Dulce Candy," 280

Nader, Ralph, 261
Nagin, C. Ray, 388
National Association for the Advancement of Colored
        People (NAACP), 132–136, 311
National conventions, 246
National Football League, 203–204, 204f
National Gazette, 214
National Hurricane Center, 389
National Industrial Recovery Act (NIRA), 78–80
National Organization for Women (NOW), 146
National Performance Review, 406
National Recovery Administration (NRA), 78–80
National Security Act, 398
National Security Council, 398
National security issues, 372–376, 373–375f
National versus state law, 62f, 63–66, 65f, 88
National Voter Registration Act of 1993, 168–169
National Woman Suffrage Association, 145
Native peoples. *See* Indigenous peoples
Natural rights, 6, 7, 25, 127
Nava, Pedro, 284
Necessary and proper clause, 45, 68, 72–73
Negative campaign ads, 276
Negative freedoms, 93
Nelson, Candice, 344
Nelson, Kjersten, 231
Net neutrality, 227
Neustadt, Richard, 379
Neutrality test, 105
New Deal, 78–81
New federalism, 84
New Hampshire primary, 244
New Jersey Plan, 42–43, 44t
New media, 218
New Orleans, 387–390, 388f
News anchors, 216–217
News media
    bias and, 221–224f, 221–225
    campaign ads, 276
    changing sources of, 226–227, 227f
    defined, 211
    editorial choices about, 192f
    federal bureaucracy and, 406
    historical development of, 213–220, 215–220f
    influence of, 211–213, 212f
    mass media, 214–215
    negative campaign ads, 170
    presidency and, 370–371, 370f
    public opinion influenced by, 201
    regulation of, 225–228, 226–227f

technology adoption and, 217, 218f
    Trump's use of, 240
    The War of the Worlds, 229–231, 230f
    See also Social media
New York assembly, 316
New York Times, 221, 358, 373
New York Times v. United States (1971), 107
Niche journalism, 218
Nichols, Sheila, 315
Nineteenth Amendment, 145–146
Ninth Amendment, 99, 99t, 114–117
NIRA (National Industrial Recovery Act), 78–80
Nixon, Joy, 252
Nixon, Richard, 84, 216, 363, 365, 377
Nomination process, 243–247, 244–245f, 247f
Nonattitudes, 189
Nonpartisan blanket primaries, 282
Norms, 334
North Carolina, 290, 291f
Norton, Eleanor Holmes, 342
Novotny, Patrick, 213
NOW (National Organization for Women), 146
NRA (National Recovery Administration), 78–80

Obama, Barack
    al-Awlaki killing, 372–374, 373f, 376
    marijuana and, 65–66
    net neutrality, 227
    sexual assault on campus, 174
    Supreme Court nominations, 413–414, 416
    tax cuts by, 239
Obergefell, James, 117–118, 118f
Obergefell v. Hodges (2015), 118, 149
Obscenity, 109
Occupy Wall Street (OWS), 238, 314–316f, 314–317
O'Connor, Sandra Day, 4
Office for Civil Rights, 174
Office of Management and Budget (OMB), 368
Ohio Company, 12
Olson, Mancur, 305
O'Malley, Martin, 203
OMB (Office of Management and Budget), 368
Open primaries, 244, 244f
Open rules, 337
Open seat elections, 282
OpenSecrets.org, 307
Oral arguments, 429–430
Original jurisdiction, 418, 428
Outside lobbying, 313
Oversight, 328–329
OWS (Occupy Wall Street), 238, 314–316f, 314–317

PACs (political action committees), 276, 312, 343
Page, Benjamin, 190
Paine, Thomas, 14, 14f, 17
Pamphlets, 213. *See also* "Letter from Birmingham Jail"
Paper money versus hard money, 37

Pardons, 364
Parks, Rosa, 137–138, 138f
Partisan attachment, 167
Partisan bias, 222
Partisan gerrymandering, 288
Partisan identification, 198–200, 199f
Partisan press, 214
Partisanship
    Congress and, 323–324
    Ferguson shooting and, 199, 199f
    news media and, 222, 223f
    racism as a "big problem" and, 204, 205–206f
    See also Political parties
The Party Decides (Cohen et al.), 246–247
Party establishment, 238
Party identification
    changes over time, 249, 250f
    defined, 197, 248
    public opinion surveys and, 190
Party platforms, 255
Party systems, 256–258, 257f
Paterson, William, 42–43, 43f
Path dependence, 397
Patronage, 396, 403
Paul, Alice, 147
Paul, Rand, 96, 359
Paulson, Henry M., Jr., 299, 300f
Peace and Freedom Party, 260t
Pelosi, Nancy, 284, 300, 300f
Pence, Mike, 367f
Pendleton Act (Civil Service Reform Act), 397–398
Pennsylvania, 324–325, 325f
Pennsylvania Evening Post, and Daily Advertiser, 213–214
Pennsylvania Packet, and Daily Advertiser, 214
Penny press, 214–215, 215f
People's mic, 315–316, 318f
Perez, Paulina, 31f
Personal Responsibility and Work Opportunity Reconciliation
    Act (PRWORA), 84
Pew Research Center, 70
Peyote, 104f, 105
Philadelphia Convention. *See* Constitutional Convention
Philosoraptor, 111, 111f
Pinckney, Charles, 214
Pitkin, Hannah, 346, 351
Plain sight, 112
Plaintiffs, 424
Plea bargaining, 424
Plessy, Homer, 75, 75f, 131
Plessy v. Ferguson (1896), 75, 75f, 131, 134, 135
Pluralism, 302
Plurality, 286
Pocket vetoes, 339
Polarization and gridlock, 255–256
Polarization of parties, 347–348, 347f
Police, 96, 196, 198, 198f
Police patrol oversight, 329, 405

Police powers, 68
Policy. *See* Domestic public policy; Economic policy;
    Foreign policy
Policy agenda, 302
Political action committees (PACs), 276, 312, 343
Political ambition, 342
Political campaigns. *See* Campaigns
Political culture, 6–10
Political efficacy, 166
Political ideology, 199, 248. *See also* Democratic Party;
    Political parties; Republican Party
Political institutions, 21–22f, 21–23
Political knowledge, 189–190, 189f, 219, 219f
Political mobilization, 167–168
Political movements. *See* Social movements
Political participation
    carrying the weight in, 178–179
    concealed carry weapons activism, 155–160, 157f
    defined, 155
    fluidity of, 162f
    forms of, 160–163, 161–162f
    prevention of sexual assaults and, 171–175f, 171–176
    young Americans and, 176–178, 177f
    See also Voters and voting process
Political parties
    Congress' organization and, 331–332, 332f, 345
    control by over time, 258, 258f
    defined, 237
    history of, 256–258, 257f
    nomination process, 243–244, 244–245f, 247f
    numbers of, 259, 259f
    party identification and, 248–249, 249–250f
    polarization of, 255–256
    presidency and, 369
    recruitment of candidates, 242–243
    responsible party model, 241
    roles of, 241–247, 243–247f
    state versus national, 242, 243f
    third-party candidates, 260–261, 260t, 261f
    2016 presidential election and, 237–240, 238–240f,
        251–253f, 251–254
    two-party dominance, 256–261, 257–259f, 260t, 261f
    See also Democratic Party; Partisanship; Political ideology;
        Republican Party
Political patronage, 396, 403
Political polarization, 255–256, 347–348, 347f
Political propaganda, 13–14
Political science, 7
Political socialization, 197–198
Politico report, 301
Politics, defined, 3
Polls, 193–196, 194f
Pompeo, Mike, 358–359
Popular vote, 279
Populism, 238
Pornography, 109
Positive freedoms, 93, 123

Power elite, 302
Prayer in schools, 103–104, 103f
Precedent, 429, 434
Presidency
   about, 357
   approval ratings, 371–372, 371f
   character and personality and, 379–380
   commander in chief, 363–364
   Constitution and, 361–365, 361f, 365t
   diplomacy, 363
   eligibility for, 362
   federal bureaucracy and, 405
   institutional and informal influences on, 366–372,
      368f, 371f
   national security issues and, 372–376, 373–375f
   powers and roles, 45–46, 361–365, 365t, 394
   Supreme Court nominations and, 432
   unilateral actions, 377–379, 378–379f
   vetoes, 339
   war powers, 363–364
   See also Executive branch; Federal bureaucracy;
      specific presidents
The Presidential Character (Barber), 380
Presidential debates, 216
Presidential election of 2016
   about, 237
   campaign contributions, 307
   challenge to party establishment in, 236f, 237–240,
      238–240f
   constituency changes, 267–272, 268–273f
   cost of, 275
   implications for political parties of, 251–253f, 251–254
   media use and, 211–212, 212f, 222f
   national conventions, 247f
   party identification and, 249
   Russian involvement in, 212–213, 212f, 221, 329
   third-party candidates in, 261
   votes, 254
Presidential pardons, 364
Presidential primary elections, 244, 244f
President pro tempore, 332
Press. *See* News media
Press secretary, 369
Primary elections, 244, 244f, 252, 282–283
Priming, 231
Principal-agent problem, 391–392, 392f
Printz v. United States (1997), 87
Prior, Markus, 231
Prior restraint, 107
Privacy rights, 115–117
Private bureaucracies, 390–391
Private contractors, 401–402
Privatization, 406
Privileges, 8
Probable cause, 112
Problem of moral hazard, 433
Procedural justice, 110

Prohibition Party, 260t
Project Veritas, 221
Proportional representation systems, 259
Protests, 177–178, 177f, 317–318. *See also* Civil rights; Occupy
   Wall Street (OWS); Social movements; Standing Rock
PRWORA (Personal Responsibility and Work Opportunity
   Reconciliation Act), 84
Public good, 305
Public interest groups, 306–308
Public opinion
   defined, 183, 188
   democratic representation and, 202–205, 202f, 204–206f
   fluidity of, 183–187, 184–186f
   formation of, 187–190, 189f
   measuring, 193–196, 194f
   presidency and, 370–371
   socialization and ideology and, 197–201, 198–201f
   Supreme Court and, 438
   transmission of, 191–196, 192f, 194f, 275
   Trump and, 371
   See also Ferguson shooting
Public Opinion (Lippmann), 188
Public opinion surveys, 184, 190
Public policy. *See* Domestic public policy; Economic policy;
   Foreign policy
Puerto Rico, 386–387, 387f, 407
Purposive benefits, 306
Push polls, 196

Question order effects, 195
Question wording effects, 195
Quid pro quo sexual harassment, 148
Quiet vetoes, 339
Quotas, 141

Race of interviewer effects, 195
Racial and ethnic gerrymandering, 288, 291f, 350–351
Racial and ethnic minorities
   Hurricane Katrina and, 408, 408f
   as majority of population, 245f
   NFL protests and, 203–204, 204f
   Occupy Wall Street and, 316
   projected population change of, 271f
   public opinion and, 200, 200–201f
   racial identity and, 149–150
   voting and, 166, 167f
   See also African Americans; Ferguson shooting; Latinos/
      Latinas; Segregation; Slavery
Racial discrimination, 127–131
Radio, 215–216
Radio Act of 1927, 226
Radio addresses, 216
Raich, Angel, 62f, 63–66, 88
Random digit dialing, 194–195
Random selection, 193
Ranked choice voting, 261
Rational basis standard, 147

Rational-legal authority, 391
Rauch, Jonathan, 242
Reagan, Ronald, 84, 399, 406, 415–416, 415f
Realignment, 256, 270–272
Reasonable cause, 112
Reasonableness standard, 147
Reasonable suspicion, 112
Recess appointments, 362–363
Reconstruction amendments, 129–130
Recruitment of candidates, 242–243
Redistricting, 283, 286–290, 287f
Red tape, 404, 405f
Reed, Esther de Berdt, 18, 18f
Referral to committee, 337
Reform Party, 260t
Regents of the University of California v. Bakke (1978), 141
Registration requirements for voting, 168–169, 169f
Regulators, 38
Regulatory capture, 311
Rehabilitation Act, 124
Rehnquist, William, 87
Religion
    American political culture and, 9–10
    demographics of, 10f
    establishment clause and, 102–105
    extracurricular clubs, 4–5, 8, 103f
    free exercise clause, 102
Represent, 323
Representation. *See* Congress
Representative bureaucracy, 403
Representative democracy, 21f, 22
Republican National Committee (RNC), 253, 271
Republican Party
    delegates, 246
    history of, 257
    ideology of, 199
    political ideology and, 248, 249f
Republic of Liberia, 49f
Republics, 31, 55
Reserved powers, 68, 69f, 117
Resolution of Interposition, 135–136
Respondents to surveys, 70, 193
Responsible party model, 241
Retrospective voting, 275
Revolving door phenomenon, 309, 310f
Right to bear arms. *See* Second Amendment
Riot Act (1786), 38
RNC (Republican National Committee), 253, 271
Robinson, Jo Ann, 137–138
Roe v. Wade (1973), 116–117, 147
Roll-call votes, 338
Roosevelt, Eleanor, 369, 369f
Roosevelt, Franklin
    court-packing plan, 80, 80f
    Executive Order 9066, 378, 379f
    federal bureaucracy and, 398
    fireside chats, 216, 217f

New Deal and, 78–81, 78f
    term limits and, 362
Roosevelt, Theodore, 397f
Rosenberg, Gerald, 136
Rossiter, Clinton, 361
Roth v. United States (1957), 109
Rubio, Marco, 268, 268f, 278f
Rulemaking, 403
Runoff elections, 286
Russell, Tory, 207
Russia
    Cold War and, 398
    election interference by, 212–213, 329, 359
    Syrian chemical attack and, 358, 359
    Trump and, 221, 329
Rutledge, John, 49
Ryan, Paul, 331f

Salience of opinions, 195–196
Same-sex marriage, 114–117
Samples, 193
Sample size, 380
Sampling error, 193
Sanders, Bernie
    challenge to party establishment by, 238–239, 240, 254
    Democratic Party impacted by, 251–252, 251–252f, 262
    Latinos/Latinas and, 269
    popular support for, 239, 239f
Sasse, Ben, 253
Scalia, Antonin, 64, 416
Scalise, Steve, 331f
Scanlon, Mary Gay, 324–325, 325f
Schattschneider, E. E., 302
Schechter, Martin, 78–80, 79f
Schechter Poultry Corp. v. U.S. (1935), 79–80
Schenck, Charles, 106–107
Schenck v. United States (1919), 106–107
Schlozman, Kay Lehman, 160, 313
School choice, racism and, 140
School IDs to prove residence, 168
Schools. *See* Education; School choice
Schroeder, Pat, 342
Schuyler, Robert Livingston, 32
Scientific polls, 193–195
SCLC (Southern Christian Leadership Conference), 23–25
Scott, Dred, 127, 128f
SDGU (self-defense gun use), 157–158
Search and seizure, 111–112
Secession, 20, 128–129, 129f
Second Amendment
    about, 99t
    gun control, 86–87, 111, 111f
    selective incorporation of, 101t
Second Continental Congress, 19–20, 34
Second New Deal, 80
Section 504, 124
Sedition Act of 1918, 106

Segregation
  Brown v. Board of Education, 132–136
  Civil War aftermath, 128–131
  de facto segregation, 140
  de jure segregation, 140
  integration timeline in the south, 137f
  legal segregation, 75, 130–131
  separate but equal, 75, 131, 134–135
Select Bipartisan Committee to Investigate the Preparation
    for and Response to Hurricane Katrina, 408
Select committees, 333
Selective benefits, 305–306
Selective incorporation of Constitution, 99–100, 101t
Self-defense gun use (SDGU), 157–158
Self-incrimination, 113
Self-selected listener opinion polls (SLOP), 194
Senate
  constituencies, 286
  Constitution and, 327
  filibuster, 338–339
  House of Representatives compared to, 328t
  state representation debates, 43, 289–290
  statistics on, 327f
  Vice president and, 366
  See also Congress
Senate majority leaders, 332
Senate minority leaders, 332
Senatorial courtesy, 330, 430
Seneca Falls Convention, 144–145
Senior Executive Service (SES), 402
Sensationalism, 215, 216f
The Sentiments of an American Woman (Reed), 18
Separate but equal, 75, 131, 134–135
Separation of powers, 47, 47t, 405–406
SES (Senior Executive Service), 402
SES (socioeconomic status), 165
Sessions, Jeff, 66, 88
Seventh Amendment, 99t, 101t
Seven Years' War, 12
Sexual assault, 155–160, 171–175f, 171–176
Sexual harassment, 146–148
Shaheen, Jeanne, 348f
Shapiro, Robert, 190
Shaw, Bernard, 217f
Shaw v. Reno (1993), 290, 291f
Shays, Daniel, 37, 38
Shays' Rebellion, 37–39, 37f
Shepard, William, 38
Shuttlesworth, Fred, 24f
Signing statements, 377
Sinclair, Barbara, 335, 337, 338
Single-member plurality system, 259
Sit-ins, 138
Sixth Amendment, 99t, 101t, 113
Skocpol, Theda, 397
Slander, 108
Slaughterhouse Cases (1873), 75, 100

Slavery
  Constitutional Convention and, 48–51, 50–51f, 127
  Declaration of Independence and, 19–20
  Madison and, 33
  rights in colonial America, 16–17
  Thirteenth Amendment and, 129
  women in favor of abolishing, 142–144
SLOP (self-selected listener opinion polls), 194
Smith, Patty, 346f
Social benefits, 306
Social contract, 6, 7
Social equality, 7
Socialism, 199
Socialist Party USA, 260t
Socialist system, 22f, 23
Social media
  campaigns, 280
  equal time and, 228
  Ferguson shooting and, 201
  impact of, 218–220
  Trump's use of, 240, 358
Social movements
  defined, 297
  Occupy Wall Street, 238, 314–316f, 314–317
  Standing Rock, 94–96f, 94–97, 149
  tactics compared to interest groups, 317–319
  See also Protests; Public opinion
Social Security Act, 80
Socioeconomic status (SES), 165
Sodomy, 116
Soft news, 222
Solicitor general, 419, 429
Sons of Liberty, 14–16
Sotomayor, Sonia, 412f, 413–415
Southern Christian Leadership Conference (SCLC), 23–25
Sovereignty, 34–35, 86
Soviet Union. *See* Russia
Spanish-American War, 215, 216f
Speaker of the House, 331–332
Special committees, 333
Special interests. *See* Interest groups; Occupy Wall Street
    (OWS); Social movements
Speedy trials, 113
Split-ticket voting, 249
Spoils system, 396
Spyer, Thea C., 114, 115f
Stability of opinions, 195–196
Staff, 333
Stamp Act, 15
Stamp Act Congress, 15
Standard operating procedures, 391
Standing, 429, 438
Standing committees, 333, 334t
Standing Rock, 94–96f, 94–97, 149
Stanton, Elizabeth Cady, 144–145
Stare decisis, 434
State and local bureaucracies, 390, 400, 400f

State government, 40–44, 44t
State of the Union address, 364
State sovereignty resolutions, 86
States' rights, 74
Statutes, 328
Steamboat monopoly case, 73
Stereotypes, 188
Stewart, Maria W., 149
Strategic model of judicial decision making, 434, 435f
Straw polls, 193–194, 194f
Strict scrutiny, 147
Strolovitch, Dara, 313
"Strong Women Fight Back" video, 157
Students, voting by, 168
Subprime mortgage crisis, 297–301, 298–300f
Substantive representation, 351–352
Suffrage, 142–146, 168. *See also* Voters and voting process
Sulkowicz, Emma, 171–173, 171f, 175
Superdelegates, 246, 247f, 251, 252
Superdome, 388
Super PACs, 276, 312
Supremacy clause, 67
Supreme Court
    analyzing decisions of, 82
    case selection by, 428–429
    Clarence Thomas hearings, 341–342
    court-packing plan, 80, 80f
    decision making theories and process, 433–439, 435–437f
    defined, 413
    federalism shaped by, 72–73
    gerrymandering, 290
    Hughes Court, 437, 437f
    judicial review, 46–47
    Judiciary Acts and, 418–419
    lobbying, 311
    National Industrial Recovery Act and, 79
    nomination process, 413–417, 415–416f, 432
    oral arguments, 429–430
    original jurisdiction, 428
    as policymaker, 435, 438–439
    process of cases, 431f
    role in judicial system, 426–428, 427f
    social change and, 137
    standards used for different types of cases, 147–148
    visual presentation of, 419, 419f
    Warren Court, 436, 436f
    See also specific court cases; specific justices
Surveys, 70, 184, 190, 193
Suspect classifications, 147
Swain, Carol, 351
Swann v. Charlotte-Mecklenburg Board of Education (1971), 140
Sweatt, Heman, 134
Sweatt v. Painter (1950), 134
Swing states, 272
Symbolic speech, 108
Syria, 357–358, 359, 360f, 374

Talk radio, 216
Taney, Roger Brooke, 127, 375–376, 375f
TANF (Temporary Assistance for Needy Families), 84
Taxation, 14–15, 85, 86f
Tea Act, 15
Technology adoption, 217, 218f
Telecommunications Act of 1996, 226
Telegraph, 215
Television, 216–217
Temporary Assistance for Needy Families (TANF), 84
Tenth Amendment
    about, 99, 99t
    reserved powers, 68
    reserved powers and, 117
    same-sex marriage and, 114–117
    state sovereignty, 86
Tenure of Office Act, 394
Term limits, 327, 362
Terrell, Anton, 239
Texas, 288
Texas v. Johnson (1989), 108
Thayer, James Bradley, 433
Theodorice, Willy, 2f
Third Amendment, 99t, 101t
Third-party candidates, 260–261, 260t, 261f
Thirteenth Amendment, 129
Thomas, Clarence, 341–342
Thompson, Nato, 172
Thornburg v. Gingles (1986), 290
Three-fifths Compromise, 49–51, 50–51f, 129
Title VII, 146, 148
Title IX, 173–174
Tocqueville, Alexis de, 302
Top-two primary systems, 282–283
Totalitarian governments, 21, 21f
Trade, 240
Treaty of Paris (1783), 12, 20
Truman, David, 304
Truman, Harry S., 378–379, 398
Trump, Donald
    candidacy of, 238f
    celebrity status of, 228
    Charlottesville protests and, 205
    conflict by, 357–360, 359–360f
    Dakota Access Pipeline and, 97
    fake tweets by, 210f
    federal bureaucracy and, 399, 399f
    FEMA and, 389
    filibuster and, 339
    horse race phenomenon and, 225
    immigration and, 269, 269f
    marijuana and, 66, 88
    media relationship, 221, 221f
    net neutrality, 227
    NFL protests and, 204
    as party outsider, 239–240, 262
    picture, 356f, 363f

platform lacking, 255

public opinion and, 371

Republican Party rules benefitting, 253–254, 253f

Russia and, 221, 329

Syria and, 357–358, 359, 360f, 374

turnover in administration, 358, 359f

women inspired to run because of, 325

See also Presidential election of 2016

Trust, 34, 37, 223, 224f

Truth, Sojourner, 148–149, 149f

Turf wars, 394

Twenty-fifth Amendment, 366–367

Twenty-second Amendment, 362

Twenty-sixth Amendment, 168

2008 housing crisis, 297–301, 298–300f

2016 presidential election. *See* Presidential election of 2016

2018 midterm election, 292, 323–326, 324–325f. *See also* Women in Congress

Tyranny, 54–56

Tyranny of the majority, 55–56

Tyranny of the minority, 55–56

Uncle Sam recruitment poster, 189f

Unfunded mandates, 85–86

Unicameral system, 34

Unitary systems, 66, 67f

United Farm Workers, 125

United States v. Darby (1941), 87

United States v. Lopez (1995), 86–87

United States v. Miller (1939), 111

United States v. Nixon (1974), 377

United States v. O'Brien (1968), 108

United States v. Windsor (2013), 115, 117

Unite the Right, 205, 206f

Unjust versus just laws, 25

Unorthodox lawmaking, 335

Unsoeld, Jolene, 342

U.S. Constitution. *See* Constitution of the United States

U.S. Department of Education, 174

U.S. Supreme Court. *See* Supreme Court

Validity of polls, 193–199

Vazquez, Yamiles, 387f

Vehar, Fabiola, 266f

Venegas, Rodrigo, 316

Verba, Sidney, 160

Vetoes, 339, 364, 365

Vice presidency, 332, 366–367, 367f

Vieth v. Jubelirer (2004), 290

Vinson, Fred, 135

Virginia Company, 11

Virginia Plan, 42, 44t

Voluntary associations, 297. *See also* Interest groups; Social movements

Volunteerism, 303–304f

Voters and voting process

African Americans, 166, 167f

decision to vote, 163–170, 164f, 166–167f, 169–170f

eligibility for, 165

Latinos/Latinas, 272, 273f

methods of voting, 259, 259f, 261

Nineteenth Amendment, 145–146

registration requirements, 168–169, 169f

rights for women, 142–146, 168

split-ticket voting, 249

turnout of young adults, 176–178, 177f

Voter turnout

factors that shape, 163–170, 166–167f

other countries compared to United States, 164f

reasons for lack of, 274

young Americans and, 170f, 176–178, 177f

Voting Rights Act of 1965, 138

Wall Street. *See* Banking; Occupy Wall Street (OWS)

War-making power of Congress, 363–364

The War of the Worlds, 229–231, 230f

War powers, 376

War Powers Resolution (WPR), 363–364

Warrants, 112

Warren, Earl, 135

Warren, Mercy Otis, 57, 57f

Warren Court, 436, 436f

Washington, George

Constitutional Convention attendance, 40, 41f

correspondence with Madison, 32, 38–39

federal bureaucracy and, 394–396

personality of, 380

on political parties, 241, 256

presence of, 39

as president, 46f, 361f, 362

Seven Years' War, 12

Watchdogs, 231

Watergate affair, 365

Wealth inequality, 238, 315, 315f. *See also* Occupy Wall Street (OWS)

Weber, Max, 391, 392f

Weighting of surveys, 193

Welles, Orson, 229–231, 230f

Whig Party, 256–257

Whips, 332

"White Clergymen Urge Local Negroes to Withdraw from Demonstrations," 24

Whitefish Energy, 407

White House Office, 368–369

Whitney, Katherine, 158

Wickard v. Filburn (1942), 64–65, 87

Wilcox, Clyde, 343

Wilentz, Sean, 260

Wilson, Darren, 183

Wilson, Edith Bolling Galt, 369

Wilson, James, 40, 43, 361

Wilson, James Q., 392, 392f, 406–407

Wilson, Woodrow, 338

Windsor, Edith, 114–115, 115f

Winthrop, John, 10

Wire service, 215

Wisdom of crowds, 190
Women
  American Revolution and, 17–18
  first wave of civil rights, 142–146
  party affiliation and, 200, 200f
  second wave of civil rights, 146–147
  2018 midterm election, 324–325f, 324–326
  voting and gender, 166–167
Women in Congress
  Iwo Jima metaphor, 342
  1992 elections, 340–344, 341–344f
  numbers of, 349–350, 349–350f
  support for, 322f
  2018 elections, 292, 353
  year of the woman, 324, 326, 340

Wong, Alia, 178
Worcester, Samuel, 438f
WPR (War Powers Resolution), 363–364
Writs of certiorari, 429
Writs of habeas corpus, 110, 375–376
Writs of mandamus, 421, 422
Wyoming Territory, 145

Year of the woman, 324, 326, 340
Yellow journalism, 215, 216f
Youngstown Sheet & Tube Co. v. Sawyer (1952), 378–379

Zaller, John, 190
Zuccotti Park, 314–317, 314f, 316f. *See also*
  Occupy Wall Street (OWS)